# THE FORMS OF THE OLD TESTAMENT LIT

*Now available

# PSALMS

## PART 2

—— and ——

# LAMENTATIONS

## ERHARD S. GERSTENBERGER

*The Forms of the Old Testament Literature*

VOLUME XV

*Rolf P. Knierim, Gene M. Tucker, and
Marvin A. Sweeney, editors*

WILLIAM B. EERDMANS PUBLISHING COMPANY
GRAND RAPIDS, MICHIGAN / CAMBRIDGE, U.K.

© 2001 Wm. B. Eerdmans Publishing Co.
255 Jefferson Ave. S.E., Grand Rapids, Michigan 49503 /
P.O. Box 163, Cambridge CB3 9PU U.K.

Printed in the United States of America

06 05 04 03 02 01     7 6 5 4 3 2 1

ISBN 0-8028-0488-8

# CONTENTS

# ABBREVIATIONS AND SYMBOLS

## I. Miscellaneous Abbreviations and Symbols

| | |
|---|---|
| cf. | compare |
| ch(s). | chapter(s) |
| D | Deuteronomic source |
| diss. | dissertation |
| Dtr | Deuteronomistic source |
| E | Elohistic source |
| ed(s). | editor(s), edited by, edition |
| e.g. | for example |
| esp. | especially |
| et al. | *et alii* (and others) |
| *Fest.* | *Festschrift* |
| Heb. | Hebrew |
| i.e. | *id est* (that is) |
| LXX | Septuagint |
| MS(S) | manuscript(s) |
| MT | Masoretic Text |
| NF, NS | Neue Folge, New Series (in serial listings) |
| no. | number |
| NT | New Testament |
| OT | Old Testament |
| P | Priestly source |
| p(p). | page(s) |
| repr. | reprint |
| tr. | translated by |
| v(v). | verse(s) |
| vol(s). | volume(s) |
| → | The arrow indicates a cross-reference to another section of the commentary |
| §(§) | section(s) |

## II. Publications

| | |
|---|---|
| AB | Anchor Bible |
| *ABD* | *Anchor Bible Dictionary* |
| *AHW* | W. von Soden, *Akkadisches Handwörterbuch* (3 vols.; Wiesbaden: Harrassowitz, 1965-81) |
| *AJSL* | *American Journal of Semitic Languages and Literatures* |
| Alt, *KS* | A. Alt, *Kleine Schriften zur Geschichte des Volkes Israel* (3 vols.; Munich: Beck, 1953-59) |
| AnBib | Analecta biblica |
| *ANET* | J. B. Pritchard, ed., *Ancient Near Eastern Texts Relating to the Old Testament* (3rd ed.; Princeton: Princeton University Press, 1969) |
| AnOr | Analecta orientalia |
| AOAT | Alter Orient und Altes Testament |
| *ARE* | J. H. Breasted, ed., *Ancient Records of Egypt* (5 vols.; Chicago: University of Chicago Press, 1906-7) |
| *ASTI* | *Annual of the Swedish Theological Institute* |
| ATANT | Abhandlungen zur Theologie des Alten und Neuen Testaments |
| ATD | Das Alte Testament Deutsch |
| *ATR* | *Anglican Theological Review* |
| *AUSS* | *Andrews University Seminary Studies* |
| *BASOR* | *Bulletin of the American Schools of Oriental Research* |
| BBB | Bonner biblische Beiträge |
| BDB | F. Brown, S. R. Driver, and C. A. Briggs, *Hebrew and English Lexicon of the Old Testament* (rev. ed.; Oxford: Oxford University Press, 1957) |
| BE | Biblische Enzyklopädie |
| *BeO* | *Bibbia e oriente* |
| BETL | Bibliotheca ephemeridum theologicarum lovaniensium |
| BEvT | Beiträge zur evangelischen Theologie |
| *BHH* | B. Reicke and L. Rost, eds., *Biblisch-historisches Handwörterbuch* (4 vols.; Göttingen: Vandenhoeck & Ruprecht, 1962-66) |
| *BHK* | R. Kittel, ed., *Biblia hebraica* (Stuttgart: Württembergische Bibelanstalt, 1937) |
| *BHS* | K. Elliger and W. Rudolph, eds., *Biblia hebraica stuttgartensia* (Stuttgart: Deutsche Bibelstiftung, 1977) |
| *Bib* | *Biblica* |
| *BibLeb* | *Bibel und Leben* |
| BibOr | Biblica et orientalia |
| BibS(N) | Biblische Studien (Neukirchen, 1951-) |
| *BJRL* | *Bulletin of the John Rylands University Library of Manchester* |
| *BK* | *Bibel und Kirche* |
| BKAT | Biblischer Kommentar: Altes Testament |

| | |
|---|---|
| *BLit* | *Bibel und Liturgie* |
| *BM* | *Beth Mikra* |
| *BN* | *Biblische Notizen* |
| *BO* | *Bibliotheca Orientalis* |
| *BR* | *Biblical Research* |
| *BRL* | K. Galling, ed., *Biblisches Reallexikon* (2nd ed.; Tübingen: Mohr, 1977) |
| *BSac* | *Bibliotheca Sacra* |
| *BT* | *Bible Translator* |
| *BTB* | *Biblical Theology Bulletin* |
| *BTS* | *Bible et terre sainte* |
| *BVC* | *Bible et vie chrétienne* |
| BWANT | Beiträge zur Wissenschaft vom Alten und Neuen Testament |
| *BZ* | *Biblische Zeitschrift* |
| BZAW | Beihefte zur Zeitschrift für die alttestamentliche Wissenschaft |
| BZNW | Beihefte zur Zeitschrift für die neutestamentliche Wissenschaft |
| *CBQ* | *Catholic Biblical Quarterly* |
| CBQMS | Catholic Biblical Quarterly Monograph Series |
| *CJT* | *Canadian Journal of Theology* |
| CT | Cahiers théologiques de l'actualité protestante |
| *CTM* | *Concordia Theological Monthly* |
| Eissfeldt, *Intro.* | O. Eissfeldt, *The Old Testament: An Introduction* (3rd ed.; tr. P. R. Ackroyd; New York: Harper & Row, 1965) |
| Eissfeldt, *KS* | O. Eissfeldt, *Kleine Schriften* (5 vols.; Tübingen: Mohr, 1962-73) |
| *EstBib* | *Estudios bíblicos* |
| *EsTe* | *Estudos teológicos* |
| *ETL* | *Ephemerides theologicae lovanienses* |
| *ETR* | *Études théologiques et religieuses* |
| *EvQ* | *Evangelical Quarterly* |
| *EvT* | *Evangelische Theologie* |
| *ExpTim* | *Expository Times* |
| *FAT* | *Forschungen zum Alten Testament* |
| FOTL | Forms of the Old Testament Literature |
| FRLANT | Forschungen zur Religion und Literatur des Alten und Neuen Testaments |
| *FuF* | *Forschungen und Fortschritte* |
| *GKC* | E. Kautzsch, ed., *Gesenius' Hebrew Grammar* (tr. A. E. Cowley; 2nd ed.; Oxford: Clarendon, 1910) |
| *GTJ* | *Grace Theological Journal* |
| *HAL* | *Hebräisches und aramäisches Lexikon zum Alten Testament* (ed. W. Baumgartner et al.; 3rd ed.; 5 vols.; Leiden: Brill, 1967–96) |
| *HAR* | *Hebrew Annual Review* |
| HAT | Handbuch zum Alten Testament |

| | |
|---|---|
| HBS | Herders Biblische Studien |
| *HerTS* | *Hervormde theologiese Studies* |
| HO | B. Spuler, ed., *Handbuch der Orientalistik* (Leiden and Cologne: Brill, 1952) |
| HSM | Harvard Semitic Monographs |
| *HTR* | *Harvard Theological Review* |
| *HUCA* | *Hebrew Union College Annual* |
| *IDB* | *Interpreter's Dictionary of the Bible* |
| *IDBSup* | Supplementary volume to *IDB* |
| *Int* | *Interpretation* |
| *JANESCU* | *Journal of the Ancient Near Eastern Society of Columbia University* |
| *JAOS* | *Journal of the American Oriental Society* |
| *JBL* | *Journal of Biblical Literature* |
| *JCS* | *Journal of Cuneiform Studies* |
| *JEOL* | *Jaarbericht van het Voorazietisch Egyptisch Genotschap ex oriente lux* |
| *JETS* | *Journal of the Evangelical Theological Society* |
| *JJS* | *Journal of Jewish Studies* |
| *JNES* | *Journal of Near Eastern Studies* |
| *JNSL* | *Journal of Northwest Semitic Languages* |
| *JQR* | *Jewish Quarterly Review* |
| JSNTSup | Journal for the Study of the New Testament, Supplements |
| *JSOT* | *Journal for the Study of the Old Testament* |
| JSOTSup | Journal for the Study of the Old Testament, Supplements |
| *JSS* | *Journal of Semitic Studies* |
| *JTS* | *Journal of Theological Studies* |
| *KAI* | H. Donner and W. Röllig, *Kanaanäische und aramäische Inschriften* (2nd ed.; 3 vols.; Wiesbaden: Harrassowitz, 1966-68) |
| *KD* | *Kerygma und Dogma* |
| KHK | Kurzer Hand-Kommentar zum Alten Testament |
| Mowinckel, *PsSt* | S. Mowinckel, *Psalmenstudien* (6 vols.; 1921-24; repr. Amsterdam: Schippers, 1961) |
| Mowinckel, *W* | S. Mowinckel, *The Psalms in Israel's Worship* (2 vols.; tr. D. R. Ap-Thomas; New York: Abingdon, 1962) |
| *NBL* | *Neues Bibellexikon* (ed. M. Görg and B. Lang; Zurich: Benziger, 1988–) |
| NEB | New English Bible |
| *NGTT* | *Nederduitse gereformeerde teologiese Tydskrif* |
| NIB | New Interpreter's Bible |
| *NorTT* | *Norsk teologisk tidsskrift* |
| *NovT* | *Novum Testamentum* |
| NRSV | New Revised Standard Version |
| *NRT* | *Nouvelle revue théologique* |
| OBO | Orbis biblicus et orientalis |
| OBT | Overtures to Biblical Theology |

| | |
|---|---|
| *OrAnt* | *Oriens antiquus* |
| *OTE* | *Old Testament Essays* |
| OTL | Old Testament Library |
| *OTS* | *Oudtestamentische Studiën* |
| *OTWSA* | *Ou-Testamentiese Werkgemeenskap in Suid-Afrika* |
| *PEQ* | *Palestine Exploration Quarterly* |
| POS | Pretoria Oriental Series |
| *RA* | *Revue d'assyriologie et d'archéologie orientale* |
| *RAC* | *Reallexikon für Antike und Christentum* |
| *RB* | *Revue biblique* |
| *RevExp* | *Review and Expositor* |
| *RevistB* | *Revista bíblica* |
| *RevQ* | *Revue de Qumran* |
| *RHPR* | *Revue d'histoire et de philosophie religieuses* |
| *RHR* | *Revue de l'histoire des religions* |
| *RivB* | *Rivista biblica* |
| *RLA* | *Reallexikon der Assyriologie* (Berlin, New York, and Leipzig: de Gruyter, 1932-) |
| *RSO* | *Rivista degli studi orientali* |
| *RSP* | L. R. Fisher and S. Rummel, eds., *Ras Shamra Parallels* (3 vols.; AnOr 49-51; Rome: Pontifical Biblical Institute, 1972-81) |
| *RSR* | *Recherches de science religieuse* |
| RSV | Revised Standard Version |
| *RTP* | *Revue de théologie et de philosophie* |
| *RTR* | *Reformed Theological Review* |
| *SAHG* | A. Falkenstein and W. von Soden, *Sumerische und akkadische Hymnen und Gebete* (Zurich: Artemis, 1953) |
| SBB | Stuttgarter biblische Beiträge |
| SBLDS | Society of Biblical Literature Dissertation Series |
| SBLMS | Society of Biblical Literature Monograph Series |
| *SBLSP* | *Society of Biblical Literature Seminar Papers* |
| SBM | Stuttgarter biblische Monographien |
| SBS | Stuttgarter Bibelstudien |
| SBT | Studies in Biblical Theology |
| *SEÅ* | *Svensk exegetisk årsbok* |
| *Sem* | *Semitica* |
| *SJOT* | *Scandinavian Journal of the Old Testament* |
| *SJT* | *Scottish Journal of Theology* |
| *SK* | *Skrif en Kerk* |
| *STU* | *Schweizerische theologische Umschau* |
| TBü | Theologische Bücherei |
| *TDOT* | G. J. Botterweck and H. Ringgren, eds., *Theologisches Wörterbuch zum Alten Testament* (Stuttgart: Kohlhammer, 1973- ); Eng., *Theological Dictionary of the Old Testament* (tr. D. E. Green et al.; Grand Rapids: Eerdmans, 1974-) |
| TEV | Today's English Version |

| | |
|---|---|
| *TGl* | *Theologie und Glaube* |
| *THAT* | E. Jenni and C. Westermann, eds., *Theologisches Handwörterbuch zum Alten Testament* (2 vols.; Munich: Christoph Kaiser, 1971-1976) |
| ThSt(B) | Theologische Studien (founded and edited by K. Barth) |
| *ThStK* | *Theologische Studien und Kritiken* |
| *TLZ* | *Theologische Literaturzeitung* |
| *TQ* | *Theologische Quartalschrift* |
| *TRE* | *Theologische Realenzyklopädie* (ed. G. Krause and G. Müller; Berlin: de Gruyter, 1977–) |
| *TTZ* | *Trierer theologische Zeitschrift* |
| *TUAT* | *Texte aus der Umwelt des Alten Testaments* (ed. O. Kaiser, Gütersloh: Gütersloher Verlagshaus, 1981-1997) |
| TUMSR | Trinity University Monograph Series in Religion |
| *TWAT* | *Theologisches Wörterbuch zum Alten Testament* (→ *TDOT*) |
| *TynBul* | *Tyndale Bulletin* |
| *TZ* | *Theologische Zeitschrift* |
| *UF* | *Ugarit-Forschungen* |
| *VC* | *Vigiliae Christianae* |
| *VD* | *Verbum domini* |
| *VieS* | *Vie spirituelle* |
| *VT* | *Vetus Testamentum* |
| *VTSup* | *Vetus Testamentum, Supplements* |
| WMANT | Wissenschaftliche Monographien zum Alten und Neuen Testament |
| *WO* | *Die Welt des Orients* |
| *WTJ* | *Westminster Theological Journal* |
| *WuD* | *Wort und Dienst* |
| *WZHalle* | *Wissenschaftliche Zeitschrift der Martin-Luther-Universität* |
| *ZÄS* | *Zeitschrift für ägyptische Sprache und Altertumskunde* |
| *ZAW* | *Zeitschrift für die alttestamentliche Wissenschaft* |
| *ZKT* | *Zeitschrift für katholische Theologie* |
| *ZNW* | *Zeitschrift für die neutestamentliche Wissenschaft* |
| *ZTK* | *Zeitschrift für Theologie und Kirche* |

# EDITORS' FOREWORD

This book is the fifteenth in a series of twenty-four volumes planned for publication. The series eventually will present a form-critical analysis of every book and each unit of the Old Testament (Hebrew Bible) according to a standard outline and methodology. The aims of the work are fundamentally exegetical, attempting to understand the biblical literature from the viewpoint of a particular set of questions. Each volume in the series will also give an account of the history of the form-critical discussion of the material in question, attempt to bring consistency to the terminology for the genres and formulas of the biblical literature, and expose the exegetical procedure in such a way as to enable students and pastors to engage in their own analysis and interpretation. It is hoped, therefore, that the audience will be a broad one, including not only biblical scholars but also students, pastors, priests, and rabbis who are engaged in biblical interpretation.

There is a difference between the planned order of appearance of the individual volumes and their position in the series. While the series follows basically the sequence of the books of the Hebrew Bible, the individual volumes will appear in accordance with the projected working schedules of the individual contributors. The number of twenty-four volumes has been chosen for merely practical reasons that make it necessary to combine several biblical books in one volume at times, and at times to have two authors contribute to the same volume. Volume XIII is an exception to the arrangement according to the sequence of the Hebrew canon in that it omits Lamentations. The commentary on Lamentations appears here in the second of two volumes on the book of Psalms.

The initiation of this series is the result of deliberations and plans that began some twenty years ago. At that time the original editors perceived the need for a comprehensive reference work that would enable scholars and students of the Hebrew scriptures to gain from the insights that form-critical work had accumulated throughout seven decades, and at the same time to participate more effectively in such work themselves. An international and interconfessional team of scholars was assembled and has been expanded in recent years.

Several possible approaches and formats for publication presented themselves. The work could not be a handbook of the form-critical method with some examples of its application. Nor would it be satisfactory to present an encyclopedia of the genres identified in the Old Testament literature. The reference work would have to demonstrate the method on all of the texts, and identify genres only through the actual interpretation of the texts themselves. Hence, the work had to be a commentary following the sequence of the books in the Hebrew Bible (the Kittel edition of the *Biblia hebraica* then and the *Biblia hebraica stuttgartensia* now).

The main purpose of this project is to lead the student to the Old Testament texts themselves, and not just to form-critical studies of the texts. It should be stressed that the commentary is confined to the form-critical interpretation of the texts. Consequently, the reader should not expect here a full-fledged exegetical commentary that deals with the broad range of issues concerning the meaning of the text. In order to keep the focus as clearly as possible on a particular set of questions, matters of text, translation, philology, verse-by-verse explanation, etc. are raised only when they appear directly relevant to the form-critical analysis and interpretation.

The adoption of a commentary format with specific categories for the analysis of the texts rests upon a conclusion that has become crucial for all form-critical work. If the results of form criticism are to be verifiable and generally intelligible, then the determination of typical forms and genres, their settings and functions, has to take place through the analysis of the forms in and of the texts themselves. This leads to two consequences for the volumes in this series. First, each interpretation of a text begins with the presentation of the *structure* of that text in outline form. The ensuing discussion of this structure attempts to distinguish the typical from the individual or unique elements, and to proceed on this basis to the determination of the *genre,* its *setting,* and its *intention.* Traditio-historical factors are discussed throughout this process where relevant; e.g., is there evidence of a written or oral stage of the material earlier than the actual text before the reader?

Second, the interpretation of the texts accepts the fundamental premise that we possess all texts basically at their latest written stages — technically speaking, at the levels of the final redactions. Any access to the texts, therefore, must confront and analyze that latest edition first, i.e., a specific version of that edition as represented in a particular text tradition. Consequently, the commentary proceeds from the analysis of the larger literary corpora created by the redactions back to any prior discernible stages in their literary history. Larger units are examined first, and then their subsections. Therefore, in most instances the first unit examined in terms of structure, genre, setting, and intention is the entire biblical book in question; next the commentary treats the individual larger and then smaller units.

The original plan of the project was to record critically all the relevant results of previous form-critical studies concerning the texts in question. While this remains one of the goals of the series, it had to be expanded to allow for more of the research of the individual contributors. This approach has proved to be important not only with regard to the ongoing insights of the contributors but also in view of the significant developments that have taken place in the field in recent years. The team of scholars responsible for the series is committed to following a basic design throughout the commentary, but differences of emphasis and even to some extent of approach will be recognized as more volumes appear. Each author will ultimately be responsible for his own contribution.

The use of the commentary is by and large self-explanatory, but a few comments may prove helpful to the reader. This work is designed to be used alongside the Hebrew text or a translation of the Bible. The format of the interpretation of the texts, large or small, is the same throughout, except in cases where the biblical material itself suggests a different form of presentation. Individual books and major literary corpora are introduced by a general bibliography referring to wider information on the subjects discussed and to works relevant for the subunits of that literary body. Whenever available, a special form-critical bibliography for a specific unit under discussion will conclude the discussion of that unit. In the outline of the structure of units, the system of sigla attempts to indicate the relationship and interdependence of the parts within that structure. The traditional chapter and verse divisions of the Hebrew text, as well as the versification of the *New Revised Standard Version,* are supplied in the right-hand margin of the outlines.

In addition to the commentary on the biblical book, this volume includes a glossary of the genres discussed in the commentary. Many of the definitions in the glossary were prepared by Professor Gerstenberger, but some have arisen from the work of other members of the project on other parts of the Old Testament. Each subsequent volume will include such a glossary. Eventually, upon the completion of the commentary series, all of the glossaries will be revised in the light of the analysis of each book of the Old Testament and published as Volume XXIII of the series. The individual volumes will not contain special indices, but the indices for the entire series will be published as Volume XXIV.

The editors acknowledge with appreciation the contribution of numerous persons and institutions to the work of the project. All of the contributors have received significant financial, secretarial, and student assistance from their respective institutions. In particular, the editors have received extensive support from their universities. Without such concrete expressions of encouragement the work scarcely could have gone on. At Claremont, the Institute for Antiquity and Christianity has from its own inception provided an atmosphere that stimulates not only individual but also team research. Emory University and the Candler School of Theology have likewise provided tangible support and encouragement.

ROLF P. KNIERIM
GENE M. TUCKER
MARVIN A. SWEENEY

# Author's Preface

More than a decade has elapsed since FOTL XIV appeared from Eerdmans, representatives of whom I had a chance to talk to almost annually at the Frankfurt Book Fair. Also, the Claremont headquarters of the FOTL project held the line open to Germany by timely communications. So I kept in touch with general developments of the American theological book market and the destinies of the form-critical project in particular. The flow of literature on the Psalms and cultic poetry has acquired almost torrential dimensions. To my knowledge, no previous decade has brought forth so many full-fledged commentaries on the Psalter as well as all sorts of articles and monographs on detailed problems of individual texts and themes as the 1990s. New avenues are being tried out, for example, in some holistic or literary molds of interpretation, in terms of intercultural comparisons of sacred songs, or their spiritual and theological dimensions. All of these very different modern studies on ancient prayers prove the great need of our own time for communications with the Ground of Being (P. Tillich), the Holy One, the personal and communal God, the father of Jesus Christ, who — in the Psalter — is mostly the God of exilic and postexilic Israel. They certainly reveal overwhelmingly the unfathomable richness of the Hebrew Psalms. It is amazing how much these ancient texts can mean to so many different people. In all this extended ecumenical concert of psalm interpretations and notwithstanding the beauty, wealth, and perspicuity of other exegetical methods from which I gratefully acknowledge to have learned and profited enormously, I still think that a form-critical and social-historical analysis like the one begun with FOTL XIV may be helpful to recognize the multiple roots of psalmody in different types of human organization and ritual practice. It may enable us to discover the multilayered spirituality of generations of psalmists and psalm users of ancient times. The final converging point of collecting and redactional activities, as I see it, is the worship ceremonies of the early Jewish communities of the sixth to second centuries B.C.E. Use and re-use, oral and scribal tradition have shaped individual texts, intermediate collections, and the Psalter as a whole, and deserve specific attention. My emphasis, however, remains with distinct genres and the individual psalms that have survived as well-definable specimens of praise and lament, reflection and exhortation, encompassing the experiences of faith of many generations of Israelite and Jewish communities. The use of these songs, prayers, sermons, and meditations seems to be more important than the authorship of the texts. That means, in my opinion, that a text may change locales in the course of transmission, but it cannot lose its life setting, i.e., being anchored in communicative processes of some social/ecclesiastical organization. Texts are not freelancing autonomous powers, but belong to determined people. Exegesis needs to respect this social contextuality in order to understand better what ancient texts are talking about, and how we in our own time and environments may articulate our own search for truth, life, and justice, that is, for God.

My work with this form-critical commentary on the Psalter and Lamentations has come to a provisional end. Many people have taken part in my efforts over the years. I am most grateful to all friends, parishioners, students, and colleagues in Germany, the United States, and Brazil with whom I had the chance to study this unique treasure, the book of Psalms. We discussed many texts and issues, and ever so often marveled at the human and theological insights of our ancient forebears (cf. Ps 139:6). Four student assistants I should like to mention — *pars pro toto* — in gratitude, who actively helped me with my manuscript during the last years before my retirement in 1997: Kerstin Ulrich, Julia Conrad, Michaela Geiger and Stephan Koopmann. They not only collected bibliographical information, corrected my typescript, and made technical suggestions, but were deeply involved in the subject matter, debating with me essentials of interpretation. To all those who already used the first volume, FOTL XIV, and quite often inquired for the second one, I now should like to say: Here it is, finally.

*Giessen/Marburg, January 2001*                    ERHARD S. GERSTENBERGER

# Additional Bibliography

## A. Commentaries
### (cited by author's name and pages only)

L. C. Allen, *Psalms 101–150* (Word Biblical Commentary 21; Dallas: Word Books, 1983); L. Alonso Schökel and C. Carniti, *I Salmi* (Rome: Pontifical Biblical Institute, 1992); R. Bratcher, et al., *A Translator's Handbook on the Book of Psalms* (New York: United Bible Societies, 1991); W. G. Braude, *The Midrash on Psalms* (2 vols.; New Haven: Yale University Press, 1959); P. C. Craigie, *Psalms 1–50* (Word Biblical Commentary 19; Dallas: Word Books, 1983); M. Dahood, *Psalms* (3 vols.; AB 16, 17, 17A; Garden City, N.Y.: Doubleday, 1965-70); J. Day, *Psalms* (Old Testament Guides; Sheffield: Sheffield Academic Press, 1991); A. Deissler, *Das Buch der Psalmen* (3 vols.; Düsseldorf: Patmos, 1963-65); B. Duhm, *Die Psalmen* (2nd ed.; KHK XIV; Tübingen: Mohr, 1922); J. H. Eaton, *Psalms. Introduction and Commentary* (Torch Bible Commentaries; London: SCM, 1967); A. C. Feuer, *Tehillin: A New Translation with a Commentary* (3rd ed.; New York: Ktav, 1991); M. Girard, *Les Psaumes redécouverts* (3 vols.; Montreal: Bellarmin, 1994); M. Goulder, *Psalms of the Sons of Korah* (JSOTSup 20; Sheffield: JSOT Press, 1982); idem, *The Prayers of David* (JSOTSup 102; Sheffield: JSOT Press, 1990); H. Gunkel, *Die Psalmen* (4th ed.; 1926; repr. Göttingen: Vandenhoeck & Ruprecht, 1956); F.-L. Hossfeld and E. Zenger, *Die Psalmen: I Psalm 1–50* (Neue Echter Bibel; Würzburg: Echter, 1993); idem, *Psalmen 51–100* (Freiburg: Herder, 2000); L. Jacquet, *Les Psaumes et le coeur de l'homme: Étude textuelle, littéraire et doctrinale* (3 vols.; Gembloux: Duculot, 1975-79); H.-J. Kraus, *Psalmen* (5th ed.; BKAT XV/1-2; Neukirchen-Vluyn: Neukirchener Verlag, 1978); Eng.: *Psalms: A Commentary* (tr. H. C. Oswald; 2 vols.; Minneapolis: Augsburg, 1988-89); J. Limburg, *Psalms* (Louisville: Westminster John Knox, 2000); J. L. Mays, *Psalms* (Interpretation; Louisville: John Knox, 1994); Y. C. McCann, Jr., *The Book of Psalms* (NIB IV; Nashville: Abingdon, 1996) 639-1280; M. Oeming, *Das Buch der Psalmen*, vol. I (Stuttgart: Kath. Bibelwerk, 2000); W. O. E. Oesterley, *The Psalms* (London: SPCK, 1939); G. Ravasi, *Il libro dei Salmi* (3 vols.; Bologna: Edizione Detzariane, 1981-84); H. Schmidt, *Die Psalmen* (HAT I/15; Tübingen: Mohr, 1934); L. Schottroff, et al., eds., *Kompendium feministischer Bibelauslegung* (2nd ed.; Gütersloh: Chr. Kaiser, 1999); K. Seybold, "Psalmen-Kommentare 1972-1994," *Theologische Rundschau* 60 (1995) 113-30 (review of recent commentaries); idem, *Die Psalmen* (HAT I/15; Tübingen: Mohr, 1996); C. Stuhlmueller, *Psalms* (Old Testament Message; Wilmington, Del.: Glazier, 1983); M. E. Tate, *Psalms 51–100* (Word Biblical Commentary 20; Dallas: Word, 1990); A. Weiser, *Die Psalmen* (ATD 14-15; Göttingen: Vandenhoeck & Ruprecht, 1950); Eng.: *The Psalms: A Commentary* (tr. H. Hartwell; OTL; Philadelphia: Westminster, 1962); A. Wünsch, ed., *Midrasch Tehillin* (Trier: Sigmund Mayer, 1892).

# B. Cultic Poetry and Ceremony

R. Albertz, *Religionsgeschichte Israels* (Göttingen: Vandenhoeck, 1992); Eng. *A History of Israelite Religion in the Old Testament Period* (2 vols.; OTL; London: SCM; Louisville: Westminster, 1994); Y. Avishur, *Studies in Hebrew and Ugaritic Psalms* (Jerusalem: Magnes, 1994); A. Berlin, *The Dynamics of Biblical Parallelism* (Bloomington: Indiana University Press, 1985); J. Black, et al., *Gods, Demons, and Symbols of Ancient Mesopotamia* (2nd ed.; London: British Museum, 1998); J. Blenkinsopp, *Sage, Priest, Prophet: Religious and Intellectual Leadership in Ancient Israel* (Louisville: Westminster John Knox, 1995); E. Blum, *Studien zur Komposition des Pentateuch* (BZAW 189; Berlin: de Gruyter, 1990); H. J. Boecker, *Redeformen des Rechtslebens im Alten Testament* (2nd ed.; WMANT 14; Neukirchen-Vluyn: Neukirchener Verlag, 1970); R. N. Boyce, *The Cry to God in the Old Testament* (SBLDS 103; Atlanta: Scholars Press, 1989); R. L. Bunzel, *Zuni Ceremonialism* (1932; repr. Albuquerque: University of New Mexico Press, 1992); W. Burkert and F. Stolz, eds., *Hymnen der Alten Welt im Kulturvergleich* (OBO 131; Fribourg: Universitätsverlag; Göttingen: Vandenhoeck & Ruprecht, 1994); O. Camponovo, *Königtum, Königsherrschaft und Reich Gottes in den frühjüdischen Schriften* (OBO 58; Fribourg: Universitätsverlag, 1984); R. J. Clifford, *The Cosmic Mountain in Canaan and the Old Testament* (HSM 4; Cambridge: Harvard University Press, 1970); G. W. Coats, *Rebellion in the Wilderness* (Nashville: Abingdon, 1968); J. S. Croatto, *Exodus, a Hermeneutics of Freedom* (tr. S. Attanasio, Maryknoll, N.Y.: Orbis, 1981); P. R. Davies, *Scribes and Schools* (Louisville: Westminster John Knox, 1998); A. Deissler, "Vorstufen der Mystik in den Psalmen," in *Von der Suche nach Gott* (ed. M. Schmidt, et al.; Stuttgart–Bad Cannstatt: Frommann-Holzboog, 1998) 39-50; J. H. Eaton, *Psalms of the Way and the Kingdom* (JSOTSup 199; Sheffield: Sheffield Academic Press, 1995); D. N. Fabian, "The Socio-Religious Role of Witchcraft in the Old Testament Culture: An African Insight," *OTE* 11 (1998) 215-39; J. C. Faris, *The Nightway, a History: And a History of Documentation of a Navajo Ceremonial* (Albuquerque: University of New Mexico Press, 1990); J. L. Foster, *Hymns, Prayers and Songs* (Writings from the Ancient World 8; Atlanta: Scholars Press, 1996); D. N. Freedman, *Pottery, Poetry, and Prophecy* (Winona Lake, Ind.: Eisenbrauns, 1980); A. Gamper, *Gott als Richter in Mesopotamien und im Alten Testament* (Innsbruck: Universität, 1966); F. García Martínez, *The Dead Sea Scrolls Translated* (2nd ed.; Leiden: Brill; Grand Rapids: Eerdmans, 1996); E. S. Gerstenberger, *Leviticus: A Commentary* (OTL; Louisville: Westminster John Knox, 1996); idem, *Yahweh the Patriarch* (Minneapolis: Fortress, 1996); J. C. L. Gibson, *Canaanite Myths and Legends* (Edinburgh: T. & T. Clark, 1978); R. Girard, *Le bouc émissaire* (Paris: Grasset, 1982); Eng.: *The Scapegoat* (tr. Y. Freccero; Baltimore: Johns Hopkins University Press, 1986); M. P. Graham, ed., *Worship and the Hebrew Bible* (JSOTSup 284; *Fest.* J. T. Willis; Sheffield: Sheffield Academic Press, 1999); R. L. Grimes, *Beginnings in Ritual Studies* (1982; 2nd ed.; Columbia: University of South Carolina Press, 1995); K. E. Grözinger, *Musik und Gesang in der Theologie der frühen jüdischen Literatur* (Tübingen: Mohr, 1982); B. Haile, *Love-Magic and Butterfly People* (American Tribal Religions 2; Flagstaff: Museum of Northern Arizona Press, 1978); idem, *Waterway: A Navajo Ceremonial Myth Told by Black Mustache Circle* (American Tribal Religions 5; Flagstaff: Museum of Northern Arizona Press, 1979); idem, *The Upward Moving and Emergency Way* (American Tribal Religions 7; Lincoln/London: University of Nebraska Press, 1981); idem, *Women Versus Men: A Conflict of Navajo Emergence* (American Tribal Religions 6; Lincoln/London: University of Nebraska Press, 1981); C. A. Hammerschlag, *The Dancing Healers* (San Francisco: Harper & Row, 1988); M. Haran, *Temple and Temple-Service in Ancient Israel* (Oxford: Oxford University Press, 1978); F. Hartenstein, *Die Unzugänglichkeit Gottes im Heiligtum* (WMANT 75; Neukirchen-Vluyn: Neukirchener Verlag, 1997); M. Hengel, *Judentum und Hellenismus* (Tübingen: Mohr, 1988); F. F. Hvidberg, *Weeping and Laughter in the Old Testament* (tr. N. Haislund; Leiden: Brill; Copenhagen: Nyt Nordisk Forlag, 1962); B. Janowski, *Sühne als Heilsgeschehen* (Neukirchen-Vluyn: Neukirchener Verlag, 1982); idem, *Rettungsgewissheit und Epiphanie des Heils* (Neukirchen-Vluyn: Neukirchener Verlag, 1989); J. Jeremias, *Theophanie: Die Geschichte einer alttestamentlichen Gattung* (2nd ed.; Neukirchen-Vluyn: Neukirchener Verlag, 1977); O. Kaiser, *Die mythische Bedeutung des Meeres in Ägypten, Ugarit und Israel* (Berlin: Töpelmann, 1959; 2nd ed., 1962); idem, *Der Gott des Alten Testaments* (2 vols.; Göttingen: Vandenhoeck & Ruprecht, 1993-98); idem, ed., *TUAT;* O. Keel, *The Symbolism of the Biblical World* (tr. T. J. Hallett; New York: Seabury, 1978); C. Keil, *The Tiv Song* (Chicago: University of Chicago Press, 1979); M. Klinghardt, "Prayer Formularies for Public Recitation: Their Use and Function in Ancient Religion," *Numen* 46 (1999) 1-52; M. Klopfenstein, *Scham und Schande im Alten Testament* (Zurich: Theologischer Verlag, 1972); I. Knohl, *The Sanctuary of Silence* (Minneapolis: Fortress, 1995); M. Köckert, *Vätergott und Väterverheissungen* (Göttingen: Vandenhoeck & Ruprecht, 1988); K. Koenen, *Jahwe wird kommen zu herrschen über die Erde* (BBB 101; Weinheim: Beltz Athenäum, 1995); idem, *Heil den Gerechten — Unheil den Sündern* (BZAW 229; Berlin: de Gruyter, 1994); D. Mathias, *Das 'Gottesvolk' in der Sicht der Geschichtssummarien des Psalters* (Berlin: Evangelische Verlagsanstalt, 1991); S. M. Maul, *Zukunftsbewältigung* (Mainz: Philipp von Zabern, 1994); M. Mauss, *The Gift, Forms and Functions of Exchange in Archaic Societies* (New York: Norton, 1967; 2nd ed. New York: Routledge, 1990); C. S. McClain, ed., *Women as Healers: Cross-Cultural Perspectives* (New Brunswick/London: Rutgers University Press, 1991); T. N. D. Mettinger, *King and Messiah* (Lund: Gleerup, 1976); idem, *The Dethronement of Sabaoth* (Lund: Gleerup, 1982); M. Metzger, *Königsthron und Gottesthron* (AOAT 15.1.2; Kevelaer: Butzon & Bercker; Neukirchen-Vluyn: Neukirchener Verlag, 1985); P. D. Miller, *The Divine Warrior in Early Israel* (HSM 5; Cambridge: Harvard University Press, 1973; 2nd ed. 1975); J. C. de Moor, *An Anthology of Religious Texts from Ugarit* (Leiden: Brill, 1987); idem, *The Rise of Yahwism* (2nd ed.; Leuven: Peeters, 1997); H. P. Nasuti, *Defining the Sacred Songs* (JSOT 218; Sheffield: Sheffield Academic Press, 2000); J. H. Newman, *Praying by the Book* (Early Judaism and Its Literature 14; Atlanta: Scholars Press, 1999); N. Nicolsky, *Spuren magischer Formeln in den Psalmen* (BZAW 46; Giessen: Töpelmann, 1927); M. Pope, *El in the Ugaritic Texts* (VTSup 2; Leiden: Brill, 1955); H. D. Preuss, *Verspottung fremder Religionen im Alten Testament* (Stuttgart: Kohlhammer, 1971); S. J. Rasmussen, *Spirit Possession and Personhood among the Kel Ewog Tuareg* (Cambridge: Cambridge University Press, 1995); G. A. Reichard, *Prayer: The Compulsive Word* (American Ethnological Society Monograph 7; New York: Augustin, 1944); idem, *Navajo Religion* (1950; repr. Princeton: Princeton University Press, 1990); T. Römer, *Israels Väter* (OBO 99; Göttingen: Vandenhoeck & Ruprecht, 1990); S. Safrai, *Die Wallfahrt im Zeitalter des Zweiten Tempels* (orig. Hebrew 1965; tr. D. Mach; Neukirchen-Vluyn: Neukirchener Verlag, 1981); W. Sallaberger, *Der kultische Kalender der Ur III–Zeit* (Berlin: de Gruyter, 1993); K. Schlosser, *Die Bantu-Bibel* (Kiel: Schmidt und Klaunig, 1977); H. Schmidt, *Die Thronfahrt JAHWES am Fest der Jahreswende im alten Israel* (Tübingen: Mohr, 1927); L. A. Schökel, *A Manual of Hebrew Poetics* (orig. Spanish 1987; tr. A. Graffey; Subsidia Biblica 11; Rome: Pontifical Biblical Institute, 1988); W. Schottroff, *Gedenken im Alten Orient und im Alten Testament* (WMANT 15; Neukirchen-Vluyn: Neukirchener Verlag, 1964); S. Schroer and T. Staubli, *Die Körpersymbolik der Bibel* (Darmstadt: Wissenschaftliche Buchgesellschaft, 1998); H. Seidel, *Musik in Altisrael* (Frankfurt/Bern: Peter Lang, 1989); A. Sendrey, *Music in Ancient Israel* (New York: Vision, 1969); J. van Seters, "Confessional Reformulation in the Exilic Period," *VT* 22 (1972) 448-59; idem, "The Place of the Yahwist in the History of Passover and Massot," *ZAW* 98 (1986) 31-39; M.-J. Seux, *Hymnes et prières aux dieux de Babylonie et d'Assyrie* (Litérature ancienne du Proche Orient 8; Paris: Cerf, 1976); L. W. Simmons, *Sun Chief* (New Haven: Yale University Press, 1942); M. Smith, *Palestinian Parties and Politics That Shaped the Old Testament* (1971; repr. London: SCM, 1987); M. S. Smith, *The Early History of God: Yahweh and the Other Deities in Ancient Israel* (San Francisco: Harper & Row, 1991); idem, *The Ugaritic Baal Cycle* (VTSup 55; Leiden: Brill, 1994); O. H. Steck, *Friedensvorstellungen im alten Jerusalem* (ThSt[B] 111; Zurich: Theologischer Verlag, 1972); K. van der Toorn, *Family Religion in Babylonia, Syria and Israel* (Leiden: Brill, 1996); idem, et al., eds., *Dictionary of Deities and Demons in the Bible* (Leiden: Brill, 1995); R. J. Tournay, *Seeing and Hearing God with the Psalms* (JSOTSup 118; Sheffield: Sheffield Academic Press, 1991); E. Turner, *Experiencing Ritual: A New Interpretation of African Healing* (Philadelphia: University of Pennsylvania Press, 1992); R. M. Underhill, *Singing for Power* (1938; repr. Tucson: University of Arizona Press, 1993); M. Weinfeld, *Social Justice in Ancient Israel and in the Ancient Near East* (Jerusalem: Magnes; Minneapolis: Fortress, 1995); R. A. Werline, "The Development of Penitential Prayer as a Religious Institution in Second Temple Jerusalem" (diss., University of Iowa, 1995); R. R. Wilson, *Prophecy and Society* (Philadelphia: Westminster, 1980); L. C. Wyman, *The Mountainway of the Navajo* (Tucson: University of Arizona Press, 1975); W. Zwickel, *Der Tempelkult in Kanaan und Israel* (*FAT* 10; Tübingen: Mohr, 1994).

# C. Psalms

A. Brenner et al., eds., *Wisdom and Psalms* (The Feminist Companion to the Bible, Second Series 2; Sheffield: Sheffield Academic Press, 1998); C. C. Broyles, *The Conflict of Faith and Experience in the Psalms: A Form-Critical and Theological Study* (JSOTSup 32; Sheffield: Sheffield Academic Press, 1989); W. Brueggemann, *The Psalms and the Life of Faith* (ed. P. D. Miller; Minneapolis: Fortress, 1995); idem, *Abiding Astonishment: Psalms, Modernity and the Making of History* (Louisville: Westminster John Knox, 1991); idem, *Theology of the Old Testament* (Minneapolis: Fortress, 1997); M. J. Buss, "The Psalms of Asaph and Korah," *JBL* 82 (1963) 383-92; T. W. Cartledge, "Conditional Vows in the Psalms of Lament: A New Approach to an Old Problem," in *The Listening Heart* (Fest. R. E. Murphy; ed. K. Hoglund, et al.; JSOTSup 58; Sheffield: Sheffield Academic Press, 1987) 77-94; E. Cortese, "Sulle redazioni finali de Salterio," *RB* 106 (1999) 66-100; L. D. Crow, *The Songs of Ascents* (SBLDS 148; Atlanta:

Scholars Press, 1996); P. Fiedler, "Zur Herkunft des gottesdienstlichen Gebrauchs von Psalmen aus dem Frühjudentum," *Archiv für Liturgiewissenschaft* 30 (1988) 229-37; P. W. Flint, "The Book of the Psalms in the Light of the Dead Sea Scrolls," *VT* 48 (1998) 453-72; N. Füglister, "Die Verwendung und das Verständnis der Psalmen und des Psalters um die Zeitenwende," in *Beiträge zur Psalmenforschung* (ed. J. Schreiner; Forschungen zur Bibel 60; Würzburg: Echter, 1988) 319-84; E. S. Gerstenberger, "Der Psalter als Buch und als Sammlung," in *Neue Wege der Psalmenforschung* (ed. K. Seybold and E. Zenger; Herders biblische Studien 1; Freiburg: Herder, 1994) 3-13; S. E. Gillinghan, "The Exodus Tradition and Israelite Psalmody," *SJT* 52 (1999) 19-46; H Gunkel and J. Begrich, *An Introduction to the Psalms* (tr. J. D. Nogalski; Macon: Mercer University Press, 1998); M. R. Hauge, *Between Sheol and Temple: Motif Structure and Function in the I-Psalms* (JSOTSup 178; Sheffield: Sheffield Academic Press, 1995); T. R. Hobbs and P. K. Jackson, "The Enemy in the Psalms," *BTB* 21 (1991) 22-29; P. R. House, ed., *Beyond Form Criticism* (Sources for Biblical and Theological Study 2; Winona Lake: Eisenbrauns, 1992); J. H. Hunter, "The Literary Composition of Theophany Passages in Hebrew Psalms," *JNSL* 15 (1989) 97-107; B. Janowski, *Rettungsgewissheit und Epiphanie des Heils: Das Motiv der Hilfe Gottes 'am Morgen' im Alten Orient und im Alten Testament,* I: *Alter Orient* (WMANT 59; Neukirchen-Vluyn: Neukirchener Verlag, 1989); K. Jolly, "Elves in the Psalms," in *The Devil, Heresy, and Witchcraft in the Middle Ages* (*Fest.* J. B. Russel; Leiden: Brill, 1998) 19-44; J. Kellenberger, "The Fool of the Psalms and Religious Epistemology," *International Journal for Philosophy and Religion* 45 (1999) 99-113; K. Koenen, "Maśkîl-'Wechselgesang.' Eine neue Deutung zu einem Begriff der Psalmenüberschriften," *ZAW* 103 (1991) 109-12; idem, *Gottesworte in den Psalmen* (Neukirchen-Vluyn: Neukirchener Verlag, 1996); idem, *Jahwe wird kommen, zu herrschen über die Erde* (Weinheim: Beltz Athenäum, 1996); S. Kreuzer, *Die Frühgeschichte Israels in Bekenntnis und Verkündigung des Alten Testament* (BZAW 178; Berlin: de Gruyter, 1989); M. Krieg, *Todesbilder im Alten Testament* (ATANT 73; Zurich: Theologischer Verlag, 1988); J. Kühlewein, *Geschichte in den Psalmen* (Calwer Theologische Monographien A, 2; Stuttgart: Kohlhammer, 1973); E.-T. Lamp, "Öffentlichkeit als Bedrohung — Ein Beitrag zur Deutung des 'Feindes' im Klagepsalm des einzelnen," *BN* 50 (1989) 46-57; G. Langer, "Zum Problem des Umgangs mit Macht am Beispiel der Psalmen," in *Ein Gott — eine Offenbarung* (*Fest.* N. Füglister; ed. F. V. Reiterer; Würzburg: Echter, 1991) 165-87; J. D. Levenson, *Sinai and Zion* (New York: Harper & Row, 1985); C. Levin, "Das Gebetbuch der Gerechten," *ZTK* 90 (1993) 355-81; F. Lindström, *Suffering and Sin: Interpretation of Illness in the Individual Complaint Psalms* (Stockholm: Almquist and Wiksell, 1994); N. Lohfink, *Lobgesänge der Armen: Studien zum Magnifikat, den Hodajot von Qumran und einigen späten Psalmen* (SBS 143; Stuttgart: Katholisches Bibelwerk, 1990); idem, "Psalmengebet und Psalterredaktion," *Archiv für Liturgiewissenschaft* 34 (1992) 1-22; O. Loretz, *Die Königspsalmen: Die altorientalisch-kanaanäische Königstradition in jüdischer Sicht,* part 1 (Ugaritisch-Biblische Literatur 6; Münster: Ugarit-Verlag, 1988); F. Matheus, *Singt dem Herrn ein neues Lied. Die Hymnen Deuterojesajas* (SBS 141; Stuttgart: Katholisches Bibelwerk, 1990); J. L. Mays, "The Place of the Torah Psalms in the Psalter," *JBL* 106 (1987) 3-12; J. C. McCann, "The Psalms as Instruction," *Int* 46 (1992) 117-28; idem, ed., *The Shape and Shaping of the Psalter* (JSOTSup 159; Sheffield: Sheffield Academic Press, 1993); J. Milgrom, *Leviticus 1–16* (AB 3A; New York: Doubleday, 1991);

M. Millard, *Die Komposition des Psalters* (*FAT* 9; Tübingen: Mohr, 1994); P. D. Miller, *Interpreting the Psalms* (Philadelphia: Fortress, 1986); idem, *They Cried to the Lord* (Minneapolis: Fortress, 1994); idem, "Deuteronomy and Psalms," *JBL* 118 (1999) 3-18; H. P. Nasuti, *Tradition History and the Psalms of Asaph* (SBLDS 88; Atlanta: Scholars Press, 1988); B. C. Ollenburger, *Zion: The City of the Great King* (JSOTSup 41; Sheffield: Sheffield Academic Press, 1987); P. R. Raabe, *Psalms Structures: A Study of Psalms with Refrains* (JSOTSup 104; Sheffield: JSOT Press, 1990); G. A. Rendsburg, *Linguistic Evidence for the Northern Origin of Selected Psalms* (SBLMS 43; Atlanta: Scholars Press, 1990); C. Rösel, *Die messianische Redaktion des Psalters* (diss., Marburg, 1997); L. Ruppert, "Klagelieder in Israel und Babylon — verschiedene Deutungen der Gewalt," in *Gewalt und Gewaltlosigkeit im Alten Testament* (ed. N. Lohfink; Freiburg: Herder, 1983) 111-58; A. Schenker, "Gelübde im Alten Testament. Unbeachtete Aspekte," *VT* 29 (1989) 87-91; J. Schreiner, "Gottes Verfügen durch 'Geben' und 'Nehmen' in der Sicht der Psalmen," in *Ein Gott — eine Offenbarung* (*Fest.* N. Füglister; ed. F. V. Reiterer; Würzburg: Echter, 1991) 307-31; H. Seidel, "Lobgesänge im Himmel und auf Erden," in *Gottesvolk* (ed. A. Meinhold and R. Lux; Berlin: Evangelische Verlagsanstalt, 1991); K. Seybold, "Zur Vorgeschichte der liturgischen Formel 'Amen,'" *TZ* 48 (1992) 109-17; idem, "Das 'Wir' in den Asaph-Psalmen," in *Neue Wege der Psalmenforschung* (ed. K. Seybold and E. Zenger; Freiburg: Herder, 1994) 143-55; idem, *Studien zur Psalmenauslegung* (Stuttgart: Kohlhammer, 1998); K. Seybold and E. Zenger, eds., *Neue Wege der Psalmenforschung* (Herders biblische Studien 1; Freiburg: Herder, 1994); U. Simon, *Four Ways of Approaching the Book of Psalms* (Albany: SUNY Press, 1990); W. M. Soll, "Babylonian and Biblical Acrostics," *Bib* 69 (1988) 305-23; H. Spieckermann, *Heilsgegenwart: Eine Theologie der Psalmen* (FRLANT 148; Göttingen: Vandenhoeck & Ruprecht, 1988); idem, "Psalmen und Psalter," in *Perspectives in the Study of the Old Testament* (*Fest.* A. S. van der Woude; ed. F. García Martínez; Leiden: Brill, 1998) 137-53; S. R. A. Starbuck, *Court Oracles in the Psalms* (SBLDS 172; Atlanta: Scholars Press, 1999); K. van der Toorn, "Ordeal Procedures in the Psalms and the Passover Meal," *VT* 38 (1988) 427-45; R. J. Tournay, *Voir et entendre Dieu avec les Psaumes ou la liturgie prophétique du second temple à Jérusalem* (Cahiers de la RB 24; Paris: Gabalda, 1988); Eng.: *Seeing and Hearing God with the Psalms* (JSOTSup 118; Sheffield: Sheffield Academic Press, 1991); J. Vermeylen, "L'usage liturgique des Psaumes dans la société israélite antique," *Questions liturgiques* 71 (1990) 191-206; A. Wénin, "Vulnerabilité et mal dans les Psaumes," *La Maison-Dieu* 217 (1999) 37-49; G. Willems, "Les psaumes dans la liturgie juive," *Tijdschrift voor filosofie en theologie* 4 (1990) 397-417; G. H. Wilson, "The Use of Untitled Psalms in the Psalter," *ZAW* 97 (1985) 404-13; idem, "The Shape of the Book of Psalms," *Int* 46 (1992) 129-42; idem, "The Use of Royal Psalms at the 'Seams' of the Hebrew Psalter," *JSOT* 35 (1986) 85-94; T. Wittstruck, *The Book of Psalms* (2 vols.; New York: Garland, 1994); R. Youngblood, "Divine Names in the Book of Psalms: Literary Structures and Number Patterns," *JANESCU* 19 (1989) 171-81; E. Zenger, "Was wird anders bei kanonischer Psalmenauslegung?" in *Ein Gott — eine Offenbarung* (*Fest.* N. Füglister; ed. F. V. Reiterer; Würzburg: Echter, 1991) 397-413; idem, "'Selig, wer auf die Armen achtet,'" *Jahrbuch für Biblische Theologie* 7 (1992) 21-50; idem, *Ein Gott der Rache?* (Freiburg: Herder, 1994); Eng.: *A God of Vengeance?* (tr. L. Maloney; Louisville: Westminster, 1996); idem, ed., *Der Psalter in Judentum und Christentum* (Herders biblische Studien 18; Freiburg: Herder, 1998).

# PSALMS

# THE INDIVIDUAL UNITS OF BOOK 2 (Psalms 61–72)

### Psalm 61:
### Complaint of the Individual;
### Congregational Psalm of Confidence with Intercession

#### Text

There are minor uncertainties in vv. 3c (third part of a tricolon) and 8b, but they do not pose serious problems to formal analysis.

#### Structure

|  |  | MT | NRSV |
|---|---|---|---|
| I. | Superscription | 1 | - |
| II. | Invocation | 2-3b | 1-2b |
|  | A. Initial plea | 2 | 1 |
|  | B. Description of praying | 3ab | 2ab |
| III. | Petitions and affirmations of confidence | 3c-6 | 2c-5 |
|  | A. Petition | 3c | 2c |
|  | B. Affirmation of confidence | 4 | 3 |
|  | C. Petition (wish) | 5 | 4 |
|  | D. Affirmation of confidence | 6 | 5 |
| IV. | Intercession | 7-8 | 6-7 |
|  | A. Plea | 7a | 6a |
|  | B. Wishes (benedictions) | 7b-8 | 6b-7 |
| V. | Vow | 9 | 8 |

The SUPERSCRIPTION is very akin to the headings of Psalms 4, 6, 54, 55, 57, 76, although not identical with any one of them; cf. also Hab 3:19 (→ Pss 4:1; 54:1); for *lamnaṣṣēaḥ* cf. Seybold, 38.

3

There is a regular but complex INVOCATION (vv. 2-3b) featuring first a typical initial plea by the suppliant to be heard (v. 2). The verbs used (*šm'* and *qšb*, Hiphil, "hear" and "hearken," respectively) are parallel, as quite often in liturgical language, especially in prophetic books (cf. Isa 49:1; Jer 6:10, 16-19; 18:19; Mic 1:2) and in educational discourse (Prov 4:1; 7:24). The verbs are paired also in Pss 10:17; 17:1; 66:19, but there is a tendency to add '*zn*, Hiphil, "listen," or to alternate it with *šm'* in the book of Psalms (cf. R. Mosis, *TWAT* VII, 197-205). Together with the grammatical objects "my cry" and "my prayer," these verbs make a strong, noisy, most urgent opening statement, befitting an individual complaint (see "Introduction to Cultic Poetry," section 4B). The divine addressee, however, remains vague with the generalized appellation '*ĕlōhîm* (missing altogether in the Greek Codex Vaticanus; see *FOTL* XIV, 37).

In second place we find the invocation bolstered by what H. Gunkel called the "description of praying" (v. 3a), strange only because of its geographic boundary: "From the rim of the world [land?]. . . ." What kind of liminality is intended? Is there a real, worldwide distance between the sufferer and God (cf. 46:10 [RSV 9]; 48:11 [RSV 10]; Isa 41:9; 42:10: these are all far-ranging affirmations)? Does our text intimate the boundary of Israel's promised land? Or are we facing a metaphor hinting at spiritual estrangement? The "end of the earth" may connote strangeness and danger, being lost perhaps even in the nonworld, the realm of death (cf. Deut 28:49; Isa 5:26; 43:6; Tate, 112). And it surely has a liturgical dimension: the praise of Yahweh goes out all the way to the limits of habitable soil (cf. Ps 48:11 [RSV 10]), and it echoes from there (cf. Isa 42:10). Or else: it fills the boundaries of his dominance (cf. Deut 32:8-9; 2 Kgs 5:15-19; for geographical allusions in the Psalms → Ps 42:7 [RSV 6]). So why not read this invocation in a liturgical context?

Another item has already been included, even if ephemerally, in this invocation: "when [or 'since'] my heart is being weakened" (v. 3b), a touch of COMPLAINT. The verb '*ṭp* in all its modifications denotes weakness and anxiety (Qal: Isa 57:16; Ps 102:1; Hithpael: Jonah 2:8 [RSV 7]; Pss 77:4 [RSV 3]; 107:5; 142:4 [RSV 3]; 143:4; Lam 2:12), more exactly, the point of dying by sheer exhaustion. Most of the mentioned passages talk of the deadly weakness of *rûaḥ*, "spirit, breath of life," and *lēb*, "heart"; in v. 3b it means exactly the same withering away of vital energy. Lam 2:12, using '*ṭp*, Hithpael, and *špk*, Hithpael ("to pour out one's life"), describes dying children, and Psalm 102 in its superscription offers a prayer for this very situation of extreme danger. Psalm 61, therefore, is intended and liturgically used as a COMPLAINT, although the element proper is missing. A fleeting hint at the suppliant's situation, woven into INVOCATION, in this case is entirely sufficient to make the text a prayer of the suffering individual in his or her primary group.

The INVOCATION (vv. 2-3b), then, is nicely articulated and well balanced. The first line features two cola (or semi-stichoi) with three and two accents, respectively. They present the forceful plea to be admitted to a hearing with God. The second line consists of three staccato cola with two stressed syllables each. The first and the last colon are prepositional and subordinate expressions. They frame the strong, fully verb-centered middle colon "to you do I cry," highlighting the lamentful purpose of the invocation.

4

PETITIONS and AFFIRMATIONS OF CONFIDENCE alternate line by line in vv. 3c-6. Each plea (vv. 3c, 5) is followed by a *kî* phrase that does not necessarily give the cause for asking favors but may at times be an exclamation "yea!" (for the exclamatory or hymnic *kî* cf. 3:8 [RSV 7]; 16:1; 17:6a; 106:1). Repeated pleas with *kî* phrases of varying contents are not uncommon in complaints (cf. 6:3 [RSV 2]; 25:5-6, 19-21; 31:3-5 [RSV 2-4, translating the first *kî*, v. 3, by "yea," the second, v. 4b, by "for"]; 71:3-5). The two petitionary lines are different in our case. V. 3c now has one imperfect (jussive) expression: "lead me" (*nḥh*, Hiphil; cf. 31:4 [RSV 3]; 73:24; 139:10; 143:10). The comparison "a rock higher than myself" (v. 3c) being rather awkward, we may assume with LXX that there was another imperfect in the first colon: "lift me up upon a rock" (cf. 27:5). The two pleas would be matched by two cohortatives in v. 5: "I want to stay . . . ; I want to hide . . . ," expressions from the vocabulary of sanctuary worship (*'ōhel*, "tent," and *kĕnāpayim*, "wings"; cf. 17:8; 27:5; 57:2 [RSV 1]; 91:1-4). Psalms 42/43 and 84 are fine examples of the Israelites' longing for the temple of Yahweh (cf. Knohl, *Sanctuary,* 192-96; listing at Additional Bibliography, section B; → 63:2 [RSV 1]). V. 4 reinforces the temple imagery. God and his abode are the safe place the persecuted one craves (cf. 46:2 [RSV 1]; 62:3, 7-8 [RSV 2, 6-7]; 63:8 [RSV 7]; 91:4). V. 6 leads ahead, announcing the vow that will be taken up in v. 9. The perfect forms of the verbs ("you heard," "you gave") indicate confidence based on worship, not in individual feelings. The complaining prayer has not yet been closed after v. 6, as v. 9 proves clearly (against H.-J. Kraus and others). But the interplay of petition and trust is such that assurance of being heard and helped by God becomes prominent.

Quite strange is the INTERCESSION for the monarch in an individual prayer (vv. 7-8; cf. 63:12 [RSV 11]). The little passage seems to separate v. 9 from v. 6 ("vow" in both lines) — a forced breakup. Also, worship in Israel while the monarchies lasted was probably neatly divided into familial, local, regional, and central cultic performances (cf. Gerstenberger, *Yahweh;* Albertz, *History,* both listed in Additional Bibliography, section B). The move toward centralization of cultic affairs was successful only after the fall of the Judean kingdom. The overall evidence of the Psalter would testify to a late merging of different traditions from diverse levels of worship. From a number of sources within the OT we may glean the fact that Davidic kingship was still considered a living reality in the cultic realm even in exilic/postexilic times (cf. Deut 17:14-20; 2 Samuel 7; Ezekiel 34; Hag 2:23; Zech 4:1-10). The Psalter is full of poems supporting this belief (cf. Psalms 2; 20; 21; 45; 72; 89; 110; 132). There is no reason, therefore, to deny the possibility of an exilic accretion of a "royalistic" text in Psalm 61, along a nostalgic vein. Standard pleas were voiced on behalf of that king who had been and hopefully would be again the chosen channel of God's grace, for a long life blessed by God, and a firm government (cf. 21:5 [RSV 4]; 89:25, 29, 30, 37 [RSV 24, 28, 29, 36]). Appropriately, we also should compare the (exilic?) story and psalm about King Hezekiah's cure (Isaiah 38). God sends the message through Isaiah: "Behold, I will add fifteen years to your life" (v. 5b [MT]; longer text in 2 Kgs 20:5). Much the same words are used in Ps 61:7a. Additional close similarities with → Psalm 89 mentioned before may lead to the conclusion that vv. 7-8 have been composed in the wake of exilic experiences, even if older royal language may have been used or imitated (cf. T. Veijola, listing at Psalm 89; and the discussion about a "messianic redaction" of parts of the Psalter: Rösel, *Redaktion;* McCann [ed.], *Shape,* both listed in Additional Bibliography, section C). "Sitting before God" (v. 8 [RSV 7]) seems to suggest an obedient, Dtr posture (cf. Deut 17:18-19). Formally, this intercession voices a direct plea to God for his life-preserving action and three wishes in the third person of the beneficiary: the good words of the congregation go directly to the Deity, bypassing the absent royal figure. The suggestion that in Persian times there also has been, as a "natural" obligation for all subjugated people, continuous intercession on behalf of the Great King of the empire, has to be considered seriously too (cf. Seybold, 241, 249; Ezra 6:10; 7:23).

The final Vow, articulated in a very personal and perennial way (v. 9), belongs to the inventory of elements in individual complaints. No matter how much the supplicant is asking for God's amazing grace, he also has to put in his own, though tiny, offer to God, gift for gift, song of praise and sacrifice for being heard (cf. Mauss, *Gift;* Reichard, *Prayer,* both listed in Additional Bibliography, section B). Vows are first-person pledges of something God will appreciate, originally a sacrifice, here possibly a song of praise alone (Leviticus 27; cf. O. Kaiser, *TWAT* V, 261-74). The element is an appropriate finish to individual prayer (cf. 7:18 [RSV 17]; 13:6; 35:28; 54:8-9 [RSV 6-7]; 56:11-14 [RSV 10-13]; 109:30; 116:18-19).

## *Genre/Setting*

This little psalm (9 poetic lines) has preserved some main features of the old COMPLAINT OF THE INDIVIDUAL that used to be recited by a supplicant under directions of a ritual expert (see "Introduction to Cultic Poetry," section 4B). The complaint element itself, however, is little developed (cf. in contradistinction 22:7-9, 12-19 [RSV 6-8, 11-18]; 38:3-21 [RSV 2-20] passim; 55:4-22 [RSV 3-21] passim; etc.). Consequently, petition remains a rather abstract call for safety and protection. It is hard to imagine how a prayer so vague in regard to the situation of distress could have been employed in any specific healing ceremony. Furthermore, the language and theological horizon point to a temple-oriented spiritual community of later days. There is one reference to those who "fear the Name" (v. 6b), reminiscent of the "fearful of Yahweh" (cf. 22:24, 26; 25:12; 31:20; 33:18; 34:8, 10; etc.; altogether 27 occurrences in the Psalter, mostly in definitely late texts. For *yr'*, "fear" and its semantic field cf. H. F. Fuhs, *TWAT* III, 869-93). The inclusion of intercession for state authorities also may indicate late instead of early origins. Therefore, as in → Psalm 12 and other examples, we may designate Psalm 61 a CONGREGATIONAL PSALM OF CONFIDENCE, derived from the pattern of the COMPLAINT OF THE INDIVIDUAL, and still used in common worship for the benefit of each member of the congregation (→ Psalms 4; 11; 23; 62; 131).

Asensio proposed to consider Psalms 61–63 a liturgical unit. There certainly are affinities between the three poems (e.g., emphases on the trust motif;

6

unusual mention of the king; dominance of "I" form; some common use of vocabulary and imagery). On the other hand, we may find as many dissimilarities (meter; vocabulary [hapax legomena in Psalm 63]; metaphors; style; liturgical elements; participating personnel [only 62:9 (RSV 8) has congregational first person]; roles and description of enemies; etc.). The matter has to be decided on liturgical considerations. Since we do not know the real agendas of early Jewish worship services (cf. Elbogen, *Gottesdienst;* listing at "Introduction to Cultic Poetry") we can only guess: the individual literary units of the book of Psalms were used in varying combinations in community services. The same assertion is valid against growing tendencies to treat the Psalter, in its ultimate "edition," as a uniform book for meditational reading, as N. Füglister, N. Lohfink, E. Zenger, P. D. Miller, and J. C. McCann, with varying emphases, propose in many publications (see Additional Bibliography, section C; and Gerstenberger, "Psalter"; → Psalms 72 and 73). While the archaic form elements of a petitionary ritual have largely been preserved, the generalizing tendencies in our psalm now point to a congregational service, perhaps with a communal recitation of the prayer. The "I," in this case, is each individual participant of the service. Prayers in the "I" form can be standard expressions for the worshiping group — down to our own Sunday services (cf. Klinghardt, "Prayer Formularies," Additional Bibliography, section B).

## Intention

The main emphasis is on confidence in God, who is experienced in the sanctuary and within the worshiping community. The communal prayer for all members wants to reassure everyone of a safe enclave in the midst of tribulations and solicits, in return, praises to God and continuous dedication to him, on an equal basis for everybody in need of divine assistance. Thinking about God in terms of nearness and intimacy, almost of physical touchability and most personal, warmest care, seems to be a pattern typical for family religion. State and heavenly deities normally keep an awe-inspiring distance (cf. Mayer).

## Bibliography

F. Asensio, "Teologia biblica de un tríptico: Salmos 61, 62 y 63," *EstBib* 21 (1962) 111-125; P. Auffret, "Essai sur la structure littéraire du psaume 61," *JANESCU* 14 (1982) 1-10; idem, "'Alors je jouerai sans fin pour ton nom.' Étude structurelle du psaume 61," *Science et Esprit* 36 (1984) 169-177; idem, "L'étude structurelle des psaumes: réponses et compléments 2," *Science et Esprit* 49 (1997) 39-61; W. H. Bellinger Jr., "How Shall We Read the Bible? The Case of Psalm 61," *Perspectives in Religious Studies* 20 (1993) 5-17; V. M. Beltram, "Cuatro padres ante un Salmo. El Salmo 61 comentado por Hilario, Ambrosio, Jerónimo y Agustín," *Teologia y Vida* 20 (1979) 63ff.; T. W. Cartledge, "Conditional Vows in the Psalms of Lament: A New Approach to an Old Problem," in *The Listening Heart (Fest.* R. E. Murphy; ed. K. Hoglund, et al.; JSOTSup 58; Sheffield: JSOT Press, 1987) 77-94; J. H. Eaton, "Music's Place in Worship: A Contribution from the

Psalms," in *Prophets, Worship, and Theodicy* (ed. J. Barton, et al.; Leiden: Brill, 1984) 85-107; E. S. Gerstenberger, "Der Psalter als Buch und als Sammlung," in *Neue Wege der Psalmenexegese* (ed. K. Seybold and E. Zenger; Herders biblische Studien 1; Freiburg: Herder, 1994) 3-13; D. Lenhard, *Vom Ende der Erde rufe ich zu Dir. Eine rabbinische Psalmenhomilie (PesR 9)* (Judaistische Studien 8; Frankfurt: Gesellschaft zur Förderung Judaistischer Studien, 1990); W. R. Mayer, "Ich rufe dich von ferne, höre mich von nahe," in *Werden und Wirken des Alten Testaments* (*Fest*. C. Westermann; ed. R. Albertz, et al.; Göttingen: Vandenhoeck & Ruprecht, 1980) 302-17; B. Weber, "Psalm LXI — Versuch einer hiskianischen Situierung," *VT* 43 (1993) 265-68.

# Psalm 62:
# Homily of Confidence

## Text

Some parts are garbled, especially the second line of v. 4 and v. 5. For the rest there is a clear although quite unaccustomed meaning to be discovered.

## Structure

|  | MT | NRSV |
|---|---|---|
| I. Superscription | 1 | - |
| II. Proclamation (Legitimation) | 2-3 | 1-2 |
| III. Censure | 4 | 3 |
| IV. Accusation | 5 | 4 |
| V. Proclamation (Legitimation) | 6-8 | 5-7 |
| VI. Exhortation | 9-13 | 8-12 |
|    A. Admonition | 9, 11 | 8, 10 |
|    B. Adage | 10 | 9 |
|    C. Assertion | 12 | 11 |
|    D. Aside (Prayer) | 13 | 12 |

"Jeduthun" is spelled slightly differently in two identical SUPERSCRIP-TIONS (→ Psalms 39; 77). The word is a personal name in 1 Chr 9:16; 16:38, 41-42; 25:1, 3, 6, etc., but could be a technical term referring to a liturgy or tune in the Psalm headings.

Being used to meeting songs and prayers in the Psalter we are puzzled by eloquent oratory, which in the very last verse (only formally?) turns into an address to God. Otherwise, the psalm seems a discourse directed to an audience; note the frequent direct address of a plurality of persons (vv. 4, 9, 11). Only once is the first person plural used (v. 9c; cf. v. 12, where a number of Hebrew MSS put the verb *šm'* into first plural instead of first singular). Strangely enough, there is no invocation to start out with, nor do we find clear-cut elements of complaint, thanksgiving, or hymn.

The psalm begins rather abruptly with a confessional statement apparently directed to a congregation (vv. 2-3), repeated and enlarged in due course to indicate its importance (vv. 6-8). In fact, these five lines constitute the very heart of our psalm. They disclose a single speaker anxious to asseverate the fountain of his ultimate trust. God (Yahweh?), "no one but he" (cf. vv. 3, 7), is the backbone of the speaker's life. Four of these lines open up with the emotional *'ak,* which may be translated either by emphatic "yes," "indeed" (cf. Weiser, 291) or by exclusive "only" (cf. Kraus, 594; and most translators; by contrast, A. Even-Shoshan, *Concordance* [Jerusalem: Kiryat-Sefer, 1983] 56, opts for positive accentuation). The frequency of this particle in Psalm 62 (6 times) is unparalleled (cf. 4 times in 39:6-7, 12 [RSV 5-6, 11]; however, these are only parallels to sapiential use, as in 62:10). "Confessional" *'ak* cannot be found in other psalms either (cf. 23:6; 37:8; 58:12 [RSV 11]; 68:7, 22 [RSV 6, 21]; 139:11). Thus there is unaccustomed rhetoric here, exalting God, the "rock," "help," "fortress" of the persecuted individual (vv. 3, 7; → Psalms 18; 31; 71; 91; the expression "he is my rock" has formulaic qualities; cf. 31:4; 71:3; Eichhorn, *Gott*). The "I," however, seems exemplary rather than existential. It is not invoking God, but being used as a model of piety (cf. the enigmatic *dûmîyāh napšî,* "my soul waits in silence" [? v. 2, similarly v. 6], which seems to be a stronger synonym for *bṭḥ,* "trust," vv. 9, 11) for those who are seeking their salvation elsewhere. This is a true piece of ostensive PROCLAMATION in a homiletic, not a petitionary, context. This is not to deny traces of plaintive utterances in our psalm; they are clearly of secondary import, though, and are apparently used to undergird confessional affirmations (cf. vv. 4-5). Vv. 2-3 and 6-8 on the surface could be refrains of a song or liturgy. They frame the attacks against the enemies (vv. 4-5) as if confidence in God could smother the evildoers. But unlike 42:6, 12; 43:5 our verses do not really close a strophe, nor do they in any way show any internal dialogue like the one in Psalms 42 and 43.

Following the pattern of psalms of contest (→ Psalms 4; 11) the speaker turns sharply against what seems to be his audience (vv. 4-5). Only the first line is fully intelligible, chiding, as it were, the murderous pursuits of treacherous listeners (v. 4: second person plural). We have to remember the strong social legislation in Israel, which protected the weak (cf. Deuteronomy 15; 24; Leviticus 19; 25, etc.), to classify this element as a CENSURE of society at hand. Unfortunately, the metaphors used to substantiate the verdict are not very lucid for us. An "inclining wall" and a "collapsed stone wall" (v. 4c) in our understanding hardly portray the treachery and viciousness of oppressors and exploiters. Still, comparable imagery plays some role in the complaints of Jeremiah (cf. Jer 15:20: *ḥômat něḥōšet,* a "bronze wall"; Am 5:19; Isa 30:12-13: misguided trust is "like a crack in a high wall"). To make it more difficult, however, v. 5 switches into third person plural, denouncing the wicked for violence and treacherous slander (*ndḥ* Hiphil is formulaic in Dtr language: "expel"; cf. Deut 30:1; Jer 8:3; 16:15; 23:3, 8; 24:9; etc. To be addicted to lying [vv. 5, 10] and to pretend to be good but act maliciously [v. 5] are common accusations against a rotten society; cf. Pss 4:3 [RSV 2]; 5:7 [RSV 6]; 58:4 [RSV 3]; Hos 12:2; Prov 19:22; Pss 35:12-18; 41:7 [RSV 6]). The orator uses standard vocabulary apparently to intimidate his audience, presupposing a congregation of sinners, who disregard and violate human beings (cf. *'al 'îš*, "against anyone," v. 4). The message of putting all trust in God — a rhetorical device of all ages — is repeated and amplified in vv. 6-8, to lead into a calmer EXHORTATION (vv. 9-13). The orator uses several patterns of discourse to drive home his homiletical intentions. First, there is again the direct admonition to trust in God alone (vv. 9, 11; cf. vv. 2-3, 6-8). The key term is nothing less than *bṭḥ*, "to trust" (vv. 9, 11, admonition and warning), accompanied by parallel expressions. Thus v. 9b equates "pouring out one's heart" (cf. 102:1 [RSV superscription]) with "trusting." And v. 11 juxtaposes "trusting in God" with "trusting in extortion, robbery, and wealth," social and economic crimes corrupting society (cf. Isa 30:12: "you trust in extortion and falsity and rely on them"). This cluster of social ills may indicate the state of affairs after the defeat at the hands of the Babylonians (cf. E. S. Gerstenberger, *TWAT* VI, 441-46; Ezek 18:10-18; Ps 146:7-9; Lev 19:11-14; Deut 28:29-34). Aiming at individual behavior and responsibility — that much is certain — the discourse nevertheless applies to the whole audience. A few words attached to v. 9 testify to the communal situation: "God is our refuge" (v. 9c) may be either a congregational response to the sermon, or a real allocutional phrase whereby the preacher, formerly a distinct "I," now identifies with his audience. The trust motif altogether is an important theme in the OT, most of all in exilic-postexilic literature (cf. E. S. Gerstenberger, *THAT* I, 300-305), and it certainly lends itself to preaching purposes (cf. 2 Kings 18; Jer 7:1-15). "Trusting" becomes a synonym for "constituting one's identity" (cf. J. Limburg, *ABD* V, 534-35; Miller, *They Cried,* 178-232; listing in Additional Bibliography, section C).

To support the direct exhortative discourse the speaker (or the redactor?) puts in another *'ak* sentence drawn from wisdom sources (v. 10), a real ADAGE. We came across a close formal and substantial parallel already (39:6-7, 12 [RSV 5-6, 11]). The book of Qohelet is full of similar affirmations (without the *'ak* introduction, however). Drawing on generalizing wisdom resources, at this point, the psalmist undergirds the analysis of vv. 4, 5 above and lends more weight to the thesis that we are dealing with a theological discourse rather than a prayer formula. The remaining two elements, ASSERTION and prayer-styled ASIDE (vv. 12-13), pointing away from the congregation, again legitimate the orator. Reference to God's communication by way of an indeterminate number scheme (v. 12 [RSV 11]) is a sapiential and obviously a homiletical device (cf. Job 4:12-16; 33:14; etc.). And to turn to God directly at the end of the sermon even today proves the close relationship of orator and God. The final line (v. 13bc [RSV 12bc]) gives strength to the whole speech: whoever will trust in God will receive just retribution. Possibly, the very act of trusting already conveys the reward.

## Genre

Official speech before a congregation instead of prayer seems an odd classification in the Psalter, and most form critics would not agree with it. As a rule, they understand the suppliant as voicing his personal confidence in God (e.g.,

Gunkel, 263; Mowinckel, *W* I, 220; Anderson, I, 450; Tate, 119-21; Mays, 215-17). Yet "structure" tells a different story. Language, form elements, internal structure, imagery, and theological outlook make the poem an allocution to a listening audience, a true HOMILY with a strong, confessional, outreaching "refrain" in vv. 2-3, 6-8. There are precedents for this mode of liturgical communication in psalmic texts. For example, thanksgiving songs include a joyful, exhortatory speech by the one saved (cf. 22:23-25 [RSV 22-24]; 32:6-11). In hymns we find didactic thrusts (cf. Psalms 8; 19; 78). Liturgical customs and speech forms may have influenced or even produced much of OT literature outside the Psalter (cf. E. S. Gerstenberger, "Predigt," *TRE* XXVII, 231-35; F. B. Craddock, *ABD* V, 451-54). Large parts of the so-called Priestly as well as Dtr and prophetic traditions are in fact couched in direct-address form. Not only the prophets but also Moses articulates God's own words to the congregation (SPEECH OF GOD). In the psalms the divine voice is raised as well, directly, it seems, but in reality it is mediated through an official speaker (cf. v. 12; 50:1-6; 81:6-7 [RSV 5-6]; 82:1-2; Koenen, *Gottesworte;* Miller, *They Cried,* 135-77, both listed in Additional Bibliography, section C). The pervasive force of this model of communication throughout the canonical Hebrew literature — "ordained" men speaking for and in the place of God himself — has not as yet been thoroughly studied. In our instance, the speaker emphasizes his decision for Israel's God, apparently defended under pressures from co-religionists. And he chastises and admonishes his congregation as a person authorized by God (cf. vv. 12-13). A vivid example of this kind of preaching could be Joshua's sermon: "Now therefore revere Yahweh and serve him in sincerity and faithfulness . . . as for me and my household, we will serve Yahweh!" (Josh 24:14-15 et passim). Traces of similar confessions and legitimations of preachers can also be found in the prophetic literature (cf. Mic 7:7; Hab 2:1; Isa 49:1-3; 50:4-9 [with following exhortation, vv. 10-11]) and in some narrative contexts (cf. Deut 32:1-3 [a song understood as "instruction"!]; 2 Sam 22:2-5). The congregational preacher of exilic-postexilic times (besides the suppliant of complaints and thanksgivings) may loom behind all these confessional and legitimizing discourses in the first person singular.

## Setting

Where, we must ask, would such homilies have taken place in early biblical times? The only feasible answer may be: in Jewish community worship starting with the exile and developing into synagogue meetings. The verbal element — Torah, Prophets, and Psalms — became dominant at that period, when sacrifices had ceased or receded into the background and when leaders emerged able to mediate the will of Yahweh, as Moses, Joshua, Ezra, and their successors did. They would stand in front of the congregation (cf. Exod 19:14-15; Deut 1:1, 3; 29:1 [RSV 2]; Josh 24:1-2; Neh 8:1-4). In this solemn ceremonial situation, which reflects exilic and postexilic customs, the "I" of the speaker, the "you" (second person plural) of the audience, the evident authority of God, who communicates with the people by way of his mediators, the "we" and "us" of the congregation (cf. Scharbert, "Das 'Wir,'" listed at "Introduction to Psalms") appear almost naturally. The emphasis on the exclusive trust in Yahweh, in whom the people are united (and nothing else besides him could tie them together), the strong accentuation of social justice demanded by their unique Lord, the depth of wisdom placed at the disposal of those confiding in God — all these spiritual and theological features belong in the realm of a communicative worship. Therefore the life setting of our HOMILY was the early Jewish congregation of Yahweh believers. There it still may be found around the world in Jewish and Christian congregations.

## Intention

What are sermons up to? Do they communicate the true and living Word of God? Are they to be channeled through licensed preachers only (cf. Num 12:2)? Modern questions confirm the lasting significance of the ancient postures: homilies pretend to communicate life-giving and life-preserving force from God; they want to nurture, correct, and edify the congregation of the faithful. This is achieved by presenting glorious examples of trust in God, and — unfortunately or laudably so? — also by denouncing and eventually destroying opponents, evilmongers, enemies of flesh and blood, those responsible for the ills of this world (cf. Gerstenberger, "Enemies"; listing at "Introduction to Psalms").

## Bibliography

D. Bland, "Exegesis of Psalm 62," *Restoration Quarterly* 23 (1980) 82-95; D. Eichhorn, *Gott als Fels, Burg und Zuflucht* (Bern/Frankfurt: P. Lang, 1976) 36-38; M. R. Hauge, *Between Sheol and Temple: Motif Structure and Function in the I-Psalms* (JSOTSup 178; Sheffield: Sheffield Academic Press, 1995) 243-80; A. M. Honeyman, "ID, DU and Psalm 62,12," *VT* 11 (1961) 348-50; Z. Kameeta, "Why, O Lord: Psalms and Sermons from Namibia," *Risk* 28 (1986) 1-62; F. de Meyer, "La dimension sapientale du Psaume 62," *Bijdragen* 42 (1981) 350-65; K. Seybold, "Asyl? Psalm 62 — Zeugnis eines Verfolgten," *Zeitschrift für Mission* 18 (1992) 2-5; B. Weber, "Ps 62,12-13: Kolometrie, Zahlenspruch und Gotteswort," *BN* 65 (1992) 44-47; R. Zadok, "Onomastic, Prosopographic, and Lexical Notes," *BN* 65 (1992) 47-54.

# Psalm 63:
## Thanksgiving Prayer

### Structure

|  | MT | NRSV |
|---|---|---|
| I. Superscription | 1 | - |
| II. Invocation | 2 | 1 |

|  |  | 2a | 1a |
|---|---|---|---|
| A. | Appellation | 2a | 1a |
| B. | Description of longing | 2bcd | 1bcd |
| III. | Affirmation of confidence | 3-5 | 2-4 |
| IV. | Thanksgiving | 6-9 | 5-8 |
| V. | Imprecation and intercession | 10-12 | 9-11 |
| A. | Imprecation | 10-11 | 9-10 |
| B. | Intercession | 12ab | 11ab |
| C. | Imprecation | 12c | 11c |

Verse 1 constitutes one of the thirteen "historical" SUPERSCRIPTIONS connecting a specific psalm with the biography of King David, the royal singer and organizer of worship of old (see 1 Sam 16:21-23; 2 Sam 1:17-27; 3:33-34; 1 Chr 16:4-42). The mention of arid lands in v. 2 may have prompted the reference to David's sojourn in the wilderness (see 1 Sam 23:14; 24:2; → Psalm 3).

Psalm 63 has its own delicate vocabulary, which has some affinities with the wording and outlook of Psalms 42/43; 73; 84. Verbs of intense longing for and intimately relating to God dominate the first part of the poem: *šḥr,* Piel, "search eagerly"; *ṣm',* "to thirst"; *kmh* (unique occurrence in Hebrew Scripture), "to desire" (all v. 2); *ḥzh lir'ôt,* "to look in order to behold"; *šbḥ,* Piel, "to praise" (v. 3); *dbq,* "to stick to" (v. 9). Localities mentioned include the holy precincts (v. 3), the waterless desert (v. 2), and the private home of the worshiper (v. 7). God is addressed consistently in vv. 2-9, and the mood is deeply spiritual, almost mystical.

Formal elements do not stand out that sharply as in other "I" psalms; this gives rise to speculations about a possible synthesis of biographical experiences and ideological constructions (see Hauge, listed at Psalm 62). The INVOCATION comprises the direct appellation "God" (not "Yahweh"; → FOTL XIV, 37) and a strong personal confession: "You are my God!" (see 22:11 [RSV 10]; 118:28; 140:7 [RSV 6]; Vorländer, *Gott* [listed at "Introduction to Cultic Poetry"]). This formula reflects age-old family and clan customs to adopt a protective deity, as Jacob did during his flight to Haran (Gen 28:20-21; later on many times ridiculed; see Isa 44:17; Jer 2:27; → Psalm 22). Besides the shorter name *'ēlî,* the longer form *'ĕlōhay,* "my God," also is used in the formula (see Pss 31:15 [RSV 14]; 143:10). Personal confession is the basis for expressions of longing in v. 2; "waterless, arid land" is probably a metaphor corresponding to the verb "thirst" in the preceding line. It may also intimate the dust-dry netherworld (Barth, *Errettung;* listing at "Introduction to Psalms"). Ps 42:2-3 (RSV 1-2) employs animal imagery instead. Expressions of longing like this also have a plaintive touch about them. They reveal a severe want of the presence of the protective deity and an extreme longing for the place the deity can be venerated (v. 3; cf. Psalm 84; Ruppert). The worship situation thus comes to the fore; cf. the technical expression for "praying" in v. 5b ("lifting up my hands").

Three lines of AFFIRMATION OF CONFIDENCE blend into the statements of longing (vv. 3-5). Two lines start with the autonomous *kēn,* "thus," "so" (vv. 3, 5), not aligned to any other particle (as, e.g., in 18:50 [RSV 49]; 48:9, 11 [RSV 8, 10]; 65:10 [RSV 9]; 128:4) or phrase. The perfect with following infinitive, "I [may] see you in order to behold your power" (v. 3), expresses trust based in real spiritual experience, as in 3:8 (RSV 7); 61:4 (RSV 3). The middle line between the two *kēn* phrases has hymnic, emphatic *kî*, "surely," as an opening exclamation (v. 4; see 52:11 [RSV 9]; 54:8 [RSV 6]; 69:17 [RSV 16]; 100:5; 106:1; 107:1; 109:21). These and other passages demonstrate the formulaic use of *kî tôb*, "surely good (is the Lord, etc.)," in ceremonial agendas, the exact parallels of the prayer formula in v. 4a ("Surely, good is your steadfast love") being 69:17 (RSV 16) and 109:21. A fuller liturgical form, of course, is the hymnic CALL TO WORSHIP: "Give thanks to Yahweh, for he is good; his steadfast love endures forever!" (→ 106:1; 107:1; 118:1; 136:1-3). The second *kēn* line (v. 5) sounds like a Vow to praise (in the future), but in a noncomplaint context it seems reasonable to think of an actual practice and future commitment (see 61:9 [RSV 8]).

That this indeed is the case comes to the fore in the following THANKSGIVING section (vv. 6-9). The regular thanksgiving song recounts past troubles and hails salvation brought forth by God (see "Introduction to Cultic Poetry," section 4C). In Psalm 63, however, there are only vague hints at God's help, and no traces of concrete dangers luckily overcome. The feeling of thankfulness is a general one. When the officiant recites the prayer, he is imagining the faithful on his bed, during the night (v. 7; see 6:7 [RSV 6]; 41:4 [RSV 3]; 119:148; 132:3). In particular, 119:147-148 testifies to nightly meditations, presumably at home. Incubation in the temple may loom behind, as well; see 5:4 (RSV 3; → Psalm 5, "Setting"; cf. Janowski, *Rettungsgewissheit*). Only v. 8a refers to God's help, though in most general terms (see 22:20 [RSV 19]; 40:18 [RSV 17]; 70:6 [RSV 5]; 121:1-2). Closest parallels of the expression "You have been my help" (v. 8a) can be found in 27:9 (in the parallel line: "God of my help") and 94:17 ("If Yahweh had not been my help . . ."). Both instances portray a highly trustworthy Deity, not an individual rescue operation. Ensuing avowals (vv. 8b, 9) underscore the permanent meanings: the "I" is "glued to God" (v. 9a: verb in perfect tense), and "jubilates in the shadows of your wings" (v. 8b: verb in imperfect tense). Intertwining artfully God's and the suppliant's actions, v. 9b says: "Your right hand upholds me" (*tmk;* cf. 16:5; 41:13 [RSV 12]; Isa 41:10; 42:1). The whole element therefore voices thanks and praises to God for securities and blessings granted in abundance (cf. "fat" and "oil" as metaphors of overflowing grace, v. 6a; equally in Pss 36:6-10 [RSV 5-9], which reads like a commentary on our vv. 6-9; 65:12 [RSV 11]; 133:2; the fat belongs to Yahweh, Lev 3:16; Tate, 128). Liturgically, thanksgiving and trust are the gravitational center of Psalm 63.

In the absence of acute dangers and without the slightest intimation of enemies in vv. 2-9, the sudden shift to IMPRECATION (vv. 10-12) is irritating to the modern reader. But we are dealing with liturgical literature, and the breaks and jumps of logical reasoning are due to ceremonial necessities or else to redactional carelessness. That the former holds true can be deduced from frequent abrupt changes in the Psalms (see 22:22-23 [RSV 21-22]; 31:19-20 [RSV 18-19]; etc.). Specifically, the unmitigated, unwarranted transition from thankful and hymnic language to denunciation and condemnation also occurs, for example, in → Psalms 104 and 139 to the point that some editors of the book of Psalms did weed out such offensive polemics. Exilic and postexilic agendas for worship probably included IMPRECATION in an effort to ward off possible interference with peace and justice by prophylactically denouncing evilmongers. There was no doubt whatsoever that they existed, and painful experience proved this fact all along. IMPRECATION thus should be understood as a liturgical companion to PETITION on the one hand and INTERCESSION on the other. There was, in OT complaint and petitionary services, an inherent need to combat the roots of evil, sometimes to be located in evil-wishing or cursing neighbors (cf. v. 12c; 62:4-5 [RSV 3-4]; 109).

The element at hand (vv. 10-12) in the Hebrew text starts out with a death wish against unknown and unnamed criminals: "They [shall go] to hell [*lĕšô'āh*, "to destruction"]! They seek my life. To the netherworld with them!" (v. 10). The curse character of IMPRECATION is obvious; it is also apparent in the death wishes of v. 11. Unmotivated, as far as we can see, there follow an INTERCESSION for the king and a blessing for those who support him ("swear by him," v. 12; see 61:7-8 [RSV 6-7]) only to be topped by another malediction (v. 12c; *skr*, Niphal, "to be stopped," another hapax legomenon in Psalm 63). Again, as in → Psalm 61, mention of the king does not automatically place the text in the time of the Judean monarchy. Obligatory, nostalgic, or messianic uses of the designation are possible.

The sequence of liturgical elements does not need to be rearranged to make sense. Although invocation, confidence, and imprecation are standard in complaint songs, they serve different ends here. Invocation does not aim at pleading for help but at expressing deep loyalty to God. Affirmation of confidence does not prepare petition but — together with the following expressions of gratitude — portrays the worshiper as totally aligned with God (cf. the last line: "My self sticks to you, your right hand upholds me," v. 9; in this instance "stick" or "be glued to" expresses most intimate communion; cf. Gen 2:24; Deut 4:4; Ps 119:31; Ruth 1:14). Imprecation does not mean to destroy specific enemies but appears to be a precautionary measure, possibly reflecting severe inner-Jewish tensions. Intercession comes in, as in Psalm 61, as a *superadditum* due to some extraordinary situation.

## Genre/Setting

Structure, vocabulary, imagery, and theological outlook all point to communal use of this prayer. The "I" form does not serve individuals in their concrete plights and in familial ritual centered around one person. Rather, all the generalizing, liturgical features betray communal use, probably by one officiant, for the congregation or with groups of sufferers (cf. "Introduction to Psalms," section 2). The worshiping community, it is true, does consist of worshiping individuals (as in our own parishes today). Therefore the "I" is perfectly appropriate. Psalm 63 is a PRAYER OF CONFIDENCE (→ Psalm 23, which is still more directed to individual needs, and Psalm 12 with similar grades of congregational use). The emerging synagogal assembly of Yahweh believers has brought forth not only homilies like Psalm 62, but also confessional prayers reflecting the strong individual/communal identification with the God of the congregation. For the possibility that Psalms 61–63 once formed a liturgical unit →

Psalm 61: *Genre/Setting.* If this compilation or the grouping together of Psalms 61–63 reflects a joint use of these texts, we should think of a worship setting, and Psalm 62 still may be considered a sermon, while Psalm 63 could be the prayer response of the audience. Our psalm seems to be oriented toward the sanctuary (vv. 3-5, 8) but does count on private spiritual experiences (v. 7) as well. Also, references to Zion or Jerusalem are missing. Therefore we do not have sufficient evidence to label the text a "prayer of one looking for asylum" (Delekat; Seybold, 248; cf. idem, "Asyl?"; listing at Psalm 62). Temple language and concepts have probably been taken over into the assemblies of Judean communities in exile or in the province. "Seeing God" (v. 3) by visiting his/her statue in the sanctuary is a common Near Eastern experience; it may have lost its real dimension in Israel's aniconic worship, as the expression is now used metaphorically. With good reasons, Smith *(Pilgrimage Pattern)* insists that the phrase had a real meaning also in OT texts.

## Intention

Official prayers of trust, thanksgivings, and praise of course represent the congregation over against the Deity worshiped in joint ceremony. They are strong expressions of common faith and expectation, extraordinary means of group identification. On the other hand, the very personal and emotional model of the "true confider in Yahweh," formally presented to God, becomes the stimulus and matrix for every single member of the congregation. Ultimate trust belongs to God alone and to nothing else (cf. Ps 62:11 [RSV 10]). The prayer has a clear message: "Your steadfast love is better than life" (Mays, 217-18).

## Bibliography

P. Auffret, "'Ma bouche s'adonnera à la louange': Étude structurelle du Psaume 63," *Église et théologie* 20 (1989) 359-84; N. Baumert, "Omeiromenoi in 1 Thess 2:8," *Bib* 68 (1987) 552-63; W. Beyerlin, *Die Rettung der Bedrängten in den Feindpsalmen* (FRLANT 99; Göttingen: Vandenhoeck & Ruprecht, 1970) 135-38; R. Bothe, "Meditation über Psalm 63:7," *Evangelische Aspekte* 8 (1998) 3-4; A. R. Ceresko, "A Note on Psalm 63: A Psalm of Vigil," *ZAW* 92 (1980) 435-36; E. Jacob, "Prier avec les Psaumes," *Foi et Vie* 84 (1985) 58-66; R. Gelio, "Osservazioni citiche su uno *ḥazah* 'gioire' usato per lo piu in contesto liturgico (Is 28,15; Es 24,11; Sal 63,3; 27,4; Gb 8,17)," *Ephemerides liturgicae* 100 (1986) 73-95; B. Janowski, *Rettungsgewissheit und Epiphanie des Heils* (WMANT 59; Neukirchen-Vluyn: Neukirchener Verlag, 1989); J. L. Mays, "The David of the Psalms," *Int* 40 (1986) 143-55; G. von Rad, "'Gerechtigkeit' und 'Leben' in der Kultsprache der Psalmen," (1950), repr. in idem, *Gesammelte Studien zum Alten Testament I* (TBü 8; Munich: Chr. Kaiser, 1958) 225-47 (Eng.: see listing at "Introduction to Psalms"); L. Ruppert, "Dürsten nach Gott," in *Die alttestamentliche Botschaft als Wegweisung* (ed. J. Zmijewski; Stuttgart: Katholisches Bibelwerk, 1990) 237-51; M. S. Smith, *The Pilgrimage Pattern in Exodus* (JSOTSup 239; Sheffield: Sheffield Academic Press, 1997) 100-109.

# Psalm 64:
# Complaint of the Individual

## Structure

|  | MT | NRSV |
|---|---|---|
| I. Superscription | 1 | - |
| II. Invocation and plea | 2-3 | 1-2 |
| III. Complaint | 4-7 | 3-6 |
| IV. Announcement of destruction; imprecation | 8-9 | 7-8 |
| V. Announcement of salvation; beatitude | 10-11 | 9-10 |
| A. Announcement of salvation | 10 | 9 |
| B. Announcement of bliss; beatitude | 11 | 10 |

The SUPERSCRIPTION, as in → Psalm 13, has only a technical term and a standard reference to David's real or spiritual authorship. The Hebrew text attributes 73 psalms to the second king of Israel, the Greek tradition (LXX) 84, proof of a growing Davidic theological consciousness.

The INVOCATION begins with a call to God (not Yahweh! v. 2a: so-called Elohistic Psalter, Psalms 42–83; see FOTL XIV, 37) alerting God to an individual sufferer in deep trouble. In contexts of complaint prayer, śîaḥ, "concern," indicates life threats and intense suffering (see 1 Sam 1:16; Job 7:13; Pss 55:3 [RSV 2]; 102:1 [RSV superscription]; 142:3 [RSV 2]). 'ĕlōhîm is called upon, although Yahweh comes to be named in v. 11 (in a redactional phrase?). The opening half-line thus resembles 61:2a (RSV 1a); see also 4:2d (RSV 1d); 17:1, 6b; 27:7a; 28:2a; 54:4a (RSV 2a); 84:9a (RSV 8a); 102:2a (RSV 1a); 130:2a; 143:1a. Yet in all these passages the verb šm' is accompanied by other expressions of pleading. As a rule INVOCATION is an important preliminary act in any ritual (see, e.g., 5:2-3 [RSV 1-2]; 102:2-3 [RSV 1-2]; Evans-Pritchard, *Nuer Religion,* 208-11 [listing at "Introduction to Cultic Poetry"]: invocation is a statement of intention to the deity who receives the sacrifice). If it is shortened to one verbal phrase, as in 64:2a, this must be a liturgical sign of urgency (see 6:2a [RSV 1a]: only appellation "Yahweh"; 69:2a [RSV 1a]; 109:1).

The following cola (vv. 2b, 3) are actually full-blown PETITIONS. They do not tarry with INITIAL PLEA, asking for permission to enter into the presence of the Lord, to speak to him and bring problems to his attention. Rather, they put all anxious expectations held by the worshiping group into three calls for help. More precisely, the suppliant requests protection from enemies, pictured as "terrible foes" (*paḥad 'ôyēb,* v. 2b), "gang of evildoers" (*sôd mĕrē'îm,* v. 3a), and "calamity-mongers" (*pô'ălê 'āwen,* v. 3b). The exact designations are not frequent in Hebrew Scripture, but they belong to the large field of enemy imagery (see Mowinckel, *PsSt* I; Keel, *Feinde;* listing at "Introduction to Psalms"; → Psalms 22; 69). The sheer number and horrible creativeness of naming enemies (Keel lists 99 expressions for the Psalter, *Feinde,* 93-98) suggest their importance, reflecting contemporary social reality as well as mythical/magical beliefs. Potentially, a sick or stigmatized person could be surrounded by ill-intentioned foes, and be victim to that well-known scapegoat effect virulent in small communities (cf. Girard, *Scapegoat* [*Bouc émissaire*], Additional Bibliography, section B). What these mortal adversaries do at this point is only hinted at: they terrorize, design plots, agitate (in Hebrew three nouns with the preposition *min,* "from," meaning: "Keep me safe from such machinations." Cf. Mowinckel's designation: "protective psalm," *W* I, 219-20).

The psalm does not voice any other demands on God. The next element simply describes profusely in ever so potent words how the enemies act and what they are up to (COMPLAINT, vv. 4-7). In spite of martial metaphors the emphasis is not on physical violence. No, the foes harass their (innocent?) victim with slander, evil words. Mowinckel (*PsSt* I) was certainly correct in thinking inclusively of malice wrought by black magic (see also Fortune, *Sorcerers;* listing at "Introduction to Cultic Poetry"; also many entries in Additional Bibliography, section B). By word of mouth they cause sudden destruction; they act in secret, and even boast of their hidden art (v. 6). They keep their practice clandestine (v. 7 is somewhat corrupt and hard to understand). All in all, well-known schemes of conspiracy against others, mobbing and discrimination, marginalization and arbitrary incrimination (key words: "tongue" = evil speech; "bitter words" = poisoning rumors; "bad words" = damaging discourse, in vv. 3, 5) are denounced, giving us information about the negative side of ancient Israelite society (→ Psalms 36; 55; 69; on slander: B. Kedar-Kopfstein, *TWAT* IV, esp. 601-5; R. Mosis, *TWAT* IV, 111-30; on black magic see Mowinckel, *PsSt* I; J. K. Kuemmerlin-McLean, *ABD* IV, 468-71). Military jargon ("arrows," "shooting," "ambush," "snares"; on the last cf. Keel, *Symbolism,* 89; Additional Bibliography, Section B) is customary in the genre, adding to the poignancy of our prayer. In addition, words or thoughts of the foes are quoted verbatim (v. 6c; by emendation of the Hebrew text some modern exegetes extend the quotation into v. 7ab) — a common feature in individual complaints (→ 3:3 [RSV 2]; 22:9 [RSV 8]; 35:21). The DESCRIPTION OF ENEMIES and their evildoing is thus quite an important element in some complaints or sapiential diatribes (→ 10:3-11; cf. 7:13-16 [RSV 12-15]; 11:2; 57:5, 7 [RSV 4, 6]; 120:4; 140:2-6 [RSV 1-5]). It does have both psychological and social functions, serving as it were to articulate all that is hurting and revulsive, even within one's own being, and to tear or purge it out of the social group.

The following lines (vv. 8-10) have four *waw*-consecutives, i.e., "narrative" verbal forms, which obviously in this case do not refer to the past but anticipate future action. Follow-up verbs in each instance are in the perfect or imperfect form. The imperfect seems normal to IMPRECATIONS: see 35:26; 55:24; 63:11, and well-wishes: see 35:27; 40:17. Gunkel emends to an imperfect; Kraus keeps the narrative and takes them to be reports of past events. Mays: "The psalmist describes what God will do" (*Psalms,* 219). Seybold (p. 251) relies on preserved jussives in vv. 9b and 11a, emending to their likeness all the annoying consecutive imperfects. An explanation is given by Michel (*Tempora,* 15-30; listing at "Introduction to Psalms"): he investigates 65 cases of unexpected consecutive imperfects in the Psalter. They do not narrate events in the past but indicate consecutive action in any tense, depending on context (cf. 30:12 [RSV 11]; 92:10-12 [RSV 9-11]).

The first two lines (vv. 8-9) take up military imagery and appear to be de-

18

nunciations of evildoers. God kills them by arrow, analogous to their schemes (v. 8; cf. v. 4). But in v. 9 the subject changes to a plural: "they make him stumble on account [by means?] of their tongue" (v. 9a). Who is doing what? The MT is: "They will make him stumble, their tongue over them," which does not make much sense. The phrases would be a belated accusation of the enemies. A rearrangement of two consonants yields this sentence: "He will make them stumble because of their tongue," a parallel threat to that of v. 8a. In terms of formal consistency this emendation seems more likely. Because of the peculiar verbal forms we may call this section an ANNOUNCEMENT OF DESTRUCTION, with an affinity to IMPRECATION (→ 109:6-19; 63:10-11 [RSV 9-10]).

Also, consecutive imperfects continue into v. 10, the subject of this phrase being the positive crowd, "all men," as it were. They either are to "fear" God (MT) or to "see" him (other Hebrew MSS). The difference in Hebrew is only one *yod;* the sequence "see" *(r'h)* and "proclaim" *(ngd,* Hiphil) or of close synonyms is attested more frequently (see, e.g., 40:6 [RSV 5]; 66:5-8 [RSV 4-7]; 69:33 [RSV 32]; 71:17 [RSV 16]; Isa 41:19-20; 48:6; inverted order, e.g., Ps 97:6). A formulaic expression even states: "see and fear" (40:4 [RSV 3]; 52:8 [RSV 6]; Isa 41:5), and fear does not normally lead to eulogies. Be that as it may, vv. 10-11 are the other side of the coin: while vv. 8-9 denounce enemies, vv. 10-11 indirectly praise God, who saves from their power. This fact is demonstrated by those faithful (only v. 11a mentions the *ṣaddîq* as *pars pro toto* in the singular; all other phrases use plural forms) who acknowledge the saving acts of their God, and happily sing his glory. The last element of our psalm mirrors an announcement of destruction and is therefore an ANNOUNCEMENT OF SALVATION. The final phrase in essence comes close to being a BEATITUDE (which, of course, is normally introduced by *'ašrê,* "happy"; see 1:1; 128:1).

## *Genre/Setting*

Invocation, petition, and complaint are characteristic of the COMPLAINT OF THE INDIVIDUAL; imprecation and well-wishing basically do not disturb the picture (see "Introduction to Cultic Poetry," section 4B; "Introduction to Psalms," section 2). The end of Psalm 64, however, seems to be more generalized, ridiculing not personal but communal enemies, addressing itself to a larger audience (cf. "all men" in v. 10a; "the upright of heart" in v. 11b), using sapiential language and concepts, lacking the individual suppliant's voice. According to the basic liturgical pattern of individual complaints, we would expect deft, extensive imprecations of foes and warm, personal vows of thanksgiving. The elements at hand (a) echo faintly the vigorous denunciations, and (b) dissipate into a vague benediction for all humankind. Our conclusion is: the older genre COMPLAINT OF THE INDIVIDUAL has been adapted somewhat to the needs of later community life and worship. The essentials of the older genre have been preserved, however. This leads me to believe that the early Jewish community did practice petitionary rites for individual sufferers in worship services, a kind of communal care for the miserable (→ Psalm 12). Jeremias, on the other hand (*Kultprophetie,* 119-20; listing at "Introduction to Psalms"), considers the *waw-*

consecutive imperfects of vv. 8-9a typical modes of communication by cultic prophets (visualized events are experienced as having occurred).

## Intention

The original complaint of the individual had been a liturgical prayer for the suffering person to be spoken in a small prayer service (→ e.g., Psalms 3–7; 31; 35; 38). Psalm 64 probably aims at a larger congregation assembled for worship. It wants to communicate to everyone in the community that God is ready to defend the faithful against any attacks by slanderers, who are so dangerous in close-knit groups. To denounce their disastrous activities and demonstrate how they surely must fail is at the same time an effort to strengthen straightforward solitary relations within the congregation.

## Bibliography

G. W. Anderson, "Enemies and Evildoers in the Book of Psalms," *BJRL* 48 (1965) 16-29; M. L. Barré, "A Proposal on the Crux of Psalm LXIV 9A," *VT* 46 (1996) 115-19; W. H. Bellinger Jr., "Psalms of the Falsely Accused: A Reassessment," *SBLSP* 25 (1986) 463-69; C. Curti, "Una duplice interpretazione di Ps LXIV,9 negli esegeti greci e latini," *Academia Nacionale dei Lencei, Rendiconti delle scienze morali* 33 (1978) 67-82; A. Strobel, "Le psaume LXIV," *RB* 57 (1950) 161-73; R. J. Tournay, "Le Psaume 149 et la 'vengeance' des pauvres de YHWH," *RB* 92 (1985) 349-58.

## Psalm 65:
## Hymnic Prayer

### Structure

|  | MT | NRSV |
|---|---|---|
| I. Superscription | 1 | - |
| II. Praise of God | 2-4 | 1-3 |
| A. Invocation | 2ab | 1ab |
| B. Adoration | 2c-3 | 1c-2 |
| C. Confession of sin | 4ab | 3ab |
| D. Assurance of forgiveness | 4c | 3c |
| III. Communal petition | 5 | 4 |
| A. Beatitude | 5ab | 4ab |
| B. Petition (wish) | 5cd | 4cd |
| IV. Hymn | 6-9 | 5-8 |
| A. Praise of God | 6ab | 5ab |
| B. Hymn to the Creator | 6c-8 | 5c-7 |
| C. Description of jubilance | 9 | 8 |

| V. Communal thanksgiving | 10-14 | 9-13 |
|---|---|---|
| A. Praise of the Sustainer | 10-12 | 9-11 |
| B. Description of jubilance | 13-14 | 12-13 |

Standard elements, as frequently used in books 1 and 2 of the Psalter, make up the SUPERSCRIPTION (→ Psalms 4; 13–15). "A Song" (šîr) seems to be an addition possibly precipitated by the very last word of the psalm: "they sing." Not knowing the particular technical meaning of the Hebrew substantive šîr (43 times in the Psalter; see G. Brunert, et al., TWAT VII, 1263), we may conjecture that it stresses the hymnic quality of a poem (→ Psalms 30; 45; 67; 68; 149 and their superscriptions). LXX imaginatively extends the heading: "Of Jeremiah and Ezekiel, under the rule of deportation, when they were about to march out"; cf. similar prophetic references in LXX Psalms 145–148 ("of Haggai and Zechariah").

The psalm at hand is form-critically an intricate specimen, abounding in direct-address discourse to God and revealing its communal background by first-person plural speech and deep identification with worship and sanctuary. The opening part (vv. 2-4) in a very concise and at times obscure way touches on vital concerns of a worshiping community, employing — for a hymn proper this is strange (one would expect "summons to praise") — direct-address prayer language (see Crüsemann, Studien, 174-202; listing at "Introduction to Cultic Poetry"). The INVOCATION ("God in/on Zion": the concept of Yahweh dwelling there is well attested [Isa 31:9; Joel 4:17, 21 (RSV 3:17, 21); Pss 99:2; 102:22 (RSV 21)] but the appellation mentioned seems oddly unique; cf. Ps 84:8), the normal start of a prayer, is reworked into a hymnic address. What does the first line mean: "To you silence is praise, O God on Zion!" (v. 2ab; thence J. Rist's hymn: "Man lobt dich in der Stille")? The second line (vv. 2c, 3a) also starts with "To you," the third (v. 3b) with "Toward you." The whole passage sounds very intimate, its main topics being "praise," private "vows" as response to "prayer" (tĕpillāh, v. 3a), "sins" and "atonement" ('āwôn, peša', kpr, v. 4). First person singular and plural do, however, collide in v. 4: MT has "prevail over me," some Hebrew MSS and LXX read "over us." Immediately afterwards "our sins" are mentioned. This is to say: In a peculiar way the God of Zion is approached not by merely citing his qualities, attributes, or deeds, but by lauding human chances to interact with him. "All humankind," it says in v. 3b, is motivated to draw close, the term kol bāśār being a certain leitmotiv for Israel's universal outreach of later days: Isa 66:23 is a global call and apparently a first trace of regular services of Jewish congregations: "From new moon to new moon, and from sabbath to sabbath, all flesh shall come to worship before me, says Yahweh" (see also Isa 40:5; 49:26; Jer 32:27; Ezek 21:4 [RSV 20:48]; Zech 2:17 [RSV 13]; Ps 145:21). The ADORATION is intimately tied to the community experience incorporating individual lives. The CONFESSION OF SINS, with — occasionally — immediate ASSURANCE OF FORGIVENESS (v. 4), in a comprehensive way, becomes a hallmark of postexilic worshiping; see, e.g., Ezra 9; Nehemiah 9; Daniel 9; Psalms 78; 106. But PRAISE OF GOD, in this sense, seems to be the appropriate formal designation for the entire unit, vv. 2-4. The subelements mentioned are tied into the movement toward that merciful and blessing God (not even called Yahweh). It is visibly a congregational motion as v. 4b already shows. The lone "I" ("overwhelm *me*") of v. 4a is firm evidence of a liturgist leading the worship.

Within the Psalter '*ašrê* words (BEATITUDES) are quite frequent (see, e.g., 1:1; 32:1-2; 41:2; 112:1, 5; 119:1-2; 128:1; altogether 27 instances). As a rule, they exalt an exemplary person using third-person language. Here the addressee is God, who allows people to be called "happy" by admitting them into his presence (v. 5ab). And by implication, the worshiping community cherishes the benefit of this privilege, asking to be further awarded such favors mediated through the sanctuary (v. 5cd). Thus an original element BEATITUDE ("Happy the man who . . .") is transformed into a direct-address WISH or PETITION: "Happy the one whom you chose . . . , so we may take our fill from the goods of your house" (see similar assertions directed to God in 84:5-6 [RSV 4-5]; 84:13 [RSV 12]; 94:12). The shift toward first-person cohortative plural discourse (v. 5c) indicates an appropriation of the beatitude for a new genre and life situation. This type of blessing, once probably taken from wisdom or educational contexts, consequently turns into a liturgical device in HYMNIC PRAYER.

The following section is a true HYMN of what Crüsemann calls the "participial" type (vv. 6-9), framed by "direct address" praise (see his *Studien*). The wording of v. 6 is awkward; perhaps some lexeme has been lost or the unconnected *nôra'ôt*, "dreadful deeds," has to be drawn into the previous line, as LXX does. The verb *ta'ănēnû* (imperfect: "you answer us") may state a fact or wish. These options may not even be mutually exclusive. Past wonderful experience with God wants to be renewed. The basis for asking (repeated invocation in v. 6b; cf. v. 2b) is God's creational activities, exemplified by a triad of nominal expressions (vv. 6c-8). Similar eulogies, even in a basic triadic composition and including the middle attribution *mēkîn*, "the one who establishes" (*hārîm*, *tēbēl*, *hā'āreṣ*, "mountains," "earth," "land," respectively), are found with slight variations in Jer 10:12; 51:15; Ps 147:8 (see C. Koch, *TWAT* IV, 95-107). For other participial laudations of God's acts in the past see Pss 104:2-4; 136:4-17; "Introduction to Cultic Poetry," section 4D. The outcome of God's mighty performances as Creator is the general acclamation of all humankind, from the farthest corners of the world, and nature itself, personified in morning and evening (v. 9), a truly encompassing view. Interestingly, the divine acts are entitled "signs" (*'ôtôt*), a loaded theological term with some repercussions in traditions outside the Psalter (see, e.g., Gen 9:12-17; Exod 4:8-9; Num 14:11; Deut 4:34; Isa 8:18). In the Psalms, disregarding 65:9, the word is used far less frequently to indicate divine signs, occurring only in 78:43; 86:17; 135:9. None of these passages, however, speaks of creational works as "signs." So our verse stands out in its own way.

Hymnic affirmations continue in vv. 10-12, but style and vocabulary vary somewhat. Second-person address of God is carried over, to be sure, from vv. 6ab, 9 into this COMMUNAL PRAISE (the three lines in between introduced by a singular participle are objective affirmations of the Creator; they may represent the fragment of a pure hymn; thus Seybold, 253). But the glorifying sentences now for the most part carry finite verbs: perfect, imperfect, one consecutive imperfect; seven verbs altogether describe God's action;

22

there are only three short nominal clauses plus two verbal ones with different subjects, stating what God has been doing. God has graciously provided plentiful rain and fertility throughout the past year (v. 12). Small wonder that Psalm 65 has been understood and used as a thanksgiving hymn and prayer after harvest. Bucolic descriptions of this type are rare in the OT; see the third person, partly participial, presentation of the watering of the earth in 104:10-18, or the first-person speech of Yahweh, who will make the desert blossom (Isa 41:17-20).

Psalm 65 concludes with a DESCRIPTION OF JUBILANCE in the natural world, comparable to the conclusion of section IV (v. 9). In contrast to human responses to God's considerate care (vv. 2-5, 9ab), now nature — pastures, hills, meadows, plains — sings its praise, a familiar idea in OT hymns (see 96:11-12; 98:7-8; 148:1-10). Of course, nature's jubilation is part and parcel of the responsiveness of the whole creation, which is on the one hand larger than humanity, on the other subjugated to humanity (see Psalm 8) and therefore lauding the Creator vicariously, for the sake of humanity. The objective third-person style of this element reveals the human vantage point and, liturgically speaking, recitation by singer, congregation, or choir.

## *Genre*

Observing speaker(s), direction of speech (addressee), subunits and their liturgical functions, style, and vocabulary, we are led to define Psalm 65 as a COMMUNAL HYMN. Its background is a community without large-scale political interests but a group nourishing concerns for human and environmental welfare. Direct address of the "God on Zion" (v. 2b) pervades almost the whole poem (vv. 2-6, 9-12), a very personal way of relating to the Deity. The appearance of hymnic participles in vv. 6c-8 and the absence of hymnic imperatives should not lead us to postulate fundamentally opposed prototypes of extant praise texts (against Crüsemann). Rather, hymnic form elements are varied, and they were used according to liturgical needs.

The interests of the individual are visible (e.g., v. 2c: "fulfill vows"; v. 3a: "accept prayer"), but the "I" of the individual seems precarious (v. 4b: "prevail over me"), because communal "we" comes in at crucial points (v. 4b: "our sins"; v. 5c: "we want to take a fill"; v. 6: "you listen to us"; "God, our helper"; cf. Gunkel, 273). All theological concerns merge in a worshiping group oriented toward the sanctuary on Mount Zion. But the rain had been falling in the countryside, yielding bountiful produce. This locale appears to be strong on the mind of the worshipers. The needs of their community and the well-being of the land were most noticeable matters for those who chanted this hymn (see Scharbert, "Das 'Wir,'" listed at "Introduction to Psalms").

The liturgical movement of our psalm is from a very condensed, theologically loaded initial PRAISE OF GOD, spoken or sung by a leader of ceremony, over congregational interludes (PETITION; HYMN: note firm first person plurals in vv. 5c, 6b), toward the final choruses to be classified as COMMUNAL THANKSGIVING, especially after rich harvests.

23

## Setting

A debate has been waged about the proper life situation of Psalm 65: was it a hymn for temple services in Jerusalem, or may we connect it with local harvest celebrations? Evidence for an exclusive tie to the Jerusalem temple is weak or nonexistent in spite of the mention of Zion in v. 2. Local or communal services in places outside Jerusalem, while not attested explicitly, are not unlikely. There may have been worship services even in the fields or at local shrines (see Lev 23:40-43; Judg 21:19-21; 1 Sam 9:12), in particular after the harvest had been brought in and sustenance for the coming year granted by a beneficent, gracious Deity.

## Intention

As a communal hymn the primary aim of singing the praises of God who helps his followers and provides food for all is the upkeep of the congregation of believers. No animosity transpires in the poetic lines. All human beings seem to be in the same predicament: either they keep on wholesome terms with their deity and prosper, or they do not pay attention to the Lord of nature, in which case they wither. But this possibility is not considered in our psalm.

## Bibliography

D. Cohen, "Dir gebührt Lobgesang," *BM* 89/90 (1982) 105-14 (Heb.); F. Crüsemann, *Studien zur Formgeschichte von Hymnus und Danklied in Israel* (WMANT 32; Neukirchen-Vluyn: Neukirchener Verlag, 1969), 201-02; M. D. Futato, "A Metereological Analysis of Psalms 104, 65, and 29" (diss., Catholic University, Washington D.C., 1984); M. Hadas-Lebel, "Jacob et Esau ou Israel et Rome dans le Talmud et le Midrasch," *RHR* 201 (1984) 396-92; N. Lohfink, "Herausgeführt in die Freiheit, Ps 65," *Geist und Leben* 38 (1965) 81-84; J. Overduin, "Hymns for September, October, and November," *Reformed Worship* 28 (1993) 35-39; G. Rinaldi, "Gioele e il Salmo 65," *BeO* 10 (1968) 113-22; S. Schroer, "Psalm 65 — Zeugnis eines integrativen JHWH-Glaubens?" *UF* 22 (1990) 285-301; M. B. Ströle, "Psalmengebet: Psalm 65," *Erbe und Auftrag* 55 (1979) 382-83; V. H. Todd, "Biblical Eschatology: An Overview," *Cumberland Seminarian* 22 (1984) 3-16; D. Weber, "Gedanken zur Textgestaltung von Augustinus: Enarrationes in Psalmos 64 und 68," *Augustinian Studies* 27 (1996) 47-58.

## Psalm 66:
## Communal Thanksgiving Hymn

### Structure

| | MT | NRSV |
|---|---|---|
| I. Superscription | 1a | - |
| II. Call to worship | 1b-4 | 1-4 |
|    A. Summons to praise (imperatives) | 1b-2 | 1-2 |
|    B. Quoted praise | 3 | 3 |
|    C. Summons to praise (jussives) | 4 | 4 |
| III. Praise of God | 5-7 | 5-7 |
|    A. Summons to acknowledge God's power | 5 | 5 |
|    B. Remembrance of God's victories | 6 | 6 |
|    C. Praise of God's government | 7ab | 7ab |
|    D. Intimidation of God's enemies | 7c | 7c |
| IV. Communal thanksgiving | 8-12 | 8-12 |
|    A. Summons to peoples | 8 | 8 |
|    B. Account of deliverance | 9 | 9 |
|    C. Direct-address hymn | 10-12 | 10-12 |
|       1. Account of trouble | 10-12b | 10-12b |
|       2. Account of salvation | 12c | 12c |
| V. Individual thanksgiving | 13-20 | 13-20 |
|    A. Account of vow | 13-15 | 13-15 |
|    B. Account of trouble and salvation | 16-19 | 16-19 |
|       1. Account of trouble | 16-18 | 16-18 |
|       2. Account of salvation | 19 | 19 |
|    C. Blessing to God | 20 | 20 |

The name of David is lacking in the SUPERSCRIPTION, although most neighboring poems are attributed to him (Psalms 51–65; 68–79). A few Greek MSS add "David" in Psalm 67. Does this mean that both Psalms 66 and 67 have been added later to the David collection? Only three words in the heading feature a musical-technical meaning (→ "Introduction to Psalms," section 1).

The SUMMONS TO PRAISE and CALL TO WORSHIP (vv. 1b-4) are common introductions to communal hymns (→ "Introduction to Cultic Poetry," section 4D). The first, extended line (vv. 1b-2) uses three imperatives, two of which are well-known technical terms: hārî'û, "make noise" (see 47:2 [RSV 1]; 81:2 [RSV 1]; 95:1, 2; 98:4, 6; 100:1) and zammĕrû ("sing, play"; see, e.g., 30:5 [RSV 4]; 33:2; 47:7, 8 [RSV 6, 7]; 68:5, 33 [RSV 4, 32]; 98:4, 5; 105:2; 135:3; 147:7; Isa 12:5). The third expression is singular and uncertain: śîmû kābôd tĕhillātô, "put up glory, his song" — for God (cf. Psalm 29; the Syriac version smooths it into "sing the glory of his song"). The call goes out into "all the land" or "all the world" (v. 1b), appropriate for a faith that incorporates humankind and the nations (cf. vv. 5, 8). The threefold opening is followed by a special summons to acknowledge the terrible power of God (v. 3; cf. v. 5). The words to be used are quoted literally, and this little "inset" hymn is cast in

direct-address language: "How frightful are your deeds!" Challenging participants in ritual to voice their approval and enhance God must have been a liturgical custom, especially in hymnic and thanksgiving contexts (cf. 40:17 [RSV
16]; 70:5 [RSV 4]; 96:10; 107:1-2; 118:2-4; 124:1; 129:1). Only the last two
examples spell out longer quotations of past experiences. For the rest of the
sampled texts the summonses go for short, hymnic statements with a confessional character. "God is great!" (40:17 [RSV 16]; 70:5 [RSV 4]); "God
reigns!" (96:10). So we may surmise that also in our case the solicited hymn, to
be sung by the congregation, is articulated in v. 3 alone. The adjoining verse
takes up "all the earth" from v. 1 and continues the call to worship, using the
jussive mood of three verbs (*šḥh*, Eshtaphel, "to prostrate oneself"; and twice
*zmr*, Piel, "to sing, play"), and, significantly, the direct-address style, as in the
quoted hymn. We have another proof of interchanging or gliding hymnic articulations.

The ensuing PRAISE OF GOD (vv. 5-7) is descriptive throughout, not employing any prayer language. God's great deeds are at stake, in nature and history, as we would say today. But the discourse remains allusive; it does not
spell out clear-cut motifs. Also, these verses do not seem consistent in a literary sense. The beginning of v. 6 is made up by a third-person verb without a
nearby grammatical subject: *hāpak*, "he turned over." The logical point of reference, "God" in v. 5a, is one phrase removed, the liturgical situation providing coherence of subjects. The next line, v. 7, opens with a hymnic participle:
*mōšēl*, "reigning," which still depends on the remote subject "God." Perhaps
both lines were taken from an independent poem and fitted into the present
context. This impression is deepened by the absence of any subject, not even a
remote point of reference, in v. 6b: "They went through the river on foot" remains indefinite as to the actors. Again, only the informed audience or worshiping congregation can identify the wandering people. One more irregularity: v. 6c looks like an incongruous appendix to the hymn at hand: "There let
us rejoice in him" (see below).

As the text stands now, however, the SUMMONS TO ACKNOWLEDGE God's
power (v. 5: "mighty deeds of God"; "horrible action," both expressions are
pretty rare; cf. 46:9 [RSV 8]; 9:12 [RSV 11]; 77:12-16 [RSV 11-15]; 78:11;
103:7; 105:1-2; quite often "wondrous works" are cited in parallel phrases)
aims at generating fear and awe, an essential ingredient of Israelite and ancient
Near Eastern religion (see Becker, *Gottesfurcht*). The REMEMBRANCE OF VIC-
TORIES (v. 6) keeps history and more ancient myths alive, for the benefit of
present communion. The line in question, on account of its vocabulary and outlook, seems to lean more on the tale of Israel's crossing the Jordan River (Josh
3:1–5:1) than on the exodus story (Exodus 14–15; but cf. *yabbāšāh*, "dry land,"
and *ʿbr*, "pass through," in 14:16, 22, 29; 15:16, 19). Perhaps both victories are
fused into one tradition of God's overcoming the waters on behalf of the people. The descriptive song is interrupted only once, at the end of v. 6: "There let
us enjoy him [or 'it'] greatly." A strangely personal expression that may come
from D sources (cf. joy at worship in Deut 12:7, 12, 18; 14:26; 16:11, 14;
26:11) extending into the Psalms (cf. Pss 33:21; 34:3 [RSV 2]; 67:5 [RSV 4];
90:14; 97:12; 118:24). Cultic joyful celebration in this fashion, drawing history

into the very presence of the jubilating community, on the other hand may also have been projected into the liberating stories of the ancient past (v. 6; note *šām*, "there"), which, of course, always had been commemorated in sacred ceremonies (see Exod 12; 23:15; Deut 16:1, 3, 6, 12). The supreme authority of God is asserted in hymnic fashion by v. 7ab (cf. similar participles: Pss 22:29 [RSV 28]; 59:14 [RSV 13]; 89:10 [RSV 9]), while a warning against rebels concludes the element (v. 7c: *sôrĕrîm*, "rebellious ones," was originally a social and political term: Deut 21:18-21; Isa 1:23, and turned into a religious concept; see Pss 68:7, 19 [RSV 6, 18]; 78:8; Isa 30:1; 65:2; Jer 5:23; 6:28; Hos 4:16; Zech 7:11; L. Ruppert, *TWAT* V, 957-63; Hos 4:16, however, is hardly the turning point from one to the other meaning).

Using the verb *brk*, Piel, "to bless," the COMMUNAL THANKSGIVING starts with a SUMMONS TO PEOPLES. They are to tune in on the praise of Israel's God, even singing "his song" (v. 8; cf. 2). The Piel of *brk* not only denotes God's favorable act for his clients but is frequently employed also for humans blessing the Deity (see 68:27 [RSV 26]; 96:2; 100:4; 103:20-22). Divine economy of power and glory includes the worshiping community, peoples, and heavenly beings (→ Psalms 29; 96; 148). The reason for the large-scale, ideal convocation to worship is obviously the deliverance only hinted at in v. 9: a very condensed notion of historical deliverance. A concrete victory song would spell out the details of God's intervention (→ Psalm 68). Reduction of the ACCOUNT OF DELIVERANCE to a one-line general statement (v. 9; cf. 96:3) is tantamount to a tight sublimation of past experience. "He put us back to life" (v. 9a) and "He did not let our feet slip" (v. 9b) are fairly rare expressions of personal and communal salvation from danger. For the former see 56:14 (RSV 13): "You have rescued me from death . . . to exist before God in the light of life" (almost identically 116:8-9 says: ". . . in the lands of life"). The personal tone of such affirmations apparently led LXX to put first person singular instead of MT plural in v. 9.

The metaphor of the slipping foot also occurs with individual supplication (see 38:17 [RSV 16]; 94:18; 121:3). But there are triumphant hymns extolling Israel's feet as instruments of dominion (cf. 47:4 [RSV 3]). Our v. 9 is exactly pointing in the direction of regained strength, even if not in the military sense. Both lines, vv. 8 and 9, are definitely spoken by the community or on its behalf, the first-person plural suffix occurring three times. This kind of collective locution is unique, due to the singular mode of socio-religious organization (see Scharbert, "Das 'Wir'"; listing at "Introduction to Psalms"). So far the speaking "we" maintain their objective pose in relation to God, facing and addressing, so to speak, within their worship liturgy attentive peoples all over the world.

This attitude changes in vv. 10-12, and, for that matter, also in vv. 13-15. The congregation turns to God, speaking to him directly. Significantly, prayerful direct address is carried on first by the collective "we" (vv. 10-12), thereafter by an unidentified "I" (vv. 13-15). The old debate, whether we are dealing with two separate psalms (cf., e.g., Duhm; Gunkel; Oesterley; Westermann; Crüsemann, *Studien* 174-91 and 229 n. 1 versus propagators of at least a "liturgical composition": Mowinckel, *W* II, 28; Schmidt; Leslie; Weiser; Tate) seems superfluous in the face of these stylistic and ceremonial facts: vv. 10-15 are dif-

27

ferentiated by the grammatical number of speaker(s), but tightly sewn into one liturgical quilt by consistent prayer address to God.

Deictic *kî* opens v. 10 in good hymnic fashion (→ Psalm 33, call to worship; Psalm 136; cf. also 9:5 [RSV 4]; 24:2; 30:2 [RSV 1]; 117:2). In generalized, metaphorical language the community recounts its hardships, occasioned by God himself as a test of loyalty (vv. 10-12b). The key words of v. 10 are *bhn*, "test," and *ṣrp*, "purify by melting," quite common in some prophetic discourses (see Jer 6:27-30; 9:6 [RSV 7]; 17:10; 20:12; Isa 1:25; 48:10, but also Pss 17:3; 26:2; 81:8 [RSV 7]; 139:23). The concept of testing and purifying faith is certainly common in OT personal piety, but also apt to be applied to the community as a whole. Isa 48:10, if slightly emended in its Hebrew wording, sounds like a compact version of our vv. 10-11, put into first-person form with God speaking: "Behold, I have refined *(ṣrp)* you like silver, I have tested you in the furnace of misery." These ideas set the tone for the two following lines mentioning a pair of calamitous situations each. It is hard to imagine that vv. 11a and 12a should deviate from the pattern of an ACCOUNT OF TROUBLE. Some versions and modern translators give a positive meaning to v. 11a: "you brought us into a fortress" *(měṣûdāh* can signify "net" or "fortification"), and v. 12a: "you let a man ride in our front" (purportedly referring to Moses' leadership in the exodus; cf. Tate, 145-46). But the parallel cola of each line are not at all ambivalent. An antithetical reading of the two lines would imbalance the liturgical element, which testifies to severe trials of the community (v. 10) only to be stopped by a liberating ACCOUNT OF SALVATION (v. 12c). This third colon of v. 12 is in fact the culminating point of the liturgical subunit, corresponding to affirmations of being heard and helped in complaint songs (cf. 22:22 [RSV 21]). "You brought us into open space" (v. 12c; cf. *yṣ'*, Hiphil, in 18:20 [RSV 19]; 25:15, 17; 31:5; 68:7 [RSV 6]; 105:37, 43; 107:14, 28; 136:11; 142:8 [RSV 7]; 143:11). Every one of these passages has to be understood against the background of constricting experiences of misery and oppression, the counterconcepts to "open space" = liberty being "narrowness," "danger" (cf. H.-J. Faber, *TWAT* VI, 1113-22). Again, all the circumstances mentioned in vv. 11, 12ab are to be considered background to v. 12c; they belong to the categories of "fire" and "water," dreadful forecastings of Jewish destiny through Christian history (v. 12b; cf. 6). The condensed hostile powers threaten to destroy the community of faithful; cf. Isa 43:2, which communicates assurance in such terrible trials: "When you [i.e., Israel] pass through waters, I will be with you; and through the rivers, they shall not overwhelm you; when you walk through fire you shall not be burned, and the flame shall not consume you."

So far, then, the hymn unfolds regularly, even if not according to "pure" form-critical standards by way of a CALL TO WORSHIP, general PRAISE, and condensed THANKSGIVING to the Deity. There can be hardly any doubt about its collective use. Individual parts were recited by different groups or persons; thus the summons to praise probably pertained to the liturgist, the shouts of adoration (e.g., v. 3, perhaps 5b), and most of the praising and complaining "we" statements came from the congregation (vv. 8-12). Vv. 5-9 sound more like an INSTRUCTION, and were very likely recited by officiants.

The rest of the psalm (vv. 13-20) is obviously modeled according to the

INDIVIDUAL THANKSGIVING in the "I" form (see "Introduction to Cultic Poetry," section 4C). However, there are intimate compositional and liturgical ties to the preceding sections. Therefore, while an original autonomy of the text and erroneous joining with the communal praise and thanksgiving cannot be totally excluded, we have strong indications of conscious redactional or liturgical composition. First, vv. 13-20, bare of any introductory elements, do not represent a complete thanksgiving agenda (see Psalms 30; 116). Second, an AC-COUNT OF VOW, i.e., execution of promise, vv. 13-15, and an ACCOUNT OF TROUBLE AND SALVATION, with a jubilant address of the congregation (vv. 16-19), seem to be inverted to fit the liturgical order of the communal thanksgiving. The proper response to v. 12c should not be another reference to past troubles: vv. 16-19 could not follow v. 12c. Third, liturgical proceedings occur in their traditional line at least until v. 15 (→ Psalm 107). Fourth, the nature and quantity of sacrifices to be offered exceed private conditions and befit the community: 'ôlôt, "holocausts," were costly and not really adequate to the festive occasion of personal thanksgiving (what would guests eat after the service?), and although declared opportune for individuals (Leviticus 1; 6:1-6 [RSV 8-13]), emphasis was on atonement for sins. The recognizable practice of familial thanksgiving does not point to private full-fledged "burnt offerings" (see 1 Samuel 1–2; Gerstenberger, *Leviticus,* on Leviticus 3, Additional Bibliography, section B). Unless 'ôlôt in vv. 13 and 15 has an uncommonly restricted meaning (burning of the fat parts of the animal only), the term does not fit a private context. Holocausts of individuals (cf. Pss 40:7 [RSV 6]; 51:18, 21 [RSV 16, 19]; Mic 6:6; G. A. Anderson, *ABD* VI, 870-86) may be products of theological imagination rather than empirical facts. They seem to have been more or less restricted to official ceremonies, and possibly even to very special occasions. In any case, the amount of animals promised in v. 15 ("fatlings," "rams," "bulls," "goats") transcends normal private capacities. We have to think either of joint offerings of the congregation or exaggerated metaphorical language.

We cannot help, therefore, but consider seriously Mowinckel's thesis: the "I" speaking "is the *leading man of the people,* the king or a corresponding figure among the people" (Mowinckel, *W* II, 28). Just as Jephthah took a vow to offer a "holocaust" if he would win the battle, having to execute it afterward (Judg 11:30-39), or as Ezra and Nehemiah had been acting on behalf of the people (see, e.g., Ezra 9–10; Nehemiah 8–10), thus the liturgists of Psalm 66 may have visualized a bipartite ceremony from the beginning. The people would voice their gratitude (vv. 1-12), but to make a vow and execute its sacrifices would be the responsibility of the leader (cf. Num 21:2: Israel vows! See O. Kaiser, *TWAT* VI, 261-74). Religious leadership in Israel, beyond the bounds of familial cult and through changing social structures, always remained fairly hierarchical, with single mediators communicating between people and God (see Blenkinsopp, *Sage*).

If this thesis should be correct, the repeated ACCOUNT OF TROUBLE AND SALVATION (vv. 16-19) would not be so surprising after all. In liturgical terms it may have been considered the personal experience of the leader, who had to prove his blamelessness in order to be granted God's blessing (v. 18: formally a PROTESTATION OF INNOCENCE; cf. Psalms 18; 45; 72). He also is entrusted with

29

the office of intercession like Moses (e.g., Exodus 32): only in the "I" section of the psalm is *těpillāh,* "prayer," mentioned (vv. 19, 20; against *těhillāh,* "praise," in vv. 2, 8) with concomitant vocabulary of "crying to God," and God "listening" to the supplicant (vv. 17-19). The concluding line, a BLESSING of God from the human side, has deep roots in archaic religious experience, reflecting a later suppressed notion of God's dependence on human acknowledgment (→ BLESSING FORMULA). Another possible explanation of the INDIVIDUAL THANKSGIVING as an integral part of a communal hymn would be: the individual sacrifices and thanksgivings reflect congregational practices of all members taking part in communal feasting, family by family (cf. 1 Sam 1:1-4; 2:12-17).

## Genre

Psalm 66 is a COMMUNAL THANKSGIVING HYMN. It draws on forms and traditions, both familial and collective, extant in Hebrew Scripture. Throughout the diverse elements is noticeable a process of sublimation and abstraction. No specific historical event has prompted the psalm; past experiences as gleaned from written or oral traditions have been synthesized into brief allusions. The forms of personal thanksgiving have been modified to adapt to the community situation (not vice versa, as claimed by Weiser, 306-9). The exilic and postexilic congregation, cloaked in liturgical language and traditions of the past, affirms its faith in God, sings praises because of God's help and sustenance, and after having established its "we" identity has the leader recite vows and commitments. A host of sacrifices, and every one of them a "whole burnt offering," could signify full spiritual and physical dedication. O'Brien points out the relationship between vow inscriptions, found often on votive stelae, and the thanksgiving rite, promised for the case of being heard and rescued. One example of an inscription found on the island of Malta (*KAI* 47): "To the Lord Melqart, Lord of Tyre, that which your servant *'bd'sr* and his brother *'srśmr*... vowed, because he heard their voice. May he bless them" (quoted in O'Brien, 285).

## Setting/Intention

Where else than in congregational worship could a hymn like this have been composed and used? Prominence of the "we" passages suggests a strong community feeling. This would be true also if the "we" parts had been spoken by an officiant (cf. Ezra 9; Nehemiah 9). Chances are, however, that such communal expressions of praise and thanks were intoned by choirs or partly even by the attending people. By contrast, priestly ceremonies tend to concentrate on sacrosanct rites around the altar, preferring to exclude laity. Therefore, the dominating "we" hymn and the spiritualized individual thanksgiving as a liturgical unit may belong in a congregational worship either within temple precincts or far from the Jerusalem temple. The liturgy was performed in times of hardships (for exiled or repressed Jews under Babylonian and Persian rule, pressures were probably always just around the corner), in order to celebrate small, daily victories of survival, and to strengthen one another in the community and in relation with a dependable Deity.

## Bibliography

J. Becker, *Israel deutet seine Psalmen* (SBS 18; Stuttgart: Katholisches Bibelwerk, 1966) 57-58; idem, *Gottesfurcht im Alten Testament* (AnBib 25; Rome: Pontifical Biblical Institute, 1965); F. Crüsemann, *Studien zur Formgeschichte von Hymnus und Danklied in Israel* (WMANT 32; Neukirchen: Neukirchener Verlag, 1969) 175-84, 228-31; H.-J. Kraus, "Gilgal — Ein Beitrag zur Kultusgeschichte Israels," *VT* 1 (1951) 181-99; A. Lauha, *Die Geschichtsmotive in den alttestamentlichen Psalmen* (Helsinki: Finnische Literaturgesellschaft, 1945) 69-70; J. M. O'Brien, "'Because God Heard My Voice': The Individual Thanksgiving Psalm and Vow-Fulfillment," in *The Listening Heart (Fest.* R. E. Murphy; ed. K. Hoglund, et al.; JSOTSup 58; Sheffield: Sheffield Academic Press, 1987) 281-97.

## Psalm 67:
## Communal Thanksgiving Hymn

### Structure

|  | MT | NRSV |
|---|---|---|
| I. Superscription | 1 | - |
| II. Imploration | 2-3 | 1-2 |
|    A. Plea for blessing | 2 | 1 |
|    B. Plea for acknowledgment | 3 | 2 |
| III. Call to worship | 4-6 | 3-5 |
|    A. Summons to praise | 4 | 3 |
|    B. Motives for joy | 5 | 4 |
|    C. Summons to praise | 6 | 5 |
| IV. Longing for well-being and acknowledgment | 7-8 | 6-7 |

SUPERSCRIPTIONS including reference to the instrument *nĕgînōt*, "stringed one," occur seven times in the Psalter (with Psalms 4; 6; 54; 55; 61; 67; 76; see Stauder, *Musik,* 174-207 [listing at "Introduction to Cultic Poetry"]; Sendrey, *Music,* 300-301; Seidel, *Musik,* 222 [listing at Additional Bibliography, section B]; → Psalm 150). Apart from this name the scribal heading of Psalm 67 contains but three standard terms that seem to be put in quite arbitrarily (→ Psalms 65; 66; 68; etc.). The surprising lack of attribution to David has also been noted in the heading of → Psalm 66.

The IMPLORATION (vv. 2-3) differs from PETITION or INITIAL PLEA in complaint contexts. The latter form elements call to attention special calamities and ask for remedy, or they beg for audience, while the former is basically a general prayer for help or BLESSING. God is addressed indirectly; the liturgy uses jussives (third person singular) with first-person plural suffixes: "May God be merciful *(hnn)* with us, may he bless *(brk)* us, may he let his face shine *('ûr)* among us" (v. 2). The phrases are strongly reminiscent of the Aaronite blessing, except that the powerful words there are conferred on the congregation by a priest (Num 6:24-26; same verbs plus one in a different order from Ps 67:2: *brk*, Piel, "bless"; *šmr*, Qal, "keep"; *'ûr*, Hiphil, "let shine"; *hnn*, Qal, "be merciful"). The opening prayer line of Psalm 67, in contrast, is spoken by the congregation itself (or by its representative using inclusive language? cf. the modification to that effect of the Aaronite blessing in some Protestant liturgical traditions). The general well-being of the faithful community is to be a signal to "all the people" of "the earth" (v. 3) to make known the way and potential of God (note the universal horizon). He is to be proclaimed by the very existence of that "we" congregation, which is obviously neither a political nor a military entity. The situation of vv. 2-3, then, is that of a religious body existing among a plurality of ethnic groups within a universal empire. Strangely enough, but in line with liturgical custom of congregational worship, the second line of the psalm (v. 3) uses direct-address prayer language (see below).

Those *gôyim*, "nations," in v. 3a (cf. R. E. Clements, *TWAT* I, 965-73; D. L. Christensen, *ABD* IV, 1037-49) strike the notion of global proclamation kept up and increased in vv. 4-6, a comprehensive CALL TO WORSHIP. The synonomous terms now put to the front are *'ammîm*, "peoples," and *lĕ'ummîm*, "societies," the trouble being that we hardly understand the differences among the three designations (cf. H. D. Preuss, *TWAT* IV, 411-13; E. Lipiński, *TWAT* VI, 177-94: the experts confirm the ambiguities of the three terms, their converging development, but they all fail to take seriously the outward-directed meanings). The distribution of the words is almost a "graphic happening," a feast of interethnic relations in letter and liturgy: four occurrences of *'ammîm* encircle a tripartite nucleus of *lĕ'ummîm*, *'ammîm*, *lĕ'ummîm* (vv. 4-6). The psalmist is very conscious of other ethnic groups in the Babylonian and Persian empires. They are summoned to sing praises to the God of Israel (vv. 4, 6): the jussive *yôdû*, "they shall praise/give thanks," occurs four times to frame two lines of a reinforced call to praise and motive thereof; cf. 45:18 (RSV 17); 89:6 (RSV 5); 99:3; 107:8, 15, 21, 31; 138:4; 140:14 (RSV 13); 145:10. The direct summons to the congregation at hand is, of course, in the imperative plural; cf. 30:5 (RSV 4); 33:2; 118:1, 29; 136:1-3, 26. Although many passages in the Psalter talk about subduing and destroying foreign nations (see Psalms 2; 18; 68; 110), quite often the foreign nationals are included in the jubilant announcement of worship to Israel's God (cf. 99:1-3; 138:4-6; 148:11; Isa 2:1-4; 19:19-24; with threats: Isaiah 60). There is nothing but exuberant joy in store for the people at this moment, with no specific references to divine victories or demonstrations of power. This may be gleaned from v. 5, perhaps with one reservation: the idea of God's "judging rightly" could still hide a prediction of punishment. *špt* in the sense of "global judgment" (cf. Pss 9:8-9 [RSV 7-8]; 58:11-12 [RSV 10-11]; 75:3-11 [RSV 2-10]; 82; 96:13; 98:9) is as outspoken as it can be. The understanding is, however, that the "righteous ones" may always look on investigation and sentencing with calmness and joy, a bold hope not warranted by human juridical performance. Jubilance may draw its full justification from abundance of crops, however (v. 7), a yearly demonstration of blessing, in which other peoples participate (v. 5: should "judge with equity" in this case also have this connotation?).

The closing lines of Psalm 67 revert to the circle of the faithful (vv. 7, 8a) and to articulating a hope of universal acknowledgment (v. 8bc). The blessing received and further expected has been made manifest through a plentiful harvest (v. 7a; cf. Psalm 65; Crüsemann, *Studien*, 199-202). The motif may have been used as an example of divine competition (cf. Hosea 2). The God of Israel has proven his power and benvolence, therefore let all the people fear him (v. 8bc). Liturgically, drawing back to the opening clauses, repeating them in a way (*brk*, in vv. 2, 7, 8), and setting again the stage for the congregation's self-affirmation are evidence enough for a careful structuring of the text (cf. Auffret) pointing to a live worship situation.

The "direction" of speech (Westermann, *Praise*, 30-35, 53, 64, 66, 135, 155; listing at "Introduction to Cultic Poetry") is always important in analyses of liturgical texts; thus we have to evaluate the second-person address of God. This important stylistic feature comes up in v. 3: the congregation, looking for the blessing of God, speaks to him face to face, a posture prevalent through v. 6. That means that worshipers deal with their Deity in prayer language, and their topics are "God's blessing" in the context of a world of "other peoples" (cf. Beyerlin, *Lichte*, 1-50). Everything said on first sight seems to be imbued with a highly utopian character, with wishful thinking, and perhaps urging God to accomplish such marvelous harmony of unison religious praise. The extant text communicates the strong conviction that God is worthy of every nation's praise. Seen through nationalistic glasses and presupposing aggressive monotheism, as happened in later interpretation, the particular faith of one tiny group of people living in an immense and pluralistic empire makes the model valid for humankind. This certainly would be a projection and usurpation, taking hostages spiritually, so to speak, borne of a peculiar situation of Yahweh communities in the sixth and fifth centuries B.C.E. (→ Psalms 96–99), with tremendous consequences for later Christian political history. Looking more closely at the original situation of the hymn, though, we may detect the overwhelming gratitude to God for yearly sustenance to be shared, quite naturally, by all the other ethnic groups because of their similar experiences of being benignly blessed year after year (cf. Schroer; listing at Psalm 65).

## Genre/Setting/Intention

The small poem is not a full-grown hymn, nor is it a petitionary prayer. Rather, it has thanksgiving and imploring qualities oscillating between the two sentiments. The most likely place in worship for this psalm would have been the opening or closing phases. The universal horizon is to bolster the magnitude of that God adored in that particular community. Thus the COMMUNAL THANKSGIVING HYMN is a means of self-assurance and comfort in a world that was unperspicuous in its vastness and complexity. The harvest season has been

33

the most likely time of use, as in fact it still is in Christian hymnals. Affinity with Yahweh-kingship hymns (→ Psalms 93; 95–99) is obvious (cf. Prinsloo, 238-39, who rejects tight genre classifications, but favors a definition of purposes in different settings). Beyerlin's theological interpretation is this: "The Psalm responds to a liability of the Yahweh community in regard to the nations" (*Lichte*, 13).

## Bibliography

P. Auffret, "'Qu'il nous bénisse, Dieu!' Étude structurelle du Psaume 67," *BN* 69 (1993) 5-8; W. Beyerlin, *Im Lichte der Traditionen: Psalm LXVII und CXV, ein Entwicklungszusammenhang* (VTSup 45; Leiden: Brill, 1992); H. Blocher, "God, Our God," *European Journal of Theology* 4 (1995) 19-25; H. G. Jefferson, "The Date of Psalm 67," *VT* 12 (1962) 201-5; O. Loretz, "Die Psalmen 8 und 67," *UF* 8 (1977) 117-21; R. Meynet, "Le psaume 67: 'Je ferai de toi la lumière des nations,'" *NRT* 120 (1998) 3-17; W. S. Prinsloo, "Psalm 67: Harvest Thanksgiving Psalm, (Eschatological) Hymn, Communal Prayer, Communal Lament, or . . . ?" *OTE* 7 (1994) 231-46; A. Rose, "L'influence des Septante sur la tradition chrétienne III: Aperçus sur Psaume 67," *Questions Liturgiques et Paroissiales* 47 (1966) 11-35; H.-M. Wahl, "Psalm 67. Erwägungen zu Aufbau, Gattung und Datierung," *Bib* 73 (1992) 240-47; B. Weber, "Psalm LXVII: Anmerkungen zum Text selbst und zur Studie von W. Beyerlin," *VT* 43 (1993) 559-66.

## Psalm 68:
## Victory Songs; Communal Hymn

## Text

All commentators deplore the bad state of text-preservation. Cf., e.g., Gunkel, 283: "The corrupted text extraordinarily impedes the understanding of details in this psalm; it can be reconstructed only hypothetically." He continues to point out the subsidiary value of metrical and form-critical considerations. Likewise Mowinckel, *Psalm [68]*; Schmidt, 126-27; Seybold, 262-63; and most other exegetes take note of this enigmatic state of affairs. Albright ("Catalogue") was so frustrated with the text that he declared it a kind of archival list, containing only first lines (incipits) of liturgical songs without any substantial coherence. Opposed are "liturgists," who make ceremonial sense of breaks, jumps, and bolts (cf., e.g., Mowinckel, Hauge, Vogt, et al.). In addition, the extant text obviously incorporates archaic as well as fairly late vocabulary, imagery, and theological interests, which at times are hard to identify and keep apart (cf. Haupt, Gunkel, et al.). The only way to proceed is to analyze as closely as possible the individual units of this psalm and then come to tentative conclusions in regard to genre and function of the whole composition.

## Structure

| | MT | NRSV |
|---|---|---|
| I. Superscription | 1 | - |
| II. Prologue | 2-4 | 1-3 |
| III. Hymnic introduction | 5-7 | 4-6 |
| A. Summons to worship | 5 | 4 |
| B. Hymnic praise | 6-7 | 5-6 |
| IV. Hymnic address | 8-11 | 7-10 |
| V. Battle hymn | 12-15 | 11-14 |
| VI. Mountain hymn | 16-19 | 15-18 |
| VII. Congregational response | 20-21 | 19-20 |
| VIII. Divine oracle | 22-24 | 21-23 |
| IX. Account of procession | 25-28 | 24-27 |
| X. Hymnic address, petition | 29-32 | 28-31 |
| XI. Hymnic close | 33-36 | 32-35 |
| A. Summons to worship | 33-35a | 32-34a |
| B. Hymnic praise | 35b-36 | 34b-35 |

There is a slight possibility that vv. 2-4 are not the beginning of the hymn proper (which would start only, with a regular SUMMONS TO PRAISE, in v. 5), but a PROLOGUE to be read or sung in the worship service before the intonation of the victory song. Evidence for this classification includes (a) that v. 2 is a quotation from Num 10:35, the famous old spell-like saying about the ark, and (b) the late, general juxtaposition of rĕšā'îm and ṣaddîqîm in vv. 3c, 4, which seems to function as a heading for the whole poem (see Levin, "Gebetbuch," 364; he also calls the opening verses "prologue"). On (a): Of 24 affirmations on God or Yahweh "rising" against his foes, only Num 10:35 and Ps 68:2 have the sequence of these three verbs: qûm-pûṣ-nûs ("rise — disperse — flee"; cf., e.g., Isa 14:22-23; 28:21; 31:2; 33:10; Pss 7:7 [RSV 6]; 10:12; 12:6 [RSV 5]; 44:27 [RSV 26]; 74:22; 76:10 [RSV 9]; 82:8; 102:14 [RSV 13]; Job 31:14). On (b): The opposition of "wicked" and "righteous" reflects an inner-Jewish theological dichotomy (Levin) not to be identified with those outer conflicts of some parts of the hymn proper. This pattern of internal religious strife is present in other late layers of Psalter redaction (cf. Psalms 1; 119; 146; also Hab 1:4, 13; 2:4-19; etc.). Notably, the "wicked" are threatened with decay ('bd, v. 3c), the "righteous" are promised enduring bliss (śmḥ, v. 4; cf. 1:3-6; 37:16-20; 49:14-15 [RSV 13-14]; 73:27-28; 83:14-16 [RSV 13-15]; 92:10-16 [RSV 9-15]; 102:27-29 [RSV 26-28]; 112:1-10). In spite of this argumentation, we may stick for good reasons — maintaining a merely literary argument — to the traditional view that vv. 2-4 are an integral part of the psalm, being a liturgical adaptation of the "dictum of the ark" (Num 10:35). In this case, however, we face a rather young layer of the psalm, representing the structure and cult of an early Jewish confessional community rather than age-old features of a tribal society (see below, Genre/Setting). Liturgically speaking, however, the prologue would serve as a kind of introit to the service or an intimidation of the wicked, separating right from the beginning the sheep from the goats.

The HYMNIC INTRODUCTION comprises two distinct elements: a SUM-MONS TO WORSHIP (v. 5) and an initial HYMNIC PRAISE with a warning against "rebellious ones" (vv. 6-7). The first item already has some peculiarities. Two of the four imperatives are well attested in hymnic openings (v. 5a: šîr, "sing," and zmr, Piel, "play"; cf. 33:2-3; 105:2; 149:1-3, and the renewed call to "sing" and "play" here in v. 33). The third is a unique and isolated expression in the Psalter: "Put up (highways) to the rider in the desert" (v. 5b), which does not make easy sense; we need to turn to Second and Third Isaiah to find similar phrases (cf. Isa 40:3; 57:14; 62:10), referring most logically to the people in exile who want to return to their homes. Ugaritic texts have a divine epithet for Baal: "rider of the clouds," which is probably the meaning of Heb. rōkēb ba'ărābôt, v. 5b (cf. v. 34a: rōkēb baššāmayim [emended text: cf. BHS]; Miller, Warrior, 105, Additional Bibliography, section B). Then the summons to worship would presuppose another meaning of sll, e.g., "lift up; praise," or else another verb misspelled by later scribes, e.g., hll, "praise." Conjectures in all these directions abound (overview in Tate, 163, 170-75, 176). The fourth imperative (of 'lz, Qal, "to jubilate") is also unique in hymnic introductions; once we find a jussive in a similar function (Ps 149:5), and also one imperative singular (Zeph 3:14). A few consonants preceding the imperative seem to be disconnected or inserted: they say literally "in Yah is his name" (v. 5c; NRSV emends: "his name is the Lord [= Yahweh]"). Some emendation is necessary to make this fragment intelligible; and we have to doubt whether it refers to Yahweh, since this particular divine name does not occur frequently in our psalm (cf. vv. 17, 21, 27, and one more yāh, v. 19; contrast 'ĕlōhîm [22 times], 'ădōnāy [6 times], and other designations overwhelmingly used for God ). All in all, the SUMMONS TO WORSHIP is a little unusual, beginning with standard imperatives, then apparently introducing rare or archaic words to evoke the hymnic response of the congregation.

The preliminary PRAISE (vv. 6-7), we might say, is inspired by an inward vision or evaluation of the community. Socially underprivileged groups are mentioned, first orphans and widows (v. 6a), and second the "lonely ones" and the "bound ones" (v. 7). Again, the first pair constitutes traditional clientele in pentateuchal laws especially of D provenance, prophetic writings, and some special psalms, occasionally named "prayers of the poor" (cf. Lurje, Studien; Munch, "Problem" [listing at "Introduction to Psalms"]; Hossfeld and Zenger, 83-88, 231-39; J. D. Pleins, ABD V, 402-14; cf., e.g., Deuteronomy 15; Am 2:6-8; 5:11-15; Psalms 9/10; 37). The other pair of miserables is much less defined in Scripture: "lonely or destitute ones" who are brought home by God (v. 7a)? Only Ps 25:16 gives an inkling of the kind of loneliness that might be intended by yāḥîd: "I am isolated and downtrodden," i.e., socially despised and marginalized, with family solidarity no longer effective. Perhaps the story of Abraham's sacrifice of Isaac has an echo of this meaning, too: the word yāḥîd is employed first of all in the sense of "only" son; but on second thought the son is no longer protected by parental love (cf. Gen 22:2, 12, 16). The beloved only son becomes the destitute, forlorn sacrifice. Only this story would lend itself to an interpretation of the "lost one" to be brought back home. The final group of needy people are the 'ăsîrîm, "bound ones." Indeed, they play a large role in

36

some prophetic traditions (cf. Zech 9:11-12; Isa 42:6-7; 49:8-9; 61:1), and also occur in a few psalms (Pss 79:11; 102:21 [RSV 20]; 107:10; 146:7). What kind of captivity are we facing in these texts? Political and economic motivations, individual and collective aspects seem intertwined. For a historical background we probably should look into exilic-postexilic life conditions of the Israelite community. The exilic Isaiah's kerygma of liberation seems to be behind our passage (cf. Isa 42:10-16; 43:1-7; 61:1-2; etc.).

The groupings of miserables to be helped and saved by God is contrasted by those *sôrărîm,* "rebellious ones" (v. 7c), whom we meet as well in v. 19 and in 66:7. In prophetic writings they appear as rebellious sons or leaders (Isa 1:23; 30:1; 65:2; Hos 9:15; Jer 6:28). Altogether, these passages may be read in the light of internal schisms within the religious community. They are not denunciations of foreign groups (cf. L. Ruppert, *TWAT* V, 957-63). This fact, together with the descriptions of internal social discriminations in vv. 6-7 and the designations used for *'ĕlōhîm* in vv. 6-7 (see below), all directed toward the very congregation of the faithful, make the HYMNIC INTRODUCTION a clear case of a late congregational hymn.

Divine epithets of vv. 6-7 comply fully with this interpretation. The Deity to be extolled is father to the fatherless (and mother to the motherless; cf. Gilkes, "Mother"), v. 6a. The epithet "Father" seems to have been used very early in family religion and very late in Israelite religion (cf. Gerstenberger, *Yahweh,* 1-12; van der Toorn, *Family Religion,* 226; both in Additional Bibliography, section B; Fischer, 111-20). God is *dayyan,* "attorney," for the widow (v. 6a), a rare and possibly late designation in the Hebrew OT (cf. 1 Sam 24:16; "judging" and "administering the law" are normally expressed by lexemes of the root *špṭ*). God is, of course, living in his holy abode, mentioned without big attributes in v. 6b. The next line has two participles in the causative Hiphil to hail the saving works of God. Both hardly allude to exilic topics: "he who lets settle down" *(môšîb),* "he leads out of" *(môṣî')),* being, so to speak, privatizing actions, aiming at a person's own home or one's own happiness, respectively (v. 7). The group of nouns and participles of the root *'sr,* "to bind, keep captive," may, of course, indicate prisoners of war (cf. Pss 79:11; 102:21; Zech 9:11-12), but need not be interpreted that way. There are sufficient instances of a spiritual, private meaning (cf. Pss 107:10; 146:7), and our present context supports this interpretation. Indeed, vv. 6-7 seem to have their closest formal and substantial parallels in congregational hymns like Psalm 113 or 146:6-10. The HYMNIC PRAISE as a whole thus radiates the values, concepts, and interests of a community of parishioners, not a people at arms.

Change of style, from neutral praise to direct address in vv. 8-11, signalizes a liturgical shift, but may also indicate literary stratification. The HYMNIC ADDRESS or DIRECT-ADDRESS HYMN is here theophanic in essence (see Jeremias, *Theophanie,* 123-27, 179-80 [Additional Bibliography, section B]), celebrating nature's reaction to the coming of God. The almost literal correspondence of vv. 8-9 with Judg 5:4-5 cannot be coincidental:

| Judg 5:4-5 | Ps 68:8-9 |
|---|---|
| Yahweh, when you came out from Seir, when you stepped forth from the land of Edom, the earth trembled, the heavens dropped water, the clouds dropped rain. The mountains quaked before Yahweh, the one from Sinai — before Yahweh, the God of Israel. | God, when you came out in front of your people, when you stepped forth in the desert, the earth trembled, the heavens dropped water, . . . . . . . . . . . . . . . . . . . . . . . . . . . . . . . . . . . . . . . . . . . before God, the one from Sinai — before God, the God of Israel. |

We can be assured that we are dealing with an old hymn handed down with slight variations in Israel (cf. Freedman, *Pottery,* 104-7; notable is the change from "God" to "Yahweh" or vice versa). Jeremias considers vv. 8-9 and Judg 5:4-5 the oldest forms of a very archaic REPORT OF THEOPHANY (Jeremias, *Theophanie,* 7-16 [Additional Bibliography, section B]; cf. younger parallels: Deut 33:2; Hab 3:3; Mic 1:3-4; Am 1:2; Pss 46:7 [RSV 6]; 50:2-3; Isa 63:19b–64:1). In Ps 68:8a, however, the starting point of God's journey, i.e., his abode, is missing (Judg 5:4: Seir, Edom), perhaps being intimated only by the rare term *yĕšîmôn,* "desert" (apparently charged with theological connotations: 13 times; cf. Deut 32:10; Isa 43:19-20). Two more peculiarities call for comment. In conformity to the general pattern of Psalms 42–83, the divine name is not used in 68:8-9, not even by later redaction. "Sinai" and the "God of Israel" are in view in v. 9, and there was no need to call him by his proper name, as in Judg 5:5. Furthermore, the reaction of nature — trembling of the earth, dripping water from the skies — was originally meant to portray fits of fear in creation (for ancient Near Eastern parallels see, e.g., Lipiński, "Juges 5,4-5"). But in our context (gently?) dripping and flowing water immediately connotes God's blessing: vv. 10-11 celebrate abundant rain and fertility bestowed on God's own *naḥălāh,* "hereditary land" (v. 10b), that will satiate all living creatures. Evidently, the horrible performance of God has exactly this finality, as in Ps 104:5-13. Thus we should rethink the "originality" of theophanic hymns. Possibly, vv. 8-11 constitute an old or new fertility song that borrowed theophanic features from a battle or victory tradition. As noted earlier, there is a marked affinity of such concepts to the Baal literature of Ugarit (cf. Smith, *History,* 49-51, with references to F. M. Cross and biblical parallels like 18:6-19 [RSV 5-18]; 29; 89:7-19 [RSV 6-18]).

Ba'lu gave forth his holy voice,
Ba'lu repeated the utterance of his lips.
His holy voice made the earth quake,
the utterance of his lips the mountains.
The sea-shores all got agitated [this line according to Olmo Lete, 209];

the heights of the earth rocked. (*KTU* 1.4 VII 29-35, according to de Moor, *Anthology,* 63; listing at Additional Bibliography, section B)

Vv. 12-15 are back to a neutral, third-person style again (which will last until v. 19). The passage may be an old, badly preserved victory hymn of the descriptive type, similar to Judg 5:19, 30. Victory over "the kings," sending out messengers of joy, division of spoils, and snowfall on Mount Zalmon (cf. Judg 9:48) are recognizable features. V. 14a may be a fragment from Judg 5:16a, erroneously mingled into our text. Is the larger part of the unit (vv. 12-14) an archaic oracle, issued before the battle against Sisera, and preserved through commemorations of that event (thus Kraus, et al.)? *'ōmer,* "word, speech" (v. 12a), may signify "audio communication by God" (cf. Ps 77:9 [RSV 8]; the synonyms *'emer* and *'imrāh,* however, are much more frequent: Num 24:4, 16; Josh 24:27; Pss 107:11; 138:4/Isa 5:24; Ps 119:11, 38, 67, 158, 172; 147:15). But the phrase *ntn 'ōmer/'emer/'imrāh* does not occur again in Hebrew Scripture. If we are dealing with an oracle we have to assume a mediator like Balaam (Numbers 22–24) to be the "hearer" of the divine word, but he is not mentioned in Psalm 68.

The division of spoils is part of victory's aftermath (cf. Judg 5:30). "Dove wings" may refer to precious amulets of some sorts (cf. Keel, *Tauben*). That it should be the task of women seems strange, being normally an act performed on the battlefield itself (v. 13, according to most translations; the expression *nĕwat bayit,* "pasture/living place of the house," does not make sense. It is often changed to *na'weh bayit,* "beauty of the house" = housewife, but as such is unique and perhaps to be emended: "[in] the living room of the house," however, still sounds unusual). In any case, there is a strong air of victory celebration around this element. And its final line commemorates snowfall on Mount Zalmon, "black mountain" (cf. the only other occurrence of this name in Judg 9:48, probably another location). The psalm with this reference enters the mythology of mountains, the pillars of the earth, and the abodes of divinities (cf. vv. 16-17; S. Talmon, *TWAT* III, 478-83).

The following hymn to the Lord of the mountain (vv. 16-19) clearly reveals its mythological background. Mount Bashan in Transjordan is seen in competition with the mountain that Yahweh chose as his residence (cf. de Moor, *Rise,* 162-207; Additional Bibliography, section B). The direct address of the abode of a deity (vv. 16-17) was not uncommon in the ancient Near East (cf. Hittite prayers; see A. Ünal, TUAT II, 791-817; Marduk and Enlil also are sometimes designated "Great Mountain"). In this case the transmitters must have been thinking rather of Mount Zion or Mount Sinai, dwelling places of Israel's God, the latter peak being mentioned in v. 18 (the Hebrew text, at this point, does not have "coming from" Sinai; this is a modern emendation, by analogy to Deut 33:2, presupposing another division of consonants: *bā['] missînay* instead of *bām sînay).* The subject is Yahweh's ascendence to his new seat, a violent, battle-torn change of holy mountains (v. 19). Direct address to the former holy places (v. 17a) is paralleled with direct address to victorious Yahweh venerated by his defeated enemies (v. 19). The profane battle of vv. 12-15 is linked up to a mythological war in regard to possession of the holy mountain (vv. 16-19, esp. vv. 18, 19ab; cf. Stolz, *Strukturen;* listing at "Introduction to Cultic Poetry"). What seems to be a mere contest among divine dwelling places turns into a (primordial?) war of God against hostile powers culminating in a stunning victory over all his foes who are taken captive. They explicitly include humans who have to pay tribute to Israel's God (v. 19ab). The last line of our section (v. 19cd) reverts to third-person discourse, warns against internal rebellion like v. 7c, and seems anticlimactic in every respect. It could be a later accretion. The ascension of Yahweh to his new seat on Mount Zion, very significantly, is the topic of the so-called Psalms of YAHWEH'S KINGSHIP (Psalms 47; 93; 96–99: cf. discussions there). V. 19 therefore plays an important role in determining the genre of Psalm 68 (as to sacred mountains in general see Clifford, *Mountain,* Additional Bibliography, section B).

Unexpectedly, the language of battle and victory is interrupted by a COMMUNAL BLESSING and PRAYER (vv. 20-21, note the first person plural). The language is entirely indicative of a congregational assembly. BLESSING FORMULAS abound in the Psalter; they literally "pay tribute" to the Deity who helps and protects the faithful. While the victory is celebrated, the congregation responds from its daily experiences (cf. 1 Sam 25:32; 1 Kgs 1:48; 5:21; Pss 28:6; 31:22 [RSV 21]; 66:20; 124:6; Ruth 4:14), drawing the message of victory into its own realm of life and faith, mincing mythological and historical language into small portions (cf. *yôm yôm,* "daily," Gen 39:10; Exod 16:5; Ps 61:9 [RSV 8]; Esth 3:4; Neh 8:18), a crucial liturgical intervention. We find similar appearances of the people, i.e., the worshiping community, in → Psalms 8; 33; 46; 90; 103; 118; 132; 135; 147 (cf. Scharbert, "Das 'Wir'"; listing at "Introduction to the Psalms"). Salvation from death is at the same time a very personal and a communal and mythic experience.

A praise of God's immense power of destruction, opening with adversative or hymnic *'ak,* "but" or "indeed" (v. 22), introduces a new liturgical unit (vv. 22-24; some exegetes, however, defend a closing position for v. 22, which may be viable). The description of God's enemies is archaic ("hairy skull"), and the idea of his cracking their heads also goes back to very ancient mythical concepts (cf. *Enuma elish:* Marduk defeats Tiamat this way: "The lord trod on the legs of Tiamat, / With his unsparing mace he crushed her skull. / When the arteries of blood he had severed, / The North Wind bore [it] to places undisclosed" [E. A. Speiser, *ANET,* 67]). This hymnic introduction prepares an ORACLE of God (vv. 23-24; cf. 12-15), mediated through whom and addressed to which audience? The prophetic formulaic introductions *(ně'um yahweh* or *kōh 'āmar yahweh)* are missing. We find a simple opening: "The Lord said" (v. 23a; cf. 12: "The Lord gave his saying"), which may have been standard in ancient times, before more elaborate formulas were applied to prophetic words. But can we count on prophets delivering messages in cultic assemblies? We probably should first opt for the more neutral designation "mediator" (Wilson, *Prophecy,* 21-28; listing at Additional Bibliography, section B), avoiding the stereotyped and much later concept of the canonical "Word-of-God messenger," and then freely admit communication from God to his people by way of priests or liturgists in early Jewish assemblies. Consequently, we may identify two cultic but probably "nonprophetic" oracles in Psalm 68, namely vv. 12-15 and 23-24 (→ Psalm 12). Both texts promise victory over unnamed enemies, the first probably in neutral, the second in direct-address discourse. "Bathing your foot in the blood" of the slain and "letting the dogs have their share of the enemy" (v. 24) are stereotyped expressions of victory (cf. Isa 63:3, 6; 1 Kgs 14:11; 16:4; 21:19; 22:38; 2 Kgs 9:10, 36). The later congregation will share this experience only spiritually, to be sure. The first line of the oracle (v. 23), on the other hand, communicates future salvation for God's community. Because of the most likely parallelism of the two cola at hand, and because of the restricted and hardly fitting meaning of the mountain name *bāšān*, one should consider the interpretation suggested by one Ugaritic text: "snake" or "primordial dragon" (cf. Albright, Dahood, Fensham, et al.). In this case we hear a message about a mythical salvation of the adherents of this God, which, of course, had to be specified in the contemporary wording. The bloody victory over the enemies is such a concretization. In other words, it is hard to tell whether the transmitters and redactors in using the key word *'āšîb*, "I will bring back" (cf. Gen 28:15; Jer 12:15; 16:15; 23:3; 24:6; 33:11; Ezek 34:16; etc.), wanted to hint at the liberation from Egypt or from Babylonia as a basic pattern of God's historical intervention.

The DESCRIPTION OF A PROCESSION (vv. 25-28), initiated by the verb "they see" (passive in LXX: "it is seen" = NRSV), brings in a visual, narrative element (cf. P. B. Duff, *ABD* V, 469-73). The discourse is direct address of God with an "I" appearing as speaker (v. 25: "my God, my King"). Obviously, an official is reporting to an audience. Three groups of participants stand out: singers, instrumentalists, and young women with their little drums (v. 26). If v. 27 is not a later insertion (*maqhēlôt*, "gathering," seems inappropriate for a procession; cf. 26:12), it may refer to the hymn singing. Four tribes are mentioned next as marching in the procession (v. 28: Benjamin, Judah, Zebulun, Naphtali. Could the last two names echo the lauding of Judg 5:18, and the first one be an extract of Judg 5:14?). This detail gave rise to much speculation about geographical and historical situations of the ceremony in question. Does our passage reflect premonarchical conditions? What does a concern like this for professional and political order of procession demonstrate? Illuminating texts are not easily available. The naming of only four tribes could indicate a regional alliance, perhaps centered at Mount Tabor, with its sanctuary and religious rites (Kraus, et al.). The Chronistic writings betray deep interest in liturgical personnel and procedures (cf. 1 Chronicles 16, etc.), but they do not employ the vocabulary and imagery found in Ps 68:25-28. And women marching with men toward the sanctuary seems to be an unusual arrangement, at least in strictly patriarchal setups (for women as singers and dancers in victory celebrations see Exod 15:20-21; 1 Sam 18:6; Judg 11:34; P. A. Bird, *ABD* VI, 951-57). Processions mentioned in prophetic books do not note any particular sequence of pilgrims (cf. Isa 2:3; 49:22; 62:10-12; Mic 7:12). There is, however, a question of ranking in the tradition of leaving Mount Sinai (Num 10:11-28), and several strands emphasize the superior importance of the weak (cf. 1 Sam 9:21; Mic 5:1; Bächli). These references do not account for the professional and gender sequence in v. 26 that seems to imitate the order of troops on the warpath. As a description of ceremonial proceedings the passage does fit well into the context (cf. Pss 24:7-10; 45:15-16 [RSV 14-15]; 55:15 [RSV 14]; 66:13-15; 132:6-8), and we may surmise that some sort of procession was the contemporary background for Psalm 68.

Vv. 29-32 switch into prayer language again. God is approached directly with entreaties (imperatives in vv. 29-31; best emendation of v. 29a: "Summon your might, God!"; the imperfects of v. 32 are apparently announcements of future submission of Egypt and Cush = Sudan). The element thus is clearly PETITION, not on the personal but on the political level. In spite of some textual uncertainties its main thrust is clear. The community (note the first person plural in v. 29) demands Egypt, the "beast of the reeds" (v. 31a), be defeated. Other enemy nations are vaguely referred to (v. 31d). If v. 32 is a later insertion, specifying Egypt as the main foe, the pleas in v. 31 had been less concrete before the accretion. In this case the enemies would have gone unnamed, being depicted only as powerful and greedy (v. 31c is much debated, however; cf. *HAL* 1193) and obsessed by warfare. Jerusalem is at stake (v. 30a). So far, this name has not been mentioned overtly. There has been only one allusion to Zion in v. 17. Although petition is not the rule in victory songs or communal hymns, in liturgical use of such texts entreaty for further protection and elimination of enemies would be very natural indeed (cf. Judg 5:31). One situational aspect becomes evident: the praying community is oriented toward the Jerusalem temple, whence it is expecting God's decisive help against foreign domination.

In true hymnic style the last section of Psalm 68 gets back to a SUMMONS TO WORSHIP and other expressions of adoration and praise (vv. 33-36). The BLESSING FORMULA at the very end of the psalm (v. 36d) takes up that of v. 20, being a proper ending of a communal hymn (cf. Pss 72:18-19; 106:48; 135:21). Looking at the passage more closely one discovers that the imperatives of v. 33 correspond exactly to those in v. 5a. In fact, v. 33 is a slightly enlarged version of v. 5a. The title "rider of heavens" (v. 34a) connects with v. 5b, "rider of the clouds." The following praising treatise on God's superior *'ōz,* "power" (vv. 34b-36), expands the topic of v. 29, a communal refrain, as well as the subject matter, e.g., of Psalms 29 and 148. As to the contents of the concluding element: the addressees are not members of a congregation, but international entities. The summons to worship for them is an order to surrender (cf. the ultimatum of Ps 2:10-12).

## Genre

Psalm 68, complex as it is, comprises a number of apparently unconnected form elements; the overall impression indeed is that of a broken text. We suggested already, in accord with some exegetes, various stages of growth. In order to determine its possible liturgical coherence and generic type, one should first investigate the latest redactional composition or layers and then proceed toward an evaluation of the whole psalm, considering, however, different stages of its development.

Phrases or lines of the psalm that seem to be completely unconnected with their context, granted that it be a liturgical one, may be attributed with some confidence to the latest redactional work. Thus vv. 7c, 9c, 14a, and 19cd are probably written additions at a late stage of transmission, when the psalm was already being read and meditated on in congregational services. Such ultimate remarks were supposed to clarify and emphasize certain points of theological interest. Vv. 7c and 19cd in this fashion are warnings against the *sôrărîm*, "troublemakers," within the congregation who disobey the community rules. V. 9c, *zeh sînay*, "the one from Sinai(?)," may well be an attempt to emphasize Yahweh's place of origin over against the later mention of Mount Bashan (v. 16). In the case of v. 14a the best explanation would be to assume a disconnected gloss taken over accidentally from Judg 5:16. Most of these latest additions are exhortatory in character, highlighting the early Jewish parenetical thrust of common worship.

Another layer of redactional work reflects the conscious creation of texts partially on the basis of already existing Scriptures and in the light of the congregation. Exactly these two characteristics are decisive: reference to Scripture and service to the Jewish community. Vv. 2-4, in quoting Num 10:35 and exposing the typical contemporary view as to "godless" and "just ones," share both features. Vv. 6-7 draw on D (cf. Deut 10:18; 16:11, 14; 24:19-21; 26:12-13; 27:19; etc.) and possibly Isaianic (cf. Isa 10:4; 14:17; 24:22; 42:7; 49:9; 61:1; also Pss 69:34; 79:11: 102:21; 107:10) affirmations. Vv. 8-9, as shown above, are dependent on Judg 5:4-5. The congregation of worshipers shows up in vv. 20-21 by virtue of an ostentatious "we" discourse, which is contrasted by the "I" of v. 25. The congregation is also visible behind the petition in vv. 29-32 and the summons to praise in vv. 33-36. The petition uses again a first-person plural pronoun (v. 29) and concentrates on Jerusalem (v. 30) and the spiritual or future political submission of Egypt and the Sudan (v. 32) in a move to affirm the universal rule of Israel's God. This very same motif orients the final section: all the "kingdoms of the earth" are drawn into recognizing and venerating the superior power of Israel's God (vv. 33-36). At this level Psalm 68 is a COMMUNAL HYMN, proclaiming the incredible faith of exilic-postexilic Jewish communities in the universal sovereignty of Yahweh, the exclusive God, creator of the world and governor of all its history (cf. Isa 40:12-31; 45:14-25; Psalms 2; 48; 96–99; 135; etc.). Israel's political reality being far from ideal at that time, the hymn carries a touch of eschatological expectation (Gunkel).

A third layer can be seen in those sections that do not bear the stamp of Jewish community life and theology but seem to be more archaic, going back, as it were, to old songs of fertility rites, war, victory, competition between sanctuaries, and so on. Of course, one may doubt whether they formed a comprehensive liturgical text before the community remodeled the whole to serve its own ends. If this were the case, the liturgists of the congregation put together sacred songs and fragments of old to suit their multiple purposes. The Jewish community presumably being a more homogeneous organism than earlier, more or less syncretistic sanctuaries, the variety of units at hand would rather speak in favor of an older complex festival, as Mowinckel envisions it. If this is correct, the units vv. 5, 10-11, 12-15, 16-19ab, 23-24, and 25-28 constitute the nucleus of Psalm 68, addressing themselves, after a standard summons to

43

praise (v. 5), to God, the raingiver, the one who wins victory, who prefers the sanctuary at hand, who is superior to primordial powers, who is led in solemn procession into his abode. In a noncentralized and not theologically homogenized society of preexilic provenience, a plurality of divine functions is perfectly feasible. A yearly festival at a local or regional sanctuary, or several of them, could be the point of origin for such hymns.

## Setting

If the different layers of Psalm 68 are to be identified as distinct genres, as proposed above, the settings are to be localized within varying rituals of specific communities. The people of preexilic times used to celebrate their great festivals at sanctuaries like Shiloh, Gilgal, Nob, Bethel, Tabor, and Dan (cf. only 1 Samuel 1–2 for Shiloh). Each sacred place cherished its own liturgical traditions, especially for those yearly events of profound impact. Attention is directed, in the nucleus of Psalm 68, toward the God of war and fertility (cf. Gerstenberger, *Yahweh*, 38-54) who is allied to that people in whose sanctuary he has chosen to dwell (v. 17: the name "Yahweh" may be a secondary modification). There are two oracles of victory in this ancient collection of songs (vv. 12-15 and 23-24) and ample affirmations about God's terrible power. Thus the procession in his honor, at the same time being a commemoration of mythical and historical victories under his leadership, is fully justified (vv. 25-28).

Interestingly enough, the name Yahweh appears only three times in the whole psalm (vv. 17, 21, 27), plus twice the short version "Yah" (vv. 5, 19). By contrast, *'ĕlōhîm* appears alone 22 times, not counting composite and other designations (e.g., *'ēl yiśrā'ēl, 'ădōnāy, šadday, rōkēb bā'ărābôt, 'āb, dayyan,* etc.). These statistics cannot be explained by the hypothesis of an "Elohistic redaction of Psalms 42–83" (cf. "Introduction to the Psalms," section 5). Rather, the evidence proves little concern for the exclusive and elusive personal name of Israel's God. At the first stage of Psalm 68, this seems all the more plausible, because Israel's religious history apparently moved from pluralism to monism (cf. Gerstenberger, *Yahweh:* Additional Bibliography, section B; Schroer, "Zeugnis"; listing at Psalm 65). The setting of the oldest psalm recognizable in our song may be the pre-Yahwistic tribal society (in v. 18 *sînay* is ambiguous, too, and not a full proof of Yahweh's identity).

With the second and third stages of our psalm we enter the time and realm of Jewish community services, either in Judah or in Babylonia. At this point Psalm 68 more and more serves as a memory of the glorious past, and as a wondrous manifestation of the newly discovered (cf. Isaiah 40–55) claim for Yahweh's universal rule. Tiny groups of defeated and deported Judahites dared to challenge the world powers of their day, by singing psalms like the one at hand and reading passages from prophetic books in their worship meetings. This leads us to a brief discussion of intention.

## Intention

In changing situations and with reference to different social organisms, the psalm in its distinct layers and liturgical functions served one and the same purpose: to strengthen the Israelite and Jewish communities of faith. "The God of Israel gives strength and power to the people" (v. 36bc). Memory and tradition, praise and petition are employed to this end.

## Bibliography

J. Aistleitner, "Zu Psalm 68," *BZ* 19 (1931) 29-41; W. F. Albright, "A Catalogue of Early Hebrew Lyric Poems (Psalm LXVIII)," *HUCA* 23 (1950/51) 1-39; idem, "Notes on Pss 68 and 134," *NorTT* 56 (1955) 1-12; P. Auffret, "Le Dieu d'Israel, c'est lui: Étude structurelle du Psaume 68," in idem, *Merveilles à nos yeux* (BZAW 235; Berlin/New York: de Gruyter, 1995) 1-30; A. Caquot, "Le psaume LXVIII," *RHR* 177 (1970) 147-182; C. Carniti, *Il Salmo 68 — studio letterario* (Rome: Libreria dell' Ateneo Salesiano, 1985); U. Cassuto, "Psalm 68" (1940), in idem, *Biblical and Oriental Studies* (tr. I. Abrahams; 2 vols.; Jerusalem: Magnes, 1973-75) 1:241-84; A. Ceballos Atienza, "La argumentación teológica-bíblica en la Bibli Parva de San Pedro Pascual," *EstBib* 42 (1984) 89-136; S. L. Cook, "Apocalypticism and the Psalter," *ZAW* 104 (1992) 82-99; J. B. Curtis, "Har-Basan, the Mountain of God (Ps 68:16[15])," in *Proceedings of the Eastern Great Lakes and Midwest Biblical Society* 6 (1986) 85-95; idem, "The Celebrated Victory at Zalmon (Ps 68:12-15)," in *Proceedings of the Eastern Great Lakes and Midwest Biblical Society* 7 (1987) 39-47; B. D. Eerdmans, "Psalm 68," *ExpTim* 46 (1934-35) 169-72; O. Eissfeldt, "Der Gott des Tabor und seine Verbreitung," *Archiv für Religionswissenschaft* 31 (1934) 14-41 (repr. in *KS* II, 29-54); J. A. Emerton, "The 'Mountain of God' in Psalm 68:16," in *History and Traditions of Early Israel* (ed. A. Lemaire; VTSup 50; Leiden: Brill, 1993) 24-37; F. C. Fensham, "Psalm 68:23 in the Light of the Recently Discovered Ugaritic Tables," *JNES* 19 (1960) 292-93; I. Fischer, *Wo ist Jahwe?* (SBB 19; Stuttgart: Katholisches Bibelwerk, 1989); J. P. Fokkelman, "The Structure of Psalm 68," in *In Quest of the Past* (ed. A. van der Woude; OTS 26; Leiden: Brill, 1990) 72-83; C. T. Gilkes, "Mother to the Motherless, Father to the Fatherless: Power, Gender, and Community in an Afrocentric Biblical Tradition," *Semeia* 47 (1989) 57-85; D. W. Goodwin, "A Rare Spelling or a Rare Root in Ps 68:10," *VT* 14 (1964) 490-91; S. Grill, "Der Berg Salmon Ps 68:15," *TZ* 17 (1961) 432-34; C. Grottanelli, "Da Myrrha alla mirra: Adonis e il profumo dei re siriani," in *Adonis* (ed. S. Ribichini, et al.; Rome: Consiglo Nazionale delle Ricerche, 1984) 35-60; D. Gualandi, "Salmo 68," *RivB (Italiana)* 6 (1958) 210-18; M. R. Hauge, "Some Aspects of the Motiv 'The City Facing Death' of Ps 68:21," *SJOT* 1 (1988) 1-29; P. Haupt, "Der achtundsechzigste Psalm," *AJSL* 23 (1906/7) 220-40; B. S. J. Isserlin, "Psalm 68, Verse 14," *PEQ* 103 (1971) 5-8; S. Iwry, "Notes on Psalm 68," *JBL* 71 (1952) 161-65; H.-J. Kraus, "Die Kulttraditionen des Berges Tabor," in *Basileia (Fest.* W. Freytag; ed. J. Hermelink et al.; Stuttgart: Evangelischer Missionsverlag, 1959) 177-84; J. P. Le Peau, "Psalm 68: An Exegetical and Theological Study" (diss., University of Iowa, 1981); C. Levin, "Das Gebetbuch der Gerechten," *ZTK* 90 (1993) 355-81; E. Lipiński, "Juges 5,4-5 et Psaume 68,8-11," *Bib* 48 (1967) 185-206; B. Margulis, "Ps. LXVIII,18-

19 and the Tradition of Divine Rebellion," *Tarbiz* 39 (1969) 1-8; P. D. Miller, "Two Critical Notes on Psalm 68 and Deuteronomy 33," *HTR* 57 (1964) 240-43; idem, *The Divine Warrior in Early Israel* (HSM 5; Cambridge: Harvard University Press, 1973) 102-13; S. Mowinckel, *Der Achtundsechzigste Psalm* (Oslo: Dybwad, 1953); F. Mussner, "Die Psalmen im Gedankengang des Paulus in Röm 9–11," in *Freude an der Weisung des Herrn* (*Fest.* H. Gross; ed. E. Haag, et al.; Stuttgart: Katholisches Bibelwerk, 1986) 243-63; G. del Olmolete, *Mitos y leyendas segun la tradición de Ugarit* (Fuentes de la ciencia biblica 1; Madrid: Cristiandad, 1981); J. P. M. van der Ploeg, "Notes sur quelques psaumes," in *Mélanges bibliques et orientaux* (*Fest.* M. Delcor; ed. A. Caquot, et al.; Kevelaer: Butzon und Bercker, 1985) 425-30; E. Podechard, "Psaume 68," *RB* 54 (1947) 502-20; A. Rose, "Les sens de Hagios et de Hosios dans les Psaumes selon la tradition chrétienne," in *Saints e santeté dans la liturgie* (ed. A. Triacca and A. Pistoia; Rome: CLV-Edizioni Liturgiche, 1987) 305-23; R. Rubinkiewicz, "Ps LXVIII,19 (= Eph IV,8): Another textual tradition or Targum?" *NovT* 17 (1975) 219-24; O. Schroeder, "Versuch einer Erklärung von Ps 68,14b.15," *ZAW* 34 (1914) 70-72; J. Schildenberger, "Psalm 68. Gott inmitten seines Volkes," *Erbe und Auftrag* 57 (1981) 443-47; M. S. Smith, *The Early History of God* (San Francisco: Harper & Row, 1990); J. A. Soggin, "Bemerkungen zum Deboralied Richter Kap. 5," *TLZ* 9 (1981) 625-39; F. Stolz, *Jahwes und Israels Kriege* (Zurich: Theologischer Verlag, 1972); R. A. Taylor, "The Use of Psalm 68:18 in Ephesians 4:8 in the Light of the Ancient Version," *BSac* 148 (1991) 319-36; R.-J. Tournay, "Le Psaume 68 (67)," *Vivre et Penser* 2 (1942) [= *RB* 51] 227-45; idem, "Le Psaume LXVIII et le livre des Juges," *RB* 66 (1959) 358-68; J. Vlaardingerbroek, "Psalm 68" (diss. Amsterdam, Free University, 1973); E. Vogt, "'Die Himmel troffen.' Psalm 68,9," *Bib* 46 (1965) 207-9; idem, "'Regen in Fülle.' Psalm 68,10," *Bib* 46 (1965) 359-61; idem, "'Die Wagen Gottes, zehntausendfach, Tausende *šin'an.*' Psalm 68,18," *Bib* 46 (1965) 460-63; M. Wilcox, "The Aramaic Targum to Psalms," in *Proceedings of the 9th World Congress of Jewish Studies* (ed. R. Giveon, et al.; Jerusalem: World Union of Jewish Studies, 1986) 143-50.


# Psalm 69:
# Complaint of the Individual

## *Structure*

|  | MT | NRSV |
|---|---|---|
| I. Superscription | 1 | - |
| II. Invocation and complaint | 2-5 | 1-4 |
| III. Confession and petition | 6-7 | 5-6 |
| IV. Complaint | 8-14ab | 7-13ab |
| V. Petition | 14cd-19 | 13cd-18 |
| VI. Complaint | 20-22 | 19-21 |
| VII. Imprecation | 23-29 | 22-28 |
| VIII. Vow | 30-32 | 29-31 |
| IX. Blessing | 33-34 | 32-33 |
| X. Hymnic closure | 35-37 | 34-36 |

The structure of our psalm, at first sight, is very lucid, fitting well into the molds of an individual complaint, with the possible exception of the last two sections. The BLESSING of the poor and the universal SUMMONS TO PRAISE (vv. 33-37) seem to exceed the concerns of the individual and his family group, at least at the point of a complaint-and-petition service (Becker; see "Introduction to Cultic Poetry," section 4B). But there are other examples of a wider horizon in complaints of the individual, giving rise to the idea of a communal reworking of the texts (cf. Pss 31:24-25; 102:13-23).

The word *šôšannîm* is unusual in an otherwise common SUPERSCRIPTION (v. 1; without this term: → Ps 11:1; etc.). By itself *šûšan* means "lily"; in ritual contexts it may signify a musical instrument or a certain melody. But the meaning remains obscure; cf. 45:1; 60:1; 80:1 (RSV superscriptions in each).

There is no distinct INVOCATION or initial "plea to be heard." Rather, the address of God immediately fuses with the urgent petition for deliverance (v. 2a) and without hesitation flows into a lengthy COMPLAINT (vv. 2b-5). The opening call to be saved may be found in the body of plaintive prayers (cf., e.g., 3:8 [RSV 7]; 6:5 [RSV 4]; 31:17 [RSV 16]; 109:26; 119:94, 146). Obviously, it was customarily used as a cry for help, thus becoming a popular formula (cf. 119:146). Sometimes it occurs already in opening lines (7:2 [RSV 1]; 54:3 [RSV 1]; 86:2), lending a sense of urgency to initial pleas. The metaphor of the muddy netherworld (cf. watery abyss: Jonah 2:3-7) and the description of ceaseless crying and begging for help from God as well as reference to the many enemies that threaten the suppliant, also leveling false accusations against him — all these facets combine perfectly with the opening part of a plaintive and petitionary prayer (see "Introduction to Cultic Poetry," section 4B). A petition oriented to this first round of complaints follows in vv. 14-19, after an interlude.

Looking back to divine scrutiny (*yāda'tā*, "you know," v. 6; cf. v. 20, possibly reflecting ancient praxis of verification of guilt, ordeal, etc.), the next unit represents itself as a strange mixture of CONFESSION and (negative) PETITION (vv. 6-7). Its closest parallels come from the so-called confessions of Jeremiah. Formally and in regard to vocabulary employed there, a number of affinities show up; cf. only *'attāh yāda'tā* in Jer 12:3; 15:15; 17:16; 18:23. More important, the whole concept of the suppliant being persecuted because of zeal for Yahweh and the temple, and his vicarious suffering (cf. v. 10) are reminiscent of some prophetic traditions, including besides Jeremiah the "servant of Yahweh" of Isaiah 53. "Stupidity" (*'iwwelet*, v. 6) is almost entirely a sapiential expression (of 25 occurrences, 23 are in the book of Proverbs, 2 in the Psalms; cf. Ps 38:6 [RSV 5]; the adjective *'ěwîl*, "dumb," likewise appears only a few times in prophetic books: Isa 19:11; 35:8; Jer 4:22; Hos 9:7; and once in Ps 107:17). "Tresspasses/guilt" (*'ašmāh;* related to *'āšām*, "sacrifice for guilt") is very rarely used outside sacrificial and priestly contexts (besides v. 6 only Am 8:14; cf. late occurrences of *'āšām*, outside Priestly writings, in Ps 68:22; Isa 53:10; Jer 51:5). Notable, however, is the late usage in the Chronistic tradition, e.g., Ezra 9:6, 7, 13, 15. To sum up: v. 6 seems to be a confession of guilt, clad in late terminology. Together with the two negative wishes or petitions (v. 7), which in essence mean to intercede for other members of the congregation ("those who hope for you; those who seek you," v. 7), we get the impression that someone of central importance for the people, like Moses himself (cf. Exod 32:30-32) or the servant of Yahweh (cf. Isa 53:4-12), has been offering this prayer to God. The malaise to be averted is expressed by two common verbs, *bôš,* Qal, and *klm,* Niphal, "be ashamed" and "be dishonored," respectively (cf. Klopfenstein, *Scham,* Additional Bibliography, section B). In the context of vv. 8 and 10 the words may acquire a specific meaning (see below).

A subsequent COMPLAINT (vv. 8-14ab) spells out the peculiar relationship of the suppliant with Yahweh. In the fashion of the Jeremiah tradition (suffering for Yahweh's sake) the psalmist portrays a spokesman of God being castigated for fulfilling his task. This jeremiad evolves around the terms *ḥerpāh* and *kĕlimmāh* ("shame, reproach," vv. 8, 10, 11), bordering the direct accusation against God: "For your sake did I bear reproach," v. 8; "the insults of those insulting you fell upon me," v. 10. Affirmations like these are rare in Hebrew Scripture; they match with some phrases in the confessions of Jeremiah: "Acknowledge that for your sake I bore reproach" (Jer 15:15b); "Every day I have been ridiculed, everybody is laughing at me" (20:7b). To conclude from these correspondences that Jeremiah was the author of our psalm would be unwarranted. In the light of the late composition of the book of Jeremiah, one would have to argue the other way around: the "confessions" of the prophet are psalmlike compositions of later transmitters (cf. E. S. Gerstenberger, "The Woe-Oracles of the Prophets," *JBL* 81 [1962] 249-63). We are left, then with our question: What figure is intended to loom behind vv. 6-13? In the absence of any theory or theology of the "Word-of-God messenger" within our passage, we may surmise that all individuals with zeal for Yahweh could be indicated as defenders of temple and customs (v. 10a). Consequently, the two sections under discussion are typical of the confessional situation of early Judaism. We need not go down to the late Hellenistic age with the vivid reports about the central role of the temple and the stories of heroic confessions of faith (cf. 2 Maccabees 7; Duhm [265-66, 269] places our psalm in the period of severest conflict between pro- and antihellenistic factions in Israel, ca. 168 to 160 B.C.E.; 1 Macc 7:1-25; 9:54-57 = Alcimus, treacherous high priest who persecuted the pious ones).

The PETITION in vv. 14cd-19, opening with a fresh invocation, is more or less in accordance with standard individual complaints, although each psalm shows its own peculiarities, too. In our case various imperatives, cries for help and acceptance, abound, and one specific passage (vv. 15-16) is intimately tied to some of the opening complaints (vv. 2-3), entreating God to save the suppliant from the watery abyss (symbolizing death; cf. Barth, *Errettung;* listing at "Introduction to Psalms"). Five decisive words used in the opening section to describe the awful conditions of the netherworld recur in vv. 15-16 ("sink in," "deep waters," "sweep over," "flood," "abyss"), another one is replaced by a synonym ("mire"). Thus the liturgical tie to initial complaints is strong (cf. Allen, 578). Strangely enough, there is barely any reference to the persecutors in vv. 14-19 (cf. v. 5), because the only word in this respect in the former part (*miśśōnĕʾay,* "from those who hate me," v. 15b) seems misplaced and secondary, and the only one in the latter (*ʾōyĕbay,* "my enemies," v. 19b) is quite general. Both expressions do occur, however, in v. 5, with much more coloring to them. Vv. 14, 17-19 otherwise do not ponder the ill fate of the suppliant, but concentrate completely on imploring God for help. While ties to vv. 2-5 in this fashion are obvious, we do not find any connection to vv. 6-13. Naming the pleader "servant" (v. 18a) in a way could be understood to point to the "servant" figure of vv. 6-13, but this would be quite a hidden meaning. Explication of the calamity at hand in v. 18b is absolutely vague: ṣar lî, "I am miserable."

In regard to the imperatives of petition, already mentioned, we note the preponderance of "answer me" (vv. 14, 17, 18). This cry to be heard and attended was originally part of the initial plea. "When I call, answer me, O God of my right" (Ps 4:2 [RSV 1]), is a proper opening line of an individual complaint (cf. also 55:2-3 [RSV 1-2]; 86:1; 102:3 [RSV 2]). Increasingly this typical introductory plea has been used to summarize petition as a whole (cf. 13:4 [RSV 3]; 27:7; 108:7 [RSV 6]; 119:145; 143:1, 7).

For the remaining features we may note the explicit designation of the unit as "supplication" (těpillāh, v. 14; cf. 66:19; 80:5 [RSV 4]; 102:1, 18 [RSV superscription, 17]), the use of a typical verb of petition nṣl, "deliver, tear away from," in v. 15 (cf. F. L. Hossfeld and B. Kalthoff, TWAT V, 570-77), three negative, preventive pleas in vv. 15-16, and insistent calls for divine attention, rapprochement, and helpful action in vv. 17-19. Besides "answer me" we find the following pleas: "turn toward me" (v. 17b), "do not hide your face" (v. 18a), "come close to me, redeem me" (v. 19a), "set me free" (v. 19b). All these expressions are characteristic of PETITION in complaints, in both individual and congregational contexts (cf. 44:27 [RSV 26]; 86:16; 143:7). Interestingly enough, however, clusters of these specific verbs found in vv. 17-19 occur in acrostic psalms of later epochs, namely Psalms 25 and 119. Considering only the relevant imperatives we discover that "come close to me" (from qrb) as a plea to God is unique in the Psalter, meeting a counterpart only in 119:169 ("let my clamor come close to you"). All the other verbs are represented in imperative or jussive form within Psalm 119 (cf. vv. 132, 19, 154, 134, listing the verbs in the sequence of 69:17-19). Similarly, the pair pnh/pdh, "turn to"/"rescue," providing an inclusion for our segment vv. 17-19, is present in 25:16, 22. Taken together, the above observations could suggest layers of growth in this petitionary passage, with vv. 15-16 antedating vv. 14, 17-19. Note also the emphatic use of "Yahweh" in vv. 14 and 17, in a prayer that mostly addresses 'ělōhîm (vv. 2, 6, 7c, 14c, 30, 33, 36).

Vv. 20-22 renew the COMPLAINT element with some vocabulary used already in vv. 6, 8, 10, 11. Yet the central concern of vv. 6-13 is missing: there is no hint at the suppliant's suffering for the sake of his God, or on account of his religious zealousness. Rather, this complaint section portrays a typical situation of a normal member of society: for some reason he/she has become suspect of carrying a spiritual disease, of being the target of divine revenge, thus endangering his/her family or community (cf. 88:19 [RSV 18]; Job 19:6-22; 30; see "Introduction to Psalms," section 2). Family solidarity, essential for survival, has given way to distrust and hostility. Therefore, the craving for human support, even traditional signs of sympathy ("condolence [by waving one's head], comfort," v. 21cd; "bread of pity" [bārût], v. 22a), have not been extended to the one in sorrow and anxiety. Social ties are broken; this is cause for alarm and physical suffering (v. 21ab). A vivid description of social ostracism is given in 41:7-10 (RSV 6-9). Treacherous friends increase the pain by their calumny. The same phenomenon is alluded to in v. 22 ("gall instead of bread, vinegar for my thirst"; cf. Matt 27:34, 48). Job's friends, being, as it were, bad counselors, at least did not exploit the sufferer (cf. Job 1–2). After all, the little passage of complaint is talking about a plain suppliant, contending with his fellow men. It is not portraying a special figure of a confessor or servant of the Lord.

After passing through various stages of liturgical complaint and petition, the following unit (vv. 23-29) is a full-fledged IMPRECATION against enemies (see Psalm 109). Giving only one line of motivation for all the brutal denunciations (v. 27), the list includes harsh maledictions, which should reveal, however, some connection with alleged crimes of the opponents. Their sacrifices (v. 23; cf. emendation of šālôm to šelem, "offering," and the parallelism with šulḥān, "sacrificial table") will attract disaster instead of divine benevolence. Blindness and fragility (v. 24), destruction of living quarters (v. 26; the designation ṭîrāh is rare) may have been evil wishes of the enemies against the sufferer. The repeated address of God (vv. 25, 27, 28) assures the proper understanding of who is responsible for punitive action. The suppliant is certainly incapable of executing any of his imprecations.

The last line (v. 29) is the most enigmatic (cf. Herrmann, Smith). Why does the passage culminate in a wish to blot out the enemies from the "book of life"? And what is this book about? Being a list of the "justified" or "righteous" (ṣaddîqîm; cf. Exod 32:32-33; Isa 4:3; Jer 17:13; Ezek 13:9; Dan 7:10; 10:21; 12:1; Mal 3:16), i.e., of confessing members of the Judean community, the concept is exilic or postexilic in origin. There are very few and dim traces of this idea in the psalms (cf. Pss 87:6; 139:16). Vv. 28-29, then, using the late concepts of the just community and its just members (see 68:4 [RSV 3]; cf. Levin, "Gebetbuch," Additional Bibliography, section C) may be a timely addition to the section in question, which originally ended in v. 27. Further evidence of this confessional grouping comes up in vv. 33-34.

The Vow (vv. 31-32, in the strict sense), based on declarations of humility and confidence (v. 30), is a fitting close to any individual complaint (cf. 7:18 [RSV 17]; 56:13-14 [RSV 12-13]; 70:6a, c [RSV 5a, c]; 71:22-24; 109:30-31). The confession of lowliness and forlornness (v. 30a) is formulaic: 40:18 (RSV 17); 70:6 (RSV 5); 86:1; 109:22. In any ritual of petition, sacred or profane, historical or contemporary, it would serve as a signal of submission and dependence on the one approached in supplication (cf. Gerstenberger, Mensch, 21-22, 126). A glorifying expression of trust (it may also be read as a petition; v. 30b; for śgb, Piel, "protect," cf. 20:2 [RSV 1]; 59:2 [RSV 1]; 91:14; 107:41) provides a further foundation of the following vow (vv. 31-32). It is explicitly a promise of a thanksgiving song (v. 31a; in this case šîr, "song," must be a synonym of tôdāh, v. 31b, which originally indicated a "thanksgiving sacrifice"; cf. 66:13-15). The wordplay is obvious: a šîr is better than a šôr, "bull" (v. 32a; cf. Allen). The other possible explanation would be: šîr and tôdāh in v. 31 indeed originally meant "song" and "sacrifice," and v. 32 is a later view along the line of 40:7 (RSV 6) and 50:7-15, which relativize sacrifice probably in the wake of the destruction of the temple and worship services far from Jerusalem (cf. Keel, *Welt,* 306-8). First-person singular cohortatives of *hll,* Piel, "praise" (v. 31), are not too frequent but they are significant; cf. 22:23 (RSV 22); 35:18; 109:30; 145:2; 146:2 (all occurrences are either in the context of a vow or of hymnic praise; *gdl,* Piel, does not appear in this fashion). Thus the pledge "I will praise" is well established as a genuine expression of vow in complaint liturgies, besides formulations like "I will give thanks" (*'ôdeh;* cf. 35:18; 109:30); "I will extol" (*'ărômēm;* cf. 30:2), etc. The term "parted" or "cleft hoof," used in v. 32b beside the hapax legomenon "horned" (*maqrin,* Hiphil participle from *qrn*), plays a large role in the dietary rules of Leviticus 11 and Deuteronomy 14 (cf. Gerstenberger, *Leviticus,* 134-40; Additional Bibliography, section B). It is imaginable that the allusion has been consciously made, perhaps in order to relativize even further the importance of sacrifice and meat consumption (cf. Ps 50:7-15).

Vv. 33-34 are BLESSINGS or well-wishes for "oppressed ones," "god-seekers," "poor people," "imprisoned ones"; this section places the whole prayer into that congregation of worshipers who consider themselves "miserable," and some of the OT psalms testify to the existence of such communities (Psalms 9/10; 37; 68:6-7 [RSV 5-6]; 73; cf. Lohfink, *Lobgesänge;* Zenger, "Selig," both in Additional Bibliography, section C; J. D. Pleins, *ABD* V, 402-14). Every one of those names occurs in various passages within the book of Psalms, often signaling the conditions of the exilic or postexilic Jewish community (cf. *'ănāwîm,* "oppressed ones": 22:27 [RSV 26]; 37:11; 76:10 [RSV 9]; 147:6 — *dōrĕšê yahweh,* "seekers of Yahweh," etc.: 9:11 [RSV 10]; 34:11 [RSV 10] — *'ebyônîm,* "poor": 9:19 [RSV 18]; 12:6 [RSV 5]; 140:13 [RSV 12] — *'asîrîm,* "bound or imprisoned ones": 68:7 [RSV 6]; 79:11; 102:21 [RSV 20]; 107:10 [RSV 9]). Most frequent are the words for "oppressed ones" and "poor," the first and third of our list. They also appear in couplets, making fine parallels. But there are no clusters of these appellations outside Psalm 69, serving as a sort of self-designation of the Jewish community. The closest we can get is the list of the preferred partners of Yahweh in 146:7-9 and the enumeration of four social groups in → 68:6-7 (RSV 5-6; only the "bound ones" coincide with 69:34b). Nine classes of persons are mentioned in Psalm 146, and again only one of them corresponds with our list of four: the imprisoned ones (v. 34b — 146:7c). Nevertheless, the enumeration of Psalm 146 has a similar profile: the worshiping community comprises all sorts of weak and underprivileged people, who apparently constitute the congregation. And "bound ones" is common ground for the three passages mentioned — evidence of exilic origin or mentality? With vv. 33-34 we thus make a transition into the realm of the larger community, as the suppliant usually experiences it when inviting his people for a thanksgiving ceremony (cf. Ps 22:23-27 [RSV 22-26]). In our case this larger community to be invited by the suppliant upon deliverance is nothing else than the early Jewish congregation, which strongly favors all underprivileged.

In accordance with the congregational horizon and extending it toward the whole world, the now concluding passage vv. 35-37 summons everyone to the PRAISE of God, who will gather his believers at Zion and reconstruct the province of Judah. Exilic or postexilic expectations are clearly visible in these announcements. Formally, the section is a little hymn, with a summons to praise (v. 35), hymnic affirmations (v. 36ab), and a promise to the deported that they may occupy again their home country (vv. 36c, 37). Such a cosmic and international dimension of feasting is hardly feasible in small family and clan circles. Its background must be the Jewish community that had to find ways of manifesting their faith in Yahweh over against imperial, provincial, and local supremacies. Hymnic elements as signs of orientation toward community can be found in individual complaints more often: 22:28-32 (RSV 27-31); 31:20-22 (RSV 19-21); 40:14 (RSV 13); 102:13, 17-23 (RSV 12, 16-22).

## Genre

A more detailed analysis with conclusions in regard to genre and setting can be found in Gerstenberger, "Psalm 69"; the most profound investigation of the literary growth and liturgical use of our text, coming to very similar conclusions, is that of Tillmann (vv. 6-14ab, 20-30 for him are additions in the mold of postexilic, "Jeremianic" confessions; they make the text a community prayer [pp. 118, 134, 247]). Considering the observations made above and also acknowledging that individual complaints in ancient times have been part of small-group healing rituals extant, e.g., in Babylonian incantations (cf. Gerstenberger, *Mensch*), we cannot avoid a "separatist" conclusion: there was apparently an old INDIVIDUAL COMPLAINT song describing the suppliant's plight in metaphorical terms as "going down to hell," sinking into the mire of the netherworld, the abyss closing the gate behind him. This psalm would roughly comprise vv. 2-5, 14b-16, 21-27, 30-32, altogether 23 poetic lines. The average length of old complaint prayers in Babylonia and Israel is approximately 10 to 20 lines, so the text isolated would not exceed very much the established size. It also would contain all the elements necessary for a ritual prayer: invocation, complaint, petition, complaint, imprecation, vow. The rest of the psalm (21 poetic lines of a total of 44, much later organized in 37 verses) belongs to a layer of interpretation and adaptation of that original prayer, remodeling significantly the image of the sufferer. He is no longer a man at the brink of death, being devoured by abysmal powers, but a conscious adorer of Yahweh bearing responsibility for temple, community, and the proclamation of the universal God. He is a confessing believer constantly seeking integration with his community of faith (cf. vv. 6-13, 14a, 17-19, 20, 28-29, 33-37) and defending himself against the persecutions of apostates.

Looking at our psalm in this way we find it difficult to follow any interpretation adhering to the idea of one unified text. Thus, e.g., the perfect correspondences that Allen discovers between vv. 1-14 and 15-33 seem partially artificial. That there has been a measure of compositional ordering is patent from the text. But liturgical ends and existing text material to be reworked did not permit freelance poetic modeling. The genre, however, stayed just about the same in spite of changes of social setting. Complaints of the individual were to be found not only in family religions but also in parochial settings (→ Psalm 12), although, evidently, in a different liturgical setup and with all the connotations and implications given by being a suppliant embedded in a larger, not familial, but confessional community.

## Setting

Naturally, changing texts may indicate changing settings. As different groups of people and different social structures experience their specific dangers and anxieties, they produce their distinct prayers, and the texts under scrutiny disclose these divergent circumstances. Complaints of the mythological and general type (fear of death, social marginalization) seem to sprout from small-group, familial ritual (cf. "Introduction to Psalms," section 2). "Confessional" complaint with a background of the faith community (note the plural designations of members of the congregation in vv. 7, 29, 33-34), on the other hand, proves deep moorings in early Jewish assemblies. While the familial setting of complaint and supplication is well attested by Babylonian incantations, the use of individual/communal prayer in congregations of the sixth to third centuries B.C.E. is little investigated. The psalms of individual complaint were presumably sung and/or read in local assemblies of Judahites in Judah and abroad. Mentioning the temple, Zion, or Jerusalem in these texts does not make them psalms exclusively of a central temple community. It is well known that the dispersed faithful oriented themselves quite intensively toward their spiritual center Jerusalem (cf. Psalm 137; Elbogen, *Gottesdienst* [listing at "Introduction to Cultic Poetry"]; Haran, *Temple;* Hauge, *Sheol,* both Additional Bibliography, sections B and C; P. J. King, *ABD* III, 764-65). Details of liturgical uses are hard to ascertain; reduction to meditative reading, as Füglister proposes for the time of Jesus, would be extremely doubtful for the preceding centuries. The community setting of the complaint suggests that the conscience of a martyr for God's sake is being rehabilitated by the orthodox congregation. Early Christians saw the life and passion of Christ prefigured especially in the Psalter; therefore they even used certain psalms (e.g., 22; 31; 69) as a description of what had happened to their Master, drawing on and quoting freely the old prayers (for Psalm 69 cf. Matt 27:34, 48; Mark 15:36; Luke 23:36; John 19:29; Rom 11:9-10; etc.).

## Intention

Complaints and supplications are necessary religious and liturgical expressions in almost any social environment boasting some organization. Prayers of this type permit in the first place articulation of personal and social ills, of injustices and imbalances endemic in a particular social and religious structure. Second, liturgical outbursts like Psalm 69 provide much-desired power against the harmful forces at hand that threaten individuals, eliminate solidarity, destroy communion, and let life be swallowed up by death. In this regard the help of

53

God, sought with great fervor, includes destruction of enemy power. In other words, complaints and supplications are corrective forces of the highest quality within their respective communities, be they small-scale and intimate or confessional and semipublic.

## Bibliography

L. C. Allen, "The Value of Rhetorical Criticism in Psalm 69," *JBL* 105 (1986) 577-89; M. L. Barré, "The Formulaic Pair *ṭwb (w)ḥsd* in the Psalter," *ZAW* 98 (1986) 100-105; J. B. Bauer, "Exegesegeschichte und Textkritik, Ps 68 (69),32," *ZAW* 102 (1990) 414-17; J. Becker, *Israel deutet seine Psalmen* (SBS 18; Stuttgart: Katholisches Bibelwerk, 1966) 45-48; C. Bryan, "Shall We Sing Hallel in the Days of the Messiah?" *Saint Luke's Journal of Theology* 29 (1985) 25-36; M. Casalis, "Angústia versus esperança," *EsTe* 25 (1985) 281-88; F. Cassou, "En quête de Dieu — Psaume 69: proposition de structure," *Foi et Vie* 87 (1988) 49-57; J. H. Coetzee, "Lyding 'om u ontwil' in Psalms 44 en 69," *SK* 9 (1988) 1-9; J. H. Eaton, "Music's Place in Worship," in *Prophets, Worship, and Theodicy* (*OTS* 23; ed. J. Barton, et al.; Leiden: Brill, 1984) 85-107; E. S. Gerstenberger, "Psalm 69: Complaint and Confession," *Covenant Quarterly* 55 (1997) 3-19; M. Hahn, "Die Flut will mich ersäufen," *Zeitschrift für die Praxis des Religionsunterrichts* 23 (1993) 68-75; M. Haran, "The Shining of Moses' Face," in *In the Shelter of Elyon* (JSOTSup 31; *Fest.* G. W. Ahlström; ed. W. B. Barrick, et al.; Sheffield: JSOT Press, 1984) 159-73; W. Herrmann, "Das Buch des Lebens," *Das Altertum* 20 (1974) 3-10; Z. Kameeta, "O Lord: Psalms and Sermons from Namibia," *Risk* 28 (1986) 1-62; A. Pezhumkattil, "The Image of the Servant of the Lord in Psalm 69,2-30 in Comparison to the other 'Servant' Psalms" (diss., Pont. Univ. Gregoriana, Rome, 1986); G. Pfeifer, "Ich bin in tiefe Wasser geraten und die Flut will mich ersäufen (Psalm 69:3)," *VT* 37 (1987) 327-39; H. Schmidt, *Das Gebet des Angeklagten im Alten Testament* (BZAW 49; Giessen: Töpelmann, 1928); B. Sirch, "Deus in adiutorium meum intende," in *Liturgie und Dichtung I* (ed. H. Becker, et al.; St. Ottilien: EOS, 1983) 315-43; C. R. Smith, "The Book of Life," *GTJ* 6 (1985) 219-30; N. Tillmann, *'Das Wasser bis zum Hals'* (Münsteraner Theologische Abhandlungen 20; Altenberge: Oros-Verlag, 1993); E. Vogt, "Ihr Tisch werde ihnen zur Falle," *Bib* 43 (1962) 79-82.

## Psalm 70:
## Complaint of the Individual

### Structure

| | MT | NRSV |
|---|---|---|
| I. Superscription | 1 | - |
| II. Invocation, petition | 2 | 1 |
| III. Imprecation | 3-4 | 2-3 |
| IV. Praise of God | 5 | 4 |
| V. Self-abasement, confidence, petition | 6 | 5 |

Psalm 70 in its substance and line by line, with only minor deviations, is identical with 40:14-18 (→ Psalm 40). The text has been used in its own right, however, as a plaintive petition, and therefore deserves a separate treatment. In Psalm 40 the text is used as an appendix to a thanksgiving hymn. All psalmic texts being communal and liturgical in essence, we should not be taken by surprise with doubled transmissions and varying uses.

The SUPERSCRIPTION is identical with that of → Psalm 38. Schottroff (Gedenken, 336-37; listing at Additional Bibliography, section B) suggests a semantic and ritual connection of lĕhazkîr, "to remember," with that part of a sacrifice which "remembered" or "called upon" the name of Yahweh (cf. Lev 2:2, 9, 16; 5:11-13; etc.). Although such liturgical annotations were late additions to the psalms, Schottroff allows that they retained some authentic information about the original use of the psalms (Gedenken, 336).

INVOCATION and PETITION (v. 2) form a self-sufficient opening line. Appellation to 'ĕlōhîm (not yhwh as in Ps 40:14 [RSV 13]) comes first, as it should according to postulated etiquette (exceptions from this rule: e.g., 12:2 [RSV 1]; 69:2 [RSV 1]). The imperative rĕṣeh, "be gracious" (40:14 [RSV 13]), is not present in our psalm, nor is the outright complaint section of 40:13 (RSV 12). Thus if Psalm 70 has been taken from Psalm 40 and made an independent prayer, the opening line was consciously remodeled to serve a new purpose. Omitting the first imperative would support this theory, the infinitive lĕhaṣṣîlēnî, "to save me" (v. 2a), now being dependent on the verb at the very end of the line (ḥûšāh, "make haste," v. 2b, which also closes the first line of v. 6; 40:18b [RSV 17b] differently). The alteration of divine appellations ('ĕlōhîm, yahweh, v. 2) in one and the same line is difficult to assess. Ps 40:14-18 (RSV 13-17) has yhwh in decisive positions (vv. 14, 17 [RSV 13, 16]). Only the personal confession uses 'ădōnāy and 'ĕlōhay in direct and confidential address (40:18 [RSV 17]). Psalm 70, in contradistinction, brings in yhwh only in second place (v. 2b, and in 6d after a twofold 'ĕlōhîm, vv. 5c, 6b). The evidence of Hebrew MSS proves, however, that there has been a lot of exchange of wording between 40:14-18 and 70 during scribal transmission. Chances are, however, that Psalm 70 is more deeply entrenched in the 'ĕlōhîm tradition of Psalms 42-83 (see FOTL XIV, 37).

The first line of our prayer, then, is a call to God combined in one and the same breath with a plea for salvation, which is afterward taken up in v. 6, thus enveloping imprecations and praise with personal entreaty. The verb ḥûš, "hasten," in its imperative singular form with emphatic ending -āh, gives urgency to this petition (cf. formulaic use in 22:22b [RSV 21b]; 38:23 — both prayers use ḥûšāh in the final petition, and both employ a variety of designations for "God"; 71:12 also has the formula in the Qere; 141:1 shows the shorter version [like v. 6] in the opening position).

There is no real complaint section in Psalm 70, nor any description of suffering. Both dimensions are presupposed, however, in vv. 3-4, the IMPRECATION of those who cause anxieties and personal damage. Their malicious acts are alluded to in all three relevant lines, each time in the second half, after articulating a vehement ill-wish. They "seek my life" (mĕbaqšê napšî, v. 3b; cf. 35:4; 38:13 [RSV 12]; 40:15 [RSV 14]; and with slight variations of words or forms:

54:5 [RSV 3]; 63:10 [RSV 9]; 71:13, 24; 86:14), "they delight in my misery" (*ḥăpēṣê rā'ātî*, v. 3d; only parallel: 40:15 [RSV 14]; positive phrase: "they delight in my righteousness," 35:27), "they say: Aha, aha!" (*ha'ōmĕrîm he'āḥ he'āḥ*, v. 4b; cf. 35:21; 40:16 [RSV 15]; Ezek 25:3; 26:2; 36:2), the last exclamation being not only a manifestation of gloating but an evil and destructive force in itself.

The first half of each line carries strong expressions of distaste and condemnation to be wrought by God over the evildoers. There are five typical demands to do away with them. A frequent expression of such IMPRECATION or ill-wish to be executed by God is *yēbōšû*, "may they be put to shame," i.e., "be socially destroyed" (cf. Klopfenstein, *Scham*, 90-107, Additional Bibliography, section B). This very wish appears 16 times in the Psalter. Another good number of negative affirmations with the same verb ("I shall not be put to shame" or similarly) emphasize the firmness of that person who is protected by God (cf., e.g., 25:3; 86:17; 109:28). Some of the parallel passages stand out because they indulge in a similar array of denunciations as our vv. 3-4; cf. 31:18 (RSV 17); 35:4 (all four verbs of our v. 3); 35:26 (two verbs of our v. 3a and some similar expressions); 71:13, 24 (one verb and similar wording); 83:18 (RSV 17; two verbs of our v. 3a plus two synonyms); 129:5 (two verbs of our v. 3). These listings demonstrate the widespread use of ill-wishes against enemies and evildoers. The expression "be put to shame" and its synonyms signify social and possibly physical annihilation to be effected by divine powers or sanctions as the only possible means of defense for the marginalized sufferers (see "Introduction to Psalms," section 2; Gerstenberger, "Enemies"; listing at "Introduction to Psalms"). The quintuplet of verbs is led by "be put to shame," and possibly culminates in "be utterly destroyed" (v. 4a: *yāšōmmû* instead of *yāšûbû*), if this verb *šmm*, "be waste," or "be cut off from life," may be transplanted from 40:16a (RSV 15a; Klopfenstein, *Scham*, 97 n. 156, emends the other way around). The IMPRECATION thus constitutes the very center of this psalm, implying two sides, that of complaint and that of aggressive petition to destroy the authors of suffering. The powerful words used against them in themselves do not refer to any deity. This observation may lead us to conclude that imprecatory formulations of this type are very old, probably antedating Yahwism, and were originally administered as magic spells against enemies (cf. Mowinckel, *PsSt* I, 7, 14-23, 95-103; → Psalm 109).

Next in line is PRAISE of the God who helps his faithful (v. 5). We may call it anticipated thanksgiving, very similar to that of 35:27. The exhortation to join in praise goes to participants of the ceremony and is quite frequent in complaint psalms, whenever they anticipate being heard and helped by God. Thus the thanksgiving ceremony of Psalm 22 is introduced by a threefold summons to praise: "You who fear Yahweh, praise him! All you offspring of Jacob, glorify him; stand in awe of him, all you offspring of Israel" (v. 24 [RSV 23]). The quotation of a jubilant cry "great is God" (in 35:27; 40:17c [RSV 16c] = "great is Yahweh"; there is, of course, a tradition history of this jubilant formula from the ancient Near East to Islamic "Allah is great" as well) amounts to a powerful affirmation of divine power, counterbalancing the destructive words of the enemies of v. 4. The summons to be happy, articulated in wish form and by direct-address discourse to God (v. 5a; *śmḥ* is the more frequent expression: 43 times in the Psalter, partly of gloating enemies; directed to parishioners/congregation: 5:12 [RSV 11]; 14:7; 32:11; 34:3 [RSV 2]; 35:27; 40:17 [RSV 16]; 58:11 [RSV 10]; 64:11 [RSV 10]; 67:5 [RSV 4]; 68:4 [RSV 3]; 69:33 [RSV 32]; 85:7 [RSV 6]; 97:12; 105:3; 107:42; 119:74; 149:2; only five passages are in direct-address style), as well as description of joyful outbreaks or shouting (v. 5c), fill the first half-lines, while designation of the blissful respondents follows in corresponding second stichoi. "All who seek you" (v. 5b) is in contrast to v. 3b, "those who seek my life"; "those who love your help" (v. 5d) has a certain affinity to "those who like my grief" (v. 3d). Evildoers and godless are thus juxtaposed to the saved and happy ones, i.e., the community of God-fearing people. It is a liturgical confrontation. Imprecation and praise are mutually dependent, which seems to be a structural phenomenon in complaint songs and ceremonies (cf. "Introduction to Cultic Poetry," section 4B).

At the very end of the psalm a self-abasement formula introduces final PETITIONS: the positive one of v. 6b, and the one formulated negatively in v. 6d. That means that parallelism is again complementary, as in vv. 2-5. The MT puts "God" and "Yahweh," respectively, as recipients of petition, urging speedy salvation, nothing more. But there is a clear connection between v. 6 and v. 2, by way of the plea *ḥûšāh*, "hurry up!" (outside the twin texts only in the following complaints: 22:20 [RSV 19]; 38:23 [RSV 22]; 71:12b [Qere]; 141:1). Only in v. 2 is the plea explicitly filled with demands to help the sufferer, but this insinuation resounds also at the end of the psalm. Self-abasement (v. 6a) supports the plea, just as hymnic address does in v. 6c. The latter has all the qualities of an AFFIRMATION OF CONFIDENCE, especially by the possessive pronouns used ("you are my help and my savior"). Similar formulas in individual complaints include 16:5 (RSV 4); 22:10, 11 (RSV 9, 10); 25:5; 31:4, 5 (RSV 3, 4); 32:7; 43:2; 44:5 (RSV 4); 63:2 (RSV 1); 71:3, 5, 6.

## Genre/Setting

In spite of resorting very little to formal complaints, the psalm has all the characteristics of an INDIVIDUAL COMPLAINT, dealing, as it were, with personal calamities of people affected by unspecified ills. Clearly enough such sufferers and their ritual assistants identify the causes of harm done; and they come up with the maliciousness of unnamed personal enemies — at that time, a popular option to explain any kind of misery or bad luck. In a private prayer ceremony the hurts are to be healed, the patient is to be restored (see "Introduction to Cultic Poetry," section 4B). Anticipated praise (v. 5) visualizes a larger community of God-fearing people, the designations of which suggest not a familial or neighborhood assembly but a congregation of exilic adorers of Yahweh. The haphazard use of divine names, on the other hand, testifies to confessional flexibility.

## Intention

Cure and rehabilitation of the innocent or pardoned sufferer are to be achieved by motivating God into punitive action against the authors of mischief (→ Psalm 109).

## Bibliography

P. Auffret, "'Les oreilles, tu me (les) as ouverts': Étude structurelle du Ps 40 (et du Ps 70)," *NRT* 109 (1987) 220-47; J. M. Auwers, "Les Psaumes 70-72: Essai de lecture canonique," *RB* 101 (1994) 244-57; S. Weisblit, "Psalm 70 — A Personal Prayer," *BM* 60 (1974) 76-78.

# Psalm 71:
# Individual Complaint; Meditation

## Text

The transmission has left many textual scars. Form-critical analysis is handicapped more severely, however, by stylistic, oratorical, and structural uncertainties.

## Structure

| | | MT | NRSV |
|---|---|---|---|
| I. | Affirmation of confidence, petition | 1-3 | 1-3 |
| II. | Petition, affirmation of confidence | 4-7 | 4-7 |
| III. | Petition, wish | 8-9 | 8-9 |
| IV. | Complaint | 10-11 | 10-11 |
| V. | Petition | 12-13 | 12-13 |
| | A. Dissuasion and demand | 12 | 12 |
| | B. Imprecation | 13 | 13 |
| VI. | Meditation | 14-21 | 14-21 |
| | A. Spiritual self-portrait | 14-16 | 14-16 |
| | B. Recollection, petition, wish | 17-18 | 17-18 |
| | C. Personal hymn | 19-21 | 19-21 |
| VII. | Thanksgiving | 22-24 | 22-24 |

Designation of form elements and division of units can be tentative only, because this psalm is rather diffuse in character. While we do encounter definite patterns of speech deriving from individual complaint, especially in vv. 1-13, 22-24, the middle section (vv. 14-21) is a loose, heterogeneous discourse, preoccupied first with the personal posture of the suppliant (vv. 14-18), then with the saving power of God guarding that faithful orator (vv. 19-21). This section altogether has a musing, meditative air.

Strangely enough, Psalm 71 does not have a technical SUPERSCRIPTION. This is an extraordinary feature in the first two books of psalms (Psalms 1–72), although a rather common one in books 4 and 5 (cf. Psalms 90–150). In the first two books only six texts lack such a caption, most of them for good reasons. Psalms 1–2 are considered introductions to the Psalter, not independent prayers. Psalms 10 and 43 in reality are parts of the preceding poems, erroneously, at some point, cut off from their context and numbered individually. Also, the transmission of Psalm 33 is ambiguous. Some MSS tie it firmly to Psalm 32, and the much-related wording of 32:11 and 33:1 certainly gave basis to this union. Why, then, does Psalm 71 remain without redactional heading? And without an ordinary number in Codex Leningradensis, at that (see *BHS* apparatus)? The conclusion does not seem far-fetched: Psalm 71 (Hebrew version), too, was transmitted once as part and parcel of Psalm 70. Other indications make this suggestion probable. In the third century B.C.E., to be sure, the LXX found the text separated from Psalm 70 and without a proper heading. Therefore the Greek transmitters added their own: "For David. Of the sons of Jonadab and the first captives."

The first unit (vv. 1-3) is more or less identical with → Ps 31:2-4a (RSV 1-3a). We are dealing with a very strong petitionary block that contains INVOCATION (name of Yahweh, v. 1; initial plea: "incline your ear to me" [v. 2b], strangely placed in the middle of further-reaching petitions), AFFIRMATIONS OF CONFIDENCE ("with you I take refuge," v. 1a; "you are my rock, and my fortress," v. 3c), and regular PETITIONS to be rescued and protected. Together they occupy the largest part of the passage (six verbal expressions). Parallel transmission of the texts within the Psalter proves, to be sure, the flexible use of components of psalms in different liturgical situations (→ Psalms 14; 70; 108). If this be the case here, vv. 1-3 may have been recited also in connection with Psalm 70. Yet they do compete, in a way, with the very similar unit vv. 4-7. A doubled introduction, both parts comprising mainly PETITION and AFFIRMATIONS OF CONFIDENCE, may have been too heavy, liturgically speaking, for one and the same prayer. The present text division, on the other hand, would allow this accumulation of entreaty.

The second unit (vv. 4-7) repeats the opening statements, differing from the antecedents in small but significant highlights. This time the enemies are named (vv. 4, 7a), as usual in complaints, by their generic designations. Yet besides the common titles *rāšāʿ* ("godless," v. 4a) and *rabbîm* ("the crowd," v. 7a) two rare epithets stand out: *mĕʿawwēl*, "wrongdoer" (only occurrence of participle in Hebrew Scripture), and *ḥômēṣ*, "oppressor" (only occurrence of verb *ḥmṣ* II in Hebrew Scripture). The transmitters wanted to present the opponents, and they preferred their specific concepts of social disrupters. Furthermore, there is a marked emphasis on considering the whole life span of the suppliant. His trust in Yahweh is dated "from youth" (v. 5b), and "from the uterus," "from the womb of my mother" (v. 7). Connotations of life's long duration tie in neatly with all the anxieties in terms of old age (cf. vv. 9, 17, 18). Third, the second introductory unit places even higher emphasis on confidence. It starts out with pleas for help against the enemies (v. 4; only one verb *plṭ,* also in v. 2a), but continues with heavy AFFIRMATIONS OF CONFIDENCE (vv. 5-6, 7b: three formulas of the type: "you are my [hope] etc.," plus one with divine name: "Yahweh is my confidant," v. 5b). We rarely find such an accumulation of expressions of confidence in the Psalter (cf. 18:3 [RSV 2]; 31:5-6 [RSV 4-5]). These observations — naming of enemies, accentuating old age of suppliant, crowding the text with expressions of confidence — each in its own way suggests an original unified introduction.

Enigmatic is the suppliant's becoming a "sign" for his community (v. 7a). Within the Psalter the idea of a person becoming a symbol or portent of God's disgrace is implicit in complaints like 22:7-9, quoting enemy taunts with theological connotations (cf. 70:10-11). But the subject is not broached explicitly under the topic of "being a sign." Other parts of Hebrew Scripture, it is true, cherish this metaphor (cf. Deut 28:46; Isa 8:18; 20:3; Ezek 12:6, 11; 24:24, 27; Zech 3:8). Could there have been a prophetic influence on our psalm? But what does v. 7a mean exactly, to be begin with? The announcement of a future catastrophe would be but one possibility; vicarious suffering, as in 69:8-13, another.

After all the affirmations of confidence, liturgical custom does not prohibit a round of PETITION (vv. 8-9). At least v. 9 is clearly a dissuasive plea, trying to secure the status quo, protect the integrity of the suppliant (cf. 51:13 [RSV 11]; 2 Kgs 13:23; Jer 7:15 and v. 18; Pss 27:9; 38:22; 119:8; E. S. Gerstenberger, *TWAT* V, 1200-1208). V. 8, on the other hand, is ambiguous. The imperfect tense may serve as a wish form (cf. Michel, *Tempora,* 152-67, but he lists v. 8 under "modal uses," 144-45; listing at "Introduction to Psalms"). Most exegetes consider the phrase as either present or future indicative (the past could be considered, too), signifying a real outburst of joy because of salvation (cf. Gunkel, Kraus, Tate, et al.). Liturgically speaking the wish form would be most adequate at this point, accompanying the requests of v. 9.

Vv. 10-11, for the first time, articulate COMPLAINT, which had been only hinted at so far. The statements are typical in denouncing "enemies" (v. 10a), even quoting their malicious words (v. 11; cf. 22:7-9; 70:4). Most commentators understand *šōměrê napšî* ("guardians of myself," v. 10b) in the pejorative sense (cf. 56:7 [RSV 6]; Jer 20:10). But Ps 41:7-9 (RSV 6-8) tells us how best friends become enemies in cases of extreme illness. Therefore, the expression cited above could mean, as in most other passages (cf. 25:20; 86:2; 97:10; 121:3, 4, 5, 7; 127:1; Job 2:6; etc.), simply "guardians," their treachery being castigated afterward. Ensuing PETITIONS in their twofold orientation toward the suppliant and against the enemies (vv. 12-13) are regular liturgical complaint usage. The first line (v. 12) has its counterparts in 22:12a (RSV 11a) and 70:2b (RSV 1b), asking for God's loyalty and help. The second and third lines constitute a customary IMPRECATION (→ 70:3 [RSV 2]; 31:18; 35:4). The whole passage vv. 4-13, as interpreted above, demonstrates a liturgical agenda of trust — petition — complaint — petition, which is quite normal within the parameters of individual complaint (see "Introduction to Cultic Poetry," section 4B).

From v. 14 to v. 21 the text roams through the fields of psalmodic poetry without concentrating on clear-cut patterns of speech. The topic is clear enough: personal performance over against God, and God's positive reaction toward his adorer. Vv. 14-16 set forth the profile of an exemplary believer (cf. 73:22-25). Personal piety is at stake, as in some other meditative prayers, which apparently have developed from thanksgiving speeches in a festive community (cf. 40:6-12 [RSV 5-11]; 41:12-13 [RSV 11-12]; 56:9-12 [RSV 8-11]; 63:6-9 [RSV 5-8]; 77:6-7 [RSV 5-6]; 131:1-2). The habit to meditate on one's own life and posture over against God must have been cultivated with greater intensity in that faith community that was the backbone of Judahite existence after the defeat of 587 B.C.E. A prime example of this kind of musing over one's own relationship to God is, of course, Psalm 119. Small wonder that central terms of our passage (*ṣedeq, tĕhillāh, tĕšûʿāh, gĕbûrāh* — all near synonyms: "wondrous deeds [of Yahweh]"; cf. furthermore the verbs employed: *yḥl*, "wait"; *spr*, "tell"; *bôʾ*, "come"; *zkr*, "remember") do play an important role in Psalm 119 too. And the general theological reasoning of this longest poem in the Psalter is congruous to what we find in vv. 14-16. The person relates him/herself to God, waiting for him, telling his gracious interventions, remembering divine solidarity. V. 16 reminds one of visiting the sanctuary, with the verbs "come" and "remember = call upon" (cf. 5:8 [RSV 7]; 40:8 [RSV 7]; 42:3 [RSV 2]; 43:4; 66:13; 73:17; 118:19 for "I am coming [into the sanctuary]"; 20:8 [RSV 7]; 45:18 [RSV 17] for "calling upon [Yahweh]"). We are probably dealing with metaphorical use in our context, because the place of prayer may be remote from the temple (see Setting).

Meditation then assumes a general biographical perspective scanning the period between youth and old age (vv. 17-18). In retrospect, its main characteristics are: to be "taught" (*lmd*, Piel) by God himself and to "proclaim" (*ngd*, Hiphil) his wondrous acts (v. 17). Both affirmations lead to the conclusion that Torah instruction and communal hymn singing are hinted at. Reference to divine teaching is frequent in Psalm 119 (ten times: vv. 12, 26, 64, 66, 68, etc.) and Psalm 25 (vv. 4, 5, 9; cf. also 94:12; 143:10; R. E. Friedman, *ABD* VI, 621; A. S. Kapelrud, *TWAT* IV, 576-82, esp. 578-80: the concept of teaching the Torah is prominent in Deuteronomy). To announce Yahweh's great achievements often means exactly hymnic praise; cf. v. 18c; 9:12 (RSV 11); 19:2 (RSV 1); 22:32 (RSV 31); 30:10 (RSV 9); 50:6; 51:17 (RSV 15); etc.; and hymns are explicitly taught as a matter of sacred tradition in Deut 31:19, 22 (cf. F. García López, *TWAT* V, 188-201, esp. 198-200). Both verses, consequently, are concerned about fulfillment of primary responsibilities over against God during one's lifetime; they elaborate what was said already in v. 15a: "My mouth tells your righteousness." The petitionary line (v. 18ab) is no real PETITION, echoing, as it were, v. 9, but pleading for continuity of praising the Lord, not for a special act of salvation or restitution. Significantly, telling Yahweh's praise constitutes an inner-congregational obligation (v. 18cd: lit. "until I proclaim your power to a generation, to all that come"). The family of faith is dependent on continuous witnessing. Such activity is not only a cultic but a communal affair, constituting and preserving fellowship (cf. 64:10 [RSV 9]; 145:4-7; Exod 13:8; Deut 32:7; F. García-López, *TWAT* V, 197-201).

Vv. 19-21: musing goes on in the same vein, even though a real hymnic phrase intervenes in v. 19 (including the last word of v. 18). Two lines extol the deeds of God on high, ending in that well-known formula of incomparability:

"Who, O God, is like you?" (cf. 35:10; 89:9 [RSV 8]; 113:5; Exod 15:11; Mic 7:18; Job 36:22). The relative phrase in v. 19c, after a general praise of God's sublimeness, is a modification of hymnic style allowing for a direct-address hymn (cf. Pss 8:2 [RSV 1]; 95:3-5; Crüsemann, *Studien,* 285-94; listing at "Introduction to Cultic Poetry"). The second relative sentence (v. 20ab) retains direct address, but does not stay in the praising mode. It reverts to the suppliant's biography, acknowledging gratefully God's saving acts in the past. The last line (v. 21) follows suit in this meditative way of PERSONAL PRAISE, apparently summing up, using unique language (e.g., *gĕdullāh,* "greatness, honor," traditionally applied in relation to God; cf. 145:3, only very late becoming a human attribute: Esth 6:3; 10:2. *sbb,* "circle," appears to be an auxiliary verb, just like *šûb* in v. 20c and e, or else is to be emended into *sābîb: HAL* 698). Most commentators understand this line to be an anticipatory affirmation of well-being.

Vv. 14-21 with all their subunits may be called a confessional MEDITATION brought before God and the community or spoken jointly by the worshipers in a community service. The lines portray a paradigmatic Yahweh believer, comparable to Ps 1:1-3 (being a kind of benediction of the just one, though). Our text, in contrast, does have confessional qualities. The faithful ("I") addresses God directly throughout, naming his/her highest life aspirations and ideals, obligations and purposes. This is not an old man speaking, reviewing his life, but a confessing parishioner, accounting before God for his/her basic orientation, loyalty, identity, and perspectives.

The final unit of our psalm (vv. 22-24) falls into the pattern of promised THANKSGIVING, common in individual complaint songs (cf. 7:18 [RSV 17]; 30:12-13 [RSV 11-12]; 43:4; 86:12-13). The cultic background is obvious: to give thanks included sacrifice (v. 22a, if the verb *ydh* does suggest a thanksgiving rite = *todah;* cf. "Introduction to Cultic Poetry," section 4C); the use of sacred instruments was obligatory (v. 22a, c). Emphasis is, however, on verbal articulation, offering the proper songs of one "saved" or "rescued" (vv. 23-24ab), while the imprecation against enemies (v. 13) bears its fruits (v. 24cd). The confessors having given their life pledge (vv. 11-21) now conclude their service with an extensive thanksgiving promise (vv. 22-24).

## Genre

Exegetes as a rule are uncertain how to classify Psalm 71. Gunkel (pp. 301-2) only affirms the existence of form elements of complaint, confidence, and hymn, interpreting the whole poem in biographical terms ("The psalmist struggles to get out of his misery and arrives, ever more comforted, at a jubilant confidence," 302). Consequently, form-critical analysis loses its importance for Gunkel. He divides the texts into three thematic units: vv. 1-8, 9-16, 18-24 (ibid., erroneously omitting v. 17; Kraus, 652, copies this outline). Most commentators follow Gunkel. Mowinckel (*W* I, 220) groups Psalm 71 with the national "protective psalms" in the "I" form. We should not hesitate to leave Gunkel's biographical and Mowinckel's national interpretation. Psalm 71 is a meditative variation of an INDIVIDUAL COMPLAINT in the mood of Torah piety.

## Setting

This classification logically leads to the community life of early Jewish congregations as the most likely setting. We should not be intrigued by that frequently suggested "private" relationship of an isolated and aging "I" with his/her God; that much Mowinckel clearly recognized. After all, in the absence of direct references to the congregation there are sufficient vestiges of it, e.g., the worship to attend (v. 16), "coming generations" to proclaim to (v. 18), the "holy one of Israel" (v. 22), etc. Additionally, the "enemies" may be considered not so much in personal but in communal terms. Vv. 10-11, it is true, testify briefly to that marginalization of sufferers that is normal to individual complaints. However, the psalm treats hostility only marginally, bringing this eternal problem of any life experience into the congregational realm. Animosity by others here may have religious reasons ("shame," "disgrace," v. 13b; cf. 70:3; 69:8, 20; Klopfenstein, *Scham*, 90-107, Additional Bibliography, section B). The suppliants are pleading help from God, anyway, trying to have the offenders execrated. Because of the poem's reflective air its proper setting would be a community service. If our suppositions above are correct, a confessional meditation could be placed into a special worship service of (re-)confirming members into the Yahweh community. Some articulations of faith lend themselves to such purpose: "I shall always hope, add to all your fame" (v. 14); "I shall alert to your righteousness, yours alone" (v. 16b); "O God, who is like you?" (v. 19c); "Until old age and grey hair, O God, do not forsake me" (v. 18ab). Experience of distress and distance and overcoming both by Yahweh's intervention (vv. 20-21) do fit into the context of articulating a commitment to God. In fact, various types of assemblies to that effect are documented in Scripture; they all use the terminology of "alliance," even if in different ways: cf., e.g., Josh 24:1-28; Deut 29:1-31:13; Neh 8:1-12; 10:1-40. Our psalm may represent another kind of "confirmation of faith," or else have served as some liturgical element in a "covenant" festival.

## Intention

Using the traditional complaint song as a model, Psalm 71, along the line of Psalm 119, portrays a life dedicated to Yahweh as the highest ideal for all members of the community. Trust in this God will carry the faithful through all difficulties of a long life, and will serve well the congregation as a whole. Confessing one's faith and abiding with God and God's power over all evil forces become the commendable life project for everyone under the shelter of God's power, i.e., within the community of believers.

## Bibliography

P. Auffret, "'Ma bouche publiera ta justice': Étude structurelle du psaume 71," *Eglise et théologie* 25 (1994) 5-35; J. B. Bauer, "Psalm 70 (71),15. Quoniam non cognovi litteraturam," *Erbe und Auftrag* 58 (1982) 167-78; D. P. Beal, "Effective Church Ministry with Older Adults," *Christian Education Journal* 4 (1983) 5-17; B. Blackburn, "Psalm 71," *RevExp* 88 (1991) 241-45; M. Cogan, "A Technical Form for Exposure," *JNES* 27 (1968) 133-35; R. J. Tourney, "Notules sur les Psaumes (Ps. XIX,2-5; LXXI,15-16)," in *Alttestamentliche Studien* (*Fest.* F. Nötscher; ed. H. Junker, et al.; Bonn: Peter Hansen, 1950) 274-80.

## Psalm 72:
## Intercession, Wishes

### Text

Textual problems do not interfere much with form-critical analyses or the prima facie understanding of this psalm; those problems that do occur will be mentioned in their place.

### Structure

|  | MT | NRSV |
|---|---|---|
| I. Superscription | 1a | - |
| II. Intercession for a king | 1b-3 | 1a-3 |
| A. Petition | 1bc | 1ab |
| B. Wish | 2 | 2 |
| C. Blessing | 3 | 3 |
| III. Wishes | 4-11 | 4-11 |
| A. Justice | 4-7 | 4-7 |
| B. Power | 8-11 | 8-11 |
| IV. Positive record | 12-14 | 12-14 |
| V. Wishes | 15-17 | 15-17 |
| A. Well-being | 15 | 15 |
| B. Abundance | 16-17 | 16-17 |
| VI. Blessings | 18-19b | 18-19b |
| VII. Response of community | 19c | 19c |
| VIII. Postscript | 20 | 20 |

The psalm, with its liturgical purpose remaining in the shadows, is difficult to define in its speech patterns. Therefore the above structural outline constitutes but one possibility of subdivision. Many commentators do not try at all to find a convincing structure; others propose quite a different segmentation (cf., e.g., Gorgulho: vv. 1-4, 5-7, 8-11, 12-14, 15-17; Zenger, "So betete," 68: "a five-part structure of vv. 2-17, with vv. 8-11 in the center").

To begin with, a general observation is in order. Only the first two lines are couched in prayer language (vv. 1-2). After this God-directed opening the second person singular recurs only once more, in the first word of v. 5: *yîrā'ûkā,* "they may fear you," which, however, does not seem to make good sense, and is emended by most commentators in correspondence with LXX to ya'ărîk ('rk, Hiphil), "he may make long" (i.e., the king's life). This change ties v. 5 in with the singular verbal forms of vv. 4, 6-8, all speaking in some way of the royal figure, not of community members or opponents. With some difficulty, one could argue, however, that v. 5 is the concluding line of a strophic unit explaining and challenging the faith of the "oppressed" and "poor" of v. 4.

In any case, after a rather short venture of prayer language the rest of the psalm (until v. 17) is nothing but a discourse or enactment, not very much organized, of good wishes, an extended benediction, so to speak, in benefit of an anonymous monarchic figure. Psalms 20 and 21 are similar in their outlines, although they vary in their addressees. A prolonged speech like this from the start suggests a composite nature and several stages of development (Renaud, Tourney).

Some Hebrew MSS leave out the SUPERSCRIPTION, linking Psalm 72 to 71. The majority tradition, however, ascribes the text to Solomon, a model son of a king (cf. v. 1b), and a monarch at that, whose main concerns were justice (cf. 1 Kgs 3:16-28), peace in an immense national territory (cf. 1 Kgs 5:4 [RSV 4:24]), and prosperity (cf. 1 Kings 10). All these traits occur in our text, while his famous wisdom (cf. 1 Kgs 3:12; 5:9-14 [RSV 4:29-34]) is, curiously, not mentioned. Nonetheless, there may exist some mutual dependence between the stories about Solomon's enormous splendor and Psalm 72 (cf., e.g., the visits and tributes of kings and queens to Solomon, 1 Kgs 5:14, 15 [RSV 4:34; 5:1]; 10:1-2, 10; cf. Ps 72:8-11). Sheba and Seba (vv. 10c, 15a) refer explicitly to or are dependent on that fabulous queen who adored her colleague in Jerusalem (1 Kings 10).

The INTERCESSION for the king, formally speaking, should be restricted to v. 1 (excluding "Of Solomon"). Only in this opening line do we find the typical plea to God, issued by an unnamed speaker (intermediary? priest? congregation?) in favor of a third party. Already line two switches into the wish form, withholding, however, direct address to the Deity ("May he judge your people," v. 2a). The third line (v. 3) deals with the land, the (sacred?) mountains, their creative and protective power, and may be considered a fine conclusion of an original intercessory unit. To include in the original prayer more or all of the following wishes would possibly overstretch the genre. Ps 21:2-7 (RSV 1-6) is an example: every single praising affirmation is articulated in direct-address discourse to God. Prayer language, if intended to be heard by the Deity, should not peter out as it does in vv. 4-17 of our psalm. Therefore, I conclude that vv. 1-3 with their second-person singular signals and a powerful wish for "shalom" in "justice" (v. 3) are one nucleus of Psalm 72. The petition clearly goes for justice and righteousness, derivatives of ṣdq occurring three times in three lines, to be established among the people. And the people in v. 2 are *identified* with the "oppressed" ('ănāwîm; cf. Isa 49:13; E. S. Gerstenberger, TWAT VI, 247-70); the latter are not singled out as a special group within society at large (differently: Schwantes, Recht, 184). Therefore, we are justified in speaking of a "community of poor" in Psalm 72 and some other psalms (Gorgulho, Zenger; cf. the interpretation of Psalms 9/10; 37; 49; → 69:33-34 [RSV 32-33]).

The two blocks of WISHES (vv. 4-11) want to strengthen the king internally and externally. The passage concerned with internal affairs (vv. 4-7) starts out practically repeating v. 2, but without using direct-address lexemes, and, perhaps more importantly, introducing that social dichotomy of "oppressed" and "poor" on the one hand, and "oppressors" on the other. Here, obviously, as well as in vv. 12-14, the internal rift is presupposed. This does not mean that affirmations referring to class divisions are totally incompatible with those claiming a uniform "community of the poor." But emphases are different. The king, according to vv. 4, 12-14 has to help the underprivileged and thus balance social justice in his territory. This idea was commonly held in the ancient Near East. King Hammurapi of Babylon confesses himself to be commissioned by Anu and Enlil "to promote the welfare of the people, . . . to cause justice to prevail in the land, to destroy the wicked and the evil, that the strong might not oppress the weak" (*ANET*, 164). He accomplishes his divine task by proclaiming his laws in the land and enforcing justice among the "black-headed" people as their good shepherd. "In my bosom I carried the peoples of the land of Sumer and Akkad; they prospered under my protection; I always governed them in peace; I sheltered them in my wisdom. In order that the strong might not oppress the weak, that justice might be dealt the orphan (and) the widow . . . I wrote my precious words on my stela" (*ANET*, 178). The first wish unit takes up the original intercessory prayer for royal justice and makes it the key issue of internal well-being. The longevity of the monarch depends on it (LXX in v. 5; if MT is correct: the wish is for a God-fearing subject), as well as sufficient rainfall (v. 6) and the general state of justice and shalom ("well-being," v. 7).

The second WISH passage (vv. 8-11) enters the field of foreign policy. The monarch is to exercise his universal reign, the delineation of which is practically identical with that of Zech 9:10ef, attributed to the poor Messiah (Zech 9:9). All foreign peoples will pay homage to the king, especially the most distant nations on the islands and beyond the sea and in the far south, Tarshish, Sheba, and Seba (Ps 72:10-11). These or similar names are prevalent, apart from the Solomon story, in quite a number of fantasies about the future as transmitted in prophetic books (cf. Isa 43:3; 45:14). Also, the fate of these *gôyim* is pictured more than once: they shall lick dust (v. 9b; cf. Isa 49:23; Mic 7:17) and serve the king (v. 11b; cf. Ps 2:10-12).

And what is the function of WISHES within the Psalms? PETITIONS, BLESSINGS, and FELICITATIONS are related elements. The wish form, as we have seen, is less authoritative than petition or blessing. But it takes a similar course, being expressed by humans who consider the situation from religious perspectives, yet without involving God directly. Felicitation seems still a littler further away from divine supervision, simply expressing the highest and ethically well-founded esteem for certain attitudes and actions. Where and how the WISHES have been used will be discussed below (see Setting).

Vv. 12-14, although formally not unlike the other phrases of the wish sections (imperfect mood), stand out by their realism. While the wishes border on the utopian, and draw on horizons of time and space that transcend the possibilities of individual human beings, the passage at hand speaks in the plainest way about juridical help for the poor and oppressed. To declare this section a mere "wish" would be tantamount to denying any chance of executing justice on earth. This is the only reason to evaluate the passage as factual, and we then still need to decide whether it witnesses to the past, present, or future. Most translations opt for the future tense, some for the present or past (NRSV = present). The alternatives tie in, of course, with the option to take the king of Psalm 72 as a living head of government or a messianic figure. Suffice it to say here that in other places of Hebrew Scripture the servant of the Lord provides justice (Isa 42:1-9), or Yahweh himself does (cf. Ps 146:7-9; Isa 51:4-8). Our passage, then, establishes a real RECORD of providing justice for the afflicted, future actions included.

The concluding WISHES (vv. 15-17) are back on the utopian line. Indeed, v. 15 seems to connect directly with vv. 10-11, v. 16 continues the topic of rain and fertility touched on in v. 6, v. 17ab is linked thematically with v. 5, and v. 17cd is linked with vv. 10-11. The interlude in vv. 12-14 thus seems to be an element, liturgical or literary, in its own right.

Two *bārûk* sentences (vv. 18-19), very similar to those found at the end of three other "books" of Psalms (cf. 41:14 [RSV 13]; 89:53 [RSV 52]; 106:48), terminate the text without any mark-off sign. These formulas glorify God in general terms, a homage of the scribes who completed the work or perhaps of the congregation that sang or meditated on the texts. The response "Amen, Amen," present in all four of the *bārûk* formulas quoted above, is purportedly a liturgical response of the congregation. The final scribal remark (v. 20: "Ended are the prayers [LXX has 'the hymns'] of David, the son of Jesse") is unique in the Psalter. Parallel entries we meet, e.g., in Jer 51:64: "Thus far Jeremiah spoke"; or — at the beginning of collections — Prov 10:1; 24:23; 25:1; etc. These scribal notes (colophons) are definitely secondary additions, just like the superscriptions of individual psalms. They testify to the growth of collections and the Psalter itself.

## Genre

What was the purpose of enlarging a short prayer on behalf of the king and making it a long wish litany? Would this designation, "litany of wishes," be appropriate as a genre qualification? We carry these questions into the discussion of life setting, because the practice of using a text is decisive for determining its genre.

## Setting

We already hinted at a fundamental problem in evaluating our psalm. Was it composed and used during the period of Israelite monarchies? Many exegetes do believe in a preexilic date. Or should we rather support the growing conviction of those who consider Psalm 72 a late, postexilic messianic poem? Some important observations speak for the latter option. (a) Certain linguistic features in the text may be understood as influences of the Aramaic spoken in the

Persian Empire. (b) The successive growth of the text is a signal of late composition. (c) We discovered vestiges of early Jewish community structures and theologies. (d) A royal figure is feasible in Israelite texts of the Persian period, because hope for a renewal of the Davidic dynasty (or some substitute for it) never died out completely, and sometimes rose to fervent heat (cf. Hag 2:23; Zech 4:1-10; etc.). (e) Given the political conditions of the Persian Empire, the possibility cannot be excluded that intercession for the Great Emperor at least in periods of harmonious coexistence was customary or obligatory in Judean and Babylonian Yahweh communities (Ezra 6:10; → Pss 61:7-8 [RSV 6-7]; 63:12 [RSV 11]; 80:18 [RSV 17]; Seybold, in regard to 61:7-8 and 63:12).

Increasingly in recent years scholars have called attention to late redactional and canonical processes taking account also of the psalmic tradition (cf. G. H. Wilson, J. C. McCann, P. D. Miller, N. Füglister, N. Lohfink, et al., Additional Bibliography, section C). Most of these exegetes presuppose a change of *Sitz im Leben* when the Psalms became a book: they became reading material, be it for private or public opportunities. When did this happen? We do not know exactly. But some scholars insist on an early date — compared to monastic Christian reading and meditating habits — sometime between the second century B.C.E. and the first century C.E. If this is true, Psalm 72 was given a privileged place in the growing book of Psalms, i.e., at the end of book 2 (book 1: Psalms 1–41; book 2: Psalms 42–72). Combined, the two units constitute an expanded David collection of psalms, probably antedating the other books of Psalms (contained in Psalms 73–150). The colophon in 72:20, "Ended are the prayers of David . . . ," is unique in the Psalter (Wilson, *Editing,* 139; listing at "Introduction to Psalms"). With collections and books of psalms taking shape in a new social environment, a change of meaning of individual texts came about. Scholars visualize a royal and messianic message of the collection as a whole, from Psalm 2 at the beginning to Psalm 72 at the end, later to be continued by Psalm 89 (downfall of monarchy) and Psalm 145 (spiritual resurrection: kingdom of God); cf. Wilson, "Use"; E. Zenger, "David"; et al. The new theological perspective, then, would be truly eschatological, giving a way and justification (thus, e.g., Zenger) for a christological reading, but not limiting it to this one partisan meaning. Jewish messianism may equally draw on Psalm 72 for a theological backing.

## Intention

The dream of a renewed dynasty for the trouble-ridden Jewish community of the poor or of rich and poor motivated continued study and cultivation of royal legends, values, and hopes. The psalm wants to strengthen the rule of justice; it aims at emancipation of the oppressed ones and rehabilitation of the whole people. Whether the text served in worship services or was used in more day-to-day gatherings for educational purposes would have to be investigated further.

# Bibliography

S. Abramski, "The Beginning of the Israelite Monarchy and Its Impact upon Leadership in Israel," *Immanuel* 19 (1984/85) 7-21; J. Assmann, *Politische Theologie zwischen Ägypten und Israel* (Munich: Hanser, 1992); P. E. Bonnard, "Le Psaume 72, ses relectures, ses traces dans l'oeuvre de Luc," *RSR* 69 (1981) 259-78; F. Breukelman, "Der König im Tun von 'Mischpat w-Zedaqah'," *Theologie im Kontext* 23 (1984) 4-12; F. F. Bruce, "The Bible and the Environment," in *The Living and Active Word of God (Fest. S. J. Schultz; ed. M. Inch, et al.; Winona Lake, Ind.: Eisenbrauns, 1983) 15-29; A. Caquot, "Psaume 72:16," *VT* 38 (1988) 214-20; J.-M. Carrière, "Le Psaume 72 est-il un psaume messianique?" *Bib* 72 (1991) 49-69; E. Cortese, "Salmo 72," *Studium Biblicum Franciscanum* 41 (1991) 41-53; A. Deissler, "La composante sociale dans le message messianique de l'Ancien Testament," in *Bible et christologie* (ed. P. Grelot, et al.; Paris: Cerf, 1984) 161-72; P. Grelot, "Un parallèle babylonien d'Isaie LX et du Psaume LXXII," *VT* 7 (1957) 319-21; G. Gorgulho, "O libertador dos pobres," *EstBib* 23 (1989) 45-51; D. Jobling, "Deconstruction and the Political Analysis of Biblical Texts: A Jamesonian Reading of Psalm 72," *Semeia* 59/60 (1992) 95-127; A. R. Johnson, "The Role of the King in the Jerusalem Cultus," in *The Labyrinth* (ed. S. Hooke; London: SCM, 1935) 71-111; J. S. Kselman, "Psalm 72: Some Observations on Structure," *BASOR* 220 (1975) 77-81; J. L. Mays, "In a Vision: The Portrayal of the Messiah in the Psalms," *Ex Auditu* 7 (1991) 1-8; P. D. Miller Jr., "Power, Justice, and Peace: An Exegesis of Psalm 72," *Faith and Mission* 4 (1986) 65-70; A. Niccacci, "I monti portino pace al popolo (Sal 72,3)," *Antonianum* 56 (1981) 93-118; R. Pautrel, "Le style de cour et le Psaume LXXII," in *À la rencontre de Dieu* (ed. A. Gelin; Paris: Garland, 1961) 157-63; J. Quinones-Ortiz, "Psalm 72: On Confronting Rulers in Urban Society," *Apuntes* 13 (1993) 180-89; B. Renaud, "De la bénédiction du roi à la bénédiction de Dieu (Ps 72)," *Bib* 70 (1989) 305-26; M. Saebø, "Vom Grossreich zum Weltreich," *VT* 28 (1978) 83-91; M. Schwantes, *Das Recht der Armen* (Frankfurt/Bern: Peter Lang, 1977) 183-89; P. W. Skehan, "Strophic Structure in Ps. 72 (71)," *Bib* 40 (1959) 302-8; H. Spieckermann, "Die ganze Erde ist seiner Herrlichkeit voll: Pantheismus im Alten Testament?" *ZTK* 87 (1990) 415-36; R. J. Tournay, "Le Psaume 73: Relectures et interprétation," *RB* 92 (1985) 187-99; P. Veugelers, "Le Psaume LXXII, poème messianique?" (diss., Louvain, 1965); S. Wagner, "Das Reich des Messias: Zur Theologie der alttestamentlichen Königspsalmen," *TLZ* 109 (1984) 865-74; G. H. Wilson, "The Use of Royal Psalms at the 'Seams' of the Hebrew Psalter," *JSOT* 35 (1986) 85-94; E. Zenger, "'So betete David für seinen Sohn Salomo und für den König Messias': Überlegungen zur holistischen und kanonischen Lektüre des 72. Psalms," in *Der Messias (Jahrbuch für biblische Theologie* 8; ed. I. Baldermann, et al.; Neukirchen-Vluyn: Neukirchener Verlag, 1993) 57-72.

# CHAPTER 4

# THE INDIVIDUAL UNITS OF BOOK 3 (Psalms 73–89)

## Psalm 73:
## Meditation and Confession

### *Structure*

|  | MT | NRSV |
|---|---|---|
| I. Superscription | 1a | - |
| II. Instruction: Rule and exception | 1b-3 | 1-3 |
| III. Portrayal of godless | 4-12 | 4-12 |
| IV. Complaint | 13-17 | 13-17 |
|   A. Description of suffering | 13-14 | 13-14 |
|   B. Reflection; confession of guilt | 15-16 | 15-16 |
|   C. Account of reversal | 17 | 17 |
| V. Warning | 18-20 | 18-20 |
| VI. Personalized account | 21-26 | 21-26 |
|   A. Reminiscence | 21-22 | 21-22 |
|   B. Confidence and petition | 23-26 | 23-26 |
| VII. Imprecation and confidence | 27-28 | 27-28 |

Twelve psalms altogether have been attributed by late redactors (or by ancient tradition?) to those Levitical Asaphites known from Chronicles (cf. 1 Chr 15:17, 19; 16:4-5, 37; 25:1-2). A plain SUPERSCRIPTION "song" *(mizmôr)* of (or according to) "Asaph" can be found with → Psalms 50; 73; 79; 82. Various additions may modify this basic title (cf. with Psalms 75; 76; 77; 80; 83). Another designation within the Asaph collection (Psalms 50; 73–83) is *maśkîl lĕ'āsāp* ("instruction [?] of/according to Asaph," Psalms 74; 78). The redactors wanted to highlight sacred music and possibly sacred teaching as the main tasks of the renowned family of temple officials in the fifth and fourth centuries B.C.E.

The opening lines of the poem in some ways remind one of sapiential discourse. Exclamatory *'ak,* "only, indeed," may mark a common truth, uncontestable in its obvious validity and theological tradition. Similar use of the particle occurs in 39:6, 7, 12 (RSV 5, 6, 11); 62:2, 3, 6, 7, 10 (RSV 1, 2, 5, 6, 9); 68:7c, 19c, 22 (RSV 6c, 18c, 21). The "pure-hearted" in Israel are under special care of God. Yet the experience of some people, perhaps we may call them the Jobian minority, runs counter to this readily embraced truism. They perceive a dangerous contradiction between the community's conviction and real life. Therefore the psalm, speaking in personal "I" style, challenges cherished beliefs, protesting against the abundant gifts of resources and life opportunities that the nonbelievers, even blasphemers, receive. The first part of Psalm 73, until v. 17, then, is a piece of CONTEST literature testing a principle of faith. More closely, the subsection under discussion (vv. 1b-3) is INSTRUCTION, posing rule and exception. The "I" speaking is the exemplary believer (against Kraus, et al.) who runs into doubts; in 69:8-13 (RSV 7-12) it is the one who encounters hostility for God's sake. The adversaries are apparently senseless but well-to-do people (v. 3; cf. 5:6 [RSV 5]; 75:5 [RSV 4]). In this way the conflict between righteous sufferers and godless but opulent people is set as a problem of faith, a truly Jobian constellation, but cf. also Psalms 9/10; 37; 49. This affliction within the group has to be voiced.

PORTRAYALS of the wicked (vv. 4-12; cf. R. C. Cover, *ABD* VI, 31-40), prompted by v. 3, may serve different ends. Basically, they are necessary in any process of socialization and education to make clear that socially unjust behavior does not work out and must be ostracized. The profile of "bad man" or "bad woman" has to be delineated clearly. The main points of emphasis in such a presentation of the godless would be their misconduct and due fate. The book of Proverbs offers a great number of miniatures in this regard (cf., e.g., Proverbs 12; 21), and the book of Job gives elaborate examples (cf. Job 15:20-35; 20:5-29). Of course, the portrait may also be used by the Jobian minority, demonstrating the wicked's misdeeds and complaining about their prosperity and arrogance, in the wake of the utter lack of just retribution (cf. Job 21:7-15). Obviously, pictures like this were used widely and formed an independent genre (cf. the positive profiles in NT *Haustafeln*). The examples cited so far correspond in their topics, as well as in some formulations. They quite often have their own concluding line, like our text ("That is, what the wicked are," v. 12a). The main characteristics of the wicked are: egocentric mania for power, unsocial brutality, hideous rebellion against God, apostasy from him (cf. v. 27b). Drastic descriptions of the oppressor (*'ōšeq;* cf. E. S. Gerstenberger, *TWAT* VI, 441-46) should arouse the divine helper, but also educate listeners to learn to abhor the godless. The element has been used in some other psalms as well (cf. Pss 10:3-11; 37:12-15, 17, 20-21, 32, 35-36).

The whole problem of injustice and near loss of faith in a just Deity can arise only as far as "just" believers (the "pure-hearted" of v. 1c; cf. v. 13a), who really are "innocent" (cf. v. 13b and Psalms 7; 17; 26), become conscious of gross ethical imbalances, by way of their own suffering. Again, this is hardly the achievement of one person only but the discovery of underprivileged groups (cf. Nehemiah 5), and all individual psalms testify to accumulated experiences.

Therefore, the "I" speaking up in vv. 13-17 (COMPLAINT) cannot be one concrete person with a special biography. Rather, we face the ideal sufferer, pieced together from the collective experience of many members of the community. A believer's life full of setbacks and punishments (v. 14; full protestation of innocence intimating an oath formula in v. 15) contrasted with the bliss of blasphemers is devastating and demands a thorough explanation (v. 16). Vv. 15-16 are reflective along the wisdom line (cf. burdensome thinking in v. 16). The answers are impossible to find (cf. v. 16; Ps 139:6; Ecclesiastes). Interestingly enough, the solution lies with attending a worship service (v. 17a) and taking the sum total to the very end of the life of the wicked (v. 17b). Mal 3:13-21 (RSV 3:13–4:3) is the proper key to these theological perspectives. They definitely include an eschatological dimension. The true believers in Yahweh will have all their doings and lives recorded in a divine book (Mal 3:16). "They shall be mine, says the Lord of hosts, my special possession on the day when I act. . . . Then once more you shall distinguish between the righteous and the wicked, between the one who serves God and one who does not serve him" (Mal 3:17-18). There also is a possibility, in the light of many known cursing rituals of the period (cf. Leviticus 26; Numbers 5; Deuteronomy 27; 28; Psalm 109; etc.), that wrongdoers and apostates were effectively dealt with in public worship (note the unusual and vague designation of the place of worship, v. 17a), thus giving substance to the innocents' anticipated triumph.

Formally, vv. 13-17 function as a COMPLAINT although the latter verses (15-16) call into question that comprehensive traditional protestation of the sufferer (vv. 13-14). Still, they prepare for the PETITION (v. 24), admitting more or less directly one's deficits (CONFESSION OF GUILT). V. 17 marks the turning point in the psalm's dramatic struggle: participating in worship (miqdĕšê 'ēl, "holy quarters of El"; cf. similar plural expressions in Jer 51:51; Ezek 21:7; Ps 68:36 [RSV 35]) most probably suggests receiving tôrāh instruction about the fate of the evilmongers.

For the third time a section begins with 'ak (vv. 1b, 13, 18), a signal of sapiential discourse, sounding a stern WARNING against the godless (vv. 18-20). We are practically dealing with the second motif for portraying the wicked. Announcing their sudden and total destruction is part of the educative presentation (cf. Job 15:29-35; 20:5-29: the passage is a full denunciation of the wrongdoers, with a fitting postscript: "this is the portion of the wicked . . . ," v. 29; Pss 37:9, 10, 17, 20, 35-36, 38; 92:8 [RSV 7]). The imagery and vocabulary of these threats of annihilation correspond to the portrayal of the wicked without repeating it (vv. 4-12; note: 9 lines versus 3 in the WARNING). They call attention to the swiftness and radicalness of divine retribution and to the total weakness, falsehood, and delusive existence of the condemned ones who had been so powerful before.

The real center of the debate, however, is the performance and life of the exemplary faithful who is to benefit from reciting this psalm (PERSONALIZED ACCOUNT). In reviewing the past (a common liturgical practice for thanksgiving rituals; see "Introduction to Cultic Poetry," section 4C), the worshiper acknowledges his error. He misunderstood the situation of injustice and the apparent inactivity of God (v. 22; comparison with brute beasts is common in wisdom reflections; cf. 49:13; 92:7 [RSV 6]; Prov 30:24-31), as only proper instruction in worship can give the right insight (v. 17). The source of enlightened knowledge about the functioning of this world, of course, is solely God and the community of his adherents (vv. 23-26); in effect, it is the Torah. Such close and steadfast communion with God is a supreme value in itself. Nothing indicates a reference to the resurrection of the dead, as many interpreters claim, not even expressions of long duration or "thereafter" (vv. 23-24, 26b). The articulations of CONFIDENCE and intimate allegiance with the God of Israel in this section approximate genuine confessions of faith (cf. E. S. Gerstenberger, *TRE* XIII, 386-88). V. 23 affirms facts using a nominal clause and a perfect tense: "But I — always with you"; "You grabbed my right hand." PETITION is intended by the imperfects of v. 24. Expressions of belonging to God culminate in vv. 25-26, which — textually somewhat uncertain — have been meditated on innumerable times since: "Who is mine in heaven [but you]? [Being] with you I do not like [anything] on earth. My body and heart may faint, the rock of my heart and my portion forever is God." This is certainly a strong commitment to Israel's God.

The last two verses (vv. 27-28) could be counted as parts of the preceding block. For liturgical reasons I set them apart, however. In individual complaints the IMPRECATION is normally a separate procedure from declaring one's trust and faith. Nevertheless, v. 28 repeats the affirmations of vv. 23-26, adding for the first time, however, the name of Yahweh, and closing with a vow to communicate Yahweh's deeds to the congregation, so it seems. The two opposing groups are lastly called the "distant ones" and the "near" ones (to Yahweh; vv. 27a, 28a). V. 27b, in addition, uses the designation *znh min,* "fornicate away from," Yahweh, customary in a series of prophetic and pentateuchal texts but very rare in the Psalter (cf. Hos 1:2; 2:7 [RSV 5]; 4:12-15; 9:1; Jer 2:20; 3:6-10; Ezek 6:9; 16:15-34; 23:3-30; Exod 34:15-16; Lev 17:7; 20:5-6; Num 15:39; 25:1-2; Deut 31:16; Judg 2:17; 8:27, 33; Ps 106:39. All cited passages from the Pentateuch use *znh 'aḥărê,* "fornicate after," some deity).

## *Genre*

Genre discussions of Psalm 73 come to very different conclusions, oscillating between "wisdom psalm," "individual complaint," "individual thanksgiving," "psalm of confidence," etc. (cf. Allen; Tate, 232, who enumerates 37 literary patterns proposed for the poem; McCann; Irsigler; Würthwein). We leave behind the individualistic one-author hypothesis, quite virulent in the debate, as well as the private-reading assumption: no psalm was originally composed for a literary readership or scholarly debate. Rather, we presuppose a communal origin and use of all the texts united in the Psalter. This point of departure leads to the following observations.

A few traces of INDIVIDUAL COMPLAINT have been pointed out above. Psalm 73 as a whole does not, on their account, fall into this category, nor could we claim that the psalmist used a complete prayer of that sort. The relation to individual complaint remains ephemeral. One individual "I" speaks throughout; orientation toward a listening congregation may be presupposed. Emphatic presentation of the psalmist's case is patent, but the audience is never mentioned explicitly. Rather, the text juxtaposes the two ideal figures of the "godless" and the "pure-hearted follower of God" in a sapiential, argumentative and almost objective manner, but off and on couched in prayer language. God is the prima facie addressee (vv. 15, 18, 22, 23-25, 27-28), yet somebody is to listen to this teaching and to heed it. Sapiential, exemplary MEDITATION seems a possible classification, bearing in mind its extroverted features: the dramatic struggle for a correct estimation of God, suffering, justice, and faith. Focusing on this last perspective we may call the psalm a dramatic CONFESSION of faith (Zenger, "Psalm 73," 184: "a credal statement grown out of a crisis of faith"), probably involving Torah piety, even if explicit vocabulary in this sense is missing.

## Setting

Our psalm was certainly not meant to be recited in seclusion but in some kind of public setting. Most likely, it was the community gathering of the early Jewish period under Persian rule where the poem/meditation/confession was used. Its very topics and theological outlooks reveal this *Sitz im Leben:* the wicked and the just one; the suffering of the latter and apparent bliss of the former; the internal division into antagonistic groups; the conflict of the orthodox faithful with their traditional concepts of justice in the line of the book of Job; faith in and full communion with the Deity (named Yahweh only in the last line); the absence of a strictly temple-centered theology; the strong identification with the (correct, orthodox) community of Israel — all these vestiges testify to a strictly congregational, possibly sectarian worship setting.

Whether our Psalm comes to speak with renewed vigor in the later canonical setting of a written Psalter (cf. J. Limburg, *ABD* V, 522-36) has to be debated. McCann, Brueggemann, Zenger, et al. try to make a case for our text being the pivotal theological point of the completed book of Psalms. Like similar interpretations of Psalm 72, this view presupposes a lay readership of the Psalter. Without continuous reading practices the idea of a literary or theological center could hardly come up. Granted this, Brueggemann suggests a general theological trajectory of thought within the Psalter from complaint to praise. Israelite and Judaic thinking being much closer than ours to the troublesome, disruptive day-to-day experience of injustice, suffering, and apparent absence of God, the level of praise can be attained only in arduous conflict with opponents, circumstances, and — God. Psalm 73, looking back to the proclamation of wholeness, order, and peace in Psalm 1, as well as the struggles witnessed to in Psalms 2–72 (afflictions, doubts, sufferings), on the other side of the line aiming at Psalm 150 with its unrestricted jubilation, does mark the most sensitive and best reflected transitional point between depression and exuberance. If someone took this perspective on the whole Psalter sometime before monastic continuous reading was introduced in the European Middle Ages, Psalm 73 lost its individual significance, exclusively serving a theological vision of Israel wandering from spiritual captivity to freedom. A long and dangerous journey, indeed, which Psalm 73, incidentally, takes up after Psalm 72, which by its superscription "Solomon" suggests disastrous failure (cf. 1 Kings 11–12) in the battle for justice, faithfulness, and dignity.

## Intention

A faith community like dispersed Israel in exilic and postexilic times needed a good amount of self-discipline to stay unified in a very pluralistic culture dominated by powerful foreign elements. Insistence on concentrating one's dedication to only one God was essential for survival. Also, the portraits of good and evil personalities (and the notions of good and evil came together with religious belief) had to be taught each individual member of a congregation. "For me it is good to be near God; I have made the Lord Yahweh my refuge, that I may tell of all your works" (v. 28): full and undisturbed communion with God is the highest value for followers of Yahweh. Small wonder that pluriform visions and interests divided the people of Yahweh, recognizably so since Assyrian times (cf. Albertz, *History*, §3.5; 3.6, Additional Bibliography, section B). So, internally, the exilic and postexilic people wrestled for their right path, to be recognized by Yahweh himself. In critical moments of uncertainty (cf. vv. 2, 13-16) the worshipers had to be reassured about the solidarity of their God. This goal is to be communicated and taught by Psalm 73.

## Bibliography

L. C. Allen, "Psalm 73: An Analysis," *TynBul* 33 (1982) 93-118; P. Auffret, "Et moi sens cesse avec toi," *SJOT* 9 (1995) 241-58; E. Balla, "Das Problem des Leides in der israelitisch-jüdischen Religion," in *Eucharisterion (Fest.* H. Gunkel; ed. H. Schmidt; Göttingen: Vandenhoeck & Ruprecht, 1923) 214-60 (esp. 252-55); E. Beaucamp, "Voie nouvelle pour l'exégèse du Psaume 73," in *Studia Hierosolymitana (Fest.* B. Bagatti; ed. E. Testa; Jerusalem: Franciscan Printing, 1976) 44-46; P. Beyerhaus, "Wenn ich nur dich habe . . . ," *Theologische Beiträge* 25 (1994) 57-65; H. Birkeland, "The Chief Problems of Ps. 73,14ff," *ZAW* 67 (1955) 99-103; P. A. H. de Boer, "The Meaning of Ps 73,9," *VT* 18 (1968) 260-64; W. Brueggemann, "Bounded by Obedience and Praise: The Psalms as Canon," *JSOT* 50 (1991) 63-92, esp. 80-88 (repr. in *The Psalms and the Life of Faith* [ed. P. D. Miller; Minneapolis: Fortress, 1995] 189-213, esp. 204-10); idem, "Response to J. L. Mays, 'The Question of Context,'" in *The Shape and Shaping of the Psalter* (ed. J. McCann Jr.; JSOTSup 159; Sheffield: JSOT Press, 1993) 29-41; idem and P. D. Miller Jr., "Psalm 73 as a Canonical Marker," *JSOT* 72 (1996) 45-56; M. Buber, *Recht und Unrecht. Deutung einiger Psalmen* (Basel: Benno Schwalbe, 1952; Sammlung Klosterberg) 39-61 (repr. in *Werke II, Schriften zur Bibel* [Munich: Lambert Schneider, 1964] 971-83); idem, "The Heart Determines," in *On the Bible* (ed. N. N. Glatzer; New York: Schocken, 1968) 199-210; A. Caquot, "Le Psaume LXXIII," *Sem* 21 (1971) 29-56; R. Cortese, "E se il salmo 73 lo recitano i poveri?" *RivB* 43 (1995) 55-71; J. L. Crenshaw, "Standing Near the Flame: Psalm 73," in idem, *A Whirlpool of Torment*

(OBT; Philadelphia: Fortress, 1984) 93-109; P. Drijvers, "Psalm 73: Kan het de goeden slecht gan?" *Schrift* 68 (1980) 51-56; E. L. Ehrlich, "Und doch bleibe ich stets bei dir: Auslegung des 73. Psalms," in *Umkehr und Erneuerung* (ed. B. Klappert, et al.; Neukirchen-Vluyn: Neukirchener Verlag, 1980) 128-37; H. Gese, "Die Frage nach dem Lebenssinn: Hiob und seine Folgen," *ZTK* 79 (1982) 161-79; M. D. Goulder, "Asaph's 'History of Israel,'" *JSOT* 65 (1995) 71-81; K.-J. Illman, "Till tolkningen av Psalm 73," *SEÅ* 41/42 (1977) 120-29; H. Irsigler, *Psalm 73: Monolog eines Weisen: Text, Programm, Struktur* (Arbeiten zu Text und Sprache im Alten Testament 20; St. Ottilien: EOS, 1984); H.-J. Kraus, "Psalm 73," *Bethel* 11 (1973) 3-12; G. Kuhn, "Bemerkungen zu Ps. 73," *ZAW* 55 (1937) 307-8; D. M. Lloyd-Jones, *Faith on Trial* (London: Inter-Varsity Fellowship, 1965); J. Luyten, "Psalm 73 and Wisdom," in *La Sagesse de l'Ancient Testament* (BETL 51; ed. M. Gilbert; Paris/Gembloux: Duculot, 1979) 59-81; R. Malter, "Schöpfergott und Theodizee: Eine philosophische Meditation über den 73. Psalm und das Buch Hiob," in *Gott — das bleibende Geheimnis (Fest.* W. Seidel; ed. P. Reifenberg; Würzburg: Echter, 1996) 68-88; M. Mannati, "Les adorateurs de Mot dans le Psaume LXXIII," *VT* 22 (1972) 420-25; J. Marböck, "Hoffnung in Auferstehung und Bewährung. Eine Besinnung zu Ps 73," *Theologisch-Praktische Quartalschrift* 131 (1983) 195-203; R. Martin-Achard, *La mort en face selon la Bible hébraique* (Geneva: Labor et Fides, 1988); J. C. McCann, "Psalm 73: An Interpretation Emphasizing Rhetorical and Canonical Criticism" (diss., Duke, 1985); idem, "Psalm 73: A Microcosm of Old Testament Theology," in *The Listening Heart (Fest.* R. E. Murphy; ed. K. Hoglund, et al.; JSOTSup 58; Sheffield: Sheffield Academic Press, 1987) 247-57; D. Michel, "'Ich aber bin immer bei dir.' Von der Unsterblichkeit der Gottesbeziehung," *Pietas Liturgica* 3 (1987) 637-58; J. A. Mindling, "Hope for a Felicitous Afterlife in Psalm 16:49 and 73," *Laurentianum* 32 (1991) 305-69; P. A. Munch, "Das Problem des Reichtums in den Ps. 37; 49; 73," *ZAW* 55 (1937) 36-46; E. Nielsen, "Psalm 73: Scandinavian Contributions," in *Understanding Poets and Prophets* (ed. A. Auld; JSOTSup 152; Sheffield: JSOT Press, 1993) 273-83; E. Otto, "Der Vorwurf an Gott" (lecture given at Marburg, at a meeting of Orientalists, 1950/1951); B. Renaud, "Le Psaume 73, méditation individuelle ou prière collective?" *RHPR* 59 (1979) 541-50; H. Ringgren, "Einige Bemerkungen zum LXXIII. Psalm," *VT* 3 (1953) 265-72; J. F. Ross, "Psalm 73," in *Israelite Wisdom (Fest.* S. Terrien; ed. J. G. Gammie; Missoula, Mont.: Scholars Press, 1978) 161-75; N. H. Snaith, *Hymns of the Temple* (London: SCM, 1951) 102-19; R. J. Tournay, "Le Psaume 73: Relectures et interprétation," *RB* 92 (1985) 187-99; E. R. Wendland, "Introit 'into the Sanctuary of God' (Ps 73:17): Entering the Theological 'Heart' of the Psalm at the Center of the Psalter," *OTE* 11 (1998) 128-53; E. Würthwein, "Erwägungen zu Psalm 73," in *Festschrift A. Bertholet* (ed. W. Baumgartner; Tübingen: Mohr, 1950) 532-49 (repr. idem, *Wort und Existenz* [Göttingen: Vandenhoeck & Ruprecht, 1970] 161-78); E. Zenger, "Psalm 73 als christlich-jüdisches Gebet," *BK* 74 (1992) 184-87.

# Psalm 74:
# Communal Complaint

## *Structure*

|  | MT | NRSV |
|---|---|---|
| I. Superscription | 1a | - |
| II. Initial complaint, petition, hymn | 1b-2 | 1-2 |
| III. Complaint | 3-9 | 3-9 |
| IV. Plaintive petition | 10-11 | 10-11 |
| V. Hymn | 12-17 | 12-17 |
| VI. Petition | 18-23 | 18-23 |

While the date and setting of Psalm 74 are much debated, its structure appears to be molded lucidly and traditionally along parameters of COMMUNUAL COMPLAINT. Some traits not so well attested for this genre call for attention, however. (a) The absence of a proper invocation of Yahweh, the God of Israel, cannot be explained away simply by making responsible a phantom like "Elohist redaction." (b) A proper ending, be it vow or word of praise, is lacking after v. 23, which stops in the middle of petition. (c) There are hardly any direct references to the national community or its God-given monarch. (d) The enemies' actions are reported at length, but their identity remains obscure; and, more strangely still, they are recommended to the avenging memory of God without suffering any direct imprecatory action of the suppliants (cf. 79:10-12). These latter, in turn, hide behind designations like "flock of your pasture" (v. 1b; cf. 77:21 [RSV 20]; 78:52; 79:13; 95:7; 100:3), "your assembly" (v. 2a; frequent in Priestly literature, especially in Numbers; in this sense only in very late psalms; cf. Pss 1:5; 111:1), "tribe of your inheritance" (v. 2b; the expression itself is unique in the Psalms; cf. Isa 63:17; Jer 10:16; 51:19; and *naḥălāh*, "inheritance," meaning the chosen people in Pss 33:12; 78:71; 94:5; 106:5), and finally, as a geographic and theological marker, "Mount Zion" (v. 2c). Later on, allusions to the worshiping congregation are found in vv. 19-22, at the center of which appear the self-appellations *'ănîyekkā,* "your oppressed ones" (v. 19b), and *'ānî wě'ebyôn,* "oppressed and poor" (v. 21b; cf., in relation to groups or people, Pss 12:6 [RSV 5]; 18:28 [RSV 27]; 72:2, 4). Furthermore, there is a reference to the "alliance" (v. 20). The first person plural of the community, oddly enough, comes to the fore only in v. 9 (cf. Scharbert, "Das 'Wir'"; listing at "Introduction to Psalms").

The individual form elements may be discussed briefly. The SUPERSCRIPTION is of the simplest kind, giving, as it were, a psalm category and author or reference person. *maśkîl* appears in 13 psalm headings and once in the body of a song (Ps 47:8 [RSV 7]) and could mean a type of instruction or an "intensive" prayer (thus Mowinckel, Delekat; → Psalm 32). Five of the *maśkîl* superscriptions have an inverted word order: reference person — *maśkîl* (Psalms 32; 44; 45; 88; 99). For Asaph → Psalms 50; 73.

The first section of the song, COMPLAINT and PETITION, is complex, beginning with accusatory "why" like 22:2 (RSV 1), similarly "How long" (13:2

[RSV 1]). The plaintive "why" is quite common in complaints (cf. 44:10 [RSV 9]; 79:10; 89:39 [RSV 38]; Isa 63:17; Jer 14:8, 19; Gunkel-Begrich, *Einleitung,* 217; listing at "Introduction to Cultic Poetry"; Eng. at Additional Bibliography, section C). Psalm 22, however, in all its anguish has a proper INVOCATION, missing also in → Psalm 13. Our psalm ranks the interrogative "why" first and the appellation of *'ĕlōhîm* only second, thus giving the impression of a hasty opening that ignores etiquette. A strong COMPLAINT (v. 1bc; cf. *znḥ,* "reject," in communal songs: Pss 44:10 [RSV 9]; 60:3, 12 [RSV 1, 10]; 89:39 [RSV 38]; Lam 2:7), insistent PETITION (v. 2b; also vv. 18, 22; cf. *zkr,* "remember, heed," in communal petition: 89:51 [RSV 50]; 105:8; 106:4), and hymnic praise (v. 2bc; cf. *g'l,* "redeem," in congregational hymns: 77:16 [RSV 15]; 106:10; Isa 48:20; 63:9) follow in due course. As pointed out, the first two lines refer clearly to the community behind the psalm, without using first-person plural forms.

This kind of self-presentation is absent from v. 3, which still contains PETITION (v. 3a). Consequently there may be some doubt as to the liturgical division between elements. The entreaty for taking action (v. 3a) is probably the opening of a uniform section of COMPLAINT (vv. 3-9). Its main point is to describe the disastrous sacrilege of God's enemies who invaded his sanctuary (or sanctuaries? in v. 8 *mô'ădê,* "places of assembly of [God]," is an uncontested plural, while in v. 4 most Hebrew MSS have plural; cf. *BHS; qōdeš,* "sanctuary," in v. 3b is singular, while *miqdāš,* "sanctuary," in v. 7 again is plural with the majority of textual witnesses). In any case, the bitter complaint is about the destruction of a temple (or many sanctuaries?) by axes and fire (vv. 3-8). One more lament arises because of lack of divine communication (v. 9). The facts mentioned seem so concrete and noninventable that most exegetes have tried to identify the sacking of Zion with some historical event of this kind (against this trend argues, e.g., Willesen, postulating a cultic [New Year] commemoration of defeat). Some localize Psalm 74 sometime after the fall of Jerusalem in 587 B.C.E. (e.g., Schmidt, Kraus). The well-known Lachish Ostraca no. IV, "we are watching for the signals of Lachish," and no. III, "letter of Tobiah . . . through the prophet" (both texts *ANET,* 322), have only a vague resemblance to v. 9. The latter, at that, seems extravagant stylistically (only first-person plural expressions) and could even be a secondary addition (cf. Roberts).

An intermediary PLAINTIVE PETITION (vv. 10-11), with typical rhetorical questions of the complaint genre ("How long?" "Why?" cf. v. 1b) is a new element, because it leaves behind the description of evil machinations and want, challenging God to act immediately on behalf of his followers. In fact, the plaintive sentences urge him, and MT ends the two lines with an outright imperative: "Take your right hand out of your vestment" (v. 11b). Plaintive statements, as a rule, drive at PETITION in that they denounce a deplorable and dangerous state of affairs (cf. Gerstenberger, *Mensch,* 47-51, 98-101).

Astonishingly, from a logical point of view, but very much in line with complaint liturgies, a fine hymnic section comes next (vv. 12-17). It employs direct-address style (cf. Crüsemann, *Studien,* 285-94; listing at "Introduction to Cultic Poetry"), and — contrary to our own theological expectations postulating the exodus tradition — draws on very old mythological traditions of the creator-god smashing the primordial powers of chaos, *yām,* "sea (monster)," *tannînîm,* "dragons," *liwyātān,* "Leviathan," *nāḥal,* "torrent," *naḥărôt,* "river (demons)" (vv. 13-15). Evidently, these superhuman and divine entities correspond to those with identical names in Ugaritic literature (cf. A. Cooper and M. H. Pope, "Divine Names and Epithets," *RSP* III, 333-469; Dahood, II, 204-7; Day; Ringgren; Römer; Willesen; R. Kalmin, *ABD* IV, 295-97). This mythical hymn here functions as a powerful reminder that God once took seriously his creative potentialities over against the whole world. A good number of parallel texts in the Hebrew Bible come up with similar discourse (cf. Isa 27:1; 51:1-11; 63:7-19; Jer 10:6-24; Pss 77:17-21 [RSV 16-20]; 114; etc.). Now, in times of crisis, he is to exercise his powers and responsibilities over against his people. It is exactly this idea that the final PETITION (vv. 18-23) spells out. All the emphasis is on moving Yahweh to intervene against the enemies, perhaps also against the insensate people in Israel (vv. 18b, 22b) who possibly collaborate with outside oppressors. The group of the faithful is in the midst of danger, of trouble, awaiting rescue. With a glance at those terrible offenders (v. 23) the song comes to an abrupt end. Formally we find imperatives alternating with negated jussives: "Remember" (v. 18a) — "do not deliver" (v. 19a); "consider" (v. 20a) — "do not let be ashamed" (v. 21a); "arise," "remember" (v. 22ab) — "do not forget" (v. 23a). Petition is explicitly directed to Yahweh (v. 18a), pleading for solidarity and help for a battered people, designated as "poor," "oppressed," "miserable" but insisting on an ancient alliance (v. 20a: *běrît;* cf. v. 2a: "acquired ages ago") — all these affirmations indicating the exilic situation (cf. "perpetual ruins," v. 3a). The petition asks for a remedy in troubled times after the defeat of Judah. Could the abrupt finish (→ Psalm 88) have been liturgically ameliorated by the subsequent recitation of a hymnic element, e.g., Psalm 117?

## Genre

The starting point for our genre classification is naturally all the traits mentioned indicating a communal complaint. Apart from some uncertainties (invocation; hybrid opening; lack of confessions of guilt or innocence; abrupt ending; absence of concluding vows, praises, etc.) the formal elements are in best accordance with the general scheme of COMMUNAL COMPLAINT (cf. Psalms 44; 79; 80; 89; see "Introduction to Cultic Poetry," section 4B). The more general background of the genre includes ancient Near Eastern lamentations over the destruction of city and sanctuary; cf. Dobbs-Allsopp; → Book of Lamentations.

## Setting/Intention

A thorny problem, however, is the exact date of our psalm. Donner has argued convincingly that we should not fix our attention too much on the sixth century B.C.E. and the immediacy of Nebuchadnezzar's destruction of Jerusalem. Following Gunkel, we may assume some unknown incident of temple profanation in later times, if vv. 4-9 at all refer exclusively to one historical event. More important than dating, anyway, are the life situation and the liturgical setup in which Psalm 73 was used in ancient times. As Veijola has pointed out in his pertinent monograph (listing at Psalm 89), there were probably sacrificial ceremonies even during that period when the Jerusalem temple lay in ruins. Later on, ceremonies of mourning and remembering the defeat continued, particularly among exiles (cf. Zech 7:1-3; Lamentations 1–2; 4–5). New desecrations of Israel's meeting houses occurred and possibly entered into the tradition of these memorial celebrations or created new days of communal lament. Thus some day of mourning gave rise also to our psalm (cf. Isaiah 63–64), its main purpose being to overcome grave problems of survival in a rather hostile world. Psalm 74 wants to overcome the crisis of the community by uniting all the faithful and by pleading for a decisive intervention of Yahweh.

## Bibliography

P. R. Ackroyd, "Some Notes on the Psalms," *JTS* 17 (1966) 392-99; P. Auffret, "Essai sur la structure littéraire du Psaume LXXIV," *VT* 33 (1983) 129-48; R. Bascom, "The Targums: Ancient Reader's Helps," *BT* 36 (1985) 301-16; C. T. Begg, "The Covenantal Dove in Psalm LXXIV,19-20," *VT* 37 (1987) 78-81; G. W. Buchanan, "The Fall of Jerusalem and the Reconsideration of Some Dates," *RevQ* 14 (1989) 31-48; R. J. Clifford, "The Hebrew Scriptures and the Theology of Creation," *Theological Studies* 46 (1985) 507-23; M. Dahood, "Vocative Lamedh in Ps 74:14," *Bib* 59 (1978) 262-63; J. Day, *God's Conflict with the Dragon and the Sea* (University of Cambridge Oriental Publications 35; Cambridge: Cambridge University Press, 1985); H. Donner, "Argumente zur Datierung des 74. Psalms," in *Wort, Lied und Gottesspruch (Fest. J. Ziegler; ed. J. Schreiner; Würzburg: Echter, 1972) 41-50; F. W. Dobbs-Allsopp, *Weep, O Daughter of Zion: A Study of the City-Lament Genre in the Hebrew Bible* (BibOr 44; Rome: Pontifical Biblical Institute, 1993), esp. 154-56; O. Eissfeldt, "Gott und das Meer in der Bibel," in *Studia Orientalia (Fest. J. Pedersen; Copenhagen: Nordisk Forlag, 1953) 76-84 (repr. in Eissfeldt, *KS* III, 256-64); J. A. Emerton, "'Spring and Torrent' in Psalm 74,15," *VTSup* 15 (1966) 122-33; R. W. Engle, "Psalm 74: Studies in Context, Structure, and Meaning" (diss., Grace Theological Seminary, 1987); I. Fischer, *Wo ist Jahwe?* (SBB 19; Stuttgart: Katholisches Bibelwerk, 1989) 212-14; A. Gelston, "A Note on Psalm LXXIV,8," *VT* 34 (1984) 82-87; W. Herrmann, "Duo augmina emendantia," *VT* 41 (1991) 342-44; D. J. Human, "Die struktuur en traditsiesamestelling van Psalm 74," *SK* 14 (1993) 203-21; idem, "Die begrip 'berit' in 'n aantal klaagpsalms: 'n perspektief," *SK* 15 (1994) 280-293; idem, "Berit in Psalm 74," *SK* 16 (1995) 57-66; C. Loeliger, "Biblical Concepts of Salvation," *Point* 6 (1977) 134-45; O. Loretz, *Leberschau, Sündenbock, Asasel in Ugarit und Israel* (Ugaritisch-biblische Literatur 3; Altenberge: CIS, 1985), esp. 92-112; J. L. McKenzie, "A Note on Psalm 73 (74),13-15," *Theological Studies Woodstock* 2 (1950) 275-82; M. Metzger, "Eigentumsdeklaration und Schöpfungsaussage," in *"Wenn nicht jetzt?" (Fest. H.-J. Kraus; ed. H.-G. Geyer, et al.; Neukirchen-Vluyn: Neukirchener Verlag, 1983) 37-51; J. P. M. van der Ploeg, "Psalm 74 and Its Structure," in *Travels in the World of the Old Testament (Fest. M. A. Beek; ed. M. S. H. G. Heerma van Voss, et al.; Assen: Van Gorcum, 1974) 204-10; H. Ringgren, "Die Funktion des Schöpfungsmythos in Jes 51," in *Schalom (Fest. A. Jepsen; ed. K. H.

Bernhardt; Arbeiten zur Theologie 46; Stuttgart: Calwer, 1971) 38-40; J. J. M. Roberts, "Of Signs, Prophets, and Time Limits," *CBQ* 39 (1977) 474-81; A. Robinson, "A Possible Solution to the Problem of Psalm 74,5," *ZAW* 89 (1977) 121-22; T. Römer, "La redécouverte d'un mythe dans l'Ancient Testament: La création comme combat," *ETR* 64 (1989) 561-73; G. E. Sharrock, "Ps 74: A Literary-Structural Analysis," *AUSS* 21 (1983) 211-23; R. Sollamo, "The Simile in Ps 74:5: A Wood-Cutter Entering a Forest Wielding Axes?" *SEÅ* 54 (1989) 178-87; V. H. Todd, "Biblical Eschatology: An Overview," *Cumberland Seminarian* 22 (1984) 3-16; C. Uehlinger, "Der Mythos vom Drachenkampf: Von Sumer nach Nicaragua," *Reformatio* 39 (1990) 213-26; L. Vosberg, *Studien zum Reden vom Schöpfer in den Psalmen* (Munich: Kaiser, 1975); M. Weiss, "Die Methode der Total-Interpretation," *VTSup* 22 (1972) 88-112 (esp. 96-106); F. Willesen, "The Cultic Situation of Psalm LXXIV," *VT* 2 (1952) 289-306; W. A. Young, "Psalm 74: A Methodological and Exegetical Study" (diss., University of Iowa, 1974).

## Psalm 75:
## Exhortation, Sermon

### Structure

|  | MT | NRSV |
|---|---|---|
| I. Superscription | 1 | - |
| II. Summons to praise | 2 | 1 |
| III. Oracle | 3-4 | 2-3 |
| IV. Exhortation | 5-9 | 4-8 |
| V. Vow, imprecation | 10-11 | 9-10 |

Besides assigning the psalm to Asaph and classifying it as *mizmôr* and *šîr*, the SUPERSCRIPTION informs about the "choir leader" (?) and possibly a specific tune, *'al tašḥēt*, "do not annihilate" (v. 1). Psalms 57 and 59 include in their superscriptions the same wording. But the exact meaning in all three instances escapes us.

At first sight the reader of the poem may be confused by alternating figures raising their voices: a community speaks up jubilantly in v. 2. Thereafter, only individuals articulate themselves, and, obviously, the "I" of v. 3 cannot be the same as the "I" in v. 10. Furthermore, the identity of the person entering with "I said" (v. 5) is obscure. Theoretically it could be the speaker of v. 3 or v. 10 or a third figure not outed so far. If we presuppose a worship situation — as many commentators do — things fall in line more easily with the liturgical elements.

Congregational praise (v. 2) with a self-hortatory and/or other-directed SUMMONS also occurs as the opening line in Psalms 8; 95; etc. We may imagine a call of this sort being sounded at the beginning of a worship service or of a new liturgical section. More frequently, a leader of ceremonies calls on the congregation to give thanks and praise and the people respond (Pss 107:1; 118:1; 136:1-3). Here the cohortative "let us thank you, O God" (v. 2) may include the officiant, who later on, in the same line, dissociates himself from the congregation by reporting that "they tell your marvelous deeds." The prayer address of God, however, remains the same in both stichoi. V. 2b is awkward in the MT ("near is your name; they tell your wondrous deeds") and may have to be emended (e.g., "we call on your name; we tell of your wondrous deeds" or similarly). Anyhow, the communal character of the opening is patent.

The abrupt change of speaker and direction of oratory without any transitory formula is perplexing. This fact alone excludes a merely literary origin or style for the psalm; it is proof of liturgical composition. The voice manifesting itself in vv. 3-4 (if not in vv. 3-8) is evidently God's own, and it is equally clear that some human representative vicariously has to pronounce the divine words. The Psalter contains a surprising number of discourses like that (cf. Koenen, *Gottesworte;* Starbuck, *Oracles;* listing at Additional Bibliography, section C), and some of them are clearly marked as divine speech (cf. 12:6 [RSV 5]; 50:4-7, 16; 81:6-9 [RSV 5-8]; 82:1-2; 95:7-8). Unmarked change to divine discourse delivered by spokespersons, on the other hand, is quite in order during liturgical proceedings, because the shift becomes audible and visible all by itself (cf. 46:11 [RSV 10], to be followed immediately by a communal part, v. 12 [RSV 11]; 89:4-5 [RSV 3-4]; 91:14-16; 105:15). But prophetic pronouncements perhaps needed special framings and legitimations to identify a given communication as divine. Discourses of God within worship services go by different rules and must not be confounded with prophetic, not even cult-prophetic, speech. The concept of "cultic prophecy" as such needs revision (→ Psalm 12).

In terms of content vv. 3-4 are an announcement of an approaching, very likely eschatological, judgment (vv. 3b, 4a; cf. Psalms 50; 81). This manifestation of God is in the oracular tradition (see Glossary: ORACLE; R. D. Weis, *ABD* V, 28-29). Its universal scope ("the earth and all its inhabitants," v. 4a; cf. "the godless of the earth," v. 9d) is hymnic rhetoric. The whole psalm focuses on the "godless" (vv. 5, 9, 11) in opposition to the "righteous" (v. 11) within their own community and under the "God of Jacob" (v. 10).

"I said" (*'āmartî,* v. 5) probably indicates another shift, even if the same speaker should continue "on air." Eighteen times this very form occurs in the Psalter, and all the examples outside Psalm 75 indicate the psalmist speaking (cf., e.g., 30:7 (RSV 6); 31:5 (RSV 4); 32:5; 38:17 (RSV 16); 39:2 (RSV 1); 40:11 (RSV 10); 41:5 (RSV 4); 73:15; 89:3 (RSV 2); 116:11; 119:57). Should our v. 5 be the only exception to this rule? The ancient translators into Syriac avoided the problem by letting the community address God in vv. 4b, 5a: "You stabilized its pillars. You said to the preposterous," and then continuing with God's speech. Yet in vv. 8 and 9 God is mentioned in the third person (if the emendation *baṣṣûr,* "against the Rock [= divine name]" instead of *běṣawwā'r,* "on the neck," in v. 6b is correct, this perspective becomes dominant throughout), the discourse now instructional in character, affirming insights about God. For reasons pointed out it may be wise to consider vv. 5-9 a plain theological EXHORTATION, transmitted and duly introduced by *'āmartî,* through the officiant who is the legitimate interpreter of the divine oracle. To take up the former argument: if accentuated "I say" in the Psalter always indicates a human being speaking, and to a human audience at that ("to the vainglorious," v. 5a), then he

82

or she must be a preacher or teacher. That means that we are witnessing in vv. 3-9 a type of homiletical venture in early Jewish community service. The voice of God, recorded and recited by the leader of worship (vv. 3-4), is being interpreted by the latter. Ps 50:16a attributes to God himself the task of talking to the wicked (which seems a redactional insertion, however); 95:7-11 seems to be a midrashic paraphrase of Scripture passages; 81:7-8 draws on exodus motifs, 89:4-5 on 2 Samuel 7 — we are, with all these texts, in the middle of community processes of preaching and teaching.

The main point for the "preposterous" and "godless" — these are certainly members of the psalmist's own ethnic and religious group — to watch is their trust in power (vv. 5-6). Heb. *qeren,* "horn" (vv. 5, 6, 11), symbolizes political and economic strength. Other psalms of this genre spell out in more detail and in different ways the iniquities of the godless (cf. 10:3-11; 50:16-20; 73:3-12; 81:12-13 [RSV 11-12]). To worship other gods and to violate the norms of Yahweh's will correspond to the basic teaching of the D school. In our passage self-exaltation is chastised, which more or less coincides with the diatribes of the other psalms just mentioned. What makes our exhortation a special one is the direct address in vv. 5-6: three negative jussives and one imperfect, which probably receives negative force from the first stichos, severely admonish the wayward before three motive clauses furnish the reasons for the attack (vv. 7-9). God's sovereignty transcends that of all other powers. Alluding to them succinctly by mentioning the directions of the wind (v. 7) and not pinpointing their religious or political names may be a matter of precaution in a foreign-dominated imperium.

V. 8 coincides partly with 1 Sam 2:7 (there are more affinities between the texts: cf. the denunciation of the wicked and the fortification of the faithful in 1 Sam 2:3-10; the congruence of vocabulary and imagery) and interprets v. 3: God alone is judge. The metaphor for introducing justice (cup of foaming wine, etc., which apparently kills the wicked, or, according to an emendation proposed by Dijkstra, which is withheld from the godless, while only the bitter dregs are left for them, v. 9) appears frequently in Hebrew Scripture (cf. Isa 51:17-23; Jer 25:15-29; Ezek 23:31-35; Ps 60:5 [RSV 3]). This motif looks independent and could well have been incorporated into our psalm at a secondary stage.

The Vow to keep on praising and a sort of THREAT or IMPRECATION against the impious (vv. 10-11) bring Psalm 75 to a close. Thus the present text ends up like a complaint song, after starting like a communal thanksgiving (v. 2) and unfolding like a parenetical sermon (vv. 3-9). Since the topic is throughout that tension between groups within the congregation, and since the body of the psalm develops the idea of divine punishment of the "wicked," the closing two lines are appropriate.

## *Genre*

We opted for a homiletical structure reflecting early Jewish congregational worship. Therefore the psalm may be grouped, in a way, with EXHORTATIONS and SERMONS to be found in the Psalms (→ Psalm 62) and some other layers of the OT (cf. Deuteronomy 1–12; Isaiah 40–66; and many more prophetic texts. Note the distinction of levels: Yahweh speaks to a mediator, who in turn communicates to the congregation). To define our genres more closely: the EXHORTATION grew out of thanksgiving services, wherein the saved one proclaimed the gracious help of God and drew some conclusions from this fact for those participating in the feast of thanksgiving offering (→ Pss 22:23-27 [RSV 22-26]; 32:9-12; 66:16-19; 116:14, 18). The exhortation becomes a SERMON if there is no specific occasion for witnessing to personal salvation, but the speaker has ample opportunity to point to God's interventions for his people and, as in our case, to adduce an oracle of God from tradition (or Scripture?).

Attempts to make this psalm a "prophetic liturgy" betray a heightened sensitivity over against changing voices and worship liturgies, but they introduce, it seems to me, a foreign element, that of late and dogmatic Word-of-Yahweh prophetism into early community service (against Jeremias, *Kultprophetie,* 117-19; Johnson, *Prophet,* 4-45 and passim; listing at "Introduction to Psalms"). Even vv. 3-4 cannot easily be considered a freshly received oracle, which probably needed to be presented as such (cf. 50:16-22; 60:8-10 [RSV 6-8]; 62:12 [RSV 11]; 95:7-11; Hab 2:1-3; Job 33:14-18).

The debate whether we may expect the genre SERMON in the Psalter transcends by far the topic "Levitical preaching" and certainly has not been concluded yet (against Mathias; Koenen, 16).

## Setting

The early Jewish communities started to organize themselves in the wake of deportations and destruction of their own national identity. Nehemiah 8 demonstrates the assembly in which Torah was read and explained. Psalms and other late texts of the OT testify to other types of meetings: the people of Yahweh came together to pray, meditate, sing, and hear the will of Yahweh expounded by their leaders, be they of Levitical or scribal formation. Our psalm was apparently composed and used in the homiletical tradition of these early Jewish communities.

## Intention

There are an orthodox claim in Psalm 75 to represent the true followers of the "God of Jacob" (v. 10) and an attempt to purge the power-conscious and wicked ones. That the latter have been adherents of Babylonian astral deities (Seybold, 291-93) is a possibility, but the name *hôlĕlîm* alone (v. 5: "shining ones" [?]) does not warrant such a conclusion. Expectation of a day of reckoning (v. 3) propels this strongly exhortative sermon.

84

## Bibliography

P. Auffret, "C'est Dieu qui juge," *ZAW* 109 (1997) 385-94; U. Bach, "Der Wert des Lebens," *Junge Kirche* 55 (1994) 194-97; E. Beaucamp and de Relles, "Psaume 75 (74). La coupe de Yahwe," *Feu Nouveau* 8/16 (1965) 21-27; M. Dahood, "The Four Cardinal Points in Psalm 75,7 and Joel 2,20," *Bib* 52 (1971) 397; M. Dijkstra, "He Pours the Sweet Wine Off, Only the Dregs Are for the Wicked: An Epigraphic Note on *mizzæh* in Ps 75,9," *ZAW* 107 (1995) 296-300; A. González, "El Salmo 75 y el jicio escatológico," *EstBib* 21 (1962) 5-22; J. G. Harris III, "Prophetic Oracles in the Psalter" (diss., Princeton, 1970); J. Jeremias, *Kultprophetie und Gerichtsverkündigung in der späten Königszeit* (WMANT 35; Neukirchen: Neukirchener Verlag, 1970) 110-20; D. Mathias, "'Levitische Predigt' und Deuteronomismus," *ZAW* 96 (1984) 23-49; S. Mowinckel, *PsSt* III, 47-49; R. Tournay, "Notes sur les Psaumes," *RB* 79 (1972) 39-58; E. Wiesenberg, "A Note on *mzh* in Ps LXXV,9," *VT* 4 (1954) 434-39.

## Psalm 76:
## Confessional Hymn; Zion Hymn

### Structure

|  | MT | NRSV |
|---|---|---|
| I. Superscription | 1 | - |
| II. Hymnic affirmation | 2-4 | 1-3 |
| III. Direct-address hymn | 5-11 | 4-10 |
| A. Address to God, the Warrior | 5-7 | 4-6 |
| B. Address to God, the Judge | 8-11 | 7-10 |
| IV. Exhortation | 12-13 | 11-12 |

Psalm 76 belongs to the collection ascribed to Asaph (see Psalm 73). The technical term *binĕgînōt* refers to stringed instruments and occurs seven times in headings of psalms (see, e.g., Psalms 4; 54; 67), once in a closing line of a hymn (Hab 3:19), and several times in the body of a psalm (cf. Pss 69:13 [RSV 12]; 77:7 [RSV 6]; Lam 5:14; Isa 38:20). The instrument cannot be identified with certainty; it should be stringed, however (cf. Sendrey, *Music,* 300-301; listing at Additional Bibliography, section B; I. H. Jones, *ABD* IV, 937-38).

Four liturgical sections are recognizable in the body of the psalm, three of which begin with an affirmation about God, placing an adjective (Niphal participle) in front (vv. 2, 5, 8). The first segment thus introduced ("known is in Judah *'ĕlōhîm,*" v. 2a; cf. 9:17 [RSV 16]; 48:4 [RSV 3]) employs third-person language for God, paying homage to the God of Judah *and* Israel, both gentilic names being synonymous here, as it were, characterizing the God who chose Jerusalem and Zion for his abode (vv. 2-3). The name Yahweh does not yet appear, coming up only in v. 12, in a sort of climax. But the locale of God's dwelling and action is clear from the beginning. V. 4 takes up a special Jerusalemite tradition, which may antedate Israel's conquest of the city under David: the

God of this stronghold defeats attacking enemies, destroying their (or all?) weapons (cf. vv. 5-7); the vocabulary and imagery of such battle reports go back to primeval, mythological tales (cf. 46:3-11 [RSV 2-10]; 48:5-8 [RSV 4-7]; Stolz, *Strukturen;* listing at "Introduction to Cultic Poetry"). The glorification of the God on Zion has a confessional ring to it: he is the supreme power, and he is the Lord of the Zion community, who probably offered this song of praise to him. Thus objective praise of the god (not yet Yahweh!) on Zion constitutes the introductory HYMNIC AFFIRMATION, emphasizing the power and peace of Jerusalem (cf. Steck, *Friedensvorstellungen,* 25-51; listing at Additional Bibliography, section B).

The direct-address HYMN (vv. 5-11) exemplifies God's victorious power; it falls into two liturgical entities set apart by topic and sentence markers (Niphal participles: *nā'ôr,* "glorious," v. 5; *nôrā',* "awesome," v. 8) but united by prayer language. In one, details of a past battle are given (vv. 5-7). This part comes close to a victory hymn (cf. 68:12-15 [RSV 11-14]; Judges 5). There are no mythological figures mentioned, as in Pss 74:12-15; 77:17-19 (RSV 16-18). The enemies are human potentates fighting with their hands and armed with normal horse-and-chariot equipment. The superior power of God is acclaimed; his war cry alone paralyzed them (v. 7; on the verb *rdm,* "to dismay, fall into unconsciousness," cf. Judg 4:21; Jonah 1:5-6; Dan 8:18; 10:9: always the effect of extreme impacts of the divine). Second-person address (vv. 5, 7) is somewhat unusual in narrating hymns; dramatization of events leads to a neutral report, as in Judg 5:13-30. But Ps 77:12-21 (RSV 11-20) is a clear example of this liturgical pattern. May we surmise that direct-address hymns reflect the emotional participation of a congregation in singing praises (→ Psalm 8)? There are, in any case, more "objective," i.e., purely descriptive, hymns in the Psalter (cf. 19:2-10 [RSV 1-9]; 34:1-23 [RSV 1-22]; 136; etc.).

The second strophe of the direct-address hymn visualizes God intervening as supreme judge (vv. 8-11). The vocabulary used is juridical, the topic "divine judge" is well known from the Bible and the ancient Near East (cf. H. Niehr, *TWAT* VIII, 408-28), the solar deities being chief judges in the ancient world. The God of Israel, too, bears the title "judge" (7:12 [RSV 11]; 9:5 [RSV 4]; 50:6; 58:12 [RSV 11]; 82:1; 94:2). Justice in general, for human individuals, is the focal point, especially as thematized in Psalms 58; 82; 94 (cf. Qoh 3:17). This universal horizon (vv. 9b, 10b) and perhaps — if H.Schmidt's and H. J. Kraus's emendation is correct — the mention of the nations Edom and Hamath in v. 11 give this passage an eschatological outlook. In any case the preoccupation with "all the miserable of the earth" (v. 10b; Seybold, 295: "postexilic redaction"), suggesting a community of the poor as the place of origin for this kind of expectation, is astounding. "You are frightening," i.e., God is irresistible in his power (v. 8a): the continued message from the first part. V. 11 is textually uncertain, almost untranslatable (see conjectures in *BHK*). The second-person address of God increases in this section (vv. 8, 9, 11). Intimacy and urgency of praise befit a confessing community. Reciters or singers of the whole hymn are not made explicit. Possibly, different groups or choirs intoned the lines vv. 2-4, 5-7, 8-10 (11); note the *selah* markers, untranslated even in most modern Bibles, at the end of vv. 4 and 10.

In conclusion, a voice turns toward the congregation, asking for loyalty to Yahweh "your God" (v. 12a: second-person plural suffix). The addressees are "all grouped around him," Yahweh, as God only now is called (*kol sĕbîbāyw,* v. 12). They apparently find themselves within an international power structure (v. 13: "governors," "kings of the earth"), all subservient, in reality, to Yahweh. That means that the congregational situation becomes explicit at the end, having been presupposed at least in vv. 2-4. The EXHORTATION to the community is undergirded by hymnic affirmations that emphasize the powerful action of God (v. 13). In this fashion the last two lines prove sufficiently the psalm's moorings in congregational worship (cf. 46:9 [RSV 8]; 48:13 [RSV 12]).

## Genre

The text as a whole emits a strong feeling of allegiance with Yahweh, the God of Zion. His majesty and power is glorified in highest pitch. On the other hand, Zion remains a secondary theme. Nowhere in the psalm do we find a line addressed to the holy dwelling place or extolling the shrine or city all by themselves. Therefore, in contradistinction to Psalms 46 and 48, we should not primarily count our hymn as a "Song of Zion" (against, e.g., Seybold, 295). Again, however, the motif of divine defense of the Holy City is present (vv. 4-7), so that a vivid interest in Zion is noticeable. What to make of an ambiguous situation like this? We may resolve: the Zion tradition is subsumed to glorification of the supreme God of the Judean/Israelite community of faith. CONFESSIONAL HYMN, therefore, may be the best classification of our song.

## Setting/Intention

This glorification of God takes place in congregational worship, by a common liturgy, and it is destined to fortify the faith community around God. A leader of the assembly or a group of parishioners (perhaps also professional choirs) will recite the hymnic strophes. The first, and paramount, motif for the congregation's praise is the accessibility of Yahweh in Judah and Jerusalem. For the faithful this is a fundamental fact of their own existence, confessed in straight affirmations (vv. 2-4). Next, the subject of divine power is presented in two variations, approaching Yahweh directly (prayer language), but also in an effort to communicate God's marvelous victories and just power to the listeners, for their instruction and edification. Finally, some worship leader addresses the crowd, directly pleading for their loyalty to Yahweh, assuring them of his protection even under foreign rule.

## Bibliography

P. Auffret, "Quand Dieu se leve pour jugement," *BN* 84 (1996) 5-10; M. Dahood, "Love and Death at Ebla and Their Biblical Reflections," in *Love and Death in the Ancient*

Near East (Fest. M. H. Pope; ed. J. Marks, et al.; Guilford, Conn.: Four Quarters Pub. Co., 1987) 93-99; J. Day, "Shear-Jasub (Isaiah vii 3) and 'the Remnant of Wrath' (Psalm lxxvi 11)," VT 31 (1981) 76-78; O. Eissfeldt, "Psalm 76," in KS, III, 448-57 (repr. from TLZ 82 [1957] 801-8); J. A. Emerton, "A Neglected Solution of a Problem in Psalm LXXVI,11," VT 24 (1974) 136-46; idem, "The Site of Salem, the City of Melchizedek (Genesis 14:18)," VTSup 41 (1990) 45-71; S. L. Kelly, "The Zion-Victory Songs: Psalms 46, 48, and 76" (diss., Vanderbilt, 1968); K. Seybold, "Jerusalem in the View of Psalm 76," in The Centrality of Jerusalem (ed. M. Poorthuis, et al.; Kampen: Pharos, 1995) 7-14; T. Thorion-Vardi, "Mwr' in Pešer Habaquq VI, 5 ['fear']," RevQ 12 (1986) 282; R. Tournay, "Psaume LXXVI, 11: Nouvel essai d'interprétation," in Studia Hierosolymitana (Fest. B. Bagatti; ed. G. C. Bottini; Jerusalem: Franciscan Printing, 1976) II, 20-26.

# Psalm 77:
# Plaintive Meditation and Hymn

## Structure

|  | MT | NRSV |
|---|---|---|
| I. Superscription | 1 | - |
| II. Description of praying | 2-3 | 1-2 |
| III. Remembrance, plaintive and praising | 4-13 | 3-12 |
| A. Motifs to record the past | 4-6 | 3-5 |
| B. Complaint about people | 7-11 | 6-10 |
| C. Remembrance of God's actions | 12-13 | 11-12 |
| IV. Hymn | 14-21 | 13-20 |

The simple Asaph SUPERSCRIPTION (cf. Psalm 73) is augmented by the common lamĕnaṣṣēaḥ (cf. Psalm 4) and a technical term that may indicate a melody or ritual ('al yĕdîtûn or yĕdûtûn; cf. Psalms 39; 62).

The psalm does not open with an invocation, nor does it use, at the outset, any direct prayer language. Instead, the first section (vv. 2-3) is a DESCRIPTION OF PRAYING, tinged with an affirmation of confidence (v. 2b: "he does attend me," perfect tense) as well as complaint (v. 3c: "I do not find comfort"), as customary in individual complaint songs (see "Introduction to Cultic Poetry," section 4B). Lack of most of the significant parts of the complaint genre (invocation; affirmation of confidence; petition; vow) prohibits a classification in this category. The body of the psalm is characterized by reflective and hymnic moods and a meditative and laudatory style.

Three times the verb zkr, "remember," appears in the first person singular of the psalmist (vv. 4, 7, 12), paralleled each time by śîḥ, "contemplate" (vv. 4b, 7b, 13b), and occasionally by some other synonyms ("consider," v. 6a; "meditate," v. 13a) — a full arsenal of meditative expressions. Since "I shall remember" is placed each time in a front position of the respective lines, we may take it as a marker of subsections. A depressed mood, burdened by musing about the past, betrays the difficulties of taking proper account of experiences and the history of faith (vv. 4, 5, 8-11). The final hymn stands out as a compositional unit in its own right (vv. 14-21). Apart from the first word in v. 5 (which may have been misspelled, however) the direct-address language begins only in v. 12 to dominate the fully hymnic part.

Jussive (and imperfect) forms of *zkr,* "remember," may signify different things in different contexts. It probably referred originally to bringing a sacrifice, later on to remembering and cultically actualizing the presence of God. Thus personal and communal remembrance of ceremonial acts are the preferred references of the first-person expression (Pss 42:5, 7 [RSV 4, 6]; 63:7 [RSV 6]; 119:52, 55; 137:6; 143:5; cf. Job 21:6; Jonah 2:8 [RSV 7]; Jer 20:9). D layers look at this remembrance from a different angle. They take it as a responsibility of individuals and the congregation to "remember" and thus actualize everything Yahweh did and communicated to his people (e.g., Num 15:39, 40; Deut 5:15; 7:18; 8:2, 18; 9:7, 27; 15:15; 16:3, 12; 24:9, 18, 22).

The whole commemorative, or better, reflective, section in vv. 4-13 may be considered an introduction to the final hymn, vv. 14-21. There is a movement in vv. 4-13 of an individual mediator to find fundamental answers on behalf of a desperate community feeling forsaken by its God. This is to say: the frustrations and doubts described in vv. 8-11 are those of the congregation, not of a private person. They echo in exilic-postexilic literature (cf. 44:25 [RSV 24]; 89:47, 50 [RSV 46, 49]; Lam 2:20; 5:20; similar reproachful questions occur in individual complaints: Pss 13:2-3 [RSV 1-2]; 22:2 [RSV 1]; Job 10:18-20). The final line of the psalm clearly supports this interpretation: "You have led your people like a flock" (v. 21a).

Each passage introduced by *'ezkĕrāh* or *'ezkôr* ("I will remember," "I remember," respectively) has its own profile, though. Vv. 4-6 are descriptive and plaintive in essence, and express clearly an intention to investigate the past (v. 6). A similar idea, articulated as an exhortation to the people, appears in Jer 6:16: "Stand at the crossroads, and look, and ask for the ancient paths, where the good way lies; and walk in it." The past is the source of spiritual controversy and renewal for the congregation. The second piece — after a descriptive line portraying again the suppliant's activities "at night" "with a stringed instrument" (v. 7; cf. Ps 76:1 [RSV superscription]) — is entirely dedicated to complaining (vv. 8-11), the topic being not a personal problem but God's apparent neglect of his people. This, of course, is a communal concern, and in reflective psalms like this one the "I" may indicate a leader, or each member assuming co-responsibility for the group. Only the third summons to "remember" (v. 12) leads to the liturgical climax: Yahweh's deeds are at stake. There is a fourfold and exactly synonymous declaration of will: to make Yahweh's past actions the object of study (vv. 12-13). Twice the verb *zkr* is used (v. 12); the synonyms *hgh* and *śîh* in chiastic position take over the next line (v. 13). The very first statement (v. 12a) is couched in objective language; the three remaining phrases are all direct-address promise to God. Four synonyms designate his marvelous acts in preparation for the hymnic praise to follow.

The HYMN proper (vv. 14-21) focuses on God. No longer do we find meditative sentences concerned with the suppliant's or congregation's spiritual life. Now, everything said is positively spoken about God himself. "Your way is in holiness" (v. 14a) does not have an exact equal; cf., however, "your way is through the flood" (v. 20). The comparative formula, a rhetorical question, aims at confessing Yahweh as the supreme Deity (v. 14b; cf. Deut 3:24; often in a stereotyped way: "Who is like you?" cf. Pss 35:10; 71:19; 89:9 [RSV 8]; Exod 15:11; Mic 7:18). Affirmation of God's marvelous acts opens up a stance over against other nations (v. 15) and a remembrance of his saving interventions in the past in favor of ancient Israel (v. 16). In short, the first part of the hymn is a celebration of the national or congregational well-being. The poetic meter is regular, with 3 + 3 stresses per line. Not so the next block of the hymn (vv. 17-20). Very evenly, each line exposes oversize conglomerations of colons, three at a time. Also, the subject matter changes. Modeled like some of the Yahweh-kingship hymns (cf. 93:3-4), the text tells about the primordial encounter between God and the chaos powers (vv. 17-20). Mythological language, ignoring questions of national history, celebration of God's victory in the chaos battle — all this favors the notion that this part of Psalm 77 once had been separate (cf. Loretz, *Ugarit-Texte*).

Contents of the hymnic passage prove its distinctiveness. The turmoil of natural powers — water, clouds, lightnings, soil — is either emanations of Yahweh himself or frightened reactions to his coming. We are, therefore, in the realm of theophanic texts that have their counterparts in Ugaritic literature (cf. already Jefferson, emphasizing linguistic, literary, mythological, and theological features of Canaanite background). The hymn may be older than the rest of the psalm: vv. 14-16 are a historical prelude, vv. 17-20 are the mythical nucleus, v. 21 is a fitting close, reverting from hymnic affirmations of a primordial nature to the people of Moses and Aaron. Thus, we may say, an old Canaanite hymn, probably pertaining to the storm-god Baal, has been utilized freely by Israelite theologians (→ 74:13-15).

The HYMN proper (vv. 17-20) is put into direct-address prayer language, like its introductory and closing section (vv. 14-16, 21). This seems to be an effect of redactional work, because there are more examples of objective hymns describing God's epiphany in third-person expressions (cf. 93:3-4 [tricola, framed by direct address language in vv. 2, 5]; 96:11-13; 97:2-6; 98:7-8; 114:3-4 [taunting address of sea, mountains, and earth in vv. 5-7]). The objective stylization is quite probably the original one, while direct address was employed in later community worship.

## Genre

Neither complaint elements nor contemplations of salvation history dominate our psalm. Rather, the text is musing, in a meditative and kerygmatic way, about communal uncertainties. Has God forsaken his people (vv. 8-10)? If so, this would mean instability and collapse for his congregation. "I said: This is why I am troubled; the Most High has changed his preference" (v. 11). One voice is apparently speaking for the whole congregation, or the congregation is speaking with one voice only (Mowinckel, *W*, I, 42-46, 229-37). If this is correct, the expressions of deep and tormented reflection (vv. 4-11) are also to be intended as communal activities. In presenting them to the audience the words become instruction for the people and thereafter prayer from their common experience and consciousness. Besides the verb *zkr,* already discussed, three more expressions designate this congregational search for identity and security: *śîḥ, ḥšb,* and *hgh* (vv. 4, 6, 7, 13). The first one is no doubt the pilot lexeme of the triad, occurring three times in the reflective section. The root belongs almost exclusively to psalm contexts, with special frequency in Psalm 119 (six times; furthermore: 55:18 [RSV 17]; 143:5; 145:5). Meditation of God's words and actions is in view, and the other two verbs may be used synonymously (cf. 73:16; 119:59; 1:2; 35:28; 37:30; 63:7 [RSV 6]; 71:24; 143:5). Pondering theologically the state of the community under the impression of God's disgrace is the motivation to sing a hymn of glorification and historical as well as mythical remembrance. Thus the psalm is a MEDITATIVE HYMN testifying to the shaking of spiritual foundations in the exilic and postexilic period (Tate, 274).

## Setting/Intention

Congregational worship qualifies as the life setting and place of liturgical performance of this psalm, its intention being educative and honorific. God is extolled as the primeval Lord of all powers; therefore his community hopes he will attend their needs. When intoning the song of God's contested but everlasting care for his adorants, each of them learns to think through tribulations and uncertainties in communion, yet relevant for him/herself, the faithful individual. Then the believers immerse themselves in the great hymnic sea: hymns of glory, victory, superiority at all times have strengthened those who lacked courage and power.

## Bibliography

P. Auffret, "La droite du Très-Haut," *SJOT* 6 (1992) 92-122; L. Ben Zion, "Ephraimite Psalms," *BM* 73 (1978) 151-61; J. H. Eaton, "Music's Place in Worship," in *Prophets, Worship, and Theodicy* (ed. J. Barton, et al.; *OTS* 23; Leiden: Brill, 1984) 85-107; J. A. Emerton, "The Text of Psalm LXXVII 11," *VT* 44 (1994) 183-94; Y. Feenstra, "Le Dieu qui fait merveille (Ps 77,15)," *Revue du Clergé Africain* 22 (1967) 252-57; B. Feininger, "'Denk ich an Gott, muss ich seufzen' (Ps 77:4)," *BK* 46 (1991) 152-59; J. I. Hunt, "Translating Psalm 29," *ATR* 67 (1985) 219-27; E. Jacob, "Prier avec les Psaumes," *Foi et Vie* 84 (1985) 58-66; H. G. Jefferson, "Psalm 77," *VT* 13 (1963) 87-91; J. S. Kselman, "Psalm 77 and the Book of Exodus," *JANESCU* 15 (1983) 51-58; O. Loretz, *Ugarit-Texte und Thronbesteigungspsalmen* (Münster: Cornelsen, 1988); T. L. J. Mafico, "The Ancient and Biblical View of the Universe," *Journal of Theology for Southern Africa* 54 (1986) 3-14; W. van der Meer, "Psalm 77:17-19: Hymnisches Fragment oder Aktualisierung?" *ETL* 70 (1994) 105-11; D. A. Patrick, "Epiphanic Imagery in Second Isaiah's Portrayal of a New Exodus," *HAR* 8 (1984) 125-41; W. Schottroff, *'Gedenken' im Alten Orient und im Alten Testament* (WMANT 15; Neukirchen: Neukirchener

Verlag, 1964; 2nd ed. 1967) 131-32; S. A. Gameleira Soares, "Salmos: História, poesia e oracão," *EstBib* (Petrópolis) 10 (1986) 8-27; G. M. Stevenson, "Communal Imagery and the Individual Lament," *Restoration Quarterly* 39 (1997) 215-229; B. Weber, *Psalm 77 und sein Umfeld: Eine poetologische Studie* (BBB 103; Weinheim: Beltz/Athenäum, 1995); A. Weiser, "Psalm 77: Ein Beitrag zur Frage nach dem Verhältnis von Kult und Heilsgeschichte," *TLZ* 72 (1947) 133-40 (repr. in idem, *Glaube und Geschichte im Alten Testament* [Göttingen: Vandenhoeck & Ruprecht, 1961] 280-90); M. Weiss, "'And I Will Tell You All Your Work': Faith and Belief in Psalm 77," in *Texts, Temples, and Tradition (Fest.* M. Haran; ed. M. Fox, et al.; Winona Lake, Ind.: Eisenbrauns, 1996) 47-58.

# Psalm 78:
# Didactic Song, Homily

## *Structure*

|  |  | MT | NRSV |
|---|---|---|---|
| I. | Superscription | 1a | - |
| II. | Introduction | 1b-4 | 1-4 |
| III. | Exhortation | 5-8 | 5-8 |
| IV. | Lessons from Scripture | 9-64 | 9-64 |
| | A. The Ephraimites | 9-11 | 9-11 |
| | B. Exodus and wilderness | 12-31 | 12-31 |
| |   1. Proposition | 12-16 | 12-16 |
| |   2. Response | 17-20 | 17-20 |
| |   3. Reaction and castigation | 21-31 | 21-31 |
| | C. General reflection | 32-39 | 32-39 |
| | D. Wilderness and Egypt | 40-64 | 40-64 |
| |   1. General reflection | 40-42 | 40-42 |
| |   2. The plagues | 43-51 | 43-51 |
| |   3. Exodus and conquest | 52-58 | 52-58 |
| |   4. Warning (Shiloh's fate) | 59-64 | 59-64 |
| V. | Decision of the past | 65-72 | 65-72 |

With 76 poetic lines arranged in 72 verses, this psalm is one of the longest texts of the Psalter; only Psalm 119 is more voluminous. The inner order, symbolism, theology, and outward structure are much debated in OT interpretation. Apparent confusions may be due either to a disorderly growth of text during the ages of oral and written transmission, or to our failure to understand the life situations of psalm texts. Psalm 78 is obviously not simply a literary work obeying the rules of written discourse. Literary analysis as a rule postulates just that. Much to the contrary, the liturgical and homiletical background and use seem quite recognizable. An individual speaker presents his insights (vv. 1-2). He includes himself in the congregation (vv. 3-4); both face former generations of the fathers in faith (cf. vv. 3, 5, 8, 12, 57), not unlike the discussion in Ezekiel 18. The style, imagery, and argumentation of the whole psalm are to be classified as poetic, rhetorical, and liturgical. There are, of course, narrative sections and reflective ones, exhortative passages and confessional ones. But they all fit into a pattern of practical usage in distinction from mere literary shape. The tone is always serene, and many times urging, instructing, demanding, warning. In short, the psalm is nothing less than an extended and impressive instruction or sermon on matters of faith and loyalty to Israel's God. It does not want simply to teach history, but to exemplify present faith in the light of a few historical situations. It is not at all a "summary of salvific events," but a loose and nonchronological treatment of possible postures of faith over against that God who acted in favor of Israel. The vocabulary used and concepts communicated by the psalm are interesting. Mathias points out that the wording is under the strong influence of both wisdom and Dtr discourse throughout (pp. 58-67). In addition, we should look for favorite formulations showing up in the text. Central lexemes are those dealing with the process of teaching and receiving sacred knowledge about the wondrous deeds of God (cf. *yd'* and its derivatives: vv. 3, 5, 6, all in the programmatic opening part) and the parallel descriptions of the past generation's obliviousness and rebellion (cf. *škḥ*, "forget": vv. 7, 11; *mrh*, "rebel": vv. 8, 17, 40, 56; *nsh*, "try": vv. 18, 41, 56; *ḥt'*, "err": vv. 17, 32; *lō' he'ĕmîn*, "disbelieve": vv. 22, 32, 37, etc.). God, on the other hand, always reacts with merciful pedagogical measures (cf. *'śh pele'*, "perform astoundingly": vv. 4, 12; *'br* II, Hithpael, "become angry": vv. 21, 59, 62, as in Deut 3:26; Ps 89:39 [RSV 38]; *hrg*, "kill": vv. 31, 34, 47; *zkr*, "remember": v. 39; "be merciful": four expressions in v. 38, etc.). The drama of God willing the best for his people and they, in return, disregarding his concerns, straying away from their savior, is, of course, a Dtr pattern of evaluating the past. This pattern informs the structure of Psalm 78 not in a historicizing way but as a theological and homiletical device. We should also remember that the Deuteronomists largely employ or imitate a special rhetoric of preaching, instructing, and consoling the people of Yahweh (cf. P. D. Miller, "Deuteronomy"; listing at Additional Bibliography, section C). Psalm 78, on the other hand, seems to draw on a scriptural tradition not yet canonical but well on the way to becoming a fixed canon. This point underlines a classification as HOMILY (see Genre below).

The plain SUPERSCRIPTION is identical to the one of Psalm 74. If *maśkîl* really means some kind of didactic discourse (differently: Koenen, "Maśkîl"; listing at Additional Bibliography, section C) or song then this designation is accurate in our case. The majority of psalm headings with *maśkîl*, however, would be at odds with the corresponding psalm text itself (cf. Psalms 32; 42; 44; 88; 89).

More extensive orations need an INTRODUCTION that explicates their purpose and almost by necessity gives us clues as to speaker and audience. Vv. 1-4 fulfill these characteristics excellently (cf. 45:2 [RSV 1]). An individual presents him/herself in the first person (vv. 1-2), talking to "my people," communicating "my Torah," and demanding attention. The discourse itself is qualified not as *maśkîl* but in sapiential terminology as "proverb" or "saying" *(māšāl)* and "riddles from the ancient past" *(ḥîdôt minnî qedem)*. Especially the first line (v. 1b) calls for attention. Who may address an audience as "my people," announcing "my Torah"? Within the Psalter and the prophetic canon it is always God himself who speaks this way, even if through his prophet or messenger (cf. 50:7; 81:9 [RSV 8]; Jer 2:13; 4:22; "my Torah": Exod 16:4; Isa 51:7; Jer 6:19; 9:12; 16:11; 26:4; 31:33; 44:10; Ezek 22:26; Hos 8:1; Ps 89:31 [RSV 30]; 2 Chr 6:16; only in some wisdom contexts does *tôrātî* actually refer to human teachings: Prov 3:1; 4:2; 7:2). In the light of all these texts and the proper context of Psalm 78 (cf. v. 5) it is difficult to dissociate the programmatic statement in v. 1 from the elaborations that follow. In other words, the speaker of v. 1 is probably presenting his *tôrāh, māšāl,* and *ḥîdôt* as divine communication. This makes good sense, if he or she is the official liturgist in a communal worship service, because legitimized officiants in fact must speak out in the name of God himself. The often-stressed wisdom affinity of the above vocabulary does not impede worship rootings at all (cf. Perdue, *Wisdom;* listing at "Introduction to Cultic Poetry"; R. E. Murphy, *ABD* VI, 920-31).

As all commentators note, the second part of the introduction switches into first person plural (vv. 3-4). "We" forms, by all means, indicate congregational use of the text (see Scharbert, "Das 'Wir'"; listing at "Introduction to Psalms"; Seybold, "Das 'Wir'"; Additional Bibliography, section C). In our case, either the officiant includes himself in the congregation (cf. Neh 9:32-37; Ezra 9:6-15; Dan 9:4-19) or the whole community present responds to God in conjunction, with "one voice" (cf. Exod 24:3; Neh 8:6. All those scenes where an officiant interacts with a worshiping assembly are models of early Jewish communication patterns: e.g., Deut 29:9-28 [congregational response in v. 28]; Josh 24:14-24; 1 Kgs 8:22-61; Neh 8:1-12; Isa 63:7–64:11; Jer 14:1-22; Hos 67:1-3). Both possibilities are feasible in liturgical procedure. Because of socio-religious considerations the first alternative may be more plausible. Tradition, handed down through generations, is at stake. The songs about marvelous interventions of Yahweh, with all their power, glory, and pedagogy, must not be forgotten or neglected. Deut 32:19-22, 30 tells us in an exemplary way about the importance of "sacred songs" (*šîrāh;* "This song may become a testimony for me . . . ," v. 19b; "it will not be forgettable with his descendants," v. 21a). They contain all the tradition necessary to maintain the congregation's identity. Deut 32:1-43, consequently, is a remembrance, comparable to Psalm 78, of former generations going astray, of Yahweh's continuing mercy, and a powerful appeal to stay loyal to Israel's God in the face of many other deities.

The introduction ends with a statement of Yahweh's power, common in hymns; and the rest of the psalm is an elaboration of his marvelous deeds, not according to their historical chronology and enumeration, nor with extant canonical writings, but in line with their contents and significance for contemporary believers. This becomes evident in vv. 5-8, a general EXHORTATION to heed the revealed will of Yahweh. Thus the theological opinion is that Torah has been given to the forefathers, in order to have the following generations informed and instructed in an endless process of transmission from father to son (vv. 5-6). The "sons" (three times in vv. 5-6) are, as far as Psalm 78 is concerned, all the descendants in Israel up to the text's contemporary recitation. They should stay in a good relationship of trust with Yahweh, not forgetting either wondrous acts or commandments, and most of all not falling prey to the sins of the fathers (vv. 3-4), a steady warning throughout the Dtr History (cf. 2 Kgs 17:14; Römer, *Väter:* listing at Additional Bibliography, section B). This part of the psalm is most important in telling openly what the contemporary congregation expected and where its problems were felt. The past had been lost because of the fathers' misconduct. Now, the present may be won if the people ("the sons") keep loyal to their God. Without referring to the Sinai traditions the psalm makes fundamental statements about the situation of early Jewish congregational life. Life can be preserved if Israel remains loyal to her Lord and keeps his commandments. This is the general and central part of the homily, to be followed by a number of illustrations taken from past experience.

In vv. 9-11 "Ephraim" is enigmatic, and may indeed be a later insertion (cf. Mathias, 103-4, et al.) to motivate the denunciation of that tribe in v. 67. The final text, however, has taken up this tribal name (cf. Carroll). Closer reading reveals that v. 9 is quite different in language, conceptualization, and purpose from vv. 10-11. Rare and concrete lexemes describe Ephraim's preparation for battle and shameful retreat (v. 9; the last word, *qĕrāb,* "battle," may qualify for a late Aramaic word; cf. Zech 14:3; Job 38:23; Qoh 9:18; Pss 55:22 [RSV 21]; 68:31 [RSV 30]). In sharp contrast, vv. 10-11 use denunciatory theological language close to Dtr patterns. The basis for accusing Ephraim of treason can hardly be weakness in battle. Not keeping the covenant (v. 10a), despising Torah (v. 10b), and forgetting the wondrous assistance of Yahweh (v. 11) are invectives against the fathers in general, the "rebellious generation" (v. 8; cf. v. 7). Indeed, v. 9 was probably inserted to make Ephraim the first example of serious disloyalty against Yahweh. If one stretches one's exegetical imagination, v. 9 could be an interpretation of Judg 12:2b, Joshua accusing the Ephraimites: "I called you, but you did not deliver me from their [i.e., the Ammonites'] power."

A large block of material refers to the wilderness stories of the books of Exodus and Numbers (vv. 12-31). Yahweh "split the sea" to let Israel pass, leading his people by a column of fire and clouds (v. 13; cf. Exodus 14–15; Num 14:14). He also "split" the rock to give water to them in the wilderness (vv. 15-16; cf. Exod 17:1-7; Num 20:1-13). Both incidents, presented in narrative style, serve as a backdrop for the teachings on rebellion (vv. 17-20) and Yahweh's reactions (vv. 21-31). Hideously provoking Yahweh again (v. 17a) presupposes a certain sequence of events. But the chronological, or better, canonical, order seems unimportant; against the order in Exodus, the gift of manna (vv. 24-28; cf. Exodus 16) is made only after Moses strikes the rock. In our psalm Israel challenges God in a three-line direct-address discourse to add meat to the provision of water. As some commentators point out, the different view of the psalmist is patent: he or she takes the concession of manna in itself as a punitive measure. The greedy crowd virtually suffocates and kills itself (vv. 29-31), the wrath of God coming over them while the meat is still sticking in their mouths (v. 30b). In this manner the interpretation of selected events of the past is of supreme importance. The motto is: Yahweh performs mighty deeds to convince the forefathers in Egypt (v. 12; localization is established quite loosely, since the incidents referred to occur outside Egypt, at the Sea of Reeds and in the wilderness). They in turn do not recognize this demonstration and maintain their arrogant posture (vv. 17-18). God's verdict is unavoidable: "They disbelieve in God, and do not trust in his help" (v. 22). Therefore they are punished by an overdose of meat (vv. 29-31). The psalm, so far, makes another perfect case of remote incidents reported in the Scriptures to warn contemporary believers: to act contrary to Israel's God leads only to catastrophes.

The next passage is more reflective and less occupied with concrete historical events (vv. 32-39), a kind of wholesale evaluation of the period of the fathers. The connection with the foregoing, though, is explicit: "With all this they continued to err" ('ôd, "further," v. 32a; cf. v. 17a). Cardinal points of this theological appraisal are on the one hand Israel's treachery, on the other God's mercifulness (cf. vv. 35-37, 38-39). The last line of this section (v. 39) is in fact a sapiential statement: "He took into account that they are flesh, spirit waning away, to no return." In contradistinction to vv. 12-31 and 40-72 there is not the least reference to moments of past history. In terms of literary analysis the passage at hand could well be a distinct layer, and under liturgical aspects we might assume a different voice reciting it. Within the discourse as a whole the GENERAL REFLECTION serves apparently as a final element. Affinities to wisdom literature could be found (for v. 39 cf. 90:5-6; 103:15-16; Ecclesiastes). The vocabulary apart from v. 39 is conducive to such a comparison, too (cf. hebel, "nothingness," v. 33; pth and kzb, "betray," v. 36; lēb nākôn, "firm heart," v. 37; etc.).

The psalm does not end here, however, but returns to a more historical outlook. Some exegetes (e.g., Clifford, "In Zion") speak about a "second recital" beginning at this point. Again, the wilderness tradition comes to the fore because it contains the paradigms par excellence of ungratefulness and spiritual forgetfulness. More specifically, the plagues, known from Exodus 7–12, are quoted partially (seven out of ten) and in a different sequence. With this the psalm again disregards the literary order, jumping back into the time of sojourn in Egypt proper. The first part of the second round of historical samples starts out, proleptically, it seems, with a verdict against the forefathers and their rebellious and negligent attitudes (vv. 40-43; explicit link to vv. 17, 32-33: "again they tested God," v. 41), in order thereafter to enumerate most of the plagues wrought in Egypt by Yahweh, to achieve liberation for the enslaved (vv. 44-51). This last section has its parallel in vv. 13-16. The exodus and the conquest themes follow suit organically (vv. 52-55) as far as canonical tradition is concerned. A similar spectrum of historical situations, from the passage through the Reed Sea to the immigration into the land, may be found in Exod 15:3-18.

The people are only able to continue with their rebellion, which is, at the same time a terrible challenge to God (nsh, Piel, "to test," a key word of the psalm; cf. vv. 18, 41, 56). Clad in some Dtr vocabulary (nsh; mrh, "rebel"; šmr, "keep"; 'ēdôt, "regulations" = v. 56; k's, "despise"; bāmôt, "hill sanctuaries"; pesel, "cut images"; qn', "make angry" = v. 58, etc.), the discourse evidently describes attitudes and actions of ancient Israelites down to the settlement in the promised land. The reaction of Yahweh is anticipated: he castigates severely "his people" (v. 62a), giving them away into captivity (v. 61) or letting them be killed by the enemy (vv. 62-64). The picture of defeat and disgrace is so close to that of Lamentations (cf. Lam 1:18-19; 2:1, 21; 5:2; etc.) that one

96

wonders if the name Shiloh as the sanctuary destroyed (v. 60) is correct. Could it be a pseudonym for Jerusalem? The treatment of Shiloh in Jeremiah 26 may lead in this direction. Shiloh was the sanctuary of Eli (cf. 1 Samuel 1–2). This ancient holy place features as a kind of prototype of Jerusalem in Jer 26:6, 9, and could well have a symbolic value in our passage.

If each main unit of the psalm consists of descriptions of what God had done for his people, of how the fathers failed to respond adequately to these marvelous deeds, and of pedagogic action from the side of the insulted Deity, then the last segment (vv. 65-72) of this long composition is either a fragment or a well-planned conclusion of an impressive didactic text. Formally, the eight poetic lines at hand employ plain narrative forms, like vv. 12-16 and 40-55, telling about an important event in the spiritual history of Israel. David is elected by God in the territory of Judah. Ephraim, on the other hand, has lost her prerogatives (vv. 67-70). On the surface, this is nothing but a REPORT OF ELECTION. But because the audience or the contemporary congregation presumably identifies strongly with David, and because the fundamental issue of who is being privileged stands under discussion (*bḥr,* "elect," and *m's,* "reject," are the central verbs), a question of vital concern since the sixth century B.C.E., we must not leave this section on the merely historical plain. The reported historical decision for Judah was of crucial importance for the living generations under Babylonian and Persian rule. The Judahite and Davidic line established itself victoriously. The subunit to be analyzed therefore is more than a report. It is a living text communicating deep religious identity to all members of the David clans and of the Israelite community.

The overall structure reveals a step-by-step unfolding of religious teaching. Psalm 78 falls into handy kerygmatic units: vv. 1b-4 introduce the sermon; vv. 5-8 continue with a basic exhortation. The main body of the psalm (vv. 9-64) takes up episodes of early Israelite history in order to exemplify loyalty and disloyalty to God. Irregular in size, the subunits focus on different topics of the exodus and wilderness stories of the Bible, interspersed with theological resumés and homiletical applications, forming separate little lessons: Ephraim being disobedient, breaking the covenant (vv. 9-11); the exodus from Egypt in summary (vv. 12-16). To no avail! "Yet they sinned still more" (v. 17; cf. vv. 32, 36-39, 56-58), dire evaluations of Israel's ways with Yahweh. Rebellion in the wilderness is the next theological topic (vv. 17-31). After a reflective interlude (vv. 32-39) the preacher goes back to the plague story (vv. 40-51) and again the exodus tradition plus subsequent castigations, Israel already being settled in the good land (vv. 52-64). The closing section (vv. 65-72) is a real homage to Zion and the Davidic dynasty (vv. 65-72).

## Genre

The quest is for a good, trustworthy tradition to rely on in everyday life. A preacher picked traditional examples from the past to exemplify loyalty to Yahweh, which was absolutely necessary for any member of the early Jewish community. The historical situation of the Jews in Babylonian and Persian times at the same time required an interpretation of the lowly state of the people of Yahweh. Of course, the fathers had been oblivious and negligent of their religious duties. The discourses employed to communicate interpretations and encouragements were Scripture readings, prayers, songs, and sermons in public worship. Therefore we may call this psalm a didactic HOMILY. A reflective mood, deep theological interests, confrontation with their own people's past, use of tradition, etc., were characteristic of this kind of sermon.

The canon of Scripture was not ready yet when our psalm came into being. Consequently, there had not yet been formed a fixed interpretation of Yahweh's history with Israel. But the psalmists who created and composed the sacred texts used freely whatever tradition was known in the community. And the well-being of the people as well as the loyalty over against Yahweh have been of primary importance for the community's survival.

The problem of Psalm 78 being a literary entity is hard to solve. Analysts tend to distinguish layers, e.g., Seybold (307-8): an Ephraimite historical hymn was reworked first by Deuteronomists, introducing the Torah perspective, and second by wisdom teachers, couching the psalm in public instruction. As long as a psalm does not seriously contradict liturgical usages, in my opinion it may be taken as part of a worship agenda. The neat division of the large text into individual historical scenes with a distinct theological truth to tell displays the didactic and homiletic orientation of the psalm.

## Setting

According to all likelihood, the psalm was handed down in worship situations in the ancient Jewish community. Later on, different groups took over such texts, modified them over the years, and used them in their own meeting places. A community leader was probably responsible for the text, which grew and got reshaped thoroughly as time passed. This does not do away with the necessity to see all the background and development of a given text, from its supposed roots to present times.

## Intention

As suggested above at various occasions, edification of the community was the chief purpose of the liturgical teams, who would work on the texts to use them in solemn assemblies. This goal would include strengthening the faith and conscience of members of a Yahweh congregation.

## Bibliography

D. C. Bass, "History, the Church, and the Public," *Chicago Theological Seminary Register* 73 (1983) 6-11; A. van den Branden, "'Reseph' nella Bibbia," *BeO* 13 (1971) 211-25; A. F. Campbell, *The Ark Narrative (I Sam 4–6; II Sam 6): A Form-Critical and*

*Traditio-Historical Study* (SBLDS 16; Missoula, Mont.: Scholars Press, 1975); idem, "Psalm 78: A Contribution of the Theology of Tenth Century Israel," *CBQ* 41 (1979) 51-79; R. P. Carroll, "Psalm LXXVIII: Vestiges of a Tribal Polemic," *VT* 21 (1971) 133-50; idem, "Rebellion and Dissent," *ZAW* 89 (1977) 176-204; W. Chrostowski, "An Examination of Conscience by God's People as Exemplified in Neh 9,6-37," *BZ* 34 (1990) 253-61; R. J. Clifford, "In Zion and David a New Beginning: An Interpretation of Psalm 78," in *Traditions in Transformation* (*Fest.* F. M. Cross; ed. B. Halpern and J. D. Levenson; Winona Lake, Ind.: Eisenbrauns, 1981) 121-41; J. Day, "Pre-Deuteronomic Allusions to the Covenant in Hosea and Psalm 78," *VT* 36 (1986) 1-12; P. E. Dion, "Le 'pain des forts' (Ps 75,25a) dans un dérivé de la littérature Hénochienne," *Science et Esprit* 35 (1983) 223-26; O. Eissfeldt, *Das Lied Moses Dt 32,1-43 und das Lehrgedicht Asaphs* (Berichte über die Verhandlungen der Sächsischen Akademie der Wissenschaften zu Leipzig; Berlin: Akademie Verlag, 1958); D. N. Freedman, "God Almighty in Psalm 78,59," *Bib* 54 (1973) 268; N. Füglister, "Psalm 78: der Rätsel Lösung?" in *VTSup* 43 (ed. J. A. Emerton; Leiden: Brill, 1991) 264-97; G. Geiger, "Aufruf an Rückkehrende. Zum Sinn des Zitats von Ps 78,24b in Joh 6,31," *Bib* 65 (1984) 449-64; E. Greenstein, "Mixing Memory and Design: Reading Psalm 78," *Prooftexts* 10 (1990) 197-218; B. H. Grigsby, "If Any Man Thirsts: Observations on the Rabbinic Background of John 7:37-39," *Bib* 67 (1986) 101-8; E. Haag, "Zion und Schilo: Traditionsgeschichtliche Parallelen in Jeremia 7 und Psalm 78," in *Die alttestamentliche Botschaft als Wegweisung* (*Fest.* H. Reinelt; ed. J. Zmijewski; Stuttgart: Katholisches Bilbelwerk, 1990) 85-115; B. Halpern, "Doctrine by Misadventure: Between Israelite Source and the Biblical Historian," in *The Poet and the Historian* (ed. R. E. Friedman; Chico, Calif.: Scholars Press, 1983) 41-73; T. Hieke, "Weitergabe des Glaubens (Ps 78:1-8)," *BN* 78 (1995) 49-62; E. Hilgert, "The Dual Image of Joseph in Hebrew and Early Jewish Literature," *BR* 30 (1985) 5-21; J. Hofbauer, "Psalm 77/78," *ZKT* 89 (1967) 41-50; H. Junker, "Die Entstehungszeit des Psalms 78 und des Deuteronomiums," *Bib* 34 (1953) 487-500; R. Kessler, "Das kollektive Schuldbekenntnis im Alten Testament," *EvT* 56 (1996) 29-43; W. T. Koopmans, "Psalm 78, Canto D — A Response," *UF* 20 (1988) 121-23; A. Lauha, *Die Geschichtsmotive in den alttestamentlichen Psalmen* (Helsinki: Druckerei A.-G-. der finn. Literaturgesellschaft, 1945); A. C. C. Lee, "The Context and Function of the Plagues Tradition in Psalm 78," *JSOT* 48 (1990) 83-89; S. E. Loewenstamm, "The Number of Plagues in Psalm 105," *Bib* 52 (1971) 34-38; A. J. Levoratti, "La lectura no sacrificial del evangelio en la obra de René Girard," *RevistB* 47 (1985) 159-76; D. Mathias, *Geschichtstheologie* (listing at Additional Bibliography, section B); J. L. Mays, "The David of the Psalms," *Int* 40 (1986) 143-55; M. J. J. Menken, "The Provenance and Meaning of the Old Testament Quotation in John 67:31," *NovT* 30 (1988) 39-56; U. Moebus, "'Gott, zerbrich ihnen die Zähne im Maul!'" in *Seelsorge auf dem Feld des Denkens* (ed. T. Dietz; Marburg: Kein anderes Evangelium, 1995) 129-32; J. M. Munoz, "Estudio sobre Salmo 78," *Cuadernos Biblicos* 4 (1980) 74-101; J. Navone, "Lex Narrandi: The Sacramental Dimension of the Recital of a Community's Faith," *Journal of Dharma* 9 (1984) 246-60; S. Sabugal, "El concepto del pecado en el Antiguo Testamento," *Estudios Eclesiásticos* 59 (1984) 459-69; A. Schenker, *Hexaplarische Psalmenbruchstücke* (OBO 8; Fribourg: Univertätsverlag; Göttingen: Vandenhoeck & Ruprecht, 1975); J. Schildenberger, "Psalm 78 (77) und die Pentateuchquellen," in *Lex tua veritas* (*Fest.* H. Junker; ed. H. Gross and F. Mussner; Trier: Paulinus, 1961) 231-56; J. Schreiner, "Geschichte als Wegweisung: Psalm 78," in

*Die alttestamentliche Botschaft als Wegweisung* (*Fest.* H. Reinelt; ed. J. Zmijewski; Stuttgart: Katholisches Bibelwerk, 1990) 307-28; P. Stern, "The Eighth Century Dating of Psalm 78 Re-argued," *HUCA* 66 (1995) 41-65; C. C. Twombly, "Redemptive History and the Shaping of the Affections," *Crux* 20 (1984) 21-26; A. Wolters, "Not Rescue but Destruction: Rereading Exodus 15:8," *CBQ* 52 (1990) 223-40.

# Psalm 79:
# Communal Complaint

## Structure

|  | MT | NRSV |
|---|---|---|
| I. Superscription | 1a | - |
| II. Invocation and complaint | 1b-4 | 1-4 |
| A. Against enemies | 1b-3 | 1-3 |
| B. Own suffering | 4 | 4 |
| III. Petition | 5-12 | 5-12 |
| A. Reproachful question and imprecation | 5-7 | 5-7 |
| B. Plea for help | 8-9 | 8-9 |
| C. Reproachful question and plea for mercy | 10-11 | 10-11 |
| D. Imprecation | 12 | 12 |
| IV. Collective vow | 13 | 13 |

In spite of metrical disturbances (overstretched lines), the text is lucid throughout, and we may immediately turn to a structural analysis of this COMMUNAL COMPLAINT par excellence.

The SUPERSCRIPTION (v. 1a) is just the same as that of → Psalm 73, within the Asaph collection. The INVOCATION is the shortest possible: *'ĕlōhîm*, "O God" (cf. 72:1; 74:1; 75:2 [RSV 1]; 83:2 [RSV 1]). Noteworthy are the variations of 80:2, 4, 5 (RSV 1, 3, 4: "O shepherd of Israel"; "O God"; "O Yahweh, God of hosts"), which demonstrate options available for calling on the Deity even within the so-called Elohistic Psalter (Psalms 42–83; see "Introduction to Psalms," section 5). Outside this block of texts, it is true, the invocation "O Yahweh" is much more frequent (→ Psalms 3; 6). The terseness of the invocation may be a signal of familiarity with God, of urgency, or, who knows, of a liturgical necessity to place a laudatory piece before the complaint proper.

Immediately after the invocation the psalm turns to COMPLAINT, denouncing brutal enemies (vv. 1-3), a dominant theme in the genre, and to lamentation over the psalmist's own bitter destiny (v. 4). The actions of victorious enemies are stereotyped and tie in with descriptions found in 74:3-8; Lam 1:10; 2:7, 20-21. Also, the common Near Eastern tradition of city and sanctuary lament uses the same motifs and may be considered the fertile matrix of the OT genre (Dobbs-Allsopp, 155). Profaning sanctuaries (v. 1c) and slaying defeated opponents (vv. 2-3; cf. 2 Sam 8:2), leaving them unburied to increase their shame (cf. 2 Sam 21:5-14), were part of warfare. Nevertheless, victimized people felt the inhumanity of such barbarism, accused the victors, and complained before their own God. Physical suffering, caused by enemy action, has always been cruel, but taunting "neighbors" (v. 4) was salt in bad wounds. While a complaint against enemies (vv. 1-3) appears in direct-address discourse to God, without making explicit speaker or plaintiff, the shame suffered from onlookers all of a sudden is couched in first-person plural discourse (v. 4; cf. Seybold, "Das 'Wir'"; listing at Additional Bibliography, section C). This line corresponds almost exactly with 44:14 (RSV 13), which in turn is embedded in a whole section of "we" lament (44:10-15 [RSV 9-14]), with the gloating of enemies as a high point (44:14-15 [RSV 13-14]; Klopfenstein, *Scham;* listing at Additional Bibliography, section B). Should there be a conscious taking over of individual phrases from other psalms (cf. also v. 5 with 89:47 [RSV 46]; vv. 6-7 with Jer 10:25; v. 10 with Ps 115:2; Joel 2:17)? We should bear in mind, however, that the lines indicated in our psalm are stock phrases of lament and complaint; frequent use testifies to the formulaic character of liturgical songs and is not in itself proof of literary techniques of composition (cf. Culley, *Language;* listing at "Introduction to Cultic Poetry"). Next to complaining about the dire fate of the defeated community, a special concern for Jerusalem looms large (vv. 1, 3) and indicates the supreme religious value of this city. As Seybold has pointed out ("Das 'Wir'," 146-48), however, the community is looking at Jerusalem from a distance.

The PETITION begins with a reproachful question (v. 5), which Gunkel already declared to be a typical transition element between complaints and pleas. As indicated above, Ps 89:47 (RSV 46) is a nearly perfect parallel. The question makes God (here named Yahweh!) responsible for the ruinous situation, and by its temporal implications ("how long?") already demands help. As customary in complaints (see "Introduction to Cultic Poetry," section 4B), outright pleas move in two directions. They ask for elimination of the evilmongers (IMPRECATION, vv. 6-7; cf. Jer 10:25; Ps 83:10-19; in individual complaints see Psalms 35; 55; 109) and for rehabilitation and help in regard to the worshiping community (vv. 8-9), the same pattern being repeated once more in vv. 10-12, in a different order (reproachful question: v. 10ab; pleas: vv. 10cd, 11; imprecation: v. 12). Both sections of imprecation are based, in the final analysis, on customs to destroy the enemy by powerful and magical wishes against their evil behavior, activating as it were the wrath of the group's own deity (v. 6) and trying to revert their machinations on their own heads (v. 12; cf. Fabian, "Witchcraft," Additional Bibliography, section B). A probative means to motivate God in this way is certainly to remind him that the enemy's hostility is warring against God himself (v. 12b; cf. 74:10, 18, 22-23). The plea for the community's own salvation and restoration eventually (and in contrast to Psalm 44) has to consider faults and sins, asking for mercy (vv. 8-9), thus moving God to take action in favor of his "very downtrodden" believers (vv. 8c-9, 10cd-11).

In the final line, as in v. 4 at the end of the initial complaint, a DECLARATION OF CONFIDENCE (v. 13a) is incorporated into the closing Vow of the community (v. 13 as a whole). The element occurs more often, especially with individual complaints, in final position as a fitting close of such a liturgical agenda (cf. 7:18 [RSV 17]; 35:28; 43:5; 59:18 [RSV 17]; 69:30 [RSV 29]).

## Genre/Setting

COMMUNAL COMPLAINTS (see "Introduction to Cultic Poetry," section 4B) were part of solemn commemorations of past catastrophes (cf. Zech 7:3; Isa 63:7–64:11) or else belonged to ad hoc liturgies to avert imminent danger (cf. Joel 1–2; Jeremiah 14). In our case the psalm evidently remembers profanation of the Jerusalem temple, as well as, in stereotyped imagery, the killing of people and desecration of corpses around the city. Psalm 74 and Lamentations 1–2; 5 have essentially the same setup and outlook. Although it would be interesting to know exactly when the psalm was composed and used, dating the text is not all that important. It has presumably been in liturgical use for a long period, subsuming more than one historical incident of defeat and desacralization. The earliest recorded reference could be to the fall of Jerusalem in 587 B.C.E.; the latest would be 1 Macc 1:16-40; 2:7-13; 7:17 (quotation from Ps 79:2-3); 2 Macc 8:2-4; etc. Gunkel, et al., miss more exact descriptions of the Babylonian enemy burning the city and taking its population into captivity (cf. Lam 1:3, 5; 2 Kgs 24:10-17; 25:8-12), so they refrain from an early exilic dating. This argument is not too conclusive because psalms are by no means historical reports, but stereotyped liturgical texts. The social situation visible between the lines of the psalm itself, on the other hand, leads to the conclusion that the text is younger than the first half of the sixth century B.C.E. The Yahweh community, so it seems, has long consolidated itself. It faces a plurality of nations, indifferent or hostile to Israel. The community of believers guards itself against malevolent and mocking "neighbors," apparently within a multicultural world of one of the great empires of the day. Over against this unfriendly environment the community sticks together in a confessing religious group; the pronounced "we" forms in our text are eloquent witness of this situation (vv. 4, 8-9, 10, 12, 13). Since the psalm is a liturgical text, we are looking right into the community's worship when reading its complaints and petitions.

## Intention

Like all days of mourning and remembering in the world, commemorations of this dire sort are designed to relive the frightening past, to work through its pains and terrors, in order to restore the balance and standing of the group, and win a new future. Struggling with God, the one at least co-responsible for all calamities, also helps to verify one's own postures and possibilities in an ongoing test of faith, will, and strength to survive.

## Bibliography

P. Beentjes, "Deuterocanonieke gegevens voor een datering van psalm 79," in *Proef en toets* (ed. W. Beuken, et al.; Amersfoort: De Horstink, 1977) 25-29; F. W. Dobbs-Allsopp, *Weep, O Daughter of Zion: A Study of the City-Lament Genre in the Hebrew Bible* (BibOr 44; Rome: Pontifical Biblical Institute, 1993); D. Kirchner, "Gruppendynamische Untersuchung zu Struktur und Geschichte der Klage im Alten Testament," *TLZ* 114 (1989) 785-96; C. J. Labuschagne, "On the Structural Use of Numbers as a Composition Technique," *JNSL* 12 (1984) 87-99; W. M. Schniedewind, "'Are We His People or Not?'" *Bib* 76 (1995) 540-50.

## Psalm 80:
## Communal Complaint

### *Structure*

| | MT | NRSV |
|---|---|---|
| I. Superscription | 1 | - |
| II. Invocation, initial plea | 2-4 | 1-3 |
|   A. Invocation | 2-3a | 1-2a |
|   B. Plea | 3bc | 2bc |
|   C. Refrain | 4 | 3 |
| III. Complaint | 5-8 | 4-7 |
|   A. Invocation | 5a | 4a |
|   B. Complaint | 5b-7 | 4b-6 |
|   C. Refrain | 8 | 7 |
| IV. Entreaty | 9-16 | 8-15 |
|   A. Account of salvific acts (parable) | 9-12 | 8-11 |
|   B. Complaint | 13-14 | 12-13 |
|   C. Petition | 15-16 | 14-15 |
| V. Petition | 17-20 | 16-19 |
|   A. Complaint and imprecation | 17 | 16 |
|   B. Petition (wishes) | 18-19 | 17-18 |
|   C. Refrain | 20 | 19 |

The basic parts of the SUPERSCRIPTION are the words "to the choirmaster (?)," "of Asaph, a song" (cf. Psalms 4; 13; 73; 77; 85). Additionally, we find the terms *'el šōšannîm* ("according to lilies" [?]) and *'ēdût* ("testimony" [?]). Both of them are rather obscure in the context of psalm headings (cf. *šōšannîm* in superscriptions to Psalms 45; 60; 69). In Song of Songs, however, the literal meaning "lilies" makes good sense: cf. Cant 2:1, 2, 16; 4:5; 5:13; etc. By contrast, *'ēdût* is more frequent in exhortatory and meditative texts (cf. Pss 78:5; 81:6 [RSV 5]; 119:88, 157; 122:4; 132:12), occurring but twice in psalm headings; cf. Psalm 60.

The main structural problem of the song proper is its refrains. Are we entitled to harmonize the text by "straightening out" v. 15 and putting in a "missing" refrain after v. 11 (thus Gunkel, 353, "although vv. 11-12 belong together thematically" [!])? Hardly, because the three existing refrains (vv. 4, 8, 20) are nearly identical, while v. 15 (+ 16) is quite different in vocabulary, imagery, and contents (some exegetes, therefore, consider a loss or spoiling of the text, e.g., Seybold, 317, 319-20). This last passage begs Yahweh to turn around and attend again to his people (cf. Isa 63:15a, 17c). The three genuine refrains ask Yahweh to rehabilitate his congregation by letting his face again shine over them (cf. Num 6:25). Furthermore, these fixed phrases have been articulated in the first person plural. In this way they indeed are a fitting refrain for the worshiping congregation, unlike vv. 15-16. In addition, the entire passage vv. 9-16 does not betray any direct participation of the community, while in vv. 3c, 7, 19 the communal "we" or "us" is present. The conclusion is easy: vv. 9-16 are a text sui generis, be it a later insertion or an early compositional element (Beyerlin, *Schichten,* 14-15).

The first liturgical unit, then, is vv. 2-4, closing with the standard refrain: "Restore us, O God; let your face shine that we may be saved." Its INVOCATION (v. 2a; unusual appellation: "O Shepherd of Israel," no regular name of God mentioned) expands into hymnic attributions with typical participles, lauding God for being the owner and protector of his people (*rō'ēh,* "pasturing," and *nōhēg,* "leading"; cf. 23:1-2; 78:52), and a supreme Lord (*yōšēb hakkĕrûbîm,* "sitting on the cherubs"; cf. 18:11 [RSV 10]; 99:1). Hymnic elements especially in communal complaints enhance the Deity and prepare for petition (cf. 44:2-9 [RSV 1-8]; 89:2-38 [RSV 1-37]). The participial attribution is one typical hymnic form (cf. 104:2-4; Crüsemann, *Studien,* 95-126; listing at "Introduction to Cultic Poetry"). Conventional openings of communal complaints include very short, one-word appellations (cf. 44:2 [RSV 1]; 74:1; 79:1; 83:1 [RSV superscription]) in contrast to more expressive invocations in individual prayers.

Immediately following the hymnic attributions are three imperatives, calling on God to enter into action. *hôpî'āh,* "be radiant," could well be a cultic shout (cf. Deut 33:2; Pss 50:2; 94:1), provoking or accompanying some kind of visible theophany. In v. 3a the naming of only three tribes as the recipients of theophany is probably due to traditio-historical reasons (see Setting). The rest of v. 3 is a comprehensive PETITION to be helped at once, as is customary in any complaint. Only one phrase seems unique in this context: *'ôrĕrāh 'et gĕbûrātĕkā,* "agitate your strength," does not have an exact parallel in the OT. Analogous Qal or Hiphil imperatives are quite common, however, also in liturgical situations (cf. Judg 5:12; Isa 51:9; 52:1; Pss 7:7 [RSV 6]; 44:24 [RSV 23]; 57:9 [RSV 8]; 108:3 [RSV 2]). "Come to our rescue" (v. 3c), on the other hand, is the very essence of petition, already voiced in the initial statements (cf. derivatives of *yš',* "help, rescue," in complaints: 7:2 [RSV 1]; 12:2 [RSV 1]; 31:3 [RSV 2]; 54:3 [RSV 1]; 59:3 [RSV 2]; 69:2 [RSV 1]; 71:2; 86:2). The REFRAIN, for its part, is a genuine response of the community (first person plural) consisting of two imperatives and a conclusion in the cohortative (v. 4). The idea of a "full restitution" into a state of wholeness and wholesomeness is behind all complaints and petitions (cf. similar pleas in the plural: 67:2 [RSV 1]; 118:27a; Lam 5:21; in the singular, Jer 31:18; as hopeful affirmation, Hos 6:2-3). Asking for God's "face to shine" again reminds one of the priestly blessing in Num 6:24-26, a sacred wish upon the congregation used in worship. The almost exact repetition of this refrain in vv. 8 and 20 proves its liturgical character.

The second strophe emphasizes COMPLAINT (vv. 5-8), comprising — just like the first one — three lines plus REFRAIN. The full naming of God (INVOCATION; v. 5a: the epithet "Yahweh, God Sabaoth," is much debated; cf.

Mettinger, *Dethronement*, 19-37; Additional Bibliography, section B) again raises the question why this standard form is missing at the very beginning of the psalm. Forms and contents of ensuing COMPLAINT are traditional (see "Introduction to Cultic Poetry," section 4B; → Psalms 44; 89). The reproachful question ("how long?" v. 5b), making God directly responsible (vv. 6, 7a), denouncing enemy scorn (v. 7b): all these features make the fabric of complaint. "Tears" is the catchword of v. 6, possibly indicating ritual weeping (cf. V. Hamp, *TWAT* I, 638-43; K. H. Richards, *ABD* II, 108-10. The refrain closes this liturgical unit, suggesting that a speaker would have recited the plaintive lines, while the community (first person plural) chanted the petitionary phrases.

An inset prayer like vv. 9-16 may be a mere literary addition or possibly a ceremonial interlude. The metaphor of the fruitful and powerful vine (cf. Isa 5:1-7; Jer 12:10; Ezek 17:1-10; 19:10-14) is used throughout from v. 9 to v. 16a, to be abruptly replaced by a totally different one (the "son whom you raised for yourself") in v. 16b. Most exegetes agree that this latter phrase came in erroneously from v. 18b and should be disregarded at this point. The PARABLE of God's care for his vine is told concisely, and much along the line of Ezekiel's allegories. There is even an intermingling of vine and cedar (v. 11) as in Ezekiel 17 and 19. Within the Psalter a poetic parable seems unique (but cf. Judg 9:8-15; 2 Sam 12:1-4; Isa 5:1-6). The prayer has a distinctive COMPLAINT (vv. 13-14) with singular vocabulary and imagery. But it does fit well to the parable, including the use of a reproachful question (v. 13a) and an accusation of enemies (passers-by, v. 13b). The PETITION (vv. 15-16a) is close to Isa 63:15, 17b, pleading in this case for the restoration of the vineyard. God's dwelling in heaven (v. 15b) is a special trait not accounted for in the refrained song. A certain affinity, however, between v. 15a and the refrains of vv. 4, 8, 20 may have stimulated the junction of the two texts.

Finally, vv. 17-20 belong to the first two strophes (vv. 2-8). Again, we have three poetic lines (vv. 17-19) and a refrain (v. 20). Unfortunately, there is no proper invocation as in v. 5, and the text begins abruptly, with some textual uncertainties as to the exact formulation of the verbs. More logical would be the emendation, adopted by some commentators and translations, of passive forms to "they burned it . . . they cut it down" (v. 17). In any case, the verse complains about and denounces the enemies, turning into intense PETITION afterward (vv. 18-19). While petition in our psalm so far has been aimed at restoring the community (cf. vv. 3bc, 4, 8, also v. 19) it now becomes a fervent intercession for one single person, the "man of your right hand" and "son of man, whom you have raised" (v. 18). This is extraordinary and cryptic language that has sparked much scholarly discussion (cf. Gelston, Hill, Bittner, et al.). Analogous texts and expressions (cf. Ps 110:1; Ezek 8:2, 8; Dan 7:13-14) suggest that we are dealing with messianic terminology. Thus our communal complaint in fact culminates with an eschatological petition, asking God to protect a royal figure considered a divine savior (cf. Isa 9:5-6 [RSV 6-7]; 11:1-5; Hag 2:23; Zech 4:6-10).

All in all, the psalm gives the impression of being somewhat fragmented. The first strophe begins abruptly, in the middle we find inserted a text of its own right, the third strophe seems truncated and unusual. In spite of this, however, the poem communicates a deep sense of community feeling and a strong interest in that community's restoration.

## Genre

How to define more closely the COMMUNAL COMPLAINT at hand? Psalm 80 is not a song on occasion of military defeat, protracted drought, deadly epidemic, or any instantaneous threat to the community. Rather, the psalm faces ongoing oppression and silent destruction of the community itself. People are chronically downcast (cf. v. 6), they suffer constant aggression by hostile elements (neighbors? cf. vv. 13-14). Therefore their hope is, in the last instance, with a royal and messianic leader who will bring about a turn of their destiny. Should we not call this kind of psalm more concretely a COMPLAINT OF THE ESCHATOLOGICAL COMMUNITY (cf. D. L. Petersen, *ABD* II, 575-79)?

## Setting

The vivid structure of Psalm 80, with direct participation of the community reciting the refrains, and spiritual leaders who are able to voice laments and pleas, even to use adequate hymnic attributions and a poetic parable, certainly brings to mind worship situations as the only plausible creative background. The assembly united in worship supplies all the voices necessary to recite this psalm, including, in the first place, those pronounced first-person plural sections.

As to dating the text, we can only speculate: from premonarchic to postexilic times, everything has been suggested. Quite a few interpreters consider a North Israelite preexilic origin as likely (cf. the "northern" tribes, vv. 2-3; the possible wordplay "man of your right hand," v. 18a, with "Benjaminite" = "son of the right hand" = King Saul?). In spite of these alluring affinities we probably have to deal with a longer growth of our text, which transports the painful communal experiences of generations. Yearly commemorations of defeats and violence are condensed into mourning rites, weeping, soul searching, pleas, imprecations, articulations also of gratitude and hope to God. Thus no single historical setting can be decisive for understanding this psalm (some exegetes argue in this direction, e.g., Nasuti; Tate; Beyerlin; Seybold, 317; the last two with the help of a literary stratification, visualizing an original text of Assyrian times or older plus exilic reworkings).

## Intention

As stated above, the psalm tries to enlist, by entreaty and persuasion, the help of Israel's God (the name "Yahweh" comes up only in the very last line; there may be a conscious accretion of divine names in vv. 4, 8, [15], 20) in crucial times of outward pressures. The whole community promises loyalty to God (v. 19a) and asks for restoration and a new chance to survive (v. 19b).

# Bibliography

W. Beyerlin, "Schichten im 80. Psalm," in *Das Wort und die Wörter* (*Fest.* G. Friedrich; ed. H. Balz and S. Schulz; Stuttgart: Kohlhammer, 1973) 9-24; W. Bittner, "Gott — Menschensohn — Davidsohn: Eine Untersuchung zur Traditionsgeschichte von Daniel 7:13f," *Freiburger Zeitschrift für Philosophie und Theologie* 32 (1985) 343-72; A. Gelston, "A Sidelight on the 'Son of Man,'" *SJT* 22 (1969) 186-96; O. Eissfeldt, "Psalm 80," in *Geschichte und Altes Testament* (*Fest.* A. Alt; Tübingen: Mohr, 1953) 65-78 (repr. idem, *KS* III, 221-32); idem, "Psalm 80 und Psalm 89," *WO* 3 (1964) 27-31 (repr. idem, *KS* IV, 132-36); H. J. Heinemann, "The Date of Psalm 80," *JQR* 40 (1949/50) 297-302; T. Hieke, "Der Exodus in Psalm 80," in *Studies in the Book of Exodus* (ed. M. Vervenne; Louvain: Peeters, 1996) 551-58; idem, "Psalm 80 and Its Neighbors in the Psalter," *BN* 86 (1997) 36-43; idem, *Psalm 80* (St. Ottilien: Eos-Verlag, 1997); E. Hilgert, "The Dual Image of Joseph in Hebrew and Early Jewish Literature," *BR* 30 (1985) 5-21; D. Hill, "'Son of Man' in Psalm 80 v. 17," *NovT* 15 (1973) 261-69; V. Maag, "Der Hirte Israels," *Schweizer theologische Umschau* 28 (1958) 2-28; A. MacEwen, "'Revival' in the Old Testament," *Vox Reformata* 61 (1996) 67-82; T. N. D. Mettinger, "Härskoronas Gud," *SEÅ* 44 (1979) 7-21; M. Metzger, "Zeder, Weinstock und Weltenbaum," in *Ernten, was man sät* (*Fest.* K. Koch; ed. D. Daniels, et al.; Neukirchen-Vluyn: Neukirchener Verlag, 1991) 197-229; A. Pietersma, "New Greek Fragments of Biblical Manuscripts in the Chester Beatty Library," *Bulletin of the American Society of Papyrologists* 24 (1987) 37-61; G. T. Prinsloo, "Shepherd, Vine-power, Father: Divine Metaphor and Existential Reality in a Community of Lament (Psalm 80)," *OTE* 10 (1997) 279-302; A. Roefer, "The End of Psalm 80," *Tarbiz* 29 (1959) 113-24; J. Schreiner, "Hirte Israels, stelle uns wieder her!" *BibLeb* 10 (1969) 95-111; L. T. Tisdale, "Psalm 80:1-7," *Int* 47 (1993) 396-99; N. J. Tromp, "La métaphore engloutie. Le langage métaphorique du Psaume 80," *Sémiotique et Bible* 47 (1987) 30-43; idem, "Psalm LXXX: Form of Expression and Form of Contents," in *New Avenues in the Study of the Old Testament* (ed. A. Woude; *OTS* 25; Leiden: Brill, 1989) 145-55; M. Wagner, "Der Menschensohn des 80. Psalms," *ThStK* 104 (1932) 84-93.

# Psalm 81:
# Divine Oracles; Sermon

## Structure

|  | MT | NRSV |
|---|---|---|
| I. Superscription | 1 | - |
| II. Summons to praise | 2-6b | 1-5b |
|    A. Summons | 2-4 | 1-3 |
|    B. Motives | 5-6b | 4-5b |
| III. Oracles (sermon) | 6c-17 | 5c-16 |
|    A. Audition formula | 6c | 5c |
|    B. Account of salvation | 7-8 | 6-7 |
|    C. Torah exhortation | 9-11 | 8-10 |

| D. Account of disobedience | 12-13 | 11-12 |
| E. God's entreaty | 14-17 | 13-16 |

The Asaph SUPERSCRIPTION is composed of three parts: dedication to a choir leader (? cf. Psalms 4–6; 61–62), attribution to Asaph (cf. Psalms 50; 73–83), and, sandwiched in between, a musical-technical term, *'al haggittît*, "on the gittite [instrument]" (? cf. Psalms 8; 84; Kraus, I, 27 = *Einleitung*, §4 no. 23; Mowinckel, *W* II, 215).

The SUMMONS TO PRAISE (vv. 2-6b) is formally construed like a hymnic overture (see "Introduction to Cultic Poetry," section 4D): Imperatives in the plural call for the jubilant noise of common worship. The God of Israel is to be lauded by vocal cords (v. 2), a variety of instruments (vv. 3-4: *tōp, kinnôr, nābel, šôpār* = "tambourine, lyre, harp, trumpet," a real orchestra; cf. Sendrey, *Music,* 262-387; Seidel, *Musik;* I. H. Jones, *ABD* IV, 934-39), and the festive occasion is hinted at (v. 4; cf. Gunkel-Begrich, *Einleitung,* 60-63). In a general way, a day of the moon is to be celebrated (cf. *ḥōdeš,* "new moon," v. 4a, and the emendation suggested by a few Hebrew MSS in v. 4b: *kēseh,* perhaps "hat," becomes *kese',* "full moon"). Is there a lunar or a seasonal cycle in view?

The worshiping community becomes visible in two first-person plural suffixes ("God, *our* strength," v. 2a; "*our* feast," v. 4b). The MOTIVES for praise (vv. 5-6) are standard references to the divine ordinances since "the exodus from Egypt" (v. 6b). Three terms are used, each one tied to a different name for the early Jewish community: "statute *(ḥōq)* for Israel"; "right *(mišpāṭ)* of the God of Jacob"; "witness *('ēdût)* in Joseph" (unusual spelling: *yĕhôsēp;* cf. Layton). Note that common designations such as *miṣwāh, tôrāh,* and *dābār* are absent (→ Psalm 119). The first two terms in our text, *ḥōq* and *mišpāṭ,* are a frequent pair, especially in D traditions (cf. Lohfink). For its part, *'ēdût* in the singular is concentrated in the temple passages of Exodus 25–40, mostly in connection with the ark, and in the book of Numbers, while the plural forms are most frequent in the book of Psalms (22 times in Psalm 119 alone; H. Simian-Yofre, *TWAT* V, 1107-28, esp. 1123-28). The trio are found all in plural forms in Deut 4:45; 6:20. In our psalm, all singular lexemes, these terms indicate the basic will of Yahweh for his community, as in Pss 78:5; 19:8-10 (RSV 7-9), and not merely a reinforcement of ritual law and festive praxis (cf. the connection, on the surface, with v. 4). With this reference to the fundamentals of Israelite community life, received since liberation from Egypt (v. 6b), the stage is set for the sermon.

Indeed, vv. 7-17 are a kind of SERMON, like the one preserved in → Psalm 50 (cf. also 62:10-13 [RSV 9-12]; 75:5-11 [RSV 4-10]; 78:1-2; 95:8-11; Tate, 321), although we do encounter difficulties in structuring it as a coherent discourse akin to that of our Sunday worship services. The text seems fragmentary at times and in bad order, which led Gunkel to reorganize it completely (p. 359; cf. also Seybold, 322). Others (e.g., Kraus, 727; et al.) content themselves to piece together two apparently lost stichoi, namely vv. 6c + 11c: "I heard a voice, unknown to me: Open your mouth, I will feed you right." They suffer the inadequate, abrupt opening of the sermon (v. 7) and the postponed address "Hear, my people" (v. 9), as well as some seemingly logical disjunctions. No doubt, the passage breaks up into subunits; especially vv. 7-8 look somewhat haphazard with no proper beginning or ending. There may have been oracular elements that served as material for composition (cf. Psalms 60; 75; 91; 95). Even so, the composition as a whole makes good sense as a liturgical text in the preaching tradition of the early Jewish community. This tradition likes to indulge in salvation history, quote the divine norms given in the past, call for unwavering faith in the one God, interpret stories and affirmations of old, articulate itself in the first person of God, etc. (for a survey of these characteristics see Seybold, "Das 'Wir,'" 148-51; listing at Additional Bibliography, section C).

The sermon starts with an AUDITION FORMULA (v. 6c). In contrast to visionary experience (cf. Am 7:1, 4; Ezek 1:4), audition emphasizes aural perception. There seems to be a sapiential tradition preferring this paradigm (cf. Job 4:12-16; 33:14-18), which is also present in conventional prophetic discourse (cf. Isa 21:10; 28:22; Jer 49:14; Hab 3:2, 16) and becomes influential in later vision reports (cf. Ezek 1:28; 2:2; Dan 8:13, 16; 10:9; 12:7-8). Community worship of Jewish times recognized in some way direct communication of God with individuals, probably in leading positions. But we have to distinguish between prophetic and cultic manifestations of the divine (cf. Pss 12:6 [RSV 5]; 62:12 [RSV 11]; 85:9 [RSV 8]), and in different epochs of history at that. The debate in regard to "cultic prophecy" since Mowinckel is largely negligent of these important distinctions (cf. Gerstenberger, "Gott hilft den Unterdrückten"; listing at Psalm 12; J. Blenkinsopp, *History of Prophecy in Israel* [2nd ed.; Louisville: Westminster John Knox, 1996] 222-26).

The first section of our sermon (vv. 7-8) is a brief ACCOUNT of salvation, drawing on Israel's sacred history of liberation from slavery in Egypt: Exodus 1–6 relates incidents of the people being burdened by oppression (v. 7; but cf. also 1 Kgs 11:28), and v. 8a refers to the story of Exod 17:1-7, the "testing" of God at Meribah (cf. Num 20:2-13, 24; 27:14; Deut 32:51). This tradition is also reflected in Pss 95:8; 106:32. To reduce salvation history of old to these two sporadic references is a liturgical possibility *(pars pro toto)*. The community knows about the larger context. Therefore we need not complain too much about the fragmentary state of this passage, even if the very shortness and abruptness of the poetic narration seem unusual.

Formally, however, the introductory subunit is remarkable. The text begins with the "I" discourse of God and a third-person account of what he has done for his people (v. 7). The following lines switch into second-person direct address of the community. The direct reference is to the desperate crying of the enslaved to be liberated (v. 8ab; cf. Exod 1:23-25; 2:7; 6:5; etc.). The term for "save," "deliver" (v. 8a: ḥlṣ, Piel), is absent from the Exodus texts, but fairly frequent in the Psalter (e.g., Pss 6:5; 18:20; 34:8 — all in all nine occurrences, in different genres). Formally, there is a relationship to oracular (see Glossary: Oracle) language, which also may use neutral or direct-address diction. Also, we may remind ourselves of the stereotyped formulas introducing Moses' allocutions to his people: God talks to him first, and he directly communicates the divine will to Israel (cf. Lev 1:1-2; 4:1-2; Deut 1:3, 5 [Moses tells everything Yahweh has communicated to him before; Moses "interprets" the Torah = bēʾēr ʾet hattôrāh; cf. Deut 27:8; Hab 2:2]). Thus there is a continuum of divine and human communication in the worship situation.

The direct address of the community continues: the following section, properly introduced by a CALL TO ATTENTION ("Listen, my people," v. 9a), in content and style is very much like a Dtr speech. "Listen, Israel, Yahweh, our God, is the only God" (Deut 6:4; cf. 5:1; 9:1; 20:3), the famous central text of Judaism, in fact constitutes a close parallel to vv. 9-10. The only difference is this: while in Deuteronomy the human intermediary, Moses, remains visible at all times, Psalm 81 as well as Psalms 50 and 95 have God speak for himself. The functionary communicating the message does not introduce himself, nor does he become very transparent. In this respect, our text resembles the first lines of the Decalogue, as, indeed, this direct speech of God is being quoted in v. 11ab. Thus the passage vv. 9-11b is nothing else than a piece of Torah preaching or TORAH EXHORTATION. The sequence of vv. 6c-8 and 9-11 may seem disturbed formally and logically. But the traditional order of events is maintained: liberation from the yoke in Egypt — divine communication of Torah, supposedly on Mount Sinai.

Following the exhortation is a brief ACCOUNT OF DISOBEDIENCE (vv. 12-13), as is common in Dtr preaching. The key word "(my people) did not listen" (v. 12; cf. Deut 9:23; 18:19; 28:1, 15; Judg 2:2, 17, 20; 1 Sam 15:19; 2 Kgs 17:14, 40; etc.) is typical of these exilic circles' preaching. In fact, all the Deuteronomists' theological thinking revolves around the concepts of "listening and obeying the word of Yahweh" and the dreadful opposite: "rejecting or disobeying the word" (cf. U. Rüterswörden, *TWAT* VIII, 255-79, esp. 273-76; G. Mendenhall and G. A. Herion, *ABD* I, 1179-1202). This same theological scheme pervades much of OT Literature, also outside the Dtr and Chronistic layers of tradition, especially the prophetic canon (cf. Isa 1:10; 30:9; Ezek 2:5, 7; Zeph 3:2; etc.). Our psalm just succinctly states that Israel did not heed Yahweh's orientation (v. 12; cf. 2 Kgs 17:14; 21:8-9; Jer 3:13, 25; 7:13, 24, 26; 9:12; 11:8; etc.), and equally concise and nonnarrational is the account of consequences: Yahweh "gave them away to the obstinacy of their heart" (v. 13), a typical expression of the Dtr parts of the book of Jeremiah (8 of 10 occurrences of *šĕrîrût* are there: Jer 3:17; 7:24; 9:13; 11:8; 13:10; 16:12; 18:12; 23:17; the tenth passage is Deut 29:18: an exclusive term of this stratum and time). The parallel expression "(evil) plans" (*mô'ăṣôt*, v. 13b; cf. Jer 7:24; Mic 6:16), emerging from wisdom contexts, has been used in the same tradition. All in all, we have a very condensed homiletical discourse in vv. 12-13: "They did not obey — they were punished" (cf. also Psalms 78; 106; Deut 32:10-25; Neh 9:16-30). Direct address of the congregation is, surprisingly, missing at this point and throughout the rest of the psalm (vv. 12-17), with a solitary second-person suffix referring to the people at the very end of v. 17b. Why? Apparently, in forensic allocutions, the culprit may be treated "objectively," due to the court situation (the judges present are to listen to what the accuser says). Perhaps the neutral way of denouncing culprits entered theological discourse as a particularly stringent kind of censure; cf. the great direct-address speech of Jer 2:4-37 with interspersed third-person accusations (e.g., v. 13: "my people have committed two evils: they have forsaken me, the fountain of living water, and dug out cisterns for themselves, cracked cisterns that can hold no water").

Divine imploring discourse, administered by the preacher, makes a strong closing part of our psalm (vv. 14-17). Irreal wishes voiced in regard to "my people" communicate a sense of despair and broken relationship between God and Israel. The combination of *lû* with participle (beginning of v. 14) may express a hopeless case (cf. Num 22:29; 2 Sam 18:12); here we should expect a reading like "Would that my people listen to me" (v. 14a, assuming the imperfect or imperative of the verb *šm*ʿ), which would be a highly emotional entreaty to the congregation (cf. Gen 17:18; 30:34; 23:5-6, 13, 15-16 [partly conjectured]). The contents of the speech support the emendation of the verbal form. If Israel will stay faithful — thus the main thrust of God's talk — her fate will change immediately. She would be rescued from her enemies (vv. 15-16) and satiated with choice foods (v. 17). Basically, this argumentation is found in many other biblical texts. The promise of perfect living conditions is the reward of loyalty to Yahweh (cf. Lev 26:3-13; Deut 28:1-14). If one looks at these parallel texts, which are in the preaching mode too, the second-person address at the end of v. 17 becomes plausible and need not be altered. Rather, we should again ask why there is so much third-person neutrality in vv. 14-16. These verses deal with the "people" in a demonstrative way, as if addressing another audience. As in vv. 12-13, perhaps a fictitious court is subconsciously alluded to, as in Jeremiah 2; Isa 1:2-31; or Am 3:9-11. Anyway, the homily is aimed at the community of believers, and the DIVINE ENTREATY is meant to stir up their faith and hope. Pointing out the two choices — life with Yahweh, death without him — is the principal aim of Dtr preaching; cf. Deuteronomy 29–30; Leviticus 26; also Deuteronomy 28. Psalm 81 in the last instance presents the option for life.

## *Genre*

Are we really dealing with a SERMON of old? Considering structure and themes, as outlined above, and comparing some close parallel texts like Psalms 50; 75; 78; and 95 there should be little doubt about this genre classification, even though it does not coincide completely with our own literary typology. In Psalm 81 the homily proper starts with an introduction (vv. 5-6b), giving the reference point for all Jewish preaching (against those who understand these lines only to call attention to the festive calendar). Unusual, then, is the explicit legitimation to speak up in the first person of God (v. 6c). This AUDITION FORMULA clearly does not belong to prophetic traditions but could derive from sapiential discourse (cf. 62:12 [RSV 11]). The various elements of the divine allocution in their present order emphasize liberation from bondage (vv. 7-8), the exclusiveness of Yahweh worship (vv. 9-11), a statement of failure (vv. 12-13), and a fervent appeal to renew relationship with Yahweh (vv. 14-17). Although direct address of the community, always in the second person singular, is present only in vv. 8-11 and 17b (with the rest of the allocution seemingly talking to imaginary bystanders) we may take this variability as a sign of living discourse. To use, unashamedly and without fear, the first person of Yahweh (cf. the doubts about God speaking in his own voice: Deut 5:23-27, but v. 27 could also be a formidable legitimation of the preacher: "You [Moses] listen to everything Yahweh, our God, is saying, and then you speak to us"), not even using a messenger formula, is quite extraordinary and theologically significant. The topic of the sermon, Israel's renewed chance to find and keep her identity, is the fundamental one of most exilic preaching (see Nicholson, *Preaching;* listing at "Introduction to Psalms").

## Setting

Preaching and interpreting Israel's past history in the light of (beginning) Scripture reading is an intrinsic part of early Jewish community worship (and has remained so throughout Jewish and Christian traditions). Official preachers, who are not to be confounded with prophets, must have taken care of this congregational function. The community, for its part, was visibly tied in with the liturgy by following the summons to praise and feast (vv. 2-4).

## Intention

The constitution and maintenance of the people of Yahweh are to be achieved by this worship's praise and preaching. Edification of the community through close communion with Yahweh (Torah being the backbone of religious organization), in the face of salvation history, recognized failures, and with the divine promise of decisive improvements is the great goal of the preacher.

## Bibliography

P. Auffret, "'Écoute, mon peuple!' Étude structurelle du Psaume 81," *SJOT* 7 (1993) 285-302; R. T. Beckwith, "The Courses of Levites and the Eccentric Psalm Scrolls from Qumran," *RevQ* 11 (1984) 499-524; W. Beyerlin, *Herkunft und Geschichte der ältesten Sinaitraditionen* (Tübingen: Mohr, 1961); P. A. H. de Boer, "Psalm 91:6a: Observations on Translation and Meaning of One Hebrew Line," in *In the Shelter of Elyon (Fest. G. W. Ahlström; ed. W. B. Barrick, et al.; JSOTSup 31; Sheffield: JSOT Press, 1984) 67-80; T. Booij, "The Background of the Oracle in Ps 81," *Bib* 65 (1984) 465-75; H. Bückers, "Zur Verwertung der Sinaitraditionen in den Psalmen," *Bib* 32 (1951) 401-22; F. L. Hossfeld, "Ps 50 und die Verkündigung des Gottesrechts," in *Ein Gott, eine Offenbarung (Fest. N. Füglister; Würzburg: Echter, 1991) 83-101; A. R. Johnson, *The Cultic Prophet and Israel's Psalmody* (Cardiff: University of Wales Press, 1979) 5-17; K. Koenen, *Gottesworte in den Psalmen* (Biblisch-theologische Studien 30; Neukirchen: Neukirchener Verlag, 1996); S. C. Layton, "Jehoseph in Ps 81,6," *Bib* 69 (1988) 406-11; H. J. Levine, "The Dialogic Discourse of Psalms," in *Mappings of the Biblical Terrain* (ed. V. Tollers and J. Maier; Lewisburg: Bucknell University Press, 1990) 268-81; N. Lohfink, "Noch einmal *ḥōq ûmišpāṭ*," *Bib* 73 (1992) 253-54; S. Mowinckel, *PsSt* III, 38-40; G.-W. Nebe, "Die Masada-Psalmen," *RevQ* 14 (1989) 89-98; R. D. Patterson, "Calling on God," *Fundamentalist Journal* 3 (1984) 17; W. H. Schmidt, *Das erste Gebot* (Theologische Existenz Heute 165; Munich: Kaiser, 1970) 17-18; Z. A. Steinfeld, "The Sounding of the Shofar on the New Moon," *Tarbiz* 54

(1984) 347-65; S. Talmon, "Fragments of a Psalm-Scroll: MasPs a Ps 81:2b–85:6a," *Dead Sea Discoveries* 3 (1996) 296-314; M. Weinfeld, "The Uniqueness of the Decalogue and Its Place in Jewish Tradition," in *Ten Commandments in History and Tradition* (ed. B. Segal; Jerusalem: Magnes, 1990) 1-44 (also in *Religion and Law* [ed. E. Firmage, et al.; Winona Lake, Ind.: Eisenbrauns, 1990] 3-47); E. Würthwein, "Der Ursprung der prophetischen Gerichtsrede," *ZTK* 49 (1952) 1-16 (repr. idem, *Wort und Existenz: Studien zum Alten Testament* [Göttingen: Vandenhoeck & Ruprecht, 1970] 111-26).

# Psalm 82:
## Report of Trial; Praise and Petition

### Structure

|  | MT | NRSV |
|---|---|---|
| I. Superscription | 1a | - |
| II. Introduction, praise | 1bc | 1 |
| III. Indictment of gods | 2-7 | 2-7 |
|    A. Accusation | 2 | 2 |
|    B. Command, censure | 3-4 | 3-4 |
|    C. Verdict | 5-7 | 5-7 |
|       1. Pronouncement of guilt | 5 | 5 |
|       2. Sentence | 6-7 | 6-7 |
| IV. Petition | 8 | 8 |

The SUPERSCRIPTION (v. 1a) is nothing more than a plain attribution of the psalm to the guild of Asaph (→ Psalm 73).

Our psalm apparently belongs to a dramatic enactment of a divine trial against opponents or ill-behaved subjects; thus it does not need any of the regular opening phrases customary in complaints or hymns. Perhaps we may liturgically connect the short poem with the preceding Psalm 81, where God levies accusations against his people (81:12-13 [RSV 11-12]) to end up with a promissory exhortation (81:14-17 [RSV 13-16]). In prophetic discourse quite often the denunciation of foreign powers is a sequel to indictments and admonitions to Israel herself (cf. Isa 40:1-11; Zephaniah 1–2; Zechariah 12–14). If Psalm 82 has some liturgical link with the preceding text, the merely descriptive INTRODUCTION (v. 1bc) would not be surprising. It sets the scene "in heaven," like Job 1:6-12 or 1 Kgs 22:19. God is, in our text, "standing up in council"; why is he not "sitting," as befits the leader of the divine assembly? Most likely, the term *nṣb,* Niphal, "stand up," already suggests juridical action against the culprits (cf. v. 8: *qûmāh 'ĕlōhîm,* "rise up, God"; likewise in some psalms, e.g., 44:24-27 [RSV 23-26]). The divine council is a well-known institution in Ugaritic mythology (cf. Eissfeldt, Gordon, Mullen, Fleming). There, e.g., Baal stands up to give rousing speeches against his enemies (cf. *ANET,* 130, 132 = Baal III, 10-13).

The body of the psalm is taken up by direct address aimed at the "gods"

113

responsible for corrupted justice. The term *špṭ* pervades the whole psalm, from the first to the last line. The ACCUSATION (v. 2: accusatory question, "how long?") happens because of chronic misjudgment in favor of the "wicked" ones (v. 2b). This crime is demonstrated more clearly in a command to do justice (four imperatives in cross-position), which really implies only CENSURE (vv. 3-4). Surprisingly, we find the "poor" and "weak," the social outcasts, in opposition to the "wicked." Unless the marginalized understand themselves in this psalm as the only legitimate community (→ Psalm 37), we have to explain this crucial juxtaposition (see Setting). At this point we note a strong affinity of this censure with sapiential and D social ethos (cf. *dal,* "lowly"; *rāš,* "poor": Prov 10:15; 13:8, 23; 14:20, 31; 19:1, 7, 22; 21:13; 22:9, 16, 22, etc.; *yātôm,* "orphan"; *ʿānî, ʾebyôn,* "miserable, poor": Deut 10:18; 15:4, 7, 9, 11; 16:11, 14; 24:12, 14, 15; 27:19; etc.). A very similar command to do what is right within an accusation is Isa 1:17.

The VERDICT first declares the authorities in charge of justice to have totally failed in their job (v. 5). They "did not know or understand" (v. 5a) is sapiential language; "they go about in darkness" (v. 5b) could be of the same general origin (cf. 39:7 [RSV 6]). The statement about shaking of the world's foundations (v. 5c: *mûṭ,* "quake") here and there in the Psalms denotes universal turmoil (cf. 11:3; 46:3, 7 [RSV 2, 6]; 60:4 [RSV 2]; 93:1). All three parts of this concluding line are addressed not to the culprits but rather to an imaginary court, as verdicts normally are (cf. Boecker, "Schuldigerklärung," in idem, *Redeformen,* 135-43; listing at "Introduction to Psalms").

The two following lines (vv. 6-7) carry the SENTENCE, and they again are formulated in the second person plural as proper in an Israelite trial. V. 6 sounds like a forestalling thought: Should not divine descent of the accused make them exempt from condemnation? The conclusion is to the contrary. Like simple mortals, they have to die (v. 7). Accusation and sentencing of other deities by Yahweh, the Lord of all gods and powers, is elsewhere a topic, e.g., in Second Isaiah or Jeremiah (cf. Isaiah 46; Jer 10:6-16). Hardly in any other passage, however, is the lack of social justice made the central point of accusation. Partly for this reason, modern exegetes have been mesmerized by the problem whether Psalm 82 is talking about foreign gods or about dominant political powers acting in the name of their deities. Niehr is probably right when he evaluates this whole controversy as a "false alternative." Wherever justice was at stake in the ancient Near East, the deities played an important role, but those humans in charge were always involved with the execution of the law (Gamper, *Gott;* Weinfeld, *Justice;* listing at Additional Bibliography, section B).

The last line of the psalm proves it is anchored in community worship. A purely literary creation of the psalm therefore becomes less likely. The clear PETITION of v. 8a urges execution of divine judgment over foreign gods and peoples. God is implored to realize his jurisdictional power over the earth (cf. Psalms 24; 96). The last phrase (v. 8b) undergirds petition, attributing power to Israel's God. Power entails praise, just as praise encompasses power (cf. Psalms 29; 148). Thus the very last affirmation of the psalm is PRAISE, as the first line also, in a more neutral way, expresses a powerful act of God with praising attention.

## Genre

Psalms 50 and 81 already demonstrated the possibility of having God himself speak in community worship through a liturgist of sorts within a community service. Psalm 82, for its part, not only uses the first person of God but also portrays his action in the divine council. The concept of God's acting among a pantheon of deities was apparently common throughout Israel's history, in spite of later monotheistic restrictions of any polytheistic models (cf. only the "God alone" formulas in Deut 4:39 or Isa 44:6). The action described in our psalm seems to have been put "on stage" by the speaker in a worship service; therefore we may call the genre a REPORT OF TRIAL or even an ENACTMENT OF TRIAL. Although the heavenly council reminds one of 1 Kgs 22:19-22 — Micah's vision — we should not think of prophetic activity in the classical sense at this point (against Jeremias, *Kultprophetie;* Johnson, *Prophet;* listing at "Introduction to Psalms"; Tournay, *Seeing;* Koenen, *Gottesworte;* Starbuck, *Oracles;* listing at Additional Bibliography, section C; J. Barton, *ABD* V, 490-91); cf. Psalms 12; 75.

## Setting

As pointed out above, the place of this vivid presentation of God's saving act for his people was congregational worship. Perhaps the scene was enacted after Psalm 81, which is a serious admonition of Israel herself. Having concluded that part, the community would listen to God's forceful intervention to bring about justice for his people. There is a midrashic tradition, however, that makes Israel herself, not foreign gods or authorities, the addressee of vv. 6-7: Israel became godlike, deathless at Sinai, by the gift of Torah, but forfeited her privilege and turned mortal (Neyrey).

## Intention

The defeat of outward oppressive powers, both religious and political, especially during exilic and postexilic times was a necessity for the communities of Yahweh dispersed in the Babylonian and Persian empires. Therefore in communal liturgies throughout the Hebrew Bible coming from this period of time, we find much emphatic denunciation of strange deities, as in Psalm 82 (cf. the polemics against the "other gods" because of alleged powerlessness: 115:4-7; 135:15-18 as well as indictments in "prophetic" books: Isaiah 46; Jeremiah 50).

## Bibliography

J. S. Ackermann, "An Exegetical Study of Psalm 82" (diss., Harvard, 1965/66); F. I. Andersen, "A Short Note on Psalm 82,5," *Bib* 50 (1969) 393-94; P. Auffret, "Dieu juge. Étude structurelle du Psaume 82," *BN* 58 (1991) 7-12; H. J. Benedict, "Wenn die Götter

Unrecht stützen: Sozialgeschichtliche Bibelauslegung zu Psalm 82," *Junge Kirche* 57 (1996) 496-98; W. Boesak, "Exegesis and Proclamation, Psalm 82: God amidst the Gods," *Journal of Theology for Southern Africa* 64 (1988) 64-68; M. Buber, *Recht und Unrecht: Deutung einiger Psalmen* (Basel: Benno Schwalbe, 1952; Sammlung Klosterberg) 27-38 (repr. idem, *Werke II, Schriften zur Bibel* [Munich: Lambert Schneider, 1964] 964-70); G. Cooke, "The Sons of (the) God(s)," *ZAW* 76 (1964) 22-47; K. M. Craig Jr., "Psalm 82," *Int* 49 (1995) 281-84; F. Crüsemann, "'Meine Kraft ist in den Schwachen mächtig': Eine theologische Reflektion," *Reformatio* 38 (1989) 117-21; C. R. Dickson, "Empowerment: A Theological Perspective," *SK* 15 (1994) 248-63; idem, "The Hebrew Terminology for the Poor in Psalm 82," *HerTS* 51 (1995) 1029-45; J. Dus, "Melek Sor — Melquart?" *Archiv orientální* 26 (1958) 159-85; O. Eissfeldt, "El and Yahweh," *JSS* 1 (1956) 25-37 (German tr. in idem, *KS* III, 386-97); H.-J. Fabry, "'Ihr alle seid Söhne des Allerhöchsten' (Ps 82,6)," *BibLeb* 15 (1974) 135-47; D. M. Fleming, "The Divine Council as Type-Scene in the Hebrew Bible" (diss., Southern Baptist Theological Seminary, 1989); A. Gonzales, "Le Psaume 82," *VT* 13 (1963) 293-309; C. H. Gordon, "History of Religion in Psalm 82," in *Biblical and Near Eastern Studies* (*Fest.* W. S. LaSor; ed. G. A. Tuttle; Grand Rapids: Eerdmans, 1978) 129-31; L. K. Handy, "Sounds, Words, and Meanings in Psalm 82," *JSOT* 47 (1990) 51-66; idem, "One Problem Involved in Translating to Meaning (Ps 82:1)," *SJOT* 10 (1996) 16-27; A. T. Hanson, "John's Citation of Psalm 82 Reconsidered," *New Testament Studies* 13 (1967) 363-67; P. D. Hanson, "War, Peace, and Justice in Early Israel," *Bible Review* 3 (1987) 32-45; W. Herrmann, "Die Göttersöhne," *Zeitschrift für Religions- und Geistesgeschichte* 12 (1960) 242-51; P. Höffken, "Werden und Vergehen der Götter: Ein Beitrag zur Auslegung von Psalm 82," *TZ* 39 (1983) 129-37, esp. 120-27; H.-W. Jüngling, *Der Tod der Götter: Eine Untersuchung zu Psalm 82* (Stuttgart: Katholisches Bibelwerk, 1969); E. G. Kingsbury, "The Prophets and the Council of Yahweh," *JBL* 83 (1964) 279-86; O. Loretz, "Eine kanaanäische Short Story: Psalm 82," *UF* 3 (1971) 113-15; P. D. Miller Jr., "When Gods Meet: Psalm 82 and the Issue of Justice," *Journal for Preachers* 9 (1986) 2-5; idem, *Interpreting,* 120-24 (listing at Additional Bibliography, section C); J. Morgenstern, "The Mythological Background of Psalm 82," *HUCA* 14 (1939) 29-126; E. T. Mullen Jr., *The Assembly of the Gods: The Divine Council in Canaanite and Early Hebrew Literature* (HSM 24; Chico, Calif.: Scholars Press, 1980); J. H. Neyrey, "I said: 'You are Gods' — Ps 82:6 and John 10:34," *JBL* 108 (1989) 647-63; H. Niehr, "Götter oder Menschen — eine falsche Alternative: Bemerkungen zu Ps 82," *ZAW* 99 (1987) 94-98; R. T. O'Callaghan, "A Note on the Canaanite Background of Psalm 82," *CBQ* 15 (1933) 311-14; S. B. Parker, "The Beginning of the Reign of God: Ps 82 as Myth and Liturgy," *RB* 102 (1995) 532-59; M. C. Pecheux, "The Council Scenes in Paradise Lost," in *Milton and Scriptural Tradition* (ed. J. Sims and L. Ryken; Columbia: University of Missouri Press, 1984) 82-103; W. G. Phillips, "An Apologetic Study of John 10:34-36," *BSac* 146 (1989) 405-19; H. Plantin, "Deuteronomium och lövhyddofestens psalmer i b Sukka 55a," *SEÅ* 55 (1990) 7-38; W. S. Prinsloo, "Psalm 82: Once Again, Gods or Men?" *Bib* 76 (1995) 219-28; G. Rinaldi, "Synagoga Deorum (Salmo 82)," *BeO* 6 (1964) 9-11; Z. Rokay, "Vom Stadttor zu den Vorhöfen: Ps 82 — Sach 1–8 (ein Vergleich)," *ZKT* 116 (1994) 457-63; R. B. Salters, "Psalm 82,1 and the Septuagint," *ZAW* 103 (1991) 225-38; W. Schlisske, *Gottessöhne und Gottessohn im Alten Testament* (Stuttgart: Kohlhammer, 1973) 32-40; C. R. Seitz, "The Divine Council: Temporal Transition and New Prophecy in the Book of Isaiah," *JBL* 109 (1990) 229-

47; T. M. Siqueira, "O Salmo 82," *EstBib* (Petrópolis) 2 (1985) 11-18; E. B. Smick, "Mythopoetic Language in the Psalms," *Westminster Theological Journal* 44 (1982) 88-98; F. J. Stendebach, "Glaube und Ethos: Überlegungen zu Ps 82," in *Freude an der Weisung des Herrn* (ed. E. Haag and F.-L. Hossfeld; Stuttgart: Katholisches Bibelwerk, 1986) 425-40; M. Tsevat, "God and the Gods in Assembly," *HUCA* 40 (1969) 123-37; E. Würthwein, "Der Ursprung der prophetischen Gerichtsrede," *ZTK* 49 (1952) 1-16 (repr. in idem, *Wort und Existenz* [Göttingen: Vandenhoeck & Ruprecht, 1970] 111-26); P. J. van Zijl, "Die interpretasie van Ps 82 in die lig van nuwe navorsing," *NGTT* 11 (1970) 65-77.

# Psalm 83:
# Communal Complaint

## Structure

|  | MT | NRSV |
|---|---|---|
| I. Superscription | 1 | - |
| II. Invocation and plea | 2 | 1 |
| III. Complaint | 3-9 | 2-8 |
| A. Charge against enemies | 3-4 | 2-3 |
| B. Quotation of enemies | 5 | 4 |
| C. List of enemies | 6-9 | 5-8 |
| IV. Imprecation | 10-18 | 9-17 |
| A. Historical comparisons | 10-13 | 9-12 |
| B. Imprecation | 14-18 | 13-17 |
| V. Praise | 19 | 18 |

The last of the block of Asaph psalms (Psalms 73–83) is headed by a simple attribution to that ominous "singer" of postexilic history writings (1 Chr 15:17; 25:1, 9; → Psalm 50). Added on we find the designation *šîr,* "song," which does not mean much more than liturgical, cultic use of the poem (cf. G. Bonnert, *TWAT* VII, 1269-78).

A double but concise INVOCATION frames the first line of initial pleas. Such chiastic position of calling out the name of God, in this case *'ĕlōhîm* and *'ēl,* is unusual in opening sections of complaint songs. Together with the three-fold entreaty not to ignore the suppliant, the first line acquires a special quality. Normally, it is the positive plea to be heard and heeded that opens the plaintive prayer (cf. 4:2 [RSV 1]; 5:2-3 [RSV 1-2]; 61:2-3b [RSV 1-2b]; etc.). Here we have an exclusively negative (grammatical form) approach to God, to prevent the worst, so it seems. Other complaint songs use an avoidance formulation only as a collateral phrase (cf. 28:1; 31:2 [RSV 1]; 55:2 [RSV 1]; 102:2-3 [RSV 1-2]; 143:1-2). Closer to our psalm are the opening lines of Psalms 38 (two negative pleas) and 109 (one negative plea), with slightly different contents. All in all, such negatively formulated, almost apotropaic openings try to avert imminent danger. A prayer of this sort is not so much looking back to defeat and dis-

117

grace, as, e.g., Psalms 44; 74; 79; 89; and Lamentations 1 do, but forward to keeping away the catastrophe.

The body of the psalm consists of a COMMUNAL COMPLAINT about impending enemy action, an IMPRECATION against the adversaries, and a final PRAISE. Much of the song involves historical allusions and symbols, which seem to be taken more out of Scripture tradition than political reality. In particular, Israel's early formation plays an important role in the psalm's attack on threatening enemies.

The COMPLAINT runs from v. 3 through v. 9; we should distinguish three subelements: the charge of waging hostile machinations against anonymous adversaries (vv. 3-4), the citation of their evil words to prove their aggressiveness (v. 5), and the listing of nations and tribes who are involved in such detrimental scheming (vv. 6-9). The first two sections, then, move on generalized terrain. The opponents are called "your enemies" and "those who hate you" (v. 3), making Israel's political struggle from the beginning a case for God himself to act on. Formally, as a matter of fact, direct-address style continues from v. 2 through v. 4. The suppliants, however, never refer explicitly to themselves, i.e., with communal "we" (for a contrast see, e.g., Psalms 44; 79). Only once does the "I" of one speaker become manifest (v. 14a); or should it be considered a communal "I" (cf. theories of one leader representing the whole congregation, or the assembly speaking in the first person singular: Mowinckel, W I, 42-46, 225-39)? Direct address to God, on the other hand, continues in vv. 10, 12, 14 (singular imperatives), 16, 17 (jussives, second-person singular suffixes), 19 (full appellation in second person singular).

The accusation is "conspiracy against the people of God," as in 2:1-3, without the messianic overtones, however. Vocabulary and structure of 2:1-3 are very akin to our vv. 3-5, including the verbatim citation of the plotters in 2:3 and our v. 5. Other parallel texts include Isa 7:5-6; 17:12-13; Jer 6:23; Ezek 38:15-16; Ps 48:5 (RSV 4); and with these texts we certainly touch the wide field of concepts related to the battle around Jerusalem (cf. F. Stolz, *Strukturen;* listing at "Introduction to Cultic Poetry"). Also, on the formal side, it is noteworthy that descriptions of strategies of war, after using the verb $y'\underline{s}$, "to conspire," almost invariably lead to a quotation of the deadly counsel divulged in enemy circles (cf. Isa 7:5-6; Ezek 11:2-3; Ps 2:3). The citation of v. 5 has been terribly actualized into the twentieth century: peoples plan the annihilation of Israel. Ps 2:3 speaks of rebellion against Yahweh, Isa 7:6 of conquering Judah. To propose the extinction of Israel is an extremely brutal affirmation (cf. the verb *khd,* Hiphil, "exterminate," Exod 23:23; 1 Kgs 13:34; Zech 11:8; 2 Chr 32:21; in Esth 3:6, 13; 4:8; 7:4 different vocabulary, equally cynical, occurs: *šmd,* Hiphil, "annihilate"; *hrg,* "murder"; *'bd,* Piel, "extinguish" [all the Jews]; Esth 8:11 reverses the killing license).

In summary, vv. 3-5 are a complaint in the face of coming danger, using imagery and vocabulary of an imagined catastrophe for the community of Yahweh believers. Anxiety about being overrun by potent foes certainly has deep roots in historical experience, but the articulation of this fear is highly stylized to fit the outlook of many a contemporary community.

The next segment of the psalm (vv. 6-9) goes far in naming the enemies who threaten to extinguish Israel. This feature is not frequent in either individual or communal complaints. Of all the specimens of the first group only Ps 120:5 names, in a generic fashion, some hostile neighbors. The extant communal complaints keep as silent as the individual counterparts as far as the identity of adversaries is concerned (cf. Psalms 44; 76; 79; 80; 89). So what is the use or purpose of stringing together a total of ten enemy peoples in this part of the psalm? The custom may go back to much more ancient execration rituals, which are known to us, e.g., from Egyptian sources. Names of enemy peoples found on broken potsherds may betray a cultic ritual in which adversaries were executed in effigy (see ANET, 328-29; see also the enumeration of enemies in Merneptah's victory hymn, ANET, 376-78). If the origin and use of such lists point to ritual practice, then we should consider this genre a CULTIC LIST, not the protocol of a particular historical situation (as many exegetes do in regard to Psalm 83). There is no point asking at which juncture of history Israel was expecting the attack of those ten nations or tribes mentioned in vv. 7-9 (ten "kings" also play a part in the great vision of Dan 7:7, 20, 24). Instead, we note a certain ideal structuring of the names, and we try to understand its meaning and references.

V. 9 apparently summarizes nine of the ten peoples by calling them "sons of Lot." According to biblical evidence this title can refer only to Moab and Ammon (cf. Gen 19:36-38, a very biased, derogatory birth legend of their eponyms). Unless the designation "sons of Lot" had acquired the general meaning "son of a bitch," it could not have been used as the common denominator of so many nations. Furthermore, the list in vv. 7-9 seems composed of two separate little clusters. In v. 7 we find four names, two authentic tribal or state designations (Edom and Moab), and two gentilic appellations in the plural form (Ishmaelites, Hagrites). These last names are not very frequent in the OT (nine and six times, respectively). Apparently, two neighboring nations, known for their intimate ties with Israel as well as for persisting antagonisms — Edom and Moab (cf. Genesis 27; 36; 2 Kings 3; etc.; J. R. Bartlett, ABD II, 287-95; J. M. Miller, ABD IV, 882-93) — became standing symbols of animosity, and each of them receives a kind of tribal adjunct (Ishmaelites: cf. Judg 8:24; Hagrites), perhaps to demonstrate a comprehensive front of differently organized, i.e., settled and nomadic, peoples against Israel. The name "Hagrite," when consciously connected with "Hagar" (Genesis 16), could also be a mere synonym to "Ishmaelite."

The second cluster of adversaries is in v. 8. This time the sequence runs from "Gebal," to "Tyre," touching "Ammon," "Amalek," and "Philistine land" on the way. V. 9a, finally, calls out — and this move occupies most of the poetic line — the name of Assyria, "who came to help the sons of Lot." Of "Gebal" we know practically nothing (which led commentators to propose emendations, e.g., into gĕbûl, "territory"). All the other peoples are attested to have been fierce enemies of Israel at one time or another (cf. 1 Samuel 11; Exod 17:8-16; 1 Samuel 5; Ezekiel 27–28; etc.). The structure of the list, its climactic arrangement (two plus two adversaries, five more, final member of the war council, the imperial overlord, summary), suggest a prolonged growth of this accumulation of enemy names. There is a good possibility that they were taken successively from the ancient traditions in order to be used in this communal complaint psalm.

The larger unit IMPRECATION (vv. 10-18) has two parts to it, one with enemy names, the other contenting itself with anonymous denunciation. The neutral part (vv. 14-18) follows the named one (vv. 10-13), so that in the middle of the psalm "historical" reference abounds in complaint and imprecation (vv. 6-13), while generalized and anonymous elements envelop this concrete and seemingly historical nucleus (vv. 3-5, 14-18). Interestingly, the names of the enemies pointed out as plotters against Israel in the complaint section do not reappear in the imprecation, which would have been natural and proper to liturgy. Instead, great victories of Israel are remembered (Judges 4–5; 6–8) and the terrible fates of the the enemies' leaders — Sisera, Jabin, Oreb, Zeeb, Zebach, and Zalmunna: all of them murdered or slaughtered in that legendary past when Israel was in her formative stage — as well as of one cruel enemy tribe (Midian; cf. G. E. Mendenhall, *ABD* IV, 815-18) are activated against the potential aggressors of the preceding list. Thus there is no direct execration or magical execution of named adversaries, but an equally powerful imprecation of the type: "They may perish like those foes of old, of whose aggression tradition is telling." The supposed analogy between enemies planning the extermination of Israel and war leaders of old, who perished long ago, is taken to the point of explicitly citing their evil words (v. 13; cf. v. 5). Legendary narrations of victories were certainly kept alive even in popular tradition (cf. Isa 10:26; Josh 13:21). Naturally, historical facts, names of persons and locales have been often confused, as they are polished in transmission like pebbles in running water: is *ʾên-dôr* in v. 11 mutilated from *ʾên-ḥărōd* in Judg 7:1? Important is the act of cultic imprecation. Maybe the examples of killed enemy leaders are remembered because they are more powerful — in that their fate already had been effected by God — than a condemnation of still active would-be offenders could be. It is strange that this practice of conjuring up blessed events of the past is so little used in the Psalms. Outside Judges 4–8 the six names of defeated enemy leaders occur exclusively in our psalm, with the sole exception of Sisera, who appears once more in 1 Sam 12:9 at the side of Philistines and Moabites in a Dtr historical summary.

A citation of historical enemy words (v. 13) gives color and plausibility to the claim that the opponents of the day constitute a high security hazard to Israel, because the latter are but copies of the former. They really were and are planning the extermination of Yahweh's people. At the same time their words being made public in liturgy become vulnerable to countermeasures. Therefore, it seems, the liturgical tradition existent in all kinds of complaint psalms quite often exhibits the dangerous affirmation of enemies (cf. 3:3 [RSV 2]; 22:9 [RSV 8]; 41:6, 9 [RSV 5, 8]; 64:6 [RSV 5]; 74:8; etc.; Gunkel and Begrich, *Einleitung*, 199-200; listing at "Introduction to Cultic Poetry").

After this unique dramatization IMPRECATION goes on in more neutral but still forcefully damaging wishes toward God (vv. 14-18). A new invocation, "My God," opens the new liturgical part (v. 14a) demonstrating its ceremonial independence. In regard to contents this general devastation of opponents employs traditional concepts: God is to throw his storm and fire against the evilmongers (vv. 14-16; cf. Isa 17:13; 29:5-6; 47:14; Mal 3:19; Pss 1:4; 21:10 [RSV 9]; 79:6; 140:10-11 [RSV 9-10]). No doubt, traces of the old storm-god (Baal) are present in this powerful imprecation (cf. Psalm 29). In terms of liturgy it carries the highest energy charges, and vv. 17-18 only make explicit what the final purpose of God's action should be: shame and destruction (both are synonymous for the ancient mind; cf. Klopfenstein, *Scham;* listing at Additional Bibliography, section B) to those who plot against Israel. The name itself of the worshiping community, by the way, is extant only in the enemy citation of v. 5 ("Israel"), but all the concrete nominations in vv. 6-13 testify to this and no other people. The outward world is deadly hostile to the worshipers; therefore it has to be warded off and destroyed. A concurring idea comes at the end of the two lines (vv. 17, 19): "so that they will ask for your name, Yahweh," and "and they will know, (that your name is Yahweh)." Are hopes for a final conversion of heathen nations to Yahweh visible here? After all the destruction wrought upon them? Or is this outlook a mere rhetorical device to accentuate even more the abysmal destiny of the enemies?

The closing line, in any case, is full of PRAISE for this mighty God, who has the power to act on behalf of those who call to him. Obviously, this single line is a full-fledged hymn of the community, introductory *kî* being an exclamation: "Indeed!" marking the point where the congregation has to take up the hymnic phrase to be repeated endlessly by the crowd (cf. Exod 15:21; Ps 118:1; Crüsemann, *Studien,* 32-35; listing at "Introduction to Cultic Poetry"). The introductory summons ("let us praise," "give thanks," or similarly) in v. 19 is replaced by "they [the enemies sentenced to death] shall know," which makes for an excellent transition from the preceding imprecation.

## Genre/Setting

Psalm 83 is a COMMUNAL COMPLAINT (see "Introduction to Cultic Poetry," section 4B) to be sure. Its special feature, however, has become obvious from the very beginning. The community, feeling its existence threatened, counteracts in a prophylactic manner. The psalm therefore betrays a climate of anxiety and distrust on the part of Yahweh believers over against other ethnic and religious groups, which are probably politically dominant. The names of oppressive neighbors (vv. 7-9) need not reflect the contemporary historical situation (cf. Ahlström, *History,* 282-333, 371-90; Fritz, *Entstehung,* 39-50, 121-28). Nor are the examples of defeated enemy leaders in any way trustworthy sources for the reconstruction of most ancient history. Chances are that all these historical references are syntheses of oral or written tradition as it came down to the exilic and postexilic age. General fear of suffering terminal persecution and concentration on Yahweh as the only way of survival fit with the localization indicated. In those days of pressure, community worship, also because of its defensive capacities through enemy imprecation, became the salvation experience par excellence.

## Intention

A worship service in self-defense against political oppressors is in reality a force of its own, as experiences for instance in base communities in the slums of Third World countries have proved many times (cf. the Latin American experience: the fight for survival of the poor; cf. Pedro Casaldaliga, *Creio na justiça e esperança* [Rio de Janeiro: Civilização Brasileira, 1978]). Defense against superior outward pressure, on the other hand, is also intended to strengthen the congregation of Yahweh believers.

## Bibliography

G. W. Ahlström, *The History of Ancient Palestine* (Minneapolis: Fortress, 1993); P. Auffret, "Qu'ils sachent que toi, ton nom est YHWH! Étude structurelle du Psaume 83," *Science et Esprit* 45 (1993) 41-59; M. Z. Brettler, "Images of YHWH the Warrior in Psalms," *Semeia* 61 (1993) 135-65; B. Costacurta, "L'agressione contra Dios: Studio del Salmo 83," *Bib* 64 (1983) 518-41; P. R. Dekar, "Does the State of Israel Have Theological Significance?" *Conrad Grebel Review* 2 (1984) 31-46; V. Fritz, *Die Entstehung Israels im 12. und 11. Jahrhundert v. Chr.* (Biblische Enzyklopädie, ed. W. Dietrich and W. Stegemann, vol. 2; Stuttgart: Kohlhammer, 1996); B. Gosse, "Le Psaume 83, Isaïe 62,6-7 et la tradition des Oracles contre les Nations des livres d'Isaïe et d'Ezéchiel," *BN* 70 (1993) 9-12; D. J. Human, "Die begrip 'berit' in 'n aantal klaagpsalms: 'n perspektief," *SK* 15 (1994) 280-93; idem, "Enkele tradisie-historiese perspektiewe op Psalm 83," *HerTS* 51 (1995) 175-88; O. Margalith, "Dor and En-Dor," *ZAW* 97 (1985) 109-11; S. Mowinckel, *PsSt* V, 83-85; E. Zenger, "Die Gotteszeugenschaft des 83. Psalms," in *Und dennoch ist von Gott zu reden* (ed. M. Lutz-Bachmann; Freiburg: Herder, 1994) 11-37.

## Psalm 84:
## Zion Hymn, Pilgrim Song

### Structure

|                          | MT    | NRSV  |
|--------------------------|-------|-------|
| I. Superscription        | 1     | -     |
| II. Praise of Zion       | 2-4   | 1-3   |
| III. Blessing            | 5-8   | 4-7   |
| IV. Petition             | 9-10  | 8-9   |
| V. Confession            | 11    | 10    |
| VI. Praise of Yahweh     | 12-13 | 11-12 |
|   A. Hymnic attributions | 12ab  | 11ab  |
|   B. Wish      | 12cd  | 11cd  |
|   C. Felicitation | 13 | 12    |

Being the first poem of the second cluster of Korah psalms (Psalms 84–85; 87–88; cf. the earlier collection: Psalms 42; 44–49; R. R. Hutton, *ABD* IV, 100-101; Zenger, *Bedeutung;* Buss, *Psalms;* for the last see Additional Bibliography, section C) our song receives an ascription to the "choirmaster" (cf.

Psalms 4; 61) and a musical-technical note (*'al haggittît*, "on the gittite [instrument; melody]"; cf. Psalms 8; 81). The terms used hardly constitute conscious compositional markers to "bind together" the group of Korah psalms (against Zenger, *Bedeutung*, 176-77).

The first section (vv. 2-4) is a real temple hymn, praising the abode of Israel's God on Mount Zion from the perspective of an individual Yahweh adorer; note the personal confession at the end of v. 4: "Yahweh Sabaoth, my king and my God" (cf. 5:3 [RSV 2]; 44:5 [RSV 4]; 68:25 [RSV 24]; 74:12; 145:1). The full title "Yahweh Sabaoth," more likely a Jerusalem than a Shiloh epithet (cf. 2 Sam 6:2, 18; Wanke, *Zionstheologie*, 40-46; listing at "Introduction to Psalms"; differently Mettinger, *Dethronement;* listing at Additional Bibliography, section B; and J. Zobel, *TWAT* VI, 876-92), carries special weight in our hymn, framing, as it were, the affirmations about Zion (vv. 2 and 4; only eight psalms use "Sabaoth": Psalms 24; 46; 48; 59; 69; 80; 84; 89). Otherwise, personal confession to "God the King" is more or less standardized, apparently being an important element also of communal hymn singing. Psalms 44; 68; 74; and 145 are congregational songs, while Psalm 5 qualifies as an individual complaint.

Central attention is directed to the temple precincts. Astonished exclamations "How lovely!" "How great!" even in present-day Western languages function as high expressions of praise. Hebrew examples from liturgical backgrounds include 8:2, 10 (RSV 1, 9); 31:20 (RSV 19); 36:8 (RSV 7); 66:3; 92:6 (RSV 5); 104:24; 139:17. Just like our psalm (v. 2), all of these use direct-address language of the type "How wonderful are your works, God!" This means that exclamatory phrases with the rhetorical particle *māh* or *meh*, "how," were distinctive forms of individual and congregational adoration. Ps 66:3 testifies more clearly to this function: the call to worship (66:1b-4) contains an explicit summons to exclaim: "How frightful are your deeds!" Such a concise mode of expressing praise is very fit to be used by the assembled congregation, and frequency as well as typical configurations of phrases listed above prove that these shouts were applied in common worship.

The idea of community is alive also in v. 3, in spite of its very personal character. Longing ardently for the temple, and thus for the presence of Yahweh, naturally implies a community of fellow worshipers or pilgrims, as vv. 5-8 will show (cf. also references to the crowds who wander and worship together: 55:15 [RSV 14]; 122:1-2). The intensity of wanting to be with Yahweh (*ksp*, Niphal, "long for"; cf. Gen 31:30; Job 14:15; both Korah collections begin with expressions of longing for Yahweh; cf. Ps 42:2-3 [RSV 1-2]) is sometimes expressed in poetic imagery, including comparisons with animal behavior (cf. 42:2-3 [RSV 1-2]; 131:2). Our psalm gives another beautiful example, mentioning the birds that traditionally find refuge in the sanctuary (v. 4; "altar" being *pars pro toto* of the temple).

All in all, the opening part of Psalm 84 records possible exclamations of the congregation itself (first and last lines of vv. 2-4) and a recitation, in communal first person singular, of words of longing for the (distant?) sanctuary of Yahweh, where the highest aspirations of the faithful are fulfilled. The language is that of adoring prayer, and the immediate object the sanctuary as such. In ancient Near Eastern traditions the earthly "living place" of the gods has always been of eminent importance for religious reflection; therefore the genre of "temple hymn" is of long standing (cf. Sumerian examples, S. N. Kramer, *ANET,* 582-84).

The second part (vv. 5-8) is a pilgrim song in the form of BLESSINGS or well-wishes. Two felicitations (vv. 5-6; cf. 1:1; 32:1-2; 40:5 [RSV 4]; 41:2 [RSV 1]; 119:1-2; 128:1-2), spoken to God, not to human partners, introduce the element. Such *'ašrê* sayings or BEATITUDES, quite frequent within the Psalms, are often used at the very beginning of a text or at the opening of a main liturgical part. Most probably, words of being blessed of this type had to be pronounced by the leader of a liturgy. They require a certain position of prestige and an air of intimacy with the Deity to be effective. The felicitation applies to community members (v. 5) and generally to "everybody" (*'ādām,* v. 6, if two Hebrew MSS reading *hā'ām,* "the people," do not preserve the more original wording). Of course, even the general formulation is restricted by "whose strength are you" (v. 6a). The experiences alluded to are those of living in the house of God (vv. 5-6; cf. Psalms 1; 122), and of wandering toward the holy site in a long pilgrimage (vv. 7-8). "Living in the sanctuary" may be a figurative expression for "partaking of highest bliss" or else refer to (temporary) lodgings within the sanctuary (cf. 1 Sam 21:8). The pilgrimage through arid lands has its counterparts in a number of Deutero-Isaian passages (e.g., Isa 41:18-19; 48:21) and also, in a way, in the wilderness stories of the exodus from Egypt (cf. Exodus 16–17; Numbers 11; 14). The "valley of Baca" (v. 7) was either a geographical name (which we are unable to locate) or a legendary, imaginary, or mythical designation. Etymologically, there is no way of linking it with the famous "valley of tears" ("to weep" would be *bākāh* in Hebrew, not *bākā';* cf. Judg 2:4-5) of later Christian tradition. The high point of the pilgrims' song in vv. 5-8 is the poetic assertion that those on their way to Jerusalem, under the blessings of their God, receive physical and spiritual strength, rain, and comfort from above, until they arrive in the presence of the Lord at Zion (v. 8b). He "makes himself visible" is the most likely Masoretic wording, normally altered by translators into "they shall see," because of the following preposition *'el,* "toward" (cf. Nötscher, *Gott;* listing at "Introduction to Cultic Poetry"; Ps 17:15). Probably, however, *'el* should be understood generically as El, "God." The end of the journey and the cultic encounter with Yahweh (v. 8b then names him "God of gods") are the ultimate concern of the psalmist. Here the psalm could well terminate, perhaps vv. 11-13 forming a kind of epilogue.

But there is a strange interlude of a petitionary passage that may either comprise only vv. 9-10, or still include v. 11. Some commentators feel that at least vv. 9-10 are totally misplaced and cannot belong to the original pilgrims' hymn (thus, e.g., Duhm, Gunkel). PETITION as well as INTERCESSION for a king, they argue, are incompatible with such hymns, as they are with some other genres (cf. 28:8-9; 61:7-8 [RSV 6-7]). But in the absence of any evidence of misplacement there is no reason to doubt that somehow at this point the worshiping community has been offering a prayer to Yahweh, the only question being whether we are dealing with a pre- or a postexilic setting (see below). The petition at hand has an elaborated INVOCATION ("Yahweh God Sabaoth," v. 9a; cf. appellations in vv. 2 and 4), and, in chiastic position, another name, "God of Jacob" (v. 9c). Parallel to these appellations of God we find "our shield" (i.e., the king) and "your anointed" occupying the head and tail positions of v. 10. Thus the assumed worship liturgy did provide an opportunity for these interventions, just as Psalms 28 and 61 did, too (see above). It is significant that the royal figure is referred to in communal solidarity (*"our* shield"), as apparent also in 80:18-19 (RSV 17-18). Our choice will be to interpret these designations as referring either to an actual monarch or to a future messiah.

Vv. 11 and 12 are both introduced by *kî*, a chameleon particle. It surely cannot give motivations for preceding petitions in this context. But the particle may mark two liturgical units, sung by different voices. First, the community again — as in v. 3 — through the voice of individual pilgrims praises Yahweh and confesses allegiance to him in the first person singular (v. 11). The phrases may have been read or recited by the liturgist or sung by the congregation itself, thus communalizing the individual discourse or individualizing collective faith. The form is that of a sapiential comparative saying: "Better . . . than" (cf. Prov 12:9; 15:16-17; 16:32; 17:1; 19:1, 22; 21:19; 25:24), put into direct-address language and articulated in two poetic lines. Doubled dicta also occur in Proverbs (e.g., Prov 15:16-17; 16:32). Second, v. 12 contains a pure Yahweh hymn with wonderful attributions as to his power, justice, and mercy ("sun and shield"; "grace and glory": the epithets come from ancient Near Eastern tradition; cf. Keel and Uehlinger). The second line of v. 12, however, still being praise of the benevolent Yahweh, has an imperfect or jussive verb (*yittēn*, "he gives"), thus voicing the hope of the community to benefit from all the good gifts of their Lord. The concluding line (v. 13) is composed of the fourth call to "Yahweh Sabaoth" and another (third) felicitation of "the person who trusts in you" (cf. vv. 5-6), indicating the finality of the song.

## Genre/Setting

As observed quite frequently, genre classifications depend a great deal on assumed settings. In our case the basic question seems to be what kind of community we may presuppose to have created and used our psalm. Preexilic and exilic religious assemblies, we understand, were quite distinct in Israel. The mere appearance of a royal figure would seem to point to a Jerusalemite and preexilic setting. Considering that Zion was made the state sanctuary as early as in Davidic times (2 Samuel 5–6), the early dating of the psalm is apparently undergirded and, indeed, upheld by some interpreters (e.g., Goulder, *Psalms;* Seybold, 331; Additional Bibliography, section A: old pilgrimage song for sanctuary of Dan, reused for Zion). As to the festival intended in Psalm 84, scholars usually opt for the autumn celebration of Tabernacles (cf. Lev 23:33-43).

On the other hand, several weighty arguments testify in favor of a late, i.e., exilic or postexilic, origin of Psalm 84. The historical background may have been like this: in preexilic times the sanctuary had been under royal jurisdiction; the people were excluded from state rituals and worshiped in local or regional holy places. Zion theology during the monarchy probably included some celebrations of invincibility of the holy capital (later of course remembered and adapted by congregations), as in Psalms 46 and 48, but had no notion of personal encounters with Yahweh by laypeople, as in our psalm. The sanctuary on Mount Zion became an international symbol of Yahweh's presence, and therefore a visible sign of identity for the faith community, only after the end of Judean statehood. The formation of individual piety within the community of Yahweh believers, as witnessed by Psalm 84, in itself is a sure sign of exilic and postexilic developments. Finally, the resurgence of hope for a Davidic restoration and a perfect messianic kingdom can be observed in many late OT texts (cf. Isa 9:5-6 [RSV 6-7]; 11:1-9; Ezekiel 34; Psalms 2; 110). Therefore intercessions for the king in the Psalter may be late, and in most cases probably come out of Jewish communities after statehood.

Psalm 84 may have been used during pilgrimages toward the geographical center of faith. Reliable notices of religious wanderings at festive times are absent from preexilic documents, and really available only from Babylonian or Persian times (cf. Safrai, *Wallfahrt*, 7-8; listing at Additional Bibliography, section B). Another possibility is that intense longing for the presence of Yahweh was articulated liturgically in "pilgrims'" hymns even in diaspora worship. In this case the procession toward the Holy City was a spiritual affair rather than a real pilgrimage, the situation being imagined in 1 Kgs 8:48-49 (an *exilic* or *postexilic* prayer): "If they . . . in the land of their enemies . . . pray to you toward their land . . . , the city . . . , and the house which I have built for your name; then hear you in heaven . . . their prayer and their supplication, and maintain their cause."

## Intention

The hymnic prayer tells us about expectations and aspirations of the dispersed community of Yahweh believers in regard to the Holy City, idealized as a token of God's helpful presence and in memory of the lost homeland. In keeping up strong ties with Zion and the sanctuary of Yahweh Sabaoth, the dispersed communities maintained their own faith and identity.

## Bibliography

P. Auffret, "Qu'elles sont aimable, tes demeures! Étude structurelle du psaume 84," *BZ* 38 (1994) 29-43; E. Baumann, "Strukturuntersuchungen im Psalter II," *ZAW* 62 (1950) 132-36; R. Benedetto, "Psalm 84," *Int* 51 (1997) 57-61; T. Booij, "Royal Words in Psalm LXXXIV,11," *VT* 36 (1986) 117-21; G. W. Buchanan, "The Courts of the Lord," *VT* 16 (1966) 231-32; T. E. Fretheim, "The Color of God: Israel's God-Talk and Life Experience," *Word & World* 6 (1986) 256-65; L. Grollenberg, "Post-Biblical *herut* in Ps 84,11?" *VT* 9 (1959) 311-12; J. Jeremias, "Lade und Zion," in *Probleme biblischer Theologie* (*Fest.* G. von Rad; ed. H. W. Wolff; Munich: Kaiser, 1971) 183-98; W. Jetter, "Erfreuliches über den Gottesdienst: Eine Betrachtung über den 84. Psalm," in *Das lebendige Wort* (*Fest.* G. Voigt; ed. H. Seidel, et al.; Berlin: Evangelische Verlagsanstalt,

1982) 11-25; O. Keel and C. Uehlinger, "Jahwe und die Sonnengottheit von Jerusalem," in *Ein Gott allein?* (ed. W. Dietrich, et al.; Freiburg: Universitätsverlag, 1994) 269-306; S. Loersch, "'Sie wandern von Kraft zu Kraft': Glück und Segnung auf dem Pilgerweg nach Ps 84:6-8," in *Sie wandern von Kraft zu Kraft (Fest. R. Lettmann;* ed. A. Angenendt, et al.; Kevelaer: Butzon & Bercker, 1993) 13-27; D. Rappel, "A Soldier's Prayer," *BM* 57 (1974) 194-201; S. J. P. K. Riekert, "The Meaning of Public Worship: An Exegetical and Revelational-Historical Study of Ps 84," *NGTT* 18 (1977) 186-88; A. Robinson, "Three Suggested Interpretations in Ps LXXXIV," *VT* 24 (1974) 378-81; G. Voigt, "Im Hause Gottes," *Lutherische Kirche in der Welt* 44 (1997) 9-31; E. Zenger, "Zur redaktionsgeschichtlichen Bedeutung der Korahpsalmen," in *Neue Wege der Psalmenforschung* (HBS 1; ed. K. Seybold, et al.; Freiburg: Herder, 1994) 175-98.

## Psalm 85:
## Communal Complaint; Communal Prayer

### Structure

|  | MT | NRSV |
|---|---|---|
| I. Superscription | 1 | - |
| II. Retrospect | 2-4 | 1-3 |
| III. Petition | 5-8 | 4-7 |
| IV. Wishes | 9-14 | 8-13 |
|     A. Request for divine orientation | 9 | 8 |
|     B. Blessing | 10-13 | 9-12 |
|     C. Final vote | 14 | 13 |

Psalm 85 is grouped with the Korah psalms, 84 and 87–88, by the redactor's SUPERSCRIPTION, a simplified version of that found with Psalm 84. The most elaborate heading of the group is with Psalm 88, and also that exemplar contains all the words of our present superscription. It thus seems to be the standard designation of the Korah psalms (cf. also ascriptions of Psalms 42; 44–49).

The overall structure of the liturgical song is characterized by theological reminiscences, communal petition, and an extensive passage of wishes for blessing. All of these elements occur in complaint liturgies (see "Introduction to Cultic Poetry," section 4B), but fully articulated INVOCATION, COMPLAINT, CONFESSION, AFFIRMATION OF CONFIDENCE, and IMPRECATION, all vital elements in complaints, are strangely absent from our psalm.

The RETROSPECT toward a more favorable past (vv. 2-4) constitutes an important part in some communal complaints: cf. 44:2-4 (RSV 1-3); 80:9-12 (RSV 8-11); 89:2-38 (RSV 1-37), also, differently, 83:10-13. While some of these parallel texts recount past history, occasionally along Dtr lines (cf. Psalms 44; 89), our song in regard to vocabulary, motives, and theology is on a priestly path: "You did forgive [lit. 'lift'] the iniquity of your people, you did pardon [lit. 'cover'] all their sin" (v. 3; MT has singular, LXX plural forms of *'āwōn*, "guilt," and *ḥaṭṭā't*, "sin"). Affirmations about the effectiveness of Yahweh's forgiving grace in the past are part and parcel of many historical-theological retrospects to make plausible Israel's survival (cf. Psalms 78; 106; Deuteronomy 32). But their language and imagery differ from Psalm 85. Those great accounts of sin and salvation usually employ narrational discourse, stating how Yahweh reacted with longanimity and love to the apostasies of his people. In v. 3, on the other hand, we meet the language of reflected Priestly theology. Similar statements of absolution from sin in the past occur, e.g., in Neh 9:17; Ezra 9:9, 16; also, exceptionally, in Ps 78:38. Still, the specific expressions of our psalm ("lift or carry" and "cover" sin, the typical Priestly expression being "atone" = *kîpper,* without object; cf. Lev 4:20, 26, 31, 35; 5:6, 10, 13, 16, 18, 24; etc.; cf. Janowski, *Sühne;* listing at Additional Bibliography, section B) are not too frequent in Priestly or in psalm literature (Ps 32:1, 5; Exod 28:38; 32:32; 34:7; "carry guilt" for others sometimes signifies "atone for"; cf., however, Lev 10:17; 16:22; Janowski, *Sühne,* 207-8). Thus direct dependence on professional priests is unlikely. Liturgical use in community worship is a separate matter. Reflexes of such use may be identified in formulaic petitions like "Lift my sin" (cf. Gen 50:17; Exod 10:17; 1 Sam 15:25) or expressions of "absolving guilt" (using the verb *slḥ;* cf. Jer 31:34; 33:8; 36:3; Pss 25:11; 103:3). Together with a statement of Yahweh's long-standing benevolence over against Israel (v. 2; cf. postexilic usage: *šûb šĕbît* or *šûb šĕbût,* "restore the fortunes," esp. in the book of Jeremiah: Jer 29:14; 30:3, 18; 31:23; 32:44; 33:7, 11; Ezek 16:53; Ps 53:7 [RSV 6]; 126:1, 4) and another affirmation of a historical end to God's wrath (v. 4; cf. mainly prophetic passages: Isa 9:18 [RSV 19]; 10:6; 13:9, 13; Ezek 7:19; 22:21, 31; Zeph 1:15, 18; Ps 90:9), v. 3 constitutes a theological triad interpreting past history under aspects of Yahweh's benevolence (cf. *rṣh,* "to like, accept"; cf. 2 Sam 24:23; Isa 42:1; Jer 14:10, 12; Lev 1:4; 7:18; H. M. Barstad, *TWAT* VII, 640-52), forgiveness, and restraint. There is a meditative and instructional air around this retrospective introduction to our psalm. A proper INVOCATION is reduced to the simple appellation "Yahweh," put into second place in the first line, as in Ps 89:2 (RSV 1); cf. Elohim as the opening call in 44:2 (RSV 1); 83:2 (RSV 1).

The PETITION (vv. 5-8) is, line after line, emphatically communitarian: every single plea comes from the worshiping congregation aiming at Yahweh's action in Israel's favor ("turn to *us,* God of *our* salvation," v. 5a, etc.; cf. 44:25-27 [RSV 24-26]; 90:13-15; 33:20-22; J. Scharbert, "Das 'Wir' "; listing at "Introduction to Psalms"). The concentration of first-person singular possessive suffixes is a sure sign of the prayer being rooted in communal practice. Where else than in common worship could the "we" group be pronounced so forcefully? (→ Psalms 44; 80; 90; 95; 103).

Of course, the context of petition is irritating; it is not reconcilable with literary logic. The opening retrospective stated God's overwhelming benignity and forgiveness. The petition in a plaintive way, and spiced with urging, reproachful rhetorical questions (vv. 6-7a), talks about Yahweh's anger against his people and ongoing castigations that the petitioner hopes can be ended by this joint intervention. The problem is, even considering the liturgical character of the psalm, that no complaint has prepared for such petitionary prayer. Furthermore, the petition itself, in contradistinction to, e.g., Psalms 44 and 89, remains very general, abstract, and patterned by standard theological vocabulary: each line has a number of typical parallels in Hebrew Scripture, and some liturgical formulas can easily be detected in this material (*v. 5:* 6:5 [RSV 4]; 71:20; 80:15 [RSV 14]; 90:13; Isa 63:17; *v. 6:* Pss 60:3 [RSV 1]; 79:5; 89:47 [RSV 46]; 1 Kgs 8:46; Ezra 9:14; Isa 12:1; 64:8; *v. 7:* Pss 6:5 [RSV 4]; 71:20; 80:15 [RSV 14]; 90:15; *v. 8:* Pss 50:23; 59:11 [RSV 10]; 90:16; 91:16; Exod 33:18; Deut 5:24). In other words, the petition in our psalm is very generalized, does not refer back to special complaints, and is not followed by an imprecation against enemies, as is often the case with true communal complaints (cf. Psalms 44; 74; 79; 80; 81; 89). Rather, it leans toward a meditative, theologically motivated intervention with Yahweh, like 90:13-17, supposedly before the general background of misery and exploitation in exilic or postexilic times.

The third section of our psalm is the most important, because RETROSPECT and PETITION now find their liturgical conclusion. Many exegetes consider vv. 9-14 a kind of divine oracle communicated to the community by a prophetic figure (thus Gunkel, 374; Mowinckel, *PsSt* III, 54-59). If we refrain from identifying "cultic prophets" with "messenger prophets" of the prophetic canon, we are left with the solid insight that a liturgist of some sort is asking for and communicating Yahweh's will, possibly even on the basis of written Torah (cf. Psalms 12; 60; 81; 91; 95; differently also Johnson, *Prophet;* listing at "Introduction to Psalms"). V. 9 states the issue: "I should like to hear what God has to say." Similar requests are reported (by late Priestly transmitters of tradition) in episodes of Mosaic times. The REQUEST FOR DIVINE ORIENTATION occurs literally in Num 9:8. Situations of equal portent are mentioned in Lev 24:10-16; Num 15:32-36. In moments of ethical or cultic uncertainty the congregation — through its leader, liturgist, or scribe — would ask for the will of Yahweh, possibly by consulting Scripture. Thus there is no "watching out" on prophetic towers (Gunkel, et al., point to this image of Hab 2:1) hinted at in the Psalms, but strict attention to what "God is saying" through Scripture (note the importance of *dibber,* "speak," in both the relevant psalm texts and the examples from the Moses tradition, and the absence of all vocabulary of ecstatic, visionary, or dream revelation). One important type of old prophetic figures is called *hōzeh,* "visionary" (cf. 1 Sam 9:9), indicating the prevalence of this kind of divine communication. We do not learn, in preexilic literature, of a parallel designation "auditioner" of the divine word. In any case the Psalms are free of any vestiges that might refer to what we consider prophecy proper (→ Psalms 12; 50; 75; 81).

This observation is confirmed not only by the formulation of v. 9, but also by the structure and contents of vv. 10-13. No trace of "prophetic" language can be detected, and there is certainly no comparable introductory formula known from prophetic books (e.g., "thus says Yahweh"; "the word of Yahweh came to me"; "saying of Yahweh"; etc.). The passage employs kerygmatic and sapiental language, and it seems to be composed of quotations from different sources. Vv. 10 and 13 apparently once formed a coherent statement, confirming the basic benevolence of Yahweh to the "land" and people of Israel. Introduced by the exclamation *'ak,* "yes" (cf. 39:6-7 [RSV 5-6]; 62:2-10 [RSV 1-9]; 69:7, 19

129

[RSV 6, 18]), which here highlights a generally accepted truth, the two lines give a comforting assurance of the unwavering presence of Yahweh, spoken by or in the name of the congregation (cf. "*our* land" in both verses). "His help is near his faithful" (v. 10a; cf. 34:19 [RSV 18]; 75:2 [RSV 1]; 119:151; 145:18; Isa 50:8; 55:6) reflects a principle of faith articulated in worship. The consequence of Yahweh's solidarity with his congregation is expected to be a full blessing of the land and good harvests (v. 13; cf. Pss 34:11 [RSV 10]), "the land yields [or 'does not yield'] its produce" (v. 13b) being a colloquial phrase used in many literary layers (cf. Lev 26:4, 20; Deut 11:17; Ezek 34:27; Hag 1:10; Zech 8:12; Pss 67:7 [RSV 6]). Significantly, in v. 13 the expression is changed to speak about "*our* land," to correspond with v. 10. In the light of these two personalized affirmations about the land, vv. 11-12, with their rhythmic, objective, sapiential collocations, clearly stand out as a separate element, used by the congregation or the liturgist to reinforce their message. While the framing lines make affirmations about Yahweh himself, culminating with calling his name in v. 13a, now all of a sudden four different entities appear, as if they were divine impersonations. In fact, ḥesed, 'ĕmet, ṣedeq, and šālôm are sometimes mentioned in the Psalms as autonomous, almost mythological, figures (cf., e.g., 40:12 [RSV 11]; 57:4 [RSV 3]; 89:15 [RSV 14]; 91:4; 97:2; 119:165; N. Glueck, Ḥesed in the Bible (ed. E. L. Epstein; tr. A. Gottschalk; Cincinnati: Hebrew Union College Press, 1967; T. B. Dozeman, JBL 108 [1989] 207-23; and the articles in TDOT/TWAT and THAT; also J. S. Kselman, ABD II, 1084-86). Our vv. 11-12 are one of the most vivid and beautiful personifications of the fundamental life-preserving powers according to ancient Near Eastern world concepts (cf. W. Eisenbeis, Die Wurzel šalom im Alten Testament [BZAW 113; Berlin: de Gruyter, 1969]; J. Assmann, Ma'at: Gerechtigkeit und Unsterblichkeit im Alten Ägypten [Munich: Carl Hanser, 1990]). Two pairs of religious world powers meet and kiss (v. 11). They are by no means diametrically opposed powers. In fact, they function complementarily and often almost synonymously (see passages cited above). But everybody knows how difficult it may be to bring together "solidarity" and "truth," "justice" and "peace" under one roof and into one group of people. There are social distinctions and interests involved, e.g., the serious tension between familial solidarity, which supports every member with what he or she needs, and anonymous justice, which is to distribute the means of life evenly, without considering the person. So the happy unification of interpersonal values and general social requirements must be proverbial for the highest state of bliss and the greatest blessing that a community may encounter. Consequently, v. 11 in itself may be a popular saying to describe the perfect state of affairs that could come about under the auspices of the four ancient Near Eastern "graces." V. 12, then, may well be a further reflection on the preceding line, singling out 'ĕmet and ṣedeq as earthly and heavenly powers. Not that the other two "divine" qualities are less important. But the two now in focus (v. 12) are in themselves a celebrated couple (cf. 45:5 [RSV 4]; 119:142, 160; slightly modified in 19:10 [RSV 9]; 111:7) although the pairing of ḥesed and 'ĕmet overwhelmingly outnumbers our present combination. The very last verse, 14, after all, has only ṣedeq left of the quadruplet of divine and ethical powers. In this manner the wish section vv. 9-14 starts out with *šālôm* and ends with *ṣedeq*. This final emphasis on justice, also clad in a personalizing image of a herald accompanying Yahweh, reveals the thrust of this part and of the whole psalm.

## Genre

As noticed before, the psalm has some characteristics of COMMUNAL COM-PLAINT, while others are missing. With no concrete emergency alluded to, our text emphasizes wishful PRAYER. A lot of tradition is in the background: consciousness of Yahweh's benevolent actions in the past, of Israel's deviations from his will, and a necessity to improve the general situation of the community best expressed in v. 7a: "Don't you want to come back and let us live again?" The gist of the psalm is a plea for divine support. Reflections on "peace" and "justice" (vv. 9-14) prove not so much a covenant background but the general framework of ancient Near Eastern theological thinking. Divine powers cooperating with the supreme Deity are directly responsible for the community's well-being. In this regard the psalm could also be labeled a conjuration of helpful powers. As to possible "prophetic" influences, we have to take exception with traditional views: the request for God's revelation and offer of prayer occur within the bounds of contemporary worship, i.e., in liturgical and scriptural molds.

## Setting

The community behind the psalm is one dedicated loyally to Yahweh (cf. the self-designations "your people," v. 7b; "his faithful," v. 9c; "those who fear him," v. 10a). It is hearkening to the past and probably to Scripture in order to recognize the will of its God. And it is pleading for his sustained help. All these features point to the worship of early Jewish congregations in the sixth or fifth centuries B.C.E. as the original setting.

## Intention

Like many other psalms of the epoch, this communal prayer served the spiritual and material needs of the marginalized Jewish community, trying to overcome burdensome alienations and deviations from the God of all blessings.

## Bibliography

E. Beaucamp, "L'heure d'une réconciliation totale et universelle," *BVC* 24 (1958) 68-79; J. Becker, *Israel deutet seine Psalmen* (SBS 18; Stuttgart: Katholisches Bibelwerk, 1966) 58-59; J. M. Bracke, "Sub sebut: A Reappraisal," *ZAW* 97 (1985) 233-44; E. Castro, "God's Justice: Promise and Challenge," *Ecumenical Review* 37 (1985) 471-505; J. Ebach, "Was anders war, kann anders werden," *Junge Kirche* 56 (1995) 510-12; idem,

"'Gerechtigkeit und Frieden küssen sich' oder 'Gerechtigkeit und Frieden kämpfen' (Ps 85,11)," in *Gott an den Rändern* (ed. U. Bail, et al.; Gütersloh: Gütersloher Verlagshaus, 1996) 42-52; H. Falcke, "'Wenn Gerechtigkeit und Friede sich küssen," *Junge Kirche* 58 (1997) 395-97; E. S. Gerstenberger, "Gerechtigkeit und Frieden umarmen sich," *Dokumentationsdienst der Konferenz Europäischer Kirchen* 13 (1988) 6-12 (Eng.: *Documentation Service of the Conference of European Churches* 13 [1988] 7-13); N. Hoffmann, "Gerechtigkeit und Frieden küssen sich (Psalm 85,11)," *Dimensionen des Glaubens* 57 (1981) 15-21; J. S. Kselman, "A Note on Psalm 85:9-10," *CBQ* 46 (1984) 23-27; L. Kunz, "Psalm 85 als westorientalischer Nomos," *TGl* 67 (1977) 373-80; E. Lipiński, "Ps. 85: Le salut est proche," *Assemblées du Seigneur* 5 (1966) 24-31; O. Loretz, "Ugaritisch *tbn* und hebräisch *twb* 'Regen' — Regenrituale beim Neujahrsfest in Kanaan und Israel (Ps 85; 126)," *UF* 21 (1990) 247-58; D. J. McCarthy, "Psalm 85 and the Meaning of Peace," *Way* 22 (1982) 3-9; R. de Menezes, "Covenant, Law, and Cult in Relation to Righteousness," *Indian Journal of Theology* 26 (1977) 111-31; R. Meynet, "L'enfant de l'amour (Ps 85)," *NRT* 112 (1990) 843-58; S. Mowinckel, *PsSt* III, 54-59; C. R. Padilla, "The Fruit of Justice Will Be Peace," *Transformation* 2 (1985) 2-4; S. Pagán, "And Peace Will Be Multiplied unto Your Children," in *Conflict and Context* (ed. M. Branson and C. Padilla; Grand Rapids: Eerdmans, 1986) 178-84; B. Renaud, "Le psaume 85 et son caractère théophanique," in *Ouvrir les Écritures* (*Fest.* P. Beauchamp; ed. P. Bovati; Paris: Cerf, 1995) 133-49; J. T. E. Renner, "Thoughts of Peace and Not of War," *Lutheran Theological Journal* 19 (1985) 65-72; C. Thoma, "Gerechtigkeit und Frieden in jüdisch-rabbinischer Optik," *Verbum Societatis Verbi Domini* 39 (1998) 161-64; C. Trautmann, "La citation du Psaume 85 (84:11-12) et ses commentaires dans la Pistis Sophia," *RHPR* 59 (1979) 551-57; Z. Rokay, "Die Datierung des Psalms 85," *ZKT* 113 (1991) 52-61; C. C. Twombly, "Redemptive History and the Shaping of the Affections," *Crux* 20 (1984) 21-26; R. L. Underwood, "The Presence of God in Pastoral Care Ministry," *Austin Seminary Bulletin* (Faculty Edition) 101 (1985) 5-14; St. Virgulin, "'Ritorna . . . e noi ritorneremo!' (Salmi 85 e 126)," *Parola Spirito e Vita* 22 (1990) 73-84.

# Psalm 86:
## Individual Complaint, Congregational Prayer

### *Structure*

|  | MT | NRSV |
|---|---|---|
| I. Superscription | 1a | - |
| II. Initial plea | 1b-7 | 1-7 |
| III. Hymn | 8-10 | 8-10 |
| IV. Petition | 11 | 11 |
| V. Thanksgiving | 12-13 | 12-13 |
| VI. Complaint | 14 | 14 |
| VII. Affirmation of confidence | 15 | 15 |
| VIII. Petition | 16-17b | 16-17b |
| IX. Praise (thanksgiving) | 17c | 17c |

"A prayer of [or 'for, according to'] David" is a very simple SUPERSCRIP-
TION that strangely enough, among so many psalms attributed to the famous
singer-king, has only one exact parallel (Psalm 17; cf. Psalm 142). "Prayer"
(těpillāh) as a redactional designation of psalms in general is extremely rare
(only two more occurrences, Psalms 90 and 102). The collectors and editors of
the Psalter by far preferred music-technical or literal classifications of the
texts. If the meaning of těpillāh is really almost identical with "petition" (see
Psalm 17), then the redactor at this point probably visualized David in a situation calling for prayer, as the thirteen "historical" superscriptions do (see
Psalms 3; 7; 18; 34; 51; etc.). A "David" psalm in the middle of "Korah" songs
(see Psalms 85; 87) poses a puzzle. Perhaps this "intercalation" does not testify so much to rational composition of psalm collections but to chance junc-
tions of texts for practical purposes (against Zenger, "Bedeutung"; listing at
Psalm 84).

The psalm itself is composed of a mixture of elements apparently taken
from complaint and thanksgiving rituals. The INITIAL PLEA seems overstretched; the COMPLAINT is fairly underdeveloped; the formal PETITION occurs
twice (which is not unusual in complaint ceremonies) with specific (not customary) contents; the PRAISE and a special HYMN to the one, exclusive Yahweh
have an erratic air in the individual complaint liturgy.

The INITIAL PLEA to be admitted to an audience with Yahweh (cf. explicit
demands to be heard in vv. 1b and 6) extends from v. 1b until v. 7, covering
seven poetic lines. V. 2 is overcrowded with words and should be counted as
two lines to make a total of eight for this introduction. The sheer length of this
liturgical element in comparison with the other ones listed above, together with
the fact that the initial plea here includes some complaining and some more inclusive petitioning, leads us to speculate whether vv. 1b-7 were a complete
prayer at one time. The opening part of an individual complaint, asking for admission to the presence of the Lord, normally comprises two to four lines of
pleas, sometimes interspersed with fragments of other elements (cf. 5:2-4 [RSV
1-3]; 6:2-4 [RSV 1-3]; 17:1-2; 35:1-3; 88:2-3 [RSV 1-2]; etc.; see "Introduction to Cultic Poetry," section 4B).

The vocabulary of vv. 1b-7 for the most part is that of true complaint
psalms; note, e.g., the verbs in the imperative mood: "Incline your ear" (v. 1b:
cf. 17:6; 31:3 [RSV 2]; 71:2; 88:3 [RSV 2]; 102:3 [RSV 2] — exclusively in individual complaints); "protect my life" (v. 2a: cf. 16:1; 17:8; 25:20; 140:5
[RSV 4]; 141:9 — generalized petition); "save your servant" (v. 2b: cf. a
shorter version: "save me" in 3:8 [RSV 7]; 6:5 [RSV 4]; 7:2 [RSV 1]; etc.; 17
times in the Psalter — generalized petition); "have mercy on me" (v. 3a: cf. 4:2
[RSV 1]; 6:3 [RSV 2]; 9:14 [RSV 13]; etc.; 19 times in the Psalter); "make your
servant rejoice" (v. 4a: Piel singular imperative in Hebrew Scripture; closest
parallels are Qal plural imperatives, e.g., 32:11; 97:12: "rejoice"); "listen to
me" (v. 6a: cf. 5:2 [RSV 1]; 17:1; 39:13 [RSV 12], etc., 11 times in the Psalter);
"pay attention to the voice of my supplication" (v. 6b: cf. 5:3 [RSV 2]; 17:1;
55:3 [RSV 2]; 61:2 [RSV 1]; 142:7 [RSV 6]). The prevalence of standard expressions and the variety of outlooks, or rooting in different elements, suggest a
mixture of formal traditions.

If one looks at the microstructure of vv. 1b-7, the impression of mingling forms is confirmed. Most of the imperatives mentioned above are followed by an explicative *kî* phrase. Thus the first four lines with four imperative pleas all have their motive clause, with the exception of v. 2b, which suffers from a textual problem. The inserted "you are my God" interrupts the meaningful phrase "Save your servant who is relying on you," and a conjunctive *kî* would fit well into this (eighth) line of initial plea. The affirmation "You are my God" on the other hand recurs in vv. 5 and 15 (cf. also v. 10). It would make some liturgical sense, to be sure, to have an exclamation like this repeated in pivotal places of worship. Most commentators, however, consider some misplacement and put the words in front or at the end of v. 3, because the present location in the middle of a coherent plea is too awkward, even in regard to liturgy. A possible reason for repeating "you are my God" at the beginning of the psalm could be the relative weakness of its INVOCATION, which is restricted to naming "Yahweh" in v. 1b and "my Lord" in v. 3a, a rather poor introductory appellation. The *kî* phrases in vv. 1b-4 all refer to the condition of the suppliant, yet in most formulaic language and quite schematized contents. "I am oppressed and poor" (v. 1c) is a common expression in the Psalms, reflecting in some way the social and economic depression the community was experiencing at the time (cf. 25:15; 40:18 [RSV 17]; 69:30 [RSV 29]; Gerstenberger, *TWAT* VI, 247-70). "I am a faithful one" (v. 2a) stresses integration in the community of those loyal to Yahweh (cf. singular: 4:4 [RSV 3]; 12:2 [RSV 1]; 18:26 [RSV 25]; 32:6; mostly plural: 30:5 [RSV 4]; 52:11 [RSV 9]; 79:2; 85:9 [RSV 8]; etc.). "I am calling to you all day long" (v. 3b: cf. 3:5 [RSV 4]; 22:3, 7 [RSV 2, 6]; 28:1; 30:9 [RSV 8]; 88:10 [RSV 9]; 141:1; etc.) is a description of praying. "I raise my longings to you" is literally translated; in our Bibles it is often "I lift up my soul" (v. 4b: cf. 25:1; 143:8). The first colon of each of these lines calls on Yahweh for help, the second colon gives a short motivation for each request. This pattern of prayer is found in several individual complaints (cf. 6:3 [RSV 2]; 56:2 [RSV 1]; 57:2 [RSV 1]; 69:2 [RSV 1]), but a higher concentration of such phrases occurs in the acrostic 25:16-21, a section that also features four *kî* clauses (25:16, 19-21; also vv. 5-6) of the type discussed above. This last psalm has some more affinities to our prayer (vocabulary, imagery, etc.); those compositional likenesses may be all the more revealing. The didactic Psalm 119 sometimes also has petitions followed by motive clauses with *kî:* cf. 119:22, 35, 39, 45, 77, 153, 173.

After the cluster of four introductory pleas (vv. 2-4), vv. 6-7 go on to articulate the same kind of entreaties with a typical pair of imperatives, as pointed out above (v. 6ab), combined with a description of praying (v. 7a). Even a motivational *kî* phrase follows these three units, the difference from the abovementioned motive clauses being that v. 7b is extremely short and affirms a hoped-for action of God ("you will answer me"), instead of telling reasons from the life of the suppliant for approaching Yahweh. We may surmise, therefore, that vv. 6-7 do not intimately belong to the enumeration of pleas in vv. 1-4 but constitute a subunit of some sort. This impression receives support from the fact that a different kind of *kî* phrase intervenes in v. 5. Making a hymnic assertion directed to Yahweh himself ("You, Lord, are good and merciful," v. 5a), it should not be regarded as a motive clause. Rather, this *kî* belongs in the category of exclamations that mark a real hymn, a shout of praise possibly sung by the congregation (cf. Crüsemann, *Studien,* 32-35; listing at "Introduction to Cultic Poetry"). Very importantly, such phrases recur four more times in our psalm, *kî* missing only in one instance (vv. 10, 13, [15], 17c). The other way around: five times in our psalm a hymnic line enters the scene, obviously highlighting a liturgical juncture. One is reminded, in a way, of the hymnic fragments interspersed in the book of Amos (cf. Am 4:13; 5:8-9; 9:5-6). In our case, the hymnic lines are in the direct-address form and seem partially to play on well-known liturgical formulas celebrating the greatness and kindness of Yahweh (see below). As to Psalm 86, these little hymns seem to be the very pillars of the prayer.

V. 5 probably functions as an interim line, or an intermediate congregational song, after four verses of individual pleading. The qualities of Yahweh are extolled with reference to "those who call to you" (v. 5b). *qr',* "to call to," is a technical term for making petition (v. 3b; cf. 3:5 [RSV 4]; 17:6; 28:1; 55:17 [RSV 16]; 61:3 [RSV 2]; etc.). V. 5 responds to vv. 1-4 by congregational antiphonal praise. The qualities of forgiveness and lovingkindness are lauded in three expressions (*ṭôb, sallāḥ, rab ḥesed:* "good, forgiving, very steadfast," respectively). The adjective *sallāḥ* here is a hapax legomenon in Hebrew Scripture, but the verb is present in 25:11 and 103:3 (frequent in Dtr layers like 1 Kgs 8:30-50; cf. also Num 14:19-20; 30:6, 9, 13).The other two designations used of Yahweh are liturgical in character (*ṭôb:* cf. Pss 118:1, 29; 119:68; 135:3; 136:1; etc.; *rab ḥesed:* cf. v. 15; 69:14 [RSV 13]; 103:8; 106:7; 145:8). The latter attribution is firmly rooted in the great liturgical (and confessional-instructional) formula: "You, Yahweh, are a God who is merciful and gracious, slow to anger and abounding in solidarity and trust" (cf. Exod 34:6; Num 14:18; Neh 9:17; Pss 103:8; 145:8; Jonah 4:2; variations of this basic praising confession include Pss 25:8; 116:5). This praise formula is quite frequent in Hebrew Scripture, and it proves to have been very stable in its formulation. Therefore we may conclude that it has been, at some point, one of the most important liturgical elements (cf. Spieckermann). V. 5, then, may be leaning on this hallowed articulation of faith, which, however, in most passages quoted above appears in neutral, third-person forms, proclaiming Yahweh's kindness to an audience. As already stated, all hymnic phrases in Psalm 86 are in the second person singular, sung as prayer hymns by a liturgist or, more probably, by all the congregation.

The next element that clearly stands out in our psalm is a "doctrinaire" HYMN about Yahweh's unique and exclusive power over other deities and peoples (vv. 8-10). It may be called a "Yahweh-alone song" along the lines of Deuteronomy and Second Isaiah. The three poetic lines concerned give stereotyped contents in varying linguistic forms. V. 8 offers two exclamations of astonishment and reverence of the type: "There is no God like you" (2 Sam 7:22; 1 Kgs 8:23; Jer 10:6-7). A similar form is the rhetorical question: "Who is like you?" (Pss 35:10; 71:19; 89:9 [RSV 8]; Exod 15:11; Mic 7:18), from which derives the personal name Micha(yahu). Both linguistic types may originally have come out of contest situations. But the expressions of incomparability and supreme authority of Yahweh have become statements of faith with enormous weight within the tradition of Israel (cf. Johannes, *Unvergleichlichkeitsformulierungen;* listing at "Introduction to Cultic Poetry"). The middle line of our Yahweh hymn (v. 9) is prosaic in character and oversize. Submission of foreign people was originally not a theme in individual complaints, but with the upcoming confessional community in the sixth century B.C.E. in an imperial context this motif could be included in all kinds of prayers, even individual ones (cf. 59:6 [RSV 5]; 94:10; 102:16 [RSV 15]). A flat statement of Yahweh having created all nations (v. 9a) is rare in the Hebrew Bible; at best the texts speak only of their pacification and salvation (v. 9bc; cf. Isa 2:1-5; Pss 102:16 [RSV 15]).

"You are great" (v. 10a) is part of the standard affirmations in ancient Near Eastern worship (cf. Deut 10:17; Jer 10:6; Ps 48:2 [RSV 1]; 95:3; 147:5; etc.; R. Mosis, *TWAT* I, 944-51). "You alone are God" (v. 10b) may be a reflex from Dtr theology, perhaps from its literature (2 Kgs 19:19). Yet the affirmation has spread through many layers (cf. Isa 2:11, 17; 37:16, 20; Neh 9:6), being present also in the Psalms: Pss 72:18; 83:19 (RSV 18); 136:4; 148:13. The special hymnic line v. 10 extolling this time the uncomparable power of Yahweh fits well with the preceding hymnic affirmations and constitutes a high and final point of that little section. V. 5 emphasized Yahweh's benevolence; v. 10 adds his overwhelming power and exclusiveness.

V. 11, clearly a petitionary line, again oversize, goes back to personal prayer for divine guidance in the style of Psalm 119 (*hôrēnî,* "teach me"; cf. 119:33-40; the root *yrh* is behind *tôrāh,* too; does our v. 11 also presuppose Torah instruction?). We are on sapiential grounds with this very reduced and abstract PETITION; that much is clear. No emergency situation is detectable, and there is hardly any correspondence with the initial pleas of vv. 1-4, which still suggest some danger, guilt, and salvation.

The following THANKSGIVING (vv. 12-13) can be understood either as an anticipated jubilation because of imminent salvation or as a thanksgiving vow spoken in times of tribulation (cf. 22:23-27 [RSV 22-26]). In the latter case the perfect of v. 13b ("you delivered me from the deep netherworld") should be understood as the coming event of rescue. Parallel affirmations are integral parts, of course, of true thanksgiving songs; cf. 116:8, 17; 118:21; Jonah 2:7, 10 (RSV 6, 9). If our psalm is somewhat remote from concrete complaint rituals for a suffering individual (see "Introduction to Cultic Poetry," section 4B; Gerstenberger, *Mensch*), then inclusion of general thanksgiving elements is not too strange a phenomenon. The *kî* phrase in v. 13 differs from those in vv. 5, 10, 15, 17c in that it does not have an emphatic "you" address or lengthy honorary attributions, but one nominal and one verbal clause, the latter praising personal salvation. Still, it does serve the same ends as the other phrases, giving the contents of hymnic adoration and closing a subsection of the psalm.

A new round of COMPLAINT, AFFIRMATION OF CONFIDENCE, PETITION with urgent IMPRECATION, and PRAISE (or VOW TO GIVE THANKS) develops from v. 14 through v. 17. The individual parts of this setup are authentic enough to let the commentators speak either of a second psalm or a characteristic (cf. Psalms 22 and 31) repetition of the complaint ceremony (cf. Gunkel, Kraus, et al.). We note a much clearer concept of being threatened by enemies (v. 14) than recognizable in vv. 1-13, the full liturgical formula about an unbelievably gracious and patient God (v. 15) already mentioned above, and a concise petition using parts of the initial plea (v. 16; cf. vv. 3a, 2b), but dedicating two cola to a new thought: "Show me a sign of your favor, that my haters will realize it and be put to shame" (v. 17ab). Barré ("Parallel") wants to explain this sequence by painting a relationship of suzerain and vassal, or of covenant ties between Yahweh and Israel. It is probably more adequate to think of simple anthropological patterns of asking and receiving, gift and countergift, religious loyalty and disloyalty than of specific treaty conditions.

The final *kî* phrase with an assertion about Yahweh's saving and forgiving interventions puts an end to a somewhat enigmatic individual complaint psalm.

## Genre/Setting

Psalms showing a mixture of compositional elements, superseding, as it were, liturgically realistic passages and making transparent theological concerns and social structures of later Jewish community life, must be exilic or postexilic. Commentators are almost unanimous that Psalm 86 is a product of the late OT period. Its genre, then, is probably LITURGICAL PRAYER on the basis of older INDIVIDUAL COMPLAINT elements and patterns. They are visibly adapted, however, to Jewish community life in the epoch of, let us say, the Persian Empire. Emphasis on "Yahweh alone" would support this view, as do the traces of liturgical forms, individual piety within the congregation (cf. the motifs of trust, servant, supplication), grade of theological abstraction, etc.

The text lets transpire a vivid liturgical sequence of personal petitions and communal responses, among which the hymnic lines vv. 5, 10, 13, 15 are most important. The praising unit vv. 8-10 does include such a hymnic line. The passage may have been a communal part altogether.

## Intention

The principal goals are the general adoration of Yahweh in community worship and with active participation of members and the general improvement of spiritual and material welfare under the eyes of Yahweh. The message resounds in Rev 15:4.

## Bibliography

F. Asensio, "El eje ki en el movimiento progressivo del Salmo 86," *Gregorianum* 56 (1975) 527-43; idem, "El protagonismo del 'Hombre-Hijo del Hombre' dek -salmo 86," *EstBib* 41 (1983) 17-51; P. Auffret, "Essai sur la structure littéraire du Psaume LXXXVI," *VT* 29 (1979) 385-402; M. L. Barré, "A Cuneiform Parallel to Ps 86:16-17 and Mic 7:16-17," *JBL* 101 (1982) 271-75; idem, "The Formulaic Pair *ṭwb (w)ḥsd* in the

Psalter," *ZAW* 98 (1986) 100-105; G. Giavini, "La struttura letteraria del Salmo 86 (85),"
*RivB* 14 (1966) 455-58; W. E. March, "Psalm 86: When Love Is Not Enough," *Austin
Seminary Bulletin*, Faculty Edition 105 (1990) 17-25; C. S. Rademaker, "Erasmus and
the Psalms: His Commentary on Psalm 86 (85)," in *Erasmus of Rotterdam, the Man and
the Scholar* (ed. J. Weiland; Leiden/New York: Brill, 1988) 187-94; R. Ribera-Marin,
"Significat d'un poema antologic: Salm 86," in *Tradició i traducció de la paraula* (ed.
F. Raurell, et al.; Montserrat: Associació Bíblica de Catalunya, 1993) 97-115; A. M.
Serra, "Appunti critici sul Salm 86 (85)," *RivB* 16 (1968) 229-46; H. Spieckermann,
"'Barmherzig und gnädig ist der Herr . . . ,'" *ZAW* 102 (1990) 1-18; J. Vorndran, "Alle
Völker werden kommen" (Diss. Münster, 2000); D. Zeller, "Gott nennen an einem
Beispiel aus dem Psalter," in *Gott nennen: Phänomenologische Zugänge* (ed. B. Casper;
Freiburg/Munich: Karl Alber, 1981) 13-34.


# Psalm 87:
# Admission Pronouncement; Zion Hymn

## Text

Partly because of faulty transmission, the text is obscure in several places, notably in vv. 1 and 7. But the general contours of a hymn centering on Zion and the
foreign nations are clearly recognizable.


## Structure

|  | MT | NRSV |
|---|---|---|
| I. Superscription | 1a | - |
| II. Praise of Zion | 1b-3 | 1-3 |
| III. Laudation | 4 | 4 |
| IV. Confirmation of status | 5-7 | 5-7 |

The SUPERSCRIPTION in v. 1a carries a standard attribution to the "sons
of Korah" (cf. Psalm 84), the most frequent liturgical classification (*mizmôr,*
"song," 57 times in the Psalter, used only in headings and never outside the
book of Psalms; cf. Psalms 3; 15), and the additional musical or liturgical designation *šîr,* "song." This last label has been affixed by Hebrew redactors to
thirty-one psalms (cf. Psalms 30; 120–134). From our historical distance we
hardly are able to understand the exact meaning of all the technical terms in
psalm superscriptions (cf. Sendrey, *Music;* Seidel, *Musik*).
The rest of v. 1 is problematic. It could be either a fragment of a superscription, possibly indicating a tune, as in the headings of Psalms 22; 56–60;
etc., or an erratic introductory proclamation, or a misplaced part of the text that
actually should follow v. 2. As the text stands, vv. 2-3 are coherent, and v. 1b
may be aligned to them. But neither way of joining the two and a half lines can
produce a proper hymnic introduction (e.g., summons to praise or laudatory ex-

clamations). If we could reconstruct v. 1b to say: "Yahweh has founded his house on holy mountains," the continuation of v. 2 would be more plausible and more in line with hymnic patterns. The participle of v. 2a makes a clumsy opening of a hymn. Be that as it may, the PRAISE OF ZION is first articulated by a description of Yahweh's predilection for his Jerusalem sanctuary, second (v. 3; cf. v. 7b) in a direct-address praise of the "city of God," which, of course, antedates Israelite occupation by centuries (cf. Otto, *Jerusalem*, 21-41; listing at Additional Bibliography, section B). Direct praise of a (female) city is possible in such hymns ("O city of God"; direct address, e.g., Isa 62:1-9; Pss 122:2; 137:5-6; cf. personalized Jerusalem speaking in Lam 1:18-22, etc.); it has antecedents in Sumero-Akkadian hymnology (cf. Dobbs-Allsopp, *Weep;* Bibliography of Psalm 74; → Lamentations).

The LAUDATION of foreign nations (v. 4), offered in the first person by an unnamed speaker, is an extraordinary announcement. No equal formulation can be found in Hebrew Scripture. Who is speaking? According to the context the subject of the phrase could be Jerusalem or Yahweh communicating through a liturgist or another representative. The wording of v. 4a favors the first possibility, the city saying: "I consider Rahab and Babel my acquaintances," which certainly has some historical truth to it. Thus v. 4 is the pivotal line in our short psalm, giving voice to Jerusalem herself. Perhaps the end of the extremely long line ("this one was born there") has been added accidentally, the words originally belonging only to vv. 5 and 6 (lack of grammatical correspondence in v. 4). In this case v. 4 would list only the presence and good standing in Jerusalem of Egyptians, Babylonians, Philistines, and people from Tyre and Cush, without yet referring to their "birthrights." After this declaration from the side of the city herself, outward reaction (v. 5) confirms and explains her international status. Anonymous and indeterminate voices, as if coming from a great crowd, pronounce a legal conclusion: if the city acknowledges strangers, this amounts to including them among the citizens; this is articulated by the unique phrase: "To Zion will be said: everyone [lit. 'a man and a man'] was born there" (v. 5a; LXX differently: "'Mother Zion' a man will say, and a man was born in her"). Next, this extraordinary accomplishment is made official by Yahweh himself, who in his heavenly office takes account of all the nations. He enters into his list the foreigners mentioned (or all strangers?), adding the remark: "this one: born there" (v. 6b). The news is celebrated by dancing and singing. If the obscure v. 7b is to make any sense, it may be the incipit of a hymn to be sung: "All my springs are there with you," addressing once more the city of Jerusalem.

Now, the almost formulaic expressions "one by one: born in her" and "this one: born there" are certainly the heart of vv. 5-6, even more, of the whole psalm. Considering concepts and values of birth and genealogies in the ancient Near East and putting aside our norms of "free citizens in a democratic community," the formulas call attention to the fact that they do not mention father or parents, which was of utmost importance to establish patrilineal descent, but focus on the *place* of birth. The only phenomenon compatible with this idea is that of home-born slaves (*yĕlîd bayit:* Gen 14:14; 17:12, 13, 23, 27; Lev 22:11; cf. J. Schreiner, *TWAT* III, 638). It would seem to me, therefore, that the said formulas of our psalm refer to the slave status of foreigners in Jerusalem, legalizing their "right" to come to and live in the Holy City. This combines well with some Israelite hopes of receiving all nations on Mount Zion and letting them participate, in a more or less submissive way, in the teachings of Torah and the celebrations of Israel's feasts (cf. Isa 2:1-5; 49:18:23; 60:4-14; Zech 14:16-19; equal rights for strangers are postulated in Isa 56:6-8).

The formal classification of vv. 5-7 is difficult. Their discourse is descriptive; they are meant to undergird and explain the pronouncement of v. 4. CON-FIRMATION of a legal situation, or AUTHENTICATION of social or ecclesiastic standing, may be the right classification.

## Genre

Seen in the context of other Zion hymns (cf. Psalms 46; 48; 76; 84; 122; 132) that are clearly rooted in rituals and festivities around the holy site of Yahweh's choice, and some other texts focusing on Jerusalem and Zion like those cited above, Psalm 87 has the special function of clarifying the admission of foreigners to the Holy City. We may name it, by analogy to "liturgy of admission" or "entrance liturgy" (cf. Psalms 15; 24; Isa 33:14-16), ADMISSION PRONOUNCE-MENT.

## Setting

Various festivities centering in Jerusalem and on Mount Zion, including pilgrimages from far away to the Holy City (cf. Psalms 84; 120–134), brought up the question of admitting foreigners to the holy precincts. At some point of the ceremonies this issue had to be taken up and resolved. Psalm 87 together with Exod 12:43-51 and Deut 23:2-9, superseded by Isa 56:1-8, belongs to those conscious efforts to clarify the problems. Our psalm was probably part of a worship liturgy during the initial stages of some feast held regularly in Jerusalem.

## Intention

The purpose of this fragment of an ancient Jewish community worship was to clear the way for foreigners to take part in the ceremonies. No requirements are listed in Psalm 84. Presumably, they have been passed already: keep the Sabbath, perform circumcision, confess Yahweh, and call on his name (cf. Exod 12:43-51; 1 Kgs 8:41-43; Isa 56:1-8) have been varying stipulations for strangers. After they had been properly checked, the pronouncement of admission could take place, legalizing the presence of foreign people of different extractions. Apparently, the specific intention expressed by Psalm 87 is to keep strangers — in defiance of Isa 56:1-8 — on an inferior level.

## Bibliography

R. B. Allen, "On Paths Less Travelled: Discovering the Savior in Unexpected Places of the Old Testament, part 2: Ps 87, a Song Rarely Sung," *BSac* 153 (1996) 131-40; E. Beaucamp, "Psaume 87: À la Jerusalem nouvelle," *Laval théologique et philosophique* 35 (1979) 279-88; J. W. H. Bos, "Psalm 87," *Int* 47 (1989) 281-85; T. Booij, "Some Observations on Psalm LXXXVII," *VT* 37 (1987) 16-25; W. Horbury, "The Messianic Associations of 'Son of Man,'" *JTS* 36 (1985) 34-55; G. Ravasi, "L'universalisme dei Salmi 8; 47; 87," *RivB* 43 (1995) 77-92; J. Schmitt, "Psalm 87: Zion, the City of God's Love," in *The Psalms and Other Studies on the Old Testament* (*Fest.* J. I. Hunt; ed. J. C. Knight and A. Lawrence; Nashotah: Nashotah House Seminary, 1990) 34-44; M. S. Smith, "The Structure of Psalm LXXXVII," *VT* 38 (1988) 357-88; A. Stadelmann, "Psalm 87 (86) — Theologischer Gehalt und gesellschaftliche Wirkung," in *Ein Gott, eine Offenbarung* (*Fest.* N. Füglister; ed. F. V. Reiterer; Würzburg: Echter, 1991) 333-56; A. Vaccari, "Note critiche et esegetiche," *Bib* 27 (1946) 394-406; J. W. Wevers, "Psalm 87 and Its 'Sitz im Leben,'" *Theologinen Aikakauskirja* 82 (1977) 274-82.

## Psalm 88:
## Individual Complaint

### Structure

|  | MT | NRSV |
|---|---|---|
| I. Superscription | 1 | - |
| II. Invocation, initial plea | 2-3 | 1-2 |
| III. Complaint I | 4-10a | 3-8 |
|    A. Description of suffering | 4-6 | 3-5 |
|    B. Accusation | 7-10a | 6-8 |
| IV. Complaint II | 10b-13 | 9b-12 |
|    A. Description of praying | 10bc | 9bc |
|    B. Contestation of God | 11-13 | 10-12 |
| V. Complaint III | 14-19 | 13-18 |
|    A. Description of praying | 14 | 13 |
|    B. Accusation of God | 15 | 15 |
|    C. Description of suffering | 16-19 | 15-18 |

A multilayered SUPERSCRIPTION has accumulated at the head of Psalm 88. The first four words in their substance correspond exactly to the heading of Psalm 87, only the sequence of lexemes being different. To this Korah attribution have been added a musical annotation and a second authorial reference, to "Heman the Ezrahite." A legendary singer and liturgist, he is known principally from Chronicles (cf. 1 Chr 6:18; 15:17, 19; 16:41-42; etc.). His clan, the "Ezrahites," is referred to only in the superscription of Psalm 89 and in 1 Kgs 5:11 (RSV 4:31). From these scant references we are able to deduce that during the Second Temple a family of Levitical singers by this name was active in Jerusalem. Obviously, they derived themselves from ancestors like "Heman" and "Ethan."

The musical commentary may refer to "dancing" or "illness," depending on the verbal roots we want to discover in the somewhat mutilated expression *ʿal māḥălat lĕʿannôt* (*māḥălāh*, "illness," or *mĕḥôlāh*, "roundabout": cf. Psalm 53:1 [RSV superscription]; *ʾnh* IV, Piel, "sing": cf. Exod 32:18; Isa 27:2).

A classical INVOCATION and INITIAL PLEA open this prayer for extremely distressed persons (see "Introduction to Cultic Poetry," section 4B). Calling Yahweh "God of my help" befits the personal relationship presupposed in individual laments (see Pss 25:5; 27:9; 38:23 [RSV 22]; 62:2, 3, 7 [RSV 1, 2, 6]; also 42:6, 12 [RSV 5, 11]; 43:5). The appellation fills one colon, thus being a full, sonorous opening call. The mere name of Yahweh serves occasionally the important function of initiating the prayer (cf. 3:2 [RSV 1]; 6:2 [RSV 1]; *ʾĕlōhîm*: 61:2 [RSV 1]; 63:2 [RSV 1]; 64:2 [RSV 1]; etc.). Correctly addressing the Deity who may rescue one is crucial, however. Therefore individual prayers usually modulate the name of God with some attributes addressing his or her benevolence, justice, mercy, or personal relationship with the suppliant (see 4:2 [RSV 1]; 7:2 [RSV 1]; 17:1; 22:2 [RSV 1]; 27:1; 28:1; 109:1; 130:2; also 94:1 = "God of revenge"). It is notable, though, that all appellations of the Deity right away merge with descriptions of praying (v. 2b; cf. 22:3 [RSV 2]; 42:2 [RSV 1]; 61:3a [RSV 2a]; 142:2-3 [RSV 1-2]; etc.), with pleas to be heard or admitted into the presence of God (v. 3; cf. 4:2 [RSV 1]; 5:2-4 [RSV 1-3]; 17:1; 54:3-4 [RSV 1-2]; 55:2-3 [RSV 1-2]; 61:2 [RSV 1]; 102:2-3 [RSV 1-2]; 130:1-2; 143:1), or with a number of other form elements preparing the main concerns of individual prayer, namely complaint and petition (cf. Gerstenberger, *Mensch;* listing at "Introduction to Cultic Poetry"). According to the principal function of the opening lines, the INITIAL PLEA has to open a door to the Deity being approached for help. Therefore vv. 1-2 with their three modes of speech (direct appellation — depiction of suppliant's doing in the "I" form — direct plea to be heard in second-person address and first-person "sender") constitute a perfect introduction to the following complaints. There is nothing that would suggest a special urgency or an extraordinarily grave situation as far as the users of the psalm are concerned. The choice of verb indicating supplication (*ṣʿq*, "cry out," v. 2b; cf. 77:2 [RSV 1]; 107:6, 13, 19, 28; Exod 8:8; 14:10; 15:25) is normal; designations of "prayer" are standard (*tĕpillāh, rinnāh*, v. 3; these synonyms are traditionally paired; cf. Pss 17:1; 61:2 [RSV 1]; 1 Kgs 8:28b; Jer 7:16; 11:14 — the last three passages being of Dtr origin); the number of words used for the introductory segment is modest (two lines as in Psalms 4; 22; 54; 55; 64; 94; 120; 130; 130; 142); we have some much more redundant openings (→ Ps 86:1-7).

The impression of "normality" disappears when we look at the three successive and increasingly violent COMPLAINT segments (vv. 4-19), hardly interrupted by very short DESCRIPTIONS OF PRAYING (vv. 10bc, 14). At the end, we are stunned by an abrupt and — so it seems — nonliturgical closing line that leaves no room whatsoever for AFFIRMATIONS OF CONFIDENCE, regular PETITIONS and IMPRECATIONS, VOWS, or WELL-WISHES. What are the details of this setup?

The first COMPLAINT (vv. 1-10a) already articulates the anxieties of the suppliant, in an ascending line. He experiences — thus the synthesis of our preformulated, liturgical prayer, administered by ritual experts on account of preceding diagnoses (→ Psalms 7; 31; 35; 38; etc.) — unidentified threats of death (vv. 4-6). "My life is near Sheol" (netherworld, v. 4b); the reality of death is elaborated in vv. 5-6 (cf. 6:6 [RSV 5]; Jonah 2:3-7 [RSV 2-6]; Barth, *Errettung;* listing at "Introduction to Psalms"). In spite of this drastic reality, the tone of the description is still relatively controlled, almost objective. The text strictly limits itself to the suppliant's own realm. It does not involve yet the spheres of either God or humans who may have caused the suffering. There is very little reaching out yet into other fields of action or responsibilities. The suppliant seems to be isolated (v. 4), then the outward world comes in by passive formulations: "I am considered . . ." (v. 5a). Only the last line mentions Yahweh, in a subordinate phrase: "*You* no longer remember them" (i.e., the dead ones; v. 6a), "they have been cut off from *your* influence" (v. 6b). Here, in fact, for the first time in this psalm second-person direct address of God enters the text, making it a formal prayer. From now on the direct confrontation with that God ("of my help," v. 2a) gains force until the end of the psalm. The second phase of the first round of complaints already reveals this thrust. "*You* threw me into the deepest pit" (v. 7a): now Yahweh himself is named as the one responsible for the suppliant's pains. The affirmation comes in a main clause and with an active verb, God being the self-determined agent. This is a direct confrontation with Yahweh; enemies, evildoers, or other mercenaries of God's wrath are ignored. The great majority of individual complaints make human or demonic agents responsible in the first place (cf. 3:2-3 [RSV 1-2]; 5:10-11 [RSV 9-10]; 6:9-11 [RSV 8-10]; 7:2-6 [RSV 1-5]; 11:1-3; 17:9; 22:13, 17 [RSV 12, 16]; 27:2, 11-12; 31:12-19 [RSV 11-18]; 35:1-8; 38:13, 20-21 [RSV 12, 19-20]; 52:3-9 [RSV 1-7]; 54:5 [RSV 3]; 55; 56:2-3, 7-8 [RSV 1-2, 6-7]; 64; 69:5, 8-13 [RSV 4, 7-12]; 71:10-13; 94; 102:9 [RSV 8]; 109; 120; 140; 143:3; etc.). Evilmongers are accused of causing every harm. They are usually pointed out and denounced in individual complaint psalms; God's wrath is called on to destroy them. All this seems invalid in the case of Psalm 88. The suppliant is turning toward and against Yahweh himself only. Some passages of the book of Job are obviously quite close to our psalm (cf. Job 7:11-21; 13:18-28; 30:20-23; etc.). On the other hand, some communal complaints contain direct accusation against Yahweh, making him ultimately responsible for defeat and despair (cf. Psalms 44; 60:3-6 [RSV 2-5]; 89). Westermann observes: "Accusations of God loom large in communal complaints. The most frequent form is a reproachful question directed to God himself" (Westermann, "Struktur," 275; listing at "Introduction to Psalms"). In vv. 7-9 the fault is attributed to Yahweh in several ways: he has cast the suppliant into the netherworld (v. 7), so that the chaos waters can torment and swallow him (v. 8). Second, social relations around the suppliant have been impaired by God's interventions (v. 9ab), so that he feels totally cut off from his environment, blinded with sorrow (vv. 9c, 10a). Mythological concepts of death and life, the earth and the realm of the dead are always close at hand. The formal characteristics of second-person, direct-address discourse to God continue throughout this little subsegment of COMPLAINT no. I.

COMPLAINT is repeated twice in vv. 11-13 and 15-19 in modified forms and with increasing force. COMPLAINT no. II consists of three rhetorical questions, addressed to Yahweh (without mentioning his name in these phrases proper), each of them requesting a negative answer: No! In the netherworld, contact with the God of life is impossible; he does not exercise any influence on the realm of the dead — a very ancient Near Eastern religious axiom (cf. Ps 6:6 [RSV 5]; Isa 26:14; cf. Wächter, *Tod;* listing at "Introduction to Cultic Poetry"; H. Ringgren, K.-J. Illman, and H.-J. Fabry, *TWAT* IV, 763-87). Rhetorical questions like the ones at hand contest the authority and veracity of the one addressed. They are used large-scale in disputes like the one between God and the righteous sufferer incorporated into the book of Job (cf. Job 38–39; the genre has antecedents in ancient Near Eastern wisdom literature; see Lambert, *Wisdom;* listed at "Introduction to Cultic Poetry"). Other examples from Hebrew Scripture include Judg 9:9, 11, 13, and Ps 94:9-10, minor disputations between different contestants. This means that the language and ritual of complaint at times make use of the rhetoric of dispute between adversaries, being in themselves highly provocative and aggressive. Rhetorical questions aiming at undermining the opponent by dismantling his argumentation are extraordinary, though, in the individual complaint genre (see above on "accusations of God").

The reader imagines that there could be no crescendo any more in putting God himself into the stand. But COMPLAINT no. III (vv. 15-19) in fact increases once more the suppliant's diatribe. The dire description of his suffering, comparable to vv. 4-6, is now placed under the accusatory question: "Why, Yahweh, do you repudiate me?" On *znh,* "repudiate, expel," see H. Ringgren, *TWAT* II, 619-21. The term implies rejection, banishment, and intention to kill principally in communal complaints (cf. 43:2; 44:10, 24 [RSV 9, 23]; 60:3, 12 [RSV 1, 10]; 74:1; 77:8 [RSV 7]; 89:39 [RSV 38]; 108:12 [RSV 11]). The connotation of a "why" question is even more serious. God is accused of having brought about the condemnation of his client (as in vv. 7-9), and unjustly so, at that. "Why" accusations, originally used in bringing to trial suspected criminals (cf. Josh 7:19; Jer 26:8-9; Boecker, *Redeformen,* 71-94; listing at Additional Bibliography, section B), presuppose that the accused is wrong and the accuser is right. In this sense the interrogative particle is used in the Psalms and the book of Job (cf., e.g., Pss 22:2a [RSV 1a]; 44:10 [RSV 9]; similarly, the particles "how long?" 13:2-3 [RSV 1-2]; 89:47 [RSV 46]; and "where?" 89:50 [RSV 49]; A. Jepsen, "Warum? Eine lexakalische und theologische Studie," in *Das ferne und nahe Wort* [*Fest.* L. Rost; ed. F. Maass; BZAW 105; Berlin: Töpelmann, 1967] 106-13). The DESCRIPTION OF SUFFERING in this case amounts to demonstrating, still in direct address to God, that all chances to continue life have gone. The collocations are radical; they include the whole life span from youth on (cf. 51:7 [RSV 5]) and employ mythical images of being drowned in the watery abyss (v. 18; cf. v. 8; 42:8 [RSV 7]; 69:2-3 [RSV 1-2]; Jonah 2:4-6 [RSV 3-5]: "You cast me into the abyss, down to the heart of the sea; the flood was round about me. All your waves and billows passed over me. I felt cut off from your presence, never again would I see your sanctuary. The waters closed in over me, the abyss was round about me"). Strangely enough, after using these mythical metaphors, the text returns to social life, complaining about the destruction of intimate bonds of family and friends (v. 19). This is certainly not an unusual feature in individual complaints (cf. 35:11-16; 41:10 [RSV 9]), but repeating the affirmation of v. 9a, juxtaposing social disruption to abysmal threats, and ending the psalm on this note of utter abandonment seem strange. The lack of any quest for rescue or other customary elements in individual complaint reinforces our astonishment.

In this context the two lines labeled above as DESCRIPTIONS OF PRAYING (vv. 10bc, 14) need to be discussed further. Do they open sections II and III of complaint (thus the majority of exegetes), or do they actually close sections I and II, thus substituting for the missing PETITION? The sequence of complaint and petition is a traditional and, in regard to liturgical practice, a logical one. But formally, vv. 10bc and 14 are not real petitions. Furthermore, complaint no. III would not have been equipped with a like ending. Consequently, we may content ourselves with the traditional interpretation.

## Genre

The classification as COMPLAINT OF THE INDIVIDUAL is beyond doubt. The only problem is the fragmentary state of this psalm. Is Psalm 88 a collection of pure complaints, to be used in diverse liturgies in combination with pertinent elements of petition, confidence, vow? Have the appropriate but missing parts of individual complaint been lost? Would it be feasible to think of our psalm as a complete prayer, with an INITIAL PLEA and DESCRIPTIONS OF PRAYING substituting for the missing parts? Each of these alternative interpretations is able to muster some supportive arguments. We really do not know sufficient details about individual prayer services to decide the issue. I lean toward the third proposal.

With Psalm 88 it seems particularly opportune to repeat one essential observation in regard to individual complaints: the crescendo of lamentation observed in this psalm, seemingly so full of personal emotions and psychological drama, is not to be interpreted in terms of biographical experiences of just one suppliant. Individual complaints in the ancient Near East (and Hebrew Scripture, of course) are not individualistic poems of specific authors. They are prayer formulas, composed and transmitted by ritual experts. These, in turn, synthesized experiences of human sufferings, anguish, and hope into ritual texts. Thus we read today accumulated and collective — and ritually calculated — outbreaks of pain, forlornness, and typical struggles for rehabilitation or restitution.

## Setting

In preexilic times our text was probably recited in prayer services outside the sanctuary (see "Introduction to Cultic Poetry," section 4B). Very strong complaints addressed to the personal Deity and very subdued petitions testify to an intimate relationship between suppliant and God. State cults could never offer

145

such intimacy. (In the same vein, the book of Job of much later origin betrays an unusual closeness of human being and God.) From a family, clan, or village background (affiliation of the text with a Korah clan may have preserved some remembrance of this early setting; → Psalms 42; 84) the text moved into early Jewish congregations. They may have read it in special worship services on behalf of hopelessly destitute persons as an expression of extreme despair in the face of grave distress.

## Intention

Apparently, users and transmitters of Psalm 88 were equally fascinated by the extremely strong language in dealing with God. The message would be that prayer is not only pious submission to the divine will, but may be a dangerous struggle with God himself (cf. Gen 32:25-32; Job 3–27). Brueggemann has captured this theological dimension of OT complaints, expressed so radically in our text, when speaking about Israel's "counter-testimony" and appreciating the psalmist's capacity to live in the face of God's inscrutable darkness (see idem, *Theology*, Additional Bibliography, section C).

## Bibliography

P. Auffret, "'Les ombres se levent-elles pour te louer?' Étude structurelle du Ps 88," *EstBib* 45 (1987) 23-38; A. Bentzen, "Der Tod des Beters in den Psalmen" (*Fest.* O. Eissfeldt; ed. J. Fück; Halle: Max Niemeyer, 1947) 57-60; R. Bohlen, "Klagen — Leben — Hoffen — Trösten," *TTZ* 105 (1996) 275-84; A. Bonora, "Angoscia e abbandono di fronte alle more (Salmo 88)," in *Gesù e la sua morte* (ed. G. Boggio, et al.; Brescia: Paideia, 1984) 207-17; B. A. Bozak, "Suffering and the Psalms of Lament," *Église et Théologie* 23 (1992) 325-38; R. C. Culley, "Psalm 88 among the Complaints," in *Ascribe to the Lord* (*Fest.* P. C. Craigie; ed. L. Eslinger and G. Taylor; JSOTSup 67; Sheffield: Sheffield Academic Press, 1988) 289-301; J. T. Cummings, "Jubilation or Ululation: Patristic Testimony for the Old Latin Especially Psalm 88:16," *Studia Patristica* 18/1 (1985) 311-16; J. S. Custer, "Poetics and Context: Psalm 88 in the Roman and Byzantine Liturgies," *Diakonia* 21 (1987) 23-37; C. van Duin, *'Zal het sof u loven?'* (diss., Amsterdam, 1989); B. Fischer, "Liturgiegeschichte und Exegesegeschichte," *Jahrbuch für Antike und Christentum* 30 (1987) 5-13; N. Füglister, "Psalm 88: Der Rätsel Lösung?" *VTSup* 43 (1989) 264-97; P. L. Graber, "A Textlinguistic Approach to Understanding Psalm 88," *Journal of Translation and Textlinguistics* [formerly: *OPTAT*] 4 (1990) 322-39; P. Grelot, "HOFŠI (Ps. LXXXVIII,6)," *VT* 14 (1964) 256-63; E. Haag, "Psalm 88," in *Freude an der Weisung des Herrn* (ed. E. Haag and F.-L. Hossfeld; Stuttgart: Katholisches Bibelwerk, 1986) 149-70; K.-L. Illman, "Psalm 88 — a Lamentation without Answer," *SJOT* 4 (1991) 112-20; R. Martin-Achard, *De la mort à la résurrection* (Neuchâtel: Delachaux et Niestlé, 1956); idem, "Prédication: Psaume 88," *Cahier de la Revue de Théologie et de Philosophie* 11 (1984) 363-68; H.-D. Preuss, "Psalm 88 als Beispiel alttestamentlichen Redens vom Tod," in *Der Tod — ungelöstes Rätsel oder überwundener Feind* (ed. A. Strobel; Stuttgart: Calwer, 1974)

63-79; H.-P. Stähli, "Tod und Leben im Alten Testament," *TGl* 76 (1986) 172-92; M. E. Tate, "Psalm 88," *RevExp* 87 (1990) 91-96; L. Wächter, *Der Tod im Alten Testament* (Berlin: Evangelische Verlagsanstalt, 1967); G. D. Weaver, "Senile Dementia and a Resurrection Theology," *Theology Today* 42 (1986) 444-56; G. Widengren, "Konunges vistelse i dodsriket. En studie till Psalm 88," *SEÅ* 10 (1945) 66-81; D. J. C. Zub, "God as the Object of Anger in the Psalms," *Church Divinity* (1991/1992) 47-63.

## Psalm 89:
## Communal Complaint

### Structure

|  | MT | NRSV |
|---|---|---|
| I. Superscription | 1 | - |
| II. Initial praise | 2-3 | 1-2 |
| III. David oracle | 4-5 | 3-4 |
| IV. Yahweh hymn | 6-19 | 5-18 |
|   A. Summons | 6 | 5 |
|   B. Affirmations of incomparability | 7-9 | 6-8 |
|   C. Description of superiority | 10-15 | 9-14 |
|   D. Felicitation of people | 16-19 | 15-18 |
| V. Retrospective: the David story | 20-38 | 19-37 |
| VI. Complaint | 39-46 | 38-45 |
| VII. Petition | 47-52 | 46-51 |
| VIII. Praise formula | 53 | 52 |

Psalm 89 is credited by many scholars with being a "cornerstone" in the assembly of the Psalter at the end of psalmic "books," as is the case also with Psalms 41; 72; 106. A PRAISE FORMULA has been added to the psalm, marking off a book-length collection of liturgical texts of the Second Temple community. Interestingly, this enhanced position of a rather lengthy text is not at all reflected in the SUPERSCRIPTION. There we have a commonplace genre term (*maśkîl*, "didactic song"? 13 times in MT headings; see, e.g., Psalms 32; 42; 44; 74; 74; 142 — with no recognizable generic correspondence), and an unusual author or ancestor, Ethan the Ezrahite, mentioned only once outside Psalm 89, in the Solomon story of 1 Kgs 5:11 (RSV 4:31). Perhaps the late redactor of our text even received his inspiration from this passage. Both Ethan and Heman (Ps 88:1 [RSV superscription]) are listed as famous wise men of the Ezrahite clan. If the final redactors who added this superscription meant to emphasize the monarchic dimensions of the "corner-psalm," they most successfully hid their intention.

The opening lines of the psalm (vv. 2-3) are hymnic in character. Some features call for attention, however. The two cola of each poetic line share one word each with the other: *ʿôlām* in vv. 2a and 3a, *ʾĕmûnātĕkā* in vv. 2b and 3b. Since both verses are oversize (at best, we can establish cola of four [?] or even five stresses; Veijola, 34-35, measures stichoi = full lines, of the psalm, discovering three types) and v. 3 comes out rather clumsily, there may be some textual irregularity involved. With the redundancy at hand we may suspect that some scribes did confuse somewhat a shorter and more poetic wording. The text that has come down to us sounds prosaic, overburdened, and does not make the best sense. Another stylistic issue is worth mentioning: vv. 1-2a make a point of presenting a *personal* hymn of praise. *'āšîrāh* is self-exhortation, as in Exod 15:1; Judg 5:3; Isa 5:1; Pss 13:6 [RSV 5]; 27:6; 57:8 [RSV 7]; 59:17 [RSV 16]; 101:1; 104:33; 108:2 [RSV 1]; 144:9). In all these passages cultic singing is clearly intended, and for the most part it is the individual thanksgiving or the victory hymn presented by individuals (women!) that the texts allude to. In sum, INITIAL PRAISE is a composite opening of a grand liturgical poem that will include praise, complaint, and petition. Cf. the somewhat different sapiential opening of Ps 78:1-2.

Vv. 4-5 pose a considerable problem for our analysis. A speaker emerges abruptly, communicating a divine promise over David and his dynasty. Obviously, this collocation has to be evaluated in conjunction with the extensive oracular passage in vv. 20-38. The latter discourse is introduced by a historical reminiscence clothed in prayer form: "Once upon a time you spoke through a vision" (*ḥāzôn*, v. 20a; the concept was popular esp. in later OT times; cf. Ezek 12:23; Dan 8:2; A. Jepsen, *TWAT* II, 822-35). To reproduce a similar introduction for the oracle of vv. 4-5 is textually hazardous. "Yes, I said" (v. 3a) cannot easily be transferred to v. 4 and changed into "You [Yahweh] said." Liturgical presentation of the text — be it by dramatic enactment or by plain reading — does not necessarily need an explicit introduction of a new voice or impersonation (→ Ps 81:7-8). Thus vv. 4-5 are a prelude to the elaborate David oracle of vv. 20-38, and both texts are to be seen in close literary and theological contact with 2 Samuel 7, Psalm 132, and other David traditions. More specifically, vv. 4-5 summarize in free "poetic interpretation" (Veijola, 69) the promise Yahweh gave to his (in Dtr perspective) beloved firstborn servant and king of Israel. The promise itself is called an "alliance" and "oath" (v. 4; cf. L. Perlitt, *Bundestheologie* [Neukirchen: Neukirchener Verlag, 1969]), and it is guaranteed to last into the unforeseeable future (v. 5; 2 Sam 7:13, 16; Mettinger, *King*, 254-93; listing at Additional Bibliography, section B; more below in discussion of the "David story").

A full-fledged YAHWEH HYMN (vv. 6-19) separates the two oracular parts. Why? To build up "liturgical suspense"? We do not know for sure. A few Hebrew MSS and the Greek tradition take v. 6 as a SUMMONS TO PRAISE, albeit couched in direct address to God, which is a deviation from the normal pattern (cf. 33:1-3; 148:1-14 = addressing directly those agents who are to offer praises). "Heaven" and "assembly of the holy ones" stand in parallelism; they are to extol the Lord. "Holy ones" may indicate the congregation of worshipers, or the "host of heavens" (cf. v. 8; 34:10 [RSV 9]; 50:5; Zech 14:5; Noth, "Die Heiligen").

That the heavens applaud the supreme Deity is a well-known idea in Scripture (cf. Pss 19:2 [RSV 1]; 29:1-2; 50:6; 69:35 [RSV 34]; 97:6; 148:1, 4, 13), the basic concept being that of cosmological supremacy. If a summons to praise opens up cosmic dimensions, the contents of vv. 7-19 do not cause surprise. Yahweh is pictured as the only Lord in heaven and on earth, much in line with 2 Sam 7:22, the Yahweh-kingship hymns (→ Psalms 47; 93; 96–99), Dtr preaching, and Second Isaiah. Eulogy starts with a rhetorical question: "Who is comparable to Yahweh?" (v. 7), to come to a first climax in v. 9, a glorifying appellation and stunning affirmation of power and justice: "Yahweh, God of heavenly hosts, who is like you? 'Your' power and your truth surround you." This same theme is repeated and further developed in vv. 14-15, after a lustrous elaboration of Yahweh's accomplishments in creation (vv. 10-13). This means that the general background of the hymn to Yahweh is cosmological, based on creation myths.

Details of this inset hymn, which some commentators (Duhm, Gunkel, Schmidt, et al.) have considered an independent poem, include the provocative rhetorical question "Who is like Yahweh?" (vv. 7, 9; cf. the affirmation: "No one like you," 86:8; Johannes, *Unvergleichlichkeitsaussagen* 91, 125-26, 204-5). Derived from sapiential comparisons and amply used in various fields of daily life, this mode of determining a highest ranking deity in a pantheon or even a singular, and perhaps in tendency, otherworldly God was a late achievement in Israel (cf. Deut 4:32-35; Isa 40:25; 44:6-8; cf. Gerstenberger, *Yahweh*, Additional Bibliography, section B). Comparison of gods and serious competition with other deities are best understandable in the situation of exile and imperial dominion of Babylonia as well as Persia. V. 8 elaborates the preceding affirmation of incomparability. Yahweh is seen as surrounded by competing and subjugated deities (cf. Deut 32:8-9; Psalm 82). He radiates power and glory, so that all the competitors are filled with terror. The designations *'ēl na'ărāṣ . . . wĕnôrā'*, "terrifying and frightening God," reflect that concept. While the Niphal participle of *'rṣ* is a hapax legomenon, the same form of *yr'* occurs with some frequency and has become an adjective in its own right (cf. in connection with Yahweh or Elohim: Pss 47:3 [RSV 2]; 68:36 [RSV 35]; 76:8, 12, 13 [RSV 7, 11, 12]; 96:4; 99:3; 111:9; Deut 7:21; 10:17; Zeph 2:11; Dan 9:4; Neh 1:5; 4:8; 9:32). With an extended appellation, v. 9 once again challenges concurrent contenders and their potential followers: "Who is like you?" It continues with an honorable affirmation about Yahweh and thus ends the subunit. Note that 2 Sam 7:22 is very close in formulation, meaning, and intention.

After this, the hymnic part unfolds without more contesting rhetoric, in a pure and praising "objectivity" (vv. 10-15) quite homogeneous in regard to form and contents. The phrases are nonetheless direct address to Yahweh. First comes a whole series of "You are . . ." declarations (five times in vv. 10-13), reflecting awe and trust in the mighty Creator and Lord. In fact, these very lines draw explicitly on chaos-battle motifs, exalting Yahweh because he defeated the primordial powers and established that wholesome order of all life. Psalm 104 takes the same stand, but it is much more elaborate and intricate on individual acts of creation and species brought forth by the Deity. Likewise, 77:17-20 (RSV 16-19) lends more colorful details to the description of the founding battle (cf. furthermore 114:3-6; 139:13-16; etc.). Our passage is only summarizing the mythical events of creation, extolling in every colon the overwhelming power of the Creator in the face of primordial chaotic antagonists. Main stylistic features are the personal pronoun "You" with a perfect verb (e.g., "you pacified its waves," v. 10b; three more declarations of this type occur in vv. 11-13; only once with a participle: "You are reigning over the fierce sea," v. 10a); and a preposition with a second-person singular possessive suffix: "To you (belong)," followed by a noun (e.g., "heaven" and "earth," v. 12a; "power," v. 14). Whether or not this hymnic style has been developed from personal hymns, perhaps originally sung in situations of distress, we should recognize it as a distinct mode of praising Yahweh in the late periods of Israel's congregational worshiping (cf. Crüsemann, *Studien*, 292-94; listing at "Introduction to Cultic Poetry"; similar style in Psalms 66; 104). The last line of the Yahweh eulogy proper (v. 15) ably draws together the results of divine victories and demonstrations of power: Now the wholesome forces (*ṣedeq, mišpāṭ, ḥesed, 'ĕmet:* best summarized in our concepts of "justice" and "solidarity") that maintain life and well-being are the exclusive foundations of Yahweh's government (85:10-14 [RSV 9-13]).

Praising Yahweh is not altogether an end in itself. The hymn turns into a blessing of those who are privileged to be aligned to that supreme Deity. A BE-ATITUDE (v. 16; → 1:1; 119:1-2) draws this conclusion from the hymnic narration, just as 33:12 does. The laudatory phrases of vv. 10-13 are reflected in v. 18a: "*You are* the glory of their strength." In the same line appears for the first time the communal "we": "in your favor you raise *our* horn" (v. 18b; cf. v. 19). Our suspicion is that this congregational voice will appear again in the complaint section (vv. 39-52) under the guise of David and in a communal "I" (cf. vv. 48, 51). The double preposition *lĕ* in v. 19 (missing in the Syriac translation, thus designating only Yahweh himself as "our shield" and "our king"), indicating a possessive relationship, also echoes the hymnic affirmations of vv. 12 and 14, so that linguistic and ideological links are very strong with the preceding hymn. Interestingly, the benediction introduced by *'ašrê*, "happy," comprises only two lines (vv. 16-17), while the motive clauses after *kî* (vv. 18-19) switch — when talking of the "people" — from the objective third person plural into first person plural. Both segments, however, are unified by second-person discourse (prayer language) in relation to Yahweh. This means that the *'ašrê* saying is consciously used maintaining its traditional form of a blessing wish (vv. 16-17; Crüsemann, *Studien*, 187-89), while the congregation comes to the fore in additional motive clauses (vv. 18-19).

Next in line is a long, poetic narrational account, almost epic in nature (vv. 20-38). The "David story" of 2 Samuel 7 has to be compared, because it seems to be the quarry that Psalm 89 exploited; cf. the most elaborate literary study of this matter by Veijola, *Verheissung*. As many commentators annotate, the poetic lines in this part of the psalm are shorter, there are mostly 3 (seldom 4 or 2) stresses to each colon (cf. Kraus, 781). Both facts — parallelism with 2 Samuel 7 (including at least v. 9) and specific poetic meter — make the relevant parts of Psalm 89 a rather independent text, to which other elements, like the nucleus of the Yahweh HYMN (vv. 10-15) and the important COMPLAINT and PETITION (vv. 39-52) may have been added, not in terms of literary patchwork, done at the writing table. Rather, conscious liturgical composition of the different parts would be a better conceptual guide.

The narration is introduced by a citation formula (v. 20) justifying Yahweh's first-person singular discourse throughout vv. 21-38. The parallel story does not mention a vision, though, but only divine communication to the prophet Nathan at night (2 Sam 7:4; cf., however, the *post factum* designation in v. 17). More significant: the prophetic mediator is missing altogether in Psalm 89. Here, according to MT, Yahweh's communication goes to "your faithful ones" (*ḥăsîdeykā*, plural! cf. 79:2; 132:9, 16). Many Hebrew MSS and most modern translators emend the word to represent the singular, i.e., perhaps Nathan? But his name is ignored in Psalm 89. The MT plural, however, anachronistically portrays the exilic-postexilic community as the recipient of divine communication. Equally important, the figure of David is mysteriously absorbed into the history of the community of Israel in vv. 39-46.

There are too many coincidences of vocabulary and theological concepts between Psalm 89 and 2 Samuel 7 as well as other Dtr and exilic-postexilic texts (e.g., Second Isaiah; communal complaint psalms; Lamentations; cf. meticulous listings in Veijola, *Verheissung*, 48-59) to be investigated here in detail. We need to content ourselves with a few remarks about concepts and formulas. Vv. 20c-25 recount election and elevation of David to the monarchy with an eye on 1 Samuel 16–2 Samuel 5 (although few details are taken up) and with 2 Sam 7:8-9, 18; 23:2-7 as raw material to be molded poetically for liturgical use. Yahweh speaks in first-person promissory discourse. The oracle is mediated by a speaker, with the recipient, David — in marked contrast to 2 Sam 7:8-16, where it is delivered to him directly by Yahweh through Nathan — staying in the objective third person, as is the case throughout vv. 20c-38. This stylistic feature undergirds the impression that our text is a report of a long-passed vision for the transmitters of Psalm 89 (cf. *'āz*, "once upon a time," v. 20a). The vocabulary of election, consecration, strengthening, and protection in these verses is only partially that of commission reports (cf. Exod 3:6–4:17; Judg 6:12-24; Isa 6:1-13; Jer 1:4-19); more dominant are expressions of Dtr and other theologies (in relation to vv. 20cd-21 cf., e.g., the use of lexemes derived from *bḥr*, "select": Deut 17:15; 1 Sam 10:24; 16:8-10; 2 Sam 6:21; 1 Kgs 8:16; 11:34; Pss 78:70; 132:13; *rûm*, "elevate": 1 Kgs 14:7; 16:2; *mšḥ*, "anoint": 2 Sam 12:7; 19:22; 22:51; 23:1; Ps 132:10, 17). What we get in vv. 20c-25, after all, is a broad and general image of a very powerful Deity, implanting a just government through David, the chosen one among his people. National particularities are all but absent.

Divine powers conferred on the anointed (v. 22) or enacted by Yahweh himself make the king invincible (vv. 23-24). Just as God's reign is supported by "justice" and "solidarity" (v. 15), the power of his elected king depends on Yahweh's own "truth" and "solidarity" (v. 25). Earthly authority is sustained only if directly undergirded by the divine (cf. v. 25b with v. 18b).

The following thematic unit (vv. 26-30) unfolds the motif of power. David has been promised an imperial reign covering sea and rivers (v. 26: mythological; v. 28b: political allusions; cf. the growth of tradition from 2 Sam 8:15 to Josh 1:4, probably visualized Davidic frontiers; also Ps 72:8; A. R. Müller, "David," *NBL* I, 390-96; D. M. Howard Jr., *ABD* II, 41-49). The center of this section is the DESCENT FORMULA granted to David in v. 27: "You are my father, my God, and the rock of my salvation." The parallel expression in 2 Sam 7:14 — this time Solomon being the privileged one — runs: "I will be father to him, and he will be son to me." Some other phrases of similar dimensions should be compared: "You are my son; today I have begotten you" (Ps 2:7); "Sit at my right side, until I shall put your enemies under your feet" (110:1); "like dew I have begotten you" (restored text: 110:3c); finally v. 28a of our psalm: "I have made him the firstborn." Taken together, these concise divine pronouncements in regard to the Davidic ruler or dynasty testify to a very close relationship between the Judean king and Yahweh, the intimacy of father and son providing the main metaphor (cf. Frankfort, *Kingship;* Lipiński, *Royauté,* both listed at "Introduction to Cultic Poetry"). Since ancient Near Eastern theologians from the dawn of history in the fourth millennium reflected on this issue, using quite often the same father-son model, we can be assured of its great antiquity. Which formula goes back to early Israelite or even proto-Israelite royal ceremonialism is hard to decide. Theories of dramatic enactments of the sacred rites of ascending to the throne after chaos battle or seasonal rebirth, the king representing the Deity (Mowinckel, Hooke, Widengren, Volz, Kraus, etc.), are partially right, but cannot be held to explain every detail of known texts (see "Introduction to Cultic Poetry," section 4E). And the question remains wide open, to what extent exilic and postexilic theologians in Israel worked on that ancient concept of divine kingship, incorporating it into their community-oriented system. In any case, within Psalm 89 the attention is not on mythical battles and their festive enactments, but on Yahweh's great promises of the past and the sad state of his people in the present.

The promise of farthest-reaching (*lĕ'ôlām* is not "eternally") guarantees for the Davidic dynasty (vv. 29-30; cf. 2 Sam 7:16: "Your house and your kingdom shall be steadfast for all times [*lĕ'ôlām*]") had been contradicted by history itself in that the northern and southern kingdoms of Israel had been defeated and vanished from the historical scene. Therefore, later Israelite theologians had to take account of these facts. 2 Sam 7:12-16 and Ps 89:31-34, in their own specific formulations, are doing exactly this, permitting deviations of David's successors and divine castigations for the sinner, but not letting loose the basic promises Yahweh gave to the dynasty and through the dynasty to the people. Historically speaking, this insistence on guarantees for David's house and monarchy is absurd. It can be understood only in the light of the posterior identification of people, religious community, and David's ongoing reign (see below, vv. 39-46). Stylistically, our little passage dealing with David's apostate descendants is an interlude, with two lines of conditional protasis (vv. 31-32; note the language of Torah obedience, not employed in 2 Sam 7:12-16, but very much present in Deut 17:18-20; Psalm 119), one line of emphatic threat against the culprits (v. 33), and another one of glowing promise for David himself (v. 34). These last affirmations of perpetual solidarity with David overflow into fantastic assurances of ongoing, uninterrupted benevolence of Yahweh with his chosen one (vv. 35-38; cf. 2 Sam 7:14b-16, where different affirmations have been put together: the sinner will be punished "humanely," not by total destruction as Saul was; David's dynasty and "throne" will go unharmed). The passage is driving toward a climax. Yahweh confirms his unwavering determination to stay with David; the affirmations have a quality of oath with them (vv. 35-36), and the "longest-lasting" (*lĕ'ôlām;* cf. vv. 5, 29) promise reaches out for comparisons with the longevity of sun and moon (cf. vv. 37b, 38a). Again, the cosmic dimension of royal government, and implicitly of early Jewish community, comes to the fore.

In sum, the "David Report" in vv. 20-38 sticks to tradition and uses some ancient formulaic language to work out a coherent picture of salvific history in its own right, emphasizing the continuity of divine grace over Israel. The Yahweh community is the direct heir of promises given to the Davidic dynasty. Continuity of divine care for Israel is best expressed by the concept of *bĕrît,* "alliance," used in vv. 4, 29, 35, 40. This holy covenant is destined to endure forever, i.e., into the foreseeable future and beyond.

Leaping from hymnic to plaintive and petitionary elements (vv. 39-52), the modern reader, but without doubt also the ancient participant in worship, experiences a sort of cataclysm. Everything said and sung so far in this impressive psalm is turned upside down, brought to nothing. Psalm 44 is a close parallel with its hymnic introduction and terrifying reflections on defeat and suffering. In both psalms, COMPLAINT is articulated in its most severe form. Direct address to Yahweh is maintained in vv. 39-46 (cf. 44:10-15 [RSV 9-14]; 88:7-9, 15 [RSV 6-8, 14]; Isa 63:15-17), now enumerating his disastrous actions in open defiance of his benevolent announcements, thus accusing God of having perverted his promises. The style is the same as in vv. 10-15. An emphatic personal pronoun opens the diatribe; verbs in the absolute state, without any grammatical objects, heighten the sense of definiteness: "You have cast off and despised" (v. 39a). "You have broken the covenant with your servant" (v. 40a), i.e., David (vv. 4, 21, etc.). The legendary king of Judah was of course not present at the time of the Babylonian invasion; his name in vv. 39-46 stands for the community of faithful, the real bearers of divine promises (cf. v. 46, where even David's biography is implicitly paralleled with the history of the believers; v. 50, where the community claims validity and benefits from "ancient solidarities"). All in all, devastating complaints bluntly call Yahweh the only one responsible for destruction, loss of the monarchy, and utter lack of protection against enemies (cf. v. 43 with promises in vv. 23-24).

We have to imagine how a fundamental break in perspectives could be accommodated in one and the same psalm and worship service. There can be no reasonable doubt that the divergent elements have been used together, even admitting the vague possibility of one-time independence of individual psalm elements before their juncture in the present Psalm 89. Relative uniformity in styles, vocabulary, and theological concepts throughout vv. 2-52 should, however, alert us against postulating too much autonomy for individual passages (cf. Clifford, "Psalm 89"). Complaint services in exilic-postexilic times, we may learn, sometimes went to the extremes of arguing against God himself (cf. the dialogues of Job).

The PETITION (vv. 47-52), for its part, seems quite reduced, unspecific, and submissive in relation to those huge hymnic and radical plaintive sections. Vv. 48-49 seem to belong to general complaints about human life's transitoriness (cf. Psalms 39; 90). There even appears a strange "I" in vv. 48a and 51b.

Attention is focused, but in very general terms, on the hostile nations who humilated the "servants" (now plural, v. 51; paralleled with "your anointed one" in v. 52b) of Yahweh. V. 50, as already mentioned, comes to the point of asking for resuscitation of the old promises, and in its light the petition in vv. 47-52 gears in a little with preceding complaints and praises.

V. 53 does not really belong to Psalm 89, but the importance of the BLESSING FORMULA with the response of the people is obvious: Psalm 89 is the cornerstone of the so-called third book of the Psalter. The little phrase consists perhaps of a community leader's shout: *bārûk yhwh*, "blessed be Yahweh," and a response of the congregation (v. 53b).

## Genre

Tate (pp. 414-15) gives a concise overview of the genre debate, the fundamental question of which is the problem of unity of the oversize and heterogeneous psalm. If one sets it in the context of liturgical procedures within community worship of the exilic or postexilic age, the cohesion of the whole becomes plausible. In that case, still, genre designations vary between COMPLAINT LITURGY, often considered to be part of a comprehensive festival, and some kind of catechetical INSTRUCTIONAL TREATISE, presenting a decisive part of Israel's history in the molds of hymn and complaint. The truth may be somewhere in the middle. Psalm 89 gives the impression of containing succinct pieces of theological discourse, but at the same time shows strong traces of liturgical use. As for the literature, the concept of "alliance" or "covenant" with the famous king of Yahweh's choice is central to the poem. Presupposed is the continued inheritance of the guarantees of old. Where are Yahweh's help and protection now, in this disastrous situation of exile, deportation, and submission under foreign rule? The spiritual and political inheritance went into a severe "crisis" (Veijola). This crisis is worked on in a theological debate, put into conflicting psalm elements for public hearing and enactment. Psalm 89 demonstrates theology in action: there are a public recitation of old divine promises (put into new words, though) and subsequent denunciation of Yahweh for having failed to fulfill his words to David and his spiritual descendants — a COMMUNAL COMPLAINT, in other words, under the conditions of exilic-postexilic congregations.

## Setting

A historical situation cannot be fixed with certainty for the text. Communal complaints like Psalms 44, 74, or the book of Lamentations are often connected with the fall of Jerusalem in 587 B.C.E. Insinuations of concrete events, however, are rare in these texts, and they are insufficient to determine the date of text composition. Also, they would be of limited use, because the text was used and reused for decades or centuries, before becoming fixed canonically. The only thing we can say is that the final composition of Psalm 89 did happen well after the Babylonian conquest. But historical allusions have been "digested" by theological thinkers. And our psalm with all its reflections about Israel's fate at the hand of enemies is both a theological treatise and a piece of liturgy, probably part of meditative gatherings of defeated and dispersed people. Therefore we should locate its "social" or "ecclesiastical" setting within the community, although direct evidence of a "we" group is scarce (vv. 18-19, 51a). Meetings or regular worship services offered occasions to rethink the catastrophes of old.

## Intention

To secure again and maintain the grace of the Lord is the goal of our psalm. Extraordinarily, the leading officials of Israel do not speak for themselves. They provoke a debate over the most fundamental religious issue of their day. Their provisional solution is: no enemy or the guilt of the people has brought about the downfall of Israel, but solely Yahweh himself. In this spiritual context they want the congregation to "rebel" against God and exert pressures on him to take up again his covenant relationship with his chosen people. Since "your anointed" is the very last word of the prayer, after occurring in v. 39, and since the term "king" is avoided, messianic hope, similar to that found in Psalms 2 and 110, was possibly implanted in the text.

This interpretation is somewhat at odds with certain "canonical" views of the growth and division of the Psalter (cf., e.g., Goulder; Childs, *Introduction*, 517; Wilson, *Editing*, 212-15; idem, "Seams"). According to some of these exegetes, Psalm 89 is a landmark in an overall salvific history of Yahweh with his people through the Davidic dynasty (→ Psalms 2; 18; 20; 21; 45; 72; etc.). Our psalm supposedly indicates the failure of the Davidic covenant and its transfer to a future messianic king. In my opinion, the ancient promises of Yahweh have long been assimilated by the community, which is struggling to revive them in her own midst through her own institutions.

## Bibliography

S. Abramski, "The Beginning of the Israelite Monarchy and Its Impact upon Leadership in Israel," *Immanuel* 19 (1984/85) 7-21; G. W. Ahlström, *Psalm 89: Eine Liturgie aus dem Ritual des leidenden Königs* (Lund: Gleerup, 1959); W. Bittner, "Gott — Menschensohn — Davidsohn: Eine Untersuchung zur Traditionsgeschichte von Daniel 7:13f," *Freiburger Zeitschrift für Philosophie und Theologie* 32 (1985) 343-72; H. van der Bussche, "Le texte de la prophetie de Nathan sur la dynastie Davidique," *ETL* 24 (1948) 354-94; A. R. Ceresko, "Function of Chiasmus in Hebrew Poetry," *CBQ* 40 (1978) 1-10; R. J. Clifford, "Psalm 89: A Lament over the Davidic Ruler's Continued Failure," *HTR* 73 (1980) 35-47; J. Coppens, "Le messianisme royal II," *NRT* (1968) 225-51; J. L. Cunchillos, "Le dieu Mut, guerrier de El," *Syria* 62 (1985) 205-18; M. Dahood, "'Throne' in Ps. 89:37; 2 Sam 7:16; Soph 3,8 cf. UgM 127,22," *Bibliotheca Ephemeridum theologicarum Lovaniensium* 12 (1959) 276-88; idem, "The Composite Divine Name in Psalms 89:16-17 and 140:9," *Bib* 61 (1980) 277-78; D. M. Debuisson, "Une lecture du psaume 89," *Mélanges de science religieuse* 53 (1996) 275-92;

O. Eissfeldt, "Psalm 80 und Psalm 89," *WO* 3 (1964) 27-31 (repr. *KS* IV, 132-36); idem, "The Promises of Grace to David in Isa 55:1-5," in *Israel's Prophetic Heritage* (*Fest.* J. Muilenburg; ed. B. Anderson and W. Harrelson; New York: Harper & Brothers, 1962) 196-207; M. H. Floyd, "Psalm LXXXIX: A Prophetic Complaint about the Fulfillment of an Oracle," *VT* 42 (1992) 442-57; U. Glessmer, "Das Textwachstum von Ps 89 und ein Qumranfragment," *BN* 65 (1992) 55-73; H. Gottlieb, "El und Krt — Jahwe und David," *VT* 24 (1974) 159-67; S. Herrmann, "Die Königsnovelle in Ägypten und Israel," *Zeitschrift der Karl Marx Universität Leipzig*, Gesellschafts- und sprachwissenschaftliche Reihe 3 (1953/54) 33-45; G. Johannes, *Unvergleichlichkeitsformulierungen im Alten Testament* (diss., Mainz, 1968); A. R. Johnson, "The Role of the King in the Jerusalem Cultus," in *The Labyrinth* (ed. S. H. Hooke; London: SCM, 1935) 71-111; J. D. Levenson, "The Davidic Covenant and Its Modern Interpreters," *CBQ* 41 (1979) 205-219; E. Lipiński, *Le poème royal du psaume LXXXIX 1-5. 20-38* (Cahiers de la Revue biblique 6; Paris: Gabalda, 1967); C. Loeliger, "Biblical Concepts of Salvation and Melanesian Religion," *Point* 6 (1977) 134-45; H. G. May, "Aspect of the Imagery of World Dominion and World State in the Old Testament," in *Essays in Old Testament Ethics* (*Fest.* P. Hyatt; ed. J. L. Crenshaw and J. T. Willis; New York: Ktav, 1974) 57-76; J. L. Mays, "The David of the Psalms," *Int* 40 (1986) 143-55; idem, "In a Vision: The Portrayal of the Messiah in the Psalms," *Ex Auditu* 7 (1991) 1-8; T. N. Mettinger, "Yhwh Sabaoth: The Heavenly King on the Cherubim Throne," in *Studies in the Period of David and Solomon* (ed. T. Ishida; Winona Lake, Ind.: Eisenbrauns, 1992) 109-38; M. Metzger, "Eigentumsdeklaration und Schöpfungsaussage," in *'Wenn nicht jetzt'* (*Fest.* H.-J. Kraus; ed. H.-G. Geyer, et al.; Neukirchen-Vluyn: Neukirchener Verlag, 1983) 37-51; P. G. Mosca, "Once Again the Heavenly Witness of Ps 89:38," *JBL* 105 (1986) 27-37; idem, "Ugarit and Daniel 7: A Missing Link," *Bib* 67 (1986) 496-517; E. T. Mullen Jr., "The Divine Witness and the Davidic Royal Grant," *JBL* 102 (1983) 207-18; M. Noth, "Die Heiligen des Höchsten," *NorTT* 56 (1955) 146-61 (repr. in idem, *Gesammelte Studien zum Alten Testament* [Munich: Kaiser, 1957; 3rd ed. 1966] 274-90); D. Pardee, "The Semantic Parallelism of Psalm 89," in *In the Shelter of Elyon* (*Fest.* G. W. Ahlström; ed. W. B. Barrick, et al.; Sheffield: Sheffield Academic Press, 1984) 121-37; J. P. M. van der Ploeg, "Le sens et un problème textuel du Ps 89," in *Mélanges bibliques et orientaux* (*Fest.* H. Cazelles; ed. A. Caquot and M. Delcor; AOAT 212; Kevelaer: Butzon & Bercker; Neukirchen-Vluyn: Neukirchener Verlag, 1981) 471-81; G. von Rad, "Das judäische Königsritual," *TLZ* 72 (1947) 211-16 (repr. in idem, *Gesammelte Studien* [Munich: Kaiser, 1958] I, 205-13); V. Ravanelli, "Aspetti letterari del Salmo 89," *Studium Biblicum Franciscanum* 30 (1980) 7-46; B. Renaud, "La cohérence litteraire et théologique du Psaume 89," *RSR* 69 (1995) 419-33; L. Rost, "Sinaibund und Davidsbund," *TLZ* 72 (1947) 129-34; S. Sabugal, "La paternidad de Dios en la literature extraneotestamentaria," *Salmanticensis* 32 (1985) 141-51; M. Saebø, "Vom Grossreich zum Weltreich," *VT* 28 (1978) 83-91; N. M. Sarna, "Psalm 89: A Study in Inner Biblical Exegesis," in *Biblical and Other Studies* (ed. A. Altmann; Cambridge: Harvard University Press, 1963) 29-46; J. M. Schmidt, "Biblische Vorstellungen von 'Bund' als Grundlage und Orientierung für das jüdisch-christliche Gespräch," in *'Wenn nicht jetzt'* (*Fest.* H.-J. Kraus; ed. H.-G. Geyer, et al.; Neukirchen-Vluyn: Neukirchener Verlag, 1983) 153-68; W. H. Schmidt, "Kritik am Königtum," in *Probleme biblischer Theologie* (*Fest.* G. von Rad; ed. H. W. Wolff; Munich: Kaiser, 1971) 440-61; I. Shirun-Grumach, "Remarks on the Goddess Maat," in *Pharaonic Egypt* (ed. S. Israelit-Grool; Jerusalem: Magnes, 1985) 173-201; M. Simon, "La prophétie de Nathan et le Temple," *RHPR* 32 (1952) 41-58; T. M. Siqueira, "Salmo 89. A crise da promessa," *EstBib* 21 (1989) 30-38; V. H. Todd, "Biblical Eschatology: An Overview," *Cumberland Seminarian* 22 (1984) 3-16; R. Tournay, "Note sur le psaume LXXXIX,51-52," *RB* 83 (1976) 380-89; T. Veijola, *Verheissung in der Krise* (Helsinki: Suomalainen Tiedeakatemia, 1982); idem, "Davidverheissung und Staatsvertrag," *ZAW* 95 (1983) 9-31; idem, "Remarks of an Outsider Concerning Scandinavian Tradition History with Emphasis on the Davidic Tradition," in *The Productions of Time* (ed. K. Jeppesen, et al.; Sheffield: Almond, 1984) 29-51; idem, "The Witness in the Clouds: Ps 89:38," *JBL* 107 (1988) 413-17; S. Wagner, "Das Reich des Messias: Zur Theologie der alttestamentlichen Königspsalmen," *TLZ* 109 (1984) 865-74; J. M. Ward, "A Literary and Exegetical Study of the 89th Psalm" (diss., University of Michigan, Ann Arbor, 1958); idem, "The Literary Form and Liturgical Background of Psalm 89," *VT* 11 (1961) 321-39; E. J. Waschke, "Das Verhältnis alttestamentlicher Überlieferungen im Schnittpunkt der Dynastiezusage und die Dynastiezusage im Spiegel alttestamentlicher Überlieferungen," *ZAW* 99 (1987) 157-79; G. H. Wilson, "The Use of Royal Psalms at the 'Seams' of the Hebrew Psalter," *JSOT* 35 (1986) 85-94.

# CHAPTER 5

# THE INDIVIDUAL UNITS OF BOOK 4 (Psalms 90–106)

## Psalm 90:
## Meditation

### *Structure*

|  | MT | NRSV |
|---|---|---|
| I. Superscription | 1a | - |
| II. Hymnic praise | 1b-2 | 1-2 |
| III. Meditation | 3-12 | 3-12 |
| A. Description | 3-6 | 3-6 |
| B. Scrutiny | 7-10 | 7-10 |
| C. Reactions | 11-12 | 11-12 |
| IV. Petition | 13-17 | 13-17 |

Psalm 90, the first of a new "book" of Psalms, is the only one attributed to Moses. Why is this so? Perhaps the late collectors and editors of the psalms wanted to mark a new beginning of Israel, after the downfall of the monarchy, as a Torah-centered community (→ Psalm 89, Intention), or were dwelling on some affinities of Psalm 90 to the Song of Moses (Deuteronomy 32), or they simply thought of Moses as the most ancient hero of their history. He was closest to primeval antiquity, he was the most intimate with God (Exod 33:11); therefore he should have the best information about prehistoric times. The SUPERSCRIPTION, in consequence, names Moses "man of God," a title otherwise restricted to prophetical figures of the monarchic period. The psalm itself is classified *těpillāh,* "prayer," like Psalm 86 and only one more song in the Psalter (Psalm 102), perhaps because of basic human anxieties expressed throughout vv. 1-12.

A brief look at our psalm, however, suggests that the original text can be neither derived from Moses or his epoch nor interpreted as a petitionary prayer taken from emergency rituals for suffering individuals or threatened communities (see "Introduction to Cultic Poetry," section 4B). One of the most salient formal characteristics of the poem is its intense "we" oratory. Considering subject matter, theological concepts, and modes of reflection, we are led into the latest layers of the OT. Moses cannot be the author of Psalm 90. His name in the superscription is relevant for evaluating the history of interpretation of our psalm and its influence on later theological thinking. Formally "the psalm is a communal prayer composed of grateful reflection, complaint, and petitions for gracious divine action." Contents, topics, and spirituality testify, on the other hand, "that Ps 90 is a literary composition, belonging to the category of 'learned psalmography,' i.e., psalmography from the circles of sages and scribes for the use of individuals and groups, but especially for personal piety and devotion" (Tate, 437 and 439, the last citation with reference to von Rad, "Der 90. Psalm").

The introductory part of our psalm has a rare invocation: *'ădōnāy*, "my Lord" (v. 1b). This appellation is usually connected with "Yahweh" (cf. 86:1, 3; 130:1-2; Jer 1:6; 4:10; 14:13; 32:17; Ezek 4:14). Is this supposed to be a very archaic designation, as in Gen 18:30, 32; Exod 4:10, 13; 5:22? Or has there once been another epithet of Yahweh instead of MT *mā'ôn*, "(covered) dwelling" (some MSS have *mā'ōz*, "strength")? Either "dwelling" or "strength" makes an unusual Hebrew phrase with the word order: predicate noun — subject — verb — prepositional object (cf. C. Brockelmann, *Hebräische Syntax* [Neukirchen: Erziehungsverein, 1956] 49). The introduction establishing contact with God is couched in "you are" phrases (vv. 1b, 2c) characteristic of prayer hymns (cf. 89:10-13). Thematically it is dealing with God's "eternity" (in the Semitic, not the Greek, sense: long, uncontrollable duration, ages; cf. H. D. Preuss, *TWAT* V, 1144-59). Beside the direct address of the yet unnamed deity, the communal "us" (v. 1b) is noteworthy. With the first two lines the theme of Psalm 90 is set. God is permanent, he endures for ages, but what about humankind?

Transitoriness of all human life, always a problem for individuals and groups, at certain cultural junctures becomes a principal existential dilemma. It does not happen necessarily when danger of death is highest (e.g., during wars, epidemics, or famines). Thematization of transitoriness seems to accompany periods of cultural and religious weakness or uncertainty. In our case, clearly a whole community is lamenting the shortness and ineffectiveness of biographical time and experience. A first section of this fundamental MEDITATION is more descriptive and summarizes, as it were, the dire fate of living creatures (vv. 3-6). Grass and greenery wither away in one day (vv. 5b-6; cf. Isa 40:6-8). The metaphor apparently became a topic in exilic preaching; other comparisons (v. 5a: "stream"? "sleep"?) are textually uncertain. The background for such a lament is, of course, the unbelievable durability of God, for whom a thousand years are equal to one human day (v. 4; likely the introductory *kî* is exclamatory, not a causal conjunction), measures that cannot be compared or put into a reasonable relationship whatsoever. If the subject matter of this first segment is human evanescence, then v. 3 can hardly refer to death and resurrection, as some translations have it. Rather, the double use of the verb *šûb* in v. 3 reinforces the same idea: human beings return to dust (cf. Gen 3:19). Thus the verse becomes the topical heading not only of vv. 4-6 but of the meditative unit vv. 3-12 as a whole. The structure of the reflective DESCRIPTION is lucid: a general thesis (v. 3) is contrasted to an absolute antithesis (v. 4), but there is no possible synthesis. God's durability makes humans feel wretchedly unstable and insignificant. This kind of argumentation is not reminiscent of older wisdom; it does have affinities with Ecclesiastes.

Following such general affirmations, the SCRUTINY of reasons for all this fragility (vv. 7-10) does not concentrate on humankind as such but on the particular community reciting the psalm. First person plural now is the absolutely dominant verbal form, and suffixes of the same kind are attached to most nouns. Ties to the community are stressed to such an extent that the ligature seems almost compulsory. Transience, clearly recognized to be a general human destiny, is linked to 'āwōn, "guilt," of this particular group (v. 8; "known and hidden guilt" is a very ancient formula; cf. Akk. *annu idu u la idu,* "sin known and unknown": Mayer, *Untersuchungen,* 114; listing at "Introduction to Cultic Poetry"; R. C. Cover, *ABD* VI, 31-40) and to 'ap, "anger," and ḥēmāh, "wrath" (v. 7), of God. This seems inconsistent unless we assume that the community is living not in spiritual isolation but ideologically tuned to interhuman and international concerns (see PETITION below). The element under discussion exhibits traces of general lament, like Psalms 14; 39; 73. The main sentiment of vv. 7, 9, 10 is: life is passing rapidly, flying away (cf. Job 7:6-9; 9:25; 14:1-22); it is 'āmāl wā'āwen, "toil and trouble" (cf. Pss 10:17; 55:11 [RSV 10]; Isa 59:4; Job 15:35; one of Ecclesiastes' favorite terms is 'āmāl). Parallels in late wisdom writings suggest that this mode of lamenting scrutiny of human existence was fashionable in the third century B.C.E. (cf. Hengel, *Judentum;* listing at Additional Bibliography, section B).

Vv. 11-12 draw conclusions from reflections and scrutiny, first in generalized language but maintaining second-person prayer style (v. 11), then coming back to first-person group-oriented petitionary (imperative) counsel: "Teach [us] to number our days that we may bring [our] heart [into] wisdom" (v. 12; many propose to smooth the text by emending the second colon). With the final word of v. 12, ḥokmāh, "wisdom," we are manifestly in the field of sapiential discourse valid for all human beings. The rhetorical question "Who can estimate the power of your anger?" (v. 11a) derives from challenge speech in sapiential contests (cf. Job 25:3-4; 28:12, 20; 38:18, 33, 37; 41:2b, 3), in our case drawn into laudatory prayer. The contestation formula used in confrontations of wise men may be found in Job 38:3b; 40:7b; 42:4b: "I will question you, let me know" (cf. similar expressions: Job 6:24; 8:8; 11:5; 12:7; 13:22; etc.).

The psalm ends in PETITION (vv. 13-17) with clear shifts in emphasis. The reference group in vv. 3-12 had been human beings in general (cf. thematic line v. 3), and the real subject matter was their deplorable destiny of being cast away into the quickly moving current of time. We found this to be valid even though the prayer was pushing a community of first-person reciters into the foreground (vv. 7-12). From v. 13 on, however, the situation changes radically. No longer are "man" and "humankind" at the center of attention, but "your servants" (vv. 13b, 16a) and "their sons" (v. 16b). Moreover, the main theme of the preceding parts — the shortness and insignificance of life — is left behind altogether. All of a sudden the prayer laments some "years of evil" (v. 15b) that *Yahweh* is asked to end and replace with periods of bliss (vv. 14-16; Yahweh is named only here; cf. general appellations in vv. 2, 17). The community pleads for God to *return (šûb)*, as if he had been absent for a while, a typical expression of complaints (v. 13; cf. 6:5 [RSV 4]; 80:15 [RSV 14]; 85:5 [RSV 4]; Isa 63:17). The expression may pick up in a different sense the concept of *šûb*, "return," of v. 3. God is expected to fill his people with victorious joy after they passed through trouble and need (vv. 14b, 15). They want to witness his great actions of salvation (v. 16) and hope for continuous blessing of their daily work (v. 17: because of the general naming of the Deity and rather vague wish for blessings, this verse could be a closing line of section III, but only remotely so). All these features in vv. 13-17 do not agree with the thrust of vv. 1-12 and their melancholic view of transient life. Formally, part IV with its "we/us" prayer style definitely belongs to the body of Psalm 90. But perspectives change in vv. 13-17. This final PETITION is rooted in communal complaints (see "Introduction to Cultic Poetry," section 4B) adapted to the congregational situation of later times. It does not pursue the common plight of every mortal being. Yahweh has castigated his servants (v. 15); the entreaty of the community is for renewed help and blessing.

## Genre

Genre characteristics in themselves are not unambiguous in this famous reflective psalm. We noted traits of complaint and petition, praise and sapiential reflection, contest literature and theological argumentation. If one considers a possible setting in early Jewish community life, however, all these indicators fall into line and support formal evidence of congregational use ("we" discourse). Therefore a classification as communal MEDITATION seems in order.

## Setting

Lack of individual voices and strong accentuation of communal speech guarantee use of the text in assemblies (cf. P. D. Hanson, *ABD* I, 1099-1103). At the same time they do not exclude the possibility of one liturgical leader speaking for the whole congregation, including him- or herself in the first person plural. Which liturgical proceedings are we allowed to imagine? Psalm 90 being a highly reflective text, and participation of the whole community in worship services probably being restricted to short refrains and shouts of praise, thanksgiving, petition, it may be reasonable to think of professional liturgists who recited the psalm within the assembly. The time suggested by late sapiential terminology and outlook on life is the fourth or third century B.C.E., somewhere in the neighborhood of Job and Ecclesiastes (cf. J. L. Crenshaw, *ABD* III, 858-68; idem, *ABD* II, 271-80). With these books Psalm 90 shares a

161

mode of contemplating philosophically existential human problems. Questions of life and death, transitoriness and security are pondered in an almost ageless way.

## Intention

Wisdom reflection, like all scholarly effort, is proud to analyze problems and articulate insights, thereby illuminating human existence in the face of absolute values. In so doing the authors and cantors of Psalm 90, sages of their time, utilize prayer forms and the (weekly?) worship setting to communicate their higher knowledge about life and death to the community. They also add ordinary petitions to the more academic corpus of the psalm. Their intentions, without doubt, were to instruct and console the whole congregation, which was facing general human anxieties as well as special hardships under foreign rule.

## Bibliography

P. Auffret, "Essai sur la structure littéraire du Psaume 90," *Bib* 61 (1980) 262-76; P. S. Baker, "A Little Known Variant Text of the Old English Metrical Psalms," *Speculum* 59 (1984) 263-81; H. M. Barth, "Leben und sterben können . . . ," in *Ars moriendi in der Theologie Martin Luthers* (ed. H. Wagner and T. Kruse; Freiburg im Breisgau: Herder, 1989) 45-66; T. Booij, "Psalm 90:5-6: Junction of Two Traditional Motifs," *Bib* 68 (1987) 393-96; J.-P. Bouhot, "Hesychius de Salone et Augustin," in *Saint Augustin et la Bible* (ed. A.-M. La Bonnardière; Paris: Beauchesne, 1986) 229-50; M. Camroux, "The Passing of Time," *ExpTim* 95 (1984) 109-10; J. F. Creach, "The Shape of Book Four of the Psalter and the Shape of Second Isaiah," *JSOT* 80 (1998) 63-76; J. L. Crenshaw, "The Expression *mî yôdēaʿ* in the Hebrew Bible," *VT* 36 (1986) 274-88; M. Dahood, "Interrogative *kî* in Psalm 90,11; Isaiah 36,19, and Hosea 13,9," *Bib* 60 (1979) 573-74; G. R. Driver, "Old Problems Re-examined," *ZAW* 80 (1968) 174-83; G. A. Fitchett, "Wisdom and Folly in Death and Dying," *Journal of Religion and Health* 19 (1980) 203-14; J. A. Foster, "The Motherhood of God," in *Uncovering Ancient Stones* (ed. L. Hopfe; Winona Lake, Ind.: Eisenbrauns, 1994) 93-102; T. E. Fretheim, "The Color of God," *Word & World* 6 (1986) 256-65; R. W. Goetsch, "'The Lord Is My Refuge,'" *Classical Journal* 9 (1983) 140-45; S. D. Goitein, "*Māʿōn* — A Reminder of Sin," *JSS* 10 (1965) 52-53; N. Greinacher, "Psalm 90," in *Die Freude an Gott* (*Fest.* O. Knoch; ed. J. Degenhardt; Stuttgart: Katholisches Bibelwerk, 1991) 366-77; W. Harrelson, "A Meditation on the Wrath of God: Psalm 90," in *Scripture in History and Theology* (*Fest.* J. C. Rylaarsdam; ed. A. L. Merrill; Pittsburgh: Pickwick, 1977) 181-91; F. Hesse, "'Und wenn's hoch geht, so sind's 80 Jahre.' Zum Verständnis des 90. Psalms," *Pastoraltheologie* 57 (1968) 297-302; D. M. Howard Jr., "A Contextual Reading of Psalms 90–94," in *The Shape and Shaping of the Psalter* (JSOTSup 159; ed. J. McCann Jr.; Sheffield: Sheffield Academic Press, 1993) 90-94; J. Howell, "A Hermeneutical Approach to Psalm 90" (diss., Duke, 1984); W. Jens, "Psalm 90: On Transience," *Lutheran Quarterly* 9 (1995) 177-89; T. Krüger, "Psalm 90 und die 'Vergänglichkeit des Menschen,'" *Bib* 75 (1994) 191-219; J. D. Levenson, "A Technical Meaning for *nʿm* in the Hebrew Bible," *VT* 35 (1985) 61-67; H. P. Müller, "Der 90. Psalm, ein Paradigma exegetischer Aufgaben," *ZTK* 81 (1984) 265-85; R. Nysse, "The Dark Side of God," *Word & World* 17 (1997) 437-46; H. Quecke, "Ein faijumisches Fragment aus Ps 90 (91)," in *Studien zu Geschichte, Kultur und Religion Ägyptens und des alten Testaments (Fest.* E. Edel; ed. M. Görg, et al.; Bamberg: M. Görg, 1979) 332-37; G. von Rad, "Der 90. Psalm," in *Gottes Wirken in Israel* (ed. O. H. Steck; Neukirchen-Vluyn: Neukirchener Verlag, 1974) 268-83; D. Robertson, "Literary Criticism of the Bible: Psalm 90 and Shelley's 'Hymn to Intellectual Beauty'," *Semeia* 8 (1977) 35-50; J. T. van Ruiten, "Van tekst tot tekst: Psalm 90 en Jubilee 23:12-15," *Nederlands theologisch Tijdschrift* 47 (1993) 177-85; M. Schlicht, "Luthers Vorlesung über Psalm 90," *Lutherjahrbuch* 62 (1995) 242-43; W. H. Schmidt, " 'Der Du die Menschen lässest sterben': Exegetische Anmerkungen zu Ps 90," in *Was ist der Mensch?* (ed. F. Crüsemann, et al.; Munich: Kaiser, 1992) 115-30; W. Schrage, " 'Ein Tag ist beim Herrn wie tausend Jahre, und tausend Jahre sind wie ein Tag,' " in *Glaube und Eschatologie* (ed. E. Grässer and O. Merk; Tübingen: Mohr, 1985) 267-75; S. Schreiner, "Erwägungen zur Struktur des 90. Psalms," *Bib* 59 (1978) 80-90; K. Seybold, "Zu den Zeitvorstellungen in Psalm 90," *TZ* 53 (1997) 97-108; W. von Soden, "Zum Psalm 90–3: Statt dakkā lies dukkā?" *UF* 15 (1983) 307-18; S. W. Sykes, "Death and Doctrine," *Churchman* 95 (1981) 306-312; D. Winton Thomas, "A Note on Psalm 90,5," *VT* 18 (1968) 267-68; M. Tsevat, "Psalm 90:5-6," *VT* 35 (1985) 115-17; W. J. Urbrock, "Psalm 90: Moses, Mortality, and . . . the Morning," *Currents in Theology and Mission* 25 (1998) 26-29; B. Vawter, "Postexilic Prayer and Hope," *CBQ* 37 (1975) 460-70; L. Wächter, "Drei umstrittene Psalmenstellen (Ps. 26,1; 30,8; 90,4-6)," *ZAW* 78 (1966) 61-68; H. M. Wahl, "Psalm 90,12: Text, Tradition und Interpretation," *ZAW* 106 (1994) 116-23; C. Westermann, "Der 90. Psalm," in *Forschung am Alten Testament* II (TBü 55; Munich: Kaiser, 1974) 344-50; C. Whitley, "The Text of Psalm 90,5," *Bib* 62 (1981) 555-57; G. H. Wilson, "The Use of 'Untitled' Psalms in the Hebrew Psalter," *ZAW* 97 (1985) 404-13; E. Zenger, "Israel und Kirche im gemeinsamen Gottesbund: Beobachtungen zum theologischen Programm des 4. Psalmbuches (Ps 90-106)," in *Israel und Kirche heute (Fest.* E. L. Ehrlich; ed. M. Marcus, et al.; Freiburg: Herder, 1991) 236-54.

# Psalm 91:
# Benediction; Sermon

## *Structure*

|  | MT | NRSV |
|---|---|---|
| I. Felicitation | 1-2 | 1-2 |
|   A. Statement | 1 | 1 |
|   B. Exhortation | 2 | 2 |
| II. Personal blessings | 3-13 | 3-13 |
|   A. Apotropaic sayings | 3-8 | 3-8 |
|   B. Protective sayings | 9-13 | 9-13 |
| III. Divine reflection and promise | 14-16 | 14-16 |

The absence of a SUPERSCRIPTION is noticeable in a number of psalms, increasingly so within the latter part of the Psalter (→ Psalms 33; 71; 93-97); to "amend" this deficiency LXX provides a David heading.

According to form-critical standards, the first two lines are a little obscure. MT does not make good sense: "He who stays in the shelter of the Most High . . . , I will say to Yahweh. . . ." Most translators change the beginning of v. 2 in accordance with the LXX correction: ". . . he will say. . . ." NRSV opts for "You will say," in accordance with vv. 3-13. However, the opening term of v. 1 could well be that standard verbal expression, a masculine singular participle, which quite often follows benedictory *'ašrê,* "happy the one who . . ." (cf. *'ašrê* in the opening position: 1:1; 32:1-2; 41:2 [RSV 1]; 112:1; 119:1-2; 128:1; Gunkel, 406; Mowinckel, *PsSt* III, 102-3). In this case the second line need not furnish a belated subject to v. 1 but may begin with a self-exhortation (or a confessional statement) of a suppliant who asks for a helpful word in his troubles: "I speak [or 'want to speak'] to Yahweh: he is my refuge and my fortress, my God in whom I trust." Parallel expressions are frequent in individual complaints (cf. only 31:2-4 [RSV 1-3]; 71:1-3), but there they mostly occur in direct address to the Deity. All the more significant is the third-person formulation in v. 2. The suppliant, so it seems, speaks for himself, but in the direction of the officiant, professing his desire to return into the shelter of a benevolent God, portrayed in the felicitation of v. 1. First-person prayer introduced with *'ōmar,* "I say," also occurs in 102:25 (RSV 24); in both cases later tradition took issue with the verbal form, changing it into an expression that fitted the literary flow of thought. But the liturgical setup that we surmise should be held responsible for the structure of the poem.

There is a clear change of speakers beginning with v. 3. Someone is talking about what God will be doing for "you," and the addressed one must be the suppliant of v. 2 (seeking refuge in the temple? thus Delekat, *Asylie;* or preparing for battle? thus Johnson, *Prophet,* 184-91; or converting to Yahwism? thus Eissfeldt, "Jahwes Verhältnis"; for the first two references listing at "Introduction to Psalms"). The whole segment (vv. 3-13) is uniform in this regard, constantly aiming at the person who needs comfort and consolation. But it features two distinct subunits, both introduced by exclamatory or affirming *kî,* "indeed" (vv. 3a, 9a). First, the speaker communicates salvation through God's intervention as well as banishment of evil powers actually afflicting the miserable (vv. 3-8). Only in the last line of this part, in a kind of summarizing effort, are the adversaries called *rěšāʿîm,* "evil ones" (v. 8b). The second part consists of personal BLESSINGS dedicated to future protection (vv. 9-10). Thus we have a clear liturgical sequence. The suppliant needs to be liberated from the ills that beset him, and he wants to receive guarantees of further accompaniment and protection (cf. Psalm 121). APOTROPAIC and PROTECTIVE DICTA are widely used in magical and healing proceedings of all cultures (cf. Fabian, "Role"; Rasmussen, *Possession;* Reichard, *Prayer;* idem, *Religion,* 288: Navaho songs are covers! 308-13: talking prayersticks; see index, s.v. "blessing." For all books see Additional Bibliography, section B).

Analyzing the details of both subunits, we note first the language of (Priestly?) counseling (→ ASSURANCE FORMULA, "Do not fear," v. 5a). Vv. 3

THE INDIVIDUAL UNITS OF BOOK FOUR

and 8 frame this central pronouncement with consonant affirmations. Asseverative *kî,* "yes!" heralds the decisive word to the sufferer: "He [God] will save you" or rather in the present tense: "He is saving you" (v. 3a, with emphatic personal pronoun; cf. the frequent plea: *haṣṣîlēnî,* "save me," 7:2 [RSV 1]; 31:3, 16 [RSV 2, 15]; 59:2, 3 [RSV 1, 2]; 109:21; 142:7 [RSV 6]; 144:7, 11; etc.). Mythical and metaphorical concepts blend in vv. 3-8: dangers threatening the suppliant are like snares and "deadly pestilence" (v. 3b; Exod 9:1-6; 2 Sam 24:13-15; Jer 21:6, 9; etc.; cf. Kaupel, Lubetski); they are overcome by divine action. God's "wings" are tokens of protection; cf. Ps 17:8 and the tradition of winged guardians in Assyrian religious history as well as in Jerusalemite temple equipment (1 Kgs 6:23-27; W. Dommershausen, *TWAT* IV, 243-46; F. C. Fensham, "Winged Gods and Goddesses in the Ugaritic Tablets," *OrAnt* 5 [1966] 157-64). The image of God's sheltering wings is almost proverbial in the Psalms and beyond (cf. Pss 17:8; 36:8 [RSV 7]; 57:2 [RSV 1]; 61:5 [RSV 4]; 63:8 [RSV 7]; Ruth 2:12; Isa 8:8; Deut 32:11). Also, metaphors from the military world like "shield" and "wall" (v. 4c) are well adapted into liturgical language (cf. also v. 7). The focal point of the passage, however, is vv. 5-6, which may once have been independent from the present context. These verses stand out by formulaic introduction (v. 5a; cf. Isa 43:1-7; 44:2-5; Begrich, "Heilsorakel"; listing at "Introduction to Cultic Poetry"), regular structure (two lines of bicola, set in between possible tricola, vv. 4 and 7), enumeration of four most likely demonic figures (cf. Nicolsky, *Spuren;* Keel, *Welt,* 68-74; listing at "Introduction to Cultic Poetry"). This little dictum of assurance has apparently been used in critical situations of complaint and petition. After stating that the "battle" will not harm the faithful (v. 7, which seems to connect well with v. 4), the closing line in v. 8 announces victory and gloating joy over against the evildoers.

A second round of blessing follows; was it to be used subsequently or alternatively in ceremonial procedure? The opening again is with asseverative *kî,* "yes" (v. 9a; cf. v. 3a), presenting a person: "You." The following word *(maḥsî)* again has an enigmatic first-person speaker in it, just like v. 2a; the phrase means literally: "You, Yahweh, are my refuge." This reading does not correspond at all with v. 9b: "You made Elyon your habitation." The parallel cola address different parties. Most translators adjust v. 9a to 9b by simply changing the suffix of the predicate, thus gaining a human addressee: "You made Yahweh your refuge." Perhaps, however, MT is correct, and we do have a liturgical allocution: "Yes! You [say]: Yahweh is my refuge. You make Elyon your habitation." The speaker resumes the confessional statement of v. 2a, making it the condition of his new assurance speech. The consequences of taking refuge with Yahweh are greatly encouraging (vv. 10-13): no evil, not even a God-sent "blow" *(nega';* v. 10; cf. L. Schwienhorst, *TWAT* V, 219-26), will hit the suppliant. On the contrary, he will be carried safely by "angels" through rough times (vv. 11-12; cf. Luke 4:10-11; D. N. Freedman, B. E. Willoughby, and H.-J. Fabry, *TWAT* IV, 887-904). Again we may ask — especially in the light of NT quotations of the passage as in Luke 4:10-11 (par. Matt 4:6; reference to v. 13 = Luke 10:19; Mark 16:18) — whether vv. 11-12 once had been an autonomous saying, for example, a toast to a young man or woman beginning their adult-

165

life's journey, or a blessing for a recuperated patient. Separation from the context is not so clear as in vv. 5-6, however. There are hardly any formal indications, although vv. 11-12 do have a distinct subject matter. Angelology, as extant in our passage ("messengers" who carry a person on their hands are "angels" in the later sense), was a growing belief in late OT and postcanonical times (cf. Ps 34:8 [RSV 7]; Dan 3:24-28; Tobit 5–7). It does tune in also with ancient Near Eastern concepts of protective divine beings (cf. J. Black, et al., *Gods;* van der Toorn, et al., *Dictionary,* Additional Bibliography, section B).

Mediated assurance sayings come to an end in v. 13, a victory line like v. 8. Stepping on the defeated was a gesture of absolute superiority over and subjugation of enemies. Mythological and demonistic traits emerge again. Four animal or, alternatively, demonic beings (cf. Nicolsky, 24-25) are defeated and laid underfoot.

Next comes the most spectacular final part of Psalm 91. A speaker — not at all manifest in vv. 1-13 — reveals him- or herself by explicit first-person singular discourse in vv. 14-16. The anonymous voice, judging from contents and intentions, can only be Yahweh himself reflecting on his motivations and mentioning his client only in the third person, in sharp contrast to vv. 3-13. Starting with a third exclamatory *kî,* "yes" (v. 14a), Yahweh positively evaluates actions and attitudes of the supplicant and relates his own reactions — but to whom? The only feasible audience would be the congregation of worshipers or the cultic functionary, through whom Yahweh is communicating himself. For formal and situational reasons, therefore, the passage cannot be a direct "oracle," as maintained in many analyses. Equally, it is not theologically legitimate to treat these words as the genuine and direct communication of God himself falling from heaven. Scripture in no part offers an unmediated access to the eternal, unchanging reality. The eternal Word is available for us only in conditioned and definitely noneternal words, phrases, languages, mediated by transitory humans. They are highly dependent on their respective social, cultural, and historical situations. So, what are vv. 14-16 about? Exposing the profile of a real "righteous" man ("sticking to," "knowing," "calling" on Yahweh, vv. 14-15; cf. Psalms 1; 119), they have certainly been communicated by some official of the early Jewish congregation. They confirm and undergird the benedictions of vv. 3-13 and even may give a *post-festum* argument, perhaps a defensive one, why a supplicant is being helped like this, without first bringing to bear proper complaint, petition, confession of sin, absolution, etc.

## Genre/Setting

Psalm 91 in many respects is somewhat unusual. Is it possibly only a fragment for an individual complaint and petition service? Already Mowinckel suggested a similar solution. In that case we would have to imagine, along the line of individual complaint rituals (Gerstenberger, *Mensch*), that a petitionary psalm had to precede our text, which in itself takes care of only the assurance function. Alternatively, one could think of specialized psalms, which, without being "fragments," furnished good material for particular parts of worship only. In our case, words of assurance would be used to comfort frustrated sufferers who had brought their plight before Yahweh (cf. Psalm 102:1 [RSV superscription]). The existence of two subsequent "words of assurance" in vv. 3-13 strengthens the case for liturgical use of our psalm. Perhaps we should consider the term "psalm of blessing" (Mowinckel, *PsSt* V, 33-60), but the formal characteristics of blessing (cf. Deut 27:12; 28:3-6; Lev 26:3-13) are not very obvious in our case. Other attempts to fix genre and setting for Psalm 91 are less convincing, if they do not consider these liturgical possibilities of interpretation. Gunkel, et al., consider institutionalized cultic instruction to have been the proper locale of transmission. Thus Hugger speaks about an "aftermath of cultic instruction" (pp. 16-27). Stuhlmueller (p. 73) and Tate (p. 450) prefer the designation "sermon [or sermonette] of encouragment," while rabbinic interpreters call our psalm a "protective song" for encounters with evil situations. These classifications point more or less clearly to a local Jewish community and worship situation, where individuals found consolation in their distress. They were comforted by leaders or liturgists of the worship ceremony, in the name of the protective Deity. Divine assurance undoubtedly comes to a climax in vv. 14-16. Just as the preaching of Second Isaiah uses the (unchanged) oracle form ("Don't be afraid, I am with you!" cf. Isa 41:10-14; 43:1, 5; 44:2; 51:7; 54:4; →SALVATION ORACLE), our psalm employs a slightly modified version of this pattern, revealing its liturgical use: the third person of the suppliant is hardly a "descriptive vocative" (Johnson, *Prophet*) but implies transmission by the liturgist. In this fashion the whole psalm remains a BENEDICTION preached to the community in worship.

## Intention

Vv. 1-13 furnish liturgical statements to comfort those who seek refuge with their God. They deserve consolation, and we do not know on what conditions they got it (preceding complaint-petition service? cf. 1 Samuel 1-2; confession and absolution of sins? cf. 2 Sam 12:13; Job 33:26; proof of innocence, perhaps by ordeal? cf. Num 5:11-31). Divine assurance (vv. 14-16) is the ultimate confirmation of such a favorable intention. This very last part of our psalm also may try to resolve a disturbing theological question, similar to that posed in the book of Jonah: How is it possible that someone receives such unconditional promises of divine help and human prosperity? The answer given is: No, Yahweh enters into action only if a suppliant proves to be a loyal follower of Israel's God. The main part of Psalm 91, however, does not betray the least concern about God's excessive indulgence.

## Bibliography

R. Arbesmann, "The Daemonium meridianum and Greek and Latin Exegesis," *Traditio* 14 (1958) 17-31; P. Auffret, "'Car toi, tu as agi.' Étude structurelle du Psaume 91," *Bijdragen* 51 (1990) 118-38; E. Beaucamp, "Le repos dans la maison de Dieu: Ps. 91,"

*BVC* 76 (1967) 55-64; S. Beck, "A Handle in the Emptiness," *Cumberland Seminarian* 27 (1989) 87-90; U. Bergmann, "Old Testament Concepts of Blessing: Their Relevance for a Theological Interpretation of Cargo Cult," *Point* 3 (1974) 176-86; L. F. Bliese, "Figurative Language in the Psalms," *BT* 41 (1990) 445; A. Caquot, "Le Psaume XCI," *Sem* 8 (1958) 21-37; O. Eissfeldt, "Jahwes Verhältnis zu Eljon und Schaddaj nach Psalm 91," *WO* 2 (1954-59) 343-48 (repr. idem, *KS* III, 441-47); idem, "Eine Qumran-Textform des 91. Psalms," in *Bibel und Qumran* (*Fest.* H. Bardtke; ed. S. Wagner; Berlin: Evangelische Haupt- und Bibelgesellschaft, 1968) 82-85 (repr. idem, *KS* V, 45-49); J. de Fraine, "Le 'démon du midi' (Ps 91/90,6)," *Bib* 40 (1959) 372-83; S. Hidal, "Israel och hellas: tva världar eller en enda verklighet?" *Svensk Teologisk Kvartalskrift* 61 (1985) 49-58; P. Hugger, *Jahwe meine Zuflucht: Gestalt und Theologie des 91. Psalms* (Münsterschwarzach: Vier-Türme, 1971); H. Kaupel, "Ps 91 (Vulg. 90: 'Qui habitat in adjutorio Altissimi') und die Dämonen," *TGl* 16 (1924) 174-79; S. Landersdorfer, "Das daemonium meridiarum (Ps 91/90,6)," *BZ* 18 (1929) 294-300; B. A. Levine and J. M. de Tarragon, "Dead Kings and Rephaim: The Patrons of the Ugaritic Dynasty," *JAOS* 104 (1984) 649-59; M. Lubetski, "The Utterance from the East: The Sense of *hwt* in Psalms 52:4, 9; 91:3," *Religion* 20 (1990) 217-32; A. A. Macintosh, "Psalm XCI,4 and the Root *shr,*" *VT* 23 (1973) 56-62; K. Maly, *Im Geist der Bibel beten: Eine Einführung am Beispiel von Ps. 91* (Frankfurt: J. Knecht, 1983); N. Nicolsky, *Spuren magischer Formeln in den Psalmen* (BZAW 46; Giessen: Töpelmann, 1927) 14-29; R. D. Patterson, "Calling on God," *Fundamentalist Journal* 3 (1984) 17; J. van der Ploeg, "Le Psaume XCI dans une recension de Qumran," *RB* 72 (1965) 210-17; A. Quacquarelli, "Il salmo 90 (91) nei riflessi dell'arte ravennate del V. secolo," *Corsi di Cultura* 21 (1974) 237-43; W. Schottroff, "'Wohin ich getrost fliehen kann . . . ,'" *Junge Kirche* 57 (1996) 284-87; W. Speyer, "Mittag und Mitternacht als heilige Zeiten in Antike und Christentum," in *Vivarium* (*Fest.* T. Klauser; ed. E. Dassmann, et al.; Münster: Aschendorff, 1984) 314-26; A. K. Squire, "Adam's Song in a Commentary of Hilary of Poitiers (Ps 91)," *Studia Patristica* 17 (1982) 338-42; H. Vorländer, *Mein Gott,* 287-91 (listing at "Introduction to Cultic Poetry"); L. Wachinger, "Spiegelung und dunkles Wort: Tiefenpsychologische Schriftauslegung — am Beispiel des Ps 91 (90)," *Liturgie und Dichtung II* (ed. H. Becker, et al.; St. Ottilien: EOS, 1983) 335-57; F. S. Welsham, "Psalm 91 in Relation to a Malavian Background," *Journal of Theology for Southern Africa* 8 (1974) 24-30.

# Psalm 92:
# Hymnic Prayer

## *Structure*

|                                | MT   | NRSV |
| ------------------------------ | ---- | ---- |
| I. Superscription              | 1    | -    |
| II. Praise of God              | 2-5  | 1-4  |
| A. Opening                     | 2-4  | 1-3  |
| B. Personal hymn               | 5    | 4    |
| III. Denunciation of adversaries | 6-12 | 5-11 |

168

| A. Praise of God | 6 | 5 |
|---|---|---|
| B. Description of foes | 7-8 | 6-7 |
| C. Praise of God | 9 | 8 |
| D. Repulsion of foes | 10-12 | 9-11 |
| IV. Praise of the just one | 13-16 | 12-15 |

Against most rules of formulating a heading for a liturgical psalm, our SUPERSCRIPTION omits possible references to any "author." It lists only two musical technical terms, and it indicates a liturgical use for the prayer to follow: the song is to be intoned on the Sabbath day. As special hymns for this weekly event from the Qumran library prove, there were community services on Sabbath days as early as the second century B.C.E. We do not have vestiges, however, of earlier Sabbath hymns or worship services (cf. García Martínez, *Dead Sea Scrolls,* 419-31; listing at Additional Bibliography, section B; E. Haag, *TWAT* VII, 1047-57).

Our psalm seems to be a kind of confessional declaration with harsh polemics against those who do not believe in Yahweh or perhaps deviate in their worship from the God of Israel as established in the psalm-singer's community. Throughout we find "I" identifications of individual members of the congregation; only once a communal first person plural (v. 14) protrudes conspicuously from first person singulars of the suppliants (vv. 5, 11-12). Linkage with the Sabbath day was probably suggested by the retrospection on creation in v. 6.

The introductory part, PRAISE of God (vv. 2-5), is not the customary SUMMONS (see "Introduction to Cultic Poetry," section 4D), but an extended liturgical and theological evaluation of what is "good," "wholesome," "appropriate." Heb. *ṭôb,* "good (is)," v. 2, and the annexed three infinitives with the preposition *lĕ,* "to," could be a sapiential mode of judging situations and actions (cf. Ps 133:1b; Prov 21:19; 25:24; Qoh 7:2, 5; 11:7; Lam 3:25-27). There is one exact formal parallel (Ps 118:8-9). The form may come from ethical or cultic instruction (cf. 84:11). In terms of content two infinitives identify liturgical praise (*ydh,* Hiphil; *zmr,* Piel: cf., e.g., 9:2-3 [RSV 1-2]; 30:5 [RSV 4]; 42:6, 12 [RSV 5, 11]; 47:7-8 [RSV 6-7]; 107:8; 108:2, 4 [RSV 1, 3]; 118:1, 19, 21, 28, 29; 144:9), while the third employs vocabulary of various kinds of (cultic) manifestation (v. 3: *ngd,* Hiphil, "tell, communicate," 19 times in psalm texts; cf. 38:19 [RSV 18]; 40:6 [RSV 5]; 71:17-18; 142:3 [RSV 2]), filling two cola. The evaluative expression "It is good to give thanks to Yahweh" certainly mirrors the well-known liturgical shout: "Praise Yahweh: He [it] is good!" (cf. 54:8; 106:1; 107:1; 118:1, 29; 136:1). V. 4 significantly adds reference to sacred instruments, *'āśôr, nābel, kinnôr:* various types of harps and lyres (cf. Sendrey, *Music;* Seidel, *Musik;* Stauder, *Musik;* listing at Additional Bibliography, section B; and listing at "Introduction to Cultic Poetry"). This allusion can hardly be taken symbolically. As in other psalms (cf. 33:2-3; 49:5 [RSV 4]; 57:9 [RSV 8]; 81:3 [RSV 2]; 108:3 [RSV 2]; 144:9; 149:3; 150:3) the naming of instruments is a reliable indication of their being used in connection with prayer (cf. Miller, *They Cried,* 207, 361; listing at Additional Bibliography, section C).

A personal HYMN (v. 5), introduced by deictic or exclamatory *kî,* "Yes," "Indeed" (→ Pss 71:5; 108:5 [RSV 4]; 136:1-26), is the culminating point of the preceding overture. We do well imagining that this single line could be repeated many times in actual worship: "You have made me happy, Yahweh, through your action [many MSS have the plural: 'actions']; over the works of your hand I will jubilate." These affirmations remain on a very abstract level; individual thanksgiving at this point would articulate some statement of having been saved from death (cf. 30:2-4 [RSV 1-3]; 40:2-4 [RSV 1-3]; 116:8; 118:21). A personal hymn, on the other side, takes up the general language of praise about marvelous divine accomplishments in direct-address form (cf. 8:7 [RSV 6]; 44:2 [RSV 1]; 64:10 [RSV 9]; 77:12-13 [11-12]; 102:26 [RSV 25]; 138:8; 143:5), and strictly from a first-person singular speaker.

Vv. 6-10 do not show a trace of individual prayer. The "I" of the singer or suppliant comes back only in vv. 11-12. Furthermore, vv. 6-10 are introduced by an impersonal rhetorical question, and they clearly aim at a confrontation with the impious adversaries (vv. 7-8). What are the liturgical and theological reasons for such a juxtaposition of praise and condemnation?

Rhetorical questions or rather exclamations of awe and amazement belong to stock expressions of hymnic compositions. Perhaps they were germinal forms of speech in the development of songs of praise (see Sumerian and Akkadian hymns in *SAHG* and in Seux; listing at Additional Bibliography, section B). V. 6 has close parallels in Pss 8:2, 10 (RSV 1, 9); 36:8 (RSV 7); 66:3; 84:2 (RSV 1); 89:7, 9 (RSV 6, 8); 104:24; 139:17, also in some other contexts (cf., e.g., Dan 3:33; most prophetic and wisdom formulations reflect competition or controversy; cf. Isa 40:12-14; Jer 10:7; Mic 7:18; Nah 1:6; Job 9:4, 12; 11:8, 10; also Pss 86:8-10; 115:1-7). In correspondence to the rest of the psalm this exclamation is direct address to Yahweh — a demonstration of reverence and at the same time of abnegation of one's own power (→ Psalm 148). Liturgical dimensions become clearly visible, e.g., in 8:2, 10 (RSV 1, 9); 66:3; 104:24. The whole community is apparently to join in shouting: "How magnificent are your deeds . . ." (cf. esp. 66:3: "Say to God . . ."). After this seemingly selfless exaltation the poem changes into a strong denunciation of the mindless and wicked (vv. 7-8, 10). In a vicious crescendo of name-calling the adversaries are first fools (v. 7); second, godless people and evilmongers (v. 8); and third, God's own enemies (v. 10). That means that sapiential, ancient magical, and theological terminology are merging, the last being manifest in the postexilic differentiation of "godless" (*rĕšā'îm*, v. 8a) and "righteous" (*ṣaddîq*, v. 13a). The bliss and well-being of the opponents within the group thus fenced off from the community (cf. Psalms 9/10; 37; 73; 94) in this case does not become a problem, because our psalmist already knows "what will be the end of these enemies" (cf. 73:17-20): they will be permanently quenched (v. 8c), they will perish and be dispersed (v. 10). All these announcements of doom over some opponents in faith depend on "praise of God," expressed in admiring exclamation (v. 6), reinforced by a hymnic affirmation (v. 9). Praise divides a community, as in 104:35 and 139:19-22. The latter passage is explicit on this issue:

That you would kill the godless! That the bloodthirsty would let me go!
They talk blasphemically about you; lifted up for evil (are) your cities
(? v. 20b corrupt)

Should I not hate your haters? Not despise those who defy you?
I do hate them profoundly, they became enemies for me.

In fact, the godless turned away from praising Yahweh and therefore turned themselves into "enemies."
There are some textual uncertainties also in vv. 11-12, but the structure and meaning are perfectly clear. God is directly addressed, as in all the preceding lines. Additionally, an individual speaker is exposed principally in first-person suffixes, pointing back to v. 5. The style is that of a victory song: God has boosted up "my" power; "I" am looking down on "my" enemies (both lines begin with a consecutive perfect). Victorious statements like these abound in thanksgivings, battle songs, and sometimes proleptically in complaints (cf. 18:17-20, 38-46 [RSV 16-19, 37-45]; 31:20-23 [RSV 19-22]; 89:20-26 [RSV 19-25]; 1 Sam 2:2-10). If v. 5 may be considered a pure personal hymn without polemics like, e.g., Psalm 8, the continuation of "I" affirmations in vv. 11-12 is certainly deeply entrenched in the struggle against "unbelievers," just as vv. 7-10 are. A notable difference between v. 5 and vv. 11-12 is that creation terminology is employed only in the former passage. Our conclusion, then, would be: v. 5 has been reinterpreted and developed in transmission, perhaps in two subsequent stages (vv. 6-10 and 11-12).

More calmly Psalm 92 comes to an end with a little hymn about the blessed life of the righteous one (vv. 13-16). The metaphor of a flourishing tree planted by water (vv. 13-15) occurs several times in Hebrew writings (cf. 1:3; 52:10 [RSV 8]; Jer 17:6-7). Being a very meaningful image not only in arid zones, it has influenced broadly and deeply interpretation of Scripture up to our own days (cf. *Wirkungsgeschichte,* esp. of Psalm 23). Of course, there are also other songs about the "righteous" and their destiny, just as there are poems about the abominable "impious" (for the latter cf. 1:4-6; 10:2-11; 73:3-12). Hymns about the "righteous" are less obtrusive, it seems (cf. descriptive passages like 1:1-3; 91:13-16). One specimen is hidden away in an acrostic psalm (112:6-9). Another is unfolded in a huge song that purports to be a hymn to divine *tôrāh* (Psalm 119: cf. only all the affirmations about the pious suppliant, e.g., vv. 97-104; the term *ṣaddîq,* "righteous," is reserved for Yahweh, however: v. 137). Thus descriptive hymns about the "righteous" have been used freely, and one of them was attached to vv. 2-12 to counterbalance possibly harmful impressions of portraying the wicked. A righteous person, thus the comforting outlook, will preserve his or her strength into old age (v. 15; cf. 71:17-18) in order to tell of Yahweh's righteousness (v. 16). The second colon even quotes an aged witness as saying: "He is my rock, there is no vileness in him."

## Genre

The introductory and closing lines, as well as the body of the psalm, reveal sapiential theology (cf. Gunkel, 408: "Reflection is dissolving hymnic forms") and cultic, i.e., congregational, vocabulary, concepts, and settings. Language is individual, spoken without doubt in a communal environment (cf., e.g., *ngd,* "tell, proclaim," in vv. 3, 16; cultic music in v. 4, etc.). The main problem of this HYMNIC PRAYER is the superiority of Yahweh (the name occurs with great emphasis 7 times in only 15 lines) as recognized by the pious speaker and ignored by religious opponents. Therefore we might also designate the psalm a CONFESSIONAL PRAYER.

## Setting

Language (see Structure above: vv. 2-3, etc.), the concept of righteous versus godless, the complex literary character, etc., lead us to believe that Psalm 92 was composed late, perhaps in the fourth or third century B.C.E. Late dating would immediately mean that early Jewish community life, be it worship or religious education, was the original setting of our text. Schmidt (pp. 174-75), although considering the psalm a personal thanksgiving of a patient healed, does admit a communal background. The "I" of the speaker is not biographical but exemplary, involving every member of the community.

## Intention

Religious pluralism of the Persian and Hellenistic periods forced Jewish communities to identify themselves as Yahweh believers. There was no other way of maintaining the identity of the ethnic group. Yahweh worship, however, was controversial among the Jews themselves. We know of deviant or nonorthodox groups, e.g., the Samaritans and the military community at Elephantine; later on the sectarians of Qumran established themselves at the shore of the Dead Sea (cf. Smith, *Parties;* listing at Additional Bibliography, section B). Our psalm is to ward off in a very general way the erroneous glorification of Yahweh, i.e., nonorthodox worship, without identifying errors or deviations. The singers and listeners to the psalm are confident that they practice the only permissible, correct liturgy, that their faith alone is the correct one.

## Bibliography

R. T. Beckwith, "The Courses of the Levites and the Eccentric Psalms Scroll from Qumran," *RevQ* 11 (1984) 499-524; Th. Booij, "The Hebrew Text of Psalm 92:11," *VT* 38 (1988) 210-14; J. F. D. Creach, "Like a Tree Planted by the Temple Stream," *CBQ* 61 (1999) 1-11; C. Datema and P. Allen, "Leontius, Presbyter of Constantinople, the Author of Ps. Chrysostom, *In psalmum 92?*" *VC* 40 (1986) 169-82; H. Donner, "Ugaritismen in der Psalmenforschung," *ZAW* 79 (1967) 344-46; S. E. Loewenstamm, "Balloti b$^e$šämän ra$^{ca}$nän," *UF* 10 (1979) 111-13; idem, "An Additional Remark upon Ps 92,11," *UF* 13 (1981) 302; O. Loretz, "Psalm 92: Ugaritische Texte und Gattungsforschung," *UF* 25 (1994) 275-88; N. Sarna, "The Psalm for the Sabbath Day, Ps 92," *JBL* 81 (1962) 155-68; S. Schullerus-Kessler, " 'Und wenn sie gleich alt werden' — Religion in Lebenszyklen," *Diakonie* 21 (1995) 278-80; M. Weiss, " 'A Psalm Sung for the Sabbath-Day,'" in *Tehillah le-Moshe* (*Fest.* M. Greenberg; ed. M. Cogan, et al.; Winona Lake, Ind.: Eisenbrauns, 1997) 45-51 (Hebrew; Eng. abstract, 317).

# Psalm 93:
# Confessional Hymn
## (cf. Yahweh-kingship Psalms 47; 95–99)

## Structure

|  | MT | NRSV |
|---|---|---|
| I. Hymnic affirmation | 1 | 1 |
| II. Adoration (of community) | 2 | 2 |
| III. Creation hymn | 3-4 | 3-4 |
| IV. Adoration (of community) | 5 | 5 |

Psalm 93 belongs to a rather compact group of Yahweh-kingship hymns (cf. Jeremias, *Königtum;* listing at "Introduction to Psalms"). Therefore it has to be analyzed in constant reference to its companion songs Psalms 47; 95–99. Whether Psalms 93–100 constitute a liturgical, instructional, or theological block is an open question. Advocates of a textual unity of some kind are, e.g., Wilson, Willard, Howard, Zenger, Koenen, and Jeremias. In spite of missing superscriptions, we observe a strong structural, liturgical, and thematic autonomy of most texts, which should not completely exclude the possibility of later use of texts in conjunction, e.g., with worship or instruction.

Generally speaking, we find five main types of statements in this group of psalms: hymnic affirmations about superior qualities and powers of Yahweh, the God of Israel (in third person singular); communal praise of Yahweh in direct address (second person singular); descriptions of behavior of other (divine) powers; statements about activities of the congregation (mostly first person plural); summons to praise (plural imperatives).

We should note the lack of superscriptions in all the Yahweh-kingship songs with the exception of Psalm 47. The reason for this phenomenon could be very simple: the group has been inserted at a later stage after the main redactional work had been completed. In the hind parts of the Psalter headings are increasingly missing, however (→ Psalms 71; 119). Our little hymn of only five poetic lines begins right away with the principal HYMNIC AFFIRMATION "Yahweh is [or 'has become'] king" (v. 1a; cf. 47:6, 8-9 [RSV 5, 7-8]; 97:1; 98:6; 99:1). Back in the 1960s an extensive and partially heated debate was waged in regard to the exact meaning of this phrase. Does it stress the eternal kingship of Yahweh, affirming his everlasting authority over the whole creation and all other divine powers? Or does it communicate remembrances of old, when Yahweh used to assume supreme lordship annually, in the manner of dying and rising deities of the ancient Near East? (cf. Bernhardt, *Problem;* Frankfort, *Kingship;* Mowinckel, *PsSt* II; Lipiński, *Royauté,* all in listing at "Introduction to Cultic Poetry"). This scholarly skirmish was resumed in the late

1980s (cf. Bowes, Jeremias, Loretz, Irsigler). A mere insistence on grammatical structure (prepositive or postpositive position of the verb: *mlk yhwh* or *yhwh mlk*) or some fixed meaning of tenses seems inconclusive. Ps 47:6-9 (RSV 5-8), on the other hand, proves that a dynamic concept of Yahweh's taking power was possible in biblical times. Whether this can be made the crucial testimony for an annual New Year's Festival with Yahweh's ascension and being installed again as the supreme Deity is another question (Mowinckel, *PsSt* II; Loretz). On account of linguistic and theological evidence, it seems obvious that Yahweh-kingship psalms presuppose myths of primordial battle and that even the "structure of postexilic worship could be molded by the concepts of Yahweh-kingship" (Seybold, 577). To my mind, preexilic datings of this psalm group are unlikely; Yahweh, the supreme God, makes best sense in Israel's diaspora situation after 587 B.C.E., in a polytheistic, imperial society. A conscious refutation of Canaanite divine-kingship ideas is not apparent (Mosis).

The idea of God "putting on" power or majesty like clothes (v. 1) turns up in Ps 104:1-2 and Isa 51:9; 59:17. This is figurative language, to be sure, but very impressive, also by its repetitiousness. The psalm does not linger with Yahweh's appearance; a third colon (v. 1c) moves on to his creation works. The verb perhaps has to be emended to derive from *tkn*, Piel, "establish firmly," instead of MT *kûn*, Qal, "to stand firmly." If this is correct, the affirmation is about Yahweh himself: "He founded the world," as in Ps 75:4 (RSV 3) and, after emendation, in 96:10b, which is identical with our v. 1c. Objective HYMNIC AFFIRMATIONS as found in v. 1 were probably spoken by a liturgist to the congregation, and they serve objectively to strengthen the power of the deity praised.

V. 2 is different in that it articulates direct eulogies to Yahweh: "Your throne has been established of old, you are there since *time immemorial (mē'ôlām)*." This time the community must be speaking, directing itself to Yahweh; also this hymnic mode is to signal obedience and to confer power to the addressed one. It is, indeed, the execution of an old liturgical command: "Bring to the Lord power and glory!" (cf. 29:1-2; 96:7-9). Communal praise in v. 2 is matched by the same form in v. 5, so that vv. 3-4 are framed by direct ADORATION of Yahweh by the congregation. The closing line, v. 5, has three cola, perhaps in adaptation to vv. 3-4; it acclaims the Torah (in a typical postexilic expression: *'ēdôt*, "ordinances") and the temple (!), and concludes by calling on the name of Yahweh again. The first phrase is close to affirmations customarily linked with late wisdom poetry, as in 19:8 (RSV 7) and 119:144. Praise to the temple (v. 5b) is to be expected in various contexts; cf. Psalms 46; 48; 76; 84; 122; 132; 1 Kgs 8:29-51; Isa 56:1-7; Jer 7; Zech 14:8-21; etc. The background is general awe in regard to God's holiness (cf. most of the Priestly writings, e.g., Leviticus 8–10).

After looking at the framework we can easily identify a hymnic nucleus of distinctive linguistic fiber (vv. 3-4). This compact little HYMN consists of two tripartite lines each (cf. Mowinckel, *Tricola;* listing at "Introduction to Psalms"; Jeremias, *Königtum,* 16-26). The language is redundant and very rhythmic. V. 3 operates with two stock words (*ns'*, "lift up," and *nĕhārôt*, "streams") that are the backbone of each phrase. But each phrase also has one alternate word: the appellation "Yahweh," taking the place of a grammatical object, thus heightening tension: What about the streams' lifting up? Second, the suffixed noun "their voice"; third, another substantive with suffix, "their clapping." To advance a poetic line through three stages could be an archaic Canaanite pattern (thus Albright, *Yahweh;* listing at "Introduction to Cultic Poetry"; Loretz; Freedman, *Pottery,* 1-50, 179-86; listing at Additional Bibliography, section B). Hebrew poetry runs basically two parallel cola in each line. Thematically, the adoration of primordial chaos monsters like the "streams" is an ancient motif, known from Ugaritic texts (cf. Pope, *El;* Kaiser, *Bedeutung;* Smith, *Baal;* all in Additional Bibliography, section B). The second line (v. 4) follows suit: the three cola are tightly knit, forming one overarching major unit, beginning with a comparative *min:* "Greater than the roaring of floods, than the power of breakers, is the force in the height of Yahweh." Yahweh is in fact the last word of this line, hence the clumsy translation. From colon to colon the listener ascends to Yahweh, leaving behind deadly powers of destruction.

The primeval battle for an orderly and life-giving world is insinuated by this hymn. The chaos waters cannot resist the forces of the God of life; they have to concede victory to Yahweh (in Ugarit to Baal; in Babylonia to Marduk; see *Enuma elish,* tr. E. A. Speiser, *ANET,* 60-72), and in adoring the victor they yield their power to him (cf. Pss 96:11; 98:7-8). The uproar of hostility becomes praise and applause.

## *Genre*

Psalm 93, as pointed out above, is part of a somewhat dispersed collection of YAHWEH-KINGSHIP HYMNS (cf. "Introduction to Cultic Poetry," sections D and E). Special emphasis is on the mythical story of the subjugation of chaos waters (cf. Pss 77:17-20 [RSV 16-19]; Isa 17:12-14). Yahweh is praised objectively and in direct-address statements to be the supreme God over all powers. There is a confessional ring to this hymn (Mosis, 255), which — this is a remote possibility — in some core affirmations (vv. 3-4) may go back into preexilic times. "Yahweh is king!" (v. 1a) is fashioned according to ancient enthronement shouts (cf. Ugaritic parallels and 1 Kgs 1:34; 2 Kgs 11:12; Loretz, 415, 429-33). More likely, adoration of Yahweh, even in archaic poetical forms, as the supreme God constituted a vital theological concern of the Jewish community only by the end of the sixth century B.C.E. (cf. Gerstenberger, *Yahweh*). In that case, on the basis of its function, the generic description CONFESSIONAL HYMN is preferable to the traditional naming. Jeremias and most other exegetes recognize the long history of the so-called Yahweh-kingship motifs (cf. Jeremias, *Königtum*). Still, the composition and use of these hymns are likely to have begun after the exile to Babylonia. To divide the texts into an older (Psalms 93; 97; 99) and a younger (Psalms 47; 96; 98) group with distinct theological interests does not help much.

## Setting

References to the postexilic community and its allegiance to Torah and temple suggest a late origin and use of this psalm in beginning synagogue worship services, although the center part (vv. 3-4) is possibly an archaic poem remodeled by Yahweh theologians. After all, the name of the deity at the beginning and the end of this section (vv. 3a and 4c) could easily be altered.

## Intention

The struggle of maintaining an ethnic and religious identity in the pluralistic Persian Empire and under strict control of the superpower was a life-and-death issue for Jewish communities of that time. Elevating Yahweh to be the supreme Lord of all powers mythical and historical, the early Jewish congregations in a bold move challenged the political and religious superpower, establishing their own claims of survival and self-determination.

## Bibliography

P. R. Ackroyd, "Some Notes on the Psalms," *JTS* 17 (1966) 392-99; P. Auffret, "Yahwé règne: Étude structurelle du Psaume 93," *ZAW* 103 (1991) 101-9; A. W. Bowes, "The Basilomorphic Conception of Deity in Israel and Mesopotamia," in *The Biblical Canon in Comparative Perspective* (ed. K. L. Younger, et al.; Lewiston: Edwin Mellen, 1991) 235-75; J. H. Eaton, "Some Questions of Philology and Exegesis in the Psalms," *JTS* 19 (1968) 603-9; idem, "A Bloodless Compromise?" in *Crossing the Boundaries* (*Fest.* M. Goulder; ed. S. Porter, et al.; Leiden: Brill, 1994) 69-82; O. Eissfeldt, "Jahwe als König," *ZAW* 46 (1928) 81-105 (repr. in idem, *KS* I, 172-93); A. Gelston, "A Note on *yhwh mlk*," *VT* 16 (1966) 507-12; B. Gosse, "Les introductions des Psaumes 88–94 et Isaie 59,15b-20," *ZAW* 106 (1994) 303-6; J. Gray, "The Hebrew Conception of the Kingship of God," *VT* 6 (1956) 268-85; H. Gross, "Lässt sich in den Psalmen ein 'Thronbesteigungsfest Gottes' nachweisen?" *TTZ* 65 (1956) 24-40; D. M. Howard, *The Structure of Psalms 93–100* (Winona Lake, Ind.: Eisenbrauns, 1997); H. Irsigler, "Thronbesteigung in Psalm 93? Der Textverlauf als Prozess syntaktischer und semantischer Interpretation," in *Text, Methode und Grammatik* (*Fest.* W. Richter; ed. W. Gross, et al.; St. Ottilien: EOS, 1991) 155-90; B. Janowski, "Das Königtum Gottes in den Psalmen," *ZTK* 86 (1989) 389-454; H. G. Jefferson, "Psalm 93," *JBL* 71 (1952) 155-60; J. Jeremias, "Schöpfung in Poesie und Prosa des Alten Testaments," *Jahrbuch für Biblische Theologie* 5 (1990) 10-36; A. S. Kapelrud, "Nochmals Jahwä *mālāk*," *VT* 13 (1963) 229-31; O. Loretz, *Ugarit-Texte und Thronbesteigungspsalmen* (Ugaritisch-biblische Literatur 7; Münster: Ugarit-Verlag, 1988) 274-303; R. Mosis, "'Ströme erheben, Jahwe, ihr Tosen': Beobachtungen zu Ps 93," in *Ein Gott — eine Offenbarung* (*Fest.* N. Füglister; ed. F. Reiterer; Würzburg: Echter, 1991) 223-55; E. Otto, "Schöpfung als Kategorie der Vermittlung von Gott und Welt in biblischer Theologie," in *'Wenn nicht jetzt'* (*Fest.* H.-J. Kraus; ed. H.-G. Geyer, et al.; Neukirchen-Vluyn: Neukirchener Verlag, 1983) 53-68; D. Pardee, "The Poetic Structure of Psalm 93,"

*Studii epigrafici e linguistici* 5 (1988) 163-70; J. D. S. Shenkel, "An Interpretation of Psalm 93,5," *Bib* 46 (1965) 401-16; P. N. Tarazi, "An Exegesis of Psalm 93," *Saint Vladimir's Theological Quarterly* 35 (1991) 137-48; J. D. Watts, "Yahweh *Mālak* Psalms," *TZ* 21 (1965) 341-48.

# Psalm 94:
# Communal Complaint

## *Structure*

|  | MT | NRSV |
|---|---|---|
| I. Invocation, initial plea | 1-2 | 1-2 |
| II. Complaint | 3-7 | 3-7 |
| III. Exhortation | 8-11 | 8-11 |
| IV. Felicitation | 12-13 | 12-13 |
| V. Affirmation of confidence | 14-15 | 14-15 |
| VI. Prayer | 16-23 | 16-23 |
| A. Petition | 16-17 | 16-17 |
| B. Thanksgiving | 18-19 | 18-19 |
| C. Complaint | 20-21 | 20-21 |
| D. Affirmation of confidence | 22 | 22 |
| E. Imprecation | 23 | 23 |

The SUPERSCRIPTION is missing, as in Psalms 71; 93; 95–99; etc. The poem — being somewhat extravagant as to its formal elements and liturgical structure — starts out with a sort of invocation. But the appellation of the addressed Deity as well as the initial plea (if the verb has to be transposed into an imperative) are extraordinary. Nowhere else is Yahweh directly and bluntly called a "God of revenge" (v. 1; cf., however, "God of retribution," Jer 51:56, and various other expressions: Isa 35:4; 66:6; Jer 51:6; Pss 28:4; 137:8; etc.). The imperative of *yp',* Hiphil, "let shine," is used once more in an INITIAL PLEA (Ps 80:2 [RSV 1]; cf. the descriptive use of a finite verb in 50:2). The expression refers to theophany. Theophany for its part being a communal affair, this kind of plea could have been used only in congregational contexts. If at all, individual complaint in urgent cases would use imperatives of verbs of salvation in the first line (cf. 12:2 [RSV 1]; 69:2 [RSV 1]; 86:2). The second line of initial plea also fits into a communal context, calling on the "judge of the world" (cf. Gen 18:25) to execute retribution on the *gē'îm,* "the haughty ones" (a sapiential expression; cf. Prov 8:13; 15:25; 16:19; Job 40:11-12; Isa 2:12; 16:6; Jer 48:29).

The last colon of v. 2 heralds COMPLAINT (vv. 3-7), also of the communal kind. Opponents, called *rĕšā'îm,* "rebellious, wicked, godless ones" (twice in v. 3; cf. H. Ringgren, *TWAT* VII, 675-84), or *pō'ălê 'āwen,* "evilmongers" (v. 4b; also in Psalms 5; 28; 36; 59; 64; 141; cf. K. H. Bernhardt, *TWAT* I, 157-59; Mowinckel, *PsSt* I), have been besetting Yahweh's "people" (v. 5a), oppressing God's "inheritance" (v. 5b). More specifically, these adversaries have been "murdering widows, strangers, and orphans" (v. 6: clear reference to D legislation in favor of marginal groups of Israelite society; cf. Deut 10:18; 14:29; 16:11, 14; 24:17, 19-21; 26:12-13; 27:19; etc.), and, most disgraceful and criminal, they have blasphemously contradicted the powers of Yahweh (vv. 4, 6). A quotation of their words proves their utter haughtiness: "Yahweh does not perceive anything; the God of Jacob understands nothing" (v. 6; cf. similar affirmations taken from or put into the mouth of the "wicked": 10:11; 14:1; 73:10). Denial of God in these sapiential contexts amounts to negating his effectiveness and, apparently, separation from the community of his followers. In other words, all indications point to the fact that our complaint passage addresses a serious rift within the Jewish community. The adversaries accused of oppressing their co-religionists, judged from their evil deeds painted in a phantom picture, are nonbelievers, blasphemers. With this kind of argumentation and conceptual outlook (social justice), our psalm falls in line with those texts that defend the poor and needy (cf. Psalms 9/10; 37; 73; 146; etc.). Prayer language directed toward Yahweh is partially employed (vv. 3, 5, 12, 18, 19, 20). Polemics (vv. 9-11), exhortation (vv. 8, 12-15, 22), and felicitations (v. 12) are further elements of the poem, whereas one does expect, after COMPLAINT, petition. What kind of complaint are we looking at then?

EXHORTATION (vv. 8-11) seems, in a way, a logical and liturgical consequence of communitarian complaint. Apparently — as in Psalms 4; 11; 62 — the reciter directly addresses himself to participants of the assembly (v. 8) accused or suspected of apostate behavior, not denouncing them completely, but trying to argue with them, to convince them that they have done wrong. The rĕšā'îm of v. 3 are now called "stupid ones," "unwise people" (v. 8; cf. 92:7; 49:11; 73:22; Prov 12:1; 30:2; Jer 10:8). But the addressees should be the same in both lines. The psalm testifies to inner-Jewish conflicts. Instruction of deviant people within one's own group is certainly a well-known pedagogic feature in religions. In this case, the "teacher" utilizes lines from an autonomous text to make clear his point (vv. 9-11). They look like fragments taken from contest literature: rhetorical questions are posed in such a way as to show the absurdity of the opponent's opinion: "He who fashioned the ear, should he not be able to hear?" (v. 9a). Three equally constructed phrases are strung together; the fourth one is incomplete, probably having been damaged in transmission (v. 10b). The first two questions deal with ear and eye, and capacities to hear and see — in some congruence with v. 7, where God was denied the faculties of seeing and understanding. The second line, however, moves on to Yahweh's supreme authority over nations (v. 10a; it has not been contested by the "faithless" crew). The end of the questioning could have been — as suggested by modern exegetes (see BHS apparatus) — a phrase like this: "He who teaches humankind, should he not be knowledgeable?" (v. 10b). This topic again coincides with that of v. 7, as does the concluding line of our little passage, v. 11: "Yahweh is aware of human thinking, yes, it is futile," essentially an affirmation like the tenets of Ecclesiastes. Now, while there is a wide thematic coincidence between v. 7 and the sapiential vocabulary and configurations of vv. 9-11, the compact structure of these three lines; the objective formulations and the disappearance of exhortative discourse; their broad, wise approach to the matter of God's sagacity; the broken end of v. 10 — all these factors would lead to the conclusion that the three lines under discussion were an autonomous adage. This impression is greatly strengthened by several texts that use similar wording to denounce strange gods: "They have ears and do not hear" (Ps 115:6a; 135:17a; cf. the contexts: 115:4-7; 135:15-18; Preuss, *Verspottung;* listing at Additional Bibliography, section B). Popular (or learned?) wisdom of the time in this way counterbalances disturbing questions about the power and justice of God. The speaker of vv. 8-11 is apparently the liturgist or perhaps the plaintive suppliant of vv. 3-7.

After refuting adversaries the psalm portrays the "righteous" and "just" ones (vv. 12-13), with an exhortatory undertone, using the fixed form of FELICITATION modified only by second-person address to God (v. 12). Felicitation is a kind of BLESSING (see Glossary: Blessing Formula), frequently employed in the Psalms, i.e., in community worship, to encourage the faithful followers of Yahweh and strengthen them. Central to the saying is the individual person (*geber,* "man," v. 12a) who receives the promise of divine protection in trouble and who witnesses the downfall of the oppressors (v. 13b; cf. 73:17-20). He also is seen as receiving divine instruction through Torah (v. 12b). There is no reason to doubt that the written Pentateuch is being alluded to. "Your *torah*" can hardly be a collection of human instructions. The following AFFIRMATION OF CONFIDENCE (vv. 14-15) obviously considers the people or rather the congregation as a whole to be the partner of Yahweh. We note a certain discrepancy between the individual figure of v. 12 and the religious group mentioned in v. 14. On the other hand, v. 14 seems to be a direct response to v. 5, assuring that God's "people" and "inheritance" will not suffer any harm. Thus we find distinct layers of tradition not only in vv. 8-11 but also in vv. 12-15. The psalmist apparently composed a (liturgical) text from various sources.

The psalm could well end on the note of confidence as expressed in vv. 14-15, although the petitionary element appeared, so far, only in the introduction (vv. 1-2). Like so many other complaints, however (cf., e.g., Psalms 22; 31; 69; "Introduction to Cultic Poetry," section 4B), liturgical proceedings from complaint to petition or confidence are repeated in worship. This is true also for Psalm 94, the difference being a change of style in vv. 16-23, the second round of complaining. Vv. 1-15 did not reveal any kind of speaker or reciter of the text. This first part of the psalm is already, at least formally, a real PRAYER, addressing Yahweh directly (imperatives in vv. 1-2, second-person singular verbs and suffixes in vv. 5 and 12, appellation of Yahweh in vv. 1, 3; cf. Miller, *They Cried,* esp. 127-29; listing at Additional Bibliography, section C). But who has been talking? Even that moral authority chastising those defiant fools (v. 8) is not identified or legitimized by the text. All of a sudden, starting with v. 16, an "I" emerges with vehemence. Three more lines (vv. 17-19) are virtually crowded with references to one person speaking. Also, v. 22 is a very personal confession of trust. Only at the very end, actually in the very last word, of our section and of the whole psalm does a first person plural come up: "Our God." This near-absolute dominance of first person singular led most exegetes to believe that the second part of Psalm 94, in contrast to the first, was a true individual complaint. The occurrence, even if only in one instance, of the first person plural, however, should warn us about drawing hasty conclusions. Vv. 16-23 may, of course, derive from an originally private setting. As soon as it is recited together with vv. 1-15, which demonstratively expose communal dimensions, the "I" is understood in an exemplary way, meaning every single member of the assembly. The last word of v. 23, "our God," is a welcome proof of this thesis.

The second round of complaining, then, starts with a cry for (juridical) assistance, as if in a court session (v. 16; cf. Boecker, *Redeformen;* listing at "Introduction to Psalms"; Psalms 17; 35). The conjunction *lûlê'* (v. 17a) not only indicates an unreal state, but seems to leave open the possibility that help from Yahweh can fail (cf. 119:92; 124:1-3). Therefore, this line is in the middle between Petition and Thanksgiving. The following verses (18-19), however, look at real acts of salvation: imperfects in vv. 18b and 19b stress the validity of God's help, which may be experienced again and again. Fear of personal failure is voiced in complaints, becoming interwoven with petition and trust (cf. 38:16-18 [RSV 15-17]; 66:9-12; 121:3). V. 19 has a remarkable concentration of rare words (probably late usage; for "cares," "consolations," "cheer" [NRSV] cf. 139:23; Isa 11:8; Ps 119:70; Isa 66:11; Jer 16:7). Vv. 20-21, textually enigmatic, resume the Complaint, as MT stands, even with a provocative question to Yahweh: "Are you siding with the throne of wickedness?" (v. 20a). Liturgically, sharp contrasts between elements of a psalm are possible. Tension between thanksgiving and plaintive accusation, and renewed Affirmation of Confidence (v. 22) are feasible. The closing line is an Imprecation, an indispensable part of all those complaint psalms and liturgies that were recited on the basis of enemy involvement in threats and damages experienced by the community.

## *Genre*

The topic of Psalm 94 is that terrible tension within a religious community between "righteous" ones and "wrongdoers" (in later Christian tradition they came to be called "orthodox" and "heterodox"), induced by the apparent inactivity or injustice of God (v. 3; cf. Gen 4:4-5; Job 9; → Psalm 73), a conflict that threatens to tear apart the congregation (cf. Imprecation). The party of the just ones uses elements of Communal and Individual Complaint as well as Wisdom forms (see "Introduction to Cultic Poetry," sections 4B and F) to express its anguish and disgust, praying to God for help and voicing strong confidence in him. Specific petitions are not articulated. There is a double sequence of liturgical action from complaint to trust, with alternating voices. Vv. 1-15 are a general plea for assistance against haughty, oppressive, God-forgetting coreligionists threatening the whole community. Then, complaint and affirmations of confidence become individualized within the congregation (vv. 16-23), because each individual member is prone to be a victim of the "evilmongers."

## *Setting*

The setting is definitely early Jewish community life with its doctrinal rifts as they are documented historically by dissenting groups at Samaria and through the Dead Sea community of Qumran, as well as in the Psalter (cf. Psalms 9/10; 37; 49; 73) and in the Prophets (cf. Isa 66:1-5; J. Blenkinsopp, *A History of Prophecy in Israel* [2nd ed.; Louisville: Westminster John Knox, 1996] 216-22). The place of contention in our psalm still seems to be a common assembly or congregational worship, as the opponents are partly attacked directly (cf. Psalms 11; 62). Calling them "godless" and "evilmongers" in vv. 3-4, then addressing them as "stupid ones" in v. 8, and returning to harsher condemnations in v. 16, may also indicate a process of denouncement, trying to regain the apostates, and final exclusion from the community of the "righteous."

## Intention

The "just ones" are obviously under pressure from the "godless" party, which seems to be identical with the well-to-do and powerful in this early Jewish society (cf. Nehemiah 5; Smith, *Parties;* Albertz, *History,* both in Additional Bibliography, section B) who are possibly collaborating with imperial authorities. The oppressed want to be liberated from economic, political, and social oppression (there is no evidence as to religious persecution by state authorities). But they apparently hold some vague hope for a social conversion of the "wicked." If there is no betterment, however, the godless party is to be execrated.

## Bibliography

R. Albertz, *Weltschöpfung,* 126-27 (listing at "Introduction to Psalms"); A. Allgeier, "Psalm 93(94),20. Ein auslegungs- und bedeutungsgeschichtlicher Beitrag," in *Fest. A. Bertholet* (ed. W. Baumgartner, et al.; Tübingen: Mohr, 1950) 15-28; P. Auffret, "Essai sur la structure littéraire du Psaume 94," *BN* 24 (1984) 44-72; idem, "'Qui se lèvera pour moi?'" *RivB* 46 (1998) 129-56; M. Conti, "Dio difensore della causa degli oppressi secondo il Salmo 94," *Antonianum* 72 (1997) 3-37; D. N. Freedman, "Acrostic Poems in the Hebrew Bible: Alphabetic and Otherwise," *CBQ* 48 (1986) 408-31; R. A. Harrisville, "Paul and the Psalms: A Formal Study," *Word & World* 5 (1985) 168-79; K. Koch, "Gibt es ein Vergeltungsdogma im Alten Testament?" *ZTK* 52 (1955) 1-42 (repr. in *Spuren des hebräischen Denkens* [ed. B. Janowski, et al.; Gesammelte Aufsätze 1; Neukirchen-Vluyn: Neukirchener Verlag, 1991] 65-103); A. Maillot, "La justice contre la justice (Ps 94)," *BVC* 79 (1968) 54-57; F. de Meyer, "La sagesse psalmique et le Psaume 94," *Bijdragen* 42 (1981) 22-45; H. Plantin, "Deuteronomium och lövhyddofestens psalmer i b Sukka 55a," *SEÅ* 55 (1990) 7-38; N. M. Sarna, "Songs of the Heart," *Bible Review* 9 (1993) 32-40; K. Schwarzwäller, *Leerlauf?* (Neukirchen-Vluyn: Neukirchener Verlag, 1971) 62-72; J. Wehrle, "Die PV *k.* = *'mat* als Indikator für den Satzmodus in Sprechakten," in *Text, Methode und Grammatik (Fest.* W. Richter; ed. W. Gross, et al.; St. Ottilien: EOS, 1991) 577-94; P. Weimar, "Struktur und Komposition der priesterschriftlichen Geschichtsdarstellung," *BN* 24 (1984) 138-62.

# Psalm 95:
# Yahweh-Kingship Hymn; Sermon

## Structure

|  | MT | NRSV |
|---|---|---|
| I. Call to worship | 1-2 | 1-2 |
| II. Hymn | 3-5 | 3-5 |
| III. Call to worship | 6 | 6 |
| IV. Hymn | 7ab | 7ab |
| V. Sermon | 7c-11 | 7c-11 |
|   A. Exhortation | 7c | 7c |
|   B. Exposition | 8-11 | 8-11 |

We do not have any SUPERSCRIPTION in the so-called Yahweh-kingship psalms (→ Psalm 93; a rudimentary "song," 98:1 notwithstanding). Perhaps they once were used jointly in special worship services. Our present text stands out by the standard opening and abrupt close, which leave doubts as to its liturgical completeness. More than other psalms of this genre our text shows signs of communal or congregational use.

CALLS TO WORSHIP (vv. 1-2, 6) are intimately related to a SUMMONS TO PRAISE: we may imagine such admonitions to have been issued by congregational leaders or liturgists. They called out loudly to the participants in worship to get together and engage in joyful shouting, and they would supply the hymnic lines, as did Miriam when she intoned her victory song (Exod 15:21). The first two lines here apparently ask the people to draw near, either into the temple precinct, more likely for a synagogue kind of assembly a long way from Jerusalem (vv. 1-2; special mention of the "sacred songs," zĕmirôt, which the assembly will offer, v. 2b; only one more plural of this term in the Psalter: Ps 119:54; cf. 2 Sam 23:1; Isa 24:16; Job 35:10), while the repeated call (v. 6) is an orientation to assume postures of adoration. Three verbs are used in the first CALL TO WORSHIP: rnn, Piel, "jubilate," rû', Hiphil, "make noise," and qdm, Piel, "draw near." They all occur in various psalms of praise and adoration. But the first person plural, in the jussive mode, is rarely applied in our psalm literature. Indeed, to my knowledge communal hymns have not been preserved in extra-Israelite psalms, a sure sign of that special organization of early Jewish communities (cf. Scharbert, "Das 'Wir'"; listing at "Introduction to Psalms"; Seybold, "Das 'Wir'"; Additional Bibliography, section C. Seybold emphasizes the concentration of "we" psalms in the Asaph collection, the most significant specimens being Psalms 79 and 80, and beyond the Asaph group, Psalms 44; 90; 95; 103; Lamentations 5; Isa 63:1–64:11; Jer 14:7-9; Hos 6:1-3). Of the three verbs listed above only the first is used in a comparable way in 20:6 (RSV 5) and 90:14, though not in the introductory position. The third verb, qdm, Piel, appears in prayer introductions, but only in the first person singular (cf. 119:147; Mic 6:6). We can also point out other verbs, the first person singular or plural of which serves as introductory call to praise (e.g., šîr, "sing": Exod 15:1, 21; brk, Piel, "bless," in the phrase: "my 'soul', bless . . ." = "I will bless":

Pss 103:1; 104:1; *ydh*, Hiphil, "give thanks": three plural forms: 44:9 [RSV 8]; 75:2 [RSV 1]; 79:13; and forty singular forms in the Psalter, plus two singular jussives in Isa 12:1; 25:1). The last-mentioned passages from Isaiah clearly introduce communal hymns; this fact reminds us that the first person singular may indicate an exemplary person, either the leader of the assembly who is speaking for the community, or an "everyman," meaning the typical member of the group. Thus, within the forty summonses directed to a speaker's self, at least some address in reality the congregation as a whole. In any case, vv. 1-2 and 6 by virtue of their strong plural jussives make Psalm 95 one of the most community-based hymns in the Psalter, a fact that certainly has consequences for determining the life setting and theological outlook of the psalm. In terms of liturgical functioning, we may say, the first person plural probably indicates the whole community speaking, or else a functionary in the name of the congregation (cf. Sunday sermons today). The vociferous presence of the assembly apparently marks the beginning of cultic action or worship (cf. Psalm 100).

The two *kî* phrases following calls to worship are not motive clauses but true hymnic lines, as in Exod 15:21: "Yes," "indeed" — God is great! (cf. vv. 3 and 7). They do not give reasons to sing, but are the song itself, put before the participants in worship to be endlessly repeated (cf. Crüsemann, *Studien,* 32-35; listing at "Introduction to Cultic Poetry"). Superiority of Yahweh is one subject (v. 3; cf. Psalms 93; 96:4-6, 10; 97:9; 99:2) looming large in all hymns, especially the Yahweh-kingship songs. The other topic is the fact that this congregation feels intricately associated with the most powerful Deity. "He is our God, we are the people of his pasture" (v. 7; cf. Psalm 100). Praise of God and the feeling of belonging are mutually dependent.

The first hymnic line (v. 3) is elaborated into a little hymn (vv. 4-5). These two bicola explain the greatness of Yahweh; one by one they were probably repeated by the community, just like v. 3. What is strange, though, is the grammatical conjunction with the relative particle *'ăšer,* "who," atypical of poetic language (four occurrences altogether: vv. 4, 5, 9, 11, missing in some Hebrew MSS). Does the use of this conjunction betray later, rather prosaic, additions to an older text? While v. 3 exhibits the titles of Yahweh's superiority, vv. 4-5 spell out his ownership over all creation. V. 6b continues the idea of Yahweh having created the whole world, but — according to the thrust of this new hymnic intonation — it enters the claim of the community to be Yahweh's handiwork.

Hymn singing of the people apparently comes to an end in v. 7ab. The line seems broken at the end; perhaps there were originally two words with similar orthography: *yādô,* "his hand" ("sheep of his hand"), and subsequent *dĕ'û,* "take knowledge" (Gunkel). Be that as it may, a totally new segment begins with v. 7c: "Today you must listen to his voice!" The phrase sounds like the protasis of an oath, with the apodosis missing (which is customary): "Today, if you do not listen (the curse will come over you)!" Or: "Beware that you do listen (if not, the curse will come over you!" Emphasis on "today's" opportunity to listen to the will of God is found most of all in Dtr texts (cf. Exod 34:11; Deut 4:40; 6:6; 7:11; 8:19; 9:3; 11:2; 29:9-14; 30:11, 15; etc.). Insistence on the present moment in the context of religious instruction must have some fixed setting. The best explanation of this oratory, it seems to me, is to understand it as a central concern of early Jewish preaching. Ps 95:7c, then, uses some kerygmatic or homiletic vocabulary, taken from Dtr traditions. By formulating a conditioned oath to introduce God's speech (cf. other introductions: 50:10; 81:6c) the psalmist creates a very strong formula to herald God's own discourse (vv. 8-10). Then he takes up wilderness traditions about Israel's rebellion against Yahweh (cf. Exod 17:1-7; Num 20:1-13) and freely as well as succinctly interprets his material. At Massah and Meribah — thus the meaning of the names — Israel "tried" Yahweh and "quarrelled" with him (cf. also v. 9). For him, however, this event was a "hardening of hearts" (v. 8a) comparable to Isaiah's message of "fattening of hearts" (Isa 6:10). The Dtr metaphor is frequently "hardening [or 'stiffening'] of necks" (cf. Deut 9:6, 13; 10:16; 31:27; 2 Kgs 17:14; Jer 7:26; 17:23; 19:15). Evaluation of the whole wilderness period (40 years, v. 10a) leads Yahweh to the conclusion that his people do not want to follow his directions (v. 10bc). Therefore he swears not to let them come "to my tranquility" or "rest" (v. 11). On this note of negation or divine frustration the psalm ends, which is certainly puzzling. How would a sermon or a worship liturgy close on such a verdict?

God's own discourse, however, just like the divine speeches contained in Psalms 50; 81; 82; 91, poses some form-critical problems. How can we explain the existence of divine oratory at all? Who was entitled to mediate the "I" words of Yahweh to his congregation? Taking divine oratory simply at face value (cf. Koenen, *Gottesworte;* Miller, *They Cried,* 141-77, Additional Bibliography, section C) is insufficient, because human mediation is always an integral part of God's messages. Most exegetes postulate prophetic mediation. Apart from all the problems of missing prophetic profiles in the psalms, in this case we have clear indications that the speaker of vv. 7c-11 is interpreting tradition or even Scripture. He is delivering a SERMON on stories of Massah and Meribah and on the basis of contemporary "hardening of hearts" theories (cf. 2 Chr 30:6-9: "Do not now be stiffnecked" — v. 8, preached by messengers; Num 12:2; Jeremiah 28). Exegesis and interpretation are the main characteristics of vv. 8-10; we should not be misled by the formal "I" discourse of God to miss these traits of exegetical work on traditions or texts.

The question posed above, in regard to the abrupt and odd ending of the psalm, can be answered only this way: Psalm 95 is probably neither a complete hymn nor a full sermon, but a fragment of a liturgical agenda. It depended on supplementation of the very message of doom, because the initial "today is listening time" demands an offer of a real chance of survival, as in Dtr and Chronistic preaching. Liturgical considerations would let us expect, e.g., a penitential prayer after a condemnatory statement like that of v. 11.

### Genre

Taking seriously the observations above, we wonder whether we are dealing with an authentic YAHWEH-KINGSHIP SONG (→ Psalms 47; 93). Besides the lone term "king" (v. 3b: "great God — great King" are stereotyped, imperial epithets; cf. 47:3; K. Seybold, *TWAT* IV, 952-56; K. W. Whitelam, *ABD* II, 43-

44), nothing in our text reminds us of "kingship," unless creation is the work of a king of the gods (vv. 4-5; cf. Marduk). The metaphor of pastures and sheep does not necessarily signify a royal background. On the contrary, Yahweh is pictured not as a king but principally as the giver of *tôrāh;* cf., e.g., the highly revealing phrase: "they do not know my ways" (v. 10c). Thus we may put in a claim to classify our psalm as SERMON with a hymnic introduction. Dtr and, partially, Chronistic terminology, rhetoric, and theology lend weight to this classification. Cf., e.g., the great sermon of Moses in Deuteronomy 29–30, where the preacher insists that the Word of God must be accepted and obeyed "today" (cf. Ps 95:7c). Every so often, early Jewish preaching urges that one listen to God's will and not spurn it (cf. Exod 34:11-12; Deut 4:40; 5:1-3; 6:4-7; Jer 11:6-8; 25:3-7; 2 Chr 30:8; etc.: Ps 95:7-8). The sin of the fathers is a constant topic in postexilic sermons (cf. Jer 44:9-10; Nehemiah 9; Ezra 9; 2 Chr 29:6; Psalm 106; etc.; Ps 95:9). The verdict that all the people went astray in their wanderings after the exodus from Egypt with subsequent punishment by Yahweh (vv. 10-11) is a direct reflection on the wilderness tradition (cf. Coats, Additional Bibliography, section B). "To enter the rest (of Yahweh)" (v. 11b) seems to be a direct import from Deut 12:9, just as v. 8 refers to Exod 17:1-7. This means that Psalm 95 is firmly rooted in early Jewish preaching traditions. They in turn are, as far as our psalm and other sermonlike texts of the Psalter are concerned, embedded in worship and hymn singing. The abrupt close of v. 11 parallels that of 81:17 (RSV 16). Another liturgical element would probably follow the divine speech. The discussion of oracular patterns in the psalms has not come to a good conclusion yet (→ Psalms 12; 75; 81; cf. Starbuck, *Oracles,* Additional Bibliography, section C).

## Setting

Normal worship services in Jewish congregations of the fifth and fourth centuries B.C.E., held in the diaspora or "at home" on Judean soil, may have given rise to this kind of communal introit and subsequent interpretive preaching. The "we" form represents communal liturgical action. It "leads us toward a relatively novel phenomenon, which we may call a religious community lacking state or cult organization. It is probably a new kind of community of laypeople *('ēdāh),* which we may best designate as a 'people's parish'" (Seybold, "Das 'Wir,'" 148). In this sense we opt for congregational worship outside Jerusalem and its temple for a likely point of anchorage. Commentators in general acknowledge links to postexilic worship, and homiletical argumentation in the D tradition (e.g., Gunkel, 417-20; Seybold, 377-78; Tate, 499-500; Jeremias, *Kultprophetie,* 125-26, listing at "Introduction to Psalms"; Hossfeld).

## Intention

This fragmentary psalm wants to meditate on the fate of Israel in the times of Moses in order to (this has to be deduced from Dtr parallels) warn the actual generation of pitfalls and temptations along the way. Faith in Yahweh has to be maintained, even when knowing his harsh verdicts over a hardened generation. The history of the people as well as the testimony of the Torah do encourage hope, thanksgiving, and trust in Yahweh (vv. 1-7b).

## Bibliography

P. Auffret, "Essai sur la structure littéraire du psaume 95," *BN* 20 (1983) 47-69; W. E. Barnes, "Two Psalm Notes — Ps 22:17; 95:6," *JTS* 37 (1936) 385-87; J. Brand, "Sabbath-Rest, Worship, and the Epistle to the Hebrews: Celebrating the Rule of Yahweh," *Didaskalia* 1 (1990) 3-13; G. Braulik, "Gottes Ruhe — das Land oder der Tempel? Zu Psalm 95,11," in *Freude an der Weisung des Herrn* (*Fest.* H. Gross; ed. E. Haag, et al.; Stuttgart: Katholisches Bibelwerk, 1986) 33-44; G. H. Davies, "Psalm 95," *ZAW* 85 (1973) 183-95; J. D. M. Derrett, "Ho Kyrios ebasileusen apo tou xylou," *VC* 43 (1989) 378-92; P. E. Enns, "Creation and Re-Creation: Psalm 95 and Its Interpretation in Hebrews 3:1–4:13," *WTJ* 55 (1993) 255-80; J. Finkel, "Some Problems Relating to Ps 95," *AJSL* 50 (1933/34) 32-40; P. F. Gesch, "Finding Your Place in God's World," *Point* 6 (1977) 50-60; M. Girard, "Analyse structurelle du Psaume 95," *Science et Esprit* 33 (1981) 179-89; idem, "The Literary Structure of Psalm 95," *Theology Digest* 30 (1982) 55-58; F.-L. Hossfeld, "Psalm 95: Gattungsgeschichtliche, kompositionskritische und bibeltheologische Anfragen," in *Neue Wege der Psalmenforschung* (HBS 1; ed. K. Seybold; Freiburg im Breisgau: Herder, 1994) 29-44; J. Jeremias, *Königtum,* 107-14 (listing at "Introduction to Psalms"); M. Kolden, "People of His Pasture," *Currents in Theology and Mission* 18 (1991) 122-24; S. Lemming, "Massa und Meriba," *ZAW* 73 (1961) 71-77; B. Marin, "'Accoltate, oggi, la voce del Signore! Il tema dell ascolto nel Salmo 95," *Parola Spirito e Vita* 1 (1980) 59-79; S. Massouh, "Exegetical Notes: Psalm 95," *Trinity Journal* 4 (1983) 84-88; D. E. McGregor, "The Fish and the Cross," *Point Series* 1 (1982) 1-139; M. Metzger, "Eigentumsdeklaration und Schöpfungsaussage," in *'Wenn nicht jetzt'* (*Fest.* H.-J. Kraus; ed. H.-G. Geyer, et al.; Neukirchen-Vluyn: Neukirchener Verlag, 1983) 37-51; C. Petersen, *Mythos,* 177-82 (listing at "Introduction to Cultic Poetry"); J. du Preez, "Reading Three 'Enthronement Psalms' from an Ecological Perspective," *Missionalia* 19 (1991) 122-30; G. von Rad, "Es ist noch eine Ruhe vorhanden dem Volke Gottes," *Zwischen den Zeiten* 11 (1933) 104-11; C. J. Renz, "Come, Let Us Listen to the Voice of the Lord!" *Worship* 70 (1996) 140-53; C. B. Riding, "Psalm 95:1-7c as a Large Chiasm," *ZAW* 88 (1976) 418; S. Sabugal, "El concepto del pecado en el Antiguo Testamento," *Estudios Eclesiásticos* 59 (1984) 459-69; O. Schilling, "Die Anbetung Gottes — Wurzel und Konsequenz," *BibLeb* 2 (1961) 105-20; T. Seidl, "Scheltwort als Befreiungsrede," in *Das Volk Gottes — ein Ort der Befreiung* (*Fest.* E. Klinger; ed. H. Keul; Würzburg: Echter, 1998) 107-20; N. Tromp, "De bronnen van lof en dank (Ps 95,1-7a)," and "De houding van ons hart (Ps 95,7b-11)," *Ons Geestelijk Leven* 43 (1966) 308-12 and 312-16; L. Vosberg, *Studien* (listing at "Introduction to Psalms"); H. Weiss, "Sabbatismus in the Epistle to the Hebrews," *CBQ* 58 (1996) 674-89.

## Psalm 96:
## Yahweh-Kingship Hymn

### Structure

|                                | MT    | NRSV  |
| ------------------------------ | ----- | ----- |
| I. Summons to praise           | 1-3   | 1-3   |
| II. Hymn                       | 4-6   | 4-6   |
| III. Summons to praise         | 7-9   | 7-9   |
| IV. Proclamation of enthronement | 10  | 10    |
| V. Beckoning jubilation        | 11-13 | 11-13 |
|    A. Joy of nature | 11-12 | 11-12 |
|    B. Justice for nations | 13 | 13 |

A slightly shorter and somewhat modified text of the psalm has been transmitted in 1 Chr 16:23-33 (discussion of variants: Jeremias, *Königtum,* 122-23; listing at "Introduction to Psalms") as an example of Davidic/Levitical hymn singing in the First Temple. The psalm is placed between parts of Psalms 105 and 106. Would this sequence of psalms reveal a different order of psalms in the Psalter? Or simply a liturgical arrangement?

Since the Yahweh-kingship psalms do not have any regular superscriptions in the MT (only LXX provides them in Greek), the psalm starts out with a SUMMONS TO PRAISE featuring five plural imperatives, three of which are *šîrû,* "sing," the fourth and fifth are *baśśĕrû* and *sappĕrû,* "proclaim" and "tell" (vv. 1-3; Crüsemann, *Studien,* 210-66, locates the original form in personal thanksgiving songs with its obligatory "narration" of salvific experience; see esp. 265-66). A worship leader addresses an audience that seems to be global: "all the earth" (vv. 1b, 9b), "to/among all people/nations" (cf. vv. 3, 7a, 10a). With this emphasis on proclamation and the wide horizon of addressees the psalm from the outset has a universal and extroverted character. Given the modest reality of exilic/postexilic Jewish congregations, though, we may surmise that proclamations of this sort were used not in public (of police-controlled imperial states) but rather in closed worship services, by and for the gathered crowd. A certain sense of mission to other ethnic groups and of superiority over them is apparent in vv. 3, 4, 10, 13-14, and especially in v. 5 (satirical polemics, as in → 115:4-8; 135:15-18).

The verb *šîr,* usually parallel with "play," "make noise," "jubilate," "praise," "extol," etc., frequently denotes "hymn singing" in the strict sense; the noun *šîr* is almost a genre term for "hymn" (cf. 21:14 [RSV 13]; 27:6; 68:5, 33 [RSV 4, 32]; 98:1; 105:2; 137:3-4; 144:9; 149:1 — the noun being frequent in superscriptions; cf. Psalms 45; 46; 48; 65–69; on the whole, 31 occurrences). It is a "new" song the leader of the assembly is calling for (cf. Isa 42:10; Pss 98:1; 144:9; 149:1) that is equivalent to "vigorous," "powerful," because hymns live from their inherent energy; cf. Deut 31:19-22, 30; 32:44; 2 Chr 20:21-22 (cf. Miller, *They Cried,* 178-232; Brueggemann, *Psalms,* 112-32, both in Additional Bibliography, section C). The contents of the hymn are Yahweh's glory and wondrous deeds (v. 3; the name of Yahweh is mentioned three times in conjunction with *šîr* in vv. 1-2). Thus the topic and mode of proceeding are set from the beginning of the psalm.

The HYMN proper (vv. 4-6), i.e., those lines exalting God that are to be sung one by one and repeatedly so by the choir or congregation, are partly introduced by exclamatory *kî*, "yes" (vv. 4-5; cf. Exod 15:21; Ps 118:1). The first of these (v. 4) is little different from → 95:3, celebrating, as it were, Yahweh's superiority over all the gods. A phrase like "great is Yahweh" (v. 4a) seems to have an archetypal weight and persistence; its tradition history has already lasted thousands of years (note also the Muslim praise: *Allah akbar,* "Allah is great," and occasionally some human echo: "I am the greatest"). The designation *gādôl,* "great," in regard to deities and kings is fundamental for hymnic discourse in the Hebrew Bible (cf. Deut 7:21; 10:17; Pss 21:6 [RSV 5]; 48:2 [RSV 1]; 77:14 [RSV 13]; 86:10; 99:2; 135:5; 145:3; 147:5). Interestingly, the stock phrase in v. 4a occurs in two more psalms: 48:2 (RSV 1) and 145:3, with only the second colon varying in all three cases. Our v. 4b in contradistinction to the two passages cited, but in full accordance with 95:3b, moves toward comparison with other gods. This very motif dominates v. 5, turning into sharp polemics: "All the gods (*'ĕlōhîm*) of the nations are 'nobodies' (*'ĕlîlîm)*" (v. 5a). Israelite polemics against "strange" gods are the outcome of a prolonged battle for survival in a multireligious, autocratic imperium (cf. Isa 40:18-25; 44:9-20). To claim superiority for Yahweh was the only means of defense against the Babylonian and Persian oppressors. Some of the Yahweh-kingship psalms indulge in this kind of refutation of foreign powers, being, as it were, documents of this crucial age (cf. Pss 93:3-4; 95:3; 97:7, 9); but few of them ridicule deities of other people as does v. 5 (cf. only 97:7). For this kind of ridicule over against other gods we have to compare especially some passages in Second Isaiah: Isa 40:18-25; 44:9-20. Derogatory *'ĕlîlîm* is used in some other contexts: cf. Lev 19:4; 26:1; Isa 2:8, 20; 10:10-11; 19:1, 3; Hab 2:18 (Preuss, *Verspottung;* Additional Bibliography, section B). The last line of the hymn is pure praise of Yahweh "in his sanctuary" (differently in 1 Chr 16:27).

From the liturgical point of view the repeated SUMMONS TO PRAISE (vv. 7-9) does not come as a surprise. Yet the formulations used are somewhat extravagant. Like Ps 29:1-2 or Deut 32:3, our psalm employs an archaic imperative of the root *yhb,* "bring," in order to admonish unnamed beings to honor Yahweh alone (vv. 7-8). Formulations of vv. 7-9a, in fact, are near identical with those of Ps 29:1-2. Are we facing a kind of sacred plagiarism? Hardly so, if judged again from a liturgical point of view. Standard articulations of faith were used freely in worship; they were not considered "property" of individual "authors." The phraseology suggests something like taking one's own powers and privileges to the divine overlord, in order to strengthen his supreme authority. In essence, this is still the main concern of any kind of submission, obedience, and praise — transfer of power. Subordinated entities render to the superior authority whatever they can muster in terms of influence or power. Psalm 96 asks all the world to join in adoration of Yahweh, to partake in his worship and be happy (v. 9). Here is an ecumenical dimension of the psalm viewed and experienced by an impotent people, a negligible religious community within an immense, imperial power structure. Parts of vv. 9-11 correspond literally to

29:1-2. Jeremias (*Königtum,* 125) affirms that 96:1-9 "on the whole wants to be a 'modern' exegesis of Ps 29:1-2," which would be true only on a strictly literary level of transmission. The most important statement of the hymn is the PROCLAMATION and therefore acknowledgment of Yahweh's, the supreme king's, government by all powers and all humankind (v. 10). Also this very verse seems to be patched together from different literary sources (v. 10a, cf. 97:1; 99:1; v. 10b, cf. 93:1; v. 10c, cf. 7:9 [RSV 8]; 1 Sam 2:10). This impression may be totally wrong from the liturgical perspective. Textual uncertainties, including the different wording and position of our verse in the duplicate text of 1 Chr 16:23-33 (exactly in v. 31), may be due to growing ignorance in biblical tradition as to its cultic importance. In reality, the verse is of central importance to the whole psalm (cf. Howard, 65; listing at Psalm 93). After summoning all powers of the earth (not the ones of heaven, as in Psalms 29; 148) to subjugate themselves to Yahweh, the overlord, and enhance his prestige (vv. 7-9), the speaker suggests a witness for the lordship of Yahweh by Israel (v. 10). It is this tripartite poetical line that is on everybody's mind and can be shouted as a communal refrain: "Tell the peoples that Yahweh has become king: Yes, he has established the earth. He will judge the earth in solidarity; he will bring justice to the nations" (v. 10; cf. Psalms 24; 93:2; 82). The universal outlook of this verse and of the total psalm is quite obvious. Proclamation of Yahweh's kingship serves as a catalyst for the whole text, supporting its hymnic structure. The creation of the world and the capacity to judge all nations are the pillars of God's authority. But what did it mean to the worshipers of Persian times to witness Yahweh's supreme authority in a superior political system? The books of Esther and Daniel may partly answer that question. As little opportunity as may have existed for Yahweh believers to engage in active mission strategies, the problem of the public appearance of the Jewish faith and of open conflicts with "official," i.e., imperial, religion was clearly at hand. This general experience of Jews in the Persian Empire was apparently the background of a kind of "mission order" in vv. 3, 10: "Tell (it) among the nations" (cf. Matt 28:19-20).

What follows is a description of consequences deriving from Yahweh's supreme government (vv. 11-13). Phrases are formed as affirmations, with a wishful and exhortatory undertone: "Heavens are to be glad, earth is to burst out in joy" (v. 11a). Most verbs are plain imperfects, though. Just as in all preceding verses, there is no indication of who is speaking and no direct address of the Deity. Important is the outbreak of joy, as in a cosmic feast, in the face of God's reign. Parallel passages of the Psalter include 97:1, 8, 12; 67:5-6 (RSV 4-5); 68:4 (RSV 3); 69:33 (RSV 32); 70:5 (RSV 4). Quite close are, as well, admonitions to rejoice in Deuteronomy; they let transpire festive merriment of worship and seasonal gatherings (cf. Deut 12:7, 11-12, 18; 14:26; 16:10-11, 13-14; etc.). Our verses are BECKONING all the world to participate: first, primordial creatures, heaven, earth, and sea (v. 11); then secondary entities like cultivated land and its inhabitants, namely humankind and domestic beasts, as well as the trees of the forest (v. 12; cf. Psalm 148). The list is very interesting in terms of inherent concepts of nature (cf. Russ). V. 13 picks up the proclamation of Yahweh's government (v. 10), announcing the coming of this (new?) king.

Debate has been going on rather inconclusively about the nature of God's appearance. Is it a seasonal celebration in a festive context, or is it an eschatological coming at the end of history? A short verse like ours can hardly provide sufficient information to resolve the question. In general, it seems certain that in prophetic contexts expectancy of a day of final judgment (cf. Ezekiel 38; 39; Zechariah 14) has slowly grown out of short-term prospects, seasonal and otherwise, of Yahweh's coming (cf. Am 5:18-20; Zeph 1:7-18). Judgment of nations in the Psalms appears to stay in a realistic middle ground, proclaiming just judgment of the people now.

## Genre

Psalm 96 is part of the block of YAHWEH-KINGSHIP PSALMS (→ Psalm 93). But, like its companions, it has a character of its own (cf. the formal analysis of Jeremias, *Königtum,* 121-31). While Psalms 47 and 93 celebrate the initiation of Yahweh's government, and Psalm 95 is involved with inner-Israelite opposition of the (postexilic) time, our psalm is oriented toward the world of "natural" (i.e., divine) and political powers, summoning them to praise Yahweh alone (cf. Psalms 29; 98). This is the concern of a true HYMN. That the composition draws on various sources of tradition does not contradict our genre definition, which is essentially liturgical. May we call it an eschatological hymn (e.g., Gunkel, 421)? Was it part of the liturgy of Yahweh's annual enthronement (e.g., Mowinckel, *PsSt* II)? The "coming" of Yahweh and his "judging the earth" (vv. 10c, 13) indeed may refer to political and social upheavals of the late sixth and fifth centuries B.C.E., expressing hopes of a fundamental change in world domination (cf. the preaching of Second Isaiah; Jeremias, *Königtum,* 131).

## Setting

Seasonal festivals (cf. Leviticus 23; Deuteronomy 16) or regular worship services in the exilic-postexilic era certainly gave occasion to confess Yahweh as the creator of heaven and earth and dominator of all the nations (cf. Otto) — a risky undertaking in the political environment of the day. Challenging the power of imperial deities had to be considered a subversive act by the authorities in charge. Apparently, early Jewish worship to the exclusive and jealous God Yahweh often (but not necessarily always; cf. Psalms 85; 104; etc.) had also a polemic quality. Given the rootage of the Psalm in early Jewish community life, we need to acknowledge its great importance for establishing that community's identity.

## Intention

As mentioned in the structure analysis, polemics against other gods in the first place was a means of self-defense in early Jewish Yahwism. To face an exclusive (even if religiously tolerant) imperium and its hegemonistic economy, administration, and military strategy required a comprehensive and absolute denial of obedience, and an equally absolute allegiance to another power that would be able to hold its ground. Yahwism, at this point, was the only possible alternative in downtrodden and dispersed Israel. The claim of Yahweh's universal reign was a bulwark against Israel's disintegration (→ Psalms 47; 93; 95–100).

## Bibliography

W. A. M. Beuken, "Psalm 96: Israel en de volken," *SK* 13 (1992) 1-10; A. Feuillet, "Les psaumes eschatologiques du règne de Yahweh," *NRT* 73 (1951) 244-60, 352-63; B. Fischer, "Liturgiegeschichte und Exegesegeschichte: Interdisziplinäre Zusammenhänge," *Jahrbuch für Antike und Christentum* 30 (1987) 5-13; B. Gosse, "Les citations de Psaumes en 1 Ch 16,8-36," *Église et théologie* 27 (1996) 313-33; C. Houtman, "De jubelzang van de struiken der wildernis in Psalm 96,12b," in *Loven en geloven (Fest.* N. H. Ridderbos; ed. C. Houtman, et al.; Amsterdam: Uitgeverij Ton Bolland, 1975); J. I. Hunt, "Translating Psalm 29," *ATR* 67 (1985) 219-27; H.-J. Kraus, *Die Königsherrschaft Gottes im Alten Testament* (Tübingen: Mohr, 1951); M. Lee, "An Exegetical Study of Psalm 96" (Th.M. thesis, Calvin Theological Seminary, 1996; cf. *Calvin Theological Journal* 32 [1997] 220); A. C. Lovelace, "Make Joyful Noise to the Lord: Biblical Foundations of Church Music," *Point* 2 (1973) 15-27; R. Martin-Achard, "Israël, peuple sacerdotal," *Cahiers de la Revue de Théologie et de Philosophie* 11 (1984) 129-46; H.-D. Preuss, *Die Verspottung fremder Religionen im Alten Testament* (Stuttgart: Kohlhammer, 1971); H. Ringgren, "Behold, Your King Comes," *VT* 24 (1974) 207-11; M. Russ, "'Singt ihm einen neuen Gesang!'" in *Wort Gottes in der Zeit (Fest.* K. H. Schelkl; ed. H. Feld, et al.; Düsseldorf: Patmos Verlag, 1973) 15-21; H. Schmidt, *Die Thronfahrt Jahwes zum Fest der Jahreswende im alten Israel* (Tübingen: Mohr, 1927); G. H. Wilson, "The Qumran Psalms Scroll Reconsidered," *CBQ* 47 (1985) 624-42.

## Psalm 97:
## Yahweh-Kingship Hymn

### Structure

|  | MT | NRSV |
|---|---|---|
| I. Hymn | 1-6 | 1-6 |
| A. Enthronement shout | 1a | 1a |
| B. Beckoning to jubilate | 1ab | 1ab |
| C. Description of theophany | 2-5 | 2-5 |
| D. Summons to proclaim | 6 | 6 |
| II. Victory song | 7-9 | 7-9 |
| A. Imprecation | 7 | 7 |

| | | |
|---|---|---|
| B. Jubilation | 8 | 8 |
| C. Praise | 9 | 9 |
| III. Exhortation, sermon | 10-12 | 10-12 |
| A. Admonition | 10a | 10a |
| B. Consolation | 10b-11 | 10b-11 |
| C. Beckoning | 12 | 12 |

With a superscription missing, the psalm plunges in medias res: *yhwh mālak,* "Yahweh is reigning as king" or "Yahweh became king" (v. 1a), is an ENTHRONEMENT SHOUT (cf. 2 Sam 15:10; 1 Kgs 1:34, 39 [here the shout is: "The king may live!"]; 1 Kgs 1:18; 2 Kgs 9:13). The two historical reports that transmit an identical enthronement shout invert the word order: *XY mālak,* "XY has become king" (2 Sam 15:10; 2 Kgs 9:13). Still, the similarity to the phrase used in psalmic first lines (Pss 93:1; 97:1; 99:1) and some other places (47:9 [RSV 8]; 96:10) is undeniable, and even most painstaking grammatical investigations of the matter cannot do away with the impression that the two expressions are very close in meaning (K. Seybold, *TWAT* IV, 952-53). In any case, the shout is used in three psalms as a heralding manifestation of Yahweh's power. Yahweh's kingship is their main topic; therefore the enthronement shout is put in the very first line. BECKONING JUBILATION, as in → Ps 96:11-12 and many other passages, is a logical consequence in coronation ceremonies. All subjects are liable to acknowledge the lordship of a new king and swear obeisance. In our case, Yahweh being the universal and even cosmic overlord (cf. the global expressions in the Yahweh-kingship hymns: "earth," "islands" = marking the fringes of the world: v. 1; "world," "earth": v. 4; "the whole earth": vv. 5b; 9a; etc.), heaven and earth, and all the gods therein, have to pay attention and bow down to him (vv. 6; 9b → Psalms 93; 96; 98; 99). In historical reports we also hear about the rejoicing connected with the enthronement of a new king (cf. 1 Sam 10:24; 1 Kgs 1:40, 45). Monarchies until our own day teach their subjects to be happy and thankful for and with the royal family. Like other hymns of this type praise and joy therefore include "all the land" and its fringes (v. 1). This means that a universal reign of Yahweh is intended and confessed against all other claims.

The THEOPHANY (vv. 2-5) has a standard way of being depicted: fire, thunder, clouds belong to the paraphernalia of God's coming (→ Ps 18:8-16 [RSV 7-15]; Habakkuk 3; Jeremias, *Theophanie;* listing at Psalm 18). Parallelism of two pairs of metaphors, one mythological ("clouds, darkness," v. 2a) and one ethical ("justice, right," v. 2b), is remarkable; cf. the first couplet in Deut 4:11; Ezek 34:12; Joel 2:2; Zeph 1:15; and the second one in Pss 89:15 (RSV 14); 119:121; Prov 1:3; 2:9. To describe Yahweh's clouded appearance is not enough. Most important is the effect of his coming, with fire (or lightning?) preparing his way among enemies and "natural" powers like earth and mountains (vv. 3-5). The latter even "melt away like wax" (v. 5a; cf. Ps 68:3 [RSV 2]; Mic 1:3-4; Judg 5:4-5), marking the violent upheaval of all nature — which in the mythical past used to be hostile to the God of life — at the coming of Yahweh. Similarly, the coming of weather- and storm-gods (e.g., Baal, Hadad) in ancient Near Eastern texts can be described in terms of uproars in nature (cf., e.g., H. L. Ginsberg, *ANET,* 135: "Baal gives forth his holy voice, Baal discharges the utterance of his lips. His holy voice convulses the earth, . . . the mountains quake"). Theophany, then, is a piece of dramatic enactment of primeval battle for control over the universe. In later times, the imagery of this battle was used to paint eschatological clashes, but at this point, eschatology does not yet appear to be in the making. PROCLAMATION of Yahweh's victory (v. 6) does not belong to the original theophanic record, but is a later accretion to the form (cf. Jeremias, *Theophanie,* 4). The line states the consequences of theophany, expecting universal publication of Yahweh's appearance. Heaven or, more precisely, heavenly powers are to praise him (v. 6a) and the nations are to listen (v. 6b). This is much the same pattern as in v. 2: a mythical and a historical colon are dramatically glued together. All in all, the report of Yahweh's appearance is no longer located in ancient war preparation (Jeremias) but apparently functions as festive rhetoric in a late, i.e., postexilic, celebration of Yahweh's royal power. The speaker of these verses does not reveal himself, though, nor does he or she address Yahweh directly.

The next element comes close to a VICTORY SONG (vv. 7-9) especially in lines two and three. Zion and the women of Judah are beckoned to jubilate, as after a battle won (v. 8ab: imperfect consecutives with exhortatory character: → Ps 96:11-12; G. Vanoni, *TWAT* VII, 808-22), and after that the psalm changes to direct address of Yahweh (vv. 8b, 9). Indeed, the last line is a real hymnic statement of Yahweh's superiority over all the other gods (v. 9b), expressed by a rare Niphal form of *'lh,* "to make oneself [or perhaps 'to be'] superior" (cf. 47:10d [RSV 9d]). All this may be understood before the background of mythical battle (vv. 2-5). Yet there is no explicit reference to primordial action in vv. 7-9, and the hymn remains concentrated on Yahweh's royal power, which is sufficient cause for all Judah to extol the Lord in extreme joy (cf. 68:2-4). The first line of our inset hymn, however (v. 7), contains a threat and exhortation against enemies and apostates. These collocations (imperfect, imperative — according to LXX) are the least fitting for a victory hymn. They do ward off continuing danger arising from dissenting "brethren," as in 96:5. V. 7, indeed, is an IMPRECATION of sorts, spoken in long-range self-defense. By these modulations of the older form of the victory hymn (→ Psalms 18; 68; Judges 5) we get an impression of later use and composition.

The last section (no. III) draws practical, homiletical conclusions from the preceding ones. The addressees are plainly the members of the congregation: they love Yahweh (cf. v. 10a), and they are finally called the "just" or "righteous" ones (v. 12a). Whenever participants of the assembly are focused on, either the accusatory or parenetic character becomes plain. In this case it is the latter. The imperative of MT ("hate evil," v. 11a; cf. Am 5:15; NRSV emends into descriptive language: "The Lord loves those who hate evil") is a strong admonition, connecting with the apostates of v. 7. Comforting assurances of God's guaranteed help (vv. 10bc, 11) make possible a resounding "hail" to the righteous (v. 12: imperatives to "be glad" and to "thank"). Exhortations in front of listeners who seem to be worshiping together call for attention. The admonitions to express existential joy are prominent in our psalm (lexemes of the root *śmḥ* in vv. 1, 8, 11, 12; cf. 96:11). Thus the whole passage is close to a SERMON.

## Genre/Setting

In line with other YAHWEH-KINGSHIP HYMNS (→ Psalms 93; 95; 98), our song celebrates Yahweh, the universal God, who is the greatest among all other deities of the pluralistic and imperial world of the day. Such adoration of Yahweh's supreme authority probably took place in regular Jewish communal worship of Persian times. The last section gives a pedagogical/homiletical finish to the psalm, so it may be seen as a real SERMON to the congregation (cf. Psalms 91; 95).

A long debate has been going on (→ Psalm 93) about whether Israel, in preexilic times, celebrated a special Yahweh enthronement festival (Mowinckel). The evidence of our Yahweh-kingship psalms on the whole is negative. The extant texts may contain some ancient concepts and even formulas (e.g., "Yahweh reigns!" v. 1a). In general, however, all the relevant psalms prove to be late, i.e., exilic/postexilic, compositions, with strong indications of congregational (not dynastic) origin. Furthermore, religious-historical considerations should lead us to the conclusion that the Yahweh-kingship hymns were designed and used only in Israel's late periods of history. The theological concept of Yahweh being the overlord over all nations and other gods is hardly rooted in Israelite monarchic experience. David and Solomon may have reigned over a large territory between Egypt and the Euphrates (cf. Ps 89:26 [RSV 25]; Josh 1:4; 2 Kgs 5:1; etc.; A. R. Müller, "David," NBL I, 390-96; M. Weippert and B. Janowski, "Königtum," NBL II, 513-20; K. W. Whitelam, ABD IV, 40-48), but their monarchy did not acquire that universal quality inherent in Mesopotamian and Persian traditions (common title: "King of the Four Quarters of the World"). With this decisive experience missing, the God of Israel during the monarchies hardly rose up to be the universal "King of the gods." At least we do not have any authentic proof for Yahweh's absolute sovereignty. His title 'elyôn, "the highest," is of Canaanite derivation and still limited in scope to the Syrian-Palestinian scene (cf. H.-J. Zobel, TWAT VI, 131-51; H. Niehr, Der höchste Gott [BZAW 190; Berlin: de Gruyter, 1990]). Only by way of entering the Babylonian-Persian world, so it seems, did Israel experience the universal horizon of world dominance and concomitant theological claims of the supreme God's absolute government over all creation and all nations and kingdoms on earth. Judged from this religious-historical angle all predications of Yahweh as the supreme and absolute God in the OT must be of exilic/postexilic provenience (J. J. Scullion, ABD II, 1041-48; W. Dietrich, et al., eds., Ein Gott allein? [Fribourg: Universitätsverlag, 1994]).

## Intention

Applauding Yahweh, the Most High, the congregation strengthens their exclusive Lord. At the same time the community is fortified and blessed by this overwhelmingly powerful God, who appears among his believers to smash enemies and subdue dissidents in their own ranks. The righteous are encouraged to express contentment, joy, and exultation.

# Bibliography

S. L. Cook, "Apocalypticism and the Psalter," *ZAW* 104 (1992) 82-99; J. Gray, "The Hebrew Conception of the Kingship of God — Its Origin and Development," *VT* 6 (1956) 268-85; D. Michel, "Studien zu den sogenannten Thronbesteigungspsalmen," *VT* 6 (1956) 40-68 (repr. *Zur neueren Psalmenforschung* [ed. P. H. A. Neumann; Darmstadt: Wissenschaftliche Buchgesellschaft, 1976] 367-99); S. Morag, "'Light Is Sown' (Ps. 97,11)," *Tarbiz* 35 (1963/64) 140-48; W. S. Prinsloo, "Psalm 97," *HerTS* 51 (1995) 1088-1113; H. H. Schmid, "Jahwe und die Kulttraditionen von Jerusalem," *ZAW* 67 (1955) 168-97; I. Shirun-Grumach, "Remarks on the Goddess Maat," in *Pharaonic Egypt* (ed. S. Israelit-Groll; Jerusalem: Magnes, 1985) 173-201; A. Weiser, "Zur Frage nach den Beziehungen der Psalmen zum Kult," in *Fest. A. Bertholet* (ed. W. Baumgartner, et al.; Tübingen: Mohr, 1950) 513-31; H. L. Wright, "The Psalter on the Way," *Reformed Liturgy and Music* 19 (1985) 129-31.

# Psalm 98:
# Yahweh-Kingship Hymn

## Structure

|  | MT | NRSV |
|---|---|---|
| I. Superscription | 1a | - |
| II. Summons to praise | 1bc | 1 |
| III. Hymn to Yahweh | 1de-3 | 1-3 |
| IV. Summons to praise | 4-6 | 4-6 |
| V. Beckoning acclamation | 7-9 | 7-9 |
| A. Of primordial powers | 7-8 | 7-8 |
| B. Motive: Yahweh's judgment | 9 | 9 |

Is it a tiny remnant of an earlier SUPERSCRIPTION or the beginning of a later redactional comment that we meet in v. 1a? The lone word *mizmôr,* "song," only classifies the psalm in the main line of redactional labeling: 57 texts of the Psalter are tagged this way, but nowhere does the word appear alone. The name of David or another singer is usually attached to it. So we may wonder about this stray designation in a group of psalms that for some reason seems to be left without superscriptions (→ Psalm 93).

Looking at the text as a whole, we notice a strong affinity to → Psalm 96 and other Yahweh-kingship hymns in regard to vocabulary, structure, and theological concepts. The opening line corresponds largely to 96:1, and the two closing lines are almost identical to 96:13. Vv. 2, 4-5, 7-8 are, as far as content goes, reminiscent of 96:3, 7-9; and v. 7a again is identical with 96:11b. Someone working exclusively along literary methods could perhaps conclude that Psalm 98 is a mechanical extract from Psalm 96. But probably not a single psalm is a purely literary product. All the texts united in the OT Psalter grew out of some community enterprise, mostly of the liturgical and/or educational

195

type, during the history of ancient Israel. Every one of them seems to be linked to some cultic and spiritual tradition within that history. The evidence of Psalm 98 clearly leads beyond copying one particular psalm. There are, e.g., affinities to other songs of the Psalter and to Second Isaiah. And, to be sure, the other Psalms of the Yahweh-kingship group (Psalms 47; 93; 95; 97; 99) also show a great deal of linguistic, thematic, and theological correspondences. With a high degree of certainty, however, the common matrix of these and many other texts of the Psalter is communal worship of exilic/postexilic times. Therefore it seems unwarranted to speak of an "anthological" character of specific psalms, as long as evaluating exegetes cling to a merely literary hypothesis. Also, the marked affinities among Yahweh-kingship songs do not necessarily lead to the conclusion that redactors composed or remodeled the group to form a coherent text for reading purposes (against Howard, *Structure,* e.g., 178-79, speaking in this sense about "concatenation of words," "common themes and theology," etc.; listing at Psalm 93).

The introductory SUMMONS TO PRAISE (v. 1), a call for a "new song" to Yahweh, is formulated just like Ps 96:1a, the difference being v. 1b: in our psalm the hymnic shout of the congregation is listed right after the summons to praise: "Yes, he works wonders!" (for this form, introduced by exclamatory *kî,* cf. Exod 15:21; Pss 95:3-4; 118:1; Crüsemann, *Studien,* 32-35; listing at "Introduction to Cultic Poetry"). In Psalm 96 the summons to praise occupies three full lines; here it has only half a line. Then the HYMN of the people is quoted, first a very brief shout, functioning like 96:4-6. In continuation of this short congregational hymn, we find elaborated praise of great saving acts of God (vv. 1de-3). These hymnic lines lack introductory *kî,* but may have been sung by the assembly as well, perhaps one by one, in ample repetition. All verbs are perfects, resuming Yahweh's way of acting on behalf of his people Israel. His right hand "saves" (v. 1d = third person feminine singular because of "hand"; cf. nominal expressions of the root *yšʿ* in vv. 2a, 3d; the same figurative language occurs also in Isa 51:9; 59:16; 63:5), he "makes known his help" (v. 2a) and "reveals his justice" (v. 2b) to all the world (cf. Isa 52:10). The idea of God communicating himself to humankind is not totally foreign to the Psalms (cf. Pss 77:15 [RSV 14]; otherwise Israel testifies to the glory of Yahweh: 47:2 [RSV 1]; 96:3). But this kind of direct language, especially articulated with the verb *gālāh,* Piel, "tear away, reveal" (v. 2b), is very unusual.

The last act of Yahweh in the sequence under discussion is "remembering" (v. 3a). All previous enactments were done to the benefit of Israel, or "in memory of the people." Exactly that purpose is formulated in v. 3ab, pinpointing the sharp contrast between the nations and the people of Yahweh. Furthermore, v. 3cd, the final line of our hymnic element (identical with Isa 52:10cd), tells about the nations: they have to acknowledge Yahweh's interventions. Only in this last line is the community outing itself as the speaker: "*our* God" has performed mighty deeds. The "we" form is telling (→ Psalm 95): the hymn in vv. 1c-3 is a truly congregational element of liturgy, unthinkable in authentic royal celebrations of a national shrine. No concretizations of divine "help" or "salvation" (vv. 1d, 2a, 3d) are necessary in a hymn like this. Every participant knows the incidents of sacred history and the promises for the future hinted at by these mentionings. The juxtaposition of Israel and the nations is confirmed (v. 3cd; cf. v. 2b and Isa 52:10): Israel is facing the rest of the world (cf. Psalm 97).

Next, another SUMMONS TO PRAISE comes into the agenda directed to the nations around Israel (vv. 4-6). Structurally, we find the same phenomenon in 96:7-9. Repeating the summons (or other form elements of psalms) is an appropriate feature of liturgical texts. Repetitions support intended effects; within hymns they offer opportunity for much "joyful noise" by which a deity can be pleased. In our case, the second round of summonses follows a different pattern from 96:7-9. There we observe an archaic sequence of imperatives: "bring to Yahweh . . ."; here we notice two main orders: "Make joyful noise" *to Yahweh,* or *before King Yahweh,* respectively (vv. 4a, 6b). These imperative phrases envelop section IV, embracing, as it were, calls to make merry, to jubilate, and to play sacred instruments (vv. 4b-6a; while the verbs *rnn,* "jubilate," and *zmr,* "play," are frequent in hymns, the first imperative in the series, *pishû,* "make merry," is represented only here in the Psalter; the six other occurrences of the verb in the Hebrew canon are in Isa 14:7; 44:23; 49:13 [Qere]; 52:9; 54:1; 55:12, i.e., almost exclusively in Second Isaiah). As to the instruments named see Pss 33:2; 57:9 (RSV 8); 71:22; 92:4 (RSV 3); 147:7; 149:3; 150:3. Most frequently "harp" and "lyre" are mentioned, serving predominantly, it seems, small-group services (see "Introduction to Cultic Poetry," sections 1 and 5; "Introduction to Psalms," section 2). In our psalm "trumpet" and "horn" are added as proper instruments, apparently for worship in larger communities (→ Psalm 150).

The closing element of Psalm 98 (vv. 7-9) has much affinity, as already pointed out, to 96:11-13, although the vocabulary of vv. 7-8, except for three words of v. 7a, has nothing to do with that of Psalm 96, with solely v. 9 being very close even on that count. First, natural powers: sea, world, streams, mountains, are called upon (imperfect or jussive forms) to get busy joining in applause and jubilation for Yahweh (vv. 7-8; cf. 96:11-12: here the powers are heaven, sea, cultivated fields, trees; 93:3: streams and sea are to praise him). After that, the coming of Yahweh to execute justice over all the nations is given as the point of reference and the reason for jubilation, just as in → 96:13.

## Genre

The general tone of jubilation in Psalm 98 is indicative of the genre HYMN. As in → Psalms 47; 93; 96; 97; 99, the outlook is universalistic, i.e., it includes the realms of nature and politics. Yahweh is extolled as the ultimate ruler over all the world and all the nations. The key word "king" comes up once (v. 6b), and the psalm is found in a cluster of other KINGSHIP HYMNS. Therefore we may put it more precisely into this category, knowing full well that thematic coincidence does not reflect so much a genre as the setting and use of given texts.

## Setting

As our hymnals often contain songs for special occasions and festive events, we may speculate whether the Yahweh-kingship hymns were linked with a yearly festival, e.g., of the enthronement of Yahweh, or the beginning of the New Year. Theories to that effect abound (→ "Introduction to Cultic Poetry," section 2). What we can exclude with some degree of certainty in regard to the kingship psalms is a preexilic feast held at Jerusalem (or Samaria?) with the participation of the reigning king (and all the ritual of the dying-and-rising God, sacred marriage, etc.). Yahweh-kingship psalms as extant in the Psalter are much too young to reflect that monarchic state of affairs. Connotations are rather with community life in exilic-postexilic times, as pointed out many times in the structure analyses. Therefore I conclude that Psalm 98, along with the other texts of the group, was used whenever opportune to celebrate Yahweh's supreme authority even over the imperial forces of the day that dominated the whole known world. The festive calendar of the year gave ample opportunity to rally behind Yahweh's overlordship, and Sabbath worship services, probably arising in the Persian epoch, were good occasions as well (cf. Lev 23:1-3; Gerstenberger, *Leviticus,* 340-42; listing at Additional Bibliography, section B; E. Haag, *TWAT* VII, 1047-57; J. C. Vanderkam, *ABD* I, 814-20).

## Intention

A feast of triumph over dominating powers was to remind early believers in Yahweh that they were neither lost nor forgotten, but would be saved one day from their miserable and humiliating situation. Yahweh, after all, had been experienced by the community of his followers to be superior to all the extant powers, religious, political, or economic, of the world. The same message was preached by the witnesses collected in Second Isaiah (Isaiah 40–55).

## Bibliography

E. Beaucamp, "L'univers acclame le justicier d'Israel: Psalm 98," *BVC* 70 (1966) 36-40; E. F. Davis, "Psalm 98," *Int* 46 (1992) 171-75; H. Gollwitzer, "Singt dem Herrn einen neuen Gesang," *EvT* 48 (1988) 489-91; B. Gosse, "Le psaume 98 et la rédaction d'ensemble du livre d'Isaïe," *BN* 86 (1997) 29-30; F.-M. Hofmann, ed., *Tu deinen Mund auf für die Stummen* (Gütersloh: Mohn, 1986); T. Longman III, "Psalm 98: A Divine Warrior Victory Song," *JETS* 26 (1983) 267-74; W. S. Prinsloo, "Psalm 98: Sing'n nuwe lied tot lof van die koning, Jahwe," *HerTS* 50 (1994) 155-68; H. Ringgren, "Behold Your King Comes," *VT* 24 (1974) 207-11.

THE INDIVIDUAL UNITS OF BOOK FOUR

## Psalm 99:
## Yahweh-Kingship Hymn

### *Structure*

|  | MT | NRSV |
|---|---|---|
| I. Hymnic affirmations | 1-2 | 1-2 |
| II. Summons and responses | 3-4 | 3-4 |
| III. Refrain of community | 5 | 5 |
| IV. Historical lesson | 6-8 | 6-8 |
| V. Refrain of community | 9 | 9 |

The text is not easy to analyze. There are abrupt shifts in phraseology, meter, and grammatical subjects that cause a fragmentary appearance. Furthermore, repetitions of various expressions lead to different conclusions as to their structural significance. Are we really hearing an echo of the trisagion of Isa 6:3 in our psalm (cf. three times "He is holy": vv. 3, 5, 9)? Is this shout of adoration the most important instrument for structuring the text (thus, e.g., Jeremias, *Königtum*, 114-21; listing at "Introduction to Psalms")? Or should we stay with that other opinion which declares the refrain of the community (vv. 5, 9) to be the end of two distinct strophes (thus Gunkel, 429; Mowinckel, *PsSt* II, 180, 218)? While the first option seems to be borne out by literary and systematic considerations, the second one is carried predominantly by liturgical reasoning. This kind of argument may not be overlooked as long as we stay with the hypothesis that all psalms arose from and were used in community activity. We will try to make plausible, therefore, a worship structure of Psalm 99.

The missing SUPERSCRIPTION is in line with the format of other Yahweh-kingship hymns (→ Psalm 93). Two opening lines give strong HYMNIC AFFIRMATIONS about Yahweh taking on kingship at Mount Zion over all nations and the whole universe (vv. 1-2; → Psalms 47; 93; 95–97; Zion only in 97:8). His royal power is painted (apart from the shout of enthronement, v. 1a; cf. 93:1; 97:1) in distinct expressions and symbols: he is the one "sitting on cherubs" (v. 1b; cf. Metzger, *Königsthron*, 309-67; listing at Additional Bibliography, section B), he is "great" (v. 2a; cf. 47:3 [RSV 2]; 95:3; 96:4; and the superlative in 97:9), he is "elevated on high" (v. 2b; cf. 113:4; 138:6; Isa 57:15). Such affirmations are fundamental to hymns; they establish spiritual realities basic to any praise and jubilation. The language is strictly "objective," Yahweh being depicted in his enormous power, which makes "the earth/people tremble" (v. 1a) and his followers happy (vv. 3-4). Who may have intoned this universal praise? Choir or liturgist is the best choice for cultic agents.

The following section is the hardest one to describe. It starts by calling on "them," i.e., the nations of v. 2b (?), to extol "your" name. That means that a speaker in front of a community assembled in worship reaches out, enticing foreigners not present to give due recognition to Yahweh. Phrases and concepts used in vv. 3-4 do not combine into epic strophes; they are of the staccato type: short, erratic, abrupt. And lines of communication shift around among speaker,

199

PSALMS

community, God, and the nations. "They shall praise your name! Great and terrible (he is)! Holy he is!" (v. 3). The objective posture of vv. 1-2 has been given up. The speaker turns to Yahweh directly, then he gets back to a neutral "he" (which, however, also could refer to "your name," "it" being great and terrible; cf. Deut 28:58; Mal 1:14; Ps 111:9). The next colon does not have a verb (v. 4a). Is the jussive "they shall praise" (v. 3a) still orienting the words "and the power of a king, loving justice"? One would expect a direct address of God, parallel to "your name" in v. 3a, or perhaps determination of "king" by the definite article. The earthly monarch does not appear in this context. Shift from "you" to "he" in prayer, on the other hand, is possible (cf. 93:1-2), and an indeterminate reference may be feasible in the sense of (obvious) "royal power." Be that as it may, the best solution would be to think of rather disconnected liturgical utterances, with interspersed shouts of choirs or congregation. "Holy is he!" may well be such a liturgical response, because it recurs two more times at odd places beyond the limits of a line. Also, the sudden shift back into second-person address (vv. 4b, 5b) could be understood more easily if more than one voice was involved in presenting this living praise. (For a general background of the Jerusalem temple theology cf., e.g., Haran, *Temple;* Knohl, *Sanctuary;* Hartenstein, *Unzugänglichkeit;* Kaiser, *Gott* II, 104-18; all in Additional Bibliography, section B).

REFRAINS sometimes mark off liturgical sections in the psalms; cf. Psalms 42/43; 56; 59; 67; 80; 107. They are reliable indications of liturgical diversity of voices. In our psalm the imperative *rômĕmû*, "extol," is followed by the grammatical object "Yahweh *our* God" (vv. 5a, 9a, and without preceding imperative, as appellation, v. 8a, as grammatical subject, v. 9c). All along in the Psalms the first-person plural attributions are noteworthy. They indicate participation of the congregation (→ 95:1-2). Without explicitly stating the change, the text leaves no doubt who is involved in praise and adoration now: no longer the surrounding nations, but those people who are descendants of "Jacob" (v. 4c) and are willing and able to call Yahweh "our God." In this fashion the call to laud him and actively venerate him in worship may be a pure SUMMONS directed to the congregation by a liturgist, but it may as well have been taken up by all the members in mutual exhortation: "Extol (all of you) Yahweh, our God." Note the fourfold occurrence of "Yahweh, our God" (*yhwh 'ĕlōhēnû;* statistics: 194 occurrences of "our God" in Hebrew Scripture; combination of "Yahweh, our God" 11 times in the Psalter: 20:8 [RSV 7]; 94:23; 105:7; 106:47; 113:5; 122:9; 123:2, but cf. also "Yahweh, our Lord," e.g., 8:2, 10 [RSV 1, 9], while the expression "Yahweh, our king" was hardly used; cf. only 47:7 [RSV 6]; Isa 33:22). All these passages are significant in terms of congregational activities. In our case, "Yahweh, our God" may have had the quality of a popular shout within the worship liturgy.

The third block of our song (vv. 6-8) is not as erratic as the second. Explaining the issue of intercession by referring back in history to Moses, Aaron, and Samuel, it is rather didactic in tone. Apparently, the community of the time felt a need to deal with possible failures to live up to the ordinances of Yahweh. V. 4bcd celebrated the giving of *tôrāh* by Jacob's God, although in terms not customary in D or Priestly writings (*mĕšārîm,* "that which is straight," normally

200

does not signify anything like "written law"; *mišpāṭ* and *ṣĕdāqāh,* "right and justice," occasionally refer to *tôrāh;* cf. F. Garcia-López, *TWAT* VIII, 597-637). Just as in Psalm 19 joy about the gift of divine orientation immediately raises doubts about the worthiness of Yahweh's servants (19:12-13 [RSV 11-12]), our psalm brings up the problem of communication between Israel and Yahweh, particularly in times of crisis, as v. 8bc shows. This part of the psalm, i.e., vv. 6-7, is certainly not apt to be shouted by a choir or crowd. It is a HISTORICAL LESSON, offered by the speaker or leader of the congregation. Very seldom in the Psalms or anywhere else outside the Pentateuch do we meet exemplary wise or gifted figures like Moses, Aaron, and Samuel (v. 6; cf. Jer 15:1; Ezek 14:14; Mommer, Schiller). They were privileged to call to Yahweh and be heard. To narrow this activity of "crying to the Lord" down to intercession and institutionalized lament (cf. Jeremias, *Königtum,* 118-21) is too strict a limitation of the three figures. Obviously, each one of them represents a major tradition of Israel's heritage: the juridical, priestly, and prophetic strains of sacred knowledge that were drawn together in the exilic-postexilic faith (cf. Blenkinsopp, *Sage;* listing at Additional Bibliography, section B). Notably, the monarchic strand is missing — in a *kingship* song! And in the middle of a collection of songs, which to a large extent are attributed to David! The pillars of early Jewish spiritual life, as far as "intellectual leadership" (Blenkinsopp) and institutionlized offices are concerned, were apparently sages (lawgivers), priests, and prophets — nobody else (cf. Scoralick).

The tradition of the cloud out of which Yahweh would manifest himself (v. 7a; cf. Exod 19:9; Deut 5:22; Ezek 1:4) gives color and substance to the teaching (cf. Psalm 95 with its references to the exodus story). Then the congregation in a typical direct-address response confirms the message of the teacher. Yahweh did communicate with the ancestors (v. 8ab), and he is a forbearing and avenging God, depending on the specific situation (v. 8cd). V. 8, therefore, is a prayer and confession of the community, formed as a sapiential conclusion of the historical retrospective. We know from other writings of the epoch that the question of being able to call on Yahweh and being heard by him was a very important theological issue in later times (cf. 1 Kings 8; Nehemiah 9; Ezra 9), which, however, was divided among the three offices indicated. The "scribes" had not yet emerged as a distinct authority.

## Genre/Setting

Psalm 99 is the last in the series of Yahweh-kingship psalms that exhibit some common characteristics, such as references to Yahweh's ascension to the heavenly throne, general praise of his supreme authority, insistence on Israel's privileged status, expectancy of divine judgment of enemies and apostates, etc. In general, all the relevant texts (→ Psalms 47; 93; 95–99) carry praise elements and may be considered HYMNS. But each one by itself has distinct generic features. Psalm 99 lauds Yahweh's overlordship (vv. 1-2), extols the giving of *tôrāh* to "Jacob" (vv. 3-4), and gives a lesson to the community on God's communication to his people (vv. 6-8), letting the congregation participate with hymns and shouts of adoration (vv. 3b, 5, 9). This complex structure is far from plain hymn singing as designated by Gunkel (cf. Gunkel and Begrich, *Einleitung* §2; listing at "Introduction to Cultic Poetry"). As far as we can discern, worship assemblies in the exilic-postexilic age developed this type of hymn inspired by congregational values and concerns, and, of course, adapted to communal ceremonial structures with their liturgists, choirs, teaching. Emphasis on Torah (cf. Psalms 95; 119) brings to mind the religious situation of early Jewish congregations from Babylonia to Egypt that defined themselves by way of Yahweh's revelation through Moses and other ancient leaders.

## Intention

Praising Yahweh leads the congregation to acknowledge his gift of just and righteous rules. Worshipers are to recognize this basic fact in Israel's spiritual life. Communication of the will of God is effectuated by leaders working in the succession of Moses, Aaron, and Samuel, in other words, in the legal, sacerdotal, and prophetic line of tradition (and Moses is the greatest among them! cf. Blenkinsopp, *Sage;* Davies, *Scribes,* both in Additional Bibliography, section B). The community is to give thanks for historical revelations and actual spiritual leadership, following in the footsteps of the ancestors.

## Bibliography

J. H. Eaton, "Proposals in Psalm 99 and 119," *VT* 18 (1968) 555-58; A. Feuillet, "Les Psaumes eschatologiques du règne de Yahweh," *NRT* 73 (1951) 244-60, 352-63; S. Lach, "'El nose,'" *Analecta Cracoviensia* 13 (1981) 129-41; P. Mommer, "Samuel in Ps 99," *BN* 31 (1986) 27-30; W. S. Prinsloo, "Psalm 99: Die Here, ons God, is heilig," *HerTS* 49 (1993) 621-36; J. Schiller, "Bemerkungen zur Analyse und Interpretation von Psalm 99," *BN* 91 (1998) 77-89; H. H. Schmid, "Jahwe und die Kulttraditionen von Jerusalem," *ZAW* 67 (1955) 168-97; R. Scoralick, *Trishagion und Gottesherrschaft: Psalm 99 als Neuinterpretation von Tora und Propheten* (SBS 138; Stuttgart: Katholisches Bibelwerk, 1989); C. F. Whitley, "Psalm 99,8," *ZAW* 85 (1973) 227-30; R. N. Whybray, "'Their Wrongdoings' in Ps. 99,8," *ZAW* 81 (1969) 237-39; M. Wilcox, "The Aramaic Targum to Psalms," in *Proceedings of the 9th World Congress of Jewish Studies* (ed. R. Giveon, et al.; Jerusalem: World Union of Jewish Studies, 1986) 143-50.

## Psalm 100:
## Introit Hymn

### Structure

|  | MT | NRSV |
|---|---|---|
| I. Superscription | 1a | - |
| II. Summons to worship | 1b-3a | 1-3a |
| III. Response of congregation | 3bc | 3bc |
| IV. Summons to worship | 4 | 4 |
| V. Response of congregation | 5 | 5 |

Being a very small hymn of limited function (nonetheless with great influence on later tradition of hymn singing), Psalm 100 consists essentially of two lines of SUMMONS TO WORSHIP with appropriate responses of the community assembled to enter a sanctuary. The text has a general SUPERSCRIPTION (v. 1a) indicating only the most comprehensive designation for cultic "songs" (*mizmôr;* cf. Psalm 98) and a definition of purpose (*lĕtôdāh,* "for thanksgiving"). The redactor gathered this last piece of information from v. 4a, c, where the substantive *tôdāh* and the verb *ydh* (Hiphil imperative) appear. The *tôdāh* was originally a thanksgiving sacrifice (cf. 30:13 [RSV 2]; 66:13-15; 116:17-19; 118:21). In later times, with the partial cessation of the temple cult, a thanksgiving song would take the place of the animal offering (cf. 51:8-15; 51:17-19 [RSV 15-17]). For this reason, we cannot interpret either heading or summons to give thanks (v. 4) as referring to real sacrifices.

The first line of the SUMMONS TO WORSHIP (vv. 1b-3a) has four plural imperatives. The second line (v. 4) follows suit with another series of three imperatives, the last one in v. 2 and the first one in v. 4 being identical: *bō'û,* "enter." The summons to enter thus gets the strongest emphasis, stringing together the two chains of imperatives. While a number of passages talk about "entering the sanctuary" (cf. 40:8 [RSV 7]; 42:3 [RSV 2]; 43:4; 66:13; 86:9; 118:19-20), the direct order to do so is rare, and not customarily found in summonses to praise or worship (cf. only 96:8; 2 Chr 30:8, in a sermon preached at the time of King Hezekiah). Also, a direct exhortation to "serve" Yahweh (imperative: *'ibdû*) is found only once in the Psalter (Ps 2:11), but several times in sermonlike literature of exilic or later origin (cf. Josh 24:14; 1 Sam 7:3; 2 Chr 30:8; 35:3; admonitions in imperfect or jussive forms are frequent in Dtr layers). Last in line of the opening summons is "Know that Yahweh is God" (v. 3a), connoting confessional and theological perspectives. This in itself seems extraordinary for a summons to worship (see below). The first imperative of the introductory summons is *hārî'û,* Hiphil of *rû',* "make noise" (v. 1b; cf. Pss 47:2 [RSV 1]; 66:1; 81:2 [RSV 1]; 98:4, 6; Isa 44:23), a quite common expression to incite hymnic praise.

The last two imperatives of the second series are *hôdû* and *bārăkû,* "give thanks" and "bless," respectively (v. 4b). The first one is frequent in praise texts, indeed, it is one of the basic forms of praise (cf. Ps 106:1a: "Praise Yahweh: he is good" = 107:1; 118:1; 136:1-3; etc.). The second verb is best

203

known from the Qal passive formula: "Blessed be Yahweh" (*bārûk yhwh;* cf. 28:6; 72:18; etc.; Towner, "Blessed"; listing at "Introduction to Cultic Poetry"). Our imperative derives from the Piel stem, meaning actively blessing God (cf. 68:27 [RSV 26]; 96:2; 103:1-2, 20-22; 134:1-2; 135:19-20), a formula of intense liturgical use. What we have, then, are two series of summoning imperatives, some of which are very common vocabulary in hymns, while the others — "serve the Lord," "enter the sanctuary," "know Yahweh" — have a special ring about them.

There seems to be a pastoral urge to participate in the veneration of Yahweh alone. Joshua 24 and 2 Chr 30:1-12; 35:1-19 apparently outline the scenario presupposed in Psalm 100: the right service to Yahweh is contested by other religious opportunities. In their summons to worship, leaders of the congregation admonish all to dedicate themselves to Yahweh, performing the right service to him. The locale of this summons is obviously in front of some sanctuary, not necessarily the Jerusalem one. The liturgists urge people to "enter" with thanks and praise. The word *tôdāh,* "thanksgiving," is matched by the parallel *tĕhillāh,* "hymn" (v. 4; cf. 34:2; 66:2; 71:8, 14; 79:13; 106:47; 147:1 — none of these passages exactly equates the two terms; 79:13 coming closest to an identification).

Having discussed the two lines of summons, we now want to investigate those verses that follow the imperative phrases. V. 5 is clearly a standard hymn, introduced by exclamatory *kî,* "yes," as found many times in praise contexts. The *kî* verse states a brief hymn to be repeatedly sung by choir or congregation (cf. 33:4; 96:4-5). The line in question here (v. 5) contains stock phrases of Israelite hymnology, perhaps the most original and ancient ones (cf. 106:1; 107:1; 118:1; 136:1-3). The fixed form found in the passages cited has been slightly modified in v. 5. Still, at least v. 5a is perfectly fit to be chanted by a group: "Good is Yahweh, forever his grace." The rest of the verse could have been sung by another group: "From age to age his trustworthiness." The other hymnic line (v. 3 or part thereof) differs, however. We do not have an introductory *kî,* nor handy liturgical formulas, not even uniform phrases. Instead, the line starts with an imperative phrase that is hardly a summons to worship in the traditional sense, but rather a disciplinary admonition: "Know that Yahweh, he is God!" (v. 3a). A censuring, demanding order, it seems, exact parallels of which are hard to find (cf. 46:11 [RSV 10]; Jer 21:34). Also, the *šĕmaʿ yiśrāʾēl* in Deut 6:4 has a similar tenor. We should note that general phrases constructed with an imperative of "to know" presuppose that very knowledge asked for from the listener, and many times the order has a threatening undertone (cf. Num 32:23; Judg 18:14; 1 Sam 12:17; 14:38; 23:22-23; 1 Kgs 20:7; 2 Kgs 5:7; 10:10; Isa 33:13; Jer 5:1; Ps 4:4 [RSV 3]; Job 19:6). The second colon of v. 3 differs in style and content. "He has made us, not we ourselves" (or, as the Qere proposes: "He has made us, we are his [property]"). This, taken in itself, is not an admonition but a confession, a statement of belonging, possibly spoken by the people ("we" discourse; cf. Psalms 90; 95). The third colon, oddly put into the next line by the scribe of Codex Leningradensis, seems to repeat a formulaic expression from 79:13; 95:7. It could be a later addition to the text, also because the parallel v. 5 has only two cola. Basically, we are faced with two options: either v. 3 was recited completely by one speaker, who first gave a stern admonition, then turned to a prolonged confessional statement ("we" form). Or we consider v. 3a — functionally comparable to the exclamatory *kî* of v. 5a — a prelude of a hymnic shout of the congregation comprising v. 3b or 3bc. Considering the introit character of our psalm and the locale at the entrance of the sanctuary, I lean to the latter interpretation.

## Genre/Setting

INTROIT is probably the best description of the genre of Psalm 100. We know introits from our own church services; the function and setting of this psalm may have been just the same as that of comparable texts in worship today. Whether the song was composed for a literary context (e.g., Psalms 95–99, alternatively 93–100 or 90–110, etc.; thus Lohfink; Jeremias; Howard; Zenger; Koenen, *Jahwe*, 76-78; listing at Additional Bibliography, section C) remains a matter of debate. The hypotheses mentioned presuppose a purely anthological literary origin for our psalm, generally proven by close correspondences in particular with Psalms 95; 96; 98 (cf., e.g., Jeremias). The evidence adduced can be interpreted, however, in favor of the communal and liturgical origin and use of the song. Take, for example, that crucial v. 3: 95:7ab says: "For he is our God, and we are the people of his pasture, and the sheep of his hand" (two or three cola?). The line was probably shouted by the congregation ("we"). Our v. 3 runs: "Know that Yahweh is God. It is he that made us, and we are his; we are his people, and the sheep of his pasture" (three cola). According to our analysis only v. 3bc is the response of the congregation ("we"), while v. 3a is summons, remembrance, exhortation. Seen in the context of living worship, the agents and liturgical constellation become transparent. Literary analysis fails to take seriously the first-person plural forms, which can hardly be explained as stylistic features. If the congregation in this fashion articulated itself, the theological conclusion of a "universalization of covenant" (Lohfink, Jeremias) becomes unfounded as well. In actual worship it seems possible to begin with a universal summons (v. 1b) and immediately afterward to focus attention on the congregation at hand (vv. 2-3). Chances are, therefore, that our psalm functioned as just another element for community worship in early Judaism, quite probably in the INTROIT category.

## Intention

The formal purpose of the psalm is to begin a service by entering the sanctuary, let the congregation express their joy and gratitude to God, while filing into the assembly hall or precinct. We noted some additional didactic and theological concerns like propagating correct faith and worship to the congregation. Late Israel's services did show a strong influence of wisdom teachings. The congregation, then, sings to all the world its confidence of being attended by Yahweh himself, the shepherd of his people, of being at home in his sanctuary and worship service. Thanks and praise are due to this gracious Lord (cf. Miller, *They Cried*, 205-12, Additional Bibliography, section C)

## Bibliography

P. Auffret, "Essai sur la structure littéraire du Psaume 100," *BN* 20 (1983) 7-14; W. Brueggemann, "Psalm 100," *Int* 39 (1985) 65-69; J. Jeremias, "Ps 100 als Auslegung von Ps 93–99," *SK* 19 (1998) 605-15; K. Koch, "'Denn seine Güte währet ewiglich,'" *EvT* 21 (1961) 531-44; M. Kube, "Monument sinfonischer Chormusik: Max Regers 100. Psalm," *Musik und Kirche* 68 (1998) 120-25; J. O. Lewis, "An Asseverative *lō'* in Psalm 100:3?" *JBL* 86 (1967) 216; N. Lohfink, "Die Universalisierung der 'Bundesformel' in Psalm 100,3," *Theologie und Philosophie* 65 (1990) 172-83; J. L. Mays, "Worship, World, and Power: An Interpretation of Ps 100," *Int* 23 (1969) 315-30; S. Poque, "Les Psaumes dans les Confessions," in *Saint Augustin et la Bible* (ed. A.-M. la Bonnardière; Paris: Beauchesne, 1986) 155-66; W. S. Prinsloo, "Psalm 100: 'n poëties minderwaardige en saamgeflansde teks?" *HerTS* 47 (1991) 968-82; E. Sánchez, "Translation of Psalm 100 Taking Account of Its Stucture," *BT* 46 (1995) 243-45; W. M. Schniedewind, "'Are We His People or Not?'" *Bib* 76 (1995) 540-50; B. Weber, "Psalm 100," *BN* 91 (1998) 90-97; E. Zenger, "Das Weltenkönigtum des Gottes Israels," in *Der Gott Israels* (ed. N. Lohfink and E. Zenger; SBS 154; Stuttgart: Katholisches Bibelwerk, 1994) 151-78; G. Ziegler, "Der jubilus," in *Origines* (ed. W. Geerlings, et al.; Bonn: Borengässer, 1995) 95-100; W. Zimmerli, *Erkenntnis Gottes nach dem Buche Ezechiel* (Zurich: Zwingli, 1954).

# Psalm 101:
# Reflection, Confession, Instruction

## Structure

|  | MT | NRSV |
|---|---|---|
| I. Superscription | 1a | - |
| II. Introduction | 1bc | 1 |
| III. Confession of innocence | 2-5 | 2-5 |
| IV. Affirmation of righteousness | 6-8 | 6-8 |

A very modest and common SUPERSCRIPTION (v. 1a; cf. the two elements: *dāwid*, "David," and *mizmôr*, "song," alone are used, e.g., with Psalms 15; 23; 24; 29; 110; etc., together with other designations in many more headings, e.g., with Psalms 3–6; 8–9; etc.) for the first time since Psalm 86 establishes a David connection, and for the first time since Psalm 90 again links a psalm to a person at all.

The introductory line (v. 1bc) is hymnic. A single voice, thereafter being heard throughout the whole psalm, volunteers to sing and play (cultically?) to Yahweh. Explicit mention of God's name occurs only once more, in the closing line of the poem (v. 8cd). Only in v. 1bc and in the enigmatic v. 2b is Yahweh addressed directly: "I will sing to you," and "when will you come to me?" (NRSV: "When shall I attain it?" i.e., the "blameless way" of v. 2a). And only v. 1a serves as a kind of thematic indicator for the whole psalm: "Of solidarity and order will I sing." All these observations lead to the question whether vv. 2-7 were once an independent (sapiential) poem. Solidarity and order (*ḥesed* and *mišpāṭ*) in any case are programmatic concepts, which are not repeated in the psalm, but they do correspond with expressions like *tām*, "without blame, perfect" (vv. 2, 6), and contradict all the negative clichés of evil, crookedness, lies, etc., used in our psalm to denounce deviant attitudes (cf. vv. 3-5, 7-8).

An outstanding stylistic feature, then, is the first person singular: who is singing to Yahweh about "solidarity and justice"? Tradition has it that Psalm 101 is a royal, perhaps even Davidic, song comparable in a way to 2 Sam 23:2-7 (cf. Gunkel; Weiser; Kraus; Kenik; Brueggemann; Allen; et al.; Seybold, 393: "a royal declaration referring to principles of employment politics"). The monarch is supposed to give a self-portrait, in accordance with divine responsibilities conferred upon him, of justice and order in his imperium (cf. Pss 45:5-8 [RSV 4-7]; 72:1-14) or to lament the existence of evildoers in his kingdom or city. The text itself, however, not considering the superscription or exegetical tradition, suggests another interpretation.

A self-portrait the psalm does offer, to be sure. The "I" presenting him- or herself is depicted in two different postures. First (vv. 2-5), the person is seen in his or her own environment and pursuit of individual righteousness. The task is to find the right path and to abstain from evil. The comprehensive vision of living correctly is expressed in v. 2, using the imagery of "path" and "walking" (for *hlk*, Hithpael, in this ethical sense see 26:3; 56:14 [RSV 13]; 116:9; 119:45; Prov 20:7; 23:31). Pursuing the right path is considered the highest human prudence and virtue (*śkl*, Hiphil, "to be prudent"; cf. Pss 2:10; 14:2; 119:99; Prov 1:3; 15:24; 19:14; 21:16). Exemplary behavior is first of all confined to one's own household and family (v. 2d; cf. King David, sitting in his house and committing evil, 2 Samuel 11; the expression *bĕqereb bêtî*, "in the midst of my house," is repeated in v. 7a, it is true, but in a different context). The following five lines explicate the ethical goal from its negative side: to live correctly implies most of all to refrain from evil and the many temptations to do wrong. Except for v. 5ab (which, incidentally, has a companion in v. 8ab), each line has a negated phrase of the type: "I do not get in touch with evil or evildoers." Thus in the first full part of Psalm 101 the person speaking declares his or her blamelessness along the lines of ancient Near Eastern wisdom. In the OT we find this ethos of abstention from evil in poems like Psalm 1 and 119, and, of course, in Proverbs and Job, as well as in exhortatory discourses of *tôrāh* (cf. the Decalogue, Exod 20:2-17; Leviticus 19).

The second part of our portrait of the blameless definitely turns toward public life. What is the righteous one to do in larger society? He watches out for the "faithful" (v. 6a: *ne'ĕmānîm*, Niphal participle of *'mn*) in order to live with them and have them as servants (or better: "attendants"? NRSV: to "minister," v. 6d: *šrt*, Piel). Both terms in no way suggest a distinct royal (administrative; military) background. Many things may be called "faithful," "trustworthy," in-

207

cluding houses, families, cities. David himself in one instance is called "faithful to Saul" (1 Sam 22:14), but this singular occurrence does not make the term a political one. "To serve" in this special wording is pretty much a cultic expression (cf. 1 Sam 2:11, 18; Deut 10:8; 17:12; 18:5, 7; 21:5; etc.) at some later point — and this means for the OT: after the monarchy had collapsed — adopted also for court scenarios, e.g., 1 Kgs 1:4, 15; 10:5; 1 Chr 27:1; 28:1; 2 Chr 9:4; 17:19; 22:8. Within the Psalms it is unique in v. 6d. Some exegetes, therefore (and for the violent language against the evildoers in vv.7-8), hold vv. 6-8 to be an oracle of Yahweh for a royal suppliant (cf. Kselman, and already K. Budde, *ZAW* 35 [1915] 191-92). The vocabulary and concepts of vv. 6-8, however, do not indicate monarchic life or a shift toward a divine proclamation, but testify only to certain, little-accustomed ideas about the righteous in his relation to the outside world. He "will be attended" only by faithful ones; that means that he takes seriously separation from the wicked and impure. V. 7ab basically expresses the same line of thought as v. 6cd. There will be no intrusion of wicked ones. On the active side, the righteous also will take any measure available to him in order to cleanse his community (here: the "city of Yahweh," v. 8c; cf. 48:2, 9; 87:3; Isa 60:14) from evildoers. We are reminded of other psalms that talk about active involvement of Yahweh believers when it comes to combating evildoers; cf. Pss 18:38-46 (RSV 37-45); 69:10 (RSV 9); 118:7, 10-12; 139:19-22; etc. In particular, those confessional "portraits" of the righteous in the Psalter (→ Psalms 1; 92; 112; 119; cf. B. Johnson, *TWAT* VI, 917-19; Levin, "Gebetbuch"; listing at Additional Bibliography, section C) all include serious ponderings about the deserved fate of the "unjust" ones. The righteous have not always been so peaceful-minded as in Psalm 131. Therefore, it is feasible to take Psalm 101 as a double-sided portrait of the *ṣaddîq*.

But where does the inspiration for such a portrait come from? We noted already strong affinities of our psalm with some other didactic poems focusing on the righteous member of the congregation. A comparison, e.g., with → Psalm 119 (or Psalms 92; 112, for that matter) would strengthen the case. This immense poem about the righteous and his nourishment by Yahweh's declared and written will betrays a very similar interest in the individual believer, in his integrity, obedience, and abstention from evil, and even the destruction of the wicked or godless (cf. 119:21, 53, 78, 113, 119, 139). Likewise, there is much consciousness of the didactic effects these reflections and confessional statements should have (cf. public consequences of private obedience in vv. 5, 8). If we ask further, what could have been the starting point for this late poem, we may point out companion psalms as possible germinal or collateral texts. Evaluating the first two psalms, for example, we note that Psalm 1 has a strong affinity to the first block of Psalm 101. The righteous one has to abstain from "sinners" (Ps 1:1). Psalm 2, on the other hand, is a strong witness of combat on behalf of Yahweh and a world united under his supreme rule. Perhaps the authors and transmitters of Psalm 101 had in mind ideas like those exhibited in diverse texts when they composed this reflective and didactic confession. The verb *ṣmt,* Hiphil, "to silence" (vv. 5, 8), has similar connotations, even though not used in the first person singular of the believer, in 18:41 (RSV 40); 54:7 (RSV 5); 73:27; 94:23; 143:12. And 119:139 expresses about the same idea in regard to the faithful one as do our vv. 5 and 8 in relation to the enemies: "My zeal consumes me [ṣmt, Piel], because your foes forget your words." Psalm 92, on the other hand, presents the "righteous" as the one who sings out his praise to Yahweh (92:2-3 [RSV 1-2]; note *ḥesed wĕ'emûnāh*, v. 3 [RSV 2], compared to *ḥesed ûmišpāṭ* in 101:1), assails the wicked ones (92:7-10, 12 [RSV 6-9, 11]), and glowingly depicts the blessings on the faithful (92:13-16 [RSV 12-15]). Our Psalm 101 does not differ in substance, but only stylistically, employing, as it were, the personal "I" form throughout that seems to have been borrowed from the PROTESTATION OF INNOCENCE (→ Psalms 7; 17; 26). Psalm 112, for its part, is a more objective picture of the righteous, put into an acrostic poem, and lacking hymnic elements, but still juxtaposed in some way to the "unjust" or "godless" (112:8, 10).

## Genre

Psalm 101 takes us not into the royal world of dynastic autocracy but into the midst of the theological anthropology of early Jewish communities. The portrait of a "righteous" man who knows himself to be on the correct path corresponds to the description of Job: "He was blameless *(tām)* and upright, one who feared God, turned away from evil" (Job 1:1b). His behavior, consequently, was self-confident: "I put on righteousness *(ṣedeq)*, and it clothed me; my justice *(mišpāṭ)* was like a robe and a turban" (29:14). Moreover, the righteous was convinced of his responsibility to engage actively in the battle for justice: "I broke the fangs of the unrighteous, and made him drop his prey from his teeth" (29:17; cf. Pss 3:8 [RSV 7]; 5:7 [RSV 6]). This way, our text cannot be considered a picture of the ideal monarch or of anybody protesting his or her innocence and receiving a divine oracle. Most likely, it purports to be a portrait of the ideal believer in Yahweh. As such, our psalm is a didactic text, in that it exemplifies the REFLECTION, CONFESSION, and INSTRUCTION (cf. also "Introduction to Cultic Poetry," section 4F) of the early Jewish community. If the MT of v. 2b is correct, it may even develop the picture of an exemplary wise man, who may count on the visit of God at night or in some vision to communicate wisdom; at least some wise "friends" of Job claim such revelatory encounters (cf. Job 4:16-17; 33:19-24).

## Setting

Descriptions of ideal types of persons are customarily used in educational discourse. Reflection about the righteous and unrighteous had been going on from early times in the exilic and postexilic Israelite community, and education of young and older people had always been closely linked with congregational assemblies and worship services. Language, imagery, theology, confrontations of just and unjust clients of Yahweh — all this points to the early Jewish community, not to monarchic society, as the original setting. Therefore portrayals of ideal types and their opposites were probably articulated and used in exilic-postexilic worship assemblies (cf. Psalms 1; 23; 92; 112; 119; etc.).

## Intention

The righteous "I" was depicted in the community to be internalized and lived up to by everyone in the group of Yahweh believers. Similar intentions can be found in "secular" wisdom literature of the ancient Near East and the Bible. There the "prudent" one is portrayed as gaining life and well-being (cf. Proverbs 1–9). General wisdom reflections, of course, greatly influenced the thinking of the early Jewish community (cf., e.g., Perdue, *Wisdom;* listing at "Introduction to Cultic Poetry").

## Bibliography

P. Auffret, "Au milieu de ma maison," *SJOT* 11 (1997) 124-37; E. Beaucamp, "L'espoir d'une ère de justice et de paix," *BVC* 73 (1967) 32-42; J. Begrich, "Sofer und Mazkir," *ZAW* 58 (1940/41) 1-29; T. Booij, "Psalm 101:2: 'When Wilt Thou Come to Me?'" *VT* 38 (1988) 458-62; A. Deissler, "La composante sociale dans le message messianique de l'Ancien Testament," in *Bible et christologie* (ed. P. Grelot, et al.; Paris: Cerf, 1984) 161-72; O. Kaiser, "Erwägungen zu Psalm 101," *ZAW* 74 (1962) 195-205; H. A. Kenik, "Code of Conduct for a King: Psalm 101," *JBL* 95 (1976) 391-403; J. S. Kselman, "Psalm 101: Royal Confession and Divine Oracle," *JSOT* 33 (1985) 45-62; J. E. Weir, "The Perfect Way: A Study of Wisdom Motifs in Psalm 101," *EvQ* 53 (1981) 54-59.

## Psalm 102:
## Complaint of the Individual; Communal Prayer

### Structure

|  | MT | NRSV |
|---|---|---|
| I. Superscription | 1 | - |
| II. Invocation, initial plea | 2-3 | 1-2 |
| III. Complaint | 4-12 | 3-11 |
| IV. Communal prayer | 13-23 | 12-22 |
| A. Hymnic introduction | 13 | 12 |
| B. Reminder, petition | 14-16 | 13-15 |
| C. Affirmation of confidence | 17-19 | 16-18 |
| D. Hymn | 20-23 | 19-22 |
| V. Complaint | 24 | 23 |
| VI. Petition | 25ab | 24ab |
| VII. Communal prayer | 25c-29 | 24c-28 |
| A. Hymn | 25c-28 | 24c-27 |
| B. Wish | 29 | 28 |

The SUPERSCRIPTION here is unique in the Psalter (cf., e.g., Brüning, 104-8). Collectors and redactors neither indicated a supposed author of the prayer nor added any liturgical or musical-technical information. They either invented those purely functional affirmations about the "oppressed" in his state of abandonment (*'tp;* cf. Ps 61:3; Isa 57:16; in the Hithpael, Pss 77:4 [RSV 3]; 107:5; 142:4 [RSV 3]; 143:4) and his desire to "pour out his anxiety before Yahweh" (cf. 142:3 [RSV 2]; 1 Sam 1:16), or they inherited it together with the traditional text. In itself, the heading looks archaic; it seems related to functional descriptions in Babylonian incantations (cf. Gerstenberger, *Mensch,* 78-82; listing at "Introduction to Cultic Poetry"). Babylonian incantations, for example, normally contain at the end or beginning of the ritual text or its subsections a generic designation (e.g., *namburbi,* "dissolution"; *šu-illa,* "hand raising"; *šiptum,* "incantation," and a type of prescription determining the use of the texts; cf. Maul, *Zukunftsbewältigung,* 163-90; listing at Additional Bibliography, section B). In a comparable fashion our heading mentions the "prayer," *tĕpillāh,* derived from *pll,* "to entreat" (cf. headings of Psalms 17; 86; 90; 142). This designation in most cases means "petitionary prayer" (cf. Isa 1:15; Jer 7:16; 11:14; Pss 4:2 [RSV 1]; 6:10 [RSV 9]; 55:2 [RSV 1]; 66:20; 84:9 [RSV 8]; 86:6). Second, it lists the supplant and the purpose of the psalm in rather elaborate, emotional, narrative language (NRSV: ". . . of one afflicted, when faint and pleading before the Lord"). Chances are that this prescription is a late, psalmodic phrase to be distinguished from factual, terse scribal colophons or superscriptions (e.g., "Prayer for a sufferer when ailing"). But the ancient structure of genre-prescriptive definition is quite visible. In this way we have a unique, patient-centered heading within the Psalter, standing out from all the rest of musical-technical, generic, historical-biographical, etc., designations.

The main problem of Psalm 102 is the juncture of individual and communal elements, the latter tending to the hymnic side. According to social-historical considerations this fusion heralds a special kind of society, perhaps in between family and clan structures and state organization (cf. "Introduction to Cultic Poetry," section 4B; "Introduction to Psalms," section 2). The first two subunits, however, are the classical individual INVOCATION and COMPLAINT (vv. 2-3, 4-12). A very short appellation of Yahweh (v. 2a; cf. 3:2 [RSV 1]; 6:2 [RSV 1]; 38:2 [RSV 1]; 79:1; 141:1; etc.) and a rather prolonged initial plea for audience (v. 2) and, negatively, for not being shunned by God (v. 3ab) but finding open ears and prompt positive answers (v. 3cd) constitute the three-line opening of the prayer (for close parallels cf. 4:2 [RSV 1]; 5:2-3 [RSV 1-2]; 17:1; 54:3-4 [RSV 1-2]; 55:2-3 [RSV 1-2]; 61:2-3 [RSV 1-2]; 86:1; 130:1-2; 143:1-2). The term *tĕpillāh* occurs again in v. 2a, indicating petitionary prayer, and there are all indications of personal anguish being presupposed, not communal calamity. As is customary, the invocation uses direct-address forms (second person singular) for God.

The COMPLAINT section (vv. 4-12), even using mostly generalized language and being a liturgical text, tells explicitly of personal anxieties in the face of transitoriness and frustrations of human life (cf. Psalms 39; 90; 139). Still, the classical descriptions of personal suffering (vv. 4-8; cf. parts of Psalms 22; 38; 69), reference to brutal enemies (v. 9), and God's own adverse actions against the suppliant (cf. v. 11: the only line in the complaint with direct-

211

address forms) are present. The main thrust of the complaint, however, seems to be the quick passage of (very burdensome) time, which is a sapiential theme: the complaint section is framed by laments over the swift passage of "my days," compared to the "withering away of greenery" (vv. 4-5, 12; cf. 39:7-9 [RSV 6-8]; 90:3-6, 10; Isa 40:6-8). Other complaints of the individual lack this type of general lament, spelling out instead phenomena of sickness, persecution, social marginalization, and threatening death (cf. Pss 22:13-19 [RSV 12-18]; 38:4-18 [RSV 3-17]; 69:2-5, 8-13 [RSV 1-4, 7-12]).

Unexpectedly the psalm continues with definitely COMMUNAL PRAYER (vv. 13-23), implying a shift in style and a profound change of topic (cf. Seybold, Allen, Culley, et al.). Formally, after a short HYMNIC INTRODUCTION in direct address, befitting a community that approaches its deity (cf. 44:2-9 [RSV 1-8]; 89:2-15 [RSV 1-14]), a PETITION for reconstruction of Jerusalem is articulated with urgency. Yahweh is entreated personally, directly: "You should rise (and) have pity on Zion" (v. 14a; cf. 12:6 [RSV 5]; 44:24-27 [RSV 23-26]). The use of imperfects or jussives instead of imperatives is a little strange in petition. Nevertheless, the demanding quality of plain imperfects should not be doubted in this context. Time has come for the destinies of the community to change (v. 14b; cf. Isa 40:2). Two kinds of arguments are listed in favor of Yahweh's immediate intervention — the existence of a community of his "servants" deeply attached to the holy place, and the position of this community in the midst of the "nations" — and they constitute one unit (vv. 15-16). The self-designation as "servants" is very common besides other names (cf. 34:23 [RSV 22]; 69:37 [RSV 36]; 79:2, 10; 89:51 [RSV 50]; 90:13, 16; etc.). The servants of Yahweh are surrounded by other nations and religious groups; they desperately need recognition from outside (v. 16). A second round of arguments apparently concerns trust in Yahweh and his old promises in favor of Zion. Four perfect verbs tell about his actions that the faithful must consider certain and can absolutely rely on: Yahweh "builds" Zion, he "appears in his glory," he "turns" to their prayer and does "not disdain" it (vv. 17-18). Certainty about God's basic disposition to reconstruct Jerusalem is so strong that the fact deserves a written testimony for future generations (v. 19): the formula is clear evidence of the late origin of the text (cf. Childs). In our opinion, the reconstruction of Jerusalem, by itself, has nothing to do with the preceding complaint of an individual sufferer. One plausible connection between the two, however, is visible in v. 18: just as the *těpillāh* of the individual *'ar'ār,* "naked, despoiled," person, is heeded by Yahweh (cf. v. 2), the prayer of the community will not fail to move him. The term "prayer," it seems, occurring for the second time in the body of the psalm, holds together the two disparate parts. In the process of worship "prayer" then turns to "praise" (v. 22; cf. Westermann and Brueggemann for the overall "trajectory" of the Psalter and its individual collections). All the arguments in favor of Zion do not so much need the personal-address form (exception: v. 16b, where a Qumran fragment has a third-person suffix) but tend to refer to Yahweh in the "objective" third person.

Communal prayer, so insistently pleading on behalf of Yahweh's sacred city, comes to a provisional end in a HYMN (vv. 20-23). An introductory *kî* announces the song about the superior reign of Israel's God, who — from his

212

heavenly abode — attends to the crying of his people (vv. 20-21; cf. Exod 3:7; Ps 79:11). Of three infinitives with the preposition *lĕ*, the first two indicate activities of Yahweh himself; the third is one step removed from the heavenly source of praise: the faithful ones are to tell and sing his fame in the city (v. 22). Still another phrase depends on actions that start out in the heights (v. 23). An infinitive with the preposition *bĕ* and unclear grammatical affiliation talks about the "nations getting together" "to serve Yahweh." This bold vision of an international pilgrimage toward Jerusalem sounds Isaianic, better Deutero-Isaianic, or late prophetic (cf. Isa 2:1-5; 49:7-23; 60–62; Zechariah 14). Does the preposition *bĕ* mean a special event at some point of historical or posthistorical time? Or is it introducing a circumstantial or conditional clause? Unfortunately, there is no way of telling with certainty. Indications of timing are all but absent from our communal prayer. "The future generation" comes to the fore only in v. 19.

Very brief phrases, which seem fragmentary, resume COMPLAINT and PETITION of the individual in vv. 24-25ab. No matter how we may read the text, it has a first person singular speaking, beseeching God to prolong his or her life (v. 25b). This, of course, is pure prayer discourse for the individual sufferer, an unexpected turn after the communal prayer had been presented. But the interlude is short. The psalm comes back to hymnic affirmations as soon as v. 25c. Thematically, the HYMN in vv. 25c-28 is juxtaposed to the individual lamenting transitoriness of life. God is creator of everything, therefore he is superior to creation in terms of longevity. All things "fade away, but you last" (v. 27a), a motif classically treated in Psalm 90. There is much poetic power in the metaphors of garments falling apart. "You are the same, your years will not come to an end" (v. 28). This analysis is opposed to human experience, whereby life is counted only in days swiftly running by. "A thousand years are to you like the day that slipped away yesterday" (90:4ab). The hymn is no end in itself, though. V. 29 closes the hymnic element as well as the whole psalm by adding a WISH. In fact, the expectation to be established in the land as the people of Yahweh (note the self-designation *'ăbādeykā*, "your servants," v. 15) is of utmost importance for the transmitters of the psalm. Wishes are mild or cautious forms of petition; v. 29 makes the final element of Psalm 102 a communal prayer, corresponding to vv. 13-23.

## *Genre*

There has been much speculation about the forms and genre of Psalm 102, because in our own way of thinking individualistic and collective concerns are difficult to reconcile. Formal analysis proves different roots and developments of the distinct speech patterns of the psalm. Invocation and complaint surely go back to ancient services for the individual sufferer (cf. Gerstenberger, *Mensch;* listing at "Introduction to Cultic Poetry"). Prayer for the restoration of Jerusalem as such needs to be located in congregational worship. How, after all, did they grow together? How could they be composed into one unit? Modern exegetes as a rule consider congruence or discrepancy of thoughts, concepts, and emotions only in order to evaluate a piece of literature. Such lines of reasoning are insufficient. We have to inquire about and take account of the use of biblical texts, if we really want to understand them. How do INDIVIDUAL COMPLAINT and COMMUNAL PRAYER go together?

## Setting

In the history of genres, petitionary prayer of and for the individual sufferer probably antedates any forms of communal praying. At least for ancient Israelite society we may insist that this is a plausible theory, because the Hebrew Bible tells us how Israel grew together and developed from individual families and clans. The religious community uniting around Yahweh and his *tôrāh* was certainly a latecomer on the scene. Thus we may surmise that Zion theology and hope for restoration in vv. 13-23 are sufficient proof of the lateness of these respective parts. If this is true, the individual complaint elements — invocation, complaint proper, and rudimentary petition — are older than communal prayer. The consequence would be that exilic-postexilic congregations used (as they in fact did on a very large scale) familial religious traditions to express their spiritual concerns. Suffering the pressures of their time and environment, the faithful of Yahweh in Jerusalem and the diaspora would take up in their services the forms of individual complaint (cf. "Introduction to Cultic Poetry," section 4B), modify them for their purposes (→ Psalm 12), and add to them liturgical expressions of trust, praise, hopes, and desires, in order to approach Yahweh in their assemblies. Individuality of articulation was no handicap to reciting first-person singular prayers in the congregation (as it is no barrier at all in our own days). The reason is simple: faith in Yahweh worked not only on a communal basis, but also — and necessarily so — in relation to each member of community (cf. Ezekiel 18; etc.). The congregation consisted of persons who had made a personal decision to stay with their God of old. Countless Jews, even in that early time, left that community of faith. Whoever stayed on became him- or herself a sustainer of Yahweh's community. Psalm 102 is deeply rooted in this community and personal faith. The real congregational worship postulated as a background for our psalm apparently included both personal and communal concerns. This means that suffering members were comforted, and common hopes for restoration were kindled in one and the same assembly. Why should this have been impossible? We are doing the same in our worship services until this very day. If this be true, strained explanations of why the mixture of prayers in Psalm 102 came about are unnecessary (cf. Steck, Culley, Brüning, most commentators; Culley's three-level performance [individual — group — cosmos] is a purely spiritual and linguistic design that cannot be applied to ritual practice). Becker is basically correct when he speaks of an interpretive growth of psalms (idem, *Israel,* 43-45; listing at "Introduction to Psalms"). Only he does not sufficiently ponder the new social conditions of the Jewish community as the matrix for changes in worship, theology, text production, and text use.

## Intention

The fundamental goal of our prayer is perseverance of Yahweh and the Zion community under adverse conditions of (probably) Persian times. The individual complaint of familial tradition is considered a proven *tĕpillāh* that may be used in the entreaty before God. It will fortify each individual member of the congregation, and it will help to undergird praise and prayer of the community itself. Looked at closely, even hymns have a petitionary touch to them (cf. Psalms 19; 33; 104).

## Bibliography

L. C. Allen, "The Value of Rhetorical Criticism in Psalm 69" (listing at Psalm 69); R. Brandscheidt, "Psalm 102. Literarische Gestalt und theologische Aussage," *TTZ* 96 (1987) 52-75; C. Brüning, *Mitten im Leben vom Tod umfangen* (Frankfurt: Anton Hain, 1992); G. Brunert, *Psalm 102 im Kontext des vierten Psalmenbuches* (Stuttgart: Katholisches Bibelwerk, 1996); B. S. Childs, "Analysis of a Canonical Formula: 'It Shall Be Recorded for a Future Generation,'" in *Die hebräische Bibel und ihre zweifache Nachgeschichte* (*Fest.* R. Rendtorff; ed. E. Blum, et al.; Neukirchen-Vluyn: Neukirchener Verlag, 1990) 357-64; R. C. Culley, "Psalm 102: A Complaint with a Difference," *Semeia* 62 (1993) 19-35; R. Dittmann, "Fire, Smoke, and Ashes," *Pro ecclesia* 4 (1995) 398-403; R. P. Gordon, "K/kI/ky in Incantational Incipits," *UF* 23 (1992) 161-63; J. Haddix, "Lamentation as Personal Experience in Selected Psalms" (diss., Boston University, 1980); C. B. Houk, "Syllables and Psalms: A Statistical Linguistic Analysis," *JSOT* 14 (1979) 55-62; R. W. Klein, "Theology for Exiles: The Kingship of Yahweh," *Dialog* 17 (1978) 128-34; J. H. le Roux, "God alles, die mens niks: gedagtes rondom Luther se 'Die Sieben Busspsalmen' van 1517," in *Martin Luther Lives* (ed. J. Hofmeyr; Pretoria: University of South Africa, 1983) 26-38; F. Sedlmeier, "Zusammengesetzte Nominalsätze und ihre Leistung für Psalm CII," *VT* 45 (1995) 239-50; idem, "Psalm 102,13-23: Aufbau und Funktion," *BZ* 40 (1996) 219-35; O. H. Steck, "Zu Eigenart und Herkunft von Ps 102," *ZAW* 102 (1990) 357-72; idem, "Zukunft des einzelnen — Zukunft des Gottesvolkes," in *Text, Methode und Grammatik* (*Fest.* W. Richter; ed. W. Gross, et al.; St. Ottilien: EOS, 1991) 471-82; A. Urban, "Verrinnendes Leben und ausgeschüttete Klage," *BibLeb* 10 (1969) 137-45.

## Psalm 103:
## Communal Hymn

### Structure

|  | MT | NRSV |
|---|---|---|
| I. Superscription | 1a | - |
| II. Summons to praise | 1b-2 | 1-2 |
| III. Hymn 1 (promissory) | 3-5 | 3-5 |

| IV. Hymn 2 (penitential) | 6-14 | 6-14 |
|---|---|---|
| A. Retrospect | 6-7 | 6-7 |
| B. Grace formula | 8-9 | 8-9 |
| C. Communal praise | 10 | 10 |
| D. Comparisons | 11-13 | 11-13 |
| E. Acquaintance formula | 14 | 14 |
| V. Hymn 3 (sapiential) | 15-18 | 15-18 |
| VI. Hymn 4 (glorifying) | 19-22 | 19-22 |
| A. Hymnic affirmation | 19 | 19 |
| B. Summons to praise | 20-22 | 20-22 |

A rudimentary SUPERSCRIPTION calls attention to the fact that redactional headings have not been applied to the psalms uniformly (cf. Psalms 93–97; 104–105; Wilson, "Untitled Psalms," Additional Bibliography, section C). Reduction of the superscription to just the name of a supposed author is rare (see Psalms 25–28; etc.). But Davidic connections in general are highly prized by redactors, as thirteen "biographical" ascriptions (→ Psalms 3; 7; 18; etc.) and a host of other references to the legendary musician-king prove.

The SUMMONS TO PRAISE here amounts to a personal self-exhortation as sometimes used in hymnic texts (bārăkî napšî, "my self may praise," is tantamount to "I will praise": Pss 16:7; 26:12; 34:2 [RSV 1]; 63:5 [RSV 4]; 104:1, 35; 132:15; 145:1, 2). This first-person singular discourse may indicate a strictly personal hymn, presented to the Deity by an individual, e.g., together with a thanksgiving offering (cf. Crüsemann, Studien, 285-96, 302-4; listing at "Introduction to Cultic Poetry"). In our case, however, individual discourse is linked to communal praise (cf. vv. 10-14). Thus the "I" framing the whole psalm (vv. 1-2, 22c) probably exposes the individual member of the community as the real protagonist of worshiping jubilation. In other words, the congregation is offering to each member a communal hymn in the "I" form (cf. Mowinckel, W I, 42-46; II, 74, 141-43). Perhaps a liturgist or leader of the community would intone the summons, so that everyone would be touched by personal responsibility to praise the God who had proved benevolent to all his followers (cf. vv. 6-14).

The first hymnic section after the summons to praise is geared to the needs of the individual member of the community (vv. 3-5). In five determined participles the help and blessings of Yahweh are sung out jubilantly. Remission of sin is first, and satisfaction with goods is last in the series (vv. 3a, 5a). In between are announcements of being healed, redeemed, and adorned (vv. 3b, 4). Very important for this promissory HYMN is that every single affirmation is dedicated to the individual participant of worship. The literary device to achieve this end is the continued speech to the "self" (nepeš is not "soul"). The last colon of the chain sums up, formally, the speaker telling him- or herself: "He rejuvenates your strength like an eagle" (v. 5b; cf. Isa 40:28-31). In reality, this little hymn is a comforting song for the afflicted members of the Yahweh community. The five participles with their resumé have possibly been recited by a choir, the leader, or — who knows — perhaps by the congregation itself. The three-word cola, each with a participle (with definite article; cf. Pss 33:15;

144:10; more frequently, hymnic participles are not determined; cf. 33:5, 7; 104:2-4; 136:4-25) at the beginning and a fitting substantive as grammatical object, constitute compact and chantable units. The substantives, for their part, all carry the personal suffix "your," in the feminine form (reference to "self," *nepeš*, feminine), i.e., "your guilt," "your infirmities," "your life," "your life span," "your youth." Only once is the suffix attached to the verb: "He crowns *you* with solidarity and mercy" (v. 4b). This colon with its different grammatical structure occupies exactly the middle position of the hymnic participial exclamations in vv. 3-5, thus demonstrating the unity of this section.

Mentioning Yahweh and his great "feats" (v. 2b: *gĕmûlîm;* only plural in Hebrew Scripture) now turns liturgical attention to his works of justice and equity beyond the personal realm of the speaker or singer (vv. 6-14). Here invariably appears the problem of misery and failure of the congregation. Two undetermined participles, i.e., without the article, tell the past story, how Yahweh came to establish justice and righteousness through Moses (vv. 6-7), to the benefit of the oppressed people (v. 6b, *ʿăšûqîm;* cf. Ps 146:7; Jer 50:33; Qoh 4:1). The terminology of "poor," "marginalized," and "oppressed" in later periods was often used in parallelism with "righteous" and "God-fearing" (cf. Psalms 9/10; 37). Here, in didactic retrospective, the intended background may be the slavery in Egypt. But as Deut 28:29, 33 would suggest, violence suffered can also be individualized and projected into the exilic period as a just payment for disobedience and apostasy, according to Deuteronomists and other Israelite theologians. Two participles of this type are rounded out with a liturgical formula that appears, with small variations, some ten times in Hebrew Scripture (see Exod 34:6; Pss 86:15; 145:8; Neh 9:17, 31; Spieckermann, 1-2; listing at Psalm 86). The GRACE FORMULA in v. 8, therefore, has a tradition history all its own (extending into our present-day worship services): "Yahweh is merciful and gracious, slow to anger and full of loyalty." Spoken by the liturgist it becomes a strong assurance of divine benevolence and help for every member of the congregation. In our psalm the formula is typically expanded (v. 9), drawing theological conclusions from divine assurance. God's wrath cannot last forever! As a visible response ("we" discourse) the congregation affirms the good news (v. 10): "He does not deal with us according to our sins" (cf. J. S. Kselman, *ABD* II, 1084-86).

Typical for exilic-postexilic communal hymns and prayers is an inherent consciousness of guilt and transgressions (see Nehemiah 9; Ezra 9; etc.). The act of erring or straying from Yahweh is not depicted or discussed at this point; it would be a matter for complaint psalms (see Psalms 78; 106). Still, vv. 9-10 presuppose the consequent state of affairs, expressing strong confidence that Yahweh will soften his stance and forgive (v. 9). This expectation becomes the central theme in vv. 10-14, a passage permeated with communal "we," "us," "our" discourse (vv. 10, 12b, 14), therefore, in all likelihood, to be attributed to the congregation. The key word of v. 8, *raḥûm*, "gracious," "forgiving," turns up again in the metaphor of a lenient human father (v. 13). From the liturgical statement of Yahweh's longanimity and steadfastness (v. 8) flows the general insight that he will forgive (v. 9) as well as a stimulus to reflect on one's own sins (v. 10). This line may be called an implicit confession of guilt. Instead of declaring one's spiritual deficits and asking for redemption, our psalm is fully certain that Yahweh will not repay according to the norms of justice, but according to fatherly love. Three main concepts of "failing" God are mentioned (vv. 10, 12b: *ḥāṭā', 'āwōn, pešaʿ;* cf. Knierim, *Hauptbegriffe;* listing at "Introduction to Psalms"). Poetic and human metaphors explain the situation. Heaven is not only in "geographical" terms superior to earth; it also is a dominant life-preserving force (v. 11). Sunrise and sunset are eternally opposed to each other, not only because of immense distances between them, but also because of irreconcilable connotations and meanings. Yahweh loves the community of the God-fearing (v. 11b); he will take away the evil threatening Israel. He will act not as judge but as father, within a familial context of full empathy for the miserable. He is able to do this because he is fully aware of his people being only mortal creatures, and therefore simply "dust" (v. 14).

The second HYMN (vv. 6-14) is a complex unit with different form elements and probably a colorful transmission history. Various liturgical entities are involved. Its central concern is God's ordinances and Israel's failure to live up to them — a common liturgical scenario in the Hebrew Bible (cf. Psalms 1; 19; 78; 106; 119; Nehemiah 9; Ezra 9; Daniel 9). The structure of the subunit is designed to lead up to the congregational confession in vv. 10-14 with its distinct communal language. In terms of liturgy, vv. 6-9 apparently reflect the voice of one or more reciters, while vv. 10-14 are the communal response, touched off by the negative phrase emphasizing Yahweh's forgiveness (v. 9), taken up by the assembly in v. 10.

The following unit (vv. 15-18) is formally an homage to human beings who are weak and transient but by eternal grace are made partners of the enduring God. OT anthropology of exilic-postexilic times comes to the fore (cf. Brueggemann, *Theology,* 487-88; listing at Additional Bibliography, section C). Astonishingly, the affirmations of this little HYMN include the vocabulary of Yahweh's particular alliance with historical Israel (v. 18; for covenantal worship in Hebrew Scripture see, e.g., Exod 24:3-11; 19:7–20:21; Joshua 24; Deuteronomy 29–30). But they transcend by far the boundaries of ethnic or religious groups potentially to take in every human being (v. 15: *'ĕnôš*) with their human destiny ("like grass" and "flower") if they become Yahweh-fearing people (v. 17b). The ordinances set forth by Yahweh (vv. 17c-18) refer back to jurisdiction in favor of the oppressed in v. 6. Now, the language, imagery, and theology of vv. 15-18 exactly in their "mixture" of motifs are typical for late OT reflection. The question "What about human existence?" is raised explicitly several times in Scripture, receiving different answers: Pss 8:5 (RSV 4); 144:3; Job 7:17; 15:14. Here as well as in many other contexts it is unspokenly present. Humans are like greenery: they flourish and die without leaving traces (vv. 15-16; cf. Pss 90:5-6; 102:12 [RSV 11]; 144:4; Isa 40:6-8; Gen 3:19). The book of Job has some poetic elaborations on the theme of human transitoriness, notably 14:1-12 (here vv. 1-2):

A human, born of a woman, lives a short time and is full of unrest.
He sprouts like a flower, and withers away; he fades like a shadow, and nothing is left.

The deepest concern of these ancient poets of the first millennium B.C.E. (for ancient Near Eastern parallels see Lambert, "Babylonian Theodicy," in *Wisdom,* 63-91; listing at "Introduction to Cultic Poetry"; J. L. Crenshaw, *ABD* VI, 444-47) is the swiftness of life, imminence of death, instability of human existence, and work. Psalms 39; 49; and 90 deal with this existential problem, which in some variation indeed is a basic one for all humanity. Psalm 90 even links the enigma of human guilt with the phenomenon of transitoriness (90:7-9). Our psalm does not succumb to melancholy when reflecting on the brevity of life. On the contrary, it overcomes fear by clinging to the presence of Yahweh even in the midst of life's rapid currents (vv. 17-18). God's solidarity and righteousness are perfectly stable; they endure over time and they are manifest in his ordinances given to those who will heed them.

We have discussed three separate hymns now, beginning with the song of basic assurance for every member of the congregation in vv. 3-5, continuing with a collective penitential liturgy (vv. 6-14), and coming to a sapiential, reflective, and covenantal doxology (vv. 15-18). Thus Psalm 103 is nothing less than a considerable agenda of worship probably used in assemblies of Yahweh believers (see Setting/Intention).

The grand finale of the psalm is a glorifying HYMN to Yahweh (vv. 19-22). His name is now mentioned in every single line, and the rest of the first as well as the second cola of vv. 20-22ab call upon diverse entities to give praise to him, the overlord. This act of "praising" is originally a type of "blessing" (*brk,* Piel), i.e., of conferring or yielding one's own power to a superior authority (cf. C. A. Keller and G. Wehmeier, *THAT* I, 353-76; C. Westermann, *Segen;* Brueggemann, *Psalms,* 112-32; listing at Additional Bibliography, section C). The SUMMONS TO PRAISE, for its part, is dependent on a HYMNIC AFFIRMATION that in fact Yahweh has taken over the overlordship in heaven (v. 19). This fact being established, all other powers (heavenly messengers, v. 20; heavenly hosts, i.e., deities, v. 21; all created things, v. 22ab) are admonished to surrender their power (note, though, that mythical forces like waters and primeval beasts, and human enemies are missing). Such a call to yield power must be very ancient and pre-Israelite (cf. ancient Near Eastern royal inscriptions and vassal treaties, e.g., *ANET,* 265-317, 531-41). Also within the Psalter we find more or less archaic evidence of calls to adore Yahweh (see Psalms 29; 82; 148). The crescendo of pure praise concerning transference of power is a final chorus of large dimensions that contrasts with the very personal beginnings of the psalm. But one last phrase or chanted line (v. 22c) repeats exactly the initial colon: "Praise, my self, Yahweh." The psalm comes back to the individual member of the congregation who is participating in common worship.

## Genre

Commentators have observed all along that Psalm 103 is a multilayered song, almost a worship liturgy in itself or a complex literary poem (cf., e.g., Seybold, 402: three stanzas focusing on the singer, the community, and the cosmos, with interspersed Scripture quotations in vv. 7-8 and 15-16). It gives comfort to the individual worshiper, moves through guilt feelings of the congregation, and comes up with resounding praise to Yahweh. The psalm quite naturally draws on motifs of salvation history (particularly the giving of divine ordinances) and at the same time proves well versed in international wisdom traditions and the discussion of basic philosophical issues of human existence. Since plaintive, petitionary, and thanksgiving overtones, if at all present, are very subtle, and the praising tenor sounds stronger and stronger, trumpetlike in the final section, we certainly may call the psalm a HYMN. This hymn is not uniform, however; it serves changing purposes, as indicated above. Why is this so?

## Setting/Intention

Looking at the use of a text in many cases can answer questions of multiplicity of forms or variety of (theological) outlooks. Psalm 103 reflects the views and social realities of a complex body of Yahweh believers in a pluralistic imperial society of the ancient Near East. Individual members of this religious community certainly crave attention in their basic human needs for physical and spiritual well-being, and they get it in this psalm. The community wrestles with its sense of failure and sin, and it is made aware of the forgiving God. The individual, again, feels threatened by death and is horrified by quickly vanishing life spans. He or she is calmed by the message of God's nearness and help. The final chorus lifts up all human problems into the higher spheres of time and space inaccessible to either individual or collective beings. Psalm 103, in other words, exhibits a lot of pastoral care, which to my mind took place within the worship service or the regular assemblies of the community. Only in this setting was the individual the responsible subject of worshiping one specific God, and the community was absolutely necessary to transmit the message of Yahweh, the supreme Deity. The psalm's intention, consequently, is a double one: take care of the individual believer and build up the community of the "God-fearing" people.

## Bibliography

P. Auffret, "Essai de structure littéraire du Psaume 103," *Folia Orientalia* 23 (1985) 197-225; E. Beaucamp, "Guérison et pardon (Ps 103)," *BVC* 29 (1959) 13-25; O. Betz, "Jesu Lieblingspsalm. Die Bedeutung von Psalm 103 für das Werk Jesu," *Theologische Beiträge* 15 (1984) 253-69; W. Brueggemann, "Remember, You are Dust," *Journal for Preachers* 14 (1991) 3-10; E. P. Dion, "Psalm 103: A Meditation on the 'Ways' of the Lord," *Eglise et Théologie* 21 (1990) 13-31; J. Doignon, "Sur la 'descente' du Christ en ce monde chez Hilaire de Poitiers," *RHR* 207 (1990) 65-75; R. Gögler, "Inkarnationsglaube und Bibeltheologie bei Origenes," *TQ* 165 (1985) 82-94; J. Herrmann, "Der 103. Psalm," in *Dienst unter dem Wort (Fest.* H. Schreiner; ed. K. Jansen; Gütersloh: Mohn, 1953) 82-93; L. C. Hoch, "Psicologia a serviço da libertação," *EsTe* 25 (1985) 249-69; F. D. Hubmann, "Gedanken zu Ps 103," *ZKT* 116 (1994) 464-71; E. Kellenberger, *ḥesed we'ĕmet als Ausdruck einer Glaubenserfahrung*

(ATANT 69; Zurich: Theologischer Verlag, 1982); K. Koch, "Redemption and Creation in Psalms 103–105," in *For the Sake of the Gospel* (*Fest.* S. Amirtham; ed. G. Robinson; Madurai: TTS Pub., 1980) 64-68; A. M. Malingrey, "Fragments du commentaire de Jean Chrysostome sur les psaumes 103 à 106," in *Texte und Textkritik* (ed. J. Dummer; Berlin: Akademie-Verlag, 1987) 351-78; J. Marböck, "Im Horizont der Gottesfurcht," *BN* 26 (1985) 47-70; J. L. Mays, "Psalm 103: Mercy Joined to Lovingkindness," *Austin Seminary Bulletin:* Faculty Edition 105 (1990) 27-32; M. Metzger, "Lobpreis der Gnade: Erwägungen zu Struktur und Inhalt von Psalm 103," in *Meilensteine* (*Fest.* H. Donner; ed. M. Weippert, et al.; Wiesbaden: Harrassowitz, 1995) 121-33; D. F. O'Kennedy, "The Relationship between Justice and Forgiveness in Psalm 103," *Scriptura* 65 (1998) 109-21; N. H. Parker, "Psalm 103 — God Is Love," *Canadian Journal of Theology* 1 (1955) 191-96; M. T. Porcile Santiso, "Solitude and Solidarity," *Ecumenical Review* 38 (1986) 35-47; G. Rice, "An Exposition of Psalm 103," *Journal of Religious Thought* 39 (1982) 55-61; K. D. Sakenfeld, *The Meaning of Hesed in the Hebrew Bible* (HSM 17; Missoula, Mont.: Scholars Press, 1978); J. Scharbert, "Formgeschichte und Exegese von Exod 34,6f und seiner Parallelen," *Bib* 38 (1957) 130-50; W. Th. in der Smitten, *Varia Theologica* (Niederkrüchten: Selbstverlag, 1977) 16-23; R. E. Sonafrank, "'Bless the Lord, O my Soul!' Psalm 103," *Hymn* 40 (1989) 30-31; H. Spieckermann, "Barmherzig" (listing at Psalm 86); T. M. Willis, "'So Great Is His Steadfast Love': A Rhetorical Analysis of Psalm 103," *Bib* 72 (1991) 525-37; G. H. Wilson, "The Use of 'Untitled' Psalms" (listing at Psalm 90).

## Psalm 104:
## Personal and Communal Hymn

### Structure

|  |  | MT | NRSV |
|---|---|---|---|
| I. | Summons to praise, hymnic address | 1 | 1 |
| II. | Hymn to cosmic ruler | 2-4 | 2-4 |
| III. | Hymn to sustainer | 5-23 | 5-23 |
|  | A. Creation | 5-9 | 5-9 |
|  | B. Provision | 10-18 | 10-18 |
|  | C. Regulation | 19-23 | 19-23 |
| IV. | Adoration | 24-30 | 24-30 |
| V. | Wishes | 31-32 | 31-32 |
| VI. | Vow | 33-34 | 33-34 |
| VII. | Imprecation | 35ab | 35ab |
| VIII. | Summons to praise | 35c | 35c |

One of the most debated and used psalms of the Psalter to this very day, our text starts and finishes with a very personal, self-addressed SUMMONS TO PRAISE (v. 1a, 35c); an identical opening is utilized in Ps 103:1b, 2a. While in the latter text dialogue with the psalmist's self continues after the overture, our present psalm immediately moves on to extroverted praise: Yahweh — in

221

chiastic position to the first colon's appellation — is called "my [personal] God" (cf. H. Vorländer, *Gott;* listing at "Introduction to Cultic Poetry"; Qumran texts have: "our God") and addressed directly as to his overwhelming majesty. Thereafter, second-person singular address or prayer discourse recedes, or at least is no longer explicit (a fact blurred by most modern translations) from v. 2 to v. 23, with the exception of vv. 7-9, one suffixed noun (v. 13b), and one verbal form in v. 20a (third person singular in the Syriac version). Grammatically, a combination of second-person pronoun with participle ("you are the one who is wrapped in light," etc.) is feasible; see Judg 6:36; Gen 43:5; 2 Kgs 4:16; etc. But there is a certain tension between v. 1 and its emphatically direct address of Yahweh on the one hand, and the series of six unspecified participles (vv. 2-4) plus the third person singular perfect (v. 5a, emended into a participle by some Greek MSS) on the other. A formal observation like this supported by other evidence indicates a composite structure of the psalm at hand. Different voices probably used to intone those distinctly formulated parts.

Six participles, then, describe the majesty and creative power of the cosmic overlord, three with and three without the definite article. The personal-address pronoun "you," however, is missing. All affirmations are neutral: "who clothes . . . , who stretches . . . , who constructs. . . ." The present context, for want of another reference, lends itself to connect the participles with the preceding colon: "You put on majesty and glory" (v. 1c). But the Hebrew styles of the two passages differ; the hymnic participles, as a rule, are construed objectively, in the third person and with third-person references. Second Isaiah contains many examples; see Isa 40:22-23, 26, 28-29; 42:5; 43:16; 45:6-7, 18; 51:15 (Crüsemann, *Studien*, 92-95, from this evidence already argues for the original autonomy of these formulations). They probably need a special notifier, a fitting personal pronoun, when shifting into second-person direct address discourse (cf. Ps 145:15b). Ps 65:6-9 (RSV 5-8), however, has a parallel structure to our text: a direct address of Yahweh, continued by participles, and coming back to second person singular, i.e., prayer language. The vast majority of hymnic participles no doubt have objective connections (cf. 1 Sam 2:6-8; Am 4:13; 5:8; 9:5-6; Jer 10:12-13; Job 5:9-16; 9:5-10; Pss 18:33-35 [RSV 32-34]; 144:1-2; 146:5-9a). Their relative independence of context, their stereotyped formulation, and their related contents make it plausible to think in terms of a fixed liturgical language pattern. In this case, the introductory element of Psalm 104 is followed by a traditional hymnic text, which may have been sung by a separate choir.

The largest part of the hymn, vv. 5-23, is stylistically not at all homogeneous. Some textual uncertainties make it even more difficult to determine formal patterns. Thus the verbal forms of vv. 5-6 (*yāsad, kissîtô*) are dubious. These two lines strike a new topic: creation of the earth as the basis of future life; they seem to provide a transition to vv. 7-9, which depict dramatically the active role of Yahweh in creation (cf. 77:17 [RSV 16]; Job 38:8-11). The formal expression of Yahweh's leading engagement in driving away death-prone primeval powers is direct-address discourse. Each line contains at least one reference to Yahweh's most vigorous moves against chaos waters, be it in the form of second-person nominal suffixes (e.g., "*your* scolding," v. 7a) or in second-person singular verbal expressions (e.g., "*you* founded," v. 8b). Still, in spite of these praising attributions to Yahweh, there is much descriptive language in the whole passage vv. 5-9, increasing ever more beyond this limit. Descriptions inform about what the chaos powers have been doing in the battle for creation and life. They "stand" upon the mountains (v. 6b), they "flee" (v. 7a), they "run away" (v. 7b; cf. 48:6 [RSV 5], the only other occurrence in Psalms), they "may not cross a boundary" or "come back" (v. 9). Between vv. 7 and 9 the information is about the firm land emerging: "Mountains rose, valleys caved in" (v. 8a). Thus the desire to praise the Creator implies curiosity about what has been going on in the wake of his appearance. We may say that a scientific interest of sorts informs the section under debate, while the preceding part (vv. 2-4), with its stereotyped participial expressions, is dedicated exclusively to the cosmic Overlord himself.

Three more participles (one with the definite article, two without), all being elaborated by descriptive phrases in the sense outlined above, appear in the following lines (vv. 10a, 13a, 14a). Of course, we are dealing with another phase of creation in vv. 10-18, only vaguely corresponding to the daily work periods mapped out in Genesis 1 (cf. Croatto, *Hombre*). While vv. 5-9 depict the consolidation of firm ground (earth = second day of Gen 1:6-8), the section at hand now is talking about the organization of the land so that it may sustain life. It is a matter of providing the right amount of water for every plant and every living creature, and a matter of God's creative will (vv. 10-18). Significantly, only one phrase with a second-person form (nominal suffix, v. 13b) appears in this section, and this incidence is textually uncertain and may amount to a scribal alteration. The backbone of the passage is the participles: they tell what Yahweh has done, or rather, what he is doing continually, to sustain life. The descriptive phrases, indicating consequences and materializations of God's deeds, follow from his efforts to provide. He gives fountains of water, and all living beings drink (vv. 10-11), while the birds sing (v. 12) — a bucolic still life. In a similar way, watering by precipitation makes the flora grow (vv. 13-14ab). Elaborating on that idea, all kinds of foods are cultivated by sufficient rain (vv. 14c, 15), a relative indicator of the geographical horizon that the psalm grew up and became used in: a non-Egyptian environment, to be sure. Then attention goes to the rugged mountains with their majestic cedars and wildlife untouched by humans. All this also depends on rainfall (vv. 16-18). Egypt, e.g., never flourished from rain but from the Nile River. Thematically, this last passage is autonomous; perhaps it was intoned by a separate group of singers or participants in a service.

Strangely enough, the poem now reverts to moon and sun, the heavenly providers of light. The reference to the moon's creation is merely rhetorical, though. The interest lies exclusively on its functions: to divide the year into months, just as the sun is responsible for daylight (vv. 19b, 22a). Under this aspect, the world is divided into creatures of the night and creatures of the day (vv. 20-23). Human beings simply belong to the latter category (v. 23). Therefore, mention of the moon and sun in v. 19 (parallel to the creation story; cf. Gen 1:14-19) is merely an introduction to this night-and-day division of the living world. The very same concept is present in the famous Hymn to Aton, the sun-god, venerated exclusively by Pharaoh Akh-en-Aton:

When thou settest in the western horizon,
The land is in darkness, in the manner of death.
They sleep in a room, with heads wrapped up,
Nor sees one eye the other.
All their goods which are under their heads might be stolen,
(But) they would not perceive (it).
Every lion is come forth from his den;
All creeping things, they sting.
Darkness *is a shroud,* and the earth is in stillness,
for he who made them rests in his horizon.
At daybreak, when thou arisest on the horizon,
When thou shinest as the Aton [i.e., sun] by day,
Thou drivest away the darkness and givest thy rays.
The Two Lands are in festivity *every day,*
Awake and standing upon (their) feet,
For thou hast raised them up.
Washing their bodies, taking (their) clothing,
Their arms are (raised) in praise at thy appearance.
All the world, they do their work. (Tr. J. A. Wilson, *ANET,* 370)

Distinct notes of this Egyptian poem obviously preclude direct literary dependence of Psalm 104. On the other hand, similarities of concepts and wordings (cf. "creeping things" and "lions" in vv. 20-21; darkness and sunrise, vv. 20, 22; humans coming out for their day's labor, v. 23) extending over still larger parts of our psalm and the Aton hymn clearly prove a common background of both texts (cf. Uehlinger). The night-life versus day-life pattern may be of Egyptian origin (for Egyptian hymnology see, e.g., Auffret, *Hymnes;* J. Assmann, *Ägyptische Hymnen und Gebete* [Zurich: Artemis, 1975]; Hornung, *Gesänge;* J. L. Foster, *Hymns, Prayers and Songs* [Atlanta: Scholars Press, 1996]).

The next element is an outburst of jubilant ADORATION (vv. 24-30). Excited exclamations introduce the passage (vv. 24-26), in the same fashion as the Egyptian counterpart: "How manifold it is, what thou hast made!" (*ANET,* 370). The passage of our psalm is pointedly put into second-person address style (which the Egyptian hymn favors throughout). Psalm 104, in a way, alternates objective description with direct address. The latter form is present in vv. 1bc, 7-9, ephemerally also in vv. 13, 20, and massively so in vv. 24-30. The topics of adoration include the sea, living beings in the sea, ships, primeval monsters (vv. 25-26; Uehlinger suggests a Phoenician origin of these motifs). To come to the central point: Yahweh takes care of all of them (vv. 27-28; also in the Egyptian hymn: "Thou suppliest their necessities: Everyone has his food" = focused on humans; *ANET,* 370). Provision with all necessary goods is contrasted with abandonment: if the provider-God turns away, everything will perish again (v. 29) as in the fall of every year. But Yahweh may send his "breath" and re-create the "face of the earth" (v. 30) in a yearly rhythm. In other words, from a form-critical perspective: exclamations of astonishment (vv. 24-26), which may have an autonomous function as in Pss 8:2, 10 (RSV 1, 9); 36:8 (RSV 7); 66:3; 92:6 (RSV 5), here are expanded by praising affirmations about the utter dependence of nature on the divine forces of life (vv. 27-30). Short phrases with exclamatory "how" or "this is" were probably shouted by groups or the community at large, as → 66:3 would suggest. The elaboration, then, could be a liturgical matter of the congregation, too, or it was presented by an official singer or reciter.

Approaching the end of the psalm we find diverse elements of a wishful or petitionary character (vv. 31-35). A double wish for Yahweh to be strong and enjoy his creation (v. 31) is bolstered by a lone participial praise followed by a synonym parallel to a plain imperfect verb (v. 32). Expressions of joy are rarely attributed to the Deity (cf. 2:4: he "laughs at and taunts" the enemies; 37:13; 59:9 [RSV 8]). The verb śmḥ, Qal, "be joyful," save for Isa 9:16 (RSV 17; here it may be misspelled for ḥml, "have pity"), occurs nowhere else with Yahweh as the subject. Vows as in vv. 33-34 are usually part of complaint songs, and the same is true for IMPRECATIONS (v. 35ab). How do these forms enter a true hymn? On closer scrutiny, the vows are formulated in the first person singular, but they do not exactly promise a thanksgiving offering as in individual complaints (→ Pss 7:18 [RSV 17]; 66:13-15). Singing and playing in v. 33 are clearly hymnic activities, probably in front of or on behalf of the community (cf. Exod 15:21). In v. 34, however, śyḥ occurs, though it seems to be a term of complaint contexts; cf. 55:3 (RSV 2); 64:2 (RSV 1); 102:1; 142:3 (RSV 2); etc. In consequence, we have to consider that individual and communal concerns were linked with congregational praise in the services of old (cf. 139:19-24). Imprecation, in this context, is largely a communal issue. "Sinners" and "godless," mentioned in v. 35, are the opponents of the community, not personal enemies as in individual complaints.

The psalm ends in a short SUMMONS TO PRAISE, addressed as in v. 1 to the proper self of the psalmist. Psalm 103 has an identical frame. In both cases we interpret the first person not so much in individualistic terms, but as a signal indicating the state of affairs in the congregation. Every single member is called on to join in this hymn.

Looking back at the overall structure of Psalm 104, then, we may venture the following conclusions. The text before us is quite complex. Literary analysis can hardly explain its origin and use, let alone postulate a private production of texts as if composed under present-day conditions. Most likely, therefore, changing styles and outlooks within the psalm are due to an interplay of liturgical voices. For example, the liturgist opens and closes with a rousing SUMMONS TO PRAISE, self-addressed and directed to Yahweh (v. 1), including him- or herself in the worshiping community. The body of the psalm is a grand HYMN to God (vv. 2-30). Individual voices, choirs, and congregation may have alternated in singing Yahweh's glory. First, he is the creator of the cosmos (vv. 2-4; choir? all worshipers?). Second, he is eulogized as the founder of the earth and the sustainer of all life (vv. 5-23; varying voices; did the liturgist take on the direct-address praise of vv. 7-9, and choruses chant vv. 10-18 and 19-23?). Third, jubilant exclamations of joy and satisfaction at the beauty, wisdom, and abundance of life mark the final section (vv. 24-30, recited again by the liturgist alone, or by groups of the assembly?). As pointed out above, the final elements of WISH, VOW, IMPRECATION, and SUMMONS (vv. 31-35) go back to congregational worship patterns. They again may have been recited by liturgists (vv. 31-32; 35?) and the attending crowd (vv. 33-34, perhaps in a confessional mood). The stray attachment *hallĕlû-yāh* (v. 35d) appears to be a scribal note (cf. Psalms 106; 111–113).

## Genre

We are dealing with a hymn in the Egyptian tradition, but mediated by the Canaanite culture and religion (cf. Uehlinger, connecting particular ships and Leviathan in vv. 25-26 to ancient Syrian motifs; Dion, pointing to an association of Hittite storm- and Egyptian sun-god in several Boghazköi letters, etc.), which may have grown together from various parts, namely some enumerations of participles, "objective" praises of the majestic creator and ruler of all the world, of loosely formulated affirmations about the heavenly sustainer, and direct-address eulogies of the God who keeps the world going in a yearly rhythm of dying and resurrected nature (on "mixed style" cf. Mowinckel, *W* II, 74: conditioned by "the psychology of religious life"). "Individual hymn" would be a designation much too narrow for our psalm. The individual is certainly included in this magnificent praise. But the congregation is involved all over the text and its subdivisions. Therefore we call it a PERSONAL AND COMMUNAL HYMN.

The concepts of God and humankind are noteworthy in our psalm, and they are reflective of its time and place of origin. There is no mention of Yahweh warring for Israel, or of the congregation's holy land or temple. Even the sinners and wicked of v. 35 are left totally unspecified. Their profile probably was perfectly clear in ancient worship (and may have had that anti-Israelite touch), but it could not have been omitted in any purely literary text, and we are unable to determine its contents from our vantage point today. God is a cosmic ruler and provider, and his creation is a wondrous symphony of life. Each being has its place to exist freely. Humankind, nonaggressive as it were, is but one creature among many (vv. 14-15, 23), and does not enjoy particular privileges in a harmonious, pacified world (cf. Gerstenberger). Government over this world remains completely in the hands of God (vv. 27-30), and all notions of sin, destruction, alienation, as well as all visions of a radical renovation of the earth are far away (Krüger speaks of marginal "ambivalences"). The creation story of Genesis 1 has some deep-rooted affinity with Psalm 104 (Croatto, Allen), but there are a lot of important differences, which may even be considered a critique of the pentateuchal concepts (e.g., Seybold, 409). In any case, the major characteristics of God, humankind, and world seem to be aligned to international wisdom rather than national Torah and election theology. This sapiential branch of thinking did come up in Israel by way of exilic experience (universal imperium, plurality of nations, cohesiveness of nature, wealth and beauty of life). Yahweh, in assuming the various roles of a supreme God, becomes a monistic supreme ruler.

## Setting

The community that brought forth such a mixture of texts was probably that of exilic-postexilic times, drawing freely, it seems, on diverse traditions. Main proof of this parish background is the communal involvement of the "I" speaking in the hymn. It may certainly represent the liturgist, but with equal certainty we insist on its paradigmatic significance for every member of the congregation. The collective "we" does not appear. Nevertheless, mood and insights, verve of praise and human solidarity as well as the theological concepts mentioned are all communal traits. Psalm 104 does not betray any special seasonal setting, unless we take vv. 28-29, with its pattern of dying and resurrecting nature, as indication of the fall or New Year Festival.

## Intention

Hymnic praise, aligned to some (perhaps secondary) flurries of petition and imprecation, make the poem an expression of communal awe to their particular God, who is venerated as the creator and sustainer of the whole world. Every single living being is dependent on this supreme God. Cosmic conscientization is intended, in an astonishing way, as it appears from our modern perspective. Knowing about the problems of survival after centuries of ruthless exploitation of this planet, we can only admire in our psalm a complete absence of presumptuous claims, and a deep solidarization of humans with all other creatures.

Sometimes a close alignment of our liturgical agenda to Psalm 103 is maintained. Exegetes declare both texts to be "twin psalms" (e.g., Dion, 69) using a term of W. Zimmerli. If it were true that both psalms had been composed together and placed into the Psalter side by side (cf. analogies of forms, structure elements, some theological concepts) in order to complement each other liturgically and theologically, etc., the deficit of salvation theology in Psalm 104 might have been balanced by the Torah consciousness of Psalm 103 (cf. 103:7). Joint use of both songs cannot be proved, however, and remains speculative. In any case, the form, structure, and content of Psalm 104 suggest an independent origin and handling of our psalm.

## Bibliography

M. Ahrens, "Natur pur? Probleme mit Psalm 104," *Junge Kirche* 57 (1996) 348-53; F. Asensio, "El protagonismo del 'Hombre-Hijo de Hombre' del Salmo 8," *EstBib* 41 (1983) 17-51; J. Assmann, "Die 'Häresie' des Echnaton: Aspekte der Amarna-Religion," *Saeculum* 23 (1972) 109-26; P. Auffret, *Hymnes d'Egypte et d'Israel* (Göttingen: Vandenhoeck & Ruprecht, 1981); idem, "'Avec sagesse tu les fis,'" *Église et théologie* 27 (1996) 5-19; G. M. Augustyn, "Loof die Here vir sy ekosisteem," *SK* 18 (1997) 245-57; D. G. Barker, "The Waters of the Earth: An Exegetical Study of Psalm 104:1-9," *Grace Theological Journal* 7 (1986) 57-80; J. B. Bauer, "Der priesterliche Schöpfungshymnus in Gen 1," *TZ* 20 (1964) 1-9; K. H. Bernhardt, "Amenophis IV. und Psalm 104," *Mitteilungen des Instituts für Orientforschung* (Berlin) 15 (1969) 193-206; T. Booij, " 'The Earth Is Satisfied with the Fruit of Thy Work,' " *Bib* 69 (1988) 409-12; C. Brüning, " 'Sendest du deinen Geist aus, so wird das Angesicht der Erde erneuert' " *Erbe und Auftrag* 74 (1998) 121-38; M. A. Bullmon, "The Tour Most Important," *Trinity Journal* 19 (1998) 139-62; E. B. Celada, "El salmo 104, el himno de Amenofis IV y otros documentos egipcios," *Sefarad* 30 (1970) 305-24; 31 (1971) 3-26; R. E. Clements, "The Use of the Old Testament," *Southwestern Journal of Theology* 28 (1985) 36-45; R. J. Clifford, "A Note on Psalm 104,5-9," *JBL* 100 (1981) 87-89; S. L. Cook, "Apocalypticism and the Psalter," *ZAW* 104 (1992) 82-99; P. C. Craigie, "The Comparison of Hebrew Poetry: Psalm 104 in the Light of Egyptian and Ugaritic Poetry," *Semitics* 4 (1974) 10-21; J. S. Croatto, *El hombre en el mundo I — Creacíon y designio* (Buenos Aires: Edit. La Aurora, 1974); C. Dahlgrün, " 'Voll ist die Erde deiner Werke,' " in *Theologisches geschenkt* (ed. C. Bizer, et al.; Bovenden: Foedus, 1996) 23-31; J. Day, "Echoes of Baal's Seven Thunders and Lightnings," *VT* 29 (1979) 143-51; A. Deissler, "Mensch und Schöpfung," *Oberrheinische Pastoralblätter* 61 (1960) 15-22, 42-45; idem, "The Theology of Psalm 104," in *Standing Before God* (*Fest.* J. M. Oesterreicher; ed. A. Finkel, et al.; New York: Ktav, 1981) 31-40; J. D. M. Derrett, "Birds of the Air and Lilies of the Field," *Downside Review* 105 (1987) 181-92; P. E. Dion, "YHWH as Storm-God and Sun-God: The Double Legacy of Egypt and Canaan as Reflected in Psalm 104," *ZAW* 103 (1991) 43-69; O. Eissfeldt, "Alexander von Humboldts 'Kosmos' und der 104. Psalm" (1959), in *KS* III, 471-80; L. R. Fisher, "Creation at Ugarit and in the Old Testament," *VT* 15 (1965) 313-24; N. Füglister, "Schöpfungssprache in den Psalmen: Der Psalm 104 als Paradigma," in *Schöpfung und Sprache* (ed. W. Strolz; Freiburg: Herder, 1979) 45-80; E. S. Gerstenberger, "Versöhnung mit der Natur: Anfragen an gottesdienstliche Texte des Alten Testaments (Ps 8 und 104)," in *Versöhnung mit der Natur* (ed. J. Moltmann; Munich: Kaiser, 1986) 141-49; N. C. Habel, "The Survival of Yahwism," *Point* 6 (1977) 186-96; W. Harrelson, "On God's Care for the Earth, Psalm 104," *Currents in Theology and Mission* 2 (1975) 19-22; S. Herrmann, "Die Naturlehre des Schöpfungsberichtes," *TLZ* 86 (1961) 413-23; Y. Hoffman, "Psalm 104: A Literary Examination," in *Sha'arei Talmon* (*Fest.* S. Talmon; ed. M. Fishbane, et al.; Winona Lake, Ind.: Eisenbrauns, 1992) 13-24; E. Hornung, *Gesänge vom Nil* (Zurich/Munich: Artemis, 1990); V. Howard, "Psalm 104," *Int* 46 (1992) 176-80; P. Humbert, "La relation de Genèse 1 et du Psaume 104 avec liturgie du nouvel-an Israëlite," *RHPR* 15 (1935) 1-27; B. Janecko, "Ecology, Nature, and the Psalms," in *The Psalms and Other Studies* (ed. J. Knight, et al.; Nashotah: Nashotah House Seminary, 1990) 96-108; B. Janowski, et al., eds., *Gefährten und Feinde des Menschen* (Neukirchen-Vluyn: Neukirchener Verlag, 1993); J. Jeremias, "Schöpfung in Poesie und Prosa des Alten Testaments: Gen 1–3 im Vergleich mit anderen Schöpfungstexten des Alten Testaments," in *Schöpfung und Neuschöpfung* (ed. I. Baldermann, et al.; Neukirchen-Vluyn: Neukirchener Verlag, 1990) 11-36; R. K. Johnston, "Wisdom Literature and Its Contribution to a Biblical Environmental Ethic," in *Tending the Garden* (ed. W. Granberg-Michaelson; Grand Rapids: Eerdmans, 1987) 66-82; O. Keel, "Die höchsten Berge sind dem Steinbock: Über das Verständnis von

Natur und Boden im Alten Testament," *Reformatio* 37 (1988) 34-39; J. Knöppler, "Kein Platz für einen Schöpfer?" *Glaube und Denken* 10 (1997) 47-77; R. G. Kratz, "Die Gnade des täglichen Brotes. Späte Psalmen auf dem Weg zum Vaterunser," *ZTK* 89 (1992) 1-40; T. Krüger, "'Kosmo-Theologie' zwischen Mythos und Erfahrung. Psalm 104 im Horizont altorientalischer und alttestamentlicher Schöpfungskonzepte," *BN* 68 (1993) 49-74; G. Leonardi, "Note su alcuni versetti del Salmo 104," *Bib* 49 (1968) 238-42; G. Liedke, "'Tier-Ethik' — Biblische Perspektiven," *Zeitschrift für evangelische Ethik* 29 (1985) 160-73; J. Limburg, "Down-To-Earth Theology: Psalm 104 and the Environment," *Currents in Theology and Mission* 21 (1994) 340-46; J. Marböck, "Im Horizont der Gottesfurcht: Stellungnahmen zu Welt und Leben in der alttestamentlichen Weisheit," *BN* 26 (1985) 47-70; G. Nagel, "A propos de rapports du Psaume 104 avec les textes égyptiens," in *Fest. A. Bertholet* (ed. W. Baumgartner, et al.; Tübingen: Mohr, 1950) 395-403; G. W. Nebe, "Psalm 104:11 aus Höhle 4 von Qumran (4QPsd) und der Ersatz des Gottesnamens," *ZAW* 93 (1981) 284-90; E. von Nordheim, "Der grosse Hymnus des Echnaton und Psalm 104," *Studien zur altägyptischen Kultur* 7 (1979) 227-51 (repr. in *Theologie und Menschenbild* [*Fest.* E. Link; ed. G. Dautzenberg, et al.; Frankfurt: Lang, 1978] 51-74); R. North, "Psalm 8 as a Miniature of Psalm 104," in *The Psalms and Other Studies* (ed. J. Knight, et al.; Nashotah: Nashotah House Seminary, 1990) 2-10; M. Orfali, "Anthropomorphism in the Christian Reproach of the Jews in Spain," *Immanuel* 19 (1984/85) 60-73; E. Otto, "Schöpfung als Kategorie" (listing at Psalm 93); D. J. Parkander, "Exalted Manna: The Psalms as Literature," *Word & World* 5 (1985) 122-31; S. Paulsen, "Schöpfungsverständnis im 'Psalm des Volkes' (Ps 104) und im 'Psalm der Theologen,'" *Ministerial Formation* 53 (1991) 27-30; G. von Rad, "Das theologische Problem des alttestamentlichen Schöpfungsglaubens," in *Werden und Wesen des Alten Testaments* (ed. P. Volz, et al.; BZAW 66; Berlin: Töpelmann, 1936) 138-47; M. L. Ramlot, "Hymne à la gloire du Créateur, Psalm 104," *BVC* 31 (1960) 39-47; D. B. Redford, "The Monotheism of the Heretic Pharaoh: Precursor of Mosaic Monotheism or Egyptian Anomaly?" *Biblical Archaeology Review* 13 (1987) 16-32; B. Renaud, "La structure du Ps 104 et ses implications théologiques," *RSR* 55 (1981) 1-30; J. W. Rogerson, *The Old Testament View of Nature* (OTS 20; Leiden: Brill, 1977); A. Rose, "Les Psaumes et la Sainte Trinité selon la tradition," in *Trinité et liturgie* (ed. A. Triacca, et al.; Rome: CLV Edizioni Liturgiche, 1984) 255-82; P. M. Schafran, "Is Mankind the Measure?" *Perspectives on Sciences and Christian Faith* 47 (1995) 92-102; T. Seidl, "'. . . Mit der Urflut hast du die Erde bedeckt wie mit einem Kleid,'" *BN* 25 (1984) 42-48; K. Seybold, "Psalm 104 im Spiegel seiner Unterschrift," *TZ* 40 (1984) 1-11; O. H. Steck, "Der Wein unter den Schöpfungsgaben," *TTZ* 87 (1978) 173-91; W. Strolz, "Die Vertrauenswürdigkeit der Natur, Psalm 104," in idem, *Gottes verborgene Gegenwart* (Freiburg: Herder, 1976) 12-31; R. E. Timm, "Let's Not Miss the Theology of the Creation Accounts," *Currents in Theology and Mission* 13 (1986) 97-105; V. A. Tobin, "Amarna and Biblical Religion," in *Pharaonic Egypt* (ed. S. Israelit-Groll; Jerusalem: Magnes, 1985) 231-77; C. C. Twombly, "Redemptive History and the Shaping of the Affections," *Crux* 20 (1984) 21-26; C. Uehlinger, "Leviathan und die Schiffe in Ps 104,25-26," *Bib* 71 (1990) 499-526; A. van der Voort, "Genèse 1 à 2,4a et Psaume 104," *RB* 58 (1951) 321-47; M. K. Wakeman, *God's Battle with the Monster* (Leiden: Brill, 1973); B. K. Waltke, "Creation Account in Genesis 1:1-3," *BSac* 132 (1975) 25-36; 133 (1976) 28-41; E. Zenger, "'Du kannst das Angesicht der Erde erneuern' (Ps 104,30)," *BLit* 64 (1991) 75-86. W. Zimmerli, "Zwillingspsalmen," in idem, *Studien zur*

229

*alttestamentlichen Theologie und Prophetie: Gesammelte Aufsätze* II (TBü 51; Munich: Kaiser, 1974) 261-71.

## Psalm 105:
## Hymn, Instruction

### Structure

|  | MT | NRSV |
|---|---|---|
| I. Summons to worship | 1-6 | 1-6 |
| A. Exhortations | 1-5 | 1-5 |
| B. Appellation | 6 | 6 |
| II. Praise of Yahweh acting in history | 7-45ab | 7-45ab |
| A. Covenant remembrance | 7-11 | 7-11 |
| 1. Confession | 7 | 7 |
| 2. Recitation | 8-10 | 8-10 |
| 3. Divine promise | 11 | 11 |
| B. Account of wanderings | 12-15 | 12-15 |
| C. Account of Joseph | 16-23 | 16-23 |
| D. Account of plagues | 24-36 | 24-36 |
| E. Account of exodus | 37-42 | 37-42 |
| F. Conclusion (gift of land) | 43-45ab | 43-45ab |
| III. Summons to praise | 45c | 45c |

The SUMMONS TO WORSHIP (vv. 1-6) is greatly extended in this psalm without a SUPERSCRIPTION (→ Psalms 71; 91; 93–97). Five lines are filled with imperatives demanding acts and attitudes of adoration and service to the Lord: "give thanks," "proclaim" (v. 1); "sing," "reflect" (v. 2); "praise," (be "joyful") (v. 3); "seek Yahweh," "look for him" (v. 4); "recall his marvelous deeds and words" (v. 5) — a good selection of relevant cultic proceedings and rituals. Small wonder that the last exhortation introduces the psalm as a whole, being, as it were, a communal act of worshiping remembrance (*zkr,* "remember"; Yahweh's remembrance is mentioned in vv. 8, 42; cf. W. Schottroff, *Gedenken;* listing at Additional Bibliography, section B). Only the last line of the section (v. 6, a distinct APPELLATION) reveals the addressees of all this calling to worship. Clearly, the early postexilic community is being exhorted; *zera' 'abrāhām* and *běnê ya'ăqōb* are popular designations of the Jewish community at that time; cf. Gen 13:16; 17:9-10; 22:17; 35:11-12; Josh 24:3; Isa 41:8; 45:19, 25; etc. (cf. H. D. Preuss, *TWAT* II, 663-86). The postexilic, lamenting community insists that "you [Yahweh] are our Father, though Abraham does not know us" (Isa 63:16; 64:7; cf. I. Fischer, *Wo ist Jahwe?* [Stuttgart: Katholisches Bibelwerk, 1989] 111-20, 193-98; T. Römer, *Väter;* Additional Bibliography, section B).

The corpus of the psalm, PRAISE OF YAHWEH (vv. 7-45ab), seems a well-reflected theological summary of parts of Israel's salvation history, leading to the bestowal of the land. The introduction (vv. 7-11) and conclusion (vv. 43-45ab) correspond at exactly this point, namely promise and gift of a homeland for God's people. The two parts envelop ACCOUNTS OF SACRED HISTORY, from the wanderings of the "arch-parents" (vv. 13-15; I. Fischer, *Die Erzeltern Israels* [BZAW 222; Berlin: de Gruyter, 1994]) through Joseph and plague stories to the exodus and desert wanderings (this last part in vv. 37-42). Naturally, we wonder, what parts of the canonical tradition does the psalmist draw on, how much of this historical overview may be taken from unknown sources, and which are the liturgical and theological interests patent in the specific composition of Psalm 105 (cf., e.g., Allen, Kraus)?

Fundamental for the community of faith is the covenant sealed with Abraham, Isaac, and Jacob (vv. 8-10). In a highly condensed theological INTRODUCTION this covenant is declared valid into the distant future of a thousand generations (v. 8; cf. Deut 5:10; 7:9) as the basis for Israel's existence and all her claims and obligations. The original foundation of this alliance is reported with a perfect form (v. 9: "he made," lit. "cut," the covenant with Abraham and Isaac; cf. Gen 15:17-19; 17:7-8, 19, 21). Then the relationship is transferred to Jacob (consecutive imperfect, v. 10; cf. Gen 28:3-4; 35:11-12, where the same transfer is stated). This means that vv. 8-10 are a precise summary of Genesis 15–35, taking as the main point the essential promise of Yahweh to give the "land" to the descendants of those ancestors. God's words are quoted verbatim, with introductory *lē'mōr,* "namely" (v. 11): "To you [singular] shall I give the land Canaan, as your [plural] hereditary lot." This phrase seems a condensed extract from the promises to Abraham and Isaac cited above. Especially Gen 17:8 contains all the necessary information extant in v. 11, being, however, a much more extensive, prosaic statement: "I will give to you, and to your descendants after you, the land of your sojournings, all the land of Canaan, for an everlasting possession; and I will be their God." Interestingly enough, the section under discussion is introduced by a confessional statement of the congregation, carrying the only explicit reference to the "we" group: "Yahweh is the one, *our* God" (v. 7a). Together with an acknowledgment of his supremacy (v. 7b) the line is a praising CONFESSION, and we may indeed think about giving this generic name to the passage as a whole. Contents are conducive to such a designation, because the "founding fathers" and the promise they received constitute prime material for Israel's basic affirmations. If this is true, vv. 7-11 are at least functionally to be compared to Deut 6:4-5, 20-24. Other parallels include Isa 63:16; Neh 9:7-8.

The HISTORICAL ACCOUNTS to follow in vv. 12-42 (v. 12 MT has third person plural, linking it to the following; 1 Chr 16:19 reads second person plural, thus tying it to v. 11) vary greatly in scope and elaboration of plot, but all of them seem to lean on Scripture in its final or near-final form. References to diverse parts and layers of Genesis are so numerous as to presuppose a later stage of redaction of the Pentateuch. At the same time the psalmist is still quite free to organize scriptural witness at will (cf. the sequence of plagues in vv. 28-36).

Israel's ancestral parents are pictured, even if briefly, in vv. 12-15. Their small number is implicitly the topic of all the Genesis narratives (cf. Gen 12:2; 15:2-5); it is finally stressed in Exod 1:5 at the end of that period of "wanderings." So we have a real retrospective evaluation of the "parents' stories" beginning with v. 12: a small group, the ancestors, "sojourned" in Canaan (*gûr* with all its legal implications and in juxtaposition to "possessing" is the central concept of this period in Genesis; cf. Gen 12:10; 20:1, 23, 34; 26:3; 32:5; 35:27; 47:4; D. Kellermann, *TWAT* I, 979-91; C. Bultmann, *Der Fremde im antiken Juda* [Göttingen: Vandenhoeck & Ruprecht, 1992]). The psalmist then sweepingly states (at the same time summarizing and interpreting literary traditions) their unrestful destiny moving from "nation to nation" (v. 13; a conceptualization dreadfully abused as recently as in Nazi propaganda: Jews are homeless, therefore unreliable and treacherous), emphasizing the special protection of Yahweh for his people (vv. 14-15). The first of these two lines probably refers to the salvation of Israel's ancestral mothers (cf. Fischer, *Die Erzeltern Israels*), significantly preceding protection for her menfolk (v. 15). Naming the fathers "anointed ones" and "prophets" also is an act of interpretation reverting, as it were, to Gen 20:7, where Abraham is called "prophet." From a later perspective and after the failure of the monarchy, the highest honorary titles were "prophet" (as interpreter of *tôrāh*) and "anointed" as the coming ruler of the kingdom of God (cf. Pss 2:2; 18:51 [RSV 50]; 28:8; 84:10 [RSV 9]; 89:39, 52 [RSV 38, 51]; 132:10, 17). Divine guidance and shelter thus receive highest attention in this small section on ancestral parents. And the little summary of Genesis stories is geared to the possession of the land of the fathers (v. 12) (cf. Römer, *Väter;* Blum, *Studien;* Köckert, *Vätergott;* Mathias, *Gottesvolk* — all in Additional Bibliography, section B), a typical theme in exilic and postexilic writings.

Much more space and attention is given to the Joseph cycle (Genesis 37–50) and the plagues and exodus stories (Exodus 1–17; subsequently dealt with in vv. 16-41). But the closing line of these lengthy expositions again refers back to Abraham, to whom all promises were first given (v. 42). Father Abraham thus is overtly a special figure for early Jewish identity, encompassing the whole salvation history (vv. 6, 9, 42; cf. John 8:37-40; Gal 3:6-9; R. E. Clements, *TWAT* I, 53-62; J. van Seters, *Abraham in History and Tradition* [New Haven: Yale University Press, 1975]).

The historical part is of epic broadness. Some narrational verb forms (imperfect consecutive: vv. 16, 20, 23, 24, 29, 33, 35-37) communicate this impression. The question arises how close our psalm keeps to the pentateuchal sources. If indeed the authors or transmitters of the psalm did have access to the written books, they certainly selected only a few aspects of the full stories, condensing and interpreting them rather freely. There are hardly any traits not present in the writings we know. Thus Joseph's being put into "irons" (v. 18) is not mentioned in Gen 39:20, but seems to be gleaned from psalmic traditions (cf. Pss 107:10; 149:8). Literary creativity can be observed in vv. 21-22 when compared with Gen 41:43-46 (Joseph's renewed installation as vice-regent), or vv. 28-36 viewed in concordance with Exodus 7–11 (the plagues). In both cases, the subject matter of the exodus stories is present, but the psalmist's formulations, as well as, e.g., the sequence of the plagues, are quite independent of the pentateuchal sources. They possibly betray their origin in early Jewish communities (cf. designation of the people as *ʿăbādîm*, "servants," v. 25; cf. Pss 34:23

[RSV 22]; 69:37 [RSV 36]; 79:2, 10; 89:51 [RSV 50]; 90:13, 16; 102:29 [RSV 28]; 113:1; 123:2; 134:1; 135:1, 9, 14). Many more details prove the interpretive reworking of original accounts by psalmists and their congregations, e.g., in v. 20b ("ruler of nations" is a title befitting Persian great kings; cf. allusions to that period in 2 Chr 9:26; 20:6), v. 22 ("instruction" is probably extrapolated from Jewish communities), v. 25 (new vocabulary in comparison to Exod 1:6-14), vv. 32-33 ("hail" instead of "their" normal "rain" corresponds to Judean climatic conditions, as well as arboriculture of "vine" and "figs"; notably, Exod 9:25 reports destruction only of "humans," "cattle," "greenery," and "trees" in general), v. 42 ("holy word" for the promise to Abraham reflects late theological usage).

Epic accounts of Israel's salvation history are part of the hymnic tradition (cf. Psalms 78; 106; 132; 135) but also of some collective complaints (cf. Psalms 44; 89). Emergence of the people of Yahweh in Egypt, dramatic memories of the exodus from the west (excluding, however, Sinaitic events; cf. Exodus 19–24, which irritated many modern scholars already), giving of the land as the high point of a long story — all these items of sacred history were of enormous importance for that community of Judahites which subsisted in Babylonian and Persian times under political and economic pressures hardly to be underestimated. The gift of the land, a dream to be fulfilled anew ever since Second Isaiah preached release and return from captivity, is the focus in the final section of the psalm (vv. 43-45). Yahweh himself leads his people to freedom (v. 43; chronologically, the exodus has been reported already in v. 37) and fulfills his promise by handing over to them the territory that the Babylonian exiles yearn for (v. 44), so that they may stick to "ordinances" and "rules" given by him (v. 45). To live in the promised land and to be under the direction of Yahweh's Torah is the highest blessing imaginable for the psalmist.

The whole song ends in a shout of joy and adoration: "Hallelujah!" just like Psalms 104 and 106. This special expression of praise to Yahweh here may be an original piece of liturgy. It is conceivable, however, that the collector or redactor of this section of psalms put in the hallelujah as a kind of liturgical comment and praise. Textual uncertainties as well as a somewhat awkward connection of the shout with the body of the psalm (cf. 104:35cd; 106:48, the latter verse clearly being a redactional divider of "books") may point in that direction.

For our purposes it is important to visualize a possible liturgical sequence of the elements just described. The SUMMONS TO PRAISE (or to WORSHIP) is a regular introductory part of collective hymns (cf. "Introduction to Cultic Poetry," section 4D). The most natural setup would be a leader of ceremonies calling on the congregation to extol the Deity. In our case the assembly apparently does respond: "He is Yahweh, our God, his justice is throughout the earth" (v. 7). The first person plural stands for the people in worship ($\rightarrow$ Psalm 95). Perhaps after this confessional line the congregation recited, bicolon by bicolon, the highly important summary and apex of salvation history, the covenant story (vv. 8-10), the theme of many a pentateuchal text (cf. Genesis 15; 17; Exodus 19–20; 24:1-9; etc.). This section ends with a verbal quotation (marked by the introductory formula: "saying") of divine promise of land, in direct address to the congregation: "To you I shall give the land of Canaan, as your portion for an inheritance" (v. 11). This formula certainly goes back to promises to the parents of Israel as preserved in the book of Genesis (cf. Köckert, *Vätergott*) and — in a liturgical context — was spoken by an officiant. The section as a whole amounts to a COVENANT REMEMBRANCE topic also of some Dtr chapters (cf. Deuteronomy 29–30; Joshua 24). The ACCOUNTS OF SACRED HISTORY, in narrative episodes, poetically condensed, were supposedly presented by special lecturers functioning like Ezra in Neh 8:3. The conclusion (vv. 42-45ab), aiming at exhortative extrapolation (v. 45ab), may have been part of this historical remembering. A final SUMMONS TO PRAISE, even if different from the introductory summons (v. 45c), was sung by the assembly.

Literary analyses concentrate on the textual basis, coming up with similar divisions and with intricate semantic and syntactic cross-references and intertextual relations; cf., e.g., Auffret (overview of subdivisions, pp. 9-10). Hardly any scholar, however, wants to cling exclusively to a literary description of the text (cf. Mowinckel, *W* II, 112: noncultic, learned psalmography). Most interpreters think of some kind of liturgical use (cf., e.g., Baumgärtel, Weiser, Clifford, Allen, Seybold). The quotation of our psalm in 1 Chr 16:8-22, an account of hymnic temple worship, helps to foster this view.

## Genre/Setting

The extensive hymnic part in vv. 1-11 clearly manifests the juxtaposition of a liturgical speaker, summoning a congregation to give thanks and praise to Israel's God Yahweh, and the worshiping community. The congregation addressed is even named "seed of Abraham, his servant," and "sons of Jacob, his elected" (v. 6), apparently with high honorific titles. This same body of worshipers takes up the summons to praise with a confessional response: "He, Yahweh, is our God; his rules govern the whole world" (v. 7). Vv. 8-11, on the other hand, seem to introduce the accounts of sacred history, as outlined above. Together with vv. 42-45 they envelop the strict historical scenes of vv. 12-41. A certain hiatus of both blocks of material may be seen in the heavy preoccupation with Abraham and Jacob on the side of the "envelope" and with Joseph and the exodus on the side of the "historical body" of the psalm. We also noted that the exodus is mentioned twice, in vv. 37 and 43, the latter occurrence being out of line with the sequence of events. Taken together, vv. 8-11 and 42-45 also could form a more original hymn of the congregation, dealing with the promises to the ancestral fathers, who sealed the covenant with Yahweh, received the ordinances to live by (v. 10), and heard the promise of a sacred homeland (v. 11). Exactly this promise is the content of the hymnic line v. 42: "Yes, he remembered his holy word, his servant Abraham." Then vv. 43-44 are perfectly in line with the thrust of vv. 8-11, and the great historical inclusion from the early roamings of the fathers in Canaan to the miracle in the wilderness (vv. 12-41) makes a colorful historical weaving to illustrate Yahweh's further interventions to secure the land for his people. From a generic point of view, a compact hymn of or for the people assembled in worship, comprising vv. 8-11 and 42-45,

234

makes more liturgical sense than does an elaboration of endless, meticulous details of written sacred history. The latter, consequently, may have been put in
not only for illustration but also for teaching or preaching purposes
(Wolverton). As a marginal note we may pay attention to 1 Chr 16:8-22, which
is a quote of our vv. 1-15, indicating at least a liturgical viability to separate the
story of Abraham and Jacob from the exodus part in vv. 16-41. Cf. "Introduction to Cultic Poetry," section 4D.

## Intention

The hymnic introduction (vv. 1-6) and the congregation's response (v. 7), together with a possible original praise of Yahweh's promise, deliverance, and
gift of covenant and homeland (vv. 8-11, 42-45), were full of thanksgiving and
eulogy celebrating the fundamental beliefs of the early Jewish congregations.
At the present stage of textual and liturgical development the accounts of Genesis and Exodus stories have come in purporting to give more detailed instruction as to the beginnings of Yahweh's history with his Abrahamite and Jacobite
people. They additionally enumerate historical events known from Scripture,
interpreting them with some liberty and without being too particular, e.g., about
the "canonical" sequence of the plagues. Still, they want to inform the congregation; they possibly want to correct a little the one-sided emphasis on Abraham and Jacob, introducing, as it were, Joseph, Moses, and Aaron as protagonists of some importance. Their narrational, and perhaps scribal, zeal is linked
to didactic or instructional finalities. Seybold, summarizing the objectives of
the psalm, declares: "The aim and purpose of the worship service involved is a
reflection on the wondrous and salvific acts of Yahweh in past history" (v. 5;
*Psalmen*, 415).

## Bibliography

P. Auffret, *Essai sur la structure littéraire du Psaume 105* (*BN* Beiheft 3; Munich: Görg,
1985); F. Baumgärtel, "Zur Liturgie in der 'Sektenrolle' vom Toten Meer," *ZAW* 65
(1953) 263-65; T. Booij, "The Role of Darkness in Psalm CV,28," *VT* 39 (1989) 209-14;
J. Brinktrine, "Zur Übersetzung von Ps 105 (104), 18," *ZAW* 64 (1952) 251-58; A. R.
Ceresko, "A Poetic Analysis of Ps 105, with Attention to Its Use of Irony," *Bib* 64 (1983)
20-46; R. J. Clifford, "Style and Purpose in Psalm 105," *Bib* 60 (1979) 420-27; G. Coats,
"Despoiling the Egyptians," *VT* 18 (1968) 450-57; F. C. Fensham, "Neh 9 and Pss 105;
106; 135; and 136," *JNSL* 9 (1981) 35-51; N. Füglister, "Psalm 105 und die Väterver-
heissung," in *Die Väter Israels* (ed. A. Müller, et al.; Stuttgart: Katholisches Bibelwerk,
1989) 41-59; E. Hilgert, "The Dual Image of Joseph in Hebrew and Early Jewish Literature," *BR* 30 (1985) 5-21; S. Holm-Nielsen, "The Exodus-Tradition in Psalm 105," *ASTI*
11 (1977/78) 22-30; A. Lauha, *Die Geschichtsmotive in den alttestamentlichen Psalmen*
(Helsinki: Finnische Literaturgesellschaft, 1945); A. C. O. Lee, "Genesis 1 and the
Plagues Tradition in Ps CV," *VT* 40 (1990) 257-64; G. C. Lindeque and A. P. B. Breytenbach, "'n vertelkundige ontleding van Psalm 105 met besondere verwysing na die

funksie van vertelde ruimte," *HerTS* 47 (1991) 415-30; B. Margulis, "The Plague Tradition in Ps 105," *Bib* 50 (1969) 491-96; D. Muñoz Leon, "El IV de Esdras y el Targum Palestinense: Las cuatro últimas visiones," *EstBib* 42 (1984) 5-20; T. G. Smothers, "A Superior Model: Hebrews 1:1–4:13," *RevExp* 82 (1985) 333-43; M. Wittenberg, "Aspekte israelitischer Geschichtsbetrachtung in den Psalmen 105-107," in *Kontinuität im Umbruch* (*Fest.* Augustana Hochschule; ed. W. Andersen; Munich: Claudius, 1972) 23-50; W. J. Wolverton, "Sermons in the Psalms," *CJT* 10 (1964) 166-76; W. Zimmerli, "Zwillingspsalmen" (listing at Psalm 104).

## Psalm 106:
## Communal Confession of Guilt; Hymnic Instruction

### *Structure*

|  |  | MT | NRSV |
|---|---|---|---|
| I. | Introduction | 1-7c | 1-7c |
|  | A. Summons to give thanks | 1 | 1 |
|  | B. Rhetorical question | 2 | 2 |
|  | C. Felicitation, beatitude | 3 | 3 |
|  | D. Petition | 4-5 | 4-5 |
|  | E. Confession of guilt | 6-7c | 6-7c |
| II. | Accounts of failures and deliverances | 7d-39 | 7d-39 |
|  | A. Salvation at the Sea of Reeds | 7d-12 | 7d-12 |
|  | B. Rebellion in the wilderness | 13-15 | 13-15 |
|  | C. Uprising of Korah's clan | 16-18 | 16-18 |
|  | D. The golden calf | 19-23 | 19-23 |
|  | E. Inspection of Canaan | 24-27 | 24-27 |
|  | F. Consulting Baal of Peor | 28-31 | 28-31 |
|  | G. Murmurs at Meribah | 32-33 | 32-33 |
|  | H. Sparing the inhabitants | 34-36 | 34-36 |
|  | I. Sacrificing children | 37-39 | 37-39 |
| III. | Summary | 40-46 | 40-46 |
|  | A. Banishment from the land | 40-42 | 40-42 |
|  | B. Repeated acts of mercy | 43-46 | 43-46 |
| IV. | Petition and vow | 47 | 47 |
| V. | Blessing and communal response | 48 | 48 |

The traditional division of the Psalter into five books takes Psalm 106 as the last song of book 4 and v. 48 as a dividing device of redactional origin (cf. similar additions to the text in 41:14 [RSV 13]; 72:18-20; 89:53 [RSV 52]). The BLESSING FORMULA in v. 48ab is a standard one (→ 28:6; 72:18-20), and the response of the congregation saying "Amen, Amen," also appears sometimes in this book-dividing function (cf. 41:14 [RSV 13]; 72:19; 89:53 [RSV 52]: in all these cases the summons to the audience "all the people say" [only here, v. 48c] is missing in MT [i.e., Codex Leningradensis], while the asseverative shout "amen" is doubled). "Hallelujah," on the other hand, seems an accretion typical of the group Psalms 105–106, where affiliation of the shout with the beginning or end of a psalm remains uncertain (LXX in our case links *hallĕlûyāh* with 107:1). Why this lively and liturgical interlude between two psalm books? It seems so unlike scribal customs; scribes obviously prefer archival notes like colophons on clay tablets (cf. H. Hunger, *Babylonische und assyrische Kolophone* [AOAT 2; Neukirchen: Neukirchener Verlag, 1968]) or Masoretic remarks in Hebrew Scripture (cf. G. E. Weil, ed., *Massorah Gedolah* [Rome/Stuttgart: Institutum Pontificium/Societas Biblica Virtenberg-ensis, 1971]). The evidence suggests a certain affinity of the redactional processes of the Psalter to liturgical agendas. That means that the Psalter was used in worship services of old, perhaps not only as far as the individual texts go but even in blocks of material (as reading pericopes as in 105:12-41? cf. Zenger, listing at Psalm 107, etc.).

The opening of the psalm, we assume, occurred with a shout of praise, "Hallelujah!" (v. 1a; E. Gerstenberger and B. Lang, *NBL* II, 18-19). This exclamation does not occur in the Psalter before 104:35 (see also 105:45), and we mentioned already the uncertainty in regard to its exact location at the beginning or end of a given psalm. Now, 106:1 is the first example of this shout opening a collective song to be followed by a whole range of alike overtures (cf. Psalms 111–113; 117; 135; 146–150). "Hallelujah" in all the cases mentioned stands quite isolated; it may have been intoned by a choir or the gathered assembly of faithful, more probably by an officiant leading the worship ceremony.

The INTRODUCTION of the psalm (vv. 1b-7c) combines a mixture of forms and affirmations. The first full line (v. 1bc) uses a common hymnic or thanksgiving introduction identical to that of 107:1; 118:1; 136:1. Such a line in itself already constitutes a little HYMN: a liturgist summons his people to "render thanks," and the congregation responds with the shortest possible praise: "yes, his solidarity endures forever." Second, a wondering exclamation is voiced, a rhetorical question full of admiration (v. 2), as often in hymnic contexts (cf. 8:2, 10 [RSV 1, 9]; 36:8 [RSV 7]; 66:3; 92:6 [RSV 5]; 104:24). The liturgist is the most likely orator of a line like this, and the same may be true for the following FELICITATION (v. 3). The phrase introduced by "happy the one" is mostly used to congratulate individuals (cf. 1:1; 32:1-2; 34:9 [RSV 8]; 40:5 [RSV 4]; 84:6, 13 [RSV 5, 12]; 94:12; 127:5; 128:1-2; Prov 3:13; 8:34; 28:14; etc.). A strong minority of felicitations is directed to a group of people or an assembly, however (cf. Pss 2:12; 33:12; 84:5 [RSV 4]; 89:16 [RSV 15]; 119:1-2; 144:15). But there are texts with changing addressees (e.g., Psalm 84), showing the same flexibility as our v. 3, which has a plural in the first and a singular (some MSS plural) in the second colon. The evidence permits the following conclusion: The form served originally in private contexts to pronounce a sort of blessing over individuals (→ Ps 1:1; 119:1-2). It was adapted to congregational life, that is, to the collective religious sphere, to indicate the blessed state of the community (BEATITUDE; note the expressions "keep righteousness" and "do justice," drawn into the context of faith in Yahweh [vv. 1-2] in v. 3). Within the community, according to its individualizing structure in which every member was responsible in person to his or her God, the singular comes back (→ 33:12; 146:5).

So far, we are listening to the voice of one liturgist (or more) who acts in front of a congregation (vv. 1-3) summoning the assembly to give thanks, to acknowledge the unsurpassable greatness of their God, and pronouncing the bliss of the faithful upon them. What about vv. 4-5, a clear PETITION, as if taken from a complaint setting? The MT has two clear singular suffixes in v. 4 ("remember me," "help me"), while ancient versions (and a good part of modern translations), perhaps impressed by references in v. 6, read the plural instead ("remember us," etc.). Obviously, an inner tension exists in v. 4, too. Literally, the first colon runs: "Remember me by [through?] the favor of your people." Does this mean to say, ". . . because/when you are favorable to your people"? In this case an individual suppliant pleads for mercy on account of the privileged position of the community. This interpretation is corroborated by the three infinitives of v. 5 that all visualize participation in the blessings of the people of Yahweh. The community is designated by high-flung names: "Your elected ones" (*bĕḥîrîm:* plural of the congregation only in 105:6, 43; 1 Chr 16:13 [= Ps 105:6]; Isa 65:9, 15, 22; otherwise, a prominent individual is called "elected" by this choice designation; cf. 2 Sam 21:6; Isa 42:1; 43:20; 45:4). This means that two texts are the principal bearers of this concept of an "elected plurality of faithful," i.e., descendants of Jacob: Psalm 105 and Isaiah 65, with Psalm 106 perhaps being dependent on both passages. The second honorific name is "your nation" (*gôy;* the word was used for Israel in certain epochs and layers of tradition; cf. P. Hanson, *The People Called* [San Francisco: Harper & Row, 1986]; R. E. Clements, *TWAT* I, 965-73; it occurs in various contexts and connotations; cf. Deut 4:7-8 [important passages of Deuteronomy use *'am,* however; cf. Deut 7:6]; Isa 26:2; Exod 19:6 [in contrast to Deut 7:6: *gôy qādôš*]; etc.). In direct connection with Yahweh, however, *gôy* is rarely used. Thus personal suffixes attached to *gôy* and relating to Yahweh occur only in Ps 106:5 and Zeph 2:9 (in parallelism with *'am*). The third expression, in an overlong, three-cola line, is "your heritage" (v. 5c: *naḥălāh*), used mostly for the land of Israel or Yahweh (cf. E. Lipínski, *TWAT* V, 342-60). The phrase is structured differently, though. Instead of an infinitive plus a construct cluster prefixed by the preposition *bĕ,* this third part has only an infinitive with a simple noun, introduced by the preposition *'im.* These features may indicate later accretion. On the whole, therefore, vv. 4-5 constitute a liturgical interlude, a special PETITION, pleading for the individual member's entrance into the community of faithful.

In terms of form-critical and liturgical arrangement the INTRODUCTION, at least as far as vv. 1-5 are concerned, looks somewhat fragmented and forlorn. Seybold (pp. 421-22) holds that these verses, a conglomerate of four sayings, really close off the preceding Psalm 105. Our text, in this case, would begin only with the collective confession of guilt (v. 6). Of course, transmission of written texts may lead to alterations. Thus the felicitation in v. 3 may have originated as a scribal annotation at the margin of the scroll (for a comprehensive view of beatitudes cf. Janzen, listing at "Introduction to Psalms"). On the other hand, we do not know the details of worship liturgies in early Judaism. The individual voices of vv. 1-5 may in fact have constituted elements of a ceremonial agenda. We simply cannot tell. And the diversity of forms testifies more against than in favor of literary composition. Ps 78:1-4, after all, proved to be an extraordinary introduction of a "historical" hymn, too, presenting the teacher and leader of the congregation in his role as instructor.

The following part, in contradistinction, is explicitly communal in form and outlook. "We" references abound in vv. 6-7a; direct address to Yahweh prevails in v. 7a-c. Form and content make v. 6 a classical, triadic CONFESSION OF GUILT. The closest parallels are 1 Kgs 8:47 and Dan 9:5, 15, where, in a larger context of acknowledging God's grace, which overcomes just punishments, the same kind of confession is voiced with four and two verbs, respectively: "We have erred, sinned . . ." (ḥṭ'; rš'; the third verb is relatively rare: 'wh, Qal and Hiphil; cf. 2 Sam 7:14; 19:20; 24:17). The same spirit of contrite submission is extant also in Ezra's great confession of sin (cf. Ezra 9:6-7, 10-11, 15). The formulaic expression "We have erred" (with ḥṭ' in the perfect) has 24 occurrences in the Hebrew canon, most of them in Dtr layers of literature (cf., e.g., Deut 1:41; Judg 10:10, 15; 1 Sam 7:6; 12:10; Jer 3:25; 8:14; 14:7, 20; 16:10). Tendencies to accumulate articulations of "sin" point to a later, more spiritualized theological thinking (cf. Num 12:11; Jer 16:10). The outright tripartite formula of v. 6 we find in only two other passages: 1 Kgs 8:47 (= 2 Chr 6:37) and Dan 9:5 (cf. Knierim, Hauptbegriffe; listing at "Introduction to Psalms").

The concept of sinning "together" with the ancestors (v. 6a) is common in ancient Near Eastern genealogical thinking. Ezra 9:7 puts it this way: "From the time of our fathers until this very day we have been in great culpability." According to the LXX, Isa 64:4 runs: "We have sinned against you from time immemorial," and Dan 9:16 laments the disgrace of Jerusalem contracted "on account of our sins and the misdeeds of our fathers." Of course, late, Dtr historical writings attribute the defeat at the hands of the Assyrians and Babylonians to accumulated guilt (cf. 2 Kgs 17:7-23; 23:26-27; 24:3-4). V. 7, in any case, elaborates on the theme of "our fathers"; it thus may be understood either as an exposition of v. 6a or as an introduction to vv. 7d-39. Because of the direct address to God in v. 7a-c, and absolutely neutral, narrative (consecutive imperfect) style in vv. 7d-39, I want to draw a line between vv. 6-7c and 7d-39. The former passage is formally and theologically "we" discourse, prayer, and confession of guilt, while the latter must be classified as epos, historical narrative, and exemplary illustration.

With this we turn to the ACCOUNTS of failures and deliverances outlined above (vv. 7d-39). The predominant verbal tense is the consecutive imperfect, the narrative form par excellence. In general, the psalm chooses specific incidents of the exodus and wilderness traditions, reports on Israel's failure to respond to Yahweh in a fitting, i.e., faithful, manner, and continues to narrate the unexpected merciful and kind reactions of Israel's God. The same general pattern comes to the fore in Psalm 78 even to the point of considering temporary, severe castigation of Israel through defeat and exile a means of divine education (cf. vv. 40-42; 78:59-64). In the same vein, the great communal confessions of guilt in Ezra 9, Nehemiah 9, and Daniel 9 stress the unbelievable contrast between Israel's negligence and apostasies and Yahweh's merciful longanimity (cf. also Psalm 103). In this particular scheme of sin and grace, we encounter a firm, exilic pattern of prayer oscillating between praising God and blaming the community of faith.

The first of nine segments (vv. 7d-12) clearly refers to the exodus event itself, as we read it in Exodus 14–15. Indeed, according to some source (is it the Yahwistic or the Priestly layer? or just a tradition-historical redaction? cf. van Seters, "Reformulation"; Blum, *Studien,* Additional Bibliography, section B), the people are clamoring, full of fear and lacking essential trust in their God (Exod 14:11-12). The term used to describe the rebellious act (*mrh,* "be obstinate") does not occur in the book of Exodus; it seems to be concentrated in Deuteronomy, Ezekiel 20, Psalms 78 and 106 (cf. vv. 33, 43). Anyhow, emphasis in this exodus scene is on Yahweh's gracious saving act (vv. 8-11), exposed in some detail with vocabulary partially uncommon to the written story of the exodus, at least to the prose version of Exodus 14 (e.g., God "chides" the sea and lets Israel pass through "the chaos flood" in v. 9: the language is reminiscent of mythological tales; cf. Nah 1:4; Gen 1:1; Exod 15:5; the designation of "foes" in v. 10 derives from history writing and complaints; cf., however, Exod 15:6, 9 for *'ôyēb,* "enemy"; the principal verb of v. 11, *ksh,* Piel, "cover," occurs twice in Exod 15:5, 10; that "not a single one" of the Egyptians survived is said in Exod 14:28). The final line of the exodus passage, featuring Israel's reaction to that wonderous salvation, seems to point to Exod 14:31 (v. 12a; "they believed") and to Exod 15:21 or 15:1-18 (v. 12b; "they sang his praise"), the latter being more probable, taking into account the affinities of vocabulary already mentioned.

The incidents to follow (vv. 13-39) for the most part deal with Israel's wanderings in the desert as reported in Exodus 16–18 and Numbers 11–36. The sequence of events is neither chronological nor thematic. Apparently, the psalmist only wanted to give the impression of repeated apostasy and disobedience, and an even more insistent repetition of God's benevolent interventions and corrections. Vv. 13-15 lean on Num 11:4-6, 31-35, with v. 13 giving an introductory evaluation of the fathers' negligence, v. 14 quoting the main points of accusation ("craving" for food; "testing" God), and v. 15 telling how Yahweh fulfilled their desires, at the same time punishing the greedy ones. The short passage is much in the line of Ps 78:17-31. But why is it so reduced in size? Does the psalmist or liturgist who recited the text count on everybody's knowledge of the tradition?

Another group of three lines makes up the next subunit (vv. 16-18). This time the event referred to is that of Numbers 16, the uprising against Moses and Aaron by some Levites, among them Dathan and Abiram. These four names are even mentioned in vv. 16-17, a rare occasion within any genre of psalms. Psalm 106 has the only reference to Dathan and Abiram in the Psalter; even inside the Pentateuch, except for Deut 11:6, the two names are mentioned only in Numbers 16. That v. 18 adds punishment by burning, after the culprits have been swallowed by the earth already, may be a conscious reference to the parallel story in Lev 10:2. In short, contesting the supreme authority of Moses and Aaron (and their successors, of course) among the people of Yahweh is a criminal offense of grave consequences. Therefore annihilation of the evildoers is a reward for the righteous.

Next come vv. 19-23, with a resumé of the golden calf story (cf. Exodus 32). Here the reaction of Yahweh is not sheer love and forgiveness, but wrath and aggression, stopped only by the intervention of Moses standing "in the breach" to protect the people (cf. Ezek 22:20). Veneration of the calf is ridiculed in v. 20 in the manner of Second Isaiah (cf. Isa 40:18-25; 44:9-20). The description of the incident is neutral (v. 19), changing into a reproach (v. 20; *mûr*, Hiphil, "exchange their glory"; cf. Jer 2:11; Hos 4:7), and then into outright accusation (vv. 21-22; "they forgot their Savior-God"; cf. Pss 50:22; 78:11; frequently in Dtr circles: Deut 8:14; Judg 3:7; 1 Sam 12:9; Jer 2:32; 3:21; also in Isa 17:10; Jer 23:27. "Forget," *škḥ*, is tantamount to "forsake," "break off relations"). The matter the people has been leaving behind is described by God's "great deeds," "wondrous works," "terrible feats" — very general, i.e.: theologically loaded designations of God's actions in favor of Israel (cf., e.g., in the book of Psalms: *gĕdōlôt*, 71:19; *niplā'ôt*, 9:2 [RSV 1]; 26:7; 71:17; 72:18; 75:2 [RSV 1]; 78:4, 11; 96:3; 98:1; 105:5; 107:8, 15, 21, 24, 31; *nôrā'ôt*, 65:6 [RSV 5]).

Rejecting the gift of the land (v. 24) is obviously an allusion to the tradition of Numbers 14, where the Israelites refuse to obey the counsel of the spies to go ahead with the invasion of Canaan (vv. 24-27; cf. Num 14:7-9). A shortened version of this story has been transmitted in Deut 1:24-27, including even that conspicuous expression of v. 25: "murmuring in one's tents" (the finite verb *rgn*, Niphal, "mumble," only in these two passages), which is absent from Numbers 13–14. The outcome of such detachment is all but benevolence from the side of Yahweh. He kindles his terrible wrath, kills his people in the desert, and expels them from the promised land (vv. 26-27). This course of events is totally anachronistic in the sense of canonical narration. We have here a case of theological condensation of history: exilic deportations are joined together with frustrated entrance into the land (Num 14:30; Deut 1:35; cf. Lev 26:33; Ezek 20:23) to make up a single and definite divine castigation for "despising" this highest gift of Yahweh, in the eyes of the exiles. The psalmist is clearly interpreting Scripture traditions from his remote angle.

A more friendly conclusion — at least for the majority involved — is reported in regard to Israel's apostasy to Baal of Peor (vv. 28-31; cf. Num 25:1-13, esp. v. 2; Deut 4:3). Phinehas, because of his zeal for Yahweh, becomes a hero, and a great example of a truly faithful follower (cf. Abraham in Gen 15:6; the declarative phrases are nearly identical: "it was reckoned to him as righteousness"). Phinehas is even to be a prototype "for generations without end" (cf. v. 31b), an idealization not found elsewhere in the canon. Again, we witness profound interpretive theological thinking in Psalm 106.

Only two lines refer to Israel's remonstration at Massah and Meribah (vv. 32-33; cf. Num 20:3-13; Exod 17:1-7; Pss 81:8 [RSV 7]; 95:8). Since there is nothing but the event itself alluded to — and no divine reaction visible — the scene seems incomplete or fragmentary. As it stands now, the text emphasizes the imagined pain of Moses, who has to bear the brunt of Israel's resistance against Yahweh. Moses' "talking rashly" (v. 33b; *bṭ'*, Piel, occurs just one more time, in Lev 5:4) is an interpretation gleaned from Exod 17:4, considered an improper discourse in the face of God, rather than from Numbers 20. Possibly,

Moses is censured a little more in Psalm 106 than Aaron, who gains the extremely honorific title of "holy one of Yahweh" in v. 16, balanced in v. 23 by the eulogy to Moses, "his elected one."

With vv. 32-33 open-ended the narration of concrete biblical episodes peters out. What follows in vv. 34-39 are two general examples of deviant behavior. The passages are close to Dtr teaching or preaching. Thus vv. 34-36 focus on "not having exterminated the inhabitants of the land." The divine commandment to do so is listed, e.g., in Exod 34:11-16; Deut 7:1-5; 12:1-3; affirmations of nonfulfillment are found in Joshua 9; Judg 1:17-35; 2:23–3:6. On the other hand, vv. 37-39 thematize the sacrifice of sons and daughters according to the alleged ways of the Canaanites. This topic is prefigured, e.g., in Lev 18:21; 20:2-5; Deut 18:10; 2 Kgs 16:3; 17:17; Jer 7:30-31; 19:5. These sermonizing summaries, in consequence, seem to presuppose both Dtr and Priestly writings and to interpret sample items.

Consecutive imperfects continue also through vv. 40-46, two segments of the psalm that summarize all that has been said before, driving home the lesson of this epos. The vocabulary is traditional and well in line with the historical accounts. The pattern adopted — sin of Israel and redemption of Yahweh — is common in the Psalter as well as in the historical parts of the Pentateuch. Nevertheless, this SUMMARY and evaluation of historical accounts offers the opportunity to the psalmist to pronounce more lucidly his concerns. The first subunit (vv. 40-42) accounts for the disaster of foreign domination presumably experienced after the Babylonians captured Judah, leading only to the Persian yoke thereafter. No names are mentioned any more; the situation must have been understood by hearers of the psalm or participants in assemblies. V. 43 is a crucial interpretive line. It appears overlong; perhaps the third, textually uncertain colon had been a gloss once to indicate the presence of stern judgments of Yahweh, thus highlighting passages like vv. 24-27. The first two cola testify only to Yahweh's unfounded mercy when once again helping his querulous people. But it is exactly this continuing help and forgiveness that is being focused on in vv. 44-46. Yahweh is seen as being mindful of the community's crying out for deliverance (v. 44; cf. Exod 3:7-8; Ps 12:6 [RSV 5]). He remembers his covenant (v. 45a; cf. v. 4; 25:6; 98:3; 105:5, 42). The only passages in the psalms where "remember" *(zākar)* has the object *běrît,* "covenant," though, are 105:8; 106:45; 111:5. The expression is more prosaic and homiletical, it seems; cf. Gen 9:15-16; Lev 26:42, 45; Ezek 16:60, and perhaps taken into some liturgical texts from there. Yahweh's final act in the narrational parts is described in v. 46: "He gave them over to mercy, before all their captors." Does this really mean to say: "He caused them to be pitied by all those who held them captive"? Perhaps *rahămîm,* "mercy," signals the mercy of Yahweh that operates through their overlords, as indeed is the case, with much the same wording, in 1 Kgs 8:50.

The final part of our psalm is without doubt a communal PETITION. Direct-address prayer style immediately gets our attention; it corresponds to the form of vv. 6-7c. First-person plural suffixes reveal the supplicating congregation; second-person singular suffixes indicate the addressee, Yahweh. Two imperatives urge him to deliver his people, as if vv. 44-46 had not just been spoken. The liturgical reality, however, permits or even demands such juxtapositions: certitude of God's saving intervention and immediately afterward strong petition for deliverance from evil. Petition having been voiced, the last line of the psalm proper visualizes, with two infinitives, the purpose of keeping God's people alive: the result is the glory of Yahweh and the triumph of the congregation involved in hymn singing (*šbḥ*, Hithpael, "to boast of," only in this verse and in its copy at 1 Chr 16:35).

As already indicated, v. 48 is a hymnic marker of the end of a collection (Psalms 90–106), the so-called fourth book of psalms. It has to be evaluated together with 41:14; 72:18-20; 89:53, which are very similar in form, vocabulary, and content, serving the same divider function. 1 Chr 16:34-36, however, shows that the division of psalm texts was not so clear-cut as one might wish. The passage there is a composition of Pss 105:1-15 + 96 + 106:1 (or 107:1, or 136:1) + 106:47-48. Obviously, vv. 47-48 of our psalm are taken to be a unit, but we cannot be sure whether the Chronicler considered it to be the last part of an extensive composition, a psalm all by itself, or a dividing text between two psalm "books."

Although we face difficulties in trying to recognize liturgical procedures in Psalm 106, the worship structure still seems to be the best explanation of the poem. CONFESSION OF GUILT by the congregation sets the tone (vv. 6-7c); historical remembrance here becomes the showcase of pitfalls for the congregation, to be overcome by the grace of God (contrast Psalms 105 and 136, where the covenant stays a firm and steady light for the people; parallels: Psalm 78; Ezra 9; Nehemiah 9; Daniel 9; cf. Kessler). With all this, history becomes the material for INSTRUCTION (cf. McCann, "Psalms," Additional Bibliography, section C; Kühlewein, *Geschichte,* Additional Bibliography, section C; Mathias, *Gottesvolk,* Additional Bibliography, section B).

## Genre

Our long text contains a diversity of genre elements and is far from being homogeneous, form-critically speaking. A preliminary issue in the genre discussion is the use of Scripture in the text, recognized in all relevant studies on the psalm. Are we dealing with a mere scribal compilation of chance references to the ancient traditions of the exodus? Use of Scripture is evident, just as in Psalms 78 and 105. But we must not project our scrapbook habits of accumulating random texts for private purposes into the ancient world. Psalms, to be sure, have been composed and collected for liturgical reasons. This hermeneutical guideline is valid also for scribal compilations. Therefore we should look for clues in the realm of liturgical structure and composition. The opening part (vv. 1-7c) is hymnic, petitionary, and confessional in character, being matched by the closing verse (v. 47). In between these "corner posts" is a long, didactic elaboration of exemplary failures and deliverances in Israel's early history. Closeness to the canonical tradition as well as liberal use of its individual episodes make it difficult to recognize the main thrust of this lesson in history. In my opinion it comes to the fore in vv. 43-46 and 47. The message is: Yahweh's untiring care for his people does overcome sufferings and captivity under foreign powers. The land, forfeited by neglect and fear (vv. 24-27), will be open again to receive the returnees (vv. 46, 47). The most deplorable failure of the "fathers in Egypt," not to have been aware of Yahweh's power and solidarity (vv. 6-7c), will be corrected. Thus the whole psalm may be seen as COMMUNAL CONFESSION and HYMNIC INSTRUCTION (cf. "Introduction to Cultic Poetry," sections D and F).

## Setting

Although we are not able to determine every single liturgical move, the different elements of Psalm 106 do fit into Israel's communal worship service of postexilic times, when Scripture use was already at the center of the people's assemblies. The elements outlined above represent various liturgical stances by liturgists, congregation, reciters of history, etc. The introductory summons to give thanks (v. 1b) may have been answered in the manner of Psalm 136 by all the congregation: "Yes, [he is good,] his care endures forever" (v. 1c). The shouts of vv. 3-4 were likely uttered by a liturgist, while the individual petition of vv. 4-5, being in balance (note the phrase structures and the communal concerns) with the communal petition of v. 47, also may be attributed to a leader of the community or to some prominent member. Vv. 6-7c should have been a matter for all the assembly, and vv. 7d-46 probably came from a professional teacher. All in all, Psalm 106 gives a vivid impression of a many-voiced meeting of Judahites gathered in foreign lands to remember the wondrous assistance and care of Yahweh and the failures of the fathers to respond properly to Israel's caring God.

## Intention

These failures of the fathers serve as a warning not to ignore or forget Yahweh, but to trust in him while subsisting with difficulties in an alien empire. The Yahweh congregation has to take on its spiritual heritage, confess its historical guilt, and rely on the gracious God who has proven his "steadfast love" to his people. This emphasis on trust becomes stronger, indeed, if we give credit to the hypothesis that Psalms 105 and 106 were meant to be read or used in conjunction (Zimmerli: "twin psalms"). No doubt, both liturgical agendas are of similar form and substance. Against all those who place primary significance on integral and cross-readings of the book of Psalms and its individual clusters and collections, I would maintain the basic autonomy of each individual text (→ Psalms 72/73; 89/90; 107; 120–134). Each one of the so-called twin psalms has its own liturgical profile, structure, and theological message. Later reading habits (beginning with Christian monastic communities? against Füglister, Additional Bibliography, section C) joined all psalms into one continuous document of personal edification. The parameters of interpretation changed. Integralists and holists in Psalm exegesis are discovering vast new horizons today, but it is our distinct vantage points that furnish such new meanings in old texts. We cannot claim to unearth hidden, unheard-of ancient ideas. On the whole — and this is valid for all exegesis — our "eisegetical" endeavors have to stand a critical dialogue and be challenged by the original affirmations of authors, redactors, and ancient texts (cf. Croatto, *Hermeneutics,* Additional Bibliography, section B).

## Bibliography

F. Baumgärtel, "Zur Liturgie in der 'Sektenrolle' vom Toten Meer," *ZAW* 65 (1953) 263-65; A. Bentzen, "Die Schwindsucht in Ps. 106,15b," *ZAW* 57 (1939) 152; W. Beyerlin, "Der nervus rerum in Psalm 106," *ZAW* 86 (1974) 50-64; A. M. la Bonnardière, "La Chananéene, préfiguration de l'Eglise," in *Saint Augustin et la Bible* (ed. A. M. la Bonnardière; Paris: Beauchesne, 1986) 117-43; G. J. Brooke, "Psalms 105 and 106 at Qumran," *RevQ* 14 (1989) 267-92; G. W. Coats, *Rebellion in the Wilderness* (Nashville: Abingdon, 1968); M. D. Gray, "Psalm 106:15b. Did the Children of Israel Get What They Asked For?" *SJOT* 7 (1993) 125-33; J. Hoftijzer, *Die Verheissungen an die drei Erzväter* (Leiden: Brill, 1956) 72-73; B. Janowski, "Psalm CVI,28-31 und die Interzession des Pinchas," *VT* 33 (1983) 237-48; R. Kessler, "Das kollektive Schuldbekenntnis im Alten Testament," *EvT* 56 (1996) 29-43; R. Knierim, *Die Hauptbegriffe für Sünde im Alten Testament* (Gütersloh: Mohn, 1965) 28-37; A. Lauha, *Die Geschichtsmotive in den alttestamentlichen Psalmen* (Helsinki: Finnische Literaturgesellschaft, 1945); P. D. Miller Jr., "Enthroned on the Praises of Israel," *Int* 39 (1985) 5-19; R. W. L. Moberly, "Abraham's Righteousness (Genesis 15:6)," in *Studies in the Pentateuch* (VTSup 41; Leiden: Brill, 1990) 103-30; J. P. Oberholzer, "Opmerkings oor die teologie von Psalm 106," *HerTS* 44 (1988) 380-87; F. Refoulé, "Note sur Romains 9:30-33," *RB* 92 (1985) 161-86; N. H. Richardson, "Psalm 106 — Yahweh's Succoring Love Saves from the Death of a Broken Covenant," in *Love and Death in the Ancient Near East* (Fest. M. H. Pope; ed. J. Marks, et al.; Guilford, Conn.: Four Quarters Pub. Co., 1987) 191-203; S. Sabugal, "El concepto del pecado en el Antiguo Testamento," *Estudios Eclesiásticos* 59 (1984) 459-69; H. W. Titus, "God's Gift to Man: Laws, Not Paradigms, for Public Policy," *Transformation* 2 (1985) 10-12; H. G. M. Williamson, "Laments at the Destroyed Temple," *Bible Review* 6 (1990) 12-17; G. H. Wilson, "The Qumran Psalms Scroll Reconsidered: Analysis of the Debate," *CBQ* 47 (1985) 624-42; E. Zenger, "Komposition und Theologie" (listing at Psalm 107); W. Zimmerli, "Zwillingspsalmen" (listing at Psalm 104).

# CHAPTER 6

# THE INDIVIDUAL UNITS OF BOOK 5 (Psalms 107–150)

### Psalm 107:
### Instruction to Give Thanks

### *Structure*

|  | MT | NRSV |
|---|---|---|
| I. Introduction and purpose | 1-3 | 1-3 |
| II. Examples of thanksgiving | 4-32 | 4-32 |
| (To sing praises after having been:) | | |
| A. Lost in the desert | 4-9 | 4-9 |
| B. Imprisoned | 10-16 | 10-16 |
| C. Sick with guilt | 17-22 | 17-22 |
| D. Shipwrecked | 23-32 | 23-32 |
| III. Meditation, counsel | 33-42 | 33-42 |
| IV. Challenge | 43 | 43 |

Like many songs in book 5 of the Psalter, Psalm 107 is without any superscription and is unique in form and structure. The subject matter is thanksgiving throughout, to be sure, but modulations of this theme are wide and far-reaching (cf. Beyerlin, 1-6, for an overview of hypotheses and models of interpretation). While the INTRODUCTION talks about those who returned from captivity, the four neatly organized strophes give examples from a wider range of life situations, and the final MEDITATION muses over the fate of those who stayed in foreign lands and the blessings of those who may qualify as poor and pious in the community of faith.

We first follow the buildup of form elements as they now stand in the final composition and later discuss the possible growth of literary layers and traditions. The problems of the psalm begin already with its first lines, the INTRO-DUCTION to the song (vv. 1-3). Three more psalms of the Psalter open with that formulaic liturgical line: "Give thanks to Yahweh, yes, he is good; yes, forever endures his steadfast love" (Psalms 106; 118; 136). The frequency of this standard thanksgiving phrase testifies to its liturgical background, use, and transmission. Where else than in praising situations of the community could its roots be? The question where and when (once or twice, depending on those two $k\hat{\imath}$ phrases in v. 1) the congregation responded to a SUMMONS of this type is not decisive; the formulaic phrases are styled purely in liturgical terms. They are part of a most stable and important treasure of worship formulas that have been transmitted almost without alterations through the centuries down to our own days (cf. a few more examples: "Yahweh is merciful and gracious, slow to anger and abounding in steadfast love" — Pss 103:8; 145:8; Exod 34:6; Nah 1:3; Spieckermann [listing at Psalm 86]; the Aaronite blessing in Num 6:24-26 or the famous praise: "Everyone is waiting for you . . . ," Pss 104:27; 145:15-16).

The crucial issue is our evalutation of vv. 2-3. Is this renewed summons a merely fictional and literary device, or does it extend the liturgical summons of v. 1? The verb '$mr$, "tell," in a third- or second-person plural form is quite often employed within hymnic contexts, notably at the end of some prayers, when — so to speak — "bystanders" are drawn into the community of worshipers (cf. 35:27; 40:17 [RSV 16]; 70:5 [RSV 4]), or else at the very beginning of a hymn, when the community itself is addressed and summoned to praise (66:1b-3; 96:10; 118:1-4; 124:1b-5; 129:1b-3; 145:6-7, 10-11). All the examples cited, with the sole exception of our vv. 2-3, either directly provide the line the audience has to recite, or at least hint at the contents of what has to be said (thus 145:6, 11). In 35:27; 40:17 (RSV 16); 70:5 (RSV 4) the community hymn is "Great is Yahweh"; in 66:3a it runs "How frightful are your deeds"; in 96:10: "Yahweh is king." So far, the quotations of hymnic response strangely enough are not presented with introductory $k\hat{\imath}$, as we would expect in the wake of Crüsemann's hypothesis (cf. his *Studien*, 32-35; listing at "Introduction to Cultic Poetry"). Only 118:2-4 meets this standard: Israel, the Aaronites, and all the Yahweh-fearing members of the congregation are exhorted to sing praises to the Lord. Finally, 124:1b-5 and 129:1b-3 have a peculiar sentence structure: the summons to "speak up" goes to "Israel" as a whole, but it is placed into the very text that should be recited by the congregation: "If Yahweh had not been with us — Israel is to say — if Yahweh had not been with us . . ." (124:1b-2a), and the phrase rolls on over three more lines, picturing what would have happened without the intervention of Israel's God. A similar construction is found in 129:1b-3, the contents of which are plaintive, however, instead of intrinsically hymnic, as in Psalm 124. The last two specimens of SUMMONS TO SPEAK, then, entice liturgical response in a rather sophisticated, perhaps literary, manner. The conclusions we may draw from this comparison are these: the summons to speak in a worship liturgy almost inevitably presupposes a text to be spoken. This text is normally quoted verbatim by the psalmist. Could it have been forgotten or left out in vv. 2-3? Or is it feasible that the author or redactor of Psalm 107 wanted the congregation to recite the whole psalm, at least vv. 4-22? In that case, he or she probably had composed the four strophes with their quite regular refrains, and possibly on the basis of older themes and poems.

To investigate this possibility more closely: Who are those people being addressed in vv. 2-3? They are named "the delivered ones of Yahweh" (v. 2a: *gĕ'ûlê yhwh* is a singular expression in the Psalter and rare in most other books of the Hebrew canon, with only three more occurrences in the later chapters of Isaiah [Isa 35:9-10; 51:10-11: *gĕ'ûlîm* parallel to synonym *pĕdûyîm;* 62:12: *gĕ'ûlê yhwh* parallel to *'am haqqōdeš,* "people of the Holy One"]. All three passages are highly charged with eschatological expectations). The concept of *gĕ'ûlîm,* "ransomed" or "redeemed ones," is specifically linked to Yahweh's being the *gō'ēl,* "redeemer," of Israel (cf. Isa 41:14; 43:14; 44:6, 24; 47:4; 48:17; etc.; Pss 19:15; 78:35) so that we can hardly avoid interpreting vv. 2-3 in the light of the Isaian message. This means that our psalmist addresses a community of faithful who understand themselves as the "rescued ones" and who ideally gather at one place from all the nations around (v. 3). Although v. 3 is in some disarray ("sunrise," "sunset," "north," and "sea" [*yām?* perhaps misspelled for "south," *yāmîm?*]), the intention is clear: Yahweh's faithful come together from all corners of the world, and the four strophes coming up in vv. 4-22 are in a way corresponding to this universal coherence of the Yahweh community.

The four segments forming the body of Psalm 107 — vv. 4-9, 10-16, 17-22, 23-32 — give examples of thanksgiving situations; they vary a little in length (6, 7, 6, 10 lines, respectively) but adhere to a strict pattern. At the outset each one names a group of people who went through extreme suffering at the brink of death and were rescued by Yahweh himself. Only the first strophe has a finite verb in this crucial place; the other three parts open with a participle (vv. 10, 23) or noun (v. 17). The participle describing a typical emergency is the most fitting category of words in the overall structure of these passages and may have been the original incipit in all four of them. "Those who went astray in the desert" (v. 4a), "those who were sitting in darkness and shadows" (v. 10), "those who were sick with their guilt" (v. 17), "those who went to sea on ships" (v. 23) are pictured before the eyes of the congregation with impressive dramatic force. Two to five lines of the poem are spent to describe their dire straits, hunger and thirst (vv. 4-5), God's castigation of the rebellious (vv. 10-12), terminal sickness (vv. 17-18), and, with heaviest emphasis, the perils of the sea (vv. 23-27). This compilation looks like a catalogue of standard dangers, yet closer scrutiny reveals certain imbalances. Thirst and hunger as well as sickness are elementary hazards for any living being, while imprisonment because of disobedience against Yahweh (vv. 10-12) is explicable only from special historical situations, and threats to seafaring people (vv. 23-27) seem somewhat inopportune in relation to landbound Israel or Judah (but cf. the book of Jonah). The next phase in each drama of salvation is marked by a stereotyped phrase using narrative forms for the expression of crying (consecutive imperfect): "They cried to Yahweh in their agony, he delivered them from their distress" (vv. 6, 13, 19, 28; three synonyms are used for "deliver": *nṣl, yšʿ* [twice], *yṣʾ,* all in plain imperfect). After one more line (only in the last strophe two lines: vv. 29-30) describing the details of each saving act partly with narrative forms, partly with plain imperfects, the psalmist passes on to his main exhortation, uniform for all four cases: "They should render thanks to Yahweh for his loyalty, for all his wondrous help he bestows on humans" (vv. 8, 15, 21, 31). After this stereotyped affirmation one more closing line in each of the four passages either exemplifies Yahweh's wondrous help (vv. 9, 12, both lines introduced by *kî*, which can be taken as a marker of a hymnic phrase) or elaborates on the thanksgiving motif (vv. 22, 32: important information about the setting). Now, it is clear that the two stereotyped lines contain the essence of the psalmist's intention; they are the skeleton of the psalm. Therefore they need to be investigated formally and in regard to their liturgical function.

A group of Yahweh believers is in extreme distress; they turn to their God in lament (the verb *ṣ'q* or *z'q* is a technical term for "crying for help" in a regular complaint worship; cf. G. F. Hasel, *TWAT* II, 628-39, esp. 636-39; Miller, *They Cried,* 55-134; listing at Additional Bibliography, section C; Pss 34:18 [RSV 17]; 77:2 [RSV 1]; 88:2 [RSV 1]), are saved by their Lord, and are therefore summoned to give thanks — in the fashion of thanksgiving worship (and sacrifices, v. 22) we meet in Psalms 30; 32; 40; 116; 118; 1 Samuel 1-2; etc. (cf. "Introduction to Cultic Poetry," section 4C). Each of the four sections forms a coherent liturgical, poetic, and logical structure, the subject looming in front, the individual descriptions and explanations following, and the two standard lines quoted above supporting the whole edifice. Each passage thus seems to be an artistic construction, hardly apt to be sung by an untrained group (with the possible exception of the *kî* lines in vv. 9, 16, which are placed to indicate real psalm responses by the congregation). The impression of skillful organization and poetical artisanship is enhanced by numerous affinities, especially in the first three strophes, with Isaian and Joban motifs and vocabulary (cf. Beyerlin, 13-31). Also, original situations of individual life threats are transferred to a plurality of sufferers — note the initial expression "those who went astray," "those who sat in darkness," etc. — to include collective experiences of the community (against Beyerlin), perhaps on a high level of metaphoric abstraction (cf., e.g., v. 11, a genuinely collective misdemeanor [Deut 1:26, 43; 9:7, 23-24; Ezek 20:8, 13, 21; Pss 78:17, 40, 56; 106:7, 33, 43], and the pluralization of individual experiences and affirmations in Psalms 12; 102). If it suffered more redactional reworking than the other parts, or even was composed in a second try, the fourth strophe (vv. 23-32) certainly belongs in this scheme, because it participates in the overall pattern carried by the skeleton phrases in vv. 28, 31, and it ties in with the fourfold division in v. 3 (the key word *yām*, "sea," was perhaps placed in connection with the fourth strophe, which deals with the "sea").

The four examples of how to behave in situations of extreme danger seem to constitute something like a textbook for liturgists. They are composed not in dry factual words (as, e.g., ritual instructions in Babylonian incantations) but in a poetical and highly liturgical language suggesting ceremonial use.

For vv. 33-43 scholars have long postulated some contacts with wisdom language and ideology (e.g., Beyerlin, 29-31). Especially v. 43, a final exhortation to heed the lesson given in the psalm, is typical for an instructional situation. We have a close parallel in the redactional remark in Hos 14:10 (RSV 9). Our psalm muses over God's power to create deserts and flowering landscapes (vv. 33-35; for a parallel affirmation concerning the social sphere cf. 1 Sam 2:3-8) and applies this insight loosely to the situation of the first strophe (v. 36; cf.

v. 40). Obviously, here the concept of "losing one's way in the wilderness" is linked to the people's wanderings, which ended in "founding a sheltering city" that becomes home to the homeless (vv. 36-38; elaboration of v. 9?). It seems that the desert situation in this sense is paradigmatic for the ultimate part of Psalm 107; the transmitters do not care to comment on the other strophes of suffering and redemption. What they do want, however, is to sketch the history of ancient Israel further, indicating the developments after the settlement: the burden of wickedness pressed them down, they "dwindled" and "bowed" (v. 39); God punished the leaders but built up the "poor" again (vv. 40-41); the latter phrase has not been prepared by the strophes on danger and salvation, being concerned instead about the surviving community of the "righteous" (v. 42). As the "leaders" are sent back into the wilderness (v. 40b) to resume their death-stricken life and perhaps perish there, and the "poor" or "just ones" alone remain (vv. 41-42), we may interpret this to signalize the condensed experience of Israel's history. Whether this may coincide also with the portrait of the ones who despised the "words of God" and therefore were "humiliated" (vv. 11-12) is an open question. On the whole, the treatment of these historical and theological aspects of Israel's history points beyond older wisdom reflection, which had been limited to nonhistorical themes. Therefore I should like to call this segment MEDITATION and CHALLENGE instead of some strictly sapiential specification.

Does Psalm 107 thus prove itself to be a uniform liturgical text, or the remains of a coherent liturgical agenda? The structure seems homogeneous, leaving few points open to doubt. The coherence of the INTRODUCTION (vv. 1-3) can be seen in the light of other psalms starting with a SUMMONS TO GIVE THANKS and continuing with an EXHORTATION TO RECITE (yō'mĕrû, "they shall say"). Transition from INTRODUCTION to examples may be continuous if the strophes thereafter are understood to be the texts proper of communal singing or communal presentation. The four existential examples are of a different quality, to be sure. They draw on life situations that are generalized (plural forms) and in a way idealized to serve as models for the postexilic community of faith and their experiences. (1) Elementary thirst and hunger in the desert becomes transparent for the wanderings of early Israelite parents as well as migrations between places of captivity and the Judean homeland. (2) Theological conclusions in the Dtr way of thinking lead to a general conviction of those who rebelled against the "words of God" — a very late concept in OT history. (3) Human experience of guilt and sickness is taken as the background of Yahweh's intervention by sending "his word" to heal his faithful (v. 20; cf. Isa 55:11). Again, the motif perhaps lets shine through ancient traditions like Exod 15:26; Num 21:4-9; Deut 32:39. (4) The image of dreadful, chaotic waters threatening life is present in the shipwreck passage. Knowledge of chaos water was not limited to sea experiences; every thunderstorm was a life demonstration of destructive potentiality and danger for the ancients. (Interestingly, Loretz [418] takes vv. 23-32 to be an old Canaanite hymn about Baal-Zaphon being the saving patron of seafarers and the nucleus of the whole psalm.) In sum, we realize that all four strophes have been paradigms of historical and actual perils. Each one of them has been construed on top of deep insights; none of them corresponds to individual dangers or threats as they are formulated in individual complaint or thanksgiving psalms (cf. Pss 38:4-9 [RSV 3-8]; 69:2-5 [RSV 1-4]; Jonah 2:3-7a [RSV 2-6a]). The subject matter of each strophe is different, but the mode of fashioning a poetic and theological unit is very homogeneous.

If we consider vv. 1-32 a coherent liturgical agenda, the rest of the psalm (vv. 33-43) may fit into this picture. Of course, we note the differences between the two blocks of material. The latter is not a commentary on the former, but — if originally belonging to it — does strike other notes than the preceding verses. Liturgically speaking, we would not expect it to be otherwise, because liturgy is not a lecture or a mathematical exposition. Possibly, a simple reflection on the bliss of those who found places to dwell outside the desert in fertile lands (vv. 33-38) has been the first stage of this MEDITATION. It would be a reflection of the first strophe in the interpretation of some congregational worshipers and a celebration of their own joy. Continuing, then, with the serious trouble of the people of faith, which ends up with the expulsion of leaders and the survival of the "poor" (vv. 39-42), could well be a new interpretation because of a changed situation or point of view (cf. a rather strange juxtaposition and linkage of the last word of v. 38 and the first of v. 39, both from the root *m't*, "diminish"). On the whole, the meditation part communicates concern with the Yahweh community in the wake of difficult external and internal developments.

## *Genre*

The psalm has hymnic elements and communicates, for the most part, the joy of the liberated that has to be articulated in cultic praise. Nevertheless, it is not exactly a hymn, but rather a REFLECTION ON PRAISING. The first and the last lines of the psalm best express this mood. They call everyone in the assembly to give thanks (v. 1) by considering the (world)wide range of Yahweh's redeeming acts in a community of worldwide migration and immigration, a community that consists of righteous people of faith (v. 42) who are simply marveling at the course of events (v. 43). The psalm wants to induce this attitude of sacred astonishment, leading to gratitude and praise, by calling attention to Yahweh's manifold loyalty to his followers; therefore it may be called an INSTRUCTION TO GIVE THANKS.

## *Setting/Intention*

Worship services of postexilic congregations, either in Jerusalem or outside in the diaspora, constitute the general background of most of the psalms. In this case, the community of those who believe in Yahweh is clearly visible in the text. But it is not that assembly directly involved in prayer or praise as in, e.g., Pss 104:1, 7-9, 24-30; 106:4-7, 47; etc. Rather, the gathered people are admonished to reflect on their history and experience to discover for themselves that praiseworthy life of those who follow Yahweh. The gist is educational, instruction being part of worship.

Looking at the tradition history of thanksgiving (see "Introduction to Cultic Poetry," section 4C), we may say that individual *tôdāh* rituals were the starting point of the kind of praise we meet in Psalm 107. To offer a sacrifice of gratitude after being saved was an age-old religious obligation in the ancient Near East and in other cultures (→ Psalms 30; 66; 116). Early Jewish communities took over thanksgiving rites from family religion, adapting them to the needs of a congregation (→ Psalm 118). Naturally, community concerns like, in our case, salvation from Babylonian captivity, blended with the original private interests.

Psalm 107 opens a new book, the fifth, of the Psalter. Modern "holistic" readers of the Psalter pay much (in my opinion, too much) attention to this very late redactional division of the canonical collection of Psalms. Redactional activities, by and large, were not able to thoroughly mold transmitted texts to interconnect them and give them new meanings. For example, Zenger makes Psalms 107 and 145 the cornerstones of book 5, on very general observations ("both celebrate the universal benevolence and power of Yahweh," "Komposition," 106). The first line of Psalm 107 is to be the "dominant theme" of the entire book, and since it coincides with 106:1bc he suggests that we have to read the last book of the Psalter "as a running commentary to the preceding four books of psalms, which want to be understood as a unit" (ibid.). Much more cautiously Wilson declares Psalms 107 and 145 a "wisdom frame" around book 5 ("Shaping," 78). If there were conscious redactional efforts to structure those "books" within the Psalter in terms of theological perspectives and logical consistency, they appear at best very subdued and controversial in the present texts.

## Bibliography

C. Barth, *Errettung* (listing at "Introduction to Psalms"); A. Berlin, "Jeremiah 29:5-7: A Deuteronomic Allusion," *HAR* 8 (1984) 3-11; W. Beyerlin, *Werden und Wesen des 107. Psalms* (BZAW 153; Berlin: de Gruyter, 1978); E. M. Curtis, "Old Testament Wisdom," *Christian Scholar's Review* 15 (1986) 213-27; R. Glöckner, "Neutestamentliche Wundergeschichten und frühchristliche Gebetsparänese," in *Die Mysterien des Lebens Jesu und die christliche Existenz* (ed. L. Scheffczyk; Aschaffenburg: Paul Pattich, 1984) 57-74; R. Helms, "Fiction in the Gospels," in *Jesus in History and Myth* (ed. R. Hoffmann and G. Larue; Buffalo: Prometheus, 1986) 135-42; J. Jarick, "The Four Corners of Psalm 107," *CBQ* 59 (1997) 270-87; O. Loretz, "Baal — Jahwe als Beschützer der Kaufleute in Ps. 107," *UF* 12 (1980) 417-19; T. McElwain, "A Structural Approach to the Biblical Psalms: The Songs of Degrees as a Year-End Pilgrimage Motif," *Temenos* 30 (1994) 113-23; J. Mejia, "Some Observations on Psalm 107," *BTB* 5 (1975) 56-66; R. P. Meye, "Psalm 107 as Horizon for Interpreting the Miracle Stories of Mark 4:35–8:26," in *Unity and Diversity in New Testament Theology* (*Fest.* G. L. Ladd; ed. R. A. Guelich; Grand Rapids: Eerdmans, 1978) 1-13; J. W. Michaux, "Le chemin des sources du salut, Ps. 107 (106)," *BVC* 83 (1968) 46-55; W. L. Michel, "*Ṣlmwt,* 'Deep Darkness' or 'Shadow of Death'?" *BR* 29 (1984) 5-20; P. D. Miller, "The End of the Psalter: A Response to Erich Zenger," *JSOT* 80 (1998) 103-10; C. de Moor, "The Art of Versification in Ugarit and Israel, III: Further Illustrations of the Principle of Expansion (Ps. 107,4-32)," *UF* 12 (1980) 311-15; D. A. Patrick, "Epiphanic Imagery in Second Isaiah's Portrayal of a New Exodus," *HAR* 8 (1984) 125-41; J. W. Roffey, "Beyond Reality: Poetic Discourse and Psalm 107," in *A Biblical Itinerary (Fest. G. W. Coats; ed. E. Carpenter; JSOTSup 240; Sheffield: Sheffield Academic Press, 1997) 60-76; R. Schatz, "The Commentary of R. Israel Ba'al Shem Tov to Psalm CVII," *Tarbiz* 42 (1972/73) 154-84; M. Schiltknecht, "Er tötet und macht lebendig. Meditation zu Psalm 107," *Reformatio* 26 (1977) 636-38; F. Schnider, "Rettung aus Seenot. Ps 107,23-32 und Mk 4,35-41," in *Freude an der Weisung des Herrn (Fest. H. Gross; ed. E. Haag and F.-L. Hossfeld; Stuttgart: Katholisches Bibelwerk, 1986) 375-93; M. H. Snaith, *Five Psalms* (London: SCM, 1938); D. Winton Thomas, "Hebrew *'oni,* 'captivity,'" *JTS* 16 (1965) 444-45; M. Weinfeld, "A Comparison of a Passage from the Shamash Hymn (lines 65-78) with Psalm 107," *Archiv für Orientforschung*, Beiheft 19 (1982) 275-79; G. H. Wilson, "Shaping the Psalter," in *The Shape and Shaping of the Psalter* (ed. J. C. McCann; JSOTSup 159; Sheffield: Sheffield Academic Press, 1993) 93-107; E. Zenger, "Komposition und Theologie des 5. Psalmenbuches 107–145," *BN* 82 (1996) 97-116 (Eng.: "The Composition and Theology of the Fifth Book of Psalms: Psalms 107–145," *JSOT* 80 [1998] 77-102).

# Psalm 108:
## Communal Complaint

### Structure

|  |  | MT | NRSV |
|---|---|---|---|
| I. | Superscription | 1 | - |
| II. | Hymn | 2-7 | 1-6 |
|  | A. Summons to praise | 2-3 | 1-2 |
|  | B. Vow to give thanks | 4-5 | 3-4 |
|  | C. Wish and petition | 6-7 | 5-6 |
| III. | Yahweh oracle; sermon | 8-11 | 7-10 |
| IV. | Complaint | 12 | 11 |
| V. | Petition | 13 | 12 |
| VI. | Affirmation of confidence | 14 | 13 |

There is no question about the evidence at hand: the two main parts of Psalm 108 — after a common "Davidic" SUPERSCRIPTION (cf., e.g., the headings of Psalms 3–6; 62–68; 101; 109; 110; 139–141; 143) — are extant also in 57:8-12 (= vv. 2-6) and 60:7-14 (= vv. 7-14), notwithstanding small deviations from our text. This fact in itself may irritate those readers who cling to a modern (and very wrong) concept of psalm authorship, as if the psalms were private compositions or literary pamphlets under some copyright rules. Much in contrast to our customs, psalms were liturgical texts to be used in worship gatherings or related ceremonies. And according to the needs and insights of the congregations and their leaders, the songs and prayers were freely combined in specific liturgical situations. Other examples of "double" use of some psalm texts can be studied with Psalms 14 and 53; 70; 18 (see 2 Samuel 22), etc. Each compilation of psalm texts, however, has to be analyzed and evaluated in its own right.

The first block of Psalm 108 is really a personal HYMN (vv. 2-6). Classical form elements include a SUMMONS TO PRAISE (vv. 2-3), in this case addressed to the self presenting the song. Such self-exhortation does not occur too often (see 103:1-2; 104:1a). It should point to the individual in a festive crowd, not the isolated singer in his home. One addresses oneself to God (v. 2a), at a proper place of worship, referring to cultic instruments (v. 3; cf. 81:3-4 [RSV 2-3]; 92:4 [RSV 3]; 144:9). The following VOW TO GIVE THANKS (including the offering formula itself, v. 4a; cf. 66:13; 116:14, 17) is dressed in prayer language with direct address of Yahweh. The singer visualizes large crowds; in times of euphoria the worshipers may have imagined national gatherings (v. 4; cf. hymnic outbursts to the "nations," gôyîm, in 82:8; 86:9; 96:10; 102:16; etc.; cf. Gunkel, 247). Greatness is attributed to Yahweh's solidarity and loyalty over against Israel (v. 5) — a truly hymnic line that may represent the very text to be articulated by participants in the service.

At the docking point of the two parts (vv. 6-7) we may study the effects of new "joints" of texts. Taken by itself, v. 6 is a wish or request, in spite of the imperative, to enhance the glory of God. Linked to v. 7 the hymnic wish is given a definite purpose, articulated quite differently from v. 6. "In order to have your beloved ones saved" (v. 7a) is the wording, complemented by direct PETITION for help and a plea to be answered (v. 7b; 'nh, "respond," is a masculine singular imperative with a first-person singular suffix). The singular form of the speaker or reciter is in concordance with vv. 2-6, of course, but not so with the congregational "we"; cf. vv. 12-14. Modern translators wrestle with the singular, and usually prefer the plural. Putting the two texts vv. 2-6 and 7-14 that close together and molding a good linkage between them, the psalm becomes a liturgical unit by being used in worship. "Yahweh's beloved ones" (v. 7) clearly is a self-designation of the community (cf. Deut 33:12; Jer 11:15; H.-J. Zobel, TWAT III, esp. 474-79).

The rest of the song (vv. 8-14) has been discussed in some detail with → Psalm 60. Formal use of oracular discourse (vv. 8-10) does not invalidate a genre classification like "sermon." Divine words in the psalter cannot be taken separately from their liturgical contexts. Every single pronouncement of Yahweh had to be communicated by officiants within the worship liturgy (cf. Koenen, 49-54, who ignores this rule). Therefore, v. 11 probably continues the "I" speech of God. His speaker communicates the divine concern that ancient Israelite sites already occupied by Jacob (Gen 33:17-20: thus Koenen, 51) and other territories have apparently not been given back to his people — an exilic and postexilic preoccupation. The congregation then enters with reproachful COMPLAINT: "Isn't it you yourself, God, who rejected us? You, God, did not march out with our army" (v. 12; cf. Pss 44:10 [RSV 9]; 89:44 [RSV 43]), immediately followed by communal PETITION (v. 13). An AFFIRMATION OF CONFIDENCE (v. 14) is a fitting end of a complaint psalm. Marked use of first-person plural suffixes in vv. 12-14 assigns this closing part of the song to the congregation (or — less likely — to its spokesman), justifying once more our separating v. 12 from vv. 8-11.

The "new" song composed of parts of Psalms 57 and 60 (cf. also 1 Chronicles 16 with its "new" composition made up of pieces of Psalms 105; 96; and 106) has a clear structure. From a hymnic introduction (vv. 2-5), including already a preliminary petition (v. 6), the liturgy moves to an ancient, unfulfilled promise of Yahweh to provide land (vv. 8-11), and then to some basic elements of complaint, petition, and confidence (vv. 12-14). Comparable are other communal complaints like Psalms 44 and 89, which also start out with praises to the loyal Yahweh. In our case, especially complaint may be considered much reduced in comparison to the other elements. But we unfortunately do not know how a communal part like vv. 12-14 was performed in reality. There is a chance that the assembly repeated individual lines often.

## Genre

Hymnic elements are not totally foreign to complaints of the people, as Psalms 44 and 89 prove. The singular speaker of vv. 2-8 in the context of vv. 12-14 and with that communal background appearing already in vv. 2 (sacred instruments), 4 ("crowds"), and 7 ("your beloved ones") may be understood as the leader of ceremonies. Equally, remembrance of divine promises fits into the pattern of complaints (cf. 89:4-5 [RSV 3-4]; 105:8-11, ending in an oracle-type promise of land). Therefore we may count Psalm 108 under COMMUNAL COMPLAINTS. Why has there been a liturgical fusion of two fragments of psalms? Because the elements put together suited the needs of a specific worship situation: hymnic praise, dedication to Yahweh, memory of divine promises, etc., were necessary ingredients of communal complaint in the exile (cf. Psalms 44; 89). The specific Edomite orientation may betray a south Judean localization.

## Setting

A historical situation is usually hard to determine for any given psalm. God leading the army into battle (v. 12b) sounds like a preexilic experience for Israel. But this unique piece of evidence does not prove an early date of composition for Psalm 108. The place of performance of any of the communal complaints must have been the assembly of people for worship or mourning. As mentioned above, the first person singular in vv. 1-7 and first person plural in vv. 12-14 indicate participation of individuals in a group affair. According to the contents of these verses the congregation consists of individual members who are responsible for faith and worship. To many exegetes the pronounced appearance of Edom as the "archenemy" is disconcerting. The relationship of Judah and Edom having been quite ambivalent in history (cf. E. A. Knauf, *NBL* II, 468-71; J. R. Bartlett, *ABD* II, 287-95), we would have to look for a period when Edomite power had hurt Judah, and for this reason hatred in the Yahweh community had risen high against the southern neighbors. In fact, during the war against the Babylonians (589-587 B.C.E.) the Edomites seem to have been allied with the superpower, sacking Judean territory (cf. Obad 1–14; Dicou, 182-83). But it was not this incident alone that overshadowed occasional brotherly relations to Esau's offspring (cf. Gen 33:1-16; Deut 23:8; D. V. Edelman, *"You Shall Not Abhor an Edomite, For He Is Your Brother"* [Atlanta: Scholars Press, 1995]). Hatred against Edom was apparently promoted in worship (thus Kellermann, *Israel*, 228: Edom singled out in a scapegoat function). "The Jerusalem lament cult . . . [was] the 'motor' for the production of oracles against Edom" (Dicou, 192; cf. Lam 4:21-22; Isa 34-35; 49:7-22; 63:1-5; Mic 7:7-10; Ezek 35-36; Am 9:11-12; Mal 1:2-5; Ps 137:7-9).

## Intention

Complaints with strong elements of praise and remembrances of history are designed to strengthen the community of faith, promote its sense of solidarity among its members and of being protected by their mighty God Yahweh (v. 4; *'ĕlōhîm* in vv. 6, 8, 14 is "preserved" [Gunkel, 474-75] from the context of Psalms 57 and 60). Projection of hatred against a selected people or group, unfortunately, is part of this process of consolidation (cf. Girard, *Violence;* listing at Additional Bibliography, section B). Since we do recognize some historical roots of our communal complaint, and furthermore suspect a contemporary cultic stimulus for hating Edom in a specific exilic situation, there is no real need to make Psalm 108 an "eschatological" text (thus Becker, 67).

## Bibliography

J. R. Bartlett, *Edom and the Edomites* (JSOTSup 77; Sheffield: Sheffield Academic Press, 1989); J. Becker, *Israel deutet seine Psalmen* (SBS 18; Stuttgart: Katholisches Bibelwerk, 1966) 65-67; S. L. Cook, "Apocalypticism and the Psalter," *ZAW* 104 (1992) 82-99; B. Dicou, *Edom, Israel's Brother and Antagonist* (JSOTSup 169; Sheffield: Sheffield Academic Press, 1994); U. Kellermann, "Erwägungen zum historischen Ort von Psalm LX," *VT* 28 (1978) 56-65; idem, *Israel and Edom* (diss., Münster, 1975); K. Koenen, *Gottesworte in den Psalmen* (Biblisch-theologische Studien 30; Neukirchen-Vluyn: Neukirchener Verlag, 1996); S. Mowinckel, *PsSt* III, 64-78; C. R. North, *"'e'lōzeh 'ăhallĕqāh šĕkem* (Psa. lx 8 // Psa. cviii 8)," *VT* 17 (1967) 242-43; R. J. Tournay, "Psaumes 57, 60 et 108: Analyse et interprétation," *RB* 96 (1989) 5-26; G. H. Wilson, "The Qumran Psalms Scroll Reconsidered: Analysis of the Debate," *CBQ* 47 (1985) 624-42.

## Psalm 109:
## Complaint of the Individual; Counter-Curse

### Structure

|  |  | MT | NRSV |
|---|---|---|---|
| I. | Superscription | 1a | - |
| II. | Invocation, initial plea | 1b | 1 |
| III. | Complaint | 2-5 | 2-5 |
| IV. | Imprecation | 6-20 | 6-20 |
| V. | Petition | 21-29 | 21-29 |
|  | A. Plea for help | 21 | 21 |
|  | B. Complaint | 22-25 | 22-25 |
|  | C. Plea for help | 26 | 26 |
|  | D. Ill-wish, imprecation | 27-29 | 27-29 |
| VI. | Vow | 30-31 | 30-31 |

This clear-cut individual complaint voices overwhelming disgust for and aggression against enemies. There is no other example of individual complaint with an equal share of imprecative and ill-wishing affirmations. Many times it is labeled a "curse psalm" (*Fluchpsalm;* cf. S. S. Johnson, *ABD* I, 1218-19) by modern exegetes, and accordingly it is treated with caution or disregard in Christian tradition much to our own disadvantage, exempting us from facing the realities of human life. Attempting to neutralize the brutality of sanctions against the persecutor, some commentators and translators of the psalm (e.g., Kraus, 918, 922; Lohfink) make vv. 6-19 the imprecations of persecutors against the supplicant, an interpretation that is unfounded given the textual evidence.

The SUPERSCRIPTION falls into the plain category of David ascriptions (→ Psalms 13; 19; 20; 21; 108; 110), but the INVOCATION is surprising: "God of my praise!" ('*ĕlōhê tĕhillātî,* v. 1b) defining the Deity as receptor of the supplicant's hymns. Hymnic presentations in the cult are rarely marked explicitly as originating with the believer (cf. 71:6c); the due tribute of praise is normally declared God's own property, as in 22:26: "My praise comes from you" (cf. many occurrences of *tĕhillāh* with suffixes indicating the divine proprietor or addressee: 9:15 [RSV 14]; 34:2 [RSV 1]; 35:28; 48:11 [RSV 10]; 51:17 [RSV 15]; 66:2, 8; 71:8, 14; 79:13; 102:22 [RSV 21]; 106:2, 12, 47; 111:10; 149:1). In fact, all hymns address or belong to Yahweh (22:4 [RSV 3]; 145:21). Expressions like "my song" and "my eulogy" are quite rare, indeed (cf. 28:7; 71:6). That hymns have their legitimate place also in complaint services is impressively demonstrated by the passages listed above (→ e.g., Psalms 35; 51; 71; 79; 102). Still, the invocation "God of my praise" is unique in the Psalter. It highlights the spiritual fact that distress may even provoke memories of gratitude and praise (cf. Daniel 3 and the apocryphal Song of the Three Jews, inserted after Dan 3:23 in LXX). The INITIAL PLEA comes out very reduced, limiting itself to the negative aspect only (v. 1b: "Do not be silent"). In complaints there is frequently a positive demand to be heard or admitted into the presence of God ("Introduction to Cultic Poetry," section 4B). Here more substantial pleas appear at the end of the prayer (vv. 21, 26-29).

The psalm seems to move hastily on to COMPLAINT (vv. 2-5, to be repeated in vv. 22-25). Few psalms go into this liturgical field so fast (cf. Psalm 88). The impression of urgency may be caused by the special type of suffering at hand and by the fact that in these cases preliminary ritual investigations like "asking God" about the causes of suffering (cf. 1 Kgs 14:1-2; 2 Kgs 1:2) have cleared the way so that longer preludes are unnecessary or counterproductive. The first complaint section, the text of which seems somewhat garbled in the Hebrew MSS (fragmentation, redundancy, lack of order), conjures the image of a person haunted by malevolent neighbors. He accuses his persecutors of having received "hatred for my love" (v. 5b after slight conjecture). Twice more this negative compensation formula is used: "evil for good" (vv. 4a, 5a). It is extant in several other individual complaints (cf. 35:12; 38:21 [RSV 20]; 41:10 [RSV 9]; also in narratives: Gen 50:20; Judg 11:27; 1 Sam 24:12). This very formula is sufficient evidence to suggest conflicts within the intimate circle of people living together, of fear, suspicion, and outright hatred executed against a particular person. The psalms just cited paint a vivid picture of a terrible infighting (→ Psalms 35; 41), consisting of slander and "evil words," corroborated by some texts from contest literature (cf. Job 19:13-19; 29-30; Ps 88:9, 19 [RSV 8, 18]; Babylonian *namburbi* texts: see Caplice, listing at "Introduction to Cultic Poetry"; Maul, listing at Additional Bibliography, section B). Social anthropology tells us that human groups under certain conditions are prone to single out this or that member to heap on him their own collective frustration (cf. Fortune, *Sorcerers;* listing at "Introduction to Cultic Poetry"; Girard, *Scapegoat;* listing at Additional Bibliography, section B). Studying more closely the description of the persecutors (vv. 2-3), we notice that they are accused in many instances of using their tongues to damage their victim (cf. Pss 10:4, 6-7; 12:3-5; 42:11; 55:4; 59:8, 13; 2 Sam 16:5-8). The power of words, considered curses, was feared very much in ancient cultures. "Among such curses were counted all sorts of evil words, calumnies, abusive terms, threatenings, bad wishes, the cultic words of other religions" (Mowinckel, *W* II, 3). According to ancient belief they destroy a person's well-being, health, and life prospects. One who has been ostracized by the community and complains about such deadly verbal harassment is practically charging persecutors with demonic conspiration (cf. Mowinckel, *PsSt* I). Vice versa, we may surmise that this person has been accused of the same crime, because defense and accusation often correspond to each other. If one grants that the attacks mentioned in vv. 2-3 were launched because of suspicion of sorcery or black magic, then the counterattack in vv. 6-20 seems much more plausible (cf. vv. 17-20).

The IMPRECATIONS or BAD WISHES of Psalm 109 are the most elaborate and the roughest in the OT (but cf. Pss 137:9; 139:19; 2 Sam 23:6-7; Isaiah 13–23: prophetic "words against the nations" are, however, more descriptive than wishful). Interestingly, they focus on one individual "hater," "enemy" (only direct designation: "my juridical opponents," *śôṭĕnay,* v. 29; for the many names of the enemy cf. Keel, *Feinde;* listing at "Introduction to Psalms"), and his family, while vv. 2-5 and 25-29 deal with a plurality of persecutors and slanderers.

This difference in conceptualization in itself should not provoke a discussion about the unity of Psalm 109. Liturgical texts may easily switch from singular to plural passages, and vice versa, in keeping with the liturgical agenda. Curses against culprits have traditionally been administered on an individual basis, aiming at each one responsible for his or her evil works. This was probably considered a more effective counteroffensive against the authors of the suppliant's suffering (cf. J. Scharbert, *TWAT* VII, 40-49).

Neither is the shift from plural to singular discourse sufficient evidence of a complete reversal of speakers. Notably N. Lohfink ("Drei Arten") takes vv. 6-19 to be a citation of enemy words against the suppliant (NRSV follows suit in putting a textually nonexistent "They say" in front of the long passage, and framing it by quotation marks). As a rule, however, enemy quotations in the Psalms are carefully identified (cf. 2:1-3; 3:3 [RSV 2]; 10:4, 6, 11, 13; 12:5 [RSV 4]; 22:8-9 [RSV 7-8]; 35:21, 25; 41:6-9 [RSV 5-8]; etc.). Being evil words capable of doing damage even in liturgical contexts, they needed to be handled with care. For this same reason, such bad words were usually mentioned only in passing, and given the most unobtrusive and general gist of their poisonous speech. It is almost unimaginable that ancient writers or redactors would extensively quote their hateful opponents, copying meticulously all their — presumably false — accusations against the righteous suppliant. To have such an enormous listing of serious indictments as in vv. 6-19, allegedly (Lohfink, et al.) directed against the psalmist, would certainly cause a liturgical disaster. No worship service of any kind could stand such a quantity of foreign, hostile words within its agenda. Another possibility suggested by Lohfink ("Drei Arten," 326) is that Psalm 109 could be a literary work using consciously literary techniques in order to overcome traditional formal patterns. In that case, I believe, the basic aversion to exaggeratedly quoting enemy opinions would still hold, unless the author were a masochist. Texts of this provenance, however, would hardly have gotten a chance to be transmitted and canonized.

Formally and according to varying levels of authorization we may distinguish the following types of "evil words": (a) Direct (eventually: nominal) curse against a person having committed a capital crime, more specifically, a grave offense against God himself. "Cursed be the one who fashions an idol or a graven image" (Deut 27:15: *'ārûr hā'îš 'ǎšer ya'ǎśeh pesel ûmassĕkāh*). This kind of condemnation was apparently restricted to the highest spiritual authorities (but in Deuteronomy 27 it needs confirmation by all the congregation saying "Amen"). (b) A lesser kind of chastisement, opposed to beatitudes (→ Ps 1:1), was the *hôy* formula, now found principally in prophetic writings (cf. Am 5:18; 6:1; Isa 5:8, 11, 18, 20, 21-22, etc.; e.g., *hôy gibbôrîm lištôt yāyin,* "Woe to the heroes in wine drinking," Isa 5:22). It did not have those sacral undertones or that cultic embellishment, but seems to have emerged from wisdom traditions (cf. E. S. Gerstenberger, *JBL* 81 [1962] 249-63; against W. Janzen, *Mourning Cry and Woe Oracle* [BZAW 125; Berlin/New York: de Gruyter, 1972] and those who follow him, I am not yet convinced of its origin in mourning rites). Still, the word had a maledictive force and certainly was feared for that. (c) The evil wish over some wicked person, pronounced directly against the trespasser. "May they die childless" (Lev 20:20, 21: against sexual offenders, man or woman); "All your enemies . . . may become like Nabal" (Abigail to David, 1 Sam 25:26); "This year you shall die" (the prophet to Hananiah, Jer 28:16). (d) Wishes against evil persons making God the executioner; cf. Jer 29:22: "Yahweh make you like Zedekiah and Ahab, whom the king of Babylon roasted in the fire." (e) Some enemy or evil may overcome the target person: "May fire go forth from the citizens of Shechem . . . and devour Abimelek" (Judg 9:20; cf. v. 57, where this pronouncement is called a "curse," qĕlālāh). The agent of castigation need not be named; the evil word is then put into the passive: "They shall be exterminated" (Lev 20:18); "He shall be put to death" (Lev 20:9-13).

In vv. 6-20 we find, most of all, phrases of the last two categories. Evil wishes to be executed by Yahweh seem to have entered the scene only secondarily. The passage commences with an imperative (v. 6a), the only one in the section, without naming an addressee: "Put over him a criminal." The second colon interprets this to mean: "A plaintiff right next to him may stand up against him" (v. 6b). The imbalance of sentence structures and the overwhelming majority of neutral phrases not mentioning the Deity lead to an initial suspicion that v. 6a has been altered in the course of tradition to suggest Yahweh's involvement. This impression gains force with vv. 14-15, which (quite awkwardly in v. 14: "to/with Yahweh") introduce Yahweh by name to guarantee nonforgiveness for the culprit (v. 16 is a lengthy prosaic justification of this merciless attitude); it was probably added only at a late stage. At the end of our segment the name of Yahweh once more seems to have been inserted (v. 20a), because the line is oversize and the expression "from Yahweh" does not fit well into the phrase. This means that the central part of Psalm 109 was apparently worked over along the centuries of transmission to be finally adapted to strict Yahwism. The older layer of evil words did not refer to any deity, but used the type of evil wishes described above under (e): Human agents are to harass and damage the persecutor (e.g., vv. 6b, 8b, 11), anonymous force may spoil his endeavors and destroy his family (e.g., vv. 7, 8a, 9, 13; cf. Kilpp, 217: rooted in family experience). Most of all, the slanderous and cursing words he used against the suppliant are to turn against the persecutor himself and finish with him (vv. 17-19). This passage, because of its coherence, vocabulary, and archaic outlook (cf. K. Koch, "Gibt es ein Vergeltungsdogma im Alten Testament?" *ZTK* 52 [1955] 1-42), may constitute an old magic anti-curse formula (cf. Wright, 397-400, setting it apart for its special analogical way of speech). The original compact saying could have run like this: "He loved curses — may they enter his body! He wore curses like shirts — may they invade his intestines like water!" (cf. the respective parts of vv. 17-18).

The latter third of our psalm carries the designation PETITION, which is the decisive element in individual complaints (Gerstenberger, *Mensch;* listing at "Introduction to Cultic Poetry"). Formally, these pleas for help are spiced with some other forms, which, however, are subservient to petition. New and forceful INVOCATIONS emphasize the importance of this part ("Yahweh, my Lord," v. 21a; "Yahweh, my God," v. 26a). Note also the second-person singular prayer language (the personal pronoun "You" in vv. 21, 27, 28) and the emphatic imperatives calling for divine help (vv. 21, 26: typical verbs are nṣl, "rescue"; *zr,* "help"; *yš*, "save"; all with first-person suffixes of the suppliant). The two lines of crying out for support, both "heavy" with invocations, liturgically speaking (vv. 21 and 26), are separated by a renewed COMPLAINT (vv. 22-25). These latter lines are obviously intended to make urgent the PLEAS for help. They describe the precarious state of the suppliant, surprisingly using very general vocabulary. A formulaic expression serves as a general label: "I am oppressed and poor" (v. 22a; from here, it seems, v. 16b copied these words). As a rule, it indicates social exploitation and marginalization, not demonic or magic persecution (cf. 35:10; 37:14; 40:18 [RSV 17]; 70:6 [RSV 5]; 86:1; Deut 15:11; 24:14; Jer 22:16; Job 24:14; Prov 31:9). Thus this second complaint seems less specific than the first one (vv. 2-5). On the other hand, marginalization is certainly a consequence of slandereous accusation of every kind. The prayer therefore may well use general descriptions of suffering. The patient is the object of public fear and contempt (v. 25); he feels the uselessness of his (rehabilitative) fasting (v. 24) and the physical effects of being shunned (v. 23).

Petitions to be saved from deadly dangers in ancient Israelite rituals had to be supplemented by IMPRECATIONS against those who caused anxiety and misery — if they could be identified (if not, the only way to react was a "curse against unknown persons"; cf. Judg 17:2). Vv. 27-29 come in for exactly this reason: to complement petition. The struggle for the suppliant's well-being is a partisan one. Saving him from trouble alone is useless if the causes of his agony persist. The enemies are to realize that Yahweh is helping the patient (v. 27); this in itself promotes their defeat. All of their evil activities are to be frustrated, to the jubilance of the suppliant (v. 28). Small wonder that in confrontation with the adversaries the suppliant intimates again that they are doing damage by magic: they curse (v. 28a), and they are to "wear" their own wicked machinations (v. 29) — this line refers back to the anti-magic saying of vv. 17-18.

A Vow to offer thanks (vv. 30-31) closes this anti-curse psalm, which uses a strong dose of evil words in counteracting vicious slanderers (as to the vow → 7:18 [RSV 17]; 52:11 [RSV 9]; 57:10 [RSV 9]; as to the whole prayer → Psalms 35; 41; 55; 59; 140). After the suppliant was saved by the Deity, thanksgiving would be celebrated with a multitude of neighbors, friends, and relatives (v. 29b), i.e., possibly in the same group that had stigmatized the victim. In consequence, an act like this would have amounted to a ceremony of rehabilitation of the cursed suppliant.

## Genre/Setting

The psalm is built around real "curses" or evil words, used to defend a marginalized person falsely accused of black magic, against public opinion ready to condemn and perhaps to kill a suspect like this. (Every now and then, even in our age, there are televised news stories about tribal medicine men pointing out witches and sorcerers to be killed by the community.) This general background explains the preponderance of "curses" in our psalm. It is a true COMPLAINT OF THE INDIVIDUAL, to be sure, because the main concern of this prayer is to rehabilitate particular persons in a hopeless situation. Since the psalm serves specific cases only, however, we may define the subgenre as an "anti-defamation" song, or still better, a COUNTER-CURSE. Other subgenres of the individual complaint deal with false accusations in court (see Psalms 7; 17; 26), cases of grave illness (see Psalms 22; 38; 102), or heavy guilt (→ Psalm 51). Our prayer grew out of a special situation involving cursing and sorcery, comparable to the Babylonian series *namburbi*, "untying" (cf. Caplice, listed at "Introduction to Cultic Poetry"; Maul, listed at Additional Bibliography, section B), which deals with undoing magical spells. The original life setting, therefore, was the incantation of a sorcery expert to heal or protect a suspect who could claim to be innocent (cf. Gerstenberger, *Mensch*). Healing rituals for individual patients were held at the home of the sick or persecuted, perhaps also at local sanctuaries. Later, prayers like Psalm 109 were drawn into the Yahweh community. We noticed vestiges of a certain "Yahwehization" of the text indicative of this process. The early Jewish community must have continued to offer services for people accused of sorcery, either separately or within the regular assembly of worshipers. Psalm 109 was used in this fashion until it fell into disgrace, because of its personal condemnations.

## Intention

To understand a psalm of cursing we have to remind ourselves of the worldviews and life patterns of ancient Near Eastern people. The whole world was governed by divine and demonic forces. Evil words were part and parcel of life's reality (modern mobbing or slander can give us a slight notion of the destructive power of demonic speech in antiquity). The only remedy against murderous gossip or witchcraft was a powerful attack from the side of the righteous deity. He or she needed to be called on and motivated to act against the evil forces, and that is what our psalm does in its supposed ritual frame. With beliefs in demons and magic words gone, and with the establishment of post-Enlightenment societies of a rationally and scientifically oriented democracy, we must not confide in antidemonic curses but in the realization of human rights and equal chances for everyone unmasking those powers that denounce, oppress, exploit, and massacre human beings and nature — which is as hard to achieve as eliminating demonic forces. According to all we know, male and female members of the congregation used individual complaints and thanksgivings in Israelite and early Jewish periods. This means that the prayer formulas collected experiences also of women (cf. 1 Sam 2:2-10; Tanner; Bail, in Brenner, et al., eds., *Wisdom*, 245-63; listing at Additional Bibliography, section C; Gerstenberger, *Yahweh*, 55-66; listing at Additional Bibliography, section B).

## Bibliography

M. L. Barré, "The Formulaic Pair *ṭwb (w)ḥsd* in the Psalter," *ZAW* 98 (1986) 100-105; F. Baumgärtel, "Der 109: Psalm in der Verkündigung," *Monatsschrift für Pastoraltheologie* 42 (1953) 244-53; A.-M. la Bonnardière, "La Chananéenne, préfiguration de l'Eglise," in *Saint Augustin et la Bible* (ed. A.-M. la Bonnardière; Paris: Editions Beauchesne, 1986) 117-43; W. Brueggemann, "Psalm 109: Three Times 'Steadfast Love,'" *Word & World* 5 (1985) 144-54; T. W. Cartledge, "Conditional Vows in the Psalms of Lament: A New Approach to an Old Problem," in *The Listening Heart (Fest.* R. E. Murphy; ed. K. Hoglund, et al.; JSOTSup 58; Sheffield: JSOT Press, 1987) 77-94; H. L. Creager, "Note on Psalm 109," *JNES* 6 (1947) 121-32; W. Dürig, "Die Verwendung des Fluchpsalms 108 (109) im Volksglauben und in der Liturgie," *Münchener Theologische Zeitschrift* 27 (1976) 71-84; D. G. Firth, "Context and Violence in Individual Prayers for Protection," *SK* 18 (1997) 86-96; E. A. Gosselin, "David in tempore belli: Beza's David in the Service of the Huguenots," *Sixteenth Century Journal* 7 (1976) 31-54; M. Z. Kaddari, "hll = 'Bore,' 'Pierce'? Note on Psalm 109:22," *VT* 13 (1963) 486-89; N. Kilpp, "Eine frühe Interpretation der Katastrophe von 587," *ZAW* 97 (1985) 210-20; E. J. Kissane, "The Interpretation of Psalm 109 (108)," *Irish Theological Quarterly* 18 (1951) 1-8; F. Lindström, *Suffering* 218-38 (listing at Additional Bibliography, section C); N. Lohfink, "Drei Arten, von Armut zu sprechen," *Theologie und Philosophie* 72 (1997) 321-36; H. Pirmin, "'Das sei meiner Ankläger Lohn . . .': Zur Deutung von Ps 109:20," *BibLeb* 14 (1973) 105-12; W. Schottroff, *Der altisraelitische Fluchspruch* (WMANT 30; Neukirchen-Vluyn: Neukirchener Verlag, 1969); idem, "Fluch," *NBL* I, 683-85; J. Shepherd, "The Place of Imprecatory Psalms in the Canon of Scripture," *Churchman* 111 (1997) 27-47; B. L. Tanner, "Hearing the Cries Unspoken," in *Wisdom* (ed. A. Brenner, et al.) 283-301 (listing at Additional Bibliography, section C); M. J. Ward, "Psalm 109: David's Poem of Vengeance," *AUSS* 18 (1980) 163-68; D. P. Wright, "Ritual Analogy in Psalm 109," *JBL* 113 (1994) 385-404; E. Zenger, *Ein Gott der Rache?* (Freiburg: Herder, 1994).

## Psalm 110:
## Divine Proclamation; Messianic Promise

### Structure

|  | MT | NRSV |
|---|---|---|
| I. Superscription | 1a | - |
| II. Oracle and interpretation | 1b-3 | 1-3 |
| A. Revelation formula | 1b | 1a |
| B. Divine invitation | 1c-1e | 1b-1d |
| C. Interpretation | 2-3 | 2-3 |
| III. Oracle and interpretation | 4-7 | 4-7 |
| A. Oath introduction | 4ab | 4ab |
| B. Divine installation | 4cd | 4cd |
| C. Interpretation | 5-7 | 5-7 |

SUPERSCRIPTIONS like the one in v. 1a ("to/for David, a song") belong to the most common kind of David attributions (see headings of Psalms 15; 23; 24; 29; etc.). Two major "David" collections precede our poem (Psalms 3–41; 51–72); a few more texts in the Masoretic tradition are linked with David afterward (cf. Psalms 86; 101; 103; 108; 109; 131; 138–145). Attribution to David in the last three books of the Psalter thus seems haphazard and may be due to chance redactional or scribal decisions (or errors). At least we seem not to be able to discover any compositional or theological scheme in these stray David headings (against Zenger, "Komposition"; listing at Psalm 107).

The text of Psalm 110 is partially obscure, first, because of textual corruptions, and second, because of unintelligible allusions to mythical, ritual, and theological details. What can be made out with certainty, however, are two pronouncements of Yahweh (vv. 1, 4) concerning an unnamed royal or messianic figure. A speaker mediating these words of God each time gives a short introduction and a somewhat more extensive commentary. He does not introduce himself (as, e.g., in 45:2 [RSV 1]), but his figure looms behind the words, for example, right at the beginning ("Whispering of Yahweh for my lord," v. 1b: *nĕ'um yhwh la'dōnî*), where "my lord" is certainly a human authority. The beginning of the psalm is rather curious, though. How can a text of any kind, let alone a liturgical piece, commence so abruptly, without any preparatory remark or introductory formula? Furthermore, "Whispering/word of Yahweh" is an expression almost totally unknown outside prophetic literature: I count about 350 cases in the prophetic canon, and a few more in connection with prophetic figures in narrative contexts (e.g., Num 24:3-4, 15-16). Very rare are usages for the king's discourse (2 Sam 23:1) or to signify general human speech (see Prov 30:1). In the Psalter there is but one more passage with an isolated *nĕ'um* (Ps 36:2 [RSV 1]).

Given the abrupt start with a "prophetic" marker, the contents of the divine oracle are still more surprising. "Sit at my right hand, until I put your enemies as a footstool for your feet" (v. 1c-e). Yahweh speaks to the addressee (called "my lord" in v. 1b), who must be an Israelite royal figure. He is offered the highest possible dynastic honor: to sit next to God on the divine throne as divine regent or vice-deity. Egyptian texts and iconography abound in references of this sort (cf. Keel, *Welt,* nos. 333, 341, 342, 353, etc.; listing at "Introduction to Cultic Poetry"; Mesopotamian sources more often portray the ruler standing before the enthroned deity; see King Hammurapi before the sun-god Shamash on his famous obelisk). The oracle itself is probably supposed to mark the beginning of a reign; at least it is promising in character and expecting a victorious government for the one enthroned. The wording is compact, three cola with two stresses each. Formally the divine pronouncement (imperative) is an INVITATION to the throne for a pretender or incumbent to take office. Divine oracles, as such, occur — in Middle Eastern cultures and elsewhere — spontaneously or by means of institutionalized divination (cf. J. K. Kuemmerlin-McLean, *ABD* IV, 468-71; K. Engelken, *NBL* III, 46-49). Important oracles, especially to heads of dynasties, were transmitted, modified, and interpreted (cf. Ps 89:4-5, 20-38 [RSV 3-4, 19-37]). Sometimes, they were invented ad hoc to legitimate new situations and incumbents. The history of oracular forms within and without the OT still needs much more attention, including, if possible, anthropological data (cf. T. W. Overholt, *Prophecy in Cross-Cultural Perspective* [Atlanta: Scholars Press, 1986]; J. Blenkinsopp, *A History of Prophecy in Israel* [2nd ed.; Louisville: Westminster John Knox, 1996]).

Following that terse saying three poetic lines continue to address the enthroned human figure (vv. 2-3; second-person singular suffixes). Yahweh, however, is mentioned only in the third person, so he can no longer be the speaker. Poetic lines are longer now; the first and the third may have three cola, with a two-cola exemplar between them. The promise to defeat enemies is repeated (v. 2b); eager warriors are to join the king in battle, as in Judg 5:9, 18 (v. 3ab). The final line, v. 3cde, is very difficult textually. It does not make sense in its Masoretic shape. Speculations are that the phrase was originally another divine oracle: "From the womb of Shachar [in Hebrew tantamount to "dawn," but in Ugaritic a well-known goddess; see L. Ruppert, *TWAT* VII, 1226-33] I have generated you." This assertion would stand in line with Pss 2:7; 89:27 (RSV 26), but it would have been modified in the course of transmission because it intimates a sexual relationship of Yahweh with the goddess.

The second oracle is constructed quite similarly. An oath formula plus a favorable comment introduce a personal assurance of Yahweh directed to the same figure prominent in vv. 1-3. Thereafter the promissory discourse continues, while God again is referred to in the third person. Only the very last line (v. 7) seems to deal with the addressee as a subject in his own right.

The details are these. The oath introduction (v. 4a) corresponds with the REVELATION FORMULA of v. 1b, only surpassing it in force and weight. After all, a solemn oath is always a matter of life and death. The addition "he will not withdraw from it" (v. 4b), obviously a spokesman's comment, is a kind of tautology, or even an anticlimax after the foregoing strong affirmation. The remark shows, however, that the whole oracle of Yahweh has been communicated and worked over by some mediator, be it priest, prophet, Levite, or leader of worship. V. 4cd, then, contains a surprising divine announcement. While the oracle of v. 1 suggested a victorious battle with a following enthronement, the new pronouncement of Yahweh through his spokesman installs the receiver of this message as "priest forever, according to the order of Melchizedek." If v. 1 intimated a royal figure, then v. 4 indicates a priestly one, and of Jerusalem stock at that (cf. Gen 14:18). Priest and king do have some affinities in the ancient Near East (cf. H.-P. Müller, et al., *TWAT* IV, 926-68), but OT writers rarely focus on this connection, transmitting only chance references of royal-priestly activities (cf. David in 2 Sam 6:14; Solomon in 1 Kgs 8:63; etc.). Therefore the priestly role of the Davidic king is treated with caution, also by modern interpreters, being classified as alien to Israelite theological thinking (cf. Müller, *TWAT* IV, 944-47; Mettinger, *King*, 264-65; listing at Additional Bibliography, section B). Still, the evidence of Ps 110:4 is obvious, and the problem is when and where to locate the merging of political and sacral offices in Judean kingship and priesthood, respectively. Vv. 5-6 return to the warrior images, promising divine help in battle — an age-old concept in the Near East (cf. Miller, *Warrior*, listing at Additional Bibliography, section B). The mediator is speaking; he describes mighty interventions of the "Lord" Yahweh (v. 5a: many Hebrew MSS have *yhwh* instead of '*ădōnāy;* even the latter expression alone refers to Yahweh; cf. v. 4). At the very end mention is made of "drinking from the brook" (v. 7). The phrase is possibly a remnant of a coronation rite (cf. 1 Kgs 1:38, Gihon being the sacred spring). All in all, the segment vv. 4-7 is an oracle mediated and interpreted by a divine spokesman.

What about these oracles, then? Although the (Judean) king is not mentioned explicitly in Psalm 110, he or a comparable stately figure must be the addressee. Several related texts containing divine promises in oracle form for the king are quite explicit at this point: 2:6-9; 89:20-38 (RSV 19-37); 132:11-12; 2 Sam 7:8-16; 23:3-7. There was a tradition in Israel that insisted on direct communication between the monarch and "his Lord" Yahweh, mediated probably through court prophets or mantic priests. Who else than figures like Nathan or Gad (2 Sam 7:4; 24:11) could have been the intermediaries of the Davidic king? But a thorough reworking of old oracles, an interpretive modeling of perhaps ancient words (cf. v. 2: universal outlook; world government from Zion; vv. 5-6: final battle against nations = features incompatible with preexilic Judean theology), forbids dating our psalm into monarchic times. Rather, it should be localized in the exilic/postexilic messianic expectation.

## Genre

The psalm looks fragmentary, no doubt. It is built around a nucleus of two (or originally three) oracles that seem to be archaic in form and content. "Sit at my right side, until I put your enemies as a footstool for your feet" (v. 1c-e); ("From the womb of dawn did I beget you," v. 3de); "You are a priest forever according to the order of Melchizedek" (v. 4cd) — these oracles taken by themselves may well be pieces of ancient inauguration rituals. The tradition of Melchizedek, priest-king of Jerusalem who blessed Abraham (Gen 14:18-20), is probably behind our psalm. Only these two Melchizedek passages are extant in OT writings; but later on the tradition was unfolded by Jewish authors, being prominent also in the letter to the Hebrews (cf. F. C. Horton, *The Melchisedek-Tradition* [Cambridge: Cambridge University Press, 1976]; M. C. Astour, *ABD* IV, 684-86). The writings of Qumran reveal a book dealing with Melchizedek's eschatological role (García Martínez, *Scrolls,* 139-40, listing at Additional Bibliography, section B). The debate of the 1950s and 1960s, however, ignored that priestly figure. On the one hand, it focused on the solemn act of installing Judean kings (1 Kgs 1:38-40; 2 Kgs 11:12; cf. the debate about their "coronation ritual": von Rad, Ringgren, Widengren, etc.). This discussion was brought to a certain close by S. Herrmann. On the other hand, Mowinckel's theory of the New Year Festival, including symbolized death and reinstallation of God and the human king, has been examined extensively. As the "prophetic" framing and interpretation of basic oracles make it difficult to place the text in monarchic times, one should consider seriously a genre classification of MESSIANIC PROMISE. Because of its fragmentary state, our psalm probably had to be used in connection with other songs focusing on "royal" figures (cf. Psalms 2; 20; 21; 45; 132). The dual function of monarch and priest is visualized, e.g., in Zech 4:11-14; 6:9-15; the latter passage talks about the high priest Joshua apparently assuming royal functions (cf. Schreiner). Although the concept of "priest-king" is a very old one, going back to the Sumerians of the third and second millennia B.C.E., in our psalm it seems to be tied to eschatological battle, which in itself is a Persian idea unthinkable in Judah before the takeover by

Cyrus. Schreiner ("Psalm CX," 220: Psalm 110 "legitimates the new institution of the high priest") may be right when pointing to the "coronation" of the high priest Joshua and possible messianic speculations originating from this incident as the most likely background for 110:4.

## Setting

The Jewish community of the Second Temple periodically developed fervent expectations of a restitution of the Davidic empire (cf. Ezekiel 34) or, more generally, hopes for a thorough change of all political, social, and economic affairs connected or not with the emergence of a special messianic figure (cf. Isa 9:1-6 [RSV 2-7]; 11:1-9; 49; 60–62; Hag 2:23; Zechariah 1–7; 12–14; S. Mowinckel, *He That Cometh* [tr. G. W. Anderson; Nashville: Abingdon, 1955]; K. Seybold, *Bilder zum Tempelbau* [Stuttgart: Katholisches Bibelwerk, 1974]; R. Smend, "Eschatologie," *TRE* X, 256-64; D. L. Petersen, *ABD* II, 575-79). Strictly "messianic" psalms (→ Psalms 2; 89) belong in this context. We do not know exactly how they were recited in the assembly of believers. Still, we may be sure that promises of a prospective new regent of Yahweh on Zion would excite the whole community. These words were probably made public in connection with some cultic service, not necessarily on the occasion of important feasts. There is a cryptic air about Psalm 110. Very likely, songs like this had to use veiled language, in order not to arouse distrust and draw the attention of Persian officials. Since messianic expectations within the early Jewish community were oscillating between royal and priestly types, sometimes envisioning two different persons sharing leadership along these lines (cf. Zech 4:11-14), Psalm 110 in taking up the Melchizedek strand of Genesis 14 became an influential synthesizer of such futuristic concepts, well into the Christian tradition (cf. Mays). In the NT, in any case, it is the most quoted OT text. Early Christians considered our psalm an excellent theological condensation of Christ's authoritative offices (cf. Hengel, Dautzenberg, Bateman, Clements, et al.).

## Intention

Messianic texts want to kindle hope for betterment and the strength to fight for it. Messianic promises typically arise in downtrodden groups or nations (→ Psalm 2). The focus on the divine savior of the faithful, acting both politically and spiritually, after the battle and final victory, envisions an ultimate, urgently longed-for rehabilitation of the community.

## Bibliography

A. del Agua Pérez, "Derás cristológico del Salmo 110 en el Nuevo Testamento," in *Simposio Biblico Espanol* (ed. N. Fernández Marcos, et al.; Madrid: Universidad

Complutense, 1984) 637-62; idem, "Procedimentos derásicos del Sal 2:7b en el Nuevo Testamento," *EstBib* 42 (1984) 391-414; R. J. Allen, "Twelve Steps to the Old Testament Sermon," *Preaching* 10 (1995) 24-34; J. Alonso Diaz, "Cómo y cuando entra en la línea del messianismo clássico el aspecto sacerdotal?" *EstBib* 25 (1966) 283-98; H. U. von Balthasar, "Sedet ad dexteram Patris," *Communio* 13 (1984) 1-34; H. W. Bateman, "Ps 110:1 and the New Testament," *BSac* 149 (1992) 438-53; J. Becker, "Zur Deutung von Ps 110:7," in *Freude an der Weisung des Herrn* (*Fest.* H. Gross; ed. E. Haag, et al.; SBB 13; Stuttgart: Katholisches Bibelwerk, 1986) 17-31; M. Black, "The Theological Appropriation of the Old Testament by the New Testament," *SJT* 39 (1986) 1-17; T. Booij, "Psalm CX: 'Rule in the Midst of Your Foes!'" *VT* 41 (1991) 396-407; K. Bornkamm, "Teilhabe an Christi Thronen zur Rechten Gottes," in *Kirche in der Schule Luthers* (*Fest.* J. Heubach; ed. B. Hägglund; Erlangen: Martin Luther Verlag, 1995) 23-36; J. W. Bowker, "Psalm CX," *VT* 17 (1967) 31-41; C. Breytenbach, "Das Markusevangelium, Psalm 110,1 und 118,22f: Folgetext und Prätext," in *The Scriptures in the Gospels* (ed. C. Tuckett; Leuven: Leuven University Press, 1997) 197-222; W. P. Brown, "A Royal Performance," *JBL* 117 (1998) 93-96; G. B. Caird, "Son by Appointment," in *The New Testament Age* (ed. W. Weinrich; Macon, Ga.: Mercer University Press, 1984) 73-81; T. Callan, "Psalm 110:1 and the Origin of the Expectation That Jesus Will Come Again," *CBQ* 44 (1982) 622-36; A. Caquot, "Remarques sur le Psaume CX," *Sem* 6 (1956) 33-52; R. E. Clements, "The Use of the Old Testament in Hebrews," *Southwestern Journal of Theology* 28 (1985) 36-45; J. Coppens, "La portée messianique du Psaume CX," *Analecta Lovaniensia Biblica et Orientalia,* third series 1 (1956) 5-23; G. Dautzenberg, "Psalm 110 im Neuen Testament," in *Liturgie und Dichtung* (ed. H.-J. Becker, et al.; St. Ottilien: EOS, 1983) 141-71; M. Dietrich, "Der König wäscht sich und ist rein . . . ," *Mitteilungen für Anthropologie und Religionsgeschichte* 12 (1997) 33-56; H. Donner, "Der verlässliche Prophet: Betrachtungen zu 1 Makk 14,41ff und zu Ps 110," in *Prophetie und geschichtliche Wirklichkeit im alten Israel* (*Fest.* S. Herrmann; ed. R. Liwak, et al.; Stuttgart: Kohlhammer, 1991) 89-98; G. D. Driver, "Psalm CX — Its Form, Meaning, and Purpose," in *Studies in the Bible* (*Fest.* M. H. Segal; ed. J. M. Grintz, et al.; Jerusalem: Kiryat Sepher, 1964) 17-31; L. Dürr, *Psalm 110 im Lichte der neueren altorientalischen Forschung* (Vorlesung der Akademie Braunsberg, 1929-30; Münster: Aschendorf, 1929); Y. Elitzur, "Melkizedek between Genesis and Psalms," in *Proceedings of the 9th World Congress of Jewish Studies* (ed. R. Giveon, et al.; Jerusalem: World Union of Jewish Studies, 1986) *59-*63; D. Fleming, "The Biblical Tradition of Anointing Priests," *JBL* 117 (1998) 401-14; T. E. Fretheim, "Divine Foreknowledge, Divine Constancy, and the Rejection of Saul's Kingship," *CBQ* 47 (1985) 595-602; J. H. Gammie, "A New Setting for Psalm 110," *ATR* 51 (1969) 4-17; G. Gerleman, "Psalm 110," *VT* 31 (1981) 1-19; M. Gilbert and S. Pisano, "Psalm 110 (109),5-7," *Bib* 61 (1980) 343-56; J. Gray, "Canaanite Kingship in Theory and Practice," *VT* 2 (1952) 193-220; V. Hamp, "Ps 110,4b und die Septuaginta," in *Neues Testament und Kirche* (*Fest.* R. Schnackenburg; ed. J. Gnilka; Freiburg: Herder, 1974) 519-29; E. R. Hardy, "The Date of Psalm 110," *JBL* 64 (1945) 385-93; D. M. Hay, *Glory at the Right Hand* (SBLMS 18; Nashville/New York: Abingdon, 1973); M. Hengel, "Psalm 110 und die Erhöhung des Auferstandenen zur Rechten Gottes," in *Anfänge der Christologie* (*Fest.* F. Hahn; ed. C. Breytenbach, et al.; Göttingen: Vandenhoeck & Ruprecht, 1991) 43-73; idem, "'Setze dich zu meiner Rechten!' Die Inthronisation Christi zur Rechten Gottes und Psalm 110,1," in *Le Trône de Dieu* (ed. M. Philonenko; Tübingen: Mohr, 1993) 108-

94; H. Herkenne, "Ps 110/109: 'Dixit dominus domino meo,'" *Bib* 11 (1930) 450-57; S. Herrmann, *Königsnovelle;* see listing at Psalm 2; K. Homburg, "Psalm 110,1 im Rahmen des judäischen Krönungszeremoniells," *ZAW* 84 (1972) 243-46; idem, "Setze dich zu meiner Rechten!" *EsTe* 11 (1971) 29-33; T. Ishida, *The Royal Dynasties in Ancient Israel* (BZAW 142; Berlin: de Gruyter, 1977); H. G. Jefferson, "Is Psalm 110 Canaanite?" *JBL* 73 (1954) 152-56; E. E. Johnson, "Hermeneutical Principles and the Interpretation of Psalm 110," *BSac* 149 (1992) 428-37; R. Kilian, "Relecture in Psalm 110," in *Sendung und Dienst im bischöflichen Amt (Fest.* J. Stimpfle; ed. A. Ziegenaus; St. Ottilien: EOS, 1991) 285-302; idem, "Der 'Tau' in Ps 110,3 — ein Missverständnis?" *ZAW* 102 (1990) 417-19; E. Kissane, "The Interpretation of Psalm 110," *Irish Theological Quarterly* 21 (1954) 103-14; R. Kolb, "The Doctrine of Christ in Nikolaus Selneckers Interpretation of Psalms 8, 22, and 110," in *Biblical Interpretation in the Era of the Reformation (Fest.* D. C. Steinmetz; ed. R. A. Muller; Grand Rapids: Eerdmans, 1996) 313-32; L. Krinetzki, "Ps 110 (109): Eine Untersuchung seines dichterischen Stils," *TGl* 51 (1961) 110-21; T. C. de Kruif, "Priest-King Melchizedek: The Reception of Gen 14,18-20 in Hebrews Mediated by Psalm 110," *Bijdragen* 54 (1993) 393-406; L. Kunz, "Psalm 110 in masoretischer Deutung," *TGl* 72 (1982) 331-35; C. P. März, "Melchisedek: Bibeltheologische Überlegungen zu den Melchisedek-Bezügen im Hebräerbrief," in *Geglaubt habe ich, deshalb habe ich geredet (Fest.* A. Bsteh; ed. A. T. Khoury; Würzburg: Echter, 1998) 229-50; F. Manzi, "La figura di Melchisedek," *Ephemerides Liturgicae* 109 (1995) 331-49; idem, "La risurrezione di Gesù Cristo segundo Matteo," *RivB* 46 (1998) 277-315; C. Markschies, "'Sessio ad dexteram . . . ,'" in *Le Trône de Dieu* (ed. M. Philonenko; Tübingen: Mohr, 1993) 252-317; J. L. Mays, "In a Vision: The Portrayal of the Messiah in the Psalms," *Ex Auditu* 7 (1991) 1-8; H. E. Medico, "Melchisédech," *ZAW* 69 (1957) 160-70; W. van der Meer, "Psalm 110: A Psalm of Rehabilitation?" in *The Structural Analysis of Biblical Poetry* (ed. W. van der Meer and J. C. de Moor; JSOTSup 74; Sheffield: JSOT Press, 1988) 207-34; T. N. D. Mettinger, *King;* listing at Additional Bibliography, section B; H. Möller, "Der Textzusammenhang in Ps 110," *ZAW* 92 (1989) 287-89; M. Naumann, "Messianic Mountain Tops," *Springfielder* 39 (1975) 5-72; G. von Rad, "Ritual"; see listing at Psalm 2; A. Rebic, "Psalm 110,1: Zur Bedeutung von 'sedet ad dexteram Patris' im Alten Testament," *Communio* 13 (1984) 14-17; H. Ringgren, "König und Messias," *ZAW* 64 (1952) 120-47; H. H. Rowley, "Melchizedek and Zadok, Gn 14 and Ps 110," in *Fest. A. Bertholet* (ed. W. Baumgartner, et al.; Tübingen: Mohr, 1950) 461-72; idem, "Melchizedek and David," *VT* 17 (1967) 485; M. Saucy, "Exaltation Christology in Hebrews: What Kind of Reign?" *Trinity Journal* 14 (1993) 41-62; G. Sauer, "Die Psalm II and CX," *Zeitschrift der Deutschen Morgenländischen Gesellschaft* 118 (1968) 259-64; J. de Savignac, "Essai d'interpretation du Psaume CX à l'aide de la littérature égyptienne," *OTS* 9 (1951) 107-35; J. Schaberg, "Mark 14:62: Early Christian Merkabah Imagery?" in *Apocalyptic and the New Testament* (ed. J. Marcus, et al.; JSOTSup 24; Sheffield: JSOT Press, 1989) 69-94; C. Schedl, "'Aus dem Bach am Wege . . . ,'" *ZAW* 73 (1961) 290-97; J. Schildenberger, "Der Königspsalm 110," *Erbe und Auftrag* 56 (1980) 53-59; S. Schreiner, "Psalm CX und die Investitur des Hohenpriesters," *VT* 27 (1977) 216-22; A. Serina, *La figura di Melchisidec nel Salmo 110,4* (diss., Rome, 1965/ 1966); D. S. Shapiro, "Psalm 110," *BM* 57 (1974) 286-89; J. P. Sterk, "An Attempt at Translating a Psalm," *BT* 42 (1991) 437-42; H.-J. Stoebe, "Erwägungen zu Psalm 110 auf dem Hintergrund von 1 Sam 21," in *Fest. F. Baumgärtel* (ed. L. Rost; Erlangen:

Universitätsbund, 1959) 175-91; H. Strauss, "Exegetische Erwägungen zu Psalm 110," *Este* 9 (1969) 3-7; R. J. Tournay, "Les relectures du Psaume 110 (109) et l'allusion à Gédéon," *RB* 105 (1998) 321-31; M. Treves, "Two Acrostic Psalms," *VT* 15 (1965) 81-96; T. C. Vriezen, "Psalm 110," *Vox Theologica* 15 (1944) 81-85; S. Wagner, "Das Reich des Messias: Zur Theologie der alttestamentlichen Königspsalmen," *TLZ* 109 (1984) 865-74; B. K. Waltke, "'He Ascended and Sitteth . . .': Reflections on the Sixth Article of the Apostles' Creed," *Crux* 30 (1994) 2-8; G. Widengren, *Psalm 110 och det sakrala kungadömet i Israel* (Acta Universitatis Upsaliensis 7; Uppsala: Lundequist, 1941); idem (amplified translation of the foregoing), "Psalm 110 und das sakrale Königtum in Israel," in *Zur neueren Psalmenforschung* (ed. P. H. A. Neumann; Darmstadt: Wissenschaftliche Buchgesellschaft, 1976) 185-216; H. W. Wolff, "Psalm 110:1-4," in *Herr, tue meine Lippen auf,* vol. 5 (ed. G. Eichholz; Wuppertal: Emil Müller, 1961) 310-23.

## Psalm 111:
## Acrostic Hymn

### Structure

|  | MT | NRSV |
|---|---|---|
| I. Summons to praise | 1a | 1a |
| II. Thanksgiving | 1bc | 1bc |
| III. Hymnic affirmations | 2-9 | 2-9 |
| IV. Praise of wisdom | 10 | 10 |

In Hebrew ACROSTICS the overarching structure is determined by devices related to alphabetical order (→ Psalms 25; 34; 119; Lamentations). Thus the poetic lines of such a psalm have been arranged to begin, in a regular sequence (each line, every second line, two to eight lines forming one block, etc.), with consecutive letters of the alphabet. In Psalms 111 and 112, which are obviously in a special relationship to each other, every line is headed by a word the first consonant of which is in neat alphabetical sequence with the other "acro"s or "head" items.

A SUMMONS TO PRAISE (v. 1a) has not been included in the alphabetical setup; it has a clear introductory function, exhorting a community to sing out loudly. Taking this exhortation seriously, we have to consider even such an artistic, if not artificial, poem a liturgical text (see below, Genre/Setting). "Praise you God" *(hallĕlû-yāh)* must be a very old shout of the people to eulogize their God Yahweh, and it has become, in the course of Jewish-Christian history, a standard formula of praise until this day. There are various expressions in the Psalter to indicate this extolling of Yahweh ("I shall praise you"; "they shall praise him," "praise the name of Yahweh," etc.), but the concise formula "hallelujah" (NRSV: "Praise the Lord") does not occur in Psalms 1–103. Beginning only with Psalm 104, and ending with Psalm 150, we find frequent use of precisely this summons, in all, 25 times. In some cases the exhortatory shout either introduces (Psalms 111; 112; 113) or closes (Psalms 104; 105; 106; 115; 116;

117) a psalm with some uncertainties of allocating it to the beginning or end of the text (and frequent variations in the LXX Psalter). It is often found at both the beginning and the end of a psalm (Psalms [106]; 113; 135; 146; 147; 148; 149; 150). The latter is a closed group being completely wrapped in "hallelujahs"; traditionally, however, Psalms 113–118 are called the "Hallel" psalms, which served particular ends in Jewish liturgy (cf. Mark 14:26; Elbogen, 496; listing at "Introduction to Cultic Poetry"). In general, there is a crescendo of summons to praise of all sorts starting with Psalm 104 (cf. Brueggemann, *Psalms,* 112-32, 189-213), reaching a climax in Psalms 148 and 150. The verb *hll*, Piel, "praise," is virtually never used with a divine name other than "Yahweh." It seems to be a specific articulation of faith in the God of Israel. Religious use of the word and of many synonyms is known, however, from other Semitic languages as well (H. Ringgren, *TWAT* II, 433-41; etymological equivalents in Ugaritic, Syriac, Akkadian, and Arabic).

With the dominant pattern of alphabetical order at hand it is difficult to establish any substructure. Twenty-two short phrases beginning with subsequent letters are lined up without fault from *aleph* in v. 1b to *taw* in v. 10c. The meter is unusual. Psalmists and scribes in this exceptional case (Psalms 111 and 112 are unique at this point) did not stick to their custom of writing two cola per poetic line. Instead they wrote half-lines (cola), but reserved one full line for each colon, thus making a single colon an acrostic unit. In this manner they doubled the opportunities to exercise their art and, at the same time, shortened the poem considerably (which may have had desirable effects for anybody's learning it by heart). One may speculate about the use of alphabetical order. Notwithstanding that the sequence of letters may not have been noticed by illiterate users of the song, the alphabet in itself is a literary device presupposing and promoting knowledge of a certain system of writing. From this observation we may deduce outlines of an early Jewish community extensively using written testimony, the written word of Moses, written communication, perhaps written worship agendas, etc. — it was basically a literate group of people.

The first subunit of Psalm 111 after the opening summons to praise comprises only the next two lines of v. 1. It is a personal thanksgiving, recognizable by the opening statement "I will thank Yahweh" (cf. Pss 7:18 [RSV 17]; 9:2 [RSV 1]; 109:30; 118:19). This objective way of addressing oneself to God is contrasted sharply with a frequent formula put into prayer language: "I will thank you, Yahweh" (cf. 18:50 [RSV 49]; 35:18; 43:4; 52:11 [RSV 9]; 57:10 [RSV 9]; 71:22; 86:12; 108:4 [RSV 3]; 118:21, 28; 119:7; 138:1; 139:14). The first form clearly addresses the congregation, giving exemplary praise and stimulating everybody to join. The situation is one of hymn singing. The latter, direct-address formula reflects thanksgiving for personal salvation or protection, originally being the offertory word of the adorant when consecrating the animal to be sacrificed (cf. 118:21; Crüsemann, *Studien,* 267-68, listing at "Introduction to Cultic Poetry"). Now, our *aleph* and *bet* lines constitute a subjective declaration of intent, in rather "objective" words, which nevertheless becomes a hymnic invitation "within the community of righteous" (v. 1c). Orientation to the congregation is kept up in the whole poem; there is not a single occurrence

271

of direct address of Yahweh. Psalm 111 is thus a true hymn (see Genre), not a prayer.

HYMNIC AFFIRMATIONS (vv. 2-9) are all about Yahweh, whose name is mentioned twice in this section (vv. 2a, 4b). After he has been nominated as the receptor of praise (cf. already v. 1b) phrase after phrase extols his wondrous works, but in very general terms, as most hymns do. Sometimes the faithful people enter the scene, thus in vv. 2b, 5a, 6, 9a, always on the receiving side. Yahweh alone is really in focus; he receives the honorary designations; he is the uncontested agent of all the hymnic affirmations, those unspecified wondrous, mighty, benevolent acts. Most of the phrases are well known from other Hebrew texts, and ancient Near Eastern hymns as well. Thus we have descriptions of Yahweh's greatness and power in nominal clauses like "great are the works of Yahweh" (v. 2a; cf. "great works" of God in Exod 34:10; Deut 11:7; Judg 2:7, 10), "his doing is glorious and majestic" (v. 3a; cf. Pss 96:6; 104:1), "forgiving and merciful is Yahweh" (v. 4b; cf. Exod 34:6; Joel 2:13; Jonah 4:2; Pss 86:15; 103:8; 145:8; Neh 9:17, 31; 2 Chr 30:9; Spieckermann, listing at Psalm 86; J. S. Kselman, *ABD* II, 1084-86), "holy and dreadful is his name" (v. 9c; cf. Exod 34:10; Deut 7:21; 28:58; Pss 68:36 [RSV 35]; 89:8 [RSV 7]; 96:4; 99:3. Several prayers use "great and dreadful" as a stereotyped pair; see Neh 1:5; 4:8; 9:32; Dan 9:4). On the other hand, there are assertions about Yahweh doing wondrous and helpful things for the "just ones" (v. 1c). These affirmations are made in verbal sentences like "he established remembrance of his marvelous deeds" (v. 4); "he remembers always his covenant" (v. 5b; cf. v. 9b). Such affirmations stay very general, emphasizing the reliability of Yahweh's favor. Some phrases point a little more to events of sacred history: "He gave food to the ones who feared him" (v. 5a); "he sent redemption to his people" (v. 9a). Sacred tradition seems to be much condensed in these announcements. The most unusual statement is that of v. 6, however: "The power of his works he made known to his people, in order to hand over to them the heritage [= land] of the nations." This couplet of lines is located exactly in the middle of the poem, being preceded and followed by ten lines on each side. Furthermore, v. 6 is the only passage in vv. 2-9 tying together two lines into a grammatical and meaningful entity by making v. 6b dependent on 6a (infinitive). This means that the celebration of Yahweh's power and glory revolves around the gift of the (holy) land, which, of course, is an eminent theme of exilic and postexilic theology.

Strong vocabulary affinities with different layers and bodies of OT literature suggest that the authors of our psalm were familiar with much of the writings as we have them now (Allen, 90, deduces right away from this involvement in formulaic language a cultic setting of our psalm). Curiously enough, the use of rare expressions like *pědût,* "redemption" (v. 9a; occurs only three times more: Ps 130:7; Exod 8:19; Isa 50:2), *děrûš,* "sought for" (only once more: Isa 62:12), underscores the impression of Psalm 111 being rooted in later canonical history.

Our psalm concludes with an authentic wisdom counsel (v. 10; cf. Prov 1:7; 9:10; 15:33) summarizing in one sentence the only responsible position a human being may assume before God. A PRAISE OF WISDOM befits this posture; the very last line denominates the prayer as a "hymn" *(těhillāh).*

## Genre

Our preconceived idea is this: acrostic poems generically must differ from complaints, thanksgivings, and hymns. Their formal orientation is, in the first place, with alphabetical order, not a ritual but a literary and aesthetic category. Yet a closer look at acrostics in the Psalter reveals in each case a certain affinity to specific genres of psalms. Our example at hand is no doubt a HYMN, as v. 10c says explicitly and v. 1 indicates by a SUMMONS TO PRAISE and a THANKS-GIVING FORMULA (the latter expression is very close to a eulogy of Yahweh). Joining hymnic affirmations about Yahweh, then, even if supposedly taken from Scripture and lacking thematic coherence (because of alphabetic formation?), the psalmist arrives at a body of text to be considered hymnic (see "Introduction to Cultic Poetry," sections D and E; Psalms 9/10; 25; 119). The fixed alphabetical format does not preclude a generic profile.

## Setting

Acrostic organization of a text presupposes literacy at least of the spiritual leadership of the congregation. In exilic and postexilic times the Jewish community grew into literacy, with the sacred writings taking a central place in the group's worship and life. Therefore, acrostic poems may be taken as typical phenomena of an educated membership dealing continuously with the written word. Worship services were based on readings, meditations, and prayers rather than sacrificial acts. The Torah became the visible centerpiece of worship sessions. Instruction from the written word and intense study of its implications were essential preoccupations of the Jewish community. Small wonder, then, that hymn singing also tuned in with the written religious culture directly eulogizing Torah (cf. Psalms 1; 19; 119) or using its contents to formulate praises.

## Intention

The little psalm lets shine forth the glories of the God of Israel in both content and literary style. It is a witness to Yahweh by the community of faithful, and a guideline for each individual member to orient one's life toward God's superior powers. The psalm apparently was composed or at least placed together with its companion Psalm 112 (Zimmerli: "Zwillingspsalmen" = twin psalms; cf. Seybold, 440).

## Bibliography

P. Auffret, "Essai sur la structure littéraire des Psaumes CXI et CXII," *VT* 30 (1980) 257-79; idem, "Grandes sont les oeuvres de YHWH," *JNES* 56 (1997) 183-96; M. D. Koster, "Gods grote werken/Gods grote daden," *Nederlands Theologisch Tijdschrift* 33 (1979) 10-26; D. Pardee, "Acrostics and Parallelism: The Parallelistic Structure of

Psalm 111," *Maarav* 8 (1992) 117-38; J. Schildenberger, "Das Psalmenpaar 111 und 112," *Erbe und Auftrag* 56 (1980) 203-7; R. Scoralick, "Psalm 111 — Bauplan und Gedankengang," *Bib* 78 (1997) 190-205; T. L. Wilt, "Alphabetic Acrostics: Perhaps the Form Can Be Represented," *BT* 44 (1993) 207-12; W. Zimmerli, "Zwillingspsalmen"; listing at Psalm 104.

## Psalm 112:
## Acrostic Felicitation

### Structure

|  | MT | NRSV |
|---|---|---|
| I. Summons to praise | 1a | 1a |
| II. Felicitation, beatitude | 1b-4 | 1b-4 |
| III. Portrait of the righteous | 5-9 | 5-9 |
| IV. Portrait of the unjust | 10 | 10 |

Psalms 111 and 112 are close to each other in almost every respect: acrostic structure, half-line style, closeness to Scripture, life orientation of hearers/presenters, community mooring, etc. They really may be called "twin psalms" (Zimmerli, listing at Psalm 104), also in regard to content: while the first psalm extols Yahweh, the second is dedicated to Yahweh's partner in covenant, the Yahweh believer (Seybold, 440: Psalm 111 gives "theology," Psalm 112 "anthropology"). The hymn to God and the felicitation of the faithful are two sides of the same coin. Therefore, there is no need to repeat everything said on structure with regard to Psalm 111. We concentrate on specific traits of this anthropocentric song.

The psalm initiates with a communal SUMMONS TO PRAISE, as in → Ps 111:1a; 113:1a, and immediately turns to FELICITATION or BEATITUDE (vv. 1b-4). The typical opening is "happy the one who . . ." *('ašrê [hā]'îš ['ăšer])*. I surmise that the form was originally used in educational contexts to congratulate someone for his or her becoming behavior; the form was later incorporated in liturgical texts lauding certain stances and actions of religiously accepted comportment (→ 1:1). The Psalter is rich in examples of this one-time autonomous form, counting 26 occurrences of *'ašrê* altogether, representing various stages of formal modification: 1:1; 2:12; 32:1-2; 33:12; 34:9 (RSV 8); 40:5 (RSV 4); 41:2 (RSV 1); 65:5 (RSV 4); 84:5, 6, 13 (RSV 4, 5, 12); 89:16 (RSV 15); 94:12; 106:3; 112:1; 119:1-2; 127:5; 128:1-2; 137:8, 9; 144:15; 146:5 (cf. Mowinckel, *PsSt* V; idem, *W* II, 44-51). In the present context the first line of the acrostic proper (v. 1b) is an authentic beatitude: "Happy the one who fears/adores Yahweh"; that does not need amplification. A person affiliated with Yahweh and under Yahweh's protection is to be congratulated. The only exact parallel is 128:1a, but several *'ašrê* words in a similar way declare Yahweh believers as happy (cf. 2:12; 84:5, 13 [RSV 4, 12]; 106:3; 119:1-2; 146:5). Explications of ensuing happiness are not necessary, because any felicitation is self-evident (cf., e.g., 119:1-2), but they certainly fit neatly with the original saying. Everyone hearing a beatitude like this is curious to know the good consequences for the one lauded (cf. Matt 5:3: "Blessed are the poor in spirit, *for theirs is the kingdom of heaven*"). This is the reason we find a variety of amplifications of *'ašrê* words in the Hebrew writings. In our case, six lines beginning with the letters *gimel* through *ḥet* do spell out the "wages" of belonging to Yahweh's followers. One preceding line beginning with *bet* appears to be a duplication of the original *yārē' 'et yhwh*, "fearing Yahweh" (v. 1b), because it employs a verbal adjective as well (*ḥāpēṣ*, "liking," v. 1c). Now, this enumeration of blessings coming upon the faithful is cleverly articulated and arranged according to the values cherished at that time. Powerful progeny organized in an enduring clan (v. 2) in antiquity was perhaps the highest of all earthly desires. Economic well-being is essential for families and individuals, and the concept of "justice" *(ṣĕdāqāh)* in this context is plainly a synonym for this earthly blessing (v. 3). Note that our verse corresponds directly with 111:3: God's "glory and majesty" equate on the human side with "plenty and richness" (v. 3a). V. 3b being identical to 111:3b, we also have to parallel God's and humans' *ṣĕdāqāh*. Yahweh's glory remains steadfast, and — because of God's grace — the high standard of living for the "just ones" as well. Repeating the same line once more in v. 9b, the psalmist still includes the "poor" in his concept of *ṣĕdāqāh*. V. 4 climaxes the favorable perspective for the believer. He will be illuminated in darkness (v. 4a), without doubt metaphorical for "suffering." V. 4b does not have a clear subject, but it corresponds largely with 111:4b. Perhaps the name Yahweh, provided by the ancient versions, was erroneously replaced by *wĕṣaddîq*, "and the righteous one." All in all, this beatitude sings praises of that "one who fears Yahweh," in consequence being interpreted as the "one who loves his commandments" (v. 1c), who belongs to the "just ones" (v. 4a), and, possibly, is a "righteous one" (v. 4b). Already in this first part of the psalm we have a portrait of a member of the Jewish community in postexilic times.

This portrait is followed up by a new round of descriptive affirmations about the *ṣaddîq*, "the righteous one" (vv. 5-9 = eleven lines; *ṣaddîq* in v. 6, the center of the psalm with 10 lines preceding and 10 lines following). The section starts — parallel to v. 1b — with "Good [for?] a man who is merciful and prone to give loans" *(ṭôb 'îš ḥônēn ûmalweh)*. Some translations render it "Happy the man who . . . ," assuming that the actual wording has come about because of the alphabetical order, the synonym *ṭôb* substituting for *'ašrê*. This assumption is not unreasonable, but we have no parallel texts (the *ṭôb . . . min*, "better . . . than" sayings of Prov 19:1, 22; 28:6 are somewhat comparable in sentence structure, but serve a different function). Be that as it may, v. 5a strikes a new chord in putting up a new grammatical subject, qualifying the "man" to be lauded by his social consciousness. This social orientation eventually becomes important in our segment, vv. 5-9. The favorable consequences of being benevolent to others are introduced by *kî*, "for" (v. 6a), missing in v. 2. Utter fearlessness (vv. 7a, 8a, referring back to "fear of Yahweh," v. 1b) and unshakable solidity, most of all in spiritual and confessional terms, are the hallmarks of the "righteous one" (vv. 6-8). A key phrase is v. 7b: "His heart is steady in trusting Yahweh" (cf. *bṭḥ* in 4:6; 9:11; 13:6; 21:8; 22:5-6; 2 Kgs 18; Jer 7:4-15; etc.;

275

E. S. Gerstenberger, *THAT* I, 300-305). Trust in Yahweh is a result of "fearing him," i.e., belonging to him as an active worshiper. The believer's steadfastness endures even in conflicts (v. 8b). After thus reemphasizing the blessings on the worshiper, the psalm comes back to his social obligations (v. 9ab). Wealth, that important blessing to the faithful (v. 3a), is not granted for one's own consumption alone, but needs to be distributed to the poor (v. 9a; cf. Prov 11:24; Gerstenberger, *THAT* I, 23-25). The other one, be it neighbor or "stranger in your gates," clansman or member of underprivileged minority group, takes part in *ṣĕdāqāh*, "justice" (v. 9b, repeating v. 3b). His share in goods and living standards is as important as the believer's.

A man who models himself on this ideal is to be congratulated on account of his practicing faith and may stand upright, not bowing in front of anybody (v. 9c). The third colon of v. 9 thus finishes up with the PORTRAIT OF THE RIGHTEOUS actually being the second sketch of the ideal member of the congregation in this psalm.

A negative picture of the *rāšā'*, "wicked, godless" (v. 10a), as opposed to the *ṣaddîq*, "just one" (v. 6b), is apparently in order. Why is that so? Because of our binary type of thinking (brain structure) that needs oppositions in order not to get lost in shades and degrees of truth? Or is this kind of antagonistic juxtaposition of good and evil a result of daily experience of suffering from innumerous conflicts and contradictions? The PORTRAIT OF THE UNJUST given in the three cola of v. 10 is quite vague, reporting only his disgust and frustration. Summarizing, the last colon (*taw* line) simply postulates ultimate failure of the *rĕšā'îm* (cf. Prov 10:24; 11:23, which give a double prognosis for *ṣaddîqim* and *rĕšā'îm*). Three cola for a portrait of the wicked over against eight plus eleven cola for the just one — the imbalance of these passages is obvious. More often, Hebrew writings give detailed profiles of the *rĕšā'îm*. But this is a matter of genre discussion.

## Genre

Indeed, catalogues describing the godless are fairly frequent in the Hebrew Bible (→ Psalms 10; 37; 109), while the characteristics of the just ones appear only sparsely. Ps 1:1-3 pictures the just one in what he avoids and what he does: study of Torah. Ps 25:12-15 examines the destiny of the Yahweh believer. Psalm 37 shows just ones and godless ones in confrontation. Psalm 119 in all its enormous textual volume hardly raises the question of characterizing the two opposed types. Thus the topic of "just" and "unjust" persons before God is taken up by some acrostics and some other psalms as well (cf. Psalms 58; 73; 94; 109; also so-called entrance liturgies posing the question, "Who may approach God?" determine admission standards: Psalms 15; 24; Isa 33:14-16) not to speak of regular individual complaints, which struggle with their personal enemies and persecutors. Our psalm takes the difficult approach of an acrostic composition and should be labeled an ACROSTIC FELICITATION, because the just one is at the center of interest. Outside the Psalter some texts try to delineate the just one: Ezek 18:5-24; Job 31; and others. All these texts are didactic in form and content. Looking at Psalm 111 from this angle we note that it is didactic, too, sketching briefly some central traits of Yahweh, the only God to be venerated among Judeans. This obviously demonstrates that hymns can be wonderful texts for instruction.

## Setting/Intention

Who felt the need to catalogue qualities, actions, and destinies of the opposing groups of people within the community of faith in Judah and the diaspora? Main motivations probably came out of didactic situations. Think of congregations of Yahweh believers at that time who did not have a national political organization of their own but were living with dispersion or diaspora codes of faith and behavior; catalogues were the only means of forming a consciousness of identity and delimiting the true body of members. Very likely, this was done in instructional settings. Both Psalms 111 and 112 are didactic in nature. They tell the community some basic insights of why and how to praise Yahweh, concentrating on his gift of a land to live in. The two acrostics are material for instructing the community, especially youngsters to be introduced to life and worship of that religious group.

## Bibliography

P. Auffret, "En mémoire éternelle sera le juste," *VT* 48 (1998) 2-14; M. Conti, "Beatificazione del giusto e rovina dell' impio secondo il Salmo 112," *Antonianum* 69 (1994) 433-41; E. Fudge, "The Final End of the Wicked," *JETS* 27 (1984) 325-34; R. A. Harrisville, "Paul and the Psalms: A Formal Study," *Word & World* 5 (1985) 168-79; S. Mowinckel, "Marginalien zur hebräischen Metrik," *ZAW* 68 (1956) 97-123; G. W. Nebe, "Qumranica 2," *Zeitschrift für Althebraistik* 10 (1997) 134-38; St. K. Sherwood, "Psalm 112 — a Royal Wisdom Psalm?" *CBQ* 51 (1989) 50-64; B. Smilde, "Psalm 112, gelezen, gezongen, gepraktizeerd: hymnologische bespiegelingen rond een vergeten psalm," in *Ars et musica in liturgia* (*Fest.* C. Honders; ed. F. Brouwer, et al.; Metuchen: Scarecrow Press, 1994) 167-86; Y. V. Smirnov, "The Righteous Lamp of Life," *Journal of the Moscow Patriarchate* 11 (1983) 34-35; H. Thomas, "Psalm 1 and 112 as a Paradigm for the Comparison of Wisdom Motifs in the Psalms," *JETS* 29 (1986) 15-24 (cf. also Bibliography at Psalm 111).

## Psalm 113:
## Communal Hymn, Praise from Below

### Structure

|  | MT | NRSV |
|---|---|---|
| I. Summons to praise | 1 | 1 |
| II. Hymnic wish | 2-3 | 2-3 |

| III. Yahweh hymn | 4-9b | 4-9b |
|---|---|---|
| A. Praise | 4 | 4 |
| B. Challenge | 5 | 5 |
| C. Exaltation | 6-9b | 6-9b |
| IV. Summons to praise | 9c | 9c |

Three imperatives in the plural (*hallĕlû,* "sing praises") constitute a SUMMONS TO PRAISE (v. 1); the first of these has with it the object *yāh,* for "Yahweh," an opening equal to Pss 106:1a; 111:1a; 112:1a. *hallĕlû-yāh* is an autonomous nondirective shout of exaltation that also can serve as a closing element of a hymn (cf. 113:9c [LXX connects it with the following psalm]; 104:35d; 105:45c; 106:48d; 115:18c; etc. [ancient versions partially differ in all instances]). Versatile in character, this general summons is indicative of cultic ceremonialism in ancient Jewish communities. The two remaining imperatives also point to Yahweh (grammatical object), but one addresses directly the "servants of Yahweh" (ancient versions read an absolute form = vocative: "praise Yahweh, you servants"), the other adds "the name" in front of "Yahweh." In this fashion, the last two summonses focus on the congregation, which is seen in a specific role as adorants of Israel's God: *ʿăbādîm,* "servants," suggests submission, loyalty, dedication; cf. 34:23 (RSV 22); 69:37 (RSV 36); 90:13, 16; 102:15, 29 (RSV 14, 28); 105:25; 119:91; 134:1; Isa 49:1-7. We find an almost identical summons to praise in Ps 135:1 (three plural imperatives of *hll,* Piel).

While repeated exhortations to raise voices in honor of Yahweh are liturgically lucid, HYMNIC WISHES (vv. 2-3) are less plausible in the context of worship. They do not have an identifiable addressee or speaker. We may imagine that they were interjections of somebody in worship, perhaps to be in part responded to by the congregation. The phrases are formalized, precise, and rather short. Both lines elaborate the last colon of v. 1, introducing the "*name* of Yahweh" as the object to be extolled. Two passive participles take up this orientation, holding chiastic positions at the beginning and the end of the unit: "Blessed be the name of Yahweh" (v. 2a) and "Praised be the name of Yahweh" (v. 3b). They both seem adequate liturgical formulas, yet they are not frequent in Hebrew Scripture. The D theology of the "Name" of Yahweh dwelling at his "place" may loom behind this emphatic presentation (cf. Deut 12:5, 11, 21; 14:23-24; 16:2, 6, 11; etc.; G. von Rad, "Deuteronomiumstudien," in idem, *Gesammelte Studien zum Alten Testament* II [Munich: Chr. Kaiser, 1973] 109-53, esp. 127-32).

The Pual participle of *brk* is used but once more in this way (Job 1:21); the "blessing" (= extolling) of Yahweh is normally expressed by the Qal passive participle: *bārûk yhwh* (Pss 18:47 [RSV 46]; 28:6; 31:22 [RSV 21]: sixteen times in the Psalter alone; → 72:18-19). The other participle (v. 3b) is from *hll,* Pual, of which we have four more examples in the Psalter: 18:4 (RSV 3); 48:2 (RSV 1); 96:4; 145:3. Additional formulaic phrases affirm extension in time. V. 2b, "from now on until eternity," has exact parallels in 115:18; 121:8; 125:2; 131:3 (besides related expressions of long duration: 41:14 [RSV 13]; 45:7 [RSV 6]; 48:15 [RSV 14]; etc.). "From sunrise to sunset" (v. 3a) covers one full daylight's span of time (cf. 50:1; Mal 1:11), i.e., the period of possible economic and/or liturgical activity. We get the impression that the composers of Psalm 113 have purposefully joined liturgical formulas, not using the most common ones, to formulate, in an indirect way, eulogies to Yahweh. Introductory yĕhî (jussive of hyh), "may it come to pass," is rarely used in this context, although some hymns or prayers abound with wish formulations, like Psalms 20; 72; 109; 122 (mostly in relation to human entities, though). For positive wishes with yĕhî or wîhî see 9:10 (RSV 9); 33:22; 72:16-17; 90:17; 104:31; 119:76, 80; 122:7; negative ones, e.g., in 81:16 (RSV 15); 109:12-13; other forms in 33:8; 67:5 (RSV 4); 96:11-12; etc. Only in rare cases is God made the object of a wish (cf. 104:31) as he is in vv. 2-3, probably because this form of speech was considered too weak. To Yahweh honor and eulogy were not ephemeral gifts but essential tributes.

This very idea is borne out fully in the HYMN proper (vv. 4-9b). Now Yahweh is praised as sovereign of the nations and lord of the heavens (v. 4; cf. 99:2; 138:6; Isa 57:15 and Pss 36:6 [RSV 5]; 50:4; 57:6, 11-12 [RSV 5, 10-11]; 115:15-16; 148:4). In consequence, the community cries out a challenge to all the world: "Who is like Yahweh, our God?" (v. 5a). Notable is the first-person plural suffix, which occurs only in this instance, revealing the community background of the psalm (→ Psalms 8; 90). The rhetorical question provoking the answer "not a single one!" (cf. 8:2; 84:2; 92:6) is followed by a string of four participles, all Hiphils and all adorned with an archaic -î ending, exposing the qualities and wondrous acts of Yahweh (vv. 5b-9; the exchange of vv. 5b and 6b adopted by many translators is unnecessary). The passage is a good example of what has been called a "participle hymn" (Crüsemann, Studien, 83-154; listing at "Introduction to Cultic Poetry"). Yet putting one's praises into opportune participles is but one mode of speaking and singing. Adjectives also are very handy for this task (cf. v. 4; 86:10; 111:4b; 112:4b; 118:1; 135:3; 136:1; etc.) as well as nominal clauses (cf. 111:2a, 3) or even plain wishes (vv. 2-3). Formulations in our verses are different: those participles that explain Yahweh's own position and action are determined by definite articles: "The one who takes place on high" (v. 5b), "the one who looks down" (v. 6a; cf. allusions to Yahweh's lofty seat, 2:4; 14:2; 104:3). The other participles, telling about Yahweh's social actions, are not determined: "who raises the lowly from the dust" (v. 7a; cf. 1 Sam 2:8) and "who provides the home for the barren woman" (v. 9a). In fact, the correspondence with the vocabulary and ideas of the Song of Hannah (1 Sam 2:2-10) is striking (cf. Willis, Freedman, Marcus, Hurvitz). Vv. 7-8 are almost identical with 1 Sam 2:8. This does not automatically mean that our psalmist copied from the Samuel text. Why would he have contented himself with the particulars of vv. 7-9 (rehabilitation of "lowly," "poor," "barren woman")? This sort of parallelism of two texts may indicate a common stock of hymnic material, at the disposal of ancient liturgists (cf. Culley, Language, listing at "Introduction to Cultic Poetry"). In the same manner we use traditional texts available in liturgies and hymnbooks for our worship services. The present case of hymnic lines concerned with lower-class and marginalized people points to the social reality of at least some contemporary Yahweh congregations (→ Psalms 37; 73; Hossfeld and Zenger, 1993, 14-15; Lohfink,

*Lobgesänge,* listing at Additional Bibliography, section C). Placing the poor in the roles of the powerful (v. 8) means a reversal of the social order. The psalm ends, as mentioned above, in a general SUMMONS TO PRAISE, which was possibly responded to by the congregation singing their own repeated hallelujahs.

## Genre

Psalms 113–118 in later liturgical use formed one block of texts, the Great Hallel (cf. Matt 26:30; Elbogen, *Gottesdienst,* 125, 130, 136-38, listing at "Introduction to Cultic Poetry"; Zenger, "Composition," 91-92, listing at Psalm 107). The songs are indeed closely related to each other, all of them being praises of God and thanksgivings to him. Psalm 113 is a normal HYMN of the community, and a poor one at that. There is no direct address of Yahweh, in the second person; there are no reflections on creation or salvation history. The sheer necessities of life inspire this kind of hymn singing. Yahweh is pictured as the superior one governing the earth from high up beyond the skies. This fact is important not in itself but as a symbol of God's unlimited redeeming power. He is able to straighten out bad social conditions. Indeed, 1 Samuel 1–2 gives a vivid impression of life situations in which this sort of praise could be sung. Because Yahweh is the protector and provider for the discriminated, miserable, and barren ones, he is lauded and hoped for. No trace of politics, power struggles, or triumph over enemies can be detected in the text.

## Setting

Summoning a community to hail Yahweh, and this community manifesting itself briefly but authentically in saying: "Yahweh our God" (v. 5a) together with the use of familiar forms of hymn singing (see "Introduction to Cultic Poetry," section 4D) are sufficient proof for a *Sitz im Leben* in early Jewish worship services, perhaps in diaspora congregations. Early Jewish liturgical use of the Hallel psalms is in the Passover liturgy.

## Intention

To strengthen Yahweh in his superior reign, by singing hymns and bringing adoration and strength to him, means also to guarantee survival for lowly and oppressed believers. That is what this hymn is trying to accomplish.

## Bibliography

Y. Bazaq, "The Six Sections of the Hallel: Numerological Ornamentation and Formal Structure of Psalms 113–118," *BM* 34 (1989-90) 182-91 (Heb.); P. C. Craigie, "Psalm 113," *Int* 39 (1985) 70-74; D. N. Freedman, "Psalm 113 and the Song of Hannah," *Eretz*

*Israel* 14 (1978) 56-69; P. L. Graber, "The Structural Meaning of Psalm 113," *Journal for Translation and Textlinguistics* 4 (1990) 340-52; A. Hurvitz, "Originals and Imitations in Biblical Poetry: A Comparative Examination of 1 Sam 2:1-10 and Ps 113:5-9," in *Biblical and Related Studies (Fest.* S. Iwry; ed. A. Kort, et al.; Winona Lake, Ind.: Eisenbrauns, 1985) 115-21; H. B. Kossen, "The Peace Church in a World of Conflict," *Conrad Grebel Review* 2 (1984) 1-9; J. A. Loader, "A Structural Analysis of Psalm 113," *OTWSA* 19 (1976) 57-68; D. Marcus, "The Barren Woman of Psalm 113,9 and the Housewife: An Antiphrastic Dysphemism," *JANESCU* 11 (1979-81) 81-84; G. T. Prinsloo, "Yahweh and the Poor in Psalm 113," *OTE* 9 (1996) 465-85; H. Quecke, "Zur sahidischen Psalmenzählung," in *Nubia et Oriens Christianus (Fest.* C. D. G. Müller; ed. P. Scholz, et al.; Cologne: Dinter, 1987) 205-9; R. Rutherford, "Psalm 113 (114-115) and Christian Burial," *Studia Patristica* 13/2 (ed. E. Livingstone; Berlin: Akademie Verlag, 1975) 391-96; K. K. Sacon, "A Methodological Remark on Exegesis and Preaching of Psalm 113," *Nihon no Shingaku* 25 (1986) 26-42; I. W. Slotki, "Omnipresence, Condescension, and Omniscience in Ps. 113,5-6," *JTS* 32 (1931) 367-70; C. J. Weborg, "God's Break-in: Occasion for Praise," *Ex Auditu* 8 (1992) 135-39; J. T. Willis, "The Song of Hannah and Psalm 113," *CBQ* 35 (1973) 139-54; G. J. Zemek, "Grandeur and Grace: God's Transcendence and Immanence in Psalm 113," *Master's Seminary Journal* 1 (1990) 129-48.

## Psalm 114:
## Communal Hymn, Proclamation of Yahweh's Reign

### Structure

|  | MT | NRSV |
|---|---|---|
| I. Account of exodus, claim | 1-2 | 1-2 |
| II. Dramatization | 3-8 | 3-8 |
| A. Mythical account | 3-4 | 3-4 |
| B. Ridicule | 5-6 | 5-6 |
| C. Exhortation | 7-8 | 7-8 |

The opening is unusual: vv. 1-2 conjure a historical situation and draw dogmatic conlusions from it. An infinitive with the temporal preposition *bě* (cf. Ps 126:1b) introduces the sentence of the first line (v. 1): "When Israel moved out of Egypt." "Israel" recurs in v. 2b, but in v. 2a (anachronistically?) the people are named Judah, revealing late, Judahite origin of the whole assertion. The infinitive construction with concomitant subordination of the second poetic line (narrative style) is rare in the Psalter (cf. 95:7d-9; 105:12-13; 137:1-2) and signals a particular historical reflection and theological reasoning. Sacred history is a matter of serious study. The result in our case is a firm and straight affirmation of Judah's (!) election by Yahweh (v. 2). "Israel" in this context is therefore tantamount to "Judah," revealing a late exilic-postexilic stage in OT thinking. To separate a "modernizing" v. 2 from a more archaic body of the psalm (Ruppert) may be accurate in terms of literary growth. Alternatively, however, the whole psalm may have been composed around v. 2, the missing name of Yahweh being no obstacle (hymns may reveal their main agent belatedly, i.e., in v. 7).

Strong affirmations pertaining to this and no other divine overlord mark such a theological position. "His holy property/sanctuary" (*qadšô*, v. 2a) and "his political properties" (*mamšĕlôtāyw*, v. 2b; one of two plural forms; see 136:9) are designations of the Yahweh community (see 103:22; 145:13 for the latter; and Ezra 8:32; Lev 19:2 for the former, the noun *qōdeš* used mostly for space and equipment reserved to Yahweh). The congregation itself, then, is declared the "sanctuary" of God (cf. Lev 19:2). This, indeed, is a very bold statement in the Priestly line of theological thinking (cf. Gerstenberger, *Leviticus,* 96-127, 261-62; Knohl, *Sanctuary,* 148-57; listing at Additional Bibliography, section B). Vv. 1-2 seem to be an opening statement of didactic rather than liturgical qualities, an announcement of claims against concurrent entities, a theological conclusion drawn from ancient history. The prelude of our psalm is a dogmatic statement or theological CLAIM.

What follows, judging from speech forms, has characteristics of a DRAMATIZATION exposing the elements of MYTHICAL ACCOUNT, RIDICULE, and EXHORTATION (vv. 3-8). Someone first recounts the agitation of primeval chaos waters and emerging mountains. No doubt, the language and metaphors of "sea" *(yām),* "Jordan" *(yardēn),* and "mountains" or "hills" *(hārîm, gĕbāʿôt)* (vv. 3-6) all point back to a creation myth. From other psalms (cf. 77:17-18 [RSV 16-17]; 93:3-4; 104:7-9) as well as from Ugaritic and Akkadian texts we are familiar with the raging floods that finally have to give in and flee in the face of the good creator deity. The description of the early events involving Yahweh and Israel makes use of that mythological language enriched by metaphors of theophanic origins (both fields of discourse are related to each other; cf. Jeremias, *Theophanie,* see Bibliography of Psalm 18). The uproar of primeval powers in the present context is juxtaposed to the exodus event, not to creation. The composers of our psalm apparently interpret Exodus 14–15 and Josh 3:9-17 side by side. The waters seem to behave more civilly in both narratives, and the verbs denoting "fleeing" and "turning around" (v. 3) are not used in these accounts, with the waters being subjects. But cultic dramatization wants it this way, personalizing the enemies of Yahweh in a continuing battle for the world order, designing a cosmic picture even in a historical situation. In this fashion, even the river Jordan acquires primeval qualities resembling the "Lord River" in the Baal myths.

The dramatical setup becomes clear with the taunting RIDICULE of vv. 5-6. Ancient ritualized warfare included verbal exchanges before the battle started (cf. 1 Sam 17:41-47; 2 Sam 2:12-16) as well as severe taunts of the victorious party against the defeated one (cf. Judg 5:27; Isa 14:4-23). Asking another person "What is wrong with you?" in times of peace is a manifestation of sympathy and concern (cf. Gen 21:17; Josh 15:18; Judg 18:24; 2 Sam 14:5; 1 Kgs 1:16; etc.). But given a situation of bloody conflict and the defeat of one party, the same question asked by the victors is deadly irony. Thus in Baal's fight against Yam, the god of the sea, we meet a very similar figure of speech:

Baal's enemies take to the woods, Hadd's foes to the sides of the
mountain,
Quoth Puissant Baal: "Baal's enemies, why do you quake; Why do
you quake?" (H. L. Ginsberg, *ANET* 135)

Mountains and hills jumping like lambs (cf. Ps 29:6; 1 Chr 15:29; Qoh
3:4) should be taken as an expression of joy. Mountains are no longer part of
chaos; they are created bodies, greeting their creator in awe and festive action.
The psalmist does not hesitate to mingle the battle of creation and theophanic
motion and to connect them with Israel's exodus from Egypt, which may have
been celebrated dramatically at an early Jewish festival (Mowinckel, *PsSt* II).
What is the lesson to be learned from Yahweh's primeval victory, which,
theologically speaking, was restaged in the exodus from Egypt, thus becoming
the foundation event for the Judahite community of faith? The last section of
the psalm is an EXHORTATION to all the world to pay homage to the God of Jacob (v. 7). The universal outlook is remarkable. Some Yahweh-kingship songs
use similar phraseology and theological concepts: 96:7-10; 97:1-6. "Earth,
world" (*'ereṣ*, v. 7a), the civilized world of humans, is to be distinguished from
the watery chaos powers (vv. 3, 5) and the created but uninhabitable mountains
(vv. 4, 6). After addressing the world the psalmist reverts to sacred history and
scriptural witness, reinterpreting it profoundly. The last line carries a true
hymnic element, extolling Yahweh in a participial phrase because of his water
wonders during the exodus (Exod 17:1-7; Num 20:2-13; cf. Ps 107:35; Isa
35:7; 41:18; Deut 8:15). The quality and quantity of the miracle are enlarged
when rocks and stones are transformed into water.

## *Genre*

Form critics have observed that Psalm 114 conveys a mood of hymn singing but
does not have many formal characteristics of hymnic language. The summons
to praise is missing as well as the typical descriptions of Yahweh's superiority
and success. There is but one hymnic participle (v. 8a: "he who turns the rock
into a lake"), and, of course, there are Yahweh's victory over primeval powers
(vv. 3, 5) and his coming in glory (vv. 4, 6) behind the scenes. Thus the occasion of lauding Judah's God is modeled into a dialogical structure with several
voices taking part: liturgist (narrator), challenger, exhortator. They enact that
moment when Yahweh defeated chaos and had his reign proclaimed over all the
earth, coinciding with the liberation of Israel from Egypt. This event is articulated as a COMMUNAL HYMN characteristic of exilic-postexilic Judahite theological thinking. Lubsczyk holds that Psalms 114 and 115 according to LXX
reading should be joined into one covenant liturgy (most other exegetes consider both psalms "totally different" texts; thus Ruppert, 81).

## Setting

Some early Jewish festival is behind a hymnic intonation like this. Scholars like to think about the Passover celebrations, because of the exodus theme in vv. 1-2, 8, and later use of the Hallel psalms (→ Psalm 113; 118) in Jewish Passover liturgies (cf. Halbe, et al.), or they prefer an enthronement ritual linked to the New Year ceremonies in the fall (cf. Mowinckel, *W* I, 114-15). The psalms do not offer sufficient information to decide which festival was the origin for this notion of Yahweh's taking over his dominion. What we can say is this: the early Jewish community, with or without its temple intact, proclaimed Yahweh's lordship in its services. Dtr vocabulary and spirituality are visible in our short psalm (Lohfink, "Ps 114," 204, has a list of 11 coincidences), and influences of Second Isaiah (Zenger, based on Schröten, *Entstehung;* listing at Psalm 118) may help us to identify a Jewish congregational theology of the postexilic age.

## Intention

A sovereign Deity has elected a special community of faith to let it partake in the benefits of his government, or perhaps more: finally to execute his reign through the elected people (cf. Psalm 2; Isa 49:22-23). The eulogy of Yahweh's power is to maintain and strengthen the confessing community.

## Bibliography

P. Auffret, "Notes conjointes sur la structure littéraire des Psaumes 114 et 29," *EstBib* 37 (1978) 103-13; A. Berlin, "Jeremiah 29:5-7: A Deuteronomic Allusion," *HAR* 8 (1984) 3-11; K. Burba, "Psalm 114: Wir singen ihn täglich," *Luther* 62 (1991) 12-20; B. Bureau, "Exercices spirituels et exercice rhétorique dans commentaires antiques et médiévaux du Ps 113:1-6," *Revue théologique de Louvain* 29 (1998) 46-67; 180-201; S. A. Geller, "The Language of Imagery in Psalm 114," in *Lingering over Words (Fest.* W. L. Moran; ed. T. Abusch, et al.; Atlanta: Scholars Press, 1990) 179-94; G. Glessner, "Aufbruch als Heimat: Zur Theologie des 114. Psalms," *ZKT* 116 (1994) 472-79; J. C. Greenfield, "A Mandaic 'Targum' of Psalm 114," in *Studies in Aggadah, Targum and Jewish Liturgy* (ed. J. Petuchowski; Jerusalem: Magnes, 1981) 23-31; J. Halbe, "Das Passa-Massot-Fest im deuteronomischen Festkalender," *ZAW* 87 (1975) 147-68; idem, "Erwägungen zu Ursprung und Wesen des Massotfestes," *ZAW* 87 (1975) 324-46; J. H. Hunter, "Theophany Verses in the Hebrew Psalms," *OTE* 11 (1998) 255-70; O. Kaiser, *Bedeutung* (listing at Additional Bibliography, section B); H.-J. Kraus, "Gilgal — Ein Beitrag zur Kultusgeschichte Israels," *VT* 1 (1951) 181-99; idem, "Zur Geschichte des Passah-Massot-Festes im Alten Testament," *EvT* 18 (1958) 47-67; F. Langlamet, *Gilgal et les récits de la traversée du Jourdain* (Cahiers de la *RB* 11; Paris: Gabalda, 1969); A. Lauha, *Geschichtsmotive* (see Bibliography at Psalm 78); N. Lohfink, "Ps 114 & 115 und die deuteronomische Sprachwelt," in *Freude an der Weisung des Herrn (Fest.* H. Gross; ed. E. Haag, et al.; Stuttgart: Katholisches Bibelwerk, 1986) 199-205; H. Lubsczyk, "Einheit und heilsgeschichtliche Bedeutung von Ps. 114/115 (113)," *BZ*

11 (1967) 161-73; A. A. Macintosh, "Christian Exodus," *Theology* 72 (1969) 317-19; G. T. Prinsloo, "Tremble before the Lord," *OTE* 11 (1998) 306-25; F. Refoulé, "Note sur Romains 9:30-33," *RB* 92 (1985) 161-86; B. Renaud, "Les deux lectures de Ps. 114," *RSR* 52 (1978) 14-28; L. Ruppert, "Zur Frage der Einheitlichkeit von Psalm 114," in *Altes Testament — Forschung und Wirkung (Fest.* H. Graf Reventlow; ed. P. Mommer, et al.; Frankfurt: Peter Lang, 1994) 81-94; V. E. Schmitt, "'Wer ist dieser Gott?' Israel besingt seinen Schöpfer," *Geist und Leben* 53 (1980) 18-24; K. L. Schmitz, "World and Word in Theophany," *Faith and Philosophy* 1 (1984) 50-70; E. Vogt, "Die Erzählung vom Jordanübergang Jos 3–4," *Bib* 46 (1965) 125-48; M. Weiss, "Psalm 114," *Tarbiz* 49 (1979/80) 527-35; G. H. Wilson, "The Use of 'Untitled' Psalms in the Hebrew Psalter," *ZAW* 97 (1985) 404-13.

# Psalm 115:
## Communal Hymn, Polemics against Idols

### Structure

|  | MT | NRSV |
|---|---|---|
| I. Abnegation, summons to praise | 1 | 1 |
| II. Communal complaint, response | 2-3 | 2-3 |
| III. Derision of idols | 4-7 | 4-7 |
| IV. Denunciation of idolaters, imprecation | 8 | 8 |
| V. Summons to trust | 9-11 | 9-11 |
| VI. Blessing | 12-15 | 12-15 |
|   A. Communal wish | 12a | 12a |
|   B. Blessing | 12b-15 | 12b-15 |
| VII. Praise of Yahweh | 16-18 | 16-18 |
|   A. Affirmation of overlordship | 16 | 16 |
|   B. Affirmation of loyalty | 17-18b | 17-18b |
|   C. Summons to praise | 18c | 18c |

Apart from Ps 135:15-18 (which corresponds almost word for word to vv. 4-6, 8), there is no parallel to our text in the Psalter. Individual parts of Psalm 115 are therefore enigmatic and not easy to classify. The overall structure also is difficult to analyze and to locate in a special setting.

What does the opening element (v. 1) stand for? The imperative of v. 1b seems to suggest the form "petition" as in complaint psalms ("give honor/recognition to . . . "; cf. 89:51-52 [RSV 50-51]). But the contents ("Yahweh, give honor to your name" — "not to us": what does this mean to say?) advise against this classification. Rather, the statement is a theological, not a liturgical, one comparable to the general idea that Israel failed completely, but nevertheless has been sustained by Yahweh (cf. Neh 9:16-35; Dan 9:4-19). "Not we — but you, Yahweh" deserve homage — this kind of discourse sounds like a confession of guilt and at the same time a sophisticated hymnic reference; cf. Ps 100:3: "Understand that Yahweh is God; he has made us — not we ourselves —

his people and the sheep of his pasture." Another way of expressing the one-sideness of divine help and forbearance is to emphasize that Yahweh acted "re-gardless [or 'not because'] of Israel's merits" to do her good (cf. Deut 7:7-8; Isa 48:11; Ezek 36:32; etc.). Therefore, our v. 1 is a hymnic statement, or a SUM-MONS TO PRAISE, if one considers also that "to give glory *(kābôd)*" can hardly be made a petition of human clients (cf. Ps 8:6 [RSV 5], where divine qualities are bestowed by surprising grace, not on request; 29:1-2; 96:7-8: deities and na-tions "bring glory").

In contrast to the unspeakable glory and power of Yahweh, his faithful community suffers shame and pain from gloating strangers in a pluralistic soci-ety probably of Babylonian or Persian times (v. 2). The cynical question "Where is their/his/your God?" is a standard taunt either taken from real experi-ence or created in theological reflection and controversy with real or imagined opponents (v. 2b; cf. 2 Kgs 18:34-35; Pss 42:4, 11 [RSV 3, 10]; 79:10; Joel 2:17. Narrational texts sometimes give modified taunts of the nations: Ezek 36:20; Num 14:16; Isa 36:7-20; etc.). The question of the community is why God allowed this to happen (v. 1a), a typical accusatory charge against a deity supposedly failing in her/his responsibilities during complaint services; → Pss 22:2 (RSV 1); 44:10 (RSV 9). The answer follows directly, using a type of con-cise communal confession: "Our (!) God is in heaven; everything he likes he ef-fectuates" (v. 3; cf. E. S. Gerstenberger, "Bekenntnis, AT," *TRE* XIII, 386-88; for the formula of legal power see Hurvitz). The first person plural is conclusive for communal discourse (→ Psalms 46; 90).

Instead of following suit with laudatory affirmations about God, the stronghold of Israel's faith, the psalm continues with strong polemics against idols and idol makers along the line of Second Isaiah (vv. 4-8; cf. Isa 40:18-25; 44:9-20; Jer 10:3-16; Preuss, *Verspottung,* listing at Additional Bibliography, section B). Since Ps 135:15-18 is almost identical with our passage, we may first compare the two psalm sections. Both texts focus on handmade "idols" (*'ăşabbîm:* v. 4a; 135:15a). Subjects in both versions are the *gôyim,* "nations," with the difference that v. 4 has to connect with this subject word in v. 2a, while 135:15 simply runs "the idols of the nations." Because they are manufactured of most precious metals, they lack all vitality and power. The word *'ăşabbîm* itself seems to underline this postulate: it does not refer to techniques of producing idols like *massēkāh,* "molten image," or *pesel,* "carved image," nor to forbidden religious praxis like *tĕmûnāh,* "likeness, appearance," or *şelem,* "statue," but seems to be oriented to homophonous Heb. *'eşeb II,* plural *'ăşābîm,* "insults." Handmade images are, in the opinion of those who recited this psalm, a terrible nuisance, a sacrilege. This is the basic affirmation of the two texts as well as those parallels from Isaiah and Jeremiah cited above. Examples of such denun-ciatory talk are given by three lines in vv. 5-7 and only two lines in 135:16-17. Wording of the two common lines is so stereotyped that I am inclined to think of a popular provenance. Mouth, eyes, ears, and nose are correctly modeled to make statues in the likeness of human beings, but they do not function at all. Each of the four phrases comprises exactly four words to express the existence of communicative organs and to declare their uselessness. In a literal, hebraizing translation: "Mouth they have, not can they speak" (v. 5a; the other three sentences are exactly alike; 135:16-17 deviates only in v. 17b). Possibly, these four cola in two lines were proverbial at that time and were incorporated into the polemical section by some redactor or composer (cf. also Deut 4:28). Now, in v. 7 our psalm has a surplus over against the text of 135:15-18. Mentioning, in a three-cola line, the hands, feet, and throat of the idols, the text enters into another dimension, that of free locomotion, and repeats the first item of v. 5a, phonetic expression, with different vocabulary. A formal observation also calls for attention: each of the three cola has only three words to it, and the LXX works on adjusting this picture to the four-word pattern of vv. 5-6. With 135:16-17 moving immediately to v. 18 (= our v. 8) and the special features of v. 7 in our mind, we may conclude that this latter line is a secondary accretion to the preceding block of four sensual failures of dead idols. The concluding line is again common to both texts (v. 8 and 135:18). The verdict over manufactured gods is applied to the manufacturers. A wish form of the verb *hyh,* "to be," is used (imperfect or jussive of the third person plural). The DERISION of idols and idol manufactoring leads to the DENUNCIATION of idolaters, and that equals IMPRECATION. Bitterly aggressive satire like this presupposes a climate of religious tensions, conflicts, and forced theological reflection. Because of its compactness, uniformity, and rhythm the passage lends itself, liturgically, to be chanted by choirs or congregation.

In providing the key word "trust," the end of v. 8 is a "road sign" toward the next section focusing on "trust" in Yahweh (vv. 9-11). Nowhere in the Hebrew Bible do we find an exhortation using so often the verb *bṭḥ* with the following preposition *bě,* "to confide in." The closest parallel at this point is the narrative about Hezekiah's trust in Yahweh, 2 Kings 18 (= Isaiah 36; 2 Chr 32:1-19). The SUMMONS TO TRUST in imperative form, however, is fairly rare: in the plural, Pss 4:6 (RSV 5); 62:9 (RSV 8); Isa 26:4; in the singular, Pss 37:3, 5; Prov 3:5 (extant jussive forms are negated, advising against trust in the wrong entities). Taken together with analogous expressions like "seek shelter," "wait for," "be quiet with," "take refuge to" — all directed to Yahweh or his holy abode — as well as with other exhortations to participants of worship, evidence for an ancient liturgical practice of admonition can be multiplied (cf. Pss 11:1; 22:24 [RSV 23]; 32:9; 37:7, 34; 55:23 [RSV 22]; 62:11 [RSV 10]; 66:16; 75:5-6 [RSV 4-5]; 78:1; etc. Perhaps divine warnings as in Psalms 50 and 81 may be taken as proof, too). In any case, our passage is an important piece of exhortatory discourse in the Psalms. Three groups within the congregation are called with exactly the same words to "confide in Yahweh," and they apparently have to respond all in the same way: "Their help and their shield is he" (vv. 9b, 10b, 11b).Why are third-person and not first-person plural suffixes attached to the nouns? This, indeed, is a tricky question. Either the liturgy used "alienating" forms of speech, as sometimes was done in deference to a high authority, when suppliants or interlocutors referred to themselves in this neutral way; or the psalmist could not pull out of his neutral, external position, presenting a learned psalm, a piece of literature only, not to be used in worship. I believe the first option is closer to reality.

The text so far reminds one of lively ceremonial procedures also in the light of its partial parallel, Psalm 135. There we find four groups called upon to "bless" or "hail" Yahweh, not to "confide in" him. Four rubrics in 135:19-20 are organized more regularly: three times the group addressed is called "house of" (Israel, Aaron, Levi), and the fourth group is called "those who fear Yahweh" just like the last one of our list (v. 11a). Now, our present psalm has only two of the three names mentioned above (Israel, Aaron: vv. 9a, 10a), and the first one is missing *bêt,* "house," in some MT MSS (other Hebrew texts — even v. 12a — and all the LXX tradition do have *bêt yiśrā'ēl,* "house of Israel," as all Hebrew MSS have *bêt 'ăhărōn,* "house of Aaron"). Granted that the full denominations with *bêt* are original, what is the significance of these groupings and their being called upon separately? How do the listings differ among themselves? The absence of "house of Levi" in Psalm 115 may be accidental (note the mutilation of v. 9a), or it may signify ignorance of or disregard for the Levi group. The problem between Aaronites and Levites may be studied in Numbers 16 and the books of Chronicles. They were, for some time during the Second Temple period, rival priestly clans. The range and background of "house of Israel" and "Yahweh-fearers" are less known. Could the first one be "Israel's laymen," and the second one "the proselytes" from other nations (thus Acts 10:2, 22; 13:16, 26; Gunkel, 498)? Both definitions are to be doubted for the centuries B.C.E. (cf. J. Becker, *Gottesfurcht im Alten Testament* [AnBib 25; Rome: Pontifical Biblical Institute, 1965]). In vv. 9-11 a certain segmentation of the congregation addressed is clear (cf. also Ps 118:2-4, with its identical sequence of "Israel, . . . house of Aaron, . . . Yahweh-fearers"). Perhaps it reflects a liturgical division of the congregation, but all of them have to intone the same hymnic half-line. This means that the summons to trust really implies also a summons to praise (cf. 135:19-20, where plural imperatives of *brk,* "bless," take the place of our exhortation to "trust in Yahweh"). Vv. 9-11, then, reveal a clear antiphonal structure: someone voices a summons to the plenary "Israel" and two subgroups of the congregation, and the ones addressed respond by a set liturgical phrase: "He is their help and their shield" (in Hebrew only three words: *'ezrām ûmāginnām hû*).

Psalm 135 closes with a summons to bless or praise, but Psalm 115 continues after the SUMMONS TO TRUST. There is a new start with v. 12, which some MSS understand as the beginning of a new psalm. But the first line is incomplete; LXX adds a first-person plural suffix to the second verb "he may bless us." Thus v. 12a becomes a statement of faith and hope: "Yahweh has been mindful of us," leading toward a WISH to be blessed by Yahweh (→ Psalms 91; 121; 128; C. A. Keller and G. Wehmeier, *THAT* I, 353-76; Westermann, *Segen* [= *Blessing*]). The verb is *brk,* Piel, "to bless"; the subject of the three following complete phrases (vv. 12b-14), echoing the communal petition, is Yahweh. The verbal expression (third masculine singular imperfect) always stays the same: "He may bless." The congregation is calling their Protector (Davies, "Minder"; listing at Psalm 121) to bless her, but indirectly so, in wish sentences. Or else the liturgist takes up the communal wish for blessing (v. 12a), repeating the petition, in a third-person, neutral form. As hinted at above, the same threefold division of groups in the congregation as in vv. 9-11 comes to the fore again (vv. 12bc, 13a). After the last colon of the series (v. 13a) an interesting characterization of the community is added: "the small ones together with the great ones" (v. 13b). This circumscription may mean younger and older worshipers, or it could indicate social status, which coincides better with the term *gādôl*, "great" (cf. R. Mosis, *TWAT* I, 928-56).

A WISH FOR BLESSING, or indirect blessing, continues into v. 14, but now in direct-address style: an official communicates God's blessing (or quest for blessing) to the community (second-person plural suffixes; → Pss 91:3-13; 121:4-8; Num 6:24-25). The partition into a nondirected wish form (vv. 12b-13) and a direct, comforting application (vv. 14-15) may be a liturgical device. First, the officiant mentions the separate groups seeking God's grace — in neutral language. Afterward, he speaks directly to all of them as they participate in the service, unified by their faith in Yahweh. Our worship language today quite often follows the same rule, e.g., in intercessory prayer.

V. 15 may still cause a little doubt as to its precise meaning. Taken literally, it seems to draw an overall conclusion: a participial phrase affirms the status of being blessed by Yahweh — unless we have to understand that participle to continue the wishful discourse that preceded. Since a simple assertion "You are blessed" would be strange after all the prayerful wishes to receive blessings from the Lord, I would choose the second option, knowing full well that the simple addition of the verb *hyh* in the form "may you [be blessed]" would have made the case clearer (cf. "holy may you be," Lev 19:2 — with the auxiliary verb *tihyû*, "may you"). Still, the abundant wish forms of vv. 12-14 may influence the meaning of v. 15. Yahweh as the creator of the universe (v. 15b) is asked to grant further blessing. Vv. 12b-15, then, were probably spoken by a liturgist.

At the end, the psalm reverts to the issue of praising Yahweh (vv. 16-18). A hymnic line (v. 16) eulogizes the Lord of the heavens (cf. v. 3) who granted the earth to be a human possession. This assertion is the basis for the praise emanating from the community (v. 18ab), the dark background of this bright and lovely song of praise being the netherworld, unable to emit praises to the living God at all times (v. 17; cf. 6:6 [RSV 5]; 88:11-13 [RSV 10-12]; etc.). This statement, of course, in the last resort has been part and parcel of complaints. Decisive, however, is praise coming from the community of faithful. For the third time in this psalm the community as a whole voices its participation (v. 18a; cf. vv. 3a, 12a). The strongly emphasized personal pronoun "we" ("bless Yah" [short form of "Yahweh"]) demonstrates the value of being a group of followers of this great God. We may understand the imperfect phrase as open to the future: "We shall/want to bless Yahweh," a declaration strengthened by a concluding SUMMONS TO PRAISE, "hallelujah." If taken more in the past sense the psalm as a whole could be understood as actual hymnic praise, including the exhortation of vv. 9-11.

## Genre

Hymnic elements seem to struggle with several other modes of liturgical speech: complaint, polemic, exhortation, wish. Yet the psalm may be declared a real HYMN of the community. Vv. 1, 3, 16-18 strike the tone of praise; vv. 3, 12, 18 reveal the community of Yahweh believers and their worship service as the fertile matrix of our text. (Anderson, 786; Allen, 109; et al., view an inverse development of our text: from complaint to praise.) Hymnic praise — this much is clear from the evidence — does not go uncontested and unmolested by daily affairs. Obviously, the contemporary Jewish congregation had to suffer attacks from the outside, considered heathen religion a senseless adoration of dead idols (resulting, in reality, in oppressive discrimination by the powerful foes or rulers), needed internal stimulation to confide in Yahweh alone, and surely was in need of his blessing. In all these external and internal difficulties praise of Yahweh "in heaven" (vv. 3, 16), i.e., in an untouchable reigning position, provides necessary support. Beyerlin recognizes a strong internal affinity ("blessing") of Psalm 115 to Psalm 67.

## Setting

Worship assemblies of some kind, as with most other psalms, have been the place of origin and use of such liturgical poetry. The character of these gatherings is hard to determine. We do not necessarily have to think of important annual festivals where Judahites of the later periods of OT history met. Local reunions of Yahweh believers in nonfestive times were sufficient to voice in communion the power of God in heaven. Congregational groups were present at these meetings comparable to the situation in Priestly writings or Chronicles (e.g., Lev 9:1-7: Moses-Aaron-Israelites; 1 Chr 16:1-6: David-Israelites-Levites-priests; cf. J. P. Weinberg, "Die Agrarverhältnisse in der Bürger-Tempel-Gemeinde der Achämenidenzeit," *Acta Antiqua* 22 [1974] 473-586). This (weekly?) assembly also was the place of common learning, of instruction and exhortation.

## Intention

Hymns sung in the middle of daily anguish and toil are intoned in self-defense and stubborn resistance to powers encroaching on one's own spiritual living space. Second Isaiah gives a number of examples of this situation of marginalized communities of faith (cf. Isa 40:18-25; 44:9-20; 46:1-7; 47:1-15; Preuss, *Verspottung*, listing at Additional Bibliography, section B; he does not consider, though, the situation of the oppressed minority acting in utter self-defense). Reassurance of Yahweh's power to enact "what he likes," the active defense against pagan (and Jewish?!) fabricators of idols, and the fortification of one's own community of the faithful are the goals of the worshiping group, which receives encouragement by way of this liturgy full of blessing (cf. Frettlöh).

## Bibliography

U. Bergmann, "Old Testament Concepts of Blessing: Their Relevance for a Theological Interpretation of the Cargo Cult," *Point* 3 (1974) 176-86; W. Beyerlin, *Im Lichte,* 51-

137; see listing at Psalm 67; M. L. Frettlöh, "Von der Macht des Segens," *Junge Kirche* 56 (1995) 638-41; idem, "Gott segnen," *EvT* 56 (1996) 482-510; R. Hammer, "Two Liturgical Psalms: Salvation and Thanksgiving," *Judaism* 40 (1991) 484-97; A. Hurvitz, "The History of a Legal Formula: *kōl ᵃšer ḥāpēṣ 'āśāh* (Pss cxv 3; cxxxv 6)," *VT* 32 (1982) 257-67; Z. Kameeta, "Why, O Lord: Psalms and Sermons from Namibia," *Risk* 28 (1986) 1-62; H. Lubsczyk, "Einheit und heilsgeschichtliche Bedeutung von Ps. 114/ 115 (113)," *BZ* 11 (1967) 161-73; K. Luke, "The Setting of Psalm 115," *Irish Theological Quarterly* 34 (1967) 347-357; J. Mayonet, "Convention and Creativity: The Phrase "maker of heaven and earth" in the Psalms," in *Open Thou Mine Eyes (Fest.* W. G. Braude; ed. H. Blumberg, et al.; Hoboken: Ktav, 1992) 139-53; M. Metzger, "Eigentumsdeklaration und Schöpfungsaussage," in *'Wenn nicht jetzt' (Fest.* H.-J. Kraus; ed. H.-G. Geyer, et al.; Neukirchen-Vluyn: Neukirchener Verlag, 1983) 37-51; N. P. Moritzen, "Psalm 115," *Zeitschrift für Mission* 10 (1984) 2-4; H. D. Preuss, *Verspottung fremder Religionen im Alten Testament* (BWANT 92; Stuttgart: Kohlhammer, 1971); C. Westermann, *Der Segen in der Bibel und im Handeln der Kirche* (Munich: Chr. Kaiser, 1968 (Eng.: *Blessing in the Bible and the Life of the Church* [Philadelphia: Fortress, 1978]); M. Wilcox, "The Aramaic Targum to Psalms," in *Proceedings of the 9th World Congress of Jewish Studies* (ed. R. Giveon, et al.; Jerusalem: World Union of Jewish Studies, 1986) 143-50.

## Psalm 116:
## Thanksgiving of the Individual

### *Structure*

| | MT | NRSV |
|---|---|---|
| I. Declaration of being heard | 1-2 | 1-2 |
| II. Account of trouble and salvation | 3-4 | 3-4 |
| III. Responses of community | 5-7 | 5-7 |
| IV. Thanks and vow of the saved one | 8-9 | 8-9 |
| V. Account of trouble and salvation | 10-11 | 10-11 |
| VI. Vow and fulfillment | 12-15 | 12-15 |
| VII. Account of salvation | 16 | 16 |
| VIII. Vow and fulfillment | 17-19 | 17-19 |

Quite a few exegetes assess any given psalm primarily as a poetic text composed by some unknown individual. Consequently, they look principally for a coherent poetical and thematic structure. With Psalm 116 such interpreters encounter certain difficulties in establishing a logical, poetic, and theological order, because the structure of the text seems haphazard. I shall try to understand the psalm — in accordance with what has been said in the introductions (*FOTL* XIV) — as a liturgical piece serving certain functions in worship, knowing full well that some enigmas of the text will remain.

The introduction is enigmatic already. How can a psalm, and an individual thanksgiving at that, open up with a declaration of love (to Yahweh? Cf.

291

v. 1a in MT: "I love, because Yahweh has heard")? The verb *'hb,* "to love," used without a direct object, i.e., in an absolute state, does not make sense. The first person of the suppliant does not make much sense either. A minimal emendation is: "I love Yahweh, because he has heard. . . ." The sequence of events in vv. 1-2 (declaration–confession of having been heard–account of crying to the Lord) also seems odd. To express "love" (= allegiance) for Yahweh or his presence seems to be a late usage (cf. Deut 6:5; 11:1; 13:4; Ps 119:47, 48, 97, 113, 119, 127, 140, 159, 163, 167; in Psalm 119 the verb "love" is, in fact, restricted to use in relation to God's word and will; there are rare parallels in the rest of the Psalter: 26:8; 31:24). What we can glean from the text in regard to its form and function is this: an individual is articulating his/her experience of having been heard, while in deep distress, by Yahweh. The opening word for such a DECLARATION OF BEING HEARD could have been *'ăhallēl,* "I shall praise," *'āšîrāh,* "I shall sing," *'ărûmēm,* "I shall extol," *'ôdeh,* "I shall give thanks," or *'erḥōm,* "I shall love" (only occurrence: 18:2 [RSV 1], with suffix "you"; the absolute use without object is not attested for any of these verbal expressions, however; cf. 56:5, 11 [RSV 4, 10]; Exod 15:21; Pss 30:2 [RSV 1]; 111:1; 18:2 [RSV 1]). To call attention to Yahweh's audience is a fitting start for a thanksgiving song (cf. 30:2-4 [RSV 1-3]; 118:5; Jonah 2:3 [RSV 2]; "Introduction to Cultic Poetry," section C). It may also be used to close a prayer (cf. Ps 66:19-20).

Equally opportune for a personal thanksgiving, in fact, indispensable for such a ritual, is an ACCOUNT OF TROUBLE AND SALVATION (vv. 3-4). In our case, the text is short and concentrated, but in essence it is replete with characteristic phrases to be uttered at this point of the ceremony: the saved one was close to death, better, he already had fallen prey to death and the netherworld; he was suffering deepest agony (v. 3; cf. Jonah 2:6 [RSV 5]: "Waters surrounded me, threatening my life, the deep engulfed me"; Ps 88:6 [RSV 5]: "I am 'abandoned' like the slain in their graves"; Chr. Barth, *Errettung,* listing at "Introduction to Psalms). Anguished crying to God, the only possible savior (v. 4), is a standard topic of complaints (cf. 5:3 [RSV 2]; 22:2-3 [RSV 1-2]; 102:2-3 [RSV 1-2]; 142:2-3 [RSV 1-2]; etc.). Consequently, looking back at the occasion of a thanksgiving feast is to recall these decisive moments and ceremonies of crying out to the name of the Savior-God. To quote, in condensed form, the words of the suppliant's prayer (v. 4b) is a proven means of re-creating the times of anguish (cf. 30:10-11 [RSV 9-10]; 32:5). So far, then, we find our text elements in line with a thanksgiving ceremony for someone saved from death, be it physical or social.

Next, in a worship service of gratitude (cf. 107:1-32) we would expect explicit praises and thanksgivings of the saved person. In fact, this element is the most important one in ceremonies of rendering thanks. Vv. 5-9 do fall into this category, although they do not yet include the offertory formula (cf. v. 17a; Crüsemann, *Studien,* 267-82; listing at "Introduction to Cultic Poetry"). Thus the very act of giving thanks, e.g., the handing over of a sacrificial animal or the recitation of a relevant prayer, appears to be postponed. Furthermore, the individual lines of this section seem to represent different speakers, ideas, and liturgical moments: the only first person plural of the whole psalm, i.e., the community speaking, comes to the fore in v. 5. Modifying an old liturgical praise formula (v. 5a; cf. 103:8; 111:4; 112:4; Exod 34:6; Neh 9:17, 33), the congregation puts in a response, aware of Yahweh's miraculous grace, justice, and mercy (*ḥannûn,* "gracious," and *ṣaddîq,* "just," are adjectives; *mĕraḥēm,* "showing mercy," is a Piel participle rarely used in liturgical formulas: perhaps a conscious modification?). Continued praising affirmations in vv. 6-7 now expose an "I" as speaker. The connection to v. 5 is made by a participle extolling Yahweh the "guardian of [lit. 'protecting'] the weak ones." This participle combines well with *mĕraḥēm,* the last word of v. 5: Yahweh's ongoing, continuing mercy and protection are better expressed in this way than by adjectives. The question, however, is simply: Who formulated the phrases of vv. 6-7? The main verbs in these two lines (*yš',* Hiphil imperfect, "save," v. 6b; *gml,* Qal perfect, "grant") seem to affirm Yahweh's support in general terms. Also, each of the three lines in vv. 5-7 has its center in the name of Yahweh, a liturgical point of gravitation. Possibly, then, all three lines were sung by the community signifying that the whole assembly was grounded in trusting Yahweh's unfathomable benevolence (vv. 5, 6a), and each member ("I") adopted the experience of being saved for him/herself (vv. 6b-7).

Vv. 8-9, on the other hand, exhibit quite a different character. The saving act of Yahweh, alluded to in v. 8 ("you rescued me from death," v. 8a), no longer affirms continuous and general help but a specific act of salvation. In addition, the phrase is clad in prayer language ("you, God"), like vv. 16-17, the center of individual thanksgiving. The introductory *kî* (v. 8a) is apparently emphatic, not motivational, heading an independent liturgical unit, the exclamation of the suppliant (as in v. 2a and possibly in v. 7b). The song shouted by the saved one continues into v. 9, which is a grateful acknowledgment of newly granted life after the threats of death have disappeared. Thus vv. 8-9 are a continuation of the announcement in vv. 1-2: Yahweh hearkened to the cries of the afflicted, yes, he saved him/her and bestowed new life on the hopelessly lost one (vv. 8-9). The interruption of this sequence of thoughts by a retrospective account of trouble and salvation (vv. 3-4) and intervening responses of the community (vv. 5-7) is due to liturgical procedure.

Having voiced the bliss of a new life the psalm might come to an end, it seems; indeed, LXX tradition starts a new text (no. 115; the juncture of MT Psalms 114 and 115 is presupposed in LXX with that counting). The first colon of v. 10 is suspiciously similar to v. 1a (Auffret, Barré, et al.): a first-person singular verb used absolutely without any additions expressing spiritual concerns and affinities. Perhaps late redactors have manipulated older introductory formulas in order to stress further allegiance of Yahweh believers to the Lord; after all, both '*hb,* "to love" (v. 1a), and '*mn,* Hiphil, "to believe" (v. 10a), are important concepts of later days (cf. Deut 6:5; Isa 7:9: even this last passage is late exilic or postexilic, exactly because of the absoluteness of the concept of "believing"; thus O. Kaiser, *Jesaja* [5th ed.; ATD 17; Göttingen: Vandenhoeck & Ruprecht, 1981] 117-20, 135-49). The somewhat modified opening of both sections of the psalm should not confound our structural analysis. Obviously, vv. 10-11 constitute a repetition of the ACCOUNT OF TROUBLE AND SALVATION expressed a little differently in vv. 3-4. Such redundancy is quite genuine in liturgical texts because it occurs frequently in ceremonial procedure. And, as stated before, the climax of personal thanksgiving will be reached only in vv. 16-17. Therefore we should not be surprised about this retrospective. What does call for attention, though, is wisdom language in part of the wording. While remembrances of the "bygone days" (either of the unmolested or molested times), including quoted thoughts or affirmations, are standard in thanksgivings (cf. 30:7 [RSV 6]; 32:5; Isa 38:11; Jonah 2:5 [RSV 4]), sapiential formulations ("all humans are liars," v. 11b) certainly grew out of a special environment and mode of thinking. A renewed retrospective in a complaining tone, opened by a statement of faith (vv. 10-11) in comparison to v. 3, that impressive and traditional description of anguish, seems rather vague (in spite of v. 10b: "I am greatly oppressed"). We get the impression of a secondary formulation on the basis of some sapiential reflection.

The rest of the psalm is back to the thanksgiving agenda. There is a dramatic change of voices and scenes, but the dominant speaker is the suppliant. He/she begins with the rhetorical question that is well known from Mic 6:6-8, only it does not receive an answer in our passage (v. 12; all commentators point out Aramaic influence with the word *tagmûlōhî*, "his benevolent deeds"). Why should there be an answer if everything is clear: salvation of the miserable and readiness to offer thanks in return? Therefore two cultic actions are put into effect, accompanied by proper ritual words: the saved one has to raise and empty a "cup of salvation" (v. 13; cf. Jewish Sabbath rituals; see below, Setting) and to bring the prescribed offering (v. 17). These features seem to be very old and traditional, but they may have been enacted in a symbolic way, especially in the latter instance, during times of bloodless worship services. Both rites are accompanied (if the preserved text is correct; some commentators argue that v. 14 is an erroneous duplicate of v. 18: thus, e.g., Gunkel, 503) by assertions to fulfill the vow (done in times of misery) in front of "all his people," i.e., Yahweh's congregation (strange hapax legomenon: *negdāh-nā'*, "in view of"). Our text becomes transparent for thanksgiving rites as hardly any other psalm text does. At the ceremony the host who invited friends to celebrate his/her salvation from death greets the assembly with a full cup (of wine? prototype of communion, as stressed by Christian exegetes). The thanksgiving banquet is testified to, e.g., in Ps 22:26-27 (RSV 25-26) and 1 Sam 1:3-5; 2:12-15 (see below, Setting). Sacrifice of an animal promised to God (v. 17) is the basis for the communal and communicative celebration.

If the rites mentioned above were the heart of the thanksgiving ritual for somebody saved from death, we still need to explain the remaining lines in Psalm 116, i.e., vv. 15-16 and 19. In varying degrees these lines constitute enigmas, most of all v. 15. The text may be corrupt; if it is meaningful it is talking about Yahweh's consideration for martyrs and martyrdom. This may have been the meaning in later times, e.g., during the Maccabean revolt. Given the objectivity of the phrase (no address of Yahweh; no first person singular or plural of speakers), the line seems interjected, possibly to bring to mind those who died in the service of Yahweh. In the light of other Aramaic influences on the psalm, the emendation of Barré (pp. 69-73) also has some plausibility. Instead of the difficult *hammāwtāh*, "the dying," he postulates Aramaic *hemānûtāh*, "faith/

trust" ("of the devoted ones"). If authentic to this text and liturgy, the phrase could indicate a confirmation of the suppliant's faith.

V. 16 is unusual, because it starts out like a cry for help to Yahweh (cf. v. 4b; Exod 32:31; Dan 9:4). In the body of the sentence, however, it becomes clear that no renewed complaint or petition follows but a confession of faith, a firm statement of allegiance to Yahweh. Taken as such, the verse may have belonged to the ritual from the beginning, or else it was added in times when confessions of this type became necessary and opportune in worship ceremonies. Parallel texts are: declarative formulas of submission to some human authority like 2 Sam 15:34; and, on the religious plane, declarations of submission to God (cf. Pss 119:125; 143:12; 1 Kgs 18:36). The combination of "your servant" with "son of your maidservant" occurs but one time elsewhere in Hebrew Scripture: Ps 86:16. The emphasis of our v. 16 is unmatched anywhere; it duplicates the formula "I am your servant," adding "son of your maidservant." Mentioning both parents seems to be a special wisdom trait (cf. Prov 1:8; 4:3; 6:20; 23:22, 25; 30:11, 17; etc.). We can imagine that a confession of this intensity was part of a regular thanksgiving service.

There remains only v. 19, which seems to be a simple elaboration of v. 18, localizing the place of worship in the Jerusalem temple. The psalm in itself does not mention Yahweh's abode or the Holy City. V. 14, the geminated line of v. 18, does not allude to any place of worship. V. 19 probably arose in a situation when Jerusalem and its temple became the focal points of Jewish faith for all communities in the dispersion. To construct a synonymity between "in the courts of Yahweh's house" (v. 19a) and "in the lands of life" (v. 9b; thus Barré) is a haphazard undertaking, to say the least. The summons to praise *(hallĕlû-yāh)* in MT closes off the psalm, while LXX makes it the introit of Psalm 117.

Liturgically speaking, the sequence of elements within Psalm 116 may well reflect some worship ceremony of and for an individual fulfilling a vow of thanksgiving within a congregation of faithful (O'Brien): starting with a statement of intent and a report of personal distress and Yahweh's salvific intervention (vv. 1-4), the saved one receives spiritual support from the worshiping community, reaffirming God's wonderful benevolence (vv. 5-6, possibly including v. 7). The individual at hand — looking back to his or her positive experience with Yahweh — promises faithfulness to God (vv. 8-9). The following part of the psalm repeats this liturgical sequence of thanksgiving-confirmation-vow, as quite often is the case in worship liturgies of complaint and petition (cf. Psalms 31; 38; 40; etc.). The suppliant declares the intention to give thanks and refers back to times of trouble and salvation (vv. 10-12). Next, references to worship are portrayed, including a sacred meal and the promised vow (cf. "cup of salvation," vv. 13-14). This latter element is taken up, and extensively so, in vv. 16-19, after a proverbial interlude (v. 15); it has possibly been adorned with a temple-oriented stanza (v. 19). Most exegetes, however, seek to divide the psalm into three or four more even parts (cf. Mays, 369; Allen, 114; Seybold, 454-56; but Prinsloo does have seven similar parts like ours).

# Genre

Notwithstanding some textual problems and some uncertainties of meaning and liturgical procedure as well as a good deal of liturgical modification during the transmission, we may call Psalm 116 a classic example of PERSONAL THANKSGIVING (cf. the tradition history of rituals and concepts: Chr. Wolff and H.-J. von der Minde, *ABD* VI, 435-41), which, of course, took place within a community of worshipers. The saved individual had to celebrate with neighbors, friends, and co-religionists (cf. Pss 22:23-27 [RSV 22-26]; 40; 107; 118; etc.). The psalm patently shows some liturgical movement, from recalling danger and distress to fulfilling vows and praising Yahweh for his generous help, and in a doubled liturgical ceremony. Modifications of and accretions to older versions of this psalm may be credited to changing needs of the communities that embraced the grateful saved person.

# Setting

Originally and up to monarchic times, thanksgiving services in Israel were probably held in family and neighboring circles, in homes or at local sanctuaries. With the emergence of an exclusively Yahweh-centered Jewish community (cf. Gerstenberger, *Yahweh,* listing at Additional Bibliography, section B), ceremonies for suffering and healed persons passed into the administration of local congregations (→ Psalms 12; 118) that adapted them to their needs and expectations. Thus the personal gods in ancient days responsible for the welfare of families and their individuals were replaced by Yahweh alone, and the symbols and theology of the Yahweh community (Jerusalem!) were placed beside much older ritual signs (e.g., thanksgiving sacrifice, cup of salvation). The saved person retains a good deal of the initiative in the ritual, although community and choirs take over an increasing part of liturgical responsibility. The main words and actions are spoken or performed by the saved one him/herself. It is astonishing to see that there is no trace of priestly prerogatives in the psalm. Older texts already pointed out above corroborate family privileges in bringing thanksgiving offerings (cf. 1 Sam 1:3-5; 2:12-15). Apparently, and astonishingly so, old rights held by laypeople of doing worship were preserved well into the period of the Second Temple and the diaspora community (cf. Lev 7:11-21: priests are restricted to blood rites at the altar; the rest of the ritual remains with the family; cf. Gerstenberger, *Leviticus,* listing at Additional Bibliography, section B). Wherever animal offerings were impossible, congregations would use prayers and songs as substitutes for bloody sacrifice (cf. Pss 40:7 [RSV 6]; 50:5-15).

Older or perhaps even contemporaneous customs of fulfilling a vow like our (post)exilic psalm have come to light, e.g., in Phoenician and Punic votive inscriptions: both categories of texts "may be understood as two related yet distinctive literary manifestations of a shared setting: that of vow fulfillment" (O'Brien, 282-83). The use of the Hallel songs (Psalms 113–118) in the later Jewish Passover liturgy (cf. Mishnah *Pesaḥim* 10:1-9) reaffirms their general liturgical functions as praise and thanksgiving.

296

## Intention

All thanksgiving is "returning thanks, praises, allegiance" to the donor of good gifts or blessings and the divine helper in times of trouble (cf. Psalm 107). The rhetorical question of v. 12 is correct: persons and their groups do owe recognition and thanks to the Deity who stepped in to cure and save (cf. Mauss, *Gift;* listing at Additional Bibliography, section B; Brueggemann, *Psalms;* listing at Additional Bibliography, section C).

## Bibliography

N. Airoldi, "Salmi 116 e 130. Saggi di traduzione," *Augustianum* 13 (1973) 141-47; P. Auffret, "'Je marcherai à la face de YHWH': Étude structurelle du Psaume 116," *OTE* 10 (1997) 161-77; idem, "Essai sur la structure littéraire du psaume 116," *BN* 23 (1984) 32-47; M. L. Barré, "Psalm 116 — Its Structure and Enigmas," *JBL* 109 (1990) 61-78; T. Booij, "Psalm 116:10-11," *Bib* 76 (1995) 388-95; J. A. Emerton, "'How Does the Lord Regard the Death of His Saints in Psalm 116:15,'" *JTS* 34 (1983) 146-56; S. B. Frost, "Asseveration by Thanksgiving," *VT* 8 (1958) 380-90; H. L. Ginsberg, "Psalms and Inscriptions of Petition and Acknowledgment," in *Louis Ginzberg Jubilee Volume* (New York: Ktav, 1945) I, 159-71; H. Gressmann, "Der Festbecher," in *Beiträge zur Religionsgeschichte und Archäologie Palästinas (Fest. E. Sellin; ed. W. F. Albright and A. Jirku; Leipzig: Deichert, 1927) 55-62; K. Hagen, "'Omnis homo mendax': Luther on Psalm 116," in *Biblical Interpretation in the Era of Reformation (Fest. D. C. Steinmetz; ed. R. A. Muller; Grand Rapids: Eerdmans, 1996) 85-102; M. Harl, "L'éloge de la fête de pâques dans le prologue du sermon In sanctum pascha de Grégoire de Nysse," in *The Easter Sermons of Gregory of Nyssa* (ed. A. Spira, et al.; Cambridge: Philadelphia Patristic Foundation, 1981) 81-100; R. A. Harrisville, "Paul and the Psalms," *Word & World* 5 (1985) 168-79; W. Kasper, "The Unity and Multiplicity of Aspects in the Eucharist," *Communio* (U.S.) 12 (1985) 115-38; M. Kiley, "'Lord, Save My Life' (Ps 116:4) as Generative Text for Jesus' Gethsemane Prayer (Mark 14:36a)," *CBQ* 48 (1986) 655-59; N. Ludwig, "Precious in the Sight of the Lord," *Epiphany* 5 (1985) 32-41; D. Lührmann, "Confesser sa foi à l'époque apostolique," *RTP* 117 (1985) 93-110; J. M. O'Brien, "'Because God Heard My Voice': The Individual Thanksgiving Psalm and Vow-Fulfillment," in *The Listening Heart (Fest. R. E. Murphy; ed. K. Hoglund, et al.; JSOTSup 58; Sheffield: JSOT Press, 1987) 281-98; W. S. Prinsloo, "Psalm 116: Disconnected Text or Symmetrical Whole?" *Bib* 74 (1993) 71-82; C. J. Simon, "We the Living, We the Dying (Death in Psalm 116 and Two Recent Novels)," *Perspectives* 8 (1993) 13-16; H. Spieckermann, "Lieben und Glauben: Beobachtungen zu Psalm 116," in *Meilenstein (Fest. H. Donner; ed. M. Weippert, et al.; Wiesbaden: Harrassowitz, 1995) 266-75; W. S. Stafford, "Repentance on the Eve of the English Reformation. John Fisher's Sermons of 1508-1509," *Historical Magazine of the Protestant Episcopal Church* 54 (1985) 297-338; G. Vanoni, "'Geglaubt habe ich, deshalb habe ich geredet'," in *'Geglaubt habe ich . . .' (Fest. A. Bsteh; ed. A. T. Khoury; Würzburg: Echter, 1998) 511-35.

# Psalm 117:
# Communal Hymn

## *Structure*

|  | MT | NRSV |
|---|---|---|
| I. Summons to praise | 1 | 1 |
| II. Hymn proper | 2ab | 2ab |
| III. Summons to praise | 2c | 2c |

The shortest psalm of the whole Psalter may be regarded as a tiny fragment of a hymn. Yet it does contain essential elements of a real song of praise, and tradition both in the Hebrew as well as the Greek line acknowledging its independence takes it seriously, so that we have to consider it as a possibly autonomous text. The mere number of words or lines does not account for the usefulness and practicality of a given song. Exod 15:21 and 1 Sam 18:7 are examples of very short psalmic compositions the texts of which were probably repeated endlessly by the crowds. Thus one-line shouted phrases could very well serve as those joyful noises to the Lord Yahweh (cf. Pss 33:3; 98:4-8; 118:1-4; Lev 23:24; Isa 51:11; 52:8-9).

The *hallĕlû* introduction by itself is a shortened and formulaic expression of praise coming up in the Psalter from Ps 104:35 onward (cf. 105:45; 106:1, 48; 111:1; 112:1; 113:1; etc.). V. 1a employs the more extensive (full divine name, with accusative particle) and more variable form: "Praise Yahweh, all you nations" (cf. 22:27 [RSV 26]; 113:1; 135:1; 146:1; 147:12; 148:1-13; 150:1-6). Most noteworthy in our psalm is that the SUMMONS TO PRAISE goes to all the "nations" *(gôyim),* not to Israel alone or to the powers of the natural world. The second colon, in synonymous parallelism to the first one, reinforces the "call to worship" by using the rare verb *šbḥ,* Piel, "to praise," in the masculine plural imperative and with third-person singular (= Yahweh) suffix. This verb has only three more occurrences in the Hebrew Psalter (63:4 [RSV 3]; 145:4; 147:12) and two more in Ecclesiastes (Qoh 4:2; 8:15); the Hithpael form is used in Ps 106:47 = 1 Chr 16:35. The verb in its meaning "praise" is used only eight times in all the Hebrew Bible. The synonym to "nations" in the second colon (v. 1b) is *hā'ummîm,* "the peoples" (definite article; only other occurrences Gen 25:16; Num 25:15; synonym: *lĕ'ōm,* "nation"; see H.-D. Preuss, *TWAT* IV, 411-13). Now, addressing the nations around Israel, and all of them in their totality, is a feature of some Yahweh-kingship hymns (see Psalms 96; 98) as well as some messianic songs (see Psalms 2; 110) or other royal texts (see Psalms 18; 45; 144). Does Psalm 117 belong in the context of any of these "monarchic" songs? Placement in the middle of two personal thanksgivings (which are rather unpolitical in outlook) seems odd, though, under this hypothesis.

The second verse opens with Heb. *kî,* which — in hymnic contexts — rarely gives the *reason* for singing Yahweh's praise, but introduces the hymn itself with its emphatic shout: "Yes," "Sure" (cf. Crüsemann, *Studien,* 32-35, 41; listing at "Introduction to Cultic Poetry"; Allen, 117). Other examples showing impulsive shouts of *kî* and hymnic lines to be repeated by the crowds include Pss

106:1; 107:1; 118:1-4; 136; Exod 15:21. Taking these passages as evidence and models of short hymns to be sung by people, we are entitled to interpret v. 2ab as such a popular hymnic line. The first person plural in v. 2a supports this understanding. Two essential truths are concisely expressed in this line: "His benevolence reigns over us; Yahweh's loyalty endures forever" (v. 2ab). The affirmations are about the *ḥesed* and *'ĕmet* of Yahweh, basic qualities — according to Hebrew Scripture — of Israel's God (see, respectively, H.-J. Zobel, *TWAT* III, 48-71; A. Jepsen, *TWAT* I, 313-48). The word pair is present in many psalms (cf. 25:10; 57:4 [RSV 3]; 85:11 [RSV 10]; 89:15 [RSV 14]) and — by varying combinations — in some prophetic texts (cf. Jer 9:23; 16:5; Hos 12:7 = influences of liturgical language? cf. N. Glueck, *Ḥesed in the Bible* [ed. E. L. Epstein; tr. A. Gottschalk; Cincinnati: Hebrew Union College Press, 1967]; J. S. Kselman, *ABD* II, 1084-86). The line is constructed skillfully: six words (disregarding the particle *kî*), with *ḥesed* and *'ĕmet* juxtaposed chiastically, and also *'ālēnû*, "over us" (i.e., Israel), and Yahweh in juxtaposition. Ending the little song with *hallĕlû-yāh* (v. 2c) is a feature known from MT versions of Psalms 104; 105; 113; 116; 146–150.

## Genre/Setting

Hymns small or great were sung at festive occasions by the community assembled in worship. In this universalistic HYMN (cf. "Introduction to Cultic Poetry," section 4D) Yahweh believers look out toward a pluralistic world of many ethnic and religious groups, including them all in their praise of their benign and loyal God. The attitude and theological position are characteristic of emerging Jewish thought. From depression of exilic experiences the dispersed Yahweh communities developed a firm conviction of the superiority of their God and faith (cf., e.g., Psalms 2; 95–100; 148).

## Intention

Stressing allegiance to Yahweh and reaching out toward the nations — while living in a multinational empire — are the specific concerns of the congregation intoning Psalm 117. Its isolated position between individual thanksgivings, Psalms 116 and 118, and possible links to other groups of "national" psalms remain obscure. J. Schröten believes (p. 107, listing at Psalm 118) that our text was composed specifically for the Hallel collection, Psalms 113–118, in order to "widen" the circle of users over the groups mentioned in 113:1. But the chance mention of *gôyim* in 118:10 can hardly have been the motive for placing Psalm 117 here.

## Bibliography

P. Auffret, "Louez YAHWEH, toutes les nations!" *BN* 74 (1994) 5-9; R. C. Brand Jr., "The Place of Praise," *ExpTim* 97 (1985) 82-84; E. W. Bunkowske, "Was Luther a Missionary?" *Concordia Theological Quarterly* 49 (1985) 161-79; R. Martin-Achard, *Israel et les nations — la perspective missionnaire de l'Ancien Testament* (Cahiers théologiques 42; Neuchâtel/Paris: Delachaux & Niestlé, 1959); O. Rickenbacher, "Quelques problèmes du Psaume 117 en malgache," in *Etudes bibliques* (*Fest.* D. Barthélemy; ed. P. Casetti, et al.; Fribourg: Universitätsverlag, 1981) 309-16.

# Psalm 118:
## Thanksgiving of the Individual

### *Structure*

|  |  | MT | NRSV |
|---|---|---|---|
| I. | Summons to give thanks and responses | 1-4 | 1-4 |
| II. | Account of trouble and salvation | 5-18 | 5-18 |
| | A. Complaint and account of rescue | 5 | 5 |
| | B. Affirmation of confidence | 6-7 | 6-7 |
| | C. Instruction | 8-9 | 8-9 |
| | D. Account of crisis | 10-13 | 10-13 |
| | E. Victory hymn | 14-18 | 14-18 |
| III. | Thanksgiving ceremony | 19-28 | 19-28 |
| | A. Introit | 19-20 | 19-20 |
| | B. Sacrificial formula | 21 | 21 |
| | C. Communal hymn | 22-27 | 22-27 |
| | 1. Song of cornerstone | 22-23 | 22-23 |
| | 2. Festive shout | 24 | 24 |
| | 3. Supplication | 25 | 25 |
| | 4. Blessing | 26 | 26 |
| | 5. Petition | 27a | 27a |
| | 6. Summons to celebrate | 27bc | 27bc |
| | D. Sacrificial formula | 28 | 28 |
| IV. | Summons to give thanks | 29 | 29 |

The SUMMONS TO GIVE THANKS is the overall frame of our psalm (vv. 1, 29). No addressee being mentioned in this general admonition ("Give thanks to Yahweh"), we have to conclude that all the congregation of worshipers is aimed at. In fact, this general type of summons is formulaic, occurring in various psalms and even some narrative contexts (cf. 30:5 [RSV 4]; 33:2; 97:12; 100:4; 105:1; 106:1; 107:1; 136:1-3, 26; 1 Kgs 8:33, 35 [perfect mode]; Isa 12:4; Jer 33:11; 2 Chr 20:21). The frequency of use in late Hebrew Scripture is significant. We are really dealing with a standard liturgical formula of the early Jewish community worship. There is no need to make explicit reference to that worshiping community. The people addressed are simply that particular group to whom belong the Scriptures, the only source of knowledge about the great deeds of Yahweh. So the imperative plural has no other possible point of reference than the congregation. Not only is the summons itself standardized and well established in that community, but the whole opening (and closing) lines of our psalm are formulaic. Several of the above-mentioned psalms use exactly the same opening, viz. 106:1; 107:1; 136:1. Furthermore, some other contexts quote essentially this summons to thank: Jer 33:11; 2 Chr 20:21. Still other texts use modifications of the introductory thanksgiving formula; see Pss 30:5 (RSV 4); 33:2; 97:12; 100:4; Isa 12:4; etc. All this evidence suggests widespread use of the SUMMONS TO PRAISE in the plural form directed toward a worshiping community.

Analysis of the whole line (v. 1) in the light of parallel passages yields the following result: the second colon ("everlasting is his grace") is the RESPONSE of the community. Some officiant would shout the summons, and the assembled worshipers would take up the second half-line and bring it home: "everlasting is his grace," *lĕ'ôlām ḥasdô,* possibly not one time only but repeatedly. All the relevant texts witness to this use, and corroboration can be found in vv. 2-4, where three groups of community members are called upon to articulate exactly that part of the general introductory line (cf. also the groups in 115:9-11; 135:19-20). We may take this colon as an authentic hymnic response anchored in ancient Jewish worship services (→ Psalm 136). Is this genre designation valid also for the expression "he is good" (or "it is good") in v. 1a? The formulaic line does not always contain this exclamation or statement. MT has it in all the cited psalm openings. But after the first line of the psalm has been said, the little expression (in Hebrew: *kî ṭôb*) seems to be forgotten. Only our psalm (vv. 2-4) and Psalm 136, which repeats the chant of the congregation 25 times, do not have a trace of *kî ṭôb* after the opening line. We may surmise, then, that the one-word phrase presented with *kî* in v. 1a does not constitute a hymnic element, but a motive clause to legitimate the summons to thank. Support could come from passages like 135:3-4, where the summons line (135:3) contains two evaluations of praising ("extol Yah, because Yahweh is good; play to his name, because this is pleasant"). In this case the full name "Yahweh" may have been inserted (some versions omit it); the original meaning was: "Hallelujah, because this is good. . . ." The second colon: "because this is pleasant," proves the suggested solution, because Yahweh may not be called that way. The hymnic line to be sung by the congregation is apparently cited in 135:4: "Yes, Yah has elected Jacob for himself, Israel for his possession." In consequence, we should translate our v. 1: "Give thanks to Yahweh, for this is good. Yea, everlasting is his grace." Gen 1:4-25 with its sixfold declaration "that it was good," *kî ṭôb,* may be an echo of such a liturgical use.

After this general invitation to give thanks, which envelops the whole ceremony, three "factions" of the community are called upon to articulate the common praise monotonously in the same fashion (vv. 2-4). The identity of the groups mentioned is more or less obscure. Aaronites (v. 3) are all those who trace their lineage to the high priest of Israel (cf. Num 26:59-60; 1 Chr 5:29-40; 6:35-38; etc.). That one particular group should have been called "Israel" (v. 2) or "house of Israel" (Ps 135:19) is unlikely, because the patriarch so named was the father of all Israelites. Equally uncertain is the designation of only one group or faction of the congregation by "Yahweh-fearers." "To fear Yahweh" is the obligation of all believers (cf. 22:24, 26; 25:12, 14; 34:8, 10; 52:8; 112:1;

145:19; Prov 3:7; 24:21). In most cases, the name "fearer of Yahweh" indiscriminately means "Yahweh believer." Only later times, as visible in NT texts (see Acts 2:5; 13:43; 17:4; etc.), reserved this designation for "proselytes" who could not be identified by Jewish genealogy. Some late psalms prepare for this understanding of the term by inferring a special piety with the "Yahweh-fearers" (cf. Pss 34:8, 10 [RSV 7, 9]; 119:74, 79). H. F. Fuhs counts 115:11, 13; 118:4; 135:20 among the "dubious" cases (*TWAT* III, 888).

For all these reasons we cannot be sure of the "factions" and liturgical groupings within the community; it may be that only the Aaronites (and sometimes the Levites) were singled out in worship, while all other designations in reality were general names (a) for the whole of dispersed Israel (v. 2), (b) for the congregation participating in worship (v. 4). If this is correct the hierarchy visible in the listings would be: Israel as a whole–priestly offspring–all the congregation gathered, and in fact the *yir'ê yhwh* in all relevant passages occupy the last spot (115:11; 118:4; 135:20b).

The first part of the psalm is mainly dedicated to re-creating the past experience of misery and salvation (vv. 5-18), letting shine through some ritual activities of the actual worship service, while the second part (vv. 19-28) more directly reflects the thanksgiving ceremony proper. The ACCOUNT OF TROUBLE AND SALVATION (a fairly limited exposition of how the patient suffered and was rescued) is a fixed element of thanksgiving songs (see "Introduction to Cultic Poetry," section 4C), but in our psalm motifs otherwise rarely mentioned, as well as unknown liturgical procedures, come in additionally.

The first line of the retrospective (v. 5) already comprises everything we expect of this element: descriptions of the suppliant crying out in anguish and of being saved by Yahweh are typical of remembered complaints (cf. 30:3 [RSV 2]; 32:3; 66:17; 116:4, 11; Jonah 2:3 [RSV 2]; Isa 38:13-16. In our case *mēṣar*, "distress," is unusual, with only two more occurrences in the Hebrew Bible: Ps 116:3; Lam 1:3; the text in v. 5b is somewhat corrupt; cf. the parallel statement in Ps 4:2c [RSV 1c]).Of course, the retrospective uses first-person discourse, quoting more or less what had been said in the complaint ceremony held at the time of deepest despair.

Unparalleled in other thanksgiving songs are the next two subunits, AFFIRMATION OF CONFIDENCE and INSTRUCTION. These elements are not simply reminiscences of past distress and complaint ceremony. True, an affirmation of confidence is an important part of any service for the suffering individual (cf. "Introduction to Cultic Poetry," section B). But the main formulation of trust: *yhwh lî*, "God (is) with me" (vv. 6a, 7a), seems to include the experience of being saved. It has a triumphant ring about it that is normally missing in authentic complaints "from the depths" (130:1). There, help is normally expected as still coming from God (e.g., "with you there is redemption," 130:4) but not having arrived yet. Or past experience with Yahweh is adduced (cf. 22:5-6, 10-11 [RSV 4-5, 9-10]). Straightforward affirmation that "God is on my side," as in our passage, is unique in the Psalter. All parallel phrases express more hope than certainty (cf. 18:19b [RSV 18b]; 30:11b [RSV 10b]; 32:7; 40:18bc [RSV 17bc]; 59:17cd [RSV 16cd]; 61:4a [RSV 3a]; 63:8a [RSV 7a]; 71:3a). Note in particular 94:16-17, where the concept of divine help is thematized: "Who will be with me?" (v. 16); "If Yahweh had not been my help . . ." (v. 17). Further-more, 54:6 (RSV 4) and 56:5c, 12b (RSV 4c, 11b), which seem to be closely re-lated to our v. 6, have more cautious formulations ("God is helping me," 54:6a [RSV 4a]; similarly in our v. 7a). Affirmations of security ("I do not fear; what harm can humans do?" v. 5) in the last instance lean on the institution of the ORACLE OF SALVATION (cf. Isa 41:14; 43:1; etc.). This means that a flat affirma-tion of God's helpful presence carries with it the experience of being saved, at the same time including the experience of the community at large of having been helped through. In our double line affirming trust, therefore, we hear the voice of the saved one as reflected in the common worship liturgy; the two lines are not a quotation from an earlier complaint service.

This is true even more in vv. 8-9, an INSTRUCTION — given to whom? This type of discourse does not occur in complaint psalms. The form is that of a "better . . . than" *(ṭôb min)* saying known from wisdom literature, more particu-larly, from collections of proverbs (cf. Prov 15:16-17; 16:32; 19:1, 22; Qoh 4:6, 13; 6:9; 7:1-5; etc.). In the Psalter this saying is used only in strictly educational contexts (cf. Pss 37:16; 84:11 [RSV 10]). And this is valid also for vv. 8-9. They are educational in the context of thanksgiving. In other words, the "better-than" sayings interrupt our account of trouble and salvation, drawing "ethical" conclusions from the suppliant's story to be applied daily in the lives of all members of the congregation. The "I" of the saved one does not appear in those neutral proverbs designed to regulate public life in small communities (cf. E. S. Gerstenberger, *TRE* XXVII, 583-90; J. L. Crenshaw, *ABD* V, 513-20). There-fore they were probably pronounced in the worship service by some officiant or some educational authority, possibly even by the assembly itself. Liturgically, anyway, vv. 8-9 are a distinct and regularly structured subunit. The wording is exactly alike in the two lines, save for the last word of v. 9. This little change signals a climax: trust in human beings is not comparable to confidence in God; not even trust in "noblemen" *(nědîbîm;* the word is seldom used, and fairly late: cf. 107:40 [= Job 12:21]; 113:7-8; 146:3; Num 21:18) may compensate for di-vine sheltering. All in all, instruction that tries to draw conclusions from Yahweh's saving interventions is part of the ceremony (→ Ps 32:8-9).

The next subunit, vv. 10-13, for its part, is back again to give a broader version of trouble and salvation, functioning basically as v. 5 does. The differ-ences are patent, though. While v. 5 focuses on the suppliant's (liturgical) cry-ing for help, vv. 10-13 paint the picture of the beleaguered and persecuted suf-ferer who — in the name of Yahweh — fights back against the evildoers. The text at times seems corrupted or reworked, but the basic structure is clear. Three lines (vv. 10-12) tell, each time in the first colon, the trouble of the sufferer, the key word being *sbb,* "encircle." Evilmongers close in on the miserable; this is a much-used image, perfectly understandable for moderns, and deeply meaning-ful for psychological or psychotherapeutic interpretation (cf. 18:6 [RSV 5]; 22:13-14, 17 [RSV 12-13, 16]; 59:4, 7-8, 15 [RSV 3, 6-7, 14]; 88:18 [RSV 17]; 143:3). The second colon in the same lines is stereotyped: "In Yahweh's name I repelled [imperfect: *'ămîlēm*] them." The meaning of the verb *mûl,* Hiphil, is guesswork, however. Its Qal forms signify "circumcise." Does the Hiphil inti-mate "cut off," or does it derive from another verbal root (thus *HAL* 527;

G. Mayer, *TWAT* IV, 734-38)? We cannot tell whether the usage presupposes concepts of war or battle. The mention of *gôyim,* "strangers" (v. 10a), who turn out to be the grammatical subject of vv. 10-12, is also debatable. Earlier the persecutors were called "those who hate me" (v. 7b). In the present text *gôyim* cannot signify "nations," because that does not make sense in a personal complaint (cf. 59:6 [RSV 5]). An older term for "enemies" may have been used (commentators suggest that in the course of tradition *kĕlābîm,* "dogs," as, e.g., in Ps 22:17 [RSV 16] was replaced by *gôyim,* "stranger, heathen," in the derogatory sense known from NT times). Or, in case "nations" was the original wording, the collective experience of the congregation, living in the midst of hostile ethnic groups, as well as reminiscences of military clashes, may have been synthesized in this triumphant passage. Be that as it may, the language in vv. 10-12 is highly formalized, betraying ritualized performance. Obviously, the saved one had to recite, perhaps enact, this account of trouble and salvation, leaving his/her mark in the first-person singular forms.

That threefold staccato account of past danger and resistance in MT is topped by a line seemingly too offensive to be taken seriously: "You have knocked me, to fall down" (v. 13a). Our translations prefer an emendation according to LXX that renders a passive verb: "I was pushed down." As a matter of fact, the second colon of v. 13 evaluates the situation in a diametrically opposed sense: "(But) Yahweh did help me." MT must not be wrong in putting these mutually exclusive affirmations into one line. According to some complaint songs (e.g., Psalms 44; 88) it is God himself who inflicts suffering and pain, defeat and disgrace. In our psalm the (second) account of trouble and salvation might want to communicate that there is a highest degree of affliction, a deepest point of despair: the attack on the sufferer by Yahweh himself (cf. Psalm 88; the book of Job; and also v. 18a here). Astoundingly, the same God, Yahweh, is the one who saves the afflicted (v. 13b). With this witness of having been rescued the ACCOUNT OF CRISIS terminates to give way to a VICTORY HYMN (vv. 14-18).

This new subunit again uses much formulaic liturgical language seemingly bordering on the sphere of political and military discourse. V. 14 is a formulaic phrase also used in victory celebrations (cf. Exod 15:2; Isa 12:2). The formulation as such does not show a martial background. Indeed, the strict employment of the first person singular should advise against this interpretation. The words and concepts in vv. 14-15 are civil ones. "Power," "song" (*zimrāh* need not be divided into two lexemes, since "song" in itself is a synonym of "force"; against *HAL* 263), "help" — all concepts in v. 14 — and "jubilation," "help," "tents of the righteous" — all concepts of v. 15ab — in no way suggest military origin or exclusively military use. To choose but one term as an example: "the tents of the righteous" need not refer to a military camp, as some modern translations suggest (in the context of a militarizing modern interpretation: RSV has "Hark, glad songs of victory in the tents of the righteous"). Wherever the plural of *'ōhel* appears in the Psalter it has the quality of "living quarters," not necessarily implying a nomadic lifestyle (cf. 69:26 [RSV 25]; 78:51, 55; 83:7 [RSV 6]; 84:11 [RSV 10]; 120:5). Is the following line exhibiting three stereotyped cola (vv. 15c, 16) the ultimate source of warlike imagery and interpretation? No doubt, the "right hand of Yahweh" can be his powerful weapon against enemies (cf. 18:36 [RSV 35]; 44:4 [RSV 3]; 74:10-11; Exod 15:6). But the range of meaning is much wider; God's "right (hand, arm)" is a metaphor for creative power, fatherly care, love, guidance, etc. (cf. the variety of applications in Pss 48:11 [RSV 10]; 63:9 [RSV 8]; 77:11 [RSV 10]; 80:16 [RSV 15]; 89:14 [RSV 13]; 98:1; 138:7; 139:10). I do not want to exclude the possibility that the threefold shout "The right (hand) of Yahweh performs powerful deeds" (*ḥayil* is as close to a military term as can be [cf. Exod 14:4], but may indicate many other facets of power: economic, sexual, physical, magical, etc.) may have been a battle cry of sorts (cf. Judg 7:18). If so, that martial background need not penetrate into our passage. The continuation of our triumph, anyway, does not refer to enemies or battle, but concludes with a very civil expression of hope (v. 17: AFFIRMATION OF CONFIDENCE; cf. vv. 6-7) and a summarizing retrospective (v. 18) that takes up again the struggle for survival (vv. 10-13) and triumph of salvation (vv. 14-17). Thus the first part of the psalm (vv. 5-18) is a mixture of retrospective on complaint ritual and thanksgiving proceedings.

The second part (vv. 19-28) according to Crüsemann's observation (*Studien*, 220-21, 264; listing at "Introduction to Cultic Poetry") is formally marked by the festive procession entering the sanctuary. This may be an imaginative or symbolic procedure (our congregations today as a rule do not move from their seats when singing an introit or advent songs of the coming of the Lord). Originally, however, there must have been a custom to call on the doors of the temple to open (vv. 19-20; cf. Psalms 15; 24), and a real INTROIT was practiced. (Does this mean that the first part of the psalm was recited in the precincts of the sanctuary?) The theme of personal thanksgiving is struck for the first time in v. 19b (singular of *ydh*), after the general summons to give thanks in v. 1 (plural). Now, in v. 21, the celebration comes to its climax. The saved person in this ancient ritual handed over his animal to be dedicated as a *tôdāh*, "thanksgiving sacrifice" (cf. Lev 7:11-21). The formula spoken by the donor of the animal is essentially: "I will give you thanks" (v. 21a; perhaps also: "I will give thanks to him," i.e., God; cf. Pss 18:50 [RSV 49]; 35:18; 43:4; 71:22; 86:12; 138:1-2; Isa 12:1; 38:15b; Crüsemann, *Studien*, 221-23, 267-68; Gunkel, 507). For the client of Yahweh saved from the brink of death the SACRIFICIAL FORMULA is the high point of the thanksgiving ceremony. The phrase, which has a confessional ring about it, is repeated once more in v. 28: "You are my God; I will thank you; my God, I will extol you." The announcement of the formula (v. 19b) and the twofold repetition demonstrate the central importance of this personal act of thanksgiving. The synonym "extol, praise" (*rûm*, Polel, v. 28b; cf. Exod 15:2; Pss 30:2 [RSV 1]; 34:4 [RSV 3]; 107:32) may occasionally substitute for *ydh*. The two lines pointed out, vv. 21 and 28, are the last words the saved one had to contribute to the ceremony. For the rest (vv. 22-27) choir or congregation seem to be responsible, because the "I" of the individual devotee is totally missing, communal "we" coming to the fore instead (vv. 23, 24, 26, 27). That shift of liturgical agents being clear enough, and some subunits standing out fairly well, we still cannot understand completely what is being said or sung in these lines. The history of Christian interpretation insisted on christological foreshadowings (cf. Matt 21:9, 42; 23:39; Acts 4:11; 1 Peter

2:7), thus obscuring original meanings. First, there is a song of the cornerstone (vv. 22-24, including FESTIVE SHOUT, v. 24, unique in Hebrew Scripture, 1 Kgs 14:14 notwithstanding) intoned by a group of people. The language is metaphoric; a parable of the despised stone seems to be behind the saying in v. 22. A neglected person acquires crucial importance: why should the parable not mean the same supplicant who was saved, thus demonstrating the benevolence and power of Yahweh (thus Gunkel, 509)? Another possibility is that of Isa 52:13–53:12: some member of the community is utterly despised but turns out to be the chosen "lamb of God." In this case, a messianic interpretation would not be compulsory or automatic, but it certainly would (in conjunction with v. 26) enter the scene. Considering the whole psalm and its setting I opt for the "small" solution: the worshiping congregation treats the saved one as a rehabilitated, important member. This person had been marginalized and suffered contempt, exactly because of his/her suffering; Yahweh has readmitted him/her into the community of the faithful and "righteous" (vv. 15, 20).

A lone "cry for help" (SUPPLICATION) interrupts once more the liturgical events. We cannot determine its purpose or legitimation. Possibly, these elementary shouts (v. 25; cf. 116:4, 16) were once scribal glosses proving existential excitement on the part of the transmitters of Scripture. Presently, the line serves as a reminder that Yahweh's help is continuously wanted (cf. 40:12 [RSV 11]; 138:7-8a; similarly in hymns: 104:35; 139:19). In this sense the renewed cry for help may have had a liturgical purpose in the offertory ceremony.

BLESSING has been an opportune element to close worship services down to our own days (cf. 2 Sam 6:18; 1 Kgs 8:55, 66). Here a group of priests(?) extends blessings to a plurality of persons (v. 26b), probably the whole congregation, or each one who had "entered" the sanctuary "in the name of Yahweh" (v. 26a). In this sense we are dealing with the final blessing of the worship service. Apparently, v. 27a contains fragments of the blessing itself (cf. Num 6:24-26); the text seems shortened and mutilated. V. 27bc, then, would be a summons to continue with other festival activities. We do not know what the ornamentation with twigs was all about (spring or Passover ceremony? autumn ritual?). The term *ḥag,* "feast," may hint at a dancing ritual (Gunkel, 509; B. Kedar-Kopfstein, *TWAT* II, 730-44). Doubled closing lines (vv. 28, 29) ending the personal and communal thanksgiving service make the psalm a well-rounded unit, especially since v. 29 is identical with v. 1. Thus a communal summons to give thanks constitutes the frame for individual praise, as in Psalm 8. And individual, joyful offering is embedded in the liturgies, concepts, and experiences of the celebrating community (cf. Mays).

One question, in particular, does arise after this overview of formal elements in Psalm 118: Are we able to discern purely literary language over against liturgical usages? Do we have to admit final stages of redactional comments serving readers of the Psalter instead of participants in worship? The literary viewpoint looms large in various scholarly investigations (cf., e.g., Schröten, 74-77; Levin, "Gebetbuch," 367, 370-74; listing at Additional Bibliography, section C). Linguistic evidence for either theory is hard to adduce. But general considerations about production and use of sacred texts in antiquity may invalidate the "reader concept" of the Psalter. Collections of prayers, songs, and meditations during the period concerned (fifth to second century B.C.E.) were probably nothing but liturgical handbooks and not yet reading texts to be used privately, for solitary edification.

## Genre

Our psalm abounds in liturgical forms and rhythmic, repetitious, formulaic phrases and shouts; we cannot have serious doubts about its use in worship ceremonies probably of early Jewish times (sixth to third century B.C.E.). Most exegetes will acknowledge such liturgical use at least in regard to a basic poem of individual thanksgiving contained in the body of Psalm 118, i.e., in vv. 5-28. Recognizably individual features and rites are presupposed, fitting well into the structure of individual thanksgiving. But of course we cannot tell whether the psalm preserved the right order and the full ceremony, and furthermore whether its users interpreted transmitted texts correctly. The nucleus of Psalm 118 is certainly a personal thanksgiving: an account of trouble and salvation (vv. 5, 10-13, 18) and thanksgiving sacrifice, be it real or symbolic (vv. 21, 28), are characteristic of that genre (see "Introduction to Cultic Poetry," section 4C). But the psalm, with equal certainty, does not represent a "private ceremony." All personal concerns and actions are deeply embedded in communal worship. This is quite obvious by various form elements pointed out as collective discourse: summons to give thanks, instruction, victory hymn, song of cornerstone, blessing (e.g., vv. 1-4, 15-16, 20, 22-25, 26-27). Our psalm, consequently, is a fine example of how individual and family rituals were incorporated into the communal worship of the early Jewish community (→ Psalms 8; 12; against, e.g., Schröten, 75, who limits her analysis to the poet's text). Language, vocabulary, and concepts are in no way individualistic but corporate. The speakers presupposed are the patient saved by Yahweh, and various voices speaking to the congregation. The "I" stands for the saved one, and for each individual member of the community, hardly for the worshiping group as a whole. Whenever the worshiping group does manifest itself, it uses first-person plural forms. One verse or another, however, may have been spoken by a leader or officiant (cf. vv. 8-9, 20, 22, 26). Yet there is hardly sufficient evidence to attribute some initial form of the psalm to a royal figure (cf. Psalm 18; against Allen, 124).

## Setting

Worship services in early Jewish communities must have been more varied than we tend to believe or deduce from texts like Nehemiah 8. Torah reading was certainly the backbone of congregational life. But besides gatherings to listen to *tôrāh* (cf. Deuteronomy 29–30) to be held every seven years (Deut 31:9-11), the people of Yahweh practiced quite a number of other ceremonies, e.g., seasonal festivals (Exod 23:14-17), Feast of Purim (Est 9:17-32), virginity rites (Judg 11:39-40), rituals when women were suspected of adultery (Num 5:12-

28), sacrifices for many occasions (Leviticus 1–7). Complaint and thanksgiving services for individuals in the proper setting of their respective social entities are testified to most of all in the Psalms (cf. Gerstenberger, *Mensch,* listing at "Introduction to Cultic Poetry"). We have to locate Psalm 118 in this framework of exilic and postexilic thanksgiving rites within Jewish congregations of "righteous" Yahweh believers (cf. Psalm 107). The offertory proper was combined with days of feasting in the circle of friends, family, and co-religionists. The saved one would invite a "large congregation" and pay for eating and drinking (→ 22:26-27 [RSV 25-26]). Thus Mays is perfectly right when he reads Psalm 118 in the context of early Jewish community life, the backbone of which was Torah. But this social setting was certainly not the only and exclusive one. There are recognizable older rites of bringing personal offertories in previous periods. And the "canon" cannot be made the guarantee of a uniform, homogeneous, normative set of rules, ceremonies, or doctrines to adhere to through the ages.

## Intention

Members of the Jewish community of faith who had vowed a thanksgiving sacrifice (and feast) while in danger of death needed institutional and ritual opportunities to fulfill their promises. Thanksgiving services offered the opportunity to do so (cf. already Absalom, who seemingly waited four years to bring his promised sacrifice: 2 Sam 15:8). The ritual of thanksgiving was, at the same time, the act of rehabilitation of a formerly ostracized member, comparable to cleansing rituals (cf. Leviticus 12–15). It also served all members of the community to incorporate themselves into the larger religious body of Yahweh believers, scattered through a sometimes cold, hostile, multicultural, and quite stratified religious world. Communicating among themselves in a world like this, with not only grievances and defeats but also victorious experiences, was especially important for oppressed minorities prone to be melted down into an anonymous mass of subjects.

## Bibliography

M. Alexandre, "Pâques, la vie nouvelle," in *The Easter Sermons of Gregory of Nyssa* (ed. A. Spira, et al.; Cambridge: Philadelphia Patristic Foundation, 1981) 153-94; E. Beaucamp, "Plaidoyer pour le Psaume 118," *VieS* 116 (1967) 64-77; idem and A. Rose, "Le Psaume 118 (117)," *Feu Nouveau* 9 (1966) 11-26; O. Becker, "Psalm 118,12," *ZAW* 70 (1958) 174; H. Beintker, "'Verbum Domini manet in aeternum': Eine Skizze zum Schriftverständnis der Reformation," *TLZ* 107 (1982) 161-75; U. Bergmann, "Old Testament Concepts of Blessing"; see listing at Psalm 115; A. Berlin, "Psalm 118:24," *JBL* 96 (1977) 567-68; C. Brown, "The Gates of Hell: An Alternative Approach," *SBLSP* 26 (1987) 357-67; J. Ching, "No Other Name," *Japanese Journal of Religious Studies* 12 (1985) 253-62; J. Driscoll, "The Psalms and Psychic Conversion," *Cistercian Studies* 22 (1987) 91-110; G. R. Driver, "Psalm 118,27," *Textus* 7 (1969) 130-

31; M. Durst, "Der Kölner Hilarius-Codex," *Jahrbuch für Antike und Christentum* 33 (1991) 53-80; J. H. Eaton, "Music's Place in Worship: A Contribution from the Psalms," in *Prophets, Worship, and Theodicy* (ed. J. Barton, et al.; Leiden: Brill, 1984), 85-107; L. Finkelstein, "The Origin of the Hallel," *HUCA* 23 (1950/51) 319-37; J. A. Fitzmyer, "Aramaic Evidence Affecting the Interpretation of Hosanna in the New Testament," in *Tradition and Interpretation in the New Testament* (*Fest.* E. E. Ellis; ed. G. Hawthorne, et al.; Grand Rapids: Eerdmans, 1987) 110-18; M. H. Floyd, "How Can We Sing the Lord's Song?" *Reformed Liturgy and Music* 20 (1986) 95-101; R. C. Fulton, "Victory from Death: What Makes the Rejects Sing?" *Currents in Theology and Mission* 14 (1987) 278-82; M. Giesler, *Christ the Rejected Stone: A Study of Ps 118,22-23* (Pamplona: Ediciones Universidad de Navarra, 1974); W. Grudem, "Does *kephalē* ('Head') Mean 'Source' or 'Authority Over' in Greek Literature?" *Trinity Journal* 6 (1985) 38-59; R. M. Hals, "Psalm 118 (Luther's Exposition)," *Int* 37 (1983) 277-83; R. Hammer, "Two Liturgical Psalms: Salvation and Thanksgiving," *Judaism* 40 (1991) 484-97; T. Harding, "Psalm 118: Can We Sing the Lord's Song Sitting Down?" *Touchstone* 4 (1986) 38-46; M. R. Hauge, "Some Aspects of the Motif 'The City Facing Death' of Ps 68:21," *SJOT* 1 (1988) 1-29; P. Haupt, "'Schmücket das Fest mit Maien!'" *ZAW* 35 (1915) 102-9; E. Jenni, "'Vom Herrn ist dies gewirkt': Ps 118,23," *TZ* 35 (1979) 55-62; S. Kim, "Jesus — the Son of God, the Stone, Son of Man, and the Servant," in *Tradition and Interpretation in the New Testament* (*Fest.* E. E. Ellis; ed. G. Hawthorne, et al.; Grand Rapids: Eerdmans, 1987) 134-48; E. Kutsch, "Deus humiliat et exaltat," *ZTK* 61 (1964) 193-220; S. E. Loewenstamm, "'The Lord Is My Strength and My Glory,'" *VT* 19 (1969) 464-70; U. Luck, "Die Bekehrung des Paulus und das paulinische Evangelium," *ZNW* 76 (1985) 187-208; H. S. Mays, "Psalm 118 — the Song of the Citadel," in *Religions in Antiquity* (*Fest.* E. R. Goodenough; Supplement to *Numen* XIV; Leiden: Brill, 1968) 97-106; J. L. Mays, "Psalm 118 in the Light of Canonical Analysis," in *Canon, Theology, and Old Testament Interpretation* (*Fest.* B. S. Childs; ed. G. M. Tucker, et al.; Philadelphia: Fortress, 1988) 299-311; J. B. McCandless, "Christian Commitment and a 'Docetic' View of Human Emotions," *Journal of Religion and Health* 23 (1984) 125-37; J. Meysing, "A Text-Reconstruction of Psalm 117 (118),27," *VT* 10 (1969) 130-37; A. A. Milavec, "Mark's Parable of the Wicked Husbandman as Reaffirming God's Predilection for Israel," *Journal for Ecumenical Studies* 26 (1989) 289-312; B. J. Oosterhoff, "Het loven van God in Psalm 118," in *Loven en geloven* (ed. A. Ridderbos-Boersma; Amsterdam: Ton Bolland, 1975) 175-90; J. J. Petuchowski, "'Hoshi'ah na'" in Psalm cxviii 25," *VT* 5 (1955) 266-71; H. de Poitiers, *Commentaire sur le psaume 118* (Paris: Cerf, 1988); H. Ringgren, "The Use of the Psalms in the Gospels," in *The Living Text* (*Fest.* E. W. Sanders; ed. D. Groh, et al.; Lanham, Md.: University Press of America, 1985) 39-43; W. Robinson, "Psalm 118: A Liturgy for the Admission of a Proselyte," *Church Quarterly Review* 144 (1947) 179-83; A. Rose, "Quelques orientations de la tradition chrétienne dans la lecture du psaume 118," in *Liturgie und Dichtung* (ed. H. Becker, et al.; St. Ottilien: Eos, 1983) 209-26; J. A. Sanders, "A New Testament Hermeneutic Fabric: Psalm 118 in the Entrance Narrative," in *Studies in Memory of W. H. Brownlee* (ed. C. A. Evans, et al.; Atlanta: Scholars Press, 1987) 177-90; H. Savon, "Le temps de l'exégèse allégorique dans la catéchèse d'Ambroise de Milan," in *Le temps chrétien* (ed. J.-M. Leroux; Paris: Centre National de la Recherche Scientifique, 1984) 345-61; H. Schmidt, "Erklärung des 118. Psalms," *ZAW* 40 (1922) 1-14; H. Schröer, "Gott ist mein Psalm: Teilhabe und Freigabe," in *Ja und Nein* (*Fest.*

W. Schrage; ed. K. Wengst, et al.; Neukirchen-Vluyn: Neukirchener Verlag, 1998) 55-64; J. Schröten, *Entstehung, Komposition und Wirkungsgeschichte des 118. Psalms* (BBB 95; Weinheim: Beltz/Athenäum, 1994); idem, "Das Spiel mit Anspielungen: Psalm 118 im Neuen Testament," *BLit* 69 (1996) 228-37; J. R. Wagner, "Psalm 118 in Luke — Acts," in *Early Christian Interpretation of the Scriptures of Israel* (JSNTSup 148; ed. C. Evans, et al.; Sheffield: Sheffield Academic Press, 1997) 154-78; G. H. Wilson, "The Qumran Psalms Scroll Reconsidered," *CBQ* 47 (1985) 624-42; H. W. Wolff, "Psalm 118," in *Herr, tue meine Lippen auf* (ed. G. Eichholz; 2nd ed.; 5 vols.; Wuppertal: E. Müller, 1961) V, 251-57; H. L. Wright, "The Psalter on the Way," *Reformed Liturgy and Music* 19 (1985) 129-31.

# Psalm 119:
## Acrostic Prayer; Instruction

### Structure

Preliminary remark: Psalm 119 is an acrostic poem, each eight-verse unit of which is artistically formalized to begin every line with the same letter of the alphabet. The psalm thus arrives at the enormous length of eight times twenty-two (number of Hebrew letters) lines, that is, 176 poetic bicola (corresponding exactly to the number of verses). The dominant formal law governing the psalm is, of course, this special acrostic scheme. Another principle of poetic technique is the placement of as many as ten synonyms of *tôrāh* in each block. Within this pattern, however, other formal and generic concerns are operative that permit comparisons with several specific genres, excluding others. Therefore I give the normal structural outline of the psalm and then discuss first its form-critical characteristics and second, under "Genre," the acrostic pattern extant also, in various modifications, in Psalms 9/10; 25; 34; 37; 111; 112; 145; Lamentations 1–4.

| | | MT | NRSV |
|---|---|---|---|
| I. | (Aleph) | 1-8 | 1-8 |
| | A. Beatitude | 1-3 | 1-3 |
| | B. Prayer, adoration, promise, petition | 4-8 | 4-8 |
| II. | *(Bet)* Promise, praise, petition | 9-16 | 9-16 |
| III. | *(Gimel)* Petition, complaint, promise | 17-24 | 17-24 |
| IV. | *(Dalet)* Complaint, petition, promise, confidence | 25-32 | 25-32 |
| V. | *(He)* Petition | 33-40 | 33-40 |
| VI. | *(Waw)* Petition, confidence, promise | 41-48 | 41-48 |
| VII. | *(Zayin)* Petition, complaint, promise | 49-56 | 49-56 |
| VIII. | *(Ḥet)* Promise, complaint, praise, petition | 57-64 | 57-64 |
| IX. | *(Ṭet)* Praise, petition, complaint, promise | 65-72 | 65-72 |
| X. | *(Yod)* Praise, petition, promise | 73-80 | 73-80 |
| XI. | *(Kaph)* Complaint | 81-88 | 81-88 |
| XII. | *(Lamed)* Praise, promise, complaint | 89-96 | 89-96 |
| XIII. | *(Mem)* Confession | 97-104 | 97-104 |

| | | |
|---|---|---|
| XIV. *(Nun)* Promise, complaint, petition | 105-112 | 105-112 |
| XV. *(Samek)* Promise, petition, confession | 113-120 | 113-120 |
| XVI. *(Ayin)* Petition, complaint, promise | 121-128 | 121-128 |
| XVII. *(Pe)* Praise, petition, complaint | 129-136 | 129-136 |
| XVIII. *(Ṣade)* Praise, complaint, promise | 137-144 | 137-144 |
| XIX. *(Qoph)* Petition, promise | 145-152 | 145-152 |
| XX. *(Resh)* Petition, complaint, praise | 153-160 | 153-160 |
| XXI. *(Śin/Shin)* Complaint, confession, promise | 161-168 | 161-168 |
| XXII. *(Taw)* Petition, promise | 169-176 | 169-176 |

The overall structure — disregarding for the moment the alphabetical order — is peculiar: Psalm 119 starts out with a double BEATITUDE (vv. 1-3), a distinct opening form, but it does not have, form-critically speaking, a definite end. Vv. 169-176 obey the last letter of the alphabet only; there is nothing to correspond to the well-known felicitation at the beginning. Such "beatitudes" are frequent in the Psalter. They go back to nonsacral felicitations of praiseworthy human qualities and behavior (cf. Prov 3:13; 8:34; 28:14), used in educational contexts to mold positively the character of young people. A basic form was probably the expression for "happiness" preceding a general term for a human (mostly male) being and a relative clause stating the model constellation of that being: *'ašrê 'ādām 'ăšer . . .* ("Happy a human being who . . ."). Another possibility of formulation was *'ăšrê* with a following active participle indicating the ideal type of action ("Happy the ones doing . . ."). Our psalm uses the second option, expanding a simple saying, "Happy the ones who are on the right path" (v. 1a; perhaps a singular felicitation antecedes this plural one), first by indicating the *tôrāh* as that "right path," namely "(happy) . . . those walking according to Yahweh's Torah" (v. 1b). The following two lines are not independent sayings but seem to be further elaborations of the theme struck in v. 1. The personal suffixes in both verses all point back to Yahweh in v. 1b ("*his* testimonies" and "seek *him*" in v. 2; "*his* ways" in v. 3). Furthermore, vv. 2b-3 spell out the qualities of that perfect adorer of Yahweh's Torah: He/she clings to it "wholeheartedly" (v. 2b; cf. 13 more occurrences of the singer's *lēb/lēbāb*, e.g., vv. 7, 10, 11), and he/she refrains from evil (v. 3a; cf. that motif in wisdom and torah contexts, e.g., Psalms 1; 19; 37; etc.). Notwithstanding that beatitudes do appear in pairs (cf. 32:1-2; 128:1-2), we should consider the doublet as an expanded form. All the more significant is this introduction to Psalm 119. The composers and transmitters thought the form to be fit to represent the program of the whole psalm. In fact, it does so beautifully. Life oriented by Yahweh's will is at stake, and the *tôrāh* is the vehicle of his will. Also, the plural of the blessed followers of Yahweh is highly important. Beatitudes of the Psalter (→ Psalm 1) normally speak in individual terms, the same way as their didactic antecedents in other layers of OT literature. Vv. 1-3 consciously chose the plural to make clear from the beginning that all believers in Yahweh are indicated as addressees. In the light of the first-person singular designation of the speaker throughout Psalm 119, this is rather surprising. Looking at vv. 1-3, then, we learn from the start that the "I" of our grand poem is not an isolated and concrete human being, but a model representation for all the members of that community of faith (for the central importance of Psalm 119 cf., e.g., Levenson, Mays).

Another aspect of the introductory elements calls for attention. The psalm on the whole is full of prayer language and personal prayer forms. But it is notoriously negligent of or cautious about proper appellations of the name Yahweh or formal invocations of that holy name, as we know them from complaints, thanksgivings, or hymns (cf. "Introduction to Cultic Poetry," section 4). Limitations of the acrostic patterns cannot be made responsible for this lack. V. 4 (after neutral language about Yahweh in vv. 1-3) starts out with an emphatic "you" (Yahweh). Metrical considerations cannot have prevented insertion of the tetragrammaton in this crucial line either. The authors were content with Yahweh's appearance in a construct relationship of v. 1 ("Torah of Yahweh"), which does not substitute for a well-educated opportune address of the divine partner in dialogue. They apparently did not care or were hypersensitive in regard to direct appellations, and the irregular handling of Yahweh's name in the text proves this negligence. The first mention of Yahweh after v. 1 is in v. 12, although he has been addressed up to that point eight times, i.e., in every single line from v. 4 through 11. After this first direct appellation of v. 12, the name reappears in vv. 31, 33, 41, 52, 55, 57, 64, 65, etc. There is no premeditated order in this sequence, except to say that the makers and users of our psalm did not care to create any regularity at this point, or that they wanted the irregularity of Yahweh's appearance. Nevertheless, quite regularly they stylized the text as a personal prayer of one individual talking to his God.

Form elements recognizable in this large poem seem to be taken from traditional prayers of the individual, but modified to the purposes of this psalm. Some forms of collective origin, for instance, hymns with their typical summons to praise, affirmations of Yahweh's mighty deeds in mythical times and history, are conspicuously absent from Psalm 119. Every line seems consciously designed from the perspective of an individual speaker, who raises his/her voice from within a Torah-oriented community (cf. Deissler).

COMPLAINTS OF THE INDIVIDUAL do occur with some frequency (see vv. 19a, 20, 23a, 25a, 28a, 51a, 61a, 69a, 70a, etc., with the highest concentration in the *kaph* strophe, vv. 81-88). Taken together, these statements of distress are mainly concerned with (a) the suppliant's suffering from unwarranted attacks by godless and haughty people; (b) his longing for certitude, guidance, acceptance by God; and (c) his pain caused by obstinate opponents of Yahweh. Typical examples are: (a) v. 95a ("The godless lie in wait for me to kill me"); v. 157 ("Many are those who persecute and encroach on me"); v. 141 ("I am small and despised"); (b) vv. 81-82: ("I long for your salvation, I wait for your word. My eyes crave your word, begging: When will you comfort me?"); v. 25a ("I stick to the dust") and v. 28a ("I weep because of my sorrow") — in both lines want of God's word is put forth as the reason for misery; (c) v. 139 ("My zeal consumes me, because my foes forget your words"); v. 70a ("their heart is numb like fat"), v. 126 ("It is time for Yahweh to act, for they have broken your order"). The vocabulary of complaint comes in large part from sapiential sources. Existential dangers are alluded to, but they seem to be located in the realm of religious intolerance of the ruling groups: note that the designation of "enemies" leans toward the *śārîm*, "leaders" (vv. 23, 161), and *zēdîm*, "haughty ones" (vv. 21, 51, 69, 78, 85, 122), with the general label of *rĕšā'îm*, "godless," still present (cf. vv. 6, 53, 61, 95, 110, 119, 155), but the older names of *'ôyĕbîm*, "enemies," *śônĕ'îm*, "haters," *pô'ălê 'āwen*, "evilmongers," etc., in full decline (only vv. 3, 98; for enemy designations cf. Keel, *Feinde;* listing at "Introduction to Psalms"). The complaint has obviously moved from the family network into a different social organization and to a different plane of thinking and conflict. But the predominance of complaint language indicates that from time immemorial petition — induced by complaint — is the basis of human prayer (cf. Bowra, Heiler, et al., listing at "Introduction to Cultic Poetry").

PETITION is the most important element in individual (and communal) complaints (cf. Gerstenberger, *Mensch*, listing at "Introduction to Cultic Poetry"). Original forms and functions of petition include direct imperative address of the Deity to tear the suppliant out of his/her misery, to restore health and good fortune, and to destroy those who caused anxiety and suffering (→ Psalms 3–7). Petitionary discourse is strong in Psalm 119, but it, too, seems partly transposed to that other plane of religious life we noted before. "Teach me your ordinances" (v. 12b; *lmd*, Piel, "teach," also in vv. 12, 26, 64, 68, 108, 124, 135, 171 — except for the last passage all imperative petitions); "Deal bountifully with your servant, that I may live and observe your word. Open my eyes that I may behold wonderful things from your Torah" (vv. 17-18); "Do not abandon me for good" (v. 8b); "Do not let me go astray from your commandments" (v. 10b). We see positive requests to be helped, guided, and nurtured by Yahweh, and negative petitions to ward off catastrophes that may be threatening the suppliant by his/her own fault or that of God. A third type of petition is labeled "imprecation" in complaint psalms (→ Glossary; Psalm 109). Psalm 119 also has what appears to be some remnants of this form element: "You rebuke [Hebrew: perfect] the haughty ones, they are cursed [Hebrew: participle], they leave your commandments" (v. 21); "May the haughty ones be put to shame, since they betray me with lies" (v. 78). "You discard [Hebrew: perfect] all those who leave your ordinances, because lies are their betrayals. You 'count' as dross all the godless on earth" (vv. 118-119a; further imprecative statements vv. 53, 84, 113, 115, 126, 150, 155, 158). This is only a sampling of forms pertaining to the petition category. Vv. 33-40 are a cluster of petitions, typical in the sense pointed out above, adherence to Yahweh's will as revealed in *tôrāh* being the main concern. The absence of references to special calamities from which to be saved is as noteworthy as the negligence of rules regarding personal conduct, social responsibility, and cultic purity. We note a complete concentration on religious ideals concerning Torah piety.

Traces of PRAISE formulations are spread through the whole long poem, but rather sparsely so (cf. vv. 7a, 12a, 50, 64a, 68a, 75a, 86a, 89-92, 96b, 129a, 137-138, 140a, 142, 144a, 156a, 160). Yahweh is lauded mainly as the giver of the all-important *tôrāh* (in compact form vv. 89-92, 137-144). Again, we sense the central importance of the revealed "Word of God," and the negligence of his saving acts in both family and national realms. Therefore, we cannot simply maintain that most of the genre elements of the extant categories of psalms have been used and mingled in Psalm 119. Just as complaint and petition were modified in this poem, also and more profoundly praise and thanksgiving have been altered in their form and content compared with such expressions of praise and their respective genres (cf. "Introduction to Cultic Poetry," section 4D, and exemplary hymns like Psalms 8; 19; 34; 46; 96; 103; 104; 136; 148; etc.).

What I have labeled as PROMISE is the most frequent and apparently also the most important element in our psalm. The name chosen may not be adequate for what I am trying to communicate. "Promise" in this context does not mean a limited and materialized offer of something or some kind of (sacrificial or economic) promissory note or obligation. No, it means a complete self-dedication to Yahweh, assurance of total commitment to the cause of that God, which may take the forms of assertion, comparison, or confession. Essential features of promises in this sense are the centrality of the suppliant's ego, his/her attempt to relate to Yahweh, the sense of absolute loyalty, the double aspect of describing a spiritual reality and vouchsafing an ideal not yet achieved. Thus vv. 6 and 8a already contain our element: "I will not be put to shame, as long I do watch out for all your commandments," and "I will keep your ordinances." The following line is an ethical reflection seemingly of general validity, but we probably do not miss the point when taking the term *na'ar,* "young man," as a circumlocution for "I," the suppliant: "Whereby a young man can keep blameless his life? By keeping your word" (v. 9). And immediately the assertion of complying to that finality: "I do seek you with all my heart" (v. 10a), "I do guard your words in my heart, that I may not trespass against you" (v. 11). After one praise to Yahweh (v. 12) the rest of the *bet* block is more or less of this promissory kind, voicing the actual state of affairs and, at the same time, expressing the willingness and desire to perfect the ideal behavior and stature of the faithful one. Occasional allusions to imperfection (cf. vv. 25, 50, 67a, 131) are background material; assertion of keeping loyalty to God (cf., e.g., vv. 10a, 11a, 13-16, 24, 30-32, 44-48, 55, 57-60, etc. — the perfect tense being the standard verbal form) and denouncing all evil and deviant people (cf. vv. 21, 53, 78, 158; some imperfects, or wish forms) are the heart of the psalm. For the suppliant there may enter even a ritual note of boasting (cf. vv. 97-100). "I have more wisdom than all my teachers" (v. 99a) is a most "unwise" assertion, but it is giving credit to the ideal of a Torah-oriented young believer and student of God's ways. All in all, this model behavior and this paragon of a Yahweh follower are displayed over and over again, so that we may see in Psalm 119, most of all, a portrait of the perfect practitioner of true faith.

## Genre

Acrostic stylization is the outward frame of the psalm; of course, this feature looks very prominent. It is surely an indication of literary erudition and poetic competence. Still, setting and intention do play an important role in determining the genre, too. Acrostic artistry does — as already pointed out — organize blocks of eight lines the first words of which all begin with the same letter of the Hebrew alphabet. To achieve such a homogeneity of initial sounds and at the same time an aesthetic literary manifestation the authors and traditionists were not extremely creative or successful. Many times the same words recur in a given eight block of lines (cf., e.g., the eight prepositions *bĕ* in the *bet* strophe; eight copulas *wĕ* in the *waw* part; five *derek*, "way," in the *dalet* block; five *ṭôb*, etc., in the *ṭet* listing). On the other hand, certain catchwords that one would expect do not occur at all in pole positions, e.g., *qādôš*, "holy"; *tôrāh*, "instruction"; *'ĕlōhîm*, "God"; *'ĕmûnāh*, "loyalty, truth"; *rĕšā'îm*, "godless"; *ṣaddîqîm*, "righteous"; etc. While one may get the general impression of a rather disorderly choice of first words, we sometimes note a careful structuring of these expressions, as in vv. 57 and 64, the first and last lines of the *ḥet* strophe: "My share is Yahweh" (v. 57a) seems to be echoed by "your solidarity, Yahweh" (v. 64a). Possibly, these expressions were even meant to be read in an overarching linkage: "My share, Yahweh, is your solidarity, Yahweh." Other formal features include the variety of the synonyms for *tôrāh* within the first and especially the second colon of each line (cf. Deissler, 74-86; Levenson, 561-63). In our psalm "torah" is apparently not totally fixed on the written Pentateuch, but includes oral tradition as extant in the teaching of the elders (vv. 99-100; thus Levenson).

Poetical devices are not sufficient to determine the genre of this psalm. We have to take into account contents and purposes, too. The overwhelming preponderance of "I" discourse (PROMISES), the equally astounding prevalence of personal prayer language from v. 4 to v. 176, together with the general thrust of presenting a model of a Yahweh believer and student of Torah lead to the conclusion that we have in Psalm 119 a PORTRAIT OF A CONFESSOR. There are some relations to well-known confessions of the innocent (cf. 7:4-6 [RSV 4-5]; Job 31). These also employ "I" discourse, but they stress exemption from a series of concrete, criminal accusations. Accusatory PORTRAITS OF THE GODLESS (cf. Pss 10:3-11; 94:3-7) are the other side of the coin, summarizing bad behavior of opponents and enemies. Our psalm is essentially confined to portraying but one characteristic of the believer, painting him as a tireless student and adept of torah (cf. 1:2), a propagator of faith among the faithless (cf. v. 46), and a zealous defender of Yahweh's ordinances (cf. v. 53). The "godless," principally called *zēdîm* (see above) and *rĕšā'îm* (seven times: vv. 6, 53, 61, 95, 110, 119, 155), are internal opponents and heterodox groups. Strangely enough, though, the customary juxtaposition with the *ṣaddîqîm*, "righteous," is missing. The term is used only one time (v. 137), in relation to Yahweh himself. The psalm does not introduce a substitute for this important young concept either (cf. Levin, "Gebetbuch"; listing at Additional Bibliography, section C; Hossfeld and Zenger, 45-49; listing at Additional Bibliography section A). It vaguely describes the group or community the suppliant considers his "home" in some rare allusions to "those who fear you" (vv. 63, 74). So we are left with rather extensive descriptions of opponents but with almost no reference to the suppliant's own "we" group, and a first-person plural form in fact does not occur in the whole long poem.

## Setting/Intention

The use of a text is decisive for recognizing its genre and meaning. I doubt that Psalm 119 was intended primarily to be a private prayer, in spite of continuous prayer language. It seems to me that the large poem, being a PORTRAIT OF A YAHWEH CONFESSOR, served as a model text for all members of the community. It was probably recited in worship, formally as a prayer but with the clear intention to instruct everyone, especially younger people, as to the correct postures over against Yahweh and his will. The psalm belongs to the didactic strands of early Jewish worship, being a beautiful example of endeavors to orient members toward the Lord of all justice and bounty articulated within the Torah (cf. F. García López, *TWAT* VIII, 597-637).

## Bibliography

Y. Amir, "Psalm 119 als Zeugnis eines protorabbinischen Judentums," in idem, *Studien zum Antiken Judentum* (Frankfurt: Peter Lang, 1985) 1-34; F. Asensio, "Los zedîn del salmo 119 en el área 'dolo-mentira,'" *EstBib* 41 (1983) 185-204; S. Bergler, "Der längste Psalm — Anthologie oder Liturgie?" *VT* 29 (1979) 257-88; T. Booij, "Psalm 119:89-91," *Bib* 79 (1998) 539-41; J. Chopineau, "Midrache des lectures," *Foi et Vie* 84/6 (1985) 1-4; F. Crüsemann, *Die Tora* (Munich: Chr. Kaiser, 1992); J. D. Currid, "Recognition and Use of Typology in Preaching," *Reformed Theological Review* 53 (1994) 115-29; A. Deissler, *Psalm 119 (118) und seine Theologie* (Munich: Karl Zink, 1955); F. Diedrich, "'Lehre mich, Jahwe!' Überlegungen zu einer Gebetsbitte," in *Die alttestamentliche Botschaft als Wegweisung* (*Fest.* H. Reinelt; ed. J. Zmijewski; Stuttgart: Katholisches Bibelwerk, 1990) 59-74; J. Dupont, "Le 'suspice me' d'un vieux moine," in *La parola edifica la comunità* (*Fest.* J. Dupont; ed. E. Bianchi; Magnano: Ed. Qiqájon, 1997) 257-63; J. H. Eaton, "Proposals in Psalms 99 and 119," *VT* 18 (1968) 555-58; L. O. Erikson, "Vägen i Psaltaren 119," *SEÅ* 63 (1998) 31-40; D. N. Freedman, "The Structure of Psalm 119," *HAR* 14 (1994) 55-87; idem, *Psalm 119: The Exaltation of Torah* (Winona Lake, Ind.: Eisenbrauns, 1999); B. Heyne, "Zu Ps. 119, 75 und 67," *ZAW* 51 (1933) 312; C. B. Houk, "Acrostic Psalms and Syllables," in *The Psalms and Other Studies* (ed. J. Knight, et al.; Nashotah: Nashotah House Seminary, 1990) 54-60; A. Hurvitz, "*sswy twrh* in Ps 119: The Origins of the Phrase and Its Linguistic Background," in *Studies on Hebrew and Other Semitic Languages Presented to Chaim Rabin* (ed. M. Goshen-Gottstein; Jerusalem: Academon Press, 1990) 105-9; H.-J. Kraus, "Freude an Gottes Gesetz," *EvT* 11 (1951) 337-51; idem, "Zum Gesetzesverständnis der nachprophetischen Zeit," in idem, *Biblisch-Theologische Aufsätze* (Neukirchen-Vluyn: Neukirchener Verlag, 1972) 179-94; S. M. Lehmann, "Psalm 119," *Jewish Biblical Quarterly* 23 (1995) 55-56; J. D. Levenson, "The Sources of Torah: Psalm 119 and the Modes of Revelation in Second Temple Judaism," in *Ancient Israelite Religion* (*Fest.* F. M. Cross; ed. P. D. Miller, et al.; Philadelphia: Fortress, 1987) 559-74; J. L. Mays, "The Place of the Torah-Psalms in the Psalter," *JBL* 106 (1987) 3-12; A. MacEwen, "'Revival' in the Old Testament," *Vox Reformata* 61 (1996) 67-82; H. P. Müller, "Die hebräische Wurzel *ṣyḥ*," *VT* 19 (1969) 361-71; P. Opitz, "Ein Torahpsalm als ABC des christlichen Glaubens," in *Calvin's Books* (*Fest.* P. de Klerk; ed. W. H. Neuser, et al.;

Heerenveen: Groen, 1997) 117-31; G. Östborn, *Tora in the Old Testament: A Semantic Study* (Lund: Gleerup, 1945); J. P. M. van der Ploeg, "Le Psaume 119 et la sagesse" (1979), in *La Sagesse de l'Ancien Testament* (ed. M. Gilbert; 2nd ed.; Leuven: Peters, 1990) 82-87; M. L. Potter, "The 'Whole Office of the Law' in the Theology of John Calvin," *Journal of Law and Religion* 3 (1985) 117-39; G. von Rad, "'Gerechtigkeit' und 'Leben' in der Kultsprache der Psalmen" (1950), repr. in idem, *Gesammelte Studien zum Alten Testament* I (Munich: Chr. Kaiser, 1958) 225-47; A. Robert, "Le Psaume 119 et les sapientiaux," *RB* 48 (1939) 5-20; V. Sasson, "Two Unrecognized Terms in the Plaster Texts from Deir Alla," *PEQ* 117 (1985) 102-3; J. Schildenberger, "Psalm 119: Das grosse Bekenntnis der Liebe zu Gottes Weisung," *Erbe und Auftrag* 57 (1981) 360-62; J. Schreiner, "Leben nach der Weisung des Herrn: Eine Auslegung des Ps 119," in *Freude an der Weisung des Herrn* (*Fest.* H. Gross; ed. E. Haag, et al.; Stuttgart: Katholisches Bibelwerk, 1986) 395-424; W. M. Soll, "The Hermeneutics of an Acrostic Lament," *Dissertation Abstracts* 43/4 (1982) 1183; idem, "The Question of Psalm 119:9," *JBL* 106 (1987) 687-88; idem, *Psalm 119: Matrix, Form, and Setting* (CBQMS 23; Washington, D.C.: Catholic Biblical Association, 1991); L. Steiger and R. Steiger, "'Es ist dir gesagt, Mensch, was gut ist': J. S. Bachs Kantate BWV 45, ihre Theologie und Musik," *KD* 32 (1986) 3-34; G. Toloni, "Un problema di semantica," *RivB* 42 (1994) 35-43; G. Vermes, "'The Torah Is a Light,'" *VT* 8 (1958) 436-38; R. E. O. White, "The Student's Psalm?" *ExpTim* 102 (1990/1991) 71-74; R. N. Whybray, "Psalm 119, Profile of a Psalmist," in *Wisdom, You Are My Sister* (*Fest.* R. E. Murphy; CBQMS 29; Washington, D.C.: Catholic Biblical Association, 1997) 31-43.

# Psalm 120:
# Complaint of the Individual

## Structure

|  | MT | NRSV |
|---|---|---|
| I. Superscription | 1a | - |
| II. Invocation and confidence | 1bc | 1 |
| III. Petition | 2 | 2 |
| IV. Contest, challenge of opponents | 3 | 3 |
| V. Curse | 4 | 4 |
| VI. Complaint | 5-6 | 5-6 |
| VII. Affirmation of righteousness and denunciation | 7 | 7 |

Psalm 120 begins the series of prayers entitled "Psalms of Ascent" (Psalms 120–134): each song, and very regularly so, bears the superscription *šîr hamma'ălôt* [alternatively: *lamma'ălôt*], "song of the ascents [alternatively: 'for the ascents']." Only a few headings exhibit a slight accretion: "of/for David," "of/for Solomon" (cf. Psalms 122; 124; 127; 131; 133). This fixed formulaic superscription suggests a separate collection and handling of the combined texts. To what end? Are we dealing with a real "hymnal" for pilgrimages "going up to Jerusalem"? They may have been collected on the basis of D regulations to celebrate seasonal feasts at the "place that Yahweh will elect" (cf. Deut 12:5, 7, 11, 14, 18, etc.). Although historical proof of such sacred wanderings is quite late (first century B.C.E.; cf. Safrai, 8; listing at Additional Bibliography, section B), so may be the collection of "Psalms of Ascent," while individual psalms in this body of texts may go back to much more ancient times (cf. Seybold). What does the stereotyped title mean in terms of structure, content, and intention of the individual song, then? We postpone the discussion of this matter to the section on Setting, because the generic diversity of the texts obviously demands an evaluation in its own right.

H. Gunkel (p. 537) calls Psalm 120 "rather odd," considering its form, structure, and locality. The first poetic line — emended by Gunkel — is already enigmatic: to Yahweh "I call, and he answered me" (v. 1c). This is usually a statement of thanksgiving (consecutive imperfect of 'nh, "answer," is rare in the Psalter, but should indicate the past tense; cf. 3:5 [RSV 4]; 119:26; 138:3). Of the three passages indicated, the clearest example of a thanksgiving context is 138:1-3. The other two occurrences may be taken in the sense of anticipated realization, as AFFIRMATION OF CONFIDENCE (cf. 7:2 [RSV 1]; 31:2-3 [RSV 1-2]), which probably holds true also in our case. With all other elements of thanksgiving lacking, the psalm is really a complaint song (against Seybold, et al., who consider vv. 2-7 as a remembrance of distress and complaint), confidence being an integral sentiment of that genre (see "Introduction to Cultic Poetry," section 4B).

The PETITION (v. 2) comes as a standard imperative — and just one — of a person asking to be "torn out of" calamity (nṣl, Hiphil; cf. Pss 7:2 [RSV 1]; 22:21 [RSV 20]; 25:20; 31:3, 16 [RSV 2, 15]; 39:9 [RSV 8]; 51:16 [RSV 14]; 59:2-3 [RSV 1-2]; 69:15 [RSV 14]; etc.). The second colon of v. 2, indicating the kind of threat to be rescued from, is plaintive already, anticipating the full complaint of vv. 5-6. The specific grievance is with murderous slander, virulent in "primitive" (cf. Fortune, Sorcerers; listing at "Introduction to Cultic Poetry") as well as "modern" societies (cf. phenomena of "mob," "witch hunt," "blackmail," "character assassination," etc.). Our text has two descriptive affirmations: "lying lips" and "deceitful tongue" (vv. 2c, 3c), reinforced by "peace haters" in v. 6b. Now, these allusions are quite concrete and unusually fixed on a determined social mechanism of marginalization and threat against deviant members of a group.

The CONTEST and CURSE (vv. 3-4) of the marginalized suppliant over against his persecutors indicate the ritual implications of the psalm. Opponents of the sufferer are either present in the service or are talked to and condemned in absentia (→ Psalms 4; 11; 62). The rhetorical, challenging, and defensive question (v. 3) derives from CONTEST discourse, implying God's curse. Apparently, the oath formula "May God do to you this or that [and continue to do so]" (cf. 1 Sam 3:17; 14:44; 25:22; 2 Sam 3:9, 35; etc.) looms behind that question (Gunkel, 538). The ill-wish or curse itself (v. 4) draws on war experiences. Furthermore, "arrows" and "glowing coal" are frequently used metaphorically to indicate the fierce power of evil or any other words (cf. Pss 64:4; 140:4; Prov 25:22). The two cola of three words each are not complete sentences, but rather exclamations. As such, they may represent old cursing formulas, which carry their destructive powers within themselves. One might expect a more elementary form in this case: *ḥiṣṣê šĕnûnîm/gaḥălê rĕtāmîm,* "sharp arrows/coal of broom" (the latter may have been used for burning rituals; cf. Galling, *Reallexikon,* 5-6, 9-10; G. A. Anderson, *ABD* V, 870-86).

Vv. 5-7 are COMPLAINTS, although of an uncommon type as far as the Psalter is concerned. The opening formula *'ôyāh lî,* "woe to me," with the mourning cry itself extended by the syllable *-āh,* is unique in the whole Hebrew canon, while the shorter version *'ôy lî* or *'ôy nā' lî* occurs six times in Isaiah and Jeremiah (Isa 6:5; 24:12; Jer 4:13; 10:19; 15:10; 45:3). Crying out because of one's own desperate situation, bewailing, so to speak, one's own ill-fated life or situation, is a strong signal of anxiety. Strangely enough, this expression of anguish is not used in individual complaints outside Psalm 120. Also, the first-person plural wail (*'ôy lānû*) has not been incorporated in communal complaints of the Psalms proper (cf. the following passages outside the Psalter: 1 Sam 4:7-8; Jer 4:13; 6:4; Lam 5:16). Without doubt, however, the cry that in most cases gives the reason for moaning in a *kî* phrase, as in v. 5a, reflects real usage in everyday life. By saying "woe to me/us" the ancient Israelites made public their grief in a ritualized form. Vv. 5-6, however, spell out that grievance in a single-minded fashion. Wicked slanderers, nobody and nothing else, are causing the calamity at hand. The much-debated question is only whether the lexemes *mešek* and *qēdār* (NRSV Study Bible [ed. W. A. Meeks et al.; New York: HarperCollins, 1993], 918: "Meshech" — "distant region in eastern Asia Minor"; "Kedar" — "Arab tribes inhabiting the northern regions of the Arabian peninsula") in v. 5 represent real tribal names. In my opinion, it is futile to speculate about the historicity and geographical location of such hostile tribes. Arguing from the very nature of psalm texts that were used by many people in succeeding generations (see "Introduction to Psalms"), one must admit that any possible reference to a concrete situation must have acquired symbolic value in order to stay meaningful to the users of the text. We may surmise, therefore, that the complaint gives voice proverbially to how much a given suppliant is suffering from ostracism among his or her neighbors, all the more so whenever a foreigner becomes the target of communal disdain. Here could be hidden a special subtlety: a member of the Israelite/Jewish community formally complains about some legendary inhumane people who do not let a stranger live in peace. But he or she does so within the community where the prayer was certainly used. Bringing to bear this extraterritorial symbolism is in a way similar to speaking about the memory of slavehood in Egypt (cf. Exod 22:20; Lev 19:34; Deut 5:15; etc.).

Grammatically and in regard to contents and meaning, v. 7 is somewhat difficult: "I am peace" (v. 7a) and "they are for war" (v. 7b) are atypical expressions. If v. 6b refers to "haters of peace," one would expect the statement "I do love peace" in v. 7a, and in continuation of this line, "while they prefer strife" (v. 7b). "When I speak out" (v. 7a) seems a forlorn interpolation. Cody gives a fanciful translation of MT ("I am peace itself, and so, whenever I spoke, they would turn to strife"), which nevertheless may come close to some original meaning. Form-critically, the last line belongs to complaint, but evaluated in itself it is an AFFIRMATION OF RIGHTEOUSNESS turning into DENUNCIATION of opponents in its second half. There is a deeply human desire to point out, in times of conflict and disgrace, the impeccability of one's own self, and the total wickedness of some opponents. This self-righteous attitude, to some degree necessary in certain situations of brutal injustice, has been molded into liturgical shape, of a black-and-white type, e.g., in protestations of innocence (→ Psalms 7; 17; 26), discourses of contest (→ Psalms 4; 11; 62; the book of Job), and cursing rituals (→ Psalm 109).

## *Genre*

Since the consecutive imperfect in v. 1c is not sufficient to make the whole psalm a thanksgiving song, our text, on the strength of prevailing complaint elements, should be classified as a COMPLAINT OF THE INDIVIDUAL. The special function of this prayer may have been to ward off social discrimination and slander (see "Introduction to Cultic Poetry," section 4B; Mowinckel, *PsSt* II).

## *Setting*

It is highly unlikely that Psalm 120 was composed and used in strange territories among "the barbarians" of Meshech and Kedar (the location of which is not at all certain: Isa 21:16-17 leaves the impression of a wild and doomed people of "archers"; cf. v. 4). Some traditions of nomadic tribes have probably been proverbialized in our Psalm, so that we may take v. 5 in a symbolic sense. In this case, the setting is just the community transmitting that song to be used in prayer services for those who were suffering from social marginalization (→ Psalms 3; 88).

Were there a special setting for the whole collection of "Psalms of Ascent" and a marked influence of this setting on the individual texts of the collection? Most exegetes, intrigued by the uniformity of superscriptions, take this supposition for granted. We may distinguish two typical opinions: (a) Psalms 120–134 were composed from scratch for a specific liturgical procedure, either peregrinations to Jerusalem ("to go up," *'lh*, is a technical term for journeying to the Holy City; cf. Safrai, *Wallfahrt;* listing at Additional Bibliography, section B) or singing "ascent hymns" on the steps leading to the temple. (b) The individual texts are older than the pilgrimages to Jerusalem; they came from different backgrounds and were secondarily adapted to be used in "ascent" liturgies of some kind (Seybold, *Wallfahrtspsalmen*). To exemplify such hypotheses with only a few instances: Seidel has it that every single psalm was construed around a general insight or theological affirmation (e.g., 120:1; 128:1) meditated on by pilgrims at daily rest stops. Seybold considers the fifteen texts to be reworked by late redactors (who can be neatly distinguished by literary analysis) to fit the peregrination situation, giving theological instruction to the pilgrims. Zenger (p. 92; listing at Psalm 107) also discovers a rather literary and theological structure in Psalms 120–134. To him there are subgroups recognizable, three with five psalms each, clustering around a central poem, namely Psalms 122; 127; 132: "With their different emphases (122: Jerusalem; 127: the temple; and 132: David), these three psalms produce a coherent theological view that acclaims Zion as the place of blessing and salvation to which Israel should go in 'ascents' or a 'pilgrimage' (executed as a second exodus from exile or foreign land)." In effect, he presupposes a community of readers finding new meanings in the canonical psalm text.

Such systematizations of settings and meanings are clearly possible in retrospect, as their sheer existence proves. But they hardly seem plausible for the ancient texts. To my mind, the individual use of the psalms is predominant even in the last phases of collection and canonization (and to this very day).

## Intention

Voicing complaints of the individual in proper rituals is a prerogative of the sufferers unjustly accused and pushed beyond the fringes of society (→ Psalms 7; 17; 26). Thus a correction of majority behavior is really aimed at, an essential condition for the rehabilitation of the victimized member of the community. In the context of assumed pilgrimages the outlook of the song may be wider, surpassing individual needs and encompassing humiliations and defeats of the religious community of those fearing Yahweh, being on their way to recovering safety and trust in their Lord.

## Bibliography

E. Beaucamp, "L'unité du recueil de montées. Psaumes 120–134," *Studium Biblicum Franciscanum* 29 (ed. E. Testa, et al.; Jerusalem: Franciscan Printing, 1979) 73-90; A. Cody, "Psalm 120(119),7," in *Ein Gott, eine Offenbarung* (*Fest.* N. Füglister; ed. F. Reiterer; Würzburg: Echter, 1991) 51-64; L. D. Crow, *The Songs of Ascents* (SBLDS 148; Atlanta: Scholars Press, 1996); K. Deurloo, "Gedächtnis des Exils (Psalm 120–134)," *Communio Viatorum* 34 (1992) 5-14; M. D. Goulder, "The Songs of Ascent and Nehemiah," *JSOT* 75 (1997) 43-58; C. Keet, *A Study of the Psalms of Ascents* (London: Mitre Press, 1969); M. Mannati, "Les Psaumes Graduels constituent-ils un genre littéraire distinct à l'intérieur du psautier biblique?" *Sem* 29 (1979) 85-100; D. F. O'Kennedy, "Vergifnis vooer gehorsaamheid," *In die Skriflig* 31 (1997) 163-74; H. Seidel, "'Wallfahrtslieder' (Ps. 120–134)," in *Das lebendige Wort* (*Fest.* G. Voigt; ed. H. Seidel, et al.; Berlin: Evangelische Verlagsanstalt, 1982) 26-40; K. Seybold, *Die Wallfahrtspsalmen* (Neukirchen-Vluyn: Neukirchener Verlag, 1978); H. Viviers, "Trust and Lament in the *ma'alot* Psalms (Psalms 120–134)," *OTE* 5 (1992) 64-77; idem, "Klank — inhoud — chiasme in die *ma'alot* — psalms (Ps 120–134)," *SK* 13 (1992) 65-79; idem, "Why Was the *ma'alot*-Collection (Ps 120–134) Written?" *HerTS* 50 (1994) 798-811; idem, "The Coherence of the *ma$^a$lôt* Psalms," *ZAW* 106 (1994) 275-89.

# Psalm 121:
# Pilgrimage Song, Words of Assurance

## Structure

|  | MT | NRSV |
|---|---|---|
| I. Superscription | 1a | - |
| II. Affirmation of confidence | 1bc-2 | 1-2 |
| A. Plaintive question | 1bc | 1 |
| B. Affirmation of confidence | 2a | 2a |
| C. Glorification | 2b | 2b |
| III. Consolation, words of assurance | 3-8 | 3-8 |
| A. Basic comfort | 3-4 | 3-4 |
| B. Daily protection | 5-6 | 5-6 |
| C. Blessing for journey | 7-8 | 7-8 |

The SUPERSCRIPTION is that of → Psalm 120 (a slight variation being the preposition *lĕ* instead of the definite article), standard wording for the whole collection 120–134. Seybold suggests that originally there had been but one collective superscription for the whole series of psalms (*Wallfahrtspsalmen,* 73; listing at Psalm 120).

The body of our psalm consists of consoling, personal ASSURANCES (vv. 3-8). The first part (vv. 1b-2) is introductory to these words of comfort. In a rhetorical question the suppliant or pilgrim asks for help, *'ezer,* "support," being the key concept of the two preliminary lines. Looking out for help and expecting it from God are a common concept in Hebrew Scripture; cf. the following passages with *'ezer* and the synonym *'ezrāh:* Exod 18:4; Deut 33:7; Dan 11:34; Pss 22:20 (RSV 19); 27:9; 35:2; 38:23 (RSV 22); 40:14, 18 (RSV 13, 17); 70:2, 6 (RSV 1, 5); 71:12. Most of the Psalm texts cited are petitions for divine help. Only the book of Job has one interrogatory phrase seemingly expressing a desperate need for help, to no avail (Job 6:13). Judging from this evidence we may consider vv. 1b-2 a PLAINTIVE QUESTION, comparable to a series of questions for God introduced with "why?" "when?" "how long?" (cf. Pss 13:2-3 [RSV 1-2]; 22:2 [RSV 1]). By putting a circumstantial clause in front of that question (v. 1b) the author is perhaps indicating the geographical location: pilgrims are approaching Jerusalem and watching out for their God. The hills around the Holy City with their sanctuaries do not offer any divine helpers (Gunkel, 540; Willis, "Attempt"). An AFFIRMATION OF CONFIDENCE (v. 2a) is the answer to the question posed. Interestingly enough, in comparison to vv. 3-8, this affirmation is given by the suppliant him- or herself, thus becoming a strong confession of faith in Yahweh. Parallel formulations in the Psalter are: "You are my helper" (40:18 [RSV 17]; 70:6 [RSV 5]). Emendation of v. 2a into second-person address ("your helper") and into first-person suffixes in v. 3 ("my foot," "my guardian"), in order to create a line-to-line dialogue (thus Gunkel, H. Schmidt, et al.), is haphazard because there is no textual evidence for it whatsoever. This solemn affirmation of an individual carries with it a highly liturgical epithet of Yahweh: "creator of heaven and earth" (v. 2b). The title has ancient antecedents in Mesopotamian and Syrian religions (cf. W. H. Schmidt, *Alttestamentlicher Glaube in seiner Geschichte* [6th ed.; Neukirchen-Vluyn: Neukirchener Verlag, 1987] 197-206; Habel, "Yahweh"). In the Psalter it appears concentrated in 115:15; 121:2; 124:8; 134:3 (cf. H. Ringgren, *TWAT* VI, 417-18). Appealing for personal help to the highest creator-deity presupposes access to this supreme God, no easy venture in a world governed by a hierarchical pantheon (cf. Psalm 82; Deuteronomy 32). Individualization of religion in the ancient Near East apparently took place already during the second millennium B.C.E. (Jacobsen, *Treasures,* 145-64; Vorländer, *Gott,* both in Listing at "Introduction to Cultic Poetry"); in Israel it came to its high point during exilic and postexilic times. The title "Creator of the Universe" was probably given to Yahweh only in the Babylonian and Persian environments. But it became extremely influential in Jewish and Christian liturgy and theology (J. J. Scullion, *ABD* II, 1043-44; Brueggemann, *Theology,* 145-64; listing at Additional Bibliography, section C).

The string of ASSURANCES (vv. 3-8) is to be divided into three units, which display certain differences in their formal structure. Vv. 3-4 depend directly on the confessional affirmation of v. 2. An official voice addresses the suppliant, first in second-person discourse extending a (negatively formulated) wish to the client: Yahweh may not take a minute's break in protecting him. The word *nûm,* "snooze off," is rare in the OT (see Isa 5:27; 56:10; Ps 76:6); it may be colloquial for *yšn,* "sleep." While the first line is a wish to ward off the danger of God forsaking his or her follower (twice *'al* with jussive), and while the Deity here is called "your guardian" (v. 3b), the second line does not have any personal-address suffixes or verbal forms. It is formulated quite neutrally and objectively; only the exclamation "behold" (*hinnēh,* → Psalm 133) could be interpreted to aim at the suppliant (which is not necessarily the case). The objective phrase is a daring affirmation about God's untiring watch over his or her client, an affirmation made in the name of the "guardian of Israel" (v. 4b). The whole sentence, taking up the verb *nûm* from v. 3b, reinforces it by the factual statement "he does not sleep" (*yšn;* combining *lō'* with imperfect form) in order to mention the divine agent only at the very end of the line: "the guardian of Israel" (v. 4; linkage with "your guardian" of v. 3b). Personal assurance is thus undergirded by a homiletical/doctrinal statement having as its background the community of faithful called Israel.

The two remaining assurances (vv. 5-6, 7-8) are construed in the personal-address mode throughout. General statements are missing as well as exclamations or other attention markers. Every single line goes directly to the suppliant; note the grammatical singular: in three out of four lines Yahweh is the dominant substantive. At this point we discover a small difference between the two units. Vv. 5-6 have the name Yahweh twice in successive cola of v. 5. On the other hand, the divine name is missing in v. 6. But both lines nicely unfold the concept of divine protection during the (demonic?) heat of the day and the (demonic?) light of the moon (cf. 91:4-6). The starting point of this sequence is the concept of *šōmēr,* "guardian" (v. 5a), taken over from vv. 3-4. Metaphoric interpretation adds "Yahweh is your shadow" (v. 5b), in order to explain this day-and-night protection in v. 6.

Finally, vv. 7-8 are built most regularly and autonomously. Each of the two lines opens with "Yahweh"; the verbal chain is homogeneous: three times imperfect forms of *šmr* are at the center of positive wishes or blessings. Exegetes have long noted a certain affinity to Num 6:24-26, the Aaronite blessing: "Yahweh bless you and keep you" (*yĕbārekĕkā yhwh wĕyišmĕrekā*, Num 6:24; cf. F. García López, *TWAT* X, 280-306, esp. 301-3). In the case of this most important liturgical formula Yahweh is mentioned three times in three consecutive lines, with two verbs in each line describing his gracious actions in favor of the community and its members. Among those six different verbs *šmr*, "to keep," "to guard," occupies the second place. Our psalm text, on the other hand, dwells on *šmr* exclusively, puts Yahweh to the front, and introduces space and time as fundamental extensions of God's personal care (v. 8). We get the impression that vv. 7-8 are variations on Num 6:24.

It is somewhat difficult to say how the parts of Psalm 121 interrelate. The plaintive question and the first word of assurance undoubtedly belong together (vv. 1b-4). The following two units display varying degrees of autonomy: vv. 5-6 are connected to the preceding lines by the key word *šōmĕrekā* (v. 5a). As noted above, vv. 7-8 constitute a rather independent saying, well balanced in itself, with a certain affinity to Num 6:24-26. Various interpretations are possible: Psalm 121 may be a composition for compact liturgical use, a potent discourse of assurance to participants in Yahweh services. Or it may be a compilation of some specimens of such words of comfort, to be used alternatively in special situations.

## Genre

H. Schmidt identified the genres "greetings and congratulations" within the Psalter ("Grüsse und Glückwünsche"; listing at "Introduction to the Psalms"). Almost all form critics since Gunkel believe that the largest part of Psalm 121 was pronounced by cult officials to console laypersons seeking assurance from God. Thus the first person singular in vv. 1-2 would indicate the suppliant (or suppliants using collectively individualizing language). Vv. 3-8, addressing the worshiper directly, would come from cultic functionaries (cf. Mays, 390: "litany performed by two persons"). This opinion is still sustainable; therefore we may label the text WORDS OF ASSURANCE. In the context of the Psalms of Ascent (Psalms 120–134; cf. above Psalm 120, Setting) our little composition becomes a PILGRIMAGE SONG.

As suggested by the close parallelism of the verbs *brk*, "bless," and *šmr*, "guard" (Num 6:24, also extant on amulets from Ketef Hinnom; cf. D. Conrad, *TUAT* II, 929), there is a strong affinity between WORD OF ASSURANCE and BLESSING. The comforting words directed to the suppliant by a liturgist at the same time carry the protective power of God, which is one characteristic of blessing (→ Psalm 91).

## Setting

Many are the attempts to localize this psalm: most commentators dwell on the first line talking about help expected in vain from "the mountains." Sometimes a forlorn wanderer in bedouin territory is visualized (e.g., Morgenstern); quite often, the "mountains" are identified with the hills around Jerusalem, the suppliant being a just-arrived pilgrim (e.g., Gunkel, H. Schmidt, Keet, Willis). In fact, *hārîm*, "mountains," may signify or connote "sanctuaries on mountaintops" (cf. Deut 12:2; Jer 2:20; Ezek 18:6, 11, 15; etc.), but in a general way is not limited to the hills around Jerusalem. This fact alone may bring to mind that the psalm was used, during its transmission, in various liturgical, perhaps also private (thus Volz: a father blesses his son leaving for the pilgrimage), situations. Since neither Jerusalem nor Zion is mentioned explicitly, the blessings may have been used in local services before they were incorporated into the songbook of pilgrims heading for the Jerusalem temple.

## Intention

Stabilization of Yahweh believers is the paramount interest of the words of assurance and blessings. No matter how much they may fear bad or demonic influences from all sides, they are assured to be safe under the protection of this singularly mighty God Yahweh (cf. Psalm 91). The protective Deity, responding to the existential needs of the confessing faithful, vividly communicated in liturgical formulas, is at the center of this outstanding psalm, which resounds through the centuries of its cultic and spiritual use until our days (cf. Westermann; Miller, 294-99; listing at Additional Bibliography, section C).

## Bibliography

D. G. Barker, "'The Lord Watches over You': A Pilgrimage Reading of Psalm 121," *BSac* 152 (1995) 163-81; B. F. Bernard, "The Sleeping God: An Ancient Near Eastern Motif of Divine Sovereignty," *Bib* 68 (1987) 153-77; A. R. Ceresko, "Psalm 121: A Prayer of a Warrior?" *Bib* 70 (1989) 496-510; J. F. Creach, "Psalm 121," *Int* 50 (1996) 47-51; P. R. Davies, "Yahweh as Minder," *OTE* 11 (1998) 427-37; O. Eissfeldt, "Psalm 121," in *Stat crux dum volvitur orbis* (*Fest.* H. Lilje; ed. G. Hoffmann, et al.; Berlin: Lutherisches Verlagshaus, 1959) 9-14 (repr. idem, *Kleine Schriften* III, 494-500); H. W. M. van Grol, "De exegeet als restaurator en interpreet, een verhandeling over de bijbelse poetica met Ps 121 als exempel," *Bijdragen* 44 (1983) 234-61; C. Keet, *A Study of the Psalms of Ascents* (London: Mitre, 1969); B. A. Levine and J. M. de Tarragon, "Dead Kings and Rephaim: The Patrons of the Ugaritic Dynasty," *JAOS* 104 (1984) 649-59; J. Limburg, "Psalm 121: A Psalm for Sojourners," *Word & World* 5 (1985) 180-87; C. Loeliger, "Biblical Concepts of Salvation," *Point* 6 (1977) 134-45; J. Magonet, "Convention and Creativity: The Phrase 'Maker of Heaven and Earth' in the Psalms," in *'Open Thou Mine Eyes . . .'* (*Fest.* W. D. Braude; ed. H. Blumberg, et al.; Hoboken: Ktav, 1992) 139-53; J. Morgenstern, "Psalm 121," *JBL* 58 (1939) 311-23; K. A. Plank, "Ascent to Darker Hills," *Literature and Theology* 11 (1997) 152-67; P. H. Pollock, "Psalm 121," *JBL* 59 (1940) 411-12; W. S. Prinsloo, "Psalm 121: 'n triomflied van vertrouwe," *NGTT* 21 (1980) 162-68; P. Volz, "Zur Auslegung von Ps 23 und 121," *Neue Kirchliche Zeitschrift* 36 (1925) 576-85; M. Weippert, "'Ecce non dormitabit neque dormiet qui custodit Israel.' Zur Erklärung von Psalm 121,4," in *Lesezeichen für Annelies Findeiss* (Heidelberg: Selbstverlag Dielheimer Blätter, 1984) 75-87; C. Westermann, *Blessing in the Bible and in the Life of the Church* (Philadelphia: Fortress, 1978); J. T. Willis, "Psalm 121 as a Wisdom Poem," *HAR* 11 (1987) 435-51; idem, "An Attempt to Decipher Psalm 121:1b," *CBQ* 52 (1990) 241-51.

# Psalm 122:
# Pilgrimage Song; Hymn to Jerusalem

## Structure

|  | MT | NRSV |
|---|---|---|
| I. Superscription | 1a | - |
| II. Account of pilgrimage | 1b-2 | 1-2 |
| III. Praise of Jerusalem | 3-5 | 3-5 |
| IV. Hymn to Jerusalem | 6-9 | 6-9 |

As with Psalms 124; 131; 133 of the "ascent" collection of songs (→ Psalm 120), the SUPERSCRIPTION is slightly augmented by adding the name David (in one case it is the name of Solomon: Psalm 127). Some Greek MSS in all these instances stay with the shorter and stereotyped heading: "Song of Ascents." The addition of a royal name probably sneaked in only by scribal habit and negligence, because there are so many psalms attributed to David, e.g., Psalms 3–41. Psalm 127 may have been linked to Solomon because the first line contains the conspicuous expression "built a house," with Yahweh acting as supervisor (127:1).

The song starts out with allusions to the beginning of a pilgrimage (v. 1bc). *bêt yhwh nēlēk,* "let us go to Yahweh's house" (v. 1c), sounds like a popular shout to rally for the journey (cf. similar summonses in daily affairs: Gen 37:17; 2 Kgs 6:2; 1 Sam 9:6, 9, 10; religious events: Exod 3:18; 5:3, 8, 17; Zech 8:21; differently Hos 6:1). The topic "rejoice about Jerusalem" (v. 1b) is a theme of Trito-Isaiah and his time (cf. Isa 56:7; 60:4-5, 15; 62:6-12; 65:18-19; 66:10), going back to the first decades of the Second Temple. Commencing on this personal note of joy suggests individual action embedded in communal liturgy: cf. the "I" discourse in v. 1b, which is amalgamated immediately by "we" speech in vv. 1c, 2a, a clear example of interplay between person and group, i.e., probably officiant and congregation.

The other significant detail of the introductory ACCOUNT OF PILGRIMAGE is the direct address of Jerusalem (v. 2b; cf. 87:3; 137:5). Late prophetic texts and Lamentations use this mode of formulation with some frequency (cf. Isa 60:4, 15; 62:6; Ezek 16:3; 23:22; Zech 9:9; Lam 2:13-14, 17-19). In our case it serves as a form of hymnic praise (cf. Crüsemann, *Studien* 285-94; listing at "Introduction to Cultic Poetry") to be fully unfolded in vv. 6-9. Direct-address hymns to objects or entities other than Yahweh himself are extraordinary in a monotheistic faith. We should also note that our psalm praises the city of Jerusalem throughout, because it is the city of "Yahweh's house" (v. 1c; cf. Isa 56:8). But Zion is not mentioned at all, in spite of being so prominent in the Zion hymns proper (cf. Psalms 48; 87).

The hymn has two parts, both being dedicated in their first lines (vv. 3, 6) to Jerusalem, the extraordinary city. Vv. 3-5 sing praises to this singular place of Yahweh's presence using objective affirmations and descriptions. Jerusalem is pictured as the center of the tribes' life (vv. 3b-4). Pilgrimages are hinted at: they all "go upward" (*'lh*) to meet there, in later times a technical term for seasonal peregrinations. Even if somewhat corrupt, v. 3b is understood correctly in our translations ("built as a city that . . ."), the only purpose of Jerusalem being to host the multitudes (cf. Psalm 87). Reference to tribal structure is probably evidence not of an early date of this psalm but of the contrary. It seems that connotations and identifications with the twelve tribes of old gained enormous significance during the exile and later on. So restitution of the people after the collapse of the monarchies meant revival of the tribes (cf. Numbers 1–3; 1 Chronicles 1–9; M. Oeming, *Das wahre Israel: Die genealogische Vorhalle* [BWANT 128; Stuttgart: Kohlhammer, 1990]). The proper designation of the multitude at this point seems to be *šibṭê yāh*, "tribes of Yah" (v. 4b), over against the customary name "tribes of Israel." D phrases talk about Yahweh acting among "your tribes" (cf. Deut 12:5, 14; 16:18), addressing the community at large. But the formulation found in v. 4b is unique in the Hebrew canon (cf. the title of Gottwald's study). Not even the full form *šibṭê yhwh* is attested anywhere. Qumran texts read the following two words in v. 4c as *'ădat yiśrā'ēl* instead of MT *'ēdût lĕyiśrā'ēl* ("obligation for Israel"), thus giving the first designation "tribes of Yah" a fitting apposition: "assembly of Israel."

Strangely enough, the fact to be commemorated in particular (v. 5) is not that Yahweh took his lodgings in Jerusalem or in his "house" (v. 1c). Rather, the motif of "thrones of judgment," which have been or will be put up in this city, becomes the subject of praise (*yāšĕbû kissĕ'ôt lĕmišpāṭ*, "thrones are sitting for judgment," is an unusual formulation, though; cf. Metzger, *Königsthron;* listing at Additional Bibliography, section B). What seems clear is that the remembrance of David and his dynasty is celebrated, perhaps in a messianic way. Thus the psalm gets an eschatological ring (cf. H.-J. Fabry, *TWAT* IV, 259-60, not admitted for Psalm 122: pp. 262, 263).

"Justice" *(mišpāṭ)* is an age-old prerequisite and responsibility of kingship in Mesopotamia and Egypt as well as in Canaanite and Syrian territories (cf. Fabry, *TWAT* IV, 247-72; Psalms 45; 72), to the extent of considering the king's jurisdiction a direct realization of Yahweh's reign — and this expecially in exilic or later texts (cf. 1 Chr 28:5: Solomon, to sit "on the throne of Yahweh's kingship"). This idea ties in very well with the messianic expectation of justice being established by the future king (cf. Isa 9:5-6 [RSV 6-7]; 16:5; Jer 33:15, 17). The Yahweh-kingship psalms are connected with these hopes for renewal, even though they do not expect a messianic figure (cf. Pss 96:10;

97:2; 98:9; also 89:15 [RSV 14]; Mettinger, *King* [listing at Additional Bibliography, section B], with largely preexilic datings, which is hardly correct). Having sung the glory of Jerusalem in a more objective, descriptive way, the congregation (or the choir) now turns to a direct-address praise (vv. 6-9). Each one of the four lines comprising this hymnic unit ends with a second-person feminine singular suffix referring to the Holy City attached to some noun or preposition. That means that all second colas end homophonously in *-ayik* (vv. 6b, 7b) or *-āk* (vv. 8b, 9b). In addition, v. 7a also has a suffix of the same category (only vocalized *-ēk*). Further poetic and stylistic features include the alliteration of *š* sounds in vv. 6-7 (five *š* occurrences), the conjunction *lĕmaʿan* opening the final clauses of vv. 8 and 9, and first-person singular and plural suffixes and verbal forms dominating vv. 8-9. All these formal characteristics make the unit more sophisticated and better organized than the preceding one (vv. 3-5). Undoubtedly, it receives a higher degree of attention and liturgical weight. Starting out with an imperative directed to the congregation (v. 6a), the singer(s) turn(s) to Jerusalem herself (cities are feminine in Hebrew), wishing first all the best to her friends (v. 6b) and second extending a blessinglike well-wish to the city herself (v. 7; "walls" and "palaces" also in 48:4, 14 [RSV 3, 13]; Zech 9:4). *yĕhî šālôm bĕhêlēk,* "may peace/well-being be within your walls" (v. 7a), amounts to a blessed greeting that corresponds exactly to the initial request to "seek Jerusalem's peace" (v. 6a). The beautiful little hymn is the climax and termination of the psalm, also in that it takes up the expression *bêt yhwh* of v. 1c in its last line (v. 9a). Thus, succinctly, the temple of the city receives a lot of emphasis, after all.

## Genre

HYMN TO JERUSALEM is a just name for Psalm 122. The Holy City and its prominent temple are focal points in our text (cf. Psalms 48; 87; 137, the last song mentioning both Jerusalem and Zion). Those Zion hymns are certainly closely related to Psalm 122. Still, both go back to different traditions. Jerusalem as a city was apparently famous for her invincibility guaranteed by her deities of old (cf. Yahweh versions of this mythical tradition: Ps 48:5-12 [RSV 4-11]; 2 Kgs 19; B. S. Childs, *Isaiah and the Assyrian Crisis* [SBT 2/3; London: SCM, 1967]; Stolz, *Strukturen;* listing at "Introduction to Cultic Poetry") already before Zion was used as a temple precinct by Israelites (cf. 2 Samuel 24). Therefore the very city, with the temple of Yahweh and "the thrones of David's family" in it, becomes an object of hymnic praise. Set, as it is, in the pilgrimage or "ascent" tradition, Psalm 122 becomes a true PILGRIMAGE SONG.

## Setting

Since there are clear allusions to undertaking a journey to that celebrated, unique Yahweh sanctuary at Jerusalem (vv. 1b-2), we may assume that Psalm 122 was rooted in the pilgrimage tradition from the beginning. It testifies to a deeply, almost mystical personal attachment to that place elected by Yahweh. Both the city and, within the city, the temple of Yahweh became unifying symbols of Israel's (and Judah's) faith in the only authentic Deity, who held all the power of the world in his hands. Therefore he had to be praised (v. 4cd) also via the election and utilization of that age-old Jebusite city (cf. 2 Sam 5:6-10). "Jerusalem, du hochgebaute Stadt, ich wollt ich waer in dir" (Melchior Franck, 1663, translated by Catherine Winkworth, 1858: "Jerusalem, thou city fair and high, Would God I were in thee!") — the topic passed into our modern hymnbooks for use in worship services — without being connected any more to peregrinations to the Holy City. But at the beginning the pilgrimages to the center of Jewish faith probably gave rise to this psalm. Whether it marks the hour of arrival at the Holy City (cf., e.g., Allen, 157) remains uncertain. The time of the psalm — because of its theological expectations and its fully developed spiritual preponderance of Jerusalem — in all likelihood is postexilic, i.e., the Second Temple period.

## Intention

Jerusalem and Zion songs express — into our own days — the strong desire of early Jewish people from the fifth century on to visit the city of David, where the roots of ancient Israel's political and religious strength are (cf. the celebrations of the 3000th "anniversary" in 1996 and continuing strife about the possession of the integral city). The fate of this "elected" city is intimately tied to the destiny of the whole people (cf., e.g., E. Wiesel, *A Beggar in Jerusalem* [1968], trans. L. Edelman [New York: Random House, 1970]; A. Elon, *Jerusalem, City of Mirrors* [Boston: Little, Brown and Co., 1989]). And the holy place in itself has become internalized as a credal element and a part of pious existence.

## Bibliography

H. Donner, "Psalm 122," in *Text and Context* (*Fest.* F. C. Fensham; ed. W. Claassen; Sheffield: Sheffield Academic Press, 1988) 81-91; J. Jeremias, "Lade und Zion. Zur Entstehung der Zionstradition," in *Probleme biblischer Theologie* (*Fest.* G. von Rad; ed. H. W. Wolff; Munich: Kaiser, 1971) 183-98; E. Levinas, "Leçon talmudique: Les villes-refuges," in *Jérusalem l'unique et l'universel* (ed. J. Halpérin, et al.; Paris: Presses Universitaires de France, 1979) 35-48; R. R. Marrs, "Psalm 122:3-4: A New Reading," *Bib* 68 (1987) 106-9; J. McCann, "Preaching on Psalms for Advent," *Journal for Preachers* 16 (1992) 11-16; B. Ognibersi, "Sal 122,8: angusio de pace ou intercessione de pace?" *Lateranum* 64 (1998) 215-20; A. Strus and A. Schökel; "Salmo 122: Canto al nombre de Jerusalém," *Bib* 61 (1980) 234-50; J. T. Willis, "Isaiah 2:2-5 and the Psalms of Zion," in *Writing and Reading the Scroll of Isaiah* (VTSup 70; ed. C. Broyles, et al.; Leiden: Brill, 1997) 295-316.

# Psalm 123:
## Communal Complaint; Psalm of Confidence

### Structure

|  | MT | NRSV |
|---|---|---|
| I. Superscription | 1a | - |
| II. Introduction, summons | 1bc | 1ab |
| III. Communal prayer | 2-4 | 2-4 |
| A. Affirmation of confidence | 2 | 2 |
| B. Petition | 3 | 3 |
| C. Complaint | 4 | 4 |

For the SUPERSCRIPTION see Psalms 120–122. The song proper opens with a first-person statement similar to that of 121:1b (RSV 1a). Psalms 120 and 122 are introduced with first-person discourse as well; is this merely coincidental? In contradistinction to Psalm 121, though, there is no plaintive note in the initial affirmation. Our psalmist simply raises his eyes to the Lord in heaven (v. 1c), betraying a popular concept of Yahweh's residing in his heavenly abode (cf. 11:4; 14:2; 73:25; 115:3, 16). "Raising one's eyes to heaven" indicates that this affirmation is directed to God himself (prayer language), without mentioning his name yet. Appellation by name follows later (v. 3a; v. 2e does mention Yahweh in a neutral way), but personal address "to you I lift up my eyes" is highly emphasized already in v. 1b, four lines earlier. If this is so, the exclamation *hinnēh*, "behold" (v. 2a), must be directed to Yahweh also, even if v. 2e points to Yahweh in the third person.

After that call to attention *(hinnēh)* we find two comparative statements introduced by *kě*, "as" (vv. 2a, c), and the situation explained by those comparisons is introduced by *kēn*, "so, that way" (v. 2ef). As in 122:1-2, the first person singular of the opening line soon gives way to the first person plural (v. 2ef, to be continued in vv. 3-4). That means that the individual speaker merges with the congregation (Mays, 394). To put it in liturgical terms: the introductory line may have been sung by an officiant, the congregation responding by collective AFFIRMATION OF CONFIDENCE, etc. (vv. 2-4), using prayer language as well (cf. the imperatives of v. 3). The same transition from singular to plural occurs in 122:1-2. Comparisons used are taken from private life: male and female slaves are dependent on the mercy of their proprietors. They observe their "hands," symbol of power and benevolence (cf. 104:27-28; Sir 33:22; Schroer and Staubli, *Körpersymbolik*, 185-204, listing at Additional Bibliography, section B). In the same way Yahweh believers watch out for the hand of their God to open and give nourishment, gifts, and help (v. 2ef).

Scenes from daily life and interhuman relations are used sometimes in the Psalter to depict the relationship of the suppliant to Yahweh. Thus Ps 131:2 utilizes the image of a sheltered babe to show the contentedness and calmness of the believer. Here too the affirmation is explicitly marked as a comparison by the particle *kě*, "as." In our case, a double line (two bicola) expresses the comparison. Male and female slaves are adduced who expect sustenance and benevolence from their master or mistress, respectively. Transferred into plain meaning for the worshiping congregation, both sexes are subservient to Yahweh the overlord, as, in fact, v. 2ef spells out neatly: "Thus our eyes are directed toward Yahweh, our God, until he will bestow mercy on us." The appellation "Yahweh, our God," is a CONFESSIONAL STATEMENT. There are more than 70 instances in the Hebrew Bible, heavily concentrated in Dtr layers (see Deut 1:6, 19, 20, 25, 41; 2:29, 33, 36, 37; 1 Kgs 8:57, 59, 61, 65) and the Psalter (see Pss 20:8 [RSV 7]; 94:23; 99:5, 8, 9; 105:7; 106:47; 122:9). While other formulations like "Yahweh, your God," betray a preacher's voice addressing an individual or an audience, our present expression clearly comes from a worshiping group of people praying in unison. The only other alternative would be that of an official liturgist speaking on behalf of the people. But the first option is more plausible because the "we" suffixes sound very strong and determined. The confessional line (v. 2ef) centers around the name of Yahweh; it has a 4-and-2-beat rhythm and is quite feasible as a kind of communal response. If this is correct, then the foregoing two lines — although not showing any sign of a possible speaker — are communal discourse, too. They in fact lead up to the confession by using the impressive metaphorical affirmation of confidence. In retrospect, then, v. 1bc may have been recited by an individual voice, and the exclamation *hinnēh* (v. 2a) marks the transition to communal prayer.

The rest of this little and intimate psalm is plain PETITION and COMPLAINT (vv. 3-4), all in the communal "we" mode of discourse. Part of the vocabulary is well known from complaint psalms. Details include the petition for mercy with the verb *ḥnn*, "be favorable" (in the Psalter mostly imperative singular with first-person singular suffix: cf. 4:2 [RSV 1]; 6:3 [RSV 2]; 9:14 [RSV 13]; 25:16; 27:7; 30:11 [RSV 10]; 31:10 [RSV 9]; etc.). First-person plural suffixes can be found in communal prayer outside the Psalter (see Isa 33:2). Duplication of the imperative in our v. 3a makes the petition more urgent.

To be saturated by shame (v. 3b; cf. 4a) or other evils is a strong expression in complaints, lamentations, and wisdom contexts (cf. Ps 88:4 [RSV 3]; Lam 3:30; Job 10:15). The "careless" and "haughty" (v. 4b, c; only occurrence in the Psalter) and related concepts are characteristic of proverbial and homiletical discourse (cf. Prov 15:25; 16:19; 29:23; Isa 9:8 [RSV 9]; 32:9-14; Am 6:1; Zeph 3:11; Job 12:5; Pss 10:2; 73:6; W. Thiel, *TWAT* VII, 928-29). What kind of theology and anthropology is behind these concepts? It is possibly an elementary aversion against social imbalance deeply ingrained in Hebrew Scripture (Weinfeld, *Justice;* listing at Additional Bibliography, section B). The thrust of the denunciation in this case would be against internal opponents. In an alternative setup all complaints of vv. 3-4 would be directed against outward enemies gloating about that impotent Jewish community and its God. In any case, the overall juxtaposition of Psalm 123 is that of full confidence in Yahweh (vv. 1-2) within a context of ongoing molestation and ridicule on account of faith in Yahweh (vv. 3-4; cf. Brueggemann, *Theology,* 373-85; listing at Additional Bibliography, section C).

## Genre

A prayer so small and simple as Psalm 123, talking calmly about believers and God and making trust the main theme, may be legitimately called a PSALM OF CONFIDENCE (cf. Psalms 16; 23; Westermann, *Praise*, 55, 80; listing at "Introduction to Cultic Poetry"). On the other hand, petition and complaint elements are characteristic for INDIVIDUAL and COMMUNAL COMPLAINT, a genre classification preferred by quite a few exegetes (cf. Allen, 160; Gunkel, 544-45; Mowinckel, *W* I, 216; Anderson, 856-57; et al.).

## Setting

Because of the strong emphasis on "we" discourse (Scharbert, "Das 'Wir'"; listing at "Introduction to Psalms"), we have to visualize our psalm as having been used in congregational worship. Perhaps it was once part of complaint services in public calamities, together with a more extensive description of the emergency (cf. Psalm 44; Isa 63:7–64:11; Jeremiah 14; see "Introduction to Cultic Poetry," section B; P. A. Hanson, *ABD* I, 1099-1103), destined to voice the element of confidence. Complaint psalms and liturgies, as a rule, include expressions of confidence in juxtaposition with plaintive elements (cf. Pss 22:5-6, 10 [RSV 4-5, 9]; 31:4-7 [RSV 3-6]). Why not imagine a complementary liturgical use of small texts like Psalms 23; 62; 123 to highlight the basic trust of the suppliants? Seen in the context of pilgrimages to Jerusalem ("Psalms of Ascents," → Psalm 120), the song expresses the desires of the wandering group. Mays (pp. 394-95) imagines a definite moment when it came to be intoned: "Pilgrims stand within the gates (122:2) and their first word to the LORD is a prayer for grace." The taunting by the haughty ones (v. 4), then, perhaps would be directed against those who ventured on a peregrination of obedience and hope.

## Intention

By itself the psalm expresses the confidence of the congregation in God, taking in the experiences and hopes of all its members, the "haughty" ones posing a painful problem. By doing so, the text also induces new hopes among those who suffer irritations from people outside the core community of faithful, be it from hostile foreigners or dissident parishioners.

## Bibliography

C. Curti, "Due frammenti esegetici sul salm 123," in *Paideia Cristiana* (*Fest.* M. Naldini; ed. G. Privitera; Rome: Gruppo Editoriale Internazionale, 1994) 131-40; H. Goeke, "Gott, Mensch und Gemeinde in Ps 123," *BibLeb* 13 (1972) 124-28; F. M. Th. de Liagre Böhl, "Hymnisches und Rhythmisches in den Amarnabriefen aus Kanaan," in idem, *Opera Minora* (Groningen: Wolters, 1953) 375-79.

# Psalm 124:
## Thanksgiving of Community

### Structure

|  | MT | NRSV |
|---|---|---|
| I. Superscription | 1a | - |
| II. Affirmation of confidence | 1b-5 | 1-5 |
| A. Irreal conditions | 1b-2 | 1-2 |
| B. Summons to recite (interspersed) | 1c | 1b |
| C. Irreal consequences | 3-5 | 3-5 |
| III. Hymn | 6-7 | 6-7 |
| IV. Well-wish | 8 | 8 |

The SUPERSCRIPTION is within the pattern of the Psalms of Ascent (→ Psalms 120; 122). "If Yahweh had not been with us" — the first two lines open with this conditional phrase (vv. 1b, 2a), which discusses the irreal case of God acting in a way he really did not do. This kind of retrospective reflection on "What would be our situation, if something had happened differently in the past?" (always in the sense: if something had gone wrong) was apparently quite popular. We find similar phraseology (with *lûlē'*, "if not"; the formulation *'im lō'*, "if not," is mostly reserved for oath formulations; cf. Ezek 17:16, 19; → Ps 127:1), e.g., in Gen 31:42; 43:10; Deut 32:26-27; Judg 14:18; 1 Sam 25:34; 2 Sam 2:27; 2 Kgs 3:14; Isa 1:9; Pss 106:23; 119:92, but only the two Psalm passages, Gen 31:42, and Isa 1:9 deal with the same subject matter: God's forbearance over against a querulous people or person. The interspersed SUMMONS TO RECITE is a special formulaic expression of call to worship (→ Ps 118:1-4). In this case, as in 118:1-4; 129:1, the hymnic line to be sung by the congregation is intoned in the first place by the liturgist. Then he or she calls upon all people present to join in ("let Israel say") and the thematic first line is repeated, a ritual procedure described also in Exod 15:20-21; 1 Sam 18:6-7. *'nh* in the first passage means "to intone a song" (as a cantor). Since the hymnic SUMMONS TO PRAISE seems usually to have been expressed by the imperatives of *šîr*, "sing," *ydh*, Hiphil, "give thanks," *hll*, "praise," *rnn*, "extol" (cf. 33:1-3; 81:2; 98:1; 105:1-2; 106:1; 113:1; 117:1; 148:1-4; etc.; Gunkel-Begrich, *Einleitung*, 33; listing at "Introduction to Psalms") the formulas construed with a verbal form of *'mr*, "speak" (either jussive or imperative), may well be a subordinate type to the aforementioned more musical and theological phrases.

Granted, then, that Yahweh did stay at the side of his elected ones (in spite of their obstinacy), they now gratefully meditate on the dreadful consequences of a potentially unfavorable attitude of God in the past. Three almost uniformly structured lines answer the question posed (vv. 3-5): the main clauses are all introduced by *'ăzay*, "in that case, then." This conjunctive particle is normally spelled a little shorter, namely *'āz;* the unique forms of vv. 3-5 seem more emphatic. Interestingly, v. 3 stays with the historical situation hinted at in v. 2b: "They, i.e., the enemies, would have devoured us." The other two lines (vv. 4-5) take up mythological language speaking about "waters" that flood and swallow people (cf. similar metaphors in Isa 8:7-8). Although connections with Exodus 14–15, the drowning of the Egyptians, are feasible, the main signification points to primeval floods. Enemies are equated with dreadful chaos waters, as extant in complaint psalms (cf. Psalm 69; Jonah 2). Such paralleling is done in some prophetic texts, too (cf. Isa 17:12-14), not to speak of the Psalms themselves alluding to those powers (cf. Pss 93:3-4; 96:3; 98:7-8; Kaiser, *Bedeutung;* listing at Additional Bibliography, section B; Stolz, *Figuren;* listing at "Introduction to Cultic Poetry").

In conjunction the two elements together of naming the irreal case of abandonment and its horrible consequences form an AFFIRMATION OF CONFIDENCE to Yahweh, with grateful or even hymnic undertones. We see a liturgical movement going on in this block of verses: the "Israelites" in their totality (represented in the congregation) are summoned to articulate their agenda (v. 1c). In accordance with other texts that single out special groups to speak up in liturgy (cf. 115:9-11; 118:2-4), v. 1c here may include all the groupings of the Judahite community. V. 2b, for its part, visualizes the uprising of an unidentified "man," "people," against the congregation — which seems fairly strange. Only in the following line are they described as those who want to devour the faithful (v. 3). But the situation remains obscure; we do not know whether inner or outward enemies are pictured as the evil attackers. Antagonistic powers, human or mythical, are mentioned in abstract terms, summarizing experiences of generations. Liturgically, the stereotyped, uniform structure of vv. 3-5 insinuates repetitious chanting.

The historical or social background does not become more lucid in vv. 6-7, a HYMN introduced by *bārûk yhwh,* "blessed be Yahweh" (v. 6a). This BLESSING FORMULA is frequent in the Psalms (15 times; cf. 18:47 [RSV 46]; 28:6; 72:18-19; 119:12) and in some other parts of Hebrew Scripture (cf. Gen 9:26; 24:27; 1 Kgs 1:48; 8:15, 56; Ruth 4:14; Ezra 7:27; 2 Chr 2:11; 6:4; 9:8, often in greeting situations; → Psalm 72). Again, the "negative" action of Yahweh is praised: he did not abandon his congregation ("us"!) or deliver them to the bestial opponents (v. 6). On the contrary, his faithful escaped their enemies' fury. The metaphor employed is not exactly congruent with the enemy vocabulary in vv. 2-4, but it is poetically suggestive: the hunter's net was torn, the birds gained their freedom (v. 7; cf. *paḥ,* "bird trap," 69:23 [RSV 22]; 91:3; 119:110; 141:9; metaphor of bird, i.e., believer: 11:1; 102:8). Constant use of the first person plural makes all this allusive discourse a firm part of communal experience. Indeed, Psalm 124 is one of the strongest and most homogeneous "we" psalms in the Psalter (cf. Scharbert, "Das 'Wir'"; listing at "Introduction to Psalms"). This fact alone indicates congregational origin and use. The last line is at the same time a kind of blessing on the community, as well as a WELL-WISH on all participants, and a communal affirmation of confidence. Evoking the name of Yahweh and his solemn attributes as a creator ("of heaven and earth": sacred formula, extant, e.g., in 102:26 [RSV 25]; 115:15; 121:2; 134:3; 136:5-6; Exod 20:11; 31:17; cf. R. Bartelmus, *TWAT* X, 204-39) the congregational part comes to a close, not in an official word but with the people's own formula (note the difference from Num 6:22-27; Ps 121:3-8). The concise phrase in v. 8 has been adopted into Christian worship, particularly by John Calvin (Mays, 397), being part, as it were, of service liturgies, e.g., as an introit or a word of assurance from the pulpit.

## Genre

What could be the genre classification of a psalm so extravagant in its formal appearance? The initial summons to the congregation (v. 1c) suggests a hymnic situation; reference to near catastrophes and God's gracious forbearance point to thanksgiving motives. *bārûk* formulas are testimonies to an atmosphere of gratitude and praise as well. Taken together with the overall emphasis on having escaped grave dangers and being safe now, the evidence favors COMMUNAL THANKSGIVING. The alleged nonexistence of collective thanks is unconvincing (against Allen, 163: "individual language in plural dress"; Westermann, *Praise,* 102-11; Crüsemann; et al.). But we should remind ourselves: typical introductions of giving thanks, descriptions of distress now overcome, expressions of vows to be consummated, affirmations of loyalty and support, are lacking in this psalm (see "Introduction to Cultic Poetry," section 4C). There is no liturgist expressly mentioned acting in front of a group. But the congregation as a whole responds to a summons by singing a meditative/hymnic litany of having escaped deadly snares in its history.

## Setting

Therefore the setting is supposedly the worship service of the Jewish community, and the agents are all the members united in prayer. History, at this point, has been condensed into the vexing experiences of having escaped; the formulations of our little hymn do not suggest mighty interventions of Yahweh. Perhaps we are dealing with an early type of congregational hymn or response meant to be intoned as part of a more extensive liturgy. Inclusion of the psalm in the collection of pilgrimage songs may be due to the communality of the text, the retrospect on a difficult past and the exhilarating longing for relief and betterment through the walk to the Holy City.

## Intention

Like other expressions of gratitude toward Yahweh, the guardian of his community, our psalm is to extol God's patience with his faithful, thus reassuring them in the perils of a hostile world (*'ādām,* "human being," v. 2b, in this case meaning "everyman," "anybody," who became Israel's enemy).

## Bibliography

J. Chopineau, "Pourquoi le Christ est-il venu?" *ETR* 60 (1985) 165-77; J. Magonet, "Convention" (see listing at Psalm 121); J. Schreiner, "'Wenn nicht der Herr für uns wäre!' Auslegung von Psalm 124," *BibLeb* 10 (1969) 16-25; I. W. Slotki, "The Text and the Ancient Form of Recital of Psalm 24 and Psalm 124," *JBL* 51 (1932) 214-26.

# Psalm 125:
# Song of Confidence

## Structure

|  | MT | NRSV |
|---|---|---|
| I. Superscription | 1a | - |
| II. Felicitation | 1bc | 1 |
| III. Assurance to community | 2 | 2 |
| IV. Threat to evildoers | 3 | 3 |
| V. Petition | 4 | 4 |
| VI. Imprecation | 5ab | 5ab |
| VII. Well-wish | 5c | 5c |

The SUPERSCRIPTION is the standard one of the Psalms of Ascent (Psalms 120–134; → Psalm 120; 122). The song begins with something like a FELICITATION: a participial expression defines the faithful ones, who "trust in Yahweh" (v. 1b). In fact, a plurality of believers is called upon, while more frequently the word *bōṭēaḥ*, "trustful one," occurs in the singular (13 plural over against 23 singular forms in Hebrew Scripture). Sometimes the plural term is found in prophetic denunciations (cf. Isa 32:9-11; 42:17; Jer 7:8, 14; Am 6:1) or other expressions aiming at unfounded trust (cf. Isa 36:6; Ps 49:7 [RSV 6]). Nowhere but in Psalm 125 is the plural form connected with really good trust in Yahweh. Still, the designation, prefixed by the definite article, seems to be of a common type in early Jewish communities; cf. *hahōlĕkîm bĕtôrat yhwh*, "the ones who live by Yahweh's torah" (119:1); *yir'ê yhwh*, "the ones who fear Yahweh" (22:24 [RSV 23]; 115:11; 118:4). Identification of the community happened through Yahweh and his manifest will.

The trustful ones in MT are compared with steadfast Zion, the mountain of God's choice and habitation (v. 1c; cf. Psalm 48; Isa 4:1-5). The invincibility of his abode was part of the Jerusalemite traditions even before the Israelites took over the city (cf. B. S. Childs, *Isaiah and the Assyrian Crisis* [SBT 2/3; London: SCM, 1967]; Stolz, *Strukturen;* listing at "Introduction to Cultic Poetry"). "To be unshakable" (*mûṭ*, Niphal, "tumble," with negation) is also affirmed in regard to the earth itself (cf. Pss 93:1; 96:10; 104:5), and it is a hoped-for estate in spiritual and material life (cf. 15:5; 16:8; 21:8 [RSV 7]; 62:3, 7 [RSV 2, 6]; 112:6; Prov 10:30; 12:3). The parts compared — believers and Mount Zion — in our present estimation are in a certain tension, grammatically and semantically. Not so, apparently, for the Yahweh faithful of old. The plurality of members is conceptualized in one community and enclosed in the singularity of the mountain, and the vividness of the believers has its equal in personified Zion. We may surmise that the subject "those who trust in Yahweh" is close to a beatitude in form and meaning (→ Ps 1:1). Our initial line v. 1bc in any case is conveying FELICITATIONS to those who belong to the blessed group of believers.

If the line under debate is the opening of our psalm, the following line merely elaborates on the first one, repeating words of assurance to the troubled community ("his people," v. 2b). The point of comparison is now the enclosure of Jerusalem. The mountains around are like guardians for the city; in the same way Yahweh is believed to shelter his congregation. Note the key word *sābîb*, "all around" (twice in v. 2; cf. Ps 34:8 [RSV 7]; Josh 21:44), not frequently used in connection with Yahweh's protective activity.

Two lines of comforting and promising speech or song prepare, by juxtaposition, two more of denigrations. There seems to be no need to introduce specifically any opponents to the state of bliss imagined in vv. 1-2. The "rod of wickedness" shows up abruptly (v. 3a), and we have to speculate as to its historical, social, or religious identity. The expression as such is unique; similar wordings are used in Ezek 7:11; Sir 32:23. The thrust of v. 3 is to ward off evildoers, more precisely, to cut short their influence, in order not to lead into temptation the *ṣaddîqim*, the "just ones" (v. 3c; cf. v. 3b). This juxtaposition is clear enough! The outlines of the "wicked," however, are not clarified at all. They hold sway over the "heritage of the just ones" (v. 3b). They obviously perform iniquities attractive to the *ṣaddîqîm* (v. 3cd). Looking toward v. 5 we may add two more, but equally vague, characteristics: They "turn aside to their crooked paths" (v. 5a; the only other occurrence of "crooked paths," Judg 5:6, is more than obscure), and they are condemned together with the "evilmongers" (v. 5b: *pō'ălê hā'āwen;* cf. S. Mowinckel, *PsSt* I). What is certain is the function of v. 3: *kî lō'* in this context is a negative wish formula "May it not be that" (cf. the apotropaic formula of not wanting to get involved: *ḥālîlāh lî,* "be it far away from me," Gen 44:17; 1 Sam 24:7; 2 Sam 23:17; Job 27:5). The two lines in question, then, constitute a precative THREAT TO EVILDOERS. Significantly, they do not carry any reference to Yahweh, in contrast to vv. 1-2, 4-5, where every single line (alternatingly in the a and b cola) is equipped with the holy name. This makes me believe in the original autonomy of the middle segment of Psalm 125 (cf. Beyerlin, 35-43).

Next come two lines of PETITION and its defensive counterpart, IMPRECATION (vv. 4-5ab). "Do the best, Yahweh, for the good ones" (v. 4a) is a classic expression of asking favors from a deity. The verb *ytb,* Hiphil, is occasionally used in such imperative petitions (cf. 51:20 [RSV 18]), and Yahweh himself is called the "doer of good" (119:68). Now, petition for one's own sake is objectified by choosing honorific names: "the good ones," "those honest in their hearts" (v. 4), corresponding, of course, to the "trustful ones" of v. 1b. Dignity and merit are thus introduced into the song. Formal petition is not so frequent in psalms of confidence (see below, Genre), but it is certainly not alien to that class of songs (cf. "Introduction to Cultic Poetry," section 4B). If this is true, imprecation, too, has a right to appear in this context (v. 5). "Yahweh may make them go away" (v. 5b; is the wording perhaps euphemistic for "destroy"?). Normally, foes are denounced in more devastating terms in complaint psalms (cf., e.g., Psalm 109). Here the note of trust and well-being dominates the whole poem.

Whether the final greeting (WELL-WISH) of Israel is authentic or a later addition is a hard question to decide. "Israel" plays a role in many psalms; sometimes it seems to be the name of the whole ecclesiastical body of faithful, living in Judah and the diaspora (cf. 118:2; 124:1c). Taken that way, the greeting would make good sense in a situation of pilgrimage to the central place, Jerusalem (v. 2a). Here all Israel and all the world would meet in festive union (cf. Psalms 84; 87).

## Genre

Structure analysis of Psalm 125 has to acknowledge first of all the objective, neutral way of its presentation. Neither speaker nor audience is identifiable. It seems to be a text without addressees or protagonists, much in contrast to Psalm 124. Is SONG OF CONFIDENCE, therefore, the right category for this poem? Some scholars vehemently deny this option (e.g., Beyerlin [pp. 75, 79], who chooses the term *Vergewisserungsrede,* "address of assurance," instead [77-78], although the functions of both are quite comparable). We need to compare other examples of the genre in question, e.g., Psalms 23; 62; 131 (see also FOTL XIV, 13). Normally, songs of confidence betray an atmosphere of calmness and security, intimacy and personal relations; the words spoken are directed more to participants in worship, praising Yahweh's trustworthiness, rather than to the deity him- or herself (exception, e.g., 62:13 [RSV 12]). Songs of confidence portray the suppliant's sense of being sheltered in the midst of danger and turmoil. Thus the introductory vv. 1b-2 qualify for this genre. Since the following apotropaic and petitionary elements, reminiscent of complaints, save v. 4a, do not fall into direct prayer language (second-person address of Yahweh) but stay in descriptive discourse, we may judge them to be subordinate to the AFFIRMATIONS OF CONFIDENCE at the beginning of the psalm, determining the whole song.

## Setting

Like other specimens of the genre, our psalm of confidence belongs in the context of synagogal worship of the Yahweh community. Its members, united in prayer, receive the comforting words of Yahweh's steadfast protection, probably spoken to them by a cult official (leader? priest?). There is not a single "we" or "us" (or communal "I," for that matter) in the text, excluding the possibility of the congregation itself having recited these verses. Also, the second-person address is missing almost completely (on both counts the opposite is true, e.g., for Psalms 121–124). In the context of the Psalms of Ascent, the song would serve as a real word of assurance for the pilgrims on their way or at their arrival (cf. Mays, 398) incorporating one imperative petition (v. 4) like an ASIDE.

## Intention

Those who trust in Yahweh, and for this reason are the "just ones," "the good ones," "the honest ones," are confirmed in their position as members of that community which Yahweh loves and protects. Unfortunately, in the course of Jewish-Christian tradition this edifying purpose of trust and assurance has often been tied to or complemented by condemnations of opponents, be they oppressors and persecutors or simply dissidents (cf. v. 5). Dire necessities may have paved the way for such binary ethics, but also, surely, staunch self-righteousness. If the foreign occupation thesis is correct (on the basis of v. 3, "scepter of wickedness . . . on the land allotted to the righteous," thus Allen, 167-68; Gunkel, 549; et al.), the psalm sounds a warning against the imperial government and those Israelites who cooperate with the foreign powers.

## Bibliography

W. Beyerlin, *Weisheitliche Vergewisserung mit Bezug auf den Zionskult: Studien zum 125. Psalm* (Fribourg: Universitätsverlag; Göttingen: Vandenhoeck & Ruprecht, 1985); C. B. Reynolds, "Psalm 125," *Int* 48 (1994) 272-75; Z. Zevit, "Psalms at the Poetic Precipice," *HAR* 10 (1987) 351-66.

## Psalm 126:
## Communal Thanksgiving

### Structure

|  | MT | NRSV |
|---|---|---|
| I. Superscription | 1a | - |
| II. Praise of liberation | 1b-3 | 1-3 |
| A. Report of Yahweh's intervention | 1b-2 | 1-2 |
| B. Response of community | 3 | 3 |
| III. Petition | 4 | 4 |
| IV. Farmer's song | 5-6 | 5-6 |

Our psalm displays that basic redactional SUPERSCRIPTION typical for Psalms of Ascent (Psalms 120–134; → 120; 122). Structural analysis is difficult because of textual and grammatical problems. First, as to the Hebrew text we are not too sure about the spelling and meaning of the key expression *šûb šĕbût*, "to restore fortune," "to bring back captives," or similarly (cf. Bracke). Second, the temporal relationship between praise of the liberating event in vv. 1-3 and petition in v. 4 remains enigmatic.

Rhetorically speaking, the psalm breaks into two parts: communal first person plural in vv. 1-4 signals a different discourse from the impersonal and descriptive farmer's song in vv. 5-6. This difference is substantial as well: while the community expresses its own exuberant joy based in immediate experience, the sowers and reapers of vv. 5-6 are depicted symbolizing very general human truths. Within the larger congregational segment (vv. 1-4) we need to differentiate elements according to liturgical functions. The first three lines of the song form one unit (vv. 1b-2). The poem opens with a temporal clause (infinitive construct with particle bĕ, "when"); a similar construction is found in 114:1. Does it refer to a historical moment, when Zion was "brought back" (differently Beyerlin, 41-42, who proposes a hapax legomenon šîbāh I, "restoration," for v. 1, adopted by HAL 1369. In contrast, v. 4 supposedly has šĕbût, "captivity")? And what exactly would such a restoration mean: rebuilding the temple, resettlement of the city of Jerusalem, liberation from foreign rule? Reversal of divine judgment? How would it relate to Israel's captivity in Babylon?

The temporal clause may refer to past or future; also emphatic 'āz, "then," twice in v. 2, could point in both directions. Hebrew verbal forms in poetic texts do not indicate time levels or time sequences (cf. Michel, Tempora; listing at "Introduction to Psalms"). The only way to reason is by content and liturgical considerations. If Psalm 126 points to the future (Gunkel, Mosis, et al., consider it eschatological in outlook) it would stand in the Dtr tradition (cf. Deut 30:1-3; Jeremiah 30–33), which in talking about the future, in reality is looking back already to some fulfillment of Yahweh's promise. The same basic pattern can be found in some prophetic writings. The Deuteronomists were conscious of decisive changes in Babylonian/Persian politics; they may have witnessed already waves of exiles coming back and the temple being reconstructed. Universalistic features like participation of nations, paradisiacal peace, and final destruction of evil (cf. eschatological outlooks in Isa 2:1-5; 24–27; 60–62) are missing in Psalm 126. Everything is geared around that incredible joy of experiencing a profound change of destiny, wrought by Israel's God. Even if the song celebrates a continuing series of divine interventions, hoping for further fulfillments of promises, it does look back to realizations already performed by Yahweh. Thus vv. 1-2 should be taken as allusions to the turning point of captivity and oppression. V. 2ab describes the joy of the congregation in commemoration of that initial liberation. Liturgically speaking, hymns of joy looking back at events are basic to worship; eschatological anticipations really do require a larger set of concepts than recognizable in our text.

The third line (v. 2cd) looks at the nations that have to acknowledge the superior power of Yahweh. This motif is present in other passages of the Psalter and Prophets (cf. Isa 61:9; 66:19; Jer 31:10; Ezek 36:23, 36; Pss 96:3; 113:4; 117:1). The nations acknowledge Yahweh in liturgical statements, e.g., in Pss 72:17; 96:10. Pentateuchal tradition as well cites foreign tribute to Yahweh (cf. Exod 9:27; 10:16; 12:36; 14:18; Num 24:3-9). In our case the formula placed in the mouth of the nations runs: "Yahweh has done great things" (v. 2d: higdîl yhwh; cf. Joel 2:21; Ps 138:2). This hymnic phrase is taken up by the congregation — enemies provide Israel's hymn! — and made into a victorious song (v. 3): "Yahweh did great things/acting in our favor/(therefore) we are happy." This line is in fact a little hymn by itself, sung by the congregation. The first colon is a liturgical shout honoring Yahweh, comparable to "Yahweh is king," "Yahweh is great," "Yahweh is exalted," "Yahweh is holy," etc. (cf. 47:3, 9

[RSV 2, 8]; 48:2 [RSV 1]; 96:10; 99:3, 5, 9). The second one expresses the communal embrace of the divine deed; the third — in parallelism to v. 1c — the exuberance of the faithful. The first person plural of *hyh*, "to be," with attributive adjective is extremely rare in the Psalter, the only other occurrence outside Psalm 126 being in 79:4, a plaintive context (cf. Lam 5:3; Neh 3:36). Next, the communal plea takes up the unresolved issues of liberation, asking Yahweh to complete his work in favor of his community (v. 4). This finishing line of the congregational song is a true PETITION, as extant in complaint psalms. In other words, hymns sung in gratitude for past help may voice ongoing concern and ask for continuing support of God (cf. Ps 104:27-32; note the explicit expression of joy in v. 34).

The rest of Psalm 126 seems to be a popular wisdom song concerning the farmer and his experiences of sowing and harvesting. The day-to-day routine of human toil to make the earth render fruit (cf. Gen 3:17-19) has been condensed into touching words of suffering and joy. Vocabulary, style, rhythm, mental stance — everything is different in these three lines (vv. 5-6). There is a short reference to the situation at large and the sole agents of this metaphor: nothing but an active participle in the plural ("those sowing": professions are commonly designated by participles; cf. Gen 4:2; Isa 28:24) in the manner of sapiential or proverbial speech, which uses plural forms extensively (cf. Prov 10:14, 21, 24, 27, 28; 11:3, 6, 10, 11, 20, 23) beside singular expressions. Short stories, fables, etc., tend to have the protagonists introduced like that (cf. Judg 9:8a; 2 Sam 12:1b). Conceptualization then focuses on the opposition of sowing and harvesting, the first act being burdened with memories of failures and therefore executed under heavy ritual observances. Weeping seems to have been a general obligation for the sowers (cf. Gunkel, 552; Hvidberg, 15-49; listing at Additional Bibliography, section B). Also, from modern tribal people living in arid or semi-arid territories we have similar information about extensive ritual accompaniment of agricultural procedures (cf. Simmons, *Sun Chief,* 229-32; listing at Additional Bibliography, section B): e.g., sowing and planting is done in anxiety of not succeeding; bringing in a good harvest is followed by exuberant feasts. Jubilation *(rinnāh)* is the dominating word in Psalm 126 (vv. 2, 5, 6); it envelops the FARMER'S SONG vv. 5-6, while the tears (vv. 5, 6) are a strong contrast. In MT parallel expressions talk about "lifting up" the seeds as well as the sheaves (v. 6b, d). All in all, the beautiful, concise summary of a farmer's burden and blessing is attached to the thanksgiving part to adapt it to agricultural celebrations or to illustrate by analogy the difficulties and utter relief of exilic existence. This appendix also serves to demonstrate the continuing struggle, in spite of Yahweh's saving interventions of the past. The natural cycle of toil for survival, after all, does not stop either at one particular harvest festival. This means that one historical reversal of fates, like the return of some captives from exile, does not yet end, once and for all, the fateful course of human suffering and joy.

## Genre

Of course, the definition of genre is a precarious task, because we do not know exactly the ramifications of this psalm's employment. But we insist on communal usage: first-person plural forms abound in the first part, and they normally indicate congregational worship (cf. Scharbert, "Das 'Wir'"; listing at "Introduction to Psalms"). The very center of the song is vv. 3-4, a hymnic line followed by a petition. Since the hymn is responding to Yahweh's astounding act of liberation and reconstruction, it does imply gratitude of his faithful. Petition does not negate God's help in the past, but tries to revive and reinforce it. Also, the farmer's song suggests most of all sentiments of obligation. Therefore COMMUNAL THANKSGIVING is an appropriate tag for our psalm.

Beyerlin (pp. 23-32) ably argues that the expression "we are like dreamers" (v. 1d) must not be interpreted in modern, irrealistic terms. According to ancient beliefs, dreams were part of reality. If, however, v. 1bc points to initial realizations of God's promises in the past, we have to interpret the phrase as saying: "We *were* overwhelmed by this event like dreamers who did not at all expect a total change like that." That means that dreams in the ancient Near East do not so much stress the anticipatory quality but the unexpected, stunning grace of God's new reality (cf. Gen 28:10-15; 37:5-10; 40:5-19; 41:1-32). Beyerlin, Mosis, et al. also emphasize the intertextual connotations in Psalm 126, proving its late origin. The book of Joel (cf. Joel 2:20-21; 4:1b [RSV 3:1b] with vv. 1, 2d, 3) seems to stand behind the psalm, and perhaps some pentateuchal and more prophetic traditions as well. Still, intertextual affinities do not make the psalm a mere literary product. Liturgical pieces composed for worship services may lean on written traditions.

## Setting

The most probable social and historical location of the psalm is the "we" community of Yahweh followers in exilic-postexilic times celebrating, as it were, the beginning of liberation and reconstruction. The books of Ezra, Nehemiah, and Chronicles do give a vivid impression as to the origin and scope of such festivities. Be it the legendary edict of Cyrus, which later on was believed to have instigated liberation and the return to Judah (Ezra 1–2), be it the reconstruction of the temple (Ezra 4–6), the resettlement of Jerusalem, or the dedication of its fortifications (cf. Nehemiah 3–6) — all these milestones in restoring Judah's dignity and "independence" are the background of our psalm. There were, in early times of the dispersion, days of mourning and lamenting (Zech 7:1-3). Later on, feasts of liberation were probably introduced, celebrating salvation from Babylonian oppression (cf. Isaiah 40–55; 60–62; Ezra 6:19-22; Nehemiah 8). The emotional effect of a Torah-reading service, by the way, is comparable to the peasant's experience while sowing and reaping, and the congregation's ordeals in history: there are weeping and laughter in the congregation (Neh 8:9-12: "all the people wept," v. 9; "all the people went . . . to make great rejoicing," v. 12).

We can imagine the psalm to have been sung at seasonal worships of the postexilic period. It became included in the pilgrimage collection of songs because of its impressively dense synthesis of spiritual insights and feelings.

## Intention

Almost all commentators agree that our psalm has to be dated in exilic and postexilic times. This nearly uncontested view leads to the conclusion that the song expresses the sentiments of joy and gratitude of the emerging Jewish communities in the Persian Empire, possibly in the Mesopotamian diaspora. Hardships and frustrations were dire reality to those who united in worship to Yahweh. But all members concerned (and there are no inner-Jewish opponents in the text) may rely on Yahweh's decisive help in "turning" to the good all difficulties at hand. The psalm strengthens trust in Yahweh, a feeling of identity, and the determination to endure and work hard for a final liberation of the people.

## Bibliography

E. Baumann, "Strukturuntersuchungen im Psalter II," *ZAW* 62 (1950) 140-44; S. Ben-Chorin, "Das Volkslied der Juden," in *Liturgie und Dichtung* I (ed. H. Becker, et al.; St. Ottilien: EOS, 1983) 47-54; W. Beyerlin, *'Wir sind wie die Träumenden'. Studien zum 126. Psalm* (Stuttgart: Katholisches Bibelwerk, 1978); J. M. Bracke, "*šûb šᵉbût:* A Reappraisal," *ZAW* 97 (1985) 233-44; M. Brod, "Der 126. Psalm," *Münchener Jüdische Nachrichten* 9 (1967) 2; E. Dietrich, *šûb šᵉbût: Die endzeitliche Wiederherstellung bei den Propheten* (BZAW 40; Giessen: Töpelmann, 1925); F. E. Dobberahn, "Los que siembram entre lagrimas cosecharan entre canciones," *RevistB* 54 (1992) 1-14; A. M. Harman, "The Setting and Interpretation of Psalm 126," *RTR* 44 (1985) 74-80; F. Hvidberg, *Weeping and Laughter in the Old Testament* (Leiden: Brill, 1962); O. Loretz, "Ugaritisch *ṯbn* und hebräisch *ṯwb* 'Regen' — Regenrituale beim Neujahrsfest in Kanaan und Israel (Ps 85; 126)," *UF* 21 (1990) 247-58; R. Mosis, "'Mit Jauchzen werden sie ernten: Beobachtungen zu Psalm 126," in *Die alttestamentliche Botschaft als Wegweisung (Fest.* H. Reinelt; ed. J. Zmijewski; Stuttgart: Katholisches Bibelwerk, 1990) 181-201; A. G. Núñez, "Cual torrentes del Neguev (Salmo 126)," *EstBib* 24 (1965) 349-60; A. Rose, "Le psaume 126 (125). Joie d'un peuple que son Dieu fait revivre," *Feu Nouveau* 9 (1966) 16-26; J. Strugnell, "A Note on Ps. 126:1," *JTS* 7 (1956) 239-43; J. Witvliet, "Hymns for December, January, and February," *Reformed Worship* 25 (1992) 23-28.

## Psalm 127:
## Community Instruction

### Structure

|  | MT | NRSV |
|---|---|---|
| I. Superscription | 1a | - |
| II. Sayings | 1b-e | 1 |
| III. Exhortation | 2 | 2 |
| IV. Felicitation | 3-4 | 3-4 |
| V. Beatitude | 5 | 5 |

Only two of 150 psalms are attributed to Solomon in MT, the other one being Psalm 72. Obviously, our poem provoked this secondary alignment by the expression *bnh bayit*, "to build a house" (v. 1b). The "house" was identified as the "house of Yahweh," the temple, which, of course, Solomon ordered to be constructed in Jerusalem (cf. 1 Kings 5–6; 8). Thus the SUPERSCRIPTION at hand reveals a special stage of interpretation of the psalm. Besides the name of Solomon it does not show any extras beyond the normal heading of all the Psalms of Ascent (Psalms 120–134; → 120; 122).

One of the issues under debate is exactly the meaning of this "house construction." Many exegetes are intrigued by the private air of the whole psalm; consequently they consider the building process a normal human activity to create dwelling space for people (cf., e.g., Gunkel, Keel, Sedlmeier). Others, notably Fleming, conclude from the frequent parallelism of "house" and "city" (vv. 1b, 1d; cf. Jer 26:6, 9, 12; 1 Kgs 8:44, 48) that these terms in conjunction always allude to Yahweh's temple and city. This interpretation is difficult to maintain, however, because Yahweh's abode as a rule is referred to in a determined way as "the house," "this house," "my house," "Yahweh's house," etc. (cf., e.g., the passages cited above and Isa 37:14, 31; 38:20, 22; 56:5, 7; 66:1, 20). Considering the uniqueness of Yahweh's temple it would hardly have been feasible to refer to it as an indefinite "house" in an indefinite "city," as actually has been done in v. 1. Furthermore, common people (cf. "you," plural, in v. 2a) can hardly be expected to lose sleep and eat bread with sorrow on account of temple construction, which was definitely the responsibility of the royal head of state (cf. 2 Sam 7:1-3; 1 Chr 22:1-19). Therefore, I suggest that the Solomonic perspective of the MT superscription is a later interpretation derived from a theological understanding of the text. The original psalm itself apparently talked about plain house building.

Having taken this traditional stand we need to check the overall structure of the psalm. In sharp contrast to, e.g., Psalms 123; 124; 126, our poem does not show a trace of communal discourse. The language remains neutral and proverbial except for one occurrence of direct address of a plurality of listeners (v. 2a), one exclamation to solicit attention (v. 3a), and one announcement of felicity (v. 5a). On the whole it is descriptive, aiming at no one in particular. The sequence of sayings seems loosely knit, but there is no formal evidence of a decisive break between, e.g., vv. 2 and 3. A string of more or less independent sayings may have been used in worship contexts. (Because of formal affinities to 124:1-2 it may be intriguing to speculate about a missing formula of summons in v. 1: "Unless Yahweh builds a house — let Israel say — unless Yahweh builds a house, those who build it labor in vain.")

The first element of the psalm proper comprises two homogeneous lines (v. 1ab, cd). The negated conditional conjunction *'im . . . lō'*, "if . . . not," introduces the protasis, with the subject unusually inserted between the two lexemes *'im yhwh lō'. . .* , "if it were not Yahweh, who. . . ." The word order stresses the name of Yahweh; he is the only God able or willing to do the business at hand. A regular sequence of words, *'im lō' yhwh, . . .* would have run counter to normal usage in Hebrew Scripture that reserves *'im lō'* mainly for oath and oathlike discourse signifying strong affirmation (cf. Num 14:28; 2 Sam 19:14; Jer 15:11; 49:20; 50:45; Ezek 20:33; 33:27; 34:8; 35:6; Ps 137:6). Our SAYINGS point to possible or irreal alternative developments as in Ps 124:1-2. They do affirm one correct option, in the face of its awful counterpart. Only three out of more than thirty occurrences of *'im lō'* have a comparable meaning (Isa 10:9; Mal 3:10; Job 9:24). The insertion of Yahweh's name thus may be motivated by semantic considerations. Both lines, after the initial collocation, exhibit almost identical word order. A verb in the third person singular with an accusative object complements the first colon (v. 1b, d). The second colon opens with the word *šāw'*, "in vain," in pole position, followed by a finite verb and the subject of the main clause. Small but notable differences are, first, the grammatical number (v. 1c has a plural verb and noun; v. 1e, singular forms); second, the third-person singular suffix with plural noun plus suffixed preposition *bě* to refer back to "house" in v. 1c. Notwithstanding these little differences we may say that the two Yahweh sayings are very similar in their structure and meaning, and possibly independent from each other. What they communicate is the necessity of Yahweh's cooperation and blessing in daily human affairs. Like true proverbs each one has a well-balanced message: if Yahweh (or another personal God?) does not accompany house building or city watching, all human troubles are in vain (v. 1bc, de). "An Gottes Segen ist alles gelegen" (God's blessing is paramount) runs a German saying, often carved into the beams of a frame-structured house. The motif may be present in Prov 10:22, if one prefers this translation: "It is only God's blessing that makes rich, [one's own] travail does not add a thing." And Qoh 2:22-26 seems to be a more radical elaboration of the same thought: What is the outcome of human toil and trouble? "Pain, . . . vexation; even in the night his mind does not rest" (Qoh 2:23). Eating and drinking may be a reward, but even "that comes from the hand of God" (v. 24). "To the man whom he likes does he give wisdom, knowledge, and joy" (v. 26a). That is to say: everything depends on God's favor and blessing (cf. Sir 11:11). In our paired sayings, Yahweh is called by name, demonstrating a specific theological concern of Yahweh believers. But apart from this particularity the idea is generally known in the ancient Near East as well as in other religions: ultimate success for human endeavors comes only from the deity (see comparative texts in Gunkel, Fleming, et al.). "House" and "city" — being undetermined — refer not to Yahweh's abode and presence (against Fleming) but to people's living spaces and their respective social organizations. Bringing up progeny (vv.

3-5), the best proof of God's blessing, happens exactly in the shelter of "house" and "city."

While the sayings of v. 1 are strictly proverbial in character, giving self-sufficient orientation as to right attitudes in life, v. 2 has some exhortatory language, addressing a group of people, picking up the catchword šāw', "in vain" (v. 1c, e; "in vain for you . . . ," second person plural, v. 2a). Obviously, a speaker is applying the gist of the preceding statements to some audience, being characterized by its anxious struggle for subsistence (v. 2bc: three designations are used: early rise–late rest–"sorrow bread," reminiscent of Gen 3:17; 5:29). "He," however (referring back to Yahweh in v. 1), "gives to his beloved in sleep" (v. 2d: most commentators agree on that reading, which faces two textual problems: šēnāh, "sleep," is here spelled with ' instead of h, and yĕdîdô is singular in MT, Leningrad Codex [= Solomon?] but plural in a few other Hebrew MSS and LXX). Citizens and members of the community are talked to in this EXHORTATION, a well-known genre of synagogue worship services.

The second part of our psalm begins with soliciting attention, but without using forms of outright summons, such as plural imperatives. The exclamation hinnēh (cf. Pss 121:4; 123:2; 128:4) is nondirective, announcing a general and recognized truth to listeners. Objective language, stressing the great value of (male — suggested also by military imagery in v. 4a; furthermore: only boys stayed in the father's family) offspring (vv. 3-4), articulates a terse saying (v. 3) that is immediately followed by a comparison exemplifying and enhancing the proverb (v. 4). Both together already make a FELICITATION of sorts praising a great gift of God that is a good example of a blessing not automatically available to human endeavor. Ancient people were quite convinced that only God could give children (cf. Gen 30:1-2). There is a rhetorical progression in the two consecutive lines just dealt with to be topped by a BEATITUDE, regularly introduced by 'ašrê (v. 5; → Ps 1:1). Now, beatitudes must not be misunderstood as merely descriptive statements. They have qualities of blessings, in that their pronouncements also transport the very advantages that they address. The man called "happy" or "blessed" ('ašrê) receives the positive influence of the saying. Under this perspective it is small wonder that liturgical texts like the Psalms contain a large number of beatitudes (cf., e.g., 2:12; 32:1-2; 84:6, 13 [RSV 5, 12]; 94:12; 106:3; 119:1-2; 128:1; 137:8, 9; 146:5; the sum total is 26). They seem to be rhetorical and liturgical devices of preachers or other officiants of the congregation. That litigation with "enemies" in the "city gate" is given as the prime example of family strength on account of many sons seems strange to us. We should not make the promised "sons" into recruits for the citizens' defense corps, though. Military images in v. 4a and the "enemies" in v. 5d cannot turn the psalm into a collective song concerned only with communal affairs. The domestic air too strongly witnesses against this kind of interpretation.

## Genre

Psalm 127 talks about basic human experiences, and together with poems like Psalms 128 and 131 belongs to those texts that exhibit traits of family and clan life. They may reflect women's experience and may have been composed by women (→ Psalm 131). Exhortation, felicitation, and beatitude could be subsumed under the genre COMMUNITY INSTRUCTION. This category of texts (→ Psalms 20; 34; 37; 50; etc.) was part of the congregational worship service. In this case it is done by using popular sapiential sayings, expanding their message, and painting positive images of personal faith in Yahweh, the God of the Jewish community.

Arguing from contents and ancient Near Eastern parallels, Keel makes a good case for our psalm being a personal HYMN, giving praise and thanks to God, who "provides sound sleep and children" (essentials of a wholesome life) to stressed and worried believers. He points out a generic parallel in 33:16-19, which, though part of a "communal hymn," exhibits all the characteristics of INSTRUCTION, too. The truth of the matter is that the genres of wisdom poetry should not be taken per se as "noncultic" or "inappropriate" for Jewish worship services, as most exegetes do. Psalm 127 is clad in wisdom language and form elements, but nevertheless was part of worship liturgies. Inclusion in the "Ascent" collection of psalms remains unexplainable from any literary or thematic point of view.

## Setting

Worship was the opportune place for instructing people in the ways of Yahweh. The threefold, emphatic placement of Israel's God in our psalm suggests that the extant form of Psalm 127 is deeply rooted in that congregational, probably postexilic, situation, when Yahweh became the exclusive deity of reconstructed Judah (cf. Gerstenberger, *Yahweh;* listing at Additional Bibliography, section B). The little text itself probably served only as part of a worship liturgy, within a consoling instruction done by a speaker for the congregation. The house-building and child-rearing functions in oriental antiquity were the — highly regarded — domains of first wives. House cults honoring family gods were probably administered by women (cf. Gerstenberger, *Yahweh,* 55-66). Therefore the "family hymns" (Psalms 127; 128; 131) may go back to pre-Yahwistic female domestic traditions.

## Intention

Consolation of parishioners who press for action and changes, possibly experiencing deep frustrations, may be seen as the main purpose of this liturgical piece. Yahweh is a benevolent God, and in the last instance he alone decides about failures and successes in the human realm. Reminding God-fearing people of their own limitations is a basic task of religious instruction.

# Bibliography

T. A. Boogart, "John Calvin on Sleep," *Perspectives* 12 (1998) 17-21; R. Borger, "Keil-schrifttexte verschiedenen Inhalts," in *Symbolae Biblicae et Mesopotamicae (Fest. F. M. Th. de Liagre Böhl; ed. M. A. Beek, et al.;* Leiden: Brill, 1973) 38-55; F. Bussby, "A Note on *šēnā'* in Psalm 127:2," *JTS* 35 (1934) 306-7; J. A. Emerton, "The Meaning of *šēnā'* in Psalm cxxvii 2," *VT* 24 (1974) 15-31; D. J. Estes, "Like Arrows in the Hand of a Warrior (Psalm CXXVII)," *VT* 41 (1991) 304-11; D. E. Fleming, "House/'City': An Un-recognized Parallel Word Pair," *JBL* 105 (1986) 689-93; idem, "Psalm 127: Sleep for the Fearful, and Security in Sons," *ZAW* 107 (1995) 435-44; W. Grudem, "The Courage to Say 'No,'" *Christianity Today* 29 (1985) 58; L. E. Goodman, "Bahya on the Antinomy of Free Will and Predestination," *Journal of the History of Ideas* 44 (1983) 115-30; L. Hall, "Implementing Christian Education in the Home," *Journal of Christian Education* 1 (1981) 48-52; V. Hamp, "Der Herr gibt es den Seinen im Schlaf," in *Wort, Lied und Gottesspruch (Fest. J. Ziegler; ed. J. Schreiner; Würzburg: Echter, 1972) 71-79; M. G. Huyck, "Psalm — City: A Study of Psalm 127," *Worship* 40 (1966) 510-19; H. Irsigler, "'Umsonst ist es, dass ihr früh aufsteht . . .', Psalm 127 und die Kritik der Arbeit in Israels Weisheitsliteratur," *BN* 37 (1987) 48-72; O. Keel, "Psalm 127: Ein Lobpreis auf Den, der Schlaf und Kinder gibt," in *Ein Gott — eine Offenbarung (Fest. N. Füglister; ed. F. Reiterer, et al.; Würzburg: Echter, 1991) 155-163; J. Keller, "The Coherence of Religious Discourse," *ATR* 67 (1985) 349-60; O. Loretz, "Syllabische und alphabethische Keilschrifttexte zu Psalm 127," in *Ana sadê labnani lu allik (Fest. W. Röllig; ed. B. Pon-gratz-Leisten, et al.; AOAT 247; Kevelaer: Butzon und Bercker; Neukirchen-Vluyn: Neukirchener Verlag, 1997) 229-51; P. D. Miller Jr., "The Human Sabbath: A Study in Deuteronomic* Theology," *Princeton Seminary Bulletin* 6 (1985) 81-97; M. J. van Niekerk, "Psalms 127 and 128," *OTE* 8 (1995) 414-24; B. A. Ntreh, "Towards an African Biblical Hermeneutical," *Africa Theological Journal* 19 (1990) 247-54; O. Rickenbacher, "Psalm 127," in *Stilfiguren der Bibel (ed. W. Bühlmann, et al.; Fribourg: Schweizerisches Katholisches Bibelwerk, 1973) 100-102; M. Schwantes, "A herança de Javé," *EsTe* 27 (1987) 175-80; F. Sedlmeier, *Jerusalem — Jahwes Bau,* 166-71 (see listing at Psalm 147); H. Strauss, "'Siehe, Jahwes Erbbesitz sind Söhne.' Psalm 127 als ein Lied der Ermutigung in nachexilischer Zeit," in *Altes Testament und christliche Verkündigung (Fest. A. H. Gunneweg; ed. M. Oeming, et al.; Stuttgart: Kohlhammer, 1987) 390-98.*

# Psalm 128:
# Felicitation

## Structure

|  | MT | NRSV |
|---|---|---|
| I. Superscription | 1a | - |
| II. Beatitude | 1b-2 | 1-2 |
| A. Impersonal | 1bc | 1 |
| B. Direct address | 2 | 2 |
| III. Blessing | 3-4 | 3-4 |

| | | |
|---|---|---|
| A. Direct address | 3 | 3 |
| B. Announcement | 4 | 4 |
| IV. Blessing | 5-6a | 5-6a |
| A. Direct address | 5a | 5a |
| B. Promise | 5bc-6a | 5bc-6a |
| V. Well-wish for Israel | 6b | 6b |

For the SUPERSCRIPTION see Psalm 120. This little psalm is full of direct-address speech for an individual person in vv. 1-3 (see Psalm 121), communicating an atmosphere of intimate family relations. The second part, without giving up personal discourse, includes Zion, Jerusalem, and Israel in its horizon (vv. 5-6). Polarization of the individual and the Zion community of faith, however, is natural in postexilic times, because the early Jewish congregation was a special, nonpolitical organization of Yahweh believers. Personal faith in and confession of the God of Israel were basic to this religious community. At the same time personal life and destiny were centered on Yahweh and his Torah (cf. v. 1c; → Psalm 119). They, in turn, "belonged" to the Zion community.

The form elements are fairly well distinguished within the overall structure of the psalm. *'ašrê* is the typical incipit of a BEATITUDE (v. 1bc; → Ps 1:1). Characteristically, too, the type of person "beatified" is described by participles or adjectives, in our case *yĕrē' (yhwh)*, "Yahweh-fearing," and *hahōlēk (bidĕrākāyw)*, "he who lives (in his paths)." Formally, all the criteria of a traditional beatitude are fulfilled. Beatitudes confer extraordinary bliss on a person who lives up to certain standards of ethical and religious behavior, as implied in the descriptive designation.

There seems to have existed an objective way of delineating that model character: "Happy the man, who . . ." (cf. Prov 28:14a; Pss 32:1bc; 41:2a [RSV 1a]; from Isa 56:1 and 2 we could reconstruct a concise beatitude: *'ašrê 'ĕnôš 'ōśēh ṣĕdāqāh*, "happy the man who lives righteously"). These archaic *'ašrê* words — BEATITUDES — are not specifically Yahwistic; they are found in other ancient cultures as well and extend through apocryphal and pseudepigraphal literature into the Greek NT (cf. Matt 5:3-10; Dupont, "Beatitudes"; listing at Psalm 1; Janzen, *"'ashrê"*; listing at "Introduction to Psalms"). They have been used in many societies for didactic and ethical purposes, to standardize behavior and bestow positive powers upon those who complied with the accepted norms. What we find in the Psalter are mostly Yahweh-oriented sayings (cf. Pss 1:1; 32:2; 34:9 [RSV 8]; 40:5 [RSV 4]; 112:1; 119:1-2; 146:5), indicating extensive use of the form in the postexilic community. This observation is valid also for v. 1. As far as contents and theological outlook are concerned the opening line of our psalm is very close to 112:1; 119:1-2. Strict adherence to Yahweh and his will is the issue, in accordance with the life and theology of the period. As in the parallel passages just mentioned the saying in Psalm 128 is the heading for the whole text to follow. Unexpectedly, though, the rhetoric after v. 1 changes immediately into second-person address: "That which the labor of your hands has produced you will eat/happy you are and well off" (v. 2). Direct application of the beatitude in second-person address to a particular person is a rare feature (to Israel: Deut 33:29; Isa 32:20; to a nation: Qoh 10:17). In our case the change has been provoked by the blessing style of the psalm (cf. Psalms 91; 121). Starting with v. 2 to the end of Psalm 128, the second-person singular address prevails.

While v. 2 is manifestly a direct interpretation of the beatitude in v. 1 (the one who clings to Yahweh will be blessed and achieve good results in his work), being rounded off by the repetition 'ašreykā, "happy you are" (other occurrences of second-person suffixed forms: Deut 33:29; Qoh 10:17; Isa 32:20), vv. 3-6 are freer allocutions to the individual listener. He is being assured strong progeny by a fecund wife (v. 3). Vivid metaphoric language, terse formulations, and correspondence to the highest-ranking dreams of ancient heads of family suggest that this verse in itself may have been a potent well-wish or BLESSING, perhaps to newlywed men or women (cf. Ruth 4:11-12; Gen 24:60; 28:2-3; Seybold, 490: "Matrimonial blessing"). The words of Rebekah's brother, on the occasion of her departure from Haran, are explicitly declared to be a "blessing," and as such they are in rhythmic language: "Our sister, you may grow into thousands and thousands and your offspring may conquer the gates of their foes" (Gen 24:60). The idea of numerous progeny is present, comparable to our v. 3, and dominance over potential rivals is one of the main concerns of Ps 127:3-5, a closely related felicitation and blessing. The compiler of Psalm 128, then, apparently uses traditional motifs or sayings from the realm of family life to affirm his/her liturgical ends. He/she closes this element by an ANNOUNCEMENT TO COMMUNITY (no direct address) to the effect that the "Yahweh-fearing man" will earn all these favors from God (v. 4). This hinnēh ("behold") phrase ties together the preceding parts and consciously places the subject yĕrē' yhwh, "the Yahweh-fearing," at the very end of the line, taking up again the same expression from its front position in v. 1b, the original beatitude.

Another unit is added to the beatitude-blessing complex of vv. 1-3. This time not human words and will are mustered to bring good luck to the person qualified, but Yahweh himself is called on to perform his blessing from Zion (v. 5a). God seated on Zion is a favorite concept of the book of Isaiah (cf. Isa 4:5; 8:18; 18:7; 24:23; 33:5, 20; 52:8; 56:7; 60:14; 62:11; 66:20; etc.; see E. Otto, *TWAT* VI, esp. 1020-26). Another strand of Zion theology runs through the Psalter (cf. Psalms 46; 48; 87; 132). BLESSINGS from Yahweh and Zion are mentioned principally in the Psalms of Ascent (132:15; 133:3), with an exact repetition of v. 5a in 134:3a. To look for Mount Zion as the fountainhead of blessing may have been a very popular attitude, attested also in Hebrew inscriptions (cf. graffiti of Khirbet Beit Ley, published by J. Naveh, *Israel Exploration Journal* 13 [1963] 74-92; Seybold, *Wallfahrtspsalmen,* 79-83; listing at Psalm 120). Direct blessings through Yahweh ("he may bless you," v. 5a) also have been found in scribblings of the Israelite monarchic period that may belong to the type: "Yahweh and his Asherah may bless you," "Yahweh of Samaria may bless you," or similarly (cf. J. Renz and W. Röllig, *Handbuch der althebräischen Epigraphik,* vol. I [Darmstadt: Wissenschaftliche Buchgesellschaft, 1995] 61-62, 208; Z. Meshel, *Kuntillet 'Ajrud* [Jerusalem: Israel Museum, 1978] Inscriptions section E). With these archeological testimonies at hand we may say that blessings in the name of Yahweh were not necessarily administered only by priests, although the Aaronite blessing of Num 6:24-26 appears to be a strictly priestly formulation. It starts out with a formula very close to v. 5a: *yĕbārekĕkā yhwh wĕyišmĕrekā,* "Yahweh may bless you and keep you" (Num 6:24). Considering the context of our psalm we may surmise that the more private blessings of vv. 1-4 are now (vv. 5-6) superseded by an official communication of Yahweh's grace.

Two imperatives spell out the contents of that special divine blessing, linking, as it were, the private part with the communal perspectives and theology. "You shall see . . ." (vv. 5b, 6a) Jerusalem prospering and "sons of your sons," i.e., several generations to come. Thus the destiny of the Holy City and the personal fate of the believer are intimately twisted together: an unmistakable sign of early Jewish theological thinking. The psalm ends, like Psalm 125 (cf. also 122:6), with an appropriate well-wish for Israel, i.e., the religious community at large in which the individual believer is embedded.

## Genre/Setting

"Greetings" and "Blessings" are the genre categories used by H. Schmidt (see his "Grüsse," listing at "Introduction to Psalms") in regard to Psalm 128. Many interpreters banish our psalm from liturgical contexts to a mere literary wisdom sphere, which is unwarranted (→ Psalm 127). Seybold (*Wallfahrtspsalmen;* listing at Psalm 120) et al. try to specify and explain our psalm and those like it (esp. Psalm 121) from ceremonial procedures during the pilgrimage to Jerusalem (e.g., departure, arrival, entrance to the temple). This may well be the case, and Seybold is correct also in distinguishing between original elements and one or more redactional reworkings, which adapted older texts and layers to the festive occasion of a *hajj* (Muslim pilgrimage to Mecca) to Jerusalem. On the other hand, all the texts assembled in the collection of Psalms 120–134, including our BLESSINGS and WELL-WISHES, were probably used also in congregational worship outside the festival season, because life and liturgy even in the diaspora were linked with the Holy City at all times (cf. Elbogen, *Gottesdienst;* listing at "Introduction to Cultic Poetry").

Just as in Psalm 127, the close companion text of Psalm 128, there may have been an earlier stage of our poem, linked to female domestic cult practice (cf. Gerstenberger, *Yahweh,* 55-66; listing at Additional Bibliography, section B). At that stage reference to Jerusalem and Israel (vv. 5-6) would probably have been missing.

## Intention

If, then, Psalm 128 was part of communal liturgy (and otherwise it would not be part of the Psalter), the most amazing fact is the "pastoral care" for individual members visible in our psalm. "He" (females and children were included in this patriarchal language) was to be reassured in his personal and familial well-being and at the same time made aware of communal hopes and responsibilities, which always enveloped the interests of his own little group.

351

# Bibliography

M. C. Brettler, "Women and Psalms," in *Gender and Law in the Hebrew Bible and the Ancient Near East* (ed. V. H. Matthews, et al.; Sheffield: Sheffield Academic Press, 1998) 25-56; P. D. Miller Jr., "The Human Sabbath" (see listing at Psalm 127); R. T. Osborn, "Work in a Christian Perspective," *Quarterly Review* 5 (1985) 28-43; G. Wehmeier, *Der Segen im Alten Testament* (Basel: F. Reinhardt Kommissionsverlag, 1970).

# Psalm 129:
# Communal Thanksgiving

## Structure

|  | MT | NRSV |
|---|---|---|
| I. Superscription | 1a | - |
| II. Complaint | 1b-3 | 1-3 |
| III. Affirmation of confidence | 4 | 4 |
| IV. Imprecation | 5-8b | 5-8b |
| A. Evil wish | 5 | 5 |
| B. Metaphor | 6-7 | 6-7 |
| C. Prohibition | 8ab | 8ab |
| V. Blessing | 8c | 8c |

The SUPERSCRIPTIONS of the Psalms of Ascent are discussed with Psalms 120 to 122, etc. Several details of Psalm 129 fit into neither the thanksgiving nor the complaint category (see below, Genre), but the extant elements for their part best comply with the plaintive-and-beyond discourse known from that spectrum of the Psalter (see "Introduction to Cultic Poetry," section 4C).

The psalm begins abruptly; it lacks the introductory appellation or invocation customary in complaints. This fact alone should make us wary in regard to easy genre classification. Twice a plaintive colon of exactly the same wording opens the line (vv. 1b, 2a: "often they have afflicted me from my youth"; *rabbat,* "often," a "late adverbial form" [Gunkel 539], also used in a similar context in 120:6; 123:4). The metaphor "youth" is taken from individual biography and applied to the people of Israel (cf. Hos 2:17; 11:1; Jer 2:2; 22:31; 32:20; etc.); thus the psalm summarizes all of Israel's history, in a wailing mode of reflection, which we may designate as COMPLAINT. We find a second colon inserted in the first poetic line summoning "Israel" to testify to the sad fact of having been mistreated by anonymous foes. This SUMMONS to tell the sorrows of the people to Yahweh is used similarly in hymnic contexts (cf. 118:2; 124:1: "Israel now says: . . ." — a fixed formula for communal recitation in 118:2-4 together with other congregational groups), sufficient proof for liturgical practice. After the complaining statements the psalm falls into a triumphant declaration of victory over foes (v. 2b), only to add another line of

352

pessimistic historical summary (v. 3). Again a metaphor of the personal realm gives painful vividness to the psalm: long furrows plowed into the back of a person is reminiscent of slaves beaten by their owners and overseers (cf. Exod 5:14; Isa 50:6; 53:4-5). Thus the retrospective on the youth and adulthood of Israel leaves the impression that continuous suffering has been going on over the centuries, but — miraculously — the people of Yahweh have resisted the pressure. This kind of picture of the past can have been nurtured only from the sixth century on.

In terms of liturgical setup the first line was probably intoned by a cantor, and the congregation fell in to repeat and continue the chant (vv. 2-3). The congregation called "Israel" is using the first-person *singular* forms: "Often have they attacked me from my youth." More frequently the more natural plural comes to the fore (cf. Psalms 123; 126). Here personification of the collective and identification with the group are so strong that the singular prevails (cf. Mays, 404, et al.). In looking back from this perspective even the singulars in 121:1-2; 122:1; 123:1; etc., may be communal "I"s, because they shift into the plural in the last two texts.

The AFFIRMATION OF CONFIDENCE (v. 4) opposes the dreadful "plowers" of the past with mighty Yahweh, who already has cut apart the fetters or who always will do such a feat for his beloved people. "Yahweh is righteous" could be a formulaic liturgical expression; the concise form, *yhwh ṣaddîq*, hardly occurs; among all relevant passages (see Isa 45:21; Jer 12:1; Zeph 3:5; Pss 7:12 [RSV 11]; 11:7; 119:137; 145:17; Lam 1:18; Dan 9:14; Ezra 9:14; Neh 9:33; 2 Chr 12:6) only a few qualify in the strict sense, listing the short liturgical shout: Pss 11:7; 145:17; Lam 1:18; Dan 9:14; 2 Chr 12:6. Related is the prayer-style address: "You, Yahweh, are righteous" (Ps 119:137; Ezra 9:15; Neh 9:33).

The perfect form *qiṣṣēṣ*, "cut off" (cf. Ps 46:10 [RSV 9]), like the other perfects in vv. 1-3, does not establish a time level, but may indicate the autonomous quality of God's action. "Ropes of the godless" (v. 4b; cf. 119:61) seems a highly charged theological concept, quite different from mythological expressions like "cords of death" (18:5-6 [RSV 4-5]; 116:3). These distinct concepts indicate varied contexts and theologies. They seem to belong to postexilic times. V. 4 is considered part of the historical retrospect by Gunkel, Michel, Allen, et al.; this way it becomes a thankful affirmation.

The second part of our psalm is mostly imprecative (vv. 5-8b). Shifting toward this particular stance, the text indicates the liturgical situation: pure thanksgiving cannot yet take place; danger to the community continues. A historical summary of suffering and salvation does not solve present calamities. Therefore a ritual defense still has to be organized. V. 5 is a common BAD WISH, one of the various types of CURSES. Parallel passages include 35:4; 40:15 (RSV 14); 70:3 (RSV 2). In each case a doubled expression of being put to shame (cf. Klopfenstein, *Schande;* listing at Additional Bibliography, section B) is directed against the evildoers (cf. 109:6-20). Vv. 6-7, thereafter, add a powerful metaphor; comparisons like this in antiquity may have worked like actions performed in effigy. Grass on the (flat) roof did not have a chance to resist burning sunshine for very long (v. 6a). It serves as a symbol for losing life's battle, being so insignificant in dying that not even professionals at reaping grass would take notice (v. 7). In addition, another ill-wish is pronounced: there should be no sympathizers passing by and uttering greetings to the doomed ones; they are definitely excluded from Yahweh's compassion (v. 8). Sympathy, after all, was an obligation among neighbors (cf. 41:7-10 [RSV 6-9]; 69:21 [RSV 20]). All in all, the series of three ill-wishes in vv. 5, 6-7, 8 together are a sort of IMPRECATION even though no explicit cursing is involved (→ Psalm 109). Solemn curses using the strongest possible vocabulary of damnation were considered dangerous in themselves. They were apparently confined for the most part to official rituals at special occasions (cf. Deut 27:14-26; 28:15-43), and, we may understand, with special precautions. As a rule, within the psalms reflecting more or less regular worship services of a more private and synagogal character, the way to articulate imprecations is by evil wishes that are to be implemented, of course, by Yahweh himself (this last idea is rarely explicit; cf. Pss 5:8 [RSV 7]; 11:6; 58:7 [RSV 6]; 109:6, 14-15, 20; etc.).

Our psalm ends appropriately with a direct-address BLESSING (v. 8c) expressed, interestingly, by first-person plural speakers: "We bless you in the name of Yahweh" (cf. 121:5-8; 124:8; 125:5c; 127:5; 128:5a). The plurality of blessing people is unique. They must be official liturgists leading the service who already summoned the congregation "Israel" to sing her song (v. 1c). Otherwise, the whole text vv. 2-8b does not show a trace of cult officials speaking. Only the community itself is reflected in the first person singulars of vv. 1b-3.

## Genre

The psalm, oscillating between thanksgivings and complaints, is to be evaluated for what form elements it uses and those that do not appear. In the latter category of missing parts — as far as communal thanksgiving or complaint is concerned — we noted already the invocation and initial plea. Also, neither petition nor outright thanksgiving formula occurs. Yet THANKSGIVING is the most appropriate name for this unusual song, because it contains central statements about wondrous perseverance in past history (v. 2b) and about Yahweh's decisive help (v. 4) side by side with imprecations (vv. 5-8b) and divine blessing obviously in ongoing affliction. The "I" form of vv. 1-3 should not mislead us to look for some genre fitting for an individual biography (against Seybold, 491: "witness of a person maltreated all his life").

## Setting

Musing about past calamities and miraculous survival was certainly one train of thought among the communities of Jews under foreign rule after 587 B.C.E. Such reflections probably took place in the gatherings of the displaced as well as the assemblies of those left in their homelands. The blessing at the very end of the psalm may be interpreted also as a well-wish for participants of a pilgrimage to Jerusalem. Zion, after all, is mentioned in v. 5, signaling at least the vital importance of that holy place of Yahweh's abode for contemporary believers.

## Intention

Commemorating the arduous past and delighting in survival, furthermore, looking forward toward the destruction of opponents and the (final) victory of Yahweh's righteousness, the community reassures itself of its existence and dignity.

## Bibliography

P. Auffret, "YHWH est juste: Étude structurelle du Ps 129," *Studi epigraici e linguistici* 7 (1990) 87-96; E. Cardenal, "I Cry in the Night from the Torture Chamber (Psalm 129)," in *Mission Trends 3: Third World Theologies* (ed. G. Anderson, et al.; New York: Paulist; Grand Rapids: Eerdmans, 1976) 39-40; W. Herrmann, "Psalm 129," in *Von Gott reden (Fest.* S. Wagner; ed. D. Vieweger, et al.; Neukirchen-Vluyn: Neukirchener Verlag, 1995) 123-32; A. J. O. van der Wal, "The Structure of Psalm 129," *VT* 38 (1988) 364-67.

## Psalm 130:
## Individual and Communal Complaint

### Structure

|  |  | MT | NRSV |
|---|---|---|---|
| I. | Superscription | 1a | - |
| II. | Invocation | 1b | 1 |
| III. | Initial plea | 2 | 2 |
| IV. | Confession of guilt | 3 | 3 |
| V. | Affirmation of confidence | 4 | 4 |
| VI. | Personal prayer | 5-6 | 5-6 |
| VII. | Exhortation of community | 7-8 | 7-8 |
| | A. Exhortation | 7 | 7 |
| | B. Assurance | 8 | 8 |

A regular SUPERSCRIPTION heads this psalm: *šîr hamma'ălôt,* "song of ascents," being the stock designation of Psalms 120–134 (v. 1a; → Psalm 120). The rest of v. 1 together with v. 2 constitutes a fairly common INVOCATION and INITIAL PLEA (see "Introduction to Cultic Poetry," section 4B). The name of the Deity, in this case as in other individual complaints, does not occur at the beginning of the song but follows a plaintive or petitionary address (cf. 4:2a [RSV 1a]; 5:2a [RSV 1a]; 12:2a [RSV 1a]; 26:1a; 35:1a; 51:3a [RSV 1a]; 55:2a [RSV 1a]; 59:2a [RSV 1a]; 61:2a [RSV 1a]; 65:2 [RSV 1]; 69:2a [RSV 1a]; 140:2a [RSV 1a]). We would expect the appellation of the Deity to come first. The openings just listed tell us that such a "running start" of a petitionary prayer was possible, perhaps within a more extensive liturgy of complaining and pleading. Here it is a DESCRIPTION OF PRAYING or, rather, of crying out "from the depths" (v. 1b: *mimma'ămaqqîm;* Christian tradition renders it often, in the wake of the Vulgate, *de profundis.* There is a long history of praying these words in Jewish and Christian communities; cf. Kurzke, Jeremias, etc.). The other four occurrences of this term specify the "deep places" as filled with chaos waters (69:3, 15 [RSV 2, 14]; Isa 51:10; Ezek 27:34; cf. Jonah 2:3-7 [RSV 2-6]). We may assume the same mythical background in v. 1b. Form-critically, the description of praying (v. 1b) is unique in this front position, as the examples cited above for the most part are of an appellative and petitionary kind.

The second verse is clad in traditional pleas of being heard and attended to; especially the imperative of *šm'*, "listen," is frequently used in initial pleas (cf. Pss 4:2 [RSV 1]; 17:1; 28:2; 61:2 [RSV 1]; 64:2 [RSV 1]; 102:2 [RSV 1]; 143:1). The parallel expression, "Let your ears be attentive" (v. 2b), has no equal in the Psalter. There the equivalent plea is articulated mostly with the verb "incline [your ears]" (cf. 17:6; 71:2; 86:1; 88:3 [RSV 2]; 102:3 [RSV 2]). Only in 2 Chr 6:40 and 7:15 do we meet again the allocution construed with "attentive ears" significantly in phrases exceeding the original text of 1 Kings 8. This fact should give sufficient weight to the hypothesis that the formulation is a late one, at the earliest from the fourth century B.C.E.

Instead of more detailed complaints, affirmations of confidence, or petitions — as they would be in order in a traditional complaint psalm, our text continues with a kind of CONFESSION OF GUILT, stylized as a rhetorical question: "If you would guard iniquities, who could stand up, O Lord?" The form presupposes intensive reflection about the significance of "guilt" in the past, about possibilities of forgiveness from the side of Yahweh, and liturgical practice. The question is answered immediately by a *kî* phrase, which may be adversative or simply assertive: "But with you there is foregiveness" (v. 4), a clear AFFIRMATION OF CONFIDENCE. The word *sĕlîhāh,* "pardon," again is attested only in quite late texts (Neh 9:17; Dan 9:9). Also, the simple verb *slḥ,* "to pardon," is more or less characteristic of exilic or postexilic layers; cf., e.g., concentrations in 1 Kgs 8:30-50 (par. 2 Chr 6:21-39); Lev 4:20–5:26. In the Psalter, the verb (Qal form; no other stem manifest in the Psalter) is used only twice, in 25:11, a late acrostic text, and in 103:3, as a participle describing Yahweh. The two terms studied above, then, again testify to late exilic discourse.

Vv. 5-8 express a peculiar type of spirituality. Believers are waiting and hoping for salvation. Again an impressive metaphor is used: as guards during the night long for daybreak, thus the faithful ones anxiously look out for Yahweh. The expectancy is first articulated in regard to the individual believer (vv. 5-6; cf. the longing described in Psalms 42; 84), thereafter (vv. 7-8) in regard to Israel, the community at large. Or could the "I" also be understood in collective terms, as in 129:1-3? Here the individual praying in and with the congregation is the more likely concept. The verbs for hoping, waiting, trusting, etc. (*qwh, yḥl, dmm, bṭḥ,* etc.) signalize a complete "theology of hope" (J. Moltmann) concentrated in the Psalms and in psalmlike prophetic texts on the one hand and wisdom discourse on the other (cf. G. Waschke, *TWAT* VI, 1225-34). This peculiar way of theological thinking — waiting for Yahweh to redeem his faithful — was widespread in exilic and postexilic times and applies to the destiny of individuals and of the community in general. Exactly this double perspective is visible in our psalm.

The individual part (vv. 5-6), availing itself of the verbs *qwh*, Piel (twice), and *yḥl*, Hiphil (both: "waiting and hoping for"), in its anthropological and theological profile is related to several other songs (cf. Psalms 25; 27; 37; 62; 71; communal "we" in Isa 25:9; 26:8-9, 16; 59:9, 11). In particular, waiting and hoping for Yahweh and "his word" (v. 5b) seems to be an indicator of late theology; cf. Pss 119:40, 43, 49, 74, 81-82, 114, 147. The communal part (vv. 7-8) takes up the verb *yḥl* from v. 5b, exhorting Israel to put her confidence in Yahweh alone (v. 7a; the same phrase occurs in 131:3a). This form element seems to be decisive for the subunit; therefore we call it an EXHORTATION. The overextended line v. 7 puts a motive clause after the summons: Yahweh is the sole source of *ḥesed*, "solidarity," and *pědût*, "redemption" (v. 7bc). The latter expression, echoing in *yipdeh*, "he will pardon" (v. 8), is rare in Hebrew Scripture (three more occurrences: Ps 111:9; Exod 8:19; Isa 50:2). The exhortation proper and the motive clause (v. 7) supported by a factual but in essence promissory statement (v. 8) are linked to the preceding confession of guilt (v. 3) in a way that makes one ask for the coherence of the individual and the communal parts of the song. Against those who consider this element to be a secondary accretion, we may argue for its authenticity: especially the word of assurance at the very end is a fitting response to the questions raised by the individual voice in vv. 1-6. Without such a response the song would be truncated.

## *Genre*

With some essential elements of complaint (e.g., petition) missing and the ambivalence of individual and collective prayer at hand, defining the genre is difficult (cf. discussion of general patterns in "Introduction to Cultic Poetry," section 4B). Considering the changed social and ecclesiastical organization (see Setting) during the exile, we may say that Psalm 130 is an individual and communal COMPLAINT song expressing the anxiety of later times to be heard and pardoned by almighty Yahweh. As the great prayers of communal confession (Nehemiah 9; Ezra 9; Daniel 9; Psalms 78; 106; see Kessler) clearly demonstrate, there was rampant in those days a common feeling of guilt besetting individuals in their communities. Typically, Ezra and Nehemiah are portrayed as personally shocked, but speaking for their people.

Christian tradition singled out seven psalms for special penitential rites (Psalms 6; 32; 38; 51; 102; 130; 143), first attested in the Psalms commentary of Cassiodorus, politician and theologian in Italy of the sixth century C.E. Luther's popular interpretation of these psalms appeared in 1517 (cf. Jeremias, Kurzke, Leaver, et al.).

## Setting

Psalm 130 is a complaint song, but it is not really molded in the traditional forms and structures of individual complaint geared to specific calamities of a person in his or her natural group (→ Psalms 6; 38; 102; changes over against earlier complaints are analyzed by Jeremias; the late vocabulary of the spirituality of the poor is demonstrated by Lohfink; growing wisdom influences are central to Sedlmeier; linguistic artistry comes into focus with Vanoni, etc.). Rather, it belongs in the assembly of the Yahweh community attending to general griefs of the period, namely the "depths of guilt" (cf. vv. 1b + 3 + 8) assailing religious consciousness. The formal structure of individual complaint has therefore been modified to fit the requirements of a communal setting (→ Psalms 12; 69; 102; etc.). The individual, in any case, looms large in the context of his community, because confession to Yahweh since the exilic age has been, after all, an individual decision.

## Intention

While traditional complaints emphasize petition trying to move God into saving action on behalf of a supplicant, our psalm expresses fervent hopes for Yahweh to continue in his merciful compassion with Israel even in periods of deepest despair. The final subunit, vv. 7-8, gives resounding comfort to all those who are aware of their iniquities and long for Yahweh's mercy.

## Bibliography

N. Airoldi, "Note critiche ai salmi," *Augustinianum* 10 (1970) 174-80; R. Arconada, "Psalmus 129/130," *VD* 12 (1932) 213-19; G. Begrich, "Ruf aus der Tiefe," *Christenlehre — Religionsunterricht — Praxis* 51 (1998) 3-5; J. Brosseder, "Aus tiefer Not schrei ich zu dir," in *Liturgie und Dichtung* I (ed. H.-J. Becker, et al.; St. Ottilien: EOS, 1983) 645-57; C. H. Cornill, "Psalm 130," in *Beiträge zur alttestamentlichen Wissenschaft* (*Fest.* K. Budde; ed. K. Marti; Giessen: Töpelmann, 1920) 38-42; R. S. Dietrich, "Six Psalms: Brief Encounters," *Saint Luke's Journal of Theology* 29 (1986) 265-70; A. Gerstmaier, "Die Deutung der Psalmen im Spiegel der Musik: Vertonungen des 'de profundis' (Ps 130) von der frühchristlichen Psalmodie bis zu Arnold Schönberg," in *Liturgie und Dichtung* II (ed. H. Becker, et al.; St. Ottilien: EOS, 1983) 91-130; O. Hofius, "Vergebungszuspruch und Vollmachtsfrage," in *'Wenn nicht jetzt'* (*Fest.* H.-J. Kraus; ed. H.-G. Geyer, et al.; Neukirchen-Vluyn: Neukirchener Verlag, 1983) 115-27; E. Jacob, "Prier avec les Psaumes," *Foi et Vie* 84 (1985) 58-66; J. Jeremias, "Psalm 130 im alttestamentlichen Kanon und in Luthers Nachdichtung," in *Von Wittenberg nach Memphis* (*Fest.* R. Schwarz; ed. W. Homolka, et al.; Göttingen: Vandenhoeck & Ruprecht, 1989) 120-36; R. Kessler, "Schuldbekenntnis" (see listing at Psalm 106); H. Kurzke, "Säkularisation oder Realisation: Zur Wirkungsgeschichte von Psalm 130 ('de profundis') in der deutschen Literatur von Luther bis zur Gegenwart," in *Liturgie und Dichtung* II (ed. H. Becker, et al.; St. Ottilien: EOS, 1983) 67-89; R. A.

Leaver, "Luther's Catechism Hymns," *Lutheran Quarterly* 12 (1998) 171-80; S. Lee, "Deliverance from Depth," *CGST Journal* 24 (1998) 55-72; N. Lohfink, "Lexeme und Lexemgruppen in Psalm 25," in *Text, Methode und Grammatik* (*Fest.* W. Richter; ed. W. Gross, et al.; St. Ottilien: EOS, 1991) 271-95, esp. 278-90; R. R. Marrs, "A Cry from the Depths," *ZAW* 100 (1988) 81-90; P. D. Miller Jr., "Psalm 130," *Int* 33 (1979) 176-81; D. Olivier and U. Weisgerber, "Aus tiefer Not schrei ich zu dir," in *Dank an Luther* (ed. A. Aarflot, et al.; Göttingen: Vandenhoeck & Ruprecht, 1984) 90-98; R. J. Pettey, "Psalm 130: A Song of Sorrow," in *The Psalms and Other Studies* (*Fest.* J. I. Hunt; ed. J. Knight, et al.; Nashotah: Nashotah House Seminary, 1990) 45-53; S. Porúbčan, "Psalm cxxx 5-6," *VT* 9 (1959) 322-23; D. Rappel, "Psalm 130 — ein unvollendetes Gleichnis," *BM* 110 (1986/87) 217-20; J. H. le Roux, "God alles, die mens niks: Gedagtes rondom Luther se 'Die sieben Busspsalmen' van 1517," in *Martin Luther Lives* (ed. J. Hofmeyr; Pretoria: University of South Africa Press, 1983) 26-38; S. Sabugal, "El concepto del pecado en el Antiguo Testamento," *Estudios Eclesiásticos* 59 (1984) 459-69; W. H. Schmidt, "Gott und Mensch in Ps 130," *VT* 16 (1966) 241-53; F. Sedlmeier, "'Bei dir, da ist die Vergebung, damit du gefürchtet werdest': Überlegungen zu Psalm 130," *Bib* 73 (1992) 473-95; M. A. Smith, "Psalm 42 and 130 — Hope for the Hopeless," *RevExp* 91 (1994) 77-80; J. Tromp, "The Text of Psalm cxxx 5-6," *VT* 39 (1989) 100-103; G. Vanoni, "Wie Gott Gesellschaft wandelt: Der theologische Grund der YHWH-Furcht nach Psalm 130,4," in *Biblische Theologie und gesellschaftlicher Wandel* (*Fest.* N. Lohfink; ed. G. Braulik, et al.; Freiburg: Herder, 1993) 330-44; P. Volz, "Psalm 130," in *Fest.* K. Marti (ed. K. Budde; Giessen: Töpelmann, 1925) 287-96; Chr. Zippert, "'Aus tiefer Not schrei ich zu dir,'" *Musik und Kirche* 66 (1996) 270-73.

# Psalm 131:
## Song of Confidence, Confession of Faith

### *Structure*

|  | MT | NRSV |
|---|---|---|
| I. Superscription | 1a | - |
| II. Declaration of innocence | 1b-e | 1 |
| III. Affirmation of confidence | 2 | 2 |
| IV. Exhortation of community | 3 | 3 |

The SUPERSCRIPTIONS with the Psalms of Ascent (Psalms 120–134) we have dealt with in → Psalms 120 and 122. The latter also carries the augmented form "Song of Ascents, of David" (though *lĕdāwid* is missing in the LXX tradition), like Psalms 124 and 133. The editors of the collection found some association with Israel's great king in these texts. In this case it may have been David's humility, patent, e.g., in 2 Sam 7:18-22.

The little poem in itself, one of the shortest in the Psalter (cf. Psalms 117; 134), to modern exegetes is a jewel of simplicity (cf. Gunkel, Quell, Miller). The reason for this estimation is obvious: our psalm in its first four lines talks exclusively about personal attitudes using strictly domestic imagery. Only line five looks beyond this private realm toward the community of Israel.

Formally, v. 1b-e is a DECLARATION OF INNOCENCE of the basic type: "I am not such a one (as I am reputed to be)." We meet this element in the Psalter's protestations of innocence (sometimes called "psalms of the falsely accused": Psalms 7; 17; 26) or in Job's long defense speech (Job 31; cf. also the Egyptian Book of the Dead, ch. 125: *ANET,* 34-36). Three times a negation is articulated: "My heart is not arrogant, my eyes are not haughty. I am not living in a grand style" (v. 1b, c, d). The opponents, of course, those who really are contemptuous and full of false pride and brutal self-esteem, are human types attacked in wisdom literature: the *zēdîm,* "insolent," of Psalm 119 or the *rĕšā'îm,* "godless," in Psalms 1; 37; etc. Also, in prophetic denunciations the "high things" and every kind of "loftiness" will be torn down (cf. Isa 2:12-18; Ezekiel 17; 27; 31). "Six things Yahweh hates, . . ." and the first of the series is "haughty eyes" (Prov 6:16-17). Looking at our v. 1, then, we do not have the impression that the supplicant is under special accusation of a misdemeanor. He or she is simply disproving the possibility of belonging to that human type hateful to Yahweh. The supplicant wants to comply with the ideal of lowliness frequently found in sapiential and late OT literature (cf. Moses, the perfectly humble man: Num 12:3; E. S. Gerstenberger, *TWAT* VI, 247-70, esp. 265). Also, in some psalms the lowly and poor are the preferred partners of Yahweh, the keeper and savior of the weak ones (cf. Psalms 9/10; 37; 49; 73; 146; Lohfink, *Lobgesänge;* listing at Additional Bibliography, section C). We note that the first subunit of Psalm 131 uses the form of protestation of innocence to deny affinity with that bad model of a human being, the "haughty one," discounted also in Egyptian and Mesopotamian wisdom. Interestingly, the lines concerned with this issue are preceded by an appellation of the divine name (v. 1b). That means that the declaration of innocence is not directed toward any human jury but to the supreme judge himself. On the other hand, there is no other trace of prayer language in the whole psalm apart from this appellation. Yahweh is mentioned once more (v. 3a), but in the third person. Perhaps the first and the last lines containing his name were considered sufficient liturgical identification of God. The statements of innocence and confidence in between were apparently spoken in a subdued voice, possibly in conjunction with other prayers.

The second element is formed like an oath that consciously leaves out the protasis ("I will be struck") for being too dangerous to pronounce. It therefore opens with "if I have not done this or that" (v. 2ab). In our case, the supplicant testifies by his conditional curse that he or she really has abrogated haughtiness. The oath underlines the declaration of innocence. Saying this we presuppose that *šwh* and *dmm* in v. 2 are synonyms signifying something like "adopting a humble attitude" (which is not so clear because *šwh* is a rare verb in the Hebrew Bible meaning "equalize," "compare"; cf. Isa 28:25; Ps 18:34 [RSV 33]; cf. M. Sæbø, *TWAT* VII, 1177-82). The state of mind of the supplicant is then compared to that of a young child seeking comfort at the mother's bosom (v. 2cd). Although there is no explicit statement to this effect, we may surmise that in the last instance God is compared with a mother taking her frightened children on her lap and to her bosom (cf. Hos 11:1-4; Isa 66:13; H. Schüngel-Straumann, "Gott als Mutter in Hos 11," *TQ* 166 [1986] 119-34).

The final unit is a summons to wait and hope for Yahweh, similar to the one found in Ps 130:7 (cf. also 62:9 [RSV 8]; 115:9-11, the imperative in these passages being from *bṭḥ*, "trust in," not from *yḥl*). Its liturgical character is obvious. The twofold occurrence in consecutive psalms of v. 3a (see 130:7a) may indicate formulaic use (thus Culley, *Language;* listing at "Introduction to Cultic Poetry"). Likewise, v. 3b is a liturgical formula, utilized until our own days ("from now on until eternity"; see 113:2; 115:18; 121:8; 125:2; further occurrences with variations, e.g., "from eternity to eternity," 90:2; 103:17; etc. "Eternity," Heb. *ôlām*, in every case means "time unfathomable"; cf. J. Barr, *Biblical Words for Time* [2nd ed.; SBT 1/33; London: SCM, 1969]; H. D. Preuss, *TWAT* V, 1144-59, esp. 1149: "from now on and forevermore" = liturgical "formula" "mainly in younger texts," namely Isa 9:6 [RSV 7]; 59:21: Mic 4:7; Pss 113:2; 115:18; 121:8; 125:2).

## Genre

Psalm 131 no doubt has confessional qualities. The suppliants (I choose the plural, indicating two dimensions: a sequence of users as well as group use at the same time, although no communal first person is used) deny vehemently that they belong to the haughty ones. They do it by confirming their absolute trust in Yahweh, like that of a child with his or her mother. Believers in Yahweh do claim the status of well-protected and comforted children, since Yahweh is something like mother and father to them (cf. Isa 66:13; Pss 27:10; 103:13), although the appellation "father" or "mother" is seldom used in Hebrew prayer language (cf. Isa 63:16; 64:7; Gerstenberger, *Yahweh;* listing at Additional Bibliography, section B). Therefore the double designation is justified: Song of Confidence and Confession of Faith. The little text was probably used in worship services in conjunction with personal or communal complaints or thanksgivings. It clearly belongs to some other psalms, which draw heavily on intimate-group vocabulary and concepts. Consequently, they may derive from original domestic cult rituals, once under the rule of women (→ Psalm 127).

Beyerlin, in his meticulous monograph, concludes that Psalm 131 is an "individual confession of trust," and at the same time, a "sapiential, didactic, parenetic witness" (*Wider die Hybris,* 88), but he argues most of the time on the basis of biographical experiences the "author" must have been passing through (cf. p. 105). We should keep in mind, though, that psalms are anonymous, liturgical texts, not to be measured by the yardstick of modern "authorship." They belonged to the community or to those leaders of congregations (e.g., "sons of Korah," "sons of Asaph," etc.) who administered the rituals of worship. Therefore they do not contain unique historical or biographical events but a synthesized, amalgamated treasure of spiritual knowledge, gathered through generations.

361

## Setting

Quell, Miller, et al. have ventured the hypothesis that our psalm was composed by a woman, and Bail (pp. 188-89) basically agrees (only insisting on a liberating rather than submissive tone in our psalm). The conducive line, of course, is v. 2cd. One may argue that the metaphor of a child seeking shelter with his or her mother betrays female origin. By using this metaphor God may become a female deity — this observation may undergird said argumentation. Miller argues on the basis of social roles in a patriarchal society, which taught "submission and humility" to females, in particular as far as official religious matters were concerned, theology being a "male task" ("Things Too Wonderful," 245-46. Moses, David, Job, etc. are at times portrayed as utterly humble; cf. Num 12:3). On the other hand there is no firm proof of female authorship possible, "authorship" in itself being too modern a concept when applied to psalm literature. Also, any male person observing the role of mothers in protecting their children might use the image (cf. Isa 49:15-17). Official Yahweh religion from the beginning in principle seems to have been a male affair (cf. Gerstenberger, *Yahweh*). If we may consider previous stages of Psalm 131 wherein the name of Yahweh was possibly not present, the likelihood of female composition might be stronger. Private worship of family gods (cf. van der Toorn, *Religion;* listing at Additional Bibliography, section B) within the clan group has been a stronghold of women (cf. Gerstenberger, "Spiritualität"; → Psalm 127).

## Intention

Painting a model of human humility in the face of Yahweh, the psalm invites members of the community to trust in their God and to learn the right posture over against God. If they took over these affirmations themselves and made them their own confession, the deepest purpose of this song would be achieved.

## Bibliography

U. Bail, "Die Psalmen," in *Kompendium* (ed. L. Schottroff, et al.) 180-91 (listing at Additional Bibliography, section A); W. Beyerlin, *Wider die Hybris des Geistes: Studien zum 131. Psalm* (Stuttgart: Katholisches Bibelwerk, 1982); P. A. H. de Boer, "Ps CXXXI,2," *VT* 16 (1966) 287-92; W. A. van Gemeren, "Psalm 131:2 — kĕgāmûl: The Problems of Meaning and Metaphor," *Hebrew Studies* 23 (1982) 51-57; E. S. Gerstenberger, "Weibliche Spiritualität in Psalmen und Hauskult," in *Ein Gott allein?* (ed. W. Dietrich, et al.; Fribourg: Universitätsverlag, 1994) 349-63; V. Guroian, "Seeing Worship as Ethics: An Orthodox Perspective," *Journal of Religious Ethics* 13 (1985) 332-59; W. B. Hunter, "Contextual and Genre Implications for the Historicity of John 11:41b-42," *JETS* 28 (1985) 53-70; E. Jacob, "Prier avec les psaumes," *Foi et Vie* 84 (1985) 58-66; E. Jüngel, "Psalm 131," in *Einfach von Gott reden (Fest. F. Mildenberger;* ed. J. Roloff, et al.; Stuttgart: Kohlhammer, 1994) 240-42; O. Loretz, "Zur Parallelität zwischen KTU 1.6 II 28-30 und Ps 131,2b," *UF* 17 (1986) 183-87; A. Maillot, "Israel.

Sompte sur le seigneur (Ps 131)," *BVC* 77 (1967) 26-37; P. Miller, "Things Too Wonderful: Prayers of Women in the Old Testament," in *Biblische Theologie und gesellschaftlicher Wandel* (*Fest.* N. Lohfink; ed. G. Braulik, et al.; Freiburg: Herder, 1993) 237-51; E. Peterson, "My Eyes Are Not Raised Too High," in *A Chorus of Witnesses* (ed. T. Long and C. Plantinga Jr.; Grand Rapids: Eerdmans, 1994) 179-88; W. S. Prinsloo, "'Nie my wil nie, O Here,'" *SK* 7 (1986) 74-82; G. Quell, "Struktur und Sinn des Psalms 131," in *Das ferne und nahe Wort* (*Fest.* L. Rost; ed. F. Maass; BZAW 105; Berlin: de Gruyter, 1967) 173-85; B. P. Robinson, "Form and Meaning of Psalm 131," *Bib* 79 (1998) 180-97; A. Rose, "Les psaumes 44 et 131 dans la liturgie mariale," in *La mère de Jésus-Christ* (ed. A. Triacca, et al.; Rome: CLV Edizioni Liturgiche, 1986) 255-65; L. Ruppert, "Psalm 131," in *Von der Suche nach Gott* (*Fest.* H. Riedlinger; ed. M. Schmidt, et al.; Stuttgart-Bad Cannstatt: Frommann-Holzboog, 1998) 207-22; H. S. Shoemaker, "Psalm 131," *RevExp* 85 (1988) 89-94.

## Psalm 132:
## Zion Psalm, Messianic Hymn

### *Structure*

|  |  | MT | NRSV |
|---|---|---|---|
| I. | Superscription | 1a | - |
| II. | Remembrance | 1b-5 | 1-5 |
|  | A. Petition | 1b-2 | 1-2 |
|  | B. David's vow | 3-5 | 3-5 |
| III. | Description of procession | 6-7 | 6-7 |
| IV. | Communal prayer | 8-10 | 8-10 |
| V. | Divine oracle | 11-12 | 11-12 |
|  | A. Introduction | 11ab | 11ab |
|  | B. Oracle | 11c-12 | 11c-12 |
| VI. | Divine oracle | 13-18 | 13-18 |
|  | A. Introduction | 13 | 13 |
|  | B. Oracle | 14-18 | 14-18 |

Psalm 132 is now part of the collection of "Songs of Ascents," pilgrimage hymns (Psalms 120–134), as the SUPERSCRIPTION points out (→ Psalm 120). Like most or all of the other psalms of this group, it had its own tradition history before becoming incorporated into the collection. Noteworthy are the strong affinities of our psalm with parts of the David tradition (cf. 2 Samuel 6–7) and the structuring of the song around citations of oaths: David begins swearing allegiance to Yahweh; the king will provide a temple for his Lord (vv. 3-5). Two oaths of Yahweh himself constitute the center of vv. 11-18: the Lord of Zion will take care of David's dynasty, and he will bless his people from Zion (vv. 11c-12 and 14-18; W. H. Mare, *ABD* VI, 1096-97). Altogether, and in terms of literary volume, the first two oaths comprise three poetic lines each, the third oath has five lines and seems to carry the highest emphasis (vv.

14-18). Besides David and Yahweh speaking in the psalm, a group of people comes to the fore in vv. 6-7 with a communal "we" discourse; the same speakers supposedly direct themselves toward Yahweh in a petitionary way (vv. 1b-2, 8-10). Thus we have to take into account at least three protagonists in this dramatic setup: congregation–the historical David–Yahweh, Lord of Zion. (Bee, Houk, Huwiler, et al., investigating the text from morphological, linguistic, and literary perspectives, come to similar divisions and interesting correspondences of textual elements.) A form-critical and social analysis of the individual parts of Psalm 132 reveals the following.

The song opens with a plea to Yahweh to remember the bygone time of David (v. 1bc), specifically the efforts of the great king in regard to the construction of a temple (vv. 2-5). This endeavor is considered to have been a "burden" or "slavish toil" for the king (v. 1c: *'unnôtô*, Pual infinitive of *'nh* III; the stem is rarely but significantly used; cf. Lev 23:29; Isa 53:4; Ps 119:71. In Ps 22:25 [RSV 24] we find a synonym *'ĕnût*, "affliction," referring to misery pitied by God). Formally, this petition — spoken by the community or its leader — uses the masculine singular imperative and the name of Yahweh, which, in turn, serves both as the addressee of the plea and as invocation for the whole prayer. Pleas to "remember" past positive actions of people for God may be constructed with the accusative of the memorable action plus the dative *(lĕ)* of the person concerned, as in our v. 1bc (cf. similar style in prosaic passages like Exod 32:13; Deut 9:27). The person referred to may appear in a suffix to the accusative (cf. Lam 3:19) or be described in a relative clause (Isa 38:3; 2 Kgs 20:3). Formal analogies we also find in a peculiar first-person prayer, interspersed in some parts of the book of Nehemiah (Neh 5:19; 13:14, 22b, 31b: the basic form seems to be: "Remember to the good for me what I have done!"). In any case, the plea for remembrance is an outright PETITION drawing on general concepts of the time that attributed supreme importance to God's memory: if God did not remember, oblivion was the result (cf. Schottroff, *Gedenken;* listing at Additional Bibliography, section B). The verb *zākar* signifies reactivation of past potencies, which, in consequence, cannot be considered as "bygone" and "disappeared" in the strict sense. The past is still existent, and it may be a distant past that still exercises its influences in the present.

What is to be remembered by Yahweh? David's toil in favor of Yahweh's abode on Zion! The tradition used in vv. 2-5 has a peculiar shape and flair not to be found in the historical accounts of 2 Samuel 6–7 or, for that matter, in 1 Chronicles 13–29, that enormous accumulation of material centering on the construction of the temple. Our psalm talks about an "oath" David supposedly swore in regard to finding a proper site for the temple (v. 5a). The main narrative tradition in the historical books of the OT does not use oath formulas, nor does it articulate the specific problem of finding the right spot for the temple. Both 2 Sam 6:17 and 1 Chr 15:1 let the ark come to rest at a definite but unspecified place in Jerusalem. Later on, the construction of a temple seems to be located at the same site where the ark had been housed in a tent (cf. 2 Sam 7:2; 1 Kings 6). Only in 2 Sam 24:18-25 is the holy temple ground revealed to David in connection with atoning sacrifices he had to deliver. Even in this passage, however, there is no question of searching for a site agreeable to Yahweh. In contrast, our psalm dramatizes David's efforts to find adequate temple grounds (vv. 3-5). He vows abstention from sleep until a successful encounter (cf. Gunkel, 566, adducing many examples from the history of religions for this kind of vow). Restless activity of a monarch in favor of his temple-building project is a topic in Mesopotamian literature from Sumerian times (cf. Keel, *Welt*, 248-58; listing at "Introduction to Cultic Poetry"; R. E. Averbeck, *A Preliminary Study of Ritual and Structure in the Cylinders of Gudea*, vol. 1 [diss., Dropsie College, 1987]). The long temple hymn of Gudea of Lagash even contains a related passage:

> . . . to build the house for his king
> he [i.e., Gudea] does not sleep during the night,
> he does not slumber at noontime. (*SAHG*, 154)

Significantly, David in our passage wants to construct a temple for Yahweh, who is denominated "mighty of Jacob" (*ʾăbîr yaʿăqōb*, vv. 2b, 5b), seemingly an archaic or archaizing name of Israel's God. This name is extremely rare in Hebrew Scripture and unknown in narrative David traditions; cf. Gen 49:24; Isa 49:26; 60:16, all in all five occurrences, and one more with "Israel" instead of "Jacob" (Isa 1:24).

Abruptly, the community speaks up, telling a rather cryptic story of finding the ark somewhere in "Ephrathah" or the "jungle" (v. 6; the latter part of the text is uncertain; cf. Robinson; an allusion to Kiriath-jearim, as in 1 Sam 6:20–7:1; 2 Sam 6:2? thus Gunkel, 566; on the ark see Davies; C. L. Seow, *ABD* I, 386-93), enigmatic references that we do not understand in their significance for ancient worshipers. Has the text been spoiled by a "Davidic" reading (cf. Ephrathah in Ruth 4:11; Mic 5:1 [RSV 2])? To "hear" and "find" is a peculiar combination of verbs and concepts. Does it come from the wisdom tradition (cf. Prov 2:1-5; 8:32-35)? The third-person feminine singular suffix with both verbal forms does not have a point of reference in the preceding text, nor in the following, because the "ark" is grammatically masculine (to postulate feminine gender in exceptional cases as *HAL* 83 and many commentators do is a result not of insight but of despair. A hypothetical feminine "oath" is difficult, too, against Huwiler, et al.). As the text stands now the most likely object to be found would be the dwelling place for Yahweh (cf. v. 5); liturgically speaking, the mentioned suffix must not point exactly to *māqôm* or *miškānāh* (v. 5: "place," "habitat"; the Hebrew text has the feminine plural) but to an indefinite "it," i.e., "that thing sought after." And v. 7 most naturally supports this interpretation ("Let us go to his habitat"). It definitely does not speak about the ark but about the temple already in existence, and people speaking in the first person plural are willing to go to that place of worship (v. 7a, *nābôʾāh*, "let us go/enter," is a typical summons to tend to religious duties and approach the Deity in veneration; cf. Hos 6:1; Ps 122:1bc). All of a sudden, it seems, the text is being articulated by worshipers on their way to the holy place. The speech form of vv. 6-7 is unmistakably communal ("we" forms; → Psalm 124); the act indicated in v. 7b is that of cultic prostration, done in the presence of the suppliants, not in the Davidic past. This means that we are witnessing parts of a "live" worship, not simply historical remembrances. Even dramatizing psalm texts are not to be confounded with mere "objective" accounts (cf. Psalm 95, which also has first-person plural summons to worship: vv. 1-2, 6-7). All the more curious is the appearance of the ark in v. 8; it occurs nowhere else in Psalm 132. This unique poetic line resembles Num 10:35b, while the following v. 9 simply talks about "your priests" and "your faithful ones" without any more concern about the ark. V. 10, finally, focuses on the "messiah," the anointed one (v. 10). In terms of topics or subject matter, we may say, the ark is rather isolated in v. 8. It has possibly been placed here because everybody knew of the Davidic tradition making this king the glorious conqueror of Jerusalem, the one who found the right temple ground (and really built the temple?), where Jewish people down to our own day may celebrate their festivals.

Things become still more complicated, when we discover that 2 Chr 6:41-42 is largely identical with our vv. 8-10:

> Now rise up, O Yahweh God, and go to your resting place,
> you and the ark of your might.
> Let your priests, O Yahweh God, be clothed with salvation,
> and let your faithful rejoice in your goodness.
> O Yahweh God, do not reject your anointed one.
> Remember your steadfast love
> for your servant David.

This passage occurs in the chapter on Solomon's dedication of the temple (2 Chronicles 6). The verses concerned (2 Chr 6:41-42) are absent in 1 Kings 8; they are partially congruent with our vv. 8-10. What to make of these coincidences? The ark is placed in the temple by Solomon in both text groups (cf. 1 Kgs 8:1-11; 2 Chr 5:2-11a). Only in 2 Chr 6:41-42 a special word of stimulation and petition is pronounced over against Yahweh.

Formally here, vv. 6-10 fall into two different elements. The first one (vv. 6-7) is a self-presentation of the community — a DESCRIPTION OF PROCESSION — that may have had introductory functions. The second (vv. 8-10) is a COMMUNAL PRAYER with some incorporated wish formulations (cf. v. 9). Yahweh is directly addressed, and the high point is apparently the consideration of and intercession for the (Davidic) Messiah (v. 10b). The profile of early Jewish organization and theological hope shines through these lines. "We" discourse in vv. 6-7 suggests strong participation of the assembly of the faithful; division into "priests" and "loyal ones" (ḥăsîdîm, vv. 9, 16: cf. 30:5 [RSV 4]; 31:24 [RSV 23]; 52:11 [RSV 9]; 85:9 [RSV 8]; 89:20 [RSV 19]; 97:10; 116:15; 145:10; 148:14; 149:5, 9) is another characteristic of late Israelite community structure. The head of the royal dynasty, David, is considered a present or future figure in v. 10. All divine blessings and promises are channeled through him. This observation, of course, raises the question of the messianic outlook in Psalm 132 (see Genre).

The second part of Psalm 132, vv. 11-18, is occupied by two oracles of Yahweh (vv. 11c-12, 14-18; cf. Starbuck, Oracles; listing at Additional Bibliography, section C). The introductory phrase v. 11a corresponds exactly to v. 2a: just as David took an oath for Yahweh, now Yahweh binds himself by solemn promise on behalf of David. V. 11ab apparently serves as a kind of heading for both oracles, because v. 13 is nothing more than an intermediary justification of the second word of God. The first oath (vv. 11c-12) is concerned about dynastic continuity along the line of 2 Sam 7:12-16; Ps 89:4-5, 29-38 (RSV 3-4, 28-37). While 2 Samuel 7 in its earliest layer talks only about the immediate successor of David, Psalm 89 from its retrospective vantage point looks at the whole dynasty and its endless duration, which naturally includes exilic and postexilic times. Thus the old dynastic promise nourishes messianic hopes. Our passage is very much like the divine announcements of → Psalm 89. The formulations are different, to be sure, but vocabulary and general outlook, theological conceptualization and communal hopes are much the same in both psalms. For generations to come the throne of David is guaranteed by Yahweh's oath. Significantly, the possibility of disloyalty of Davidic kings to Yahweh is discussed in both psalms (v. 12ab; 89:31-34 [RSV 30-33]). In the present text v. 12ab states a flat condition, the keeping of the covenant, to make Yahweh's promise work. Ps 89:34-38 (RSV 33-37), on the other hand, takes pains not to let the covenant fall down at any price (but the continuation, 89:39-46 [RSV 38-45], is all the more shocking).

The second oracle (vv. 14-18) is introduced by a descriptive line containing strong theological affirmations: Yahweh prefers to dwell on Zion! (Cf. *bḥr* and *yšb* in connection with Yahweh's preference for "Jerusalem": Zech 1:17; 2:14-16; 3:2; Ps 9:12 [RSV 11]). From a fictional preceding vantage point Deuteronomy always talks about "the place" that God will "elect"; cf. Deut 12:5, 11, 14, 18, 21, 26, etc., while later Dtr sources frequently choose "the city" as the proper expression, sometimes adding the name "Jerusalem"; cf. 1 Kgs 8:44; 11:32, 36; 14:21; 23:27. Quoting a word of Yahweh in the first person the Chronicler seems to summarize the second part of our psalm: "I chose Jerusalem, to let my name dwell there, and I chose David, to lead my people Israel" (2 Chr 6:6; cf. 1 Kgs 8:16, where the first part is missing in MT).

In our psalm, for a difference, the order of naming the elected ones is inverted (David: vv. 11-12; Jerusalem: vv. 13-14). Otherwise the statement in Chronicles corresponds with Psalm 132, and it has been transmitted in oracle form, too. In Psalm 132 the oracle itself starts out with a demonstrative clause (v. 14) pointing exactly at Yahweh's abode. "My resting place" (*měnûḥāh*, v. 14a) takes up the expression of v. 8, but there are no inherent connotations of the *ark* coming to rest (cf. Num 10:33). It may seem strange that Yahweh speaks so positively about dwelling at a specific place on earth, *'wh*, Piel, "want," "desire," being a strong expression (vv. 13b, 14b; nowhere else in connection with God). In other layers of OT tradition there are equally strong reservations about God's habitation in a humanmade building (cf. 1 Kgs 8:27; Isa 66:1). This positive attitude over against Zion-Jerusalem links our psalm with Zion hymns like → Psalms 46; 48.

Yahweh next is quoted as blessing the city and her inhabitants, the poor, the priests, the loyal ones (vv. 15-16), giving us an idea that the presupposed social structure is that of the exilic-postexilic community. The climax, however, is in vv. 17-18, a divine promise for the future. The "sprouting horn for David" without doubt refers to a messianic incumbent (cf. Jer 33:15, 17; Ezek 29:21; Isa 11:1).

The basic form-critical question at this point is: How did this oracle discourse, i.e., that manner of Yahweh speaking directly to a person or to the community, come about? By which type of mediation was it communicated to those concerned? Direct speech of God to the people was considered extremely dangerous in ancient Israel, so that some kind of mediation was deemed necessary (cf. Exod 20:18-21; Deut 5:23-27). In consequence, diverse "men of God," "messengers," etc., spoke in the name of Yahweh, and often quoted him verbatim and in the first person singular. The psalms give us a good number of examples (cf. Psalms 50; 60:8-14 [RSV 6-12]; 82; 89; 95:8-11; 110). Divine speech, however, is not a handy genre designation. The tenor and life setting of the examples mentioned above are very diverse. Still, it is valid to ask about the means and communication processes by which the words of God were transported to the audience, and what this audience was like in those days. Traditional anwers postulating the office of "cultic prophet" in Israel seem to be inadequate (→ Psalms 12; 50; 95).

The large prose tradition within Hebrew Scripture — and this is valid for Dtr as well as Priestly layers of literature — abundantly used divine "I" speech. Narratives about the "arch-parents" (I. Fischer, listing at Additional Bibliography, section B) of Israel are customarily composed around Yahweh's direct address to a patriarch or his wife (cf. M. Köckert, *Verheissungen;* listing at Additional Bibliography, section B). Examples are Gen 12:1-3; 15:1-6; 17:1-22; 26:24; 28:13-15; 35:9-12. Large parts, thereafter, of the Pentateuch have been transmitted as authentic words of Yahweh mediated by Moses, thus most of Exodus 25–40, Leviticus, Numbers, and Deuteronomy. Within this vast material we also find speeches of Yahweh modeled after an oath formula (cf., e.g., Num 14:20-25, 26-35). Still another large area of literature must be consulted in this search for formal analogies: the prophetic books. By their very nature and task at least some of the prophets were destined to speak in the name of the Lord, quoting his words as exactly as possible. It is in this section of the Hebrew Bible that we also find substantial parallels to the oracles of Psalm 132, addressing themselves to the promise of a Davidic offspring (cf. Isa 11:1; Jer 22:3-5; 33:15; Ezek 29:21; 34:23; etc.). Here we should look for illuminative texts and structures. The general impression we get may be this one: kerygmatic types of divine speech in the Bible, i.e., those texts that carry a direct message to an audience, probably reflect discourse patterns used and perused in the early Jewish parish assemblies (cf. E. S. Gerstenberger, "Predigt II," *TRE* XXVII, 231-35).

## Genre

The central features of Psalm 132 are Yahweh's promises to the exilic or postexilic community of loyal believers, i.e., the communities of early Judaism. Most of all, the divine announcements of blessings and well-being include the proclamation of another Davidic king (vv. 10, 12, 17-18). Therefore the classification as MESSIANIC HYMN seems justified. Zion, however, plays an important role in this concert of hopes. ZION SONG also is an adequate designation for our psalm, which in Christian tradition was very much used in the christological interpretation of the OT. Other genre classifications in OT research include "royal hymn."

## Setting

Various theories have been built up around our psalm, frequently starting from the ark in v. 8 and postulating annual celebrations of the Davidic traditions preserved in 2 Samuel 5–7 and related historical accounts. Mowinckel, Bentzen, et al. connect the text with a yearly "enthronement festival," celebrating death and resurrection of God and his king on Zion. Since the ark is only loosely connected with Psalm 132 and the center of attention is focused on David and Zion, we may shift emphasis a little more in that direction. Still, preexilic "royal ideology" hardly plays a role in this psalm. Its setting is not really recognized unless we abandon the preexilic use and origin of the psalm. Traces of late community organization and of messianic hopes for a restoration of the Davidic monarchy make it necessary to think of early Jewish congregational activities as the matrix for our song. In this case one can imagine Zion and David festivals in situations of resurging hopes among believers for a powerful restoration of the lost monarchy.

## Intention

Messianic impetus in Israel usually grew out of precarious outside circumstances and growing hope inside a religious group for a total change to the better. Along this line we may surmise that community leaders or officiants in worship reunions would synthesize old traditions into contemporary sacred songs. The David traditions utilized in Psalm 132 differ from the ones we have in the books of Samuel. But they serve as welcome background to proclaim in the contemporary life experience a resounding message of hope. This seems to be the uppermost purpose of this influential song (→ Psalms 2; 110).

## Bibliography

A. Ammassari, " 'Ricordati, O Signore, per amore di David . . .': Esegesi storica di un Salmo," in *La religione dei Patriarchi* (ed. idem; Rome: Città Nuova, 1976) 9-135; F. Asensio, "El Salmo 132 y la 'lampara' de David," *Gregorianum* 38 (1957) 310-16; J. M. Auwers, "Le Psaume 132 parmi les graduels," *RB* 103 (1996) 546-60; R. E. Bee, "The Textual Analysis of Psalm 132: A Response to C. B. Houk," *JSOT* 10 (1978) 49-53; idem, "The Use of Syllable Counts in Textual Analysis (Ps 132)," *JSOT* 10 (1978) 68-70; A. Bentzen, "The Cultic Use of the Story of the Ark in Samuel," *JBL* 67 (1948) 37-53; C. Brekelmans, "Ps 132: Unity and Structure," *Bijdragen* 44 (1983) 261-65; G. H. Davies, "The Ark in the Psalms," in *Promise and Fulfillment (Fest.* S. H. Hooke; ed. F. F. Bruce; Edinburgh: T. & T. Clark, 1963) 51-61; O. Eissfeldt, "Psalm 132," *WO* 2 (1957) 480-83 (repr. in idem, *KS* III, 481-85); T. W. Fretheim, "Psalm 132, a Form-

Critical Study," *JBL* 86 (1967) 289-300; idem, "Divine Foreknowledge, Divine Constancy, and the Rejection of Saul's Kingship," *CBQ* 47 (1985) 595-602; H. Gese, "Davidsbund" (see listing at Psalm 2; repr. in idem, *Vom Sinai zum Zion* [Munich: Kaiser, 1974] 113-29); S. Herrmann, "Königsnovelle" (see listing at Psalm 2); D. R. Hillers, "Ritual Procession of the Ark and Psalm 132," *CBQ* 30 (1968) 48-55; C. B. Houk, "Psalm 132: Literary Integrity, and Syllable-Word Structures," *JSOT* 10 (1978) 41-48; idem, "Psalm 132: Further Discussion," *JSOT* 6 (1978) 54-57; E. R. Huwiler, "Patterns and Problems in Psalm 132," in *The Listening Heart* (*Fest.* R. E. Murphy; ed. K. Hoglund, et al.; JSOTSup 58; Sheffield: JSOT Press, 1987) 199-215; A. R. Johnson, "The Role of the King in the Jerusalem Cultus," in *The Labyrinth* (ed. S. H. Hooke; London: SCM, 1935) 71-111; A. van der Kooij, "David, 'het licht van Israel,'" in *Vruchten van de uithof* (ed. J. Doeve, et al.; Utrecht: Theologisch Instituut, 1974) 49-57; A. Laato, "Psalm 132 and the Development of the Jerusalemite/Israelite Royal Ideology," *CBQ* 54 (1992) 49-66; G. Lawless, "Psalm 132 and Augustine's Monastic Ideal," *Augustinianum* 59 (1982) 526-39; J. A. Loader, "Theologia religionum from the Perspective of Israelite Religion," *Missionalia* 13 (1985) 14-32; J. L. Mays, "In a Vision: The Portrayal of the Messiah in the Psalms," *Ex Auditu* 7 (1991) 1-8; idem, "The David of the Psalms," *Int* 40 (1986) 143-55; C. B. McCarthy, "Psalm 132: A Methodological Analysis" (diss., Marquette University, 1968); J. G. McConville, "1 Chr 28:9 — Yahweh 'seeks out' Solomon," *JTS* 37 (1986) 105-8; M. Metzger, "Himmlische und irdische Wohnstatt Jahwes," *UF* 2 (1970) 139-58; P. Nel, "Psalm 132 and Covenant Theology," in *Text and Context* (*Fest.* F. C. Fensham; ed. W. Claassen; Sheffield: Sheffield Academic Press, 1988) 183-91; M. Noth, "Gott — König — Volk im Alten Testament," *ZTK* 47 (1950) 157-91 (repr. in idem, *Gesammelte Studien zum Alten Testament* [TBü 6; Munich: Kaiser, 1957] 188-229); idem, "Jerusalem und die israelitische Tradition," *OTS* 8 (1950) 28-46; idem, "David und Israel in 2 Sam 7," in *Mélanges bibliques* (*Fest.* A. Robert; ed. J. Trinquet; Paris: Bloud et Gay, 1958) 122-30; B. G. Ockinga, "An Example of Egyptian Royal Phraseology in Psalm 132," *BN* 11 (1980) 38-42; C. L. Patton, "Psalm 132," *CBQ* 57 (1995) 643-54; J. R. Porter, "The Interpretation of 2 Sam 6 and Ps 132," *JTS* 5 (1954) 161-73; G. von Rad, "Erwägungen" (see listing at Psalm 2); idem, "Ritual" (see listing at Psalm 2); A. Robinson, "Do Ephrathah and Jaar Really Appear in Psalm 132,6?" *ZAW* 86 (1974) 220-22; L. Rost, "Sinaibund und Davidsbund," *TLZ* 72 (1947) 129-34; J. Schreiner, *Sion — Jerusalem, Jahwes Königssitz* (Munich: Kösel, 1963); M. Simon, "La prophétie de Nathan et le temple," *RHPR* 32 (1952) 41-58; G. H. Wilson, "The Qumran Psalms Scroll Reconsidered," *CBQ* 47 (1985) 624-42; M. R. Wilson, "Real Estate Theology: Zionism and Biblical Claims," *Transformation* 2 (1985) 12-18; R. R. Wilson, "The City in the Old Testament," in *Civitas: Religious Interpretation of the City* (ed. P. Hawkins; Atlanta: Scholars Press, 1986) 3-13; D. Zamagna, "O Salmo 132," *EstBib* 21-23 (1989) 39-44.

## Psalm 133:
## Announcement of Blessing

### *Structure*

|                      | MT    | NRSV |
| -------------------- | ----- | ---- |
| I. Superscription    | 1a    | -    |
| II. Exclamation      | 1bc   | 1    |
| III. Metaphors       | 2-3b  | 2-3b |
| IV. Hymn to Zion     | 3cd   | 3cd  |

Four psalms among the Songs of Ascent carry an enlarged SUPERSCRIP-
TION: *lĕdāwid*, "to [or 'from'] David" is added to the standard heading
(→ Psalms 120; 122). We are unable to recognize a firm principle for these additions, and the main Greek tradition did not follow suit, leaving these four
songs (Psalm 122; 124; 131; 133) just with the standard heading.
The little psalm opens with a "profane" EXCLAMATION, praising brotherly
neighborhood and peaceful coexistence (v. 1bc). The interrogative *mah*, "how,"
with a following adjective or verb of (positive) evaluation may be found in proverbial sayings and popular songs. "A word at (the right) moment: How good!"
(Prov 15:23b). "How wonderful is your love, my sister!" (Cant 4:10). "How beautiful is your walking" (Cant 7:2). The closest parallel to the opening line of our
psalm is Cant 7:7: "How beautiful and pleasant are you" — a repetitious eulogy
just as in our psalm (cf. also Ps 135:3: "lovely" in relation to hymn singing). The
Song of Songs lets it be spoken to a person in direct address, however, while our
psalm word is clad in neutral language lauding a harmonious familial and neigh-
borly situation (v. 1b). Still, the saying of the psalm is quite close to sapiential and
popular usage, it seems, while most of the other wondrous exclamations within
the Psalter strictly extol Yahweh and his works: "How precious is your trustworthiness, God!" (36:8 [RSV 7]); "How great is your goodness, Yahweh" (31:20
[RSV 19]); "Yahweh, our Lord, how majestic is your name over all the earth!"
(8:2, 10 [RSV 1, 9]); "How terrifying are your deeds!" (66:3). "How lovely are
your dwelling places, Yahweh of hosts!" (84:2 [RSV 1]). The form and character
of all these exclamations resemble FELICITATION and BEATITUDE. To emphasize
again, v. 1bc belongs to the "profane" type of popular sayings extolling felicitous
interhuman relations. From this mundane introductory note to the last line of
Psalm 133, a veiled plea for Yahweh's blessing from Zion (v. 3cd), we notice a
considerable tension mediated by two metaphoric comparisons.
The rhetorical question, introduced by *mah*, "how," is preceded by the
strangely redundant *hinnēh*, "behold" (v. 1b). The particle serves several functions; in this case it is used by an unidentified speaker and directed to an unidentified audience, apparently calling for special attention. Within the Psalms
of Ascent there are six other passages of this kind: 121:4; 123:2; 127:3; 128:4;
132:6; 134:1b, and they all seem to have an instructional function. The Psalter
outside Psalms 120–134 offers some more examples (see 7:15 [RSV 14]; 11:2;
33:18; 52:9 [RSV 7]; 73:12). Considering the double exclamatory opening we
may surmise that the saying of v. 1bc surely has some educational quality.

Those two lines just mentioned, each one introduced by comparative *kĕ* (vv. 2ab, 3ab), no doubt were happy and illuminating similes for a contemporary audience, but for us it is rather difficult to see the point of comparison. First, the interposed cola of v. 2cd may be a mere apposition to the preceding, thus pinpointing the metaphor of perfumed lotion to Aaron and his anointing (cf. Lev 9:12). If this is correct, the mentioned line may well be an afterthought of some transmitter, because it breaks out of those general experiences of flowing liquids reflected in vv. 2ab, 3ab. If taken as a comparison in its own right (there is no comparative particle *kĕ,* though), the intermediate line probably means the flowing down of Aaron's beard itself; but such a historicizing allusion may still be a later addition (cf., e.g., Keel, 8-9; Seybold, 26). In both cases, probably, priestly interests among the Aaronites motivated such a commentary. We are left, then, with two metaphors demonstrating the flow of blessed and life-giving liquids down from the top to the lower margins, from head to beard, from Hermon to Zion (thus at least in MT; and the final line seems to presuppose this reading. Is Mount Hermon considered superior to Zion in this context? cf. the "mountain of the north" in 48:2-3 [RSV 1-2]). Now, these metaphors cannot very well explain the peaceful coexistence of "brothers." On the contrary, that blissful state could only be a consequence of blessings from above. They in turn are visualized in v. 3cd. The inner logic of the psalm, therefore, runs counter to the sequence of the text. First, there is the blessing of Yahweh from Zion, then this blessing runs down to all who meet at the sanctuary, therefore they may be called "happy" (although the standard expression of BEATITUDE, *'ašrê,* is missing; cf. 1:1). The few lines of Psalm 133 lead in a liturgical manner to Yahweh's favorable "command" (*ṣwh,* Piel, v. 3c: in connection with "blessing" also in Lev 25:21; Deut 28:8), building up, as it were, the expectations of the community: people know about undisturbed togetherness, and wonder sometimes, how to achieve it — by the grace of Yahweh!

## *Genre*

The last line of Psalm 133 being the climax and key to the whole text, I propose ANNOUNCEMENT OF BLESSING as a genre designation (for "blessing" see W. J. Urbrock, *ABD* I, 755-61). The audience addressed from the beginning but not explicitly mentioned receives this proclamation of Yahweh's grace. Yahweh's faithful are to learn that Zion is the source of blessing. Saying this I do put aside the interesting idea of Seybold (*Wallfahrtspsalmen,* 26-27; see listing at Psalm 120) that there had first been a felicitating text consisting of vv. 1bc, 2ab, 3ab, 3e, with no traces of religious conceptualization, a simple WISDOM SAYING, which later on was molded into a congregational blessing by adding vv. 2cd, 3cd. I hold more likely the genesis sketched above: the announcement of blessing in v. 3cde was the liturgical point of departure, attracting diverse popular sayings and metaphors used for illustration of Yahweh's blessings. Gunkel's observation (p. 570) that "a living together of brothers" (v. 1) originally implied economic cooperation in a large family (cf. Deut 25:5) is helpful to understand the social-historical dimensions of the saying. We have to add a reference to the ideal of communal solidarity fostered in early Jewish congregations (cf. Leviticus 25) to grasp later social implications.

Berlin holds a similar view on the psalm, relating the metaphors, however, more to the promised land and Zion ("main theme is the unification of the land. . . . Ps 133 describes the land in terms of human features," p. 145). Loretz names the poem a "Trinklied" ("drinking song") coming out of a special sacred festival. He too denies a family background of the first line. Zenger, for his part, reviews principal lines of interpretation and highlights the spirit of brotherhood glowing within this little poem.

## Setting

Are we allowed to point to the congregation of Yahweh believers as the place of origin and transmission for Psalm 133? The general justification of answering in the affirmative lies in the fact that the Psalter hardly contains any texts not used in worship assemblies of the postexilic period. More specific evidence includes the message of the closing line v. 3cd, secondary priestly interests patent in v. 2cd, and the development from "profane" to more "spiritual" outlooks, which in reality reflects a process of assimilating the "profane" into the "spiritual." Thus the psalm was probably composed and used in the communal situation of postexilic Judaism. This does not preclude the notion, however, that the image of "brothers living peacefully together" goes back to real family experience. According to ancient Israelite ideals even married brothers cultivated paternal family inheritance as long as possible (cf. Gen 13:5-6). The present place of Psalm 133 in the collection of Psalms of Ascent is warranted by the concluding line, the blessings of Yahweh on Zion, the destination of pilgrimages.

## Intention

Pointing toward Jerusalem as the source of divine blessings, our psalm wants to alert the congregation as to the effects of orienting themselves toward the God on Zion, from "whom all blessings flow." These blessings are said to reach the lowlands of human relations and fertilize them. Congregational brotherhood has always been highly valued in Jewish-Christian tradition, many times supplementing or replacing family relations. In fact, due to centuries-old structuring of both religious bodies along the values of (patriarchal) clanlike lineage systems, the intimate group perspectives of love and solidarity have dominated by far the social teachings of Jewish and Christian corporations (the latter, however, after the Constantinian turnover were superseded by state law).

## Bibliography

P. Auffret, "Essai sur la structure littéraire du psaume 133," *BN* 27 (1985) 22-34; A. Berlin, "On the Interpretation of Psalm 133," in *Directions in Biblical Hebrew Poetry* (ed. E. Follis; Sheffield: JSOT Press, 1987) 141-47; A. Goldberg, "Form-Analysis of Midrashic Literature as a Method of Description," *JJS* 36 (1985) 159-74; H. C. Gossmann, "Unter Geschwistern," *Zeitschrift für Mission* 23 (1997) 221-23; H. Gunkel, "Psalm 133," in *Beiträge zur alttestamentlichen Wissenschaft* (*Fest.* K. Budde; ed. K. Marti; BZAW 34; Giessen: Töpelmann, 1920) 69-74; O. Keel, "Kultische Brüderlichkeit — Ps 133," *Freiburger Zeitschrift für Philosophie und Theologie* 23 (1976) 68-80; O. Loretz, "Die Ugaritistik in der Psalmeninterpretation," *UF* 4 (1972) 167-69; idem, "*marzihu* im ugaritischen und biblischen Ahnenkult," in *Mesopotamia — Ugaritica — Biblica* (*Fest.* K. Bergerhof; ed. M. Dietrich, et al.; Neukirchen-Vluyn: Neukirchener Verlag, 1993) 93-144; S. Norin, "Psalm 133, Zusammenhang und Datierung," *ASTI* 11 (1977/78) 90-95; J. P. M. van der Ploeg, "Notes sur quelques psaumes," in *Mélanges bibliques et orientaux* (*Fest.* M. Delcor; ed. A Caquot, et al.; Neukirchen-Vluyn: Neukirchener Verlag; Kevelaer: Butzon & Bercker, 1985) 425-30; J.-M. Rosenstiehl, "Un commentaire du Psaume 133 à l'époque intertestamentaire," *RHPR* 59 (1979) 559-65; D. T. Tsumura, "Sorites in Psalm 133,2-3a," *Bib* 61 (1980) 416-17; W. G. E. Watson, "The Hidden Simile in Psalm 133," *Bib* 60 (1979) 108-9; G. Wilson, "The Qumran Psalms Scroll Reconsidered: Analysis of the Debate," *CBQ* 47 (1985) 624-42; E. Zenger, "Vom Segen der Brüderlichkeit," in *Der Weg zum Menschen* (*Fest.* A. Deissler; ed. R. Mosis, et al.; Freiburg: Herder, 1989) 173-82; Z. Zevit, "Psalms at the Poetic Precipice," *HAR* 10 (1987) 351-66.

# Psalm 134:
# Blessings

## Structure

|  | MT | NRSV |
|---|---|---|
| I. Superscription | 1a | - |
| II. Summons to praise | 1b-2 | 1-2 |
| III. Blessing | 3 | 3 |

Psalm 134 is the last song in the collection called "Songs of Ascent"; its SUPERSCRIPTION is the normal one of the preceding specimens in that cluster (→ Psalm 120). The psalm at hand is very short, comprising only 23 words (over against 17 in Psalm 117), all phonemes counted.

The structure of our little psalm is lucid enough: the first three lines are a SUMMONS TO PRAISE, more exactly to BLESS (vv. 1b-2), being issued by an unidentified speaker and directed to the "servants of Yahweh" (v. 1c). The fourth and closing line (v. 3) addresses individuals (second-person masculine singular suffix in v. 3a with the verb *brk*, Piel, "to bless") qualifying for a straight BLESSING. Each of these details needs some scrutiny and explication.

The verb used to articulate the summons to praise is the same as the one expressing Yahweh's blessing, an important and conscious coincidence, it seems. The "servants of Yahweh" are called upon to "bless Yahweh," their God (vv. 1b, 2b; for other summonses with *brk* instead of *hll* or *ydh* see 103:1-2, 20-

22; 104:1; 135:19-21). Indeed, this phrase contains the central affirmation of section II of the psalm, being its first and last colon. What does it mean to "bless Yahweh"? According to ancient beliefs the deity expected praise and acknowledgment from his or her followers. This kind of reverence was not a formality but full of substantial significance. Applause and veneration in effect constituted authority and power of the supreme Deity, as many psalms clearly demonstrate (→ Psalms 29; 96; 98; 148; etc.). Indeed, Yahweh could be visualized as "enthroned on the praises of Israel" (22:4 [RSV 3]). These very ancient concepts, found widely also in ancient Near Eastern religions before Israel (cf. the hymnic traditions of Mesopotamia and Egypt, e.g., in *ANET;* Seux; Kaiser, ed., *TUAT* II; Burkert and Stolz; listing at Additional Bibliography, section B; → Psalms 29; 104), were kept in vigor even in less mythicizing times. As Mauss puts it in his classical study of the implications of giving and receiving (*The Gift;* listing at Additional Bibliography, section B), there is a deeply entrenched sense among humans to balance gifts with countergifts, and this basic scheme also applies for theological thinking, in spite of all Protestant insistence on "grace alone." The full verbal expression "Bless the Lord" was also condensed into a short version: "Blessed be Yahweh" (*bārûk yhwh;* see Blessing Formula). The imperative "bless" (v. 1a) is preceded by the deictic exclamation *hinnēh,* "behold," which seems rather odd at this place. Normally, the lexeme seems to have an instructional intention (→ Ps 133:1). Some commentators believe it to have originated by scribal error due to the influence of Psalm 133. As the texts stands now, we may consider *hinnēh* as a reinforcement of the imperative "bless!"

The addressees of the summons are called "servants of Yahweh," and they are described as performing nightly cultic ministrations at "Yahweh's house" (vv. 1cde, 2a). "Servants" (*'ăbādîm*) in late psalm recitation became a designation for the faithful community at large (cf. 19:12, 14 [RSV 11, 13]; 34:23 [RSV 22]; 69:18, 37 [RSV 17, 36]; 79:2, 10; 86:4, 16; 90:13, 16; Gen 50:17; Exod 32:13; Deut 9:27; Isa 54:17; etc.; H. Ringgren [*TWAT* V, 982-1012] largely ignores this usage; he points out individual self-designation of suppliants in the Psalms and Dtr reference to the prophets as "servants" of Yahweh [pp. 1000, 1002-3]). "To stand in the house of Yahweh at night" (v. 1cd; the longer text of LXX has likely been influenced by Ps 135:2) need not refer to priestly or Levitical activity (cf. Deut 10:8; 18:7; priests are likely to be linked to the altar, and the Second Temple is called a "prayer house" for all people: 1 Kgs 8:29-53; Isa 56:7; against Gunkel, 572-73), but does describe the general attitude of adoration (cf. Deut 29:9; Neh 8:5-7 [the people also raise their hands in prayer]; 9:3; in contrast the people are "sitting" while waiting for a decision, Ezra 10:9). Nightly hymn singing of the community is also attested in Isa 30:29: "There you shall sing in the night as at a holy feast." In short, there is no evidence for the hypothesis that vv. 1-2 address priests. On the contrary, all the congregation is called upon to praise and thus strengthen Yahweh in his sovereignty and power. The "servants" of Yahweh stand in his house (the parallel affirmation in Ps 135:2 speaks more precisely about the temple "courts") praising him in joint adoration — a self-portrayal of the temple community.

Part III of our psalm then inverts the direction of blessing (cf. 133:3cde), that spiritual transference of power. Now the officiant of the service speaks in the name of Yahweh, communicating to each individual member of the congregation the strengthening patronage of Israel's God, residing on Zion (v. 3). "Yahweh may bless you" is the most compact expression of this divine attention and influence. Exactly this formula occurs with some frequency in Dtr discourse: cf. Deut 14:24, 29; 15:4, 10; 16:15; 23:21; 24:19. Other examples include Ruth 2:4, a beautiful specimen of a divine blessing used as a greeting formula (a different wording in Ps 129:8b), the Aaronite blessing of Num 6:24, and, of course, the other extant passage of the Psalter identical with v. 3a, Ps 128:5. My conclusion is this: "Yahweh may bless you" can be a down-to-earth greeting and a highly cultic blessing, depending on the communicative situation. Several inscriptions found on Israelite territory in recent decades contain wishes for blessing: "He may bless you and guard you . . ." (cf. Renz and Röllig, I, 62, 454, 455; Conrad, *TUAT* II, 561-64, 929). In our psalm, obviously, the wish has cultic implications. "From Zion," it is true, is possibly matched by "from Samaria," etc., in a few inscriptions. Hymnic attribution "he who made heaven and earth" (v. 3b), however, sounds like a genuine cultic formulation (cf. H. Weippert, *Schöpfer Himmels und der Erden* [Stuttgart: Katholisches Bibelwerk, 1981]).

## Genre

Psalm 134 is a doubled blessing going two ways, from the community to Yahweh, and from Yahweh on Zion to the community. Perhaps we should call the psalm a BLESSING EXCHANGE, a two-way blessing, for that is what it really represents. Psalms 103 and 104 in part use a similar vocabulary, but the blessing of Yahweh for his people is implicit, not made explicit by the formulaic expression "may he bless you." This very formula proves to be a long-standing element of worship, as pointed out in regard to 121:7; 128:5; Num 6:24; and the extrabiblical texts cited above. The exact wording "he [God] may bless you" (*yĕbārekĕkā*) within the Psalter occurs only in v. 3 and 128:5. Otherwise it is a favorite expression of Deuteronomy, in narrational and preaching discourse (cf. Deut 14:24, 29;15:4, 10; 16:15; 23:21; 24:19). Its use among people for a greeting can be deduced, e.g., from 2 Kgs 4:29.

## Setting

One wonders why our psalm insists on that explicit two-way concept of Yahweh and the community blessing each other. There may be special liturgical or festive reasons for this scheme that we do not know. The psalm in itself except for the redactional heading does not suggest any special linkage with the pilgrimage to Jerusalem. But if we consider a later use of Psalms 120–134 for festive wanderings to the Holy City, then Seybold's suggestion makes sense: our collection of psalms may reflect in a way the procession toward Jerusalem, arrival, stay, and departure from there (Seybold, *Wallfahrtspsalmen,* 72; see listing at Psalm 120). On the other hand, those who locate the psalms gathered in this collection at the steps of the temple precincts, visualizing choirs to have performed a kind of graded ascent to the holy grounds, also may be right (cf. Seidel; see listing at Psalm 120). And there are other more or less plausible theories about the "life situation" of these psalms (e.g., Keet, *Study,* 162-68: festival of firstfruits; Viviers, "Coherence," 288: "meditation book" or "'book of confidence'" for cultic and private use, composed by one gifted poet; etc.; for both see listing at Psalm 120).

## Intention

Distinguishing between uses before and after completing the "Ascents" collection we may say that Psalm 134 first wanted to be an incentive for the community to enter the cultic realm of blessing. Stimulating communal acknowledgment of Yahweh by the faithful gathered in worship was tantamount to getting ready to receive the good gifts of Israel's God. Later, in the situation of pilgrimage this same scheme was applied by those who came to Jerusalem from far away, to pray at the temple. Pilgrims, of course, needed special comfort and strength on their way to and from the dwelling place of their God.

## Bibliography

W. F. Albright, "Notes on Psalm 68 and 134," in *Interpretationes ad Vetus Testamentum* (*Fest.* S. Mowinckel; ed. N. A. Dahl, et al.; Oslo: Fabritius & Sonner, 1955) 1-12; P. Auffret, "Note on the Literary Structure of Ps 134," *JSOT* 45 (1989) 87-89; F. Horst, "Segen und Segenshandlung in der Bibel," *EvT* 7 (1947) 23-27 (repr. in idem, *Gottes Recht: Gesammelte Studien zum Recht im AT* [ed. H. W. Wolff; TBü 12; Munich: Kaiser, 1961] 188-202); J. Magonet, "Convention and Creativity: The Phrase 'Maker of Heaven and Earth' in the Psalms," in *"Open Thou Mine Eyes . . ."* (*Fest.* W. G. Braude; ed. H. Blumenberg, et al.; Hoboken: Ktav, 1992) 139-53.

## Psalm 135:
## Hymn to Yahweh

### Structure

|  | MT | NRSV |
|---|---|---|
| I. Summons to praise | 1-3 | 1-3 |
| II. Hymnic chant I | 4 | 4 |
| III. Hymnic chant II | 5 | 5 |
| IV. Praise of Yahweh | 6-12 | 6-12 |
| V. Prayer chant | 13 | 13 |
| VI. Hymnic chant III | 14 | 14 |
| VII. Polemics against other gods | 15-18 | 15-18 |
| VIII. Summons to praise | 19-21 | 19-21 |

A SUPERSCRIPTION is missing (cf. Psalms 1–2; 71; 93–97; etc.). The song is composed of hymnic elements (vv. 1-14, 19-21) and a polemical passage (vv. 15-18) also found in 115:4-8 (hymnic vv. 19-21 have their counterpart in 115:9-11 as well). Correspondences with Psalm 134 occur in vv. 1-2, 19-20; with 136:17-22 in vv. 10-11. Affinities to other Hebrew writings abound (Allen, 224: "heterogeneity" of the text; Crüsemann, *Studien*, 127-29, overstresses, however, the basic difference between "imperative" and "participle" hymns; see listing at "Introduction to Cultic Poetry").

The SUMMONS TO PRAISE (vv. 1-3) with the imperative of *hll*, Piel, "acclaim, eulogize," is a common hymnic overture in the ultimate sections of the Psalter. In the final collection of psalms this imperative plural *hallĕlû*, "praise," occurs but once (22:24 [RSV 23]) before 104:35; and this particular psalm being introduced by the imperative singular of *brk*, "bless" (104:1), the *hll* summons in the plural may well belong to Psalm 105, as LXX has it. Anyway, Psalms 104–106 in the MT tradition show traces of *hll* framing, while Psalm 107 opens with the imperative plural of *ydh*, Hiphil, "give thanks." (Some exegetes want to make this a generic difference.) Thereafter, clusters of songs increasingly use the *hll* type of opening: Psalms 111–117; 118 apparently joins the group with a *ydh* imperative plural (thus Psalms 113–118 are known to have been used in the synagogue as the "great Hallel" collection, particularly in the Passover liturgies; cf. Matt 26:30; → Psalm 113), Psalms 146–150, the so-called final Hallel, with Psalms 148 and 150 practically consisting of *hll* summonses to the exclusion of other imperatives (→ Psalm 146). There is an explosion of hallelujah singing toward the end of the Psalter (cf. Brueggemann, *Psalms*, 189-213; listing at Additional Bibliography, section C).

Psalm 135 is placed in the midst of non-*hll* psalms (Psalms 119–145) presenting itself only at the beginning (vv. 1-3) as a solitary example of the category in question among wisdom and complaint genres. It ends up with a hymnic summons of the *brk* type (vv. 19-21) and is followed by a solid thanksgiving song introduced by *ydh*, Hiphil, plural imperatives ("give thanks," 136:1-3) and later by an individual thanksgiving (Psalm 138). The opening of our psalm consequently, in spite of seeming dislocation, fits into the general array of hymnic elements (see "Introduction to Cultic Poetry," section D).

But some details are noteworthy. V. 1 looks like an almost exact copy of 113:1 with only the sequence of cola changed around. V. 2a has its parallel in 134:1d, but the continuation in v. 2b is surprisingly different, resembling 92:14 (RSV 13); 116:19a. Fragments of v. 3 seem to be echoed in 54:8 (RSV 6); 66:2, 4; 68:5 (RSV 4); 133:1; 136:1. It would be misleading, however, to think in terms of literary dependencies from one psalm to the other, one "author" to the next. Individual authorship in the modern sense should not be made a criterion in psalm analysis. Liturgical language is always very traditional, time and again using proven as well as approved formulas and texts. Unless there are errors or interests of copyists involved in those text similarities, we have to assume communal worship to be the fertile ground of such usage. One item, however, does call for special attention in vv. 1-3. All of a sudden a first-person plural suffix appears in the midst of a summons to praise (v. 2b: "house of our God"). Similar ruptures happen in 18:32 (RSV 31); 50:3; 92:14 (RSV 13), the last passage also mentioning the temple in connection with "our God." The isolated expression "house of our God" outside the Psalter is heavily concentrated in Ezra 8:17-33 and Neh 10:33-40 (RSV 32-39). What does this evidence mean to us? The formulation "our God" may have been formulaic and used with frequency, sneaking in perhaps at times when "God" was spoken about. Still, the occurrence of a "we" form in the middle of plural summons to praise and once more in v. 5b (*ʾădōnênû,* "our Lord") definitely points to communal usage, strange as it may seem when considering a summons of one liturgical leader directed to the worshiping congregation. A possible explanation is this: the leader calling the congregation to praise Yahweh may use first-person plural forms integrating him- or herself with the audience. In v. 5a the "I" giving testimony to the greatness of Yahweh apparently, too, is part of the "we" group of v. 5b; this time the individual may be the member of community closing ranks with the group.

Two lines, each one headed by the particle *kî,* follow the summons to praise (vv. 4-5). In hymnic contexts the likelihood that *kî* introduces not a motive clause but, as an exclamatory particle, the hymn proper (cf. Crüsemann, *Studien,* 32-35; listing at "Introduction to Cultic Poetry": "Yes . . .") is strong indeed. It may well apply in our case, too, and in a double way at that. The *kî* lines at hand are quite different in liturgical respects. We have first a confessional shout of the community, lauding Yahweh's choice of Jacob/Israel (v. 4). Now, this combination of the two names of the community's ancestor is an honorific self-appellation. Early Jewish faith preferred to anchor Jewish identity with this remote antecedent, according to Genesis tradition, the grandson of Abraham (cf. Pss 14:7; 53:7 [RSV 6]; 78:5, 21, 71; 105:10, 23; 147:19; also in the Dtr tradition: Römer, *Väter;* listing at Additional Bibliography, section B). The topic, poetic formulation, and theological outlook of v. 4 would make it an ideal communal hymn to be shouted by the community, notwithstanding its neutral wording (no "we" discourse; cf. election vocabulary, esp. *sĕgullāh,* "property," in Exod 19:5; Deut 7:6; 14:2; 26:18). While v. 4 thus may be an "objective" praising line for the congregation, v. 5 refers explicitly to the members of the worshiping assembly, and, interestingly enough, both in singular and plural first persons. This line assumes a confessional stance: "Yes, I know that Yahweh is great, our Lord is superior to all gods!" The combination of singular and plural, in fact, is an excellent example of the contemporary structure of the community: early Jewish associations practiced a spiritual group life in which the individual was responsible for his and her credal stand. The worshiping assembly consisted of (as it does in Jewish-Christian tradition to this very day) persons forming a cohesive group. As far as v. 5 is concerned, it may have served as a second hymnic line, probably for all people gathered. Two hymnic affirmations to be sung by the congregation, without intermediary summons, may seem strange, but is surely possible under the assumption that all these *kî* lines were first intoned by a liturgical leader (cf. Exod 15:21; Ps 118:2-4) and then repeated again and again by the crowd.

This liturgical system may have worked also with more extensive hymnic texts, whenever they were sung not by choirs but by the people. General knowledge of the liturgical agenda cannot be presupposed, nor the existence of hymnals for popular use in the precincts of the temple. Consequently, we may imagine a leader pronouncing a hymn line by line, and the congregation responding. This may well be true for vv. 6-12, which enumerate standard eulogies of Yahweh, telling in a loose sequence some of his mighty manifestations. Indeed, the disparity of articulation (adjective, participles, verbs in the perfect tense, verbs in the perfect with prefixed relative particle šĕ-) as well as fragmentary contents (considering the wealth of traditions in the OT) call for our attention. First, there is a general affirmation of Yahweh's superior power to perform anything he likes (v. 6), which is expressed in so many words also of royal potentates (Qoh 8:3b). When speaking about Yahweh such statements seem kerygmatic or confessional in character (cf. Isa 55:11; Joel 1:14). There are many other ways to pronounce the sovereignty of God and deride other powers as inferior (cf. Isa 40:22-26; 46:5-10: the latter passage ends: "everything to my liking I perform"; Job 38–41; Psalms 29; 82; 96; 97; 104; etc.). The special manner of emphasizing that the supreme authority is able to execute any project is a theologoumenon by itself that plays a vital role in subsequent discussions about the omnipotence of God. Formally, v. 6 falls into three parts (oversize line? prosaic diction?), because the composer took pains to delineate the universal realm of Yahweh's reign, and because he or she uses a three-word complex to specify the grammatical object: "Everything he likes" (kōl 'ăšer ḥāpēṣ) instead of speaking in tight poetic language (cf., e.g., 95:3-5, where a few small words have possibly inflated a text still more terse). Yahweh governs in heaven and on earth (v. 6b), which is a comprehensive formula of universal rule (cf. 134:3b). Possibly, some transmitter has added, rather redundantly, "over the seas and all the (chaotic) depths" (v. 6c).

The general eulogy is followed by hymnic affirmations about Yahweh differently formulated and apparently taken from different traditions (there may be a chance that the composers already used Hebrew Scripture). One verse in three parts again (tricola? prosaic style?) deals with creational topics like clouds, rain, lightnings, winds (v. 7; cf. Psalm 104) — traditional fields of activities for ancient Near Eastern weather-gods like Baal and Hadad (cf. Smith, History; listing at Additional Bibliography, section B). The next two lines enter the field of salvation history, but very cautiously so, being dedicated exclusively to the liberation from Egypt (vv. 8-9; cf. the richness of salvation history in Psalms 78; 105; 136). Both v. 8 and v. 10 begin with that aramaizing manner of prefixing a relative pronoun to a verbal form, šĕhikkāh, "he who smote"; perhaps these two lines, which also preserve a compact poetical form, were the nucleus of this hymn. V. 9, in contrast, seems overstretched in an effort to describe exactly who were the recipients of Yahweh's miraculous signs in Exodus 5–12: the Egyptians, Pharaoh, and his officials (v. 9bc). Thus vv. 8-9 now form a pair, with one line referring to Exod 12:29 and the other possibly to Exod 11:9 or, more likely, to Dtr reflections and preaching about the exodus theme (cf. Deut 4:34; 6:22; 7:19; 13:2; 26:8; 28:46; 29:2; 34:11; see also Neh 9:10). The next thematic unit comprises three lines (vv. 10-12; v. 11 was apparently also augmented by an enumerating explanation) dealing with victories in the East Jordan area (cf. Num 21:21-31; for the enemy kings Sihon and Og see also Ps 136:19-20; Deut 1:4; 2:24, 26, 30-32; etc.) and the gift of the homeland. Significantly, the same matter in the same sequence of events and with the same vocabulary is also treated in → Ps 136:17-22. If there has been a "literary" connection between the two adjacent passages, priority of composition may go to Psalm 136, because it looks to be the more complete and uniform text. Psalm 135, on the other hand, may have borrowed considerably also from Psalm 115, since v. 6 of our present psalm does have some affinity with 115:3, and vv. 15-20 look almost like a copy of 115:4-8. The giving of the land in v. 12 (136:21a, 22a) in particular carries much weight; the words in both versions are almost identical, only the very last lexeme differing slightly, perhaps due to scribal error in one or the other direction: 'ammô, "his people," in v. 12; 'abdô, "his servant," in 136:22a. The affirmation runs: "He gave [them] their [i.e., the enemies'] land as inheritance, an inheritance for Israel his people" (v. 12), a chiastic, concise, and well-built saying with three words to each colon (in Hebrew; cf. more elaborate, prosaic but substantially equal formulations: Deut 4:38; 15:4; 19:10; 20:16; 21:23; 24:4; 25:19; 26:1; 29:7, the last passage even presupposes explicitly the East Jordan conquest). As already stated in other cases of apparent borrowings (→ Psalms 31 and 71, or 57; 60; and 108; etc.), we have to think about liturgical backgrounds and worship-oriented text production when interpreting these resemblances.

The "objective" hymnic part closes with v. 12, and the psalm for a short while turns to adoration in the form of prayer (v. 13). Crüsemann calls this "direct-address discourse" (> Psalm 8). In our case the name of Yahweh is eulogized, perhaps an indication of the late origin of the psalm (cf. Exod 3:15). The divine "name" (Heb. *šēm*) gradually assumed the hypostatical qualities of Yahweh himself. Our verse already attributes age-long persistence to that proper name (cf. 44:9 [RSV 8]; 52:11 [RSV 9]; 72:17 [the king's name]; 83:19 [RSV 18]). V. 13 may have been spoken in a worship liturgy by the official leading the service. But in v. 14 another line introduced by *kî* (cf. vv. 4-5) comes up. It is neutral in language and conceptualization, asserting Yahweh's juridical authority over his people (not over all the nations). The expectancy is to have in Yahweh a merciful judge and a just one, as far as the defense of Israel against dominant groups is concerned. The *kî* at the beginning of the line could be prompting the congregation to join in the ritual again. If this is true, we would have three lines (vv. 4-5, 14) of explicit congregational hymn singing in Psalm 135.

POLEMICS against other gods and a final SUMMONS to worship (vv. 15-20) occur in slightly changed parameters over against → Psalm 115. The difference between the two psalms is that Psalm 115 makes conflict and incompatibility between gods and Yahweh the main theme (cf. the overarching "plot" description in 115:2-3), while Psalm 135 is much more reserved in tackling these problems explicitly. But vv. 4-5 (at least in retrospect from vv. 15-18) also pose a main issue: Yahweh has elected Israel, and he is superior to all the other gods (cf. esp. v. 5b). By way of extolling the unlimited power of Yahweh (v. 6) and lauding him for his works and acts (vv. 7-12), the deities of the contemporary (Babylonian or Persian) imperium are challenged, and all of a sudden they are also denounced and ridiculed (vv. 15-18). That this kind of attack is comparable with polemic passages of Second Isaiah has been observed earlier

(→ Psalm 115). That one polemical line of 115:4-8, i.e., 115:7, is missing in Psalm 135 has also been mentioned in commenting on Psalm 115. Has our song preserved an older and shorter version of the diatribe against other gods? Or was the line about dysfunctional "hands" and "feet" of idols (115:7) deemed unnecessary after strong affirmations about the deities' mouths, eyes, ears, and noses (vv. 15-18)? The final SUMMONS TO BLESS (vv. 19-20) is not so close in its formulation to similar affirmations of Psalm 115. Still, the affinity of mind and interests between the two passages is clearly visible (cf. vv. 19-20 with their counterpart 115:9-11). We may note that the summons to praise here is articulated by the verb *brk*, Piel, "to bless" (cf. hymns with *brk* introductions, e.g., 67:2 [RSV 1]; 96:2; 103:1-2; 104:1, 134:1-2), which stands in a certain tension with the *hll* opening of our psalm. To close a psalm by a renewed summons to praise is a regular characteristic of hymns. But as a rule the same verbs occur at the beginning and end of such a hymn (cf. 103:1-2, 20-22; 104:1, 35). The final shout of v. 21, "hallelujah," may be redactional (cf. LXX, linking it to the following psalm); MT scribal tradition detaches it from the body of the text.

Looking back at the structure of our song, we cannot help recognizing its diversities of forms and content, meter and poetic style. Also, frequent intertextual ties seem to link Psalm 135 with other psalms and the Pentateuch. Most commentators admit, however, a "skillful" (Allen, 226) work of composition. From a liturgical point of view, at least, the apparent discrepancies are not so grave. We can imagine alternating voices shouting and singing, intoning and reciting parts of the text (Seybold, 503: "cantata"). Even the oversize lines (vv. 6-7, 9, 11; note, however, that, e.g., Mowinckel [*Tricola*, 29, 54; see listing at "Introduction to Psalms"] deletes and reorganizes words, to come up with regular bicola) may not be just literary in character but recitable liturgical affirmations. In this fashion the liturgist may have sung vv. 1-3, 19-21, and intoned, with the congregation repeating after him, vv. 4-5, 6-12, 13-14, 15-18. Other attributions are possible and are widely proposed, but the basic liturgical model of cantor and audience alternating seems quite plausible in this psalm.

## Genre

The category of HYMNS is a large one, comprising a great variety of contents and occasions to acclaim God's actions, essence, and attributes (see "Introduction to Cultic Poetry," section D). Psalm 135 concentrates on Yahweh's deeds for Israel (vv. 8-14), to the exclusion, even ridicule, of any other deities (vv. 15-18). "Yahweh will judge his people, he will have compassion on his servants" (v. 14) corresponds literally to Deut 32:36, and in both passages the affirmation is an accentuated assertion of trust, hope, and praise, in consequence of the preceding extolment. Therefore we may call the song a HYMN TO YAHWEH alone, apparently in the wake of exilic Dtr theology (on "exclusiveness" of God see J. J. Scullion, *ABD* II, 1041-48). Derision of foreign gods, i.e., those of the politically dominant nations, constitutes the other side of the coin. Ancient people (who knows, even modern ones) would live in binary, mutually exclusive systems, requiring condemnations of evildoers and unjust ones (→ Psalms 109;

115). Chances are that the composers and transmitters of Psalm 135 already used extant sacred pentateuchal and psalmic texts in arranging this piece of liturgy (cf. Newman, *Praying;* listing at Additional Bibliography, section B).

## Setting

The historical situation to be deduced from the psalm's outlook and theological interests is that of a multireligious society with competing religious and political systems. Israel seems to be struggling to maintain her identity as a Yahweh community. The temple functions (v. 2) as a sacred place where Yahweh's people adore his name in prayer and commemoration (cf. 1 Kgs 8:22-53; Isa 56:7: "house of prayer"; no trace of sacrifices in Psalm 135). Perhaps the reference to the "house of our God" may be understood as a symbolic reference to the distant Jerusalem center, too. In that case the psalm could have been recited in the diaspora as well. Prayer services of Jewish congregational assemblies, in any case, are the particular background of Psalm 135.

Recent discussions have emphasized the contextual meaning of our liturgy in the Psalter. Close affinities exist with Psalms 134 and 136; the latter is often called a "twin" of Psalm 135. Zenger reviews theories about the composition of the fifth book of Psalms, and puts up his own vision: Psalms 135 and 136 are climactically attached to the Psalms of Ascent (120–134), meant to bring in the praise of all the nations in a universal eulogy of the overall Lord ("Composition," 92-93; see listing at Psalm 107). Apparently, wishful theological thinking orients this interpretation, because the "ones standing in the temple courts" (v. 2b) are certainly not "heathen" foreigners, but exclusively faithful Judahites (cf. vv. 2a, 19-20).

## Intention

Wrestling with the problems of religious plurality in a politically and economically "globalized" empire, the leaders of the congregation (scribes, priests, officiants) and perhaps the members, too, wanted to promote and guarantee exclusive veneration of Yahweh as a means of preserving Israelite identity. They emphasize the unique power of Israel's God and his marvelous concern for his people. Defeating legendary kings and handing over their territory to the Israelites (vv. 10-12; cf. the Dtr tradition history of Sihon and Og: Josh 2:10; 9:10; 12:2-6; 13:10-12, 21, 27, 30; Judg 11:19-21; Neh 9:22) for the contemporary community is the most trustworthy signal of Yahweh's support and benevolence, which, apparently, needs to be demonstrated again and again. Preservation of land, temple, and community over against pressures from other gods and aligned nations is the goal of this hymn.

# Bibliography

E. Baumann, "Strukturuntersuchungen im Psalter II," *ZAW* 62 (1950) 144-48; T. E. Fretheim, "The Color of God: Israel's God-Talk and Life Experience," *Word & World* 6 (1986) 256-65; R. Lux, "'Die Rache des Mythischen.' Überlegungen zur Rezeption des Mythischen im Alten Testament," *Zeichen der Zeit* 38 (1984) 157-70; D. E. McGregor, "The Fish and the Cross," *Point Series* 1 (1982) 1-139.

# Psalm 136:
## Communal Thanksgiving

### Structure

|                                | MT    | NRSV  |
| ------------------------------ | ----- | ----- |
| I. Summons to give thanks      | 1-3   | 1-3   |
| II. Thanks for creation        | 4-9   | 4-9   |
| III. Thanks for liberation     | 10-15 | 10-15 |
| IV. Thanks for protection      | 16-22 | 16-22 |
| V. Thanks for sustenance       | 23-25 | 23-25 |
| VI. Summons to give thanks     | 26    | 26    |

One of the psalms without a SUPERSCRIPTION (→ Psalms 33; 71; 93), our song begins immediately with a threefold SUMMONS TO GIVE THANKS (vv. 1-3). The verb used is typical: Hiphil plural imperative *ydh,* "to thank" (cf. 30:5 [RSV 4]; 33:2; 97:12; 100:4; 105:1; 106:1; 107:1). In particular, Psalm 118 will prove to be a close parallel to our psalm (cf. for the time being 118:1, 29). Leaving aside, at this point, the stereotyped second colon of each line (*kî lĕʿôlām ḥasdô,* "his solidarity forever!"), we notice that the three summonses of vv. 1a, 2a, and 3a call for a eulogy of Yahweh, the supreme Lord; only the first colon differs a little from the two others in adding an exclamation (or motive clause?) *kî ṭôb,* "yes, good (he is)." The expression is formulaic (cf. 34:9 [RSV 8]; 52:11 [RSV 9]; 54:8 [RSV 6]; 63:4 [RSV 3]; 84:11 [RSV 10]); indeed, it seems to belong intimately to the longer hymnic affirmation "good he is, indeed, his solidarity forever!" (cf. 69:17 [RSV 16]; 100:5; 106:1; 107:1; 118:1, 29). Pondering all these examples of attributing goodness to Yahweh himself (cf. also Jer 33:11, a clear quotation of this liturgical expression; Nah 1:7), we realize a certain ambiguity of the formula in terms of its functions. *kî ṭôb* has some motivational force, but it may certainly serve as a cultic shout, even as a clear-cut interjection, in some contexts (cf. Pss 52:11 [RSV 9]; 54:8 [RSV 6]; 69:17 [RSV 16]; etc.). For our passage, therefore, we may claim that exclamatory function, too. Since the congregation apparently responded with *kî lĕʿôlām ḥasdô,* it is an open question whether *kî tob* was shouted by the officiant, by the people, or by both. The whole psalm obviously — MT separates every single summons from the congregational response by a wide lacuna, dividing the text into two columns — is a liturgical interplay between officiant and community.

The body of the hymn (HYMNIC AFFIRMATIONS or THANKSGIVINGS; cf. J. Limburg, *ABD* V, 522-36; Brueggemann, *Psalms,* 112-32, 189-213; see Additional Bibliography, section C) has 22 verses corresponding to 22 poetic lines, a conspicuous number: the total of letters in the Hebrew alphabet (cf. Psalms 25; 34; 119; 145, with slight irregularities in some texts). Thematically, there are two blocks of six (vv. 4-9, 10-15) and one of seven (vv. 16-22), as well as an appendix of three (vv. 23-25) lines.

The name of Yahweh has been accentuated so strongly in the opening part that it does not need to be repeated any more in vv. 4-25. The imperative summonses of vv. 1-3 are valid at least for vv. 4-22, so that the officiant or choir has only to formulate the praising colon: "to the one who alone does wonders" (v. 4a; the Hebrew text of Sirach 51 repeats the imperative "Give thanks" in every single line), and the congregation will sing the antiphone, v. 4b. All these praises are oriented quite naturally, in a liturgical sequence, to the one deity named at the beginning. The summons at the end of the psalm (v. 26) does not repeat the name of Yahweh either but chooses a new, summarizing title for him ("God of heavens").

Stylistically and liturgically all the eulogies are tuned to Yahweh, who is referred to in hymnic participles (cf. Gunkel, Westermann, Crüsemann, et al.) usually augmented by a prefixed *lĕ,* "to" (vv. 4-7, 10, 13, 16-17). Thus the summons to give thanks is followed by a long string of specifications: "To the one who wisely created the heavens" (v. 5a), "to the one who killed the Egyptian firstborn" (v. 10), "to the one who led his people in the wilderness" (v. 16), etc. This participial construction is typically hymnic (cf. "Introduction to Cultic Poetry," section 4D), and it constitutes the backbone of Psalm 136. All in all, as already indicated, we find eight of these expressions (vv. 4-7, 10, 13, 16-17), and one line commences with a plain participle without the preposition *lĕ* (v. 25); two lines are nothing but appositions (accusative objects) to participial phrases (vv. 8-9). This makes a total of 11 out of 22 lines composed in the manner of a participle hymn. The rest of the hymnic lines exhibit various verbal forms: consecutive imperfects (vv. 11, 18, 24), copulative perfects (vv. 14-15, 21), plain perfect (v. 23). Some other lines are fully dependent on one of these syntactic forms (vv. 12, 19-20, 22). Thus the first thematic block, eulogies on Yahweh the creator (vv. 4-9), is made up (not using a formalistic yardstick) completely of the participle type, God being the subject of all sentences.

The second block, liberation from Egypt, has two leading lines with participles (vv. 10, 13), but narrative and explicative verbal forms intervene. The third block, Yahweh's victorious leadership in the desert, puts two participles in front (vv. 16-17), but tells stories afterward. The last, the smallest subunit, has apparently lost track of the initial summons and the participle-with-*lĕ* construction, continuing the preceding hymnic affirmations with a relative clause (v. 23), referring to the salvation story (v. 24) and ending with a simple participle (v. 25). The grammatical subject remains throughout Yahweh, who is applauded all the time. Taking a purist view on style and form one might be tempted to conclude that our thanksgiving hymn developed from a pure participial construction into some degenerated form of mixed hymn. But this conclusion, I am certain, is unwarranted. While there may have been a preponderance of participial constructions in ancient hymn compositions as far as eulogizing Yahweh's qualities and performances was concerned, it is hard to believe that other modes of expressing thanks and praises were completely ruled out in hymnic attributions (cf. Psalms 8; 33; 104). Absolute uniformity of expression would be disastrous also in evensong liturgies. Since the specifying laudatory cola in Psalm 136 were likely sung or shouted by an individual voice, there was no eminent need for uniformity of wording. Another argument in our case concerns the shape and substance of the participial phrases themselves, which are not of perfect guise linguistically or structurally, as a closer look at the individual blocks of material will reveal.

The half-lines in vv. 4-9 are dedicated to the theme of creation. Three times a line opens with *lĕʿōśēh,* "to the one who made" (vv. 4, 5, 7), which seems rather awkward, considering the wealth of creation vocabulary (e.g., verbs like *brʾ,* "create"; *kûn,* "establish"; *yṣr,* "fashion"; etc.; cf. the respective articles in *TDOT* or *THAT*). The composers could easily have employed a diversity of verbs and images in this unit, which also limits creation to the making of cosmological entities. V. 4a, as it were, still poses as a broad general statement: "to do wondrous things" may mean anything on earth and in heaven Yahweh has accomplished (cf. in the Psalms: 40:6 [RSV 5]; 72:18; 75:2 [RSV 1]; 78:4, 11; 96:3; 98:1; 105:5; 106:7, 22; 107:8, 15, 21, 24, 31. Outside the Psalter: Exod 34:10; Josh 3:5; Job 5:9; 9:10; 37:5, 14; 42:3). Perhaps it served as an introduction for the whole range of laudations. But vv. 5-9 mention only creation of heaven, earth, and celestial bodies, in simple straightforward language. Are these factual, nonpoetic statements (cf. for contrast the language of Psalm 104; Job 38–41) dependent on Genesis 1, as many commentators suggest? The answer is impossible to find, because the mere enumeration of Yahweh's making the universe is not sufficient proof of literary dependence on the Priestly creation story. On the other hand, the detailed description of the "large lights, sun . . . moon, and stars, governing the night" does have a noteworthy affinity to Gen 1:16, only the latter text is more logical: "God made the two big lights: the larger one to govern the day, and the smaller one to govern the night, and [he made] the stars." MT's psalmic version does not keep separate the stars from the big lights (editors of *BHS* therefore want to delete the word). The argumentation could be, therefore, that vv. 7-9 are a somewhat clumsy condensation of Gen 1:16. We have to remember, however, that liturgical practice does not always allow for the finest possible language.

The second subunit (vv. 10-15) concentrates on the exodus story (cf. Exodus 12–15), presenting itself as eclectic, like the creation hymn of vv. 4-9. The psalm mentions the killing of the firstborn in Egypt (v. 10; cf. Exodus 11–12), omitting, in contrast to Ps 105:28-34, and in accordance with Ps 135:8, the preceding nine plagues. Then, after stating the exodus in a rather D manner (vv. 11-12; cf. Deut 4:34, 5:15; 7:19; 9:29; 26:8), the passage focuses on the division of the Reed Sea and the victory over Pharaoh (vv. 13-15). While the last line seems to be formulated in contact with Exod 14:27, the expression of v. 13 is unique in the context of the exodus story: Yahweh "cuts apart" the Sea of Reeds as if it were a piece of wood (cf. 2 Kgs 6:4). One is reminded of Marduk's cutting asunder the body of Tiamat after his victory over this chaos power (cf. *ANET*, 67 = *Enuma elish*, end of tablet IV). Perhaps there are mythological concepts behind our passage. On the whole, we have a formidable selection of exodus motifs in vv. 10-15, but not by a long shot the whole story. Other psalms are more elaborate, but also more mythological, about this very important event in Israel's salvation history (cf. 77:17-21 [RSV 16-20]; 106:8-11; 114:1-4; Exod 15:1-10).

Our third segment (vv. 16-22) has more general opening lines about Yahweh's leadership in the wilderness (v. 16; cf. Deut 8:2; 29:4; Jer 2:6; Am 2:10) and his slaying "great kings" (v. 17; cf. Ps 135:10: "mighty kings"). Generalizing reports or legends about victories over many kings have been brought together by the Deuteronomist in Joshua 10–12. There we find similar statements to our psalm: "All the kings he [i.e., Joshua] captured, and he smote them and killed them" (Josh 11:17b); "These are the kings of the land, whom the Israelites killed, and whose territories they occupied" (12:1a), "altogether they were 31 kings" (12:24b). Sihon, king of Heshbon, and Og, king of Bashan (cf. Rendtorff; J. C. Slayton, *ABD* VI, 22), play a role in these lists of defeated legendary adversaries (12:2-6; cf. Rendtorff), although their annihilation was past history already at the time of Joshua (cf. Num 21:21-34). But these two enemies who denied Israel free passage through their territories and had to suffer the consequences in the theological and homiletical tradition of old served as examples for the multitude of other local kings (cf. Deut 1:4; 2:26–3:11; 29:6; 31:4; Judg 11:19-21). This is exactly what happens also in vv. 18-20 of our psalm. The legendary, even mythological figures (cf. their designation as "giants" in Josh 13:12) have been made into exemplary prototypes of enemies, no doubt also with an eye on the great kings of Babylonia and Persia. The ancient potentates were defeated by Yahweh and the Israelites, and their lands were given to the people of Yahweh (vv. 21-22), a theme that is also the main concern of the book of Joshua (cf. Josh 10:42; 11:16, 23; 12:1; 13:1-33) as well as that of other Dtr material (cf. Num 21:31, 35; Deut 2:31).

On all counts the ultimate and much smaller unit (vv. 23-25) is something peculiar in this hymn. Stylistically the unit employs the only relative clause and, due to a different word order (preceding infinitive clause), the only plain perfect tense in our psalm (v. 23a). In addition, there is that singular unprefixed participle already mentioned (v. 25a). In terms of speaker reference vv. 23-24 are the only lines in the whole liturgy that reveal a first person plural, i.e., a communal voice intoning the song. Furthermore, thematically and theologically the three cola under scrutiny are not dealing with historical situations; they are apparently portraying their own, i.e., postexilic, times. Contemporary debasement and lowliness, as well as contemporary salvation experiences of the Yahweh community, are intimated in vv. 23-24, while v. 25 is a surprising outlook on Yahweh's universal benevolence in the spirit of Psalm 104. Thus the concluding colon of the array of 22 lines is the only one to open up this universal horizon. We may say that all the thanksgiving and praising done in the hymn leads up to this climax of contemporary, i.e., early Jewish, congregational praise. The enveloping summons to give thanks (v. 26) remembers and echoes the initial cluster of hymnic stimulations.

So far we have analyzed only the first cola of all the extant lines. Stereotyped *kî lě'ôlām ḥasdô,* "yes, his solidarity forever," which accompanies the text from beginning to end, being clearly marked by MT as a separate column, remains to be discussed. The introductory *kî,* "yes," should mark the hymnic response of a choir group or the whole congregation. We already referred to a number of psalm texts that prove a widespread use of this liturgical stereotype, which we may call a SELF-ASSURANCE FORMULA (cf. Pss 106:1; 107:1; 118:1-4; Jer 33:11). Asserting line by line the steadfast loyalty of Yahweh with his people, the liturgical litany presented here is the essential part of our psalm. In Ps 118:1-4 the response is demonstrably put into the mouths of parts of the congregation. In our present text we do not find that group differentiation. Therefore we may assume that the formula was chanted by all members assembled in worship. "Solidarity" of Yahweh with his community (often translated as "steadfast love," "grace," etc.) was the most essential guarantee of survival for all believers (cf. N. Glueck, *Hesed in the Bible* [ed. E. Epstein; tr. A. Gottschalk; Cincinnati: Hebrew Union College Press, 1967]; H.-J. Zobel, *TWAT* III, 48-71, esp. 63-64). The concept plays a large role in cultic texts, also in relation to covenant theology (without being fixed to them; cf. L. Perlitt, *Bundestheologie* [Neukirchen-Vluyn: Neukirchener Verlag, 1969]). Its ultimate rootage is probably family relationships and responsibilities. Remarkable poetic and linguistic analyses include those of Alonso Schökel and Auffret; the geometric vision of Bazak (e.g., "vv. 1-9 are a 'big triangle composed of three small triangles containing three verses each,'" p. 130), which he represents in a diagram, hardly works in ritual proceedings.

## Genre

COMMUNAL THANKSGIVING LITURGY would be a fair title of Psalm 136. It is the most elaborate responsorial psalm text we have in the Hebrew Bible. Sirach 51 is another piece like it in the apocryphal literature. The *hôdû* ("give thanks") summons is characteristic of this psalm type. Although thanksgiving is a genre of its own, growing out of particular situations of concrete gratitude (see "Introduction to Cultic Poetry," section 4C), every thanksgiving has a hymnic quality. This is particularly obvious with communal thanks to God. While individual thanksgivings have a more or less elaborate element, the "account of trouble and salvation," the communal branch of the genre likes to tell of historical instances of salvation, and may add some hints of contemporary divine deeds of liberation or atonement (cf. v. 24a). But, as a rule, this element does not play a larger role in these songs of gratitude. The general summons to give thanks assumes virtually completely the function of calling for eulogy and praise.

## Setting

Speculations have revolved around the possible feast or worship service in the course of which our psalm may have been sung. The four thematic units in this psalm discussed above are no unambiguous indication of a special occasion or feast opportune for this liturgy. For example, we are hardly able to pinpoint the Passover celebrations as the exclusive setting, because remembrance of the exodus and the killing of the firstborn may have been considered appropriate also at other assemblies and worships of the year, especially in a thematic cluster of the type of Psalm 136. Therefore we better not try to localize a fixed place in the festive cycle, but think of regular services of parishioners who wanted to express their general gratitude to the benign overlord Yahweh, who granted land, security, and help to his followers. Psalm 136 does have a certain affinity with Psalm 135, but both texts show their own profile, more so than we would expect from a "twin" composition. Psalm 135 focuses on overcoming and degrading Israel's enemies. Psalm 136, for its part, sticks closer to canonical salvation history, dwells more intensely on Yahweh's rescuing his people, and more openly admits congregational participation in the liturgy.

## Intention

Articulating this sense of general gratitude for the whole creation, the special acts of salvation that the people of Yahweh experienced in the past, and finally, but importantly so, giving thanks because of contemporary experiences of being rescued by God's intervention, the hymnic song wants to confirm the congregation's deep sense of dependency and joy. Yahweh's solidarity endures for sure, into a long and dark future, and this hope and certainty carry the whole congregation.

## Bibliography

L. A. Alonso-Schökel, "Psalmus 136 (135)," *VD* 45 (1967) 129-38; M. E. Andrews, "Praise in Asia: An Interpretation of Psalm 136," *East Asia Journal of Theology* 1 (1983) 107-11; P. Auffret, "Note sur la structure littéraire du psaume CXXXVI," *VT* 27 (1977) 1-12; idem, "Rendez grâce au Seigneur!" *BN* 86 (1997) 7-13; J. Bazak, "The Geometric-Figurative Structure of Psalm CXXXVI," *VT* 35 (1985) 129-38; B. C. E. Birch, "Old Testament Foundations for Peacemaking in the Nuclear Era," *Christian Century* 102 (1985) 1115-19; N. Carroll, "The Roman Catholic Tradition (Ps 136 in an Original Musical Arrangement)," in *Sacred Sound and Social Change* (ed. L. Hoffman, et al.; Notre Dame: University of Notre Dame Press, 1992) 221-34; J.-C. Margot, "'And His Love Is Eternal' (Psalm 136)," *BT* 25 (1974) 212-17; P. D. Miller, "Psalm 136," *Int* 48 (1995) 390-97; J. Obermann, "An Antiphonal Psalm from Ras Shamra," *JBL* 55 (1936) 21-44; R. Rendtorff, "Sihon, Og und das israelitische 'Credo,'" in *Meilenstein* (*Fest.* H. Donner; ed. M. Weippert; Wiesbaden: Harrassowitz, 1995) 198-203; D. Saliers, "The Methodist Tradition (Ps 136 in an Original Musical Arrangement)," in *Sacred Sound and Social Change* (ed. L. A. Hoffman, et al.; Notre Dame: University of Notre Dame Press, 1992) 235-54; C. Schedl, "Die alphabetisch-arithmetische Struktur von Psalm CXXXVI," *VT* 36 (1986) 489-94; B. Steinberg, "The Jewish Tradition (Ps 136 in an Original Musical Arrangement)," in *Sacred Sound and Social Change* (ed. L. Hoffman, et al.; Notre Dame: University of Notre Dame Press, 1992) 255-73; K. H.

Ting, "'That You Be Trustworthy' (Ps 136:1-9)," *Chinese Theological Review* 6 (1991) 127-33; A. Wyton, "The Episcopal Tradition (Ps 136 in an Original Musical Arrangement)," in *Sacred Sound and Social Change* (ed. L. Hoffman, et al.; Notre Dame: University of Notre Dame Press, 1992) 274-83.

## Psalm 137:
## Communal Complaint

### Structure

|  |  | MT | NRSV |
|---|---|---|---|
| I. | Complaint | 1-4 | 1-4 |
|  | A. Account of trouble | 1-2 | 1-2 |
|  | B. Taunt of enemies | 3 | 3 |
|  | C. Plaintive answer | 4 | 4 |
| II. | Vow | 5-6 | 5-6 |
| III. | Imprecations | 7-9 | 7-9 |
|  | A. Implicit curse against Edom | 7 | 7 |
|  | B. Implicit curse against Babylon | 8-9 | 8-9 |

In the last third of the Psalter, songs without a redactional heading (SU-PERSCRIPTION) are not rare (cf. Psalms 104; 105; 107; 114; 115; 116; 118; 119; etc.; → Psalms 71; 93). What is more disconcerting is the lack of an adequate opening of the song. If it is supposed to be a communal complaint, we should expect at least some kind of INVOCATION or INITIAL PLEA or perhaps INITIAL COMPLAINT (see "Introduction to Cultic Poetry," section 4B). Nothing of this kind is visible in the text. Instead, we find a narrational opening in the first person plural, telling in a moving way about the despair of those who had been deported to Babylon, apparently after the defeats of Judah and Jerusalem at the hands of Nebuchadnezzar in 597 and 587 B.C.E. The preponderance of first person plurals in this section is remarkable: in five poetic lines we find nine "we/us" references, a very high concentration indeed (cf. Psalms 90; 124; 126). Of course, there is no detailed or historiographic ACCOUNT OF TROUBLE, but only a highly schematized and condensed extract of the Babylonian situation (vv. 1-2): the rivers or canals are significant (v. 1a), with their unusual willow trees, barely known in the hills of Judah (v. 2a). The author mentions the longing for Zion and the deep sadness of being so far away, causing the strongest feelings of homesickness (v. 1bc); the captives have musical instruments (*kînnôr*, "harp") and like to sing nostalgic songs (v. 2b). All this evokes a rather folkloristic air, as if the psalm was offering a popular song about the ill-fated exiled Judahites. Every culture probably knows equivalent tearful texts of past suffering and heroism; the Portuguese *fado* comes to mind or elegiac African songs. The impression of dealing with popular poetry and not with liturgical elements is strengthened by vv. 3-4, where a little dramatic plot evolves from the preceding static situation. "Our captors" (*šôbênû:* Qal plural participle of *šbh*, with first-person plural suffix) "demand from us!" (v. 3ab). The expression "captor" is rare in Hebrew Scripture; the exact form of our passage, with first-person plural suffix, occurs but once. The only other suffix is that of the third person masculine plural ("their captors"; cf. Ps 106:46; Isa 14:2; Jer 50:33; 2 Chr 30:9). The expression is represented more frequently in Solomon's prayer at the dedication of the temple, a great piece of Dtr literature (1 Kgs 8:46; 2 Chr 6:36; "if they plead with you in the land of their captors, . . . grant them compassion in the sight of their captors," 1 Kgs 8:47, 50). Everywhere the context suggests that captivity is a state of hardship and injustice, violence and shame, and that the captors are dominant and cruel lords of their subjugated people who may, however, be moved to clemency by Yahweh himself (Ps 106:46; 2 Chr 30:9). In our little scene (vv. 3-4: liturgical unit, because of first person plural; against Mowinckel, et al.) the victors are apparently thought to mock the depressed slaves, challenging them sadistically to sing a "song of Zion" for them. The answer is plainly negative. "How can we sing that Yahweh song on foreign soil?" (v. 4). This response of the community sounds, first, as if the "Zion song" solicited by the captors had a special quality of a Yahweh-oriented and Yahweh-symbolizing cult song that — this is a second problem — cannot be performed outside Yahweh's territory (cf. the same problem in 2 Kings 5). Typically, the PLAINTIVE ANSWER of the community is introduced by the lament particle *'êk*, "how" (v. 4a), which has the ring of doubt, protest, and dirge about it (cf. Gen 44:8; Judg 16:15; 2 Sam 1:19; Pss 11:1; 73:19, also the longer form *'êkāh* in Lam 1:1; 2:1; 4:1-2).

All in all, the introductory part of Psalm 137 is peculiar, indeed, as an element of a communal complaint. Apart from this generic difficulty, however, the psalm is lucidly structured. The narrational and dramatic introduction in vv. 1-4 forcefully and diligently poses the problems (a) of the Jewish captivity and suffering under foreign domination, and (b) of the Jewish relationship to Zion and Yahweh. The last issue is taken up by the following subunit, vv. 5-6, while the problem of suffering is saved for vv. 7-9.

The Vow of vv. 5-6, a fitting element for COMPLAINT songs, takes on the form of an oath, that is, a conditional self-damnation (see glossary: OATH FORMULA; G. Giesen, *NBL* I, 488-89). Three times the text begins with "If I do (not) do . . . ," twice pronouncing the consequences of the specified failure. Actions and attitudes sworn to and thus guaranteed by the firmest commitment center on Jerusalem, the name of the Holy City being solemnly exhibited in the first and last line of the oath. The speaker — here we have an individual voice in sharp contrast to the dominant communal orientation of vv. 1-4 naming Zion as the symbol of identification — pledges allegiance to the city of Yahweh's presence. As the long history of tradition through the ages of islamization, crusades, imperialism, Zionism, decolonization, and founding of the new state of Israel amply and painfully demonstrates, allegiance to Jerusalem has stayed a very powerful sentiment in various conflicting groups (cf. the history of Zionism; and A. Elon, *Jerusalem* [Boston: Little, Brown, 1989]; E. Otto, *Jerusalem* [Stuttgart: Kohlhammer, 1980]). What did it mean at the time our psalm was first recited? Do we have to deal with a private emotion, a political statement, or a religious confession to keep spiritually and perhaps physically close to

God's holy place? Postexilic evidence suggests that the city had become pre-eminent in the minds of deported Jews (cf. Neh 1:3-4; 2:3), and the Nehemiah memoirs (Nehemiah 1–7) witness to the zeal for the city's reconstruction in the face of many difficulties. Also, the → book of Lamentations testifies to the shock of seeing Jerusalem and Zion destroyed and humiliated. Within the Psalter the ZION HYMNS are strong evidence of a living faith in the presence of God on that sacred mount, which probably has pre-Israelite roots (cf. Isaiah 24–27; 29; 36–37; 60–62; etc.; Stolz, *Strukturen;* listing at "Introduction to Cultic Poetry"). We may conclude from all these assorted texts that Jerusalem, after having been a Jebusite holy site for some centuries and the capital of the Davidic dynasty for about four hundred years, became the Holy City and a highly important symbol of Jewish identity in exilic/postexilic times. Granted that this may be the basis to start from, we also are able to deduce that vv. 5-6 cannot represent merely private sentiments of a chance suppliant. Comparable to the desire to go on a pilgrimage to Jerusalem and the house of Yahweh (cf. Psalms 84; 87; 132), the oath of allegiance to the Holy City must have some communitarian and confessional implications. The individual speaking in vv. 5-6, after all, is a member of the Yahweh community (though Yahweh's name does not appear in our passage).

Vows function, within the pleading discourse of COMPLAINTS, as a kind of offering to the Deity. The individual member of the congregation pledges allegiance, in direct address, to Jerusalem (→ Psalm 122). This pledge includes veneration and orientation to Yahweh's city and temple.

The name of Yahweh is present again in the last, cursing, section of the psalm (vv. 7-9: IMPRECATIONS). In the ancient Near East, cursing was a widespread phenomenon (see Glossary: CURSE). The direct condemnation of enemies and evildoers is rare in the Psalter (→ Psalm 109); there is no direct-address curse of the pattern: "Cursed be you" (cf. 2 Sam 16:5-10, Shimei curses David, but the exact cursing words are not transmitted). Only in Deuteronomy 27 and 28 do we find some authentic curse formulations, uttered in a ritual way, against some potential trespasser (27:15-26) and even directly against an audience (cf. 28:16-19: "Cursed shall you be" or "cursed are you": *'ārûr 'attāh*). Mostly, the complaint psalms do not talk that bluntly. According to ritual procedure they prefer indirect ways of counteracting evil influences, choosing among various options to destroy the opponents: by formulating ill-wishes against enemies, by inciting Yahweh to punish them, or by praising anyone who might avenge harm done to the suppliant. This is the case also with v. 7. There is a strong bid to Yahweh to "remember" what the Edomites did on a certain "day of Jerusalem" (v. 7ab; cf. Kellermann, Hartberger). A quotation of their hateful war cries is to support the plea revealing their barbarism (v. 7cd). Yahweh is called on to remember this dark day when, it seems, Edomites sacked Jerusalem (the historical event is unknown; speculations are that the Edomite onslaught occurred in connection with the Babylonian wars at the beginning of the sixth century B.C.E.; cf. U. Kellermann, *Israel und Edom* [diss., Münster, 1975]; → Lam 4:21). Now, this imprecation uses direct-address speech to Yahweh, employing the imperative masculine singular: "Remember!" (v. 7a). Going only that far and not adding any details of what punishment or revenge the people want, it proves a certain automatism of "recalling": Yahweh, only being reminded of the sacrilege against his Holy City, will certainly punish the adversaries severely. Asking for that kind of remembrance (cf. the verb *zkr* used in *malam partem:* Neh 6:14; 13:29; Jer 14:10; Hos 7:2; 8:13; 9:9; and in *bonam partem:* Neh 5:19; 13:14, 22, 31; → Ps 132:1) makes the curse an implicit matter.

The second imprecation (vv. 8-9) is against Babylon, the capital of the world power, and *pars pro toto* for the whole empire. This time, the implicit curse is hidden in a direct word against Babylon, but this saying is formally a positive beatitude (*'ašrê*, vv. 8b, 9a; cf. 1:1; 119:1-2; 128:1-2). Only its contents are disastrous: "Happy is the one who takes your young children, smashing them on the rocks" (v. 9), one of the most cruel, vengeful ill-wishes in the Bible. No matter how bestial were the sackings of the Edomites, this wish for the annihilation of children is a deplorable example of deep-rooted ethnic hatred, as shocking as those massacres among antagonistic cultural and religious groups we have to witness in our days.

The two different forms of hidden curse stand side by side. The sayings against Babylon seem late and clumsy: in two "beatitudes" we find three relative clauses of a younger type (the relative particle *'ăšer* is shortened to *šě-* and prefixed to the verb: vv. 8b, 8c, 9a). Especially v. 8 appears to be overloaded with words and very prosaic in its diction, including a lone and stealthy "to us" (only first person plural in vv. 5-9). The direct address of Babylon in an "objective" speech form (felicitation, beatitude) also calls for explication. This form is apparently used in a secondary, nonauthentic way. The Edom saying, on the other hand, poses as a plea to Yahweh plus an incentive for him to take action (v. 7); it is terse and poetic in style, not concerned with the virtual opponent but with God's reaction. For all these reasons, some scholars think that the Babylon saying may be a later addition or a secondary attribution, and that the original ill-wish and cursing text referred to Edom only (cf., e.g., Kellermann). The present setup of the text, however, presupposes the Babylonian background (vv. 1-4). If the psalm had undergone a longer compositional molding with different elements glued together from a late perspective on captivity and longing for Jerusalem, which is possible, it would still be hard to make plausible.

Hartberger extensively compares Jeremiah 51, a long diatribe against Babylon, with our psalm (pp. 73-100). Vocabulary and outlook do surprisingly correspond. Babylon is directly addressed and threatened, e.g., Jer 51:13-14, 20-23. The last-mentioned four verses, furthermore, dwell on the verb "smash" (*npṣ*, Piel: 9 occurrences, plus participle/noun = "smasher" = "hammer," Jer 51:20a; note the wordplay. This verb occurs a total of only 21 times in the OT. Cf. the only other occurrence in the Psalter: Ps 2:9). Military and civilian people are "smashed" in Jer 51:20-23, although not "babes" as in Ps 137:9. There is some talk about "rocks," too, in Jer 51:25-26, supposedly the foundation of the city of Babylon (which does not fit geographically, but seems to be a standard concept for high-ranking, powerful cities). There are more affinities between Jeremiah 51 and Psalm 137, but what do they teach us? Literary dependence of one text on the other being dubious, the best answer may be: both passages come from a common pool of sentiments and liturgical action. Both were probably recited or enacted in public worship. We may also draw on frequent Edom sayings witnessing to the same phenomenon (Obad 11-14; Lam 4:17-22; Jer 49:7-22). Ogden, on the basis of Hayes, wants to draw together prophetic oracles and communal laments, the first ones being the divine answer to complaints and petitions of the congregation.

The structure traced above presupposes some kind of liturgical presentation of the text. Most exegetes, in fact, favor a worship setting of Psalm 137. Yet there are analyses of the text from poetic and literary points of view (cf., e.g., Freedman; Halle and McCarthy; etc.). Discovery of a concentric setup (Freedman, 203: "envelope construction") or an even syllable count in all subsections probably applies less to liturgically enacted texts than to written testimony already used for private edification, and considered inspired by God. Such an attitude and practice in regard to the Psalter may be assumed only in a very late period of canonization, at the beginning of the Christian era, not in the formative phase of the Psalm collections.

## *Genre*

The denomination of Psalm 137 as COMMUNAL COMPLAINT is haphazard, to be sure. We have to take account of the elements and vestiges of complaints that the text presents, and those that it lacks. Modifications of standard forms also have to be recognized. As already pointed out, the invocation and initial plea are missing; the psalm does not have an adequate introduction to make it useful in complaint liturgies. Even worse: the complaint itself is formulated in a strange narrative style (vv. 1-4); instead of affirmations of confidence we have a vow of allegiance (not a vow to give thanks! vv. 5-6), and instead of a proper petition we get only imprecations against two different national groups (vv. 7-9). The ill-wishing element is part of the complaint ritual, to be sure, but it is usually only one of two complementary forms, the other being positive petition for help, salvation, blessing, etc. Here it remains solitary; petition for one's own sake is missing.

We cannot help but conclude that earlier complaint patterns (see "Introduction to Cultic Poetry," section 4B) have been decisively altered, probably being adapted to different community structures. Remembrance of sadness and longing (vv. 1-4) has possibly been gleaned from a popular song from outside liturgical agendas. The vow of allegiance to Jerusalem (vv. 5-6) could have been part of diaspora gatherings; conjured castigations ("drying" up of right hand; tying up of tongue; cf. Ezek 3:26; Job 29:10) do not suggest a sacral background. This is true even for the third section of the psalm (vv. 7-9). Turning to Yahweh does not make a full liturgical text yet; using the form of beatitude does not tie the text to ritual procedure. What may have been the origin, composition, and use of Psalm 137?

To mention other attempts at genre classification: interpreters have alternately stressed the folkloristic, lyrical, hymnic, imprecational, and literary aspects, and made one of them the determining quality. Since the psalm seems to contain its own genre names ("Zion song," v. 3; "Yahweh song," v. 4), and vv.

5-6 in fact being a direct-address Zion hymn, some experts propose a genre attribution to "Zion songs" (e.g., Kellermann; Allen, 238, 241). But → Psalms 46; 48; 122 differ in their structure, and are much more removed from the basic complaint disposition.

## Setting

The spirit of Psalm 137 is communitarian, laicistic, melancholic, emotional, zealous, etc. We best think of a congregation of people under pressure from majority groups (captors, taunters) and trying to fight back. In this situation people remember oppression and despair in the exilic environment, and use it either as a memory of misery or symbolically in place of their own suffering. Jewish communities of the fifth century B.C.E. did take for themselves the liberty of composing new songs of complaint, not adhering strictly to the schemes of old. They composed, e.g., complaints on the basis of a standard sequence (complaint-allegiance-imprecation) but in a new language. Recited together with other psalms, perhaps not every one of them needed a proper invocation, etc. The setting of our song, then, may have been a more elaborate worship service, in which it was intoned to express revulsion against continuing oppression and a desire for change. Dreaming of Zion and Jerusalem is tantamount to working for liberation (cf. Gutiérrez). Since we know of special worship services to commemorate the fall of Jerusalem (Zech 7:3-6; Lamentations; cf. Kraus, 1083-84; Kellermann, 52, 54, 55), our psalm may be attributed to this event, which took place on the ninth day of the month Ab (= July/August). Nonetheless, the popularity of the song may have stimulated a much wider use.

## Intention

The community, singing that new song of Jewish frustration and suffering under imperial rule, wants to rally all her members around the hope for Yahweh's reign at Jerusalem. The Holy City at the time of our psalm had acquired a supreme value in the spiritual life of dispersed Judah. Perhaps the oath of allegiance to Yahweh's place on earth (vv. 5-6) was even used in a special public ritual to stabilize members and make them more confident. Narrational and suggestive diction, heavy emphasis on personal dedication and self-controlled participation, indicate that the individual member of the congregation was addressed and challenged. Along these lines we take the individual pledge for Jerusalem as the principal purpose of Psalm 137.

Feelings of hatred and revenge over against historical enemies have unfortunately always played a large role in the psychology and religion of God-fearing people; the history of humankind has always been a dramatical test field of how to overcome such sentiments in order to bring desperately needed peace to the nations.

# Bibliography

P. Auffret, "Essai sur la structure littéraire du psaume 137," *ZAW* 92 (1980) 346-77; idem, "Souviens-toi YHWH!" *BZ* 41 (1997) 250-52; S. Bar-Efrat, "Love of Zion," in *Tehillah le-Moshe* (*Fest.* M. Greenberg; ed. M. Cogan, et al.; Winona Lake, Ind.: Eisenbrauns, 1997) 3-11; P. W. Flint, "Translation Technique in the Sepharim Psalter," in *SBLSP* 130 (1994) 312-15; D. N. Freedman, "The Structure of Psalm 137," in *Near Eastern Studies* (*Fest.* W. F. Albright; ed. H. Goedicke; Baltimore: Johns Hopkins University Press, 1971) 187-205; K. Galling, "Erwägungen zur antiken Synagoge," *Zeitschrift des Deutschen Palästinavereins* 72 (1976) 163-78; G. Gutiérrez, "A Spirituality for Liberation," *Other Side* 21 (1985) 40-43; J. L. Gutiérrez, "Cativeiro e poesia," *EstBib* 43 (1994) 30-41; M. Halle and J. J. McCarthy, "The Metrical Structure of Psalm 137," *JBL* 100 (1981) 161-67; B. Hartberger, *'An den Wassern von Babylon . . .'. Psalm 137 auf dem Hintergrund von Jer 51, der biblischen Edom-Tradition und babylonischen Originalquellen* (BBB 63; Frankfurt am Main: Hanstein, 1986); J. H. Hayes, "The Usage of Oracles against Foreign Nations in Ancient Israel," *JBL* 87 (1968) 81-92; A. M. Isasi-Diaz, " 'By the Rivers of Babylon': Exile as a Way of Life," in *Reading from This Place* I (ed. F. Segovia, et al.; Minneapolis: Fortress, 1995) 149-63; U. Kellermann, "Psalm 137," *ZAW* 90 (1978) 43-58; R. Kirscher, "Two Responses to Epochal Change: Augustine and the Rabbis on Ps 137," *VC* 44 (1990) 242-62; H. Lenowitz, "The Mock-Śimḥâ of Psalm 137," in *Directions in Biblical Hebrew Poetry* (ed. E. Follis; JSOTSup 40; Sheffield: Sheffield Academic Press, 1987) 149-59; J. S. Lowry, " 'By the Waters of Babylon' (Psalm 137)," *Journal for Preachers* 15 (1992) 26-33; F. Luke, "The Song of Zion as a Literary Category of the Psalter," *Indian Journal of Theology* 14 (1965) 72-90; G. Ogden, "Prophetic Oracle against Foreign Nations and Psalms of Communal Lament," *JSOT* 24 (1982) 89-97; D. de Pablo Maroto, "Pueblo cautivo y peregrino (Ps 137)," in *Cristianos en tierra extraña* (ed. F. Brändle, et al.; Madrid: Editional de Espiritualidad, 1978) 25-48; J. P. M. van der Ploeg, "Notes sur quelques psaumes," in *Mélanges bibliques et orientaux* (*Fest.* M. Delcor; ed. A. Caquot, et al.; Neukirchen-Vluyn: Neukirchener Verlag, 1985) 425-30; G. A. Rendsburg, "Physiological and Philological Notes to Psalm 137," *JQR* 83 (1993) 385-99; F. Renfroe, "Persiflage in Psalm 137," in *Ascribe to the Lord* (*Fest.* P. C. Craigie; ed. L. Eslinger and G. Taylor; JSOTSup 67; Sheffield: Sheffield Academic Press, 1988) 509-27; G. Sauer, *Die strafende Gerechtigkeit Gottes in den Psalmen* (diss., Basel, 1957); W. H. Shea, "Qinah Meter and Strophic Structure in Psalm 137," in *Biblical and Other Studies* (*Fest.* S. Blank; ed. R. Ahroni; Winona Lake, Ind.: Eisenbrauns, 1984) 199-214; B. Steidle, "Vom Mut zum ganzen Ps 137 (136)," *Erbe und Auftrag* 50 (1974) 21-30; M. R. Wilson, "Real Estate Theology: Zionism and Biblical Claims," *Transformation* 2 (1985) 12-18; K. Young, "How Shall We Sing the Lord's Song?" *Church and Society* 75 (1985) 37-43.

# Psalm 138:
# Individual Thanksgiving

## Structure

|  | MT | NRSV |
|---|---|---|
| I. Superscription | 1a | - |
| II. Offertory formulas | 1b-2 | 1-2 |
| III. Account of salvation | 3 | 3 |
| IV. Summons to praise | 4-5 | 4-5 |
| V. Hymnic line | 6 | 6 |
| VI. Affirmation of confidence | 7-8a | 7-8a |
| VII. Petition | 8bc | 8bc |

The SUPERSCRIPTION being extremely short (*lĕdāwid,* "to/of David"), one has to ask whether this kind of succinctness could be a consequence of scribal negligence or redactional cuts. But the frequency of minimal headings (9 occurrences: cf. MT in Psalms 25–28; 35; 37; 103; 144; Psalm 34 has *lĕdāwid,* with a following historicizing remark) suggests the redactional possibility of labeling a psalm by adding only a kind of author's or dedicatory reference; cf. also Psalm 72 ("to/of Solomon").

The declaration to give thanks to Yahweh — originally offered at the moment of handing over sacrificial gifts (cf. Ps 116:17; Crüsemann, *Studien,* 270-74; listing at "Introduction to Cultic Poetry") — is a fitting introduction to an individual thanksgiving psalm (vv. 1-2; a proper invocation "Yahweh" is preserved in some Hebrew MSS and the ancient versions; it was possibly lost by scribal error; cf. five occurrences of the divine name in vv. 4-8). A particular verbal expression, *'ôdĕkā* (from *ydh,* Hiphil), "I give thanks to you," i.e., God (v. 1b; cf. v. 2b), seems to be an especially characteristic form element in this context (→ 118:19, 21, 28), which may be accompanied or replaced by other words of gratitude; cf., e.g., *'ărômimĕkā,* "I extol you" (30:2 [RSV 1]; 118:28; 145:1; etc.), or *'ăzammerĕkā,* "I sing to you" (Judg 5:3; Pss 9:3 [RSV 2]; 27:6; 57:8, 10 [RSV 7, 9]; 61:9 [RSV 8]; 71:22, 23; 101:1; 108:2, 4 [RSV 1, 3]; 144:9), or *'āšîrāh,* "I will sing" (cf. Exod 15:1, 21; Judg 5:3; Pss 13:6 [RSV 5]; 27:6; 59:17-18 [RSV 16-17]; 89:2 [RSV 1]; 104:33; 144:9). In our case the first three lines of the psalm (v. 2bcd is overcrowded, though, and v. 2d might be a fourth line or a gloss) describe the OFFERTORY as a cultic procedure. V. 1bc starts out with the proper formula to give thanks, as pointed out above. The second colon of this line (v. 1c) mentions "gods," here an indeterminate plural form, apparently as onlookers (cf. Psalm 82; an alternative would be to take *'ĕlōhîm* as an appellation of Yahweh: "In front, God, will I sing to you" — which is a little awkward: the suffix "you" is missing with *neged,* "in front"). In front or "over against" *(neged)* the gods the jubilant offerer wants to bring his/her gift, thus heeding and inverting the warning of the Decalogue not to adore "other gods over against me" *('al pānay).* His or her sacrifice to Yahweh shall be observed by (lesser? powerless?) other gods. According to Gunkel (p. 583), ancient Near Eastern prayers employ the same concept of praising a particular god who helped while other gods witness the ritual. V. 2a, indeed, talks about prostration in front of the temple, more specifically, the holy of holies, Yahweh's living quarters (hêkal; cf. Ezek 8:16; 41:1, 4, 20, 23, 25; Pss 5:8 [RSV 7]; 11:4; 48:10 [RSV 9]; 65:5 [RSV 4]; 68:30 [RSV 29]; 79:1). The psalm visualizes adoration in the precincts of the temple, or the worshiper is actually performing the rite of thanksgiving there (cf. 1 Samuel 1–2: families celebrate in and near the temple of Shiloh; note their sacrificial meal in 1 Sam 2:12-17. Similar procedures may be presupposed later around the second Jerusalem temple, 1 Kgs 8:31-51; Psalm 107). The THANKSGIVING (the OFFERTORY) FORMULA in v. 1b is more or less repeated in v. 2b, owing to the importance of the formal declaration of giving thanks.

A short interlude is dedicated to retrospective reflection typical of thanksgiving songs (see "Introduction to Cultic Poetry," section 4C). In the present psalm the normal ACCOUNT OF TROUBLE AND SALVATION has been reduced, however, to a mere description of crying out in anguish and being attended by the powerful and benevolent God (v. 3). Logically, this part of the thanksgiving rite had to be spoken or sung by the client him- or herself, and we do not know how often it could be repeated in a thanksgiving liturgy. Interestingly, the formulation is in direct-address or prayer language, unusual for such an "account" to the participants of worship (cf. Pss 18:17-20 [RSV 16-19]; 40:2-4 [RSV 1-3]; 116:3-4; 118:10-14: examples of "neutral" reports). But there are also some retrospective passages in prayer style, such as 30:3-5 or 116:8, proving the viability of God-directed accounts that were probably intended to be heard by the community just the same.

Vv. 4-5 are less descriptive than exhortative: imagined potentates all over the world are to join lauding Yahweh. His name is prominent in this SUMMONS TO PRAISE, as well as in the following hymnic line (v. 6). Four out of six occurrences of "Yahweh" in our psalm are in these three verses (the rest in v. 8). That "all the kings of the earth" should be included in personal thanksgiving is certainly due to much theological reflection. Yahweh is much superior to any known power (v. 8); in consequence, the highest authorities on earth have to bow down. The lowest follower of Yahweh, then, is entitled, in his community, to command the monarchs of the world to do obeisance to his mighty Overlord. Exilic and postexilic theological reflection, beginning with Second Isaiah, has produced this kind of religious confidence.

While the hypertrophic summons reaching out to the heads of nations (vv. 4a, 5a) uses jussive verbal forms in the plural, the second colon of each line begins with that ambivalent particle kî. In v. 4b the kî phrase is a motive clause, but in v. 5b it sounds like a first hymnic shout: "Yes, great is the glory of Yahweh!" This hymnic tone is clearly dominant in v. 6, which appears to be a mighty eulogy: "Aloft is Yahweh, he sees the lowly, and he knows the haughty from afar." Now, this line and perhaps v. 5b were to be sung by the congregation, which was indirectly summoned to join in thanksgiving, too. If distant kings were to exalt Israel's God, how much more so the faithful congregation of Yahweh had to do exactly this sort of eulogy.

"Great is Yahweh!" (v. 5b) and "Aloft is Yahweh!" (v. 6a) are related cultic shouts finding their parallels in so many formulaic expressions (cf. some with *gādôl*, "great," and *rām*, "high," "aloft": Pss 48:2 [RSV 1]; 77:14 [RSV 13]; 86:10; 95:3; 96:4; 99:2-3; 113:4; 135:5; 145:3; 147:5. Note the D usage of these adjectives in Deut 1:28; 2:10, 21; 9:2).

A conditional phrase opens the penultimate form element, an AFFIRMA-TION OF CONFIDENCE (vv. 7-8ab; cf. Ps 23:4). This element is well known and very frequent in individual and communal complaint songs. There it appears as an anticipatory declaration, signaling a complete trust of the suppliant and support group in the Deity's willingness and power to help. Conditional phrasing makes sure that a similar outlook into the future as extant in complaint situations is really intended in vv. 7-8. This fact seems a little odd in a thanksgiving situation: did ancient worshipers bringing their gifts and songs to the helpful deity use the opportunity for expressing new hopes in regard to continuation of divine benevolence? Why not? Any type of anniversary in our culture provokes thanksgivings for the times past and wishes for a continuing blessed time and experience. The same is true in Israelite thanksgiving. In our case, new troubles and anxieties are realistically expected (v. 7). Trust in Yahweh's further help is formulated again in direct-address language (vv. 7bcd). God's hand — a long-standing metaphor for his helping action (cf. Exod 15:6; Pss 44:4 [RSV 3]; 63:9 [RSV 8]; 80:16, 18 [RSV 15, 17]; 98:1; 118:15-16; etc.) — shall save again. The last utterances of confidence (v. 8ab) are stylistically mixed. The first colon is clad in neutral language: "Yahweh will act in my favor" — a confessional affirmation spoken to the congregation. The next colon is again prayer language, like most of the psalm: "Yahweh, your solidarity will last forever!" (v. 8b). The apparent indiscriminate use of the two modes of speech may be typical for later psalmody. It indicates changing addressees of the suppliant's speech: to congregation and to God.

Our psalm closes with an outright PETITION to be further protected by Yahweh in the future (v. 8c), a logical consequence of the preceding declarations of confidence. There is a chance that this petition may be a secondary addition (the other way around: Seybold, 512: "Prayer, remodeled to be a thanksgiving song"). Nevertheless, it is part of the text now; and orthodox or not in regard to thanksgiving structures, this plea is the end of Psalm 138. Similar petitions for protection and blessing in noncomplaint psalms include 90:13-17; 104:35; 139:19-24; etc.

## Genre

Elements of INDIVIDUAL THANKSGIVING we have found without doubt in Psalm 138, but are they sufficient evidence for this genre? We noted that the whole psalm with very small exceptions uses prayer language. Thus typical allocutions of the community in which the thanksgiving rite took place (cf. Ps 22:23-27 [RSV 22-26]) are out of sight. Thanksgiving songs normally show a narrational and exhortatory dimension indicative of this communal setting (→ Psalms 30; 32; 118). Still, extant form signals are too strong to look for another designation than thanksgiving. Variation of the structure may be due to a modified life situation. It seems that this offertory of thanks has been general-

ized, e.g., by reducing the ACCOUNT OF TROUBLE AND SALVATION (see "Introduction to Cultic Poetry," section C) to just one line (v. 3). Offering thanks now,
individuals pray collectively; comprehensive affirmations dominate the service:
the affirmation of confidence and the petition to be protected and helped in the
future are all the more understandable. Also, the larger political outlook (vv. 4-
5) fits better into a congregational horizon than into some small private experience (Dahood, for that reason, declares the psalm to be a "royal song of
thanksgiving," like → Psalm 18. But evidence is too slight for such a conclusion).

## Setting

Thanksgivings for an individual saved from grave danger were originally held
in the family circle. The narratives of 1 Samuel 1–2 contain some information
on this primitive setting. The family of one person especially blessed or miraculously rescued would bring an offering, which often corresponded to the vow
taken in the moment of despair (cf. 2 Sam 15:7; Psalm 107). As Pss 22:23
(RSV 22); 26:12; etc., indicate, the person saved would invite friends and
neighbors to the event. In this context of grateful feasting the rescued one
would tell his/her story of salvation, and the shared fine meal on the sacrificed
animal with good drinks made for a merry event. Our psalm seems to be removed from this original scene; at least it does not transpire. Instead, we may
think of a more spiritualized version of thanksgiving, perhaps without sacrifice
and in the midst of a Torah community, leaning much more to prayer, confession, and meditation. The setting of our psalm, then, would have been the congregational worship in favor of someone who had experienced special protection and help from Yahweh (cf. the "collectivization of lament" in Psalm 12).

## Intention

Offering thanks for graces received has always been a concern of ancient wor-
ship. The eulogies returned to Yahweh were a wonderful way of balancing
God-human relationships and strengthening the community of believers. In
Psalm 138 the community immediately takes part in this process of praising; it
is in no way an object of exhortation or missionary witness, as it is, e.g., in
Psalm 32.

## Bibliography

R. Glöckner, "Neutestamentliche Wundergeschichten und frühchristliche Gebetsparäne-
se," in *Die Mysterien des Lebens Jesu und die christliche Existenz* (Aschaffenburg: Paul
Pattloch, 1984) 57-74; D. M. Nelson, "The Virtue of Humility in Judaism," *Journal of
Religious Ethics* 13 (1985) 298-311.

## Psalm 139:
## Meditation

### Structure

|  | MT | NRSV |
|---|---|---|
| I. Superscription | 1a | - |
| II. Meditative prayer | 1b-6 | 1-6 |
| III. Plaintive reflection | 7-12 | 7-12 |
| IV. Acknowledgment of Creator | 13-16 | 13-16 |
| V. Adoration | 17-18 | 17-18 |
| VI. Imprecation | 19-20 | 19-20 |
| VII. Dedication, vow | 21-22 | 21-22 |
| VIII. Petition | 23-24 | 23-24 |

The hind part of the Psalter shelters again a collection of Davidic psalms (Psalms 138–145) comparable to the larger compilations, Psalms 3–41 and 51–71 (cf. also Psalms 108–110). Superscriptions vary in the present collection; in Psalm 139 we encounter a traditional bipartite heading, the first expression probably referring to choir singing, the second attributing the "song" (*mizmôr:* cf. headings of Psalms 3–6; 20–24; 62–68; 109; 110; etc.) to King David. Thus our SUPERSCRIPTION is a very common one (*mizmôr* in connection with David occurs at least 35 times in the Psalter).

The whole psalm is stylized as a personal prayer to Yahweh, featuring the first person singular of the suppliant or adorant and the second person singular of the divine addressee. The speaker reveals him- or herself as a person scrutinized (*ḥqr:* vv. 1b and 23a; cf. Ps 44:22 [RSV 21]; Jer 17:10; Job 28:27; only synonyms are used in protestations of innocence, e.g., Pss 7:10 [RSV 9]; 17:3; 26:2) and fathomed through and through by God (*yd':* vv. 1b, 2a, 23ab). The worshiping community, which may be behind the scenes, does not appear in the text, but the "enemies" do, those opponents who cause nothing but evil and deserve death (vv. 19-22). Perhaps we are entitled to conclude that the enemies, called "godless" and "bloodthirsty" (v. 19) and openly in rebellion against Yahweh (v. 20), by antagonistic contrast, mirror the community of the "just ones."

The first unit (vv. 1b-6) opens with an appellation of Yahweh, a true INVOCATION, it seems (v. 1b). This is one of two namings of God in vv. 1b-20, the other being in v. 4b. "Yahweh" in v. 21a may be a secondary addition, because the line seems overburdened and some Hebrew MSS do not show this second appellation of Yahweh. Note, however, that v. 19 has another call to "God," using the rarer form *'ĕlôah,* a designation of God concentrated in the book of Job, but fairly unusual in the Psalter (see Pss 18:32 [RSV 31]; 50:22; 114:7). Comparing our psalm with some others abounding in Yahweh titulations (cf. Psalms 121; 134; 138), the scarcity of the tetragrammaton seems peculiar in a prayer.

The invocation is followed immediately by a musing, self-centered, theologically reflected PRAYER (vv. 1-6). At stake is the general fate of humans over against the pervasive presence and superior knowledge of the Deity. The sub-

401

ject matter could be a topic in almost any religion of the world (cf. religious-historical analogies presented by Hommel, Bernhardt, Pettazoni). The move-ment of thought is constant between the divine "you" and the human "I." The vocabulary employed seems refined, intellectually high-strung. Some of the lexemes are rare (e.g., *ḥqr,* "scrutinize"; *zrh* II, "measure" [hapax legomenon in Hebrew Scripture]; *skn,* Hiphil, "know intimately" [two more occurrences in Hebrew Scripture: Num 22:30; Job 22:21]; *zûr,* metaphorically: "close in" [hapax in the Psalter]; *pilʾî,* "marvelous," only other occurrence: Judg 13:18; the noun *peleʾ* is more frequent; see Pss 77:12, 15 [RSV 11, 14]; 88:11, 13 [RSV 10, 12]). This vocabulary as well as the mode of reflection in the psalm is characteristic of late wisdom (cf. Psalms 39; 49; 90). The overwhelming pres-ence and massive superiority of Yahweh are acknowledged by awed confession of incompetence (v. 6; cf. Job's answers to God: "Alas, I am too small; what could I say? I put my hand on my mouth": Job 40:4; "I know that you can do anything you like . . . ; I have talked foolishly, things too high for me, which I do not understand," Job 42:2a, 3ab). The closeness and omniscience of Yahweh are by no means considered an absolute blessing. According to wisdom reflec-tions in the Near East and the general tenor of argumentation in vv. 1-6, 7-12, there is the problem of being smothered by a towering God; cf. the verb *zûr* (v. 5a) meaning "to enclose," like a besieged city (cf. Deut 20:12, 19; 2 Sam 11:1; 20:15; Jer 37:5; 39:1).

The next section (vv. 7-12) underlines this understanding, musing about how to escape the enclosure of God. The terrorized rhetorical question: "Where do I go? . . . Where do I flee?" (v. 7) belongs in the context of persecution, im-minent danger, and ritual proceedings to neutralize dangers (cf. Gen 37:30; Deut 1:28; 2 Sam 13:13; Jer 15:2; more intensive *ʾannāh:* Pss 116:4, 16; 118:25). The "you"-"I" dialogue continues the same way as in vv. 1-6. This time, the virtual omnipresence of God is the problem. Yahweh (although his name is not mentioned in the section) is encountered in the deepest underworld and the highest heaven (v. 8; again rare expressions are used; see below). He is present not only in remote parts of the earth, but far beyond, at the end of the sea (v. 9: note the ancient cosmology: the earth floats on top of an immense ocean). Everywhere, anywhere, God is able to take hold of a would-be refugee from his rule (v. 10; for a similar topic see the book of Jonah). Geographical or cosmographical limits do not exist for God. Neither are there any restrictive boundaries established by light and darkness for him (vv. 11-12). The wording of all these lines expresses the reflective mood of meditation, not the exuberant, extroverted attitude of the hymn or thanksgiving, nor the concrete threats of life of the individual complaint. The hypothetical case of trying to escape the influ-ence of God starts with conditional phrases (v. 9), only the first one introduced by *ʾim,* "if." Two rather rare verbs picture "ascending" to heaven (v. 8a: *slq,* hapax in Hebrew Scripture) and "arranging a sleeping place" in Sheol (v. 9b: *škn,* two occurrences; cf. Isa 58:5). Each time the conclusion to these irreal con-ditions is: God would be there, too. You cannot outrun him. Two examples of possible escapes in mythological thinking, both in the vertical dimension, are given in v. 8. The following two lines contain one more example, posing the imaginary flight on the beams of dawn, this time in the horizontal realm. It would be to no avail. The conditional phrase opened by *'im* at the beginning of v. 8 continues, without repeating that conjunction. The third case is much more elaborate, then, playing on the idea that every day the light of the dawn spreads with incredible speed from east to west.

Vv. 11-12 may be climactic to this plaintive speculation. MT reads the consecutive perfect *wā'ōmar,* "I said." That would be a factual reference to a suppliant's liturgical intervention (most translators change it to *wĕ'ōmar,* "and if I say"). Both possibilities are feasible. Clear enough, in any case, is the changed diction. While vv. 7-10 expose three hypothetical actions, v. 11 introduces a quotation, direct speech, which seems to qualify as a self-damnation: "Only darkness may overcome [or 'smash'? cf. Gen 3:15; *HAL* 1342: 'attack harshly'] me" (v. 11a; cf. Job 3:4-9; Jer 20:14, 16). Taken as a more hypothetical case, this ultimate wish for self-destruction serves as an example to get away from God. Not even this extreme step into black oblivion can be successful: under the auspices of God darkness no longer fulfills its function to hide, destroy, push into chaos, obliterate (v. 12ab, with a gloss attached at the end, 12c). Thus vv. 7-12 are a powerful poetic treatise about the impossibility of escaping from God.

The next block in our psalm (vv. 13-16) is a strange and fascinating representation of creational beliefs unheard of in the Genesis stories. Is this passage meant to provide reasons for why God has so much knowledge and power in relation to his creatures? V. 13 is a motive clause introduced with *kî,* "because." God has "formed" or "created" (*qnh;* cf. Gen 4:1b; 14:19, 22) the adorant's kidneys, and he has "woven me in my mother's womb" (*skk;* cf. Job 10:11). V. 14 is an interjected thanksgiving line with the characteristic formula *'ôdĕkā,* "I do thank you" — the response of the creature to its creator (cf. Pss 18:50 [RSV 49]; 35:18; 52:11 [RSV 9]; 57:10 [RSV 9]; 118:21; 119:7; 138:1; etc., mostly used as a response to specific divine favors). Thereafter, vv. 15-16 spell out the significance of this insight, and, indeed, all statements are in the line of the preceding affirmations (vv. 1-12) about God's knowing and being present even before the time of birth and effectively so all over the world. Again, individual formulations are extraordinary in comparison to other creational reports. Thus the psalmist maintains, "my bones were not hidden from you" (v. 15a), "I was made in a secret location" (v. 15b), "I was stamped in the depths of the earth" (v. 15c). Each of these phrases has the quality of a confessional statement. How are we able to account for this type of discourse? Appeals for personal rescue and affirmations of having been saved by God's intervention abound in individual complaints and thanksgivings (cf. 3:8 [RSV 7]; 7:7 [RSV 6]; 13:4 [RSV 3]; 17:13; 30:2-4 [RSV 1-3]; 40:3 [RSV 2]; R. Albertz, *Frömmigkeit;* listing at "Introduction to Cultic Poetry"). But personal confessions of having been created by God are rare in most OT literature. Some allusions may be found in the Psalms and in some prophetic books, but all of them are in traditional concepts (created in the womb of one's mother: cf. Pss 22:9 [RSV 8]; 71:6; Jer 1:5).

V. 16 is textually uncertain (cf., e.g., Würthwein, Mannati). It does continue, however, along the line of v. 15, adding the concept of God's keeping a book of those faithful to him (cf. Ps 69:29 [RSV 28]; Exod 32:32-33; F. L. Hossfeld and E. Reuter, *TWAT* V, esp. 942-43, about "books kept in heaven").

The summary and conclusion of the three blocks outlined above are vv. 17-18, a hymnic ADORATION of the type: "How great are your deeds!" (cf. 8:2, 10 [RSV 1, 9]; 66:3; 92:6 [RSV 5]; 104:24). Here the verb *yqr,* "be precious," is used, and the subject is the "thoughts" of God (*rē'eykā,* from *rēa'* III, a rare Aramaic word meaning "plan"; cf. v. 2; Mal 2:15). Also, the tone of the two verses is sapiential. The sheer number of things worked out by God makes a human mind numb. They are countless, like the sand along the shore (v. 18a; cf. Gen 22:17; 32:13; 41:49, proverbial down to our own days). Admiration expressed in this kind of shout is more than cheap applause; it means giving back to the one adored a share of his power and authority (cf. Psalms 29; 148).

The last parts of Psalm 139 (nos. VI and VII) seem to be disgustingly inferior to the noble, humble, and open kind of thinking presented in vv. 1-18. Some modern Bible translations do away with the vengeful sections (vv. 19-22) in order to stay with a "morally clean" text. Indeed, the switch to IMPRECATION for us is shocking, comparable to the transition of 104:34 to 35 or 137:4-6 to 7-9. This is true all the more because there are no forewarnings in vv. 1-18 of the existence of enemies and hateful adversaries of Yahweh or the supplicant. With vv. 19-22 we enter the area of demarcation over against the "godless" (v. 19a, *rĕšā'îm;* this may be considered the main designation of the opposing group; other names are *'anšê dāmîm,* "bloody boys," v. 19b; *yō'mĕrûkā limzimmāh,* "they speak against you treacherously," v. 20a; in v. 20b the emendation of Gunkel, 593, may be reasonable: *niśśĕ'û lĕšāw' 'āleykā,* "they rise in vain against you"; vv. 21-22 speak of "haters," "rebels," "enemies"; cf. Keel, *Feinde;* listing at "Introduction to Psalms"). The denunciation of personal enemies was originally part and parcel of individual complaint songs. Here, ostentatiously, the opponents are Yahweh's foes, endangering, as it were, also his faithful. This is sufficient evidence to permit one conclusion: the verses alluded to are to be located in the communal worship, because only in a communal context is Yahweh's confrontation with hostile groups thematized.

Form-critically, we have two subunits in vv. 19-22. First, an outright IMPRECATION, employing a conditional oath formulation (v. 19a), an apotropaic wish (v. 19b), and a relative clause containing the damnation of enemy conduct (v. 20; → Psalm 109; 137). Second, there is a VOW of personal allegiance implying full engagement for the cause of the Lord. In human relations, unconditioned friendship functions along this rule: "I hate whoever hates you," or "Your friend is my friend, your enemy is my enemy" (cf. the friendship story of David and Jonathan, 1 Samuel 18–20; or the declaration of Ruth to stay with her mother-in-law, Ruth 1:16-17. Also, Ps 18:26-27 [RSV 25-26] comes close to this identification of partners). By way of this declaration of solidarity (not by covenant formulas) the alliance of the believers with Yahweh is made perfect (cf. Ps 69:10 [RSV 9]).

The two final lines (vv. 23-24) are straight PETITION to be scrutinized by God, obviously aiming at acquittance from guilt or false accusation. This kind of plea is common in protestations of innocence (→ Psalms 7; 17; 26; also, some speeches of Job belong to that category). Concrete points of suspicion against the supplicant are missing. The text appeals for a general testing, so that God may "determine whether my life is going on correctly, and lead me on the enduring path" (v. 24). Vocabulary and phraseology again remind us of sapiential discourse, because specific motivations for investigation — just as in the corresponding v. 1a — are not enumerated.

Because of its meditative air, its elevated poetic language, depth of thought, and unusual modulations of form elements, Psalm 139 lends itself to other than liturgical analyses. Thus many interpreters study literary structures (e.g., Holman, Auffret) and discover a treasure of literary devices (wordplays, strophes, inclusions, symmetries, chiasms, etc.). Others dedicate themselves to its philosophical and theological insights (cf. Bernhardt, Müller, Holman, Schüngel-Straumann, et al.; main problem: the "omnipresence" of God), the result being the elaboration of a clear thought structure detached from all liturgical background (cf. G. von Rad, *Weisheit in Israel* [Munich: Kaiser, 1970] 69-73, 146; Stolz, *Psalmen;* listing at "Introduction to Psalms"). The text itself seems open to ever new expositions.

## *Genre*

Psalm 139 is one of the most intensely studied poems in the Psalter. The discussion about its genre classification has been going on for a long time with no end in sight. Elements and inklings of various categories of psalms can be detected in the different subunits. The exegete who insists that one single aspect must be determinative for the whole psalm may choose among complaint, thanksgiving, hymn, and wisdom discourse. All these avenues have been tried, to the effect that the picture of our psalm is very colorful in OT research (cf. Anderson, 904-13). One favorite genre identification is that of a COMPLAINT, meaning more precisely a defensive prayer of an innocent, persecuted, or exploited person accused before a cultic tribunal (cf. Würthwein, Mowinckel, Bullard, Beyerlin, Seybold, Holman, Coote, etc.). Text and form elements, as pointed out above, in fact show resemblances with complaint patterns. But authentic complaints of the individual (cf. Psalms 3–7; 31; 35; 38; 140–143; etc.; see "Introduction to Cultic Poetry," section B) are more specific as to the type of the calamity they are to be used against. Our psalm, together with Psalms 12; 39; 49; 90; etc., is no longer preoccupied with individual sufferings. At best, we may say that it is meditating on human destiny before God in general, doing so somewhat in analogy to complaining prayers. But the real use remains rather obscure in Psalms research.

In my opinion, we can make headway on the thorny path of conflicting views only if we agree on some basic rules, such as: (a) Differences of form, contents, and origins notwithstanding, the final text of Psalm 139 included the units analyzed above. There is not enough evidence to divide the text into independent songs. (b) Unity in use presupposed, we should not subject the whole text to the rule of one form element alone. (c) Preconceived ideas about a single author of a given psalm who would be able to guarantee the prayer's unity need to be revised. Psalms are not author-centered pieces of literature, even if they display highly poetic language. (d) Instead, we have to look, as closely as possible, for communal uses in different social and "ecclesiastical" settings. (e) In our present case the common denominator (if it can be discovered) of the different form elements could be a lead in terms of likely or correct genre attribution. Sapiential language and a reflective mood are the most salient features of most of the elements (cf. Müller, von Rad, et al.). One may still doubt whether vv. 19-22 are pertinent to the rest of the psalm, but apart from modern aversion there is no real argument for cutting out that part. Even some wisdom discourse is perceivable in this section in the midst of much standard phraseology: vv. 21b and 22a seem to go beyond fixed language patterns (v. 21b MT: *bitĕqômĕmeykā 'etqôṭāṭ*, "those who rise against you I will despise"; v. 22a: *taklît śin'āh śĕnē'tîm*, "[with] fullness of hate I will hate them"). Furthermore, we have not only the weighty contextual coherence but also the supposed liturgical balance speaking for unity of the psalm. If a group feels the need to ward off deadly enemies, it will do so in the course of worship, even in between very fine and high-ranking liturgical utterances.

What I am driving at is that the reflections in Psalm 139 about God supervising human lives everywhere and anywhere, about our incapacity to withdraw from him into God-free zones, about being created by him (and mother earth?) lead to eulogy, imprecation, and petition, i.e., to a full circle of worship. Since the "I" speaking in Psalm 139 is the conscious and responsible individual member of a larger community (invocation of Yahweh, the God of Israel, is a first guarantee for such an interpretation; the metaphor of the right path in v. 24 is the second; the reflective tone a third moment in favor of this hypothesis), we may assume that all the parts of this poem indeed serve worshiping ends. Tentatively, we may call the psalm a MEDITATION; cf. Psalms 39; 90. But what could be the proper worship situation behind our psalm?

## Setting

Worship is always held in religious groups. Individual acts of adoration are the exception. Now, our psalm is a personal prayer and meditation. What would be its place in a common assembly? Since the text is linguistically, intellectually, and theologically quite sophisticated, we may surmise it being read by a wise man, perhaps representatives of some school or learned circle (cf. A. Lemaire, *ABD* II, 305-12; Davies, *Scribes;* listing at Additional Bibliography, section B), to a public audience (at least vv. 1-16). Vv. 17-18 could be a communal response to the recitation, although the communal "we" (first person plural) is missing. Various liturgical officiants thereafter would intone imprecation, vow, and petition to be scrutinized, in order to take all burdening problems of humankind to Yahweh. The general background, I would suggest, is the exilic, or better, postexilic community in either Judah or the diaspora.

## Intention

Predominantly, the individual member of the Yahweh congregation is to be confronted with the — sometimes smothering — presence of Yahweh. He or

406

she is to establish a good relation to this personal creator-God. His supervising presence can be accepted as wholesome, not destructive ("Big Brother is watching you"), because God's scrutiny lays bare the truth of human existence. Within the sheltering presence of the community, then, the suppliant is to seek security from outward enemies (Babylonian persecution, as in Psalm 137?) and orientation under the eyes of Yahweh. Psalm 139 has this invisible double horizon: individuals wrestling with their God, but within a community of faith.

## Bibliography

L. C. Allen, "Faith on Trial: An Analysis of Ps 139," in *Vox evangelica* (ed. D. Guthrie; London: Bible College, 1976) 2-23; P. Auffret, "O Dieu, connais mon coeur," *VT* 47 (1997) 1-22; D. L. Balas, "The Meaning of the 'Cross,'" in *The Easter Sermons of Gregory of Nyssa* (ed. A. Spira, et al.; Cambridge: Philadelphia Patristic Foundation, 1981) 305-18; G. M. Behler, "'Seigneur, tu me sondes et tu me connais,'" *VieS* 50 (1959) 29-56; idem, "Der nahe und der schwer zu fassende Gott," *BibLeb* 6 (1965) 135-52; K. H. Bernhardt, "Zur Gottesvorstellung von Psalm 139," in *Kirche, Theologie, Frömmigkeit (Fest.* G. Holtz; ed. H. Benckert, et al.; Berlin: Evangelische Verlagsanstalt, 1965) 20-31; W. P. Brown, "Psalm 139," *Int* 50 (1996) 280-84; J. M. Bullard, "Psalm 139: Prayer in Stillness," *SBLSP 1975* (ed. G. MacRae; 2 vols.; Missoula, Mont.: Scholars Press, 1975) I, 141-50; C. H. Bullock, "Abortion, and Old Testament Prophetic and Poetic Literature," in *Abortion: A Christian Understanding and Response* (ed. J. Hoffmeier; Grand Rapids: Baker, 1987) 65-71; K. Cooper, "Through the Ages: A Look at How Psalm 139:13 Has Endured 600 Years of Translations," *Publishers Weekly* 238 (1991) 11-18; R. B. Coote, "Psalm 139," in *The Bible and the Politics of Exegesis* (ed. D. Jobling, et al.; Cleveland: Pilgrim, 1991) 33-38; J. H. Costen, "Viewing Life from High Places," *The Journal of the Interdenominational Theological Center* 24 (1996) 183-88; G. A. Danell, "Psalm 139," *Uppsala Universitets Arsskrift* (1951) 1-37; B. J. Diebner, "Predigen 'über' Ps 139?" *Dielheimer Blätter* 19 (1984) 107-26; T. W. Engstrom, "Procrastinating When You Would Rather Not," *Leadership* 6 (1985) 42-45; G. Etzelmüller, "Überlegungen zur Schöpfungstheologie in Psalm 139," in *Resonanzen (Fest.* M. Welker; ed. S. Brandt, et al.; Wuppertal: Foedus, 1997) 324-34; A. Glasner, "Psalm 139 and the Identification of Its Author," *BM* 60 (1974) 79-86; D. Glenn, "An Exegetical and Theological Exposition of Psalm 139," in *Tradition and Testament (Fest.* C. L. Feinberg; ed. J. S. Feinberg, et al.; Chicago: Moody Press, 1981) 161-88; W. Harrelson, "On God's Knowledge of the Self: Psalm 139," *Currents in Theology and Mission* 2 (1975) 261-65; Z. Hawkinson, "The Covenant: Being," *Covenant Quarterly* 43 (1985) 13-24; H. J. Hermisson, "Altes Testament und Märchen," *EvT* 45 (1985) 299-322; idem, "Gottes Freiheit — Spielraum des Menschen," *ZTK* 82 (1985) 129-52; J. C. M. Holman, *Psalm 139: Basic Exegesis* (diss., Rome, 1969); idem, "The Structure of Psalm CXXXIX," *VT* 21 (1971) 298-310; idem, "Semiotic Analysis of Psalm CXXXVIII (LXX)," *OTS* 26 (1990) 84-100; idem, "Psalm 139 (TM) and Psalm 138 (LXX): A Semiotic Comparison," in *Goldene Äpfel in silbernen Schalen* (ed. K. Schunck, et al.; Frankfurt: Peter Lang, 1992) 113-21; H. Hommel, "Das religionsgeschichtliche Problem des 139. Psalms," *ZAW* 47 (1929) 110-12; F. Hübner, "Psalm 139," in *Gasteiner Gespräch* (ed. H. Schnell; Hamburg: Lutherisches

Verlagshaus, 1971) 138-52; R. Kilian, "In Gott geborgen," *BK* 26 (1971) 97-102; J. Koole, "Quelques remarques sur Psaume 139," in *Studia Biblica et Semitica (Fest.* T. C. Vriezen; ed. A. S. van der Woude, et al.; Wageningen: H. Veenman en Zonen, 1966) 176-80; J. Krasovec, "Die polare Ausdrucksweise im Psalm 139," *BZ* 18 (1974) 224-48; R. Lapointe, "La nuit est ma lumière," *CBQ* 33 (1971) 397-402; M. Mannati, "Psaume 139,14-16," *ZAW* 83 (1971) 257-61; Y. Mazor, "When Aesthetics Is Harnessed to Psychological Characterization," *ZAW* 109 (1997) 260-71; H.-P. Müller, "Die Gattung des 139. Psalms," *Zeitschrift der Deutschen Morgenländischen Gesellschaft, Supplement I/1* (1969) 345-55; R. Pettazoni, *The All-Knowing God* (London: Methuen, 1956); P. J. Philibert, "Contemplation and the Life Cycle," *American Benedictine Review* 49 (1998) 123-37; R. Pytel, "Psalm 139,15," *Folia Orientalia* 13 (1971) 257-66; G. Rice, "Psalm 139: A Diary of an Inward Journey," *Journal of Religious Thought* 37 (1980/81) 63-67; idem, "The Integrity of Psalm 139,20b," *CBQ* 46 (1984) 28-30; L. Sabottka, "*rē'êkā* in Ps. 139,17: Ein adverbieller Akkusativ," *Bib* 63 (1982) 558-59; M. Saebø, "Salme 139 ig visdomsdiktningen," *Tidsskrift for teologi og kirke* 34 (1966) 167-84; H. Schüngel-Straumann, "Zur Gattung und Theologie des 139. Psalms," *BZ* 17 (1973) 39-51; C. R. Smith, "The Book of Life," *Grace Theological Journal* 6 (1985) 219-30; K. A. Tanberg, "Die Bewertung des ungeborenen Lebens im alten Israel und im alten Orient," *SJOT* 1 (1987) 51-65; J. Vandevalle, "Psalm 139 and the Atharva-Veda," *Indian Ecclesiastical Studies* 8 (1969) 83-105; M. Weiss, "From Thee to Thee I Flee in Psalm 139," in *Proceedings of the 10th World Congress of Jewish Studies* (ed. D. Assaf; Jerusalem: Magnes, 1990) 31-35; V. Weymann, "Gottes Verharmlosung als Vergiftung des Lebens," *EvT* 44 (1984) 64-77; E. Würthwein, "Erwägungen zu Psalm 139," *VT* 7 (1957) 165-82 (repr. in idem, *Wort und Existenz* [Göttingen: Vandenhoeck & Ruprecht, 1970] 179-96).

# Psalm 140:
# Complaint of the Individual

## Structure

|  | MT | NRSV |
|---|---|---|
| I. Superscription | 1 | - |
| II. Invocation and petition | 2 | 1 |
| III. Complaint | 3-4 | 2-3 |
| IV. Petition | 5 | 4 |
| V. Complaint | 6 | 5 |
| VI. Invocation and affirmation of confidence | 7-8 | 6-7 |
| VII. Imprecation | 9-12 | 8-11 |
| VIII. Affirmation of confidence | 13-14 | 12-13 |

The SUPERSCRIPTION is practically identical with that of → Psalm 139 (change of word order only). The prayer is part of the Davidic collection in Psalms 138–145. The four petitionary prayers (Psalms 140–143) are placed in the middle of this collection; naturally, they have much in common.

408

The psalm exhibits form elements of individual complaint throughout, but arrangements of subunits are somewhat peculiar (cf. "Introduction to Cultic Poetry," section 4B). Initially, we find a line of full-fledged PETITION (v. 2; no customary initial plea to be heard) that is repeated almost verbatim in v. 5. The INVOCATION is rather reduced: there is only one simple appellation of Yahweh in v. 2a. On the other hand, vv. 7-8 are much more geared to the introductory qualities of complaint. The invocation is more elaborate (v. 7a: "I said to Yahweh: You are my God"; v. 8a: "Yahweh, my Lord, my powerful help!"). Furthermore, an initial plea is extant in v. 7b, and possibly initial praise in v. 8b. Did the text get mixed up or turned around during transmission? Have two psalm fragments been glued together, and we are really dealing with two separate units? Or has there been a liturgical procedure postponing the opening statements until the middle of the ritual? In the absence of more evidence for division or fragmentation of the text, we propose to treat it as it stands now.

The two petitionary lines vv. 2 and 5 function together; slight variations emphasize liturgical and theological highlights. Actually, only the respective first cola differ, the second ones of each line being identical. The verbs of the first cola are in the masculine singular imperative addressing God, with first-person singular suffixes, meaning the suppliant ("deliver me"; "guard me"). They are common expressions in the complaint category: ḥlṣ, Piel, "rescue from" (v. 2a; cf. imperatives in 6:5 [RSV 4]; 119:153; other forms, 18:20 [RSV 19]; 34:8 [RSV 7]; 50:15; 81:8 [RSV 7]; 91:15; 116:8), šmr, Qal, "protect" (v. 5a; cf. imperatives addressed to God, 16:1; 17:8; 25:20; 86:2; 141:9; other forms, 12:8 [RSV 7]; 41:3 [RSV 2]; 116:6; 121:7-8; 145:20; etc.). Second cola verbs are in the corresponding imperfect form, with the appropriate suffix as well, and in both lines identical: tinṣĕrēnî, "guard me" (vv. 2b and 5b; cf. imperative, 141:3; precative imperfects, 32:7; 64:2 [RSV 1]; other forms, 40:12 [RSV 11]; 61:8 [RSV 7]; 141:3). The petitionary lines consequently correspond perfectly to complaint usages; some of the parallel texts given above even use the verbs in introductory passages.

The opponents referred to in our petition are characterized as "evil person" ('ādām rā', v. 2a; cf. 'ādām in a hostile sense, 116:11; 118:6; 119:134; 124:2), "wicked hands" (yĕdê rāšā', v. 5a; cf. 36:12 [RSV 11]; 71:4; 82:4; 97:10; and related passages, e.g., 17:13; 37:40; 119:53, 61), and "violent man" ('îš ḥămāsîm, vv. 2b, 5b; cf. v. 12; 18:49 [RSV 48]; Prov 3:31; 16:29; and related passages, Pss 11:5; 27:12; 35:11), relatively common expressions in a rich vocabulary of hostility (cf. Keel, Feinde; see listing at "Introduction to Psalms").

Both lines of petition are followed by a relative clause with exactly the same heading: "they who think . . ." (vv. 3a, 5a), to characterize the evil machinations of the enemies. Thus both designations of the opponents are bolstered by COMPLAINTS (vv. 3-4, 5c-6). The first instance of complaining evolves regularly in terms of rhythm and style. Two bicola formulate what the wicked ones have been planning and doing: evil machinations in general (v. 3) and vicious slander in particular (v. 4). The meter is 4 + 3 and 4 + 4 beats, respectively. The subject of the one current relative clause is the enemy, pointed out twice in v. 2. We notice that the singular nouns in the preceding line are to signalize collective entities, because the three verbs in the relative clause (vv. 3ab, 4a) and the suffix referring to them (v. 4b) are all in the plural. We get a stereotyped but clear picture of the evil ones molesting the suppliant. Verbal aggressiveness, slander, and cursing were considered very harmful because of magical, malignant potencies implied in evil words; cf. 10:7; 31:21 (RSV 20); 41:7-9 (RSV 6-8); 52:4-6 (RSV 2-4); 55:22 (RSV 21); 57:5 (RSV 4); 58:5 (RSV 4); 64:2-7 (RSV 1-6); 109:2-3; 120:2-3, and more often.

The second round of describing enemy activities and thereby raising complaints (vv. 5c-6) is much less homogeneous and balanced. It does begin, to be sure, with the same expression as v. 2a: "they who think . . ." (v. 5c). The verb *ḥšb*, "think, plan," is here followed by an infinitive construct with the preposition *lĕ*, to mark the finality of their planning. Next, a new grammatical subject is introduced, giving a new name to the enemies: "haughty ones" (v. 6a; *gē'îm;* cf. Ps 94:2; Prov 15:25; 16:19; Job 40:11-12). The metrical structure and division of cola is a mess; as MT stands in the Leningrad MS (basis for *BHS; BHK* harmonizes lines), we have three truncated lines of 4, 3 + 3, and 5 beats. (Commentators like to mold the text into two lines of 4 + 4 or 3 + 4 stresses each; cf. Gunkel, 593. Kraus, 1104, diagnoses tricola in vv. 5 and 6.) The word order and balance of phrases are precarious. Therefore, contemplating the very regular structure of vv. 3-4 in comparison, we may suspect that the text is in some disorder. Still, the basic substance of a plaintive description of enemies is there. They are depicted as hunters, the suppliant feeling him- or herself their helpless victim (hunting metaphors abound, too, in the Psalter; cf. the triad of "bird trap," "net," and "trap" in v. 6; other constellations in 9:16 [RSV 15]; 10:9; 31:5 [RSV 4]; 35:7-8; 57:7 [RSV 6]; 64:6 [RSV 5]; 91:3; 124:7; 119:110; 141:9-10; 142:4 [RSV 3]).

Petition and complaint having been uttered, an AFFIRMATION OF CONFIDENCE may be in order during a rite of pleading for a suffering individual (vv. 7-8). We already noted that the passage, strangely enough at this late point, has a certain introductory character. A quotation formula ("I said," or "I say," v. 7a) marks a traditional and concise expression of confidence (v. 7a; cf. 22:2, 11 [RSV 1, 10]; 63:2 [RSV 1]; 68:25 [RSV 24]; 89:27 [RSV 26]; 102:25 [RSV 24]; 118:28). Formally and according to contents, v. 7b is an INITIAL PLEA (cf. 28:2; 86:6; 143:1), while v. 8b spells out the affirmation of confidence of v. 7a, 8a. Formulaic expressions constitute the nucleus of the declaration of confidence: "You are my God" (v. 7a), a basic form in individual/familial confessions (cf. Vorländer, *Gott;* listing at "Introduction to Cultic Poetry"; van der Toorn, *Religion;* Additional Bibliography, section B; cf. 22:2-3 [RSV 1-2]; 63:2 [RSV 1]; 118:28). The concise formula is reinforced by a resounding "Yahweh, my Lord, my strong help" (v. 8a; cf. similar phrases of confidence: 28:7; 59:18 [RSV 17]; 62:3, 7, 8 [RSV 2, 6, 7]; 71:7; 88:2 [RSV 1]; 89:27 [RSV 26]; 118:14). V. 8a is an honorific appellation, as the second-person address in v. 8b proves. "Yahweh, my Lord," is still a personal confessional formula, much in contrast to the later "The Lord Yahweh" ("has spoken," thus often in Ezekiel and other prophets). For a strictly identical expression see Pss 109:21; 141:8; inverted word order in 71:5. The formulation echoes v. 7a: "You are my God." Praising attributes like "strength of my help" = "my strong help"

(v. 8a), as indicated above, abound in the Psalms, but the exact formulation is unique here. Some passages outside the Psalter broaden the evidence; cf. Exod 15:2; Isa 12:2 (both almost identical with Ps 118:14); 49:5; Jer 16:19.

Petition for the suppliant's sake has been voiced strongly in vv. 2 and 5; the counterpart, the IMPRECATION of evildoers, now follows in vv. 9-11 (12) — a logical sequel for the ancient mind. The evil has to be fought at its roots, i.e., right where the deadly planning is going on: in the minds and lives of the wicked adversaries. (Modern medicine, psychology, psychoanalysis, social care, etc., take similar avenues, naturally, on the basis of present-day knowledge.) The thrust of v. 9 is to ward off the machinations of these (probably unknown) enemies. Vv. 10-11 counteract the evil powers first by trying to revert them to those who created and wielded them, a common practice in ancient times (v. 10; cf. only 35:8; 109:17-19; the saying of one "preparing a pit" for his fellow man and "falling into it himself," e.g., 7:16 [RSV 15]; 57:7 [RSV 6], has become proverbial in our own culture). Second, the last in the whole series of imprecative measures calls on God to annihilate the evilmongers and destroy them for good (v. 11). This means that imprecation may take different steps, in our case in a culminating way, involving all the means at the suppliant's disposal. V. 12 stands out a little isolated, because it does not exhibit any traces of prayer language. Neither the suppliant nor God has a part in this ill-wish, which shows some proverbial qualities. Grammatical subjects of the two cola are "man of tongue" (v. 12a; cf. v. 4) and "violent man" (v. 12b; cf. vv. 2b, 5b). This reference to the first unit is hardly accidental. Apparently, someone synthesized the contents of complaint into an ill-wish against the evilmongers. The secondary nature of this verse is also evident by its heavy phraseology. The line seems overburdened (should there be 4 + 5 beats in it?). Two double-word subjects, one as *casus pendens,* followed by a third lexeme, the real subject (*rā',* "evil," v. 12b), a positive and negative wish, a "surplus" hapax legomenon at the end, which cannot easily be identified (*lĕmadhēpōt; HAL* 520: "blow after blow," from *dhp,* "beat") — all these features make it difficult to discover the role of v. 12. Has it been added to the text as a gloss? Was it used in liturgy to confirm the general thrust of imprecation? This function seems likely, but we do not know.

Finally, the composers, users, and transmitters of Psalm 140 come to a close with an AFFIRMATION OF CONFIDENCE (vv. 13-14) opened by the stereotyped "I know" (v. 13a; the Ketib could be second person; cf. the formula of certitude: 20:7 [RSV 6]; 41:12 [RSV 11]; 56:10 [RSV 9]; 119:75, 152; 135:5). The affirmation has a confessional ring about it, like 56:10 (RSV 9): "This I know: God is with me"; or 135:5: "Yes, I [personally] know: God is great — and our Lord, from all the gods." Trust in Yahweh is voiced in regard to his solidarity with the "poor" (*'ĕbyōnîm,* plural, indicating a communal setting; cf. E. S. Gerstenberger, *THAT* I, 20-25) and "oppressed" (*'ānî,* singular; cf. E. S. Gerstenberger, *TWAT* VI, 247-70) people (v. 13b; J. D. Pleins, *ABD* V, 402-14). It is for the first and only time that exactly these designations come to the fore; "I am oppressed and poor" does occur on strictly individual terms (40:18 [RSV 17]; 70:6 [RSV 5]; 86:1; 109:22; cf. 25:16; 69:30 [RSV 29]; 88:16 [RSV 15]; for poverty as subject matter see Psalms 9/10; 37; etc.). Supposedly, they are self-designations of the community that transmitted the psalm (cf. esp. Hossfeld and Zenger, 1993, 14-15; and the interpretation of, e.g., Psalms 9/10; 14; 37; etc.; Lohfink, *Lobgesänge;* Additional Bibliography, section C; and some Latin American exegetes like C. Mesters, M. Schwantes, G. Pixley, et al.). The naming of the reference group goes on in v. 14. Here they appear as "just ones" and "upright ones," to whom a glorious future is predicted. The imperfect verbs (*yôdû,* "give thanks"; *yēšĕbû,* "sit down") do not show exhortatory character. They are factual descriptions of what will happen when Yahweh attends to the clamor of his faithful.

## Genre

Without doubt our psalm is a traditional INDIVIDUAL COMPLAINT (→ "Introduction to Cultic Poetry," section 4B) used in cases of personal distress and anxiety. There is little emphasis on depicting the fate of the suppliant, however (contrast Psalms 22; 38; 69; etc.). The evilmongers are much more the focus, of course, in liturgical language and standard metaphors. Yet the trust motif stands out, as well as, in the two last lines, the moorings of the suppliant in his or her congregation.

## Setting

This last feature, indeed, should not be overlooked. Congregational worship is the living context also for individual complaint. In preexilic times this liturgical situation was normally family life and/or the local sanctuary (→ Psalms 3–7; Gerstenberger, *Mensch;* listing at "Introduction to Cultic Poetry"). Later on, individual supplication was incorporated into and adapted to the exilic and postexilic community worship, which was not tied down to the Jerusalem temple, but subsisted beside and away from that central sanctuary (→ Psalms 12; 69; 102; 120). To pinpoint the evil besetting the community is difficult. But economic exploitation and oppression, besides slander and injustice, seem to be part of the miserable situation (cf. Neh 5:1-13).

## Intention

To get down to the roots of personal calamities is a legitimate concern of every human being and his or her intimate group. In antiquity (as well as — under different plausibility rules — in our own societies) the search for reasons for all ills that befell people often produced culprits in the form of other human beings, evilmongers, bad people. With the help of the personal deity these instigators of ills were warded off, condemned, and possibly persecuted. Living conditions have changed drastically since then. While cases remain of people responsible for grave ills, the means to counteract evil powers today include political and economic action especially against dramatically increased poverty.

They are not confined to prayer (and incantations, black magic, etc., which are largely excluded in today's traditions, but regaining force in some, even rationalistic, cultures). In many instances, also, medical, psychological, and social support are called for. But the basic intention of our psalm remains noteworthy: to help the individual to recuperate his or her standing in the community of human beings.

## Bibliography

A. Y. Collins, "The Appropriation of Individual Lament by Mark," in *The Scriptures in the Gospels* (ed. C. Tuckett; Leuven: Leuven University Press, 1997) 223-41; M. Greenberg, "Psalm 140," *Eretz Israel* 14 (1978) 88-99; H. M. Pope, "A Little Soul-Searching," *Maarav* 1 (1978/79) 25-31; H. Schmidt, *Das Gebet des Angeklagten im Alten Testament* (BZAW 49; Giessen: Töpelmann, 1928).

# Psalm 141:
# Complaint of the Individual

## Text

At times (esp. vv. 3, 4c, 5d, 6-7) transmission of the psalm has caused damage to the text that leaves us guessing at the meaning of words and phrases. Modern interpreters either refrain from dealing with these verses altogether, or they try to recover some lost meaning, resulting in a large number of different proposals (cf., e.g., Gunkel, 596; Hartmann, 28-31; Seybold, 213-14). We here presuppose more or less the translations of NRSV and Jerusalem Bible.

## Structure

|  | MT | NRSV |
|---|---|---|
| I. Superscription | 1a | - |
| II. Invocation and initial plea | 1b-2 | 1-2 |
| III. Petition | 3-4 | 3-4 |
| IV. Imprecation | 5-7 | 5-7 |
| A. Concession | 5 | 5 |
| B. Condemnation | 6-7 | 6-7 |
| V. Affirmation of confidence | 8 | 8 |
| VI. Petition | 9-10 | 9-10 |
| A. Petition | 9 | 9 |
| B. Imprecation | 10 | 10 |

"Song of David" is one of the most frequent headings in the Psalter (cf. Psalms 15; 143). The SUPERSCRIPTION thus links our text with the old tradi-

413

tions of David, the musician (cf. 1 Sam 16:17-23) and organizer of temple music (1 Chronicles 16; 25). By being identified also with personal prayers, the ancient king of Judah and Israel becomes the prototype of a plain suppliant. The complaint psalm at hand opens with a proper INVOCATION and INITIAL PLEA, as many specimens of this genre do (cf. Psalms 4; 5; 17; 28; 54; 55; 61; 64; 70; 77; 88; 102). A description of crying out to God and urgent requests to be heard and rescued are typical for this opening (cf. "come quickly," v. 1; 70:2, 6 [RSV 1, 5]; 71:12 [RSV 11]; Boyce, *Cry;* Additional Bibliography, section B). What is particular, however, in our two-line introduction of the prayer is the connection made between praying and some kinds of sacrifice (v. 2). Yahweh is addressed directly in both lines, the suppliant being identified by his or her "I," also in both lines. That means that we uniformly have full prayer style in this passage. Rarely, though, do we find relations between personal prayer and sacrifice articulated as is the case in v. 2. Prayer is called by its classical names: *těpillāh* ("request," not "intercession," v. 2a; cf. Gerstenberger, *TWAT* VI, 606-17) and "lifting up of hands" (*maś'at kappayim,* v. 2b; Sumerian/Akkadian *šu illu*). These technical designations are widely used, especially the first one (cf. 4:2 [RSV 1]; 6:10 [RSV 9]; 42:9 [RSV 8]; 66:19-20; 69:14 [RSV 13]; 80:5 [RSV 4]; 88:3 [RSV 2]; 102:18 [RSV 17]; 1 Kgs 8:28-29, 45, 49; Isa 56:7; Jer 7:16; 11:14; Neh 1:6, 11; and many more times). Expressions describing the prayer gesture of "raising" or "opening" hands, well attested also in ancient iconography (cf. O. Keel, *Welt,* 287-301; listing at "Introduction to Cultic Poetry"), occur here and there, articulated with different verbs, in the OT (cf. Pss 44:21 [RSV 20]; 63:5 [RSV 4]; 88:10 [RSV 9]; 119:48; 1 Kgs 8:22, 38; Jer 4:31; Job 11:13; etc.). These standard gestures of prayer contrast with one with "incense" (*qěṭōret;* cf. Ps 66:15, the only other occurrence in the Psalter; Zwickel, *Räucherkult;* listing at Additional Bibliography, section B). The text is probably not referring to that incense offering that accompanied temple rituals (cf. Exod 30:1-10; Lev 16:12-13; Num 7:10-89 passim). The burning of herbs and spices may have been a much older custom in private worship, i.e., on house altars (cf. Gerstenberger, *Yahweh;* listing at Additional Bibliography, section B). And what about the "evening offering" in v. 2b? In this case the reference to temple ritual seems much more obvious. The expression intimates a daily cycle of sacrifices, and private persons seem to have preferred the morning hours for their ceremonial rites (cf. Pss 5:4 [RSV 3]; 59:17 [RSV 16]; 88:14 [RSV 13]; 143:8); at least the evening is not often mentioned as the time for prayer (cf. 30:6; 55:18). On the other hand, in late OT times (ca. second century B.C.E.) a domestic evening prayer had been established (cf. Dan 9:21; Ezra 9:4-5) perhaps in concordance with temple sacrifices, and our expression may refer to it. In this case a domestic mooring of the whole of v. 2 would be evident, and possibly worship at home was considered not so much as antagonistic to temple rituals but rather in harmony with them.

The meaning of vv. 3-4 is fairly clear, although some words need to be adjusted: the prayer is articulating PETITIONS to Yahweh for protection and guidance, apparently detached from the urgency of part I. At first, the suppliant pleads to God to watch over the words he may utter (v. 3), making God the guardian of his mouth, a sapiential way of thinking (cf. Sir 22:27). Proverbial wisdom usually puts it as the responsibility of everyone to guard his or her mouth (cf. Prov 10:31-32; 15:2, 28; 13:3; 16:23; 21:23; Ps 39:2 [RSV 1]). Our prayer calls on God to accomplish this difficult task. Petition goes on to ask deliverance from temptations emanating from evil examples and persons prone to attract envy by their lifestyle and luxurious living (v. 4d, *man'ammîm*, "delicious food," is a hapax, from *n'm*, "be agreeable, delicious"; other psalms call the opponents "rich" and "fat"; cf. 49:3, 17 [RSV 2, 16]; 73:4-7). Still, from a scant descriptive reference we cannot judge what kind of persons or groups are to be avoided. Other psalms simply alert us against being in the company of the "godless" or "wicked" (*rĕšā'îm*; cf. v. 4b; 1:1, 6; 37;16; 73:3, 12; 94:3; 119:115).

The question of the "wicked" in the Psalms (and other writings) is surely a thorny one. We should like to know exactly whether the group alluded to was defined more by misdeeds or by deviant cultic practice, or perhaps by confessional stance and credal formulations (as became customary later in Christian tradition). Although the Psalter testifies also to groupings of *rĕšā'îm*, in juxtaposition to the *ṣaddîqîm*, "righteous," the exact outlines of that "counter-community" are not clear (cf. H. Ringgren, *TWAT* VII, 675-84, who does not even pose the question; Levin, *Gebetbuch;* Brueggemann, *Theology,* 373-99; listings at Additional Bibliography, section C). In short, the petition of vv. 3-4 comes as a surprise after a fervent introductory plea to be saved by Yahweh. We realize that the prayer is located in a congregational environment where members are afraid of the "sins of mouth and lips" (cf. also Exod 20:16; Pss 12:3-5 [RSV 2-4]; 15:3; 50:19-20) as well as of the delusiveness of "wicked" people of different morals or beliefs. Prayer for protection from sinning is definitely a sapiential concern; cf. Psalm 119.

The problem is further ventilated in the next segment, vv. 5-7, which has strong denunciatory overtones; therefore I call it an IMPRECATION. V. 5, to be sure, only initiates the matter of delineation from the "wicked," conceding, as it were, only to good-willed people the right to criticize (cf. Prov 27:5-6; Lev 19:17; internal discipline in Christian communities comes to mind, Matt 18:15-17). This much is recognizable in the extant MT. The following two lines are in a sad state of preservation. But they at least let transpire an aggressive attitude against "them," i.e., the other, hostile party. If the first word of v. 6 in fact was *nišmĕṭû*, "they should be cast down," then it has to be understood as a threat against the wicked ones. And if in the last colon (v. 7b) the first-person plural suffix should be changed into a third-person plural suffix ("their bones," thus some LXX MSS, instead of the strange "our bones"), then the imprecatory note would be perfectly clear: "May 'their' bones be thrown to the mouth of Sheol." The first and the last colon exhibit Niphal forms expressing the passive voice, presumably of acts against the evildoers. The rest of this passage, vv. 6b and 7a, does not tune in very well with that passive and maledictory discourse.

A clear AFFIRMATION OF CONFIDENCE (v. 8) followed immediately by final, double-edged PETITIONS (vv. 9-10) rounds off the psalm. Confidence is voiced together with an elaborate invocation of God ("Yahweh, my Lord," v. 8a; cf. 69:7 [RSV 6]; 71:5, 16; 109:21; 140:8 [RSV 7]), a standard expression of "seeking shelter" with the Deity (v. 8b; cf. only first-person singular expressions of *ḥsh* in complaints: 7:2 [RSV 1]; 11:1; 16:1; 18:3 [RSV 2]; 25:20; 31:2

415

[RSV 1]; 57:2 [RSV 1]; 61:5 [RSV 4]; 71:1; 144:2; E. S. Gerstenberger, *THAT* I, 621-23; *běkā hāsîtî,* "in you I trust," may be labeled a "FORMULA OF CONFIDENCE," 622), and, at the very end, a negative plea, i.e., not to "be killed" (*'rh,* Piel, with *nepeš,* in this sense is a hapax legomenon; cf. 137:7). Asking to be spared is in line with the general outlook of the psalm that — although talking with great urgency at the beginning (cf. also *hûšāh lî,* "hasten [to save] me," v. 1b) — implores for protection throughout.

The final PETITION in its twofold shape falls into the general thought pattern. It asks for preservation of that life which is going on, not explicitly or implicitly for salvation from the pit (key word: *šmr,* "guard," v. 9a; cf. 16:1; 17:8; 25:20; 86:2; 140:5). Protection is needed, because the "evildoers" (v. 9b; cf. v. 4c) are now pictured as hunters, no longer as seducers to a different and awful kind of life as in vv. 3-4. The hunting metaphor occurs here again with three different images (vv. 9-10; → 140:6), two of which are identical with the ones in 140:6 (*pah* and *mōqēš*). Also, the probate inversion of the enemy's curse is asked for in the imprecatory part of the petition (v. 10a; → 140:10). In the end, however, the positive wish for the suppliant's well-being and safety prevails (v. 10b).

The structure, also due to bad preservation of the text, is quite different in the analyses consulted. Seybold reconstructs a basic text with strophes of four lines each ("Psalm 141," 201-2); Allen (p. 274) discovers an original "triad of prayers and wishes" (vv. 1-2, 3-5, 8b-10, with later additions).

## Genre

Our psalm is without doubt a COMPLAINT OF THE INDIVIDUAL, because it is well provided with complaint elements and vocabulary (see "Introduction to Cultic Poetry," section 4B). However, the special situation of a kind of "preventive" and "sapiential" complaint should be noticed. The complaint element proper is not very evident, in contrast to the petitions, especially the fencing-off type. Luring dangers of becoming drawn away from the community seem to be behind the text. The "wicked" are the target of accusatory discourse, because they are considered responsible for the precarious situation. A certain sapiential posture is acknowledged by most commentators; the reason for this variation of complaint may be found simply in the psalm's communal setting.

## Setting

But what could have been the liturgical context for a complaint psalm of this outlook? Obviously, the dangers involving the suppliant are of a spiritual and moral kind. The psalmist fears being dragged away from Yahweh, or rather from the right path with Yahweh, and probably from the community of the "righteous." This group of Yahweh believers does not explicitly introduce itself in the psalm; the lone first-person plural suffix in v. 7b is probably a scribal error. Nevertheless, the congregation of the "righteous" are present, testified to by the opposition of the "wicked," as well as by common prayer practice (v. 2), the "righ-

416

teous" neighbor who is willing to take on corrective functions (v. 5a), the presence and attention of Yahweh, who is the God of Israel, the usage of a formulaic prayer agenda, which was and is part of a communal collection of prayers and songs. Thus the late (postexilic) congregation of Judeans is the likely life situation of our psalm. If this is correct, the psalm does not reflect a purely individual emergency, but rather an enduring condition the members of the congregation felt uncomfortable with. Therefore the "I" form somewhat hides the collective use of this complaint (cf. Caquot). The opposition of the "evildoers," however, does testify more clearly to the colliding factions.

## Intention

Struggling with seductive groups that in one way or another appeared to deviate from "orthodox" Judaism became a characteristic of the Persian and Hellenistic epochs. Nehemiah fought against the Samaritans already, Ezra had to demarcate correct conduct in the case of mixed marriages, the Qumran community was a vivid example of schism among the Jews; in Maccabean times there were rival groups of differing religious and political orientation; Josephus and other writers tell us about Pharisees, Sadducees, Zealots, etc. Something of this type of differentiation already comes up in the Psalter (cf. Psalms 37; 49; 69; Smith, *Parties;* Additional Bibliography, section B). Psalm 141 wants to help an "orthodox" group defend itself against the wicked.

## Bibliography

A. Caquot, "L'énigme du Psaume 141," *Positions luthériennes* 20 (1972) 14-26; D. Gualandi, "Salmo 141 (140)," *RivB* 6 (1958) 219-33; B. Hartmann, "Exegetische und religionsgeschichtliche Studie zu Psalm 141:5d-7," in *Tradition and Re-Interpretation (Fest.* J. C. H. Lebram; ed. J. Henten, et al.; Leiden: Brill, 1986) 27-37; H. Junker, "Einige Rätsel im Urtext der Psalmen," *Bib* 24 (1943) 197-212; P. Nechayev, "Evening Sacrifice," *Journal of the Moscow Patriarchate* 1 (1985) 40-41; K. Seybold, "Psalm 141. Ein neuer Anlauf," in *Biblische Welten (Fest.* M. Metzger; ed. W. Zwickel; Fribourg: Universitätsverlag; Göttingen: Vandenhoeck & Ruprecht, 1993) 199-214; R. Tournay, "Le Psaume 141," *VT* 9 (1959) 58-64.

## Psalm 142:
## Complaint of the Individual

### Structure

|  | MT | NRSV |
|---|---|---|
| I. Superscription | 1 | - |
| II. Initial plea (descriptive) | 2-3 | 1-2 |

417

| III. Affirmation of confidence | 4ab | 3ab |
|---|---|---|
| IV. Complaint | 4c-5 | 3c-4 |
| V. Invocation, affirmation of confidence | 6 | 5 |
| VI. Petition and complaint | 7-8b | 6-7b |
| VII. Vow | 8cd | 7cd |

Thirteen of the David psalms carry a special heading referring to some incident of that king's "biography," as far as it is extant in 1 and 2 Samuel. Our present SUPERSCRIPTION connects the following prayer with David "while staying in the cave," no doubt a reference either to 1 Samuel 24 or to 1 Sam 22:1. The first alternative is more likely. The "editors" of Psalm 142 may have considered not only David's general situation of fugitive reflected in the psalm (vv. 5, 7-8), but also his qualms about violating the king of Israel (cf. 1 Sam 24:5-8 to vv. 3-4). A similar "biographical" superscription goes with → Psalm 57. The old, redactional genre term *maśkîl*, "instruction" (?), with 13 occurrences in psalm headings, does have sapiential connotations (→ Psalm 32; cf. the verb *śkl*, Hiphil; H. Schmoldt, *TWAT* VII, 1323-27). The term *tĕpillāh*, "prayer," on the other hand, being attached to the heading, predominantly stands for our COMPLAINT OF THE INDIVIDUAL (five occurrences in superscriptions: Psalms 17; 86; 90; 102; 142; cf. E. S. Gerstenberger, *TWAT* VI, 606-17).

The INITIAL PLEA (vv. 2-3) displays two peculiarities. For one, it lacks a proper INVOCATION; two, still worse, both lines are completely phrased in the first person of the suppliant, but in the third person of the addressee. The impression they give is curious: someone is directing his or her "prayer" to bystanders: "I cry to Yahweh, . . . I will pour out my sorrow *to him*" (vv. 2a, 3a). Only in v. 4 begins — as should be expected from the start — direct address to Yahweh. This genuine form of prayer is consistently applied thereafter (vv. 6-8). In particular, we find God addressed in v. 4b (vv. 4c-5 are exempt, because they complain about persecutors in neutral discourse; singular imperatives in v. 5 seem to be merely declamatory devices), in a full-size invocational colon, v. 6b ("I cry *to you*, Yahweh"; see Boyce, *Cry;* Additional Bibliography, section B), as well as through three imperatives of petition (vv. 7a, 7c, 8a). What can we make of an initial plea that, formally, is no plea at all, but a descriptive statement of praying? My conclusion is that "neutral" invocation may substitute for direct-address discourse whenever community ties of individual prayer predominate. If this is correct, we have a strong argument in vv. 2-3 that our psalm was part of a community service, although the text is definitely aligned to individual needs. Another possibility would be to speculate about text preservation or mutilation. A regular invocation (like v. 6a) may have been lost or misplaced in the course of transmission.

Personal concerns are aptly and traditionally formulated in the AFFIRMATION OF CONFIDENCE (v. 4ab). In fact, the main catchwords of vv. 3 and 4ab ("pour out sorrows," "become weak") recur in the heading of Psalm 102, a unique overhead description of the purpose and function of individual complaints, also designated as *tĕpillāh*, "prayer" (Ps 102:1, 2 [RSV superscription, 1]). V. 4ab is certainly plaintive in character (cf. "to faint/be faint" in 61:3 [RSV

2]; 77:4, 7 [RSV 3, 6]; 102:1 [RSV heading]; 107:5; 143:4; Jonah 2:8 [RSV 7]), but the phrase leads toward a firm declaration of confidence: "You know my ways" (v. 4b). Various parallel passages testify to this stereotyped affirmation (cf. Pss 31:8 [RSV 7]; 40:10 [RSV 9]; 69:6, 20 [RSV 5, 19]; 139:2, 4, the last instances being examples of anxiety rather than confidence), which demonstrates a superhuman and caring knowledge of God to trust in when despair takes over. Three lines of true complaining come next (vv. 4cd-5) talking about well-known phenomena of social disintegration that may befall anyone suffering bad luck, illness, or simply arousing the suspicion of his or her fellows. Interestingly enough, Psalm 142 is the third prayer in a row mentioning persecutors under the metaphor of hunting (v. 4cd; cf. 140:6; 141:9-10; but also 91:3; 119:110; 124:7). This line states but briefly the evil activities of adversaries, then the text returns to describing the sad state of the victim. In fact, suppliants often articulate alienation from their social environment (cf. 41:7-10 [RSV 6-9]; 88:9, 19 [RSV 8, 18]). In our text this happens in an almost colloquial way: "Look to the right, see: no one to recognize me! Gone my refuge, no one will accept me!" (v. 5). The topic of "not knowing," "not accepting," a sufferer is prominent in complaint literature even outside the Psalter, e.g., in the book of Job (cf. Job 19:13-22; 30:1-15). A person castigated by God falls easily into disgrace among his neighbors and relatives (cf. also Lev 13:45-46). Human contacts are broken off. Nobody cares to sympathize any more with the afflicted one (→ Psalms 41; 88). The negated verb *nkr* II, Hiphil, "recognize," and the corresponding participle are used rarely in this sense. One good parallel is Deut 33:9: formulas of nonrecognition are quoted to signal the Levite's disruption of family ties. A positive example is given in Ruth 2:19: Naomi tells her daughter-in-law: "Blessed is he who recognized you." The parallel expressions: there is "no refuge" and "no one cares for me" (v. 5cd; cf. Am 2:14; Job 11:20; Jer 30:17; 38:4; Ezek 34:6; Est 10:3), underline that meaning. It should be perfectly clear, then, that our complaint element in vv. 4cd-5 refers to broken ties of social solidarity.

The renewed INVOCATION and AFFIRMATION OF CONFIDENCE (v. 6) are quite in order for liturgical practice in complaint ceremonies. The invocation (v. 6a) is shortened and personalized ("to you") in comparison with v. 2. Seeking refuge with God (v. 6bc) is very plausible in the face of broken social relations. Phrases addressing Yahweh with personal pronouns and suffixed attributes of personal relation ("You are my refuge," v. 6b) are frequent in complaint songs (→ 31:4a, 5b [RSV 3a, 4b]; and spoken from God's side, "I am your help," 35:3). The variation of this FORMULA OF TRUST in v. 6c is difficult to explain, being perhaps a later addition. "My share in the land of the living" points to a hope beyond the threatening state of death. This hardly means belief in resurrection or transcendental bliss, but trust in victory of life over presently experienced destruction (cf. H. Ringgren, *TWAT* II, 874-98).

The imperatives directed to God in petitionary language (vv. 7-8a) are complemented one by one with a plaintive *kî* phrase (vv. 7b, 7d) or an infinitive clause (v. 8b). Their weight and function differ. V. 7a is basically an INITIAL PLEA to be heard and heeded by God (*qšb*, Hiphil, "attend to": cf. 5:3 [RSV 2]; 17:1; 55:3 [RSV 2]; 61:2 [RSV 1]; 86:6). In the majority of cases this kind of plea opens a prayer. The next demand is to be "saved" or "torn away from" (v. 7c: *nṣl,* Hiphil; cf. 7:2 [RSV 1]; 25:20; 31:16 [RSV 15]; 39:9 [RSV 8]; 51:16 [RSV 14]; 59:2-3 [RSV 1-2]; 69:15 [RSV 14]; 109:21; 119:170; 143:9; 144:7, 11). Salvation from personal enemies looms large in these petitions. The expression "Tear me from . . ." seems to occupy the very center of petitionary discourse (synonyms in parallel cola are *yš',* Hiphil, "help"; *śgb,* Piel, "protect"; *pṣh,* "liberate"; cf. 144:7, 10, 11). The last imperative derives from *yṣ',* Hiphil, "to lead out of [prison]" (v. 8a; *masgēr,* "prison," only Isa 24:22; 42:7). The verb, of course, serves as the standard expression for Yahweh's (or Moses') "leading Israel out of Egypt" (cf. Exod 3:10-12; 6:6-7, 13). In our passage, however, the motive seems related to the kerygma of liberation from Babylonian captivity (Isa 42:6-7; 61:1), which, for its part, echoes in many ways the exodus from Egypt. The affinity with exilic preaching may also be visible in v. 7b, d, the *kî* phrases emphasizing the suppliant's weakness and the oppressors' power. All in all, the PETITION of vv. 7-8a covers a large range of concerns. The element aims at better conditions for the suffering individual, implicitly for the congregation, and gives as its final purpose a breakthrough to praise (v. 8b).

Then there is an extraordinary continuation of the text, possibly a later addition: the suppliant voices his or her expectation that other "righteous" ones will "gather around" him or her (*ktr,* Hiphil; in a negative sense, Hab 1:4). The suppliant as the center of the community of believers is a concept of a later congregational structure among Yahweh believers. Ps 69:8-13 (RSV 7-12) demonstrates a frustrated "righteous" believer at odds with his environment. Psalms 1 and 119, on the other hand, present the model confessor who expects to be the rallying point of his or her fellows.

## Genre/Setting

The form of the classic COMPLAINT OF THE INDIVIDUAL (see "Introduction to Cultic Poetry," section 4B) is preserved nearly perfectly. The initial plea exhibits some modifications, to be sure, but the complaint and petition are well in line with older tradition (cf. Psalms 3–7; 31; 35; 38; 69; 102; 141). Slight formal deviations (see structure no. II) and variations of contents lead me to believe that the psalm belongs to the later, postexilic phase of Judean tradition. It may be considered a complaint within the congregation of postexilic Yahweh believers (cf. Psalms 12; 39; 90). A number of interpreters narrow down the psalm's setting to situations of persecution and imprisonment (Gunkel, 600; H. Schmidt; W. Beyerlin; Anderson, 922; Seybold, 524; etc.), which, in effect, takes v. 8 too literally.

## Intention

The prayer of the believer, offered to Yahweh within the community, is very much concerned with the spiritual and physical well-being of the individual who wants to be saved and protected by God. This implies combating opponents (but imprecations are missing), integration into the community of faith, and a role of importance within the congregation of the faithful. To achieve these goals, the suppliant first of all has to be torn out of his or her social isolation and rehabilitated to good standing in his or her community.

## Bibliography

D. L. Petersen, "Portraits of David: Canonical and Otherwise," *Iliff Review* 42 (1985) 2-21; W. S. Stafford, "Repentance on the Eve of the English Reformation: John Fisher's Sermons of 1508-1509," *Historical Magazine of the Protestant Episcopal Church* 54 (1985) 297-338.

## Psalm 143:
## Complaint of the Individual

### Structure

|  | MT | NRSV |
|---|---|---|
| I. Superscription | 1a | - |
| II. Invocation, initial plea | 1b-2 | 1-2 |
| III. Complaint | 3-4 | 3-4 |
| IV. Account of praying | 5-6 | 5-6 |
| V. Petition | 7-11 | 7-11 |
| VI. (Included: affirmation of confidence | 8b, 8d, 9b, 10b) | |
| VII. Imprecation | 12ab | 12ab |
| VIII. Confession | 12c | 12c |

This "song of David" is one of the most frequent components of SUPERSCRIPTIONS in the Psalter (about 35 occurrences). A number of times (eight) this sole expression constitutes the heading: → Psalms 15; 23; 24; 29; 101; 110; 141, with the word order inverted in some cases. Here we are reminded that our psalm belongs to the last David collection of the Psalter (Psalms 138–145).

Vv. 1-5 represent some extremely long or irregular lines nourishing suspicions of later additions or redactional reworking. As they stand now part of these phrases can hardly be considered poetical unless they are emended and rearranged. This is true already at least for part of the INITIAL PLEA (vv. 1b-2). Calling on the name of Yahweh constitutes a regular INVOCATION (cf. 3:2 [RSV 1]; 6:2 [RSV 1]; 7:2 [RSV 1]; 88:2 [RSV 1]; etc.). Appellation by naming the deity is an important feature of complaint songs (see "Introduction to Cultic Poetry," section 4B). The sequence of the two imperatives "hear" and "heed to" (v. 1bc) is traditional and formulaic (cf. 17:1 [three imperatives]; 39:13ab [RSV 12ab]; 49:2 [RSV 1]; 54:4 [RSV 2]; 84:9 [RSV 8]). The deity called upon has to be alerted to the suppliant and made willing to listen to his or her complaints.

The third member (v. 1d) in the series may look justified, in so far as we sometimes find three or more initial plea imperatives (→ 17:1), and the verb 'nh, "answer," seems to fit neatly into the sequence (cf. 55:2-3 [RSV 1-2]; 86:6-7). On the other hand, however, the third element of our opening line differs from the two preceding cola. MT has a doubled prepositional object, which is clumsy ("in your truth," "in your justice" — "answer me," v. 1d). And the preceding two pleas to God to hearken lack completely this kind of theological argumentation. They simply ask for a hearing, without referring explicitly to Yahweh's attitudes or qualities. Now, it is possible that v. 1bcd was recited as a tricolon, but it is more probable that v. 1d ("in your righteousness") is a prosaic addition (NRSV et al. rearrange MT: "give ear . . . in your faithfulness; answer me in your righteousness"). If one takes away, hypothetically, the last prepositional object, the third colon would run: "in your faithfulness answer me," a well-balanced closing of the two pleas to be heard.

The second line even more blatantly looks like a prosaic piece of a gloss. Formally, there may be 3 and 4 beats to the two cola. But the wording itself is unusually heavy to be evaluated as poetical. Job 14:3b corresponds to v. 2a, demonstrating that poetic cola should be more concise and cannot suffer a Qal form of the verb *bô'* (MT lit. "Do not come into judgment with your servant," v. 2a; cf. Qal forms in Job 9:32: "we enter into court together"; 22:4: "he will go to court with you"). It should be a Hiphil form: "do not take your servant . . ." (cf. Job 14:3). The motive clause v. 2b seems to be a sapiential statement put into prayer form (cf. Job 4:12; 9:2; 15:14). The self-designation "your servant" (vv. 2a, 12c) is sometimes used in the Psalter (cf. Pss 19:12, 14 [RSV 11, 13]; 90:16). Yet it seems a little unusual in individual complaints (cf., however, 31:17 [RSV 16]; 35:27; 69:18 [RSV 17]; 86:2, 4, 16; 109:28 = references perhaps under special circumstances. Psalm 119, on the other hand, being an INSTRUCTION, has 14 occurrences of *'ebed* in the sense of "I, the suppliant"). The theological/anthropological outlook of v. 2 is pessimistic, in line with late OT wisdom theology. The problem of "not being justified by God" in the first place is a sapiential one (v. 2b; cf. Job 9:1-2; 19:1-7; Olley). All these observations suggest that v. 2 may be a later addition or a commentary to an older stratum of introductory complaint forms.

As to contents and and basic forms, COMPLAINT (vv. 3-4) falls into traditional patterns (see "Introduction to Cultic Poetry," section 4B). Textual problems arise only from v. 3, which is clearly either oversize or fragmented at the end, because the first line of MT (Leningradensis) possibly consists of three cola, while the second line is a rudiment of two words (*kĕmētê 'ôlām*, "like those dead forever" [?]). Three cola are possible (Mowinckel, *Tricola* 29, thinks that vv. 1-3 in reality consisted of 3 + 2 lines; listing at "Introduction to Psalms"; cf. J. T. Willis, "The Juxtaposition of Synonymous and Chiastic Parallelism in Tricola in OT Hebrew Psalm Poetry," *VT* 29 [1979] 465-80).

The COMPLAINT element (vv. 3-4) uses traditional language to accuse the "enemy" of harmful activities. That hostile figure, of course, is an anonymous and to a certain extent a "projected" (Keel, *Feinde;* listing at "Introduction to Psalms") person believed to have caused the misery at hand (cf. 7:6 [RSV 5]; 9:4, 7 [RSV 3, 6]; 31:9, 16 [RSV 8, 15]; 41:6, 12 [RSV 5, 11]; 69:5, 19 [RSV 4,

18]; etc.). What are the stereotyped accusations against the enemy? First, he persecutes (in order to kill) the suppliant (v. 3a; cf. verbal expressions with *rdp*, "pursue," 7:6 [RSV 5]; 69:27 [RSV 26]; 109:16; 119:86, 161). Second, he strikes down and shatters the helpless (v. 3b; cf. *dk'*, Piel, "smash, strike down," 94:5; Isa 3:15; Prov 22:22; Job 19:2). These two cola make good sense, describing the violence of the persecutor. The third instance is less lucid in terms of an individual complaint situation. "He puts me into the dark" (v. 3c) seems to be more a divine sanction (cf. Ps 88:7, 19 [RSV 6, 18]; Lam 3:6) than that of a personal enemy. The phrase may even be gleaned from Lam 3:6. And the following two words (*kĕmētê 'ôlām*, "like those dead forever") seem to be a fragment, which needed some kind of implementation or augmentation to be meaningful (unless we want to equate "darkness" of v. 3c with "the dead in the netherworld"). Perhaps v. 3cd altogether has been added in the course of transmission. V. 4 continues complaining in traditional words. For v. 4a cf. 77:4; 102:1; 142:4; and for v. 4b, Dan 8:27. This means that the second line of complaint describes the dreadful effects of enemy activities on the suppliant, a standard concern in INDIVIDUAL COMPLAINTS.

The next element (vv. 5-6) looks like those reflections on past history, as we find them, e.g., in Ps 77:4-6 (RSV 3-5). In fact, v. 5 has words and concepts in common with that psalm. Musing over the past — presumably in a nostalgic mood — may provoke hope for the future, especially when Yahweh's helpful actions are reflected (v. 5bc; note direct-address discourse). This line, by chance, again is oversize. There are possibly three cola, the last two of which show a chiastic word order. Each part has a verb of its own, the sequence of verbs being *zkr*, "remember"; *hgh*, "muse"; *śyḥ*, Pilel, "deliberate" (v. 5). Individually they occur in prayers, but not in a row like here, and they all seem to be used in younger psalms. "Deliberate" or "speak" *(śyḥ)* is the most notorious late expression, because it is a favorite of the great Torah psalm (119:15, 23, 27, 48, 78, 148), otherwise used in the Psalter only in 77:4, 7, 13 (RSV 3, 6, 12); 105:2. "Remembering" is done in individual complaints, but only in special situations of reflection; cf. 42:5, 7 (RSV 4, 6); 63:7 (RSV 6); 77:4, 7, 12 (RSV 3, 6, 11); the last-mentioned song is very reflective indeed, and the only one employing all three verbs. "Musing," for its part, has become a technical term for the study of Torah (1:2), but is used also with other connotations (cf. 35:28; 63:7 [RSV 6]; 71:24; 77:13a [RSV 12a], the last phrase is identical with our v. 5b). In sum, the prayer line in v. 5 (direct address) comes out of that meditative practice of community worship. But there is no further elaboration in this manner; the prayer, still in second-person discourse, turns into a DESCRIPTION OF PRAYING (v. 6), and focus on ritual seems to be dominant in this section. Reviewing God's actions has been mentioned summarily, because it is part of praying to God. On the other hand, telling the Deity of one's own efforts to establish contact, including description of bodily posture, time of the day or night, emotional investment, pitch of voice, etc., is not idle talk but necessary ceremony (cf. 5:4, 8 [RSV 3, 7]; 28:2; 88:2, 10, 14 [RSV 1, 9, 13]; 102:6-8 [RSV 5-7]; etc.).

PETITION occupies the largest space in this psalm (vv. 7-11), and the last verse, exhibiting the other side of the coin, i.e., defensive and damaging petition: IMPRECATION (v. 12ab), is intimately related to this main element. This fact is entirely in correspondence with the general structure of individual complaints. Details, however, are peculiar in each specimen of the genre. Psalm 143 displays regular petitions of a special kind. As a rule, we here have imperatives directed to Yahweh and first-person singular suffixes referring to the suppliant in the first colon of each line, while the second colon either offers some motive for asking God (vv. 8b, 8d, 9b, 10b — all phrases introduced by *kî*, "because"; the conjunction also has to be supplied in v. 9b), makes a statement about the suppliant's well-being (vv. 7b, 7d), or gives some additional explanation (v. 10d). Only v. 11b continues in the demanding mode, summarizing, as it were, the whole petitionary complex. The first and the last line of positive PETITION, appropriately so, mention the name of Yahweh in an appellative form (vv. 7a, 11a). A third appellation occurs in v. 9a, perhaps in a crucial place. The contents of petition are traditional, but they also seem to exhibit a high degree of spiritualization and emphasis on Torah instruction. The enemies, focused on in v. 3, are referred to again in v. 9a, which is a colon of special appeal to Yahweh. Still, the plea for help against the enemies (cf. also v. 12ab) is not the solitary concern of the prayer. V. 9 is surrounded by other petitions.

Looking briefly at the individual lines of petition, we notice that v. 7 begins with two general pleas for an answer and an audience, such as we are accustomed to find in introductory sections (cf. v. 1). This repetition of an "initial" plea for admittance may seem strange, but liturgical agendas of all ages favor this kind of redundance as a proper means of ceremonial proceedings. The second cola of both lines are plaintive in character, stating the desperate situation of the suppliant (v. 7b) and the danger of getting lost for good, if Yahweh does not attend to the prayer (v. 7d). The following four lines (vv. 8-10) are very regular indeed, in terms of structure and contents. Suffixed imperatives open each line, followed by two more lexemes (or lexeme groups) to form the first colon. V. 8a pleads for a favorable answer of God "in the morning" (cf. Janowski, *Rettungsgewissheit,* 182-89; listing at Additional Bibliography, section C; Allen, 284: the prayer is to be recited "before dawn in the temple"); vv. 8c and 10a are entreaties for divine guidance, enveloping that special plea for help against the enemies (v. 9a, this time: plural), all using traditional vocabulary. The pleas for divine orientation and instruction are close to sapiential discourse, or dispute patterns (v. 8c, *hôdî'ēnî,* "let me know"; cf. Job 10:2; 13:23; 37:19; 38:3; 40:7; 42:4; v. 10a, *lammĕdēnî,* "teach me"; cf. Ps 119:12, 26, 64, 66, 68, 108, 124, 135, 171; Diedrich). The instructional pleas end up with a heavy emphasis, because v. 10a is undergirded by a strong affirmation of trust or faith serving as a motive clause (v. 10b: "You are my God"; cf. 25:5; 31:15 [RSV 14]). This AFFIRMATION OF CONFIDENCE has been building up from v. 8b ("in you I trust") through vv. 8d and 9b to come to its climax in 10b.

Only vv. 9a, 10, and 11a possess appellations of God, making them stand out among the series of petitions. The last two lines, furthermore (vv. 10cd and 11), employ another word order than the six preceding lines. They do not place an imperative in front, but a noun suffixed with the pronoun of the second person of the interlocutor, Yahweh ("Your spirit, the good one, may guide me . . . ," etc.). Thus the precative verbal forms (imperfects with suffixes of first person singular) take their place at the end of the colon. This means in liturgical terms that petitions gain momentum from v. 9 on, ending in a crescendo of pleading that involves Yahweh from line to line more strongly. V. 11 summarizes and heightens petitions in the name of him who may concede help and guidance. He is renowned and addressed exactly for his justice (v. 11b). The help expected is rescue from suffocating "narrowness" (ṣārāh; cf. 4:2 [RSV 1]; 31:8 [RSV 7]; 77:3 [RSV 2]; 86:7; 120:1; 119:143), an apt designation for existential trouble. The last line, finally (v. 12), contains a wholesale IMPRECATION against the evil-doers guilty of the suppliant's affliction. It is formally expressed in petitionary language, using imperfect and consecutive perfect in second-person address style to move Yahweh to destroy the opponents completely. Interestingly, the prayer adds a motive clause to this final plea, following the pattern of vv. 8-10b. "Because I am your servant" (v. 12c), then, is the closing word of our psalm, manifesting that peculiar attitude of personal dedication and trust we meet every so often in early Jewish psalmography (cf. v. 2; 31:17 [RSV 16]; 69:18 [RSV 18]; 119:17, 38, 49, 65; 135:1, 14; etc.). This self-designation has a confessional quality. Individuals may use it, probably also in the context of communal worship (cf., e.g., 31:17 [RSV 16]; 69:18 [RSV 17]; 86:4, 16; and numerous occurrences in Psalm 119). The closest parallel is 116:16: "Alas, Yahweh, I am your servant! I am your servant, son of your maidservant!").

## *Genre*

A person is praying for help and guidance in this psalm. Maybe the psalm was recited mainly in cases of social ostracism, mobbing, and unwarranted juridical persecution (Seybold, 527, et al.). The elements of INDIVIDUAL COMPLAINT are used to articulate the quest for God's intervention and guidance. Descriptions of suffering remain vague (cf. vv. 3-4; in contrast: Psalms 22; 38; 55; 59; 69). This is due partly, however, to the fact that all complaint psalms are prayer formulas using stereotyped concepts of misery, persecution, and anguish. But the reduction of the complaint to a minimum also results from spiritualization. Emphasis has shifted to God's guidance, as can be seen best in the petition. The old enemy concept survives in Psalm 143. Denunciation of and imprecation against those guilty of causing mischief and suffering are in the background of our complaint, being voiced most strongly in vv. 9a and 12ab. Yet the prayer moves beyond this frame of reference into a realm where the wholesome relation with Yahweh has high priority (cf. 73:23-26). While v. 8a can still be seen in connection with a morning sacrifice at the temple and a related salvation oracle, vv. 8c and 10a rather point to an instruction to be received in a word service, via Torah exposition. Petition for instruction and guidance (v. 10) may have had one root in sapiential academies (Diedrich, 71), but it had long been integrated into the postexilic community worship.

## Setting

The process of spiritualization visible in Psalm 143 indicates a change of life situation from the old type of individual complaint, anchored in family traditions (cf. Gerstenberger, *Mensch;* listing at "Introduction to Cultic Poetry"), to a prayer defined more individualistically and at the same time more communally. Personal relation to Yahweh, plea for orientation by God on the path of righteousness, and longing for acceptance in the "plain land" (v. 10d; most exegetes want to emend to "plain path," but cf. 26:12; 27:11; 67:5 [RSV 4], where *mîšôr* has the connotation of "justice") have become the highest aspiration. All these characteristics are signals of the religious community that fostered personal piety within the group of true believers who were bound to Yahweh, the God of Israel.

## Intention

The intention of our prayer, therefore, is to strengthen and/or recover that bond to Yahweh that may protect and nourish the believer. Learning the right path under the eyes of God is preeminent in the minds of the psalmist. What type of enemy was imagined at this point we do not know. Who would try to frustrate personal faith within the congregation of Yahweh believers? Or do we have to think of outward adversaries trying to interfere with the Yahweh service? The question pervades the exegesis of quite a number of later psalms (cf. Psalms 37; 49; 69; etc.).

The question of guilt and innocence looms large in modern commentaries. The suppliant does not dare to affirm his or her innocence, as Psalms 7; 17; 26, and, of course Job, do. Rather, there seem to be admittance of a general guilt (v. 2b) and a plea to be spared judgment (v. 2a; Mays, 433). These features, however, are most probably to be attributed not to individual experiences but to a prevalent theological attitude within the early Jewish congregations; cf. Psalms 14; 106.

## Bibliography

R. Arconada, "Psalmes 142/143 retentus, emendatus, glossatus," *VD* 13 (1933) 240-46; B. Bozak, "Suffering and the Psalms of Lament," *Église et Théologie* 23 (1992) 325-338; F. Diedrich, " 'Lehre mich, Jahwe!' Überlegungen zu einer Gebetsbitte in den Psalmen," in *Die alttestamentliche Botschaft als Wegweisung (Fest.* H. Reinelt; ed. J. Zmijewski; Stuttgart: Katholisches Bibelwerk, 1990) 59-74; F. A. Gosling, "An Interesting Use of the Waw Consecutive," *ZAW* 110 (1998) 403-10; R. B. Hays, "Psalm 143 and the Logic of Romans 3," *JBL* 99 (1980) 107-15; J. W. Olley, "Righteousness: Some Issues in Old Testament Translation into English," *BT* 38 (1987) 307-15; J. Schildenberger, "Psalm 143: Von Verzagtheit zu Vertrauen," *Erbe und Auftrag* 57 (1981) 202-4; M. L. Soards, "The Righteousness of God in the Writings of the Apostle Paul," *BTB* 15 (1985) 104-9; R. F. Surburg, "Justification as a Doctrine of the Old Testament," *Concordia Theological Quarterly* 46 (1982) 129-46.

## Psalm 144:
## Praise and Petition: Worship Agenda

### *Structure*

|  |  | MT | NRSV |
|---|---|---|---|
| I. | Superscription | 1a | - |
| II. | Praise | 1b-2 | 1-2 |
| III. | Declaration of humbleness | 3-4 | 3-4 |
| IV. | Petition | 5-8 | 5-8 |
|  | A. Petition for intervention | 5-7a | 5-7a |
|  | B. Petition for salvation (refrain) | 7b-d | 7b-d |
|  | C. Complaint (refrain) | 8 | 8 |
| V. | Vow | 9-11 | 9-11 |
|  | A. Vow to praise | 9 | 9 |
|  | B. Hymnic attribution | 10 | 10 |
|  | C. Petition for salvation (refrain) | 11ab | 11ab |
|  | D. Complaint (refrain) | 11cd | 11cd |
| VI. | Blessing | 12-14 | 12-14 |
| VII. | Felicitation | 15 | 15 |

Only the name of David, prefixed by the preposition *lĕ*, has been put down as a SUPERSCRIPTION, as in → Psalm 138. We cannot tell whether other designations have been lost. If original this very rudimentary heading may indicate an ancient classification of psalms simply as "belonging to David" or "to the David collection" (Psalms 138–145).

Psalm 144 is a curious mixture of form elements ranging from praise and blessing to urgent petition, complaint, and vow. Many exegetes therefore want to divide the text into two or three independent psalms. A detailed analysis may shed some light on this patchwork.

The first subunit (vv. 1b-2) consists of three lines, the opening one being introduced by *bārûk*, "blessed be . . ." or "praised be [Yahweh]," a standard formula of later times (→ Glossary: BLESSING FORMULA). Its contents remind us of Psalm 18: there too a king or army leader seems to speak, giving thanks for victory. Quite a few words of vv. 1-2 are found — in similar positions and functions — in that ROYAL VICTORY (THANKSGIVING) HYMN (cf. 18:35 [RSV 34] for "teaching my hands to fight" = v. 1c; 18:47 [RSV 46] for *bārûk* = v. 1b; 18:3 [RSV 2] for the series of confiding appellations = v. 2abc; 18:44-45 [RSV 43-44] for submission of people = v. 2d). Is this a case of one psalmist having copied from another? Hardly, because the process of composing psalms has to be thought of much more in terms of a broad transmission of sacred texts that to a large extent consisted of traditional vocabulary, stock phrases, and form elements (cf. Culley, *Language;* listing at "Introduction to Cultic Poetry"). This handling of tradition very likely extended into the phase of written tradition. "Intertextuality," therefore, should not be misunderstood to be a result of mere copying habits (cf. Hunter, 57-58). Conscious use of particular, already existing psalms by late composers would be very difficult to ascertain. In our present case suspicion of plagiarism could arise, though, because other elements of the text seem to lean on still other songs than Psalm 18. For the time being we content ourselves with noting the affinity mentioned above.

As the introductory element stands, it emphasizes PRAISE through a *bārûk* formula strengthened by the affirmation of confidence "my rock" (v. 1b; cf. 18:3 [RSV 2] = 2 Sam 22:3; Pss 19:15 [RSV 14]; 28:1; 62:3, 7 [RSV 2, 6]; 92:16 [RSV 15]). The praise motif is continued in those participles that describe praiseworthy actions of Yahweh (vv. 1c, 2d; the last colon is textually uncertain, but a participle seems firmly established). On the other hand, the affirmation of confidence is prolonged by five appellations of trust (v. 2: "my grace," "my fortress," "my hill," "my rescuer," "my shield") and one verbal expression ("in him I trust"). Ps 18:3 (RSV 2) has a series of seven plus one almost identical affirmations. Thus the introductory praise is complex, multiple, and impressively tight and heavy. For other strings of praising, confessional expressions see 31:2-4 (RSV 1-3); 71:3, 5; D. Eichhorn, *Gott;* listing at Psalm 18. Textually difficult is v. 2d: Is the (assumed) "king" giving thanks for having subdued his own people (MT = *'ammî*, "my people")? Or is he referring to foreign nations (thus some MSS and ancient versions)?

Vv. 3-4 lean to sapiential thinking. The question "What about human beings?" comes up literally in the book of Job in much the same way as in v. 3a. The problem of human existence is related directly to God in this sense: because of their insignificance or guilt, humans hardly merit recognition by the Deity (Job 7:17-19; 15:14-16). Ps 8:5 (RSV 4), taken all by itself, has the same undertone, only to be reversed in the following cola. Our present v. 3, therefore, falls in line with this wisdom concept of human inferiority or uncleanness. There are only slight formal differences over against the wisdom texts quoted. For one, they complete the rhetorical question with a *kî* phrase, which makes the question sound more conditional. Our text has two consecutive imperfects in place of the subordinate clause, making the phrase paratactic and more factual. Second, there is a stronger accentuation of prayer language in our text. Appellative "Yahweh" is added at the very beginning (v. 3a), while Job 7:17 is a general diatribe against God, without mentioning him by name, and Job 15:14-16 is an objective argumentation within a heated speech against Job. The third example, Ps 8:5 (RSV 4), also displays direct address of Yahweh, but without formal appellation, which is reserved to the communal voices of 8:2, 10 (RSV 1, 9). The answer to such a basic anthropological query in our psalm as well as in Joban texts is in stark contrast to that of Ps 8:6-9 (RSV 5-8). V. 4 affirms wisdom's humbleness over against the universe: humans are nothing, shadows at most ("They are like breath"; cf. *hebel*, "sigh, vanity, nothing," in Ecclesiastes, e.g., Qoh 1:2, 14; 2:1, 11-26; etc.; K. Seybold, *TWAT* II, 334-43). What in the world provokes such a statement at this point, after a jubilant praise and affirmation of confidence? Is this element counteracting exactly the triumphant tone of the preceding (royal?) self-presentation? Should we interpret it to take a conscious stand against Psalm 8 in its orgulous manifestation of human power (a case could be made in this respect on account of similar wording and the inversion of *'ādām* and *'ĕnôš* in v. 3 over against 8:5 [RSV 4])? Opposition against Psalm 8 would at least merit an open renunciation of human lordship over animals, proposed by that hymn. Nobody in antiquity, however, would have doubted that kind of human power. The next two sections (vv. 5-8, 9-11) are tied together by a common refrain (vv. 7b-8, 11) and by the fact that both begin with a proper invocation. Also, a certain affinity again to Psalm 18 may be seen in allusions to theophany (cf. vv. 5-7a) and to royal warfare (cf. v. 10). On the other hand, the two sections are not dependent on any other psalm but have a profile of their own, symbolized in the urgent plea for rescue (the verb *pṣh*, "liberate," vv. 7, 10, 11, only here in Hebrew Scripture) from the hands of some unnamed "strangers" *(bĕnê nēkār)*.

Formally, vv. 5-8 are a PETITION with a relative clause in the complaining tone (v. 8). The bulk of the element consists of imperatives, sometimes "prolonged" by petitionary imperfect forms. Looking at these requests more closely, it seems curious to ask Yahweh to "bend [*nṭh*, Hiphil imperative] heaven and descend" (v. 5a), in order to rescue one forlorn suppliant. In fact, the said verb occurs in individual complaints mostly with "bending the ears" to listen and help (17:6; 31:3 [RSV 2]; 88:3 [RSV 2]; 102:3 [RSV 2]). Descent from the heavenly abode does not normally belong to plaintive requests of individuals. What is the reason for this far-flung appellation? Psalm 18, of course, speaks in a similar cosmological context. There is a complete account of theophany in descriptive language exhibited in 18:8-16 (RSV 7-15). Some of the phrases extant in our psalm do occur there: "He bent heaven and descended" (18:10 [RSV 9]; cf. v. 5a); "he shot his arrows, and dispersed them, many lightnings, and he confused them" (18:15 [RSV 14]; cf. v. 6, with "arrows" and "lightnings" inverted); "he stretched out and grasped me, he pulled me from mighty waters" (18:17 [RSV 16]; cf. v. 7a, c, the words being near identical). An ACCOUNT OF THEOPHANY, however, we do not have in Psalm 144. The words are molded into prayer, and only part of the grand scenery remains, to the effect that the "mighty waters" (v. 7c) look out of place and are quickly superseded by hostile "strangers" (v. 7d; cf. "enemies" in 18:17 [RSV 16]). These are heavy coincidences between the two psalms, indeed, but they are still no proof of literary dependence of individual authors or of full-grown and extant texts. Anonymous and collective use of psalmic traditions is still the more likely option.

Made into petitionary prayer, the phrases conjure a universal act of rescue after having previously affirmed praise of and confidence in Yahweh's power. In essence, this kind of prayer is rare in the Hebrew Bible, but not unique. In a related way Isa 63:19b–64:2 put theophanic motifs to work in a (communal) petition ("O that you would tear open the heavens and come down," Isa 63:19c; cf. Fischer, 167-73). Thus our vv. 5-7, just like the Isaiah liturgy, utilize those motifs for their own ends (cf. the treatment of Ps 144:5-6 among "theophany reports" by Jeremias, *Theophanie*, 24-26; see listing at Psalm 18).

Without giving up prayer language, vv. 9-11 begin as a VOW with attached praise (vv. 9-10) only to turn back soon to PETITION (v. 11 tuned to vv. 7b-8). The vow seems to dominate the passage, while petition apparently backs up the vow. To offer a "new" song (v. 9a) may literally refer to a new composition, which, of course, offers new power and recognition (cf. the summons to sing a "new song," always to a community: 33:3; 96:1; 98:1; 149:1; Isa 42:10. Only in Ps 40:4 [RSV 3] is an individual singer visualized). Instruments to accompany prayer are mentioned here and there in the Psalms (cf. 57:9 [RSV 8]; 71:22; 77:7 [RSV 6]; 108:3 [RSV 2]; → Psalm 150). Anticipated praise (v. 10) grounds the vow: two determined participles stress Yahweh's record as savior. Surprisingly, the argument is a historical one. David and "the kings" have been rescued by Yahweh. Rarely, and probably quite late in the history of Israel, royal ancestors (and other heroes) of faith in Yahweh are treated as models or paradigms (cf. 132:1, 10, 17; 99:6; 133:2). The refrained petition of v. 11 lacks only reference to the "mighty waters." Otherwise it is equal to vv. 7b, 7d, 8. But at what does this complaint aim? Concreteness of the enemy description we must not expect. Designation as "foreigners" may point into the direction of ethnically different overlords, most likely in exilic or postexilic times.

The last section of Psalm 144 has a regular basic structure (vv. 12-14, and slightly modified in the closing line, v. 15). A community is speaking (or being represented by a liturgist), lauding line-by-line components and properties of his or her own group. Since all the phrases are made up of nouns and participles only, each incipit being a suffixed form (vv. 12-14: "Our sons," "our daughters," "our barns," "our sheep," "our cattle"; LXX mostly presupposes third-person plural suffixes = "their"), it is hard to tell whether the passage is descriptive or petitionary. The relative pronoun 'ăšer, introducing the entire block (v. 12a), does not make sense. Chances are that it has been corrupted from an original 'ašrê, "happy" (cf. v. 15; 1:1; possibly, another form of the verb 'šr, "be happy," was the original reading). In that case not only the closing line with its special objective (third-person) stylization but the whole six-line segment would be a felicitation. One serious argument against this proposal, however, is that there are no other examples of felicitations being voiced by someone in the first person singular or plural. "Happy be our sons," "daughters," "storage rooms," etc., would run counter to the very purpose of the genre, not only because felicitation is naturally restricted to persons, but also because it is always extended from one donor to a receiver. Felicitation cannot be a narcissistic discourse. The enigma of the 'ăšer beginning thus remains unsolved.

Clear enough, though, are five affirmations or well-wishes about the main assets of an ancient Near Eastern family: sons, daughters, stored goods, sheep, cattle (vv. 12-14) are to be lucky, strong, fruitful — in short: blessed. The nominal phrases, in theory, may be taken as factual statements: "Our sons *are* like plants" (v. 12a). More probably, they represent wishes, and although this term does not appear we may call the unit a BLESSING, because it fulfills functions of that genre of powerful utterances promoting well-being. The first two lines (v. 12), dedicated to a family's offspring, are full of metaphorical language. Sons like good plants, daughters like well-carved posts: nature and artistry are called upon to depict the ideal state of existence. For the rest, it is enough to paint the highest possible results of industry and fertility (vv. 13-14; Fiedler's conjecture of "county" for "cattle" is unlikely because of the context). A little appendix, furthermore, wants to ward off all kinds of bad luck and adversities (v. 14c). Imagining the best and keeping away the worst, in effect, is a regular pattern of psalmic asking and wishing. Interestingly enough, the last line (v. 15) summarizes the intentions of the passage by declaring the people or community "happy" who achieve such a blessed state. V. 15b is more specific, revealing a secret, as it seems: "Happy are the people who remain with Yahweh, their God" (cf. 33:12; 84:5-6 [RSV 4-5]; 146:5). The speaker seems to be the leader of ceremonies, while the preceding wishes have been recited by the assembly.

Similarly, five blessings are voiced about the community that will heed the statutes of Yahweh (Deut 28:3-6: esp. vv. 4-5 contain the blessings — fertility and wealth — mentioned in our psalm). In stark contrast, curses may befall those people who do not remain faithful to Yahweh. Deut 28:16-19 are the corresponding five maledictions to the blessings of Deut 28:3-6. Leviticus 26 adheres to a similar pattern. The blessings bestowed on a faithful community comprise fertility, well-being, and protection (Lev 26:3-13). They do not show a numerical scheme. But the pertinent curses are listed in a block of five sanctions (Lev 26:14-33; cf. Gerstenberger, *Leviticus;* listing at Additional Bibliography, section B), so we may conclude that the number five may not be accidental in this passage. It may have been a preferred figure for well-wishes, blessings, and curses. Other lists of property and utensils of well-being can be found, e.g., Exod 20:17 (house, wife, servants, cattle, donkey); Gen 30:43 (sheep, servants, camels, donkeys); Job 42:12-13 (sheep, camels, cattle, donkeys, sons, daughters). All these family goods are fruits of Yahweh's blessing (cf. Psalm 127; 128). Rituals of blessing were presumably part and parcel of family services (cf. Gerstenberger, *Yahweh,* 55-66; listing at Additional Bibliography, section B).

## *Genre/Setting*

If Psalm 144 was used as a unified liturgical text (and unless we postulate an erroneous juncture of disparate elements it certainly was used as a unit sometimes), we may not easily attribute it to one of the classical genres or situations, be it of praise or complaint. Looking for a new genre designation, we certainly have to consider a situation that might constitute a plausible, unifying background for a patchwork of forms like that studied above. Such a situation may be found in a communal worship trying to do justice to the existential needs of its members. Presumably, the life of Yahweh believers in postexilic times was moved by praise and complaint, blessing and malediction, much the same way (under the auspices of different social and cultural conditions) as that of members of a Christian congregation today. Thus the sequence of forms discovered in Psalm 144 may reflect more or less the liturgical procedure of a general worship service somewhere in Judah or the diaspora. The initial praise and confidence (vv. 1-2) are an appropriate beginning for any sort of worship. Reflection on the general state of human beings (vv. 3-4) befits a conscious faith, knowing human limitations and errors. Petition, vow, and the expectation of blessed life (vv. 5-8, 9-11, 12-15) correspond to basic activities and attitudes of the worshipers. Significantly, in the last liturgical block the community unites in looking forward to the benevolent effects of Yahweh's interactions and interventions. Before that final accord of joint singing and praying, only one voice speaks at a time. Still, the communal mooring of the prayer is obvious at every step, but it comes to the fore most cogently in the first person plurals of vv. 12-14. There are few concentrations of "we" affirmations like this one in the Psalter (cf. Psalm 126). An officiant probably pronounced the final word of blessing to the congregation (v. 15). Thus the whole psalm becomes a WORSHIP AGENDA for early Jewish communities. Therefore it would not be strange at all to discover different roots for various elements of the composition, like "theophany report," "family blessing," "complaints and petitions," etc. Even "royal" discourse has been assimilated by exilic-postexilic communities (cf. Pss 5:3 [RSV 2]; 84:4 [RSV 3]; 145:1; Seybold, 530; Allen, 289).

## Intention

Our worship agenda wants to give spiritual room to the participants of common services in honor of Yahweh, the God of the people. The individual believer takes into this house of prayer and complaint his or her daily concerns, which are taken up by the fellowship of faithful.

## Bibliography

M. Z. Brettler, "Images of YHWH the Warrior in Psalms," *Semeia* 61 (1993) 135-65; S. L. Cook, "Apocalypticism and the Psalter," *ZAW* 104 (1992) 82-99; I. Fischer, *Wo ist Jahwe?* (Stuttgart: Katholisches Bibelwerk, 1989); E. S. Gerstenberger, "Singing a New Song: On Old Testament and Latin American Psalmody," *Word & World* 5 (1985) 155-67; C. Houk, "Syllables and Psalms: A Statistical Linguistic Analysis," *JSOT* 14 (1979) 55-62; J. H. Hunter, "Interpretationstheorie in der postmodernen Zeit: Suche nach Interpretationsmöglichkeiten anhand von Psalm 144," in *Neue Wege in der Psalmenforschung (Fest.* W. Beyerlin; HBS 1; ed. K. Seybold et al.; Freiburg: Herder, 1994) 45-62; A. C. Lovelace, "Make a Joyful Noice to the Lord: Biblical Foundations of Church Music," *Point* 2 (1973) 15-27; R. J. Tournay, "Le psaume CXLIV, structure et interprétation," *RB* 91 (1984) 520-30; J. Ziegler, "Psalm 144,14," in *Wort und Geschichte (Fest.* K. Elliger; ed. H. Gese; Neukirchen: Neukirchener Verlag, 1973) 191-98.

## Psalm 145:
## Acrostic Hymn

### Structure

|  | MT | NRSV |
|---|---|---|
| I. Superscription | 1a | - |
| II. Acrostic (21 lines) | 1b-21b | 1-21b |
| A. Summons to praise | 1b-2 | 1-2 |
| B. Hymnic affirmation | 3 | 3 |

| | | |
|---|---|---|
| C. Hymnic wishes | 4-7 | 4-7 |
| D. Hymnic affirmation | 8-9 | 8-9 |
| E. Hymnic wishes | 10-12 | 10-12 |
| F. Hymnic affirmation | 13-14 | 13-14 |
| G. Adoration | 15-16 | 15-16 |
| H. Hymnic affirmation | 17-20 | 17-20 |
| I. Vow and wish | 21ab | 21ab |
| III. Postscript | 21c | 21c |

The last of the final David collection (Psalms 138–145), our song is explicitly called a *těhillāh*, "psalm of praise." This designation, strange as it may seem, occurs rarely in redactional psalm headings; in fact, our psalm is the only instance in the Psalter (first lines of the songs themselves sometimes explicitly use the term: cf. 33:1; 34:2 [RSV 1]; 65:2 [RSV 1]; 109:1; 147:1; 149:1). Contrary to many musical-technical terms in SUPERSCRIPTIONS, the significance of which is uncertain, *těhillāh* can be seen as a living and well-defined word (cf. v. 21; 66:2, 8; 100:4; 106:2, 12, 47; etc.), which in the end provided the general name for the book of Psalms (special masculine form: *těhillîm*). Proximity to the Hallelujah Psalms (cf. Psalms 106; 111; 135; 146; etc.) may have stimulated the choice of that name for our song, but most certainly the content of the twenty-one verses (= lines) was decisive.

ACROSTIC poetry has always had a certain importance in the Middle East (cf. Psalms 9/10; 25; 34; 37; 111–112; 119; Lamentations 1–4; see "Introduction to Cultic Poetry," section 4F; Freedman, "Acrostics"; Soll, "Acrostics"; see listing at "Introduction to the Book of Lamentations"). It should not be misunderstood as a playful pastime only; it served a communal purpose. In this case the whole psalm before us, without fail, is geared to praise and adoration of Yahweh. Given the rule of alphabetical beginnings, i.e., of opening each line with the proper letter of the Hebrew alphabet (there is only one letter missing after v. 13: the *nun* line; LXX has either preserved or reconstructed it: "Steadfast [*ně'emān*] is Yahweh in all his words; true in all his deeds"), adherence to a determined genre or mode of speech has to be a conscious effort. In Psalm 145 the first words of every line as well as the contents of the respective cola do correspond to the objective of praise. Many expressions belong to the top arsenal of hymn singing, and significantly, the last line's opening word is *těhillāh*, "song of praise," which happens to be spelled with initial *taw*, the last letter of the Hebrew alphabet (v. 21; the name of the psalm in the superscription derives from this incipit).

Two more formal features call for attention. The praising discourse of Psalm 145 may be divided into two main categories. There are exhortatory, urging, and wishful phrases, at the same time voicing and soliciting eulogies to Yahweh (HYMNIC WISHES); and there are general statements about Yahweh and his greatness, benevolence, and care (HYMNIC AFFIRMATIONS). These two forms dominate the whole poem, and they alternate in a way that gives a certain additional structure to the psalm besides the pervasive alphabetical order. The other noteworthy fact is that the name of Yahweh (nine times, plus *'ělôhay*, "my God," v. 1a) occurs only in the first colon of a line. The second cola are explicative in nature, expanding collocations made in the first half of the line.

The poem begins with a SUMMONS TO PRAISE, directed to the suppliant him- or herself and clothed in prayer language (vv. 1b-2). Four verbal expressions are utilized, featuring the roots *rûm*, Pilel, "extol"; *brk*, Piel, "bless"; and *hll*, Piel, "praise." They are all synonyms in hymnic discourse and are frequent in the Psalter. "I will extol you," *'ărômimkā* (v. 1b), also opens the individual thanksgiving Psalm 32 (cf. the end position in 118:28) and figures as the self-summons of a group (first person plural) in 34:4 (RSV 3). The verb comes in as a summons to other participants of worship in 99:5, 9.

"I will bless you" (vv. 1c, 2a) or "I will bless Yahweh" is a common formula of eulogy (cf. 16:7; 26:12; 34:2 [RSV 1]; 63:5 [RSV 4]) modified by the dialogical form extant in two psalms: "Bless, my self, bless Yahweh" (cf. 103:1, 2, 22; 104:1, 35). Plural summonses with this verb are frequent (cf., e.g., 66:8; 103:20-21). About *hll* calls for praise much has been said (cf. with Psalms 105; 106; 111–113; 135; 146–150). For the most part, summonses are extended to the community, in plural admonitions. But there are some first-person singular self-exhortations, too: 22:23 (RSV 22); 35:18; 56:5, 11 (RSV 4, 10); 69:31 (RSV 30); 146:2. All these parallel passages indicate that our psalm is in accordance with hymnic usage. The direct address of God in the opening parts reveals a different type of hymn singing, though. The other type, considered "normal" by most exegetes (e.g., Gunkel, Crüsemann), postulates a liturgical leader soliciting praise from the congregation. Here it is the individual singing to Yahweh — but probably also in the midst of the congregation. Personal hymnic overtones are heightened in our case by the first colon's intimate address ("my God, [you, the] king," v. 1b; a similar touch occurs in 118:28b).

The overture of a hymn is followed by a HYMNIC AFFIRMATION in honor of Yahweh (v. 3). The line belongs to a treasure of hymnic stock phrases (nearly identical with 48:2 [RSV 1]; 96:4: variations of second cola demonstrate liturgical flexibility of the formula). The alteration of direct-address praise (or summons to praise) to neutral hymnic affirmation may have liturgical implications or presuppositions. At any rate, this change is repeated by the next subunits.

Vv. 4-7 are formally a summons to praise directed to coming generations, but couched in direct-address speech to Yahweh. In this manner, summons becomes immediate praise. The verbs of the first cola (vv. 4a, 6a, 7a; perhaps by emendation also in v. 5a: "I shall meditate" would become "they shall meditate"; cf. *BHK* and *BHS*) all have *dôr lĕdôr*, "generation to generation," as subject. They call for an active, praising ministry, and they again end up with hymnic affirmations (vv. 8-9) consisting of a liturgically fixed line, v. 8 = Exod 34:6; Ps 103:8 ("Gracious and merciful is Yahweh, slow to anger and abounding in steadfast love"; cf. 86:15; Spieckermann; see listing at Psalm 86), and an elaboration about Yahweh's affection for all his creation (v. 9; cf. neutral expressions in different form elements: 77:10 [RSV 9]; Lam 3:22; 1 Chr 21:13). The alteration seems logical in terms of liturgical sequence and theological plausibility. Someone first presents praises and impulses to praise, then (someone else) responds by adducing laudable facts about Yahweh.

The same pattern is followed once more in vv. 10-12, 13-14. Now "all your works" are incited to give thanks and to praise (v. 10a). Just as in vv. 6-7, the addressees are expected to talk and proclaim Yahweh's qualities, which are immediately pictured in vv. 11-12. The main content of this proclamation at this point is the "kingdom of Yahweh" (*malkût yhwh,* vv. 11, 12, 13; J. Jeremias, *NBL* II, 520-22; idem, *Königtum;* listing at "Introduction to Psalms"; Camponovo, *Königtum;* listing at Additional Bibliography, section B; D. C. Duling, *ABD* IV, 49-52). Here we have the key word for the liturgical complement in vv. 13-14. A formal flaw could be the direct address to Yahweh in v. 13: "Your kingdom is an everlasting kingdom, and your reign endures for generations and generations" (neutral formulations of these phrases: Dan 3:32; 4:31 [RSV 34]; 6:27). Contentwise, however, the line is not beckoning human praise, but stating divine facts, even if in prayer form. The sequel to this modified hymnic affirmation is clear Yahweh phrases of the factual type in v. 14: "Yahweh upholds all who are falling, and raises up all who are bowed down." We do not have exact and comprehensive formulaic doublets of this statement (cf., however, 1 Sam 2:8; Pss 113:7-8; 146:8), but the line does have the conciseness and power of a good liturgical word. Looking back at the three rounds of praising and formulating important asseverations about Yahweh, we may conclude that the "I" of the suppliant, as well as of coming generations, and all created things have to adore and worship Yahweh (alone?) in vv. 1-14.

Vv. 15-16, then, are a kind of conclusion to the three blocks of praise analyzed above. Vocabulary and style strongly remind us of Ps 104:27-28. The very same concepts have been arranged in such a way that the line headings meet the alphabetical order calling for the letters *ayin* and *pe.* Yet we may not insist that our psalmist copied from Psalm 104. He or she, in fact, preferred participles (vv. 15b, 16a) over infinitive and imperfect in 104:27b, 28b. This way our text of v. 15a came to be overloaded: "You are the one who gives to them their food in proper time." There are at least five stresses to this oversize colon, compared to only three in the compact infinitive clause of 104:27b.

The final parts of our psalm invert the order of vv. 1-14. Now HYMNIC AFFIRMATION begins with four lines of Yahweh-centered laudatory statements (vv. 17-20, with only v. 19a lacking the name of Israel's God) and a closing line of summons to one's self (v. 21). As mentioned before, the first colon of each line sings the praises of Yahweh (he is "just," "near"; he "fulfills" prayers and "guards" the faithful). The second cola talk about the effects of Yahweh's benevolence and help on his followers (vv. 17b, 18b, 19b), while the last one pronounces doom on the "godless" (*rĕšā'îm,* v. 20b).

To close a hymn with a repeated summons to praise is a regular hymnic feature (cf. Psalms 103; 104). It is noteworthy that the closing summons does not employ direct address of God as vv. 1-2 do. Furthermore, there is a little appendix to v. 21: a free-floating "for ever and ever" (*lĕ'ôlām wā'ed).* We cannot tell whether this formulaic expression (cf. 9:6 [RSV 5]; 10:16; 21:5 [RSV 4]; 45:7, 18 [RSV 6, 17]; etc.) has been added by a redactor or was actually used for recitation. Some psalms end on a note of long endurance: 121:8; 131:3; 133:3; 139:24.

An ACROSTIC PSALM challenges interpreters to look for more poetic devices than first letters of opening lines. And, indeed, scholars are able to detect more artistic schemes in this "total, A-to-Z praise of God": repetitions of key words (root *mlk,* "king"; abstract noun *kl,* "all"; *brk,* "bless," etc.), symmetries, inclusions, chiasms, interconnecting pointers and signs, etc. (cf. Liebreich, Berlin, Watson, Kimelman, Zenger, et al.). Some of these discoveries, however, betray their origin in the searching minds of interpreters rather than in the intentions of authors and transmitters of the text.

## *Genre/Setting*

ACROSTICS are artistically composed poems, but they tend to show affinities with traditional genres (→ Psalm 119; W. Soll, *ABD* I, 58-60). In our case the song is purely hymnic in character, with a strong emphasis on personal-address forms. Presumably, Psalm 145 belongs in the Jewish community service of the Persian epoch. There are traces of late OT language, e.g., the term "kingdom of Yahweh." Every member of the Yahweh congregation is included in this resounding general praise of their God. No reference is made to either salvation history or Torah revelation. The contents of the hymn are nonspecific. The first appellation even avoids the name Yahweh, calling on the personal God and King of the worshiping group (v. 1b). Thereafter, frequent naming of Yahweh, with the highest concentration in the culminating last block (vv. 17-21), demonstrates the spiritual setting in the Jewish community. Predominant praising affirmations make the psalm an ACROSTIC HYMN.

Some exegetes consider Psalm 145 once to have been the last text of the Psalter, the Hallelujah Psalms 146–150 being a later appendix (cf., e.g., Wilson, *Editing,* 193-94; listing at "Introduction to Psalms"; Zenger, 146-50; also idem, "Composition"; see listing at Psalm 107). Form-critical observations would not support such a conclusion, because they cannot corroborate lexicographical, thematic, and theological ligations between the texts. Many exegetes advocate the ancient liturgical use of the psalm (cf. Allen, 297; Kimelman, 55-58; et al.).

## *Intention*

Exuberant praise of God is the first duty of believers in ancient Near Eastern religions. Along this line of thinking, Psalm 145 practices eulogy in a very general and all-inclusive way, teaching members of the congregation to feel part of God's sovereign rule of justice and equity (vv. 13-16). Indeed, in these verses we may localize the psalm's greatest concern. The celebration of Yahweh's kingship (cf. Psalms 95–99) certainly plays an important role in this theological context, whether it be the outcome of eschatological or plain realistic-political expectation. Zenger ("Dass alles Fleisch," 10-12), with good reasons, emphasizes the Jewish prayer tradition, from which also the Lord's Prayer derived (Matt 6:9-13; Luke 11:2-4).

## Bibliography

P. Auffret, "Essai sur la structure littéraire du Psaume 145," in *Mélanges bibliques et orientaux* (*Fest.* H. Cazelles; ed. A. Caquot and M. Delcor; AOAT 212; Neukirchen-Vluyn: Neukirchener Verlag; Kevelaer: Butzon & Bercker, 1981) 15-31; A. Berlin, "The Rhetoric of Psalm 145," in *Biblical and Related Studies* (*Fest.* S. Iwry; ed. A. Kort, et al.; Winona Lake, Ind.: Eisenbrauns, 1985) 17-22; W. Brueggemann, "Praise and the Psalms: A Politics of Glad Abandonment," *Hymn* 43 (1992) 14-19 (repr. in idem, *Psalms*, 112-32; listing at Additional Bibliography, section C); D. N. Freedman, "Patterns in Psalms 25 and 34," in *Priests, Prophets, and Scribes* (JSOTSup 149; *Fest.* J. Blenkinsopp; ed. E. Ulrich et al.; Sheffield: Sheffield Academic Press, 1992) 125-38; C. B. Houk, "Acrostic Psalms and Syllables," in *The Psalms and Other Studies* (*Fest.* J. I. Hunt; ed. J. Knight, et al.; Nashotah: Nashotah House Seminary, 1990) 54-60; R. Kimelman, "Psalm 145: Theme, Structure, and Impact," *JBL* 113 (1994) 37-58; L. J. Liebreich, "Psalms 34 and 145 in the Light of Their Keywords," *HUCA* 32 (1956) 181-92; B. Lindars, "The Structure of Psalm CXLV," *VT* 39 (1989) 23-30; C. Pearl, "The Theology of Psalm 145," *Jewish Bible Quarterly* 20 (1991) 3-9; O. H. Steck, "Das Problem theologischer Strömungen in nachexilischer Zeit," *EvT* 28 (1968) 445-58; W. G. E. Watson, "Reversed Rootplay in Psalm 145," *Bib* 62 (1981) 101-2; G. H. Wilson, "The Qumran Psalms Scroll Reconsidered," *CBQ* 47 (1985) 624-42; E. Zenger, "'Dass alles Fleisch den Namen seiner Heiligung segne' (Ps 145,21)," *BZ* 41 (1997) 1-27.

## Psalm 146:
## Communal Hymn

### Structure

|  | MT | NRSV |
|---|---|---|
| I. Opening cheer | 1a | 1a |
| II. Summons to praise | 1b-2 | 1b-2 |
| III. Admonition | 3-4 | 3-4 |
| IV. Beatitude | 5 | 5 |
| V. Hymn to Yahweh | 6-9 | 6-9 |
| VI. Wish | 10ab | 10ab |
| VII. Closing cheer | 10c | 10c |

OPENING and CLOSING CHEERS (*hallĕlû-yāh,* "praise Yah[weh]") are attached in most MT MSS, sometimes lacking in LXX, to the beginning and end of Psalms 146–150, making this group of psalms a separate collection known as the "Final Hallel" of the Psalter (cf. the "Great Hallel" = Psalms 111–118, each of which has an opening *hallĕlû-yāh;* Finkelstein). This — until our own day — liturgical exclamation has obviously been used by collectors and redactors. Its somewhat haphazard existence in different Hebrew MSS and the ancient versions obscures its functions with individual texts. Are we dealing with a live exclamation framing the presentation of a given hymn? Or are we

437

encountering a scribal divider of texts? It may be nearly impossible to find the right answer. But evidently the collectors or redactors considered *hallĕlû-yāh* a genuine opening (or closing) utterance pertaining to the psalms proper (cf. E. S. Gerstenberger and B. Lang, "Halleluja," *NBL* II, 18-19; S. R. Swanson, *ABD* I, 30). At least one psalm begins with a grammatical construction showing clearly liturgical use of the cheer "Hallelujah" (→ 147:1).

The customary SUMMONS TO PRAISE starts in v. 1b, unfolding in a three-part self-exhortation. The verbs used (twice *hll*, Piel, "praise"; plus *zmr*, Piel, "play, sing") are standard in hymns. Also, the first-person singular summons to one's self in two variations, "my self, sing," and "I want to sing," is well attested in the Psalter (see 7:18 [RSV 17]; 9:3 [RSV 2]; 27:6; 57:8-10 [RSV 7-9]; 61:9 [RSV 8]; 71:22, 23; 108:2-4 [RSV 1-3]; 138:1; cf. 103:1-2; 104:1a). The usages as summons or vow are closely related to one another. In our case, the summons of oneself is apparently presented to a community of listeners and watchers, because the direct address of Yahweh is missing in vv. 1b-2. God is mentioned in the third person. The explicit address of a community, however, occurs only in the following unit (vv. 3-4: "Do not trust in human authorities"). Still, the religious body, not mentioned explicitly, is present already in vv. 1b-2. Now, the group is openly admonished (or warned) not to abandon Yahweh (v. 3) and always to be mindful of human transitoriness and dependence on God (v. 4; cf. Gen 3:19; Ps 104:29-30). Such instructional zeal we know from wisdom texts and educational settings. In hymnic contexts it seems unusual, but some psalms do exhibit a similar tendency of instructing the congregation (cf. 19:12-13 [RSV 11-12]; 75:5-9 [RSV 4-8]; 90:12; 139:6). The educational effort may be one indicator pointing to an early Jewish congregational background.

The BEATITUDE (v. 5) with a following YAHWEH HYMN (vv. 6-9) apparently receives the greatest liturgical emphasis here. *'ašrê* forms are fairly frequent in the Psalter (cf. 1:1; 41:2 [RSV 1]; 119:1-2; 128:1-2; → Glossary: FELICITATION). They indicate efforts by the community to point out, for educational purposes, model attitudes and behavior in the light of faith in God. In our text, significantly, the one called "happy" is not identified by his or her own qualities (cf. 119:1-2), which would be the standard way of pronouncing that blessing, but by his or her affiliation to the God of Israel. This peculiarity allows a direct transition to a hymnic part (vv. 6-9), lauding Yahweh by enumerating his wholesome qualities and activities. Affiliation with Yahweh as the top criterion of bliss is also expressed in 33:12; 144:15. These two felicitations applaud "the people," though, not an individual believer.

The HYMN itself (vv. 6-9) extols Yahweh the creator of heaven and earth — a favorite theological affirmation from the exilic epoch onward (cf. "heaven": Isa 37:16; Jer 32:17; Ps 96:5, using the verb *'śh*, "make"; frequently with *nṭh*, "extend," thus Isa 40:22; 44:24; 45:12; 51:13; Jer 10:12; Zech 12:1). The second colon (v. 6b) adds "the sea, and everything in it" (cf. Neh 9:6), a very late theological statement, because originally the sea with its monsters represented opposing chaos powers, in effect unreconcilable with creation at all (cf. Pss 74:13; 77:17-20 [RSV 16-19]; 104:6-9). The third colon of v. 6, on the basis of that sweeping confession to God, the creator, emphasizes his general reliability. He keeps "fidelity" (v. 6c), obviously, to those faithful to him. The three hymnic affirmations are made using participles: *'ōśeh,* "making," governs those two cola of creation (v. 6ab), while *šōmēr,* "keeping," informs the third (v. 6c). Beginning with v. 7 the same basic structure (participles with objects) is maintained. Only the very last line (v. 9bc) switches into imperfect forms instead of participles, the result being rare expressions of benevolence to the weak ("orphans and widows he supports" = *yĕʿôdēd,* from *ʿûd* I, Pilel, "help," only one more occurrence: 147:6) and rejection of the wicked ("the path of the wicked he confounds" = *ʿwt* I, Piel, "pervert, falsify"; one more instance in the Psalter, 119:78; with God as subject: Job 8:3; 19:6; 34:12). For the rest, we find participles, praising God who cares for the poor, exploited, and deficient, i.e., the socially underprivileged and endangered. There emerges, in vv. 7-9a, a list of seven groups of quite different profiles: "oppressed ones" (*ʿăšûqîm;* cf. Ps 103:6; Qoh 4:1; E. S. Gerstenberger, *TWAT* VI, 441-46; J. D. Pleins, *ABD* V, 402-14), "hungry ones" (*rĕʿēbîm;* cf. Ps 107:5, 9, 36), "bound ones" (*ʾăsûrîm;* cf. Isa 49:9; 61:1). These three kinds of people (v. 7), we may say, are socially hurt and underprivileged. The next two groups mentioned seem to be physically deficient: "blind ones" (*ʿiwwĕrîm;* cf. Lev 19:14; Isa 29:18; 35:5; 42:7, 16, 18), "bent ones" (*kĕpûpîm;* cf. Pss 57:7; 145:14). The book of Isaiah sometimes names "blind" ("deaf," "mute") ones and "bound," "imprisoned," or "poor," "miserable" ones together (cf., e.g., Isa 29:18-19; 42:7, 18-22). We may surmise that physical deficiencies have acquired metaphorical value in such theological discourse. The sixth designation (v. 8c) does not specify any kind of deprivation, presenting, as it were, the "just ones" (*ṣaddîqîm*) as the beloved partners of Yahweh. This colon sounds like a concluding phrase placed after the list of groups of miserables. In fact, v. 9 may have come in later, because v. 9bc, as pointed out, employs a different phraseology, and v. 9a, God's care for the "strangers," seems to belong to "orphan" and "widow," making that famous D triad of socially weak persons (cf., e.g., Deut 16:11, 14; 24:19, 20, 21). On the whole, therefore, we see a conscious effort in Psalm 146 to enumerate significant underprivileged persons in the community who are under the special care of Yahweh.

The hymnic expressions derive, so to speak, from the beatitude (v. 5). There Yahweh is explicitly mentioned, and subsequent participles (vv. 6-7b) all are dependent on his attributes in v. 5b. Starting with v. 7c, however, each of the five following phrases receives the name of Yahweh again, reinforcing the hymnic thrust. "Yahweh liberates the bound ones" (v. 7c; *ntr,* Hiphil, "set free," is rare in Hebrew Scripture: Ps 105:20; Isa 58:6; Job 6:9); "Yahweh makes the blind ones see" (v. 8a); "Yahweh . . ." — the words ring out like triumphant shouts, culminating in the fourth affirmation: "Yahweh loves the righteous ones" (v. 8c). V. 9a, affirming Yahweh's protection of strangers, adds one more item, then the whole series of helpful acts to people in need fades out with traditional orphan and widow — no "Yahweh" at the beginning! — (v. 9b) and the rebuttal of the *rĕšāʿîm,* "wicked ones" (v. 9c). The hymn in vv. 6-9, we may say, concentrates on Yahweh's help for the underprivileged, and my general impression is that external pressures notwithstanding, it is internal social conflicts that produced those groups of miserables and sufferers. The "wicked," then, would be compatriots (cf. Nehemiah 5 as an illustration). And the enumeration of needy ones (vv. 7-9) — altogether eight categories of people — is like a mirror of the contemporary Yahweh community, the "righteous ones." We noticed similarities to some lists of deprived people in the book of Isaiah. Psalm 146 uses similar traditional concepts, but does not copy from Isaiah. The degree of metaphorical spiritualization in both sources should be a matter of further debate.

After that hymnic climax the psalm comes to a quick end, articulating a WELL-WISH for Yahweh's kingship (v. 10ab; cf. Pss 145:13; 95–99). Surprisingly, this wish is dedicated to Zion in direct-address speech (v. 10b). Zion has not played a role so far in this psalm; mention of Yahweh's residence throws some light on the situation, however. The community is oriented toward Jerusalem, be it from afar or from within the city walls.

The CLOSING CHEER (v. 10c) corresponds directly to the opening one. Both are a proper frame for the hymn either in a mere literary or a truly liturgical way. In the latter case someone would introduce and end the song by crying aloud: *hallĕlû-yāh!* The variety of forms and content, and affinities with many other biblical texts leave commentators puzzled (cf. Reindl, 116; Kselman, 589; etc.). Some scholars elaborate intricate chiastic and other structures (cf. Kselman, 591-96).

## *Genre/Setting*

Hymnic praise by an individual singer may be a plausible evaluation of Psalm 146 (e.g., Gunkel, Kraus, et al.). The introductory summons in the first person singular lends credibility to this classification. However, we should be wary about the setting: the person singing this Yahweh hymn is not alone. There are implicit indications of a crowd of worshipers listening to the single voice (cf. the exhortation of v. 3; didactic tendencies). And there is the orientation toward Zion (v. 10), which is certainly not a private privilege but a communal treasure. The same idea is valid for Yahweh, the God of Jacob (v. 5a) and helper of the weak ones. Everything said in the psalm points to a communal background. Therefore my contention is that Psalm 146 is a COMMUNAL HYMN, sung by individual believers within a worship liturgy of the congregation. The "I" is not identical with the community at large, it is not a communal superego. The first person singular is simply one member (and, in effect, all members present, taken individually, just as in many songs of our hymnals today) speaking for him- or herself, while others hear or sing the same words for themselves.

Recent studies in the composition of the Psalter (cf. Wilson, *Editing,* 226-28; listing at "Introduction to Psalms"; Zenger; see listing at Psalm 145; Miller) emphasize the relative compositional and theological unity of the Final Hallel (Psalms 146–150). Zenger is most outspoken in this endeavor. To him, the five relevant texts have been consciously composed and concentrically arranged around the centerpiece Psalm 148 to demonstrate the universal praise of God, the cosmic King, who shortly will initiate his reign on earth. This eschatological outlook corresponds to Psalm 2, thus enveloping all the psalmic collections

440

and providing the hermeneutical key for the whole Psalter. According to Zenger, from the beginning the Final Hallel was meant to be read and meditated on as a uniform text, just as the canonical Psalter altogether served as a reading book.

In my opinion, the uniformizing tendencies of redactional work are vastly overrated in these reconstructions. Each individual text, as it stands now, is still counted as a hymn in its own right, showing a definite profile and a rootage in community service. Strong emphasis on the hymnic genres, however, is obviously intended in this little final collection of psalms (cf. Brueggemann, *Psalms,* 112-32; listing at Additional Bibliography, section C).

## Intention

The overture of Psalm 146 (vv. 1b-2) wants to extol Yahweh alone. After a solemn warning not to go astray by trusting in human authorities (vv. 3-4), the hymn unfolds via a special beatitude. This element wants to demonstrate a model believer, whose faith is in Yahweh alone. But, astonishingly, the ensuing hymn (vv. 6-9) does not explicitly give a portrait of Israel's God in contradistinction from other deities. Instead, it propagates the Yahweh of the needy ones, who must have been the hoped-for savior in contemporary Persian times and who has become so important in Latin American liberation theology (cf. Smit, Soares). Now, this line of argumentation actually reveals speakers and listeners of the psalm. They themselves are part of one or the other group highlighted in vv. 7-9. In consequence, the hymn was a vehicle to laud Yahweh for what he had been doing in favor of the lowly ones. The intention, no doubt, was also to keep close to that benign God and prosper under his rule. A didactic intention is not excluded, in that the singing person or community "wants to induce others to assume a certain religious attitude" (Reindl, 134). These "others," naturally, are the (singing and) listening members of the congregation.

## Bibliography

W. Brueggemann, "Praise" (see listing at Psalm 145); W. J. Carl, "Psalm 146," *Int* 48 (1994) 166-69; L. Finkelstein, "The Origin of the Hallel," *HUCA* 23 (1950/51) 319-37; F. O. García-Treto, "El Senour guarda los emigrantes," *Apuntes* 1 (1981) 3-9; D. Karasszon, "Bemerkungen zum Psalm 146," in *Goldene Äpfel in silbernen Schalen* (ed. K. Schunck, et al.; Frankfurt: Peter Lang, 1992) 123-27; J. S. Kselman, "Psalm 146 in Its Context," *CBQ* 50 (1988) 587-99; J. Magonet, "Convention and Creativity: The Phrase 'Maker of Heaven and Earth' in the Psalms," in *'Open Thou Mine Eyes . . .' (Fest.* W. D. Braude; ed. H. Blumberg, et al.; Hoboken: Ktav, 1992) 139-53; P. D. Miller, "The End of the Psalter," *JSOT* 80 (1998) 103-10; J. Noret, "Fragments palimpsestes d'un commentaire inconnu du psaume 146," in *Texte und Textkritik* (ed. J. Dummer; Berlin: Akademie-Verlag, 1987) 457-68; J. Reindl, "Gotteslob als 'Weisheitslehre': Zur Auslegung von Psalm 146," in *Dein Wort beachten* (ed. J. Reindl; Leipzig: Evangelische Verlagsanstalt, 1981) 116-35; D. J. Smit, "In a Special Way the God of the Destitute, the

Poor, and the Wronged," in *A Moment of Truth* (ed. G. Cloete, et al.; Grand Rapids: Eerdmans, 1984) 127-50; S. A. Soares, "Sacia de bens os famintes," *EstBib* 46 (1995) 44-51; G. H. Wilson, "The Qumran Psalms Scroll Reconsidered," *CBQ* 47 (1985) 624-42.

## Psalm 147:
## Communal Hymn

### *Structure*

|   |   | MT | NRSV |
|---|---|----|------|
| I. | Opening cheer | 1a | 1a |
| II. | Introductory hymn | 1bc | 1bc |
| III. | Hymn to Yahweh | 2-6 | 2-6 |
| IV. | Thanksgiving song | 7-11 | 7-11 |
|  | A. Summons to give thanks | 7 | 7 |
|  | B. Praise of Yahweh | 8-9 | 8-9 |
|  | C. Affirmation of compatibility | 10-11 | 10-11 |
| V. | Hymn to Yahweh | 12-20b | 12-20b |
|  | A. Summons to praise | 12 | 12 |
|  | B. Hymnic attributions | 13-14 | 13-14 |
|  | C. Praise of Yahweh | 15-20b | 15-20b |
| VI. | Closing cheer | 20c | 20c |

The OPENING CHEER in Psalms 146–150 may substitute for a superscription (→ Psalm 146). In that case it would be an exclusively literary addition to the psalm proper. But the present text seems to be constructed in such a way as to suggest the full liturgical function of *hallĕlû-yāh*. The two *kî* phrases following the opening cheer are hymnic lines to be sung by the choir or people (cf. exclamatory, hymnic *kî* in 33:4; 100:5; 118:1-4; Exod 15:21). Although the only instance in the final Hallel Psalms with this kind of construction, v. 1 may prove the feasibility of using *hallĕlû-yāh* liturgically. The two hymnic shouts of v. 1bc extol hymn singing as such, and v. 1b at that demonstrates a communal origin by using a first-person plural suffix ("our God"). Therefore the first line needs to be taken separately, being, as it were, a kind of INTRODUCTORY HYMN, or introit.

Vv. 2-6 are a regular YAHWEH HYMN, which, however, lacks a new introduction. This fact is perhaps the reason for an unusual opening line: "Builder of Jerusalem is Yahweh" (v. 2a; Sedlmeir makes this phrase, overratedly so, the determining center of the whole psalm) is the correct translation, with *bônēh*, "builder," being a substantive rather than a participle. On the other hand, the singers of the psalm are still the same as in v. 1, since the first-person plural suffix occurs again in v. 5a. Also, phraseology and grammatical forms are not homogeneous. We may find one more substantive in the sequence of predicates (v. 3a: *hārōpē'*, "doctor") and a whole series of participles (vv. 3b, 4a, 6a, 6b)

442

interrupted by some imperfect forms (vv. 2b, 4b) and two nominal clauses (v. 5a, b). This means that our hymn is not poetically pure, but it nevertheless may represent a true text for worship services. Looking at the contents of this little hymn we are perhaps irritated by the diversity of topics dealt with. Reconstruction of Jerusalem and gathering in of the dispersed ones (v. 2) are reminiscent of the message of Second and Third Isaiah (v. 2b almost repeats parts of Isa 56:8, while "building the city or the temple of Jerusalem" is an important theme, too: Isa 45:13; 58:12; 60:10; 61:4; 65:21-22; 66:1). "Healing the brokenhearted" and "bandaging their wounds" (v. 3) are important issues elsewhere (cf. Isa 30:26; 61:1; Jer 23:9; Ezek 34:16; Pss 34:19 [RSV 18]; 51:19 [RSV 17]). It seems that all these descriptions of Yahweh's restituting activities go together, belonging to the environment of the exilic community.

The following line, however, talks about Yahweh, the cosmic overlord (v. 4). Second Isaiah, in particular, utilizes creational motifs to promote arguments in the realm of salvation history. Yahweh's power as the founder of heaven and earth proves his ability to restore Israel (cf. Isa 40:26-31; 42:5-9; 44:24-28; 45:12-13; 48:12-16; etc.). Perhaps the same idea is behind the hymnic affirmations of vv. 2-6, although no explicit reference can be found to this effect. At any rate, the center of our little hymn is occupied by Yahweh's superiority over the stars, which, at least in a Babylonian context, would stand for as many deities. V. 5 apparently draws conclusions from Yahweh's cosmic hegemony. "Great is our Lord, and full of strength" (v. 5a) — a simple statement of predominance as it is used in the Psalter and in many religions (cf. Pss 48:2 [RSV 1]; 77:14 [RSV 13]; 86:10; 95:3; 96:4; 135:5; 145:3; Dan 9:4; in Islam: *Allahu akbar,* "Allah is great"). The liturgical shout is thus variable; in its communal form, "Great is our Lord," it is unique in the Psalter (cf. 8:2, 10 [RSV 1, 9]: "Yahweh, our Lord, how majestic is your name").

Curiously, the hymn reverts to the topic of the "poor" (v. 6a; cf. 146:7-9) in a certain anticlimax, because vv. 4-5 seemed to have reached out far beyond the human sphere. V. 6, indeed, is comparable to 146:9bc not only because the rare word ʿwd, Pilel, "relieve," occurs in both passages (and nowhere else in Hebrew Scripture), but also on account of the double outlook: salvation for the poor, destruction to the godless *(rěšāʿîm).* Are we entitled to think of gradual growth in these verses of a genuine Yahweh hymn? The movement of praise seems, all in all, more coherent in vv. 2-6 than in 146:6-9, in spite of that relapse to the oppressed. V. 3 having a similar outlook on "shattered" people, we may assume that both lines describe a contemporary situation. They are probably a self-portrait of a community under outward pressure (Jerusalem is obviously in ruins; cf. Ezra and Nehemiah) and burdened with inner conflicts (oppression; cf. Nehemiah 5). The hymnic affirmations belong basically to the same context, actually being praise "from the depths" (130:1; cf. Lohfink, *Lobgesänge;* listing at Additional Bibliography, section C; Risse, 165-69). Here we may discern a movement toward Yahweh, the cosmic ruler (vv. 4-5), and a second climax in v. 6a, which shows the same grammatical structure as v. 2a (working with a participle instead of a noun: "a reliever of the oppressed is Yahweh").

THANKSGIVING SONG seems an appropriate designation for vv. 7-11, because of the technical term *tôdāh,* "thank offering" or "thanksgiving," in v. 7a.

The overture of this hymn is unique, using *'nh* I, "answer," or *'nh* IV, "sing" (thus *HAL*), instead of the customary verbs ("praise," "extol," "laud"): "Answer Yahweh with thanks" (cf. *'nh* in liturgical or ritual use: Exod 15:21; 32:18; Num 21:17; Ezra 3:11). In the second colon we find a customary parallel expression: "Play to our God on the lyre" (v. 7b). The first-person plural suffix is noteworthy, revealing the communal background of the psalm. After this SUMMONS TO GIVE THANKS, the hymn proper starts with participial phrases lauding God (vv. 8-9) for his sustaining work in the natural world. Five cola are dedicated to Yahweh providing rain and feeding wild beasts, a beautiful example of attentiveness for nonhuman life (cf. Psalm 104). Yahweh causes moisture to come down and grass to grow (v. 8, three Hiphil participles), and he "gives" directly (Qal participle of *ntn*) food to large animals *(běhēmāh)* and ravens (cf. 104:21, 27-28; 145:15-16). Changing the subject abruptly, the hymn reflects about things on earth compatible with God (vv. 10-11). The key words are *ḥpṣ* and *rṣh*, "to like, accept." What is it that Yahweh agrees on, or considers agreeable? The answer is surprising and has nothing to do with the preceding hymnic praise. First in the negative: he does not like horse power (= military might; v. 10a) or "legs of men" (v. 10b). The last expression also may refer to strength in battle (cf. Judg 15:8; Deut 28:35; Sedlmeier, 228; S. Schroer and T. Staubli, *Die Körpersymbolik der Bibel* [Darmstadt: Wissenschaftliche Buchgesellschaft, 1998] 208, 213), but it may have sexual overtones as well (cf. Isa 47:2; Cant 5:15; cf., e.g., T. Frymer-Kensky, *ABD* V, 1144-46). This means: typically male expressions of dominance — be they military or sexual — are not to God's liking. Positively speaking (v. 11), Yahweh prefers the community of faithful, who put their hopes exclusively in him. This is nothing less than a description of the early Jewish community focused on the concepts of *yārē'* *('ĕlōhîm/yhwh),* "fear, adore" (cf. H. F. Fuhs, *TWAT* III, 869-93), and *yḥl,* Piel, "wait, hope for" (cf. 33:18, 22; 71:14; 119:43, 74, 81, 114, 147; 130:7; 131:3).

A whole new HYMN TO YAHWEH unfolds in vv. 12-20b. LXX even divides Psalm 147 into two independent texts, each one with "hallelujah" and a superscription, one motive certainly being to regain concord with MT numbering. In this way 147:12-20 becomes Psalm 147 in LXX. Some modern exegetes follow suit, but evidence for the original autonomy of the second text is scanty (cf. Sedlmeier, Risse).

A SUMMONS TO PRAISE, addressed nominally to Jerusalem and Zion (v. 12), begins this section. The verbs used are of different frequency in the Psalter. *šbh* I, Piel, "praise," occurs only once more in a summons, and in parallelism with *hll* as well (v. 12; cf. 117:1). Occurring a few more times in other functions (63:4; 145:4; Qoh 4:2; 8:15), *šbh* is somewhat of a rarity in hymnic language. The contrary is true for *hll,* Piel, "praise," as we know from Psalms 106; 111-113; 148-150; etc. This verb, especially in its imperative summoning form, is the best known of all calls to praise (cf. above v. 1a). So we do have a new beginning, and LXX represents a tradition that started a new psalm with a number of its own in v. 12. In terms of forms we recognize a fresh hymnic introduction, directing itself to the Holy City "in person," and two lines of praise dedicated to the same entities (second-person feminine suffixes). That means that a speaker exhorts Jerusalem to sing praises to Yahweh (v. 12a); thereafter the same voice (?) tells jubilantly how much God has been doing for his holy place. And articulating such news or experiences, the speaker or singer explicitly addresses Jerusalem. This seems odd, liturgically speaking. A real hymn to be sung by the personified city would either be couched in neutral praises to God or use the first person singular when referring to benefits received from Yahweh, e.g., "Yes, he made strong the bars of *my* gates" (cf. v. 12a, "*your* gates"). The little book of Lamentations contains examples of both types of liturgical usage. Jerusalem speaks in the first person singular (e.g., Lam 1:12-22), and is addressed in the second person singular (e.g., Lam 2:13-18). But what kind of speech would that be, to whom and for which purposes? Our two lines (vv. 13-14), anyhow, are addressed to Jerusalem, i.e., not put into her mouth. Formally, they must have been sung over and on behalf of the city. Their contents are the firm conviction that Jerusalem is invincible, that her descendants are blessed (v. 13b), and that she had received plenty of the finest food (v. 14b). The age-old concern for security over against enemies in both lines is preeminent, though, occupying the first cola (vv. 13a, 14a; cf. Isa 60:17-18).

Vv. 13-14 are meant already to praise Yahweh, the protector and benefactor of Jerusalem. Now, in vv. 15-20 we have a different outlook. No addressee of the hymn is in sight. There are mostly participial phrases extolling Yahweh directly — for what? For giving his "word" (vv. 15, 18, 19a) to the community, and this word is specified to mean "his ordinances and his rights for Israel" (v. 19b). The possessive suffixes are important. Deuteronomy and other biblical books employ the word pair *ḥōq ûmišpāṭ*, "statute and right," as well (cf. Gen 15:25; Deut 4:1, 5, 14, 45; Josh 24:25; 1 Kgs 9:4). Vv. 15-20, therefore, are a separate little hymn about Yahweh's word, and his word is nearly identical with *tôrāh*. Not the quality of Torah is lauded, as in Psalms 19 and 119, but the coming down on earth of God's mighty word (comprehensive singular). This detail exhibits theological reflection, summarizing God's relation to Israel in a "word-event." Furthermore, revelation of the word of God is linked with meteorological phenomena: snow, hoarfrost (*kĕpôr*, only 2 other occurrences: Exod 16:14; Job 38:29), ice, cold (all in vv. 16-17; cf. Job 37:9-10). A certain parallel is offered by Isa 55:10-11, where the word is compared to fertilizing (!) rain- and snowfall. In Jer 23:29, on the other hand, the word of God comes down like a "hammer smashing rocks." All these passages testify to a theological discourse centering on the (written?) word of Yahweh as the most essential force in Israel's spiritual world. Other people are excluded from this source of life (v. 20). Exclusiveness of Torah in the possession of Yahweh's people is maintained (see, e.g., Deut 4:8; 30:11-14; 31:9-13; Neh 8:1-3; 9:13-14; Pss 19:8-11 [RSV 7-10]; 78:5; etc.). A CLOSING CHEER finalizes this hymnic text.

## Genre

COMMUNAL HYMN may be the overall designation of this three- or four-part song of praise. The divisions of the text, discussed above, are due to the liturgical agenda or redactional processes. Change of choirs or groups singing in a given worship situation is nothing to be surprised at; we still adhere to the same

445

basic pattern in our worship services. A sequence of several hymns like vv. 1, 2-6, 7-11, 12-20 may have been used in the congregation of Yahweh believers. Topics like Yahweh's creational power, Yahweh's care for the oppressed, Yahweh's election of Jerusalem, and Yahweh's gift of Torah were central and decisive for the theological thinking and religious existence of early Jewish communities in the Persian and Hellenistic ages. In other words, Psalm 147 contains a communal LITURGY with marked participation of the congregation ("we" discourse in vv. 1, 5, 7; → Psalm 126). The direct-address ZION HYMN (vv. 12-14) reminds us of → 122:3-9.

## Setting

Implicitly we have defined already the setting: community life and worship in postexilic Israel has brought forth the type of praise we encounter in Psalm 147. Vividness of liturgical changes within the psalm suggests multiple liturgical groups singing different passages. Zion and Jerusalem are not necessarily indicative of that city's congregation. We know that even distant diaspora groups felt tightly united with their spiritual home. The hymn dedicated to Jerusalem (vv. 12-14) possibly hints at such a "longing praise from afar" (cf. Psalms 84; 87; 137). The psalm's position in the Final Hallel (Psalms 146–150; cf. Risse, 196-243) should be explored with caution, in order to avoid overstretching apparent evidence (→ Psalm 146).

## Intention

Yahweh, his Holy City, and his Torah are the fundamental goods of a religious community lost in the universe of a heathen empire. They ought to be praised without end, in thankfulness and trust, so that the preserving dynamics of life may continue in the community of believers. The main concerns of this hymn, in terms of its practical theological drive, are preservation of the people and their worship in times of pressure and sufferings (cf. Bianchi, Mendecki).

## Bibliography

R. B. Allen, "The Word as Divine Light: Its Unique Wisdom," in *Celebrating the Word* (ed. E. Radmacher, et al.; Portland: Multnomah, 1987) 33-43; P. Auffret, "Essai sur la structure littéraire du Psaume 147," in idem, *Hymnes d'Egypte et d'Israel* (OBO 34; Göttingen: Vandenhoeck & Ruprecht; Fribourg: Universitätsverlag, 1981) 121-31; E. Bianchi, "Das Alte Testament und die Nichtgewürdigten der Gesellschaft," *Concilium* (D) 15 (1979) 624-29; J. Blau, "*Nawa tehilla* (Ps 147,1): Lobpreisen," *VT* 4 (1954) 410-11; P.-E. Bonnard, "Un Psaume pour vivre. Le Psaume 147 (146-147)," *Esprit et Vie* 89 (1979) 113-21; J. Cazeau, "Le psaume 147," in *Critique du langage chez les prophètes d'Israel* (ed. J. Cazeau; Paris: CNRS, 1976) 149-63; H. L. Ginsberg, "A Strand in the Cord of Hebraic Hymnody," *Eretz Israel* 9 (1969) 45-50; B. Gosse, "Le

Psaume 147," *ETR* 72 (1997) 597-600; M. Harl, "Et il rassemblera les 'dispersions' d'Israel: Une note sur le pluriel de diaspora dans le Ps 146 (147),2b," in *Le Psautier chez les Pères* (ed. J. Irigoin, et al.; Strasbourg: Centre d'Analyse et de Documentation Patristiques, 1994) 281-90; R. G. Kratz, "Die Gnade des täglichen Brotes: Späte Psalmen auf dem Weg zum Vaterunser," *ZTK* 89 (1992) 1-40; N. Lohfink, *Lobgesänge der Armen* (Stuttgart: Katholisches Bibelwerk, 1990); J. Marböck, "Der Gott des Neuen und das neue Lied," in *Ein Gott, eine Offenbarung (Fest.* N. Füglister; ed. F. V. Reiterer; Würzburg: Echter, 1991) 205-21; N. Mendecki, "Jahwe Erbauer Jerusalems und Sammler der Zerstreuten in Ps 147,2-3," *Collectanea Theologica* 56 (1986) fasc. specialis 85-88; S. Risse, *'Gut ist es, unserem Gott zu singen'* (Altenberge: Oros, 1995); F. Sedlmeier, *Jerusalem — Jahwes Bau* (Würzburg: Echter, 1996); H. W. Titus, "God's Gift to Man: Laws, Not Paradigms, for Public Policy," *Transformation* 2 (1985) 10-12.

## Psalm 148:
## Communal Hymn

### *Structure*

|       |                          | MT     | NRSV   |
|-------|--------------------------|--------|--------|
| I.    | Opening cheer            | 1a     | 1a     |
| II.   | First summons to praise  | 1b-5a  | 1b-5a  |
| III.  | Hymnic affirmations      | 5b-6   | 5b-6   |
| IV.   | Second summons to praise | 7-13a  | 7-13a  |
| V.    | Hymnic affirmations      | 13b-14a| 13b-14a|
| VI.   | Subscription             | 14bc   | 14bc   |
| VII.  | Closing cheer            | 14d    | 14d    |

OPENING and CLOSING CHEERS are discussed at → Psalm 146. If v. 14bc is a redactional subscription (Gunkel; Kraus, 1141; Wilson, *Editing,* 226-28 [listing at "Introduction to Psalms"]; Millard, *Komposition,* 144-45, Additional Bibliography, section C), which is likely, we have a clear example of a closing cheer being secondary to the psalm text. A redactional line would hardly have been placed in a living liturgical element. Perhaps v. 14 is redactional as well, because the psalm seems to close on a summons to praise with short communal response (v. 13ab). Ps 147:1, by contrast, is a case of liturgical integration of initial *hallĕlû-yāh*. This means that we have to be careful in evaluating these seemingly erratic cheers in Psalms 146–150.

The structure of the body of our hymn is very lucid. The bulk of the text falls into two parts, the first of which calls on heavenly powers (vv. 1b-6), and the second on earthly entities (vv. 7-13), and both are to sing the praises of Yahweh, creator of the universe. Looking at the first part we notice regular, if not monotonous, repetition of the imperative *hallĕlû* seven times in vv. 1b-4. The first of these is a sort of heading, corresponding exactly to the introduction of the second part (vv. 7-13), which names the "earth" instead of "heaven" (v. 7a; cf. 1b). "Praise Yahweh from/in heaven" (v. 1b), then, triggers a series of

447

six short SUMMONSES TO PRAISE, all dependent on the introductory colon. Each phrase consists only of a suffixed imperative ("praise him," the suffix referring back to Yahweh) and, as a rule, of some power nominated to do the eulogizing (e.g., "all his messengers," v. 2a; "sun and moon," v. 3a; "waters above the heavens," v. 4b). We are reminded of Psalm 29, where the "sons of gods" are commanded to bring honor and glory to Yahweh (v. 1), or Psalm 19, where the heavens are "telling the glory of God" (v. 2 [RSV 1]). Nowhere else, however, are heavenly body and powers called on so directly and specifically to join the community in hymnic praises. And this is exactly what the first part of Psalm 148 is all about. The community of Yahweh believers rejoices in the glory of their God, and incorporates the whole universe in this enterprise. The psalm apparently uses lists of heavenly entities, without, however, pursuing a systematic order. V. 1c only supplements the general statement of v. 1b, *mĕrômîm*, "heights," being a somewhat artificial synonym to "heavens" (cf. occurrences of plural: Isa 33:16; Job 16:19; 25:2; 31:2; Prov 8:2; 9:3, 14; Qoh 10:6; only the Jobian passages signify "heaven"). This usage of *mĕrômîm* is obviously late, i.e., postexilic. The general indication of cosmic heights in v. 1bc hints at the most supreme authorities imaginable. For ancient Near Eastern people of the second and first millennia B.C.E., not chthonic but celestial forces were decisive for natural and human history, becoming "parents" of humankind (cf. Jacobsen, *Treasures,* 147-64; listing at "Introduction to Cultic Poetry").

V. 2 follows this lead, but does not yet enumerate, as might be expected, "sun," "moon," and "stars" (v. 3; the triad of expressions typically signifies the totality of heaven; cf. Gen 1:16; 37:9; Ps 136:8-9), those concrete celestial bodies identified with deities in antiquity. V. 2, instead, names "his messengers" and "his hosts" (H. Ringgren, *TWAT* VI, 871-76; H.-J. Zobel, *TWAT* VI, 876-92), not meaning in this context human figures, but pointing at the submission of the highest deities under the authority of Yahweh (cf. 103:20-21; 104:4; Isa 24:21; Jer 8:2; Neh 9:6; Dan 8:10). Enumeration of celestial bodies comes next (v. 3), and the passage finishes with a summons to the highest heavens (presupposed are several layers of firmaments as extant in later Jewish, Hellenistic, and Gnostic writings; cf. R. Bartelmus, *TWAT* VIII, 204-39; J. Belzer and O. Knoch, *NBL* II, 152-56).

Vv. 5-6 are summarizing lines to conclude the first part of the hymn, no longer imperatives summoning to praise, but to a large part substantial AFFIRMATIONS OF PRAISE. They exhibit imperfect, perfect, and imperfect consecutive forms of the verbs employed, and the subject in vv. 5b, 6 is Yahweh. Especially in v. 5a we meet *hll,* Piel, third-person plural imperfect: "they shall praise the name of Yahweh," instead of the former imperatives. The very same phrase is used to introduce the concluding line of the second part (v. 13a), demonstrating the complementary character of vv. 1-6 and 7-13 (or 14a). The wish form "they shall praise" is all-inclusive, meaning the entities listed in vv. 2-4. It emphasizes the "name of Yahweh" as the authority to be praised, a phenomenon of special theological reflection (cf. F. V. Reiterer, H. Ringgren, and H.-J. Fabry, *TWAT* VIII, 122-76). The second colon of v. 5, not surprisingly, refers to Yahweh's creation, implying that all the heavens and their bodies have been brought forth by him and nobody else. V. 6, by using imperfect consecutive and perfect forms, is a very brief account of primeval events, forged into two cola stressing the permanent order of all natural things. Thus the concluding lines, vv. 5-6, summarize exhortations to the natural world to praise the Creator, and they effectively spell out his creational powers and responsibilities. Formally, the larger part of the text is sheer summons (vv. 1-5a), enumerating, probably *pars pro toto*, potential singers of praise in the universe, the heavenly realm. Actual words to be sung in praise we can find only in vv. 5b, 6. They give substance to the repeated summons, articulating basic deeds of Yahweh, the Creator; and the hymnic *kî* (cf. 100:5; 118:1-4) in v. 5b seems to mark those HYMNIC AFFIRMATIONS to be used by the adorers of the Creator (cf. v. 13b).

The second block of the summons to praise (vv. 7-13a), introduced by a matching admonition (v. 7a; cf. v. 1b), is addressed to earthly entities arranged in an interesting and more numerous listing than that of the first summons. While we count only seven concrete entries in vv. 2-4, the second summons commences already in v. 7b with specific attributes and ends up presenting 23 groups of beings (including personalized "natural" phenomena) challenged to sing praises to Yahweh (vv. 7b-12). These candidates for singing eulogies are arranged in five and a half poetic lines or eleven cola over against three lines in part I. Most of the full lines offer four appellations each; only one has five (v. 8). Small wonder, then, that the text is crowded, and individual imperatives *hallĕlûhû*, "praise him" (cf. vv. 1c-4), are missing. The introductory summons (v. 7a) has to provide the call for all 23 candidates. This is the way they are organized: certainly in a sort of hierarchy, from mythical powers, superhuman forces of nature, down to human society: chaotic powers (*tannînîm*, "sea monsters"; cf. 74:13-14; Isa 27:1; 51:9; Job 7:12; *tĕhōmôt*, "primeval floods" or "depths"; cf. Pss 33:7; 77:17 [RSV 16]; 107:26; Prov 3:20; 8:24) open the earthly choir. They are considered tamed and put to the service of the celestial overlord. Then summonses are extended to meteorological phenomena (v. 8), the mountains and big trees (v. 9), and the main categories of animals (v. 10). Only after this long list of beings worthy to be included in Yahweh's grand choir (15 entries) does the psalm get down to human societies (there is no indication that humankind's position at the end of the second summons should indicate a climax of praise, against Gunkel, et al.). The sequence in this last passage (vv. 11-12) is "kings," "nations," "princes," "judges," "young men," "young women," "old people," "boys." This is not an ascending line of dignitaries, but rather a descending one, including normal citizens, males as well as females.

Hardly one comparable text in the OT puts together such a large number of beings, and we surely do not go astray too far when suspecting popular or academic knowledge to be evident in such accumulations. In fact, we are able to find traces of similar lists especially in wisdom literature, e.g., of meteorological phenomena (v. 8; cf. Job 38:22-30, with eight entries), or of land animals and birds (v. 10; cf. Gen 1:20-25; 1:26: the lists include animals living in the water). The penultimate group are the political functionaries (v. 11); they recur in a way in lists of officials (cf. 2 Sam 8:15-18; 1 Kgs 4:1-19: here we find functions plus names of officeholders). The last group, containing plain citizens (v. 12), has counterparts here and there in laments or eschatological visions (cf., e.g., Lam 1:18-19; 5:11-14; Joel 3:1-2 (RSV 2:28-29); Isa 65:20;

Zech 8:4-5. For parallelism of, e.g., "young men," "young women," cf. Deut 33:25; Isa 62:5; Jer 51:22; Am 8:13; Lam 1:18; 2:21). These last-mentioned lists for the most part concentrate on one category of beings each. Accumulations of entities ranging from primeval monsters over various natural phenomena, wild beasts, to different classes of people are uncommon. Naturally, it would be interesting to investigate more fully what the individual components are in each subgroup of our text, and which details found in parallel texts have been left out in Psalm 148. Furthermore, the arrangement of the total accumulation of addressees is important, and it may even give some clues as to the structure of the community that produced the psalm.

We must content ourselves with a few observations on these issues. The lack of functionaries and categories known in the exilic-postexilic community seems curious. Priests and prophets, scribes and singers do not appear. Neither do chiefs of families or clans, housewives and mothers, slaves, strangers, lower-class people, handicapped, professionals, etc. All appellations, in spite of their profuseness, remain rather stereotyped and traditional. According to the pattern set by vv. 5-6 in the first part of the psalm, the second summons likewise closes with a wish in the imperfect: "They shall praise the name of Yahweh" (v. 13a; a similar structure can be found in Psalm 107: the description of suppliants is wound up by "they shall give thanks" in 107:8, 15, 21, 31), followed by HYMNIC AFFIRMATIONS probably to be sung in worship (vv. 13bc, 14a). "Yes, elevated is his name alone"; "his glory goes beyond earth and heaven."

If v. 14a is an account of some historical period or event, that colon may have been used as a hymnic expression, too. In this capacity the phrase closely resembles v. 6a, which likewise shows a consecutive imperfect and tells an unknown episode: God gave victory to Israel in the past. Arguments against this interpretation include the fact that v. 13c is a hymnic affirmation, closing the psalm by sweepingly declaring Yahweh's "glory" *(hôd)* omnipresent. The words used are "on earth and in heaven" (v. 13c); they consciously bind together the two distinct parts of the psalm, inverting, however, its order, which places heaven first and lets praise descend from the highest cosmic power to powerless humans.

V. 14a is obviously a triumphant account of Yahweh's (unspecified) help for his people. In comparison to the corresponding line of the first part (v. 6), the phrase looks fragmentary. We would expect some further articulation of God's actions, after his "name" and "glory" have been honored in two cola (v. 13b, c). Also, praise of an active intervention seems displaced behind that all-embracing colon v. 13c, terminating, it seems, the completed song. Should v. 14a be a later addition? Or has a fuller ending been lost? The third option: do we have to take v. 14bc as a continuation and conclusion of the psalm itself (thus some older scholars; cf. Gunkel, 619; more recent discussion concentrates on v. 14bc being either a scribal subscription [colophon; e.g., Ruppert, 277-78] or a superscription to the following Psalm 149 [MacKenzie, 222, because of coinciding vocabulary])? In the last case the verb *wayyārem,* "he lifted up," would govern the nouns of v. 14bc, too, which results in an awkward formulation: "he made rise . . . a song for all his faithful." Most modern exegetes consider the line in question a SUBSCRIPTION, not uncommon in ancient Near Eastern text collections. There is one more instance in the Psalter of a collector's final remark: 72:20 ("End of the prayers of David, son of Jesse"). Our present text, however, uses a singular noun only (*těhillāh*, "praise"), which can refer at best to the preceding psalm and does not make much sense as a concluding remark of a collection, lending some plausibility to MacKenzie's identification as a "superscription." Be that as it may, an authentic subscription would be a significant proof that sometime in the process of transmission a "book of Psalms" ended with Psalm 148. In today's discussion about the nature and redactional workings of the Psalter, v. 14bc is evaluated in this sense (cf. Westermann, Brueggemann, Wilson, Zenger, etc.; → Psalm 146).

Ruppert's structural analysis results in a breakdown of seven strophes ("Aufforderung," 278-79: vv. 1-2, 3-4, 5-6, 7-8, 9-10, 11-12, 13-14a), which he himself sometimes considers a little arduous. On the basis of such an exposition Ruppert recognizes three summonses to heavenly and four to earthly entities (p. 280; differently Dahood, III, 353-54: he puts in the netherworld, v. 7b), furnishing the sacred number seven. A close parallel, and more detailed at that, for listing hierarchies of eulogizers can be found in the LXX version of Dan 3:34-64.

## Genre

A neat COMMUNAL HYMN, Psalm 148 comprises praises to Yahweh on account of his great power and efficiency in nature and (Israelite) society. Heaven and earth in their plenitude are called to join in extolling the creator and sustainer of the universe. The overall scheme of praise calls for challenging the top powers first and gradually descending through the hierarchy to human, i.e., Israelite, respondents. The contours of that society are first sketched in general terms (vv. 11-12), naming political offices (v. 11) and civil states (v. 12), in short, main social stratifications. The comprehensiveness of praise calls to mind Psalms 19, 29, and 104.

Searching for the tradition history of the elements incorporated in the psalm, scholars tend to point out first, hymn singing in general, and second, onomastic wisdom literature (cf. von Rad). Both strands are undoubtedly behind Psalm 148 (cf. Ruppert, "Aufforderung," 285-95; he adds manifold intertextual references within emergent Scripture), the open question being in which proportion they mingle. Hillers, e.g., plays down Egyptian onomastic influence, contradicting von Rad. Allen, et al., admit multiple streams of intellectual and liturgical traditions. Wisdom concepts cannot be ruled out for the Psalter, as we can easily see in the great number of sapiential and yet liturgical compositions present among Israel's psalms (cf., e.g., Psalms 1; 19; 39; 49; 90; 111; 112; 119; 139).

## Setting

That the Israelite, or more precisely, the Jewish community finally emerges (v. 14abc) — having been present implicitly from the beginning (vv. 1-13; cf.

451

Gen 1:1–2:4) — instigating and exercising all the praises to be summoned from all the entities known on earth and in heaven, is a sure signal of the psalm's setting: it is the worship assembly of Yahweh's congregation of believers. All the manifold summons were probably intoned by the leading liturgists, while the hymnic affirmations may have been sung by choirs or the assembly in general.

## Intention

Comprehensive and universal praise of God is to create a meaningful and rewarding spiritual world in which individuals and religious groups may seek shelter, harboring their hopes and seeking fulfillment. We may say that a "house of praise," including everything in existence, is the finest edifice to be constructed on earth in the quest to stabilize the whole known cosmos.

## Bibliography

P. Auffret, "'Qu'ils louent le nom de YHWH,'" *Église et théologie* 29 (1998) 221-34; E. Beaucamp and J. P. de Relles, "Le choral de la création en marche: Psaume 148," *BVC* 72 (1966) 31-34; Chr. Brüning, "Psalm 148 und das Psalmenbeten," *Münchener theologische Zeitschrift* 47 (1996) 1-12; J.-L. Cunchillos, "Le Psaume 148: Hymne au dieu inaccessible — document religieux d'une mentalité conservatrice," *Proceedings of the 8th World Congress of Jewish Studies* (1982) 51-56; T. E. Fretheim, "Nature's Praise of God in the Psalms," *Ex Auditu* 3 (1987) 16-30; D. R. Hillers, "A Study of Psalm 148," *CBQ* 40 (1978) 323-34; M. Kässmann, "Covenant, Praise, and Justice in Creation: Five Bible Studies," in *Eschatology* (ed. D. Hallman; Geneva: WCC; Maryknoll, N.Y.: Orbis, 1994) 28-51; R. A. F. MacKenzie, "Ps 148,14bc: Conclusion or Title?" *Bib* 51 (1970) 221-24; W. S. Prinsloo, "Structure and Cohesion of Psalm 148," *OTE* 5/1 (1992) 46-63; G. von Rad, "Hiob 38 und die altägyptische Weisheit," *VTSup* 3 (1955) 293-301; L. Ruppert, "Aufforderung an die Schöpfung zum Lob Gottes: Zur Literar-, Form- und Traditionskritik von Ps 148," in *Freude an der Weisung des Herrn* (*Fest*. H. Gross; ed. E. Haag, et al.; Stuttgart: Katholisches Bibelwerk, 1986) 275-96.

## Psalm 149:
## Communal Hymn and Instruction

### Structure

|  | MT | NRSV |
|---|---|---|
| I. Opening cheer | 1a | 1a |
| II. Summons to praise | 1bc-3 | 1bc-3 |
| III. Hymnic affirmation | 4 | 4 |
| IV. Instruction, wish for revenge | 5-9b | 5-9b |
| V. Closing cheer | 9c | 9c |

The OPENING and CLOSING CHEERS do not exhibit particular characteristics; they are neither set apart from the context nor integrated into it more than usual (→ Psalms 146–148). After the opening cheer we find at least one line of a regular SUMMONS TO PRAISE (v. 1bc) with a proper imperative plural: "Sing to Yahweh a new song" (v. 1b). The verb *šîr,* "sing," means most of all vocal intonation, in this case, of a cultic song (cf. 13:6 [RSV 5]; 27:6; 96:1-2; 98:1; 101:1; 105:2). As the passages cited reveal, it does serve various kinds of summonses, and quite often is followed by the grammatical object *šîr ḥādāš,* "a new song" (cf. 33:3; 40:4 [RSV 3]; 96:1; 98:1; 144:9; Isa 42:10; Watson, *Poetry,* 81; listing at "Introduction to Cultic Poetry"; G. Brunert, M. Kleer, and G. Steins, *TWAT* VII, 1263-93). This rather formulaic expression may appear in company with other hymnic summonses (cf. Ps 33:1-3) or else dominate the overture of a psalm of praise (cf. 96:1-3 [three times *šîrû,* "sing," and two additional imperatives]; 98:1 [one summons only]). We may say, therefore, that "sing to Yahweh a new song" has a special dynamic with it, and may mean a characteristic kind of hymnic presentation, not necessarily a brand-new song composed spontaneously on the spot, celebrating one particular salvific event or even an eschatological happening (cf. Marböck).

The continuation of v. 1b takes up the grammatical objects of "sing!" in the parallel expression "his hymn," still adding the place of performance: "in the assembly of the loyal ones" (v. 1c, *ḥăsîdîm;* similarly 50:2; 79:2; 85:9; 148:14; cf. H. Ringgren, *TWAT* III, 83-88, "*qĕhal ḥăsîdîm* is the cultic assembly," 86). This key word in terms of → setting and theological outlook recurs twice in the psalm (vv. 5a, 9b). Several other self-designations of the community accompany and interpret the main self-designation, e.g., "Israel" and "sons of Zion" (v. 2), "his people" and the "poor ones" (v. 4). From all these epithets we may glean some information about the state of that community summoned to praise Yahweh. Interestingly, the synonymous use of "new song" and "his hymn" (determined) suggests that praise is to be voiced in a fixed form. The specification "new" (song) possibly indicates a very powerful or triumphant variety of hymn or perhaps a hymn intoned at a special juncture of worship (differently Brunert, et al., *TWAT* VII, 1278).

The imperative summons is followed by four imperfects of different verbs (v. 2: *śmḥ,* "rejoice"; *gîl,* "be glad"; v. 3: *hll,* "praise"; *zmr,* "play"). For all practical (i.e., liturgical) reasons these imperfects (or jussives) continue the "summons," even if a less direct wish form is employed. We find this phenomenon in a few other hymns as well (cf. 66:4; 105:3b; 113:1-2; 148:5, 13; for imperfects only as introduction see 97:1), but it is difficult to understand why a purely imperative summons (cf. 33:1-3; 96:1-3; 100:1b-3a; 105:1-5; 118:1-4) should be "softened" this way. Expressions (wishes) to be glad and rejoice (v. 2) do come up frequently in the body of hymns, thanksgivings, and even complaints (cf. 5:12 [RSV 11]; 9:3 [RSV 2]; 14:7; 31:8 [RSV 7]; 32:11; 34:3 [RSV 2]; 35:27; 40:17 [RSV 16]; 48:12 [RSV 11]; 53:7 [RSV 6]; 58:11 [RSV 10]; 64:11 [RSV 10]; 67:5 [RSV 4]; 68:4 [RSV 3]; 69:33 [RSV 32]; 70:5 [RSV 4]; 85:7 [RSV 6]; 96:11-12; 97:8, 12; 107:30, 42; 119:74). The overwhelming evidence of these passages would indicate that the topic "joy" rarely belongs to a hymnic overture. Note too that in our case it is continued in v. 5. Exhortation to be joyful also is a concern of the Deuteronomists (cf. Deut 12:7, 12, 18; 14:26; 16:11, 14, 15; 26:11; 27:7; Barré, 55). Furthermore, quite often the subjects of joy are the members of the community, sometimes in direct opposition to evildoers or enemies. This last observation may explain the sequence of our vv. 1-3. The imperfects of vv. 2-3 all depend on *qĕhal ḥăsîdîm*, "assembly of faithful" (v. 1c). Instead of resuming the imperative of v. 1b and making "Israel" and "sons of Zion" vocatives, the psalm treats these designations as grammatical subjects, and synonyms of *qĕhal ḥăsîdîm*. The speaker of Psalm 149 is thus not addressing him- or herself directly to the group but talking about it, perhaps a sign of a certain remoteness from an authentic situation of sung praises. The vocabulary of v. 3, however, fits well into the hymnic environment (*hll*, "praise"; *zmr*, "play": cf. 9:12 [RSV 11]; 30:5 [RSV 4]; 33:2; 47:7 [RSV 6]; 66:2; 68:5, 33 [RSV 4, 32]; 98:4-6; 105:2-3; 135:3; 147:7). Combinations of *hll* and *zmr* occur in 105:2-3; 135:3. Maybe the psalm was used in a more auditory and meditative way than we are accustomed to in other cases.

The *kî* phrases of v. 4, on the other hand, probably represent genuine HYMNIC AFFIRMATIONS, sung by the choir or congregation (cf. 118:1-4; 147:1; etc.). Contents of the two cola are praiseworthy facts, such as Yahweh's benevolence in regard to his people (v. 4a) and his "glorification" (*p'r* II, Piel, "glorify"; cf. Isa 55:5; 60:7, 9, 13; Ezra 7:27) of the "oppressed ones" (v. 4b). Allusions to the exodus experience seem to be subconscious, if present at all (against Ceresko, 182-84). Employment of the term *'ănāwîm*, "poor, oppressed ones," is challenge enough for more scrutiny of social conditions in the postexilic congregations (see below, Setting).

The second part of Psalm 149, liturgically speaking, does not have a proper beginning (contrary to, e.g., Psalms 147; 148), but ties in with the first half. Thus v. 5 corresponds in vocabulary, structure, and contents to vv. 2-3. Verbs of rejoicing (*'lz*, "be glad"; *rnn*, "jubilate") echo the ones used in v. 2; imperfect forms fashion both lines. To be "glad in honor" or "glory" (v. 5a) and to "jubilate on their beds" (v. 5b) are rather obscure affirmations (Barré, 55, thinks of public and private jubilation; the "bed" as a place of privacy also occurs, e.g., in 4:5 [RSV 4]; Hos 7:14; Mic 2:1, 5). What strikes us as more curious still is the intricate sentence structure in vv. 5-9. The term "loyal ones" (*ḥăsîdîm*, v. 5a) is the only grammatical subject for all the lines down to v. 9a. The closing affirmation v. 9b repeats the term ("his loyal ones"), making the whole passage a heroic poem dedicated to the *ḥăsîdîm*. They are admonished to rejoice (that much is clear in v. 5). They are pictured as singing praises with their double-edged swords in their hands (v. 6: *rômĕmôt*, from *rômāh*, "praise" [hapax legomenon], or perhaps a strange participial form?). This idea has certainly inspired many a Jewish (cf. the books of Maccabees) and, later on, Christian soldier (Puritans in New England sometimes sang such hymns while burning Indian villages; worship on battlefields was customary at least until World War I and survives in the West in connection with modern military actions). In terms of grammatical structure v. 5 is an apposition to the subject *ḥăsîdîm* (v. 5a), expanded into v. 6, and the following three lines (vv. 7-9), all beginning with an infinitive construct prefixed by the particle *lĕ* expressing the purpose or mode of an action. In poetry, especially of the liturgical kind, use of infinitives is rare, and of clusters of infinitives almost unthinkable. For example, the Qal infinitive of 'šh, prefixed with lĕ, occurs twice (vv. 7a, 9a), but seldom outside Psalm 149 (40:9 [RSV 8; vv. 7-8 are structurally uncertain]; 119:112, 126; 126:2, 3; 143:10). Thus there is an overextended string of phrases and lexemes attached to that solitary subject in front of the passage — an unusual way of singing praises or making poetry.

This grammatical cohesion of the individual lines makes it nearly impossible to break the psalm into two separate strophes after v. 5 (cf. Prinsloo, Füglister, et al.). Thematically, vv. 5-6 have a certain axial significance. Jubilant warriors of Yahweh, reminiscent of Holy War traditions (cf. Num 21:21-35; Deut 2:26–3:11; Joshua 6; 2 Chr 20:20-30: "Yahweh had enabled them to rejoice over their enemies," v. 27b), come up in postexilic literature like Chronicles. Most notable is an earlier motif of "war cry" and "war action," or operating by "throat" and "hand," in Judg 7:19-20, echoed in the fabulous power of hymn singing when going into battle (2 Chr 20:21-22). Some modern interpreters are repulsed by these war-promoting attitudes (cf. Füglister, Prinsloo, Anderson, et al.). They like to interpret them as utopian and eschatological features, but that is closing one's eyes to ancient (and modern) realities of theologically sanctioned violence (cf. Psalms 94; 109; Deuteronomy 20; Isa 63:1-6).

Looking at the contents of this lengthy one-way discourse, we recognize the spirit of war permeating every word. To take revenge for something the "nations" have done to Israel (not spelled out here) seems to be the main concern (v. 7; nĕqāmāh, "revenge," is explicitly mentioned, still remaining a rare word in the Psalter: 18:48 [RSV 47]; 58:11 [RSV 10]; 79:10; 94:1. Certain chapters in Isaiah, Jeremiah, and Ezekiel use the term more intensely). To take the oppressor kings captive, bind them, and execute them (vv. 8, 9a) is the highest desire of the psalmist. Gunkel (p. 620) points to the killing of captured kings (Num 31:8; Josh 10:24-27; cf. also the elimination of prisoners of war in Judg 8:18-21; 2 Sam 8:2; etc.). Barré (p. 189) links the passage to the conquest stories. Extraordinary is that obscure reference to "written ordinance" (v. 9a) justifying the killing of enemy kings. Gunkel, in his eschatological interpretation, declares scriptural announcements of final judgment to be the background for this affirmation. More logical (and less eschatological) would be the idea that the composers of Psalm 149 were thinking of biblical stories about killing hostile kings like those cited above, and/or of Dtr prescriptions to annihilate the habitants of the promised land (cf. Exod 23:23; 34:11; Deut 20:13, 16-18). If this is the case, we would have here one of the first allusions to a written Torah tradition (Füglister, 91, thinks of prophetic materials used in worship).

All the heroic accomplishments of the ḥăsîdîm are considered their "glory" (v. 9b; cf. v. 4b; 8:6 [RSV 5]). Our conclusion is that vv. 5-9 are more prosaic than poetic in character. The string of phrases is not just the result of expanding a poetic line, but of intricate compositional work. The sequence of phrases seems to be more literature than liturgy. "Literary" poetic texts, however, also may have been incorporated in liturgical agendas, e.g., as a report or instructional discourse. The genre of "reading material" or "textbook" for private edification had not been invented yet, we may assume. Consequently, we may recognize the voice of some official in vv. 5-9, giving religious instruction to the community.

Such a composite exposition, uniting hymn and instruction, may have grown from worship customs in the postexilic age (cf. Psalms 8; 34; 78; 104; 135; 136; 144; 145; 147). "Rejoice in Yahweh, O you righteous"; "Let all the earth fear Yahweh"; "We are waiting for Yahweh; he is our help and shield," 33:1a, 8a, 20: hymn singing has to have practical consequences, which in turn benefit, not always by warlike action, the community of worshipers. Disinterested eulogies to Yahweh are imagined by interpreters rather than met in the Psalms. Ancient hymn singing grew out of contemporaneous contexts of belligerence, oppression, and divine violence. Our own hymns have to correspond to our present historical, social, and ecumenical situations.

## Genre

The text has some of the ingredients of a regular COMMUNAL HYMN: summons to praise, hymnic affirmations, remarkable presentations of self-designations. We observed a tendency, though, to modify hymnic patterns to the reflective, exhortatory, and instructional side. Vv. 5-9, in addition, lean to glorification of the community of faithful. If Psalm 149 and 150 are appendices to a collection once ending with Psalm 148, there may be some conscious balancing of our text with Psalms 1-2, the "prescript" to the final collection of the Psalter. If not by formal analogies then by combative spirit Psalm 149 at least shows affinities to Psalm 2. Some modern interpreters consider the Hallel Psalms (Psalms 146–150) a solid, purely literary composition to close off the Psalter, each text having its specific function and theological meaning in the small collection as well as for the whole Psalter (→ Psalm 146).

## Setting

The self-designations referred to earlier exhibit a community defined as an assembly of faithful to Yahweh. This "ecclesiastical" group is under outside (economic? political? religious?) pressure, longing for and certain of divine relief, which will end up in a large-scale revenge of some kind over against anonymous enemies. The joy to be sung out to Yahweh and the glory to be bestowed on the *ḥăsîdîm* are possibly consequences of the "turning of fates" expected and anticipated in this "grim," "ugly" (Füglister, 82) song. That the community is calling itself "the poor/oppressed ones" (v. 4b) probably points to chronic deficiences in material and political well-being. We do have numerous vestiges of a "theology of the poor" in the Psalter (cf. Psalms 9/10; 37; 73; Zenger and Hossfeld, 1993, 14-15; Lohfink, *Lobgesänge;* Additional Bibliography, sections A and C). Psalm 149 is another piece of evidence for the struggle against superior oppressive forces in the empires of the ancient Near East. It is with remarkable confidence and unabashedness that this community sings for revenge: "Praise of God in their throats, a double-edged sword in their hands" (v. 6).

Prinsloo's contention that our psalm "gradually shook off its original cultic associations and historical context so that now we have only the text before us" (op. cit. 407) betrays a misunderstanding of "cult" and "worship setting" (cf. E. S. Gerstenberger, "Canon Criticism and the Meaning of *Sitz im Leben*," in *Canon, Theology, and Old Testament Interpretation* [*Fest.* B. S. Childs; ed. G. M. Tucker, et al.; Philadelphia: Fortress, 1988] 20-31).

## Intention

Considering the real situation of early Jewish communities lost in the jungle of vast empires, there is little reason to be surprised at the propagation of violence and revenge, which are at the forefront of our psalm's concerns. The battle for survival justifies (within limits; cf. liberation theologies) propagation of violence and calling on God to help in this struggle, as long as the suppliants are really powerless. The issue becomes highly critical, though, as soon as the downtrodden and exploited themselves become overlords, as happened on a large scale, e.g., when Christianity turned state religion in the Roman Empire. Imperial strategies for dominion must not be bolstered by religious legitimations; all sorts of violence from above against the poor are criminal.

## Bibliography

G. A. Anderson, *A Time to Mourn, a Time to Dance* (University Park: Pennsylvania State University Press, 1991); M. Barré, "Hearts, Beds and Repentance in Psalm 4,5 and Hosea 7,14," *Bib* 76 (1995) 53-62; D. L. Blakey, "Expressing Black Religion in Spirituals," *AME Zion Quarterly Review* 97 (1985) 19-22; A. R. Ceresko, "Psalm 149: Poetry, Themes (Exodus and Conquest), and Social Function," *Bib* 67 (1986) 177-94; N. Füglister, "Ein garstig Lied — Ps 149," in *Freude an der Weisung des Herrn* (*Fest.* H. Gross; ed. E. Haag, et al.; Stuttgart: Katholisches Bibelwerk, 1986) 81-105; B. Gosse, "Le Psaume CXLIX et la réinterprétation post-exilique de la tradition prophétique," *VT* 44 (1994) 259-63; H. Gunkel, "Psalm 149," in *Oriental Studies* (*Fest.* P. Haupt; Baltimore: Johns Hopkins University Press, 1926) 47-57; O. Loretz, "Psalm 149 und H. Gunkels Historismus: Zur Debatte über Gattungsforschung und kanonische Exegese," *UF* 25 (1994) 289-310; J. Marböck, "Der Gott des Neuen und das Neue Lied," in *Ein Gott — eine Offenbarung* (*Fest.* N. Füglister; ed. F. V. Reiterer; Würzburg: Echter, 1991) 205-21; C. Peters, "Psalm 149 in Zitaten islamischer Autoren," *Bib* 21 (1940) 138-51; W. S. Prinsloo, "Psalm 149," *ZAW* 109 (1997) 395-407; L. I. Rabinowitz, "The Makers of Israel: A Note on Psalm 149:2," *Dor le dor* 10 (1981/82) 122-23; J. N. Simmonds, "Musical Theatre: A Prelude to the Gospel," *Crux* 21 (1985) 10-16; R. J. Tournay, "Le Psaume 149 et la 'vengeance' des pauvres de YHWH," *RB* 92 (1985) 349-58; G. Vanoni, "Zur Bedeutung der althebräischen Konjunktion *w*. Am Beispiel von Ps 149,6," in *Text, Methode und Grammatik* (*Fest.* W. Richter; ed. W. Gross; St. Ottilien: EOS, 1991) 561-76.

# Psalm 150:
# Final Praise

## *Structure*

|  | MT | NRSV |
|---|---|---|
| I. Opening cheer | 1a | 1a |
| II. Summons to praise | 1b-6a | 1b-6a |
|   A. Praise of God | 1b-2 | 1b-2 |
|   B. Praise by instruments | 3-5 | 3-5 |
|   C. Praise for everybody | 6a | 6a |
| III. Closing cheer | 6b | 6b |

Psalm 150 is the last of the Hallel Psalms (→ Psalm 146), rounding off that bouquet of hymnic praises. At the same time it closes the whole canonical collection of psalms (LXX and other versions add several poems, but with due recognition that they are surplus texts), just as Psalm 1 introduces it. Both poems are very different in character, though. While Psalm 1 addresses itself to the individual Yahweh believer, advising him strongly to choose the right path and not to get distracted by wicked, godless people, Psalm 150 directs itself to the community, at least a plurality of listeners and active participants. There are altogether — including the cheers at the beginning and the end — twelve plural imperatives (*hallĕlû-yāh* or *hallĕlûhû*) in this psalm, and one colon apparently visualizing also individuals within the community: "Everybody praise Yah" (v. 6a: jussive singular). But the Heb. *kol* in connection with a determined unit designation (*kol hannĕšāmāh,* "all taking breath") still places emphasis on the whole unit, not on individual existence. Thus v. 6a simply summarizes all the summonses at hand. This final colon looks at a host of people constituting the congregation. Using a different word order and the imperfect singular (feminine, reference: *nĕšāmāh,* "breath") of *hll* instead of the imperative plural, the closing phrase stands out from the context. By the same token the closing cheer gets more or less separated from the psalm; it is missing from the LXX tradition.

Furthermore, Psalm 1 belongs to instructional or sapiential discourse, Psalm 150 is completely couched in hymnic language. This does not automatically mean that our text is a genuine song. We do not find hymnic affirmations in our text, only a SUMMONS TO PRAISE. The summons, however, is not the hymn proper (see "Introduction to Cultic Poetry," section 4D; Seidel, *Musik,* 166 [Additional Bibliography, section B], exaggerates: "The imperatives have lost their original functions and become praise in themselves"). There are at least two explanations of this phenomenon. First, Psalm 150 could be a merely literary text, meant to be read or meditated on only, which is improbable with all the cultic language and form elements employed. Second, the psalm may have served as a general response or introit to the recitation of other hymns or thanksgivings. This last option seems more likely.

Individual segments of Psalm 150 may be distinguished as outlined above. The OPENING and CLOSING CHEERS are standard to the Final Hallel,

Psalms 146–150 (→ Psalm 146). The first unit of the body of the psalm comprises four plural imperatives (*hallĕlû,* "praise"), aimed at the Deity to be extolled. Surprisingly, that Deity is called *'ēl,* "God," not "Yah" or "Yahweh" (v. 1b), as in most other cases. Since this reading (normalized only later on by the Syriac version into *"-yāh"*) seems authentic and inexplicable, we have to take into account a wider range of summonses than the strictly Yahwistic horizon would suggest (the root *hll* is known also in Ugaritic, Akkadian, Arabic, etc., in the sense of "jubilate"). The majority of passages place Yahweh or his name as the object of *hll;* only a few texts in the so-called Elohistic Psalter have *'ĕlōhîm* instead (cf. 44:9 [RSV 8]; 56:5, 11 [RSV 4, 10]; 69:31 [RSV 30]). Praise is solicited for God "in his sanctuary" (v. 1b; cf. Am 4:2; Pss 60:8 [RSV 6]; 108:6 [RSV 5]) or synonymously "in the fortress of his power" (v. 1c; *rāqîaʿ* normally means "firmament"; connoting Yahweh's dwelling place: Ezek 1:22-26; 10:1; cf. Hartenstein, *Unzugänglichkeit;* listing at Additional Bibliography, section B). Thereafter it is God's majesty and greatness that is indicated as the object of praise (v. 2; cf. Pss 20:7 [RSV 6]; 54:3 [RSV 1]; 65:7 [RSV 6]; 66:7; 71:16 [RSV 15]; 79:11; 89:14 [RSV 13]; Deut 3:24; 5:24; 11:2). In this way the first unit points to God the powerful and holy one.

The second unit thematizes the musical means of extolling the Lord. Eight different instruments are mentioned (cf. Seidel, *Musik;* Sendrey, *Music,* 166-387; for both see listing at Additional Bibliography, section B; V. H. Matthews and I. H. Jones, "Music and Musical Instruments," *ABD* IV, 930-39) ranging from *šôpār,* "ram's horn trumpet," to two kinds of *ṣilṣĕlîm,* "cymbals" (v. 5). These instruments certainly served different ends in the days of ancient Israel, and their use may have changed also within the span of history covered by the OT. The "ram's horn" was blown for military reasons (cf. Josh 6:4-6; Am 3:6) and at important festal occasions (cf. Lev 25:9; Pss 47:6 [RSV 5]; 81:4 [RSV 3]; 98:6). "Cymbals" may have been used of old in temple precincts (elsewhere only 2 Sam 6:5). The other instruments mentioned have their own profiles. "Lute" and "harp" (*nēbel, kinnôr,* v. 3b), melody instruments, were employed to accompany vocal presentations, in both the profane and sacred spheres (cf. Pss 33:2; 43:4; 49:5 [RSV 4]; 57:9 [RSV 8]; 71:22; 81:3 [RSV 2]; 92:4 [RSV 3]; 108:3 [RSV 2]; 144:9; 147:7; 149:3). "Hand-drums" were rhythm instruments to accompany ritual dance (v. 4a; cf. Exod 15:20; Isa 30:32; Pss 81:3 [RSV 2]; 149:3). Of the following pair of instruments, *minnîm,* "corded instrument," is hard to identify (only other occurrence: Ps 45:9 [RSV 8]), beyond being another stringed melody utensil besides *nēbel* and *kinnôr.* And *ʿûgāb,* "flute," like all the preceding types, had its ritual significance, but we have only a few texts speaking of this intrument (Gen 4:21; Job 21:12; 30:31; Ps 151:4). All in all, the few verses calling for instruments to be played to God not only give us remarkable insight into the history of Israelite music (cf. Seidel, *Musik,* 165-67, 222-25, 273), but also reveal a good deal about specific liturgical arrangements and their social and ritual backgrounds. For individual prayer held within small circles of participants the main instruments of accompaniment were *nēbel* and *kinnôr* (→ 43:4; 57:9 [RSV 8]). The hand-drum we know best from victory celebrations, women being the musicians (cf. Exod 15:20; Judg 11:34; 1 Sam 18:6-7). The cultural and social history of ancient Israel comes to the fore with an enumeration of instruments like this. We may deduce from it that cultic usage of instruments and pertinent music was natural to the psalmists. Everybody, with all known instruments, was invited to praise God in this final poem of the Psalter.

## Genre

We might call Psalm 150 a hymnic overture, because summonses to praise are not hymns in themselves. The overture to songs of praise was placed at the very end of the Psalter. Taking the vantage point of later observers, we can say that this means that the work of uncounted liturgists, collectors, redactors, and many generations of transmitters came to an end with a text of sheer summons to praise. No doubt, the whole collection in consequence has to be looked upon, first, by the trajectory of complaint to thanksgiving and praise, implying much suffering and conflict (Westermann, *Praise;* listing at "Introduction to Cultic Poetry"; Brueggemann; Zenger; Miller; et al.; see listings at Psalm 145 and 146). Second, in living liturgical situations the summons to praise (Psalm 150) may be used with other songs and prayers to make for a fine piece of liturgy. Third, the end position of our psalm seems to imply that praise of Yahweh always has to continue, and on coming to an end begin anew. Therefore we call this special psalm a FINAL PRAISE.

## Setting

It is true that the Psalter was written down sometime between 500 and 100 B.C.E. and preserved in scroll or book form. Nevertheless, to put these texts into writing has been a secondary step. First and of foremost importance has always been the practical use of the texts, mostly in worship situations. The setting even of Psalm 150 was not some scribal or school office, but the place of liturgical activities, the assemblies of the faithful (cf. Psalm 149). Our psalm was not composed for individual reading or meditation, but for communal use in worship performances (against Zenger, et al.; → Psalm 146).

## Intention

The final praise of the Psalter is to make Yahweh worshipers aware that eulogy of God is paramount to all other approaches to the Holy One. Praise to the creator and sustainer of the world transcends personal destinies and acknowledges a basic and antecedent debt, regardless of present and past sufferings and wrongs. Preestablished life and sustenance are reason enough to exalt the giver of all goods. Complaints and accusations are surely not forgotten in the Psalter, and they stay very important. Praise does not obliterate suffering, but it may erupt in the middle of suffering "like a flower of fire in the night" (Pedro Casaldaliga). And praise of God is the fundament for all human existence.

460

# Bibliography

E. Bartolini, " 'Crea in me, O Dio, un cuore nuovo," *Horeb* 6 (1997) 27-33; C. Deitering, "Movement Prayer, a Learning Experience — a Worship Experience," *NICM Journal* 7 (1982) 24-30; H. Gressmann, *Musik und Musikinstrumente im Alten Testament* (Giessen: Rickersche Verlagsbuchhandlung, 1903); I. H. Jones, "Musical Instruments in the Bible," *BT* 37 (1986) 101-16; P. S. van Koningsveld, "Psalm 150 of the Translation by Hafs ibn Albar al-Quti in the Glossarium Latino-Arabicum of the Leyden University Library," *Bibliotheca Orientalis* 29 (1972) 277-80; J. W. McKinnon, "Musical Instruments in Medieval Psalm Commentaries and Psalter," *Journal of the American Musicological Society* 21/1 (1968) 3-20; D. Macleod, "Re-discovery of Praise (Psalm 150:1, 5)," *Princeton Seminary Bulletin* 67 (1975) 69-74; H. F. van Rooy, "The Marginal Notes to the Syriac Apocryphal Psalms in Manuscript 12T4," *VT* 48 (1998) 542-54; idem, "A Second Version of the Syriac Psalm 151," *OTE* 11 (1998) 567-81; H. Sachsse, "Palästinensische Musikinstrumente," *Zeitschrift des Deutschen Palästinavereins* 50 (1927) 19-35, 117-31; H. Schweizer, "Form und Inhalt," *BN* 3 (1977) 35-47; H. Seidel, "Horn und Trompete im alten Israel unter Berücksichtigung der 'Kriegsrolle' von Qumran," *Wissenschaftliche Zeitschrift der Karl-Marx Universität Leipzig. Gesellschafts- und sprachwissenschaftliche Reihe* 6 (1956/57) 589-99; idem, "Ps. 150 und die Gottesdienstmusik in Altisrael," *Nederlands Theologisch Tijdschrift* 35 (1981) 89-100; M. S. Smith, "How to Write a Poem: Psalm 151a," in *The Hebrew of the Dead Sea Scrolls and Ben Sira* (ed. T. Muraoka, et al.; Leiden: Brill, 1997) 182-208; S. Talmon, "Fragments of a Psalms Scroll from Masada," in *Minḥa le-Naḥum (Fest. N. M. Sarna; ed. M. Brettler and M. Fishbane; JSOTSup 154; Sheffield: Sheffield Academic Press, 1993) 318-27; D. Wohlenberg, *Kultmusik in Israel* (diss., Hamburg, 1967).

# LAMENTATIONS

CHAPTER 7

# INTRODUCTION TO
# THE BOOK OF LAMENTATIONS

## Bibliography

B. Albrektson, *Studies in the Text and Theology of the Book of Lamentations* (Lund: Gleerup, 1963); B. Alster, "Edin-na ú-sag-ga," in *XXXII. Rencontre Assyriologique Internationale* (ed. K. Hecker, et al.; Berlin: Reimer, 1986) 19-31; G. A. Anderson, *A Time to Mourn, a Time to Dance* (University Park: Pennsylvania State University Press, 1991); D. H. Bak, *Klagender Gott — klagende Menschen* (BZAW 193; Berlin: de Gruyter, 1990); M. E. Biddle, "The Figure of Lady Jerusalem," in *The Biblical Canon in Comparative Perspective* (ed. K. L. Younger Jr., et al.; Lewiston, Maine: Edwin Mellen, 1991) 173-94; H. J. Boecker, *Die Klagelieder* (Züricher Bibelkommentar; Zurich: Evangelische Verlag, 1985); R. Brandscheidt, "Gotteszorn und Menschenleid," *Trierer theologische Studien* 41 (1983) 357-88; K. Budde, "Das hebräische Klagelied," *ZAW* 2 (1882) 1-52; M. E. Cohen, *The Canonical Lamentations of Ancient Mesopotamia* (2 vols.; Potomac: Capital Decisions, 1988); S. J. D. Cohen, "The Destruction: From Scripture to Midrash," *Prooftexts* 11 (1982) 18-39; J. S. Cooper, *The Curse of Agade* (Baltimore: Johns Hopkins University Press, 1983); F. W. Dobbs-Allsopp, *Weep, O Daughter of Zion* (Rome: Pontifical Biblical Institute, 1993); idem, "Tragedy, Tradition, and Theology in the Book of Lamentations," *JSOT* 74 (1997) 29-60; J. A. Durlessen, "The Book of Lamentations and the Mesopotamian Laments," *Proceedings of the Eastern Great Lakes Bible Societies* 3 (1983) 69-84; M. Emmendörfer, *Der ferne Gott: Eine Untersuchung der alttestamentlichen Volksklagelieder vor dem Hintergrund der mesopotamischen Literatur* (Forschungen zum Alten Testament 21; Tübingen: Mohr, 1998); P. W. Ferris Jr., *The Genre of Communal Lament in the Bible and the Ancient Near East* (SBLDS 127; Atlanta: Scholars Press, 1992); E. R. Follis, "The Holy City as Daughter," in *Directions in Biblical Hebrew Poetry* (ed. E. R. Follis; JSOTSup 40; Sheffield: Sheffield Academic Press, 1987) 173-84; D. N. Freedman, "Acrostics and Metrics in Hebrew Poetry," *HTR* 65 (1972) 367-92; H. Gottlieb, *A Study on the Text of Lamentations* (Åarhus: Åarhus University Press, 1978); N. K. Gottwald, *Studies in the Book of Lamentations* (2nd ed.; SBT 1/14; London: SCM, 1962); idem, "Lamentations," in

*Harper's Bible Commentary* (ed. J. L. Mays; San Francisco: Harper & Row, 1988) 646-51; I. G. P. Gous, *Die herkoms van klaagliederen* [The Origin of Lamentations] (diss., University of South Africa, Pretoria, 1988); M. W. Green, "The Eridu Lament," *JCS* 30 (1978) 127-67; idem, "The Uruk Lament," *JAOS* 104 (1984) 253-79; H. Gross, *Klagelieder* (Neue Echter Bibel 14; Würzburg: Echter, 1986); W. C. Gwaltney, "The Biblical Book of Lamentations in the Context of Near Eastern Lament Literature," in *Scripture in Context* II (ed. W. W. Hallo, et al.; Winona Lake, Ind.: Eisenbrauns, 1983) 191-211; M. Haller, *Die Klagelieder* (Handbuch zum Alten Testament I/18; Tübingen: Mohr, 1940) 91-113; C. Hardmeier, *Texttheorie und biblische Exegese* (Munich: Chr. Kaiser, 1978); M. Häusl, "Die Klagelieder," in *Kompendium feministische Bibelauslegung* (ed. L. Schottroff, et al.; 2nd ed.; Gütersloh: Chr. Kaiser, 1998) 270-77; H. Heikens. "The Alphabet in Lamentations," in *Give Ear to My Words* (ed. J. Dyk; Amsterdam: Juda Palacha Institut, 1996) 189-96; J. L. Helberg, "Land in the Book of Lamentations," *ZAW* 102 (1990) 372-85; R. A. Henshaw, *Female and Male: The Cultic Personnel: The Bible and the Rest of the Ancient Near East* (Allison Park, Pa.: Pickwick, 1994); D. R. Hillers, *Lamentations* (AB 7a; Garden City, N.Y.: Doubleday, 1973; 2nd ed. 1992); idem, "History and Poetry in Lamentations," *Currents in Theology and Missions* 10 (1982) 155-61; M. P. Horgan, "A Lament over Jerusalem (4Q179)," *JSS* 18 (1973) 222-34; J. Hunter, *Faces of a Lamenting City* (Beiträge zur Erforschung des Alten Testaments 39; Frankfurt: P. Lang, 1996); H. Jahnow, *Das hebräische Leichenlied im Rahmen der Völkerdichtung* (BZAW 36; Giessen: Töpelmann, 1923); E. Janssen, *Juda in der Exilszeit* (Göttingen: Vandenhoeck & Ruprecht, 1956); W. Janzen, *Mourning Cry and Woe Oracle* (BZAW 125; Berlin: de Gruyter, 1972); B. Johnson, "Form and Message in Lamentations," *ZAW* 97 (1985) 58-73; O. Kaiser, *Klagelieder* (4th ed.; ATD 16/2; Göttingen: Vandenhoeck & Ruprecht, 1992) 91-198; S. N. Kramer, *Lamentation over the Destruction of Ur* (Chicago: University of Chicago Press, 1940); idem, "Lamentation over the Destruction of Ur," in *ANET*, 455-63; idem, "Lamentation over the Destruction of Sumer and Ur," in *ANET*, 611-19; idem, "Lamentation over the Destruction of Nippur," *Acta Sumerologica* 13 (1991) 1-26; H.-J. Kraus, *Klagelieder, 'Threni'* (BKAT XX; Neukirchen: Neukirchener Verlag, 1956); E. Kutsch, "'Trauerbräuche' und 'Selbstminderungsriten' im Alten Testament," in K. Lüthi, E. Kutsch, and W. Dantine, *Drei Wiener Antrittsreden* (ThSt[B] 78; Zurich: EVZ, 1965) 25-42; W. G. Lambert, *Babylonian Wisdom Literature* (Oxford: Oxford University Press, 1960); W. F. Lanahan, "The Speaking Voice in the Book of Lamentations," *JBL* 93 (1974) 41-49; N. C. Lee, *The Singers of Lamentations* (diss., Union Theological Seminary, Richmond, Va.: 2000); T. Linafelt, "Surviving Lamentations," in *A Feminist Companion to Reading the Bible* (ed. A. Brenner, et al.; Sheffield: Sheffield Academic Press, 1997) 344-57; B. O. Long, "The Divine Funeral Lament," *JBL* 75 (1966) 85-86; D. Marcus, "Non-Recurring Doublets in the Book of Lamentations," *HAR* 10 (1986) 177-95; S. M. Maul, *'Herzberuhigungsklagen'* (Wiesbaden: Harrassowitz, 1988); J. A. Mayoral Lopez, *Sufrimiento y esperanza en Lamentationes* (diss., Pontificia Universidade Gregoriana, Rome, 1992); T. F. McDaniel, "The Alleged Sumerian Influence upon Lamentations," *VT* 18 (1968) 198-209; P. Michalowski, *The Lamentation over the Destruction of Sumer and Ur* (Winona Lake, Ind.: Eisenbrauns, 1989); A. Mintz, "The Rhetoric of Lamentations and the Representation of Catastrophe," *Prooftexts* 11 (1982) 1-17; M. S. Moore, "Human Suffering in Lamentations," *RB* 90 (1983) 534-55; H.-P. Müller, "Gilgameschs Trauergesang um Enkidu und die Gattung

der Totenklage," *Zeitschrift für Assyriologie* 68 (1978) 233-50; M. Neary, "The Importance of Lament in the God-Man Relationship in Ancient Israel," *Irish Theological
Quarterly* 52 (1986) 180-92; M. Noth, "Die Katastrophe von Jerusalem im Jahre 587
v.Chr. und ihre Bedeutung für Israel" (1953), repr. in idem, *Gesammelte Studien zum
Alten Testament* (3rd ed.; Munich: Kaiser, 1966) 346-71; X. H. T. Pham, *Mourning in
the Ancient Near East and the Hebrew Bible* (JSOTSup 302; Sheffield: Sheffield Academic Press, 2000); O. Plöger, *Klagelieder* (2nd ed.; Handbuch zum Alten Testament I/
18; Tübingen: Mohr, 1969); I. W. Provan, *Lamentations* (New Century Bible Commentary; Grand Rapids: Eerdmans, 1991); S. P. Reèmi, *God's People in Crisis* (International
Theological Commentary; Grand Rapids: Eerdmans; Edinburgh: Handsel, 1984);
J. Renkema, *The Literary Structure of Lamentations* (JSOTSup 74; Sheffield: Sheffield
Academic Press, 1988) 294-396; idem, "The Meaning of Parallel Acrostics in Lamentations," *VT* 45 (1995) 379-83; T. H. Robinson, "Anacrusis in Hebrew Poetry," in *Werden
und Wesen des Alten Testaments* (BZAW 66; ed. P. Volz, et al.; Berlin: Töpelmann,
1936) 37-40; W. Rudolph, *Die Klagelieder* (Kommentar zum Alten Testament XVII/1-
3; Gütersloh: Gerd Mohn, 1962); W. H. Shea, "The Qinah-Structure of the Book of
Lamentations," *Bib* 60 (1979) 103-7; W. M. Soll, "Babylonian and Biblical Acrostics,"
*Bib* 69 (1988) 305-23; A. Strobel, *Trauer um Jerusalem* (Stuttgart: Katholisches Bibelwerk, 1973); K. Volk, *Die Balag-Komposition Uru Am-ma-ir-ra-bi* (Freiburger
altorientalistische Studien 18; Stuttgart: F. Steiner, 1989); C. Westermann, *Die Klagelieder* (Neukirchen-Vluyn: Neukirchener Verlag, 1990); A. Wünsche, *Der Midrasch
Echa Rabbati* (1881; repr. Hildesheim: Olms, 1967).

## *1. The History of the Booklet*

The medieval Jewish canon (since the fifth century C.E.) places "Lamentations"
— customarily under the heading of the opening word *'êkāh*, "alas," "woe," or
under the rubric of *qînôt*, "laments" — as one of the five writings assembled in
*Megilloth*, "Scrolls" (cf. H. E. Clem, *ABD* IV, 680), in the third part of the
Scriptures, right after Psalms and Proverbs. Five more books follow the
*Megilloth:* the apocalypse of Daniel, the historical accounts of Ezra and
Nehemiah, and two volumes of Chronicles. This third part of the Hebrew Bible,
in effect, brings together loosely arranged but important materials for Jewish
worship and religious instruction; while the first part, Torah, is the fundamental
witness to Yahweh's covenant with Israel; and the second part, the Prophets, offers selections of the troublesome history of this covenant relation. Hebrew
MSS antedating the sixth century C.E. sometimes attribute Lamentations to the
prophet Jeremiah and attach it to that prophetic book (cf. Babylonian Talmud,
*Baba Batra* 14b-15a). But not even the earliest Hebrew MSS really unite Lamentations with the book of Jeremiah; they make it only an attachment, in spite
of thematic correspondences. The library of Qumran has yielded several fragments of the booklet, found in caves 3, 4, and 5 (cf. E. Tov, *Der Text der
hebräischen Bibel* [Stuttgart: Kohlhammer, 1997] 87; García Martínez, *Dead
Sea Scrolls,* 472, 481, 514; see Additional Bibliography, section B), which do
not testify, however, as to its place in the canon. In general, it may be said that
these ancient witnesses together with LXX testimony, for linguistic and theo-

logical reasons, point to a time of origin for Lamentations as a distinct book only in the third or second century B.C.E. Perhaps based on or in the tradition of 2 Chr 35:25, followed, as it were, by the Latin version (the Vulgate), the Greek tradition goes farthest in aligning the booklet with the prophet Jeremiah, without ever merging it into the prophetic book. This is the reason why in Christian Bible editions Lamentations comes right after Jeremiah.

The five booklets united in the *Megilloth,* "(festive) scrolls," are quite distinct in form, contents, and utilization. The collection of five little books used in liturgical contexts was put together only in the medieval Masoretic tradition (Kaiser, 98). Different Hebrew MSS, moreover, maintain varying orders of the writings. Codex Leningradensis begins with Ruth, Song of Songs (Song of Solomon), and Ecclesiastes. The fourth in line is Lamentations (*'êkāh;* in the Greek/Latin tradition *Threnoi,* "tears," going back to *qînôt,* "laments"). In the last place we find Esther. This may respresent a supposed chronological order of origin (Hillers, *Lamentations,* XVIII). The seasonal succession of festivals may be the paradigm for the differing chain of Song of Songs, Ruth, Lamentations, Ecclesiastes, and Esther, extant in other MSS. Still other sequences have been adopted in tradition; that means that we do not have a fixed order in the collection of the "five little scrolls" (cf. the Pentateuch as the "big five"). Why is that so? Negatively, because there has not been a common use of the booklets; they belong to separate genres and different occasions of religious practice; they were never read or used in conjunction with each other. Furthermore, the *Megilloth* being a quite late collection, Lamentations probably originated in specific observances of mourning in the exilic and postexilic periods of Judean or Babylonian communities. Commemorations of the Babylonian sacking of Jerusalem, merging with the memories of the final destruction of the Jerusalem temple in 70 C.E., are still held today in Jewish congregations on the ninth day of the month Ab (approximately July/August). The booklet serves as a Scripture lesson for this day. Biblical references to the ancient customs of mourning the fall of Jerusalem include Zech 7:3-5; 8:18; 2 Chr 35:25.

Jewish Greek and Christian traditions, as mentioned before, mostly do not adopt the *Megilloth* collection into their respective canons of Scripture. They maintain, by and large, the Jeremiah tradition. The prophet, who apparently did a great deal of complaining and lamenting (cf. Jer 4:19-31; 7:16; 9:1-2, 9; 10:19-25; 12:1-4; 14:7-14; 15:10-18; etc.; for the distinction between "complaint" and "lament" see "Introduction to Cultic Poetry," sections 4A and B) is also credited with the five songs of the book of Lamentations. For linguistic, historical, generic, and thematic reasons, modern scholarship cannot accept the authorship of the prophet Jeremiah. But the book of Lamentations is certainly part of a wider, even transcultural ancient Near Eastern tradition of dirges and lamentations, in particular over defeated and destroyed cities (cf. Dobbs-Allsopp, M. E. Cohen, Ferris, et al.). This stream of city laments, and general complaining over against the Deity, also has affected some of the Jeremianic (cf., e.g., Jer 4:19-31; 14:2-9; 31:15-20) or Isaianic (cf. Isaiah 24–27) materials.

Ancient Near Eastern ties and affinities have been debated for a long time, ever since Sumerian-Akkadian laments over destroyed cities and related genres of complaints were discovered and published (cf., e.g., Dobbs-Allsopp,

2-10). S. N. Kramer was one of the initiators of comparative investigations (see his *Lamentation over the Destruction of Ur* [Chicago: University of Chicago Press, 1940]). During the past decades, however, the material basis for these studies has been considerably widened (cf., e.g., M. E. Cohen, 13-15, who gives 39 *balag* texts in transliteration and English translation: they are part of a canonical Sumerian collection of laments, to be used by the *gala* priest at funerals, incantations, razing of temples before reconstruction, and public calamities. In addition, different types of laments, called in Sumerian *eršemmu* and *eršahunga*, have been found). In consequence of the scrutinies, direct dependence of OT lamenting and complaining on Near Eastern forerunners has to be fairly much ruled out; at least it has become less important (Westermann, *Klagelieder*, 29: "Literary dependence . . . can hardly be proven"). The suggestions seems reasonable "that the Babylonian exile provided the opportunity for the Jewish clergy to encounter the [Mesopotamian] laments" (Gwaltney, 210), and, as we have to realize, Israel had been living in a common Near Eastern cultural sphere for centuries before the exile. Therefore generic affinity of lamenting songs and customs is to be expected and beyond question. Similar life situations in related cultures and societies lead to comparable ceremonies, rituals, agendas, and their relevant texts. In this fashion form-critical research like that performed by H. Jahnow, W. C. Gwaltney, D. Hillers, C. Westermann, F. W. Dobbs-Allsopp, et al., emphasizing generic and ritual parallelism of dirges, city laments, collective complaints, etc., in Israel and the ancient Near East (cf. "Introduction to Cultic Poetry," section 4A) has to be recognized as fully justified, elucidating the biblical customs and concepts of mourning. Thus we may accept basic patterns and notions in ancient Near Eastern mourning practices, without ignoring regional and ethnic dissimilarities on account of specific regional developments.

## 2. Meter and Literary Forms

Some formal features of the five texts united in Lamentations may be discussed in advance, the most obvious being their attachment to the order of the alphabet. Playing with letters and syllables in poetic composition is a well-known device throughout the ancient Near East, whether merely the number of lines corresponds to the complete array of the alphabet, one or more lines of the poem actually begin with subsequent letters or syllables, or some name or message is hidden in the incipits read in a vertical line (cf. S. M. Paul, *IDBSup* 600-601; W. Soll, *ABD* I, 58-60; Freedman, "Acrostics"). We find several of these techniques in Lamentations, provoking most of all the question: To what ends have they been adopted? Scholarly opinion today is divided on the issue. Certainly, original poets may have left their marks on the texts to impress potential users, just as painters customarily sign their works. But this idea seems to be a rather modern one, building on extreme individualistic attitudes. We would have to consider modifications according to ancient mentalities. Pride in a well-balanced poetic work coming out of a scribal school could have been a motivation for this kind of artistry (however, the name of the writer shows up in the

469

Akkadian Jobian composition called "The Babylonian Theodicy"; see Lambert, *Wisdom Literature,* 63-91; listing at "Introduction to Cultic Poetry." The first cuneiform sign of 27 stanzas, each comprising 11 lines with identical first syllables, yields this sentence: "I, Saggil-kinam-ubbib, the incantation priest, am adorant of the God and the king," Lambert, 63. Astonishingly, the tight formal structure does not hamper the dialogue between the just sufferer and his friends at all; cf. also Soll). Thinking about this explanation, we easily proceed to the conclusion that it was not so much individualistic yearning for attention that produced an alphabetical order, but the desire to create a perfectly rounded piece of text to the greater glory of God (cf. Watson, *Poetry,* 190-95; listing at "Introduction to Cultic Poetry"; in general terms R. Alter, *The Art of Biblical Poetry* [New York: Basic Books, 1985] 111-36; et al.). Something of this sort must have motivated ancient scribes and transmitters of alphabetical poems. Other possible reasons for composing such texts were magical conceptions of the world and the divine (to exert influence by a fixed order of words) and educational purposes (to facilitate memorizing).

If the religious intention has been correctly recognized, questions as to the nature and purpose of such artistic works may be resolved, too. It is unlikely, we should think, that biblical poets wrote their texts solely to please private readers. We may assume, instead, a collective destination also for alphabetical poetry. The general use of so-called wisdom texts in worship has been under scrutiny and debate for a long time (cf. Mowinckel, *W* II, ch. 16; Perdue, *Wisdom;* listing at "Introduction to Cultic Poetry"; et al.). There have been defenders of a completely acultic scribal tradition (cf. G. von Rad, *Weisheit in Israel* [Neukirchen: Neukirchener Verlag, 1971]; A. Lemaire, *Les écoles et la formation de la Bible dans l'ancien Israël* [OBO 39; Fribourg: Universitäts-verlag, 1981]; Stolz; listing at "Introduction to Psalms"). Presuppositions include the separation of temple and "school," narrow definition of "cult" as "sacrificial ritual," highly developed individualistic piety and reading habits, nonadmission of new, exilic-postexilic structures of community and worship in Judah and the diaspora. All these axioms are implausible; therefore we opt for a liturgical use even of alphabetical compositions in the OT (cf. Perdue; listing at "Introduction to Cultic Poetry"; Hillers, *Lamentations,* XL-XLI; Ferris. Opposed, e.g., Kaiser, 102-3: Lamentations "has to be considered from the beginning a literary work, primarily oriented toward readers," but, interestingly "intentionally, recitation to listeners was not excluded"). Specimens of acrostic psalms (cf. Psalms 9/10; 25; 34; 37; 111; 112; 119; 145; also Nah 1:2-8; Prov 31:10-31; Sir 51:13-30) occur principally in the Psalter, and within that prayer book and songbook they were used in worship.

The problems of poetic meter are — this is valid for all relevant texts in the Hebrew Bible — clouded by basic uncertainties. Has an alternating or an accentuating system of measured language been used? The idea that regular alternation of stressed and unstressed syllables was the fundamental linguistic pattern for biblical poets has few adherents (e.g., G. Hölscher; S. Mowinckel; S. Segert; cf. Hillers, *Lamentations,* XXXI; Watson, *Poetry,* 103; listing at "Introduction to Cultic Poetry"). Most exegetes believe in an accentuating system, as proposed in three publications by E. Sievers (1901-7), taking the natural articulations of words as a basic design, which implies the possibility of one or more unstressed syllables between accents. For other theories like syllable- and letter-counting cf. Watson, *Poetry,* 103-6. D. N. Freedman, in his studies on Hebrew poetry (see, e.g., "Acrostics"), is a defender of syllable counting, disregarding accentuation altogether.

It was K. Budde who as early as 1882 discovered a specific uneven meter characteristic for dirges and laments over destroyed cities. Each line, he maintained, normally has five accents, the first colon featuring three, the second two stresses, thus creating a curtailed, limping, exasperated impression. H. Jahnow (pp. 91-92) comments that the cadence of three and two emphases "sounds as if the wailing woman was unable to complete regularly the second part of the line because of her emotional involvement." Budde's scheme in the meantime has been questioned profoundly, but we may still count on a certain preference for the 3 + 2 rhythm in dirges and laments (called by Budde "*qînāh* meter"). This fact, however, does not preclude the use of this poetic configuration for other types of poetry at all. Nor does it prevent other arrangements, e.g., evenly balanced lines of 3 + 3 or 2 + 2 stresses, to be employed in the book of Lamentations. Hillers points out an additional difficulty: quite a few lines in Lamentations do not feature that famous *parallelismus membrorum,* i.e., the sentence and thought parallelism of the two cola of each line. Instead, they show one single phrase occupying either both cola or the full line, making it quite hazardous to determine the caesura between the two cola (*Lamentations,* XXXV). How can we speak of a balanced or unbalanced verse, if we do not know its turning point?

Other stylistic and structural peculiarities of our booklet are of lesser significance for form-critical analysis or will be treated in the individual units. As will be seen in the analyses of individual units, the authors of Lamentations made use of a great variety of literary forms and genres.

## 3. Contents and Purposes

The booklet for the most part laments the capture and destruction of the capital city. Only ch. 3 deals with personal concerns of a suppliant, in the manner of individual complaints (see "Introduction to Cultic Poetry," section 4B) or Jobian and Jeremianic protestations against God. That a complaint of the individual takes center stage in this collection of Zion-centered laments may be significant. The redactors of Lamentations may have consciously placed it there, in order to demonstrate the sufferings of each member of the community under the onslaught of common defeat and destruction. Thus collective grief is absolutely predominant in the booklet. The poems unfold a wide spectrum of complaints about the downfall of the city, without identifying, however, the victorious enemies or the historical circumstances. (Naming the Edomites as looters of defeated Jerusalem [Lam 4:21-22] is a special case and needs to be discussed separately.) The authors and transmitters are able to do so by using very traditional, i.e., liturgical, language and imagery. Comparable to descriptions in individual and communal complaints of the Psalter this language generalizes and accumulates experiences of sufferings, avoiding allusions to the adversaries. On the whole, the only concrete names extant in the texts are those of the authors' own group: Judah, Jerusalem, Zion. That means that the continuum of life and lament is that of their own social and religious organization. Outward enemies may change; the misery of defeats and the brutalities of the victors stay just the same. We may add: they are terribly uniform through the ages. Atrocities like those mentioned in Lamentations in connection with the conquest, sacking, and burning of Jerusalem are committed in all wars to this very day. Small wonder that liturgical texts, which are to be used by generations of victims, condense such perennial traumas of warfare into stereotyped patterns.

Another phenomenon in Lamentations, except for ch. 3, is the focus on Jerusalem and Zion, with frequent female personifications of the city, so that her lamenting and pleading voice is quoted directly. The ancients quite easily gave voice and character to various entities. For them, rivers and mountains, winds and trees could behave like humans. Cities also were incorporated symbols of the people living within the walls. In the ancient Near East they were governed and represented by the main deity of the settlement, often a goddess, like Inanna of Ur, or Ishtar of Isin. Some scholars suppose that personification of Jerusalem also has to do with divine representation. A few Akkadian laments are put into the mouth of the city-goddess, who has to flee and see her temple in shambles. In a similar way Jerusalem mourns the death and suffering of her inhabitants and the destruction of her edifices.

Tying together the above observations, we have to ask: What is the book of Lamentations about? For what purpose was it composed? How do we evaluate its final form, structure, and setting? The book itself — notwithstanding varying origins and prehistories of its components — is a highly organized collection of five texts revolving around the sufferings of Yahweh's city and her inhabitants. Both concepts, of city and citizens, do not necessarily refer to the local Jerusalem congregation, but may stand for any group loyal to Israel's God, be it at home or abroad. As indicated, the central text (Lamentations 3) poses the theological problems arising from defeat and misery in relation to the typical individual believer. Has Yahweh forsaken his faithful? In the last resort, no one else but God is responsible for the precarious state of affairs. "You have seen the wrong done to me, O Yahweh; judge my cause" (3:59). "Pay them back for their deeds, O Yahweh!" (3:64). The speaker and his congregation are torn between frustration about Yahweh's sanctions ("He led me off my way and tore me to pieces, he has made me desolate," 3:11) and hope for his help ("You came near when I called on you; you said: 'Do not fear!'" 3:57). Like Psalms 44 and 89 or passages from Job and Jeremiah (cf. his "confessions"), this centerpiece of the booklet is a painful, heated challenge of Yahweh. One might imagine a dramatized performance of this part, either in an academic or a worship context. Normally, we call the theological argumentation visible here a "theodicy" dispute, the quest for God's "righteousness." But the book as a whole, by way of drastic descriptions of atrocities and sufferings, does not aim at abstract theological clarifications. It wants to alleviate acute consequences of war, terror, and oppression. Therefore the main concern also of Lamentations 3 is how to gain help from God against the enemies (3:64-66). In the fashion of exilic-postexilic times it employs language and arguments of theodicy discourse or sapiential dispute. Yet the goal is plainly to argue with and pray to Yahweh for his decisive intervention in favor of his community. The surrounding chapters underline this drive for Yahweh's favor and help. They envelop the central part, which is pointedly wrestling with God, and they — most of all — try to paint the most dire picture of what Jerusalem and Yahweh's community there have been going through. The formal elements used in these four corollary texts are acquainted more with dirge and communal complaint than with wisdom literature. We may assume, therefore, that the means of public presentation would correspond to these formal characteristics. Speakers, congregational groups, and choirs may have enacted or recited the passages telling about catastrophes that have befallen the Zion community. All in all, the five chapters of Lamentations seem to fit into one liturgical sequence, with strong emphases on descriptions of sufferings (in complaint psalms this part is contained in the complaint element proper), argumentation for God's intervention, and some final pleas (cf. 5:1, 21-22). It is logical that Lamentations could serve as a liturgy in mourning festivals probably commemorating the fall of Jerusalem in 587 B.C.E. (cf. Zech 7:3-5; 8:18; Kraus, et al.). Later on, the book came to be read in yearly commemorations of the destruction of the temple unter Titus in the year 70 C.E.

## 4. Historical Situations and Social Roots

Modern scholarship has paid much, probably too much, attention to the possible historical setting(s) of the book of Lamentations. Four of the five chapters talk about the capture and destruction of Jerusalem, but without giving clear indications of a particular historical event. There have been many sieges and sackings of the Holy City in the course of Israelite history. From a form-critical point of view the facts are obvious: Lamentations has been cast into the liturgical shape of ceremonial mourning, not into any kind of historical report. Psalms 44; 74; 79; 89 — all dealing with defeat and destruction suffered from the hand of (unnamed) enemies — also stick to ceremonial lament patterns (a possible exception is Psalm 137, explicitly naming the Babylonian context of the deportees). Occasionally, they seem to offer a little bit more concrete, narrative details of how the catastrophe happened, e.g.: "Your foes have roared within your holy place. . . . At the upper entrance they hacked the wooden trellis with axes" (Ps 74:4, 5). Still, these historical allusions, if they are at all to be classified as such, are not sufficient to pinpoint the time and place of the poem's origin. And, to repeat what was said before, the nature and use of our texts are ceremonial, not at all historiographic. We simply should not expect too much information about historical events in liturgies. There is an inherent incompatibility of the two genres involved. While history writing must dedicate itself to unique details, liturgies have to serve the cultic continuum and the needs for group identification over longer periods of time. Therefore historical events cannot serve ceremonial needs and obligations.

There is, however, a seeming exception to that rule in Lam 4:21-22:

Rejoice and be glad, O daughter Edom,
you that live in the land of Uz;
but to you also the cup shall pass;
you shall become drunk and strip yourself bare.
The punishment for your iniquity, O daughter Zion, is over,
he will keep you in exile no longer;
but your iniquity, O daughter Edom, he will punish,
he will uncover your sins.

Reference to Edom, a minor neighbor of Israel, but of "brotherly" descent (Gen 25:21-34; 36:10-14, 20-28), coming to power only since the eighth century B.C.E., curiously enough occurs also in → Psalm 137 ("Remember, O Yahweh, against the Edomites the day of Jerusalem's fall, how they said, 'Tear down! Tear down! Down to its foundations!'" v. 7). Speculations are, since the Babylonians are mentioned in the next verses (137:8-9), that the Edomites took advantage of the Babylonian conquest of Judah and Jerusalem in 587 B.C.E., acting as looters in the defenseless territory (cf. Kellermann; listing at Psalm 137; J. R. Bartlett, *ABD* II, 287-95; E. A. Knauf, *NBL* I, 467-71). Ethnic hatred between Edom and Israel seems to have deeply marked the relationship of the "brother" people for centuries. Therefore it is plausible that traces of this long-standing antagonistic relationship, perhaps beginning in 587 B.C.E., may have entered even liturgical texts. This does not mean, however, that the ceremonial use of such laments and threats was restricted to the aftermath of only one particular historical incident. As the history of the book of Lamentations proves clearly, the texts (including threats of punishment to Edom) were recited still in commemoration of Titus's destruction of the temple in 70 C.E. Edom, then, has been targeted as an archenemy over a longer period of time, entering even liturgical contexts, → Psalm 137; cf. also Obad 11-14; Ezek 25:12-13; 35:1-15; Joel 4:19 [RSV 3:19]; Isa 21:11-15; Jer 49:9, 22; Knauf, *NBL,* I, 467-71). No doubt, therefore, both Psalm 137 and Lamentations 4 contain accumulated experiences with this hostile enemy-neighbor.

Equally important or more so would be the question of the social-ecclesiastical background and context for Lamentations. Refined language, artistic composition, and overarching theological interests would indicate a social group of rather educated people. Since the period of its origin may be identified as exilic-postexilic, we would like to know whether the Judean or diaspora groups were responsible for creating the booklet. A definite answer is hard to find. The texts reveal a society of citizens, with their attachment to the Holy City, with their education and social rankings, and scarce professional profiles. But city life and customs may have been exercised in foreign lands as well as at home. Longing for Jerusalem's rehabilitation would have been a desire among those who still lived in the province of Judah as well as among the exiles. In fact, as the records of Ezra and Nehemiah have it, the concern for Jerusalem, i.e., the urge to go home and rebuild the city, was sometimes much stronger among the exiled Jews. By the same token, (yearly) laments over the fallen capital were apparently also held among the exiles (cf. Psalm 137; Zech 7:3-4). It is important to observe, all in all, that the community which brought forth and used Lamentations was a religiously defined Yahweh congregation. The booklet by itself does not indicate in the least an individual author of the texts. Its detached, autonomous existence within the canon precludes any assignment to known writers. Therefore we have to consider the individual laments and the collection as a whole as the product of communal worship rather than individual craft, notwithstanding that acrostic and other literary artistry was provided by skilled individuals. The spirit of the texts is communal and liturgical in the same sense as the architecture of medieval cathedrals incorporates the talents of great masters into a totally communal enterprise.

## 5. Theology and Ethics

Only briefly may we touch on the fundamental issues of the theological and ethical concepts visible in Lamentations, always bearing in mind the special genre and use of these collected texts. God, the receiver of laments and complaints, is portrayed as a scornful deity, who has either permitted the catastrophe to overcome his people or even actively given his mandate to the enemies castigating his own faithful, destroying his own city and abode. This pattern of thought is common in ancient Near Eastern spiritual and ceremonial history. It pervades all complaint and lament literature. Admittance of one's own guilt enters in varying measure. To take Lamentations as an example: confessions of guilt are present but do not dominate the texts, as they do, e.g., in Psalms 51; 106; Ezra 9; Nehemiah 9; Daniel 9. This fact in itself is remarkable. On the other hand, protestations of innocence, quite common in the long history of the complaining and lamenting genres (cf. Psalms 7; 17; 26; 44), are not at all extant in Lamentations. What, then, is Lamentations' stand on guilt and punishment, suffering and redemption?

Granted that traditions vary on this issue and that we cannot generalize theological affirmations of our texts, because each of them is determined contextually, we have to conclude that the mourning services witnessed to by the booklet followed an intermediate line of argumentation. The people of Yahweh did have to confess their sins ("My transgressions were bound into a yoke," 1:14), but the much more intense descriptions of disproportional sufferings bear the main emphasis. That means that Yahweh is expected to reverse the indictment, restore the fortunes of the congregation, become gracious again, and destroy the enemies. All these expectations are more subdued than overt in the texts, but they apparently direct the liturgical efforts of the lamenting community.

The lamenting process in a worship setting is on the surface the only one that according to Lamentations gives opportunities for communal action. Other fields of activity, like mutual solidarity, active resistance, and innovative reconstruction are not mentioned in the texts. This is appropriate, because Lamentations is a collection of specific articulations in a determined ceremonial situation. We would have to turn to other types of exilic-postexilic literature to learn how in reality and day-to-day decisions the congregation would take up its destiny, in work and leisure, bargaining and feasting. Narrative, prophetic, and wisdom texts dating from this period might give us an idea of the difficulties and the chances of survival (e.g., Nehemiah 5; Ruth; Isaiah 40; 49; 54–55; 58–59; Proverbs 1–9). Taking into account the broader perspectives of life under foreign rule, we certainly cannot accuse the Yahweh congregation of lethargy, inactivity, fatalism, or like attitudes. On the contrary, the remnants of the populace of Judah, defeated by the Babylonians, dispersed and decapitated in terms of national independence, struggled to find a new identity within the debris of traditional values. The people had lost "every sign that had once provided assurance and confidence in God" (Hillers, *Lamentations,* XV). They had experienced a series of "shaking of the foundations" (Ps 11:3), but they proved to be surprisingly creative under extreme pressures in building up new concepts and structures for their lives as Yahweh followers. To celebrate observances of lamenting is one decisive action in the effort to consolidate the community and win back another identity in lieu of the lost one. Therefore articulations of pain and despair have been central in ancient religious history, particularly in ancient Israelite spiritual life. But textual evidence, especially in the book of Psalms, tells us that even in darkest times of loss, defeat, and death there have been nurtured also songs of praise, to counterbalance destruction and depression (cf. Brueggemann, *Theology,* Part II; Additional Bibliography, section C). And ongoing life, even under very difficult circumstances, was proof enough for the exilic-postexilic congregations to believe in Yahweh, the savior, and nourish strong hopes for redemption, restitution, and reconstruction.

One more word in regard to the female figure of Jerusalem so prominent in Lamentations as a metaphor for the Yahweh community. Very likely, this figure — naturally given not only by the female gender of the word "city," but also by a long tradition in the ancient Near East of female deities heading a city pantheon — has to be connected with prophetic concepts of Israel being the bride and wife of Yahweh (cf. Hosea 2; Jer 2:2; Isa 49:14; 62:5; Ezekiel 16; 23; etc.). Although the image of a wife subject to her husband and punishable by him for alleged misbehavior is offensive in our eyes, legitimately so under the present conditions of life and equality of sexes (cf. Gerstenberger, *Yahweh;* see Additional Bibliography, section B), in the context of ancient Israel and its patriarchal society it was supposedly able to communicate a strong sense of allegiance between Yahweh and his people. In fact, the metaphor of God being tied to his followers by some sort of matrimonial obligations seems to modify and intensify the covenant relationship basic for the D layers of Hebrew Scripture. Matrimony is more than a treaty; it implies dimensions of personal reliance unattainable by covenant partners.

CHAPTER 8

# THE INDIVIDUAL UNITS OF
# THE BOOK OF LAMENTATIONS

### Lamentations 1:
### Communal Mourning Agenda

*Text*

Each of the 22 verses (= number of letters in the Hebrew alphabet) has three poetic lines, often in the *qînāh* ("mourning") meter, which was first described by
Karl Budde (listing at "Introduction to the Book of Lamentations"). The only
exception is v. 7 with four lines. The two cola of v. 7cd are possibly a later
gloss, because they interrupt the cumbersome retrospect of lines ab and e-h.
The two cola of every line ideally (according to some modern metrical theory;
cf. Kraus, *Threni*, 7-8; Hillers, *Lamentations*, XXX-XXXVII; Freedman; Shea;
etc.) carry three and two accents, respectively. The shortened second colon apparently heightens the sense of an abrupt end, breach of harmony, and catastrophic impact. Lamentations 1 is an acrostic poem, to be sure, but rather un-
obtrusively so. In general, only the first word of the first line of each verse
carries the letter relevant to the alphabetical sequence. Lamentations 2 has the
very same structure, while Lamentations 3, also with three-line verses, makes
every line begin with the correct letter corresponding to the alphabetical order.
Lamentations 4 has two-line verses, with the first line establishing the alphabetical order, as in Lamentations 1 and 2. The last chapter, Lamentations 5, contains one-line subunits without acrostic ambitions, but exactly fitting the number 22 in its verse count.

The acrostic effect on the formal and generic molding of the texts should
not be overrated. With only one letter necessary every two or three lines to pinpoint the alphabetic sequence, the authors had a number of choices fitting their
intentions. Lamentations 3, of course, is a little more determined by acrostic
considerations. The initial *'êkāh* in the Leningrad Codex has a special position
preceding the regular poem (cf. Lam 2:1; 4:1; no other occurrence in Lamenta-

tions). Robinson stresses the autonomy of this wailing expression ("anacrusis" = unstressed syllable in front of the text; cf. *BHK*).

## Structure

|  | MT | NRSV |
|---|---|---|
| I. Opening cry (how) | *1 (*'êkāh*) | *1 |
| II. Description of misery | 1-10 | |
|   A. Jerusalem's fate | 1-6 | |
|   B. Jerusalem's guilt | 7-10a-d | |
|   C. Direct address of Yahweh | 10ef | |
| III. Personal lament | 11-22 | |
|   A. Introduction (Narration) | 11a-d | |
|   B. Initial plea | 11ef | |
|   C. Complaint | 12-15 | |
|   D. Description of mourning | 16 | |
|   (E. Narration | 17) | |
|   F. Plea for sympathy | 18-19 | |
|   G. Prayer for help | 20-22 | |

Structuring an acrostic poem may seem a haphazard task (cf. Psalms 25; 34; 119 etc; see "Introduction to Cultic Poetry," 4F), but all texts investigated in the Psalter prove a certain affinity to cultic or liturgical procedures with some ceremonial structure. They were apparently used in community worship, and they consequently exhibit modalities of liturgical movement. First of all, the isolated shout *'êkāh*, also *'êk*, "alas," "how [terrible]," well known from lament and dirge contexts (cf. 2 Sam 1:19, 25, 27; Isa 1:21; 14:12; Jer 9:19 [RSV 18]; 48:17; Ezek 26:17; Zeph 2:15), stands out in most Hebrew MSS. While the cited passages show our interjection in tight connection with the following phrase (e.g., "How the mighty have fallen!" 2 Sam 1:19, 25, 27 — "how" serving as an interrogative particle), in Lamentations the word has taken on a more technical meaning, introducing a real dirge or lamentation. Because of its special position ahead of the poems, the editors of the Hebrew text call it an "anacrusis" = unstressed, preposited syllable in Lam 1:1 and 4:1 (T. H. Robinson, in *BHK*, puts a question mark with Lam 2:1, because of metrical considerations). Indeed, the shout heading those three chapters of Lamentations does not seem to be integrated into the sentence structure of the following units either metrically or semantically. Therefore one may consider it a merely literary addendum. In that case, the letter *aleph* would be missing from the original poem — a nearly impossible situation. If the outcry is an authentic part of Lamentations 1, it may have had the liturgical function of opening up a MOURNING AGENDA.

The chapter, taken as a unit, may be divided into two major parts, according to the different voices visible and audible in the text. Vv. 1-10 are descriptive in character. Some speaker or reciter depicts Jerusalem's distress. He or she uses standard vocabulary, metaphors, and phrases to expose despair and desolation of defeated Judah, personalized in the female figure of Jerusalem. Mourning occurs typically, at least during a first phase, in isolation (v. 1ab), without the comforting presence of friends (v. 2) and under the mocking gaze of captors and enemies (vv. 3, 5, 7). Due to the condensation of the people into one mourning figure, the contours of mourning are the personal ones, also used, e.g., in Job 1–2; 2 Sam 12:15-17; etc. There is no trace of community rites as in Psalms 44; 89; Jeremiah 14; Isa 63:7–64:12; and other communal complaints. On the other hand, personification makes identification easy. The assembled community is likely to have felt: "We are Jerusalem!"

From an "objective" description couched in ritual procedure of mourning the text moves on to a more reflective stage of lament (vv. 7-10). Jerusalem now is represented as the active participant in ritual, being called explicitly by name in vv. 7 and 8 (former mentionings include "daughter Zion," v. 6; "the city," v. 1). "Jerusalem remembers . . ." (v. 7a) — this anamnesis encompasses the state of disgrace now at hand and previous happiness, and it focuses in some detail on Jerusalem's guilt (vv. 8-9; cf. the prelude to this subject in v. 5). Looking back at the past is part of funeral songs (cf. 2 Sam 1:22-27; Isa 14:5-15) as well as of communal complaints (cf. Pss 44:2-9 [RSV 1-8]; 80:9-15 [RSV 8-14]; see "Introduction to Cultic Poetry," section 4A). "Remembering" (v. 7a) may well have a liturgical connotation (cf. W. Schottroff, *Gedenken*, 127-32; Additional Bibliography, section B). Reviewing past history emphasizes the catastrophe of Jerusalem, which seems to have occurred some time ago. The words of vv. 7-9cd do not seem to carry the excitement of actual, intense involvement, but rather a spirit of distant reflection. What could be an emotional outburst (v. 9ef: "Look, Yahweh, at my affliction, for the enemy has triumphed!") proves to be a standard plea in distress, here attributed to an agonizing Jerusalem by the narrator. For parallel expressions cf. Pss 9:14 (RSV 13); 25:18, 19; 84:10 (RSV 9); 119:153; Lam 1:11, 20; 2:20. Putting in a direct quotation of what Jerusalem is saying in times of utter despair does not undo the general descriptive style. Narratives as well as liturgical language abound in citations of direct speech. The text's return to plain description of desolation and violence (v. 10a-d) makes our case stronger: in the first part of Lamentations 1 some narrator or liturgist tries to depict — in traditional terms — the sins and sufferings of the city of Jerusalem. Sometimes scriptural references seem to underlie the formulations chosen. Thus the intrusion of enemies into the sanctuary (v. 10cd) is in line with similar statements of Pss 74:3-4; 79:1, and vividness of expression is clearly on the side of the Psalm passages.

The last line of Lam 1:10, however, is most remarkable in form-critical terms. The "narrator" is outing him- or herself, stating, in regard to the wicked intruders of the temple: "those whom you forbade to enter your congregation." Up to that point there had not been the slightest hint of anybody speaking in a cultic setting. Now, all of a sudden we find this line of prayer language, with direct address of God, bringing the first large part of Lamentations 1 to a close. The "narrator" of Jerusalem's dire fate, the theological "thinker" about reasons for her castigation, the "reciter" of ritual steps to be taken is turning toward Yahweh on his own account and for his own purposes, calling attention to the absurdity of defeat and disgrace. Such prayer language is hardly fictitious or merely a literary device, as in Augustine's *Confessions*. At least we do not know of any made-up literary situation using direct-address discourse over against Yahweh. Therefore outright prayer language is a sign of the liturgical rootings of the text.

Looking at the second part of Lamentations 1, slightly larger than the first part, we note a profound switch of positions in the intercommunicative exchange. V. 11 begins, to be true, with a descriptive statement about the inhabitants of the city, suffering from hunger (v. 11 a-d). We take this to be a kind of introduction. The last line of v. 11, however, falls into a first-person plea, akin to the one we read in v. 9ef: "Look, Yahweh, see how abominable I have become" (v. 11ef). In distinction from v. 9 this brief petition for help does not remain an episode within a longer descriptive passage. Vv. 12-22, with the sole exception of v. 17, now do continue the drama of having the city Jerusalem on stage, speaking for herself (cf. Lanahan). As an overall formal and generic designation we may use PERSONAL LAMENT for this passage. The personalized city is pleading with her God, but within the social matrix of bystanders, neighbors, friends, and foes, as customary at the time. Lament in the ancient world would not occur in isolation (restricted to one "man and his God") but inside a network of relationships. This was true for personal and collective ritual procedure. People of the environment have to take part also in ritual mourning and pleading. The lament of vv. 12-15 is to create publicity for the sufferings of "the city," even to put her case before an impartial audience. The passersby (v. 12ab) are to see and evaluate the situation. The plaintive and very subjective statement of castigated Jerusalem (vv. 13-15) is directed toward those observers. It practically accuses Yahweh of being the instigator of sanctions, without even mentioning his motives or justifications. Comparable, at this point, are all the Yahweh-oriented complaints maintaining Yahweh's exclusive responsibility for human suffering: "You have put me in the depths of the Pit" (Ps 88:7 [RSV 6]); "You have rejected us and abased us" (Ps 44:10 [RSV 9]; many more examples of direct address and other-directed speech in the diatribes of Job against his "torturer" — God; cf. Job 9–10; 19). The only difference is that the two Psalm passages quoted address Yahweh directly, while our present text involves a neutral audience. A situation of this kind, with a city defeated and put to shame and outside observers wagging their heads, is presupposed in many biblical and ancient Near Eastern texts. Suffice it to point out some prophetic examples: Jer 19:8; 22:8; 49:17; 50:13; Zeph 2:15; etc. The standard formula seems to be: "to pass by a destroyed city and be horrified." Interestingly enough, and this phenomenon is not limited to our few verses, the acrostic arrangement does not hamper in any way the flow of generically determined lines.

Before going into the questions of real setting we have to complete our structural purview. V. 16 belongs to the well-known form elements of complaints, being a "description of mourning" or "wailing." Tears are, of course, a ritual means of expressing grief, and they have to flow abundantly in any kind of ceremony of this kind (cf. Ps 6:7 [RSV 6]; 2 Sam 1:12, 24; Judg 20:23, 26; Ezra 10:1). According to ritual calculation, such mourning rites will soften up God's wrath, kindle his pity and graciousness, and regain his benevolence. The lacking "comforter," often mentioned in ch. 1 (1:2, 9, 16, 17, 21; cf. 2:13; Ps 69:21 [RSV 20]) would ideally be Yahweh himself.

V. 17 constitutes a crux for our explanation. Why does the text go back to a descriptive style, dealing with Zion and Jerusalem in the third person again? Acrostic demands on the text are not responsible for this shift. The authors could have used a first-person perfect form of the verb *prś* just as easily as the third person (cf. v. 19a: *qārā'tî*, "I called," for the *q* line). The reason for again having neutral statements about Jerusalem, instead of direct discourse of the suppliant, may be precisely a liturgical one. The first round of lamenting apparently finishes with v. 16. The second cycle of mourning, then, is introduced by a "narrator" as in vv. 1-10, with third-person descriptions (v. 11a-d). They open the plaintive prayer of vv. 11ef-16. If that is correct, the last section of the second part stands out as a lament or complaint element in its own right. Indeed, vv. 18-22 can be seen as the concluding stages of a plaintive prayer. Acknowledgment of one's own guilt (v. 18ab) is essential in certain situations (cf. Psalms 38; 51), and there seems to have been a growing tendency in emerging Judaism to assume sin and guilt as the main causes of distress (cf. Psalms 78; 106; Nehemiah 9). Strange, it seems, to insist still, at this stage of ritual lament, on trying to get the help of the "lovers" (v. 19) — they must be foreign gods (cf. Hos 2:7 [RSV 5]: "I will go after my lovers"; Jer 2:23: "How can you say: . . . I have not gone after the Baals?"; Isa 62:4: "You shall no more be termed Forsaken"). The metaphor thrives on the image of a woman-city that has irritated her real husband, Yahweh.

In the last instance the ceremony visible in Lamentations 1 comes to a proper end by a regular petition (vv. 20-22). This in itself is an interesting discovery. Normally, dirges and laments over the destruction of a city do not employ much petitionary language (see "Introduction to Cultic Poetry," section 4A). The dead person is gone and cannot be raised again. A destroyed capital cannot easily be rebuilt. Perhaps this is the reason why petitions in the final passage are veiled and indirect. Nevertheless, they constitute an appropriate closing section for a complaint or lament service. Tracing the main formal and substantial characteristics of vv. 20-22, we may emphasize the following: petition is expressed in a single imperative, "Look, Yahweh" (v. 20a), taking up previous similar pleas (vv. 9e, 11e), the implication being that Yahweh needs only to become aware of the disastrous state of affairs, and he will readily come to Jerusalem's rescue. Therefore petition does not need to spell out helpful actions or steps and measures of restitution. The text presupposes a total defeat as a fait accompli. Individual complaints in the psalms as a rule had been recited before the final blow occurred. This is valid even for Psalms 6 and 88. Dirges and communal complaints often have been used *post factum*, with little hope left in the face of a complete rupture with the past. Restitution from point zero is less definable than preservation in existing molds. Here may be the reasons for — if they happen at all — subdued petitions in laments after the destruction of cities. Sumerian and Old Babylonian examples also carry wishes and petitions for restoration, usually in general terms and all the more pronounced, if recited, e.g., in temple-rebuilding ceremonies (cf. Dobbs-Allsopp, *Weep,* 92-94). The conclusion seems clear enough: petition in mourning rites tends to be subdued and

481

general. Small wonder that in Lamentations petitions are scarce, coming up principally at the end of chs. 1 and 5 (cf. 5:21: "Restore us to yourself, Yahweh, and we will be restored; renew our days as of old" — a perfect ending of a liturgical cycle of laments; but 3:59-66 has to be considered in this context too). Scarceness of petition is not a strict law for lamentations, though. Psalms 44 and 89 and some Sumerian lamentations tell us that survivors may make extensive supplication even after the destruction of cities and the killing of populations. A good example for petitions in Mesopotamian laments is the *balag* composition AME AMAŠANA, "The Bull in His Fold" (M. E. Cohen, *Canonical Lamentations*, I, 152-74). It contains long passages of detailed entreaty for restoration to Enlil, one of the highest gods. The direct address to him runs: "You have smitten the land, until you have (completely) destroyed it" (ibid., 166). Thereafter, the priest recites a flood of petitions aimed at a new period of grace and peace.

Given the dimness of petition in Lamentations, however, the closing section of ch. 1 functions as a simple plea before Yahweh to pay attention to the castigated sufferers. This plea is heavily reinforced by renewed lamenting descriptions of misery (v. 20a-f), exposing contrition (20cd) and — metaphorically — the anguish of a mother losing her children (20ef). The first word of v. 21 is ambiguous in textual transmission. The Syriac version reads a singular imperative, thus continuing the petition before Yahweh ("listen how I am groaning"). The Greek version makes the verb a plural imperative, directed to bystanders, as in v. 12. Mainstream Hebrew MSS vocalize the verb *šm'*, "hear," to be a plural perfect form as in the following line (v. 21c: "they heard"). Be that as it may, vv. 21-22 bring to bear a typical second motif of petition, the destruction of enemies (cf. Psalms 79; 109; 137). The rationale behind this kind of denunciation is probably that the enemies have been instruments in the hands of a punishing deity. So far, so good, and they are excused. But as a rule they have exceeded their mission, taking revenge on Yahweh's people. This fact makes them liable for damages and brutalities, and their own misdeeds may come upon them.

> All my enemies heard of my trouble; they are glad that you have done it.
> Bring on the day you have announced, and let them be as I am.
> Let all their evildoing come before you; and deal with them
> as you have dealt with me. (vv. 21c-22c)

Transference of guilt and punishment is at stake, a certain scapegoat syndrome. Much of the extant ancient Near Eastern complaint and lament literature adheres to this scheme (cf. Pss 28:4; 74:18-23; 79:6, 12; 109:17; 137:8-9). Denunciation of enemies as the source of evil is part and parcel of petition in complaint and lament ceremonies.

Unlike ancient Near Eastern ritual texts, biblical prayers do not give us much information about ritual practice. What we can glean from psalms and laments themselves are chance hints about ceremonial acts, like raising hands, circling the altar, putting hands on one's mouth, cleansing body and clothes, entering gates and precincts of the temple, etc. Ritual instructions are all but missing in poetic texts. We get some of this type of literature, e.g., in Num 5:15-28; Leviticus 1–7; Nehemiah 8; but it does not include any prayers. So we are uncertain about the exact worship orders in ancient Israel. Lamentations gives us hardly any indication of liturgical customs. Ritual weeping (Lam 1:2) and stretching out hands (Lam 1:17) are but inconclusive allusions as far as liturgical procedure is concerned. But we should note, as demonstrated above, the changing voices (cf. Lanahan) and differing "directions of speech" (Westermann): turning points in their regard are possibly significant notifiers of shifts in the movement. Thus we found no formal introduction to the lament other than the disconnected wailing shout. No invocation, no call for attention, no initial plea gives that introductory flair we find in regular complaint psalms. Instead, descriptive presentations of Judah's misery dominate the first part, qualified, as it were, as a complaining discourse. Should this state of affairs from the outset bespeak a recitative function of the text? In other words, would some liturgist declaim the lament to an audience? Yet the turning point of v. 10ef shows that prayer to Yahweh is intended. In vv. 11ef, 20a, 21-22 the speech is directed toward God, while bystanders and contemporaries are addressed in vv. 12, 18, evoking the impression of a communitarian interchange. The second part of our poem (vv. 11-22) moves more and more into prayer style. Together with the use of complaint elements like initial plea, complaint, and petition, we receive the impression of communal action. Also, the alternation of first-person discourse (vv. 11-16, 18-22) and neutral third-person narration (v. 17) is a lively indicator of changing roles in a worship service. A narrator presents the miserable conditions of Yahweh's people; the community, represented as "mother" Jerusalem and her children, speaks up over against her Lord (and husband?).

## Genre/Setting

Most experts agree that the book of Lamentations, or at least chs. 1, 2, 4, 5, were used in mourning ceremonies commemorating the fall of Jerusalem and the destruction of the temple. A few passages in Hebrew Scripture would hint at these regular festive occasions, most of all Zech 7:3-5, mentioning communal services in the fifth and seventh months, Zech 8:18 adding the fourth and tenth months, of every year during the Babylonian exile (70 years). In accordance with regular mournful commemorations, the texts may have been composed along traditional lines of lamenting. Influences of regular complaint liturgies, funeral rites, contemporary theological reflection (sin and guilt), and wisdom thinking are quite natural. The genre emerging in this context may aptly be called COMMUNAL MOURNING AGENDA. Funeral songs for deceased persons are different (cf. 2 Sam 1:17-27; Jahnow), just as communal complaints (cf. Psalms 44; 80; 89) are a specific genre. Still, the setting in communal service being very likely, and commemorative feasts in exilic/postexilic times having some plausibility, we do not hesitate to place Lamentations 1 there. That means we contest the classification of the chapter (and the book) as "mere literature" (thus, e.g., Jahnow, 169; Kaiser, 101-3;, et al.).

483

The setting remains to be defined more closely, however. As we have seen in the structure analysis, various speakers or performers appear in the text. The "narrator" or "liturgist" mainly describes the miserable situation, putting in, at the side, his or her theological evaluations. Some exegetes correctly mention the instructional undertones. This voice rarely appeals to God directly (v. 10ef), pointing to the locale of a communal worship service. In synthesizing the community into one figure, that of personalized Jerusalem, the speaker prepares the way not only for the woman-city to take the stage, with all metaphorical and theological implications, but also for the assembly to identify itself thoroughly with this fictitious figure. The participants in mourning worship services should be clear, then. There were acting speakers or liturgists, and they more or less were responsible for the whole agenda. There was a voice representing Jerusalem, in person, very likely provided also by the leading speakers. There was a listening and sometimes audible community (cf. communal "we" in Lamentations 5). There were imagined neighbors and observers: the peoples Judeans had to live with in the Babylonian and Persian empires. Last but not least, there was Yahweh to confront in worship. All these voices, parties in ceremonial action, are present in Lamentations 1. They communicate in a specific metaphorical language of communal and theological mourning, representing an advanced stage of Judaic spiritual life.

## Intention

Lamentations 1 was not composed for the edification of private readers. Rather, as a part of the book of Lamentations it constitutes a liturgical entity to be recited in common worship, to instruct an assembly, and make it participate in the drama of complaint, lament, mourning, by offering that strong identification with the woman Jerusalem, who grieves in anguish over her children and at the end is acquitted of her guilt (4:22).

## Bibliography

B. Gosse, "Les 'Confessions' de Jérémie, la vengeance contre Jérusalem à l'image de celle contre Babylone et les nations, et Lamentations 1," *ZAW* 111 (1999) 58-67; B. B. Kaiser, "Poet as 'Female Impersonator,'" *Journal of Religion* 67 (1987) 164-83; R. D. Salters, "Lamentations 1:3," in *A Word in Season* (*Fest.* W. McKane; ed. J. D. Martin and P. R. Davies; JSOTSup 42; Sheffield: Sheffield Academic Press, 1986) 83-84; C. L. Seow, "A Textual Note on Lam 1:20," *CBQ* 47 (1985) 46-59.

## Lamentations 2:
## Communal Mourning Agenda

### Text

Introduced, exactly like ch. 1, with a proleptic *'êkāh,* "alas," Lamentations 2 also matches its predecessor in its acrostic structure. The first line of each block of three lines (= one verse) begins with the proper letter of the running alphabet. Only vv. 16 and 17 disrupt the pattern, inverting the order of *ayin* and *pe,* so that v. 16 starts out with *pāṣû,* and v. 17 with *'āśāh.* Furthermore, there is one other block that irregularly has four lines (v. 19).

The name "Yahweh" obviously has been replaced (unless we are dealing with another literary source in the respective verses) by *'ădōnāy,* "Lord," in vv. 1-7a (four occurrences in *BHK* and *BHS;* but Hebrew MSS reading *yhwh* abounds in the collection of Kennicott). Starting with v. 7e and down to v. 22, the use of "Lord" is insignificant (only in vv. 18a, 19d) in relation to the proper name "Yahweh" (vv. 7a, 8a, 9f, 17a, 20a, 22c; cf. also v. 6c). The tuning down of "Yahweh" to "Lord" is probably an indication of later emendation, because of theological pangs in regard to possible abuse of the Holy Name.

### Structure

|  | MT | NRSV |
|---|---|---|
| I. Opening cry (how) | *1 ('êkāh) | *1 |
| II. Description of misery | 1-10 | |
| A. Yahweh's sanctions | 1-8 | |
| B. Consequent desolation | 9-10 | |
| III. Divine lament | 11-16 | |
| A. Description of suffering | 11-12 | |
| B. Resentful address | 13-16 | |
| IV. Admonitions | 17-19 | |
| V. Plea and lament | 20-22 | |

Speakers and voices are not easily defined in Lamentations 2. But it should be clear that the passages for the most part fit into a liturgical frame. Overwhelmingly, they also remind us of complaint procedures as extant in a number of psalms (cf. "Introduction to Cultic Poetry," sections A and B).

About the introductory shout of wailing see Lam 1:1. Remarkably, the first section of our text is a drawn-out depiction of how Yahweh has punished his own beloved city of Jerusalem (vv. 1-8). There may be intended a dramatic crescendo in the sequence of punitive acts and outbursts of divine wrath. The first five verses tell how Yahweh ("the Lord") has destroyed and humiliated "his footstool" (v. 1e), i.e., Jerusalem. He is the agent, the community of Israel is the target; her palaces and fortifications fall victim to his anger (cf. v. 5). "Yahweh has become like an enemy, he has destroyed Israel" (v. 5ab). There is apparently no room for any kind of wholesome relationship between the two.

485

Vv. 6-7 disclose a tiny linguistic alteration. While so far "Israel and her belongings" were the objects of Yahweh's wrath, now he is aiming at "his" most holy property. "He has destroyed his tabernacle. . . . The Lord has scorned his altar, disowned his sanctuary; he has delivered into the hand of the enemy the walls of her (!) palaces" (vv. 6b, 7a-d). If the MT is correct, we find a culmination of punitive action exactly in the destruction of God's own abode among his people. The third-person singular possessive suffixes indicate Yahweh's special tie with his people. If it is annihilated in the storm of castigation, the relationship between God and community has come to an absolute end. Many parallel texts in the Bible and ancient Near East testify to the importance of the temple as the highest guarantee of divine grace, benevolence, and presence. Destruction of the sanctuary is a deathblow to religious faith and to the physical existence of believers.

To give a small impression of the Sumerian counterpart we may quote Cohen's evaluation and a sample from one of his texts. "The canonical lamentation of Mesopotamia . . . laments national humiliation and devastation. These texts describe the destruction of cities, the defiling of temples, and the suffering of the population. A common stylistic feature of these compositions is the use of refrains, with lengthy, repetitive lists of cities and temples which have been destroyed" (Cohen, *Canonical Lamentations,* I, 15). One text in question is the *balag* composition called IMMAL GUDEDE, "The Loving Cow" (ibid., II, 604-36). There we read:

On account of the destruction of the chamber, the bedroom of the
   Urshaba, . . .
the lament of the small city cries out all day long.
On account of the destruction of the shrine of Guabba,
Ninmar, over the shrine of Guabba, cries out all day long.
On account of the destruction of Dumusagubba,
my mother, Nanâ, cries out all day long.
On account of the destruction of the brickwork of Sippar,
Aya, the beautiful woman, cries out all day long.
On account of the destruction of the brickwork of Tintir, (the city) of
   might,
the lofty princess, the holy one, the lady of Tintir, cries out all day long.
On account of the destruction of the brickwork of Borsippa,
the lady of the Edimanki cries out all day long,
she cries out all day long.
All of them perform gestures of mourning. She cries out all day long.
They shed tears. . . . She cries out all day long.
The water does not dry out on their cheeks. She cries out all day long.
                                                                    (ibid., II, 627)

Besides the repetitiousness and formulaic nature of this liturgical text we should note that mourning ("crying out") is done by female deities. This is true for most of the extant *balag* and *eršemma* compositions. Taking into account also the peculiar *emesal* dialect used in these lamentations, experts formerly concluded that priestesses in Sumerian temples spoke a distinct gender-oriented language. This view is no longer held in ancient Near Eastern studies, but the female preponderance in wailing functions, known to this day from funerals and celebrations of national lament, is quite impressive.

Back to our chapter in Lamentations, some doubt may rest on the question whether v. 7 or v. 8 is the last in line to portray the devastating actions of Yahweh. V. 7, without doubt, is a climax in terms of contents, but v. 8 still continues in the same style as vv. 1-7: "Yahweh [did this and that]." Somehow v. 8 sounds like a summary of God's disastrous deeds against his own people and temple. Vv. 9-10, in any case, continue by giving images of the downtrodden people, the grammatical subjects of all phrases now being on the human side ("her gates," "her king," "her prophets," "the elders," etc.). The whole passage vv. 1-10 in liturgical terms amounts not only to a neutral report on misery and despair, but to a description of how Yahweh has worked havoc, giving way to his enormous wrath. The reasons for such wrath, however, are not given in a single word. They may have been too well known to composers and users of Lamentations 2. Thinking in terms of liturgical performance, we may well imagine this piece to have been recited by a "narrator" type of functionary, instructing his community about the dire state of affairs, after Yahweh's disastrous intervention against his own people and sanctuary had taken place. The presentation of Israel's "extinction" has a final ring to it. Since the whole book of Lamentations contains textual units composed and used in retrospect (we are surmising a considerable distance in time), however, the finality of destruction has already given way to the reality of survival. The very worship service in which Lamentations 2 was recited contradicts the "end of history" hypothesis. "Yahweh has abolished in Zion festival and sabbath" (v. 6cd). This was no longer true when Lamentations 2 came into being. Consequently, the harsh, catastrophic punishments are put before the congregation in order to demonstrate Yahweh's seriousness, and to solicit the renewed commitment of the congregation in order to avoid future catastrophes. The passage at hand, making Yahweh the exclusive executioner of castigation — with no mitigation by intermediary enemies — constitutes a special discourse in complaint and lamenting agendas (cf. Psalms 44; 88; Job 7:11-21; 13:18-28; 30:20-23; etc.).

The second part of Lamentations 2 is more complex and not quite as lucid, as far as ceremonial voices and standpoints are concerned. Immediately, the speaker's "I" (cf. vv. 11, 13) and the direct address of Jerusalem by second-person singular forms (vv. 13, 14, 16) call for attention. Who may be addressing Yahweh's people in this emphatic, emotional, possessive manner? The liturgist or speaker? Yahweh himself? Yahweh through his (prophetic?) speaker, the leader of congregational worship? Who may call Israel "my people" (v. 11cd)? Who should speak so loftily about "your prophets," "your enemies" (vv. 14a, 16a)? The least we must assume is that within a commemorative service this part of our chapter was most naturally represented by an authorized speaker, entrusted to communicate God's personal involvement, pain, and mercy to the assembly. The book of Jeremiah contains similar passages:

My anguish, my anguish! I writhe in pain! Oh, the walls of my heart! . . .
Disaster overtakes disaster, the whole land is laid waste. . . .
For my people are foolish, they do not know me;
they are stupid children, they have no understanding. (Jer 4:19-22)

And a little further in this prophetic book:

I am full of the wrath of Yahweh: I am weary of holding it in.
Pour it out on the children in the street . . .
for I will stretch out my hand against the inhabitants of the land,
says Yahweh. (Jer 6:11-12)

These examples demonstrate, first, the existence of prophetic voices, using freely (on explicit or implicit order of God) the "I" of Yahweh to address the people. Second, they give us an idea of how prophetic liturgists, openly or succinctly speaking in the name of Yahweh, communicated God's sympathy to the people.

In a broader tradition-historical perspective we may point to the "divine lament over/for his/her city or people" as the generic background of Lam 2:11-16. In Sumerian examples Inanna (or another deity) is personally mourning the downfall of her city and temple.

The temple of Kiš, Hursagkalama, was destroyed,
Zababa took an unfamiliar path away from his beloved dwelling,
Mother Ba'u was lamenting bitterly in her Urukug,
"Alas, the destroyed city, my destroyed temple!" bitterly she cries. . . .
Kazallu, the city of teeming multitudes, was wrought with confusion,
Numušdu took an unfamiliar path away from the city, his beloved
    dwelling,
His wife Namrat, the beautiful lady, was lamenting bitterly,
"Alas, the destroyed city, my destroyed temple!" bitterly she cries. . . .
Ninzuana took an unfamiliar path away from her beloved dwelling,
"Alas, the destroyed city, my destroyed temple!" bitterly she cries.
Isin, the shrine that was not a quay, was split by (onrushing) waters.
Ninisina, the mother of the land, wept bitter tears,
"Alas, the destroyed city, my destroyed temple!" bitterly she cries.
Enlilf smote Duranki with a mace,
Enlil established lamenting in his city, the shrine of Nippur,
Mother Ninlil, the lady of the Kiur, wept bitter tears,
"Alas, the destroyed city, my destroyed temple!" bitterly she cries.
                (Michalowski, 43 and 45; quoted are lines 115-18, 123-26, 134-
                42 of "Lamentation over the Destruction of Sumer and Ur")

The "Alas" phrase seems to be a stereotyped cultic shout, repeated many more times in this lamentation. Here it is put into the mouth of goddesses: Enlil, one of the supreme gods of Sumer, is openly pointed out (accused?) as the one who destroyed his ziggurat Duranki at Nippur, while his own wife Ninlil is the main wailing goddess.

In the OT, echoes of divine anguish occur in other prophetic passages, such as Hos 11:8-9; Am 5:1-3; Jer 2:4-32; 30:12-15; and Ezekiel 19. Viewed from this side, there is a progression of divine involvement in the liturgy at hand: Yahweh is seen castigating Jerusalem and "her" inhabitants; he is destroying "his" own sanctuary; he takes up the mourning rites over his own ("my") people. The possessive relationships in this case are revealing, possibly marking also the difference of speakers in worship.

Within the whole divine lament vv. 13-16 constitute a distinct segment. They start out with a rhetorical question: "What can I testify for you, to what compare you . . ., in order to comfort you?" (v. 13a + c). Three groups of persons are mentioned afterward who might serve as witnesses: "your prophets" (v. 14a), "all who pass along" (v. 15a), and "all your enemies" (v. 16a). Their words and deeds, however, do not bring any alleviation. The first ones, from the ranks of the people themselves, are corrupt and lead astray (cf. Jer 6:13-15; 8:10-12; Ezek 13:10-14). The second, neutral passersby, only marvel at the lost beauty and grandeur of Jerusalem, expressing their disdain. The third, enemies and evilmongers, are filled with taunting scorn, not at all refuted by the speaker. In this fashion a reproachful lament comes to its peak. What has to be done now in terms of the ongoing worship?

The concluding section of Lamentations 2 gives the answer, not in terms of logical or theological discourse, but exactly in the mold of a worship agenda. A speaker refers back to what Yahweh has done and spoken (v. 17) and immediately instructs the community how to draw ritual consequences from the situation. Admonitions of this kind fit neatly into agendas (cf. Joel 1–2), because they actually have been used extensively. (A plan of instruction is also present in our worship liturgies.) Vv. 18-19 are replete with them, the textual uncertainty whether v. 18a already begins with an imperative or with a perfect form being of little importance. All the following five lines obey the imperative mood; the sixth is an attributive sentence. These imperatives give ritual instruction for proper mourning. At the same time they alert the community to the necessity of lifting up hands and voices in order to change the destiny of the congregation. The image of babies starving to death on the road (v. 19e-h) or being eaten in utter despair by their mothers (v. 20cd) belongs, of course, to the realm of the personalized city and concomitant metaphors. The words may point toward reality. In antiquity, death from hunger was a very real possibility, as it is in many regions of the world today. But the figure of "woman Jerusalem" stands for the Jewish congregation, endangered, as it were, by wars, economic pressures, droughts, epidemics, etc.

Ancient Near Eastern laments also emphasize, at times, the motif of hunger. To give but one example from the Sumerian "Lamentation over the Destruction of Sumer and Ur" (S. N. Kramer, *ANET,* 611-19):

The (people of the) city who did not succumb to the weapons were
  overcome by famine,
Famine filled the city like water, there was no respite from it,
Famine bends low their faces, it swells their sinews,
Its people threw down the . . . , hurled the weapons to the ground,

489

Raised their hands to their necks, wept,
Take counsel among themselves, speak out eloquently:
"Woe is us, what can we say, what can we add!
Until when will we perish in the *mouth* of destruction!
Ur — inside it is death, outside it is death,
Inside it we die of famine,
Outside it we are killed by the weapons of the Elamites."
(Kramer, *ANET,* 618)

Although not much of a petition in the sense of complaint services (cf. "Introduction to Cultic Poetry," section 4B), vv. 20-22 clearly exhibit a petitionary thrust. "Look, Yahweh, and consider" (v. 20a) is — in the context of lamentations, just as in 1:9, 11, 20 — a form of asking not only for Yahweh's attention but implicitly also for his help, a surrogate petition, so to speak. In our case this first line of addressing Yahweh directly has no explicit petitionary sequel. Instead, it is followed up by two hypothetical questions, clad in conditional '*im,* "if," phrases, that express the most hideous crimes imaginable. Could it be bearable that women eat their children because of hunger, and enemies kill priests and prophets at the most holy place (v. 20c-f)? These crimes have allegedly occurred through Yahweh's punishment. Now, God has to recognize the impossibility of such judgment and suffering, and implicitly he has to alter his attitude and restore his community. Since explicit petitions are largely missing (cf. 1:21-22; 4:21), the pleading of Lamentations 2 is restricted to v. 20, which, in turn, receives strength from the laments in vv. 21-22. Once more, the suffering is exemplified by describing the bloodbaths the victors staged in the captured city. Audaciously, their deeds are fully attributed to Yahweh: "In the day of your anger you have killed them, slaughtering without mercy" (v. 21ef). Lament and accusation directed to Yahweh undergird the plea to be heeded and taken care of. Who is uttering the words of vv. 20-22 becomes clear in the first-person forms shining through in vv. 21c, 22ef. Jerusalem is speaking, the woman bereft of her "children" (v. 21b: "young boys and old men"), "priests," and "prophets," i.e., the Yahweh congregation, represented in worship by a distinct voice. Thus the shift in agenda between v. 19 and v. 20, from admonition to plea and lament, becomes obvious.

The elements of Lamentations 2 function in a liturgical fashion. They resemble, in several ways, standard parts of complaint services. But distinct modifications are discernible. First, the text again lacks a formal overture, being classified only by *'êkāh* as a mourning genre (see Lamentations 1). It starts out immediately with the "description of misery," probably recited by some professional cantor or speaker. Then, if our interpretation is correct, Yahweh's own voice is made audible by some officiant (vv. 11-16), addressing directly, in second person singular, the faithful congregation. This part, carrying God's direct message to the community, probably had high authority among listeners. The following speaker (vv. 17-19), now using Yahweh's name in the third person singular, admonishes the people. He or she gives orientation as to how to cope with the situation of want and threats. Ritual suggestions include ceremonial weeping (v. 18) and nightly prayer services, confessional statements, and supplication for the life of the young children (v. 19ef: "raising one's hands in prayer" is an expression known also in Akkadian). Exhortation like this to move into the direction of God and be his client again can easily be gleaned also from some psalms and the book of Job. The sequence of speakers so far has been: narrator of misery — provider of God's own voice — exhorter to render worship to Yahweh. This line can be continued for vv. 20-21, clearly a prayer element. Now the city speaks up on behalf of all inhabitants, in the first person singular (vv. 21-22); thus here we have an intercessor pleading or the congregation speaking in unison. All parts are liturgically connected, and the four speakers without doubt performed their parts in worship gatherings of exiled Judeans or among those left at home.

## *Genre/Setting/Intention*

Lamentations 1 and 2 certainly share to a large extent their genre ascription and setting. Both texts move from descriptive to petitionary stances, both are anchored in community worship of exilic/postexilic times. The intention is the same as well. There are a number of peculiarities in Lamentations 2, however. The Yahweh perspective is predominant in vv. 1-16. This fact presupposes special authorized speakers, perhaps of a prophetic background. Cultic prophecy, on the other hand, is a much debated and very ambiguous problem. In my opinion, it should be separated entirely from what we call "classical" or "literary" prophecy. Still, there remains the question of legitimate representation of Yahweh's voice in worship. Lamentations 2 offers, if our interpretation is correct, a relevant case in vv. 13-16. An exhortation to mourn (vv. 17-19) and a plaintive plea (vv. 20-22) follow from the preceding liturgical units. The chapter orients a Judean community to identify with the ancestors who suffered Yahweh's punishment and experienced Yahweh's concern. By doing so, this much later congregation is to cope with its own problems of God's wrath, the oppressors' violence, and immense sufferings.

Structure, genre, setting, and intention as outlined above raise more questions. Are we to consider Lamentations 1 and 2 as liturgical alternatives? Or could both chapters successively have served in one and the same worship? We do not know for sure. After all, each text seems to be a well-rounded liturgical unit. On the other hand, the distinctness of both chapters certainly makes them a fitting pair to be recited and enacted in one mourning ceremony.

## *Bibliography*

B. B. Kaiser, "Poet" (see listing at Lamentations 1); J. Renkema, "The Literary Structure of Lamentations II," in *The Structural Analysis of Biblical and Canaanite Poetry* (ed. W. van der Meer, et al.; JSOTSup 74; Sheffield: Sheffield Academic Press, 1988) 321-46.

# Lamentations 3:
# Agenda of Communal Lament

## *Text*

Lamentations 3 is an acrostic poem, like chs. 1, 2, and 4. With the two preceding texts it shares that conspicuous three-line block. But here every single line of each block begins with the correct, consecutive letter of the alphabet, not just the first line. Since each line is counted as one verse in later Masoretic tradition, we find 66 verses (3 × 22) in our Hebrew Bibles. Again, as in 2:16 and 17, the order of *ayin* and *pe* is inverted (3:46-51).

## *Structure*

|  |  | MT (= NRSV) |
|---|---|---|
| I. | Complaint | 1-18 |
|  | A. Self-presentation, complaint | 1-3 |
|  | B. Description of Yahweh's punishment | 4-18 |
| II. | Affirmation of confidence | 19-36 |
|  | A. Meditation | 19-21 |
|  | B. Confession of trust | 22-36 |
| III. | Communal confession and complaint | 37-54 |
|  | A. Theological reflection | 37-39 |
|  | B. Communal prayer | 40-42 |
|  | 1. Call to repent | 40-41 |
|  | 2. Confession of guilt | 42 |
|  | C. Direct address: complaint | 43-45 |
|  | D. Complaint about enemies | 46-47 |
|  | E. Description of mourning | 48-51 |
|  | F. Complaint about enemies | 52-54 |
| IV. | Petition | 55-66 |
|  | A. Trust of being heard | 55-58 |
|  | B. Petition for help | 59 |
|  | C. Denunciation of enemies | 60-66 |

Most commentators observe that Lamentations 3 contains elements of various genres, with a preponderance of forms deriving from the individual complaint (see "Introduction to Cultic Poetry," section 4B). We are going to test this evaluation passage by passage, comparing as much as possible the traditional elements and structures of complaint as extant in the Psalms. The possible impact of stylistic (acrostic) organization is of special interest in this context.

Complaint ceremonies for the individual normally open with an invocation of the Deity and initial plea to be heard. A self-presentation of the suppliant ("I am one who . . .") with accompanying complaints (vv. 1-3) is quite unusual. We would expect it perhaps in sapiential dialogues (cf. Job 13:18; 17:1; 19:6; 23:1; 30:1, 9; 40:3; etc.). The present introduction has not been caused by acrostic considerations; it would have been easy to start, e.g., an invocation of God with the letter *aleph*. The composer consciously chose descriptive affirmations to begin the complaint, perhaps in line with the "narrational" openings of Lamentations 1, 2 and 4, after the opening shouts. The question arises, too, why the wailing shout *'êkāh*, "alas," is missing in ch. 3. We may surmise that the self-presentation "I am the man who has seen oppression" (v. 1a) at the time was seen as an adequate introduction to a mourning rite. Speculations about its individual or collective character are precocious; they must be answered at the end of this analysis.

The description of Yahweh's action against the suppliant and consequent sufferings (vv. 4-18) corresponds in a way to 2:1-8, but it features a number of motifs apparently taken from individual complaints: violation of physical integrity (v. 4; cf. Pss 22:15-18 [RSV 14-17]; 38:4-9 [RSV 3-8]; 102:4-6 [RSV 3-5]), relegation to the darkness of the netherworld (vv. 2, 6; cf. Ps 88:4-7 [RSV 3-6]), being hit by God's arrows (v. 12; cf. Pss 38:3 [RSV 2]; 64:8 [RSV 7]), and exposure to slander and ridicule (v. 14; cf. Pss 22:8 [RSV 7]; 41:6-11 [RSV 5-10]; 69:13 [RSV 12]; 102:9 [RSV 8]). Yet, in spite of these and other affinities between the laments we are discussing and the complaints of some individual psalms, we should not draw hasty conclusions. The language of Lam 3:1-18 is — due to the strict acrostic orientation — a lot more artificial than the psalmic parallels. The degree of theological reflection seems higher. As later passages in ch. 3 will prove, behind the individual "I" lamenting God's castigation there still may be hidden the whole community. And the proper self-representation at the beginning is likely to increase that suspicion: why should a paradigmatic male character be introduced at all in the way of v. 1a? Is that gender switch from city-woman to "male" victim perhaps signifying a shifting emphasis toward the masculine population of Jerusalem?

The next passage (vv. 19-36) comprises several formal units, but may be summarized under the well-known category of "affirmation of confidence." The individual complaint genre in the psalms as a rule contains statements of this sort, and the general agreement is that in some psalms this element is quite dominant (cf., e.g., Psalms 23; 31:4-7, 15-16a [RSV 3-6, 14-15a]; 56:4-5, 10 [RSV 3-4, 9]; 62; 131). In the book of Lamentations this form element is underrepresented, and quite plausibly so. The moment of catastrophic rupture and the times of commemorating them do not lend themselves much to expressions of continuing confidence (cf. also Psalms 44; 89). Lamentations 3 is an exception to this rule, perhaps thus betraying its late origin or its complaint rather than lament character. Furthermore, the formulations of vv. 19-36 vary a great deal; traditional expressions of confidence are lacking. They have been reformulated or replaced by phrases fitting to the situation. A quick purview reveals the following: the segment begins with a call to think deeply; the verb *zākar*, "remember," has a pivotal role in the endeavor to appraise the past under Yahweh's guidance (vv. 19, 20). Looking for the spiritual history brings to mind reasons to hope (v. 21).

> Yahweh's benevolent deeds have not ceased, his mercies did not come to
> an end;
> Fresh they are every morning, great is your faithfulness. (vv. 22-23)

We may call this a confessional stance; it seems to be the center of confidence. Like the surrounding verses there is little personal sentiment in all these affirmations. They sound rather like communal formulations, used in a common worship. Vv. 25-27 employ sapiential language ("Yahweh is good to anyone who . . . ; good it is . . . ," the three lines all beginning with *ṭôb*, "good"), and the following block (vv. 28-30) continues portraying the ideal masculine believer (*geber*, "adult male," as in v. 1) who devoutly bows down under the authority of God, even suffering insults and beating. Again, this description of a standard regular male member of the community suggests communal use of the text.

After this wisdom interlude the affirmations of confidence resume. Essential statements are repeated in different wording:

> The Lord will not reject forever.
> He causes grief, but he will have compassion, because abundant is his
>     love;
> it is not his heart's desire to afflict and to grieve human beings *(běnê-ʾîš)*.
>                                                                    (vv. 31-33)

These lines take up and continue vv. 22-23. They all start out with deictic or emphatic *kî*, "yes," a formal necessity taken up with strong approval, it seems, by the composers; variation with another word would have been possible. The parishioners of old were confident that Yahweh's good relationship with his people would endure or be resumed. This trust is spelled out a little more in vv. 34-36, which stress God's keen sense of justice for everybody (note *geber* and *ʾādām*, "man," in vv. 35 and 36).

The following two blocks (vv. 37-42) within section III of our outline are hard to place form-critically. They may be part of the preceding declaration of confidence. Vv. 37-39 consist of three rhetorical questions, two of them along the hymnic, admirational line; the third almost sounds like a riddle. Very peculiar is the first-person plural communal prayer in vv. 40-42. There has not been a collective statement so far in Lamentations 3. "Let us test and examine our ways" (v. 40) therefore comes as a total surprise, as does the prayer style (second-person singular address of God, v. 42). Could all this be the result of acrostic manipulation? It is true that verbal and pronominal forms used as first words in vv. 40-42 begin with *nun,* the fourteenth letter of the Hebrew alphabet, which has to be the leading letter in this fourteenth block of Lamentations 3. But the prayer discourse of v. 42b has certainly not been prompted by literary considerations. Furthermore, first-person plural discourse and second-person singular address spill over into the next triple-line block (vv. 43-45) and the two subsequent lines (vv. 46-47). These facts indicate a shift in liturgical recitation. The assembly comes to the fore, or at least a liturgist speaking in the name of the congregation; cf. the same phenomenon in some outspoken "we" psalms (e.g., Psalms 90; 95; 126). Interestingly, the participation of the assembly, the "we" group, is prepared by a laudatory, sapiential discourse in two admiring rhetorical questions (vv. 37-38) and a general query about the very nature of human beings (v. 39). This series of rhetorical, theological inquiries provokes the soul-searching response of the congregation much as the cosmic exhibition of Yahweh's power prompts Job's confession of "guilt" (cf. Job 38–42). Right after pleading guilty, however, the community goes on to complain about the fate suffered from the hands of Yahweh, and in harsh, direct words at that (vv. 43-45): "You have wrapped yourself with anger and pursued us, killing without pity" (v. 43); "You have made us filth and rubbish among the peoples" (v. 45). This statement then leads to a denunciation of the enemies who executed Yahweh's castigation (vv. 46-47).

Surprisingly, the third line of the *pe* block (v. 48) exposes another radical shift in speaker, content, and orientation. All of a sudden an "I" is the agent and object of all the actions, and this "I" carries through the complaint section into the petition section of our text (vv. 48-63). The best explanation for such an abrupt change in my opinion is the living liturgy in which the text was "performed," i.e., read. The literary division into triple blocks of an alphabetically constructed poem is not the most important feature. Rather, the ceremonial structure needs to be uncovered. The newly emerging voice, not installed by literary devices, now takes the lead first in the complaint phase. Individual and communal concerns are indistinguishable here. The description of mourning "because of the destruction of my people" (v. 48b) and "at the fate of all the young women in my city" (v. 51b) sounds collective rather than individual. The "I" speaking can hardly be the woman-city, as in ch. 1, but it could be, on the basis of vv. 48-51 only, God himself, as in 2:11-16; that would mean a highly authorized cult official speaking in the name of Yahweh. The complaining lines proper (vv. 52-54) tell us that the speaking "I" has been the victim of enemy brutality. The details are expressed in ceremonial, not historicizing language. Being hunted, thrown into a pit, stoned, flooded by torrential waters — all these images are standard liturgical expressions of suffering life threats, be it as an individual or as a maltreated community. Saying all this one wonders whether the "I" coming to voice could possibly be identical with the "we" community of vv. 40-47.

The last line of complaint poses the starting affirmation for the final petitionary section. V. 54b states dramatically: "I thought I was lost." By the way, liturgical logic has it that a statement like this does not constitute a contradiction to earlier "affirmations of confidence" or even "acknowledgments of being saved." In complaint and lament ceremonies the movement is up and down, back and forth, between hope and despair (cf. Psalms 22; 31; 69; etc.), thus accumulating saving power and stimulating God to help the suppliants. Irredeemable loss is hinted at, e.g., in Ps 88:6 (RSV 5), Jonah 2:7-8 (RSV 6-7). But this is exactly the occasion for prayer in the psalms. Lam 3:55 follows suit: "I called on your name, Yahweh, from the depths of the pit." Then, astonishingly, the mood is that of a thanksgiving psalm (vv. 56-58, again crossing the border of a triple block). "You heard my plea" (v. 56a), "you have redeemed my life" (v. 58b). In terms of liturgical procedure this sequence of form elements: complaint — trust of being heard — petition, is not unusual (cf. Psalms 22; 31; Jonah 2; Isaiah 38). The affirmation: "You have attended me" can be an anticipatory declaration; it may be a resumé of past experience, or — as some experts have it (A. Weiser, W. Beyerlin, and K. Seybold are among them) — it may constitute a real thanksgiving discourse, making the complaint section a retrospective event. The last option is, in my opinion, the least plausible.

Our text puts positive petitions in one line, v. 59. The rest of the petitionary section (vv. 60-66) is dedicated to punishing the enemies. Modern logic, which postulates a discrepancy between acknowledging one's guilt, accepting the sanctions of Yahweh (executed by hostile people), and denouncing those enemies was unknown at the time; a different partisan rationality was working in ancient times. Asking God for help — after having confessed one's guilt — implied on the one hand active help of God and betterment of one's condition. But on the other hand, these things being two sides of one coin, the immediate causes of misery and disgrace had to be annihilated. As in any medical treatment, healing could occur only by uprooting the evil machinations of hostile powers. To eradicate once and for all these damaging, death-prone powers was the ultimate goal of many a complaint and lament ritual.

There remains for us to try to evaluate the function of form elements within Lamentations 3. Without doubt, the language of the text at times is very close to that of individual complaint psalms. Equally certain is that this language has been developed in liturgical, sapiential circles with some literary ambition. Still, the function of the form elements (which do not always coincide with literary units) proves sufficiently that our text was used and transmitted in worship situations and contexts. What kind of worship are we imagining? Since language and imagery of the individual complaint ceremony were overlaid by communal expressions, forms, and interests, we are probably safe in assuming that ch. 3 was either composed from scratch to be used in congregational assemblies, or (less likely because of the literary cohesion of the text) older individual parts were reworked to fit communal purposes. The idea mentioned above, that ch. 3 is possibly stressing the male sufferings in connection with the destruction of a city, while chs. 1 and 2 concentrate more on female perspectives, should be investigated (cf. Häusl, Linafelt).

## Genre/Setting

The most essential results of the above analysis have already been indicated. Lamentations 3 is no longer an authentic complaint psalm. Neither is it a genuine dirge or funeral song. Composed, as it were, in exilic and postexilic times, at considerable temporal distance from the fall of Jerusalem in 587 B.C.E., the text utilizes various elements from older complaint and lament rituals to form a new genre of mourning song, adequate for the ongoing commemorative services in Judean congregations in and near Jerusalem, but also in the diaspora. Commemorating the historical events that had led to the end of the Judean monarchy became the focal point of lamenting all kind of disastrous events and conditions. Lamentations 3 does not contain any specific memories of the fall of Jerusalem as they may be present, e.g., in Psalms 44; 74; 79. Language, metaphors, and substantial affirmations in our case are all stereotyped and traditional. Some researchers (e.g., Kaiser, 154-71; Hillers, 61-74) suggest even a widespread dependence of the composition on older psalmic materials. Be that as it may, the new genre of the period, connected with worship services of a commemorating, synagogal community, adhered to the basic model of complaining and lamenting. Starting without invocation (why?), it moved from extensive complains and laments in our case via affirmations of confidence toward articulations of petition. Lamentations 1, 2, and 3 all may qualify, therefore, for the title AGENDA OF COMMUNAL LAMENT.

## Intention

Basically, commemorative liturgies have an educational interest. They communicate situations of old, in order to draw conclusions for contemporary times. The lesson to be learned from catastrophes threatening to annihilate the people of Yahweh, or the community of Jerusalem, or the individual members, women, men, and children, of the diaspora are these: Confess and accept your transgressions. Trust in the forgiving grace of Yahweh. Hope for restoration of your own community and the annihilation of all hostile people. It is the gospel of survival that is preached here, under the auspices of a strong, national God, whose anger is never the last word to his followers.

## Bibliography

H. Gottlieb, "Das kultische Leiden des Königs," *SJOT* 2 (1987) 121-26; I. G. P. Gous, "Sosiologiese eksegese van die Oude Testament (Lam 3)," *SK* 14 (1993) 67-83; M. Löhr, "Threni III und die jeremianische Authorschaft des Buches der Klagelieder," *ZAW* 24 (1904) 1-16; I. W. Provan, "Past, Present, and Future in Lamentations III,52-66," *VT* 41 (1991) 164-75.

## Lamentations 4:
## Communal Lament

### Text

The fourth chapter of Lamentations differs slightly from chs. 1 and 2: it is composed of two-line units, the first line beginning, in due sequence, with the proper letter of the Hebrew alphabet. The wailing shout *'êkāh* is in pole position, just as in 1:1; 2:1; and the order of letters at one point again contradicts later standards, being *samek-pe-ayin* (vv. 15-17), as in 2:15-17; 4:43-51. Some verses are difficult to understand because of textual corruption.

### Structure

|  | MT | NRSV |
|---|---|---|
| I. Opening cry (how) | *1 *('êkāh)* | *1 |
| II. Descriptive lament | 1-16 | |
| A. General | 1 | |

The opening wailing shout in isolated position is discussed at 1:1. We find a quite remarkable and not easily explained structure. Predominant is the tone of lament, which describes and reflects a bygone catastrophe: "our end had come" (v. 18d). This is the collective experience; there was no chance of survival. But there is no petition for restoration. Variations of lament take most of the available space, and sometimes it is uncertain who is raising his or her voice. The contents of what is said at times also remains obscure.

The descriptive lament covers vv. 1-16, being introduced by some dark allusion to gold (and silver?) and precious stones lying around after the fall of a city (v. 1). This verse may be a metaphorical and sapiential heading for the whole passage, demonstrating the sudden loss of value and respect for human life in situations of war and defeat. The first part of the section (vv. 2-10) specifies the fate of the young male population (v. 2), babies (vv. 3-4), wealthy citizens (v. 5), "princes" (leading politicians? vv. 7-8), and "compassionate women" (v. 10). They all were treated inhumanly by the victors: want of basic provisions made them die in the streets, hunger being the prime example of existential need (cf. 2:11-12, 19-20). The climax of that string of deadly deficiencies, derived from age-old experiences of besieged cities, is the last verse:

> Compassionate mothers have boiled their children with their own hands; they became their food, when my people were destroyed. (v. 10; cf. Lam 2:20; 2 Kgs 6:24-29)

But who is uttering all these laments, who is reviewing the population in social groups? Only once, in passing, is the name of the city given in vv. 1-10: "the precious sons of Zion" (v. 2a). Later, in vv. 11c, 12d, it becomes definite that Jerusalem is the focal point of all the laments. The speaking voice can be heard only in four instances, where the whole society, comprising the aforementioned social factions, is called *bat-'ammî*, "my [female] people" (vv. 3c, 6a, 9d, 10d). Who could be licensed to speak of Jerusalem this way? Yahweh himself, of course, or an authorized officiant in his place, would be the most plausible choice. We may argue that if it cannot be the personalized city, that woman Jerusalem of 1:11-22, who is lamenting her children, there must be a divine or divinely appointed lamenter speaking up for the people.

The next section (vv. 11-16) is framed by two affirmations about the Deity's punitive activities: "Yahweh gave full vent to his wrath" (v. 11a), and "Yahweh himself has scattered them" (v. 16a). All the lines in between depend on these collocations, it seems, spelling out their consequences. The incredulity of all the world, which had believed in the invincibility of Yahweh's city (v. 12), as well as the drastic depiction of the trespassings of prophets and priests (vv. 13-15), who had caused Yahweh's castigation to begin with, are encompassed by Yahweh's wrath. So far, the whole section vv. 1-16 is a huge painting of Jerusalem's destitution, in all likelihood being presented to the congregation by authorized officiants in a mourning liturgy.

After v. 16 the voice changes abruptly, now speaking in the first person plural, without any apparent reason for the switch. "We" discourse — this becomes clear enough in Psalm studies (cf. Psalms 90; 95; 126; Lam 3:40-47; etc.) — is a sure sign of community involvement. Texts in first person plural can hardly be literary; they were probably recited either by the assembly or by some speaker on behalf of the congregation. What does the worshiping community have to say at this point, or what is being said on their behalf? After neutral statements of extreme gravity culminating in vv. 10 and 13-16 (Yahweh did not even exercise mercy over his most intimate servants, the priests, who sinned, defiled themselves, became dreadfully unclean, and were scattered), the community takes up the topic of suffering. The anguish of the people had been terrible, persecutions by the enemies unbearable (vv. 18-19). Very new and strange, in this context, is the reference to the messiah Israel had hoped for, who apparently was taken prisoner by the imperial forces:

> Yahweh's anointed, the breath of our life, was captured in their pits,
> the one of whom we said: "Under his shadow we want to live among the
>   nations." (v. 20)

This is the only reference in the book of Lamentations to a messiah. Is it just to an anointed king, or to a future savior? Historical identification of the messianic incident is nearly impossible. Reference to the flight of Zedekiah through Babylonian lines as narrated in 2 Kgs 25:4-6 is quite precarious. More likely, the verse contains already a more developed expectation of being saved in a reign of Yahweh to come than could be present in monarchic and early exilic times. The Psalms can tell us a lot about the emerging messianic expectation of Judaism (cf. Psalms 2; 20; 21; 45; 110; 132; etc.). Also, the incident of Hag 2:20-23 and Zechariah 4 should be considered. Messianic hopes rose high particularly in Persian times, when the temple was reconstructed and the last descendants of the Davidic dynasty were still alive. Taken as an expression of messianism at an advanced stage, v. 20 can tell us about the contours of this new, exciting belief. The community of Yahweh felt endangered in the world of the nations. Judeans, therefore, hoped for a restoration of the Davidic rule, which would guarantee a good, safe standing in the pluralistic society of old (cf. Ezek 34:11-24; Jer 23:5-6; 33:14-22; Isa 9:5-6 [RSV 6-7]; 11:1-9; etc.). It is surely an extraordinary sign of theological advance in the sense of working through contemporary events and developments that a tiny minority within an unimaginably huge empire dares to express its outlook and desires in such a fashion.

The remaining two verses (= four lines) contain an extensive denunciation of Edom and a complete absolution for Jerusalem. Nobody is able to determine how and why Edom comes in at this point. The history of relations between Judah and Edom was always precarious, changing from friendship to suspicion to open hatred (cf. Weippert). This relationship is prefigured (in reality, condensed from historical experience) in the tensions between Jacob and

Esau (Edom) in Genesis 27–36. The same abrupt appearance of Edom in the context of the Babylonian conquest can be seen in Ps 137:7; Isa 11:14; Am 9:12. The same tradition is prevalent here, threatening Edom (without previous warnings) with destruction and disgrace (vv. 21, 22cd). This message seems to be the most important of the concluding section. Sandwiched in with only one line at its disposal, Jerusalem receives remission of sins and an implicit promise of restoration (v. 22ab).

Looking at the analysis we note that the whole structure of ch. 4 again starts from descriptive lament to move not toward petition but to threats against the enemy and assurance of salvation for Yahweh's congregation (cf. Isa 40:2). Considering this closing element, we may compare our textual unit with the preaching of Second Isaiah.

## Genre

Lamentations 4 seems to be a truncated text, at least in terms of standard complaint and lament rituals. A series of laments, and a concluding, very brief announcement of clemency for Zion as well as complete condemnation (even by means of ridicule, v. 21) of one-time enemies (vv. 21, 22cd) do not constitute a genre yet, according to our perception. At best, we may classify this chapter, in contradistinction to the previous three, which betrayed a classical setup of elements, as a lament without much else, or with some promise of a light in the dark tunnel. The recapitulation of sufferings ends in a sermonlike promise to the Yahweh community.

## Setting

Of the two alternatives of localization in life situations — worship or academic discourse — we choose one: the text may have been used in synagogal worship, to set an agenda. Laments like the one we are talking about expose their communal use already by the "we" passages discernible in the text. To this very day, our agendas are witnesses for the legitimacy of such usage. Our chapter may have been used as an auxiliary text in conjunction with other complaint and lament rituals. Chs. 1–3 revealed a certain completeness of form elements for these purposes. Ch. 4, on the other hand, apparently depends on previous and contemporary rituals with their agendas. Perhaps it serves as a supplement in diverse mourning worships in Judea.

## Intention

A fragmentary liturgical piece, possibly put close to another, more complete composition for lamenting and mourning, is certainly always subservient to that larger context. What we may glean from ch. 4 in terms of specific concerns may be synthesized like this: Memories of past tragedies and defeats should be kept alive. They exhibit the real situation of human beings and God, leading in present-day situations to reflections and acts of forgiveness, justice, and peacemaking. The past with its models of life and death is thus a necessary stimulus for every present moment.

## Bibliography

J. A. Emerton, "The Meaning of *'abnê qōdeš* in Lamentations 4:1," *ZAW* 79 (1967) 233-36; S. A. Fries, "Parallelen zwischen den Klageliedern Cap. IV, V und der Makkabäerzeit," *ZAW* 13 (1893) 110-24; I. G. P. Gous, "Mind over Matter: Lamentations 4 in the Light of Cognitive Sciences," *SJOT* 10 (1996) 69-87; M. Löhr, "Sind Thr. IV und V makkabäisch?" *ZAW* 14 (1894) 51-59; M. Weippert, *Edom* (diss., Tübingen, 1971); idem, "Edom und Israel," *TRE* IX, 291-99.

# Lamentations 5:
# Communal Complaint

## Text

Lamentations 5 is the only unit in our booklet that does not formally apply acrostic stylization to its lines. But the number of lines (= verses) corresponds to the amount of letters in the Hebrew alphabet; this phenomenon is called "alphabetizing" style (cf. Psalm 33). Bergler's attempt to read the first letters of each line as a meaningful phrase (he pieces together the Hebrew consonants like this: *zōnîm 'am 'ā'îb 'ōnēš bûz šānāhāh 'ĕlōhêkā* = "the apostates, the people I despise, punishing them with disdain, as your God is lamenting," p. 317) is hardly tenable.

## Structure

|  | MT | (= NRSV) |
|---|---|---|
| I. Invocation, initial plea | 1 | |
| II. Lament | 2-18 | |
| A. Collective lament | 2-10 | |
| B. Description of social groups | 11-14 | |
| C. Collective lament | 15-18 | |
| III. Petition | 19-22 | |
| A. Hymnic address | 19 | |
| B. Plaintive question | 20 | |
| C. Petition for help | 21-22 | |

The overall picture of Lamentations 5 is that of a communal complaint, with a proper opening and closing section. The initial plea uses the imperatives of *zkr,* "remember," and *nbṭ,* Hiphil, "look," combined with *r'h,* "see"; all three verbs are not uncommon in that function (cf. Pss 25:6-7; 74:2; 98:3; 106:4; 132:1 for *zkr;* 13:4 [RSV 3]; 74:20; 80:15 [RSV 14]; 84:10 [RSV 9]; 142:5 [RSV 4]; Isa 63:15; 64:8 for *nbṭ;* Pss 9:14 [RSV 13]; 10:14; 25:18-19; 31:8 [RSV 7]; 35:8; 59:5 [RSV 4], etc., for *r'h*). Thus we have here the only regular complaint overture in the book of Lamentations, including a proper invocation of the name Yahweh. The lack of an invocation in Lam 1:1; 2:1; 3:1; 4:1 may be due to the fact that in these four chapters influences of dirge or funeral rites are stronger than in this last unit of the collection. Dirges traditionally commence with a lament over the deceased, concentrating on this topic throughout; cf. Jahnow, 92-108. Finding forms of the complaint genre in ch. 5 is proof of the mixture of styles and genres in late communal commemorations. In other words, mourning services in memory of past catastrophes developed their own genre of lament, built upon traditional forms of complaining and lamenting. Variations of late complaint, emphasizing the guilt of the fathers, can be found in Ezra 9; Nehemiah 9; Daniel 9.

The large complaining and lamenting section of Lamentations 5 formcritically falls into three parts, two of them using extensive first-person plural discourse (vv. 2-10, 15-18), with the unit in the middle describing the destiny of certain social groups, all inhabitants of the defeated city (vv. 11-14). Looking at this one first and hoping to discern some traces of the social setup, we notice four pairs of agents who apparently have become most important as victims in defeat: (1) married and unmarried women; (2) "princes" (? *śārîm* can also denote "state officials," "community leaders"; cf. H. Niehr, *TWAT* VII, 855-79, esp. 873-78) and elders; (3) young men and boys; and (4) elders and choice youngsters. That means that women have been affected in the first place; children and babies, mentioned several times in previous chapters (cf. 1:5, 16; 2:19; 4:4, 10), are ignored here. The second group looming large are males in leading positions. In the third place we find mentioned strong young warriors and young boys. Missing, again, are religious leaders, like "prophets" and "priests" mentioned quite frequently in other texts (cf. 1:4, 19; 2:6, 9, 14, 20; 4:13, 16). Compared to other lists of qualified victims in a conquered city (cf. 1:4-6; 1:15; 1:18; 2:9-10; 2:20-21; 4:2-10; 4:13), our passage is rhetorically more compact, and characterized by those omissions just mentioned. The nucleus of the suffering municipal society, however, is the same in all instances. Free women are preferred objects of the victor's greed (cf. Judg 5:30), and all men of distinction, if not all males, are targets of revenge (cf. Deut 20:13-14). This is valid more or less for all ancient Near Eastern war practices. We do not have any Judean peculiarities in Lam 5:11-14.

The two passages enveloping our list of most affected war victims are highly interesting in that they offer communal "we" discourse in rare condensation (vv. 1-10, 15-18). As stated earlier (cf. 3:40-47; 4:17-20), all first-person plural statements merit our attention, because this type of usage can hardly be a literary invention. In fact, extant hymnic, petitionary, and psalmic literature from outside the OT scarcely indulges in such speech forms. The reason probably lies in the social and ecclesiastical structure of early Jewish communities, which gave voice in their worship to collective articulation. In the book of

Psalms the "we" discourse is significant as well, and it has found a few inter-
ested scholars (cf. Scharbert, "Das 'Wir'"; see listing at "Introduction to
Psalms"; Seybold, "Das 'Wir'"; see Additional Bibliography, section C). It is
the opinion of both researchers that the prevalence of first-person plural speech
in liturgical texts has its origin in the real participation of congregational assemblies in the cult.

In consequence, we should not hesitate to apply this insight also to the
book of Lamentations. What is the worshiping community lamenting about?
The lamenting affirmations tend to fit into traditional patterns, even if they
seem to refer to historical events. The conquered people are homeless and without rights in their own territory (v. 2; cf. Isa 1:7; Hos 7:9). "Here we are, slaves
to this day — slaves in the land that you gave to our ancestors to enjoy its fruit
and its good gifts. Its rich yield goes to the kings whom you have set over us because of our sins; they have power also over our bodies and over our livestock
at their pleasure, and we are in great distress" (Neh 9:36-37).

Alien dominion was a prime concern of Jewish communities after the defeat by the Babylonians; v. 3 seems to elaborate this thought metaphorically, in
regard to the loss of self-government. Vv. 5 and 8 resume this idea. The payment for water and firewood (v. 4) is otherwise not testified to, but it could easily have been a standard experience for a subject population. Any kind of food
was difficult to get (vv. 9-10); hunger, indeed, was a big problem of besieged
and defeated citizens (cf. 4:4-5, 9-10). Astonishingly enough, one verse tells
about subjugation before Egyptians and Assyrians in order to gain food (v. 6).
This seems to be an anachronistic affirmation. The Assyrians, by the time of
Lamentations, are long gone, and the Egyptians did not exercise much influence on Judah either during the period. So the saying remains obscure; it possibly refers to Jewish immigrants to foreign parts, or to an economic dependence
on traders from outside Judah. Interspersed in this picture of suffering under a
hostile, imperial government is a confession of sin (v. 7), as customary in
exilic-postexilic liturgical literature (cf. 1:8-9, 18, 20; 2:14, 17; 3:42; 4:6, 13;
5:16; Pss 78:9-11, 17-20, 32; 106:6; Ezra 9:6-15; Neh 9:16-17, 26-28). The accumulated sin of the fathers explains the dire fate of the oppressed community.

After the liturgical interlude, demonstrating the most affected social
groups (vv. 11-14), the congregation resumes telling its experience in traditional affirmations (vv. 15-18). Festive joys are gone, because of their own guilt
(vv. 15-16). The heart-sickening fact is the devastation of Zion (vv. 17-18).

Finally, the long lament of the people is over. The composition, which
started as a communal complaint with an invocation and opening plea, and
which featured also confessions of sins (vv. 7, 16), ends up in a real tripartite
petition for help and restoration (vv. 19-21). Not improper in complaints, the
first subelement is a hymnic affirmation of Yahweh's everlastingness, i.e., his
superior power (v. 19; cf. hymnic elements in communal complaints: Pss 44:2-
9 [RSV 1-8]; 66:7; 83:19 [RSV 18]; 89:7-15 [RSV 6-14]; Isa 63:7-9). An emphatic personal pronoun, "You, Yahweh," opens v. 19. T. H. Robinson, the edi-
tor of Lamentations in *BHK,* thinks it could be a proleptic, unstressed syllable.
"You," evoking the potencies and perfectness of God, contrasts decisively the
many embarrassing "we" affirmations. A reproachful rhetorical question:

"Why have you forgotten us completely?" (v. 20a), in accordance with complaint liturgies (cf. Pss 22:2 [RSV 1]; 44:10 [RSV 9]; Jer 14:8-9), takes up previous laments and leads to the all-decisive petition:

> Restore us to yourself, Yahweh, and we will be restored;
> renew our days as of old. (v. 21)

As we noticed in Lamentations 1, 2, and 4, the petitionary element at the end of each text remained somewhat evasive, probably due to dirge influences. Here we find a clear formulation, in imperative form directed to Yahweh himself (including naming him: v. 21a), of petition. The verb used is the Hiphil of *šûb*, "to revert" (cf. Jer 31:18). Full restoration (including that of Davidic statehood?) is being requested. The verse is direct and outspoken, unlike the subdued petitions in chs. 1, 2, 4, but not elaborate. All details are missing as to how the salvation from foreign overlordship could occur, and what it should imply. Surprisingly, even any reference to enemies and evildoers is absent from the petitionary section. The plea of v. 21, in any case, bears the full emphasis of the prayer. A closing line (v. 22) can only support what has been said, be it in the form of a question ("Or do you reject us . . . ?") or a grammatically more plausible, conditional phrase: "Unless you want to reject us . . ."). Both translations are popular in our Bibles.

## Genre

Little can be added to the genre definition already given in our structure analysis. Language, form elements, composition, overall ceremonial procedure (invocation — initial plea — lament — confessions of guilt — petition — pronounced "we" discourse) all speak in favor of a classification as COMMUNAL COMPLAINT. It should be noted, however, that certain adaptations to the commemorative mourning service have taken place. There is a very extended lament section (vv. 2-18), all, save vv. 11-14, in first-person plural diction. Imprecations are missing, as are larger hymnic or confessional elements. Explicit petition is reduced to but one line. Such are the modifications visible in the text. They all serve, we may surmise, the changed conditions of mourning and lamenting in the later periods of the Hebrew Bible, i.e., the emerging Jewish community, most of all in the Persian period, and the particular types of mourning ceremonies in vogue at the time.

## Setting

Asking more precisely where the setting of our text within that community may have been, we repeat our conclusion: Lamentations 5 cannot be a product of literary activity alone. It does have umbilical connections with the spiritual life of the congregations that arose in exilic and postexilic times. Special worship assemblies apparently brought forth the communal complaint and the communal

504

lament genres. They are basically distinguishable by their position before or after the catastrophe. Commemorative services of the fall of Jerusalem and the establishment of foreign rule over Yahweh's people were probably the concrete opportunities to recite and compose such laments.

## Intention

Mourning is not meant to end in total despair. Rather, it challenges the bereaved and oppressed ones to take a stand over against their own history, assume responsibilities over against God and the world, and count on God's forgiveness and help to be restored, to take up courage again and start anew a life in communion with God.

## Bibliography

S. Bergler, "Threni 5, nur ein alphabetisierendes Lied?" *VT* 27 (1977) 304-20; G. Brunet, "La cinquième lamentation," *VT* 33 (1983) 149-70; R. Gordis, "The Conclusion of the Book of Lamentations (5:22)," *JBL* 99 (1974) 289-93; S. T. Lachs, "The Date of Lamentations V," *JQR* 19 (1966/67) 46-56; H. Wiesmann, "Die Textgestalt des 5. Kapitels der Klagelieder," *Bib* 8 (1927) 339-47; P. J. K. Zenner, "Threni 5," *BZ* 2 (1904) 370-72.

# GLOSSARY

## GENRES

ACCOUNT OF CRISIS (Krisenbericht). → Account of Trouble and Salvation.

ACCOUNT OF DELIVERANCE (Rettungsbericht). → Account of Trouble and Salvation.

ACCOUNT OF DISOBEDIENCE (Ungehorsamsbericht). Sometimes (→) retrospect or (→) historical account focuses on the apostasy of the people of Yahweh (cf. Pss 81:12-13 [RSV 11-12]; 78; 106; Ezra 9). This theological scheme may be Dtr in origin. It is characteristic of an exilic-postexilic trend.

> G. W. Coats, *Exodus 1–18* (FOTL IIA; Grand Rapids: Eerdmans, 1999) 136-40 (on Exod 17:1-7); idem, *Rebellion* (Additional Bibliography, section B); R. Kessler, "Schuldbekenntnis" (listing at Psalm 106).

ACCOUNT OF PILGRIMAGE (Pilgerbericht). Since the act of praying or some details of community worship are occasionally mentioned in the psalm text, procession to the sanctuary here and there becomes the topic of prayer or hymnic praise; cf. Pss 68:25-28 (RSV 24-27); 122:1-2; 132:3-7, a feature particularly interesting in the context of the (→) Songs of Ascents.

> L. D. Crow, *Songs,* 18-25 (listing at Psalm 120); S. Safrai, *Wallfahrt,* 17-19, 44-65, 123-24 (Additional Bibliography, section B); K. Seybold, *Wallfahrtspsalmen,* 16-19, 37-44, 53-56 (listing at Psalm 120).

ACCOUNT OF SACRED HISTORY (Darstellung von heiliger Geschichte). → Retrospect; Historical Account.

ACCOUNT OF SALVATION (Rettungsbericht). → Account of Trouble and Salvation.

ACCOUNT OF TROUBLE AND SALVATION (Bericht von Not und Rettung). An element in the (→) thanksgiving song of the individual in which an afflicted person communicates an experience of deliverance to the guests invited to the thanksgiving service (Pss 30:7-13 [RSV 6-12]; 32:3-5; 116:3-4; Isa 38:10-16). This stereotyped narrative easily turns into (→) instruction or (→) exhortation (Pss 22:23-25 [RSV 22-24]; 30:5-6 [RSV 4-5]; 32:8-11). The ritual process of giving thanks, originally implying a personal sacrifice (cf. Lev 7:11-21), later replaced by a thanksgiving hymn (cf. 50:8-15), thus centers on a liturgical exposition of salvific experience (Jonah 2:4-8 [RSV 3-7]; 1 Sam 2:4-8; Job 33:27-28).

J. Begrich, *Der Psalm des Hiskia*, 4-12 (FRLANT 25; Göttingen: Vandenhoeck & Ruprecht, 1926); H. Gunkel and J. Begrich, *Einleitung*, §7 no. 4 (listing at "Introduction to Cultic Poetry"; Eng. at Additional Bibliography, section C; S. Mowinckel, *W II*, 32-42.

ACCOUNT OF VOW (Gelübdebericht). → Vow.

ACCUSATION (Anklage). Discourse in court procedures, whether civil or criminal. The court was constituted by a convocation of elders (chiefs of the family; cf. Ruth 4:1-2). The roles of attorney and defense not being fixed, any member of the court could bring forth charges against the person under suspicion. In the Psalms we sometimes find imitations of this juridical genre (cf. Pss 50:16-21; 82:2-4; also 4:3-5 [RSV 4-6]; 58:2-3 [RSV 3-4]; → Contestation). An accusation leads to a verdict, which sometimes is anticipated in changing discourses.

H. J. Boecker, *Redeformen*, 71-94 (listing at "Introduction to Psalms").

ACROSTIC PRAYER (Akrostisches Gebet). → Acrostic Psalm.

ACROSTIC PSALM (Akrostischer Psalm). A song the structure of which is guided by alphabetic considerations, with each unit (one line: Psalms 111–112; two lines: Psalm 34; Lamentations 4; three lines: Lamentations 1–2; eight lines: Psalm 119) beginning with a successive letter of the Hebrew alphabet. The term "acrostic" is a mere technical, literary designation that does not imply a specific situation or use of the poem. Acrostics were probably composed for and used in community worship (see Psalms 9/10; 25; 34; 37; 111–112; 119; 145). The alphabetic beginning served as an adornment of the liturgical text, which at the time was already written and read to the community. The book of Lamentations is composed of four acrostic chapters and one alphabetizing poem (ch. 5). For details see "Introduction to the Book of Lamentations," no. 2.

D. N. Freedman, "Acrostic Poems in the Hebrew Bible," *CBQ* 48 (1986) 408-31; idem, "Acrostics and Meter in Hebrew Poetry," *HTR* 65 (1972) 367-92; the studies of L. G. Perdue, H. Graf Reventlow, and W. G. E. Watson cited in the listing at "Introduction to Cultic Poetry" (see also listings at "Introduction to the Book of Lamentations").

ADAGE (Sprichwort). Popular saying with generally recognized contents and semi-normative function. Truths of this type were readily used by preachers, and since homiletical texts occur also within the Psalter, it is no wonder that they appear in this context (cf. Ps 62:10 [RSV 9]).

K. F. D. Römheld, *Die Weisheitslehre im Alten Orient* (BNSup 4; Munich: Görg Verlag, 1989) 121-38. N. Shupak, *Where Can Wisdom Be Found?* (OBO 130, 337-54; Fribourg: Universitätsverlag; Göttingen: Vandenhoeck & Ruprecht, 1993); R. Scoralick, *Einzelspruch und Sammlung* (BZAW 232; Berlin: de Gruyter, 1995) 1.53-73.

ADMISSION PRONOUNCEMENT (Zulassungswort). → Entrance Liturgy.

ADMONITION (Mahnung, Mahnrede). → Exhortation.

ADMONITION OF THE BRIDE (Ermahnung an die Braut). In wedding ceremonies, at least at the royal court, the bride was admonished to "forget her own family" and accept the rules of her husband's clan (Ps 45:11-13 [RSV 10-12]; cf. the relations between husband and father-in-law, Judg 19:1-4).

K. Stone, "Women in the Royal Household," in C. Meyers et al., *Women in Scripture* (Boston: Houghton Mifflin, 2000) 298.

ADORATION (Anbetung). → Hymn of Praise.

AFFIRMATION OF CONFIDENCE (Vertrauensäusserung). A particular passage of individual and communal (→) complaint that voices trust in God (Pss 22:4-6, 10-11 [RSV 3-5, 9-10]; 31:7-9 [RSV 6-8]; 56:4-5 [RSV 3-4]; 71:5-7). "You are my God" (Pss 22:11 [RSV 10]; 25:5; 31:15 [RSV 14]; 43:2; 44:5 [RSV 4]; 63:2 [RSV 1]; 68:25 [RSV 24]; 89:27 [RSV 26]; 118:28; 140:7 [RSV 6]; cf. Pss 7:2 [RSV 1]; 13:4 [RSV 3]; 25:2; 30:3 [RSV 2]; 59:6 [RSV 5]) may thus be considered a formulaic expression of confidence (→ Formula of Confidence). Some psalms concentrate on the trust motif to the exclusion of others (Psalms 11; 23; 62; → Song of Confidence). The trust element dwells on past salvific experiences that grow out of a group's relationship with God (Smith, Alt); analogies can be found in many cultures (with Vorländer, against Begrich). In fact, all prayer is based on the suppliant's and the group's underlying trust in the accessibility and benevolence of the deity invoked. This confidence has to be articulated liturgically, although it is implicit in the fact of praying itself and in each element of the prayer.

A. Alt, "The God of the Fathers," in *Essays on Old Testament History and Religion* (tr. R. A. Wilson; Oxford: Blackwell, 1966) 1-100; J. Begrich, "Die Vertrauensäusserungen im israelitischen Klagelied des Einzelnen und in seinem babylonischen Gegenstuck," in *Gesammelte Studien zum Alten Testament* (TBü 21; Munich: Kaiser, 1964) 168-216 (repr. from ZAW 46 [1928] 221-60); E. S. Gerstenberger, THAT I, 300-305; H. Gunkel and J. Begrich, *Einleitung,* § 6 no. 19, 27 (listing at "Introduction to Cultic Poetry"; Eng. at Additional Bibliography, section C); W. Robertson Smith, *The Religion of the Semites* (London: Black, 1889) ch. 2, 28-83; H. Vorländer, *Mein Gott,* 245-48, 270-72 (listing at "Introduction to Cultic Poetry").

AFFIRMATION OF RIGHTEOUSNESS (Gerechtigkeitsaussage). → Protestation of Innocence.

AGENDA OF COMMUNAL LAMENT (Volksklageagende). → Communal Mourning Agenda.

ALPHABETIC ACROSTICS (Alphabetisches Akrostichon). → Acrostic Psalm (Poem).

ANNOUNCEMENT OF BLESSING (Segensankündigung). → Blessing Formula.

ANNOUNCEMENT OF DESTRUCTION (Zerstörungsansage). → Curse; Imprecation; Oracle of Doom.

ANNOUNCEMENT OF SALVATION (Rettungsankündigung). → Oracle of Salvation.

ANNOUNCEMENT TO COMMUNITY (Ankündigung an die Gemeinde). Within liturgical proceedings there can be found affirmations that seem to communicate information to the congregation; cf. Ps 128:4. In this case it is a statement by the psalmist explaining the consequences of a blessed life. Psalm 119 has many more examples of this kind. More kerygmatic address of the assembly we call (→) proclamation.

ANTICIPATED THANKSGIVING (Vorweggenommene Danksagung). An element in some (→) complaint psalms in which the suppliant recites partly or in full a (→) thanksgiving song, implying that Yahweh has already heard the plea and granted help (Pss 22:23-27 [RSV 22-26]; 31:22-23 [RSV 21-22]; 69:31-34 [RSV 30-33]). This element has a promissory and imploring character, which can be deduced from its use in narrative contexts of calamity (Jonah 2; Isaiah 38; LXX additions to Daniel 3). → Thanksgiving Song.

APOTROPAIC DICTUM (Apotropäischer Spruch). Ancient Near Eastern societies believed in the power of magical words. Israel was no exception to this phenomenon. Therefore prayers may contain (→) curses against evildoers, e.g. Ps 109, as well as protective sayings, like Ps 91:11: "No evil shall befall you, no scourge come near your tent." The form is a negatively articulated (→) well-wish or (→) blessing. It fends off demonic powers.

K. van der Toorn, et al., eds., *Dictionary of Deities and Demons in the Bible* (Leiden: Brill, 1995) 445-55.

509

APPELLATION (Anruf) → Invocation.

ASIDE (Nebenbemerkung). Words spoken not to the immediate partner in dialogue but to someone else (bystander) within a determined discourse. Ps 62:13 (RSV 12) is a case in point. Vv. 9-12 (RSV 8-11) address the congregation; v. 13 (RSV 12) turns to Yahweh, using direct-address speech. Liturgical considerations are presumably decisive for this shift: the (→) homily ends in a prayer.

ASSERTION (Behauptung). Any statement aiming at convincing an audience, often in theological or ethical respect. Homiletical and instructional discourse in the psalmic (and, of course, in prophetic) tradition brings about variations of such affirmations; cf., e.g., Ps 62:13b (RSV 12b): "I heard this: Power belongs to God."

ASSERTION OF INNOCENCE (Unschuldsbehauptung). → Protestation of Innocence.

ASSERTION OF INTEGRITY (Behauptung der Ehrenhaftigkeit). → Protestation of Innocence.

ASSURANCE (Zuspruch). Words of assurance are usually spoken by authorized or powerful persons to those who need help (cf. 1 Sam 1:8; 19:3; Gen 35:17; Ruth 2:8-9; 1 Kgs 17:13; 2 Kgs 6:16). Frequently priests, prophets, or other religious officials communicate divine assurance (→ Oracle of Salvation; Blessing). The borderline between private and official words of assurance is not always strictly defined; cf. Ps 121:3-8.
    J. Begrich, "Heilsorakel," 217-31 (listing at "Introduction to Cultic Poetry"); A. Schoors, *I Am God Your Saviour* (VTSup 24; Leiden: Brill, 1973) 32-175.

ASSURANCE OF FORGIVENESS (Zuspruch von Vergebung). → Oracle of Salvation.

AUTHENTICATION (Rechtliche Bestätigung). Any legal expression that establishes identities of persons or groups, e.g., Ps 87:4, 5, 6: "This one was born here" and therefore may claim citizenship; Ps 2:7: "You are my son"; Ps 89:27 (RSV 26): "I will make him the firstborn"; Ps 105:11: "To you will I give the land of Canaan"; Ps 108:8 (RSV 7): "Gilead is mine; Manasseh is mine; Ephraim is my helmet; Judah is my scepter"; negatively Ps 95:10: "They are a people whose hearts go astray"; etc. → Confirmation of Status.
    M. Görg, "Adoption," *NBL* I, 34-35; B. Lang, "Ehe," *NBL* I, 475-478.

BAD WISH (Böser Wunsch). → Curse; Imprecation.

BEATITUDE (Seligpreisung, Gratulation). At its simplest, a short, formulaic speech that extols the fortunate or blessed state of an individual or a whole people, such as Israel (cf. Numbers 22–24). Typically, the utterance begins with *'ašrê* "fortunate, blessed," followed by the subject and any special qualifiers, often in the form of relative clauses. So 1 Kgs 10:8, "Happy *('ašrê)* are these your servants who continually stand before you" (see Ps 2:12; Prov 8:34; 16:20). These basic elements can be expanded with the addition of elaborate clauses (e.g., Ps 1:1-2; Prov 3:13-14) or developed into more lengthy collections of sayings, as in the NT (e.g., Matt 5:3-11). Beatitude is related to (→) blessing and (→) praise, but remains distinct. It does not invoke God's blessing or utter his praises directly but describes a person who is fortunate by reason of upright behavior or blessings already received from God. Egyptian parallels are known. Beatitude was perhaps originally a type of spontaneous exclamation. Most examples in the OT, however, suggest that it became a form of wisdom teaching, a description turned into didactic example or precept by the "wise men" or "women" whose instructions and learning live on in the books of Proverbs and Ecclesiastes and in certain Psalms (e.g., Psalms 1; 119:1-2; 128).

G. Dupont, "Beatitudes" (listing at Psalm 1); W. Janzen, *"'ašrê"* (listing at "Introduction to Psalms"); E. Lipiński, "Macarismes" (listing at Psalm 1).

BECKONING JUBILATION (Aufruf zum Jubeln). → Call to Worship.

BENEDICTION (Segnung; Seligpreisung). → Beatitude.

BLESSING (Segen; Segnung). → Blessing Formula.

BLESSING EXCHANGE (Segensaustausch). A "two-way-blessing" (cf. Psalm 134). → Blessing Formula.

CALL TO PRAISE (Aufruf zum Lob). → Call to Worship.

CALL TO WORSHIP (Ruf zur Anbetung, Aufruf zum Lob). Many (→) hymns of praise begin with or consist entirely of a summons to join in singing, playing, giving thanks, shouting, or clapping hands in honor of Yahweh, the God of salvific deeds and supreme prestige. A basic form is:

Sing to Yahweh;
Yes, he is great!

Examples are Exod 15:21; Deut 32:43; Jer 20:13; Pss 9:12-13 (RSV 11-12); 106:1; 107:1; 117:1-2; 118:1-4; 136:1. These imperative summonses were probably voiced by an officiant, while the second line, containing the praise proper, was sung or shouted as a (→) response of the community. Crüsemann calls this simple hymn a fundamental liturgical form. More likely, it generally served as the introductory or closing part of hymn singing and thus has been linked to other forms of praise such as the (→) hymnic participles or the (→) direct-address hymn. F. Crüsemann, *Studien*, 19-65; C. Westermann, *Praise*, 123-35 (both in listing at "Introduction to Cultic Poetry").

CALLING ON YAHWEH (Anrufung Jahwes). → Invocation.

CENSURE (Tadel). → Accusation.

CHALLENGE OF OPPONENTS (Herausforderung der Gegner). → Contestation.

CHEERS (Freudenrufe; Lobrufe). People participating in official worship organized by clergy or functionaries as a rule are not given substantial influence on the proceedings, but rather relegated to (→) responses in professional (→) worship agendas. On the other hand, the popular spontaneous urge to participate may be channelled into occasional shouts and cheers. From NT sources we know the repeated liturgical exclamation by the crowds at Jesus' entry into Jerusalem: "Hosanna." Within the OT Psalter we meet, e.g., the shouting of *hallĕlûyāh*, "Praise Yah(weh)," in several groups of texts, or *bārûk yhwh*, "Blessed be Yahweh" (Psalms 103–150, passim); an expression of mourning is *'ēkāh*, "Alas" (Lam 1:1; → MOURNING AGENDA). These short exclamations lend themselves to expressing collective joy, adoration, or distress (→ Formulas: Exclamation; Festive Shout).

 J. Limburg, "Psalms, Book of," *ABD* V, 522-36, esp. 527; E. S. Gerstenberger, "Halleluja," *NBL* II, 18-19.

CLAIM, THEOLOGICAL (Anspruch). Confessional affirmations (→ Confession of Faith) implicitly carry claims of superiority and privilege over against others; cf. Pss 114:1-2; 100:3; 83; 60:10 [RSV 8]). → Account of Trouble and Salvation; Report of Election.

COLOPHON (Kolophon). → Subscription.

COMMITMENT (Selbstverpflichtung). Prayer, be it personal or communal, is never a one-sided petition, expectancy to be helped or blessed. Prayer always includes self-dedication, allegiance, offertory of the suppliant, even though the formula *do ut des* ("I give in order that you give to me") is much too simple to explain the intricate relationship of man/woman and his/her God (cf. Pss 39:2 [RSV 1]; 44:5 [RSV 4]) ch. I.

 M. Mauss, *The Gift: Forms and Functions of Exchange in Archaic Societies* (New York: Norton, 1967).

COMMUNAL BLESSING (Gemeinschaftssegen). → Blessing Formula.

COMMUNAL COMPLAINT SONG (Klagelied des Volkes, Volksklagelied). Also called "national" or "congregational complaint" and "national lament" (cf. Mowinckel, *W* I, 193-246), this group of psalms comprises — according to Gunkel-Begrich, 117 — six clear-cut biblical examples (Psalms 44; 74; 79; 80; 83; Lamentations 5). Other scholars would include more texts (see "Introduction to Cultic Poetry," section 4B; cf. T. Veijola, *Verheissung in der Krise* [Helsinki: Academia Fennica, 1982] 120-43). Formally the communal complaint unfolds liturgically very much like the (→) individual complaint. It is sung, however, in a large assembly at the occasion of a national day of fasting (cf. Joel 1–2).

P. W. Ferris Jr., *Genre,* 89-152 (listing at "Introduction to the Book of Lamentations"); P. D. Miller, *They Cried,* 55-134 (Additional Bibliography, section C); S. Mowinckel, *W* I, 193-224.

COMMUNAL HYMN (Gemeinschaftshymnus). → Hymn of Praise.

COMMUNAL INSTRUCTION (Gemeinschaftsunterweisung). → Instruction.

COMMUNAL LAMENT (Gemeinschaftsklage). → Dirge.

COMMUNAL MOURNING AGENDA (Gemeinde-Klageagende). Compositions of lament, serving congregational worship, may be called "agendas" (cf. Lamentations 1; 2; → Mourning Agenda; Cultic Drama).

COMMUNAL PRAISE (Gemeinschaftslob). → Hymn of Praise.

COMMUNAL THANKSGIVING (Gemeinschaftsdank). → Thanksgiving Song.

COMMUNAL THANKSGIVING HYMN. → Hymn of Praise.

COMPLAINT ELEMENT (Klageelement). Properly speaking, the part of (→) communal or individual complaint (song) that specifically articulates the distress threatening the worshiping group or individual. Since it is a liturgical element, it does not give biographical or historical information but uses generic cultic concepts. With Westermann, we might distinguish three dimensions of complaining: about one's own suffering, about enemy activities, and about God's negligence. But other items would also have to be included, such as one's guilt (Pss 32:3-5; 38:6, 19 [RSV 5, 18]; 51:5 [RSV 3]), betrayal by friends (38:12 [RSV 11; 55:13-14 [RSV 12-13]; 88:9, 19 [RSV 8, 18]), the transitoriness of life (Psalms 39; 90), or the wickedness of the impious world (Psalms 9/10; 37; 49; 73). Using descriptive language, the element tries to communicate to God the afflictions at hand, whether those of an individual and the larger group (22:7-9, 13-19 [RSV 6-8, 12-18]; 38:3-15 [RSV 2-14]; 69:3-5, 8-13 [RSV 2-4, 7-12]; 102:4-12 [RSV 3-11]) or those of the national organization (74:4-11; 79:1-5). Direct-address style is also used (44:10-17 [RSV 9-16]; 89:39-47, 49-50 [RSV 38-46, 48-49]), and many accusing rhetorical questions appear in this genre (13:2-3 [RSV 1-2]; 22:2 [RSV 1]; 74:1; 79:5; 80:5,

12 [RSV 4, 11]). Within the worship ritual it is preparation for (→) petition.

E. S. Gerstenberger, "Der klagende Mensch," in *Probleme biblischer Theologie* (*Fest.* G. von Rad; ed. H. W. Wolff; Munich: Kaiser, 1971) 64-72; H. Gunkel and J. Begrich, *Einleitung* § 6 no. 11 (listing at "Introduction to Cultic Poetry"; Eng. at Additional Bibliography, section C); S. Mowinckel, *W* I, 196-200; C. Westermann, *Praise* (listing at "Introduction to Cultic Poetry"); idem, "Struktur" (listing at "Introduction to Psalms").

COMPLAINT LITURGY (Klageliturgie). Any psalm that involves more than one cycle of complaint to petition; cf. Psalms 31; 69; 89. → Worship Agenda Liturgy.

COMPLAINT OF THE ESCHATOLOGICAL COMMUNITY (Klage der eschatologischen Gemeinde). → Communal Complaint.

COMPLAINT PSALM (Klagepsalm). → Communal Complaint; Individual Complaint.

COMPLAINT (SONG) OF THE INDIVIDUAL (Klage des Einzelnen). → Individual Complaint.

CONFESSION (Bekenntnis). → Confession of Faith; Confession of Sin.

CONFESSION OF FAITH (Glaubensbekenntnis). In a tribal or ethnically defined society usually the whole community shares one or more religious creed(s). There is no need for public confession of faith in order to delimit on religious terms one group over against the other. The only (→) confessional formulas used are those that assert allegiance (→ Commitment) to the personal protective divinity (personal God). After the exile, Israel ceased to be a homogeneous ethnic and political group. Now it became necessary to declare and defend membership in a dispersed, confessional body of believers. Proselytism in principle became possible (cf. Ruth 1:16; Josh 24:15, 18, 21, 24; Ps 87:47). There must have been rituals for public confession of faith (→ Confessional Formula).

E. S. Gerstenberger, "Glaubensbekenntnis," *TRE* XIII, 386-88; P. D. Miller, *They Cried,* 201-3 (Additional Bibliography, section C).

CONFESSION OF GUILT (Schuldbekenntnis). → Confession of Sin.

CONFESSION OF SIN (Sündenbekenntnis). A direct expression of guilt, the most widespread formulation (→ Confessional Formulas) of which is "I have erred" (*ḥāṭā'tî,* Exod 9:27; 10:16; Num 22:34; Deut 1:41; Josh 7:20; Judg 10:10, 15; 1 Sam 7:6; 12:10; 15:30; 2 Sam 12:13; 19:21 [RSV 20]; 24:10, 17; 2 Kgs 18:14; Isa 42:24; Jer 3:25; 8:14; 14:7, 20; Mic 7:9; Pss 41:5 [RSV 4]; 51:6 [RSV 4]; 106:6; Job 7:20; 33:27; Lam 5:16; Dan 9:5, 11,

15; Neh 1:6; 6:13). Confessions are used in both individual and collective contexts and reflect diverse situations and contents (see Knierim).

In Israel and the ancient Near East, as in other cultures, one's guilt was considered a possible cause for all kinds of calamities. Therefore (→) complaints and (→) thanksgivings, in properly diagnosed situations, allow room for a formal confession of sin (see Psalm 51). In accordance with ritual language and practice, it includes only a generalized admission of fault without reference to specific sins (2 Sam 12:13; 24:17; Pss 25:7; 38:6, 19 [RSV 5, 18]; 40:13 [RSV 12]; 69:6 [RSV 5]). If one's guilt is not involved in the suffering experienced, there will be a vehement (→) protestation of innocence instead. After the exile, communal confession played a very important role in synagogue worship (see Psalm 106; Nehemiah 9; Ezra 9; Daniel 9). In earlier times confession of sin was certainly tied to sin offerings (Leviticus 4–5; 1 Kgs 8:31ff.). In both cases referred to, it was intended to pacify the wrath of God and prepare for expiation and new blessings from the Deity.

H. J. Boecker, *Redeformen,* 111-17; K. Galling, "Beichtspiegel"; E. S. Gerstenberger and W. Schrage, *Suffering,* 122-25; R. Knierim, *Sünde,* 20-38, 193-94, 208-10; E. Lipiński, *Liturgie;* P. D. Miller, *They Cried,* 244-61 (Additional Bibliography, section C); R. Pettazoni, *Confessione* (listings at "Introduction to Psalms" and "Introduction to Cultic Poetry").

CONFESSIONAL HYMN (Bekenntnishymne). → Confession of Faith; Hymn of Praise.

CONFESSIONAL PRAYER (Bekenntnisgebet). → Confession of Faith; Petition.

CONFESSIONAL STATEMENT (Bekenntnisaussage). → Confessional Formula; Confession of Faith; Confession of Sin.

CONFIDENCE (Vertrauensäusserung). → Affirmation of Confidence.

CONFIRMATION OF STATUS (Statusfestsetzung). A definition of identity with legal implications, as in Ps 87:5-6. → Authentication; Descent Formula.

CONGRATULATION (Glückwunsch). → Felicitation Formula.

CONGREGATIONAL COMPLAINT (Gemeindeklage). → Communal Complaint.

CONGREGATIONAL PRAYER (Gemeindegebet). → Communal Complaint.

CONGREGATIONAL PSALM OF CONFIDENCE (Gemeindlicher Vertrauenspsalm). → Affirmation of Confidence.

CONTEST (Streitgespräch). → Contestation.

CONTESTATION (Streitgespräch). Psalms of contest seem to reflect an open exchange of hostility between a sufferer and his/her persecutors during a prayer service (cf. Psalms 4; 11; 62). Opponents are challenged face to face to stop their unwarranted attacks. There is hardly enough evidence, however, to postulate a regular court trial within the temple precincts (against H. Schmidt, *Gebet*, 3-6 and passim; L. Delekat, *Asylie*, 154-93 [both in listing at "Introduction to Psalms"]; W. Beyerlin, *Rettung*, 54-61 [listing at "Introduction to Cultic Poetry"]). Rather, contestation takes place in the religious and ritual context of a small-scale worship service (see "Introduction to Cultic Poetry," section 4B). On the communal level we also find situations of challenge to groups or nations not in compliance with God's will; cf. Pss 107:11-12; 114 (mythical opponents); → Yahweh-Kingship Psalms.

W. Brueggemann, *Theology*, 385-99, 407-12 (Additional Bibliography, section C); G. von Rad, *Weisheit in Israel* (Neukirchen: Neukirchener Verlag, 1970) 60-62.

CORROBORATION (Bestätigung). → Formula of Transmission.

COUNTER CURSE (Abwehrfluch). → Curse.

COVENANT REMEMBRANCE (Bundeserinnerung). → Historical Account of Sacred History.

CULTIC CALENDAR. (Kultkalender). A calendar that sets the dates of required petitionary and thanksgiving feasts. For the most part, such calendars emerge from an agricultural economy and connect the changes of the seasons to their appropriate religious rituals. Early texts mention a yearly pilgrimage to a regional shrine, which has seasonal connotations (1 Sam 1:3). Systematization developed later with three yearly "appearances" before Yahweh (Exod 23:14, 17; 34:23), and the dates were more precisely marked (Exod 23:15-16; Deut 16:1-15; Lev 23:23-44). These calendars are lists of commandments, in the imperative tone, directed to the male community. Older Canaanite prototypes give only the names of months and seasons, presupposing the ritual knowledge necessary for each ritual.

M. E. Cohen, *The Cultic Calendars of the Ancient Near East* (Bethesda: CDL Press, 1993); G. Larsson, "Ancient Calendars Indicated in the Old Testament," *JSOT* 54 (1992) 61-76; A. Strobel, "Festrechnung," *BHH* III, 2211-28; S. Talmon, *King, Cult, and Calendar in Ancient Israel* (Jerusalem: Magnes, 1986) 89-139; S. J. de Vries, "Calendar," *IDB* I, 483-88; M. Weippert, "Kalender und Festrechnung," *BRL*, 165-68.

CULTIC DRAMA (Kultdrama). Our textual tradition of religious praying and singing quite often refers to accompanying rituals of various kinds (cf. Pss 5:4, 8 [RSV 3, 7]; 22:26-27 [RSV 25-26]; 24:3, 7; 68:25-26 [RSV 24-25]; 100:4; 116:13, 18-19; 118:27; 132:6-9; 136; etc. This is in line with almost all worship in most human cultures: Words are accompanied by actions, or the other way around — sacred rites need the interpretation of concomitant words (S. Mowinckel). So we have to imagine various rituals, enactments, musical accompaniment for all of the psalms. They are, of course, connected with seasonal feasts and more spontaneous commemorations and festivities, also days of mourning and petitions. Dramatization and ritualization in any case were used more extensively in the ancient world than Christians, notably Protestants, can imagine. We should be wary, however, of theories that try to concentrate all ritual activity in one centralized (Jerusalem) cult or even into one big festival (New Year). The myth-and-ritual school, building on S. Mowinckel, V. Grønbech, et al., postulated an all-pervasive cult-dramatic network in the ancient Near East (cf. J. R. Porter, "Myth and Ritual School," *Dictionary of Biblical Interpretation* [ed. J. H. Hayes; 2 vols.; Nashville: Abingdon, 1999] II, 187-88).

M. P. Graham, ed., *Worship;* R. L. Grimes, *Beginnings*, 53-86, 161-266 (both in Additional Bibliography, section B); S. Mowinckel, *Religion*, 73-80 (listing at "Introduction to Cultic Poetry").

CULTIC FEASTS (Kultfeste; Kultfeiern). → Cultic Drama.

CURSE (Fluch). In antiquity, real curses were used in combination with ritual acts to destroy personal or national enemies and evildoers. Deut 27:15-26 is one biblical example of societal dimension: two groups pronounce covenant injunctions (against the Samaritans? Cf. also Deuteronomy 28; Leviticus 26). In the private realm we find a telling story in Judg 17:2, when a rich women curses an unknown thief. A prime example for curses used in small-group rituals is Psalm 109. R. F. Fortune (*Sorcerers;* listing at "Introduction to Cultic Poetry") describes a South Seas community where cursing is practiced. In the book of Psalms we find the slightly modified (→) imprecation against enemies. Both forms, however, work through magic and/or religious excitation of divine powers.

S. Mowinckel, *PsSt* I, 29-58; *PsSt* V, 82-96; L. Ruppert, "Fluch- und Rachepsalmen," *NBL* II, 685-86; W. Schottroff, "Fluch," *NBL* II, 683-85.

DECLARATION OF CONFIDENCE (Vertrauenserklärung). → Affirmation of Confidence.

DECLARATION OF INNOCENCE (Unschuldserklärung). → Protestation of Innocence.

DECLARATION OF VICTORY (Siegesmeldung). → Victory Song.

DENUNCIATION (Denunzierung). → Accusation.

DERISION OF IDOLS (Verspottung von Götzen). → Polemics against Idols.

DESCRIPTION OF JUBILANCE (Beschreibung des Jubels). → Hymn of Praise.

DESCRIPTION OF PRAYING (Beschreibung des Betens). → Account of Trouble and Salvation; Personal Hymn.

DESCRIPTION OF PROCESSION. Processions of the festive assembly are occasionally mentioned in the Psalms; cf. 68:25-28 (RSV 24-27); 132:6-7; 48:13-14 (RSV 12-13), proof of extensive worship rituals in Israel. → Account of Pilgrimage; Liturgy; Cultic Drama.

DESCRIPTION OF SUFFERING (Beschreibung des Leidens). → Complaint Element.

DESCRIPTION OF THE ENEMY (Feindschilderung). → Complaint Element; Portrayal.

DESCRIPTION OF UNIVERSAL RULE (Darstellung von Weltherrschaft). → Messianic Hymn; Royal Psalm.

DESCRIPTION OF WORSHIP (Beschreibung des Gottesdienstes). → Complaint Element; Hymn of Praise; Cultic Drama.

DIALOGUE AT THE GATE (Dialog am Tor). → Entrance Liturgy.

DIDACTIC POEM (Weisheitsgedicht). → Wisdom Psalm.

DIDACTIC SONG (Lehrlied). → Wisdom Psalm; Instruction.

DIRECT-ADDRESS HYMN (Hymnus in direkter Anrede). According to Crüsemann, a hymnic form directly addressed to Yahweh (e.g., Psalms 8; 104), distinct from the so-called imperative hymn (→ Call to Worship) and (→) hymnic participles. Direct address, according to Crüsemann, is an adaptation from petitionary prayer language, whereas hymn singing was originally designed to enhance the glory of God among the congregation, supposedly without human interests. Yet, since all worship aims at God and worshipers alike, Crüsemann's distinction is artificial. Facing Yahweh and offering praise to him were probably always one mode of liturgical worship in Israel.

F. Crüsemann, *Studien,* 285-94; H. Graf Reventlow, *Gebet,* 139-62; H. H. Rowley, *Worship,* 176-212; C. Westermann, *Praise,* 102-22 (all in listing at "Introduction to Cultic Poetry").

DIRGE (Leichenklage, Leichenlied). In its strict sense "dirge" means funeral lamentation. In the countries of the Near East it is customary to this day to wail over the dead body. Normally, paid women or men do the wailing. Lamentation of larger groups after a military defeat or natural disaster seems to be an adaptation of the private rites. In the OT 2 Sam 1:19-27 and 3:33-34 are two genuine examples of personal lament; the book of Lamentations echoes collective grief. Prophetic invitations of dirge using the characteristic meter of five beats per bicolon are frequent (cf. Am 5:1-3; Ezekiel 19).

K. Budde, "Das hebräische Klagelied," *ZAW* 2 (1882) 1-52; M. E. Cohen, *Lamentations,* vol. I, 11-44 (listing at "Introduction to Lamentations"); H. Jahnow, *Leichenlied,* 90-108; S. N. Kramer, *Lamentation,* 1-6 (listing at "Introduction to Cultic Poetry"). More literature in listing at "Introduction to the Book of Lamentations."

DIVINE ORACLE (Gottesorakel). → Oracle.

DIVINE PROCLAMATION (Gottesverkündigung). → Proclamation.

DIVINE SPEECH (Gottesrede). → Proclamation.

DRAMATIZATION (Dramatisierung). → Cultic Drama.

ENACTMENT OF TRIAL (Inszenierte Gerichtsverhandlung). Some psalms seem to presuppose the presence of enemies in a worshiping community (cf. Psalms 11; 62; etc.; → Contestation). If this was the case, the cultic ritual did offer an extrajuridical chance of defense, by seeking the help of Yahweh, perhaps after an ordeal had taken place. → Cultic Drama.

H. J. Boecker, *Redeformen,* 71-159; H. Schmidt, *Gebet,* 1-6 and passim (both in listing at "Introduction to Psalms").

ENTRANCE LITURGY (Tempeleinlassliturgie). A liturgy of inquiry and response used to determine the admissibility of worshipers to the temple precincts. Presumably all pilgrims, when arriving at the gate of the sacred grounds, had to declare their cultic purity in order not to disturb or frustrate ritual procedures. They would thus shout their query for admission from outside the holy precincts, and a functionary of the temple would answer from within (dialogue at the gate), enumerating the conditions of entry. This pattern of question and answer is mirrored in Psalms 15 and 24 and Isa 33:14-16, which have been used to reconstruct the liturgy itself.

K. Koch, "Tempeleinlassliturgien," 45-60; S. Mowinckel, *Décalogue,* 114-62 (both in listing at Psalm 15).

EPIC ACCOUNT (Epischer Bericht). → Historical Account.

ESCHATOLOGICAL HYMN OF PRAISE (Eschatologisches Loblied). → Messianic Hymn; Hymn of Praise.

EXCLAMATION (Ausruf). Short expression of surprise, joy, or distress, like "How good," "alas," etc. → Festive Shouts; Cheers.

EXHORTATION (Ermahnung, Mahnrede). Within the liturgical genres, the exhortation or admonition carries neither the absolute weight of prophetic or juridical speech nor the rational and scientific air of wisdom discourse. Rather, it is part of worship (→) instruction. On the basis of law and tradition, community leaders holding established offices within the congregation give instruction concerning the right path to be followed by individual members and urge compliance. Examples are Psalms 1, 50, and 95.

B. Lang, "Paränese," *NBL* III, 66-68; N. Lohfink, *Das Hauptgebot* (AnBib 20; Rome: Pontifical Biblical Institute, 1963) 90-97; J. C. McCann, "Psalms" (see Additional Bibliography, section C) 117-28; L. G. Perdue, *Wisdom*, 261-65 (listing at "Introduction to Cultic Poetry").

FELICITATION (Glücklichpreisung). Similar to (→) Beatitude, but mostly in neutral third-person articulation. Extols the blessed state of believers or highly respected members of the community.

FINAL PLEA (Schlussbitte). → Petition.

FINAL PRAISE (Schlusslob). Is Psalm 150, ending the Psalter, a redactional composition without liturgical purposes? It seems to correspond to Psalm 1 enveloping the Psalter (G. Wilson, E. Zenger; etc.). → Hymnic Praise.

HISTORICAL ACCOUNT. Eclectic summary and condensation of Israel's history of salvation and apostasy, as preserved in sacred traditions, e.g., the pentateuchal narrations. Some psalms have focused on this subject and are therefore called "historical psalms" (cf. Psalms 78; 105; 106; 135; 136). Sacred history thus becomes a didactic motif. → Retrospect. The epic account of bygone times is a close parallel to historical retrospects. It works with mythical traditions; cf. Psalms 29; 77; 114.

J. Kühlewein, *Geschichte*, 19-100 (Additional Bibliography, section C); D. Mathias, "Das 'Gottesvolk' in der sicht der geschichtssummarien des Psalters," in *Gottesvolk* (ed. A. Meinhold et al.; Berlin: Evangelische Verlagsanstalt, 1991) 193-208.

HISTORICAL LESSON (Geschichtliches Lehrstück). → Retrospect; Historical Account.

HOMILY (Predigt). → Instruction.

HOMILY OF CONFIDENCE (Vertrauenspredigt). → Instruction; Affirmation of Confidence.

HYMN OF PRAISE. (Hymnus, Loblied). Joyful song of choir or community extolling the greatness and kindness of Yahweh and his dwelling place. Seasonal and ad hoc festivals for the ancient Israelites give ample occasion to get together at holy places. Sacrifices and celebrations extend over several days. The hymns intoned vary in contents: they praise creation and Creator (Psalms 8; 19; 104), and Yahweh's glorious deeds in history

(Psalms 68; 105). They admire Mount Zion, his abode (Psalms 46; 48; 76), and celebrate at his just reign (Psalms 24; 47; 93; 96). Hymn singing always has been a vital part of Jewish-Christian worship services (see "Introduction to Cultic Poetry," section 4D).

F. Crüsemann, *Studien,* 19-154; H. Gunkel and J. Begrich, *Einleitung* § 2 (both in listing at "Introduction to Cultic Poetry"); S. Mowinckel, *W* I, 81-105; P. D. Miller, *They Cried,* 204-23 (Additional Bibliography, section C).

HYMN OF THE INDIVIDUAL (Hymne des Einzelnen). → Personal Hymn.

HYMN TO CREATION (Hymne auf die Schöpfung). → Hymn of Praise.

HYMNIC AFFIRMATION (Hymnische Aussage). → Hymn of Praise.

HYMNIC INSTRUCTION (Hymnische Unterweisung). → Instruction.

HYMNIC INTRODUCTION. Some hymnic texts perhaps served as a kind of introit for worship ceremonies; they were liturgical preparations; cf., e.g., Ps 68:5-7 (RSV 4-6); 147:1 ("Praise Yahweh! Yes, good it is to sing praises to our God; for he is gracious, and a song of praise is fitting!").

HYMNIC NARRATION (Hymnische Erzählung). → Hymn of Praise; Historical Account.

HYMNIC PARTICIPLE (Hymnisches Partizipium). A descriptive phrase that gives honor to the great and salvific deeds of Yahweh in creation and history, found within the body of many (→) hymns of praise (e.g., Psalms 33; 103–104; 135; 145–146; Job 5:9-16; 9:5-10; 12:17-25; 26:7-8). This form is characteristic of liturgical praise beyond the Psalter (Amos 4:13; 5:8; 9:6; Isa 40:22-23, 29; 42:5; 43:17; 45:7; Zech 12:1; 1 Sam 2:6-8); it is common throughout the ancient Near East. → Call to Worship.

See bibliography at Call to Worship. A. Falkenstein and W. von Soden, *SAHG,* 28-49; W. Mayer, *Untersuchungen,* 307-47 (listing at "Introduction to Cultic Poetry").

HYMNIC PRAISE (Hymnischer Preis). → Hymn of Praise.

HYMNIC PRAYER (Hymnisches Gebet). → Hymn of Praise; Petition.

HYMNIC REFRAIN (Hymnischer Kehrreim). In cultic liturgies a lead singer or choir often gives the theme or stanza of a chant and the crowd joins in with shouts, (→) exclamations, or short phrases as choreographed in Pss 118:2-4; 136:1-26 (the *kî* in Psalm 136 does not indicate a reason but marks the exclamation: "yes, his kindness lasts forever": thus Crüsemann, *Studien,* 32-35). Numerous examples of similar refrains can be found in the Psalter (cf. Pss 8:2, 10 [RSV 1, 9]; 46:8, 12 [RSV 7, 11]).

Lines sung by choir or people may become liturgical markers within a (→) worship agenda; cf., e.g., Pss 8:2, 10 (RSV 1, 9); 46:8, 12 (RSV 7, 11); 95:1-2; 99:5, 9; 103:1, 22; → Refrain.

HYMNIC REMEMBRANCE (Hymnische Erinnerung). → Hymn of Praise; Historical Account.

HYMNIC THEME (Hymnenthema). → Hymn of Praise.

IMPEACHMENT (Anklage; Verurteilung). → Accusation.

IMPERATIVE HYMN (Imperativischer Hymnus). → Call to Worship.

IMPLORATION (Flehen). → Petition.

IMPRECATION (Verwünschung, Bitte gegen Feinde). An element in Complaints that asks for elimination of the evil that threatens the suppliant. Functionally, imprecation is thus part of (→) petition. Since evil is always personalized, imprecation is directed against persons ("evildoers, enemies, godless, criminals, beasts," etc.). Demonic features easily enter this picture (Psalms 59; 91). In either imperative or jussive form, the pleas call for the destruction and elimination of the opponents in order to achieve the suppliant's liberation and restoration. Psalms 35, 52, 58, 94, and 109 are examples of enemy psalms that place special emphasis on annihilation of evildoers. Unlike (→) curse, a closely related genre, imprecation rarely addresses enemies themselves (but see Pss 4:3-6 [RSV 2-5]; 11:1; 52:3-7 [RSV 1-5]; 62:4 [RSV 3]). Rather, Yahweh is solicited to do away with the wicked and thus to establish justice. From the point of view of the weak and oppressed, only this way leads to rehabilitation.

H. Birkeland, *Evildoers,* 203-9, 354-76 (listing at "Introduction to Psalms"); E. S. Gerstenberger, "The Enemies in the Psalms: A Challenge to Christian Preaching," *Horizons of Biblical Theology* 4/5 (1982-83) 61-78; O. Keel, *Feinde,* 226-31 (listing at "Introduction to Psalms"); S. Mowinckel, *PsSt* I, 29-58; *PsSt* V, 85-96; idem, *W* II, 44-52.

INDIVIDUAL ADORATION (Anbetung des Einzelnen). → Personal Hymn.

INDIVIDUAL COMPLAINT SONG (Psalm) (Klagelied des Einzelnen). The most frequent type of complaint psalms. About forty texts are preserved in the Psalter (see "Introduction to Cultic Poetry," section 4B). One suffering individual recites this kind of prayer during a worship of the small, familial group (or later on the congregation of Yahweh-believers). Through all its liturgical elements (→ Invocation; Initial Plea; Complaint; Affirmation of Confidence) this complaint moved toward (→) petition. Some scholars therefore call the genre "petitionary prayer" (Kraus, Beyerlin, etc.). Larger congregations used very similar forms of (→) communal complaint.

A. Aejmelaeus, *The Traditional Prayer in the Psalms* (BZAW 157; Berlin: de Gruyter, 1986) 85-108; E. S. Gerstenberger, *Mensch*, 118-60 (listing at "Introduction to Cultic Poetry"); H. Gunkel and J. Begrich, *Einleitung* §6 (listing at "Introduction to Cultic Poetry," Eng. at Additional Bibliography, section C); P. D. Miller, *They Cried*, 55-134 (Additional Bibliography, section C); S. Mowinckel, *W* II, 1-25; H. Graf Reventlow, *Gebet*, 163-89 (listings at "Introduction to Cultic Poetry").

INDIVIDUAL THANKSGIVING (Individuelle Danksagung). → Thanksgiving Song.

INITIAL PLEA (Einleitende Bitte; Bitte). That part of the (→) invocation in (→) complaint songs in which the individual solicits the attention of the Deity and asks to be admitted to his or her presence (Pss 5:2-3 [RSV 1-2]; 17:1; 39:13 [RSV 12]; 55:2 [RSV 1; 143:1). This form element of (→) personal prayer corresponds to general rules of courtesy in interhuman relations, especially as far as ritualized (→) petition and court etiquette are concerned. The imperatives of initial plea ("hear," "attend," "listen," "heed"; see Pss 61:2 [RSV 1]; 102:2-3 [RSV 1-2]; 130:1-2) characteristically occur in pairs or clusters of three and four in order to heighten emphasis. They may anticipate the main contents of the petitionary prayer (Pss 4:2 [RSV 1]; 31:3 [RSV 2]; 54:3-4 [RSV 1-2]; 141:1). Motive clauses or deictic particles may underline the introductory plea (Pss 12:2 [RSV 1]; 69:2 [RSV 1]; 86:1), frequently introducing the (→) complaint element proper.

I. Lande, *Formelhafte Wendungen der Umgangssprache im Alten Testament* (Leiden: Brill, 1949) 2-38; E. S. Gerstenberger, *Mensch*, 27-37, 119-28 (listing at "Introduction to Cultic Poetry").

INSTRUCTION (Unterweisung). A discourse that gives guidance to groups or individuals in the context of communal worship. Life situations that require educative discourse are common at all social levels. They probably have their origin in family education. Basically, such instruction presupposes a relationship of father to son, master to pupil, initiated to uninformed, official to subordinate, messenger to audience. In the Psalms most instructions stem from the context of early Jewish congregational life (cf. Psalms 1; 39; 49; 53; 90; 119). Older (→) thanksgiving and (→) complaint songs contain instructional, narrative elements (→ Account of Trouble and Salvation). In later communal worship, however, due to changed social conditions (see "Introduction to Psalms," section 2), the teaching responsibilities of parochial leaders produced typical homiletic forms of speech with descriptive, meditative, and exhortative overtones, often focusing on the "Word of God" or his "marvelous deeds" (Psalms 34; 37; 50; 52; 58; 78; 95; 105). This sermonizing and instructional discourse became part and parcel of synagogal and Christian worship. Thus instructional discourses preserved in the Psalter may definitely have educational, ethical perspectives.

E. S. Gerstenberger, *Wesen und Herkunft des 'apodiktischen' Rechts im Alten Testament* (WMANT 20; Neukirchen: Neukirchener Verlag, 1965) 110-30; idem, "Predigt," *TRE* XXVII, 231-35; J. C. McCann, "Psalms" (Additional Bibliography, section C); G. von Rad, "Levitical Preaching" (listing at "Introduction to Psalms").

INSTRUCTION OF COMMUNITY (Unterweisung der Gemeinde). → Instruction.

INSTRUCTION TO GIVE THANKS (Anweisung zum Danken). → Instruction.

INSTRUCTIONAL TREATISE (Belehrung). → Instruction.

INTERCESSION (Fürbitte). If one person pleads the case of other persons we call this procedure "intercession." Moses and Jeremiah are pictured as outstanding interceders (Exod 32:11-13; Num 12:11-13; Jer 14:11-14). This role became proverbial for Moses and Samuel (Jer 15:1). The prayers spoken to God are intercessions as well. They contain (→) invocation and (→) petition. Since the psalms do not narrate interceding procedure (but cf. Gen 18:16-33; Exod 32:7-14; Num 12:11-14; Jer 14:7-14; Am 7:1-6; etc.), we have to evaluate prayer texts as to their interceding quality (cf. Psalms 20; 21). Apparently, the congregation may assume this task, often considered a typical prophetic function.

R. Albertz, "Gebet," *TRE* XII, 34-42; P. D. Miller, *They Cried,* 262-80 (listing at Additional Bibliography, section C); J. Scharbert, "Fürbitte," *NBL* I, 712-13; J. G. Williams, "Comedy, Irony, Intercession," *Semeia* 7 (1977) 135-45.

INTRODUCTORY HYMN (Einführungshymne). → Hymnic Introduction.

INTROIT HYMN (Einführungshymne). → Entrance Liturgy; Hymnic Introduction.

INVECTIVE (Anschuldigung). → Accusation.

INVITATION TO GIVE THANKS (Einladung zum Danken). → Call to Worship.

INVITATION TO THE THRONE (Einladung zur Thronbesteigung). Divine pronouncement to his elected candidate to take over royal powers; in the case of Psalm 110 it is a messianic figure (see also Psalm 2).

H. Frankfort, *Kingship,* 243-48; E. Lipiński, *Royauté* (both in "Introduction to Cultic Poetry").

INVOCATION (Anrufung). The vocative address to the Deity that is the customary opening of (→) complaint and (→) thanksgiving songs, both in ancient Israel and in other cultures (Heiler, Mayer, Reichard). OT prayers appeal mostly to Yahweh (later interpreted as Greek *Kyrios,* "Lord"; see Pss 3:2 [RSV 1]; 5:2-4 [RSV 1-3]; 6:2 [RSV 1]; 27:1; 130:1; 141:1;

142:2 [RSV 1]; Gen 24:12; Jer 20:7) or Elohim (the personal God; see Pss 22:2-3 [RSV 1-2]; 51:3 [RSV 1]; 54:3-4 [RSV 1-2]; 61:2 [RSV 1]; 64:2 [RSV 1]; 69:2 [RSV 1]; 79:1; 83:2 [RSV 1]; l09:1), sometimes using hymnic epithets (27:1; 80:2 [RSV 1]; 88:2 [RSV 1]; 90:1). Such appellation originated in human discourse of encounter and interaction (Gerstenberger, *Mensch*). It is frequently linked with or even inserted in other introductory speech forms such as the (→) initial plea (17:1; 54:3-4 [RSV 1-2]; 61:2 [RSV 1]), direct (→) petition (12:2 [RSV 1]; 35:1; 59:2 [RSV 1]), (→) affirmation of confidence (7:2a [RSV la]; 31:2a [RSV la]; 63:2 [RSV 1]), (→) complaint (22:2-3 [RSV 1-2]; 69:2 [RSV 1]; 74:1), and (→) praise (30:2 [RSV 1]; 84:2 [RSV 1]). The purpose of invocation as a whole, then, is to establish contact between suppliant and Deity within a given agenda of worship or cultic adoration.

E. S. Gerstenberger, *Mensch*, 21-25, 96-98; H. Gunkel and J. Begrich, *Einleitung*, 212-14; F. Heiler, *Prayer*, 58-59 and passim; W. Mayer, *Untersuchungen*, 211-19 (all in listing at "Introduction to Cultic Poetry"; Gunkel-Begrich Eng. at Additional Bibliography, section C); G. Reichard, *Prayer* (listing at "Introduction to Psalms"); H. Vorländer, *Mein Gott*, 232-35 (listing at "Introduction to Cultic Poetry").

KINGSHIP SONG (HYMN) (Königshymne). → Yahweh-Kingship Psalm.

LAMENTATION (Klagelied; Trauergesang). → Complaint Song; Dirge.

LAUDATION (Laudatio). Eulogy of another person or group (nation); cf. Ps 87:4. → Felicitation; Beatitude.

LITURGICAL INSTRUCTION (Gottesdienstliche Unterweisung). → Instruction.

LITURGICAL PRAYER (Liturgisches Gebet). Any type of prayer or petition predominantly used in extensive congregational worships (see Psalm 86). → Worship Agenda.

LITURGICAL SERMON (Liturgische Predigt). → Instruction.

LITURGY (Liturgie). Generally — and somewhat vaguely — any text used in worship that is recited by two or more voices in a responsive fashion (→ Response of Community). Liturgy is the ritual followed by smaller or larger religious groups in their common worship. Since there has never been a uniform divine service in Israel, but rather differentiated offices and procedures in familial, village, urban, and diaspora contexts (cf. "Introduction to Psalms," section 2), we cannot expect one standard liturgy only. The ordeal for a woman accused of infidelity (Num 5:12-28) is a long way from a quasi-synagogal Torah meeting (Nehemiah 8), the installation of a high priest (cf. Leviticus 8–9), dedication of the temple (1 Kings 8), preparation for battle (cf. Deuteronomy 20; Judg 6:36–7:8), victory celebrations (cf. Judges 5; Psalm 68), public penitence (cf. Joel 1–2), and other worshiping occasions. We should distinguish liturgies also by the religious bodies performing them, including the cultic personnel. Relevant ancient Near Eastern texts may greatly elucidate the respective ritual situations in Israel.

In so-called prophetic liturgies (e.g., Jeremiah 14; Joel 1–2; Psalms 12; 95), one of the liturgical parts was supposedly spoken by a "cultic prophet," though there is little evidence for such an OT office (cf. the interpretation of Psalm 12). No doubt liturgical texts are preserved in much of the prophetic and poetic writings of the OT. We probably do not have complete liturgies, however, but only parts, extracts, fragments, or summaries of liturgical texts. Nevertheless, the rich heritage of Israelite and early Jewish worship is visible in the OT and has greatly influenced subsequent patterns of divine service through Judaism and Christianity until today.

R. L. Grimes, *Beginnings,* 1-17, 161-266 (Additional Bibliography, section B); H. Gunkel and J. Begrich, *Einleitung,* 407-15 (listing at "Introduction to Cultic Poetry"); J. Jeremias, *Kultprophetie,* 110-25; and A. Johnson, *Prophet,* 92-95, 215-36 (both in listing at "Introduction to Psalms"); M. Klinghardt, "Formularies," 1-52; and S. M. Maul, *Zukunftsbewältigung,* 37-113 (both in Additional Bibliography, section B); S. Mowinckel, *Religion,* 98-121 (listing at "Introduction to Cultic Poetry").

LITURGY OF ADMISSION (Tempeleinlassliturgie). → Entrance Liturgy.

LOVE SONG (Liebeslied). → R. Murphy, *Wisdom Literature* (FOTL XIII; Grand Rapids: Eerdmans, 1981) 177.

MEDITATION (Meditation). Meditation is certainly a term influenced by long Western and Eastern traditions of mysticism. In the OT meditative practices are barely known (but cf. the concentration on Torah in Ps 1:2). We find, however, reflections upon the suppliant's own state (see Pss 42:6, 12 [RSV 5, 11]; 43:5 [RSV 4]) as well as thoughts about the state of humankind and the world (see Psalms 39; 49; 90), which may well be called, in a broader sense, meditation. Sometimes they use prayer style (see 77:6-11). Meditations were apparently part of the liturgical agenda of postexilic congregations, even if they were quite personal in tone and outlook; see Psalm 71. They served to clarify the position of the believer and community over against God and the world.

MEDITATION PRAYER (Meditationsgebet). → Meditation.

MEDITATIVE HYMN (Meditative Hymne). → Meditation.

MESSIANIC HYMN (Messianische Hymne). A (→) royal psalm featuring the restoration of the monarchy. After the Judean state vanished in 587 B.C.E., many royal psalms continued to be used in worship with the expectation that the monarchy would be restored. Also, new songs in the same vein were composed. It is very difficult for us to distinguish between reinterpreted old texts and new messianic compositions. Are, e.g., Psalms 2, 18, 45, 72, and 110 pre- or postexilic? A certain exuberance and the astonishingly universalistic approach seem to indicate a late origin. At any rate, the central role of the king as Yahweh's vice-regent over all the earth may be the main criterion of a messianic understanding of the text. The expectation of such a king must have been vivid in early Jewish communities and was expressed in worship. The messianic hymn blends with the (→) eschatological hymn of praise.

J. Becker, "Die kollektive Deutung der Königspsalmen," *Theologie und Philosophie* 52 (1977) 561-78; S. Mowinckel, *He That Cometh* (tr. G. W. Anderson; New York: Abingdon, 1955) 155-86.

MESSIANIC PROMISE (Messiasverheissung). → Messianic Hymn; Oracle of Salvation.

MESSIANIC THANKSGIVING SONG (Messianisches Danklied). → Messianic Hymn.

MONOTHEISTIC FORMULA (Monotheismusformel). → Formula of Incomparability.

MOURNING AGENDA (Traueragende). Mourning or lamenting took place in ancient societies whenever death and destruction had hit a community. The texts preserved in the OT dealing with these occasions are of different types. First, they have a psalm structure with hymnic, plaintive, and petitionary elements; see Psalms 44; 74; 89. Second, they show a more literary character, describing defeat and distress in a highly artistic fashion, like Lamentations 1-5. In this case, there may occur a stereotyped opening cry ("alas"), and sparse petition at the end of a unit. Apparently, such texts have been used in commemorative services accompanying and stimulating mourning activities. They were probably recited to the congregation.

See listings at "Introduction to the Book of Lamentations."

MYTHICAL ACCOUNT (Mythische Darstellung). Looking back at primordial events citations of mythical events have been instrumental in construing present reality; see Psalms 77; 114. A parallel effort and genre is (→) historical account.

O. Kaiser, *Bedeutung,* 140-52 (Additional Bibliography, section B); C. Petersen, *Mythos im Alten Testament* (BZAW 157; Berlin: de Gruyter, 1982) 57-261.

NARRATION OF YAHWEH'S HELP (Bericht von Jahwehs Hilfe). → Account of Trouble and Salvation.

NEGATIVE CONFESSION (Negatives Schuldbekenntnis). → Confession of Sin.

OPENING OF INSTRUCTION (Lehreröffnungsformel). → Call to Attention (Formula).

ORACLE (Orakel). Almost any speech of God (→ Proclamation) quoted verbatim (first-person singular discourse) in the Scriptures, allegedly given to some woman or man to be communicated to the congregation. According to Greek custom oracles were usually requested from the deity. In the OT as well as in ancient Near Eastern texts (e.g., Mari prophecies) we find solicited as well as unsolicited divine communications to clergy or to laypeople; cf. Numbers 22–24; 1 Sam 23:9-12; Am 7:1-15; Pss 75:3-4 [RSV 2-3]; 89:20-38 [RSV 19-37]; 95:8-11; etc.

K. Koenen, *Gottesworte* (Additional Bibliography, section C); H. Spieckermann, "Rede Gottes und Wort Gottes in den Psalmen," in *Neue Wege der Psalmenforschung* (ed. K. Seybold, et al.; Freiburg: Herder, 1994) 157-73; S. R. A. Starbuck, *Court Oracles* (Additional Bibliography, section C).

ORACLE OF SALVATION (Priesterliches Heilsorakel). An assurance of divine grace, expressed formally by a priest or other officiant in Israelite worship. The existence of such a liturgical practice has become a matter of debate in OT scholarship. J. Begrich postulated this form (usually initiated by the formula "do not fear"; → Assurance Formula), principally on the strength of its occurrences in Second Isaiah (Isa 41:14; 43:1; 44:2; etc.; accepted by Gunkel, Westermann, Kraus, Schoors, et al.). R. Kilian has contested the existence of such a form in the agenda of individual complaint. Frequent usage of the formula, however, would also indicate fixed cultic habits, and individual complaint must be seen in its communal setting, as Kilian himself demands. Consequently, Ps 35:3 asks for a divine response to be articulated in the worship situation (cf. also the different types of salvation oracles in Pss 12:6 [RSV 5]; 91:2-8, 9-13; 121:34). Salvation oracles, then, do not reflect a psychological change from distress to exuberant joy, but they can be regarded as potential ingredients of petitionary liturgy, similar to the "assurance of grace" or "words of assurance" following confession in Christian worship.

J. Begrich, "Heilsorakel" (listing at "Introduction to Cultic Poetry"); K. Engelken, "Orakel," *NBL* III, 46-49; R. Kilian, "Heilsorakel" (listing at "Introduction to Psalms"); P. D. Miller, *They Cried,* 135-77 (Additional Bibliography, section C); T. W. Overholt, *Channels of Prophecy* (Minneapolis: Fortress, 1989); A. Schoors, *God,* 32-175 (listing at "Introduction to Cultic Poetry").

PERSONAL HYMN (Persönliches Loblied). Although the (→) hymn of praise also may have been used in small-group worship services, some psalms were especially composed to be sung by one individual person (see Pss 8:3-9 [RSV 2-8]; 77:12-16 [RSV 11-15]; 103:1-5; 104:31-35). One of the characteristics is the direct-address style (Crüsemann). Related is the (→) thanksgiving of the individual.

F. Crüsemann, *Studien,* 285-306 (listing at "Introduction to Cultic Poetry"); P. D. Miller, *They Cried,* 178-203, 233-43 (Additional Bibliography, section C).

PERSONAL LAMENT (Persönliche Klage). → Dirge.

PERSONAL PRAISE (Persönliches Lob). → Personal Hymn.

PERSONAL PRAYER (Persönliches Gebet). → Individual Complaint Song.

PERSONAL THANKSGIVING (Persönliches Danklied). → Thanksgiving Song.

PERSONALIZED ACCOUNT (Persönlicher Bericht). → Personal Hymn.

PETITION (Bitte). The central element of all (→) complaints, in which the suppliant asks for divine help. It is usually formulated in the imperative, but the various "wish" forms (jussive, imperfect, cohortative) seem to be equivalent (against Gunkel and Begrich). Yahweh is asked to intervene in favor of his client or people (Pss 3:8 [RSV 7]; 5:9 [RSV 8]; 7:7 [RSV 6]; 22:20-22 [RSV 19-21]; 31:16-17 [RSV 15-16]; 38:22-23 [RSV 21-22]; 44:27 [RSV 26]; 51:9-14 [RSV 7-l2]; 59:2-3 [RSV 1-2]; 69:14-19 [RSV 13-18]; 74:18-23; 79:8-9; 80:4, 8, 15 [RSV 3, 7, 14]; 85:5, 8 [RSV 4, 7]; 89:48, 51 [RSV 47, 50]; 90:13-16; 109:26; 143:7-l0). The language is direct, strong, poetic, and liturgical. There are no biographical or unique petitions but general pleas to be saved, healed, or restored that have accommodated generations of suppliants. All other elements of complaint (→ Invocation; Affirmation of Confidence; Complaint Element) support the petition, the complementary element of which is the (→) imprecation.

A. Aejmelaeus, *Prayer,* 15-84 (listing at → Individual Complaint Song); E. S. Gerstenberger, *Mensch,* 77-83; W. Mayer, *Untersuchungen,* 210-90 (listing at "Introduction to Cultic Poetry").

PILGRIM(AGE) SONG (Pilgerlied). → Songs of Ascents.

PLAINTIVE ANSWER (Klagende Antwort). → Response of Community.

PLAINTIVE PETITION (Klagende Bitte). → Petition; Complaint Element.

PLEA (Bitte, Ersuchen). → Petition.

PLEA FOR ATTENTION AND MERCY (Bitte um Gehör und Gnade). → Initial Plea.

PLEA FOR AUDIENCE (Bitte um Gehör). → Initial Plea.

PLEDGE OF ALLEGIANCE (Verpflichtung). → Commitment.

POLEMICS AGAINST IDOLS (Götzenpolemik). Extant principally in Second Isaiah (see Isa 40:12-25; 44:9-20) the genre seems to be an offshoot of
exilic-postexilic controversies in pluralistic Babylonian and Persian societies about the power and authenticity of Israel's God. In blatant contrast
to actual political circumstances the Yahweh community claims supreme
authority for their own Deity, deriding the gods of the world powers as insignificant nothings. In the Psalter this attitude is partly reflected in (→)
Yahweh-kingship hymns and in rare attacks on the "other gods" (see
Psalms 82; 115; 135). Prophetic books contain oracles against foreign nations that possibly imply attacks on their gods (cf. Isaiah 13–23; Jeremiah
46–51; Ezekiel 25–32).

    H. D. Preuss, *Verspottung,* 248-53 (listing at Psalm 115).

PORTRAIT OF RIGHTEOUS (CONFESSOR) (Portrait des Gerechten/Bekenners). →
Portrayal.

PORTRAIT OF UNJUST (WICKED; GODLESS) (Portrait des Ungerechten/Bösen/
Gottlosen). → Portrayal.

PORTRAYAL (Portraitierung). Exemplary descriptions of pious and righteous
members of the Yahweh congregation or typical profiles of outcasts have
certainly had an important role in educational discourses of many cultures and religions. Based partly on Greek models, they are known in NT
contexts as "catalogues of vices and virtues." In OT wisdom literature
and psalms the genre has been taken up most of all in instructional and
complaint contexts; see Psalms 1; 9/10; 73; 94; 119; etc. Besides describing stereotyped good or bad qualities of the model and anti-model, the
wicked are often quoted with their hideously godless talk: "Yahweh does
not see; the God of Jacob does not perceive" (Ps 94:7); "In the pride of
their countenance the wicked say, 'God will not seek it out'; all their
thoughts are, 'There is no God'" (10:4).

    W. Brueggemann, *Theology* (Additional Bibliography, section C),
e.g., 135-39, 444-46, 450-91; G. Fohrer, "The Righteous Man in Job 31,"
in *Essays in Old Testament Ethics* (*Fest.* J. P. Hyatt; ed. J. L. Crenshaw
and J. T. Willis; New York: Ktav, 1974) 1-22; A. Heschel, *Who Is Man?*
(Stanford: Stanford University Press, 1966).

PRAISE (Lobpreis). → Hymn of Praise.

PRAISE FROM BELOW (Lob aus der Tiefe). Notions of human inferiority frequently mingle into hymnic adoration (see Psalm 113). More astonishing
is that sometimes the psalmic tradition consciously uses hymnic elements
even in complaint psalms and communal laments. The peak of this development seems to be hymnic praise sung against death and destruction

(see Jonah 2; Dan 3:21-25; and the apocryphal hymns for this occasion: Prayer of Azariah, Song of the Three Jews). A. Jacobs, *Es ist dunkel — aber ich singe* (Mettingen: Brasilienkunde Verlag, 1986); P. Suess, *Do grito à canção* (São Paulo: Paulinas, 1983); German tr.: *Vom Geschrei zum Gesang* (Wuppertal: Jugenddienst Verlag, 1985).

PRAISE OF WISDOM (Lob der Weisheit). → Hymn of Praise; Wisdom Psalm.

PRAISE OF YAHWEH (Preis Jahwes). → Hymn of Praise.

PRAYER (Gebet). → Individual Complaint; Communal Complaint.

PRAYER OF CONFIDENCE (Vertrauens-Gebet). → Affirmation of Confidence.

PRIESTLY ANSWER (Priesterbescheid). → Oracle of Salvation.

PROCLAMATION (Verkündigung). Much of the OT material claims to be the direct word of Yahweh, communicated to Moses (e.g., the books of Exodus through Deuteronomy) or by mediation of prophets. Even the Psalter contains a number of passages clad in the first person of Yahweh, speaking directly to Israel or its king, to other deities or to the nations at large (cf. Pss 2:6-9; 46:11 [RSV 10]; 50:5, 7-23; 60:8-10 [RSV 6-8]; 75:3-4 [RSV 2-3]; 81:7-17 [RSV 6-16]; 82:2-7; 87:6; 89:21-38 [RSV 20-37]; 91:14-16; 105:11, 15; 110:1, 2, 4; 132:11-12, 14-18). Obviously, the community at the time did not expect to hear Yahweh's voice directly, but mediated by functionaries (cf. Deut 5:23-27), probably within different worship services. Understanding the phenomenon of God's proclamation we therefore easily come to investigate liturgical and homiletical forms of communication. The relevant passages in the Psalter, consequently, are models of homilies (→ Instruction) formed in exilic and postexilic congregational worship services (see, e.g., interpretations of Psalms 50; 62; 75; 91; 110; 127).

E. S. Gerstenberger, "Predigt," *TRE* XXVII, 231-35; H. Graf Reventlow, *Gebot und Predigt im Dekalog* (Gütersloh: G. Mohn, 1962); E. W. Nicholson, *Preaching to the Exiles* (Oxford: Oxford University Press, 1970).

PROCLAMATION OF YAHWEH'S REIGN (Verkündigung der Jahwe-Herrschaft). → Proclamation.

PROHIBITION, PROHIBITIVE (Verbot, Prohibitiv). Human social life on all levels of organization uses negative sanctions to ward off danger or damage from the spiritual, moral, or material goods of the group. The speech patterns used are the prohibitive forms of language, as known best from the Decalogue. There is a long history of the genre to be reconstructed from OT and ancient Near Eastern legal and sapiential texts: from family and

531

clan norms to state decrees and religious commandments (see R. Murphy, *Wisdom Literature* [FOTL XIII; Grand Rapids: Eerdmans, 1981] 180). Educational processes seem to be the original matrix of the form.

E. S. Gerstenberger, *Wesen und Herkunft des 'apodiktischen' Rechts* (WMANT 20; Neukirchen: Neukirchener Verlag, 1965) 42-88, 110-30; idem, "Covenant and Commandment," *JBL* 84 (1965) 38-51; idem, "'He/They Shall Be Put to Death,'" *Ex Auditu* 11 (1995) 43-61; F.-L. Hossfeld, *Der Dekalog* (Göttingen: Vandenhoeck & Ruprecht, 1982) 262-79.

PROPHETIC LITURGY (Prophetische Liturgie). → Liturgy.

PROTESTATION OF INNOCENCE (Unschuldserklärung). The formulaic, ritual self-defense of one who has been falsely accused. The defense can be simple and direct: "I have not committed X" or "I am innocent and without blame" (Job 9:21; 1 Sam 12:3-5). Protest is often couched in the more emphatic form of a conditional oath: "If I have done X, may I be punished" (Ps 7:4-6 [RSV 3-5]; Job 31; → Vow). Such self-condemnation would immediately come true in case of perjury, thus proving on the spot the suppliant's treachery (cf. the ritual in Num 5:11-28). Protestation of innocence may thus become part of a (→) complaint service, if the question of one's guilt has not been satisfactorily resolved beforehand (Psalms 7; 17; 26). Communal variations include Ps 44:18-23 (RSV 17-22), which at the same time contains violent accusations against Yahweh. In the ancient Near East the genre is known from different literary and ritual contexts (see the Egyptian Book of the Dead, ch. 125, confession before the netherworld judges; Surpu II; etc.), including simple petitionary prayer (Gerstenberger, *Mensch,* 102ff.).

E. S. Gerstenberger, *Mensch,* 102-4, 130-32; H. Gunkel and J. Begrich, *Einleitung,* § 6 no. 26 (both in listing at "Introduction to Cultic Poetry"); K. Galling, "Beichtspiegel"; H. Schmidt, *Gebet,* 2-6 and passim (both in listing at "Introduction to Psalms").

PROVERB (Sprichwort). → R. Murphy, *Wisdom Literature* (FOTL XIII; Grand Rapids: Eerdmans, 1981) 180.

PROVERBIAL STATEMENT (Sprichwörtliche Redensart). → Proverb.

PSALM OF CONFIDENCE (Vertrauenspsalm). → Song of Confidence.

PSALM OF CONTEST (Streitpsalm). → Contestation.

PSALM OF SICKNESS (Krankheitspsalm). → Individual Complaint Song.

PSALM (SONG) OF YAHWEH'S KINGSHIP (Thronbesteigungspsalmen; Jahwe-König-Lieder). → Yahweh-Kingship Song (Psalm).

PSALMS OF ASCENTS (Wallfahrtspsalmen). → Songs of Ascents.

REFLECTION (Meditation). → Meditation; Wisdom Psalm.

REFLECTION ON PRAISING (Meditation über das Lob). → Meditation; Hymn of Praise.

REFRAIN (Kehrvers, Refrain). As a rule, the refrains in our psalms reflect (→) responses of the congregation or choirs in the course of a common worship; cf., e.g., Ps 99:9. Other refrains belong in the area of individual ceremony, emphasizing the importance of certain statements (cf. Psalms 42/43). Refrains neatly structure the liturgical agenda.
     W. G. E. Watson, *Poetry,* 295-99 and passim (listing at "Introduction to Cultic Poetry").

REPORT OF ELECTION (Bericht von Erwählung). Election and covenant for the people are sometimes mentioned in the Psalms, but rarely narrated (cf. Pss 50:5; 95:8-11; 78:5; 105:8-12; 135:4; etc.). On a personal basis, individual complaints presuppose a favorable action of God to help the suppliant. → Account of Trouble and Salvation. The election of a dynasty constitutes a parallel tradition.
     D. J. McCarthy, *Treaty and Covenant* (AnBib 21; Rome: Pontifical Biblical Institute, 1963) 80-95 and passim; T. Veijola, *Verheissung,* 60-69, 117-43 (listing at Psalm 89).

REPORT OF THEOPHANY (Theophaniebericht). The account of Yahweh's coming, accompanied by an upheaval of nature, in order to rule and judge peoples. The report reflects an ancient Israelite religious or military theme and was probably standardized to serve cultic ends (Jeremias, *Theophanie,* 150-64). We find traces of this genre in a great many psalms (Psalms 18; 50; 68; 77; 97; 114; Habakkuk 3). Its original setting was perhaps the preparation for holy war (ibid.), but in psalmic texts it was incorporated into worship services of praise and petition.
     J. Jeremias, *Theophanie,* 7-55 and passim (listing at Psalm 18).

REPORT OF TRIAL (Verhandlungsbericht). The idea of Yahweh judging all the world is voiced in several psalms (see 96:13; 98:9). Some more details are elaborated, e.g., in Psalms 12; 50; 82, which amount to a very fragmentary trial report. God exercises his supreme juridical powers (→ Yahweh-Kingship Psalm).
     A. Gamper, *Gott,* 101-41, 216-20 (Additional Bibliography, section B); E. Zenger, *Ein Gott der Rache?* (Freiburg: Herder, 1994) 88-108; Eng.: *A God of Vengeance?* (Louisville: Westminster John Knox, 1996).

REQUEST FOR DIVINE ORIENTATION (Bitte um göttliche Führung). Arises from special impasses and uncertainties in everyday life (cf. Lev 24:10-16; Num 15:32-36). These and other texts very likely presuppose the existence of Hebrew Scriptures, which may be consulted in questions of orientation; see Ps 85:9 (RSV 8). In earlier times people would have relied on divine (→) oracles.

RESPONSE OF COMMUNITY (Antwort der Gemeinde). The congregation's affirmative response to words said or sung by officiants or choirs. Group worship in all cultures normally functions responsively, with the officiants or choirs reciting a song and the congregation joining with affirmative responses. For example, Asaph and his brethren sing hymns (1 Chr 16:7-36a), and "all the people respond 'Amen!' and 'Praise be to Yahweh!'" (v. 36b). Other short liturgical shouts attributed to the community include "his mercy lasts forever" (Pss 100:5a; 106:1a; 107:1a; 118:1a, 29; 135:3a; 136:1a). Moreover, all first-person plural refrains may be attributed to the community (e.g., 8:2, 10 [RSV 1, 9]; 46:8, 12 [RSV 7, 11]). This dialogic structure has been continued in Jewish and Christian worship.

    I. Elbogen, *Gottesdienst,* 494-97 (listing at "Introduction to Cultic Poetry").

RETROSPECT (Rückblick). Looking back into the past in worship has different functions. From history the Yahweh faithful learn that their God once had been favorable to his people (cf. Pss 22:5-6 [RSV 4-5]; 44:2-9 [RSV 1-8]). They also are conscious of the "sins of the fathers," the rebelliousness of past generations (cf. Psalms 78; 106; etc.). Thus the retrospect generates hope, in that it may serve as a positive reminder to God (cf. Psalms 44; 89; → Historical Account), and at the same time it is a continuing burden on the soul of the believers, which has to be coped with in worship, i.e., by (→) confession of guilt and penitence rituals.

RIDICULE (Verspottung). → Contestation.

ROYAL PSALM (Königslied, Königspsalm). There were certainly many rituals connected with the royal court in Israel and Judah, as analogously can be observed at the level of "government" or "heads of state" everywhere in the world. Still one should be cautious in defining specific royal prayers or psalms. As a rule, psalm texts of that realm derived from popular or sacral genres (see "Introduction to Cultic Poetry," section 4E).

    H. Gunkel and J. Begrich, *Einleitung,* §5 (listing at "Introduction to Psalms"; Eng. at Additional Bibliography, section C).

ROYAL VICTORY HYMN (Königliches Siegeslied). → Victory Song.

SALVATION ORACLE (Heilsorakel). → Oracle of Salvation.

SAYING (Redensart). → Proverb.

SELF-DEDICATION (Selbsthingabe). → Commitment.

SELF-PRESENTATION (Selbstdarstellung). → Commitment.

SENTENCE (Urteil). → Accusation.

SERMON (Predigt). → Instruction (Homily).

SONG OF CONFIDENCE (Vertrauenslied). A subgenre of the (→) individual complaint song applied by Gunkel and Begrich (*Einleitung,* 254 n. 10) to Psalms 4; 11; 16; 23; 27:1-6; 62; 131. In fact, (→) affirmation of confidence constitutes an integral and higly important part of the complaint. If the text divisions of the OT Psalter are correct, at least some of the indicated songs of confidence formed independent liturgical units to be used in various types of worship services in Israel (cf. Psalms 16; 23; 62; 131).
See bibliography at AFFIRMATION OF CONFIDENCE. H. Gunkel and J. Begrich, *Einleitung,* 254-56 (listing at "Introduction to Cultic Poetry"; Eng. at Additional Bibliography, section C).

SONGS OF ASCENTS (Wallfahrtslieder). Psalms 120–134 are a distinct group of songs not by their individual forms and structures, which vary considerably (see the interpretation of the texts) but because of their identical (→) superscriptions and probably because of their common use during pilgrimages to Jerusalem. Motifs of wandering, protective blessings, and approaching and lauding the Holy City are prominent in these songs and are the reason for the users and compilers to integrate given psalms into the collection. → Account of Pilgrimage.
See listings at Psalm 120.

SPEECH OF GOD (Gottesrede). → Proclamation.

SUBSCRIPTION (COLOPHON) (Unterschrift; Kolophon). A concluding scribal remark at the end of a text. The Psalter certainly passed through long periods and different stages of redactional compilation (see "Introduction to Psalms"; "Introduction to the Book of Lamentations"). (→) Superscriptions are vestiges of this process. Some distinct subscriptions are extant, too, notably Ps 72:20: "The prayers of David son of Jesse are ended." Another colophon may be hidden in 148:14.
H. Hunger, *Babylonische und assyrische Kolophone* (Neukirchen: Neukirchener Verlag, 1968).

SUMMONS TO ACKNOWLEDGE GOD'S POWER (Aufforderung zur Anerkennung von Gottes Macht). → Call to Worship.

SUMMONS TO PEOPLES (Aufforderung an die Völker). → Call to Worship.

SUMMONS TO PRAISE (Aufforderung zum Lob). → Call to Worship.

SUMMONS TO WORSHIP (Aufforderung zum Gottesdienst). → Call to Worship.

SUPERSCRIPTION (Überschrift). The statements prefixed to the individual psalms, basically as literary accretions to older prayers. The scribes or collectors wanted to indicate the nature, authorship, and use of the psalm. Consequently they listed (1) musical-technical annotations (e.g., "to the choirmaster," "on stringed instruments," "according to the tune . . ."), (2) references to probable authors (David, Moses, Asaph, Korahites), (3) genre classifications (e.g., *tĕpillāh*, "petitionary prayer," in Psalms 17 and 102; *maśkîl*, "instruction," in Psalms 74 and 89; *šîr, mizmôr,* types of "songs," in Psalms 65–68 and 75), and sometimes (4) information about the life situation in which David allegedly composed or recited the text (e.g., Psalms 7; 51; 54).

Critical analysis and comparison with the ancient versions (esp. LXX) prove a cumulative growth of superscriptions in the Psalter. Perhaps we are confronted here with scribal efforts to make the text look ancient from the beginning. Today the meaning of many technical terms remains obscure.

B. S. Childs, "Psalm Titles and Midrashic Exegesis," *JSS* 16 (1971) 137-50; L. Delekat, "Probleme der Psalmenüberschriften," *ZAW* 76 (1964) 280-97; D. M. Howard, "Editorial Activity in the Psalter," in J. C. McCann, *Shape,* 52-70 (listing at Additional Bibliography, section C); H.-J. Kraus, *Psalmen* I, 14-29 (listing at "Introduction to Cultic Poetry"); S. Mowinckel, "Die technischen Termini in den Psalmenüberschriften," in *PsSt* IV; idem, *W* II, 207-17.

SUPPLICATION (Flehen). → Petition.

THANKSGIVING OF COMMUNITY (Dank der Gemeinde). → Thanksgiving Song.

THANKSGIVING PRAYER (Dankgebet). → Thanksgiving Song.

THANKSGIVING SONG (Danklied). Jubilant cultic song to celebrate victory, divine help, good harvests, and all sorts of joyful occasions. There are a personal (= small group) and a national or communal (= secondary organizations) variety to thanksgiving psalms (see "Introduction to Cultic Poetry," section 4C). Customarily, thanksgivings were connected with grateful sacrifices (cf. Lev 7:11-21), replaced in times when Israel did not have a functioning temple (exile) by songs, praises, and commitments (cf. Psalm 50). Psalm 107 is an instruction as to when to give thanks; the great prayer of dedication at the (re!)opening of the temple (1 Kgs 8:23-51) visualized prayers (and thanksgivings?) at the central holy site without even mentioning sacrifice. There are only references to prayer and supplication.

P. D. Miller, *They Cried,* 178-232 (see Additional Bibliography, section C); E. Ruckstuhl, "Danksagung," *NBL* I, 387; C. Westermann, *Praise,* 15-35 (listing at "Introduction to Cultic Poetry").

THANKSGIVING SONG OF THE INDIVIDUAL (Dankgebet des Einzelnen). →
Thanksgiving Song.

THEOPHANY (Theophanie). → Report of Theophany.

THREAT TO EVILDOERS (Drohung gegen Übeltäter). → Exhortation.

TORAH EXHORTATION (Tora-Ermahnung). → Exhortation.

TORAH INSTRUCTION (Tora-Unterweisung). → Instruction.

TORAH PSALM (Tora-Psalm, Gesetzespsalm). Psalms that focus on the Mosaic
Torah (cf. most of all Psalms 1; 19B; 119) as the only fountain of divine
revelation and guidance. They reflect early Jewish community life and
worship (→ Instruction; Proclamation).
    H.-J. Kraus, "Freude an Gottes Gesetz. Ein Beitrag zur Auslegung
der Psalmen 1; 19B und 119," *EvT* 8 (1950-51) 337-51; more literature in
listing at Psalm 119.

ULTIMATUM (Ultimatum). In warfare the party that is about to win a battle or
the campaign issues to the enemy a summons to surrender (cf. 2 Kgs
18:17-37). The discourse of the near-victor usually contains offers and
threats to the foe. In the Psalms the genre appears as a speech of the messianic king (Ps 2:10-12) with typical exhortation to submit (v. 11) as well
as warnings (v. 10) and threats for the case of disobedience (v. 12).

VERDICT (Urteil). → Accusation.

VICTORY SONG (Siegeslied). May be interpreted as a (→) hymn of praise or a
communal (→) thanksgiving song for a given special occasion. Not visible in the texts of this genre are those short chants that the women sang
whenever their men came back home from battle (1 Sam 18:7; Exod
15:21; Ps 11:34). From these primitive chants developed artistic poems
narrating the course of events and extolling the heroes (cf. Judges 5; Exod
15:1-18; Psalm 68).
    For literature see listing at Psalm 68.

VOW (Gelübde). A solemn promise to God, usually including a protasis and an
apodosis. During affliction it was customary to make a promise to
Yahweh (Gen 28:20-21; Judg 11:30-31; 2 Sam 15:7-8). Consequently,
(→) complaint songs and (→) thanksgiving songs reflect this usage and
give it a liturgical form, in which the vow may become an element of
prayer (Pss 22:26 [RSV 25; 56:13 [RSV 12]; 61:6, 9 [RSV 5, 8]; 116:14,
18). Many vows contain a proposal to celebrate — together with friends,
family, or community — a feast of thanksgiving (e.g., Psalm 107). In ancient times it included a communion sacrifice and a feast for all the guests
(Ps 22:27 [RSV 26]; 1 Sam 1:4; Lev 7:11-21). Parallel to this usage, the

habit developed of offering liturgical services in the event of salvation, cure, or rehabilitation (see Psalms 40; 50). The vow is thus a typical offer in exchange for divine help, a certain bargaining proposal. But commercial or economic concepts do not explain its full significance. Vow and fulfillment of vow are only feasible within stable personal relationships between suppliants and their God.

C. A. Keller, *THAT* II, 39-43; M. Mauss, *Gift* (see Additional Bibliography, section B); H. D. Preuss, "Gelübde," *TRE* XII, 302-4.

VOW TO GIVE THANKS (Dankgelübde). → Vow.

WARNING (Warnung; Ermahnung). → Admonition.

WELL-WISH (Segenswunsch). → Blessing.

WISDOM PSALM (Weisheitspsalm). A very general term without form-critical connotations. Psalms are cultic poems, while the many types of wisdom discourse (see R. Murphy, *Wisdom Literature* [FOTL XIII; Grand Rapids: Eerdmans, 1981] 4-12) were used in educative situations, principally outside worship. But doctrinal and instructional interests within a cultic community also led to the creation or adaptation of educative discourse for liturgy, which should not, however, be confused with a wholesale intrusion of school and teaching patterns into cultic ritual. Perhaps a better genre description for texts such as Psalms 1, 8, 37, 39, 49, 73, 90, 119, etc. would be (→) instruction of community.

J. K. Kuntz, "Wisdom Psalms" (listing at "Introduction to Psalms"); S. Mowinckel, "Psalms" (listing at "Introduction to Cultic Poetry"); R. E. Murphy, "Consideration" (listing at "Introduction to Psalms"); L. G. Perdue, *Wisdom,* 261-343 (listing at "Introduction to Cultic Poetry").

WISH (Wunsch). A less formal articulation of need, desire, hope, or good or bad fate than (→) petition or (→) blessing; cf., e.g., Pss 21:9-13 (RSV 8-12); 72:4-11; 122:6; 129:5.

WORDS OF ASSURANCE (Zuspruch). → Assurance.

WORSHIP AGENDA (Gottesdienstagenda). Any kind of more complex setup of liturgical texts, e.g., Psalm 144. → Liturgy.

YAHWEH-KINGSHIP PSALM (König-Jahweh Psalm, Thronbesteigungslied). According to the theory of Sigmund Mowinckel (*PsSt* II), shared especially by Scandinavian and British scholars, this type of psalm narrates and celebrates Yahweh's yearly ascension to the throne. The God of Israel, then, would assume the role of the dying and rising deity known from ancient Near Eastern ceremonialism and mythology (cf. "Introduction to Cultic Poetry," section 2). Most Continental scholars believe, however, that

Psalms 47; 93; 96–99 (note the hailing of Yahweh as the king, who "goes up with jubilation" and trumpets, 47:6 [RSV 5]) are regular (→) hymns of praise, not rooted in a hypothetical enthronement festival (→ Zion Hymn).

J. Jeremias, *Das Königtum Gottes in den Psalmen* (Göttingen: Vandenhoeck & Ruprecht, 1987).

ZION HYMN (Zionshymnus). A song of praise that focuses on Zion as the abode of Yahweh and the principal locale of Israelite worship (e.g., Psalms 46; 48; 76; 84; 87; 122; 132; 137). In form-critical terminology, however, these songs are true (→) hymns of praise and reflect not the theology or tradition of one particular family of singers but the early Jewish community in the dispersion and its worship oriented toward the spiritual center, Jerusalem. Nevertheless, ancient, even pre-Israelite traditions of the mountain of the gods in northern territories, known also from Ugaritic mythology, are preserved in the texts (see Ps 48:3 [RSV 2]).

Y. Avishur, *Studies;* R. J. Clifford, *Mountain,* 131-60 (for both see Additional Bibliography, section B); W. H. Schmidt, *Königtum Gottes in Ugarit und Israel* (BZAW 80; Berlin: Töpelmann, 1961) 25, 32-34, 66; J. Schreiner, *Sion — Jerusalem,* 219-35 (listing at Psalm 132); G. Wanke, *Zionstheologie,* 39-106 (listing at "Introduction to Psalms").

ZION SONG (Psalm) (Zionslied/-psalm). → Zion Hymn.


# FORMULAS

ASSURANCE FORMULA (Zuspruch-Formel). The stereotyped introduction to the "priestly salvation oracle" (Begrich; → Oracle of Salvation), "do not fear" (*'al tîrā';* e.g., Isa 41:14; 43:1; 44:2).

J. Begrich, "Heilsorakel" (listing at "Introduction to Cultic Poetry").

AUDITION FORMULA (Wortempfangsformel). Indication by way of introductory, formulaic expression of receiving or, more frequently, of having received a word of God, e.g., Pss 62:12 (RSV 11); 81:6 (RSV 5: "I heard a voice I had not known"); 85:9 (RSV 8). → Proclamation.

BLESSING FORMULA (Segensformel). An utterance that expresses the wish for good will or (divine) favor on behalf of another person or group. In some cases, as in the blessings formally given to one's children, the words are believed to set into motion what they call for. A very old blessing of the congregation is preserved in Num 6:24, "May Yahweh keep you" (*yĕbārekĕkā yhwh wĕyišmĕrekā;* cf. Gen 28:3; Ps 121:7). This formula was originally used in greetings but then came to be employed in cultic proceedings. Later, the passive form "blessed be you" (*bārûk 'attā;* cf. Deut 7:14; 28:3-6; 1 Sam 15:13; Ps 115:15) apparently became more frequent. In the Psalms the *bārûk* wish is mostly used as an expression of praise directed to Yahweh himself (Pss 18:47 [RSV 46]; 28:6; 31:22 [RSV 21]; 41:14 [RSV 13]; 66:20; 68:20-36 [RSV 19-35]; 72:18-19; 89:53 [RSV 52]; 106:48; 119:12; 124:6; 135:21; 144:1). Behind this formula we may surmise a very ancient belief that the deity needs to be strengthened by the blessings of her or his followers; see Psalm 29.

E. Salonen, *Die Gruss- und Hoflichheitsformeln in babylonischassyrischen Briefen* (Helsinki: Kirjallisuuden, 1967) 20-44, 59-60, 72-76, 85-106; W. S. Towner, "Blessed Art Thou" (listing at "Introduction to Cultic Poetry"); G. Wehmeier, *Der Segen im Alten Testament* (Basel: Reinhardt, 1970) 143-71.

CALL TO ATTENTION (Aufmerksamkeitsruf, Lehreröffnungsformel, Aufforderung zum Hören). Educators, wisdom teachers, and parents would customarily begin their discourse with exhortatory, arousing, and attention-getting "listen," "hearken," "hear." This opening phrase of educative speech has also influenced prophetic discourse (cf. Am 3:1, 13; 4:1; 5:1; 7:16; 8:4), cultic (→) exhortation and (→) instruction (cf. Pss 34:3, 12 [RSV 2, 11]; 49:2 [RSV 1]; 50:7; 81:9 [RSV 8]).

CONFESSIONAL FORMULA (Bekenntnisformel). A formal expression used in certain situations of worship to assert one's faith in and allegiance to God (→ Commitment). It is directed to Yahweh himself, but nonetheless also destined for the ears of all worshipers; the suppliant says, e.g., "You are my God" (Pss 25:5; 31:15 [RSV 14]; 44:5 [RSV 4]; 63:2 [RSV 1]; 68:25 [RSV 24]; 118:28; 140:7 [RSV 6]), or "I trust in you" (7:2 [RSV 1]; 11:1; 13:6 [RSV 5]; 25:2; 26:1; 31:7, 15 [RSV 6, 14]; 71:1; 91:2; 141:8). The whole community may articulate its faith by saying, e.g., "You are our father" (Isa 63:16; 64:7 [RSV 8]). Other formulas include acknowledgment of guilt (→ Confession of Sin: *ḥāṭā'tî*, "I have erred," 2 Sam 12:13; Ps 51:6 [RSV 4]).

E. S. Gerstenberger, "Glaubensbekenntnisse im AT," *TRE* XIII, 386-88; R. Knierim, *Sünde*, 20-38, 193-94, 208-10 (listing at "Introduction to Psalms"); H. Vorländer, *Mein Gott*, 245-48, 270-72 (listing at "Introduction to Cultic Poetry").

CRY FOR HELP (Zetergeschrei, Hilfeschrei). A short, stereotyped, and highly conventionalized articulation used in emergency situations. "Help me," "save me," are possibly basic shouts by anyone in danger, regardless of the culture. One Hebrew expression is *hôšî'ēnî*, "save me," an imperative plus personal suffix. It occurs in all kinds of distress, profane and cultic (Josh 10:6; 2 Kgs 6:26; 16:7; 19:19; Jer 2:27; 17:14; Pss 3:8 [RSV 7]; 6:5 [RSV 4]; 7:2 [RSV 1]; 69:2 [RSV 1]; 71:2; 86:2-16; 118:25; 119:94, 146).

H. J. Boecker, *Redeformen*, 61-66 (listing at "Introduction to Psalms").

540

DECLARATION OF BEING HEARD (Ausdruck der Erhörungsgewissheit). Thanksgiving songs often affirm either in an anticipatory or a realistic way that complaint and petition have reached the divine destination; cf. Pss 22:22 (RSV 21); 32:5; 40:2 (RSV 1); 116:1-2; 118:5; Jonah 2:3 (RSV 2). The formula is: "He has/you have heard me." It implies trust and gratitude over against the divine helper, and the readiness of the suppliant to respond properly to God.

DESCENT FORMULA (Abstammungsformel). Establishing relationships between humans and with God was one of the deepest concerns of ancient people. Interpersonal ties were a basic necessity for survival. Small wonder that we find, in ancient literatures, a large number of formulas defining (and often making legal) such interrelationships (marriage, adoption, friendship, alliance). Some psalms presuppose a special tie between Yahweh and the king (see Psalms 2; 20; 21; 45; 110). The tradition even makes the king a "son of God," taking up formulations from civil law: "You are my son; today I have begotten you" (2:7; cf. 89:27 [RSV 26]: "You are my father"; 110:3). Concepts of divine descent for the king were common in certain periods and regions of the ancient Near East and Egypt (→ Authentication).

ENTHRONEMENT SHOUT (Inthronisationsruf). The ascension to the throne was celebrated by the multitude by choruses of "X [Absalom, Jehu, etc.] is [has become] king" (2 Sam 15:10; 2 Kgs 9:13) or "Long live King X" (1 Kgs 1:25, 34). The first-mentioned formula is used also in some (→) Yahweh-kingship psalms ("Yahweh has become king": Pss 47:8 [RSV 7]; 93:1; 97:1; 99:1). → Festive Shout.
     D. Michel, "Studien zu den sogenannten Thronbesteigungspsalmen," *VT* 6 (1956) 40-68; S. Mowinckel, *PsSt* II, 213-19; *W* I, 109-16.

EXCLAMATION (Ausruf; Ruf). → Festive Shout; Exclamation; Cheers.

FELICITATION (Glückwunsch, Seligpreisung). The standard introduction to a (→) beatitude, "happy the one *('ašrê hā'îš)* who. . . ." Used primarily in educative discourse, it probably entered worship language with both meditative and instructional functions (Pss 1:1; 41:2 [RSV 1]; 119:1-2; 128:1-2). The opposite is "Woe *(hôy)* to anyone who. . . ."
     J. Dupont, "Beatitudes" (listing at Psalm 1); W. Janzen, *"'Ašre'"*; and W. Käser, "Beobachtungen" (for both see listing at "Introduction to Psalms").

FESTIVE SHOUT (Festgeschrei). Crowds participating in assemblies and communal ritual express their emotional involvement by intoning short songs or exclamations, like Ps 118:24: "This is the day Yahweh has made; let us rejoice and be glad in it!" (paralleled by modern battle songs of soccer fans, etc.). Quite often this vociferous participation is reduced to single yells, like "Halleluyah" ("Praised be Yahweh"; cf. openings and endings of Psalms 103; 104; 112; 113; etc.; see Exclamation; Cheers, above under Genres).

FORMULA OF CONFIDENCE (Vertrauensformel). Especially used in (→) individual complaints (→ Affirmation of Confidence). The prayer-style expression is basically: "In you I trust"; it may be put into third person: "Yahweh, in whom I trust" (see Pss 7:2 [RSV 1]; 11:1; 16:1; 18:3 [RSV 2]; 25:20; 31:2 [RSV 1]; 57:2 [RSV 1]; 61:5 [RSV 4]; 71:1; 144:2). Possible variations include "You are my refuge [castle, rock, salvation, etc.]" (see Pss 18:3 [RSV 2]; 31:4-5 [RSV 3-4]; 142:6). Such formulas occur frequently in the opening lines of a prayer — proof of a fundamental importance of trust in the relationship of the suppliant to his God. → Song of Confidence.

FORMULA OF INCOMPARABILITY (Unvergleichlichkeitsformel). "Who is like El?" (= Michael) is a Hebrew sentence-name that extols the God who has given a new baby to the family. In this context of a small group, expressions of incomparability praise the personal God. On the national level comparisons with the gods of the neighbors are the result of religious and political competition (cf. 2 Kings 5; Mic 4:5). In the exilic phase Israelite theologians articulated the exclusive reign of Yahweh over all the world (cf. Isa 44:6-20; Psalms 24; 96–99). This is the background of formulas like "Yahweh, Lord of hosts, who is like you?" (Ps 89:9 [RSV 8]); "Where is a mighty God like you?" (Ps 77:14 [RSV 13]).

  G. Johannes, "Unvergleichlichkeitsformulierungen" (listing at "Introduction to Cultic Poetry").

FORMULA OF TRANSMISSION (Überlieferungsformel). Tribal societies normally live on oral tradition. Norms and genealogies, sacred history and know-how of all kinds have to be handed down the generation line. Much depends on the accuracy of oral tradition. Therefore the trustworthiness of tradition has to be guaranteed. "We heard it with our own ears" and "Our fathers told us" (Ps 44:2 [RSV 1]) seem to be formulaic corroboration of oral tradition.

FORMULA OF TRUST (Vertrauensformel). → Formula of Confidence.

GRACE FORMULA (Huldformel). The expression known from Exod 34:6 ("Yahweh, Yahweh, a God merciful and gracious, slow to anger, and abounding in steadfast love and faithfulness") in slightly modified form also occurs in the Psalms (cf. Pss 86:15; 103:8; 145:8). Its origin is probably in the worship of the exilic-postexilic community. → Festive Shout.

  H. Spieckermann, "Barmherzig" (listing at Psalm 86).

OATH FORMULA (Eidformel). Every oath in antiquity was an act of conditional self-cursing. "May I fall dead, if I do not tell the truth" was the essence of calling on the deity in such a case. A full expression of this sort we have in

542

Ps 137:5-6, in a twofold variant, chiastically juxtaposed: "If I forget you, O Jerusalem, let my right hand wither! Let my tongue cling to the roof of my mouth, if I do not remember you." Similarly Ps 7:4-6 (RSV 3-5). The deadly consequences of neglect or lie were usually suppressed in the formula, so that only the conditional phrase or the positive pledge was cited (cf. Ps 132:2-5; Gen 21:23-24; 1 Sam 20:12-13; 1 Kgs 18:10, 15; etc.). This is valid also for God's own oath formula: Pss 95:11; 110:4. → Vow.

OFFERTORY FORMULA (Opferdarbringungsformel). → Thanksgiving Formula.

PRAISE FORMULA (Lobformel). A formulaic expression of praise such as "Hallelujah," "Amen," "Praise (be to) the Lord," used in (→) responses of the community; cf. also the so-called Hallelujah Psalms, 104, 106, 111–113, and 135. → Festive Shout.

    T. Nöldeke, "Halleluja," in *Abhandlungen zur semitischen Religionskunde und Sprachwissenschaft* (*Fest.* G. von Baudissin; ed. W. Frankenberg; BZAW 33; Giessen: Töpelmann, 1918) 375-80; H. Ringgren, *TDOT* III, 404-10.

REVELATION FORMULA (Offenbarungsformel). One would not expect many mentions of Yahweh revealing himself or communicating with persons in the Psalter, being a book of prayer and songs. Yet passages with direct Yahweh speech are quite frequent (→ Proclamation). The old formulas of prophetic revelation, however, occur rarely. For example, *ně'um yhwh*, "Yahweh's whispering," in the context of divine communication is represented only in Ps 110:1 (36:3 [RSV 2] has another subject). Overwhelmingly, this formula belongs to the prophetic books. Expressions with *'mr*, "speak," have some standing in the Psalter (cf. Pss 2:7; 12:6 [RSV 5]; 50:16; 82:6) but the precise prophetic formula "Thus Yahweh has spoken" is absent from the psalms (see M. H. Floyd, *Minor Prophets, Part 2* [FOTL XXII; Grand Rapids: Eerdmans, 2000] 650, s.v. "Oracle Formula"; M. A. Sweeney, *Isaiah 1–39* [FOTL XVI; Grand Rapids: Eerdmans, 1996] 546, s.v. "Oracular Formula").

SACRIFICIAL FORMULA (Opferformel). → Thanksgiving Formula.

SUMMONS TO WORSHIP (Ruf zur Anbetung). → Call to Worship.

THANKSGIVING FORMULA (Danksagungsformel). The expression "I will give you thanks" (*'ôděkā*, Pss 43:4; 108:4 [RSV 3]; 118:21), which originally marked the dedication of the sacrificial animal to Yahweh before it was slaughtered. The expression was later widely used to designate the act of giving thanks in worship, including by means of a (→) thanksgiving song (Pss 30:13 [RSV 12]; 35:18; 52:11 [RSV 9]; 54:8 [RSV 6]; 86:12; 111:1; 138:1).

    F. Crüsemann, *Studien,* 267-79 (listing at "Introduction to Cultic Poetry").